THE FOUNDATION CENTER'S

GUIDE TO

Grantseeking on the Web

2001 EDITION

Kief Schladweiler, Editor

Contributors

This edition of *The Foundation Center's Guide to Grantseeking on the Web* is the result of the hard work of the following individuals, and of their considerable experience exploring the World Wide Web.

Claire Acher	Caroline Herbert	Lorna Aikman Mehta
Jennifer Allen	Christine Innamorato	Margaret Morth
Jonathan Chan	John Kendzior	Mitch Nauffts
David L. Clark	Cheryl L. Loe	Janice Z. Rosenberg
Sarah Collins	Judith B. Margolin	Frederick Schoff
Phyllis Edelson	Beverly McGrath	Sherry Seward

Library of Congress Cataloging-in-Publication Data
The Foundation Center's guide to grantseeking on the web.—2001 ed. / Kief
Schladweiler, editor.
    p. cm.
   Includes bibliographical references and index.
   ISBN 0-87954-966-1 (alk. paper)
    1. Fund raising—Computer network resources—Directories. 2.
Endowments—Computer network resources—Directories. 3. Web
sites—Directories. I. Title: Guide to grantseeking on the web. II. Title:
Grantseeking on the web. III. Schladweiler, Kief. IV. Foundation Center.

HV41.2 F68 2001
025.06'65815224—dc21

                                                   2001051227

TABLE OF CONTENTS

FOREWORD

The Internet has demonstrated great power not only as a communication tool but also as a reshaper of culture. The World Wide Web is both a reflection of and an impetus for our increasingly global society. As we entered the new millennium, various groups estimated that the number of people using the Internet worldwide would reach 300 million by 2005. Some estimate that in 2001 there were already 130 million people in the United States with Internet access.

When the Web took off in 1995, we heard fears expressed that the medium would be captured by commercial, for-profit, "dot com" interests, and that the early communal, sharing ethos and culture of the Internet would be destroyed. By 1999 "e-commerce" appeared to be driving the Web. And by 2000, the narrower view of e-commerce as secure credit card transactions taking place over the Web was supplanted by the more comprehensive concept of "e-business." However, the nosedive of technology stocks on the Nasdaq in April 2000 made it clear that the large number of Web users did not necessarily translate into easy riches. Many start-ups failed as venture capital dried up and companies providing hardware, software, and services for the Web scaled back their operations.

By 2001, the primary lesson learned seemed to be that size, brand, and a pre-existing non-Web audience were the keys to success in cyberspace. However, it is still true that the very technology of the Web resists outright monopolization. While large commercial interests do have the resources to be the most visible players, many people and groups are working to ensure that any community of interest can find a place on the Web, so long as it has conviction, energy, and the basic resources needed to establish itself there.

To echo this point, in a November 1999 interview, management guru Peter Drucker declared, "The 20th century was the century of business. The next century is going to be the century of the social sector." We will have to wait and see if this bold prediction comes true. It is evident that the media are now full of news of the nonprofit world in general, and of philanthropy in particular. In any case, we are certainly seeing the continued convergence of Web technology—and the commercial sector itself—with the charitable sector. In 2001 the nonprofit sector is grappling with sophisticated economic concepts like networked markets and value chains.

In the new millennium, expectations based on effortlessly grabbing large online audiences have become more realistic. The nonprofit sector has begun focusing on capacity-building, not just on the potential reach and efficiencies gained through use of Web technology. The sector has begun to address issues surrounding models of collaboration, establishing communities of practice, knowledge management, and distributing interactive educational and service programs to those in need.

However the interplay of major social and economic forces unfolds, the original culture of the Web remains ideally suited to serve the nonprofit community. With our many Web-delivered resources and services and the third edition of this guide, the Foundation Center is both documenting and contributing to the creation of a fully networked philanthropic community. In doing so we are making use of the Web's primary strengths: the broad distribution of useful information, search tools to find the most useful information, and the ability of people and groups to readily communicate with each other. We continue to develop Your Gateway to Philanthropy on the World Wide Web. We hope it opens many doors for you as you pursue your goals.

INTRODUCTION

Scope

The Foundation Center's Guide to Grantseeking on the Web, 2001 edition, is not intended as a comprehensive index of all available philanthropic sites on the Web. (We do, however, include an extensive listing of private foundations, grantmaking public charities, corporate grantmakers, and related nonprofit Web sites in the appendices at the back of the book.) No one source can cover all philanthropic Web sites that exist, and it would be foolhardy to try. Besides, the fluid nature of the Internet ensures that sites can and will be established, terminated, or moved to a new URL location overnight.

Our aim, rather, is to provide you with an introduction to the most useful Web sites and to deliver some solid advice about how to get the most out of your online funding research time. The Foundation Center is in a unique position to offer these suggestions, since Center staff has been scouring the Web in search of useful information since 1994, when the Center launched its own Web site. We hope that this selective approach will facilitate your ability to find pertinent information quickly on grantmakers on the Web while still encouraging you to explore on your own.

The Web sites referred to as examples throughout this guide cover a wide range of subject areas aimed at a broad audience. Some are specialized sites, focusing on a specific topic, while others are portal sites with information and links that span any number of topics. Some exist for one purpose only (e.g., to raise money for a particular cause). Others have a variety of features (such as news, grants announcements, e-mail notifications, software downloads, or organizational information). But each of the sites included in this guide shares one thing in common. They all provide information and tools for finding potential funders, learning about the nonprofit sector, conducting statistical research, and connecting grantseekers and others through electronic communication, and they offer useful content.

If you are interested in the world of philanthropy, this guide will lead you to appropriate resources. With our own Web site the Foundation Center has created a specialty portal for grantseekers and others. We continue to develop and expand our online offerings while keeping pace with the burgeoning Web. Once you have become familiar with the Web resources available in your area(s) of interest, we invite you to log onto our Web site (http://www.fdncenter.org) and follow the paths that open up to you.

Features and Arrangement

This new edition of *The Foundation Center's Guide to Grantseeking on the Web* employs a number of devices to make it easier for you to find the information you need. The location of the links and abstracts to the Web sites mentioned in the book has changed from the prior edition. You will now find the full listings of sites in the appendices at the back of the book. This should help provide you with an uninterrupted reading experience while still providing the information you need to locate specific Web sites and resources. Also in the 2001 edition you will find a new chapter (Chapter 6) focusing on Web sites and strategies for researching individual donors. This chapter helps to round out a complete approach to grantseeking on the Web that includes independent foundations, community foundations, public charities, corporate funders, government funding, and individual donors.

As in prior editions, screen shots of featured Web sites help you to visualize the sites and will prepare you for when you actually visit them. (But be forewarned: Some of the sites may look different by the time you get to them, due to the nature of the ever-changing Web.) Look for sidebars throughout the text providing concise tips and easy-to-read clarification. This edition also provides a combined proper name and subject index. If, for example, you're interested in Web sites mentioned in the book regarding the environment, you can look up the term "environment" in the index. Or if you have the name of a specific Web host, look that organization up in the index. Also new to this edition is a glossary of terms relating to the Internet that may be unfamiliar to someone new to the process of grantseeking on the Web.

Tips When Grantseeking on the Web

To find a word or phrase *within* the Web page you currently have open, use your browser's "Find" option ("Ctrl+F" in most cases). This is especially useful when you are confronted with a page that contains seemingly endless text. The "Find" option lets you quickly jump to that section of the page where your word or phrase occurs so that you can judge the usefulness of the site a little faster.

As you conduct your research on the Web, it is a good idea to bookmark pages that you think you will return to again. If you are using Netscape, you will find the heading Bookmarks at the top of the screen; if you are using Internet Explorer, you will find the heading Favorites. When you come across a page you'd like to bookmark, click Bookmarks/Favorites and then select Add Bookmark/Add to Favorites from the pull-down menu.

Chapter 1 is a survey of the range of information and services available at the Foundation Center's Web site (http://www.fdncenter.org). We reorganized and redesigned our Web site in early 2001 to accommodate the growing amount of information. The Center's Web site is now organized with a focus on providing specific tools and directed information according to the needs of each visitor. Especially for first-time visitors, reading this chapter may make navigating our site even easier. And remember, the Web is vast; if you get lost following a trail of links, you can always return to http://www.fdncenter.org, Your Gateway to Philanthropy on the World Wide Web, to pick up the trail afresh.

In Chapter 2 we discuss various approaches that independent (or private) foundations are taking in utilizing the World Wide Web. From simply providing basic information to actively championing the use of new communication technologies and trying to ensure equal access for all, foundations increasingly are getting involved with the Web. You can now find independent foundations that offer annual reports, grants guidelines, grants listings, and printable grant application forms. In some cases, foundations have taken the next step and are now providing grant application forms on the Web that can either be downloaded and filled out by grantseekers or, in some cases, submitted directly to the funders online. While recent innovations such as these make it easier to apply for a grant, to be successful at grantseeking on the Web still requires "old-fashioned" research, hard work, and patience.

The Foundation Center takes great pains to present an accurate picture of U.S. philanthropy. In doing so we make a distinction between private foundations and public charities, sometimes known as "public foundations." In Chapter 3 we present the public charities on the Web that we have identified as having grantmaking programs. This group includes community foundations, a growing segment of U.S. philanthropy. Information is not available as systematically for the great variety of public charities as it is for private foundations. It is our hope that highlighting grantmaking public charities in this way will stimulate more of them to provide us with detailed information about their grantmaking activities.

Chapter 4 surveys the online world of corporate philanthropy, in addition to suggesting strategies for finding corporate funding information on the Web. Corporations describe their giving programs in a variety of ways and to varying degrees, so creativity and persistence come into play when doing corporate giving research on the Web. This chapter stresses the need to consider the different motivations and goals of corporate givers and how these can affect your funding approach. This chapter also distinguishes between corporate foundations and direct giving programs, since understanding these distinctions will have an impact on your funding research.

There is a tremendous amount of government information on the Web. Chapter 5 attempts to make sense of this vast amount of information by pointing you to selected sites, at the many levels of government, that describe a variety of assistance programs. Unlike corporations, where you may need to sift through irrelevant general company information to find information specifically about giving programs, there is a wealth of information available on the Web about government funding, much of it overlapping and duplicative. People both inside and outside of government have tried to organize this information for you. This chapter reviews the many sites detailing specific support programs as well as sites that can lead you to useful information. Exploring these sites can help you understand how

What to Look for on Grantmaker Web Sites

When visiting grantmaker Web sites, you will want to obtain answers to the following questions:

- *Does the grantmaker fund projects similar to yours?*
  Most grantmaker Web sites explicitly state the sort of projects that are funded or if the grantmaker gives grants at all. Go through the site thoroughly to get a sense of the funder's mission, founders, and history.
- *Does the Web site offer a listing of recently awarded grants?*
  If such a list is not apparent, see if the grantmaker has posted its annual report on the site. Often, annual reports will contain grants lists and relevant financial data. Some grantmakers' Web sites provide links to their grantees' Web sites. Exploring these Web sites will provide you with additional information about the kinds of projects and organizations funded by the grantmaker.
- *Does the grantmaker accept applications?*
  Some grantmakers consider projects by invitation only.
- *What are the application guidelines?*
  This information, provided on most grantmaker Web sites, will tell you in the clearest terms whether or not a project such as yours would be considered for funding. Guidelines will provide you with application procedures and deadlines and inform you as to whether you should apply directly or first send a letter of inquiry. Some grantmaker Web sites have application forms, that you can download or print from the screen. A few will allow you to apply online.
- *Are there funding restrictions?*
  These are usually stated explicitly, often in the application guidelines.
- *How do you contact the grantmaker?*
  Note the correct address, phone number, and e-mail address. Before you contact a grantmaker, become familiar with that grantmaker's preferred means of approach. Some accept e-mail inquiries and respond to phone calls, but the majority will require that you send a formal letter or proposal by post.
- *Who are the officers, trustees, and staff?*
  If this information is available, you will be able to address your inquiry to the correct person, not to an institution, when you contact the grantmaker.

Note: It is always important to try to ascertain how recently the information you are looking at was posted to the Web site. If the content is vague or not dated, you will need to confirm the data you have gathered from another source or directly from the grantmaker.

government agencies and funding programs are organized and can reveal a lot about their relationship to the nonprofit sector.

As noted, Chapter 6 is new to the 2001 edition of this book. You may already know that identifying individual donors is somewhat difficult because, unlike foundations, individuals are not required to disclose to the public their financial and philanthropic activities. Approaching wealthy public figures is often an unsuccessful strategy. Most celebrities are inundated with requests for money, and they may have no particular connection to the activities or location of your nonprofit organization. This new chapter provides recommendations and links to relevant Web sites that help you find information on individual donors. It also tackles thorny issues like privacy and fundraising ethics, and it offers a prospect worksheet for use in researching individual donors online.

Chapter 7 recognizes that the World Wide Web distributes interactive software capability as well as information and hyperlinks. This chapter surveys a variety of sites—hosted in diverse settings—that offer searchable databases that may help Web users identify potential sources of assistance or general information. Wherever possible, we have divided the world of searchable databases into the two major categories of "for-free" and "for-fee." There is some overlap of this chapter with the subject matter of other chapters because the databases covered are often within corporate, government, and nonprofit organization settings, including a few on foundation Web sites.

Chapter 8 chronicles "other" useful Web sites, many of them hosted by nonprofit organizations. These are sites that Foundation Center staff has found to be the most useful and descriptive of the nonprofit sector, including some sites concerned with philanthropy in other countries. Many of the sites covered in this chapter will provide you with links to other resources you may find useful. We explore some of our staff's picks in detail. This sampling of sites is organized according to the subject categories used at the Center's Web site to provide ready access to this growing number of resources.

Chapter 9 is a comprehensive listing of online publications (with abstracts for each) concerned with philanthropy and the nonprofit sector. Included are many field-specific newsletters and other online publications that describe the current trends and policy context for various nonprofit activities. Here you will find both online journals that have print counterparts and those that offer unique content available only on the Web. Use this chapter to identify the online publications that will keep you up-to-date concerning your particular field and interests.

Chapter 10 illustrates how interactive communication is used to build communities on the World Wide Web. The simple but powerful interactivity of Internet e-mail, electronic mailing lists, and bulletin boards allows communities of Web users to define themselves online and to establish dialogues and conversations, both private and public, that can advance their work or inform their interests. This chapter surveys a number of the community-building services available for grantseekers and other nonprofit practitioners, and it provides tips on how to begin participating in these various forums.

There is also an extensive set of appendices.

Appendix A provides a brief introduction to ten search engines that we hope will provide you with the additional tools you need to be successful at grantseeking on the Web.

Appendices B–F list the many links to private foundations, grantmaking public charities, community foundations, corporate givers, and nonprofit organizations that can be found at the Center's Web site (http://www.fdncenter.org). Brief abstracts are also provided so that you will have an idea in advance what can be found at these sites. (The Center updates grantmaker links and abstracts continually, so be sure to check the Finding Funders area of the Center's Web site for the latest listings.) Readers can save time by familiarizing themselves with the world of foundations on the Web, programs of individual foundations, and basic Web offerings by referring to these appendices prior to going online.

Appendix G is a bibliography of print and other resources about the Internet that may be of interest to nonprofit practitioners. It is a compilation drawn from the Foundation Center's *Literature of the Nonprofit Sector Online* (*LNPS*), a bibliographic database you can search for free by visiting http://lnps.fdncenter.org.

Appendix H is a glossary of selected Internet-related terms that you are likely to come across in your research. It is offered here to help clarify jargon and explain technical terminology that may be unfamiliar to you.

The Foundation Center's Web site is a specialty portal that we hope will be "Your Gateway to Philanthropy on the World Wide Web." This guide is in one sense the static form of this specialty portal. It is full of specific information about where to find Web sites that may be useful in your grantseeking efforts. We invite you to use both the print and online versions in conjunction with one another as a way to get your Web grantseeking efforts off to a flying start.

CHAPTER ONE

A Guided Tour of the Foundation Center's Web Site

The Foundation Center's mission is to support and improve institutional philanthropy by promoting public understanding of the field and helping grantseekers succeed. To achieve its mission, the Foundation Center collects, organizes, and communicates information on U.S. philanthropy, conducts and facilitates research on trends in the field, and provides education and training on the grantseeking process. The Center uses various media, increasingly electronic in nature, to achieve its mission. The Center's Web site opens virtual doors to Foundation Center resources for audiences not served in the past, and it makes grantmaker information more accessible to audiences already familiar with the Center. The Foundation Center is the nation's leading authority on institutional philanthropy and is dedicated to serving grantseekers, grantmakers, researchers, policymakers, the media, and the general public.

Technology Used on the Center's Web Site

In order to reach the widest possible audience, the Foundation Center's Web site was designed for almost everyone, from high-level computer users to novices. Dynamic HTML (DHTML) and Javascript are used to enhance site navigation via drop-down menus, floating windows, and graphical effects. Interactive features (such as specialized search engines and automated listserv subscription forms) and sophisticated, secure e-commerce software are used to expedite the delivery of information and goods to our visitors. As the site evolves, the Foundation Center will provide increasingly more personalized content to online visitors. The

Foundation Center is also in the process of making its Web site more accessible to those with disabilities. While the site has been designed to accommodate as many visitors as possible, across as many computer platforms as possible, we recommend using the latest version of either Microsoft's Internet Explorer or Netscape's Navigator to browse the site.

An Overview of the Foundation Center's Web Site

If you enter the URL (Uniform Resource Locator) or Web address (http://www.fdncenter.org) in the location window of your browser, you will see the home page of the Foundation Center's Web site.

The Foundation Center's Web site greets you with an informative and attractive home page that will quickly guide you to the information you seek, living up to its tag line, "Your Gateway to Philanthropy on the World Wide Web." Links to the six main directories of the site—*Philanthropy New Digest* (*PND*), Finding Funders, Learning Lab, Researching Philanthropy, For Grantmakers, and Marketplace—are located just below our logo.

Orientation Tools on the Center's Web Site

To familiarize yourself with the layout of our site and to find the specific information you're looking for, you may find it helpful to use one of our three site orientation tools: the Guided Tour of the Foundation Center's Web site, the Site Map, and the Foundation Center Site-Wide Search.

The Guided Tour of the Foundation Center's Web site can be found in the Virtual Classroom section of the Learning Lab directory. This feature, complete with screen shots of the site's main pages, provides an overview of what you can expect to find throughout our site. Visitors can choose to view the information either in a few small, sequential steps or in a print-friendly format with all of the content appearing on a single page.

The Site Map, which is accessible from the left menu and the bottom of every page, presents the layout of the site at a glance. Each main directory and its associated subdirectories are listed, including the individual Web sites of each of the Center's five libraries. To maximize navigational convenience, each entry in the Site Map is a link that will take you directly to the destination specified.

The Foundation Center Site-Wide Search is located directly on the Center's home page. It is also in the SearchZone, which is accessible from the left menu and the bottom of every page in the site. The Foundation Center Site-Wide Search function enables you to enter a word or phrase in a search window. The search engine will search all the text on the Center's site (with the exception of *PND*) for the keywords you entered and display the results as links with summaries.

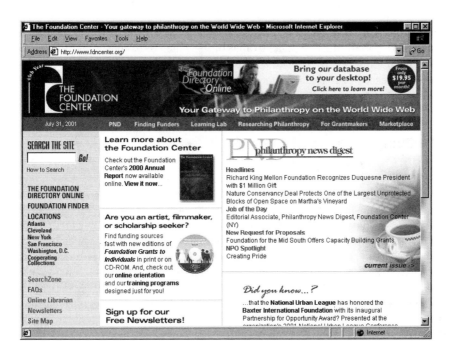

The Web site's main directories are designed to aid grantseekers and grantmakers by providing specific tools and directed information according to the needs of each visitor. Putting your cursor over the name of each directory on the top navigation bar will open up a drop-down menu of more specific areas within that directory. You can either click on the name of the directory heading itself, which will take you to the main page of that directory as well as an index of links for the content within the directory, or click on one of the specific areas from the drop-down menu, which will take you directly to that area.

In the left menu of our home page, you will find links to some of the most widely used and essential features of our site, such as our *Foundation Directory Online* fee-based subscription service, our free Foundation Finder lookup tool, the Web sites of each of the five Foundation Center libraries, and a listing of participating Cooperating Collections.

Another popular feature is our SearchZone. The SearchZone provides access to all search mechanisms on the Center's Web site from one central location, along with a help file which offers recommendations for the best search to conduct in order to find the information you seek. In addition to providing visitors with the ability to search our entire Web site (with the exception of *PND*) using the Site-Wide Search, we have created a number of specialized searches to aid you, including our new Sector Search portal, which searches a range of Web sites across the nonprofit sector.

Our Grantmaker Web Search enables you to search grantmaker Web sites selected according to criteria established by the Foundation Center. When you use this tool, you will be searching the text of our annotated links to those Web sites. The searchable annotations have been categorized by grantmaker type (private foundations, corporate grantmakers, community foundations, and grantmaking public charities) and written by Center staff members.

Also available are searchable databases. Contact information and other basic information about a particular foundation can be found in Foundation Finder. You simply enter all or part of a foundation's name to start your search. More detailed information about the nation's largest foundations can be obtained by subscribing to *The Foundation Directory Online*. The link to *The Foundation Directory Online* will deliver you to a page where you can find out more information about the service, subscribe, or log in once you have subscribed.

Other search functions that can be accessed through the SearchZone include 990-PF Search, which enables users to retrieve a foundation's IRS tax return; *PND* Search, which searches all back issues of *PND*; and *Literature of the Nonprofit Sector Online* (*LNPS*), which is a searchable database of the literature of philanthropy that incorporates the unique contents of the Foundation Center's five libraries.

Other items on the side menu include links to our answers to frequently asked questions, FAQs, a feature that first-time visitors will find especially valuable. You may also wish to contact the Online Librarian, who responds to your reference questions via e-mail; visit our Newsletters subscription page to subscribe to the Center's various free electronic newsletters; find out more about the Foundation Center itself; view postings of job openings at the Center; obtain the Center's contact information; or review information for advertisers who are interested in promoting their products on our Web site.

The Foundation Center's home page also includes a section announcing the latest developments within the Foundation Center, such as new releases, research findings, and products; a section displaying current highlights of *PND,* which is updated daily; a section on the Center's nationwide educational workshops for grantseekers; and a Did You Know? feature, which offers a fascinating new fact about philanthropy with related links each day. Clicking on the links in any of these sections will take you to more detailed information on the subject. If you are a first-time visitor to the site or have an observation to share with the Center's Web Services staff, click on Feedback at the bottom of the page and fill out the interactive form.

Most visitors to the Foundation Center's Web site have a particular question in mind that they hope will be answered over the course of their online research. We'll address many of these questions, and point out the best places on the Center's site to find answers, in the remainder of this chapter.

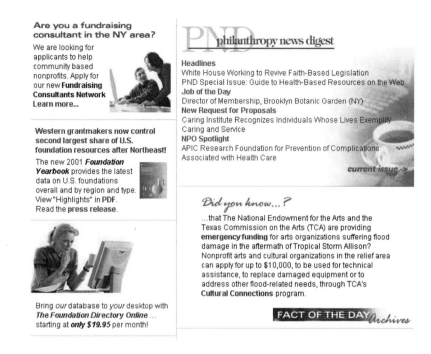

"I'm new to the grantseeking process. How do I begin?"

The Learning Lab (http://fdncenter.org/learn) should be your first stop if you want to learn about the grantseeking process—or simply brush up on your fundraising skills.

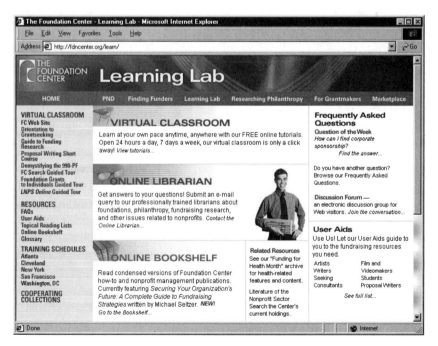

One of the Learning Lab's main offerings is its Virtual Classroom, where site visitors can take advantage of a variety of Web-based tutorials and find out about nationwide training courses taught by Foundation Center staff. In the Virtual Classroom are two resources that new grantseekers will find particularly useful. These are the Center's Online Orientation to the Grantseeking Process and the Guide to Funding Research.

The Orientation to Grantseeking introduces you to the step-by-step process of seeking funding from foundations. One of the most exciting aspects of the Web is its non-linear design, which allows you to spy an interesting link within one Web site or among the myriad Web sites that exist, and then jump to it in an instant. However, the somewhat chaotic nature of the Web can be overwhelming. Unlike other resources on the Web that offer a jumble of links to choose from, the Center's Orientation is designed in a linear format with a clear beginning and end and with links that guide you through it page by page. The Orientation will acquaint you with the following topics:

- What the Foundation Center is and the services we offer
- What a foundation is, and how foundations typically operate
- Three approaches to funding research
- Who gets foundation grants
- What funders look for in a grantee
- What types of support grantmakers typically give
- How to establish a nonprofit organization
- How to find support available to individuals
- Effective tools for funding research
- Hints on proposal writing

After a general introduction, the Orientation follows two divergent paths: grantseeking for individuals and grantseeking for nonprofit organizations. Within those paths, it branches further into specific tools, skills, and topics of interest. The Orientation provides several resources for further research on the Internet, but the bulk of its listings for additional resources are printed materials. Other areas of the Web site, which we discuss later in this chapter, have extensive lists of links to Internet resources.

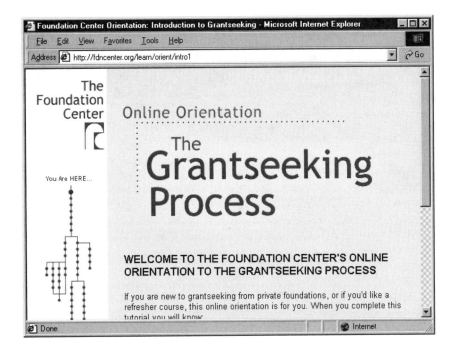

If you are familiar with the Web and the grantseeking process or have completed the Center's orientation, the Internet edition of *The Foundation Center's User-Friendly Guide to Funding Research and Resources* is a good refresher and reference as you conduct your research. The *User-Friendly Guide* contains much of the same information as the Orientation but offers it in more standard Web format. The *User-Friendly Guide* also has a glossary of common terms you will likely encounter in the course of your foray into funding research. From its table of contents and navigation frames, you can choose just the subjects you want to review and jump around if you like, without going through the material in linear fashion. In the table of contents of the *User-Friendly Guide,* you will see that you can print or save to your computer a single text file of the entire *Guide.* If you don't have regular access to a computer, you may want to consider printing the file for future reference.

Both the Orientation and the *User-Friendly Guide* offer an introduction to proposal writing, which is elaborated on in the Proposal Writing Short Course, also found in the Virtual Classroom. Use the Proposal Writing Short Course tutorial to get you through what can be a daunting process, and consider bookmarking it so that you can refer to it each time you have to write a new proposal. Remember: Even though far more time should be spent developing your program or project and researching and cultivating appropriate funders than on actual proposal preparation, you do want to approach the proposal process with care and in a systematic fashion.

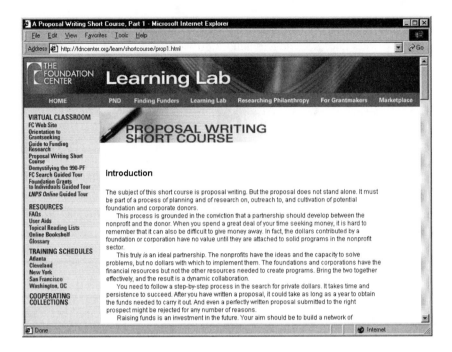

More experienced researchers will find the *LNPS* Guided Tour a useful tool. *LNPS* is a searchable database of the literature of philanthropy that incorporates the contents of the Center's five libraries. Many entries have abstracts written by Center staff. A supplementary list of new acquisitions is updated on a bimonthly basis.

Additionally, within the Virtual Classroom, visitors will find a Guide to the Foundation Center's Web Site, along with a tutorial called Demystifying the 990-PF, on using the tax form filed by foundations, and the *FC Search* Guided Tour. *FC Search: The Foundation Center's Database on CD-ROM* features a comprehensive listing of active U.S. foundations, corporate giving programs and grant-making public charities and their associated grants. It includes a Grantmaker File of approximately 60,000 records, and a Grants File with more than 243,000 grants of $10,000 or more that are awarded by the nation's largest funders. Also in the Virtual Classroom is a complete listing of the Foundation Center's training programs and seminars held in various locations across the United States—most of which are free.

The Learning Lab also offers User Aids (ready reference for nonprofit and individual grantseekers), the Online Bookshelf (offering condensed versions of Center publications available free over the Web), and a number of Topical Reading Lists (bibliographies on nonprofit topics based on Center library collections). If you have a question, check the Center's Frequently Asked Questions (FAQs). You may find that your question has already been answered here. FAQs cover a wide variety of philanthropy- and fundraising-related subjects and provide references to useful print and electronic resources.

If you still haven't found the information you need, you can submit a question to the Learning Lab's Online Librarian service, staffed by professionally trained librarians who will answer your questions about foundations, philanthropy, fundraising research, and other issues related to nonprofits. You will receive a response to your query via e-mail within approximately two business days.

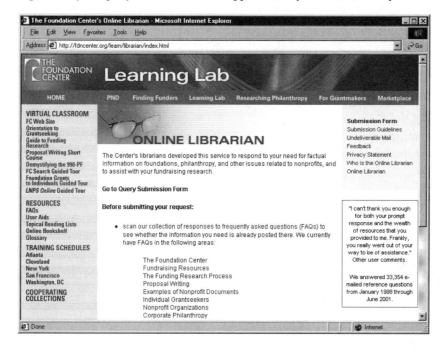

Finally, the Learning Lab provides links directly to the home pages of the Center's five libraries and to information about Cooperating Collections—the more than 200 libraries throughout the country that make the core titles of the Center's collection of print and electronic reference resources available to the public. The Collections are listed by state, and the name of the library, address, and phone number are provided. Links are supplied to Cooperating Collections that have Web sites.

Resources for Individual Grantseekers

Given the fact that the vast majority of foundation grants are awarded to nonprofit organizations rather than to individuals, individual grantseekers will appreciate two resources the Center has developed especially for them—our Foundation Grants to Individuals Guided Tour and our User Aids. The Foundation Grants to Individuals Guided Tour offers assistance in targeting funding prospects from among the Foundation Center's unique database of grantmakers who provide support for individuals. User Aids consist of lists of grantseeking resources such as Web sites, books, and periodicals specifically directed to particular groups of individuals—musicians, writers, researchers, artists, film and videomakers, students, and job seekers. There are also User Aids that provide guidance on starting a nonprofit organization, proposal writing, and researching individual donors, among others.

"How can I find information on the grantmakers that will fund me?"

If you are conducting research on potential funders, the Finding Funders directory (http://fdncenter.org/funders) is a natural place to start.

The Finding Funders section of the site contains a wealth of resources for grantseekers. Among these resources is the Center's downloadable Prospect Worksheet, which will help you focus on funders whose priorities match those of your project. It may also be helpful to examine a copy of the common grant application form, a standard application form for funding requests accepted by several regional associations of grantmakers (RAGs). The Common Grant Applications area provides a general idea of the sort of information that is important to include in a grant application and is available for downloading and printing. If there is one for your region, you may want to determine whether you should use it for the funding prospects you have in mind.

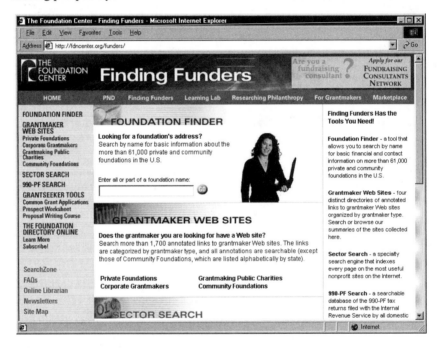

The Center's Finding Funders directory provides you with the most current and accessible information about grantmakers. This information takes several forms and is based on data that is either culled from grantmaker Web sites or that is reported by grantmakers to the IRS, through their publications, or in response to questionnaires sent to them by the Center. The different presentations of grantmaker information accommodate different research styles and different needs.

If you need information about a particular foundation, use Foundation Finder on the Finding Funders home page to look up basic information on the approximately 60,000 private and community foundations. You can search for a foundation by entering its name or a portion of its name. Foundation Finder contains basic information—address, contact person, telephone number, e-mail address, fax number, hot-linked Web address (URL), basic financial data, and type of foundation—extracted from the Center's database of grantmakers. In addition, the Foundation Center has collaborated with GrantSmart (http://www.grantsmart.org) to offer access to each foundation's Form 990-PF. The Form 990-PF will be downloaded as an Adobe PDF (Portable Document Format) file. To view these files it will be necessary to have the Adobe Acrobat Reader software (available as a free download at www.adobe.com/products/acrobat/readstep.html). You can do this by clicking on the PDF link in the Most Recent IRS Filing field of the foundation's entry. The Finder also provides an update form allowing grantmakers to correct any outdated or erroneous information in their entry.

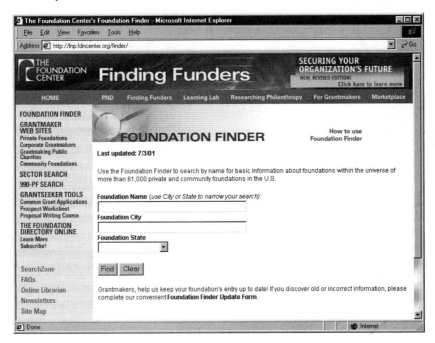

Grantmaker information is also provided through our annotated links to grantmaker Web sites. These sites are organized by four grantmaker types: private foundations, corporate grantmakers, grantmaking public charities, and community foundations. The first three categories offer searchable annotations and the fourth, community foundations, is organized by state. This link library truly serves as "Your Gateway to Philanthropy on the World Wide Web." Each grantmaker site is explored by Foundation Center staff, who then write annotations for them. Searches of our annotated links will provide you with a list of grantmakers whose Web sites might warrant a visit in the course of your research. Grantmaker Web site annotated links are updated at regular intervals and dated individually, providing you with a sense of how current the information is.

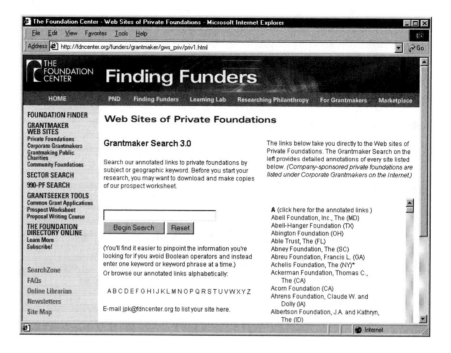

The layout of pages within the sections for private foundations, corporate grantmakers, and grantmaking public charities is identical, and the same research strategies can be used within all three sections. If you are familiar with a particular grantmaker and would like to go directly to that grantmaker's Web site, the alphabetized name list on the right side of the screen provides direct links to grantmaker Web sites. If you have heard of a grantmaker but would like some preliminary information before visiting its Web site, select the first letter of the grantmaker's name on the left to pull up a list that contains not only links to grantmaker Web sites but also descriptions of what you will find at each Web site.

If you are looking for funders focusing on a particular subject area or geographic location, you will find Grantmaker Search the most helpful. Go to the input box under the Grantmaker Search 3.0 heading and enter a word or words that describe the type of project you are seeking to fund, or enter the geographic location of the project. Now click Begin Search. You will receive a list of grantmakers for which the Center has annotated links. When you click on a grantmaker name in the search results list, you will find a description of the grantmaker and its Web site. There will also be a link to that Web site.

The directory for community foundations is not searchable in the same fashion; rather, the foundations are organized by state. You should be able to identify easily those foundations in your geographic location.

We also give you the ability to search grantmaker Web sites themselves, using our Sector Search feature. The Foundation Center has created a search application that indexes information gathered from only the most useful nonprofit Web sites. Instead of trying to retrieve useful information from a search of the entire Web, we have programmed this software to search only the Web sites of the organization type you specify (private foundations, corporate grantmakers, grantmaking public charities, community foundations, nonprofits, or government resources), thus significantly increasing your chances of finding the information you are looking for.

You can search across all categories of grantmakers, or narrow your search to just one category. For the greatest number of results, use broad search terms and conduct your search across all grantmaker categories. To narrow your search, use more specific search terms and select one category of grantmaker within which to conduct your search. Since the Sector Search will likely return broader results than the annotation-based Grantmaker Web Search, you may find you need to narrow your search terms when using this engine.

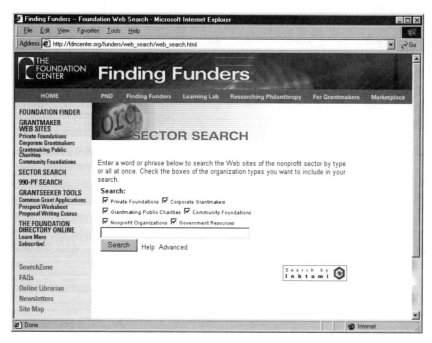

Both Sector Search and Grantmaker Web Search will provide you with a list of grantmakers on the Web that are potential funders for your organization or project, although a final determination about that will require additional research.

Detailed information about a particular grantmaker may be obtained by examining its Form 990-PF, the tax return filed with the IRS. From the Finding Funders home page, site visitors can enter a foundation's name or Employer Identification Number (EIN) in the 990-PF Search box to retrieve the foundation's Form 990-PF as a PDF file. The length of a grantmaker's return can be several pages or several hundred pages, so it might take a considerable time to download.

Another useful resource in the Finding Funders directory is the Common Grant Applications. The common grant application format has been adopted by groups of grantmakers to allow grant applicants to produce a single proposal for a specific community of funders, thereby saving time. Before applying to any funder that accepts a common grant application form, be sure to ascertain whether your project matches the funder's stated interests, and to find out whether the funder would prefer a letter of inquiry in advance of receiving a proposal. Also be sure to check whether the funder has a deadline for proposals, as well as whether it requires multiple copies of your proposal.

The Prospect Worksheet, another resource in the Finding Funders directory, is a simple form to print out and copy before starting your research. It will help keep your research organized and focused. As you locate funders whose priorities closely match your project, fill out a prospect worksheet for each one. The prospect worksheet will help you match the goals and needs of your project with the goals and interests of funders. Use this tool to record financial data; subject focus; geographic limits; types of support; populations served; the name of officers, donors, trustees, and staff; application information; sources from which you gathered information about the funder; notes; and follow-up communications.

To compile a more comprehensive and targeted list of potential funders, you might consider subscribing to *The Foundation Directory Online,* our searchable database of the nation's foundations, corporate giving programs, and grantmaking public charities. *The Foundation Directory Online* allows searches across six separate fields of data to return targeted lists of funding prospects as well as plain text searching. Searches return grantmaker profiles including address and contact information, Web site links, donors, fields of interest, types of support, names of officers and trustees, staff, financial information, and more. The first level of service contains current descriptions of 10,000 of the largest foundations in the United States. The second level of service, *The Foundation Directory Online Plus,* includes access to the database of 10,000 foundations, plus access to a grants database of information on more than 170,000 grants made by the top 1,100 foundations. The third level, *The Foundation Directory Online Premium,* provides access to the grants file plus a foundation database featuring the 20,000 largest foundations in the nation. The most comprehensive level of service, *The Foundation Directory Online Platinum,* provides access to the grants database, plus the Center's entire database of approximately 60,000 foundations, grantmaking public charities, and corporate givers. There are varying subscription fees for the different levels. To make this resource accessible to a wide audience, *The Foundation Directory Online* is offered at low monthly rates as well as a yearly subscription.

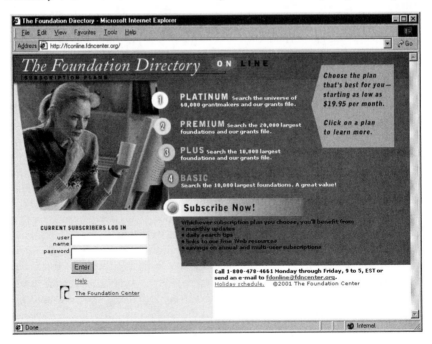

Fill out a prospect worksheet for each relevant grantmaker Web site you visit. You will have concrete results from your research on the Web that you can refer back to, and you will know what information you must find from other sources.

One final resource you may wish to consult when finding funders is the Foundation Center's *RFP Bulletin,* which can be found in the *PND* directory of the Center's site. RFPs (Requests for Proposals) are often made by grantmakers who wish to attract applicants with specific types of projects that they are interested in funding. The *RFP Bulletin* is published weekly on Friday afternoons. Each RFP listing provides a brief overview of a current funding opportunity offered by a foundation or other grantmaking organization. Interested applicants should read the full RFP at the grantmaker's Web site or contact the grantmaker directly for complete program guidelines and eligibility requirements before submitting a proposal to that grantmaker. In addition to being posted online, the content of the *RFP Bulletin* is available from the Center in the form of a free, weekly electronic newsletter. If you would like to subscribe, you may do so by entering your e-mail address in the subscribe box on the main page of the *RFP Bulletin* or by clicking on the Newsletters link, available at the bottom of every page of the Center's site and then following the easy-to-follow instructions.

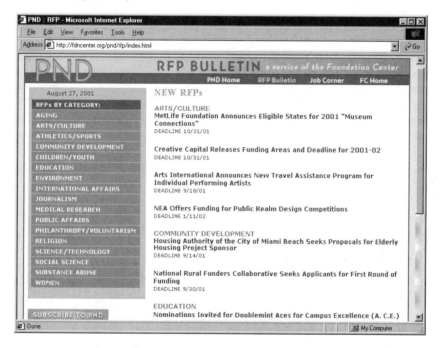

"How can I keep current with what's happening in philanthropy today?"

Philanthropy News Digest (*PND*) (http://fdncenter.org/pnd/current) is the Foundation Center's online news service. You will find it by clicking on the link on the home page. *PND* is a compendium, in digest form, of philanthropy-related articles and features culled from print and electronic media outlets nationwide. *PND* is updated daily on the Web site and delivered via e-mail every Tuesday evening.

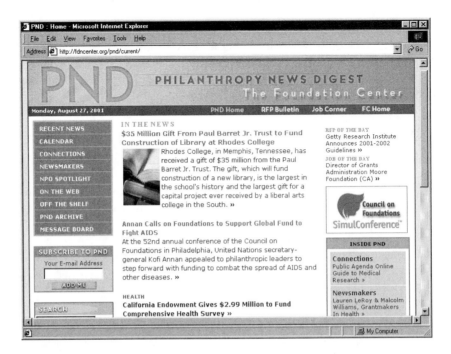

The front page of *PND* features two stories of the day followed by six to ten news headlines. Clicking on any headline on the page takes you to an abstracted version of that story, with a citation to the print or electronic source at the bottom in case you want to follow up with further research.

Besides keeping grantseekers and others abreast of recent and significant developments in the world of philanthropy, the abstracts in *PND* are accompanied by FCnotes, snapshot information regarding grantmakers mentioned in each article. This is the most current information available from the Center's database and may not yet be published in print form or available in any public database.

From the *PND* main page, you can link to several features associated with *PND*. Readers who would like to discuss and share opinions, insights, and questions related to the field of philanthropy can post to *PND*'s message board. Job seekers will find it very helpful to visit the Job Corner, which announces current full-time job openings at U.S. foundations, grantmaking public charities, and other nonprofit organizations. Those in search of grants are encouraged to consult the *RFP Bulletin,* which lists Requests for Proposals from grantmakers who are interested in funding particular types of projects. Both the Job Corner and the *RFP Bulletin* are also available via free subscription as weekly electronic newsletters. *PND*'s Newsmakers column features original *PND* news content in the form of interviews conducted with influential figures in the field of philanthropy. The NPO Spotlight highlights the interests and activities of a different nonprofit organization each week. The Connections area presents fresh links to the best the Web has to offer on issues related to the changing world of philanthropy. People seeking to continue their professional development, network with other nonprofit representatives, and learn more about the field of philanthropy may find it worthwhile to visit the Conference Calendar section, which gives the location, date, and URL of various events around the world. Finally, *PND*'s Off the Shelf (book reviews) and

On the Web (Web site reviews) sections provide recommendations of the latest online and print offerings in the nonprofit field.

Past issues of *PND* from January 1995 to the present can be searched by entering a keyword in the search box on *PND*'s Front Page. Results of your search will list the titles of abstracts, in chronological order (from most recent to oldest), in which your search terms appear. If you prefer, you can browse past *PND* issues by date, by selecting the 1995–2000 or the 2000–current archive. You can also access *PND*'s special quarterly issues that focus on a particular topic of interest to nonprofit organizations. Past topics have included international philanthropy, arts, education, and the Internet.

If you would like *PND* delivered to your e-mail box every Tuesday evening, just enter your e-mail address into the subscription box on the Front Page and click the "Add me!" button.

"I'm looking for statistics on foundation giving. Where can I find this information?"

Many excellent resources focusing on foundation giving data can be found in the Researching Philanthropy directory (http://fdncenter.org/research) of the site.

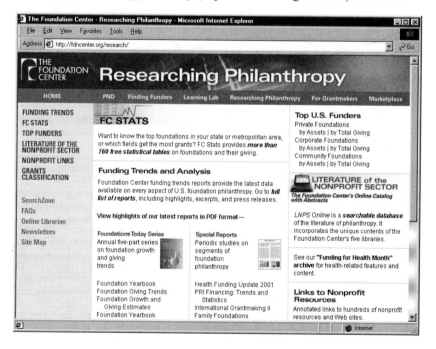

One of the most useful tools in the Researching Philanthropy directory is our FC Stats section, which can be found on the Researching Philanthropy home page. FC Stats is a free online resource that provides users with ready access to a wealth of statistical data on U.S. private and community foundations and their funding patterns. FC Stats currently offers more than 760 data tables available only from the Foundation Center. These tables and ranked lists provide the most frequently requested types of summary financial data on foundations. FC Stats is produced from the Center's research database, the authoritative national statistical data source on grantmaking foundations. The FC Stats page contains a list of the broad categories of statistical tables and ranked lists available on our Web site. To view a list of tables, click on a particular category or click on Index of Tables. If your search requires selection criteria (e.g., geographic or subject areas), click on the appropriate link to open an additional dialogue page. Tables are available in Adobe's Portable Document Format (PDF).

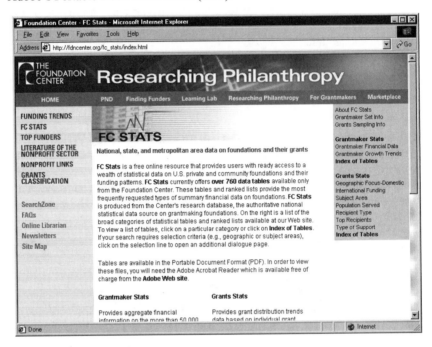

The Foundation Center's Database

The Center's research staff analyzes and interprets data on foundations stored in the Center's foundation and grants database in order to provide statistical research available on our Web site and in our other electronic and print publications. This national data source, unique for its scope, depth, and historical value, contains financial and programmatic information on the approximately 60,000 independent, corporate, community, and grantmaking operating foundations listed in the *Guide to U.S. Foundations*. In addition, it contains the 660,000 individual grant records of $10,000 or more awarded between 1990 and 1998 by a sample of larger foundations included in *The Foundation Grants Index*. These unique grant records, coded according to the Center's Grants Classification System and the National Taxonomy of Exempt Entities, provide the basis for detailed investigations of giving patterns by subject area, type of recipient, geographic location, type of support, population group, and by foundation size, type, and age.

The Foundation Center offers grantmakers, journalists, academic researchers, consultants, nonprofit executives, and many others seeking tailored information on trends in the foundation field fee-based custom statistical searches of our research database. To find out more about ordering a customized search, click on About FC Stats.

Researching Philanthropy also links you to the Funding Trends and Analysis section of the site. If you are new to this sort of research, you may find this area instructive in becoming more familiar with the foundation world and giving trends. Here you can find and view highlights of Center research publications, like the *Foundations Today* series and other special reports. Excerpts and press releases are also included. All are available in PDF format.

Site visitors can view the Center's Top Funders lists as well, which includes Top U.S. Foundations by Asset Size, Top U.S. Foundations by Total Giving, Top Corporate Grantmakers by Asset Size, Top Corporate Grantmakers by Total Giving, Largest Community Foundations by Asset Size, and Largest Community Foundations by Total Giving.

In addition, it may be useful to refer to the Foundation Center's *LNPS. LNPS* is a searchable database of the literature of philanthropy. It incorporates the unique contents of the Foundation Center's five libraries and contains more than 19,000 full bibliographic citations, of which more than 12,000 have descriptive abstracts. To further assist you in your research, there are New Acquisitions lists—including books, articles, and other resources recently added to *LNPS. LNPS* is updated on a regular basis. The following screen shot shows what a search might look like if you wanted articles from our New York library, published since 2000, on collaboration among nonprofit organizations.

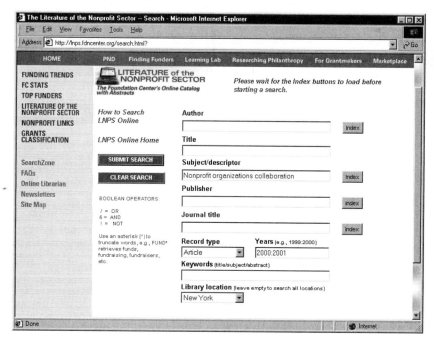

Researching Philanthropy's Links to Nonprofit Resources may be helpful as well. Links to Nonprofit Resources includes annotated links to hundreds of nonprofit resources and Web sites of interest. You may want to look through sites listed here for information from organizations doing work related to philanthropy or the Internet or for nonprofit organizations with projects similar to yours. You will find scores of links to:

- Philanthropy Resources
- Fundraising Resources
- Nonprofit Sector Information and News
- Nonprofit Resources, by Program Area
- Nonprofit Management and Staffing Resources
- Nonprofit Technology Resources
- International Resources
- General Resources (Nonprofit, Private, and Public Sectors)
- Government Resources

See Chapter 8, "Other Useful Sites for Grantseekers," for a sampling of some of the sites contained in the Center's Links to Nonprofit Resources section.

Another item in the Researching Philanthropy directory is the Internet Edition of the *Grants Classification System Indexing Manual,* which details how the Center adds value to database information through its grants-indexing procedures.

In 1989, the Foundation Center adopted a classification system derived from the National Taxonomy of Exempt Entities (NTEE), a comprehensive coding scheme developed by the National Center for Charitable Statistics. NTEE establishes a unified national standard for classifying nonprofit organizations; it also provides a more concise and consistent hierarchical method to classify and index grants. NTEE uses two- or three-character alphanumeric codes to track institutional fields and entities, governance or auspices, population groups, and religious affiliations. The universe of institutional fields is organized into 26 "major field" areas. While based on NTEE, the Foundation Center's grants classification system added indexing elements not part of the original taxonomy, including sets of codes to classify types of support, population groups served, and for international grants, geographic focus and recipient country.

"I represent a grantmaking organization. What does the Center's site offer me?"

While many of the Foundation Center's resources and services cater to grantseekers, grantmakers are an important audience as well. We have a variety of offerings in our For Grantmakers directory (http://fdncenter.org/for_grantmakers/) tailored to your special information needs.

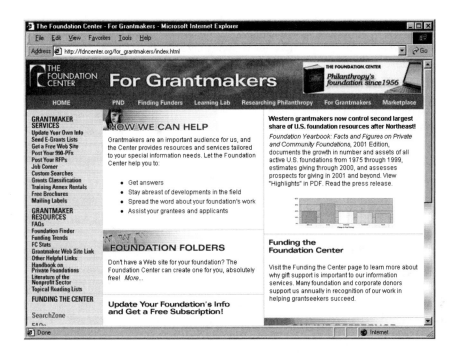

The Foundation Center is the place to find information and to communicate about institutional philanthropy. Our materials are used by grantseekers, the media, policymakers, and researchers to learn about funding programs and activities. As part of your efforts to present the work of your grantmaking organization, we encourage you to send us information about your funding programs and grants for distribution through our print and electronic publications and our Web site.

We offer eligible grantmakers free space on our Web site as part of the Center's Foundation Folder initiative. It is the Center's goal to encourage more grantmakers to develop a Web presence and to put more funding information before a wider audience. Any domestic independent, community, or company-sponsored foundation, grantmaking public charity, or affinity group can have a folder—that is, a Web site—on the Center's Web server at no charge. The Foundation Center has created folders for more than 100 grantmakers, many of which have used their folders as stepping stones to creating and maintaining Web sites on their own.

At a foundation's request we will also scan and post Form 990-PF. With new rules in effect for public availability of private foundations' information reports to the IRS (the Form 990-PF), many foundations have expressed interest in placing multiple years of their Form 990-PF on the Web in a timely fashion. The Center posts foundation Forms 990-PF in PDF format as part of the Foundation Folders initiative. In this format, the Form 990-PF has the appearance of the tax return filed with the IRS and thus meets the IRS regulations for making this document widely available to the public.

For a fee, Center staff can create mailing labels to help you distribute your materials, such as annual reports and press releases, to other grantmakers. We can also send you free sets of mailing labels for our more than 200 Cooperating Collections.

As part of *PND,* the Center posts grantmakers' Requests for Proposals, organized by subject area, every week. *PND* also features a Job Corner where you can list current full-time job openings at your organization. You may e-mail us a copy of a news item, RFP, or job description; you may also send it to us on disk via regular mail.

The Foundation Center's Web site is a ready-made system for distributing the most current information about your programs to grantseekers, policymakers, and observers of philanthropy. From your desktop, you can update the information about your grantmaking organization seen by the thousands of Web visitors who use Foundation Finder or who subscribe to *The Foundation Directory Online.* Our *Foundation Directory Online* Updater can be accessed by selecting the "Update Your Own Info" link within the For Grantmakers directory.

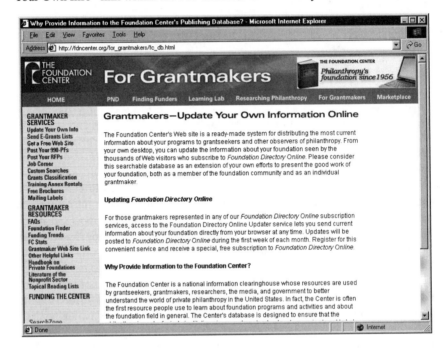

Our database of foundation grants enables grantseekers and grantmakers to identify grants made in specific areas, and it is the basis of our research on giving patterns. Electronic grants lists are an efficient way to send us specific grants information as it is described in your own systems. Several commercial software vendors have grants-tracking products that fully support our electronic grants reporting standard, but we can accept a variety of other electronic formats as well. If you are preparing to convert to a new system, we can also advise you on how to join with other foundations in adopting our classification system for your own grant records. To find out more about electronic reporting or grants classification, click on the Send E-Grants Lists and Grants Classification links from the left menu of the For Grantmakers page.

The Foundation Center offers custom searches, designed according to your specifications, of our research database. These searches can help you prepare a report for your board, identify funding partners, research philanthropic assets and giving in your locality, investigate possible new areas of funding activity, and identify potential grantees. Our database contains information on approximately 60,000 U.S. private and community foundations plus corporate giving programs and records for grants of $10,000 or more awarded by more than 1,000 of the largest foundations annually. We can perform database searches for grantmakers who want to assess philanthropic giving in a specific region or state, map funding patterns, or locate grantmakers active in a particular field. There is a charge for this service based on the data requested and staff time required. Center donors receive a discount.

Free brochures describing our various services to grantseekers are available for you to send on to applicants whose projects your foundation is unable to fund or to grantees who need to research additional funding sources.

If you have further questions about the Foundation Center and its offerings, we have compiled a special list of Grantmakers' FAQs that may prove useful to you. You may also e-mail reference questions to our Online Librarian, who will respond to you, typically within one to two business days.

There are many other Web-based resources for grantmakers beyond our own offerings, and we have compiled a list of these as well. If you select "Other Helpful Links" from the left menu of the For Grantmakers page, you will see a series of annotated links sorted into categories, such as philanthropy resources, nonprofit resources, and government resources. Web sites of regional associations of grantmakers (RAGs) and other grantmaker membership organizations are included in this listing.

Grantmakers may also wish to learn more about how they can help the Foundation Center continue to carry out its mission. For this purpose, we have developed a directory called Funding the Center (http://fdncenter.org/fundfc) that contains information about the Center's operations and the services and resources we provide to the nonprofit field. While we cover more than half of our operating budget through earned income, approximately 600 foundations and corporations provide annual support, which enables us to sustain and strengthen our existing programs. About 200 of our annual donors designate their gifts for one of our four regional offices. Special project grants permit us to develop new capacities for service.

"How can I learn about and/or purchase Foundation Center products?"

In addition to operating libraries that provide directories of grantmaker information, nonprofit literature collections, and other tools to aid grantseekers, the Foundation Center sells print, electronic, and Web-based publications about grantmakers, grantmaking in specific subject fields, nonprofit management, fundraising, and philanthropy, all of which can be ordered from the Marketplace (http://fdncenter.org/marketplace).

If you are not near a Center library or Cooperating Collection, or if you have an ongoing need for information on grantseeking, you may want to purchase Center products to continue your research. The Marketplace enables visitors to our Web site to review detailed descriptions of print and electronic products published by the Foundation Center.

If you have a particular title, author, or subject in mind, you can search our entire catalog by entering keywords into the Search Products box at the top of the left menu. Search results retrieved in response to the keywords you entered are clickable and will take you directly to the products whose descriptions best match your search terms. You can also browse our listings by product category—Funding Directories and Databases (National, Regional, International, and Subject), Fundraising, Nonprofit Management, and Research.

Once you click on a particular title, each product entry contains a detailed description of the product, its price, publication date, number of pages, and an Add to Cart button that lets you place the product in a virtual Shopping Cart. The Shopping Cart holds all the items you put aside to purchase until you have finished your search, and it lets you pay for them all at once via credit card on a secure server. You may change the desired quantity of each item in your shopping cart, and you may also remove an item by clicking the Remove box. Once you have completed any changes, click Recalculate before checking out.

Providing you with a secure online shopping experience is important to the Foundation Center. We recognize that security is an essential aspect of any online transaction, and we want to assure you that your credit card and personal information are safeguarded. To protect your credit card transaction, the Foundation Center uses industry-standard encryption software.

If you would prefer not to place an order online, just click on Print Order Form in the left menu of the Marketplace. The form will be displayed in PDF format, and it can be mailed or faxed to the Foundation Center using the contact information given.

Thousands of grantseekers take advantage of our Web-based *Foundation Directory Online* subscription service to find funders fast, benefit from monthly updating and user-friendly tools, and enjoy the convenience of round-the-clock access. Flexible monthly, annual, and multi-user subscription plans contribute to *The Foundation Directory Online*'s popularity.

Clicking on the Training Courses link in the Marketplace pulls up detailed information on the Center's fee-based seminars and training, which include proposal writing seminars, *FC Search* basic and advanced courses, and *Grantseeking on the Web* training programs. Online registration is available for all fee-based programs, which are offered in various cities throughout the country.

Fundraising professionals who would like assistance from the Center with custom research may wish to consider joining our Associates Program. Associates Program membership is a cost-effective way to supplement your staff with additional fundraising support services. Our expert researchers access the most up-to-date information in the Center's publishing and Form 990-PF databases as well as in many other resources. To find out more, click on Associates Program at the bottom of the left menu.

"What do the Center's five libraries offer to nonprofits in their region?"

If you live near one of the Center's five libraries (Atlanta, Cleveland, New York, San Francisco, and Washington, D.C.), you may want to visit that library's own home page to find out about hours, local services, and upcoming events, including training seminars and workshops. Links to each of the library home pages are accessible from the Center's home page.

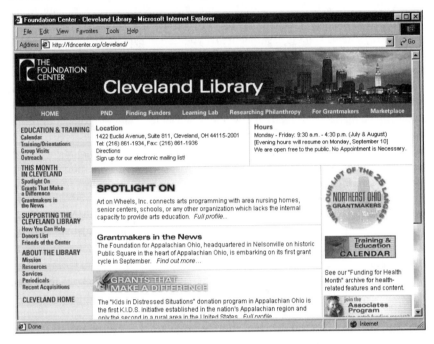

The home page of each library also serves as a source of news about local grantmaking and nonprofit activities. Three frequently updated regional features, which are presented on each library's Web site, are Spotlight On, Grantmakers in the News, and Grants That Make a Difference.

Spotlight On, which is updated at least once a month, describes the activities of different 501(c)(3) nonprofit organizations serving the regional area in which each Center library is located. The selection of organizations for Spotlight On is based on criteria such as programmatic interests, geographic focus, and size to ensure the broadest possible representation of the region's nonprofit sector.

At least once a month, Grantmakers in the News highlights regional grantmaking organizations that have undertaken new endeavors, experienced changes in their program focus or staff, participated in an interview with a Center representative, or announced their most recent award recipients.

Grants That Make a Difference features grants given to regional nonprofits that have helped make a difference in people's lives. At least once a month, Grants That Make a Difference profiles these important grants and what their recipients are doing with the funds as models for others to emulate.

At our five Foundation Center libraries, we offer free educational programs on the fundraising process, proposal writing, grantmakers and their giving, and related topics. Each library home page has a three-month training calendar, and you can register online for many of these programs. You may wish to subscribe to the free e-mail newsletter of the Center library nearest you for announcements of upcoming events and training sessions. To do this, click on Newsletters from any page on the left menu of the Center's site. Our library home pages also feature informative lead articles and new acquisitions in the monthly library newsletters, announcements of upcoming local events, and such items as up-to-date lists of the top 50 grantmakers in a particular region.

Conclusion

The Foundation Center's Web site, like the Foundation Center itself, is a multiple-access gateway to the foundations and other grantmakers who share your interest in a common cause. You should leave the Center's Web site closer to your goal of finding the funds you seek to carry out your work. The Center's site, through its information resources and organized Web link libraries, will also inform a variety of audiences about the philanthropic field in general. With an ever-increasing number of interactive features, the Foundation Center's Web site is a communication system for the field of philanthropy.

CHAPTER TWO

Independent Foundations on the Web

In 1999, 70 percent of the 100 largest foundations and roughly 400 of the more than 50,000 independent foundations in the United States had a Web site or "presence"—and only a handful of these foundations accepted proposals or applications online. At the beginning of the year 2001 approximately 80 percent of the 100 largest foundations and 1,578 of the more than 50,000 independent foundations had a Web site—and the majority of the 100 top foundations now have grant funding information on the Web, accessible to grantseekers. Some even have online application forms.

The stream of electronic communication, via e-mail, has also become a very important tool for both foundations and grantseekers. E-mail has made it easy for people in different locations to come together in ways that were not thought possible only five years ago. More than 2,000 foundations have e-mail addresses where general questions and application inquiries can be submitted. In many instances, the e-mail address will belong to a grant administrator or an information specialist.

Even with the strides made by private foundations in the last couple of years, the philanthropic field still lags behind the private sector. This is especially evident among newly established independent foundations. As the for-profit sector quickly adapts to the revolutionary impact of the Internet, the majority of newly established independent foundations have yet to take full advantage of the possibilities that the World Wide Web has to offer in terms of exposure, marketing, and public relations. In the past two years, more than 4,000 independent foundations have been established. Of this number fewer than 60 have a Web site or "presence" and only 43 have an e-mail address. Factors such as inadequate funds or lack of resources may account for the failure of newly established foundations to take full advantage of the Internet. Yet newly established independent foundations are probably among the best candidates to call upon the World Wide Web as an effective instrument for communication and exposure.

Many of those foundations that have taken advantage of the Internet are starting to utilize their Web sites in constructive, truly communicative ways. A number of foundations now post their quarterly and annual reports, newsletters, guidelines, grants listings, and even electronic application forms online. In this chapter, we'll look at Web sites of independent foundations that are using their Web sites in unique ways to delineate their mission and services more effectively to grantseekers online. Our review isn't meant to be comprehensive, nor is it intended as the final word on the subject. Our intent is to inform rather than critique, while at the same time highlighting practices and trends that seem to hold promise for foundations, the nonprofit sector, society in general, and grantseekers in particular.

Grants Information on Foundation Web Sites

In the past few years there has been an increase in the number of foundations that list some or all of their recent grants on their sites. Some sites offer grants information in the form of browsable listings. Several foundations offer grants information through searchable databases accessible directly from their sites, while others provide both. The following examples should give you a better idea of how different foundations are using the Web to communicate to grantseekers more effectively about their funding areas of interest.

Information on grantees of the Seattle-based Bullitt Foundation (http://www.bullitt.org) can be browsed by alphabetical listing, service area, program priority area, or issue. Grantee profiles include a description of the organization and contact information, including address, phone and fax numbers, e-mail addresses, and URLs. A description of the grant itself is also provided.

Two examples of searchable grants databases can be found on the Web sites of the W.K. Kellogg Foundation (http://www.wkkf.org) and the Graham Foundation for Advanced Studies in the Fine Arts (http://www.grahamfoundation.org).

The W.K. Kellogg Foundation describes the goals for its site as follows: "The purpose of this site is to inform potential grantees and others about the W.K. Kellogg Foundation's mission and current programming interests and to communicate and disseminate lessons learned, to people worldwide who share similar interests and concerns and might benefit from the foundation's knowledge and experience." In support of these ends, the W.K. Kellogg Foundation has created a searchable grants database organized around four different search approaches. By selecting Search Grants Database, you are taken to an online form where you can enter your search terms. You may also choose to browse the database by thematic coding, country, or grantee. Thematic coding allows you to browse through active grants that share the same coding within the Kellogg Foundation's system. Selecting country lets you browse according to grantee location, and the grantee option allows you to look for grants associated with a specific grantee's name.

The Chicago-based Graham Foundation for Advanced Studies in the Fine Arts clearly states the goals for its new searchable grants feature: "We have put this [grants] data online in a searchable form because we intend these abstracts to be utilitarian data rather than only historical records." The searchable grants database allows the grantseeker to search by subject, medium, or year.

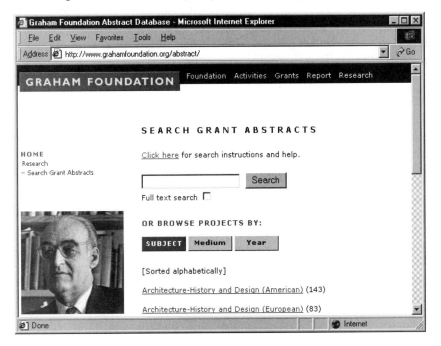

The Ford Foundation (http://www.fordfound.org), the Charles Stewart Mott Foundation (http://www.mott.org), and the Pew Charitable Trusts (http://www.pewtrusts.com) also offer searchable grants databases on their Web sites.

Many foundations also provide their grants listings online through an electronic version of their annual report. Two examples of this approach can be found at the Web sites of the Bradley Foundation (http://www.bradleyfdn.org) and the J.A. and Kathryn Albertson Foundation (http://web1.twt.jkaf.org/index.html). Both foundations offer the public the ability to obtain grants listings through a downloadable PDF version of their annual reports, which can then be viewed or printed at the grantseeker's convenience.

When you come across foundation Web sites in the course of your funding research, check to see whether there is a browsable or searchable grants database. It can help you quickly determine whether your organization's needs match the giving patterns of the foundation you are interested in approaching.

The Application Process Online

As the Internet rapidly becomes the preferred mode of worldwide communication, foundations have finally begun to use their Web sites to facilitate the application process. Some foundation Web sites offer downloadable application forms, which can be printed out, filled in, and then mailed. Others have a Web form that can be filled out online and submitted directly from the site. Most foundation Web sites that have application materials available online make a great deal of other information regarding their past giving and program areas available as well. This helps to provide grantseekers with a clearer view of who is eligible for funding and who should continue by submitting an application. In most cases, the application form serves more as a letter of inquiry than it does as a full proposal. This helps a grantmaker quickly determine whether you have done your homework and checked the guidelines and eligibility criteria made available on its site before submitting a full proposal. The following is a sampling of foundation Web sites that we've selected to illustrate the variations you may encounter.

After GTE and Bell Atlantic merged to become Verizon, a new foundation was launched in July 2000 to serve the nonprofit community—the Verizon Foundation (http://foundation.verizon.com). The Verizon Foundation is the first foundation to accept proposals and application forms online and only online. The foundation also encourages communication between grantseekers and community affairs managers in different geographical areas. Upon entering the foundation's Web site, you are given the option of viewing its grantmaking areas and public information in either English or Spanish, demonstrating the foundation's awareness of the diverse communities it serves.

Verizon's full application is available as a Web form in the Partnership Opportunities area and can be completed in approximately 45 minutes, according to the instructions. You can download a sample copy of the application to get an idea of what type of information will be required. Look carefully at the grants guidelines that provide information on eligibility criteria, how and when to apply, and a helpful hints and suggestions list. Before submitting the application form, you should take Verizon's interactive eligibility quiz. FAQs are also available to help you find the answers to basic questions you may have.

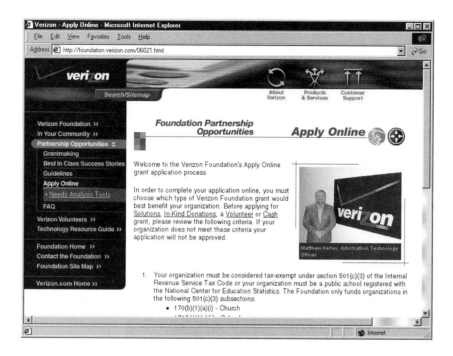

In Your Community is an interactive section of the Verizon site where you can learn about the foundation's support in your area by entering your zip code. You will find contact information for a Verizon Foundation Director of Community Affairs, a listing of grants and in-kind donations made in your specific community, and a quick form you can fill out to join an e-mail service notifying you of news, events, and special invitations to programs in your geographic area.

The Verizon Foundation has five priority funding areas: basic and computer literacy, the digital divide, workforce development, community technology development, and employee volunteerism. The foundation offers four different types of support: E-solutions, in-kind donations, volunteer support, and cash grants. E-Solutions offer technological training and support solutions for major national nonprofits with multiple points of operation throughout the United States. This grantmaking program gives the nonprofit community new tools for innovative philanthropic solutions, including a needs analysis tool that measures your organization's technology needs and "e-trainings," which are designed to close the digital divide through live training programs. Organizations interested in e-training must apply and submit to a review by the foundation.

In 2001, the Verizon Foundation became the recipient of the Council on Foundations' Wilmer Shields Rich Award for best corporate foundation Web site.

The Web site of the J. Paul Getty Trust (http://www.getty.edu/grant/apply) makes available downloadable copies of its application forms for postdoctoral fellowships, collaborative research grants, and curatorial research fellowships. You will also find listings of recent grants, back to 1995.

The California Endowment (http://www.calendow.org), in Woodland Hills, California, offers at its Web site an applicant cover sheet and a sample budget format available online as an image and in PDF format. There is also an online form to order application information through the mail (you can also order the annual report) and a mechanism for sending feedback.

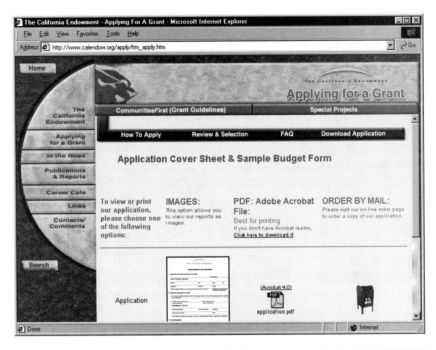

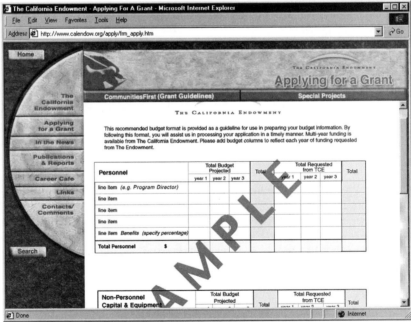

The Edward E. Ford Foundation (http://www.eeford.org), in Washington, D.C., keeps its online application information in a password-protected area on its site. Instructions read: "Schools and associations which have secured a place on an agenda for consideration by the Board of the Foundation will be issued a password to be entered below to access specific directions and necessary forms for submitting a proposal." Check the annual report or areas of interest to help determine your organization's eligibility.

The Livermore, California-based Fannie and John Hertz Foundation (http://www.hertzfndn.org) offers on its Web site an interactive application form that states "Applications are normally submitted in electronic form via the Internet. Paper application materials for those lacking Internet access may be obtained (without prejudice) from the Foundation by telephonic request." To begin the application process, registration is required.

Foundation for the Future (http://www.futurefoundation.org), in Bellevue, Washington, makes a preliminary application form available on its site. Another Washington-based grantmaker, the Brainerd Foundation (http://www.brainerd.org), which is dedicated to "protecting the environment of the Pacific Northwest," offers a great deal of information on its site, including online application forms for its Opportunity Fund Grants and Program Grants programs, proposal and reporting requirements, and a searchable grants database that catalogues past grant awards from 1998 to the present.

The Frank Stanley Beveridge Foundation's Web site (http://www.beveridge.org) is designed ". . . to determine whether your organization is eligible to receive grants from the Foundation." The site has an interactive six-step survey you can take to help determine your eligibility. Click on Determining Your Eligibility to start the survey. It queries potential grantees on their "types of support interest" and asks them to click on a map of the United States to determine if they fall within the foundation's geographic focus. If you qualify, you are taken to an electronic preliminary grant proposal. If approved, a printed grant proposal abstract and grant proposal guidelines will be mailed to you. If you do not qualify, you will receive notification to that effect.

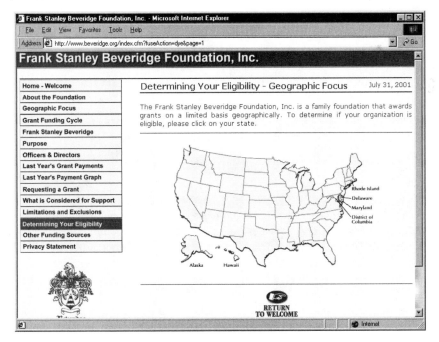

Portals, Content Aggregators, and Information-Rich Sites

A number of foundations have developed Web sites that go well beyond presenting information about their own programs. These sites offer educational and advocacy materials in support of the causes that the foundation cares about.

In the field of health care, for example, the Princeton, New Jersey-based Robert Wood Johnson Foundation (http://www.rwjf.org), the Henry J. Kaiser Family Foundation (http://www.kff.org) in Menlo Park, California, and the New York City-based Charles A. Dana Foundation (http://www.dana.org) use their sites to inform people about issues addressed by their grantmaking programs. The Dana Foundation's Web site, for instance, offers extensive information about programs, activities, foundation publications, and "material of interest to anyone concerned about brain disorders and about innovative reforms that strengthen early education." The Dana BrainWeb is a directory of links to Web sites in multiple categories related to brain disease and disorder. Additional links are added quarterly.

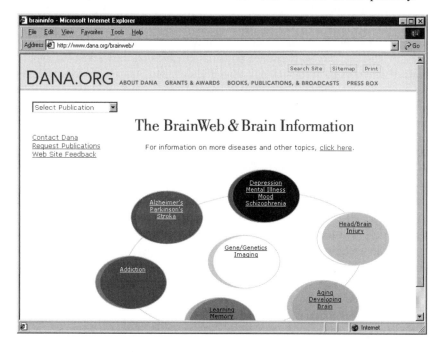

In another presentation, the Baltimore-based Annie E. Casey Foundation's Web site (http://www.aecf.org) provides a range of interactive features for those that serve disadvantaged children. The KidsCount section of the site offers statistical data in state-by-state profiles, graphs (state indicators graphed over time), maps, rankings, and raw data downloadable in a number of file formats. The Family to Family initiative offers tools for meeting the challenges of the child welfare system. Resources include a one-page fact sheet, a multi-page summary, a full implementation guide (requires registration), related links, and an online publications order form. Visitors can also access information on a range of other Casey Foundation initiatives—Casey Family Services, Juvenile Detention Alternatives, Mental Health Initiative for Urban Children, Education Reform, Jobs Initiative, State and Local Systems Reform, Rebuilding Communities, Neighborhood

Transformation/Family Development, Reforming City-Level Systems, Baltimore, and Assessing the New Federalism.

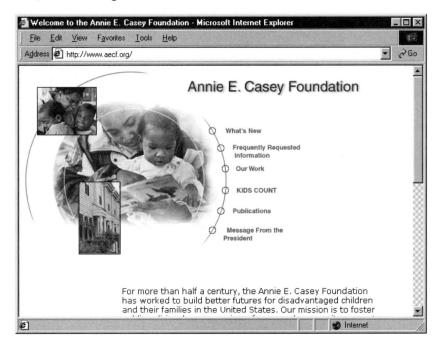

The Web site of the Washington, D.C.-based Benton Foundation (http://www.benton.org) is designed to connect people to the information and resources they need to make a difference in their communities and to use information technologies more effectively. Benton's site offers headlines, feature articles, recent publications, and e-newsletters and listservs, all designed to assist nonprofit organizations in their work. The foundation offers separate Web sites providing information on its many programmatic areas. These include Strategic Communications in the Digital Age, Communications Policy & Practice, Connect for Kids, The Digital Divide Network, One World US, Open Studio: The Arts Online (a partnership with the National Endowment for the Arts), and Sound Partners for Community Health.

The Gill Foundation (http://gillfoundation.org) in Denver, Colorado, takes information provision one step further by providing sample grant proposals in three formats (HTML, PDF, MS Word). The site also provides grantwriting workshop handouts (sponsored by the Gay and Lesbian Fund for Colorado), news releases and publications, donor and employment resources, and sample documents on employment non-discrimination policy, non-piracy software policy, and fiscal sponsorship. The OutGiving area of the site provides resources for "becoming a better donor and organization builder for your community," including opportunities for training/coaching workshops. OutGiving's Helping Hands offers numerous resources in HTML, PDF, and MS Word format, including audit tools for nonprofits, money-raising resources (including a sample corporate recognition benefits form and a list of 25 ideas for publicity about corporate sponsorship), and resources for writing better grants.

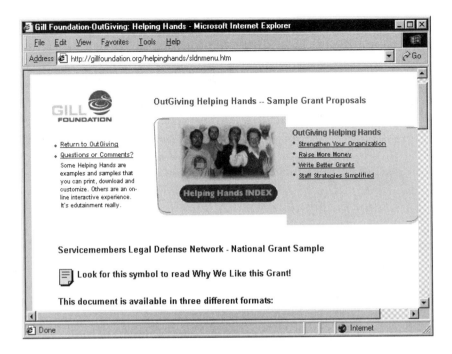

These are but a few examples of today's foundation Web sites that go beyond the mere provision of basic information about the foundations themselves. These sites demonstrate the trend of a growing number of foundations that are truly committed to using the Web to enhance their relationships with grantees and potential grantees.

Online Resource Information Centers

The Internet also has revolutionized the availability of online information to educate and inform the public about the activities of foundations. While these are not foundation Web sites per se, they may be the Web sites of a grantmaker association or membership group. They offer useful tools for unearthing information on foundations, how they work, and the people that manage them.

GrantSmart (http://www.grantsmart.org) is an informational and interactive resource center for and about the nonprofit community. Operated by Canyon Research and funded by the J.C. Downing Foundation, GrantSmart has gathered data about private foundation activities that may be of interest to grantseekers, philanthropic organizations, and individual donors. Its searchable online database allows users to access IRS Forms 990-PF filed by private foundations. You can search more than 60,000 returns by name, location, or asset size of the organization. GrantSmart and the Foundation Center have entered a collaborative partnership that makes the GrantSmart search engine available through the Form 990-PF Search feature at the Foundation Center's Web site. Foundation tax returns from the GrantSmart database are also accessible through links included in entries in the Center's Foundation Finder and *Foundation Directory Online* applications. GrantSmart also hosts a complete database of all Section 527 organizations that have filed IRS Form 8871, "Notice of Section 527 Status for Political

Organizations." Form 8871 lists contribution and expenditure information for political organizations.

The Council on Foundations (http://www.cof.org), a nonprofit membership association of grantmaking foundations and corporations, offers comprehensive philanthropic information on foundations geared to the interests of its grantmaking audience. The mission of the Council is to serve the public good by promoting and enhancing responsible and effective philanthropy. For more than 50 years, the Council on Foundations has helped foundation staff, trustees, and board members in their day-to-day grantmaking activities. Through one-to-one technical assistance, research, publications, conferences and workshops, legal services, and a wide array of other services, the Council addresses the important issues and challenges that face foundations and corporate funders.

The Council maintains an informational Web site that highlights seven primary types of nonprofit philanthropic organizations: community foundations, corporate foundations/giving programs, family foundations, private operating foundations, private independent foundations, public foundations, and international programs. The site is user-friendly, with targeted links focusing on foundations and their operation. At the Council's site you will find information on how to start a foundation and about Council publications and e-newsletters. Much of the site is available only to Council members, but some sections are open to anyone.

Each year the Council organizes workshops and lectures aimed at educating the public, policymakers, and members of the nonprofit sector about advancements or obstacles facing the philanthropic sector. In 2000 and 2001, the Council offered an Internet SimulConference featuring Webcast discussions and foundation-supported initiatives surrounding the Council's annual conference in Philadelphia.

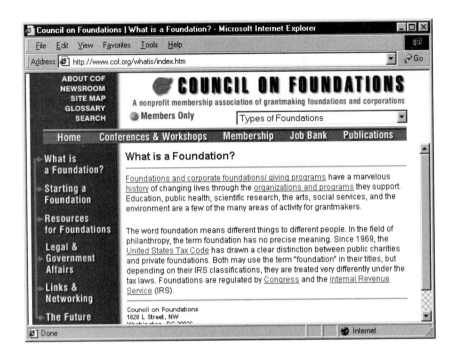

The Forum of Regional Associations of Grantmakers (http://www.rag.org) is a membership organization of 28 of the nation's largest regional associations of grantmakers, also known collectively as RAGs. RAGs themselves are associations of area grantmakers, representing more than 3,400 local grantmakers nationwide, who affiliate to enhance the effectiveness of private philanthropy in their regions. The Forum's Web site serves as a national network for other colleague organizations that collaborate with RAGs around the country. The Forum helps RAGs in providing local leadership to grantmakers in four important areas: New Ventures in Philanthropy, Public Policy, Communications/Technology, and Measuring Effectiveness. New Ventures in Philanthropy provides initiatives to help promote the creation of new foundations and corporate giving programs, and encourage new donors to endow philanthropic funds whose income and/or principal will be used for grantmaking. It does so in part by awarding grants to coalitions or organizations that promote the full range of options available for establishing foundations, giving programs, and other grantmaking funds. Measuring Effectiveness provides resources for nonprofit organizations to measure the effectiveness of funded programs, including a link to InnoNet (http://www.innonet.org), which offers an interactive evaluation tool. On the site, you will find a complete list of RAGs in the United States, information on international RAGs, and common grant application/report forms used by member RAGs. The Forum conducts research and studies of interest to those seeking information on new ventures in charitable giving. The Forum also publishes an electronic quarterly update, in its members only section, for board members and other key volunteers of its member RAGs.

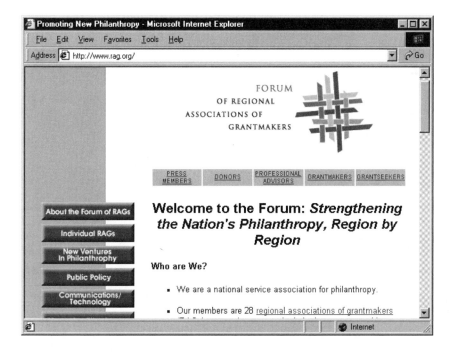

Conducting Online Funding Research Using the Foundation Center's Web Site

Going directly to individual foundation Web sites is most useful if you have already identified them as potential funders of your work. In order to facilitate your online funding research, the Finding Funders section of the Foundation Center's Web site offers several search features you can use to locate Web sites of funders you have identified as potential supporters. Two of the more useful are the Grantmaker Web Sites and Sector Search features. Grantmaker Web Sites and Sector Search offer two similar, yet distinct, ways of finding potential funders active on the World Wide Web. Both are searchable databases of the more than 1,700 grantmakers that currently have Web sites, and both allow you to search by grantmaker type.

Grantmaker Web Sites offers annotated links to hundreds of grantmaker Web sites, divided into four searchable categories: private independent foundations, grantmaking public charities, community foundations, and corporate grantmakers. The grantmaker search engine allows you to search annotations created by Center staff for grantmakers by subject and geographic keyword, making it possible for you to assemble a list of grantmakers on the Web that may be able to address your specific funding needs.

Sector Search, by contrast, is similar to a general search engine, in that it lets you search for keywords on individual Web pages. You can tailor your search to a specific grantmaker type or you can use the Advanced Search feature for a higher degree of specificity.

Remember, however, that even though these two tools represent the most complete listing of foundations on the Web, your search will be restricted to those funders with some sort of Web presence—currently, around 1,700 grantmakers of the more than 60,000 tracked by the Foundation Center. In other words, unlike the information in the Center's print directories, the *FC Search* CD-ROM, and *The Foundation Directory Online,* the comprehensiveness of the annotations in our Finding Funders directory depends solely on the availability and breadth of the online resources themselves. As more grantmakers join the online community, the Center will continue to expand its list of searchable site annotations.

(See Chapter 1 for a thorough description of Grantmaker Web Sites and Sector Search, and all of our other Web site features.)

Foundations on the Web: Design and Functionality

In terms of design, Web sites can be placed on a "generational" continuum, a concept originated by David Siegel, influential author of *Creating Killer Web Sites* (Indianapolis: Hayden Books). At one end of the scale, says Siegel, are "first-

---

What are Forms 990-PF and where can I find them?

To find detailed information on foundations that do not have Web sites or issue annual reports (most do not), you will need to refer to their IRS return, Form 990-PF. The IRS requires that every private foundation file a Form 990-PF each year. IRS returns provide basic financial data, a complete grants list, the names of the foundation's trustees and officers, and other information on the foundation. The Form 990-PF may be the only source where you will find complete grants lists for smaller foundations. The amount of detail provided on each grant will vary from foundation to foundation.

In March 2000, new disclosure regulations went into effect that require foundations to provide, at a "reasonable fee," photocopies of their three most recent tax returns—including Form 990-PF and Form 4720—as well as their original application for tax-exempt status to anyone who requests them in person or in writing. As with other tax-exempt organizations, the requirements can be satisfied by private foundations making the documents "widely available" over the Internet. Unlike other tax-exempt organizations, however, foundations will be required to make the names and addresses of their donors available to the public. Foundations will not be required to fulfill requests when they are determined to be part of a campaign of harassment.

The Foundation Center is now offering online access to more than 60,000 Forms 990-PF in PDF format through Form 990-PF Search in cooperation with GrantSmart.org. You can search by name or Employer Identification Number (EIN).

You can also look at Forms 990-PF online by linking from a foundation's record in Foundation Finder. You will need all or part of a foundation's name to search using the Foundation Finder.

Center Libraries maintain a collection of current tax returns on CD-ROM. If you happen to live near a Center library, accessing the Forms 990-PF on

generation" sites, which were designed in the Web's early days for text-only terminals, black-and-white monitors, and low-resolution color displays. First-generation sites are characterized by long lines of unbroken text, default background and hyperlink colors, the liberal use of standard HTML elements (such as bulleted lists and horizontal rules), and a hierarchical information architecture. In a first-generation site, form follows function.

Second-generation sites, which began to appear in the spring of 1995, shortly after Netscape Communications announced a set of extensions to HTML, are basically first-generation sites with more color, graphical elements (navigation bars, icons, buttons, pictures, etc.), and a greater reliance on technology. In the best second-generation sites, form is elevated to the same level as function, and the user experience is enhanced as a result.

Third-generation sites use well-executed graphic design to attract and guide visitors through the site. As Siegel puts it, "Third-generation sites form a

---

CD-ROM may be quicker and more efficient since you will not have to rely on a slow Internet connection you may have at your home or office.

Forms 990-PF, whether through the Internet or on CD-ROM at Center libraries, are updated with new returns every four to six weeks.

Copies of returns may also be ordered directly from the IRS. Write to the Ogden Service Center, P.O. Box 9941, Mail Stop 6734, Ogden, Utah, 84409. Include the foundation's full name and the city and state where it is located. The IRS will bill you for the cost of the copies.

State attorneys general (http://www.naag.org/about/aglist.cfm) may have copies of Form 990-PF returns for foundations in their states as well. If the organization you are looking for is in California, the State Attorney General's office of California (http://caag.state.ca.us/charities) has begun posting California state charity and foundation tax returns (Forms CT-2, 990, 990-EZ, and 990-PF) on its Web site.

GuideStar (http://www.guidestar.org), an online database of information on the activities and finances of more than 700,000 nonprofit organizations, run by Philanthropic Research Inc., also makes foundation Forms 990-PF accessible via the Internet. To search by EIN on GuideStar, simply click on the advanced search option and you will see an EIN search field.

The typical IRS filing deadline for most foundations is approximately six months after the end of the foundation's fiscal year. It then takes another few months for the IRS to process and scan the Forms 990-PF into a digitized format. For example, if a foundation's fiscal year ended on December 31, 2000, you can expect its Form 990-PF to become available sometime in the fall of 2002. Foundations can also request a filing extension from the IRS, which can lead to further delays in the Form 990-PF becoming publicly available. For more information, see our FAQ "What is the lag time between the close of a foundation's fiscal year and the date a copy of its tax return is available in a Foundation Center library?" (http://fdncenter.org/learn/faqs/lag_time.html).

All five Center libraries and some Cooperating Collections offer training programs on demystifying the Form 990-PF.

complete experience—the more you explore, the more the entire picture of the site comes together. Third-generation design turns a site from a menu into a meal."

Siegel developed his ideas about site design in 1995–1996, long before e-commerce began to drive Web site development in new directions. Today, e-commerce and fourth-generation sites are all the rage, though out of the reach of most organizations and businesses. While still stylish and pleasing to the eye, fourth-generation sites add a layer of technology that provides, among other things, database integration, customized page generation, transactional and streaming multimedia capabilities, and, increasingly, personalization.

EXAMPLES OF GENERATIONAL FOUNDATION WEB SITES

At the first-generation end of the spectrum, for example, you'll find the Andrew W. Mellon Foundation's Web site (http://www.mellon.org). The New York City-based Mellon Foundation, one of the largest private foundations in the country, was created in 1969 by the merger of two smaller foundations established in the 1940s by Paul Mellon and Ailsa Mellon Bruce, son and daughter of Andrew W. Mellon, the formidable American financier and patron of the arts. The foundation's broadly stated purpose is to "aid and promote such religious, charitable, scientific, literary, and educational purposes as may be in the furtherance of the public welfare or tend to promote the well-doing or well-being of mankind." Its austere Web site offers a selection of public-information materials (mission statement, program descriptions and reports, abridged versions of recent annual reports, basic contact information) and a handful of links to other sites. While there's a good deal of information on the site of interest to grantseekers, anyone hoping to find a grants list or the foundation's application guidelines will be disappointed.

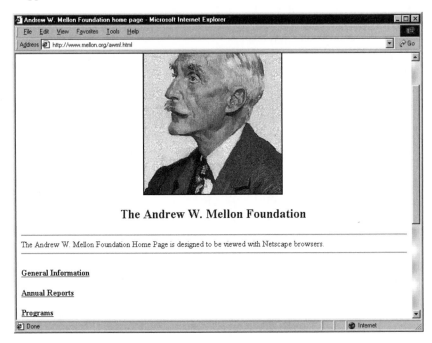

Although similarly austere in design to the Mellon site, the Annenberg Foundation's Web site (http://www.whannenberg.org) clearly reflects the St. Davids, Pennsylvania-based foundation's willingness to engage grantseekers more directly. The foundation was established in 1989 by the publisher (*TV Guide, Seventeen*) and philanthropist Walter H. Annenberg and is best known for its $500 million K–12 Challenge Grant program. It has awarded challenge grants to reform-minded school districts, local governments, and/or nonprofit stakeholders in more than a dozen cities, including Atlanta, Baltimore, Boston, Chattanooga, Chicago, Detroit, Houston, Los Angeles, Miami, New York City, Philadelphia, Salt Lake City, and San Francisco. One of the goals of the program is to replicate successful school reform programs throughout the country. One way of doing that, as the Annenberg site demonstrates, is to use the Internet's capabilities to connect people in dispersed locations to different ideas and experiences by creating links to other sites—in this case, Web sites created by stakeholders in various challenge grant locations.

The Annenberg Foundation also operates programs in math and science learning and communications policy studies. Here again it uses its Web site to make its processes more transparent to grantseekers. In addition to posting proposal guidelines, an explanation of its review procedures, and a short list of sample grants on its site, the foundation also accepts brief inquiries via e-mail.

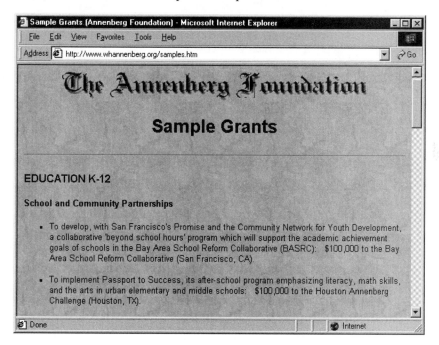

The Foundation Center's Foundation Folders Initiative

Since 1997 the Foundation Center has been helping foundations develop a Web presence through its Foundation Folders program (http://www.fdncenter.org/grantmaker/foldermenu.html). From the beginning, the program has had two goals: to provide private, community, and company-sponsored foundations with an immediate, low-cost presence on the Web and, in the process, help them become familiar with some of the issues surrounding the rapid evolution of communications technologies and media; and to put more information about foundations in front of a wider audience by making that information available on the World Wide Web. Also, starting in 2001, public charities with grantmaking programs and grantmaker affinity groups wishing to participate in the Foundation Folders program have been encouraged to do so.

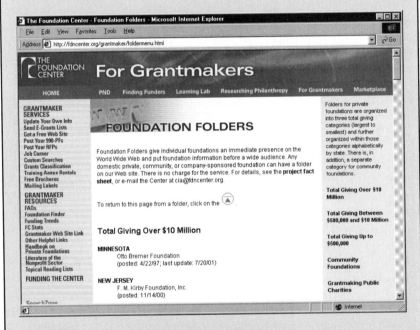

The Foundation Folders service enables eligible grantmakers (more than 100 have been created to date) to post public information materials (mission statements, program descriptions, application guidelines, grants lists, financial statements, contact information, and more) to a "folder" in the For Grantmakers area of the Center's Web site (http://www.fdncenter.org/for_grantmakers). Once a grantmaker in the program decides to establish a more permanent presence on the Web (typically, under its own unique domain name—for example, http://www.myfoundation.org), its folder on the Center's site is "retired," and a link to and description of the new site is added to the appropriate section (e.g., Grantmaker Web Sites and Sector Search) of the Finding Funders directory.

Foundation folders come in a variety of formats, from one-page fact sheets—see the folder for the Scholarships Foundation (http://fdncenter.org/grantmaker/scholarships), based in New York City—to fairly elaborate, multi-tiered mini-sites. Examples of the latter include the folder for the St. Paul-based Otto Bremer Foundation (http://fdncenter.org/grantmaker/bremer) and the Pennsylvania-based Claude Worthington Benedum Foundation (http://fdncenter.org/grantmaker/benedum).

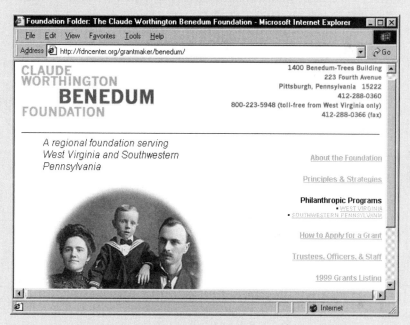

But whether a folder comprises a single page or an entire annual report, the end result is the same: the informational materials in the folder can be viewed by anyone, anywhere, who has Internet access and a Web browser. The opportunity to deliver information free on the Internet presents grantmakers—especially smaller grantmakers—with a host of challenges, and is likely to profoundly reshape the way most funders communicate with their constituencies in the next decade. At a minimum, posting public information materials to the Web ensures that those materials can be found and indexed by Web-based search engines. (See Appendix A for a listing of general search engines.) The search engines, in turn, retrieve that information, with varying degrees of effectiveness, whenever it is requested. As the information in a folder is disseminated in ever wider circles, the chances of other individuals and organizations finding and creating links to it increase. In the final analysis, it's the very simple but powerful hyperlinking capabilities of the medium that enables webs of common interest to be created and drives the exponential growth of the Web itself.

In recent years, many foundations have traded in their first-generation sites for more appealing second-generation sites. Examples of stellar second-generation Web design abound. One of the better examples belongs to the New York City-based Rockefeller Brothers Fund (RBF).

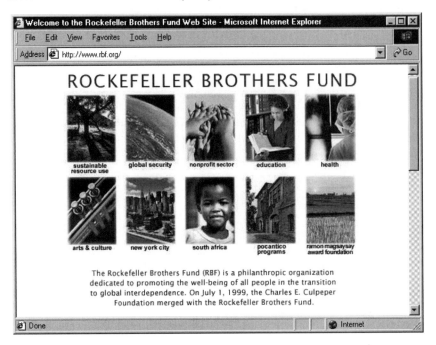

The RBF site (http://www.rbf.org) incorporates many of the hallmarks of good second-generation design—the judicious use of icons, thumbnail photos, and graphical headers; a "Web-safe" color palette; consistent navigational elements; and a well-thought-out, hierarchical architecture—with a layer of basic inter-activity to provide a satisfying, information-rich experience for grantseekers and others. Because a major objective of the Fund is to support efforts that contribute to the transition to global interdependence, the site also is offered in a fast-loading text-only version that minimizes download times and access costs for international users and others with slow and/or expensive phone connections.

Grantseekers who visit the RBF site can access a wealth of information, all logically organized and conveniently linked to relevant information located elsewhere on the site. In addition to comprehensive descriptions of Fund programs and strategies (Sustainable Resource Use, Global Security, the Nonprofit Sector, Education, Health, Arts and Culture, New York City, South Africa, and a special Asian Projects fund), the site offers lists of recent grants awarded in each program area, application guidelines, a well-organized set of links to dozens of other sites, and a list of RBF publications available free of charge via an online publications order form and, in many cases, as downloadable PDF files.

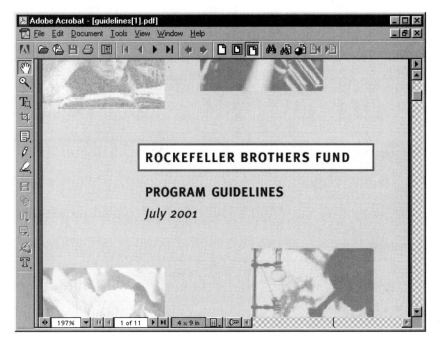

Grantseekers can see another fine example of second-generation design at the Web site of the John D. and Catherine T. MacArthur Foundation (http://www.macfnd.org), the Chicago-based foundation best known for its MacArthur Fellows Program (the so-called "genius grants"). The foundation makes grants through two major programs, Human and Community Development and Global Security and Sustainability, and two special programs—the General Program, which undertakes initiatives and supports projects that promote excellence and diversity in media, and the Fellows Program. Underlying all its programs and policies, however, are several assumptions, one of which is that the foundation's effectiveness depends on its capacity to learn from others, including its grantees.

The extent to which this assumption is embraced is underscored by the MacArthur Web site, which melds functional, low-tech design with a service-oriented approach to the foundation's audiences. Everything about the site—from its flat architecture to its use of Web-safe colors and global navigation elements—is designed to make it easy for grantseekers and other visitors to browse and find the information they're looking for. Of particular interest is the way prime real estate on the home page is used to provide shortcuts to program information, grant deadlines, and information about special grant competitions. The grouping of links to recent grants lists, program guidelines, and application instructions on most second-level pages reinforces the idea that, as far as its Web site is concerned, the foundation is committed to transparency and ease of use.

The last couple of years have seen a number of third-generation foundation Web sites come online. Large philanthropies such as the Ford Foundation (http://www.fordfound.org), the United Nations Foundation (http://www.unfoundation.org), the Open Society Institute (http://www.soros.org), and the Casey Family Program (http://www.casey.org) have unveiled meticulously designed, database-driven sites. It also has been interesting to watch the steady increase in the number of small- and medium-sized foundations that are able to leverage modest new media budgets into excellent examples of third-generation site design.

Among these are the Santa Monica, California-based Durfee Foundation (http://www.durfee.org), whose areas of interest include arts and culture, education, history, and community development, primarily in Southern California; and the Russell Sage Foundation (http://www.russellsage.org), a New York City-based operating foundation with interests in the future of work, immigration, the social psychology of cultural contact, and literacy among disadvantaged students (a joint project with the Andrew W. Mellon Foundation).

The Durfee Foundation site combines a muted, Web-safe palette with elegant graphic headers and eye-catching thumbnail graphics. The site is proof that superior Web design can be achieved, albeit on a modest scale, if the stakeholders in the site are clear at the outset about their goals for the site.

Conclusion

This brief introduction to the world of foundations on the Web is designed to give you a taste of the breadth and depth of information to be found on the various types of sites you are likely to encounter. We invite you to explore the full range of grantmaker sites available using the various search tools offered on the Foundation Center's Web site, or by other means, such as general search engines. A complete list of annotated URLs for independent foundations' Web sites will be found in Appendix B and on the Center's Web site.

CHAPTER THREE

Grantmaking Public Charities and Community Foundations on the Web

Although community foundations technically are public charities, they differ from other public charities in many respects. There is much information on the Web that provides a clear explanation of the differences. In short, for grantseekers, it is best to keep in mind that public charities have very narrowly defined interests and are not tied to a specific geographic area, while community foundations have broad interests but tend to concentrate on specified regions. Both types of public charities file Form 990 with the IRS, while private foundations file Form 990-PF. For practical purposes, paying attention to the unique features of each type of public charity can expedite grantseeking on the Web. Thus, a grant application to a public charity should emphasize the defined purpose of the project, while a grant application to a community foundation should also focus on the geographic area specified by that foundation.

What Is a Public Charity?

There are approximately 700,000 public charities registered with the IRS under Section 501(c)(3) of the Internal Revenue Code. This is more than ten times the number of private foundations. Most, of course, are not grantmakers. The relatively small number of grantmaking public charities (sometimes referred to as "public foundations") that the Center has been able to uncover differ from private foundations in several ways, primarily in their sources of support. Private foundations typically draw their funds from a single source, either an individual, a family, or a company. With the exception of those few that are endowed, the majority of public charities are supported by contributions from multiple sources, including individuals, foundations, churches, corporations, and government agencies. In some cases, income is generated from charitable activities.

There are several ways a nonprofit organization can meet the IRS definition of a public charity. One, called the "public support test," means that the organization must: a) receive no more than one-third of its support from gross investment and unrelated business income and b) receive at least one-third of its income from the public in contributions, fees, and gross receipts related to the organization's exempt purpose. A second way is for the organization to claim Automatic Public Charity Status. This status is given to organizations such as schools, churches, or hospitals that meet certain criteria. A typical example would be a church that maintains a facility for religious worship. The third way to obtain public charity status is by establishing what is called a supporting organization, or one that is organized for, and controlled by, a designated public charity (or charities). Supporting organizations have existed since 1969. They have become more popular recently because a supporting organization is not subject to the excise taxes and penalties that apply to private foundations and because the tax code provides a more liberal deduction for donations made to such an organization.

Because public charities are accountable to a broad support base, the regulations and reporting requirements for them are less stringent than they are for private foundations. Gifts to public charities are commonly eligible for maximum income tax deductibility, whereas those to private foundations are limited. Furthermore, public charities and private foundations follow different annual IRS reporting requirements.

It is important to remember that most grantmaking public charities are by definition grantseekers as well, gifts to which receive the full tax deductibility mentioned earlier. Another characteristic of grantmaking public charities is that their giving interests are typically very specific, addressing a narrow or single field of interest, a specific population group, or a limited geographic community, as is true for community foundations. For the public charities listed in this chapter, their grantmaking activity may be only a small part of their overall charitable program.

Traditionally, the Foundation Center has included community foundations in its statistical analyses and reference works about private foundations because their primary activity is grantmaking. Their more formal grantmaking operations and grant-reporting capabilities allow them to be represented logically and systematically within our databases and publications. Now that the Center is identifying and tracking other grantmaking public charities, for definitional clarity we can present community foundations as a group within the grantmaking public charity universe. The Center's links to community foundation Web sites are organized by state, as most community foundations are focused principally on a specific geographic area.

In recent years, the Foundation Center has identified more than 1,000 public charities, over and above approximately 600 community foundations, that have some sort of grantmaking program. We will not attempt to present a complete picture of the grantmaking public charity universe in this chapter. This is largely because at this time there is no simple way to systematically identify those non-private foundation charities that in fact do operate clearly defined giving programs. The Form 990, the only tool at hand, is not intended for this purpose and is only marginally helpful in this regard. We hope that our continued efforts to gather information on grantmaking public charities will stimulate those organizations that believe they qualify to be included in Center listings to contact us or forward information concerning their grantmaking programs.

Useful Web sites

There are a number of Web sites that aggregate information about the public charity universe. They are often the best starting points for your research because they present lists of useful Web links all in one location. Here are some URLs that will help you access information. Sometimes they will take you to a charity Web page, other times to a specific Web site focused on a particular aspect of your search.

Alliance of Artists' Communities (http://www.teleport.com/~aac/main.html) is a national service organization that supports the field of artists' communities and residency programs. By clicking Links on the menu, a list of organizations will pop up.

Community Foundation Locator (http://www.communityfoundationlocator.org/search/index.cfm), sponsored and maintained by the Council on Foundations, is an excellent tool for finding community foundations. Begin by clicking on a state or selecting from search options provided on the locator page. In addition to this page, as noted in the previous chapter, the Council's Web site (http://www.cof.org) provides a wealth of information about all types of grantmakers.

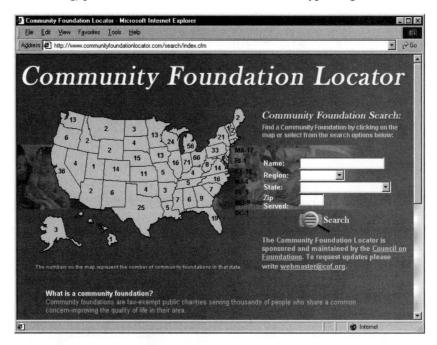

Foundations On-Line (http://www.foundations.org), a service of the Northern California Community Foundation, Inc., provides lists of community foundations, public charities, and additional sites to browse. It also provides a shortcut that can save time searching for appropriate charities.

GrantsNet (http://www.grantsnet.com), sponsored by the Howard Hughes Medical Institute and the American Association for the Advancement of Science, is a free service and an excellent source to find funding for training in the biomedical sciences and undergraduate science education.

Grantmakers in Health (http://www.gih.org) is a very good source of charity listings for grantseekers focused on health-related giving.

National Endowment for the Humanities (http://www.neh.fed.us/state/index.html) provides listings of the humanities councils maintained by all 50 states and U.S. territories. The listings are extremely useful because they describe what projects are being funded within each state or territory, and most of these sites have links that lead to other charities.

U.S. Nonprofit Organization's Public Disclosure Regulations Site (http://www.muridae.com/publicaccess) provides useful information about the regulations governing public disclosure of IRS forms concerning nonprofit organizations. It explains the different rules governing various types of nonprofits. Many areas of this site are free, but some require that you subscribe.

Looking for Funders

USING THE SEARCH CAPABILITY AT THE FOUNDATION CENTER'S WEB SITE

As noted in Chapter 1, on the Foundation Center's Web site it is possible to do structured searching of information concerning grantmaking public charities on the Web.

Grantmaker Web Sites

In the Grantmaker Web Sites area, every grantmaking public charity and community foundation listed on the Foundation Center's Web site is annotated with general information about the charity and its Web site. In the grantmaking public charities section, a time-saving search feature lets you search the text of the abstracts to learn the program interests of the charities and to become familiar with the contents of the sites without taking the time to explore them yourself. Community foundations are listed by state.

Let's say, for example, that you are interested in conservation issues and are looking for public charities or community foundations that make grants in this subject area. On the Center's Web Site, click on the Finding Funders directory and then on the left side of the following page click on the section entitled Grantmaking Public Charities or Community Foundations. Your search begins here.

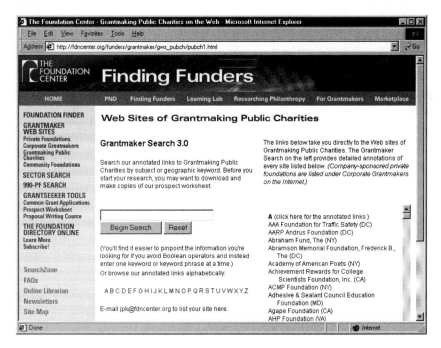

You can search grantmaking public charities by entering keyword(s) or you can simply browse the links alphabetically. Because you are interested in conservation issues, enter this term into the search box. Click the search button to perform the search. A numbered list of results will appear. Clicking on the name of any grantmaking public charity will give you a description of the charity with a link to its home page.

Sector Search
The Foundation Center also offers Sector Search (http://www.fdncenter.org/funders/web_search/web_search.html), a search engine that indexes information gathered from only the most useful nonprofit Web sites. Instead of trying to retrieve useful information from a search of the entire Web, we have programmed this software to search only the Web sites of the organization type you specify (private foundations, corporate grantmakers, grantmaking public charities, community foundations, nonprofits, or government resources), thus significantly increasing your chances of finding the information you are looking for. To search for grantmaking public charities and/or community foundations only, simply de-select the grantmaker types you wish to exclude from your search, by removing the check marks from the boxes next to those categories of grantmakers. The following screen shot shows that only the Community Foundations box remains checked.

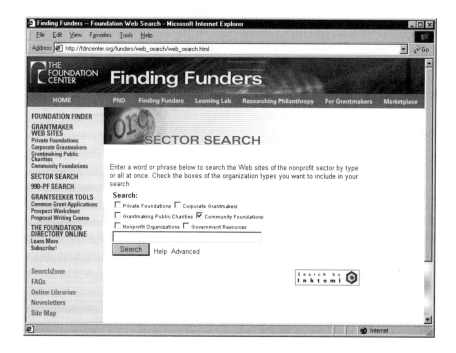

The Foundation Directory Online

For subscribers to *The Foundation Directory Online,* community foundations also will be found in all of the Foundation Center's family of *Foundation Directory Online* products, while other grantmaking public charities are covered only in the Foundation Center's *Platinum* online subscription service.

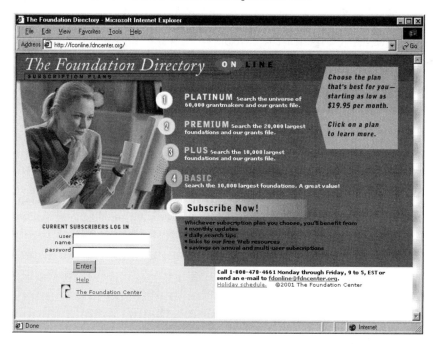

The Foundation Center continually strives to identify and describe public charities that operate grantmaking programs along with their other activities. Be sure to check the Grantmaker Web Sites, Sector Search, and *The Foundation Directory Online* areas of our Web site frequently for the latest updates. Also see Chapter 1 for a fuller description of these and all Center Web site resources.

USING A SEARCH ENGINE

An important point to keep in mind as a novice grantseeker is that searching the Web does not proceed in a straight line from point A to point B. It is very likely that in the beginning you will spend a lot of time getting used to the layered, circular approach that is required. Eventually, you will develop search strategies that suit your specific needs.

Because all search engines are not alike, it makes sense to familiarize yourself with the capabilities of each one. Where one does not provide enough information, another might. Where one delivers few "hits," another may produce thousands. When using any search engine, enter terms that best specify what you are looking for. Try to be as specific as possible. For example, if you represent an arts organization and are looking for funding for a theater, you should enter keywords such as "theater funding" or "dramatic arts" into the box next to the search button. Or you might enter "public charity," or "women's charity" as keywords if you are seeking funding for a program benefiting women. Remember, the broader the term you enter, the greater the number of search results you will receive. Because there is no immediate way to identify a grantmaking public charity, it will be necessary to investigate each site listed in the search results separately to see whether the organization actually awards grants.

If the search engine you use does not produce a satisfactory list of Web sites, you can try again, either by entering different terms or by using a different search engine altogether. Experience will enable you to learn which approach and which search engine best meets your specific research needs.

There is no substitute for a well thought-out plan for searching the Web. Discipline and persistence are required to navigate through the seemingly endless possibilities available to novice grantseekers. There are, however, several good search engines that can help you define and streamline your searches (see Appendix A).

Suggested Search Terms

Here are some specific words or phrases you may wish to include in your search strategies. Type them either separately or with another defining word in the search box. Don't stop there. Be creative. Customize your search. As you become more familiar with the kind of information you are searching for and the unique features of each search engine, add those words that appear on a regular basis to your list. You might want to begin with words such as these:

- association
- public charity
- Form 990
- fund
- community foundation
- 501(c)(3)
- arts council

- application form
- annual report
- grants list

New IRS Disclosure Rules

Revised regulations regarding the IRS Form 990 took effect on June 8, 1999. The new disclosure rule requires nonprofit organizations to respond to public requests for information by making copies available of their Forms 990 for the past three years. An organization is also required to provide a copy of its application for tax exemption (Form 1023 or 1024), if the organization filed for exemption after July 1987 or possessed a copy of its exemption application on that date. All attachments and associated schedules to the forms must be included, although non-profits do not have to provide the section listing their donor names.

Federal law has always required that most tax-exempt nonprofit organizations allow public inspection of recent, annual information returns. As a result of this new ruling, however, public access has been expanded. Copies of Forms 990 must be made readily available to anyone making a request in person to an organization's management or administrative personnel. Requests in writing must be answered within 30 days unless the organization makes these documents widely available (such as on the World Wide Web).

Organizations must comply with the regulations or face penalties. The rules also define in detail the offices of an organization to which a request may *not* be made, list circumstances under which a response can be delayed for several days, and define a circumstance of harassment (requests made to interfere with an organization's work) under which a response can be withheld.

The regulations also provide that nonprofit organizations can satisfy the "widely available" requirement by posting their Forms 990 on the World Wide Web. If an organization posts its tax return on the Web, it is free from the requirement to provide the form when requests are made in person or by mail. Because the tax form itself must be presented in its original format, most 990 documents are presented in PDF format, making the return appear as if it were a photograph. To view these files it will be necessary to have the Adobe Acrobat Reader software (available as a free download).

A Form 990 and the application for tax-exempt status are not alternatives to an annual report or an accounting audit, however. They are primarily used to help the IRS determine whether an organization qualifies for tax exemption. Secondarily, they fulfill a legal requirement for accurate financial data that is publicly available. These two legal requirements offer the public the opportunity to examine a nonprofit's financial and operational activities and heighten public accountability. Guidestar.org is one of the best places to search for a charity's Form 990. It often provides the latest tax return on file with the IRS.

USING GUIDESTAR.ORG

Finding grant money is far from easy. It usually takes many searches to find a public charity that is a grantmaker, that meets your funding criteria, and that will select your organization as an eligible recipient. You can use GuideStar to help you identify these organizations.

New Health Foundations

The dramatic increase of health conversions in the last two decades has resulted in the establishment of 138 new health foundations. These new entities were established from the sale or merger of a nonprofit hospital, health plan, or health system with another entity to become a public charity, a private foundation, or a social welfare organization. More than 45 percent of the new health foundations are public charities. The majority of these charities focus their giving on the health-related or social welfare needs of specific populations in the community that for many years were served by the facility before its conversion. For grantseekers interested in funding within the health care sector of philanthropy, the Grantmakers in Health Web site (http://www.gih.org) provides a shortcut to potential funders. An alphabetical listing of potential prospects can be accessed from this site.

GuideStar (http://www.guidestar.org) states the filing requirements of more than 700,000 nonprofit entities. Financial information is included, and for some charities program information is included. In 2000, GuideStar made all available IRS Forms 990 for public charities accessible on its site as PDF files. It is the site most commonly used by grantseekers and others seeking information on public charities.

Click on "advanced search" to use GuideStar to search by the name for the public charity or by its EIN (Employer Identification Number). You can also limit your searches by city and state, zip code, category, nonprofit type, income range, or NTEE code. Press "enter" or click "search" to submit your search, and a list of search results will appear. You may need to scroll down through a list of similar sounding names to find the specific charity you are interested in, since several

The Health Trust (http://www.healthtrust.org) of San Jose, California, is an example of a health conversion foundation with a well-developed site. Select the Site Map from the top of the page for a complete listing of the Web site's contents. You will find listings of past grant recipients and descriptions of current programs. In order to find the Trust's fiscal information for the latest tax year, you will need to refer to its Form 990 separately.

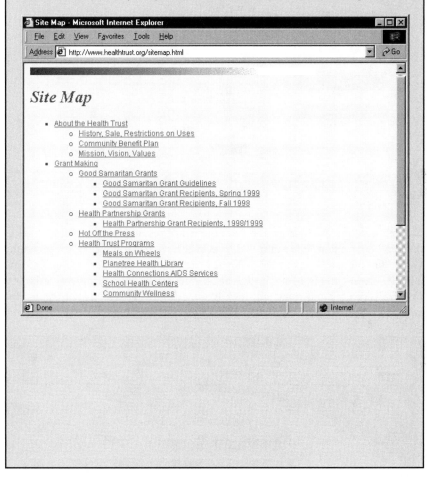

organizations may match your search criteria. When the search results page appears on the screen, you will notice five symbols in a legend across the top of the page. When these symbols appear next to an organization's name, it indicates whether there is information available about a complete report, financials, Form 990, old reports and financials, and whether the organization has a Web site. Don't rely on these notations entirely, though. If you do not see a World Wide Web icon next to the name of an organization in GuideStar, you might also want to use a search engine to try to find the Web address.

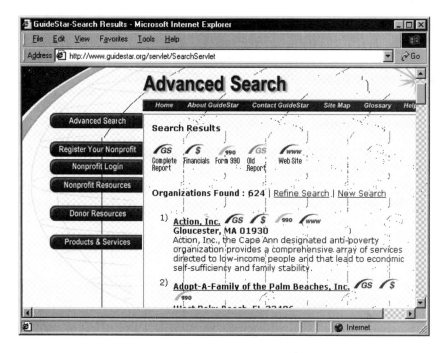

After selecting an organization from the list of results, look on the left side of the page for a menu. The Form 990, if available, is listed there. When searching GuideStar, fill in as many of the dialogue boxes as necessary. For example: to find a public charity that is an arts organization giving between $25,000 and $100,000 in New York City, the entry will look like the following screen shot. Adjust the criteria in the dialogue boxes to broaden or narrow your search.

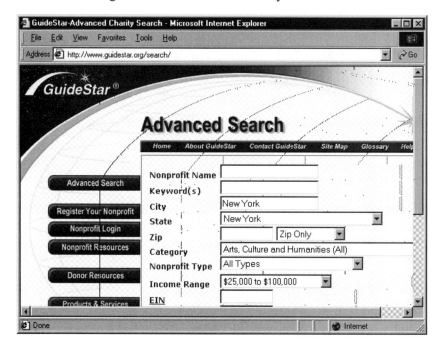

Finding Useful Information on Grantmaking Public Charity Web Sites

WEB SITE INFORMATION

An easy way to determine whether a charity is a grantmaker or not is to check whether there is a grant application form or grants list on its Web site. But don't jump to conclusions. If there is no application form or grants list on the site, the mission or program descriptions of the organization may also indicate whether it makes grants.

For public charities that appear to be grantmakers, check the annual report, if available on the site. The type of funds that the organization provides will give you an idea of your chances for getting a grant. Most funds awarded to grant-seekers come from unrestricted funds of the grantmaking organization. Grants made from restricted funds, e.g., donor-advised, or other fund, may not meet your needs. If there is no clear indication that grants are made, do not be deterred. Use GuideStar to access the Form 990, since it might contain the information you are looking for. Or check other Web pages to obtain additional information. Once you have determined that the public charity is indeed a grantmaker, but the charity states "applications not accepted," you might not want to spend further time researching this particular organization. And if it's clear from posted guidelines on the Web that you don't qualify, you shouldn't apply.

On the other hand, if it seems that you might qualify and there is an online application form, you should take this as a very good sign. The Web site should also give more detailed information about the sort of programs that are likely to be funded and the size of the grants that the organization will typically give. The preferred method of contacting the organization—by letter, e-mail, or telephone—should be noted. In some cases, application forms can be downloaded, printed, or filled in from the Web site, like the form made available on the Web site of the Theatre Communications Group (http://www.tcg.org) of New York City.

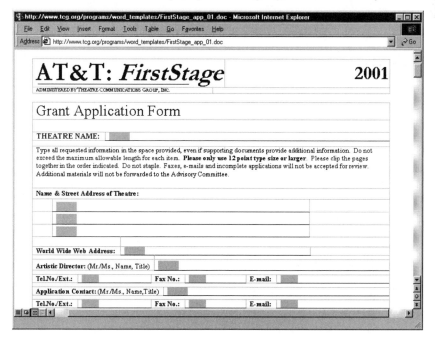

Do not neglect to scan the board of directors or staff listings of the charity. You should do this for two reasons. The first is to assess the credibility and stature of the organization. The second reason is that you may recognize the name of someone with whom you have had contact in the past. A personal connection can be valuable. A telephone call or a preliminary letter of inquiry portraying a clear idea of your program's needs is definitely worthwhile. Indeed, that enhances your chance for eventual funding, and it will also help you customize your full proposal. The following screen shot shows a list of board members for the Humanities Council of Washington, D.C. (http://www.humanities-wdc.org), with brief biographical information on each board member.

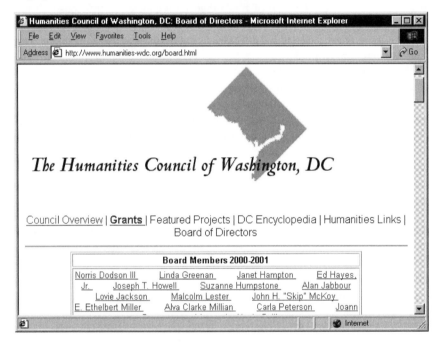

Before you exit a Web site be sure to click on available links, which may direct you to other Web sites that could be useful and should be explored. Some charities print a "last updated" line at the bottom of their Web site. If the site is not current, use caution when relying on the information provided.

THE FORM 990—AN IMPORTANT PART OF YOUR RESEARCH

More often than not, fiscal information for a nonprofit organization will not be included on its Web site. Even an annual report may not include financial data. This kind of information however, is a very important part of your research.

All public charities file an IRS Form 990, which gives information about whether the charity makes grants. Check the charity's Web site to see if it posts its Form 990. This is the best way to get the most current information. The Tides Foundation (http://www.tides.org) of San Francisco, California, for example, offers its Form 990 as well as recent grants lists on its site. If the charity you are looking at does not provide the form on its site, you may want to use GuideStar.org (see above) to obtain that information.

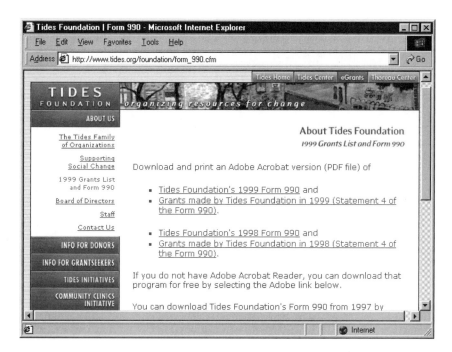

A word to the wise: If there is a current year tax return listed as well as a prior year return and the more current fiscal data do not indicate grantmaking, check the prior return. Sometimes the more recent return has not been completed or was inaccurately filled out. Checking the earlier return may provide the information you seek.

Your investigation is just beginning. To verify the grantmaking status of the organization, turn to page 2, Part II, of the Form 990. Lines 22 and 23 will state the dollar amount of grants provided for that tax year. If these lines do not give the information, line 43 may have information on awards, prizes, scholarships, etc. Read the statement attached to this line. It will say whether there were any grants, scholarships, or loans to individuals or organizations for that tax year. If the information is still not available, read Schedule A, Part IV, Line 3A to see if the organization provides grants, scholarships, loans, and the like. Again, look for a corroborating statement(s): e.g., the explanation of exempt purpose or explanation of the program achievements noted on the return.

As an illustration, the following screen shot shows the top of page 2, Part II, of the Three Guineas Fund's (http://www.3gf.org) Form 990 for 1999. By looking at line 22, you can see that $25,711 was given in grant support for that tax year. By looking further down the page to Part III, "Statement of Program Services Accomplishments," you will find that the total grants amount constituted nine separate grants in support of the Fund's mission ("to advance social justice for girls and women").

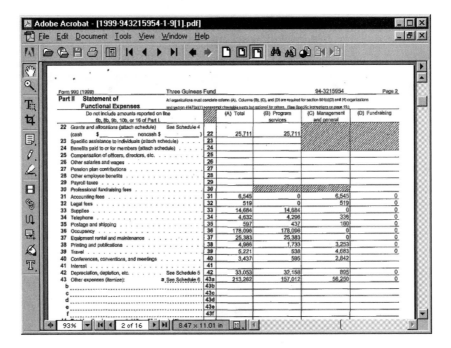

Aside from this information the Form 990, although not mandated to do so, may sometimes have grants lists attached, giving you an idea of the number of grants and amount of money awarded.

Once you have established that an organization is a grantmaking charity in your area of interest, you should make sure that you have all the information needed to meet the requirements of the grant proposal. The more information you have that corresponds to the organization's grantmaking guidelines and procedures, the greater your chance of obtaining funding. To avoid wasted effort, requests are best limited to the most likely organizations. To help you determine whether there is a match, you may want to print out and use the Foundation Center's Prospect Worksheet, available in the Finding Funders section of the Center's Web site.

Some Examples of Grantmaking Public Charity and Community Foundation Web Sites

Below are examples of several well-developed grantmaking public charity and community foundation Web sites. Please note that these are large organizations whose grantmaking programs focus on specific subject fields or geographic areas.

Ms. Foundation for Women (http://www.ms.foundation.org)

The Ms. Foundation for Women, based in New York City, has a Web site that helps to promote its charitable purpose. From the Programs area of the site, you can access the foundation's annual report (with grants listings), grants guidelines, applications, and a list of funding opportunities. The Ms. Foundation operates programs in the following areas: women's economic security; women's health and safety; and girls, young women, and leadership.

The Howard Hughes Medical Institute (http://www.hhmi.org)

The Howard Hughes Medical Institute is based in Chevy Chase, Maryland, and its mission is to support science education from the earliest grades through advanced training. Its Web site will take some time to explore thoroughly. While this site contains a wealth of information, it is necessary to click through several screens to access it. If you are looking for an application form or guidelines, these are not immediately accessible. To find the application information, select Education and Grants from the top of the home page. This will lead you to Grants and Special Programs. If you explore some of the program information, eventually you will come to find application guidelines and forms in PDF format. There are many more pages that provide relevant information for your search.

**The Virginia Beach Foundation
(http://fdncenter.org/grantmaker/vbf/index.html)**

The Web site of this community foundation was developed at the Foundation Center as part of its Foundation Folders initiative. On the left side of the page is a table of contents that makes it possible to see at a glance the topics covered. These include information about the foundation, its history, a grants list, guides for donors, a list of supporters, and an FAQ page.

The Cleveland Foundation (http://www.clevelandfoundation.org)
Based in Cleveland, Ohio, the Cleveland Foundation, America's first community foundation, has a very prominent section on its Web site concerning its grant-making activities. The site provides access to numerous forms, including the foundation's grants guidelines in PDF format, a grant request cover sheet, and a grant reporting form available as MS Word documents, so that you can enter your information directly into the forms and then save them to your computer. A project budget request form, available as an MS Excel file that can then be printed out or downloaded, similarly lets you enter your project budget information directly into the appropriate area.

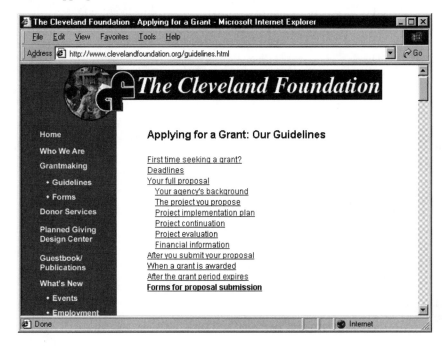

Residencies

The majority of grantmakers provide cash grants to nonprofit organizations. A typical pattern for some grantmaking public charities, however, is to give an award or awards each year in specific fields directly to individuals. Many also will provide individuals with non-monetary support. Some grantmaking public charities that support individual artists provide both cash grants and residencies, while others provide only residencies. Residencies are non-monetary grants that cover work space, food, housing, and other expenses related to the duration of the residency. If the organization you are researching appears to offer only residencies, refer to the Form 990 and/or the Web site to confirm that awards are also given.

The Djerassi Resident Artists Program (http://www.djerassi.org) is an example of a public charity that provides only residencies. You may check the Form 990 or the Web site for further information. Here is what you will find.

If you examine the Form 990, you will notice that there is no entry on Part II line 22 or 23 for grants, but Part III, Statement of Program Services, points you to Attachment B, where you will find a listing for its Artists in Residence Program and a dollar amount for the expenses. On the tax return you will also find a list of grantees. This is the kind of detective work you will need to engage in if you want to use the Web to research funding opportunities at grantmaking public charities.

In another part of the Djerassi Web site, you will see several categories across the top of the home page. Select Residencies to find out about the program. Go into Applications to find information on how and when to apply and to find the application form itself (to be printed out and mailed in). The information contained here should help you decide whether this is a good prospect for you or not.

The Robin Hood Foundation (http://www.robinhood.org)

The Robin Hood Foundation's goal is to eliminate poverty in New York City. Its Web site provides a great deal of information about its giving. In the Who We Support section, you can view a list of grant recipients in alphabetical order or by program area. The program areas are divided into the following categories: youth and after-school programs, early childhood, education, job training, and survival. There are also listings of board members, descriptions of successful ongoing programs, and a description of its funding priorities.

Conclusion

Web sites generally provide detailed information about a charity's purpose: for example, whether it gives grants on a broad basis or exists for the benefit of a specific organization. Most Web sites have internal search capabilities that will yield even more detailed information. If the description does not make it clear whether the organization gives grants, a careful look at the Form 990 can provide that information. In some cases, an even more detailed description of grant giving policies can help you select likely prospects and eliminate unlikely sources of funding. For example, most community foundations, in addition to their general funds, have donor-advised funds, which permit the donors to make recommendations as to where the donated money might be directed. Outside grantseekers will probably not qualify for these funds.

Donor-advised funds managed by financial institutions are relatively new and of increasing importance in the field. For example, in fiscal year 2000, the Fidelity Investment Charitable Gift Fund (http://www300.charitablegift.org/index.shtml) was the largest grantmaking public charity. Similar charitable gift funds have been established by other investment groups.

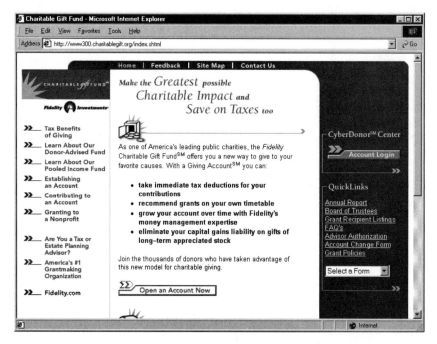

Inspection of a charitable organization's Web site will indicate that it could be a source of funding for your project. One important key phrase to look for is a description saying that the charity has "unrestricted funding." That phrase shows that the charity, independent of any advice from donors, decides where at least a portion of its funding will be directed.

To select a likely public charity for a given project, check on the amount and direction of funding that the charity typically awards. A list of the charity's recent grants will produce much of this information. The wording of the program or mission statement of the funder should be studied, to help guide the writing of a proposal or submission of an application. Directions for submission format and any deadlines should be observed carefully, as should any special instructions. For example, some funders require enclosure of a self-addressed, stamped envelope.

While submitting a number of applications to a range of different grantmaking organizations may seem to be an attractive strategy, it can be easily overdone. It is best to concentrate on meeting as closely as possible the precise criteria outlined in the guidelines of a specific public charity or charities. One well-aimed proposal can be more effective than a number of less targeted applications.

CHAPTER FOUR

Corporate Giving Information on the Web

Corporate Giving: An Overview

The motivations behind the giving policies of individual corporations vary widely and can be complex. Before delving into corporate giving research on the Web, a brief description of why and how corporations give will offer grantseekers a better understanding of what to look for when undertaking this research.

Corporate giving usually entails a combination of altruism and self-interest. Unlike foundations and other charitable agencies, philanthropy is at best a minor sideline for most corporations. Their main obligations are to their customers, employees, shareholders, and the "bottom line." They give to support employee services, guarantee well-trained potential employees, build both local and national community relations, enhance their image, return favors, secure tax deductions, and influence policy and opinion makers.

Companies understand the power of publicity and that charitable giving helps build a strong public image. Some enlightened companies view giving as essential for good corporate citizenship. However, corporations expect concrete rewards for their generosity.

Many companies use the Internet as a means to advertise their philanthropic activities. By posting grantmaking information on the Web, companies make the public aware that they are involved in improving the quality of life, particularly in areas of company operations. This exposure gives the company a positive image and improves public relations, which ultimately translates into increased profits.

TRENDS IN CORPORATE GIVING

In recent years corporations have reshaped their giving programs, narrowing their focus to specific objectives, carefully examining how grants are used, and rethinking their possible benefits. Many also have developed additional non-cash giving programs.

Companies often favor high-profile causes such as improving our nation's education system, with a focus on math, science, opportunities for minorities, and school reform. Environmental issues, low-income housing, and preventive health maintenance also are popular areas of corporate giving.

In addition, companies strive to maximize the impact of their giving. Direct involvement with students and teachers, in projects such as the adopt-a-school program and other tutoring and mentoring programs, is one approach. More and more companies also seem to be fostering collaborative donor and nonprofit efforts and taking on long-term projects. They also support volunteerism among their employees in a bid for enhanced community standing.

COMPANY-SPONSORED FOUNDATIONS AND
DIRECT CORPORATE GIVING PROGRAMS

Companies provide support to nonprofits through private "company-sponsored" foundations, direct corporate giving programs, or both. Company-sponsored foundations usually maintain close ties with their sponsoring companies, and typically their giving directly reflects their "parent's" interests. Most maintain relatively small endowments and rely on annual contributions from the company to support their programs. Some corporations build their foundations' endowments in "fat" years and tap into them in "lean" ones so that giving levels remain fairly consistent. For others, there is a direct relationship between the state of the economy, the value of company stock, and corporate philanthropic coffers, so that giving can vary greatly from year to year depending on economic conditions.

Company-sponsored foundations must adhere to the appropriate regulations governing all private foundations, including filing a yearly IRS Form 990-PF, which includes a report on contributions. As with all Forms 990-PF, these returns are publicly available on the Web and at Foundation Center libraries. These returns can be very helpful in researching individual corporate foundations.

For all other charitable activities not conducted by a company's foundation, there is much less government regulation. Corporations are not required to publicize direct giving programs or to sustain prescribed funding levels. They also may support nonprofits in a variety of ways out of operating funds, and these expenditures won't show up in their giving statistics. For these reasons, finding information on direct corporate giving programs can be difficult.

For a variety of procedural, policy, and/or legal reasons, the corporation may not be able to contribute directly to a worthy organization and will choose to provide support in some other way. This is often treated as a business expense.

"In-kind gifts," such as donated products or loaned employee services, comprise an estimated 20 percent of corporate giving, although these numbers may be inflated due to the fact that many companies report their in-kind donations at market value rather than at their cost. Whatever the true percentage of corporate giving they represent, in-kind gifts are sometimes overlooked by organizations seeking corporate support.

The Community Reinvestment Act

The Community Reinvestment Act (CRA), a federal law passed in 1977, requires banks to help meet the credit needs of their entire community, including low- and moderate-income neighborhoods. Banks failing to do so may be denied permission by the government to expand their business locations, buy or merge with other banks, or engage in interstate banking. Grantseekers looking for *loans* rather than cash or in-kind gifts, therefore, might begin by seeking out banking firms in their own communities. Whether CRA loans represent a form of corporate giving is a hotly debated topic within the philanthropic community, but some companies do include these loans, which generate interest on the companies' investment, as part of their total charitable giving.

The Community Reinvestment Act does not require banks to make unsound business decisions. Banks are not obligated to make loans to organizations or individuals believed to be a risk. The CRA points banks in a general direction in order to serve the needs of the community in which they are located, rather than directing them to make specific loans. The CRA stimulates banks to make loans for low-income family housing, invest in community development, and support small businesses.

Direct corporate giving by public companies has been a topic of controversy within the business community. Especially in lean times, shareholders sometimes complain that corporate profits belong to them and not to charity. While big business tends to agree, many enlightened CEOs realize that the long-term interests of a company and its shareholders are best met by a reinvestment of some corporate funds back into the community. Only through a healthy community, they say, can business flourish. This doesn't mean, however, that a company will not attempt to hide some or all of its charitable endeavors from the public.

For the reasons noted above, most of the corporate giving information available on the Web concerns company-sponsored foundations. Foundations usually provide much more specific information concerning their grantmaking activities, including information on application addresses, contact persons, geographic limitations, fields of interest supported, types of support offered, and so on. One of the advantages for a company that uses a direct giving program rather than a company-sponsored foundation is precisely that the company need not disclose how much or to whom it contributes. Therefore, when researching direct corporate giving programs online, grantseekers must use a little more ingenuity and adopt a well-honed and discerning selection process.

One of the basic handicaps to uncovering giving information on the Web is that companies often use their Web sites primarily as a public relations tool. They may post little more than several pages concerning some of the grants they have made in the recent past. Unfortunately, this kind of Web site can lead grantseekers to believe that they may be eligible for a grant, when in fact they are not. Sites like these often generate hundreds, if not thousands, of applications to companies that do not accept unsolicited applications or will not support the causes these proposals address.

How to Find Corporate Funders

As already noted, most corporate giving will coincide closely with other corporate activities and usually will be limited to the geographic areas where companies conduct business, including headquarters and plant and subsidiary locations. The grantseeker's search should focus on local businesses as well as on major corporations that operate in their neighborhood. Corporate directories and corporate giving studies are key resources.

In addition to the Web strategies outlined below, grantseekers should also consult public libraries for regional and business indexes. The local Chamber of Commerce and Better Business Bureau also may have such guides. Do not overlook the yellow pages and local community newspapers. In corporate grantseeking, personal contacts are essential. A grantseeker should consider board members, volunteers, and staff as assets who may have important contacts with corporate funders. These people should be encouraged to share their knowledge and to think about whom they may know who can help secure corporate funding.

UTILIZING THE WEB AS A SEARCH TOOL

All of this having been said, many companies now maintain a presence on the World Wide Web. With a little ingenuity, these sites can become important potential sources of information about corporate community involvement and grantmaking activities.

Searching: Let Others Do the Searching for You

Several portal sites are good starting points for grantseekers in search of corporate giving programs and company-sponsored foundations. Primary among these are the Foundation Center's Web site (http://www.fdncenter.org/funders/grantmaker/gws_corp/corp1.html), the U.K.-based Charities Aid Foundation's CCInet (http://www.ccinet.org/search.cfm), and the CSC Non-Profit Resource Center (http://people.ne.mediaone.net/cscunningham/Corporate.htm). These sites have extensive lists of links to corporate giving programs and company-sponsored foundations.

The Foundation Center's Web Sites of Corporate Grantmakers (http://www.fdncenter.org/funders/grantmaker/gws_corp/corp1.html) is a listing of corporate givers that can be browsed alphabetically or searched by subject or geographic keyword. (For more on this and other Center Web site features, see Chapter 1.)

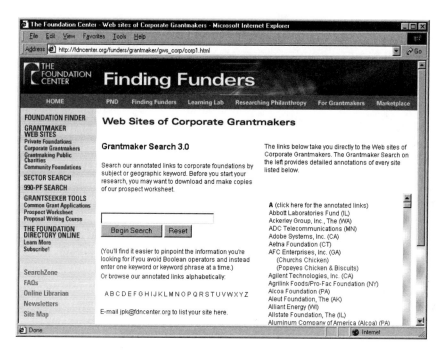

The Charities Aid Foundation's CCInet (http://www.ccinet.org), a corporate community involvement site, hosts a searchable database of more than 270 companies that offer some form of charitable giving. You can search by keyword, country, giving type (or type of support), grant area (or field of interest), by online report, or alphabetically. Entries in your search results indicate which companies have earned the CCInet Gold or Silver Hallmark Award, which are benchmarks for corporate giving. A useful key also lets you quickly identify ethics reports, social responsibility reports, environmental audits, and foundations. CCInet is based in the U.K. but includes American companies in its database.

CSC Non-Profit Resource Center's Web site (http://people.ne.mediaone.net/cscunningham/Corporate.htm) has an informative listing of links to corporate givers. Hundreds of links are coded with subject headings to identify funding areas. An icon identifies new links added to the full alphabetical list within the past month.

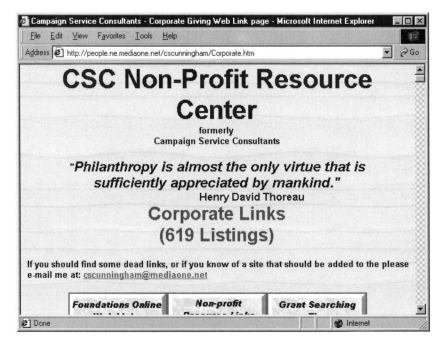

Searching: Doing It Yourself Using a Search Engine

Another way to find corporate giving information on the Internet is to use a search engine. See Appendix A for a list of some of the most useful ones. If you're new at this, try each one out to see which search engine has features you like best. The key to retrieving a reasonable number of hits that contain useful information on corporate giving, rather than a list of thousands of irrelevant Web sites, is choosing the proper search terms and knowing the rules and limitations of the search engine you are using. There are differences in how search engines work and what results you can expect from them.

The search terms you select can greatly improve your search results. Try to search initially with broad phrases such as "corporate giving," "community relations," or "company contributions." Once you have an idea about what kind of information is available on the Web, you may be able to further narrow your searches by adding words more specific to your needs (e.g., "arts corporate giving"). You may also want to try the same search using various search engines; you will often get vastly different results. Other terms to try are "in-kind gifts," if looking for product donations, or "community reinvestment act," for those seeking loans.

Searching: Uncovering Giving Information on Corporate Web Sites

A different strategy is required to research the corporate giving policies of a specific company. Often there is no "search" option within a particular Web site, although gradually this feature is becoming more available. You must be on the lookout, therefore, for broad categories that may lead you to the information you seek. Often you will find these categories among a menu list containing items such as Products and Services, Annual Report, and so on. The categories most likely to contain information on the giving policies of the company most typically will be found under headings such as Corporate Relations, Corporate Information, or About Us.

Frequently, corporate giving program information is contained on a "page within a page." In other words, you have to delve deeply, or in the case of a Web site, click often, to get to it. The best way to circumvent this sometimes tedious process is to use the site map, if one is available. A good site map will list most or all of the pages contained within the Web site. These listings are usually the simplest way to move to the subject you are looking for and are often more reliable than the hit-or-miss process of clicking from page to page.

RESEARCHING CORPORATE INFORMATION

You may want to begin with basic information about the company itself, including the areas of company operations, geographic parameters, the products and services the company provides, a list of corporate officers, and fiscal information.

A good place to start when looking for information about a public company (that is, a company whose stock is traded publicly) is the Security and Exchange Commission's (SEC's) EDGAR Database (http://www.sec.gov/edgar/searchedgar/webusers.htm). This is a text-only database that contains an archive of all the financial documents filed with the SEC since 1994.

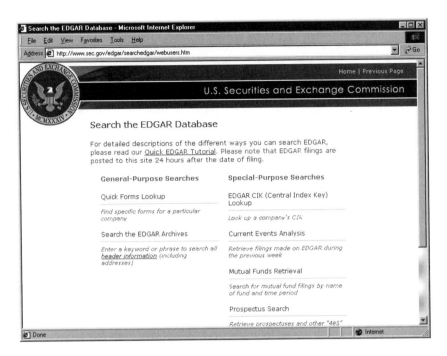

This site contains extensive information about every public company and its operations. The main challenge is digging through a lot of material that is irrelevant in order to find the information you need. This requires patience and persistence.

Another valuable site to consider when researching corporate information is Yahoo's Finance Company and Fund Index (http://biz.yahoo.com/i). This site provides a searchable database of information on most public companies in the United States and even offers a "backdoor" to the SEC's site, making a search of the EDGAR Database quicker and easier.

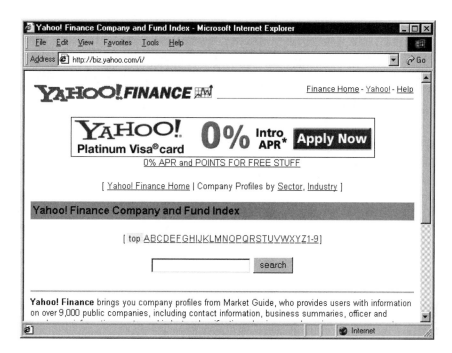

FreeEdgar (http://www.freeedgar.com) is another Internet search service that makes use of the SEC's EDGAR database. Its easy-to-use interface is considered by many to be the most user-friendly way of searching for SEC filings.

One of the most comprehensive sites for corporate information on public and private companies, not only in the United States but abroad, is Hoovers Online (http://www.hoovers.com). Hoovers boasts access to records on more than 12 million companies. (See Chapter 9 for information on e-newsletters available at Hoover's Online.)

Helpful pages for information about businesses within other Web sites include Internet Prospector's Corporations page (http://www.internet-prospector.org/company.html) and the Corporations/Execs section of David Lamb's Prospect Research Page (http://www.lambresearch.com/CorpExec.html). Both sites have links to corporate directories and other sources of business information and either one is a good starting point when looking for corporate information. Additionally, those wishing to receive or view corporate annual reports may want to visit the Investor Relations Information Network (http://www.irin.com). Here, annual reports for more than 2,500 companies can be accessed in PDF and HTML formats.

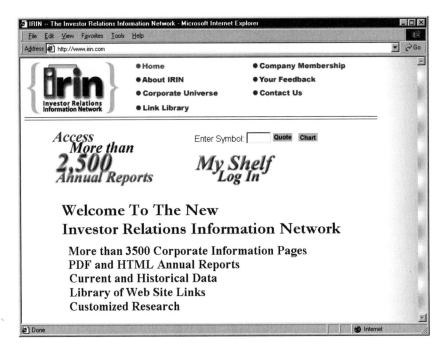

Most of the information available on these sites concerns publicly traded companies. Finding information on privately held corporations requires more research and ingenuity and may also require using a search engine to look up the company in question by name.

Perhaps the quickest and easiest way to find a public or private corporation's information is to simply type the name of a company into your browser's location bar and hope for success. Many companies have set up Web sites that usually can be accessed by the "http://www.companyname.com" format.

For example, Verizon Communications' Web site can be found at http://www.verizon.com. By clicking on the link called About Verizon, a wealth of corporate information becomes available. The company's annual report and press releases can be found within the Investor Information section of this page.

ConAgra Foods' Web site can be found at http://www.conagra.com/. By selecting About ConAgra Foods, one can access corporate facts and figures, including a listing of corporate officers in Leadership, information regarding products in Brands, and information on its giving in Social Responsibility.

CORPORATE INFORMATION: WHAT TO LOOK FOR

- Annual report
- Business statement
- Executive officers
- Press releases
- Product listings
- Worldwide locations

You should read whatever material the company provides carefully and then determine whether your organization is a logical candidate for a particular program. An inappropriate application is a waste of time for both the candidate and the corporation.

If you encounter difficulties locating corporate Web sites, try different variations of a company's name. For example, the Web site for Minnesota Mining and Manufacturing (3M) can be found alternately at http://www.3m.com and at http://www.mmm.com.

FINDING INFORMATION ON INDIVIDUAL CORPORATE WEB SITES

Corporations present their giving information in widely varying formats. Some companies provide easy access to their philanthropic activities directly from their home page, while others may have information on their grantmaking programs buried within other sections. Some companies provide no information at all on their Web sites, while others combine direct corporate giving program information with foundation information on a single page. Grantseekers must be diligent in order to find the information they need on a corporate Web site. They should also examine the information provided on a corporate site very carefully before applying for a grant.

Hidden Information

It is often the case that a company provides giving information within a section called Corporate Information or About Us. An example of a Web site containing buried corporate giving information is Compaq Computer's site (http://www.compaq.com/corporate/community).

The details on the corporation's grantmaking activities will be found in the section called Community Relations, which is itself within the section called Company Info. The links can easily be followed from the company's home page, but no reference to this path is provided. Less Web-savvy grantseekers could very well visit Compaq's Web site and entirely miss the fact that philanthropic information is available there.

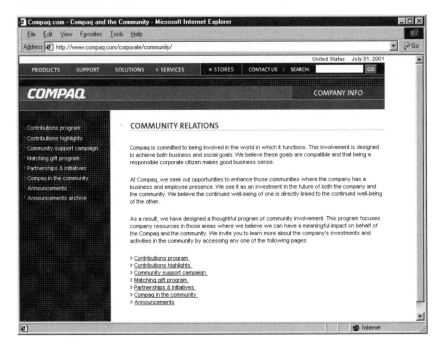

Like Compaq, the philanthropic information on Merck's Web site (http://www.merck.com) is hard to uncover.

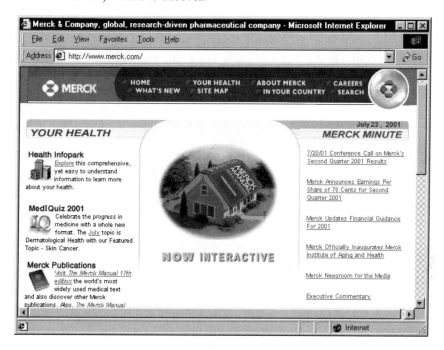

It is in the section called Corporate Philanthropy Report, which can be found in General Information, which is itself in About Merck. Once again, the information is readily uncovered if you know where to look, but Merck provides no reference on its site that this specific sequence of links must be followed.

Some companies provide site maps, which can be used as a guide to find a hidden page. For example, International Paper's home page includes a link to its site map, which clearly shows that the company has dedicated a page to its philanthropic activities (http://www.internationalpaper.com/map/index.html). Community Outreach is listed under the section called Our World and can be accessed easily with a click of the mouse once you know where to look.

More Transparent Sites

Other corporate Web sites make your search for giving far easier. For example, Dollar General's home page has a direct link to its Community Initiatives page (http://www.dollargeneral.com/DG_Community_Initiatives/dg_community_initiatives.htm). This is the area containing information on its charitable contributions and represents what you might find at a grantseeker-friendly corporate Web site.

Dollar General provides links to its guidelines for grantseekers, a description of one of its charitable programs, and selected profiles of individuals whom the company has helped.

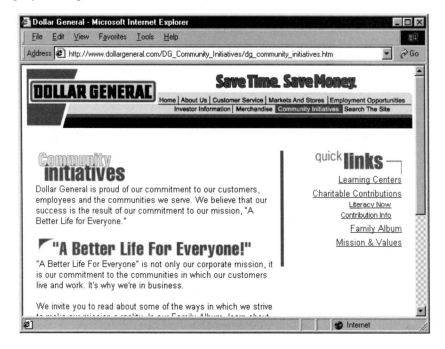

Union Pacific provides a link to its foundation directly from its home page (http://www.up.com/found). Links to company-sponsored foundations are usually easier to spot than those to the more general, and informal, direct corporate giving pages. In this case, the heading UP Foundation leaves no doubt as to the type of information that awaits you.

Union Pacific's foundation page includes links to its vision statement, history, correspondence information, guidelines, and foundation-issued press releases. This is an excellent example of a well-organized corporate giving page that provides virtually all of the information that a grantseeker would need to determine whether a company might be an appropriate source of support.

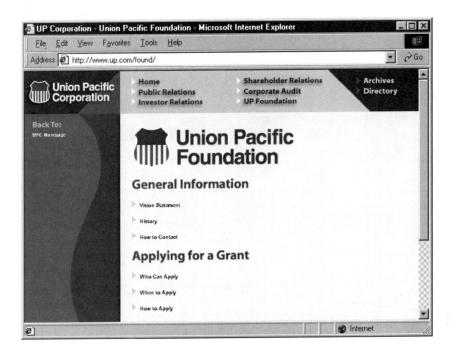

It should be noted that many companies provide information regarding their environment- and health and safety-related initiatives on their Web sites. But this is not necessarily relevant grantmaking information. Although many companies do indeed make grants to environmental organizations or to those that promote health and safety within their community, this material usually refers to a company's efforts to reduce its negative impact on the local environment or to improve health and safety conditions for its employees. Use your best judgment in deciding whether the information provided is of relevance to you as a grantseeker.

Combination Sites: Company-Sponsored Foundations and Corporate Giving Programs

As noted, many companies make charitable contributions both directly and through a company-sponsored foundation. Often, information on both arms of a company's charitable giving efforts is combined on the Web, making it difficult for the grantseeker to differentiate between the two separate grantmaking bodies. Grantseekers need to proceed with caution when visiting such sites and to conduct further research to determine the appropriate approach. Sometimes both programs are administered out of the same office and by the same staff, while at other times they act completely independently of one another. In some cases they each require separate proposals. Very often, the types of support provided and the geographic limitations established will vary widely. For instance, cash donations might be supplied by the foundation, while in-kind support is handled exclusively by the company.

CIGNA's Web site (http://www.cigna.com/general/about/community) contains information on both a company-sponsored foundation and a direct corporate giving program. In fact, the company announces this at the bottom of the first page of its Contributions Report, something many companies neglect to make so obvious. There is valuable information here on CIGNA's philanthropic endeavors, but one never knows for sure whether the information reflects donations made by the

CIGNA Foundation or by the company itself. When in doubt, a telephone call to the company is probably the grantseeker's best bet.

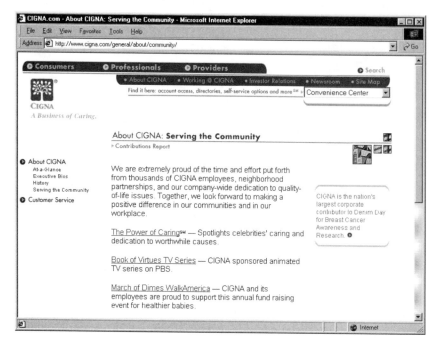

Making the Best Use of Available Resources

THE SUBJECT, GEOGRAPHIC, AND TYPE OF SUPPORT APPROACHES TO GRANTSEEKING

There are several tried-and-true approaches to corporate grantseeking research, each appropriate for a different situation. The subject approach leads grantseekers to corporations with an interest in funding programs in certain fields and to businesses whose activities are related to their nonprofit programs. Some nonprofit/corporate common interests will be obvious: A sporting goods manufacturer expresses interest in an athletic program for disadvantaged youth; a musical instruments manufacturer supports a primary school music appreciation program; a pharmaceutical company or alcoholic beverage manufacturer funds a drug education program. Because most corporate giving programs are limited to giving in communities where the company operates, a grantseeker's research should include a company's areas of operation, including corporate headquarters, subsidiaries, divisions, joint ventures, and community plants and offices. A company will often support programs that provide direct service to employees and other community residents, have potential for public recognition, and improve customer relations in specific geographic areas. A type of support approach can be equally productive. Corporations will often provide funds in a few highly specific ways, such as for capital improvements, operating budgets, and matching employee donations.

NON-CASH OR IN-KIND GIFTS

Many companies also make non-cash contributions. For example, a clothing manufacturer may have "irregulars" or extra clothing to donate to a homeless shelter. It's important to note that non-cash or in-kind giving can be much more indirect. Charities such as Gifts In Kind International (http://www.giftsinkind.org), Share Our Strength (http://www.strength.org), Volunteers of America (http://www.voa.org), and New York's City Harvest (http://www.cityharvest.org) act as pass-through organizations for corporations wishing to provide in-kind gifts and that want to make sure donations reach those who need them most in an efficient manner. By using these services first, rather than applying directly to the company, in-kind giftseekers are often then encouraged to apply to the appropriate charity.

DO YOUR HOMEWORK

It is critical that you learn as much as you can about a corporation's funding patterns before submitting a request. The funder may have an annual report or printed guidelines as well as information about the company and its giving on a Web page. These will help you target your appeal. Business reports present company philosophy and describe company plans for the community, providing vital background in linking a grant request to company interests. Economic conditions and business news also should be followed. A company laying off employees or running a deficit may not be the best one to ask for a donation.

PERSONAL CONTACTS

In terms of corporate grantseeking, how important is it to know someone? In the electronic age, actual human contact is becoming less prevalent. With e-mail, fax machines, voice mail, and the World Wide Web all competing for attention, it is sometimes difficult to get in touch directly with someone you know, much less a stranger. Personal contacts can help, but their impact varies from corporation to corporation. Seeking grants from company foundations and direct corporate giving programs with designated philanthropy personnel and explicit guidelines for grantseekers is unlikely to require personal contacts. Personal contacts may be more important when seeking support from companies with informal giving programs and no formal guidelines or staff to process requests.

PRESENTING YOUR IDEAS TO A CORPORATE GIVER

Most corporate givers will expect you to submit a proposal or a preliminary letter of inquiry by mail. A few have application forms you'll need to fill out. Even fewer have online applications. Be sure to find out in advance what is required. A proposal must be honest, clear, concise, and appropriate in tone. Draw up a realistic budget, and be prepared to divulge all sources of income and how that money will be used, since corporate grantmakers emphasize the bottom line. Many ask for evidence of fiscally responsible, efficient management. Be explicit. State program or agency goals, a plan of action, a timetable, and a method of evaluation. Be sure to submit a detailed and reasonable budget. Be brief but comprehensive.

First and foremost, the grantseeker should always consider the funder's motivation for giving. Establishing the connection with a corporate grantmaker's goals is the grantseeker's key to success. Focus on company self-interest more than benevolence. For example, a corporate giver may want to develop a trained pool of potential employees, support research for further products, expand its markets, respond to related social issues, ward off criticism of company policies, and, of course, increase sales. Consider what a business stands to gain from your program. Point out the potential benefits to the company as well as to your nonprofit and the audiences you serve.

Getting corporate support demands creativity, ingenuity, and persistence. Competition will be stiff, but gradually, the World Wide Web is making it easier for the grantseeker to put his or her best foot forward.

CHAPTER FIVE

Government Funding Resources on the Web

Grantseekers looking for federal government funding will be pleased with the wealth of resources on the Internet. Because printed government documents and information tend to be dense and laborious to search through, the Internet is the ideal place to conduct research into federal grant programs. Online government resources of interest to grantseekers include general information about government agencies, databases and statistics about philanthropy, legal and financial information, funding availability announcements, and guides to proposal writing.

Although government resources on the Internet are so plentiful as to be potentially overwhelming, a number of Web sites exist whose creators—often at universities or nonprofit organizations—have culled, categorized, organized, and annotated government and government-related sites to make things easier for the uninitiated. These sites vary greatly in design, amount and type of information, and in their usefulness to grantseekers. This chapter is intended to suggest starting points and to help identify the essential sites for uncovering government funding information.

Start at the Top

The top is a logical place to start to get the broadest possible view of resources. The executive, legislative, and judicial branches of the federal government have Web sites, as do many federal departments and agencies and state and local governments. You may want to start with the Your Government Web site (http://www.whitehouse.gov/government/index.html), which provides access to information from the White House, the President's cabinet, independent federal agencies and commissions, as well as the legislative and judicial branches.

The House of Representatives site (http://www.house.gov) and the Senate site (http://www.senate.gov) allow you to connect to your state representative or senator. These sites also include access to information about legislation recently passed and under consideration.

The frequently updated databases of THOMAS (http://thomas.loc.gov), offered by the Library of Congress, provide searchable information about the U.S. Congress and the legislative process. Included is information on congressional activity and committee reports.

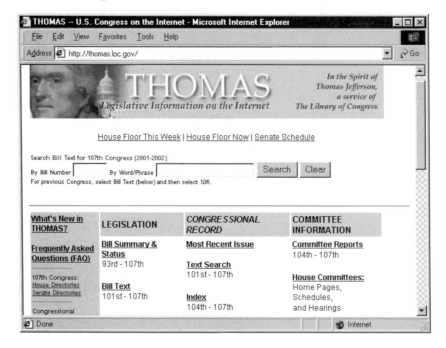

GENERAL GOVERNMENT INFORMATION SITES

In addition to the official government branch home pages, many government departments and non-governmental organizations compile links to government and related sites. One of the Library of Congress's Internet Resource Pages (http://lcweb.loc.gov/global/executive/fed.html), for example, has a comprehensive set of links organized by department and agency.

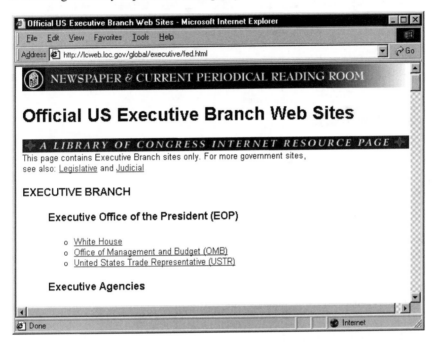

Here are some other good places to begin your search for information on government funding on the Web:

FirstGov (http://www.firstgov.gov)

This gateway site is a project of the President's Management Council. It bills itself as "your first click to the U.S. Government" and has a powerful search engine that can search 30 million pages of government information—approximately 20,000 Web sites. For example, to search for information on funding for the arts, simply enter "art grants" in the search field. The Web pages you will receive in your results list are ranked by relevancy. You can also browse government information on FirstGov by topic, such as Federal Benefits and Grants.

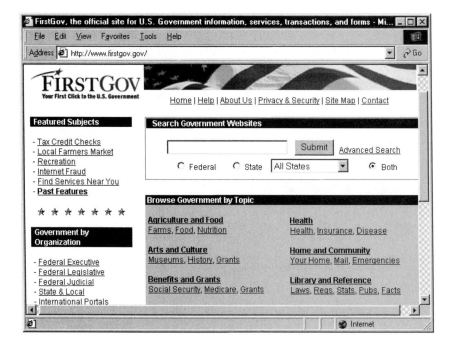

GovSpot (http://www.govspot.com)

This portal to government information online is a well-organized site produced by StartSpot Mediaworks, Inc. The main pages of the site are listed topically. For example, you can link to the FBI under the heading Justice & Military or the Department of Commerce under Matters of Money. To locate a complete list of federal agencies or state government information, look under Shortcuts. Other interesting sub-categories include Must-See Sites, Do You Know? and In the Spotlight. To find the answer to the frequently asked question, "How do I get a government grant?" look under You Asked For It. Simple navigation and use of colorful graphics make GovSpot an excellent Web site for the novice grantseeker interested in locating government information.

Federal Gateway (http://www.fedgate.org)

This search engine, which includes links to federal, state, and local government sites, states that "the entire official U.S. Government is here." It includes a unique and useful section on commonly used government abbreviations and acronyms. An area called Key Federal Documentation has a helpful user aid entitled "How to Effectively Locate Federal Government Information on the Web" that outlines the process step-by-step.

FedWorld (http://www.fedworld.gov)

Sponsored by the National Technical Information Service (NTIS), this portal site emphasizes access to technical and scientific government information and is a comprehensive, easy-to-use gateway to more than 20 full-text government databases, including U.S. Government Job Announcements and other general government Web sites.

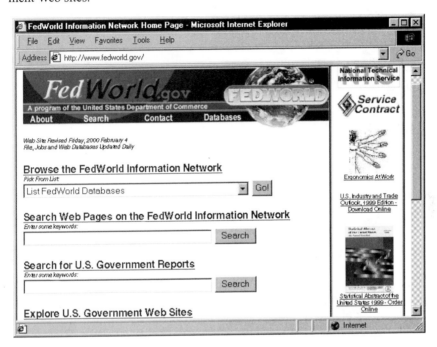

The Foundation Center's Nonprofit Links–Government Resources (http://fdncenter.org/research/npr_links/npr09.html)

The Government Resources area of Nonprofit Links in the Foundation Center's Researching Philanthropy directory provides easy access to sites highlighted in this chapter, in addition to several specific federal and state agencies of interest to grantseekers and nonprofit organizations. (See Chapter 8 for more on the Center's Links to Nonprofit Resources.)

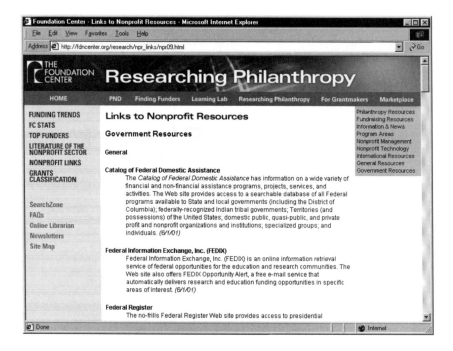

The Foundation Center's Sector Search–Government Resources
(http://fdncenter.org/funders/web_search/web_search.html)

You can search for government information on the Internet by using the Foundation Center's Sector Search and de-selecting all but Government Resources. Enter a keyword or phrase to retrieve all relevant pages on these government sites. Results can be sorted by relevancy or date.

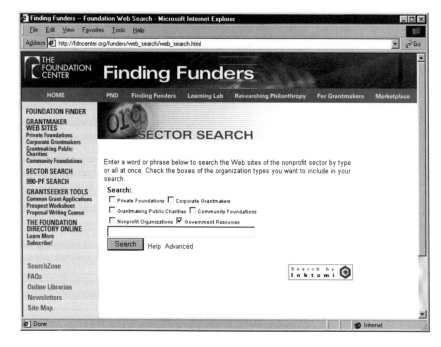

Louisiana State University's Libraries List of U.S. Federal Government Agencies (http://www.lib.lsu.edu/gov/fedgov.html)

This site provides a comprehensive list of links to government departments, agencies, and related organizations such as boards, commissions, and committees right on its main page so that you can simply search or scan for relevant words or appropriate departments.

Federal Acquisition Jumpstation (part of NASA Acquisition Internet Service) (http://nais.nasa.gov/fedproc/home.html)

Although this portal, which links to federal procurement information, is designed for the business community, it is relevant to grantseekers as well because it delineates how the government spends its money. It also includes links to specific government grantmaking agencies.

The FCIC National Contact Center (http://www.info.gov)

This site, offered by the Federal Consumer Information Center, provides information about federal agencies, programs, and services. It includes a comprehensive section with answers to often-asked questions about federal loans, grants, and assistance. Each FAQ links to general resources and specific government agencies and includes contact information. Geared toward the individual as opposed to the nonprofit organization, the site provides a toll-free number (1-800-688-9889) for members of the public to ask questions of the FCIC's knowledgeable staff.

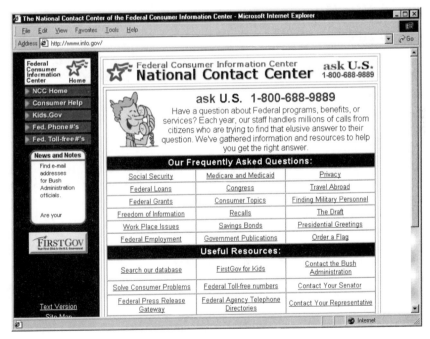

U.S. State and Local Gateway (http://www.statelocal.gov)

This Web site, an interagency project in collaboration with the National Partnership for Reinventing Government, adopts a unique approach. Developed to give employees of state and local governments easy access to federal information, it organizes its links to grants, loans, and contracts by subject category in an easy-to-read chart.

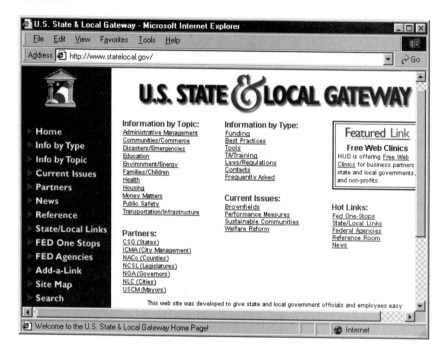

Focusing Your Research on Government Funding

Government-related sites tend to contain an enormous amount of information, much of it not very useful to the grantseeker looking for funding in a specific field. As with corporate Web sites, funding information is often buried deep within a government site and can be easily missed. In addition, funding information may not be situated in one area of the site but dispersed by department or categorized by subject matter. Because most of these sites are so information-rich, many of them have internal search engines. Grantseekers should make it a habit to use them when available. By entering the search terms "grants," "funding," "opportunities," or even "research and development," in addition to keywords describing the particular subject for which funding is sought, you are less likely to miss relevant information.

The majority of grants offered by the government—especially at the federal level—are in the fields of education, health and scientific research, human services, environment, agriculture, and industry, though not limited to these categories. The government also funds historical research, arts, and the humanities. Looking at the more specialized departments, grants are awarded in a wide range of disciplines. Federal funders generally prefer projects that serve as prototypes or models for others to replicate, whereas local government funders look for strong evidence of community support for your project.

Though a fair number of individual awards exist, as with foundation funding, the majority of government grants are awarded to eligible nonprofit organizations rather than directly to individuals.

GENERAL GOVERNMENT GRANT INFORMATION SITES

There are a number of sites that focus specifically on government funding opportunities for nonprofit organizations, researchers, and educators. These sites offer a direct avenue to federal grant information, through structured indexes or by means of site search engines.

Catalog of Federal Domestic Assistance (CFDA) (http://www.cfda.gov)

This site is part of the General Services Administration (GSA) and provides information on a wide variety of financial and other assistance programs, projects, services, and activities. The GSA uses "assistance" in a generic sense. In addition to grant programs you will also find information on other forms of aid, such as loans, surplus equipment, and training.

This is probably the government resource most familiar to grantseekers. You can submit a simple query and receive clear, detailed information, including eligibility requirements, application procedures, and examples of funded projects. New users are advised to read through the First Time User's Guide and the FAQs before beginning. Other choices from the main page are Browse the Contents and Find Assistance Programs. You'll probably want to start with Find Assistance Programs, but the Contents section is worth coming back to. Here you will find more details on how to use the CFDA, the very informative Developing and Writing Grant Proposals, and a useful link to the Office of Management and Budget (OMB) Grants Management Page (http://www.whitehouse.gov/omb/grants), which provides access to the myriad forms required for federal grant submissions. See the description in the Other Government Resources section at the end of this chapter.

There are many options for searching and browsing the Catalog from the Find Assistance Programs page. You can view lists of programs by agency and subagency (e.g., go directly to entries for the National Science Foundation), or by applicant eligibility. Many of the assistance programs listed may only be for state and local governments, so it can be helpful to limit your search to programs for which nonprofit organizations are eligible. If you're trying to plan ahead, you can even view listings arranged by application deadline.

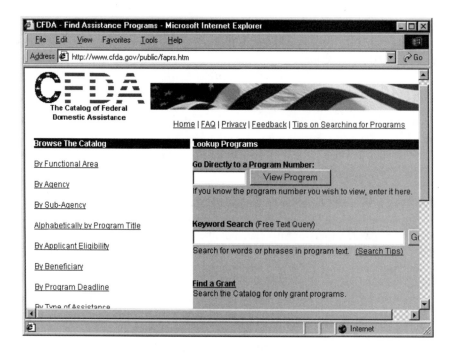

If you're not sure what to look for first, try the simple Keyword Search, which will bring up any listings in the Catalog with your keywords. The phrase "at-risk youth," for example, brings up several listings, each of which includes the sponsoring agency information, program objectives, and details on eligibility and how to apply. If a free-text search isn't specific enough for you, try the Find a Grant section, which narrows your search to only direct grant programs. In this section, you can choose from general subject categories, such as education or community development, which are then broken down into more specific areas of interest. For each topic heading you can view listings of grant opportunities only, so you don't need to wade through listings for other types of assistance, such as loans. Or for a completely different approach, try the Top 10 Percent of Programs link, which shows you the most frequently viewed Catalog programs.

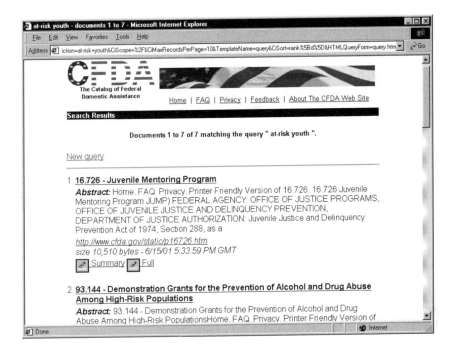

The Federal Commons (http://www.cfda.gov/federalcommons)

A relatively new government site, the Federal Commons is designed to be ". . . the world wide web information portal for the grantee organization community" and a major resource on federal grant information. The objective is to create a comprehensive grants management site for current and prospective grantees of the federal government. This is one government site to watch because eventually you will be able to apply for funding online through the Federal Commons.

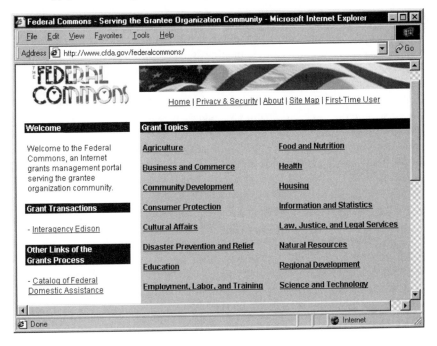

The content of this site is similar to that of the CFDA, but the program listings focus solely on grant opportunities. The main page presents a listing of topic headings. Once you click on a general heading, such as Environmental Quality, you can then view the sub-categories (water pollution, air pollution, etc.) and link directly to the grant information on each federal agency's Web site. For example, under the water pollution category, you find links for grant programs under the auspices of the Commerce Department, Department of the Interior, and the Environmental Protection Agency, among others. In addition to this directory of grant information, the Federal Commons offers links to sites of interest for current government grantees, such as the Payment Management System and the Automated Standard Application for Payment.

Federal Register (http://www.access.gpo.gov/su_docs/aces/aces140.html)

This is the official daily record of the federal government and as such it has the most current and comprehensive information regarding government-funded projects and funding availability. You can also find postings of proposed regulations and agency meetings here. The Federal Register is an essential stopping point in the grantseeker's journey because it provides information on government funding availability and new grant programs. Many government agencies, whose own compilations may not be as up-to-date, often link to this site in their grants information.

You can search the full-text of the Federal Register in a variety of ways, guided by detailed instructions and sample searches. Although there is no section devoted exclusively to grants or requests for proposals (RFPs), grantseekers can enter keywords to generate a list of potential funding notices. The official term is "Notice of Funding Availability," or NOFA. The NOFA can be a very detailed document that outlines the criteria for funding, guidelines for applications, and relevant deadlines. You will also find a contact name for the funding agency.

Grantseekers can search the Federal Register back to 1994, although the 1994 version does not include subject field identifiers. The default is to search the current year only, but you can check off multiple years. Limit your search to the Notices section only; add a date range if desired (keeping in mind that the Federal Register is published every business day); then enter search terms describing your program interests. To narrow your search to NOFAs, use the phrase "notice of funding availability" or the words "grants" or "funds" among your search terms. When viewing the results, you will note that your search terms are bolded, which makes it easier to see how relevant the notice may be.

An additional feature is the ability to browse the daily tables of contents of the Federal Register back through 1998. This can be very useful if you are looking for notices from a specific agency or department (the table of contents is listed alphabetically by government agency). When scrolling through the table of contents, look for the heading NOTICES: Grants and Cooperative Agreements; Availability, Etc. under the department/agency name.

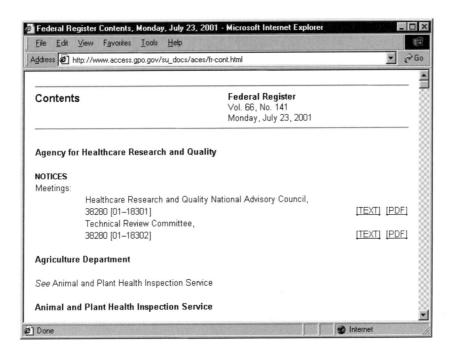

EZ/EC Notices of Funding Availability (http://ocd.usda.gov/nofa.htm)

As noted above, although comprehensive the Federal Register is not solely dedicated to serving the grantseeker. This site, developed by the Empowerment Zone and Enterprise Community Program Offices of the U.S. Department of Agriculture and the U.S. Department of Housing and Urban Development, allows grantseekers to customize a search for NOFAs, thereby making the Federal Register database more relevant and manageable. You can search for NOFAs by overall category such as Housing or Youth, or by specific agency or department.

There are two choices for viewing the results—by publication date (when the NOFA appeared in the Federal Register) or by application deadline. Although one might think that viewing NOFAs by deadline would be more useful, if you choose this option the oldest listings show up first. Since the NOFA database goes back to 1999, you will have to scroll through many programs whose deadlines have already passed. Viewing by publication date, however, brings the most recent listings to the top. (The database is actually made up of NOFA summaries, not the entire document, but each listing includes a link to the original Federal Register NOFA.)

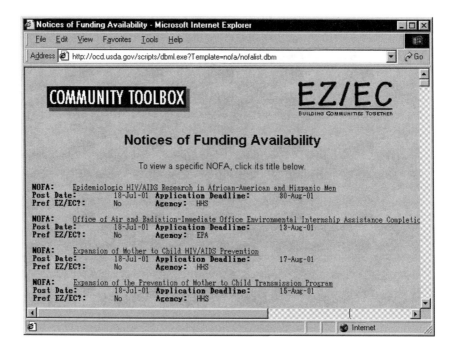

NonProfit Gateway (http://www.nonprofit.gov)

This is a "one-stop shopping" point for federal information, including funding information. Created by the White House Office of Public Liaison, this site provides extremely valuable information and services from federal agencies. You'll find links to many of the other sites discussed in this section, so this is a good site to bookmark.

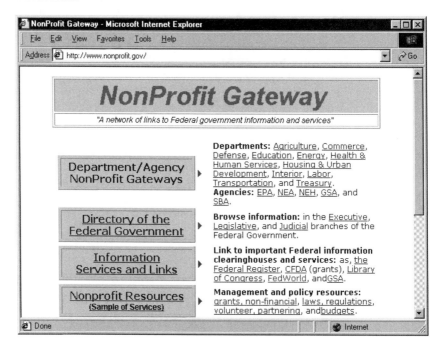

The site is divided into several major categories: Department/Agency Nonprofit Gateways, Directory of the Federal Government, Information Services and Links, and Nonprofit Resources.

If there is a specific government department or agency you're looking for, start with the Department/Agency Nonprofit Gateways section. Many departments have created their own nonprofit gateway Web sites with their relevant information, including grant and funding opportunities, all in one place. For example, if you're working for a charter school and want to see whether the Department of Education has any applicable funding programs, you could click on Education under the Department/Agency Nonprofit Gateways links to go right to the grant information.

Information Services and Links is a directory of some of the key clearinghouse sites for government information, including funding sources. We refer to many of these sites, such as FedWorld, the Federal Register, and the Catalog of Federal Domestic Assistance, throughout this chapter.

One of the most interesting and unique sections is Nonprofit Resources/ Management and Policy Resources. This is a collection of various federal departments' and agencies' charts with links to their respective Web sites, which offer informational links to Grants, Laws and Regulations, and Special Relationships such as partnerships and volunteering. This is another way to quickly link to information of importance to nonprofit organizations seeking funding. To use the charter school example again, you could go directly to the Department of Education's site on funding opportunities by linking through the Grants section of Nonprofit Resources. You could also take a look at the Department of Education's regulations under the Laws and Regulations links.

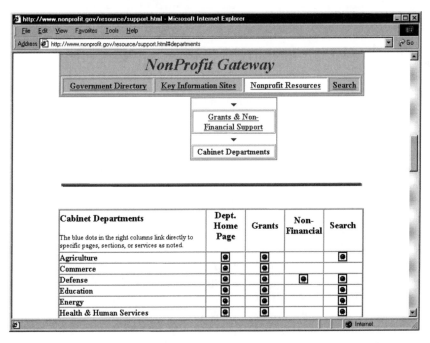

Department of Health and Human Services (http://www.hhs.gov/grantsnet)
The Department of Health and Human Services has an exemplary Web site for grantseekers. Visitors can go straight to the Electronic Roadmap to Grants, a visual representation of the grants process that includes links to information on HHS funding opportunities, how to write grant proposals, HHS standard application forms, and many other topics.

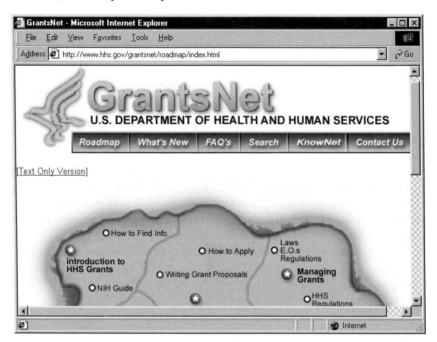

Although much of the information pertains only to HHS grants, there are some resources, especially Who's Who in Federal Grants Management, of interest to grantseekers in other fields. This is a directory, complete with phone numbers and e-mail addresses, of key personnel in many federal agencies.

NON-GOVERNMENTAL SITES

Federal Information Exchange (FEDIX)
(http://content.sciencewise.com/fedix/index.html)
Seven federal agencies contribute content to FEDIX, providing access to information on government funding opportunities for research and education organizations. Listings are arranged by participating agency: the Agency for International Development, Air Force Office of Scientific Research, Department of Agriculture, Department of Defense, National Aeronautics & Space Administration, National Institutes of Health, and the Department of Transportation.

Listings are taken primarily from Commerce Business Daily (regarding government contracts) and the Federal Register, among other sources. You can also obtain information about each agency's ongoing funding programs. Each listing includes a summary of the original posting, with links back to the sponsoring agency's pages. Your results list is displayed in order by expiration date.

You can also connect to MOLIS (http://content.sciencewise.com/molis/index.htm), the Minority Online Information Service, which serves minority populations in the education and research communities. You can search past grant awards and current opportunities offered by federal agencies to minority-serving organizations. Of special interest to individual grantseekers is a searchable database of minority scholarships. By using MOLIS you will focus on opportunities specifically for minority groups.

Grants Web (http://www.srainternational.org/cws/sra/resource.htm)

Created by the Society of Research Administrators, Grants Web is a comprehensive, well-organized site that highlights government grantmaking areas with links to federal agencies and their funding programs. Although you cannot search this site for grant opportunities, it does provide detailed lists of federal agencies and links to funding information. The site also features links to specific agencies' application forms.

University of Michigan Documents Center
(http://www.lib.umich.edu/libhome/Documents.center/fedgt.html)

The annotated links at this site provide access to some of the major government databases and funding sites, such as the Catalog of Federal Domestic Assistance, a few searchable university databases, Department of Education grant opportunities, etc. This site provides access to most of the aforementioned sites, but it is well organized and worth visiting.

Texas Research Administrators Group (TRAM) (http://tram.east.asu.edu)
TRAM offers a variety of useful resources on its Web site, which is hosted by Arizona State University East. One of the most interesting features is the Electronic Agency Forms section, where you can download copies of application forms accepted by certain government agencies. TRAM also provides links to federal agencies that have made their forms available on their own Web sites.

You also can perform a keyword search of a database of funding opportunities, culled from the Web sites of several agencies, such as NASA, the Department of Education, the EPA, and so on. The listings here are not as helpful as those found on the government sites themselves, since many seem to be out of date. A search for all listings with the word "children," for example, brought up five hits, with only one listing for 2001.

Specific Subject Areas

Grantseekers with a clearly defined project in a specific discipline or subject area may choose to go directly to the government department or agency that is most likely to offer them funding. A grant project may even be developed with a particular funder in mind. The Web sites of most government agencies have some information about funding. They usually provide links to the general grant information sites described in the previous section. The following are some of the federal government departments, independent agencies, subordinate agencies, state and local government sites, and other government sites that typically provide funding assistance and/or information. (URLs indicate grants/funding information pages, not the departmental home page.)

U.S. DEPARTMENTS

Department of Agriculture
(http://www.reeusda.gov/1700/funding/ourfund.htm)
The Cooperative State Research, Education, and Extension Service (CSREES) of the USDA administers a variety of grant programs available to researchers, educators, and small businesses.

Department of Education (http://www.ed.gov/funding.html)
The Funding Opportunities section of the Department of Education's Web site contains information on student financial assistance and links to a host of grants and contracts information.

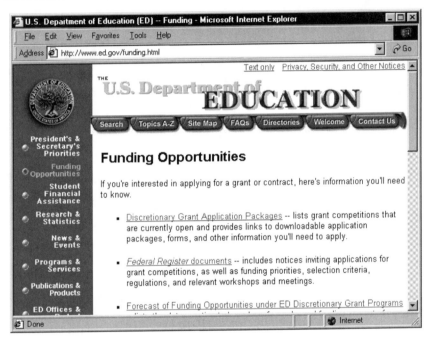

Department of Housing and Urban Development
(http://www.hud.gov/fundopp.html)
This site provides information about various types of grants, including community development, affordable housing, and research.

Department of Justice (http://www.usdoj.gov/10grants/index.html)
The funding information offered on this site includes grants offered by the Office of Justice Programs and the Community Oriented Policing Services (COPS).

Department of Transportation (http://www.dot.gov/ost/m60/grant)
This site provides information on grants, generally made to state and local governments (with some to Indian tribes, universities, and nonprofit organizations), for planning, designing, and constructing of transportation improvements. There also is a limited amount of funding available for research and development projects.

INDEPENDENT AGENCIES

Environmental Protection Agency (http://www.epa.gov/ogd/grants.htm)

This site offers information on funding opportunities for environmental causes, such as pollution prevention or environmental justice. There is an interactive grantwriting tutorial here.

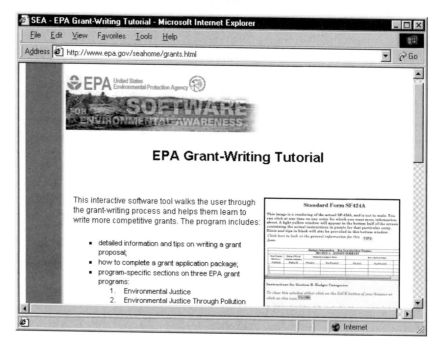

National Archives (http://www.nara.gov/nhprc)

The National Historical Publications and Records Commission (NHPRC) makes grants to archives, educational organizations, libraries, historical societies, and other nonprofit organizations aimed at identifying, preserving, and providing public access to records, photographs, and other materials that document American history.

National Endowment for the Arts (http://arts.endow.gov)

This often-visited site describes federal funding opportunities available for arts projects through national, state, and local funding programs. From the home page, click on Cultural Funding: Federal Opportunities for further information on government programs.

National Endowment for the Humanities (http://www.neh.gov)

NEH supports research, education, and public programs in the humanities. Click on Apply for a Grant to find information and application materials for this highly competitive grantmaking program. The site also lists recent NEH awards.

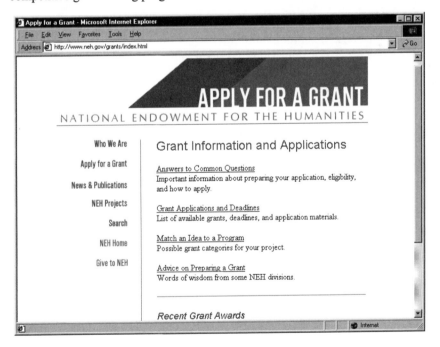

National Institutes of Health (http://www.nih.gov/grants)

This is an easy-to-use site with clear information about research training, fellowship, and career development grant programs. The Computer Retrieval of Information on Scientific Projects (CRISP), a searchable database of federally funded biomedical research projects, is accessible on the site.

National Science Foundation (http://www.nsf.gov/home/grants.htm)

The National Science Foundation (NSF) is an independent U.S. government agency responsible for promoting science and engineering through research and education projects. From the home page, you can easily find information on funding opportunities, proposal preparation, grants awarded, and more.

National Telecommunications and Information Administration (http://www.ntia.doc.gov)

This site offers information on grants, training, and research services in the telecommunications arena. The NTA administers two programs: the Public Telecommunications Facilities Program and the Technology Opportunities Program, an umbrella program under which most of the federal government's Digital Divide initiatives fall.

Small Business Administration (http://www.sbaonline.sba.gov)

This is a well-known independent governmental agency that assists small businesses through a variety of programs. You can easily navigate the site by using its search engine or by clicking on a topic such as Starting Your Business. Here you will find a startup kit, an outline for a business plan, and additional resources. Other areas of interest on the site include Financing Your Business and Business Opportunities.

Smithsonian Institution (http://www.si.edu/ofg)
The Smithsonian site offers information on its predoctoral, postdoctoral, and graduate student fellowship programs, including the Minority Internship Program and the Native American Internship Program.

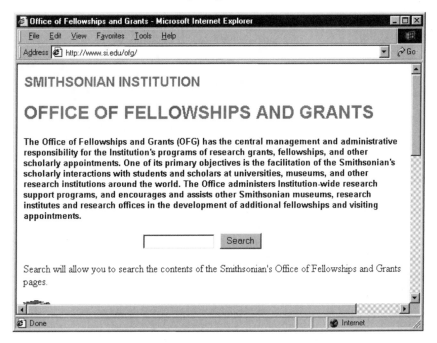

SUBORDINATE AGENCIES

Agency for Health Care Policy and Research (http://www.ahcpr.gov/fund)

On this site, Funding Opportunities describes the agency's research agenda and financial assistance for research projects. The focus primarily is on opportunities for investigator-initiated research grants.

Office of Juvenile Justice and Delinquency Prevention (OJJDP) (http://ojjdp.ncjrs.org)

This site offers comprehensive information on the grants and funding process of OJJDP, as well as statistics, publications, and national resources on juvenile justice issues.

Office of Minority Health Resource Center (http://www.omhrc.gov)

This site includes a searchable database of funding and grant resources for minority health projects.

Substance Abuse and Mental Health Services Administration (SAMHSA) (http://www.samhsa.gov/grants/grants.html)

This site has an online version of *Tips for SAMHSA Grant Applicants,* the booklet used in its Grant-Writing Technical Assistance Workshops, as well as ample information on several programs offering discretionary grants.

STATE AND LOCAL GOVERNMENT INFORMATION SITES

Virtually every branch of government—be it national, state, or local—has some sort of Internet presence these days; therefore, your grantseeking can delve even deeper if you know what you're looking for. To find state and local government resources, try these sites:

State and Local Government on the Net
(http://www.piperinfo.com/state/index.cfm)

This site consists of links to each state (plus tribal governments). In turn, each state page provides links to the branches, departments, boards, and commissions that have Web sites. It can be helpful in searching for local grantmaking bodies such as arts councils.

Grants Action News (http://assembly.state.ny.us/gan)

Grants Action News is a monthly publication of the New York State Assembly. Each issue lists funding opportunities at both the state and federal levels and provides you with eligibility requirements, funding availability, deadlines, and contact information. Each issue also features listings of learning opportunities and what's new on the Web. You can also subscribe to a free e-mail version of the newsletter.

NASCIO StateSearch (http://www.nascio.org/statesearch)

This site, offered by the National Association of State Information Resource Executives, is "designed to serve as a topical clearinghouse to state government information on the Internet." Linking to one of its 32 categories, such as Arts Commissions, State Libraries, or Education, generates a list of all departments involved in that subject, with Web presences by state.

Library of Congress: State and Local Governments
(http://lcweb.loc.gov/global/state/stategov.html)

The Library of Congress Internet Resource Page combines the information included on the previous two sites. It offers a meta-list of links to state and local government information—for example, the National City Government Resource Center, a site that provides access to cities' government information—and links to Web pages for each state.

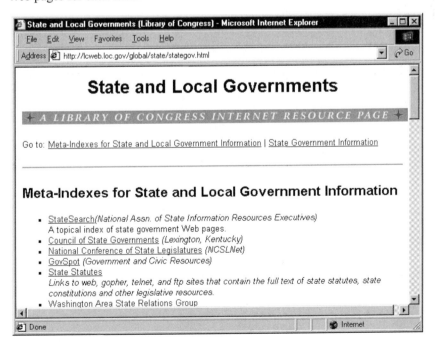

OTHER GOVERNMENT RESOURCES

In the miscellaneous category, you may find the following government-related sites useful both in your grants search and in gaining a better understanding of the nonprofit sector and its relationship to the government.

FedStats (http://www.fedstats.gov)

This site provides a variety of statistics produced by more than 100 agencies of the federal government, including the National Center for Education Statistics and the Health Resources and Services Administration. It provides links to statistics by topic or state and statistical agencies by subject or name.

Internal Revenue Service: Information for Tax-Exempt Organizations (http://www.irs.ustreas.gov/prod/bus_info/eo/index.html)

This is a very useful site for tax information. You can learn about the various types of exempt organizations, the requirements for exemption, and the annual filing requirements for tax-exempt entities. The site includes a Tax Kit—federal forms and publications for tax-exempt organizations. You also can conduct a search for any exempt organization by using the site's search engine.

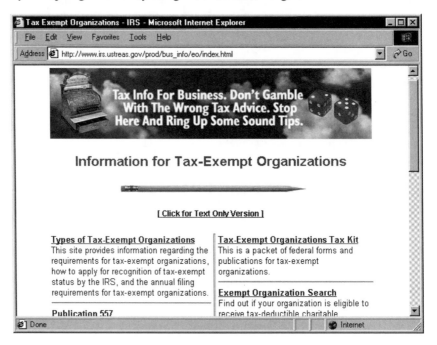

State Agencies that Monitor Charities (http://philanthropy.com/free/resources/general/stateags.htm)

The *Chronicle of Philanthropy* provides a directory of Web sites for the various state agencies that regulate charities and fundraising within their states.

National Association of Attorneys General (NAAG)
(http://www.naag.org/about/aglist.cfm).
Use this site to find a list of the chief legal officers in all 50 states.

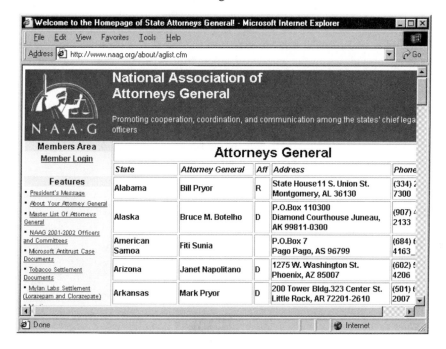

The Federal Election Commission (FEC) (http://www.fec.gov)
The FEC's Web site offers a wealth of information on contributions to presidential and congressional (but not senatorial) campaigns. You can view campaign finance disclosure filings going back to 1993 and search a database of selected contributions, by individual contributor or PAC name, in the 1997–98 and 1999–2000 election cycles. This Web site is especially useful for grantseekers researching an individual's giving patterns.

Office of Management and Budget (OMB) Grants Management page
(http://www.whitehouse.gov/omb/grants/index.html)
The Office of Management and Budget develops policy to ensure that grants are managed properly and that federal dollars are spent in accordance with applicable laws and regulations. Although OMB does not award grants, its Web site links to the Catalog of Federal Domestic Assistance and other useful sites such as GrantsNet. The site also provides links to numerous grants management forms that may be of interest to grantseekers.

U.S. Census Bureau (http://www.census.gov)
A wealth of statistical information about the United States, its people, communities, businesses, and geography can be found at this site. This is particularly useful as a source of data that can enhance and support a grant proposal.

Conclusion

The list of resources provided in this chapter is by no means exhaustive; rather, it is a guide to some of the more user-friendly stopping-off points for government grantseeking on the Web. As with any search for funding, it is essential to start with a clear idea of what you are looking for. This proves especially true when combing through the profusion of government resources. As a rule, to supplement what you've discovered on the Web, it is a good idea to contact by phone or e-mail the agency to which you are considering applying in order to obtain the most up-to-date information on its programs and procedures.

CHAPTER SIX

Online Prospecting for Individual Donors

The Internet is a veritable goldmine for prospect researchers. In fact, the advent of such an enormous compendium of information on virtually any subject readily available at the click of a mouse has totally revolutionized the strategies used by those seeking to raise funds from individuals. In this chapter we will look at some of the most useful Web sites to build your prospect files and, more importantly, to uncover relevant background information on each of your prospective donors. As a grantseeker you will find that the Internet is much more helpful for the latter function because the basic tenet of fundraising still prevails: The closer an individual is to your organization to begin with, the more likely that person is to give you money.

What Is Prospect Research?

As a prospect researcher you are looking for individuals who have the *capacity* and *willingness* to give to your organization and an *interest* in your cause or project. The research part of the equation involves gathering as much *useful* and *relevant* information as you can to measure the three factors noted above.

Another key concept to keep in mind is that in order to be *efficient* while conducting Web research, you need to be *selective*. There is so much information out there that you can easily find yourself spinning your wheels or lost in cyberspace. That is, you may find yourself wasting enormous amounts of time coming up with Web sites that produce duplicative information or, even worse, conflicting information, so that you have no idea what to believe.

Also, there may be missing items, such as a phone number, salary figure, or record of a recent contribution, that you really need in order to complete your prospect picture but that elude your best online detective work. Or you may be stymied in your efforts to prove or confirm a family relationship between two prospects. You may encounter contradictory information and need a "third opinion" or one from an authoritative source to say which is correct. While the process of researching individuals on the Web can be all-absorbing, it can also be quite frustrating.

As you begin your Web journey, you will discover that it takes a great deal of *discipline* to stay on track. Many of the sites we'll look at in this chapter offer truly fascinating information, and it's very easy to get sidetracked. For example, when you click on a site that helps you find out about real estate holdings of your prospect, the next thing you know, you'll find yourself checking on the assessed value of your neighbor's house. Unless you have unlimited time at your disposal (and what grantseeker has that luxury?), you will need to constantly remind yourself of the task at hand and continuously refocus your efforts.

Research Strategies

You might begin with a prospect worksheet that lays out the essential elements for a thorough inquiry of any individual donor. You should fill one out for each prospect on your list. We've created one for you to use (located on page 124) that includes many of the elements you will need.

The worksheet we've provided is very comprehensive. You may find that not all categories apply to your particular Web search. You may want to adapt this worksheet for your own needs or create your own. The purpose of such a research tool is to force you to be consistent and to keep a detailed history of URLs and citations to other sources you've consulted so that you can always retrace your steps. If you find yourself filling in the same or similar information repeatedly, you will need to narrow your search to Web sites with more targeted or up-to-date content. Or you may decide that perhaps you've done all you can for this particular prospect and move on to either the next step (cultivation or appeal) or to another prospect.

We recommend a three-pronged approach when researching individuals on the Web: compile, investigate, and analyze.

Compile

Much of the prospecting part of your research goes on at this earliest stage. While some prospect identification will actually take place online (and we'll show you how to use various Web sites to do that later in this chapter), most of the names on your initial prospect list will come from other sources. As noted earlier, it simply stands to reason that someone *already* involved with your organization or cause is your best source for future gifts. The greater the level of involvement (e.g., board member, volunteer, or past donor), the more likely the contribution. By the same token, the more tenuous the connection (a friend of a staff member, someone who has given to an agency similar to yours, or someone whose colleague died from the disease your agency seeks to cure), the less likely and the smaller the gift. It goes without saying that someone with absolutely no connection to your organization or cause whatsoever is highly unlikely to contribute without extensive cultivation over a period of time, even if he or she has the capacity to do so.

You'll want to compile as comprehensive a list of prospects as possible before you begin. Your list might be extensive, since it may include all alumni from your college for the past ten years or everyone who gave more than $500 to your local symphony, for example. (Competitors' Web sites, if they happen to include donor lists, are certainly a good place to look for your own prospects.) You may well use the Web to help compile such master lists. For efficiency's sake you will want to spend the greater portion of your time, however, researching those prospects with the closest ties to your organization.

Investigate

While this may seem paradoxical, it is a tried and true fundraising technique: Learn as much as you can about those prospects you already know. You can never tell when a seemingly minor detail you uncover will make or break your appeal. Is it possible that you'll actually encounter new prospective donors in the course of your Web research? Absolutely. Every fundraiser has a tale to tell regarding how they suddenly and unexpectedly came across the perfect donor in the least likely place. And the nature of the Web, with its multiple access points, interfaces, and links at all levels makes the "eureka!" phenomenon even more likely.

Nonetheless, most of your online research time will be spent using various Web sites and search engines to find out as much as possible about names you've already gathered. Here's where your prospect worksheet (located on the next page) will come in handy. It will ensure that you don't overlook a key element or fact, and it will help you avoid retracing your steps at a later time when you may be up against a deadline.

Analyze

The Internet belongs to everyone and to no one. There is no Webmaster in the sky, no content manager you can rely on to exercise overall editorial control to ensure that what you find will be up-to-date or even accurate. For this reason we recommend that you seek out the most authoritative sources possible. There's no guarantee, for example, that what you find on Hoover's reputable business information portal site (http://www.hooversonline.com) is totally correct or current, but it's far more likely that it, rather than what you come across on the Web site of some online business-related newsletter you have never heard of before, will be.

A healthy dose of skepticism is the online prospector's best friend. If you uncover "facts" about your prospect on the Web that seem too good to be true, they may well be. The best way to protect yourself is also a favorite requirement of many newspaper editors: Confirm *all* critical data in at least one other reliable source (in this case Web site) before you accept any information as valid. When visiting a Web site for the first time, *always* check to see who the host is. There's usually an About Us section that can be more or less informative. Look for the information that indicates when a site was last updated, as we've mentioned earlier. This is essential for time-sensitive materials. The more experience you have with this type of analysis, the more it will become second nature to you. Eventually you will get to the point where you can almost sense whether the information you've gathered is adequate to proceed with an appeal or whether you need to keep on digging to compile more data.

At the tail end of the analysis stage, you will want to rate your various prospects to coincide with your plans to approach them. Depending on the nature of your project, you may have a different means of approach in mind for each one (e.g., a

Prospect Worksheet—Individual Donors

Basic information:

Name (first, middle, last) _____

Title (Mr., Ms., Mrs., Dr.) _____

Former or maiden name or nickname_____

Address _____

_____

Phone number(s) _____

Alternate address _____

_____

Employment information:

Place of employment _____

(Web site, if any): http://_____

Address _____

_____

Work phone number _____

Work e-mail address_____

Position (title) _____

Since (date)_____

Salary and other benefits (estimated)_____

Other relevant employment-related data (former employment)_____

_____

Personal information:

School(s) attended _____

Board affiliation(s)_____

Foundation affiliation(s) (if any) _____

_____

Civic/volunteer interests _____

Social (include club memberships) _____

_____

Hobbies _____

Giving history (include large gifts, dates, etc.) _____

_____

Assets (real estate, stock, etc.)_____

_____

Other wealth indicators_____

_____

Family information (if applicable):

Spouse's name _____

Spouse's occupation _____

Spouse's affiliation(s) _____

Spouse's philanthropy _____

Children's school(s) _____

Other (siblings, parents, etc.) _____

Connection to your organization:

Board member (dates) _____

Volunteer (current?) _____

Current or past donor (amount and other details)_____

Friend of board member or staff (provide contact name) _____

_____

Other (shared interests, etc.)_____

Area(s) of commonality with the prospect:

Prior giving history _____

Geography _____

Subject field_____

People _____

Other_____

Sources consulted (provide URLs, dates, and other details):

Search engines (terms used) _____

Web sites _____

Databases _____

_____

Contributions lists _____

Directories _____

Newspapers _____

Other_____

History of past cultivation (if any):

Type (letter, call, invitation, meeting, etc. and dates) _____

_____

Recommended next step(s):

(Indicate deadlines) _____

_____

_____

phone call for one, a visit from a board member for another, and a letter of endorsement for a third). Or you may be making a mass appeal to a wider list (e.g., a brochure mailing, a telethon, or an invitation to a gala). Once again your prospect worksheet will come in handy. If filled in properly, it should enable you to arrange all your prospects or groups of prospects in priority order and according to recommended next steps.

TIPS TO SPEED YOU ON YOUR WAY

When researching an individual on the Web or elsewhere, clearly it is critical to be sure you're looking up the right person. The spelling or alternate spellings, including nicknames or middle names or initials, or such suffixes as "Jr." or "III" are all very important for you to have down pat *before* you begin your research. Of course the beauty of the Web is that if one form of a person's name doesn't work, you can always try another with very little time or effort expended.

A geographic location where the person either lives or works (or sometimes for people with multiple residences, where he or she vacations) can be helpful as well. It's also good to know women's maiden or former names. All of these elements will help prevent you from going down some blind online alleys before you hit on the right source.

We mentioned relevance earlier. This is an important rule of thumb to keep in mind: If you've found nothing useful after 20 minutes of searching, it's probably time to move on to a different site or to perform a new search.

Have a specific strategy in mind before you get started. How much time do you plan to spend on the Web as opposed to other, more traditional resources? While this guide is about conducting research on the Web, the Internet is not the be-all end-all of research tools. There may well be magazines, newspapers, or print or electronic directories that have the information you require. And don't overlook the value of the "invisible network," that is, people you know who may know someone who knows something about someone that might be useful to you. Lastly, that wellspring of helpful information, your local librarian, can be a wonderful resource for those seeking relevant information on prospective donors, particularly those who are famous or prominent only in your own locale.

A WORD ABOUT ETHICS

Unlike other types of prospective donors, in this chapter we are talking about individuals—people just like us—who might feel a bit uncomfortable, at a minimum, about their privacy being invaded by someone looking to solicit them for a charitable gift. While privacy matters have always been of concern to prospect researchers, the Web has made it incredibly easy to uncover information that in the past only the most persistent and creative fundraiser would have been able to unearth. Horror stories abound today about very private information, such as medical histories, banking records, or legal matters being readily accessible on the Internet to those who know someone's Social Security number. As a grantseeker you need to be highly sensitive to the appropriateness of what you uncover. First, you may not want to let your prospect know how deeply you've been delving into personal matters; but secondly, you may not want to let yourself get involved with his or her information beyond your own comfort level. If you work for a large nonprofit development office, your own organization should have standards regarding what is appropriate and what is not in terms of invading a prospect's privacy.

In response to the many issues raised regarding privacy rights and readily-available, free information on individuals, the Association of Professional Researchers for Advancement (APRA) has posted a Statement of Ethics on its Web site (http://www.aprahome.org/apra_statement_of_ethics.htm).

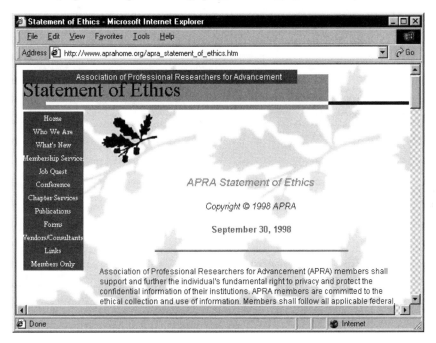

The Association of Fundraising Professionals (AFP) also posts ethical standards and a statement of principles on its site (http://www.afpnet.org/ethics/), and the ePhilanthropy Foundation has posted a code specifically related to ethical online practices on its site (http://www.ephilanthropyfoundation.org).

Search Engines

The first and most obvious place to search for online information on an individual whose name you already have is by means of a general search engine. See Appendix A for an annotated list of several of these. Be sure to follow the advice we've provided regarding correct names and forms of names and trying your search several different ways. For example, if you use Google (http://www.google.com) to find information on Brooke Astor as a prospective donor, here's what your results might look like. (Note: we got the best hits by typing "mrs. vincent astor" into the search box and selecting Google Search. If you choose I'm Feeling Lucky, your hit will be for the New York Public Library, a pet charity of Mrs. Astor.)

Each search engine has its own criteria, by means of which it generates results, and its own features for constructing your search queries. For some it's best to put the name inside quotation marks, as in "mrs. vincent astor." For others you will want to try mrs.+vincent+astor. The plus sign tells the search engine that each term you've listed must be present in your results list but not necessarily immediately adjacent to one another. This feature helps narrow your search to only the individual you have in mind, while at the same time covering variants of the name. You should also try nicknames and alternate spellings.

A search for Mrs. Astor using Alta Vista (http://altavista.com) yields the following results:

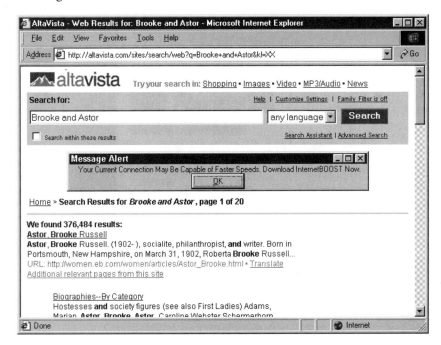

You will note that most of the hits that came up are quite different from those generated by the Google search. This is why it is recommended that you try more than one search engine and more than one variant of a name.

Be sure to learn the advanced search features of your favorite search engines and the correct search syntax for each in order to yield the most relevant results.

Incidentally, there is no foolproof way to use the Web to determine whether Mrs. Astor is a foundation's donor or board member, at least not for free. Of course, you can use a search engine and hope that her name comes up that way. You can also use Foundation Finder on the Foundation Center's Web site. However, this works only if the name of the foundation is the same as that of the individual, since you need to type in all or part of a foundation's name to search via this feature. If you subscribe to *The Foundation Directory Online,* you can type Brooke Astor into the search box to determine if she is affiliated with a foundation. Depending on whether you subscribe to *The Foundation Directory Online, Plus, Premium,* or *Platinum,* you will be searching the largest 10,000, 20,000, or all U.S. foundations (including grantmaking public charities and corporate givers), respectively. If you visit a Foundation Center library, you can perform a comprehensive search for free, using the Trustees, Officers, and Donors index on *FC Search: The Foundation Center's Database on CD-ROM.*

NEWSPAPER AND MAGAZINE SEARCHES

These online resources can be useful for anecdotal information and for biographical bits of information not available elsewhere. It goes without saying that more prominent individuals will be covered in the larger, national news sources, and the less prominent in local media. There are a variety of online sites that cover both kinds of media. If you're extremely lucky, you'll encounter an online magazine article that provides a full biographical portrait of your prospect.

For prospects active in business or finance, you might want to start with bizjournals.com. This free online resource searches some 40 business journals for articles printed in the past 30 days, and it has a very simple search interface you can use by simply typing in the individual's name.

There are also more general news search services, such as FindArticles.com, that cover a variety of different media. You may want to try more than one of these search engines. Read each home page description carefully to determine what kinds of news media are covered and how much time is permitted to elapse before items are archived. You may also find that "current" articles (those that are up to 30 to 60 days old) may be free, whereas older articles are available only to registered members or for a fee. At the top of the search screen for FindArticles.com, you can select the View Publications feature to see what publications, either by subject or alphabetically by newspaper name, are included.

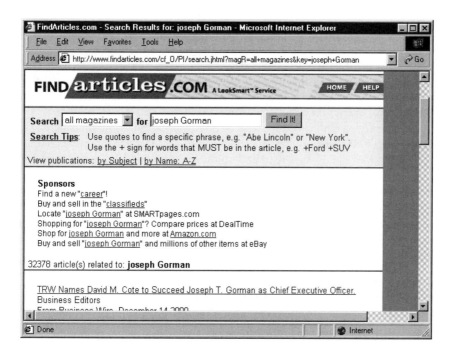

By now, you have probably noticed that most of these free online news search services have very prominent advertisements splashed across their home pages and popping up on your computer screen. Patience is required to work around these seemingly aggressive advertisers. It's one of the prices you pay for the free service. Without advertising, the online service providers would be unable to offer you this wealth of information free of charge. As you continue your Web search efforts, you will find your way around the more pesky online solicitations and learn to ignore the rest.

We mentioned the "eureka!" phenomenon earlier. By this we mean the fortuitous way in which one Web link suddenly and quite unexpectedly leads to another. For example, in the search results for TRW's former CEO, Joseph Gorman, on FindArticles.com, the very last hit on our search results list is for something called America Associates. Clicking on this link takes you to a "Dear Friends of America" letter written by Thomas J. Reese. As you scroll down you learn that this is a Catholic weekly magazine and that the letter is thanking its donors, among whom is Joseph Gorman, for 1999. This tiny nugget of information may be just the type of thing you are looking for to complete your profile of Mr. Gorman's charitable interests. Up until now it's possible you didn't even realize that he was Catholic or interested in supporting Catholic causes.

This is also a good time to illustrate how readily one can get sidetracked. For a moment you may forget the task at hand. You might well be tempted to begin exploring the other donors to this Catholic weekly magazine or, at a minimum, to scroll down the list to see whether any other names seem familiar. This side expedition may make sense as a next step, or it may not. You need to ask yourself what is the best use of your time. Perhaps you want to proceed with checking more Web sites for information on Joseph Gorman while bookmarking this list to return to later on. This is particularly true if you already have reason to believe that Mr.

Gorman is a likely prospect, while you have no idea whether this is the case for the other people on the contributions list.

The Internet Prospector Web site (http://www.internet-prospector.org/news.html) is a very useful online source for news. In fact, this is a wonderful site for varied content, and has a very helpful online reference desk to which you can submit e-mail queries on virtually any topic that a librarian will respond to. If you click on the News Online page, you will find business news, fundraising news, meta-indices to the foreign press (useful when researching executives of international companies), and a variety of news-only search engines. You may browse or search abstracts, current stories, headlines, wire services, and so on. This Web site also has extensive biographical sources. Its Hard Rock Mining feature is a three-part guide to biographical research on the Internet, which is highly informative for the novice researcher. Finding your way around this particular home page is well worth the investment of your time. In fact, some grantseekers may prefer to start their investigations here.

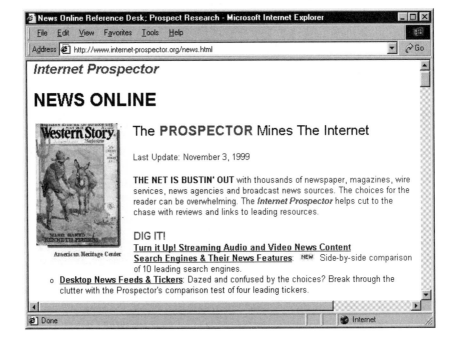

If you select the Business News option on Internet Prospector's News Only page, you will encounter a variety of databases. Hispanic business magazines and newswires are also included. There's also an often overlooked but valuable resource on this site: Pressline, which searches more than 20,000 corporate press releases—one of the very few places you'll find access to all of these. Searchable archives link to news providers' archives and search engines for a variety of media.

Sometimes you will be seeking information on a very recent newsworthy event, such as the appointment of a new CEO or a large, just-announced gift to a university. PR Newswire (http://www.prnewswire.com) is a useful source for these kinds of breaking news stories. There are three search options: all press releases for the past 72 hours, a topical search by industry or subject, and a keyword search. In addition, it is possible to search the archive for 2,000 companies included in the Company News on Call subscriber database. You can further narrow your search by state, company name, or within the last three business days. The results list you receive will be weighted by relevancy.

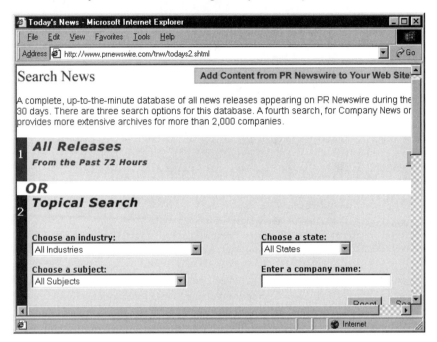

Many of the larger metropolitan newspapers have their own online search services. *The New York Times* (http://nytimes.com) and *Washington Post* (http://www.washingtonpost.com) are chief among them. Searches for current articles generally are free, whereas searches for articles more than a week or a month old may entail a fee. To access some of these, you will need to become a registered online subscriber, but generally this service is free of charge and simply requires you to fill out a brief online questionnaire and to select a password and user name. The more sophisticated of these online search services use "cookies" to remember your user name and password, so that you don't have to. A Web site's cookie will only work if you access the site with the same computer you used to register your user name and password. In addition to some of the media meta-search engines and large metropolitan newspaper sites, a search of the local hometown paper for your prospect is always worthwhile. For information on CNN's Ted Turner, for example, you might visit the *Atlanta Journal-Constitution's* Web site (http://www.accessatlanta.com/ajc). Here you can search the past seven issues or the "stacks" (the archive). On any given day you're likely to find substantial hits on Ted Turner.

Speaking of CNN, for national or international news items, don't overlook its Web site at http://CNN.com. The content changes every 15 minutes or so.

Online magazine articles are something you want to be sure to look for as well. As mentioned earlier, the truly fortunate grantseeker will find a current and comprehensive biography of a prospect in a business or other magazine via an online search service. MagPortal.com is one of these. You can select from Free Feeds in 200 categories or the Paid Feeds, which offers more traditional online magazines and more custom search engine features. As an important step in the research process, it is always worthwhile to check to see who the online provider is and to determine the database's guidelines for inclusion or exclusion. This will take a few minutes, but it will save you time in the long run.

A click on the Free Feeds section of the MagPortal.com site yields magazine titles in an alphabetical list with first and last publication date displayed. Included on this list are such magazines as *American Prospect, Boardwatch,* and *The Celebrity Café,* all of interest to the prospect researcher. Search results can be arranged by quality of match, date, publication title, and category. A recent search for Microsoft's Bill Gates yielded 820 hits. For articles from magazines with unfamiliar titles, you should be sure to investigate the publisher to check for authenticity and to see if it may have a particular axe to grind or viewpoint to put forward.

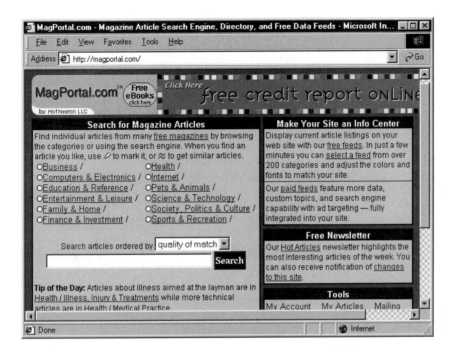

An all too often overlooked resource may be your local public library's Web site, particularly if you live in a major metropolitan area. Those who are fortunate enough to have a New York Public Library card (available to all those who live or work in New York City), for example, have free access, among a range of other searchable features, to an online database of more than 3,500 newspapers and periodicals via an online search service called Proquest Direct at the library's Web site (http://www.nypl.org). The included periodicals range from titles as specific as *Accountancy Ireland* to the more general news, business, and public interest magazines. Those who live in other urban areas, such as Los Angeles, Chicago, or Detroit, may have access, by means of their public library cards, to equally vast online resources, some of which would otherwise only be available on an expensive fee-for-service basis. These days even some smaller public libraries have Web sites that provide access to various CD-ROM and other online databases. It's worth checking to see whether your local library provides these services.

For prospect researchers, the major business publications, such as the *Wall Street Journal*, *Fortune,* and *Forbes,* each provide excellent online search features on their Web sites. Most are free or free once you register. Most also offer the options of search or advanced search. For those you plan to return to frequently, it's probably worthwhile to learn the ins and outs of the advanced search features, since this will make you more efficient each time you visit the site.

On the Forbes.com site you can search various categories, including Companies and People. On the People home page you can search by last name and/or by a company's stock symbol. The last name search is a little time consuming because you scroll down an alphabetical list. However, it yields specific information as to an individual's precise title and company affiliation.

PEOPLE, FAMOUS AND NOT-SO-FAMOUS, INCLUDING THEIR CHARITABLE GIFTS

The Church of Jesus Christ of Latter-day Saints (the Mormons) has been incredibly industrious in gathering information related to genealogy on millions of family names. The Familysearch.org Web site enables you to search a vast collection of records to determine family histories and connections. An online Social Security death index is also available at this site. Morbid as this may sound, prospect researchers frequently must determine the date of an individual's death, and this is one way to do so. Once again this is one of those Web sites where you can easily become distracted and spend hours investigating your own and others' ancestors, rather than your prospect's. If you stick to the task at hand, fascinating connections between families may emerge that are very useful for the grantseeker to know about.

Celebrities

Celebrities are very involved in charitable endeavors these days. Some have their own grantmaking organizations. Others support various causes in a variety of ways, ranging from lending their name to very publicly endorsing an organization or effort. There are a number of Web resources to help find out about celebrities' charitable activities.

The Giving Back Fund (http://www.givingback.org) is a pooled-asset community foundation primarily serving the philanthropic interests of athletes and entertainers. Its home page includes a Philanthropy Hall of Fame and the opportunity to donate to one of the charitable organizations featured on the site. Here you will find such charities as the Britney Spears Foundation, which supports a camp for underprivileged youth, and the Doug Flutie, Jr. Foundation for Autism. A click on the Nancy Kerrigan Foundation, for example, yields a great deal of information on the Olympic ice-skating champion's charitable interests.

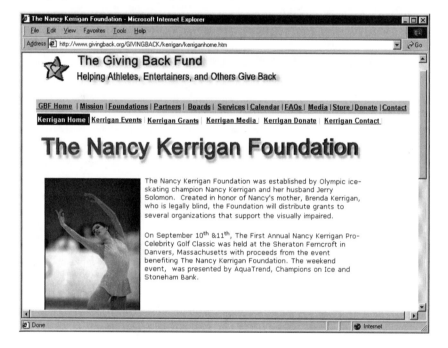

While many of these grantmaking organizations are seeking funds as well as operating their own programs, it may be a safe bet that in addition to their own organizations the celebrities involved may also be interested in supporting your program or cause, if it relates to—but doesn't compete with—their interests. Your job as a grantseeker would then be to determine the best means of approach.

You can also conduct more general searches using various online search engines. A search on the Forbes.com Web site (http://forbes.com), for example, using the term "celebrity charities," yields 124 documents listed by date, all of which describe celebrity charities covered by *Forbes.*

If you visit the People directory on Forbes.com, you can click on the Forbes Celebrity 100 list (http://www.forbes.com/celebrity100/). Choose a year from 1999 onward, and you can browse a list of the top 100 celebrities according to their "power" rank, money rank, earnings, press clips, magazine covers, TV/radio hits, and so on. You can also search the full list by name or category. This is all in good fun, but it also includes useful information for those seeking to solicit donations from celebrities.

Another useful and just plain fun Web site is Hollywoodreporter.com. Here you will find a collection of feature stories on celebrity philanthropy, a glossary entitled Terms of Endowment, the Annals of Altruism, and a Philanthropic Directory described as "our resource guide to organizations addressing a wide range of social ills and issues with the help of Hollywood time and money." While the tone is somewhat tongue-in-cheek, the information seems to be accurate and the intent—to highlight charitable activities of Hollywood celebrities—serious.

Biographies

The Arts and Entertainment (A&E) Network's Web site (http://www.AandE.com) offers a BioSearch feature covering a truly remarkable 25,000 personalities. The emphasis is clearly on celebrities, but others are here as well. A search for Michael J. Fox, for example, yields a quite well-written and comprehensive biography of this star, who has recently redirected all of his time to research on Parkinson's disease. Another search yielded information on Douglas Taylor Ross, founder of SofTech. Many of the biographic subjects are deceased, of course. This is true of most of the general biographical sites.

Speaking of the deceased, another Web site, Lives, the Biography Resource (http://www.amillionlives.com), covers only those who are no longer with us, including "individual lives of the famous, the infamous, and the not so famous." As with the Mormons' death index, this site can provide very useful background information for the prospect researcher, particularly when you are trying to track down historical and family connections.

Along the same morbid lines, a Web site called HeavenlyDoor.com (http://heavenlydoor.com/main/base/newspapers_obits.cfm) offers an extensive index of newspaper obituaries for prominent and not so prominent individuals. If you continue researching prospects for any period of time, ultimately you will need to refer to an obituary. Fundraisers know that these are often the best source for details on family connections and philanthropic initiatives.

Sometimes all you are looking for on a particular individual is an address and/or phone number. The Ultimate White Pages (http://theultimates.com/white) Web site can help you there. This is a meta-search engine that covers six different directories all at once. It does not include unlisted phone numbers, however.

Online lists of alumni may be very helpful for all prospect researchers, not just those in the field of education. Some offer biographical information, including current place of employment and residence. To access these, you might refer to Lipman Hearne's online directory (http://www.lipmanhearne.com), which has links to more than 160 alumni magazines. Yale University, for example, provides an online alumni registry. Online alumni magazines are excellent sources of information about achievements, business successes, and charitable endeavors.

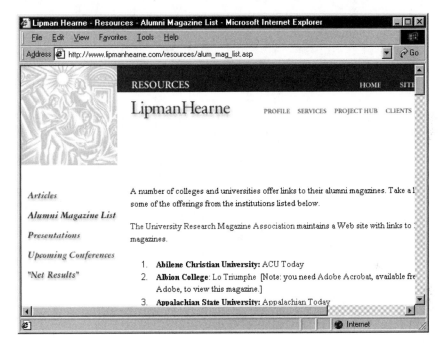

An excellent resource for finding women philanthropists is on the University of Michigan's Web site. Titled Women in Philanthropy, this site (http://www.women-philanthropy.umich.edu) includes specific information on gifts from generous women. While not comprehensive, there is a lot of information included for the online grantseeker. To search for a particular prospect, select a letter corresponding to that individual's last name. It is fascinating, however, simply to scroll down the list of charitable gifts and endeavors.

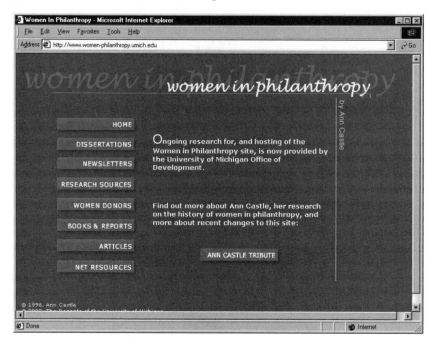

Corporate Heavy Hitters

By far the easiest category of individuals to research on the Web is corporate executives. The reason for this is that the Internet is a virtual treasure trove of information on companies and those who run them. In fact, there is so much available online today regarding corporate executives that you can easily come up with highly duplicative information in the course of visiting just a few Web sites. The best advice we can provide to grantseekers scoping out those who run our nation's corporations as possible sources of individual contributions is to find your favorite sites and stick to them, particularly once you've gained enough experience to know that a given Web site consistently provides up-to-date and accurate information and is relatively easy to search.

One site that's very popular with prospect researchers is CEO Central (http://www.surferess.com/CEO/html/biographies.html). This Web site provides not only biographies but "interesting facts and statistics" (e.g., an executive's golf handicap) and images (that is to say photos) of America's CEOs. Some of what you encounter here may come across as a rather breathless paean to captains of industry. Nonetheless, this is a useful source to become familiar with. The home page features a list of the top CEOs. Click on any of the names and you will find a thorough, well-researched biography of a luminary such as Warren Buffet of Berkshire Hathaway.

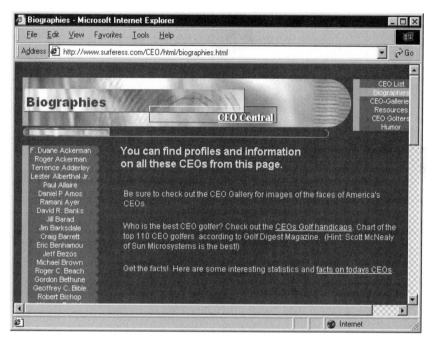

Forbes magazine's Web site (htttp://www.forbes.com), of course, is a highly useful resource on corporations and those who run them. See the description in the earlier celebrity section. The People search feature on this Web site is equally useful for those in the business sector. A search for Apple Computer's Steve Jobs, for example, yields 91 documents in the database arranged in reverse chronological order, each with its own brief abstract.

The *Forbes* Web site also boasts its frequently clicked-on Forbes 400 Richest in America list. This is divided into yearly online segments, going back a number of years. Results can be sorted by rank, worth, age, marital status, residence, and source. A quick link is also provided to *Forbes'* Celebrity 100 list from this page. A click on any of the top 400 richest listings provides you with a concise but information-packed biography of the individual in question, including an estimate of his or her net worth and a brief history of employment. Similar information is provided, along with biographical links, on *Forbes'* World's Richest People list, dating back to 1996. Many are U.S. executives.

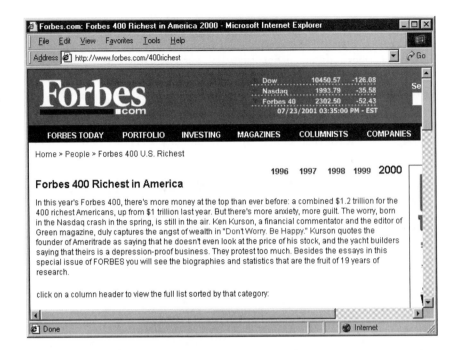

Forbes.com also offers a People Tracker service whereby you can sign up for free membership and receive customized e-mail alerts on changes in an individual's title, compensation, stock options exercised, or "breaking news" for 120,000 executives. This service might make even the most seasoned fundraiser breathe a sigh of relief, since it could save an enormous amount of effort for those in your "live" prospect file whom you are trying to monitor over a period of time.

Forbes' chief competitor, *Fortune* magazine, offers its own lists and biographical information on its Web site at http://www.fortune.com. This site includes a list of America's Forty Richest Under 40 that can be sorted by rank, name, age, company, and net worth. Online biographical sketches are available for those on the list. In addition there are numerous other searchable lists on the *Fortune* site, including Most Powerful Women in Business (the Power 50), All-star Analysts, *Fortune* e-50, and Washington Power 50. It's likely that one or another of your prospects might appear on at least one of these lists, if you are searching for those involved in industry or politics.

Another magazine, *SmartMoney,* has its own list of the 30 most influential people in the field of investing on its Web site (http://smartmoney.com).

An additional Web site to watch is that of *Worth* magazine. On this Web site (http://www.worth.com) you will find lists such as the 50 Best CEOs: 2001 and CEO Profiler (top CEOs share their thoughts on self improvement, favorite authors, and more).

Another online source for biographical snapshots of financial people is Wall Street Reporter at http://wallstreetreporter.com/html2/main.htm.

There is also a Web site for Canadian business leaders at http://www.canadianbusiness.com, which hosts a special list of Canada's Rich 100.

There are more specialized Web sites as well. One example is GoldSea 100 (http://goldsea.com/Profiles/100), which provides a list of America's top 100 Asian entrepreneurs.

If none of these Web sites pan out, you might try a large portal site such as CEOExpress at http://ceoexpress.com. Here you will find a meta-index of daily newspapers, business newspapers and magazines, tech and lifestyle magazines, newsfeeds, and Internet search engines. You can search by name, company name, or stock symbol.

If you are searching for information on an individual and you know what corporation he or she heads or works for, try going right to that company's Web site. For example, a visit to the Barnes & Noble Web site (http://www.barnesandnobleinc.com) very rapidly yields a highly informative resume of its CEO, Leonard Riggio. If he were among your top prospects, the information included here would get you well on your way to filling out your prospect worksheet.

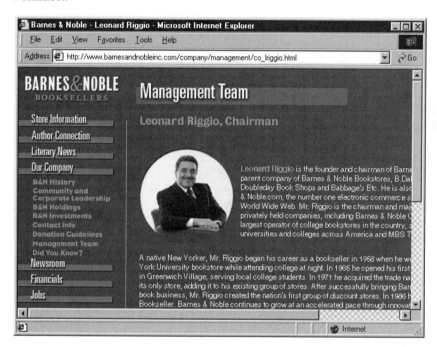

CAPACITY TO GIVE—SALARIES, ASSETS, AND RECENT GIFTS AWARDED

When researching those in the corporate sector you will want to determine their capacity to give your organization a substantial gift. One way to do this is to look at salary information. Although with most executives salary only tells part of the story, it is a good place to start. Salary surveys abound on the Internet. When referring to any of these sites, be sure to check the last date updated. Particularly in times of uncertain stock prices and company layoffs, today's millionaire could easily be tomorrow's unemployed. So it is critical to refer to the most current and trustworthy source available.

One salary survey is on the SiliconValley.com Web site (http://www0.mercurycenter.com/stech/companies/bossmakes/charts/top1000061800.htm). Another is on *Business Week* magazine's site, which posts a special report on the top paid executives at http://businessweek.com. Still another source of salary surveys is CareerJournal.com (http://www.jobsmart.org/tools/salary/sal-prof.htm).

Intended for those entering various fields, this site provides access to 300 general salary surveys, as opposed to specific individuals' salaries, but is useful if you can't find the information you need elsewhere. Here you can search by profession, such as accounting, public relations, and so on.

An additional source for salary information is the huge labor union AFL-CIO's Web site (http://www.aflcio.org/paywatch/index.htm) where you will find a feature called Paywatch. This site promises you will "learn how to track down CEO pay." We mentioned previously that it's critical that you understand whether a particular site's host may have a certain slant or perspective on the data it provides. This site is a good example, since it also has features such as Does the CEO Deserve This Big Pay Package?

Another online research strategy for determining capacity to give is to search by profession. For doctors, lawyers, and others, there are Web sites that have searchable directories. While these rarely provide any specifics on individuals' earnings, they do have useful biographical and other information. Two of these are Martindale-Hubbell's site at http://martindale.com (for attorneys) and the American Medical Association's site at http://www.ama-assn.org. Occasionally you may be searching for information on prospects and donations in the political arena. Or you may be considering asking a local politician to lend his or her name to an event your nonprofit is planning and you want to check out who's been supporting him or her in advance. A good Web site for this kind of data is Open Secrets at http://www.opensecrets.org. Here you will find a Donor Lookup feature that includes individual and "soft money" contributions.

For salary information on those in the nonprofit sector, there are a number of resources. Be forewarned, however, that since most of these derive from public information returns filed with the IRS, the data you uncover may be up to two years old. This is when it is advisable to try to refer to other resources as well, in order to determine an individual's capacity to give. A basic resource for executives of the nation's 57,000+ private foundations is the Form 990-PF that each foundation is required to file with the IRS. On this form the foundation is required to list its top officers, directors, trustees, and foundation managers, along with their compensation.

You can access Forms 990-PF readily from the Foundation Center's Web site via Foundation Finder (http://lnp.fdncenter.org/finder.html) or use the Form 990-PF search feature (http://fdncenter.org/funders/grantsmart/index.html). These are also available on the GrantSmart Web site at http://grantsmart.org.

The *Chronicle of Philanthropy* issues an annual salary survey for nonprofit executives that can be found on its Web site at http://philanthropy.com. The information is arranged by category of nonprofit and is eagerly awaited each year by those in the sector seeking to compare and contrast compensation information. Much of the data comes from direct surveying rather than the Form 990 or other public documents, so it tends to be relatively up-to-date. The *Chronicle* also publishes the names of those organizations that refuse to cooperate with its survey. Access to this part of the site is available only to *Chronicle* subscribers.

As of the writing of this chapter, GuideStar had posted a new nonprofit compensation report, compiled from Form 990 data, at its Web site, http://www.guidestar.org/services/compstudy2.stm. This study, available in several formats at various prices, includes at least one paid position at 75,000 nonprofit organizations in 14 job categories.

The NonProfit Times Web newsletter (http://www.nptimes.com) issues an annual salary survey as a special report and another special report, the NPT Power and Influence Top 50, which profiles the nation's top nonprofit executives.

An excellent and well-established resource on companies and those who manage them, including their compensation and stock holdings, is Hoovers Online (http://www.hoovers.com). One interesting feature at this site is its IPO search. Hoovers also offers a searchable database of Securities and Exchange Commission filings. If you perform such a search for Martha Stewart, for example, you very quickly find your way to a list of documents filed by her conglomerate in the last 12 months. To access her compensation information, including salary, bonus, and stock options—as well as those for the other officers and directors of her company—you will want to look for a proxy statement (Form DEF14a). This form is a quick link away, if you scroll down the list of documents. It takes a bit of getting used-to to read the Form DEF14a, but for top corporate executives at public companies whose salary information is not readily available elsewhere, this type of investigation is well worth the effort.

Regarding stock holdings, a very useful site is CNET.com (http://investor.cnet.com/?taag=stbc.gp). Here you will find a feature called CEO Wealthmeter that provides an alphabetical list by company and includes the CEO's name, the value of his/her holdings, today's change, and the CEO's latest fiscal year compensation. This is an excellent source for identifying companies' stock symbols, since a number of business sites are arranged so you can search by symbol. One other interesting feature of this site is Today's Top 5 Gainers (on the stock market) and, of course, Today's Bottom 5 Losers. The latter might be of interest to refer to just before you approach a CEO for a substantial gift.

Another way to estimate capacity to give is a more obvious one: recent gifts awarded. *Slate,* an online magazine at http://slate.msn.com, posts a list of the Slate 60: the 60 largest American charitable contributions of the year. This is fascinating reading for those seeking major gifts for their own institutions.

Fortune magazine also posts a listing of the 40 Most Generous Americans at its Web site at http://www.fortune/com. This speaks not only to capacity to give, but willingness to do so.

The Foundation Center's *Philanthropy News Digest* (*PND*) (http://fdncenter.org/pnd/current) is an excellent source for current media coverage of large gifts, not only by grantmaking organizations but by individuals. You can search the *PND* archive by an individual's name. Links to relevant foundations are provided.

The SearchZone on the Foundation Center's Web site is an excellent way to research recent gifts and affiliations of individual prospects. Here you will find Form 990-PF search, Foundation Finder, and *PND* Search mentioned above. You will also find Sector Search, a "Web crawler" that searches Web sites across the nonprofit sector, and Grantmaker Web sites, which limits your search to grantmaker sites annotated by Center staff, as well as the fee-based subscription service, *The Foundation Directory Online.*

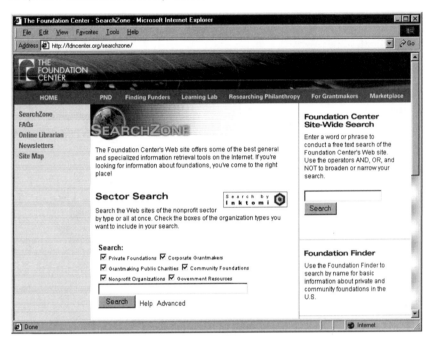

If you click on Sector Search, for example, and enter William Gates, Sr. (Bill Gates' father) in the search box, you receive 371 results, sorted by relevance. Many of the hits at the top of the results list are press announcements of recent large gifts.

An additional resource available on the Foundation Center's Web site in the Researching Philanthropy area is *Literature of the Nonprofit Sector Online*. This bibliographic database contains 19,000 records, many of which are extensively abstracted. Nearly 80 percent are from periodical articles in the fields of philanthropy and nonprofit management. A recent search using "Bill Gates" yielded 22 hits, a number of which provided valuable insights into Mr. Gates and his charitable initiatives.

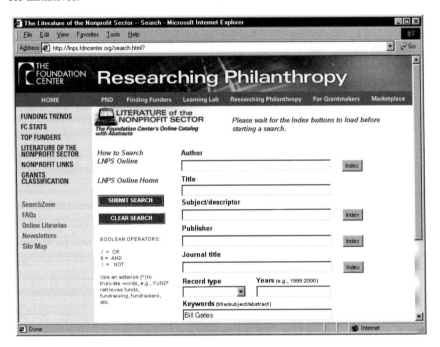

Philanthropy News Network (*PNN*) is another source of information on individual gifts and pledges. You can search the People or Giving features at the *PNN* site (http://pnnonline.org/giving) for details on large gifts derived from other sources.

The Council on Foundations Web site at http://cof.org is one additional resource you might check. A recent site-wide search on Ted Turner yielded a dozen search results, the first one referring to his "historic" commitment of $1 billion to support United Nations initiatives.

In determining an individual's capacity to give, in addition to salaries, stock holdings, and records of recent gifts, other types of assets and their value also are of interest. Real estate, yachts, and airplanes are the three types of assets about which online information is most often available. The University of Virginia has a popular feature on its Web site (http://www.people.Virginia.edu/~dev-pros/Realestate.html), whereby you can check property assessments arranged by geographic region of the country.

This site also provides other useful real estate links, including those more specific to local areas and Yahoo!'s real estate sales at http://realestate.yahoo.com/realestate/homevalues. The Yahoo! real estate page is another one of those sites where the temptation to digress from your task at hand will be great. A Web site for determining airplane ownership is at http://www.landings.com. Here you will find a database of airplane registrations. A useful site for determining yacht ownership is at http://www.yachtworld.com, which boasts the largest photo database of boats for sale on the Internet. You'll also be able to tell who owns what boat.

GATEWAYS TO PROSPECT RESEARCH

Not surprisingly, the Web sites of various university development offices throughout the country provide excellent entrees to the world of prospect research. Most are organized in highly systematic ways by topic and provide an array of links to other sites that have proven of use to university development staff over the years. It is truly amazing and of enormous benefit to the grantseeker that so much of this information is available online for free by visiting these sites, since their developers have generously decided to share their research expertise with others.

The Princeton University Web site, for example, offers an extensive list of resources its development staff has found useful in determining an individual's assets and unearthing biographical information (http://www.princeton.edu/One/research/researchlinks.html).

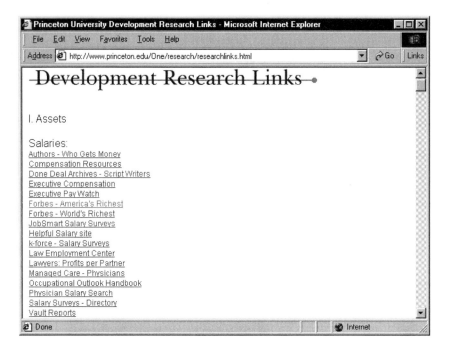

Another useful resource will be found on Syracuse University's Web site at http://web.syr.edu/~dekelley/hotlist.html. Here you will find Dorry Kelley's favorite prospect research links—"and *not* the golf variety." Northwestern University posts its research bookmarks on its site at http://pubweb.nwu.edu/~cap440/bookmark.html. Categories on the Northwestern University site include links to alumni directories, mergers and acquisitions, tax assessors' databases, and so on.

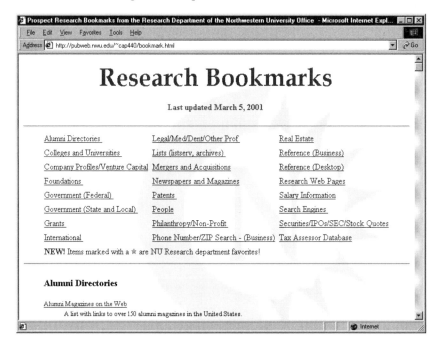

We've already mentioned the University of Virginia Web site and its prospect research area (http://www.people/virginia.edu/~dev-pros/Resources.html). On this site you will find a series of links, compiled in a very logical way (Resources for Finding Biographical Information, Resources for Finding Corporate Information, etc.) and other online resources that are extremely helpful in estimating net worth and determining capacity to give.

Another useful gateway resource to many of the Web sites featured in this chapter and others as well is the Association of Professional Researchers for Advancement's Web site, mentioned earlier for its statement of ethical standards. Here you will find Web Resources for Advancement Research (http://www.aprahome.org/links.htm), which is extremely well put together and definitely worth a visit by anyone seeking information on individual donors, especially those whose detective work has not yet yielded much useful information.

Last but certainly not least when it comes to gateways is David Lamb's Prospect Research Page (http://www.lambresearch.com), the name of which is highly deceiving, since it is certainly more than a page. David Lamb, former director of prospect research at the University of Washington and Santa Clara University, is considered by many to be the "Web Guru" of online prospect research. The site includes categories such as corporations/executives, public records, professionals, and others. This Web site is an attempt to "separate the wheat from the chaff when it comes to research resources on the Internet." These are David Lamb's personal recommendations of Web sites to visit. Since he is the expert, you may want to take them seriously.

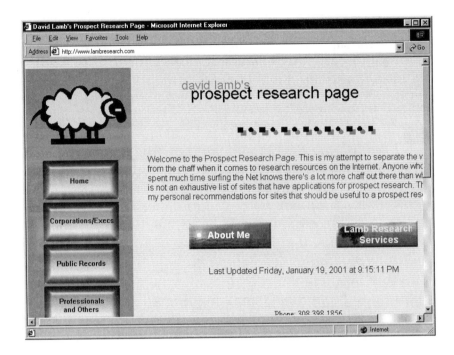

Fee-Based Services

In this chapter we have focused primarily on Web resources that are available for free to anyone seeking prospect information on potential individual donors. We would be remiss, however, if we didn't at least mention the availability of online services that provide extensive information and search capabilities on individual donors for a fee. Most require annual subscriptions or membership, and there may be individual online search charges as well. For larger organizations and those engaged in intensive campaigns to raise funds from individuals, these may be worth investigating. Chief among these are DIALOG (http://library.dialog.com/openaccess), one of the original online database providers, with access to databases in business, government, medicine, intellectual property, and many others; and Lexis-Nexis (http://web.lexis-nexis.com), with "billions" of searchable documents in disciplines related to law and business. A fee-based service called Prospect Research Online (PRO) provides a compilation of publicly available information on individuals and institutional donors on a subscription basis. For more information, visit its Web site at http://www.rpbooks.com. The Foundation Center's aforementioned family of fee-based subscriptions services, *The Foundation Directory Online,* will provide you with information on grantmakers with which your prospects are affiliated. Another fee-based service, Target America, purports to contain records on the top five percent of wealthy and generous people in the nation. And finally, the Foundation Center's Associates Program (http://fdncenter.org/marketplace; click on Associates Program), while geared to deliver information about institutional grantmakers, also provides Associate members with telephone and e-mail reference services on individual donors and offers a service whereby members can request biographical searches on individual prospects. The Associates Program recently launched its own extranet—a Web site available to members only.

Conclusion

In summary, the resources on the Web for researching individuals are quite extensive. Most of the resources you will encounter as a grantseeker are available free of charge. While in this chapter we may have only scratched the surface of what is out there, we have tried to provide a selective list of some of the better sites, guidance on the best approach to these Web sites, and research strategies to adopt. Our best advice is to utilize your individual prospect worksheet as a research tool and maintain your critical eye as you visit each site. Your most valuable resource as a grantseeker is your own time. To preserve this resource you need to adhere to the disciplined approach we described earlier. Keep in mind that the best prospects you'll uncover online have the capacity to give, an interest in your cause, and a connection to your organization.

CHAPTER SEVEN

Searchable Databases on the Web

With each passing day, more and more grantseekers are using Internet search engines as essential tools in their funding research. Because the Internet itself is indexed by search engine services, you could say that it is a sort of giant database, albeit sprawling and without the important data consistency provided by a single-source database. The good news for grantseekers is that a vast number of well-organized databases are available on the Web, some of them completely free.

As you read this chapter, please bear in mind that the list of sites it contains is by no means comprehensive. This is intended, rather, as a group of suggested starting points for the grantseeker looking for searchable, Internet-based information. These sites represent only a tiny fraction of the sites you can find on your own.

Publicly accessible databases generally offer keyword searching in one or more searchable fields and can be used effectively, even by those with little or no prior experience with online research. In addition there is further good news: Veteran information service providers, some of whom have employed database technology for decades, are now making their databases available online via the Internet, often modifying their search technology in the process—by introducing natural language searching and combining data sources, for example—to facilitate access by novice researchers. As a result of these Web-based modifications, database searching, once the sole province of prospect research professionals, has become an option for an increasingly wide and varied audience of grantseekers. In short, the Web has brought the search and retrieval of organized data sets within reach of anyone who has access to the Internet!

Internet databases cover a wide spectrum—from the funding-specific that let you search on consistently fielded data as a way to identify potential donors, to the more general and news-oriented types, which may not help you find potential donors but which certainly will help you conduct further research on the prospects you have identified from other resources. In this chapter, we describe various databases that are of particular interest to grantseekers, as well as databases of more general interest to the philanthropic community and to nonprofits.

Please note that we have differentiated between those databases that are free and those that are fee-based. Valuable information can be obtained from both categories. You shouldn't necessarily assume, however, that information that you pay for is more useful than what's out there for free. Each grantseeker must evaluate these sites on a case-by-case basis to determine how useful the information provided is going to be to his or her specific funding research needs.

Nonprofit and Foundation Databases

There are several databases containing information on nonprofit organizations and foundations that can be very useful to the grantseeker, especially in providing names, addresses, and financial information on nonprofit funders. The primary source for some of these services is IRS information, which is available to the public. (See Chapter 5 to learn more about the wealth of government information available on the World Wide Web.)

FREE DATABASES

Action Without Borders (http://www.idealist.org)
Action Without Borders is a nonprofit organization that promotes the sharing of ideas, information, and resources to "help build a world where all people can live free, dignified and productive lives." Through the site's searchable indexes, visitors can access a global directory of more than 21,500 nonprofit and community organizations in more than 150 countries, including nonprofit news sites, jobs and volunteer opportunities, and resources for nonprofit managers. Search by organization name, location, or mission keyword.

Foundation Finder—Foundation Center (http://lnp.fdncenter.org/finder.html)
More of a look-up tool than an actual searchable database, Foundation Finder serves as a wonderful, quick reference for verifying basic foundation information. If you know the name or partial name of any of the approximately 60,000 private and community foundations in the United States, Foundation Finder will provide you with that foundation's address, contact person, and basic financial information, as well as link you to its Web site, if there is one, and, for every private foundation, its most recent IRS Form 990-PF filing (in a downloadable PDF file format).

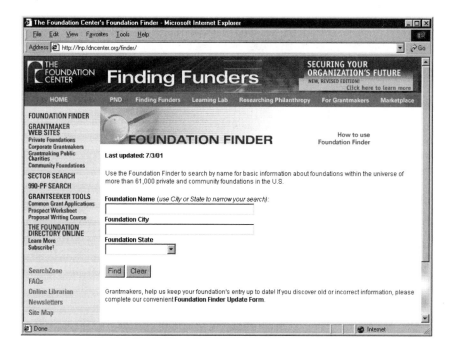

GrantSmart.Org (http://grantsmart.org)

This site features a searchable database of tax-related information for each of the more than 60,000 private foundations that file Form 990-PF with the IRS. Other nonprofit organizations are not yet indexed in the database. The database does include PDFs of the most recently filed Forms 990-PF or information from key fields within each of these tax returns. In many cases, more than one year's worth of tax returns may be available. In cooperation with the IRS, GrantSmart is developing optical character recognition (OCR) software code that will allow full IRS tax returns to be scanned and indexed into a complete, searchable database.

GuideStar (http://www.guidestar.org)

The GuideStar Web site is produced by Philanthropic Research, Inc., a 501(c)(3) public charity founded in 1994. GuideStar's mission is to promote philanthropy by helping donors, institutional funders, and charities become more informed, effective, and efficient. Its free database includes information on all IRS-registered 501(c)(3) nonprofit organizations (the organizations to which donations are tax-deductible). Currently, there are approximately 700,000 organizations in the database, including public charities and private foundations. GuideStar's search engine allows you to search for an organization by keyword or name, activity, city, state, zip code, nonprofit type, revenue range, Employer Identification Number (EIN), or NTEE code. Both Forms 990 and 990-PF are available on this site.

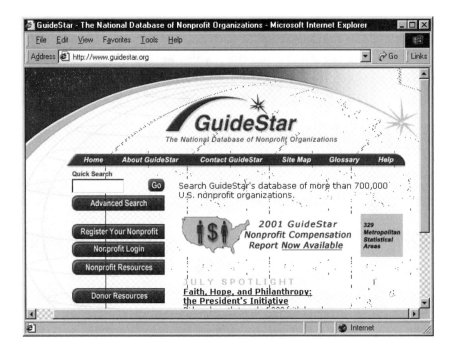

FinAid (http://www.finaid.org)

This award-winning site was started in 1994. It has a reputation for objectivity and thoroughness. The site caters to high school, college, and graduate students and contains information about scholarships, fellowships, loans, and military aid. In addition to its free databases, the site also offers a variety of useful tips, making it a good place on the Web to start a scholarship search.

FEE-BASED AND MEMBERSHIP DATABASES

Foundation Directory Online—Foundation Center
(http://www.fconline.fdncenter.org)

The Foundation Directory Online includes four levels of subscription service that provide access to varying amounts of information in the Foundation Center's database. The first level of service contains current descriptions of 10,000 of the largest foundations in the United States. The second level of service, *The Foundation Directory Online Plus,* includes access to the database of 10,000 foundations, plus access to a grants database of information on more than 170,000 grants made by the 1,100 top foundations. The third level, *The Foundation Directory Online Premium,* provides access to the grants file plus a foundation database featuring the 20,000 largest foundations in the nation. The most comprehensive level of service, *The Foundation Directory Online Platinum,* provides access to the grants database, plus the Center's entire database of approximately 60,000 foundations, grantmaking public charities, and corporate givers. There are varying subscription fees for the different levels.

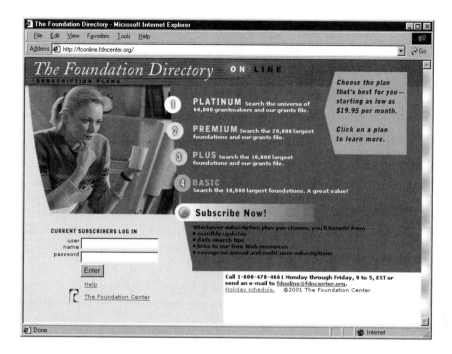

By entering specific search criteria in as many as seven fields, you can perform targeted searches that will help you identify prospective funding sources for your nonprofit organization. When conducting your searches, you have the option of sorting your results in either ascending or descending order by the grantmakers' total annual giving amount or in alphabetical order. The information available through the service is updated on a monthly basis and, like Foundation Finder, includes access to the most recent Forms 990-PF for every private foundation.

European Foundation Centre (http://www.efc.be)

The European Foundation Centre (EFC) promotes and supports the work of foundations and corporate funders active in and with the European community. A nonprofit organization established in 1989 by seven of Europe's leading foundations, the EFC today has a membership of more than 160 independent funders and serves an additional 7,000 organizations linked through networking centers in 35 countries across Europe.

The three core functions of the Centre are to represent the interests of member organizations at the level of third parties, such as national governments and European Union institutions; to convene and coordinate meetings and facilitate networking; and to provide a relevant and current information base to reinforce member organizations' programs and initiatives. The free Orpheus database includes profiles of more than 500 foundations interested in European grantmaking. The site also includes a newsroom and a variety of other free resources for grantseekers.

FOUNDATION GRANTS DATABASES—FREE

A number of foundations offer fully searchable Web sites. The Ford Foundation, W.K. Kellogg Foundation, Charles Stewart Mott Foundation, and Pew Charitable Trusts have gone one step further and provided grantseekers with specialized online databases of their grant awards.

Ford Foundation (http://www.fordfound.org)

This database covers three years' worth of all grants made by the foundation and is updated on a quarterly basis, making it one of the most current sources of information on the Ford Foundation's grantmaking activities. To access the database, click on Grants Database on the top bar. You can search the database by keyword, program area, grant year, or location. The results window includes descriptive text about the grants. Other information on Ford grants and new grantmaking initiatives can be found on the Web site in the Annual Report, the quarterly Ford Foundation Report, and the foundation's press releases.

Kellogg Foundation Online Database of Current Grants—W.K. Kellogg Foundation (http://www.wkkf.org)

The Kellogg Foundation's grants database, which is updated on a daily basis, includes all of Kellogg's grants since 1991 and is the most current source of information on the foundation's grantmaking activities. To access the database, visitors to the home page should select "grants" and then "search database." The grants database is organized around the Kellogg Foundation's program interests—Health, Food Systems and Rural Development, Youth and Education, Higher Education, and Philanthropy and Volunteerism. Within these fields the foundation may also make grants in the cross-cutting areas of leadership, information systems/technology, capitalizing on diversity, and social and economic community development. You can conduct a search of the database (by grantee name, location, program information, time frame, and purpose) or you can browse by thematic coding, country, or grantee name.

The Mott Grants Database—The Charles Stewart Mott Foundation (http://www.mott.org/grants/search.html)

The Mott Grants Database contains detailed fact sheets on each grant made by the foundation since 1995. The data is updated quarterly and is the most current source of information on Mott's grantmaking activities. Two means are provided to search for specific grant information. The first allows users to search by keyword; the second allows users to search on specific fields, such as the project description or state location of the grantee.

Pew Charitable Trusts Search Grants Database—The Pew Charitable Trusts (http://www.pewtrusts.com)

The Pew Charitable Trusts Web site allows visitors to search all its grants awarded since 1995. A synopsis of the purpose(s), the amount, and the recipient of each grant is provided. A more expanded table containing the recipient contact's name, the relevant dates, and a longer grant description is also available. The database search can be made very specific by the use of specific categories.

REGIONAL FOUNDATION DATABASES

Regional databases can be particularly useful to grantseekers looking for funding from grantmakers whose giving programs are locally focused as opposed to national. In this section we explore several regional databases that should help give you an idea of what's available. To explore additional regional resources, contact a regional association of grantmakers (RAG) (see the RAG Forum Web site at http://www.rag.org/rags/map.htm) or community foundation in your area (see the Council on Foundations' Community Foundation Locator at http://www.communityfoundationlocator.com/search/index.cfm). Some of these databases are free; others are only available to members or for a fee.

The Greater Kansas City Council on Philanthropy (http://www.kcphilnet.org)

This is a professional organization that has provided a local forum for the exchange of information on philanthropy and fundraising since 1975. This site offers fee-based access to a foundation database, a regularly-updated, cross-referenced directory of approximately 600 foundations making grants in the Kansas City region, as well as a searchable corporate giving database.

Donors Forum of Chicago (http://www.donorsforum.org)

This association of Chicago-area grantmaking institutions promotes effective philanthropy through its educational, collaborative, and networking efforts. The Donors Forum's Philanthropic Database (PhD) is a free searchable database of more than 50,000 grants awarded since 1994 by participating Donors Forum members. Representing more than $1.5 billion in grants, PhD presents specific details about philanthropic giving by almost 100 grantmakers in metropolitan Chicago. PhD does not provide funding guidelines or detailed information about individual foundations.

Associated Grantmakers of Massachusetts (AGM)
(http://www.agmconnect.org/agmwebmanager.nsf)

AGM is a statewide association whose mission is to "support and advance effective and responsible philanthropy throughout the Commonwealth." AGM's Web site offers detailed descriptions of the services it provides to grantmakers and to nonprofit organizations, information on events of interest to grantseekers and grantmakers, a catalogue of AGM books and videos for sale, and extensive links to online nonprofit and philanthropic resources. This site also includes a searchable database, which you can access if you are an Associate- or Fellow-level Partner. It contains nearly 500 grantmakers and gives these organizations the opportunity to describe, in their own words, the goals as well as the limitations of their grantmaking programs. This site also gives the grantseeking community basic information on which to build a comprehensive list of potential supporters, in order to begin a discussion of mutual interests with those organizations. This database has been designed to help fundraisers begin the process of learning all there is to know about the major Massachusetts grantmakers.

DATABASE SERVICES FOR GRANTSEEKERS—FEE-BASED

There are a small number of database services specializing in information for grantseekers. The ones described here focus on nonprofits and database management software and offer electronic services geared to the needs of grantseekers and charitable organizations.

Prospect Research Online (PRO) Rainforest Publications Books (http://www.rpbooks.com)

PRO is a service that combines information from five main areas into one comprehensive system: Corporate Research, Foundation Research, Major Gift Announcements, Executive Biographies, and Donor/Board Lists. Information is collected from a wide variety of traditional online sources and edited by PRO staff. Every week PRO subscribers receive a weekly What's New Report detailing updates to the system—new Corporate Snapshots, the IPO Watch, the Executive Alert, new Donor and Board Lists, and new Major Gift Announcements.

GrantSelect (http://www.grantselect.com)

Universities, libraries, school districts, community nonprofits, and researchers use GrantSelect, which is updated daily, to search an extensive database of funding opportunities. Offering more than 10,000 funding opportunities and a large collection of sponsored research opportunities, GrantSelect is a comprehensive tool with a range of pricing options. An E-mail Alert Service delivers funding information to users, including funds from state and federal governments, corporations, foundations, and associations.

Corporate Financial Information

Hoovers Online (http://www.hoovers.com)

This is an easy-to-use site with links to more than 4,000 corporate Web sites and more than 14,000 Company Capsules. Free Company Capsules provide news and information—company profile, key personnel, full stock quote, and selected press coverage—on more than 14,000 public and private enterprises. Subscribers (two options: personal or multi-user) get the same information but in much greater depth and detail. Hoovers also contains Capsules of a number of large non-publicly traded U.S. enterprises, including nonprofits, foundations, health care companies, cooperatives, and universities.

EDGAR Database of Corporate Information (http://www.sec.gov/edgarhp.htm)

The Securities and Exchange Commission (SEC) requires all public companies (except foreign companies and companies with less than $10 million in assets and less than 500 shareholders) to file registration statements, periodic reports, and other forms electronically through EDGAR. Anyone can access and download this information for free. Here you'll find links to a complete list of filings available through EDGAR and instructions for searching the EDGAR database.

Edgar Online (http://www.edgar-online.com)

Edgar Online is the same database as above, but the interface is more user-friendly. (Edgar Online is fee-based.)

Inc. Online (http://inc.com)

Inc. Online is an information resource for entrepreneurs and small business owners who are serious about growing their businesses. In addition to the most recent edition of *Inc. Magazine* and an archive of more than 6,500 articles on a wide variety of topics, the site offers a searchable database of America's 500 fastest-growing companies.

CORPORATE NEWS ONLINE

BusinessWire (http://www.businesswire.com)

This site includes searchable company press releases by date, industry, or company. It also includes selected corporate profiles and related URLs.

CompaniesOnline (http://www.companiesonline.com)

This site provides you with information, such as a company's address, URL, phone number, contact name and title, sales volume, and number of employees, about the companies behind the Web sites. Here you can search for information on more than 500,000 public and private companies.

PR NewsWire (http://www.prnewswire.com)

This site includes Company News On-Call, a complete, current, three-year database of all stories appearing on PR Newswire from participating companies.

Forbes People (http://www.forbes.com/people)

Forbes magazine has made available, in database format, a variety of its lists of wealthy individuals and companies including the Largest Private Companies in the United States, the Richest People in the World, the Richest People In America, etc. (See Chapter 6 for a more detailed description.)

Newspaper Searching

Newspaper Web sites are generally searchable by keyword. Articles are available until the source site deletes them (typically after one day). Archived information is generally available only for a fee from the source publication or online vendor. Many regional business newspapers are now available online (indexed at most of the major news sites) and provide excellent information on local philanthropists, corporate giving, family foundations, etc.

American Journalism Review (http://www.ajr.org)
This site includes worldwide links to thousands of news organizations online. You can also search some 18,000 links to newspapers, magazines, broadcasters, and news services worldwide, including pre-selected top sites.

Chronicle of Philanthropy (http://philanthropy.com)
Published every other week, the *Chronicle* is an important news source for charity leaders, fundraisers, grantmakers, and other people involved in philanthropic enterprise. In print, the *Chronicle* is published biweekly, except for the last two weeks in June and the last two weeks in December (a total of 24 issues a year). A subscription includes full access to this Web site and news updates by e-mail. The Web site offers the complete contents of the new issue, an archive of articles from the past two years, and more than four years' worth of grant listings—all fully searchable.

The Chronicle Guide to Grants is an electronic database of all corporate and foundation grants listed in the *Chronicle of Philanthropy* since 1995. One drawback is that the date the grant was awarded does not appear; only the date when the grant was listed in the *Chronicle* is shown. Subscriptions are available for periods of one week to one year. There is a significant discount if you are also a subscriber to the print journal.

General Information Databases

A wide range of vendors offer for-fee access to an enormous variety of databases. Most for-fee information vendors, including those that specialize in funding information, offer their database information in a variety of electronic formats, including CD-ROM and direct modem access (requiring software installation). Indexed print versions are also available for many directories. The choice of format depends largely on you and on cost effectiveness (frequency of use, expense of support systems, etc.).

Web access offers users a great deal of flexibility. For-fee database searches can, however, be quite expensive, even on the Internet. The World Wide Web has expanded rapidly, and the cost of data now varies greatly. While fee-based services are often very comprehensive and therefore efficient, the same information can sometimes be found through other sources for lower cost or even for free.

Fee-based services typically require only a user name and password for access from any computer connected to the Internet. Internet database vendors offer pricing options that can be tailored to a user's particular needs. Another benefit of these databases is that they are updated on a regular basis, some as frequently as daily. The major database vendors tend to simplify their search structures for Web presentation, gearing them toward a broad user audience as opposed to the advanced researcher. Experienced researchers may therefore prefer the wider range of search options available in direct dial-up services.

Some major database vendors offer legal and government documents, newspaper and periodical articles, and a wide variety of corporate information, including company profiles. These services are generally updated daily and offer easy-to-use search interfaces and a wide variety of search parameters. Newspaper searches, for example, can be restricted by date, source, geography, etc. You can search a single newspaper or thousands of sources at once.

The DIALOG Corporation (http://www.dialog.com/)

DIALOG has been a source for online information for more than 25 years. It offers hundreds of databases representing a broad range of disciplines, company directories, news sources, general reference, biographical information, etc.

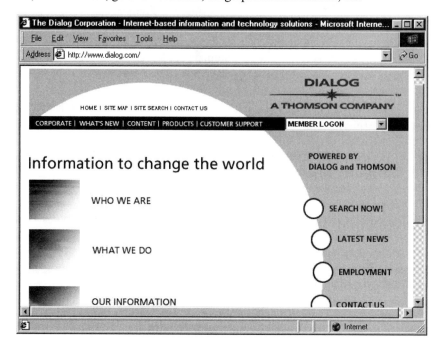

A complete listing of online databases is available at DIALOG Web (see below). The online access rates vary by database. (Prices include output and search time costs, as well as telecommunications charges.) There are annual service fees and start-up fees. Training is provided as online tutorials and/or guided tours.

DIALOG Web (http://products.dialog.com/products/dialogweb)

This is a tool for intermediate and advanced online searchers. It offers a browser-enabled interface to the full DIALOG command language, an index to most of the DIALOG databases, and a guided search component for search assistance. Other than an enhanced graphical Web interface, there are some features unique to DIALOG Web, which include a free database directory that lets you browse DIALOG databases by subject. A free preview and tutorial are available.

DIALOG Select (http://products.dialog.com/products/dialogselect)

This service is designed for novice users, utilizing pre-defined search forms in which users enter keywords and use pull-down menus to set up their searches. No prior search expertise is required.

Grantmaker/Grant Information on DIALOG

There are two Foundation Center databases in the DIALOG product line. The Foundation Directory database is known as File 26 and the Foundation Grants Index is known as File 27.

Foundation Directory—File 26—(available on DIALOG Web and DIALOG Select) is a comprehensive database providing descriptions of approximately 60,000 grantmakers, including private grantmaking foundations, community foundations, operating foundations, grantmaking public charities, and corporate grantmakers. The file covers one year's data, based on the most currently available fiscal year. The file is reloaded annually, with a semi-annual update.

The Foundation Grants Index—File 27—(available only on DIALOG Web) is an index of grants of $10,000 or more awarded to nonprofit organizations by the largest foundations in the United States. Information in File 27 includes grants found in the print *Foundation Grants Index*, beginning with those included in the 1989 edition. Each record in File 27 represents one grant.

Other DIALOG Databases

The DIALOG corporate and biographical databases are extensive and varied and can be extremely useful to grantseekers. Corporate information on DIALOG can be searched geographically, providing you with an enormous list of companies and top executives to research as potential funders for your organization. You can also use archived business newspapers and journals as well as press releases to find information on past corporate giving and company giving interests.

LEXIS-NEXIS on the World Wide Web (http://www.lexis-nexis.com)

LEXIS-NEXIS provides online access to legal, news, and business information services. There are thousands of databases accessible between the two services. The LEXIS service contains major archives of federal and state case law, continuously updated statutes of all 50 states, state and federal regulations, and an extensive collection of public records from U.S. states and larger counties. The NEXIS service is a news and business information service that contains more than 30,000 news, business, and legal information sources. These include regional, national, and international newspapers, newswires, magazines, trade journals, and business publications. NEXIS also offers brokerage house and industry analyst reports; business information from Dunn & Bradstreet; public records such as corporate filings, company records, and property records; and tax information.

Dow Jones Interactive (http://ip.dowjones.com)

Dow Jones Interactive, based on the Dow Jones News/Retrieval service, is an online business news and research tool that provides access to breaking news from more than 6,000 global sources, a custom news-tracking tool that automatically filters news and information based on an individual's needs, and a company/industry center where you can conduct in-depth research on a company, industry, or marketplace by consulting leading research and financial information providers. Dow Jones provides same-day access to full-text editions of the *Wall Street Journal, New York Times, Washington Post, Financial Times,* and *Los Angeles Times.*

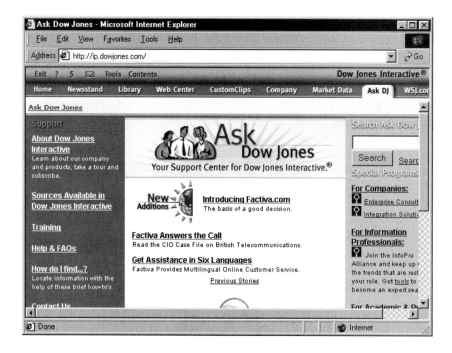

ProQuest Direct (http://www.umi.com/proquest)

ProQuest Direct provides access to a large collection of information, including summaries of articles from more than 8,000 publications, with many in full-text, full-image format.

H.W. Wilson Company (http://www.hwwilson.com)

Primarily serving librarians and researchers, H.W. Wilson offers more than 40 full-text, abstract, and index databases over the Internet, on CD-ROM, and magnetic tape. Database subjects range from Applied Science and Technology to Social Sciences. Free database trials are available.

The Gale Group (www.galegroup.com)

The Gale Group is a unit of the Thomson Corporation, an e-information publisher for libraries, schools, and businesses. Best known for its authoritative reference content as well as its helpful organization of full-text magazine and newspaper articles, the company creates and maintains more than 600 databases that are published online, in print, and in microform. In addition to serving the library community, Gale also licenses its proprietary content for integration within Web-based information services.

Target America (http://www.tgtam.com)

Target America is a fee-based database that contains information on more than 4 million records of the wealthiest and most generous people in the nation—the top five percent in terms of income, assets, and philanthropic history. Ninety-four percent of the individuals in the database give more than $5,000 a year to charities.

Database Services for Academic Professionals

There also are a number of grants databases, primarily intended for academics, that offer access to a variety of government and private funding sources. These services are fee-based, but some also offer free information.

IRIS—Illinois Researcher Information Service (http://www.library.uiuc.edu/iris)

The Illinois Researcher Information Service (IRIS) is a unit of the University of Illinois Library at Urbana-Champaign. The IRIS office compiles the IRIS Database of funding opportunities. The office also maintains a library of publications (informational brochures, application guidelines, and annual reports) from more than 2,000 funding agencies. The IRIS Database currently contains records on more than 8,000 federal and private funding opportunities in the sciences, social sciences, arts, and humanities. The IRIS Database is updated daily.

Community of Science (http://www.cos.com)

Community of Science, Inc. (COS) is an Internet site for the scientific research and development community. COS brings together scientists and researchers from more than 1,300 universities, corporations, and government agencies worldwide. Services include COS Expertise, a database of detailed, first person profiles of more than 460,000 research and development professionals; COS Funding Opportunities, an extensive source of grant information; COS Abstract Management System, an online publishing solution for universities and professional societies; and customized access to a range of professional reference databases, including U.S. Patents, MEDLINE, AGRICOLA, EiCompendex, GeoRef, and others.

InfoEd International (http://www.infoed.org/products.stm - spin)

InfoEd provides information and management software systems and services for the scientific research and development community. These systems span funding opportunities, proposal development, grants administration, and intellectual property management. A range of useful products are available through InfoEd, including SPIN, the Sponsored Programs Information Network, an up-to-date listing of national and international government and private funding sources, used by more than 800 institutions worldwide.

A FEW GENERAL SEARCH ENGINES

Keep in mind that you can always use general search engines to experiment with keyword and phrase searching, just to see what you come up with. By entering relevant terms such as "grants," "foundations," "fundraising," "philanthropy," etc., you can locate an amazing amount of useful information that can supplement your funding research very nicely. (See Appendix A for descriptions and tips on using general search engines.)

Conclusion

Initial exploration and assessment of the usefulness of Web databases will require an investment of your time and perhaps money—if you choose to sign up for subscription-based services. In conjunction with other Web resources, however, you should be able to find a great deal of useful information through these databases. And don't forget, in addition to your Web-wide database research, you can explore the wealth of free searchable resources available at the Foundation Center's Web site, especially those found in the Nonprofit Links, Grantmaker Web sites, *Philanthropy News Digest, Literature of the Nonprofit Sector Online,* and Sector Search areas.

CHAPTER EIGHT

Other Useful Sites for Grantseekers

This chapter presents a sampling of some of the unique and more useful Web sites available in the Links to Nonprofit Resources (NPO Links) section of the Foundation Center's Web site (http://fdncenter.org/research/npr_links/index.html). In general they are organized in the same way as the Web links, though a few categories are missing from this condensed version. See Appendix F for a full category listing.

A Selection of Useful Sites

In this chapter, we present a selective list of useful Web sites with annotations. These sites can be utilized whether you are looking for information on charity monitoring organizations, online giving, program evaluation, issue advocacy, nonprofit boards, nonprofit management, program areas (arts, education, environment, health, science, women and girls, etc.), international resources, or resources for individuals, among many other purposes. In collecting and providing annotations to these sites, the Foundation Center continues to function as a specialty portal, serving as "Your Gateway to Philanthropy on the World Wide Web."

Center staff continually adds to our lists of Web sites and prepares annotations for them to aid in your exploration of funding opportunities and helpful resources. Below are our recommendations of useful Web sites for grantseekers. The categories we have used to organize the sites are to a certain extent arbitrary. That is, many of the resources could fit into two or more categories, based on their features and content, since more and more sites offer multiple services and resources to nonprofit organizations and grantseekers in general. What these sites have in common is that they reward deeper investigation. They are resources that you'll want to return to time and again in searching for online information about foundations, grants, fundraising, and nonprofit management. Our goal is not to be comprehensive—which is impractical when dealing with the Web—but to point the way to a manageable number of useful sites that are representative or unique.

Philanthropy Resources

GENERAL

Chronicle of Philanthropy (http://philanthropy.com)

Like its biweekly print analog, the *Chronicle of Philanthropy*'s Web site is full of useful information for fundraisers, grantmakers, nonprofit managers, and others. The site is organized into broad topic areas—Gifts and Grants, Fund Raising, Managing Non-Profit Groups, and Technology—and includes a summary of the contents of the *Chronicle*'s current issue, with an archive of articles from the past two years, a listing of award and RFP deadlines, job opportunities in the nonprofit sector, a listing of upcoming conferences and workshops, and annotated links to other nonprofit resources on the Internet. Visitors also can sign up for free e-mail updates about changes at the site as well as breaking news stories. Some of the material is available only to *Chronicle* subscribers.

Council on Foundations (http://www.cof.org)

The Council on Foundations (COF) is a membership organization for grantmakers, providing assistance to foundation staff, trustees, and board members through one-to-one technical assistance, research, publications, conferences and workshops, legal services, and a wide array of other services. The COF Web site offers a wealth of information for and about foundations. These include: Legal and Government Affairs with excerpts from select publications and special articles on legal issues of concern to foundations; Resources for Foundations, including career and professional development, publications, and a set of useful links for grantmakers; examples of successful grantmaking; resources to aid in starting a foundation or corporate giving program; *Foundation News & Commentary,* the Council's flagship magazine; a Professional Advisors Network section; and a set of links to a wide range of grantmaking resources, with a listing of more than 30 affinity groups of grantmakers.

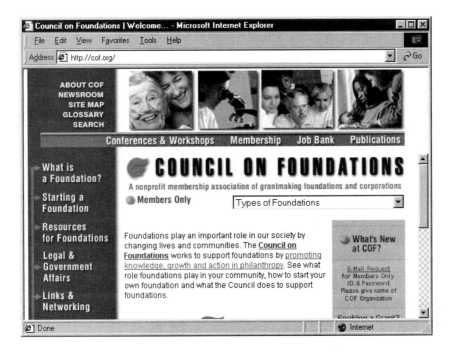

Internet NonProfit Center (http://www.nonprofits.org)

The Internet NonProfit Center aims to provide free, easily accessible information on nonprofit organizations, wise giving practices, and issues of concern to donors and volunteers. A major component of the site is the Nonprofit FAQ, which catalogs frequently asked questions—and their answers—as posed in e-mails sent to foundations, Usenet discussions, and other sources. This set of FAQs is divided into five broad categories: organization, management, regulation, resources, and development. You get to see what professionals in the field have to say on topics like special events, direct mail, corporate sponsorship, and enlisting celebrity support for an organization. The site also has a "library," which offers essays and data about the nonprofit sector.

REGIONAL ASSOCIATIONS OF GRANTMAKERS (RAGS)

National Network of Grantmakers (http://www.nng.org)

The National Network of Grantmakers is an organization of 400 members (individual donors, foundation staff, board members, and grantmaking committee members) involved in funding social and economic justice by supporting organizations working for economic and social change. The Web site provides program information, including NNG's research study on diversity in philanthropy, and its "1% More for Democracy" campaign; a section with information on events, meetings, and networking activities organized around specific themes or topics; and a section with nonprofit links, job lists, publications for sale, and a Common Grant Application form. The current issue of the quarterly newsletter also is available.

Fundraising Resources

GENERAL

CyberGrants (http://www.cybergrants.com)

This for-profit company works to bring nonprofits and grantmaking organizations together via the Internet. The site offers nonprofits the opportunity to research grant guidelines and create online proposals that are submitted directly to member grantmakers. Participating private foundations and corporate giving programs, which pay a fee, are provided with access to a grantmaking and reporting system that facilitates online proposal review.

David Lamb's Prospect Research Page (http://www.lambresearch.com)

Lamb, a former development officer at the University of Washington, has attempted to "separate the wheat from the chaff" in describing truly useful Internet sites for researching corporations, foundations, and individual donors. The site includes links to directories of doctors, dentists, lawyers, and airplane owners, as well as to online news sources and public records databases. What's nice about the Prospect Research Page is that Lamb has distilled the overwhelming number of potential sources of information on the Internet into a relatively small selection of sites, which he has thoughtfully annotated. The casual visitor can tell that he or she is in capable hands.

FundsNet (http://www.fundsnetservices.com)

Fundsnet Services Online is a comprehensive and searchable directory of funders, funding resources, and scholarship opportunities on the World Wide Web. Most links are annotated, and the Web site also includes a section organized by subject area.

Grantscape (http://www.grantscape.com)

Part of the Web site of Aspen Publishers, Inc., Grantscape is a guide to grant-seeking, taking the grantseeker through the grantseeking process step-by-step, from initial research to accepting the grant, and even dealing with rejection. The site includes a brief how-to section on proposal fundraising. Also at this site is an annotated links page to other online fundraising instructional resources and Aspen's own catalog of fundraising titles.

Internet Prospector (http://www.internet-prospector.org)

Internet Prospector is a service provided by volunteers nationwide who research the Web for corporate, foundation, and biographical information in order to find leads on prospects for nonprofit fundraisers. This service is invaluable for the prospect research community, but anyone seeking international or online news sources will find this Web site useful. You'll find an online newsletter and an archive of past issues, a guide to search engine prospecting with sample search results, tips for foundation searches, international audio and video Web content, and "Using Zip Code Demographics For Prospecting," a specialized Internet research tool.

Michigan State University Grants and Related Resources
(http://www.lib.msu.edu/harris23/grants/grants.htm)
The amount of information available on these pages is nearly overwhelming, but Jon Harrison of the University of Michigan Libraries has created a site that is well organized and cleanly designed. You won't get lost. Most valuable here are the annotated lists of resources (print, electronic, and online) for grant information in particular subject areas, from Arts and Cultural Activities to Religion and Social Change. For each subject area, Harrison gives abstracts of useful print resources, descriptions of databases, and links to online information. There is a substantial section of information on grants to individuals, including financial aid. Harrison also has assembled an impressive bibliography, with links, on grantsmanship techniques, including lots of information on fundraising research and proposal writing.

University of Virginia—Prospect Research
(http://www.people.virginia.edu/~dev-pros/webresources.html)
Assembled by the prospect researchers at the University of Virginia, this site includes sections on biographical information, corporate information, asset location and evaluation, nationwide listings of property assessors, public records, and more.

CHARITY MONITORING ORGANIZATIONS

Philanthropic Advisory Service (http://www.bbb.org/about/pas.asp)
The Philanthropic Advisory Service (PAS), a program of the Council of Better Business Bureaus' Foundation, maintains files on hundreds of national and international soliciting organizations. The Web site provides donor education information that includes reports, articles, and publications that provide "tips" to the

potential donor. The Better Business Bureau Wise Giving Guide is a new publication that combines the latest charity evaluation information completed by both the National Charities Information Bureau and PAS.

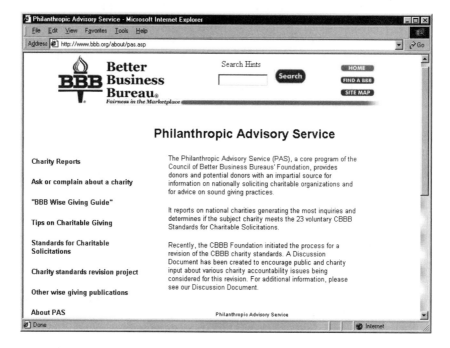

EDUCATION

The Council for Advancement and Support of Education (http://www.case.org)
The Council for Advancement and Support of Education (CASE) is an international association of education advancement officers, including alumni, administrators, fundraisers, public relations managers, publications editors, and government relations officers at more than 3,000 colleges, universities, and independent elementary and secondary schools. The CASE Web site contains job postings, discussion groups, information about CASE's awards and fellowships, training courses, member services, related merchandise, the online magazine *CURRENTS,* and news about issues related to institutional advancement at colleges, universities, and independent schools around the world.

ONLINE GIVING

4Charity.com (http://www.4charity.com)
This is a direct-donation site where users are guaranteed that 100 percent of their donations go to the nonprofit of their choice. The site earns revenue by offering advanced Internet tools and services to nonprofits and corporations.

eGrants.org (http://www.egrants.org)
Created in 1999 by the Tides Foundation, eGrants is a forward-looking organization that works to help other progressive nonprofits increase their financial support by fundraising online. eGrants provides online donation catalogs of social

change nonprofits and allows individuals, organizations, and businesses to donate money through online transactions. The Web site encourages interested organizations to contact eGrants to either establish an online presence or add their tool to an existing site.

Independent Givers of America (http://www.givedirect.org)

The Independent Givers of America is a "nonprofit tax-exempt charitable organization whose mission is to bring together generous people and deserving causes, principally but not exclusively by developing workplace-based and Internet-based systems that reduce the cost and increase the productivity of charitable solicitation." This site gives philanthropists the opportunity to set up a personal, private, online foundation and make contributions to it at any time. The site also facilitates contributions to any IRS-recognized charity, church, or school.

PROFESSIONAL ASSOCIATIONS

Association of Fundraising Professionals (http://www.afpnet.org)

The Association of Fundraising Professionals (AFP) is comprised of 25,000 individual members who work to advance philanthropy through education, training, mentoring, research, credentialing, and advocacy in 159 chapters throughout the United States, Canada, and Mexico. Visitors to this Web site will find extensive information on nonprofit philanthropy and AFP's activities and publications, including its professional advancement programs and course information, the full-text of its Code of Ethical Principles and Standards of Professional Practice, and the principles of an E-Donor Bill of Rights, created to address concerns and challenges arising from e-philanthropy. In addition, job opportunity and member services modules are made available to AFP members.

Nonprofit Sector Information and News

For general nonprofit sector information and news, see Chapter 9, Online Journals.

NONPROFIT MEMBERSHIP ORGANIZATIONS

Independent Sector (http://www.independentsector.org)

Independent Sector (IS) is committed to promoting philanthropy, volunteering, and citizen action and brings together nonprofit organizations, foundations, and corporate giving programs. The IS Web site gives an overview of its programs and includes a section on the basics of lobbying by charitable organizations, facts and figures on the size and scope of the nonprofit sector, and a statistical overview of the IS 1999 survey on giving and volunteering. The NonProfit Pathfinder, designed for scholars, researchers, practitioners, funders, and the media, is an information resource for civil society organizations. The Giving Voice to Your Heart Initiative includes five toolkits—Messages and the Media, Volunteering, Trust, Giving, and the Nonprofit Mosaic—to aid in promoting communication.

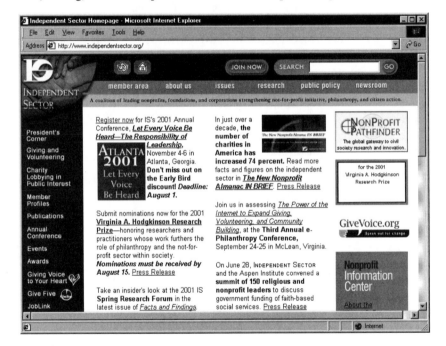

Program Areas

ArtsWire (http://www.artswire.org)

ArtsWire, funded and operated by the New York Foundation for the Arts, is a comprehensive "self-service" database of cultural resources on the Web. Offerings for artists and arts organizations include workshops, programs, telecommunications consultations, and a forum for online art. Membership privileges include Web space and an e-mail account.

Environmental Defense (http://www.edf.org)

Founded in 1967, Environmental Defense represents more than 300,000 members interested in a broad range of regional, national, and international environmental issues. The Environmental Defense Web site has information about its extensive programs, reports, brochures, fact sheets, and newsletter. Also included are practical suggestions for taking "action" to make a difference in solving environmental problems and a special section for children called "Earth2Kids."

Environmental Grantmakers Association (http://www.ega.org)

Environmental Grantmakers Association (EGA), an affinity group of the Council on Foundations, is a voluntary association of foundations and giving programs concerned with the protection of the natural environment. The Web site provides brief information on membership, EGA working groups, and member-initiated projects.

**Foundation Funding Sources for Tribal Libraries
(http://www.u.arizona.edu/~ecubbins/founfund.html)**

This site provides links to funding sources for North American Indian tribal libraries.

National Assembly of State Arts Agencies (http://www.nasaa-arts.org)

The National Assembly of State Arts Agencies (NASAA) is the membership organization of America's state and jurisdictional arts agencies. The Web site's Arts Over America section provides a directory of links to state arts agencies and regional arts organizations, an annotated list of arts-related Web sites, and links to major funders in the arts. The Artworks section has information on trends, issues, and activities influencing decision makers in the arts and government. The Web site also has publications, including a strategic planning toolkit as well as NASAA news and legislative updates.

W3C Web Accessibility Initiative (http://www.w3.org/WAI)

The World Wide Web Consortium's (W3C) Web Accessibility Initiative (WAI) promotes a high degree of usability for people with disabilities and, in coordination with organizations around the world, pursues accessibility of the Web through five primary areas of work: technology, guidelines, tools, education and outreach, and research and development. The site provides resources to aid in making a Web site accessible, including Web site evaluation, curriculum for Web content accessibility guidelines, and training and technical references. The Web site also has information on the Protocols and Formats Working Group, which reviews all W3C technologies for accessibility; the working groups that produce guidelines for Web sites, Web authoring tools, and browsers; a list of contacts, including information on how to reach WAI staff; a list of events; and a participation page that explains how to participate in WAI interest groups and working groups.

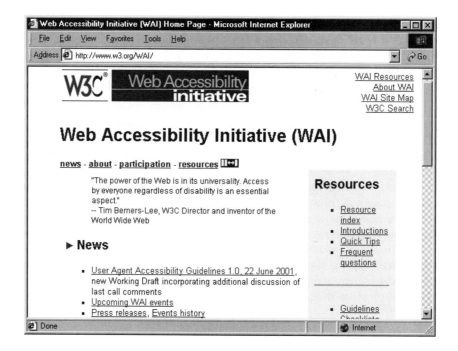

Nonprofit Management

GENERAL

Alliance for Nonprofit Management (http://www.allianceonline.org)
The Alliance for Nonprofit Management members include management support organizations, individual professionals, and a range of national, regional, umbrella, research and academic, publishing, and philanthropic organizations that provide training and consulting to nonprofits. The Alliance Web site contains a new Alliance Resource Center, which features Web sites, books, videos, and other valuable resources relating to nonprofit management and governance; the Alliance online newsletter; a job bank; and a database of Alliance member providers, searchable by geographic area, name, state, types of assistance offered, and by types of services offered.

Grantsmanship Center (http://www.tgci.com)
The Grantsmanship Center (TGCI) is a clearinghouse of fundraising information and training in grantsmanship and proposal writing for nonprofit organizations and government agencies. In addition to training program and schedule information, TGCI's Web site offers grant source information on community foundations and federal, state, and international funding; current Federal Register grant funding information, including a daily summary; TGCI's online magazine; and a listing of publications for fundraisers, including the TGCI proposal writing guide. The Web site also has a new resource, Winning Grant Proposals Online, which includes examples of effective proposal writing models, consisting entirely of recently funded, top-ranked grant proposals in a wide variety of subject areas.

BOARDS

Board Café (http://boardcafe.org)

Board Café, published by CompassPoint Nonprofit Services, is a monthly electronic newsletter for members of nonprofit boards. Each issue includes a menu of information, opinion, news, and resources, with numerous "Little Ideas," as well as one "Big Idea" that can be applied to board work. The Web site also offers a summary of past issues. (See Chapter 9 for more details on Board Café.)

National Center for Nonprofit Boards (http://www.ncnb.org)

Established in 1988 by the Association of Governing Boards of Universities and Colleges and Independent Sector, the National Center for Nonprofit Boards (NCNB) provides resources, programs, and services to the nonprofit community and publishes material on nonprofit governance, including more than 100 booklets, books, videos, and audiotapes. Visitors to the NCNB Web site will find membership, training, education, and consulting services; NCNB's Board Information Center, a free information clearinghouse on board-related topics; and Board Member Online, an abridged version of *Board Member*, the members-only periodical of the NCNB.

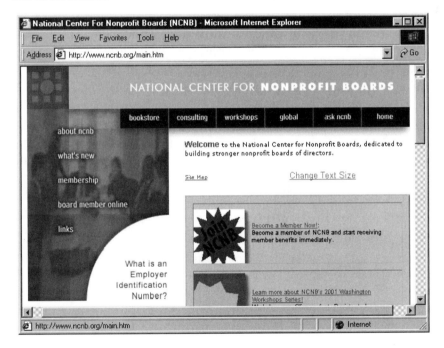

JOB OPPORTUNITIES

CharityChannel—Career Search Online
(http://charitychannel.com/careersearch)

At CharityChannel's Job search feature, you can search for positions by title, location, organization, or classification. Updated daily.

The Foundation Center's Job Corner
(http://www.fdncenter.org/pnd/jobs/index.html)

The Center's Job Corner features more than 500 current full-time job openings at U.S. foundations, nonprofit infrastructure organizations, grantmaking public charities, and other nonprofit organizations (also available as a free weekly e-mail bulletin).

Idealist—Nonprofit Jobs (http://www.idealist.org/ip/jobSearch?MODULE=JOB)

This is a searchable database of nonprofit jobs around the world. Visitors can search the database and subscribe to a free e-mail job list, and nonprofits can register and post job openings at no charge.

PROGRAM EVALUATION

American Evaluation Association (http://www.eval.org)

The American Evaluation Association (AEA) is an international professional association of evaluators who assess the effectiveness of programs, policies, personnel, products, and organizations. The AEA Web site offers a variety of evaluation-related resources, including information about the AEA's annual conference and other related events; special interest groups; published books and journals; the full-text of key documents for evaluators; a list of job postings and training institutions in the field; links to other sites of interest; and the EVALTALK Listserv, an open discussion list devoted to issues in the field of evaluation. The AEA member newsletter, first published in the winter of 2001, is also accessible from its Web site.

InnoNet (http://www.innonet.org)

Innovation Network, Inc. (InnoNet) is dedicated to building evaluation skills, knowledge, and processes within public and nonprofit organizations through the use of participatory evaluation. The InnoNet Web site provides a free, innovative "Workstation" tool to guide nonprofits and public agencies through a planning and evaluation process, resulting in a blueprint for designing, evaluating, and implementing a successful program and corresponding work plan.

VOLUNTARISM

Cybervpm.com (http://www.cybervpm.com)

Cybervpm.com is an Internet resource for volunteer programs. The Web site offers a newsletter on volunteer management, advice for volunteers, and links to other resources for volunteer programs. The Web site also includes an online discussion group for volunteer program managers, as well as an online library that is categorized by the types of resources available.

Energize (http://www.energizeinc.com)

Energize, Inc. is an international training, consulting, and publishing firm that specializes in all types of organizations with their volunteer efforts. The Web site has a free Job/Internship Bank, which includes members, interns, and community service participants; a volunteer management library of articles and books; and volunteerism information sources and links, with listings of conferences, classes, resource centers and Web sites, magazines, and products and services.

Volunteer Match (http://www.volunteermatch.org)

A service of ImpactOnline, Volunteer Match helps individuals nationwide find on-site volunteer opportunities posted by local nonprofit and public sector organizations. Volunteers can search the online database of thousands of one-time and ongoing opportunities—including walk-a-thons, beach day cleanups, tutoring, home building, and meal deliveries—by zip code, category, and date, then sign up automatically by e-mail for those that fit their interest and schedule. The Web site also has a listing of "virtual volunteering" opportunities for individuals, including those with disabilities who wish to contribute time via the Internet.

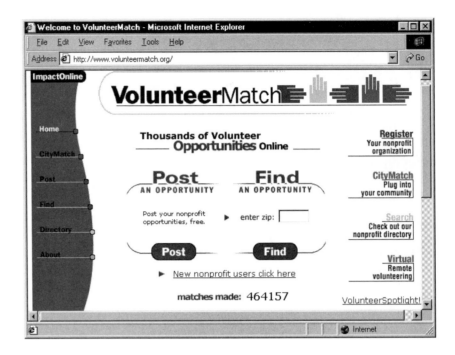

Nonprofit Technology Resources

CompuMentor (http://www.compumentor.org)
CompuMentor works to provide technology resources—person-to-person services, low-cost software, and online resources—to nonprofits and schools serving low-income communities. The Web site has software packages that can be ordered online for a fraction of the retail cost to organizations that qualify, a mentor matching program that matches skilled technical volunteers with community organizations and schools, a consulting program that includes technology planning for small and mid-size nonprofits, and information for nonprofits interested in developing a community technology center to provide access and training to low-income or disadvantaged communities.

Computer Recycling Resource List
(http://www.pnnonline.org/technology/computerrecycle1.cfm)
The Computer Recycling Resource List is a comprehensive list of organizations located in the United States that recycle and/or donate computers. The list is compiled by Lauren Matthews for Philanthropy News Network.

ebase (http://www.ebase.org)
ebase is an integrated database template based on File Maker Pro that helps nonprofits effectively manage interactive communications with their members, donors, citizen activists, and volunteers. The database is available for downloading free of charge from the Web site.

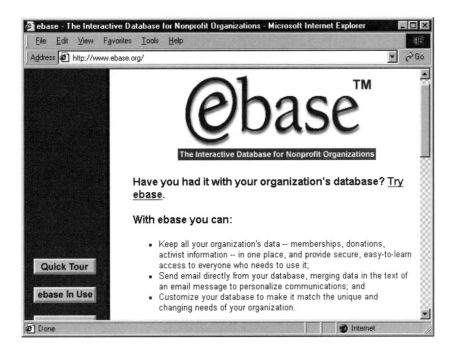

Gifts in Kind International (http://www.giftsinkind.org)

Gifts in Kind International links corporations and their product donations and services, including software and computer training, with a network of more than 50,000 nonprofit organizations. Gifts in Kind, a free global online system, matches company volunteers with nonprofits needing assistance such as community rebuilding, mentoring, coaching, technology planning, and other critically needed support.

NPower (http://www.npower.org)

NPower, based in Seattle, Washington, helps other nonprofits in the Puget Sound area use technology to better serve their communities. NPower offers a variety of technology-related services to area nonprofits, including technology assessments and planning, hands-on help with network implementation, database management, technology training classes, print and electronic technology resource libraries, and short-term technology project assistance. NPower's Tech Surveyor enables an organization to assess hardware, software, and staff technology skills. NPower also works with other organizations nationwide to help start their own NPower programs.

TechRocks (http://www.techrocks.org)

TechRocks (formerly the Technology Project), encourages and enables foundations, advocacy groups, and leading activists to use technology to achieve their goals. Visitors to the TechRocks Web site will find a free downloadable software program (ebase) that enables nonprofit organizations to manage their relationships with their members, donors, activists and volunteers; an online organization program; and additional information on cutting edge products and services to nonprofit organizations.

TechSoup (http://www.techsoup.org)
TechSoup is a Web-based resource center that offers technology assistance and solutions for small to midsize nonprofit organizations. The site offers information on where to find donated or discounted software and equipment; computer training; advice on technology funding; technology planning; and listings of available volunteers and consultants. The Web site also has a free, monthly publication, *By the Cup,* with feature articles related to nonprofit technology.

Technology Tip Sheets for Nonprofits (http://www.coyotecom.com/tips.html)
Technology Tip Sheets for Nonprofits was created by Jayne Cravens, of Coyote Communications, to help nonprofit and public sector organizations reap money-saving, program-enhancing benefits from technology. Most of the material is geared to community-based organizations, but some materials are for a broader audience. The Web site includes a What's New section.

International Resources

Canadian Centre for Philanthropy (http://www.ccp.ca)
The Canadian Centre for Philanthropy is "dedicated to advancing the role and interests of the charitable sector for the benefit of Canadian communities." Web site resources include a foundation and grants directory on more than 1,600 foundations that are actively granting in Canada; information about the Centre's publications; membership information, including the Centre's annual symposium; results of various research studies, including volunteering statistics, trends, and comparative studies; and an overview of the Centre's "Imagine" initiative, which promotes public and corporate giving, volunteering, and community support on a national level.

Charity Village (http://www.charityvillage.com)
The Canadian-based Charity Village Web site offers news, jobs, information, and resources for nonprofit managers, staffers and fundraisers, donors, and volunteers. Visitors to the Web site can access a searchable directory of annotated links to Canadian charities and nonprofit organizations; more than 10,000 positions in Canadian nonprofit organizations; an online directory of products and services especially for nonprofit executives; and a listing of educational programs and professional development opportunities, including Charity Village's own workshops and online tutorials, as well as links to dozens of courses available across the country.

European Foundation Centre (http://www.efc.be)
The European Foundation Centre (EFC) promotes and underpins the work of foundations and corporate funders active in and with Europe. Established in 1989 by seven of Europe's leading foundations, the EFC today has a membership of more than 160 independent funders and serves a further 7,000 organizations linked through networking centers in 35 countries across Europe. The Web site has a listing of member events; information on EFC's projects, activities and publications; and the EFC newsletter, *Bookshelf.*

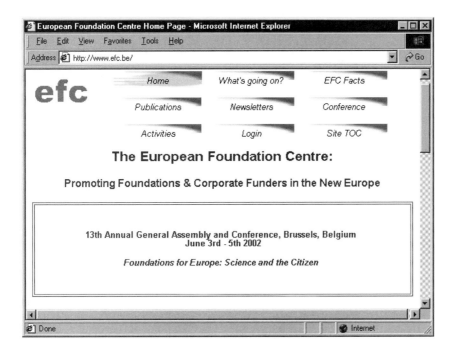

German Charities Institute (http://www.dsk.de)

This site is a clearinghouse of information on German and international charities and features a searchable directory of more than 5,000 organizations, an immense collection of links, and information about everything from volunteer opportunities to e-mail discussion groups on philanthropy and social issues. Much of the information is available in English.

Giving Wisely: The Internet Directory of Israeli Nonprofit and Philanthropic Organizations (http://www.givingwisely.org.il)

This site is the companion to the print directory, *Giving Wisely*. The site has browsable listings of Israeli foundations and nonprofit organizations. In addition to browsing, you can use the searchable database to view foundation or nonprofit profiles in full or partial format. The search features work in both Hebrew and English.

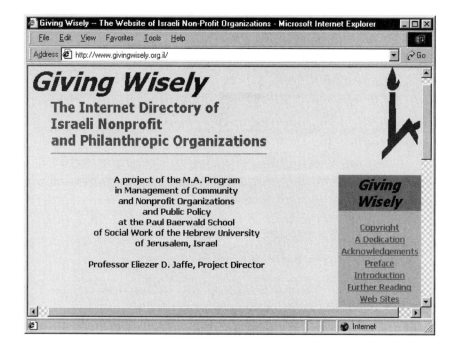

Idealist (http://www.idealist.org)

Idealist, in English and Spanish, offers a searchable network of 20,000 nonprofit and community organizations in 150 countries, which can be searched or browsed by name, location, or mission. There is also a searchable list of volunteer opportunities and hundreds of job and internship listings, events, and publications.

General Resources

PUBLIC INTEREST AND POLICY

HandsNet (http://www.handsnet.org)

HandsNet is a membership organization of more than 5,000 public interest and human services organizations. Web site features include articles and Action Alerts, providing daily news updates on human services issues and legislation; the WebClipper news and delivery service, with human services headlines from hundreds of Web sites; and information on training programs, including a Mobile Technology Classroom, management seminars, and strategic planning workshops for nonprofit professionals.

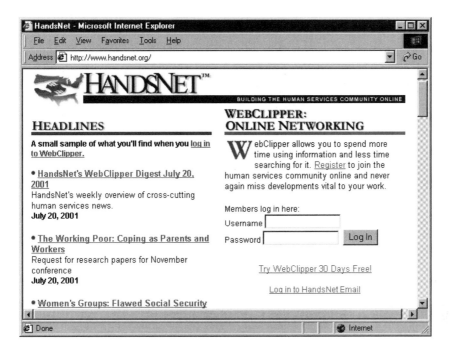

NetAction (http://www.netaction.org)

Dedicated to promoting the use of the Internet for effective grassroots citizen action campaigns and to educating the public, policymakers, and the media about technology policy issues, the NetAction site provides the Virtual Activist, an online training program; NetAction's Online Buyer's Guide; and additional reports focusing on cyber action issues.

Grants for Individuals

Michigan State University Grants and Related Resources
(http://www.lib.msu.edu/harris23/grants/3subject.htm)

Previously introduced in the Fundraising Resources section of this chapter, the MSU site includes a separate section for individuals that covers print resources as well as many federal, state, and university-based funding sources online. It is a very good place to browse for new Web-based resources.

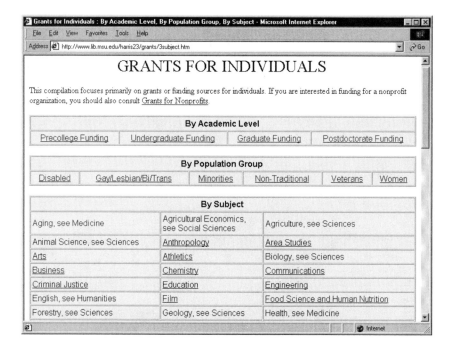

ArtsWire (http://www.artswire.org)

ArtsWire, sponsored by the New York Foundation for the Arts, is a membership organization devoted to arts advocacy that offers funding information for individual artists each week in its Web site's Current section, which includes late-breaking details on fellowships, residencies, exhibition spaces, arts events, and job listings. The site also includes an archive of Current postings going back to 1995.

Art Deadlines List (http://custwww.xensei.com/adl)

Richard Gardner's Art Deadlines List is a monthly compilation of information about juried competitions, contests, jobs, internships, scholarships, residencies, fellowships, casting calls, auditions, tryouts, festivals, and grants for artists in the visual, literary, and performing arts. Posted to the site is a free version of the list, which is also available via e-mail as a paid subscription service.

FinAid: The Financial Aid Information Page (http://www.finaid.org)

Sponsored by the National Association of Student Financial Aid Administrators and created by Mark Kantrowitz, FinAid is the most comprehensive Internet resource available on funding for education in the United States. The site runs the gamut from general information about public and private sources of scholarships and loans to scam alerts. It would be difficult to pose a question about financial aid and not find a detailed response here.

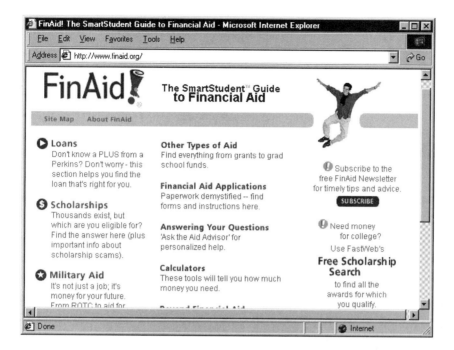

FastWeb.com (http://www.fastweb.com)
Since 1995, FastWeb has helped students find college scholarships. A student's background is matched with the eligibility requirements for scholarships from around the country. The FastFocus section gives advice on admissions, scholarships, jobs, career planning, money, and financial aid.

Conclusion

The Internet is growing so rapidly that just keeping current with what's available could be a full-time job. Surfing for new Web sites, while time consuming, is an essential part of that process. Many of the sites we've reviewed will help keep you informed about new online resources, but it's important not to understate the value of simply spending time on the Web yourself. The Links to Nonprofit Resources section of the Foundation Center's Web site is a great starting point for further exploration. We'll continue to inform you about new sites of interest as well as changes to some of your old favorites.

CHAPTER NINE

Online Journals

In today's fast-paced, information-based world, it is increasingly important for grantseekers to keep informed of recent developments in the world of philanthropy. One way to do this is by reading nonprofit journals, newsletters, and other publications. In the past a monthly print newsletter would arrive in your "snail mail" box, or you would wait until the first of the month for a favorite magazine to appear on the newsstand. Fortunately, this is no longer the case. An array of online philanthropic journals, news awareness services, and electronic publications make it easier than ever to keep your finger on the pulse of developments affecting your fundraising efforts. The range of current information now available on the World Wide Web is vast and growing daily.

Electronic publications can be useful for grantseekers in a variety of ways. These resources can make a real difference in helping you stay better informed, whether you are seeking the latest information about a particular funder, grants listings, information on nonprofit management, or for the latest news about individual movers and shakers in the nonprofit field. Content ranges from well-researched, in-depth features to abstracts of notable articles and current news headlines. Although some of the publications require a user name and password, most are open for unrestricted access.

The electronic publications described in this chapter present their information in a variety of forms. There are electronic publications that mirror their print counterparts and that post all (or nearly all) of their content online. Some journals and newsletters have created information available exclusively on the Web, while others operate e-newsletters that exist only in the form of an e-mail sent directly to your inbox. This means you don't have to visit a Web site regularly to find new content. Still others are current awareness vehicles, providing headlines on philanthropy or on programmatic areas of interest to nonprofits. Some deliver only sample articles or content as a sort of marketing tool designed to sell subscriptions to print editions. Any one of these electronic publications may also be geared toward a specific subject area or geographic focus, whether local, national, or international.

You'll find foundation-sponsored publications; government-sponsored journals relating to the federal, state, and local levels; and newsletters researched and issued by private companies and individuals. Some online publications are posted daily, some biweekly, some monthly, and some several times a year. (Most indicate prominently how often the content is updated.) More and more frequently these online publications offer the same or similar content through e-mail listservs. If you have an e-mail address, you can subscribe to the publication directly from the Web site (or by sending your e-mail address to a specified e-mail address) to receive messages ranging from notification that new content has been added to a site to the full-text of the publication itself. (See Chapter 10 for more on joining online mailing lists.)

What follows is a selective listing of some of the philanthropy-related journals now on the Web, with a brief description of each. We have organized these sites into categories for ease of reference (electronic counterparts of print publications, e-newsletters, current awareness/alert services, online exclusives, selected articles with subscription information, local/regional, international, and other sites listing online journals). A more comprehensive listing is available at the Center's Web site (http://www.fdncenter.org/research/npr_links/npr03.html). Some sites containing these journals are also mentioned in other chapters, but here we focus on the content, features, and usefulness of the online journals themselves.

Electronic Counterparts of Print Publications

Board Member Online (http://www.ncnb.org/boardmember/current.htm)

Board Member Online, published ten times a year by the National Center for Nonprofit Boards (NCNB), is "designed to give you highlights of each new regular issue of the publication, and to serve as a ready archive of past issues." The online version of *Board Member* offers access to the "members only" print publication, presenting abbreviated versions of feature articles, departments, and case studies where, each month, three different experts in the field offer possible solutions to challenges facing real board members. Issues are archived back to March 1999. *Board Member Online* also offers information on how to subscribe to the print version, how to submit articles for publication, and ordering information for special print editions that feature in-depth coverage of issues nonprofit board members face.

The Chronicle of Philanthropy (http://www.philanthropy.com)

This is the online version of the biweekly print publication, the *Chronicle of Philanthropy*, considered the "newspaper of the nonprofit world."

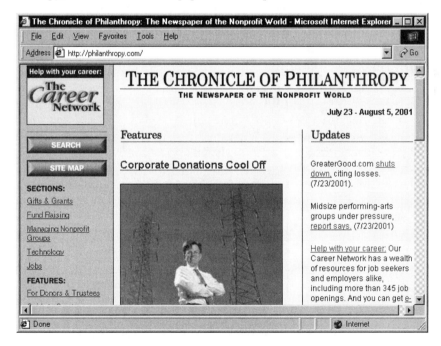

Log onto the Web site and you'll find a newspaper-like layout with news photographs and headlines from feature articles in the print edition of the *Chronicle*. There is a site-wide search engine and links to feature articles, grants listings, and current job listings from the site's main sections: Gifts and Grants, Fund Raising, Managing Nonprofit Groups, Technology, and Jobs. Other features include a section for Donor and Trustees, Guide to Grants (an electronic database of all corporate and foundation grants listed in the *Chronicle* since 1995), Ideas and Resources, the Nonprofit Handbook, Facts and Figures, Internet Resources, Events, Deadlines, Products and Services, and more. This comprehensive site also has listings of upcoming conferences in the field, news of workshops and seminars, and links to other philanthropic Internet sources. Under the Chronicle in Print heading, you can browse the titles of articles from the current and previous issues. Much of this site is available only to subscribers of the print version, although there are selected articles available for free. You can also search the job listings from the previous issue at no cost. To obtain access to the whole site, you can subscribe via e-mail, snail mail, phone, fax, or Web form. Subscribe to the *Chronicle's* free e-mail list to receive updates on what's new in the newspaper and on the site, plus special bulletins when major philanthropic news stories break.

Common Wealth (http://tap.epn.org/commonwealth)

Common Wealth is the Web site companion to the print publication, *The American Prospect* (*TAP*). Online, you will find the Common Wealth Series, which consists of full-text articles dating back to 1993 on nonprofit organizations, philanthropy, and civil society. The *Common Wealth* site itself features nonprofit news and research, an archive of past *TAP* articles, links to special reports on issues affecting the nonprofit community, original articles available only online, and links to Web sites of other organizations. *Common Wealth* is updated weekly.

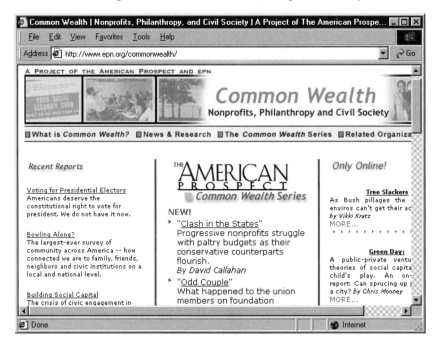

CURRENTS Online (http://www.case.org/CURRENTS)

CURRENTS Online, published by the Council for Advancement and Support of Education (CASE), focuses on educational issues with special features on fundraising. The Freebies section offers full-text access to selected articles from its current issue back to 1991. It also provides access to the *CURRENTS* index 1975–1998, which is browsable by author and topic. Get Your Own Issue provides information on how to obtain a specific issue or article from *CURRENTS* as well as subscription information for the print edition. Talk To Us gives contact information for the publication, while the Jobs section offers job postings in alumni relations, communications, development/fundraising, public relations, major gifts, annual fund, government relations, information systems, and advancement services and advancement management.

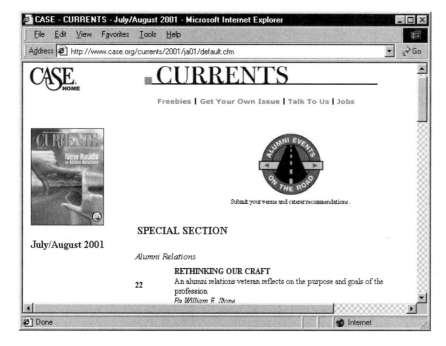

eSchoolNews Online (http://www.eschoolnews.org/funding)

eSchool News Online, "Where K–12 Education and Technology Meet," operates a Funding Center where users can find the latest information on grant programs, funding sources, and technology funding information for education. The site, which is updated daily, features educational technology funding news, a column by Deborah Ward, an independent grant writing consultant, upcoming grant deadlines, ongoing grant opportunities, a link to post-grant opportunities, recent grant awards, and a technology forum listserv, which you can subscribe to free via e-mail. The site also provides subscription information about other print publications published by eSchool News.

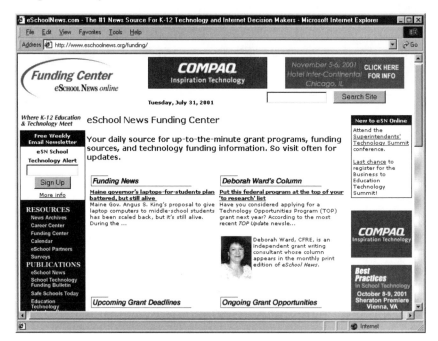

Foundation News and Commentary (http://www.foundationnews.org)

This bi-monthly print publication published by the Washington, D.C.-based Council on Foundations (COF), a membership organization for grantmakers, has a target audience consisting of grantseekers, financial advisors, policymakers, trustees and staff of donor organizations, and anyone interested in the philanthropic field. When first logging on, you will see highlights from the current issue's table of contents and the full-text of selected articles. Subscribers to the print edition receive access to the full Web content. Click on Issue Archive to view past issues dating back to March/April 1995.

Editorial content focuses on the grantmaking community and includes round-ups of trends and news in the philanthropic field, along with interviews with leaders in the nonprofit arena. It also offers analysis, commentary, and ideas—all conducive to effective grantmaking. Contents include the cover story, special features, and research. Departments, which vary from issue to issue, include Clips (a round-up of abstracts of news stories grouped by media outlet), a letters section called Feedback, reviews of new books and CD-ROM releases, and news from Affinities (special interest groups within COF) and RAGs (regional associations of grantmakers). You'll also find a helpful Government Update and Verbatim (a round-up of timely quotes from foundation executives). The People section details job changes in the foundation world. Columns include At Issue by executive editor Jody Curtis and Of All Things, a collection of foundation news stories.

There is also a link to a Job Bank that's searchable by job category, state/region, or keyword and signup form for the Jobs E-mail Notification List, which notifies you of new job postings "each time a new job opening is posted." Non-members pay a small fee to post a job listing or resume, but it is free if you are a COF member (i.e., a grantmaker). There is a toll-free number to call to obtain a subscription to the print magazine.

Grantmakers in Health Bulletin
(http://www.gih.org/info-url2678/info-url_list.htm?attrib_id=3319)
This biweekly newsletter, published by Grantmakers in Health (GIH), a
Washington, D.C.-based organization, has a mission of helping foundations
and corporate giving programs improve the nation's health by building the skills,
knowledge, and effectiveness of grantmakers in the field of health philanthropy. Through its work, GIH fosters communication and collaboration among
grantmakers and others.

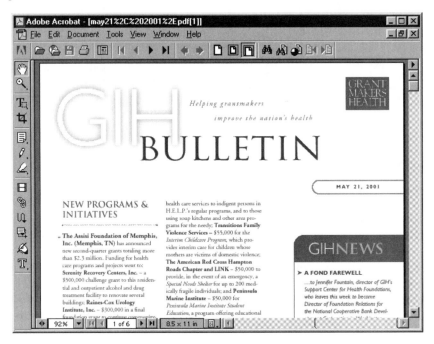

The bulletin features breaking news in health philanthropy, including New
Grants and Programs and Awards. You'll also find Surveys, Studies and Publications (linking to health-related reports), People (detailing recent personnel
appointments and promotions), Meetings (listing conferences and other gather-
ings of interest to health grantmakers), Online (reviewing new and interesting
health-related Web sites), and Positions Available (listing job openings at
grantmaking health organizations). Once a month, in Grantmaker Focus, the
activities and accomplishments of a "founding partner" are profiled. Issue Focus,
also a monthly feature, examines a single health issue or philanthropic strategy
and its implications for health grantmakers. You can access PDF files of the current issue or past issues back to October 1998. You can also browse the Issue
Focus feature separately, using the URL (http://www.gih.org/info-url2678/info-
url_list.htm?attrib_id=3320).

NonProfit Times (http://www.nptimes.com)
This Web newsletter, published 24 times a year, including six *Direct Marketing*
and six *Financial Management Editions,* presents the table of contents and
selected full-text articles from its print counterpart, published in Parsippany, New
Jersey. *NonProfit Times* bills itself as "the leading business publication for

nonprofit management" and targets its content to nonprofit executive managers (34,000 subscribers to date).

The newspaper-like home page provides selected headlines linked to complete nonprofit news features. There also are special reports available, including three popular reports issued annually. The first, Salary Survey, published in February, provides a summary of nonprofit compensation information, and information on ordering the full report and a downloadable PDF chart. The NPT 100, published in November, examines and ranks America's largest nonprofits and includes information on how to order the full report and a downloadable PDF chart. The third special report, the NPT Power and Influence Top 50, published in August, profiles the nation's top nonprofit executive leaders. The full table of contents and the full-text of selected articles from the latest issues of *Financial Management Edition* (*FME*) and *Direct Marketing Edition* (*DME*) also are available from the home page. The Executive Session columns, published in the *FME,* also can be accessed from the home page.

On the Web, you'll also have access to tables of contents and full-text lead stories from back issues dating to January 1999. The Resource Directory, updated 24 times a year, provides links to nonprofit resources. The Employment Marketplace is a good place to find job listings in the nonprofit sector. Full issues are available only through print subscriptions (information and subscription form available online).

Philanthropy (http://www.philanthropyroundtable.org)
This bi-monthly magazine is located on the site of the Philanthropy Roundtable, a Washington, D.C.-based national association of individual donors, corporate giving representatives, foundation staff and trustees, and trust and estate officers. The Roundtable believes that voluntary private action presents the best means of

addressing many of society's needs and sees that a vibrant private sector is critical to creating the wealth that makes philanthropy possible. Click on This Month in *Philanthropy* to review the magazine's full content, which includes full-text features, reviews, commentary, grants announcements, staff changes, Washington Watch, and Donor Q&A. Access to the complete content of past issues dating to winter 1997 is provided. You can sign up for an e-mail notification service, which provides daily news briefs on issues of interest to donors and alerts to upcoming Philanthropy Round Table meetings. Subscribe to the print edition by phone or fax.

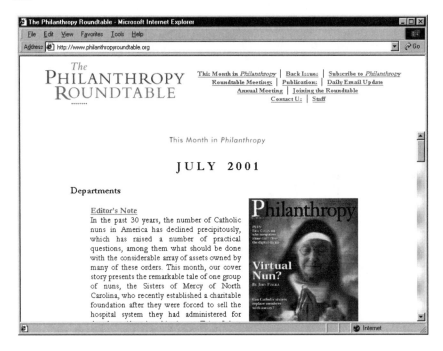

Trusts and Estates (http://trustsandestates.com)

Trusts and Estates, a magazine for estate planning and wealth management professionals, has been published monthly since 1904. The Web site for the online version is hosted by IndustryClick Financial Services. Here you will find full-text feature articles from recent issues of the publication. The site also offers exclusive online-only articles and preview articles yet to be published in the print edition. Other site features include Oddlots (containing "random samplings of news affecting the estate planning field"), information on how to subscribe to the print edition, guidelines for submitting articles for publication, an editorial index covering the years 1993 to 2000, highlights from a reader profile study, information about the magazine itself, and information for advertisers. The ability to browse back issues is currently listed as "coming soon."

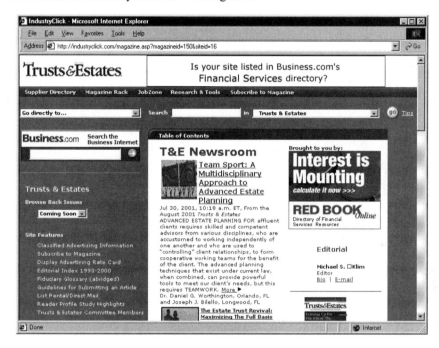

E-Newsletters

ArtsWire Current (http://www.artswire.org/current.html)

This weekly online journal of arts news and funding notices is a project of ArtsWire. The journal includes news updates on philosophical, political, social, and economic issues affecting the arts and culture community. Also featured are the ArtsWire Web Reports, notices of funding opportunities for artists, opportunities for organizations, arts events (with descriptions of events, time, date, place, and contact), and job opportunities. The Elsewhere on the Net section updates readers on Internet news relating to the arts and film showings. Scroll down to the bottom of the newsletter to find links to the archive of past issues and a search engine specifically designed to retrieve information from past issues of *ArtsWire Current* as far back as 1995. Free subscription is available via e-mail (instructions for subscribing are at the bottom of the newsletter).

Board Café (http://www.boardcafe.org)

Subscribe online to this electronic newsletter "exclusively for members of non-profit boards of directors," to have it delivered to you by e-mail the second week of each month. The publication is co-published by the Washington, D.C.-based National Center for Nonprofit Boards, whose mission is to strengthen nonprofit organizations by strengthening their boards of directors, and CompassPoint Non-profit services, formerly the Support Center for Nonprofit Management, a consulting and training organization with regional focus and national reach, with offices in San Francisco and San Jose, California. Content ("short enough to read over a cup of coffee") includes news, opinions, and information to help board members contribute and get the most out of their board service. The archive contains issues dating back to November 1997.

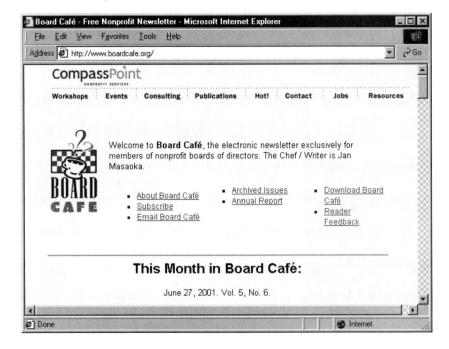

By the Cup (http://www.techsoup.org/sub_btc.cfm)

TechSoup.org, "the technology place for nonprofits," publishes the monthly e-mail newsletter, *By The Cup,* which is archived here. Each issue, dating from April 2000, has nonprofit technology news, feature articles, tips and resources, as well as highlights of the TechSoup.org Web site. To receive the most current issue, sign up for a free subscription.

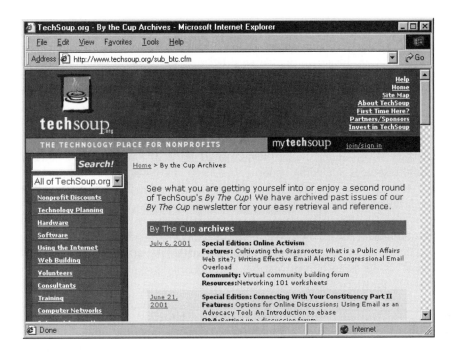

Dot.org (http://www.summitcollaborative.com/dot_org.html)

Dot.org is a new e-newsletter that serves as a practical guide with tips, tools, techniques, and case studies to help nonprofits make effective use of the Internet and other technologies. Dot.org is published by Michael Stein and Marc Osten. Back issues can be accessed in HTML and PDF formats.

Health Affairs.org (http://www.healthaffairs.org/home_p.htm)

Health Affairs, an "Internet-only publication," provides access to free full-text articles on the health care system from a variety of viewpoints, including foundations and the field of health philanthropy. The home page provides you with the editor's choice of "newsworthy articles." Each issue provides a full table of contents with the free full-text articles clearly designated. The archive dates back to Winter 1981, but the number of full-text articles drops off the further back you go.

Hoover's E-Mail Newsletters
(http://emailpreferences.com/cgi-bin/msc.pl?option=get&cn=hoovers)

Though access to much of Hoover's site requires a subscription, it does offer several free e-mail newsletters that report on the latest business news and highlights. *IPO Update* is a weekly listing of information on companies that recently filed for their initial public offering. *Hoover's Online: Week at a Glance* provides summaries of the week's business news with brief descriptions of the companies making the news. *Hoover's Industry News Digests* is delivered twice a week. There are four digests covering advertising, health care, the Internet, and telecommunications. In addition to news summaries, each e-mail newsletter provides links to the full-text of featured stories, in case you want to follow up. You can sign up for any of Hoover's newsletters as HTML or text files, except for *Hoover's Industry News Digests,* which is only available as a text file.

Ideas In Action (http://www.idealist.org/newsletter.html)

This electronic newsletter, with more than 45,000 subscribers, is published every month or so by Idealist, a global clearinghouse of nonprofit and volunteering resources on the Web. Idealist, a project of the New York City-based Action Without Borders, envisions in its mission "a global coalition of individuals and organizations working to build a world where all people can live free, dignified and productive lives." The group also trains nonprofits to use the Internet in their work. Newsletter content is targeted toward those who work for or support nonprofit and voluntary organizations. Inside the newsletter you'll find a mixture of news and helpful resources, including opportunities alerts, and links to past issues dating back to 1998. Subscribe to the newsletter by entering your e-mail address in a simple online form.

Internet Insider (http://www.efsinternet.com/internet-insider.htm)

This free e-newsletter, published twice a month "for grantseekers and fundraisers," is the brainchild of Marilyn Gross. Each issue profiles useful philanthropic Web sites, online discussion groups, publications, and more. Here you can browse past issues and find instructions for subscribing.

Internet Prospector (http://www.internet-prospector.org/index.html)

Internet Prospector, a nonprofit service to the prospect research community, is produced by volunteers nationwide who "mine" the Web for prospect research nuggets for nonprofit fundraisers. But anyone seeking tools for accessing corporate, foundation, biographical, international and online news sources will find this Web site useful.

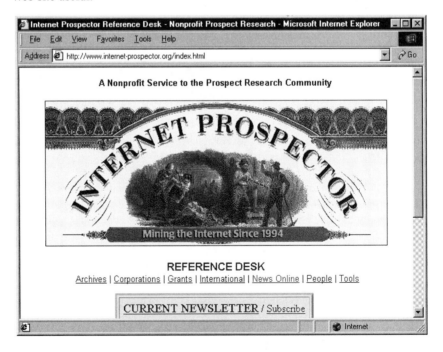

Each month's newsletter includes reviews of and annotated links to resources organized under the headings Corporations, Foundations/Grants, International, People, News Online, and Tools. There also is an archive of past issues dating back to November 1998. You can subscribe to an e-mail version of the newsletter that is sent during the first week of each month or to PRSPECT-L, a heavily used listserv for prospect researchers that incorporates *Internet Prospector* in its postings.

KDV Free Newsletter Subscriptions (http://www.kdv.com/agendas.html)

Kern, DeWenter, Viere, Ltd. (KDV), a consulting group, offers four free e-mail subscriptions on its site. *Insight on Estate Planning* (bi-monthly) features tips for reducing estate and gift taxes, marital and retirement planning, creating wills, and protecting assets. Articles present strategies for leveraging gifts, using insurance, creating trusts, timing retirement plan distributions, transferring wealth between spouses, and making charitable gifts to take maximum advantage of certain tax breaks. *KDV Nonprofit Update* (monthly) gets you nonprofit reports, guest articles, news briefs, announcements, and links of interest to the nonprofit community. There also are free classified ads for subscribers. *Nonprofit Agendas* (bi-monthly) focuses on new regulations, tax legislation, finance and governmental issues, management, fundraising, technology, and employee compensation for the nonprofit sector. *Tax Impact* (bi-monthly) is designed to help inform individuals and businesses of changing tax laws. Topics include minimizing the tax burden, creating financial plans for the future, succession plans, and tax reduction strategies. By clicking on Resources on the top navigation bar and then selecting the publication title you are interested in from under the Articles heading, you can see descriptions of articles from the latest issues.

Tech4Impact (http://www.coyotecom.com/tech4impact.html)

This e-mail newsletter is less about techno-jargon and more about the human factors in using technology, including the Internet, successfully to benefit people, communities, and the environment. The newsletter is hosted by Yahoo!'s e-groups and is sent out on the second Tuesday of the month. *Tech4Impact* is produced by Jayne Cravens, creator of coyotecom.com and contributor to the Virtual Volunteering Project and the United Nations Volunteers program.

Current Awareness/Alert Services

ChangingOurWorld.com (http://www.changingourworld.com)

"Your Online Center for Philanthropy" is presented by Changing Our World Inc., a national philanthropic services company for nonprofit corporations and individuals. The site offers analysis, commentary, interviews, and profiles on issues and people in the world of philanthropy. Select Fundraising Trends, Non-Profit News Center, or Philanthropy for more specific articles and information on those topics. ChangingOurWorld.com also offers four free e-newsletters: *Observations in Philanthropy* (biweekly), focusing on "the business of giving;" *The Next Generation* (monthly), on young people and philanthropy; *Inside Corporate Philanthropy* (monthly), on corporate grantmakers and nonprofits; and *The Internet Fundraiser* (monthly), on Web and e-mail campaigns.

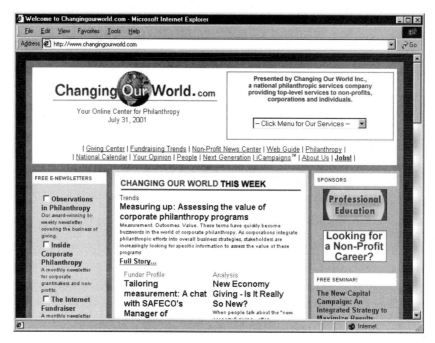

HandsNet (http://www.handsnet.org)

Washington, D.C.-based HandsNet works to "Empower organizations to effectively integrate new online strategies, strengthening their program and policy work on behalf of people in need." The site includes news headlines and features on timely surveys, data, legislation, and budget issues ranging from managed care and welfare reform to HIV prevention and neighborhood preservation. There also are alerts on pending legislation, with links to pertinent sites and direct e-mail links to relevant sources. The fee-based WebClipper Service sends members daily e-mail updates on issues they specify, ranging from affordable housing to welfare reform. There also is a professional directory, a job bank, a publications area where you can post reports for distribution on the Web, discussion groups, funding pages, action alerts, and a conference calendar. You can sign up online for a free 30-day trial of WebClipper.

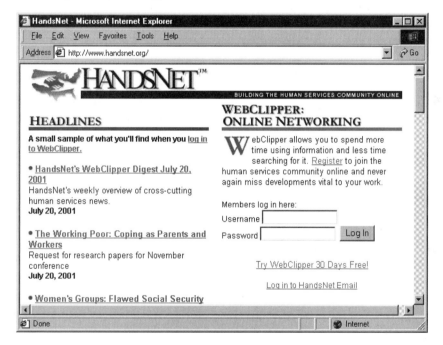

Join Together Online (JTO) (http://www.jointogether.org)

This site is a Boston-based national resource center and meeting place for communities working together with the goal of reducing substance abuse (e.g., illicit drugs, excessive alcohol, tobacco) and gun violence. *Join Together Online (JTO)* is a project of Boston University School of Public Health, funded by the Robert Wood Johnson Foundation, Joyce Foundation, and David Bohnett Foundation.

The main page offers current news releases, feature articles, links, and photo essays about substance abuse and gun violence, but each topic also has its own page with its own information. On each home page you will see the top news stories and, most relevant for grantseekers, selected funding-specific news stories and resources. Once in either the substance abuse or gun violence pages, go to the bottom of the screen, where you will find: Issues, featuring background information on substance abuse and gun violence; JTO Wire, featuring newswire stories, original features, press releases, research, and commentary; Take Action, which includes the Legislative Toolbox where you can search for elected officials and track their voting records as legislation moves through Congress; Resources, which includes a section on funding with funding news, grants announcements, feature articles and a "funding finder" that searches more than 3,000 articles; and Get Help, featuring resources for substance abusers and victims of gun violence.

For help in navigating the site you can use the site search, browse by category, or look at the site map. You can also subscribe to *JTO Direct,* a digest of important national news, funding news, and funding and legislative alerts, delivered via e-mail five days a week or once weekly.

**Nonprofit Online News: News of the Online Nonprofit Community
(http://news.gilbert.org)**

This compilation of current news and feature articles on the nonprofit sector is a program of the Seattle, Washington-based Gilbert Center, which works "to support and empower the people and organizations who are changing the world for the better." News Features includes opinions and observations by Michael Gilbert, a nonprofit communication consultant and former nonprofit executive and board member. News items range from announcements of upcoming conferences and featured speakers to notes about interesting features on philanthropic sites, news reports and surveys, books, and links to relevant articles and sites. The news follows a "weblog model of short, readable items delivered on a regular basis." You can subscribe to get a weekly e-mail version of the news site and you can access the archive back to 1997. For more recent news, use the calendar on the site to select days when items were posted.

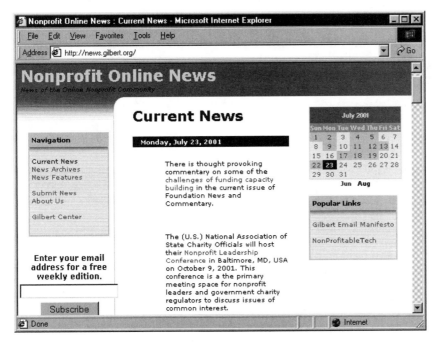

NonprofitXpress (http://npxpress.com)

This online nonprofit news awareness publication, sponsored by the A.J. Fletcher Foundation of North Carolina, "helps people understand, support and work in the nonprofit world." The site, edited by Todd Cohen, founder of *Philanthropy News Network,* focuses on nonprofit news in North Carolina, the United States, and abroad. News items are posted daily, and its archive is searchable by date, subject, geographic region, field of interest, and keyword. The site also has a searchable Announcements section where you can click through a conference calendar, profiles of people and groups, grants and gifts, and fundraising results. Users also can search through jobs listings by geographic region, title, or field of interest. Xpression, an interactive section of the site, provides access to the site's message boards, chat rooms, and user survey results. Visitors also can sign up for a free weekly e-mail newsletter. Registration is required to view the materials on this site.

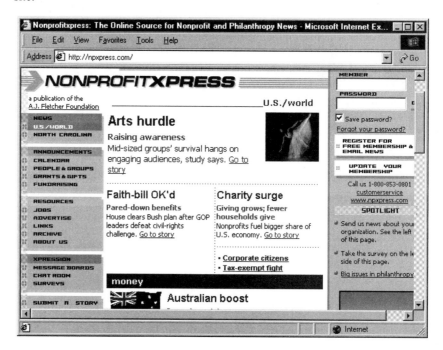

Philanthropy News Network Online (http://www.pnnonline.org)

This daily Web news service is part of *Philanthropy News Network* (*PNN*), whose mission is to deliver "news, information, and resources to all segments of the non-profit world in order to help them better achieve their goals." *PNN* was established as *Philanthropy Journal,* a column on philanthropy and nonprofit organizations by Todd Cohen, former business editor of *The News & Observer.* Cohen first launched the print publication *PNN,* then called the *Philanthropy Journal of North Carolina,* in 1993. It was published by the News and Observer Foundation.

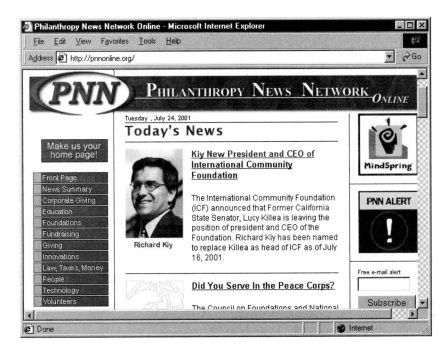

The journal's home page is designed to resemble the front page of a newspaper, with headlines linking to full-text articles. There is a daily national news summary, which is organized under the headings Corporate Giving, Education, Foundations, Fundraising, Giving, Innovations, Law, Taxes and Money, People, Technology, and Volunteers. An archive in each area allows readers to access issues dating back to February 1997 and links to other nonprofit sites. There is news about conferences and nonprofit jobs as well (searchable by region or category). You can subscribe online to the free weekly e-mail newsletter *Nonprofit Job Alert,* or post a resume. *PNN Alert,* a free, twice-weekly electronic newsletter for the nonprofit sector, has notes on fundraising, grants, corporate funding, legal and governmental issues, trends in the areas of technology and nonprofits, volunteering, foundations, sneak peeks at new features, national nonprofit job listings, tax news, and surveys of the nonprofit sector. *PNN* also produces *Nonprofits & Technology,* a free monthly national newspaper whose content focuses on technology planning, the benefits of online fundraising, virtual volunteering, and publishing on the Web for nonprofits.

Philanthropy News Digest (PND) (http://fdncenter.org/pnd/current/index.html)

A free online journal offered by the Foundation Center, *Philanthropy News Digest (PND)* is a compendium, in digest form, of philanthropy-related articles and features gathered from print and electronic media outlets nationwide. Abstracts summarize the content of each article and include complete citations to assist in locating the original article on the Web, in print, or at a library. Individual abstracts can be accessed (and printed) by clicking on a headline in the table of contents. *PND* features include the Job Corner, with more than 500 current job openings at U.S. foundations and other nonprofit organizations, and the *RFP Bulletin,* a weekly listing of current funding opportunities offered by foundations and grantmaking organizations. (You can receive both the Job Corner Alert and the *RFP Bulletin* as free weekly electronic newsletters.) You'll also find the NPO Spotlight, highlighting the activities and interests of a different nonprofit organization every week. Connections, which offers fresh links to the "best the Web has to offer" on issues related to the changing world of philanthropy; and a Conference Calendar, listing conferences taking place across the nation. The *PND* message board lets users share opinions, insights, and questions related to philanthropy with a large and growing community of consultants, development professionals, fundraisers, grantseekers, and others. Finally, *PND's* Off the Shelf (book reviews) and On the Web (Web site reviews) sections provide recommendations of the latest online and print offerings in the nonprofit field.

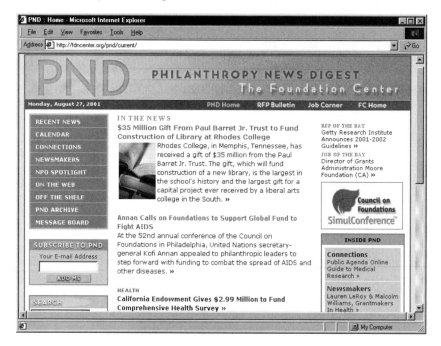

The *PND* search engine allows you to search, by name or keyword, past issues of *PND* dating back to January 1995. If you prefer, you can browse past *PND* issues by date, by selecting the 1995–2000 or the 2000–current archive. You also can access *PND* special quarterly issues focusing on timely nonprofit topics, including education and the Internet. Subscribe to *PND* for free and receive the journal via e-mail every Tuesday evening. Subscription instructions are available on the *PND* home page or on the Center's Newsletter page (http://fdncenter.org/newsletters).

Pulse! (http://www.allianceonline.org/pulse.html)

This national online Washington, D.C.-based newsletter, described as "the Online Newsletter of the Nonprofit Management Support Community," is delivered monthly via e-mail, providing readers with a timely summary of what's happening in the nonprofit sector and the management support community. Content includes a brief digest of current happenings within the sector, new ideas, conferences, awards, and postings on relevant books, videos, and Web sites. Keeping up with the Nonprofit Netizens provides information on nonprofits and their use of the Internet. Learning Tools of the Trade lists conferences, seminars, and other educational opportunities of interest to nonprofit professionals.

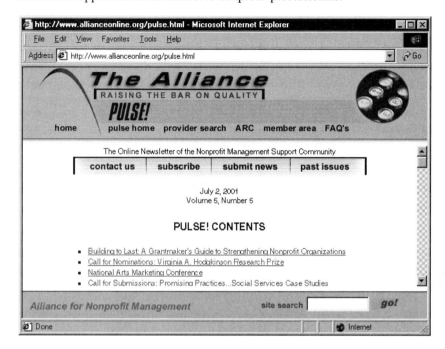

The newsletter is a free service of The Alliance, the Washington, D.C.-based organization resulting from the 1998 merger of the Support Centers of America, the Nonprofit Management Association, and the Alliance for Nonprofit Management. The Alliance's mission is to "provide leadership in enhancing a civil society by challenging and strengthening those who deliver management and governance support services to nonprofit organizations." You can subscribe to a free e-mail edition of the newsletter or submit news items to the site. A complete archive of back issues dates back to January 1997.

Online Exclusives

Alternatives In Philanthropy (http://www.capitalresearch.org/ap/welcome.html)
This monthly newsletter is published by the Washington, D.C.-based Capital Research Center (CRC), a conservative group that focuses its studies on reviving the American traditions of charity, philanthropy, and voluntarism as well as identifying private alternatives to government welfare programs. Its research is channeled into several newsletters, including *Alternatives in Philanthropy,* which is "devoted to offering fresh perspectives on prevailing trends and current issues in the philanthropic arena. [It] offers important investigative reports and discussions of broad issues in philanthropy." Online you'll also find selected full-text articles dating back to November 1995.

The Difference (http://www.e-TheDifference.com)

The Difference is the quarterly publication of the Development Research Group (DRG), an organization of executive search consultants. Look here for feature articles on new philanthropists, careers, fundraising, leadership, and philanthropy. *The Difference* also provides access to the *Fund Raising Management* magazine column, Wanted: Leadership, Experience and Change, which covers the changing recruitment environment in the nonprofit sector.

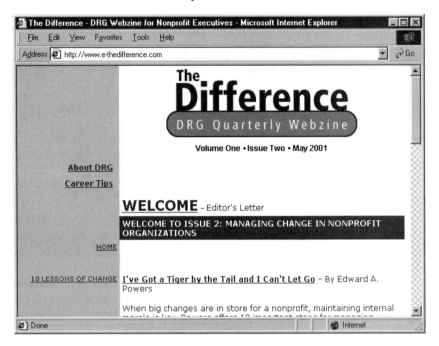

Foundation Watch (http://www.capitalresearch.org/fw)

This monthly newsletter is published by the Washington, D.C.-based Capital Research Center (CRC), a conservative group that focuses on reviving the American traditions of charity, philanthropy, and voluntarism and identifying private alternatives to government welfare programs. CRC's research is channeled into seven newsletters, including *Foundation Watch,* which monitors the activities of private foundations and analyzes their impact on American society. Specifically, the focus is on cultural activities of major foundations and the response of the donor community to the decline of federal funds for the arts and humanities. Online you'll find selected articles dating back to March 1996.

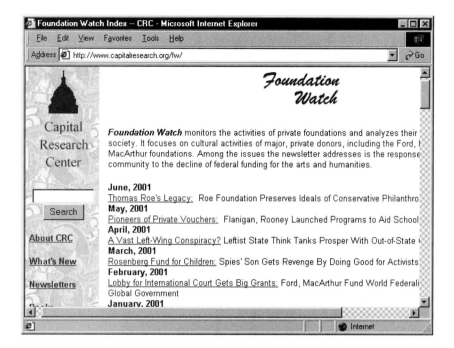

Planet 501c3: Tales from the Nonprofit Galaxy (http://www.planet501c3.org)
Miriam Engelberg's *Planet 501c3* is hosted by Compass Point Nonprofit Services in San Francisco. This monthly cartoon series takes a humorous look at the non-profit world.

Volunteer Today (http://www.volunteertoday.com)
Described as "the Electronic Gazette for Volunteerism," this monthly online newsletter is directed to those interested in volunteer management. It serves two purposes: to build the capacity of individuals to organize effective volunteer pro-grams and to enhance the profession of volunteer management. Features include volunteer news, tips and articles on Recruiting and Retention, Management and Training, Ask Connie (a volunteer manager/consultant/trainer who responds to e-mail questions), Georgean's Tech Tips, and Boards and Committees. You also can find listings of Internet resources, volunteer opportunities, a calendar of events, and a bookstore. Register online and receive an e-mail "heads-up" called *VT News,* which lets you know when each new newsletter is posted.

Selected Articles with Subscription Information

Advice at Chardon Online
(http://www.chardonpress.com/newsletter/advice.html)
This area of the Chardon Press Web site provides links to numerous useful resources and other information. There are more than 40 complete *Grassroots Fundraising Journal* articles and sample book chapters available here. In addition, you can sign up for Chardon Press' bi-monthly newsletter that includes funding tips and Kim Klein's *Grassroots Fundraising Journal* column, Dear Kim Klein, also available as a searchable archive here. You can even post a question for Klein using an online form, or you can find a Kim Klein public workshop near you.

Don Kramer's Nonprofit Issues (http://www.nonprofitissues.com)

This bi-monthly print publication, edited by Don Kramer and based in Dresher, Pennsylvania, is described as "a Newsletter of Nonprofit Law You Need to Know." Kramer, a partner in a Philadelphia law firm who has worked with nonprofits of all sizes, is a teacher, writer, publisher, board member, and one of the founders of the Pennsylvania Association of Nonprofit Organizations (http://www.pano.org). Content is targeted to nonprofit executives and their advisors and includes recent issues and news about federal and state cases and recent regulations and rulings affecting the work of nonprofit organizations. Specifically, you'll find coverage of federal tax law issues, employment law, foundation liability, volunteer law, corporate governance, funding rules, charitable giving, insurance, and copyright/trademark issues. Online, you'll find tables of contents and highlights featuring full-text articles from current and past issues. Ready reference pages (i.e., articles summarizing rules and regulations that control nonprofit activity) are available as PDF files for a fee. Subscribe online and receive a special six-month rate for first-time subscribers. Register for Thursday with the Editor, a fee-based monthly seminar conference call with the publication's editors, to discuss topics in the current issue or any other relevant subject matters. You can also subscribe online to an e-mail update and mailing list, which will alert you to site changes, new publications, and other offers.

Leader to Leader (http://www.josseybass.com/JBJournals/ltl.html)

Published by Jossey-Bass, this quarterly report is sponsored by the Peter F. Drucker Foundation for Nonprofit Management (http://www.pfdf.org) and written by top executives, authors, consultants, and social thinkers, with an interest in issues related to nonprofit management, leadership, and strategy. From this site you can access the tables of contents and links to the full-text of selected articles dating back to the summer 1996 issue. Editorials offer an insight into exactly what nonprofit leaders are planning for and how they are dealing with change and challenges. Information on how to subscribe to the print edition is also available online. *Leader to Leader* has a no-risk trial offer, and paid subscribers receive the Drucker Foundation's book, *Leader of the Future.*

The Nonprofit Quarterly (http://www.nonprofitquarterly.org)

The Nonprofit Quarterly is a 64-page publication of Boston's Third Sector New England (TSNE), whose mission is to promote "active democracy." After a simple registration, users can view the full table of contents of the current issue and access selected full-text articles. An archive, with selected full-text articles and full table of contents, is also available back to the spring 1999 issue. Users can view job postings for openings at TSNE and browse the nonprofit marketplace for services and products geared toward the nonprofit community. Visitors also can subscribe online or via e-mail, fax, or telephone.

Poets & Writers Online (http://www.pw.org/mag/index.htm)

Poets & Writers Magazine, published six times a year, has a companion Web site that offers access to selected feature articles, recent grants and awards winners, and more. Select Subscribe Now to locate information in the print version. In Current Contents you will find the table of contents from the latest issue and selected full-text articles. The Grants & Awards section lists winners of recent awards from a variety of sources. Teachers Guide provides resources for arts educators, while

Classified Ads lists such things as contests, conferences, jobs, workshops, publications, calls for manuscripts, and more. An archive of posted articles is available from January/February 1996.

Local/Regional

Food For Thought
(http://www.compasspoint.org/publications/food4thought/Food4Thought.html)
This free e-mail newsletter, published every three weeks by CompassPoint Non-profit Services, can be sent to you via either e-mail or fax. The focus of this publication is on the San Francisco Bay area. On this page you will find access to sample issues in the archive, which dates back to January 1997. If you would like to subscribe, a basic subscription form is available online.

FYI (http://www.artswire.org/nyfa/fyi)
FYI (For Your Information) is billed as the largest free arts newspaper in New York state. Though the quarterly publication is focused on New York, it has subscribers throughout the country and the world. Subscription information as well as information on workshops, calls for submissions, posting classified ads, and more is available on the site. There also is an online archive dating back to the spring 1999 issue. By selecting an issue date, you are taken to an introductory paragraph about the theme of that particular issue. Links to the remainder of the articles are then available on the left hand side of the screen.

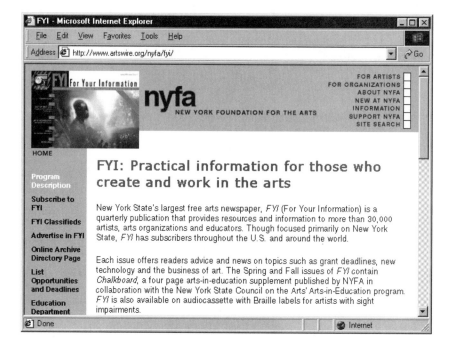

Giving Forum Online (http://www.mcf.org/mcf/forum/index.html)

This free quarterly newspaper is published by the Minnesota Council on Foundations (MCF), a regional association of grantmakers based in Minneapolis. Content includes information and news on Minnesota philanthropy, current giving issues, and grantmaking research. You'll find highlights of the latest issue plus the full-text of selected articles, arranged topically, dating back to 1995. What's New (http://www.mcf.org/mcf/whatsnew/index.html) links to the weekly *Minnesota Giving News*. Here you will find the weekly features, News Briefs, and Grants of Note. The People section provides recent news on people in Minnesota grantmaking, while Calendar lists upcoming training programs for Minnesota non-profits, and New Resources lists new publications of interest to Minnesota and national grantseekers. *Minnesota Giving News* also provides links to Minnesota grantmakers on the Web, a news archive dating back to March 1999, press releases, and job openings in Minnesota's grantmaking and related fields. You can subscribe to the newspaper using an online form.

Grants Action News (http://assembly.state.ny.us/gan)

Grants Action News is a monthly publication of the New York State Assembly. Each issue lists funding opportunities on both state and federal levels. Each listing provides you with eligibility requirements, funding availability, deadlines, and contact information. Each issue also features listings of learning opportunities and what's new on the Web. You can also subscribe to a free e-mail version of the newsletter. Instructions on how to do this are found at the end of each issue.

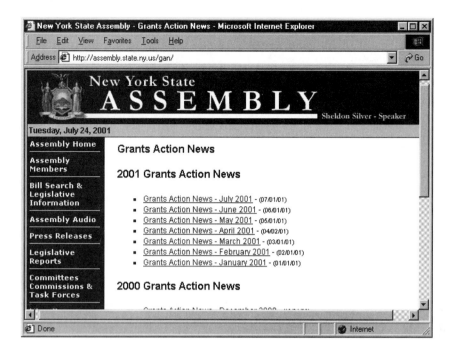

International

International Dateline
(http://www.cof.org/newsroom/newsletters/international/index.htm)
This quarterly newsletter published by the Council on Foundations provides "grantmakers and their associations with information and resources regarding domestic giving on international themes, U.S.-based cross-border grantmaking and the development of philanthropic structures around the world." Recent features of the newsletter include News and Announcements; A Conversation With . . . , which includes interviews with foundation and program representatives; a link to a conference calendar; and Legal Dimensions, an insert covering legal aspects of international grantmaking. *International Dateline* is archived back to 1997. The most recent editions are available in PDF format. The Legal Dimensions insert is archived separately, also back to 1997.

International Journal of Not-for-Profit Law
(http://www.icnl.org/journal/journal.html)
This publication of the International Center for Not-for-Profit Law, also available as a free e-mail subscription, "provides up-to-date information on legal and regulatory developments affecting the not-for-profit sector in countries around the world." Articles, country reports, case notes, and book reviews are available. Online and e-mail articles are condensed versions of the print versions. However, country reports feature links to supplementary information. Archived issues date back to September 1998.

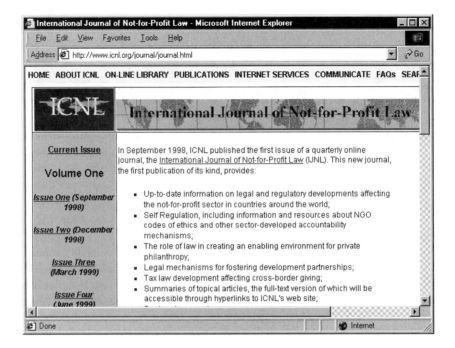

OneWorld (http://www.oneworld.net)

This site represents "an Internet community of 869 organizations leading the way for human rights and sustainable development worldwide." It is the Internet "arm" of OneWorld Broadcasting Trust, a London-based charity that was launched in 1995 and became a registered charity in 1997. Its mission is to advance information, tools, and resources about global development issues (from poverty to education) through creative and collaborative media uses.

The News section, updated daily, is focused on human rights and sustainable development and is searchable by topic and country. Facts on global campaigns, job and volunteering opportunities, articles, and press releases from partners also are available online. The Think Tank invites professional debate on global issues, such as the banning of landmines. Editions offers news of Africa, South Asia, Latin America, the United States, and the United Kingdom. OneWorld also offers Web site design and development to qualified nongovernmental organizations (NGOs). Membership is free to individuals concerned with global justice. Organizations in the areas of social justice, human rights, or sustainable development pay annual membership fees ranging from $250–$975, based on size. You can register for a free three-month trial online. Members receive regular e-mail updates from OneWorld partners on key issues.

Social Economy and Law Journal (SEAL)
(http://www.efc.be/publications/sealabstract.html)

Published by the European Foundation Centre, *Social Economy and Law* (*SEAL*) is a journal on nonprofit law focused primarily on Central and Eastern Europe and the newly independent states, with expanding coverage of the European Union. The journal seeks to promote an "enabling environment for the social economy (foundations, associations, and other nonprofit organizations) and to enhance the process of legal reform by improving the knowledge of current legal developments throughout Europe." The SEAL initiative is supported by the Charles

Stewart Mott Foundation and the Open Society Institute—Budapest. You can browse country reports, editorials, and other features back to the summer 1998 issue.

UK Fundraising (http://www.fundraising.co.uk/index.html)

UK Fundraising, "the business-to-business resource for UK charity fundraisers and the fundraising industry, published since 1994," provides summaries of news items from a variety of sources. The site, published by Fundraising UK Ltd., is updated daily and has listings of job openings, links to numerous online resources, a discussion list, and an e-mail newsletter you can subscribe to for free. The archive provides monthly highlights of news stories, features, and resources dating back to 1995. Look at the top of the page to find International News, which provides news briefs culled from a variety of new sources and is updated throughout the day.

Other Sites Listing Online Journals

About.com: Nonprofit Charitable Orgs: Nonprofit News Sources (http://about.com/careers/nonprofit/cs/nonprofitnews/index.htm)

About.com is an Internet network with hundreds of expert, topic-specific "guides." More than 700 subject areas are grouped into 36 channels, each of which is administered by a guide who has either formal training or life experience in his or her particular subject area. The guide for Nonprofit Charitable Orgs is Stan Hutton, who has been a nonprofit manager, consultant, grantwriter, and volunteer. Nonprofit News Sources includes a helpful annotated listing of online publications in the area of philanthropy, an archive of recent years' entries, relevant news headlines and features, hand-picked Net Links for exploring the nonprofit sector, job listings, and a site-wide search engine.

Charity Village: Online Publications for the Nonprofit Community
(http://www.charityvillage.com/charityvillage/ires2.html)

Charity Village, an Ontario, Canada-based site, presents this alphabetical listing of e-newsletters and other online publications that are useful to nonprofits. The scope is local, national, and international. A maple leaf icon indicates those online publications with a Canadian focus.

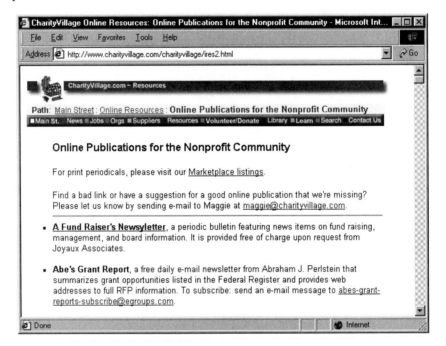

The Foundation Center—Literature of the Nonprofit Sector Online
(http://fdncenter.org/research/lnps/list.html)

Literature of the Nonprofit Sector Online (*LNPS*), the Foundation Center's online catalog of the Center's library holdings, has a separate, indexed listing of periodicals and newspapers. Links are provided to those publications with online content or information.

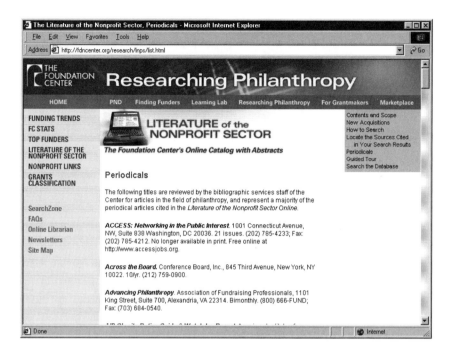

Michigan State University Libraries: Nonprofit Newsletters and Current Awareness Services (http://www.lib.msu.edu/harris23/grants/percat2.htm)
This valuable section of the Michigan State University Libraries' site provides a listing of nonprofit newsletters and current awareness services arranged alphabetically.

Conclusion

The overview of nonprofit sector online journals and news services provided in this chapter should be thought of as an introduction only. A curious mind and a focused strategy will assist you in finding additional information and/or the electronic publication that is right for you. Most of the publications listed here, and many others that you may discover on your own, have an archive of past issues and articles for you to view. Take the time to peruse these archives to find out if a particular publication is right for your needs. If there is an e-mail subscription option, you might want to subscribe to an issue or two to get a feel for the type of content provided (you can always unsubscribe later if you need to). To assess a publication's information and its relevance to you or your organization, ask the following questions: How current is the information? How much does a subscription cost? How easy is it to unsubscribe? Is there an archive of past issues? Who is the source, and do my or my organization's views, politics, and goals mirror the source's? Close reading and a critical eye are necessary for evaluating the information you seek and receive online.

The Foundation Center regularly looks for new nonprofit information and news services on the Web and posts new links and annotations to the Nonprofit Links (http://www.fdncenter.org/research/npr_links/npr03.html) section of our Web site. Please check back often to see what new publications have appeared on the scene that can help keep you well informed.

CHAPTER TEN

Building Communities: Discussion Groups, Listservs, Forums, and Message Boards

Introduction

The use of the Internet has greatly advanced the ability of grantseekers to share information, advice, and techniques with colleagues. As with a conference that goes on continuously, participants can learn efficiently from each other about useful directories, books and software, upcoming workshops and meetings, fundraising strategies, job announcements, and more. E-mail is currently the most utilized form of interactive communication on the Internet because it is ubiquitous and easy to use in a variety of ways. When setting out to discuss communities on the Internet, e-mail quite naturally became the primary focus of this chapter.

Grantseekers can communicate with each other on a wide range of nonprofit-related topics by subscribing to key mailing lists. By simply e-mailing a command to the appropriate e-mail address, a grantseeker may join a discussion group in progress and automatically begin to receive any messages posted to that list, as well as respond to messages and inquiries posted by others. There are also several relevant newsletters to which a grantseeker may subscribe electronically, newsletters that are also delivered via e-mail.

Discussion Group Basics

"Mailing list," "Listserv," "forum," and "discussion group" are common terms that are used interchangeably to describe a community of subscribers to an electronic mailing list. Mailing list manager software such as Listserv, produced by L-Soft International, and ListProc, produced by the Corporation for Research and Educational Networking (CREN), are two of the most frequently used programs by list owners to set up and administer these lists. Subscribers, on the other hand, only need e-mail access to participate. Every mailing list has two e-mail addresses. There is an administrative address for subscribing, unsubscribing, and other useful commands, which will be described below. (When sending an e-mail to an administrative address, keep in mind that it is only being read by a computer. Although the commands are simple, misspellings and even slight deviations from the prescribed format will prevent your message from getting through correctly.) The second address is the one you use to send messages to the entire list of subscribers. Keep this important distinction between the addresses in mind, in order to avoid sending an administrative message to all the other subscribers or posting your comments to a computer that won't receive them. If you wish to communicate directly with the person who manages the mailing list—often referred to as the list owner, list manager, or list administrator—you will need to send your message to that individual's personal e-mail address.

Another important distinction in mailing lists relates to whether the list is moderated or not. Unless it is stated otherwise, it is safe to assume that a list is unmoderated. This means that there is no filter on what gets posted to the list. This does not, however, mean that anything goes. Most lists have a ban on advertising and other specific guidelines as to what constitutes suitable subject matter. Violate these rules and you will likely hear from the list manager. You may also be barraged by criticism from other subscribers. If the violation is particularly egregious or persistent, the list manager can and will "unsubscribe" you.

If you subscribe to a moderated list, your messages are forwarded to the list owner, who then decides whether or not they will be posted. The moderator also reserves the right to edit your material. The moderator is usually an individual, a volunteer, or a group of volunteers. There are various reasons that lists may be moderated. Often, the list owner wants to keep the discourse tightly focused and seeks to ensure that no offensive messages are distributed to the list. Another reason might be that a list with heavy volume is receiving too many administrative commands, which are being sent mistakenly to the posting address for all subscribers to read. Subscribers may become annoyed and begin leaving the list as a result. A moderated list will introduce a slight delay in receipt of messages, though rarely more than one day, and often much less.

FINDING LISTS

There are several ways to find suitable mailing lists. Listed below are directories of mailing lists of interest to grantseekers. Once you are on a mailing list, make sure to read about other related lists that may interest you. If you are seeking a list on a specific topic and you are already on a related mailing list, it is a legitimate query to pose to the rest of the subscribers. There are also several excellent Internet sites, most of which are searchable, that contain directories of lists. You may use the indexes provided or try terms like "fundraising," "foundations," "nonprofit," or "philanthropy" in keyword searches. The following sites may be helpful.

Topica (http://www.topica.com)

Topica is a relatively new service that hosts thousands of mailing lists. You can search the site or use the indexes to locate lists of interest. The site information claims: "Over 12 million people subscribe to Topica-hosted newsletters and can manage their subscriptions through a free My Topica page. Topica's site makes it easy for readers to control their subscription options (subscribe, unsubscribe, vacation hold), find great e-mail content with a directory of tens of thousands of newsletters, and even start newsletters of their own!" Yahoo!Groups (http://groups.yahoo.com) is another example of this type of service.

L-Soft CataList (http://www.lsoft.com/catalist.html)

L-Soft International is the company that produces and sells Listserv software. Much like Kleenex has done with tissues, L-Soft has established itself as a brand name in the field. From this page on its Web site, you can browse any of the 47,184 public Listserv lists on the Internet, search for mailing lists of interest, and get information about Listserv host sites. This information is generated automatically from Listserv's lists database and is always up to date.

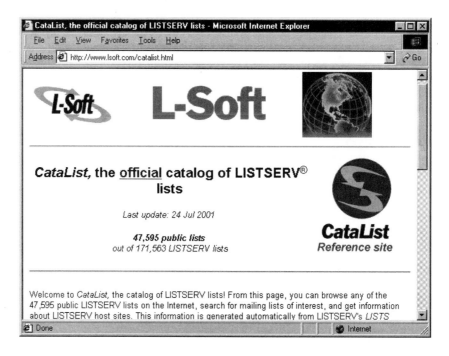

Tile.net (http://www.tile.net)

Tile.net, a part of List-universe.com's collection of Web sites, is designed to provide "A Comprehensive Internet Reference to Discussion Lists, Newsgroups, FTP Sites, Computer Product Vendors, and Internet Service and Web Design Companies."

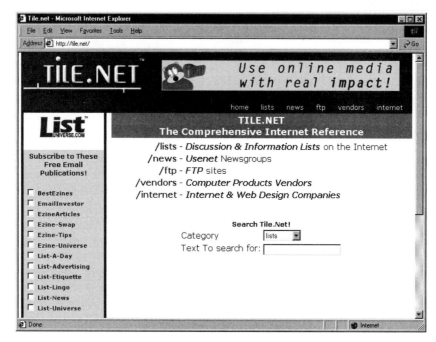

Inter-Links Internet Access
(http://www.alabanza.com/kabacoff/Inter-Links/listserv.html)
This Web area is an Internet navigator, resource locator, and tutorial provided as a public service by Robert K. Kabacoff. It contains a wide range of reference information, including a search engine for discussion lists. The Help Files found in the mailing lists on this Web site are especially useful, covering such topics as: What is a Mailing List; Subscribing, Unsubscribing, and Posting; and Other Mailing List Commands.

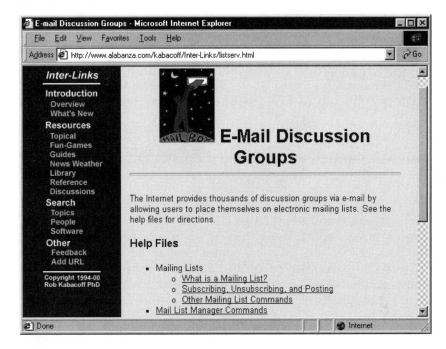

Publicly Accessible Mailing Lists (http://www.paml.net)
Developed by Stephanie and Peter DaSilva, this Web site contains a search engine and links to many useful mailing list sites. Click on Index and then Subjects for an alphabetical index of categories of mailing lists. This site allows you to subscribe to a list that sends an e-mail notice whenever a new list is added to the index.

There are also several excellent Web sites that contain lists of discussion groups of interest to the nonprofit sector. These lists include the name of the list, a brief description, and the subscription and posting addresses for the list. Jon Harrison, the Foundation Center Cooperating Collection Supervisor at Michigan State University, operates one such site. His list can be found at http://www.lib.msu.edu/ harris23/grants/maillist.htm.

Charity Village (http://www.charityvillage.com/charityvillage/stand.html)
Charity Village, a Web site for Canadian charities and nonprofits, contains a valuable list of discussion groups among its more than 1,000 pages of information.

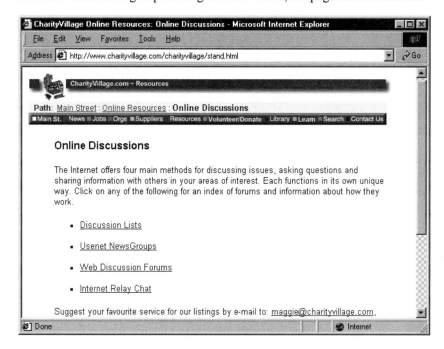

Once you find a specific list that interests you, you may want to get more information about it to determine if it is one you really want to join. In most cases you may request information directly from the list by e-mail. Many lists have an archive of previous postings, sometimes searchable, often in a Gopher file on the Internet or on a World Wide Web site. You may look in the archive to determine the level of activity and the type of discussions that have come before.

HOW TO SUBSCRIBE

To subscribe to a list, send an e-mail message to the list subscription address (administrative address) and leave the subject or "re:" line blank. In the body of the message, type "subscribe <list name>" (without the brackets or quotes). Some lists require that you include your first and last name after the list name. The subscribe command varies slightly depending on the mailing list management software used by the list owner. Shortly after sending your subscription request, you will receive an e-mail acknowledging your subscription. You should read the instructions that you receive and *print out and save them in a paper file*. The acknowledgment normally includes a description of the list, appropriate subject matter, rules, and additional commands that you may wish to use in the future—especially "unsubscribe." Keep in mind that subscription addresses can change.

SENDING A MESSAGE: DO'S AND DON'T'S

Before long you will be ready to post a message. But wait, don't be in a hurry! "Lurk" for a week or so; that is, read others' messages without posting your own for a while. One of the most valuable aspects of discussion groups is the fact that you have time to consider other postings and your own comments. Therefore, try to focus on sending concise, productive, and relevant comments or questions, not emotional ones. Be sure that your contribution is on target. Consider going to the list's archive, if it exists, to see if your topic has already been covered. Long-time subscribers can become impatient with novices who ask questions that have been thoroughly responded to in the past. If you are in a hurry, apologize up front before posting what could be an "old" topic and ask for advice about where to find the prior discussion.

Before responding to any posting to a list, think about whether you want to respond to an individual directly or post your response to the whole list. Hitting the reply button will normally mean that you are responding to the entire list. A typical mistake that a beginner makes is posting a private comment to the whole list. This can prove embarrassing. You can avoid embarrassment by making it a rule to keep personal comments or confidential information out of any e-mail. It may be unwise, for example, to send your resume over the Internet. Job announcements are frequently posted to mailing lists. We've seen people attach their resume and respond with the reply button, sending it to the entire list.

You should name the subject of your message carefully. Some lists have specific subject categories that you should use. These will be included in the initial instructions you receive upon acknowledgment of your subscription. Follow the rules. It will make it a lot easier for you and other subscribers to delete unwanted messages.

Most lists specifically forbid advertising, although some lists actually invite it. Don't delude yourself into thinking that you are simply supplying information to a community of subscribers. An advertisement will always be recognized for what it is. If you are still unsure about how your communication will be construed, you can e-mail a message to the list owner in advance and ask if your message would be acceptable.

A few other tips that will help you to be a productive member of your new list community include:

- If you ask a broad question, invite other subscribers to send their messages directly to you and offer to provide feedback to the list in the form of a summary.
- Be careful with humor. It is very easy to be misunderstood in this medium. You also risk being unsubscribed or censured by the other subscribers if your comments are seen as insulting.
- Don't post irrelevant, whimsical comments. Other subscribers will resent receiving unwanted, seemingly frivolous messages in their e-mail boxes.

MANAGING YOUR MAIL

It's useful to familiarize yourself with some easy commands that will help you keep your mailbox from overflowing, to find previous postings on a subject, and even conceal your subscription to a list. When you subscribe to a mailing list, your subscription is usually acknowledged. With the acknowledgment, you will receive a message containing the basic commands that you need. If that information is not sufficient, more information on list commands can be found by sending a message to the list's administrative address with the word "help" in the body of your message.

A quick overview of the most useful Listserv commands will include digest, postpone, index, and conceal. If you have subscribed to a list with fairly heavy volume, you may send an e-mail to the administrative address with "set <listname> mail digest" in the body of the message. This will allow you to receive batches of messages periodically rather than individually. The list manager determines the interval at which the digest will be sent—often daily or weekly. To undo this command, send "set <listname> nodigest or set <listname> mail" in a message to the administrative address. The digest command, usually included in your initial instructions after you sign on, is available for mailing lists that are managed by Listproc and Listserv.

Lists that are handled by Listproc and Listserv also offer the option of postponing your mail if you will be away for a period of time. Send an e-mail to the administrative address with the following words in the body of your message: "set <listname> mail postpone" for Listproc lists; or "set <listname> nomail" for Listserv lists. When you wish to receive messages once again, you must send a new command to the administrative address. The command for Listserv-managed lists is "set <listname> mail." Since Listproc has at least three different commands for resuming receipt of messages, you may need to send a "help" message ahead of time to the list's administrative address, in order to get the correct command.

The index command, available from all list manager software, allows you to obtain a list of archived files for the list. The command is the same for all lists. Send an e-mail to the list's administrative address with the word "index" in the body of the message.

"Conceal" is another useful command to protect your privacy. Mailing lists have a command whereby others may request that a list of the subscribers be sent to them via e-mail. In most cases this includes the e-mail address and first and last name of the person (i.e., no more than the information you provide when subscribing). With Listproc and Listserv, you have the option of sending a "set <listname> conceal yes" or "set <listname> conceal" command in order to conceal your address, so that it will not be included in any subscriber lists that are requested by others.

Listservs and Discussion Groups

CharityChannel

Grantseekers should not miss the CharityChannel Web Site at http://www.charitychannel.com/forums.

CharityChannel features an impressive collection of discussion lists for non-profit professionals. Currently there are more than 45,000 participants using the lists. With the help of many volunteers, Stephen Nill has developed and promoted these forums with clear instructions on how to use the lists, subscribe, unsubscribe, receive postings in digest forms, and access archives. At Charity-Channel, you can simply click on the Discussion Forums link for a table of available groups. You may subscribe directly from the Web site or via standard e-mail commands. To subscribe from the Web you must register first. It's a good idea to choose the option to automatically save your password in case you forget it in the future.

When you subscribe to a list from the Web site, an e-mail will be sent to you asking you to reply by e-mail or by clicking on the URL in the message in order to verify the subscription. (This will prevent others from using your e-mail address to subscribe.) You will receive a message indicating that your subscription has been accepted. From that point on, messages posted to the list will arrive in your e-mail box. You don't need to go to the Web site to participate in the forum. You may want to visit the Web site, however, for easy access to any of the lists archives or to subscribe to other lists.

Several of the CharityChannel lists are described below, along with a compilation of other mailing lists of interest to development professionals, prospect researchers, and grantseekers. Each example includes the name of the mailing list, a brief summary, subscription and posting addresses, archive address (if one exists), and other useful information, where available, such as whether the list is moderated and the volume of its "traffic." When subscribing to a mailing list, always leave the subject line of your message blank.

Alumni-L

This unmoderated list is dedicated to the interchange of ideas and information among alumni relations professionals at colleges, universities, and independent schools. Topics include alumni education, working with boards and volunteers, alumni training and workshop programs, activities of the Council for Advancement and Support of Education, cooperation with one's development office, and more. Traffic is fairly heavy on this list. It is not unusual to receive five to ten messages per day.

To subscribe to Alumni-L, just send an e-mail message to listserv@ hermes.case.edu. In the body of your message type: subscribe alumni-l <firstname lastname>. To post a message to the list, send your e-mail to alumni-l@ brownvm.brown.edu. The list owner is Paul Chewning (chewning@ns.case.org).

Charitytalk

This popular list was established in 1994 for those interested in hearing from people outside of their particular area. It invites people from almost every segment of the nonprofit sector to participate. Fund development professionals, nonprofit CEOs, college presidents, consultants, accountants, and academics are all encouraged to contribute their expertise on a wide range of topics. It is not unusual to receive five to ten messages in a single day from this list. Brief, tasteful commercial messages are permitted.

To subscribe to Charitytalk, send an e-mail message to listserv@ charitychannel.com. In the body of your message type: subscribe charitytalk <your name>. To post a message to the list, send your e-mail to charitytalk@ charitychannel.com.

The list is administered by CharityChannel. You may also subscribe or access the archive on the Web at http:www.charitychannel.com/forums.

Consultants

Originally established in 1997, Consultants is now among the CharityChannel forums. Its audience has remained the same—fundraising consultants or those interested in consulting. The purpose of the list is to discuss issues related to philanthropy and its associated services. Points of discussion may include such business aspects of consulting to nonprofit organizations as marketing, client/consultant relations, fees and collection, ethics, strategies, and resources.

To subscribe to Consultants, send an e-mail message to listserv@ charitychannel.com. In the body of your message type: subscribe consultants. To post a message to the list, just send your e-mail to consultants@ charitychannel.com.

The list is administered by CharityChannel. You may also subscribe or access the archive on the Web at http:www.charitychannel.com/forums.

Fundlist

This list is primarily for fundraising professionals whose emphasis is on education. Fundlist is heavily used, with a wide range of topics in the areas of annual campaigns, planned giving, development, ethics, policy/procedures, and many others. The list often generates 20–25 messages per day.

To subscribe to Fundlist, send an e-mail message to listproc@ listproc.hcf.jhu.edu. In the body of your message type: sub fundlist <firstname lastname>. To post a message to the list, send your e-mail to fundlist@

listproc.hcf.jhu.edu. The list manager is Stephen A. Hirby (listmaster@ listproc.hcf.jhu.edu).

Fundsvcs

This list is for those interested in the more technical aspects of fundraising services. It is designed as a companion to, and not a replacement for, Fundlist. Fundsvcs is "nuts and bolts" oriented with discussion of federal tax and accounting regulations, computer systems and procedures, and donor communications.

To subscribe to Fundsvcs, send an e-mail message to listserv@lists.duke.edu. In the body of your message type: sub fundsvcs <firstname lastname>. To post a message to the list, send your e-mail to fundsvcs@acpub.duke.edu. The list manager is John H. Taylor (fundsvcs-owner@duke.edu). The address of the archive is http://www.pacificgroup.com/html/fundsvcs.htm. A more current archive is also found at http://lists.duke.edu/archives/fundsvcs.html. You will need to register in order to access it.

Gift-pl

Gift-pl is the electronic mail forum for gift planners that involves the development and dissemination of information in the field. This forum is provided by the National Committee on Planned Giving (NCPG).

To subscribe to Gift-pl, send an e-mail message to listserv@iupui.edu. In the body of your message type: sub gift-l <firstname lastname>. To post a message to the list, send your e-mail to gift-pl@iupui.edu. The list manager is Barbara Yeager (byeager@iupui.edu).

Giftplan

Established in March 1997, this discussion group is now among the Charity-Channel forums. It focuses mainly on issues of planned giving in the United States and Canada. It is much broader in scope than Gift-pl, a forum provided by the National Committee on Planned Giving.

To subscribe to Giftplan, send an e-mail message to listserv@ charitychannel.com. In the body of your message type: subscribe giftplan <your e-mail address>. To post a message to the list, send your e-mail to giftplan@ charitychannel.com.

The list is administered by CharityChannel. You may also subscribe or access the archive on the Web at http://www.charitychannel.com/forums.

Grants

Introduced in November 1997, Grants focuses on all aspects of grants and foundations. Grantseeking in any field, foundation formation, foundation funding, and foundation administration are all suitable topics. As soon as it was launched, the list quickly gained in popularity across many nonprofits all over the United States. With the support of users, the list editors decided to lightly moderate the list on an experimental basis in order to maintain the quality of the postings.

To subscribe to Grants, send an e-mail message to listserv@ charitychannel.com. In the body of your message type: subscribe grants <firstname lastname>. To post a message to the list, send your e-mail to grants@ charitychannel.com.

The list is administered by CharityChannel. You may also subscribe or access the archive on the Web at http://www.charitychannel.com/forums.

Hilaros

The purpose of Hilaros is to provide a discussion forum for Christians in fundraising. The list complements other development lists. Topics include the Christian perspective on fundraising, sharing ideas and information, asking for suggestions, and prayer requests.

To subscribe to Hilaros, send an e-mail message to majordomo@mark.geneva.edu. In the body of your message type: subscribe hilaros. To post a message to the list, send your e-mail to hilaros@mark.geneva.edu. The list owner is Cliff Glovier (hilaros-owner@mark.geneva.edu).

Prspct-L

Prspct-L is a highly popular discussion list for prospect researchers and development professionals in education and service organizations. Participants share resources and techniques on a wide range of topics, including rating prospects, ethics, job announcements, and foundations. This is a busy, well-focused list, full of research leads.

To subscribe to Prspct-L, go to http://groups.yahoo.com/group/PRSPCT-L and register on the site. It is very convenient to sign up for this list on the Yahoo! site, and you have the option either to receive messages directly in your e-mail box or to access them at the Web site. You can also view and search the archive on this Web site.

NEWSGROUPS AND MESSAGE BOARDS

Newsgroups and message boards are other examples of communities on the Internet that are available to the grantseeker. In Usenet newsgroups, people with similar interests can chat about their favorite topic or exchange ideas, as they would on a mailing list. Newsgroups, however, do not operate by e-mail and are not moderated or owned by anyone. To access a newsgroup, you need to have Newsreader—software which is usually included with your ISP (Internet Service Provider) software. You must then go to the Usenet site where you can view previously posted messages, which you will find organized by topic. To participate, post an article (message). Before starting a new thread (topic), you are advised to read the newsgroup's FAQs to see if the topic has already been thoroughly covered.

Each newsgroup has a name that signifies the subject matter covered. For example, newsgroups of interest to the nonprofit sector include soc.org.nonprofit, alt.activism, and alt.society.civil-liberties, to name just three. Usenet newsgroups are hosted by a wide range of organizations, from government agencies and large universities to high schools and businesses. Among the periodic postings in newsgroups, you will find listings of active newsgroups. An official Usenet primer is available from Google Groups at http://groups.google.com, which recently bought the Deja.com Web site, which created a searchable archive of 500 million messages to Usenet since 1995. This document also contains a Newsgroup Directory link. Alternatively, you can visit http://tile.net, the Web site discussed earlier, to search for newsgroups.

Like newsgroups, message boards are available at some nonprofit-related Web sites, which allow you to participate in ongoing discussions organized by topic. It is not necessary to have additional software other than your Internet browser in order to participate in such forums. Web-based forums can be very convenient since your e-mail box won't fill up with messages that are not of interest to you. If you are seeking information or a dialogue on a specific subject, you can start your own thread, or go to the appropriate message board to see if the topic has been covered. For a message board to be successful, however, its existence must be well publicized in print and through mailing lists, or the Web site must be compelling enough to attract repeat visitors.

The Foundation Center has recently launched a public message board that can be found in the *Philanthropy News Digest* area of the Web site (http://www.fdncenter.org/pnd). The *PND* message board lets users share opinions, insights, and questions related to the changing world of philanthropy with a large and growing community of consultants, development professionals, fundraisers, grantseekers, and others.

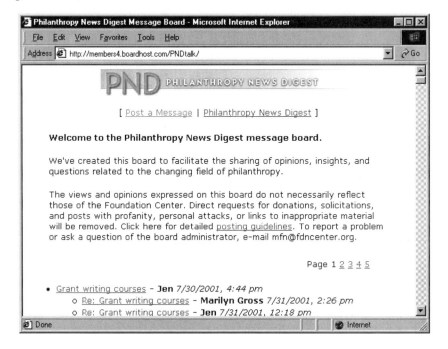

Conclusion

Clearly, grantseekers can take advantage of a number of methods to interact electronically with one another and with various other experts. Primarily e-mail based at this time, these interactions can be productive, inexpensive, and very convenient. Some of the other interactive capabilities (e.g., live chat and real-time conferencing) require more planning and organizing and may, therefore, be more suitable for specialty uses. However, many grantseekers and fundraisers have found that an easy way to get started communicating with colleagues is to subscribe to a discussion list and receive the numerous free e-newsletters available to the sector. If you lose interest in a discussion or newsletter, it's easy to unsubscribe and try another. Once you are involved in a mailing list or a newsgroup, you will find frequent postings covering technical advice and pointing the way to the growing resources available over the Internet.

APPENDIX A

General Search Engines

Here is a brief introduction to ten sites (nine search engines and one site *about* search engines), that we hope will provide you with additional information to be successful at grantseeking on the Web.

Each search engine offers different sets of parameters that you must follow in order to get the results you desire. While one search engine may automatically default to searching derivatives of a word (for example: fund, funds, funding, funder), others will not, and you will need to specify each form of a word separately. Still others will permit you to use the asterisk (*) to request all word endings after the root. Some permit you to indicate with a plus sign (+) which terms *must* be present in your results, while still other let you use the word "and." It is important to remember that search engines are not as smart as humans. That is, they don't really "know" what you are looking for or anything at all. They will only search for what you tell them to search for, within the confines of the software's programming. The burden is on you as the searcher to determine the best way to use a particular search engine. It is essential, therefore, to look for help files that are available at any search engine you visit, until you are fully familiar with its features and limitations.

Once you find a search engine you like, you might be tempted to rely on it all the time, to the exclusion of others. This would be a mistake. Although there is substantial overlap, each search engine indexes only a fraction of the total content of the World Wide Web. More importantly, search engines may index different sets of Web pages. For this reason, it is important to utilize more than one search engine to ensure the most comprehensive search results. Sophisticated Web searchers use different search engines to generate different kinds of "hits," depending on whether they want to broaden or narrow their search, focus on private or government or international sites, and so on. As you become more familiar with search engines, no doubt you will come up with your own list of favorites, depending on the circumstances.

Search Engine Watch (http://www.searchenginewatch.com)
This is *the* place to go on the Internet to find information on search engines. Search Engine Watch has at-a-glance search tip charts, a searchable database of Web search engines, reviews and ratings, and links to topical articles. You can even subscribe to a free e-mail newsletter so you can keep up with the latest changes regarding your old favorites, while keeping an eye out for new ones. Separate browsable directories are available for major and specialty search engines. If you haven't yet found a search engine to your liking, consult Search Engine Watch to identify one.

About.com (http://about.com)

About.com is an Internet directory with hundreds of expert topic-specific "guides." More than 700 subject areas are grouped into 36 channels, each administered by a guide who has either formal training or life experience in his or her particular subject matter. Each guide provides links to hundreds of the best Web sites on the Internet, as well as original content of his or her own.

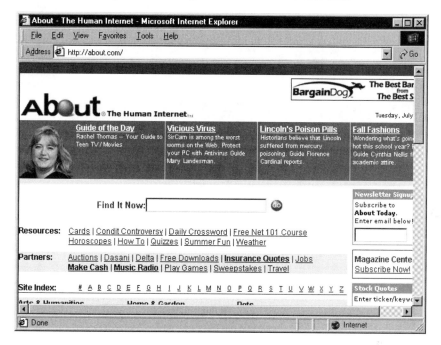

AltaVista (http://www.altavista.com)

AltaVista has one of the largest collections of Web sites in its search engine and has consistently been ranked among the best. Take the time to learn its search commands, particularly in the advanced search mode, to take full advantage of the many options available for constructing highly specific searches. You can translate from multiple foreign languages into English from sites retrieved through your search, or you can translate your own text by using Babel Fish, a free language translation service.

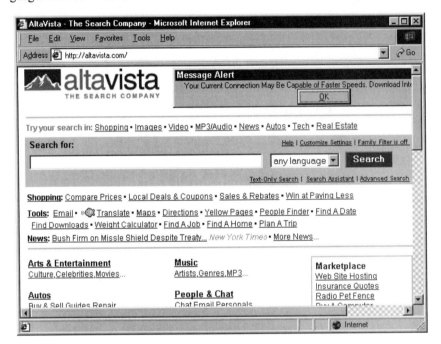

AskJeeves (http://www.askjeeves.com)

Ask Jeeves lets you search for answers the way most people want to, by simply asking a question. Instead of "techno-jargon," Ask Jeeves lets you use natural language to find the information you are looking for. The process can seem hit or miss, but more often than not, you'll retrieve links to relevant Web sites.

Google (http://www.google.com)

Google sports a simple design but packs a powerful punch. It uses a "PageRank" system that usually brings you to what you are looking for within the first page of your search results, if not the very first link. (Click on "I'm feeling lucky" for the highest ranked choice.) According to its developer, Google's system works so well because it "interprets a link from page A to page B as a vote, by page A, for page B." Google additionally ranks and reviews the content of the site, casting its "vote" to ensure quality results. Google also offers another unique feature that lets you view a cached, or stored, copy of a Web site that acts as a snapshot of a specific moment in that site's history.

Hotbot (http://hotbot.lycos.com)

HotBot, operated by Lycos, is both a search engine and a directory that has simple but powerful search features such as drop-down menus, that let you easily put together a search that's right for your needs. The ranking order of your search results is based on the number of times other HotBot users have clicked on them in the past.

Metacrawler (http://www.metacrawler.com)

As its name implies, Metacrawler is a meta-search engine that searches multiple other search engines (13 as of this writing) in one single search. Select the "Power Search" tab at the top of the page for the ability to customize your search. Here you can choose which search engines you want to include in the search, and you can use a domain/origin filter that limits your search to ".org's," ".gov's," ".com's," or to a specific country.

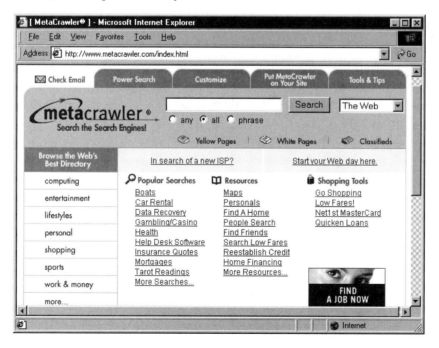

Northern Light (http://www.northernlight.com)

In addition to providing links to Web sites in your search results, Northern Light allows you access to materials not available elsewhere on the Web. Along the left-hand side of your screen you will see folders containing links to related topics and a "special collection documents" folder. While there is a fee to view actual documents in the special collections, it may be worth it, since this contains links to resources from newswires, magazines, and general and specialized databases.

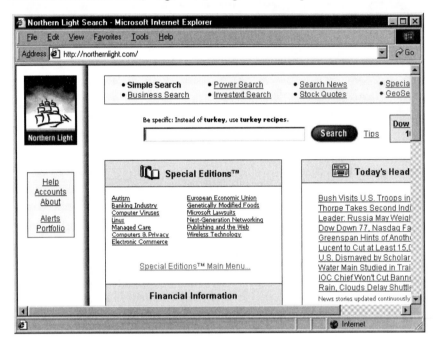

ProFusion (http://www.profusion.com)

ProFusion is a meta-search engine that also provides a topical directory listing of sites on the Web. To conduct a more structured search, click on the advanced search option to select which search engines you want ProFusion to use, including the "best" three or the "fastest" three. ProFusion also offers a unique search feature that searches "invisible Web" PDF documents.

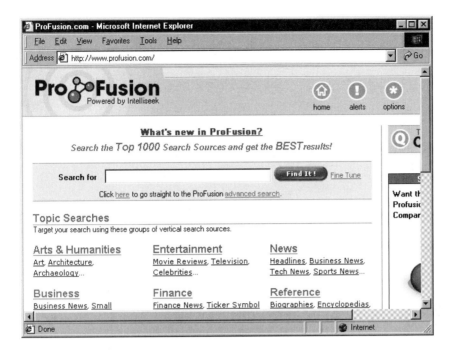

Yahoo (http://www.yahoo.com)

Yahoo, one of the most visited sites on the Web, is an excellent searchable directory. Start off with broad categories and work your way through a series of menus to find the specific information you are looking for. Yahoo also offers a search engine that you can use to search the entire site or limit to specific categories.

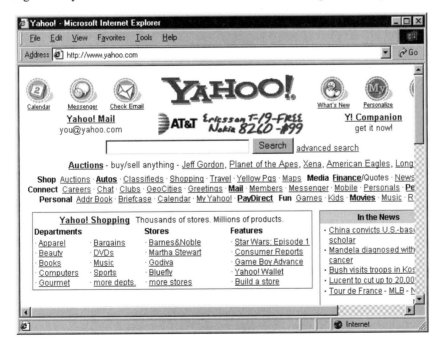

APPENDIX B

Private Foundations on the Web

Abell Foundation, Inc. (MD) (http://www.abell.org/)
The mission of the Baltimore-based Abell Foundation is "to effect positive change on the region's societal problems, with a strong focus on programs promoting educational reform, job creation and tourism; strengthening families; reducing drug addiction; and alleviating hunger and homelessness." The Foundation is committed to being an agent of change; working creatively to define issues; providing a forum to exchange ideas about them; and taking its place in the community's efforts to improve and enrich the quality of life in Maryland, and specifically in the Baltimore area. Visitors to the Foundation's Web site will find a brief history of the Foundation, general program descriptions, information about its grant policies and application procedures, a downloadable grant application form, and a number of links to other organizations of interest.

Abell-Hanger Foundation (TX) (http://www.abell-hanger.org/)
The Abell-Hanger Foundation was created by George T. and Gladys H. Abell, noted Mid-land, Texas, philanthropists. The Foundation seeks to fund organizations with projects "for the public welfare, including, but not limited to, higher education, cultural activities, health services, youth programs and the handicapped." The Foundation has specific guidelines and limitations for funding detailed on its Web site. Grants are made in the general areas of arts, culture, and humanities; education; health; human services; public/societal benefit; and religion. Block scholarships to institutions of higher learning, not individuals, are also made. Funding is limited to Texas organizations, or national groups who have a significant presence in Texas. Visitors to the Foundation's Web site will find a financial summary, the process for proposals, deadlines, and a pre-proposal questionnaire to be e-mailed to the Foundation for further information.

Abington Foundation (OH) (http://www.fmscleveland.com/abington)
The Abington Foundation, named for the place in New England where David Knight Ford's ancestors first settled, was created in 1983 to support the values that the senior Fords championed and that their descendants now uphold. The Foundation focuses its grantmaking primarily on education (pre-primary and higher), health care (with an

emphasis on geriatrics and nursing), economic independence (the promotion or sustaining of self-sufficiency), and cultural activities. Grants are primarily awarded in Cuyahoga County, Ohio. The Web site lists application deadlines and explains what to include in a grant application and whom to contact for help or questions. The site also provides information about previous grants awarded and Foundation financials.

The Able Trust (FL) (http://www.abletrust.org)

The Able Trust was created by the Florida legislature in 1990 as the Florida Governor's Alliance for the Employment of Disabled Citizens. The Trust "enable[s] over 2,000 Floridians with disabilities to enter the workforce each year," following the mission that "when people with disabilities want to work, they should." The Trust provides grants to Florida nonprofits and to Florida citizens with disabilities. The Able Trust Web site includes a link to Abilities On-line, a site providing employment information; information about VOICE (Volunteers and Organizations Initiating Commitment and Education); a link to the *Florida Grantor* newsletter; links and resources about disability; and current news and grant information in the What's Happening section. Select applications can be downloaded from the Trust's Web site using PDF.

The Abney Foundation (SC) (http://www.abneyfoundation.org/)

The Abney Foundation was established in 1957 in Greenwood, South Carolina, by Susie Mathews Abney, the widow of the founder of Abney Mills. The Foundation's mission is "to make grants for innovative and creative projects, and to programs which are responsive to changing community needs in the areas of education, health, social service and cultural affairs." The Foundation's primary focus is on higher education; the Abney Foundation Scholarship has established endowments at 12 colleges and universities throughout South Carolina. The Foundation also makes grants to organizations that serve South Carolina. Generally these grants are made once a year. The Foundation's Web site contains grant application guidelines, contact information, a listing of the 12 schools with scholarship endowments and an In the Spotlight section that highlights one of these schools, an article on the Foundation's founder, links, and contact information.

Francis L. Abreu Foundation (GA) (http://www.abreufoundation.org)

Located in Atlanta, Georgia, the Francis L. Abreu Charitable Trust was established under the will of May Patterson Abreu in honor of her husband, Francis, who died in 1969. The Abreu Charitable Trust benefits others "by providing grants to arts and cultural programs, education, health associations, human services and children and youth services primarily in the metro Atlanta area." Forms of support awarded by the Trust include capital campaigns, program development, seed money, and matching funds. To apply, interested parties must complete an application form, which may be printed from the Foundation's Web site, and supporting documentation. Details are provided online.

Achelis Foundation (NY) (http://fdncenter.org/grantmaker/achelis/)

Established in 1940 by Elisabeth Achelis, a native of Brooklyn Heights and a founder of the World Calendar Association, the Achelis Foundation today concentrates its grantmaking in the greater New York City area. Areas of foundation interest include youth, rehabilitation, biomedical research, child welfare, science education, major cultural institutions, health and hospitals, social services, alcohol and drug abuse, father absence and responsible fatherhood, and education (including charter schools, public school reform, and parental school choice). Other interests include literacy, volunteerism, homelessness, entrepreneurship and economic development, environment (science education and land conservation), welfare reform, and job training with employment in the private business sector. Visitors to the Foundation's folder on the Center's Web site will find a brief history of the Foundation; a statement from Foundation president John N. Irwin III; application guidelines and procedures; recent grants lists; a listing of the Foundation's trustees, officers, and staff; and contact information.

Thomas C. Ackerman Foundation (CA) (http://ackermanfoundation.org)

The Thomas C. Ackerman Foundation was founded in San Diego, California, in 1991 after the death of lawyer and professor Thomas C. Ackerman. The Foundation seeks to support the interests of its benefactor and namesake by making grants to support education, programs for the prevention of child abuse and cruelty to animals, the local arts, the educational institutions that he attended, and his church located in the San Diego area. The Foundation may also support programs that aid the welfare of seniors. The Foundation does not support projects that may become dependent on the Foundation for the organization's continued existence. See the Web site for other exclusions. The site also provides a complete summary of the application process, including an online application; latest fiscal information; summary of recent grants; and complete contact information.

Acorn Foundation (CA) (http://www.commoncounsel.org/pages/foundation.html)

Created in 1978, the Acorn Foundation is a member of the Common Counsel Foundation of Oakland, California. The organization "supports projects dedicated to building a sustainable future for the planet and to restoring a healthy global environment." Areas of interest include remedying and limiting pollution from industrial, chemical, and nuclear sources; advocating environmental justice; and preserving and restoring habitats supporting biological diversity. The Foundation makes grants twice a year and has no geographic limitations. Applications should be submitted to the Common Counsel Foundation and will be considered for all member foundations. The CCF offers applications guidelines and deadlines and a link to the National Network of Grantmakers Common Grant Application, which is also accepted. The Foundation does not support educational, medical, or cultural institutions or emergency funding.

The Claude W. and Dolly Ahrens Foundation (IA) (http://www.ahrensfoundation.org)

The Ahrens Foundation was founded in 1992 by Claude W. Ahrens, who wanted to give back to the native Grinnell Area, with specific support in the areas of parks and recreation. The Foundation gives grants to nonprofit organizations in Iowa that are requesting funds for specific projects to improve their communities. To apply for a grant, organizations should send a short letter of introduction describing the project and its goals. Should the Foundation be interested and request a full application, details about what to include in the application are listed on the Web site. The site also contains a mailing address and lists of previous grantees.

The J.A. & Kathryn Albertson Foundation (ID) (http://www.jkaf.org)

Established in 1966 by Joe Albertson and his wife Kathryn, this family foundation based in Boise, Idaho is committed to "fostering the improvement of education in Idaho through the promotion of research, experimentation, and innovation in an educational environment." Funding is focused in five areas: student learning, teaching excellence, preparation and advancement of educational practitioners, performance of educational systems, and early childhood education. In addition to grantmaking, the Foundation has a Center for Educational Excellence committed to the professional development needs of educators and to the promotion of the field of education in Idaho. Points of interest on its Web site include a description of its grantmaking approach, grant guidelines and instructions, a calendar of and contact information for the Center for Educational Excellence events, downloadable publications (newsletters, brochures, and annual reports), an electronic free publications request form, general contact information, and links to related sites. Online event registration for the Foundation's events and activities is currently under construction.

Alcoholic Beverage Medical Research Foundation (MD) (http://www.abmrf.org)

The Alcoholic Beverage Medical Research Foundation (ABMRF) states that it "fundamentally exists to improve the quality of people's lives at home and in the workplace" through financial support of innovative biomedical, behavioral, and social science research on alcohol consumption and abuse prevention. Headquartered in Baltimore, Maryland, the Foundation was first established in 1969 as the Medical Advisory Group under the administrative auspices of The Johns Hopkins University School of Medicine to provide independent medical advice on the health effects of alcoholic beverages to members of the Beer Institute. It merged in 1982 with a parallel group in Canada to become ABMRF, the largest independent nonprofit foundation in North America supporting research on the effects of alcohol on behavior and health and the prevention of alcohol-related problems. Primary research interests include factors influencing the transition from moderate to excessive use of alcohol, effects of moderate use of alcohol on health and behavior, mechanisms underlying the biomedical effects of alcohol, and alcohol and youth, traffic accidents, and work-related issues. Lower priority areas for support are treatment research and complications of advanced alcoholism. The Web site contains highlights of ABMRF-funded research, grant information and guidelines, a downloadable grant application and guidelines, abstracts of the *ABMRF Journal,* annual reports, summaries of recent conferences, highlights of grantee publications in various journals, a list of publications supported in part by ABMRF, contact information, and related links. The site also contains short, professional bios of each member of the Foundation's management and board of trustees and of each member of the Foundation's two advisory boards, which review grant applications and advise the Foundation of research.

Allegheny Foundation (PA) (http://www.scaife.com)
The Allegheny Foundation is one of the Scaife Foundations of Pittsburgh, Pennsylvania. It funds programs in the western Pennsylvania area that involve historical preservation, civic development, and education. The one simple page on the Foundation instructs potential grantees to send an initial letter of inquiry with the listed attachments. While grants are normally determined at a board meeting in November, proposals are accepted throughout the year and addressed as soon as possible. The Annual Report can be downloaded in PDF format.

Paul G. Allen Charitable Foundation (WA) (http://www.paulallen.com/foundations/)
The purpose of the Bellevue, Washington-based Paul G. Allen Charitable Foundation is to "improve the quality of life in the Pacific Northwest through programs designed to create new opportunities for community service." To that end, the Foundation funds projects in whole or in part in the areas of education, environmental research, youth services, social services, and aid to the disabled and disadvantaged. Ordinarily, the Foundation does not consider grant requests for operating, administrative, or overhead expenses; for contributions to general fund drives, annual appeals, or federated campaigns; for the benefit of specific individuals; for conduit organizations; to institutions "whose policy or practice unfairly discriminates against race, ethnic origin, sex, creed or sexual orientation;" to sectarian or religious organizations; or to organizations currently funded by any other Paul G. Allen foundation. In addition to a fair amount of biographical information about Microsoft co-founder Allen, "The Wired World of Paul Allen" Web site provides examples of recent grants and projects supported by the Foundation, grant application guidelines, a description of the application process, and a downloadable application form.

Paul G. Allen Foundation for Medical Research (WA)
(http://www.paulallen.com/foundations/)
The purpose of the Bellevue, Washington-based Paul G. Allen Foundation for Medical Research is to "promote innovative medical research in a variety of fields, including biochemistry, biomedical engineering, virology, immunology, cell and molecular biology, pharmacology and genetics." Projects that "develop new insights into the prevention or successful treatment of cancer" are of special interest. Ordinarily, the Foundation does not consider grant requests for operating, administrative, or overhead expenses; for contributions to general fund drives, annual appeals, or federated campaigns; for the benefit of specific individuals; for conduit organizations; to institutions "whose policy or practice unfairly discriminates against race, ethnic origin, sex, creed or sexual orientation;" to sectarian or religious organizations; or to organizations currently funded by any other Paul G. Allen foundation. In addition to a fair amount of biographical information about Microsoft co-founder Allen, "The Wired World of Paul Allen" Web site provides examples of recent

grants and projects supported by the Foundation, grant application guidelines, a description of the application process, and a downloadable application form.

Allen Foundation for the Arts (WA) (http://www.paulallen.com/foundations/)

The purpose of the Bellevue, Washington-based Allen Foundation for the Arts is to "promote a creative and flourishing arts community in the Pacific Northwest." The Foundation, which is especially interested in the performing and visual arts, also supports entities that sustain artists and art organizations. Ordinarily, the Foundation does not consider grant requests for operating, administrative or overhead expenses; for contributions to general fund drives, annual appeals or federated campaigns; for the benefit of specific individuals; for conduit organizations; to institutions "whose policy or practice unfairly discriminates against race, ethnic origin, sex, creed or sexual orientation;" to sectarian or religious organizations; or to organizations currently funded by any other Paul G. Allen foundation. In addition to a fair amount of biographical information about Microsoft co-founder Allen, "The Wired World of Paul Allen" Web site provides examples of recent grants and projects supported by the Foundation, grant application guidelines, a description of the application process, and a downloadable application form.

Paul G. Allen Forest Protection Foundation (WA)
(http://www.paulallen.com/foundations/)

The purpose of the Bellevue, Washington-based Paul G. Allen Forest Protection Foundation—the newest Allen foundation—is to assist in "the acquisition and conservation of forest land in order to preserve needed wildlife habitat and, where possible, to provide public recreational access." Rather than directly acquiring and preserving properties, the Foundation works with established conservancies (e.g., the Wilderness Society, the Nature Conservancy) to leverage, through its contributions, the expertise of these organizations to implement programs consistent with the Foundation's purpose. Ordinarily, the Foundation does not consider grant requests for operating, administrative, or overhead expenses; for contributions to general fund drives, annual appeals, or federated campaigns; for the benefit of specific individuals; for conduit organizations; to institutions "whose policy or practice unfairly discriminates against race, ethnic origin, sex, creed or sexual orientation;" to sectarian or religious organizations; or to organizations currently funded by any other Paul G. Allen foundation. In addition to a fair amount of biographical information about Microsoft co-founder Allen, "The Wired World of Paul Allen" Web site provides examples of recent grants and projects supported by the Foundation, grant application guidelines, a description of the application process, and a downloadable application form.

Paul G. Allen Virtual Education Foundation (WA) (http://www.paulallen.com/foundations/)

The purpose of the Bellevue, Washington-based Paul G. Allen Virtual Education Foundation is to "advance Internet-based distance learning [and to] support research and development of technologies and instructional strategies for computer-mediated instruction and distributed learning environments." The Foundation is especially interested in projects that "explore ways to achieve cost-effective production of innovative digital content for online learning." The Foundation does not fund individual faculty projects or capital improvements to information infrastructure or the development of instructional management or delivery technology. Nor does it ordinarily consider grant requests for operating, administrative, or overhead expenses; for contributions to general fund drives, annual appeals, or federated campaigns; for the benefit of specific individuals; for conduit organizations; to institutions "whose policy or practice unfairly discriminates against race, ethnic origin, sex, creed or sexual orientation;" to sectarian or religious organizations; or to organizations currently funded by any other Paul G. Allen foundation. Consistent with the policy of all Paul Allen foundations, institutions in the Pacific Northwest are given priority consideration. In addition to a fair amount of biographical information about Microsoft co-founder Allen, "The Wired World of Paul Allen" Web site provides examples of recent grants and projects supported by the Foundation, grant application guidelines, a description of the application process, and a downloadable application form.

Allen Foundation, Inc. (MI) (http://www.tamu.edu/baum/allen.html)
Established in 1975 by agricultural chemist William Webster Allen, the Michigan-based Allen Foundation makes grants to projects that benefit human nutrition in the areas of education, training, and research. Visitors to the Foundation's Web site will find a brief biography of Mr. Allen, a listing of the Foundation's board of trustees, a downloadable grant application form, and links to other nutrition and food science sites on the Internet. Visitors may also access a five–year archive of the Foundation's annual reports.

Alliance Healthcare Foundation (CA) (http://www.alliancehf.org/)
The San Diego-based Alliance Healthcare Foundation funds healthcare programs for indigent and underserved populations in Southern California, primarily in San Diego County. Priority is given to programs that address the issues of restricted access to healthcare, substance abuse, communicable diseases, violence, mental health, and environmental and community health problems. The Foundation also performs fundraising, advocacy, and public education campaigns to benefit the healthcare field. The Foundation's brand-new Web site provides general program descriptions; detailed application guidelines, rules, and procedures; links to related organizations and resources in the healthcare field; board and staff listings; a brief News section; and contact information.

The Herb Alpert Foundation (CA) (http://www.alpertawards.com/alpertstate.html)
In the 1980s, musician and painter Herb Alpert established the Herb Alpert Foundation, which funds projects in education, the arts, and the environment. Instead of responding to grant proposals, it is "more typical" of the Foundation to "focus on a social need, find qualified organizations that can respond in a healing manner to that need, and then creatively join in the development of responsive programs." The majority of their funding is directed toward the youngest members of American society, "in hopes that the future for them, and for the world, can be improved by an earlier intervention." Other than this, the site mainly contains information on the professional achievements of Herb Alpert. A separate award is mentioned, the Alpert Award in the Arts, which was created in conjunction with the California Institute of the arts in 1994 and awards $50,000 fellowships to emerging artists in each of five disciplines: dance, theatre, music, film/video, and visual arts. This award is administered by the California Institute of the Arts and funded by the Herb Alpert foundation to enable artists to further pursue creative expression. A link off of this Web site contains detailed information, including a mission statement, a description of the nomination process, statements from Alpert and the California Institute of the Arts, and information on past winners of the award.

Jenifer Altman Foundation (CA) (http://www.jaf.org)
Based in Bolinas, California, the Jenifer Altman Foundation was founded in 1991 shortly before its namesake, a health and environmental researcher, died. The organization is committed to "the vision of a socially just and ecologically sustainable future through program interests in environmental health, mind-body health and improved child care." Grants are made in three primary areas. In environmental health, grants focus on projects forwarding the national and international emergence of "an informed citizen movement for environmental health," specifically about manmade chemicals that affects the development of the fetus. Mind-body health supports research and demonstration programs, focusing on those dealing with cancer. Child care/local grants help improve the quality of child care, particularly in the San Francisco/Oakland Bay area. The Foundation requests that interested nonprofits submit a concept letter. If it is decided that the project matches the Foundation's interests, the grantseeker will be instructed on procedure, which will include the application cover page that is available on the site. The Jenifer Altman Foundation is run in conjunction with the Mitchell Kapor Foundation and the Starfire Fund, making co-grants with each in some categories. One application serves all three foundations.

Amateur Athletic Foundation of Los Angeles (CA) (http://www.aafla.com)
The Amateur Athletic Foundation of Los Angeles was established to manage Southern California's share of the surplus funds generated by the 1984 Olympic Games. The

Foundation focuses its grantmaking activities on sports programs for youth in southern California's eight counties: Imperial, Los Angeles, Orange, Riverside, San Bernardino, San Diego, Santa Barbara, and Ventura. At the same time, the Foundation gives special attention to women, minorities, the physically challenged or developmentally disabled, and youth in areas where the risk of involvement in delinquency is particularly high. Visitors to the Foundation's Web site will find detailed grant guidelines and application criteria, a list of the Foundation's board of directors, and links to other sports sites. The site also offers information on the Foundation's own youth sports program, historic sports art and artifact collection, sports research library, and special events.

Amazon Foundation (AZ) (http://www.amazonfound.org)
The Amazon Foundation of Arizona is primarily concerned with the advancement of women and girls in southern Arizona's Cochise, Pima, and Santa Cruz counties. The Foundation makes both grants to individuals and to nonprofit organizations that support this cause. The Foundation places emphasis on programs that deal with violence against women and girls, women's economic self-sufficiency, discrimination, and homelessness. The Foundation is especially interested in supporting the disabled; women of color; lesbians, bisexual women, and transgender people; and women in rural southern Arizona. Visitors to the Foundation's Web site will find further information on its initiatives (including information on the scholarship program), grant guidelines, a listing of recent grants, and contact information.

The Amerind Foundation, Inc. (AZ) (Operating foundation) (http://www.amerind.org)
Presently a nonprofit archaeological research facility and museum devoted to the study and interpretation of Native American cultures, The Amerind Foundation was founded by William Shirley Fulton in 1937 as a private, nonprofit archaeological research institution. Located in the southeastern corner of Arizona known locally as Texas Canyon, the Foundation commits its resources to three main concerns: the conservation and preservation of material culture, research, and education. The Amerind Foundation "strongly promotes the scholarly study and analysis of the materials in its existing collections" and "supports the active development and participation in archaeological field investigations" to reconstruct Native American cultures that have disappeared. The Foundation also "resolves to plan and support educational programs in the form of exhibits and lectures, adult and children's programs, professional services and publications, as well as other museum-related activities open to all individuals regardless of ethnic origin." In addition to the museum, the Foundation also has an archaeological library open to visiting scholars. Visitors to the Web site will find information on the history of the Foundation, current museum exhibits, a statement of purpose, contact information, publications information and online publications request form, and a list of related links. However, no specific information is provided on grants.

Amy Foundation (MI) (http://www.amyfound.org)
Named after their daughter, the Amy Foundation was established by W. James Russell and his wife Phyllis in 1976. The Foundation, based in Michigan, seeks to restore the spiritual and moral character of the nation and "reclaim" America from its perceived moral decline. The Web site states: "The Amy Foundation calls all Christians in the U.S. to the work of teaching obedience to all Christ's commands, thus making disciples through every means of communication and institutional influence open to them." To that end, the foundation has writing awards and scholarships, "specifically designed to encourage and equip both professional and nonprofessional writers to develop and utilize their skills to the reclaiming of America." The Foundation has other programs designed to carry out its mission, such as its Church Writing Group program and the dissemination of its brochure titled *The United States—A Discipled Nation in this Generation,* which outlines a biblical plan for discipling the nation by the year 2025 and is also available online. Visitors to this Web site will find writing award and scholarship criteria and rules; samples of past awarded writing; the Amy Internet Syndicate, which provides editorial opinion columns free of charge for use in any publication; an online feedback form; an online publications request form (including the

Amy Award rules and guidelines brochure and winning entries booklet); a list of resources, and links to other sites.

The Hugh J. Andersen Foundation (MN) (http://www.scenicriver.org/hja/index.cfm)

The mission of the Hugh J. Andersen Foundation is to give back to the community through focused efforts that "foster inclusivity, promote equality, and lead to increased human independence, self sufficiency, and dignity." The Foundation holds an interest in programs that serve children and youth; provide various social support services to the community at large; provide health-related services, excluding hospitals and research facilities; and provide educational opportunities and enrichment to the general community. Visitors to the Foundation's limited site will find recent annual reports, application criteria, deadlines, a copy of the Minnesota Common Grant Application Form downloadable in PDF, and contact information.

Angelica Foundation (CA) (http://www.angelicafoundation.org)

The Angelica Foundation, based in Racho Santa Fe, California, supports "progressive grassroots organizations that empower communities to become more environmentally sustainable, culturally rich and socially just." Funding is restricted to nonprofit organizations in California, New Mexico, and Hawaii as well as non-governmental organizations (NGOs) in Mexico and Central America. The funding location priority differs from year to year. The Foundation makes program and initiative grants in the areas of the environment, social justice, and the arts and supports groups that work in drug policy reform. Both types of grants are by invitation only; the program grant is usually for a two-year funding period. The Foundation posts complete application guidelines in English and Spanish on its Web site, along with a letter from the board of directors, and a recent list of grant recipients. Contact information is available online.

The Angels on Track Foundation (OH) (http://www.angelsontrack.org/)

Dennis and Vicky Moore established the Angels on Track Foundation after their son died in a collision between the car in which he was riding and a train at a railroad crossing. The mission of the Foundation is to "provide the financial backing needed to improve railroad crossing safety throughout Ohio, and to educate local highway authorities on the various programs available through state and federal funding." Located in Canal Fulton, Ohio, the Foundation aims to establish railroad safety task forces in all 88 counties in Ohio, establish a central statewide railroad safety task force, supply funding support for five upgrades each calendar year, and to "educate, save lives, and pursue all avenues available to ensure all railroad grade crossings are equipped with adequate safety devices." Consult its Web site for application instructions; a history of the foundation; information on the Foundation's railway safety film, *Without Warning*, and contact information.

Annenberg Foundation (PA) (http://www.whannenberg.org/)

The principal grantmaking focus of the St. Davids, Pennsylvania-based Annenberg Foundation is on pre-collegiate education, specifically public school restructuring and reform for grades K–12. Within these broad areas, the Foundation is particularly interested in early childhood education in relation to public education at the primary level and in child development and youth services. Visitors to the Foundation's no-frills Web site will find a brief biography of founder/donor and former TV Guide publisher Walter H. Annenberg; an overview of the Foundation's K–12 Challenge Grant program and contact information for 15 challenge grant sites and initiatives, general information about its independent Foundation-sponsored programs (the Annenberg/CPB math and Science Project and the Annenberg Washington Program in Communications Policy Studies at the University of Pennsylvania), a short list of sample grants, application procedures and proposal guidelines, and basic fiscal information.

Arca Foundation (DC) (http://fdncenter.org/grantmaker/arca/index.html)

Established in 1952 as the Nancy Reynolds Bagley Foundation, the Arca Foundation received its present name in 1968. Domestically, the Foundation's primary concern is "the overwhelming influence of private money in politics and its effect on who runs for public office, who wins, and in whose interest they govern." Arca's funding emphasizes "educational efforts to expose this legal form of corruption and suggest effective remedies at the state and national level." It also funds projects "that address the imbalance of power in society more generally, emphasizing issues of economic equity and labor rights at home and abroad." In the foreign policy field, Arca's grantmaking "reflects a focus on issues that are particularly influenced by U.S. policy in the Western Hemisphere. U.S. policy toward Cuba and Central America continues to be a central concern, alongside the human consequences of globalized production." The Foundation's folder on the Center's Web site provides a brief history of the Foundation, grantmaking guidelines and a recent grants list organized by area of interest, and contact information.

Archstone Foundation (CA) (http://www.archstone.org)
Established in 1985 as the FHP Foundation and renamed in 1996, the Archstone Foundation has refocused its grantmaking activities on "contribut[ing] toward the preparation of society in meeting the needs of an aging population." The Foundation's funding priorities for the immediate future include addressing the needs of caregivers of the elderly, end-of-life issues, and direct delivery of services to non-institutionalized seniors, with an emphasis on southern California. The Foundation's Web site offers general statements about its funding priorities and restrictions, application procedures, an Announcements area, a list of Foundation-sponsored publications, an online version of the Foundation's 1997 annual report, and contact information.

Arcus Foundation (MI) (http://www.arcusfoundation.org)
The Arcus Foundation, located in Kalamazoo, Michigan, is a family foundation established in 1997 that seeks to "contribute to a pluralistic society that celebrates diversity and dignity, invests in youth and justice, and promotes tolerance and compassion." A full list of the Foundation's values is posted on the Web site. The Foundation funds programs that fight prejudice and discrimination and protect and defend human and civil rights. It supports new, innovative, and experimental programs and projects; creative uses of resources; and collaborative efforts. The Foundation issues grants for special projects, operational funds, and capital funds. More information on funding guidelines can be found online. Those interested in applying for a grant should first send a letter of inquiry; details on what to include and a mailing address, along with details on some of the Foundation's funds, are listed on the Web site.

Ethel Louise Armstrong Foundation (CA) (http://www.ela.org)
Located in Altadena, California, the Ethel Louise Armstrong (ELA) Foundation was established in 1994. The organization "supports the work of organizations in advocacy, education, leadership development, mentoring, the arts for people with disabilities . . . , supports the work of organizations that are led by or support the work of women and girls with disabilities, and encourages distinctive projects that make a substantial difference." ELA annually awards two scholarships to women with disabilities who are pursuing advanced degrees at a school in the United States. The grant program supports groups that are either led by or work to support women with disabilities. The Foundation likes to support groups that are making a difference nationally and/or in the local community. Areas of interest include the arts, education, advocacy, mentoring, and leadership development. Application guidelines and deadlines can be found on the site, along with a list of past grant recipients. The site also includes an events calendar, related resources, and information on important issues in the movement.

Arsalyn Foundation (CA) (Operating foundation) (http://www.arsalyn.org)
The nonpartisan Glendora, California-based Arsalyn Foundation was established in 1996 to address a decline in voter participation. The organization's mission is to "foster, among young citizens, an appreciation of the value of each citizen's informed vote to the maintenance of true democracy in a representative government; and to encourage participation in the voting process as a right, a responsibility and an opportunity." The Foundation sponsors

a variety of programs to assist nonprofits throughout the country. It hosts meetings through its Technical Assistance (TA) Program to help with building organizational capacity and with networking. Through the Peer Exchange Program, the Foundation funds site visits between groups to assist in the spreading/sharing of models and methodologies. Finally, the Foundation hosts a national conference and helps cover the expenses of attendees. The Foundation is open to being approached for special projects by like-minded organizations. The Web site includes contact information, dates and deadlines for all of the participatory programs, and even an online application for the peer exchange.

The Atlanta Foundation (GA) (http://www.wachovia.com/trust/atlanta_overview.asp)

The Atlanta Foundation was established in 1921 to "assist charitable and educational institutions located in Fulton or DeKalb counties for promoting education, scientific research, for the care of the sick, aged or helpless, to improve living conditions or to provide recreation for all classes and for such other charitable purposes as will make for the mental, moral and physical improvement of the inhabitants of Fulton and DeKalb counties regardless of race, color, or creed." Visit the Foundation's Web site to view detailed information on the Foundation's programs, deadlines, recent grants recipients, financial information, and contact information.

Austin-Bailey Health and Wellness Foundation (OH)
(http://fdncenter.org/grantmaker/austinbailey/)

The Austin-Bailey Health and Wellness Foundation was founded in 1996 and strives to promote the physical well-being of the people of the Ohio counties of Holmes, Stark, Tuscarawas, and Wayne. This mission is realized by addressing the "healthcare affordability concerns of the uninsured and underinsured, the poor, children, single parents and the aging" through the Foundation's grants. The Foundation's folder on the Center's Web site provides grant guidelines, eligibility requirements and limitations, as well as a listing of previous grant recipients and the board of directors. The Foundation's Form 990-PF is also available as a PDF document to be downloaded.

Mary Reynolds Babcock Foundation, Inc. (NC) (http://www.mrbf.org/)

The Babcock Foundation was created in 1953 with a $12 million bequest from Mary Reynolds Babcock, a daughter of the founder of the R. J. Reynolds Tobacco Company. Based in Winston-Salem, North Carolina, the Foundation concentrates its activities on community-building initiatives in the southeastern United States, placing a special emphasis on activities that seek to assure the well-being of children, youth, and families; bridge the faultlines of race and class; and invest in communities' human and natural resources over the long term. The Foundation's current program, Building Just and Caring Communities, comprises three funding areas: the Organizational Development Program, which makes grants to help individual organizations in the Southeast implement concrete organizational development activities; the Community Problem Solving Program, which aims to support coalitions working on local community issues in ways that "build lasting capacity in their communities to solve problems;" and the Opportunity Fund, which provides core support to emerging organizations. Visitors to the Foundation's Web site will find detailed descriptions of all three programs, a list of recent grants, a brief history of the Foundation and a statement of its purpose and values, listings of the Foundation's board and staff, and contact information.

Helen Bader Foundation, Inc. (WI) (http://www.hbf.org/)

The Milwaukee-based Helen Bader Foundation supports innovative programs that advance the well-being of people and promote succesful relationships with their families and communities. The Foundation concentrates its grantmaking in five areas: Alzheimer's disease and dementia (geographic focus: national, with priority given to Milwaukee and Wisconsin), children and youth in Israel (geographic focus: Israel), economic development (geographic focus: Milwaukee), education (geographic focus: Milwaukee), and Jewish life and learning (geographic focus: Milwaukee and Delaware River Valley area). In addition to background information, press releases, and a biography of founder Helen Bader, the

Foundation's elegant, easy-to-navigate Web site provides general program information; application guidelines and online and downloadable application forms; recent grants list, grant summaries by program area, and profiles of featured grantees; and contact information.

The Francois-Xavier Bagnoud Foundation (NY) (http://www.fxb.org/index.html)

In 1989, the Countess Albina du Boisrouvray, along with family and friends of Francois, created the Bagnoud Foundation in memory of the Countess' only son, a helicopter pilot killed in a crash on a flying mission in West Africa at the age of 24. The Foundation "carries out various philanthropic activities;" among its programs are five fellowships in the College of Engineering at the University of Michigan and the Francois-Xavier Bagnoud Aerospace Prize, consisting of a $250,000 honorarium and sculpture, administered by the Aerospace Engineering Department at the University of Michigan. Also featured on the site is the Association Francois-Xavier Bagnoud, which, although funded by the foundation, is independent of the foundation's philanthropic activities and has at its disposal $5 million for "strictly humanitarian goals." The Association is involved in "more than two dozen initiatives involving children's rights, health and human rights, and pediatric HIV/AIDS in 17 countries." The Web site contains information and guidelines for the Xavier-Bagnoud Aerospace Prize and information on past winners of the prize, detailed information on the Association's work in each region around the world, news and press releases, downloadable application for foundation funds, and an online contact form. Also available are a calendar of events, a search engine, an archive of past news releases and information dating back to 1996, and links to related sites.

Baptist Community Ministries of New Orleans (LA) (http://www.bcm.org/)

Baptist Community Ministries (BCM) was endowed with the proceeds from the sale of Mercy + Baptist Medical Center in August of 1995. Their stated mission: "Baptist Community Ministries is committed to the development of a healthy community offering a wholesome quality of life to its residents and to improving the physical, mental, and spiritual health of the individuals we serve." This $150 million private foundation makes grants to qualifying charitable organizations in the five-parish region surrounding New Orleans. Its funding interests are primarily in education, health, public safety, and governmental oversight; grantees and programs are "evaluated considering the religious history and mission of BCM." Awards range from $50,000 for one year to nearly $2 million over four years. BCM's Web site lists goals for each funding area and provides grant information and guidelines, a summary of the grant review process, a listing of past grant recipients, and contact information.

William E. Barth Foundation (KY) (http://www.doddanddodd.com/foundation.htm)

Located in Louisville, Kentucky, the William E. Barth Foundation was established by two teachers in the Jefferson County School District in honor of their brother. The Foundation supports charitable organizations in Louisville and Jefferson Counties, with a focus on programs that address the welfare of children. The Foundation's Web site provides application guidelines, deadlines and forms that can be downloaded in Microsoft Word and Word Perfect formats, and a listing of the charitable organizations that the Foundation supports. Contact information is also available on the site.

Bartol Foundation, Stockton Rush (PA) (http://www.bartol.org/)

The Stockton Rush Bartol Foundation was established in 1984 in Philadelphia, Pennsylvania, to assure the everyday existence of the arts in the city. The foundation provides financial and technical assistance to qualifying organizations. The Foundation's priorities include organizations that serve children through arts education programs that promote social and educational development, serve communities by providing broader access to high-quality arts experiences at the neighborhood level, and/or serve the arts community by supporting cultural organizations at critical junctures in their artistic or organizational development. The Foundation does not support programs or organizations outside of the

Philadelphia area. Visit the Foundation's Web site to view other grant exclusions, application guidelines, printable application, board/staff list, and contact information.

Lee and Ramona Bass Foundation (TX) (http://www.sidrichardson.org/lrbf.htm)

Established in 1993, the Lee and Ramona Bass Foundation is based in Texas. It maintains that its funding is more effective when giving a few large grants to a select group of local nonprofit organizations. The Foundation considers projects from the following groups: education, mainly faculty development and liberal arts programs; community programs and projects, mainly the arts and environment; and national and regional conservation institutions. Visitors to the Foundation's Web site will find grant recipient guidelines, a list of past grants, contact information, and an e-mail form to order the Foundation's annual report.

The Bayer Institute for Health Care Communication (CT) (Operating foundation) (http://www.bayerinstitute.org)

The mission of the West Haven, Connecticut-based Bayer Institute For Health Care Communication is to enhance the quality of health care by improving the communication between the clinician and the patient through three major activities: education, research, and advocacy. The Institute is funded by the pharmaceutical division of the Bayer Corporation in the United States and the Healthcare Division of Bayer in Canada. The Institute works with health care organizations to conduct research and provides educational opportunities for clinicians to develop effective communication skills. Up to five grants a year are made to investigators to develop new knowledge about clinician-patient communication. The Institute also receives grants to support specific projects, enters into contracts with various organizations to develop and implement communication improvement programs, and sells materials to organizations conducting its programs. The Institute's Web site contains application instructions for the grant program, information about workshops and continuing education opportunities, and contact information.

The Bayport Foundation (MN) (http://www.scenicriver.org/bp/index.cfm)

Funded by Minnesota-based Andersen Corporation, best known for making windows and patio doors since the turn of the previous century, The Bayport Foundation supports the general operating, capital, and program funds of qualified nonprofit organizations that provide community, social, and support services to areas where Andersen Corporation employees live. These areas include St. Croix Valley, western Wisconsin, and the eastern Twin Cities areas. Visitors to the Foundation's limited site will find application criteria; deadlines; a copy of the Minnesota Common Grant Application Form, downloadable in PDF format and contact information.

Charles T. Beaird Foundation (LA) (http://www.beairdfoundation.org)

The Charles T. Beaird Foundation, founded in 1960, is dedicated to "improving the Shreveport, Louisiana area through assisting organizations to add opportunity, freedom of action and choice, self-betterment and a climate for change to the lives of the people they serve." The Foundation supports small, local programs that are "innovative and perhaps even unpopular" as well as larger national causes such as the United Way and the American Cancer Society. The Foundation provides a brief history, mission statement, and contact information on its Web site.

Arnold and Mabel Beckman Foundation (CA) (http://www.beckman-foundation.com/)

The Arnold and Mabel Beckman Foundation makes grants "to promote research in chemistry and the life sciences, broadly interpreted, and particularly to foster the invention of methods, instruments, and materials that will open up new avenues of research in science." The Irvine, California-based Foundation's no-frills Web site provides brief biographies of Arnold and Mabel Beckman; guidelines and downloadable application forms for the Beckman Young Investigators (BYI) Program, which provides research support to promising young faculty members in the early stages of academic careers in the chemical and life sciences, and the Beckman Research Technologies Initiatives; and links to Beckman

Institutes/Centers at the University of Illinois at Urbana-Champaign, the California Institute of Technology, Stanford University, the Beckman Laser Institute, and City of Hope.

The Beim Foundation (MN) (http://www.beimfoundation.org)
Established in Excelsior, Minnesota, in 1947, the Beim Foundation funds organizations primarily in Minnesota, sporadically funding in other parts of the upper Midwest as well. The Foundation's interests lie in the arts, education, the environment, and human services. Visitors to the Foundation's Web site will find an outline of project types that are considered, limitations to funding, past grant recipients, and contact information. Applications submitted via e-mail will not be considered, but the Foundation provides application procedure guidelines for mailed applications.

Beldon Fund (NY) (http://www.beldon.org/)
Beldon Fund is an environmental grantmaker headquartered in New York City. Their goals are to build a base of involved and informed activists to protect the environment and to strengthen the capacity of nonprofit organizations to effectively organize environmental activists. The primary interest of the Beldon Fund is in supporting environmental organizations working at the state level, with the following funding categories: state and regional environmental organizations, national organizations' work with state-level constituencies, progressive state-wide coalitions involving a broad spectrum of constituencies, hazardous waste and toxics use reduction, training and technical assistance, and building the organizational capacity of grantees. The Beldon Fund focuses on organizations at the state level because it believes that the need is great and that its limited resources can be used most effectively there. The Beldon Fund supports a range of approaches to strengthening the environmental movement, including outreach to new constituencies, building coalitions, encouraging greater cooperation between state and national organizations, increasing effective citizen participation in democratic political processes, and diversifying and expanding environmental groups' funding bases. The fund makes both general support and project-specific grants. The Web site features grant guidelines and application procedures, the president's statement and executive director's report, a summary of recent grants, and contact information.

The James Ford Bell Foundation (MN)
(http://www.users.uswest.net/~famphiladv/jamesfordbell.htm)
Established in 1955 by James Ford Bell, the founder of General Mills, Inc., The James Ford Bell Foundation has a long-standing historical association with the Twin Cities of Minneapolis and St. Paul, Minnesota. The Foundation is especially interested in funding projects that have historical connections to the Bell Family, such as the James Ford Bell Library, the James Ford Bell Museum of Natural History, the Delta Waterfowl Foundation, and the Minneapolis Institute of Arts. The Foundation also considers funding in these four areas: the environment, including preservation, education, and overpopulation and its impact; the arts, especially programs of historic interest to the Foundation as well as arts organizations active in the Twin Cities; social services, especially prevention and self-sufficiency in the Twin Cities; and education, consistent with the interests of the Foundation. There is an extensive biography of James Ford Bell on the Foundation's Web site that gives more detailed information on the Foundation's main programs of interest. Also available on the site are grant guidelines and limitations, detailed application procedures and deadlines, a downloadable grant application cover page available in Microsoft Word format, and contact information.

The Claude Worthington Benedum Foundation (PA)
(http://fdncenter.org/grantmaker/benedum/)
The Pittsburgh, Pennsylvania-based Claude Worthington Benedum Foundation was established in 1944 to support the areas of West Virginia and Pittsburgh, Pennsylvania. Within each area, the Foundation has distinct areas of interest. In West Virginia, areas of interest include education, health, human services, community development, economic development, and the arts. In southwestern Pennsylvania, areas of interest include regional

economic development, support for business and education development in outlying counties, the Pittsburgh cultural district, and the United Way. Visitors to the Foundation's folder on the Center's Web site will find specific program information; application guidelines; a listing of trustees, officers, and staff; recent grants listing; restrictions; and contact information.

Benton Foundation (DC) (http://www.benton.org/)

The Benton Foundation seeks to shape the emerging communications environment and to demonstrate the value of communications for solving social problems. Its mission is to promote communication tools, applications, and policies in the public interest. Through its Communications Policy & Practice arm, the foundation supports nonprofits using communications to solve social problems and strengthen social bonds. Other projects of the Foundation are Connect for Kids, an online resource for "helping Americans act on behalf of children;" Open Studio: The Arts Online, which provides community access to the arts on the Internet; Destination Democracy, dedicated to campaign finance reform; and Sound Partners for Community Health, which awards grants to public radio stations that demonstrate how community centered journalism can positively affect the ways in which local health care issues are addressed. The Foundation has created the Virtual Library, which supplies dozens of papers and policy documents online. Visitors to the site will find useful communications technology "best practices," the Benton Foundation Library, hundreds of annotated links to nonprofit and telecommunications resources on the Internet, and a listing of the Foundation's board members and staff.

H.N. & Frances C. Berger Foundation (CA) (http://www.hnberger.org/)

The H.N. and Frances C. Berger Foundation was created to provide people with the opportunity to improve their own situations, "to help people help themselves." Established as a private family foundation in 1961 by Nor and Frances Berger, the focus of its funding is on children and youth, in keeping with the Bergers' belief that the future rests in childrens' hands. To that end, the establishment of college buildings and scholarships are among its charitable projects. The foundation, located in Palm Desert, California, supports a variety of civic, educational, and community projects, with the majority of grants related to programs in the southern California area. The Berger Foundation prefers to seek out its own projects and does not solicit grant proposals. However, "those with interest in a potential dialogue" are encouraged to submit a one– to two–page request for consideration, which should include a concise statement of intent and a brief history of the organization and its activities. The Web site contains an address for contact and a brief biography of the founders.

The Grace and Franklin Bernsen Foundation (OK) (http://www.bernsen.org/)

Grace and Franklin Bernsen established their Foundation in 1968 to fund nonprofit organizations in and around their home of Tulsa, Oklahoma. The Bernsen Foundation funds grants supporting "religious, charitable, scientific, literary or educational purposes, or for the prevention of cruelty to children." A biography of the founders on the Web site contains links to recipients of the Foundation's grants over the course of its history. The Foundation's Web site also provides an annual report, grant guidelines, and contact information where all correspondence can be directed.

Frank Stanley Beveridge Foundation, Inc. (FL) (http://www.beveridge.org/)

The Florida-based Beveridge Foundation was established in Massachusetts in 1947 by Frank Stanley Beveridge, the founder of Stanley Home Products, Inc. Today the Foundation considers grant proposals in two dozen institutional/program activity areas: animal related, arts and culture, civil rights, community improvement, conservation/environment, crime, disasters/safety, diseases/medical disciplines, education, employment, food and agriculture, health (general and rehabilitative), housing, human services, mental health/crisis intervention, philanthropy/voluntarism, public affairs and society benefit, recreation, religion, science, social sciences, and youth development. The stated purpose of the Foundation's Web site, however, is to determine whether potential applicants are eligible to receive grants from the Foundation. In addition to a self-administered interactive survey to help grantseekers determine whether they meet the Foundation's basic eligibility requirements, visitors to the site will find a biography of Mr. Beveridge, a recent grants list, a listing of the Foundation's officers and directors, and contact information.

F.R. Bigelow Foundation (MN) (http://www.frbigelow.org/)
The F.R. Bigelow Foundation was founded in 1946 by the president of the St. Paul Fire & Marine Company, an insurance company now known as The St. Paul Companies, Inc., to continue the philanthropic interests of his family. Serving the greater St. Paul metropolitan area (including Ramsey, Washington and Dakota counties, but giving preference to St. Paul-based organizations), the Foundation centers its funding on education, human services, humanities, the arts, and community development. Visitors to the Foundation's Web site will find an online annual report, the details of past grants, guidelines and limitations of grants, a grant application that can be downloaded in PDF format, and contact information.

William Bingham Foundation (OH) (http://fdncenter.org/grantmaker/bingham/index.html)
The William Bingham Foundation was established in 1955 by Elizabeth Bingham Blossom in memory of her brother, William Bingham II, to continue the philanthropic tradition of the family. Initally, the Foundation's grantmaking focused on educational, cultural, and health and human service organizations in the Cleveland area. Over the years, however, the Foundation's objectives have broadened to reflect the needs of the communities in which its trustees reside. Today, the Foundation contributes to a wide variety of organizations in the areas of the arts, education, and health and human services in those communities as well as nationwide. The Foundation's folder on the Center's Web site provides a brief history of the Foundation, its program interests and grantmaking procedures, a list of grants paid in the latest year, and trustee, officer, and staff listings.

Birmingham Foundation (PA) (http://www.birminghamfoundation.org)
The Birmingham Foundation was established in 1996 to benefit the quality of life in South Pittsburgh, a community formerly known as Birmingham. The Foundation focuses on health-related and human services grantmaking in a three zip code area of South Pittsburgh. Visitors to the Foundation's Web site will find application guidelines and an outline for the initial letter of intent. The Foundation accepts a Common Grant Application form, which can be accessed and printed online from a link to the Grantmakers of Western Pennsylvania Web site. A health assessment guide and a service area guide, both of which can be downloaded in PDF format, are posted on the site. Additionally, recent and past grants and contact information are provided online.

Blakemore Foundation (WA) (http://www.blakemorefoundation.org/)
Based in Seattle, Washington, the Blakemore Foundation was established by Thomas and Frances Blakemore in 1990 to encourage the study of Asian languages at an advanced level and to increase the understanding of Asian art in the United States. The Blakemore Foundation makes approximately twenty grants each year for the advanced study of modern Chinese, Japanese, Korean, and Southeast Asian languages. These grants are intended for individuals successfully pursuing academic, professional, or business careers involving Asia who realize that language study abroad at an advanced level is essential to realize their goals. The grants cover tuition, related educational expenses, basic living costs, and transportation for a year of language study abroad. Grants to improve the understanding of Asian fine arts are made to museums, universities, and other educational or art-related institutions in the United States that have programs, exhibits, or publications dealing with the fine arts of Northeast, East, and Southeast Asia. Printable and downloadable application forms for the language grants can be found on the site. There are no formal grant applications for art grants. Visit the site for detailed grant guidelines and instructions, a history of the founders, contact information, and links to universities in Asia.

Blandin Foundation (MN) (http://www.blandinfoundation.org/)

The mission of the Blandin Foundation is to strengthen rural Minnesota communities, with a special focus on the Grand Rapids community and Itasca County. To that end, the Foundation sponsors conferences and leadership programs and provides approximately $12 million to Minnesota organizations annually. Outside of Itasca County, Blandin grants are restricted to the focus areas established by the Foundation's board of trustees: education, cultural opportunities, community leadership training, environmental stewardship, safe communities, economic opportunity, and "convening." The trustees commit most of the Foundation's grant dollars to its major partners, who have the responsibility of administering each focus area. Potential grant applicants are encouraged to review the Foundation's current focus areas and then contact the appropriate partner organization, which can be done via e-mail through the Foundation's Web site. The site also provides program descriptions, a list of grants made in the most recent year, and detailed grant restrictions.

The Arthur M. Blank Family Foundation (GA) (http://www.BlankFoundation.org)

The Arthur M. Blank Family Foundation is "committed to supporting programs and organizations that create opportunity, enhance self-esteem and increase awareness about cultural and community issues among young men and women." The Atlanta-based foundation provides funding in the following areas: arts and culture, athletics and outdoor activities, environment, fostering understanding between young people of diverse backgrounds, helping adolescents learn, and empowering young women and girls. The foundation's geographic focus includes Atlanta, Georgia; New York City; Boston, Massachusetts; and Los Angeles, California. Special consideration is given to organizations that are located in Atlanta, reach underserved youth, or improve the quality of public education. The Web site includes information about each funding area, grant application instructions and a description of the review process, a downloadable application, and a listing of grant limitations.

Blowitz-Ridgeway Foundation (IL) (http://fdncenter.org/grantmaker/blowitz/index.html)

Founded in 1984 with the proceeds from the sale of Chicago's Ridgeway Hospital, a psychiatric facility serving low-income adolescents, the Blowitz-Ridgeway Foundation continues the hospital's mission by making grants primarily for medical, psychiatric, psychological and/or residential care, and research programs in medicine, psychology, social science, and education. Preference is given to organizations operating within the state of Illinois. Visitors to the Foundation's folder on the Center's Web site will find application guidelines and procedures and a listing of recent grants.

Bodman Foundation (NY) (http://fdncenter.org/grantmaker/bodman/index.html)

The Bodman Foundation was established in 1945 by investment banker George M. Bodman and his wife, Louise Clarke Bodman, to distribute funds in the religious, educational, and charitable fields "for the moral, ethical and physical well-being and progress of mankind." Today the Foundation concentrates its grantmaking in New York City, with occasional grants directed to northern New Jersey in memory of the Bodmans. Areas of Foundation interest include funding for youth, rehabilitation, biomedical research, child welfare, science education, major cultural institutions, health and hospitals, social services, welfare reform, alcohol and drug abuse, responsible fatherhood and father absence, and education (including charter schools, public school reform, and parental school choice). Other interests include volunteerism, literacy, homelessness, entrepreneurship and economic development, environment (science education and land conservation), and job training with employment in the private business sector. Visitors to the Foundation's folder on the Center's Web site will find a brief history of the Foundation; a statement from Foundation president John N. Irwin III; application guidelines and procedures; recent grants lists; a listing of the Foundation's trustees, officers, and staff; and contact information.

Boettcher Foundation (CO) (http://www.boettcherfoundation.org/)

The Boettcher Foundation, established by the Colorado Boettcher Family in 1937, has been funding programs that promote the general well-being of Colorado residents for more than 60 years. The Foundation's four areas of giving are education, civic and cultural programs, community and social service, and hospital and health service. Additionally, the Foundation provides merit-based scholarships for Colorado high school seniors to Colorado institutions of higher learning and a Teacher Recognition Award. Honorary and Memorial Grants, mainly in honor of former board members and executives of the Foundation, are also available. Visitors to the Boettcher Foundation Web site will find extensive information on all aspects of the granting process. Guidelines, past grants in each funding area, and grant distribution information, along with the scholarship process and selection, information on past scholars and their achievements, an FAQ, financial information, and a history of the Boettcher Family are all available online.

The Bogliasco Foundation, Inc. (NY) (Operating foundation) (http://www.liguriastudycenter.org)

The Bogliasco Foundation is headquartered in New York City and grants semester-long fellowships for scholars or artists to work at the Liguria Study Center in Bogliasco, Italy, near Genoa. The Fellowship is designed for advanced creative work or scholarly research in archaeology, architecture, classics, dance, film or video, history, landscape architecture, literature, music, philosophy, theater, or visual arts. Interested applicants must submit a description of the project they will pursue while in Italy, which should result in a public presentation of some kind. The Foundation's Web site provides an overview of the facilities and resources in Bogliasco at the Study Center, an online form to request application materials, and New York contact information.

The David Bohnett Foundation (CA) (http://www.bohnettfoundation.org/)

The Los Angeles-based David Bohnett Foundation's mission is to improve society through social activism. Entrepreneur and co-founder of GeoCities, David Bohnett formed the foundation in 1999 after GeoCities became the largest community on the Internet. The grantmaking organization supports nonprofits in six key target areas including gun control, voter registration activities, animal language research, development of mass transit and non-fossil fuel transportation, and lesbian and gay organizations that provide community based social services. The Foundation encourages grant proposals from qualified nonprofit organizations with a mission that is closely aligned with the Bohnett Foundation's goals. The Foundation makes grants for general operating, seed money, capital support, matching grants, and challenge grants. Upon entering the Foundation's site, visitors can view recent grants and recipients, grant application information, proposal deadlines, and contact information.

Bonfils-Stanton Foundation (http://www.bonfils-stantonfoundation.org)

The Colorado-based, Bonfils-Stanton Foundation was established in 1963 by Charles Edwin Stanton following the death of his wife, Mary Madeline Bonfils, to support local organizations. Areas of interest of the Foundation include arts and culture, community service, education, and science, including hospitals and health services. The Foundation's Web site contains information on guidelines, deadlines, board and staff listings, and contact information.

Corella & Bertram F. Bonner Foundation (NJ) (http://www.bonner.org/)

The Bonner Foundation was established in 1989 by Corella and Bertram Bonner with "the hope and, indeed the expectation, that the impact of their support would be far reaching in the areas of hunger and education." In the years since then, the Foundation has provided $9.5 million in grants to thousands of religious, community-based hunger relief programs across the country through its Crisis Ministry Program. Over the same period the Bonner Scholars Program has awarded more than $12 million in scholarship support to more than 2,500 students at 24 colleges. The Foundation's Web site provides general information on and application guidelines for both programs, including a downloadable grant application cover sheet, as well as highlights from the Foundation's newsletter, a list of recent grants, board and staff listings, and contact information.

Mary Owen Borden Foundation (NJ) (http://fdncenter.org/grantmaker/borden/index.html)
The Mary Owen Borden Foundation was founded by Bertram H. Borden in 1934 to honor his recently departed wife. In recent decades, the Foundation has limited its new funding to New Jersey's Mercer and Monmouth counties. Its current giving is focused on disadvantaged youth and their families, including needs such as health, family planning, education, counseling, childcare, substance abuse, and delinquency. Other areas of interest for the Foundation include affordable housing, conservation and the environment, and the arts. The Foundation's folder on the Center's Web site provides general Foundation information, application guidelines and procedures, a summary of recent grants, a listing of the Foundation's officers and trustees, and contact information.

The Bothin Foundation (CA)
(http://www.pacificfoundationservices.com/bothin/index.html)
The Bothin Foundation was established in California in 1917 to support surrounding areas of Santa Barbara and San Francisco. The Foundation supports low income, at-risk children, youth and families, and the elderly and disabled. To a limited extent, grants may also be made to environmental agencies, arts organizations that serve youth predominately, and community-based capital campaigns. The Foundation will occasionally support capital or building and equipment needs but does not support endowment drives or general operating expenses. The Web site includes other explicit grantee exclusions, staff/board list, contact information, and application procedures.

Robert Bowne Foundation, Inc. (NY) (http://fdncenter.org/grantmaker/bowne/index.html)
Established in 1968 by Bowne & Co., Inc., and named in honor of the company's founder, Robert Bowne (1744–1818), the Robert Bowne Foundation concentrates its grantmaking on out-of-school programs in New York City that address the issue of youth literacy. The Foundation provides grants—ranging from $5,000 to $25,000—for special, advocacy, and research projects; for general operating expenses of relevant programs; for technical assistance in program design and reform; and for evaluation studies. The Foundation does not not support in-school projects or projects following a traditional remedial model of instruction, nor does it award grants to religious organizations or primary or secondary schools, colleges, or universities (except when some aspect of their work is an integral part of a program receiving funding from the Foundation). Visitors to the Foundation's folder on the Center's Web site will find a brief history of the Foundation, a detailed description of its program and application procedures, recent grants lists, a listing of the Foundation's trustees and staff, and contact information.

The Brackett Foundation (NY) (http://brackett.colgate.edu/)
The Brackett Foundation was established in 1997 to aid refugees in achieving an education. The Foundation supports students from nursery school through postgraduate studies. Currently the Foundation focuses on refugees from the civil war in Burma but holds a strong interest in other parts of the world. The program is divided into four major program areas that focus on four distinct demographics. To support children, the Foundation has provided funding for several development centers in Thailand, where children receive crucial childcare, food, and language and arithmetic guidance. The Beyond High School program allows a select number of students to attend college fully funded by the Foundation. The Adult Education program grants adults the necessary training needed to understand and utilize both computers and the Thai language. In India, the Foundation's fourth program supports two primary schools that allow refugees to further their education by attending high school. The Foundation's Web site provides more detailed background on the Foundation and its mission, including a picture essay. Visitors can also obtain a profile of the Foundation's trustees, annual report, and contact information.

Lynde and Harry Bradley Foundation (WI) (http://www.bradleyfdn.org)
Established to commemorate Lynde and Harry Bradley, successful turn-of-the-century Milwaukee businessmen, the Bradley Foundation furthers the brothers' mutual interest in helping to improve the quality of life in the metropolitan Milwaukee area and to

"preserving and defending the tradition of free representative government and private enterprise which has enabled the American nation . . . to flourish intellectually and economically." Like the Bradley brothers, the Foundation is "devoted to strengthening American democratic capitalism and the institutions, principles and values which sustain and nurture it. Its programs support limited, competent government; a dynamic marketplace for economic, intellectual, and cultural activity; and a vigorous defense at home and abroad of American ideas and institutions." Recognizing that "responsible self-government depends on enlightened citizens and informed public opinion," the Bradley Foundation also supports scholarly studies and academic achievement. The Foundation's Web site provides passionate descriptions of the Foundation's mission and driving philosophy, general information about its current program interests and grantmaking policies, and listings of the Foundation's board, officers, and staff.

Brainerd Foundation (WA) (http://www.brainerd.org/)

The Brainerd Foundation is dedicated to protecting the environmental quality of the Pacific Northwest—Alaska, Idaho, Montana, Oregon, Washington, and the Canadian province of British Columbia—by supporting "grassroots-oriented projects that motivate citizens to get involved in efforts to protect the environment." The majority of the foundation's grants are awarded within one of three program areas: endangered ecosystems, toxic pollution, and communication strategies. The Foundation also makes what it calls Emergency Grants, which range from $250 to $2,000 and are given to "organizations that are confronted with an opportunity to carry out important work in a hurry." Visitors to the Foundation's Web site will find detailed program guidelines and limitations, application procedures, lists of recent grant recipients, biographies of the Foundation's directors and staff, and a number of links to community resources in the Pacific Northwest.

The Braitmayer Foundation (CT) (http://www.braitmayerfoundation.org)

The Connecticut-based Braitmayer Foundation is a third generation family foundation interested in supporting organizations and programs from across the United States which enhance the education of K–12 children. Areas of particular interest for the Foundation include curricular and school reform initiatives; preparation of and professional development opportunities for teachers, particularly those which encourage people of high ability and diverse background to enter and remain in K–12 teaching; and local community efforts, including partnerships, that increase educational opportunities for students. The Foundation's Web site includes grant guidelines, a selected list of recent recipients, information about the Braimayer family, trustee listings, and contact information.

Mary Allen Lindsey Branan Foundation (GA) (http://www.wachovia.com/trust/branan_overview.asp)

The Mary Allen Lindsey Branan Foundation of Atlanta is a split-interest trust that supports public charities in Georgia through grantmaking. The Foundation places special emphasis on capital improvement projects. Included are needs of the United Methodist Church and its agencies and affiliated programs. Visitors to the Foundation's site will find grant guidelines, a grant application, financial information, recent grants awarded, a listing of committee members, and contact information.

Otto Bremer Foundation (MN) (http://fdncenter.org/grantmaker/bremer/index.html)

The mission of the St. Paul-based Otto Bremer Foundation is "to be an accessible and responsible financial resource to aid in the development and cohesion of communities within the states of Minnesota, North Dakota, Wisconsin, and Montana, with preference given to those communities served by the affiliates of Bremer Financial Corporation." Within its geographic focus, the Foundation makes grants in the areas of racism, rural poverty, community affairs, education, health, human services, and religion. Visitors to the Foundation's folder on the Center's Web site will find program and application guidelines, a summary of the Foundation's grantmaking activities, and comprehensive grants lists in each program area.

Brentwood Foundation (OH) (http://www.southpointegme.com/frames_pages/)

The Brentwood Foundation was established in 1994 following the merger of Brentwood Hospital, which was an osteopathic hospital, with Suburban Hospital, now known as South Pointe Hospital. It is a charitable trust "dedicated to the promotion and advancement of education, research, patient care and charity care in the field of osteopathic medicine." Specifically, the Foundation's mission is to provide educational opportunities designed to strengthen the capabilities of students and practitioners in the osteopathic field, support research efforts that focus on osteopathic medicine, educate the public about services and trends in the field of osteopathic medicine, and initiate and promote activities designed to advance and improve patient care in osteopathic hospitals. The Foundation limits its grants to organizations located in Ohio and strongly favors those located in the northeastern Ohio area. Additionally, the Foundation prefers to make grants for specific projects rather than for operating costs or capital. Details on how to submit an application, deadlines, and contact information are all available on the Web site.

The Bright Mountain Foundation (CO) (http://fdncenter.org/grantmaker/brightmountain/)

Founded in 1999, the Bright Mountain Foundation of Colorado is committed to providing community assistance by improving the lives of children and their families, senior citizens, and persons living with HIV/AIDS. The Bright Mountain Foundation believes that "the heart of a community is based on how the community treats its more vulnerable members." The Foundation is dedicated to helping children, senior citizens, and persons living with HIV/AIDS to enjoy safer, healthier, and more fulfilling lives in a way that promotes the potential of the individual. Visit the Foundation's folder on the Foundation Center's Web site to learn more about the Bright Mountain Foundation. Also at the site visitors will find further information about the grant programs, view grant guidelines and procedure, and receive contact information.

The Broad Foundation (CA) (http://www.broadfoundation.org/)

The Broad Foundation, located in Los Angeles, California, was established in 1999. The Foundation funds innovative efforts to dramatically improve governance, management, and labor relations in large urban school systems. The Foundation is "dedicated to building K–12 educational leadership capacity, strengthening union-management relations and supporting aggressive, system-wide strategies to increase student achievement." To apply for a grant, applicants send an initial concept paper to the Foundation via e-mail. Contact information is listed on the Web site. The site also provides more specific information about the types of grants the Foundation provides and the Foundation's staff, founders, and program areas.

The Brookdale Foundation (NY) (http://www.ewol.com/brookdale/)

Based in New York City, the Brookdale Foundation Group is comprised of The Brookdale Foundation, the Glendale Foundation, and Ramapo Trust. These three distinct entities have separate officers and boards of directors or trustees, but all are endowed by the Schwartz family and share a common focus: the needs and challenges of America's elderly population. The Foundation Group has three major funding initiatives: The Leadership in Aging Program, a fellowship in the field of gerontology and geriatrics; The National Group Respite Program, which provides small seed grants and technical assistance to foster the development of dementia-specific, social model day-service programs to meet the needs of persons with Alzheimer's and their caregivers; and the Relatives as Parents Program, to establish community-based services to grandparents and other relatives who have assumed the responsibility of surrogate parenting. However, the Foundation Group will also consider new and innovative projects to provide direct services that will improve the lives of older people. Guidelines for the three funding initiatives and instructions for application are provided as well as contact information for each program. Those interested in the Leadership in Aging program can also find lists of participating institutions, members of the medical advisory and review boards who review applications, past fellows, and senior fellows on the site. For those who wish to submit proposals unrelated to the three major initiatives, the Group provides suggestions for submission as well as a downloadable information cover sheet for general grant applications and contact information.

James Graham Brown Foundation, Inc. (KY) (http://www.jgbf.org)

Established under a trust agreement in 1943 and formally incorporated in 1954, the James Graham Brown Foundation is dedicated to fostering the well-being, quality of life, and image of Louisville (i.e., Jefferson County) and Kentucky. The Foundation does this by actively supporting and funding projects in the fields of civic and economic development, education, youth, and health and general welfare. Since the death of its benefactor, James Graham Brown, in 1969, the Foundation has awarded approximately 2,100 grants totaling more than $200 million—mainly in Kentucky, with a small percentage awarded in other parts of the Southeast. Visitors to the Foundation's Web site will find information about its proposal requirements and application procedures, a list of recent grant recipients organized by program area, and contact information.

Bruner Foundation, Inc. (MA) (http://www.brunerfoundation.org)

Based in Cambridge, Massachusetts, the Bruner Foundation administers the Rudy Bruner Award for Urban Excellence, created in 1986 by Simeon Bruner and named in honor of his late father. The Award was created by Mr. Bruner to "foster a better understanding of the role of architecture in the urban environment and has become one of America's leading forums for the discussion of issues related to urban architecture, planning, and revitalization." The Award celebrates and publicizes places that "are developed with such vision and imagination that they transform urban problems into creative solutions." The Award seeks to promote fresh and innovative thinking about cities and "to encourage us all to demand—and build—excellence in the urban environment." The site contains instructions and guidelines for applying, a list with descriptions of past award winners, contact information, and a downloadable order form for the Foundation's publications, which includes in-depth, illustrated case studies of winning projects and a distillation of selection committee discussions on the nature of the urban excellence.

Frank H. and Eva B. Buck Foundation (CA) (http://www.buckscholarships.org)

The Vacaville, California-based Frank H. and Eva B. Buck Foundation is dedicated first and foremost to the support of education. The Foundation administers The Frank H. Buck Scholarship program, under which full scholarship support is awarded annually to students "who have an overwhelming motivation to succeed in all endeavors and who have demonstrated a commitment to themselves, their families and their communities." The Foundation gives preference to the selection of scholars who reside within the boundaries of California's Third Congressional District as served by Frank H. Buck, which at that time included Solano, Napa, Yolo, Sacramento, San Joaquin, and Contra Costa Counties. Direct support is also sometimes given to educational institutions, libraries, and others in support of the Foundation's main emphasis. The Foundation also supports other charitable endeavors as determined from time to time by the board of directors. Scholarship applications may be obtained by writing, e-mailing, leaving a voice mail, or submitting a request through its online form. In addition to scholarship guidelines, visitors will find a short biography of Frank H. Buck and contact information.

Bullitt Foundation (WA) (http://www.bullitt.org/)

The Seattle-based Bullitt Foundation is committed to the protection and restoration of the environment of the Pacific Northwest. This commitment includes environmental problems that disproportionately impact lower-economic people in both urban and rural communities. The Foundation invites proposals from nonprofit organizations that serve Washington, Oregon, Idaho, British Columbia, western Montana (including the Rocky Mountain Range), and the rain forest region of southern Alaska. Within these broad parameters, the Foundation focuses its grantmaking activities in the following program areas: energy and climate change; forests and land ecosystems; growth management and transportation; public outreach, education, and capacity building; rivers, wetlands, and estuaries; sustainable agriculture; and toxic substances, mining, and radioactive waste. Visitors to the

Foundation's Web site will find program descriptions, grant application and final report instructions, detailed grantee information, a report from the Foundation's president (Denis Hayes, national coordinator of the first Earth Day in 1970), an FAQ section, board and staff listings, preliminary financial statements, and contact information.

Margaret E. Burnham Charitable Trust (ME) (http://www.megrants.org/Burnham.htm)

The Portland, Maine-based, Margaret E. Burnham Charitable Trust makes grants to organizations located in or serving the state of Maine. The subject areas supported annually include community/social services, medical, education, arts/culture, and the environment. The Trust is a member of the Maine Philanthropy Center and is linkable from the site. The limited site also includes the previous year's grant list, grant application information, deadline information, printable grant application, and contact information.

Burning Foundation (WA) (http://fdncenter.org/grantmaker/burning/)

The Burning Foundation of Seattle, Washington, is committed to helping three areas of the region. The environmental program is concerned with the preservation of the region's rivers, forests, fish population, and land. The conservation program for low-income children and youth provides grants to organizations that provide this population hands-on experience with protecting the environment in which they live. The Foundation also supports teen pregnancy prevention through school-based health and education programs, mentoring projects, and community clinic programs. Visitor's to the Foundation's folder on the Foundation Center's Web site will find further information on the above programs, application guidelines, and contact information.

Burroughs Wellcome Fund (NC) (http://www.bwfund.org/)

Established in 1955 to advance the medical sciences by supporting research and other scientific and educational activities, the Burroughs Wellcome Fund today emphasizes "career development of outstanding scientists and . . . advancing areas in the basic medical sciences that are underfunded or that have a shortage of qualified researchers." Ninety percent of the Fund's resources are distributed through seven competitive award programs, and the majority of those programs are open to scientists who are citizens or permanent residents of the United States and Canada. BWF's straightforward Web site offers complete descriptions of the Fund's programs; award eligibility requirements and guidelines; application deadlines; a listing of the Fund's board of directors, officers, and staff; a fast-loading version of its most recent annual report; and recent issues of *Focus,* the Fund's newsletter.

The Bush Foundation (MN) (http://www.bushfoundation.org/)

Archibald Granville Bush and his wife, Edyth Bassler Bush, created the Bush Foundation in 1953 to encourage and promote charitable, scientific, literary, and educational efforts. The Bush foundation, based in St. Paul, Minnesota, "is committed to enhancing the quality of life in Minnesota, North Dakota, and South Dakota by making grants to nonprofit organizations and providing fellowships to individuals in those states." The Foundation's primary grantmaking areas are human services and health, education, and arts and humanities. It's fellowship program for individuals focuses on leadership, medicine, and arts. The Foundation also supports out-of-region projects with private, historically black colleges and fully accredited, tribally controlled colleges. The Web site provides specific details on the types of grants awarded, previous grants, and what to include in each type of grant or fellowship application. Contact information, including phone numbers, address, and e-mail, is available on the site's home page.

Edyth Bush Charitable Foundation (FL)
(http://fdncenter.org/grantmaker/bush/index.html)

The mission of the Edyth Bush Charitable Foundation is "grantmaking designed to help people help themselves." To that end, the Foundation supports programs that "help underprivileged or needy people to improve themselves or relieve human suffering." The Foundation makes grants to nonprofit organizations exclusively located and/or operating within a 100-mile radius of Winter Park, Florida, with special emphasis on Orange, Seminole,

Osceola, and Lake counties. The Foundation, which was founded by the widow of Archibald G. Bush, a director and principal shareholder of the Minnesota Mining & Manufacturing Company, also has broad interests in human service, education, and health care and a limited interest in the arts. Visitors to the Foundation's folder on the Center's Web site will find a detailed account of the Foundation's application policies and procedures as well as recent grants lists by subject area.

The Morris and Gwendolyn Cafritz Foundation (DC) (http://www.cafritzfoundation.org/)

The Morris and Gwendolyn Cafritz Foundation was established in 1948 by Morris Cafritz, a civic leader who raised money for numerous charities and community projects. This Washington, D.C.–based foundation was created with the goal of "helping others less fortunate make a better life for themselves and their families, and to assist young people in achieving their full potential" and currently funds projects in four areas: arts and humanities, education, health, and community service. The foundation concentrates grants to organizations in the greater Washington area on a project basis, and generally "projects of direct assistance to the District of Columbia and its environs." The Foundation uses the Washington Regional Association of Grantmakers Common Grant Application, which can be viewed on their Web site. Also available on their Web site are grant guidelines and restrictions, the 1997 annual report, a list of e-mail links to certain staff members, information about grantees, and a list of linked resources for grantseekers.

The Louis Calder Foundation (NY) (http://www.lcfnyc.org/)

The Foundation was established in 1951 by Louis Calder to support "educational, charitable and benevolent uses and purposes." Calder was instrumental in the development of the newsprint industry in the Southwest and was also a successful pioneer in the retail gasoline market. The Foundation generally concentrates its grantmaking on organizations whose programs and projects are directed to improving the condition of young people in the City of New York and the surrounding areas. Current funding priorities are grants that support the efforts of community-based organizations whose educational programs are designed to enhance the potential and increase the self-sufficiency of New York City's children and youth. The site contains guidelines, application procedures, recent grants list, latest annual report, and links to other related sites. The Foundation requests that organizations use the New York Regional Association of Grantmakers Common Application Form, which can be downloaded from the site.

The California Endowment (CA) (http://www.calendow.org/)

Established in 1996 as a result of Blue Cross of California's conversion from a not-for-profit to a for-profit corporation, the California Endowment works to expand access to affordable, quality health care for underserved individuals and communities and to promote fundamental improvements in the health status of the people of California. Within this context, and as a new foundation keenly interested in delivering maximum benefit to its constituents, the Endowment has identified four broad areas of interest: Access, with a focus on expanding and improving access to health systems and related resources for underserved individuals and communities; Community Innovation; Health & Well-Being, especially as it relates to the promotion of prevention strategies for all populations; and Multicultural Health, with a focus on developing the field of multicultural health by supporting the theoretical and applied work of addressing socio-cultural barriers to improved health. The Foundation's Web site offers application procedures and an application cover sheet in PDF format, an online publications order form (the Endowment's publications are offered to the public at no charge), staff and board listings, contact information (including an electronic feedback form), and an extensive list of relevant Internet resources.

California Masonic Foundation (CA) (http://www.freemason.org/foundation/index.htm)

The California Masonic Foundation, located in San Francisco, California, awards scholarships to California high school students. The program is intended to assist exceptional California high school seniors who are seeking to attend a university or trade school within the United States. Scholarships are based on the whole person concept, with emphasis on academic performance and financial need. Scholarship applications can be requested by mail or downloaded from the Web site in PDF format. The Foundation also sponsors the Masonic Student Assistance Program (MSAP), a series of three-day workshops for California state educators, administrators, and support staff in schools from kindergarten through high school. These workshops teach participants how to identify kids at risk and help them on the road to a successful life. More information about MSAP is available online. Additionally, contact information, including a mailing address, e-mail form, and phone number, is available on the site.

California Wellness Foundation (CA) (http://www.tcwf.org/)

The mission of the California Wellness Foundation is to improve the health and well-being of the people of California through health promotion and disease prevention programs. The Foundation concentrates its grantmaking activities in five areas—community health, population health improvement, teenage pregnancy prevention, violence prevention, and work and health—and while it generally supports organizations located in California or projects that directly benefit California residents, national organizations providing services in California are also considered. In addition to information about its general grants program and descriptions of strategic initiatives in each of its five focus areas, the Foundation's Web site provides a listing of latest grants, links to related Web sites, and the Foundation's newsletter, which is downloadable as a PDF file.

The Campbell Foundation (FL) (http://members.aol.com/campfound)

Based in Ft. Lauderdale, Florida, the Campbell Foundation was established in 1986 by the late Richard Campbell Zahn. It was Mr. Zahn's wish that his foundation support not-for-profit organizations or individuals conducting research into the prevention and treatment of HIV, AIDS, and related conditions and illnesses. The focus of the Campbell Foundation's funding lies in alternative, nontraditional avenues of research. Visitors to the site will find grant application instructions and contact information.

Iris & B. Gerald Cantor Foundation (CA) (Operating foundation) (http://www.cantorfoundation.com/)

Established in 1978, the Iris & B. Gerald Cantor Foundation is involved with the support and promotion of the arts. The goal of the foundation, which bears the names of its founders, is to "promote and encourage the recognition and appreciation of excellence in the arts," with an emphasis on the sculptures of Auguste Rodin. The Foundation has donated more than 450 Rodin sculptures to institutions throughout the world, funded and organized Rodin exhibitions, created a Rodin Research Fund at Stanford University, and given numerous endowments to major art museums. The Foundation is also committed to supporting biomedical research and the support of healthcare initiatives for women, with an emphasis on the early diagnosis and treatment of breast cancer, which is of particular interest to this Beverly Hills–based foundation. The Foundation in its support of biomedical research makes significant gifts to endow new patient facilities, laboratories, and research fellowships at hospitals and medical centers. Visitors will find a site mostly devoted to Rodin's life and work (such as a schedule of traveling Rodin exhibitions organized by the Foundation, a suggested reading list on Rodin, the artist's biography, and a virtual gallery) but will also find information on the Cantor Foundation's activities and a biography of the founders.

Canyon Research (CA) (Operating foundation) (http://www.canyonresearch.org)

This San Diego-based foundation seeks to advance communications research and education by funding specialized research projects that focus on three areas of support: advanced computer-related communications technology, public communications policy, and domestic communications regulatory issues. Canyon Research supports these three areas of research through grants and fellowships that allow researchers to develop new and innovative technologies that in turn will create breakthroughs in computer communications capabilities. There are currently no restrictions on grant amounts and no restrictions based on geography, and typical awards are between $25,000 and $50,000. Canyon Research periodically issues a call for applications; proposals that do not fall within the specified areas of support or are not in response to a specific call for applications are unlikely to be funded. Points of interest on this Web site are the Call for Applications section (where the targeted research project is described), application procedures, grantmaking guidelines, areas of exclusion, contact information, proposals, final reports, and descriptions of past and current projects.

Captain Planet Foundation, Inc. (GA) (http://www.turner.com/cpf)

Based in Atlanta, Georgia, and established in 1991, the Captain Planet Foundation is funded by a percentage of the licensing and merchandising revenue generated by the Captain Planet character, the animated television series, and other contributions. The mission of the Captain Planet Foundation is to fund and support hands-on environmental projects for children and youths. Its objective is to encourage innovative programs that empower children and youth around the world to work individually and collectively to solve environmental problems in their neighborhoods and communities. All prospective projects must promote understanding of environmental issues, focus on hands-on involvement, involve children and young adults ages 6–18, promote interaction and cooperation within the group, help young people develop planning and problem solving skills, include adult supervision, and commit to follow-up communication with the Foundation. Visitors to the site will find an online proposal form, grant lists by state, environmental links, and contact information.

CarEth Foundation (MA) (http://www.funder.org/careth/)

The CarEth Foundation seeks to promote "a compassionate world of enduring peace, with justice, and with social, economic, and political equality for all." In support of its mission, the Foundation is currently funding programs that promote the creation of a global community of peace and justice, a genuine democracy in the United States, and peaceful conflict resolution. The Foundation is also currently interested in projects involving today's youth. Visitors to CarEth's Web site will find general descriptions of program goals, application procedures and limitations, and a list of recent grantees with links to all recipient organizations with Web sites.

CARLISLE Foundation (MA) (http://www.carlislefoundation.org)

Based in Framingham, Massachusetts, the CARLISLE Foundation evolved from CARLISLE Services, Inc., a grantmaking company founded in 1988 that acted as an intermediary between private donors and the human services community, soliciting and reviewing grant proposals and presenting them to donors for consideration. In 1991, those same donors established the CARLISLE Foundation as a more efficient and effective means for continuing their philanthropic endeavors and as a statement of their continuing commitment. CARLISLE Foundation only funds programs operating within the six New England states and "attempts to promote creative problem solving and interventions." The Foundation prefers to support new and innovative projects or those that demonstrate potential as models. Though it reviews a wide range of proposals, several areas have emerged as high priorities: substance abuse, domestic and community violence, homelessness/housing, economic development, and other services for children, youth, and family. In addition to grantmaking, the Foundation provides free technical assistance or consultation to human services organizations, whether it be assistance with proposal development or program development to fiscal or personnel management. More information about this service and application and grant guidelines are available on its site. Also of interest are descriptions of programs currently funded, a list of organizations that received prior grants, and contact information for funded projects and for the CARLISLE Foundation, complete with e-mail, telephone, and fax numbers.

Carnegie Corporation of New York (NY) (http://www.carnegie.org)

Carnegie Corporation of New York was created by Andrew Carnegie in 1911 to promote "the advancement and diffusion of knowledge and understanding." In addition to a brief history of Andrew Carnegie and his philanthropies and information about the Foundation itself, the Web site of the Carnegie Corporation of New York gives visitors general information about the Foundation's six currently supported program areas: Education, International Peace and Security, International Development, Strengthening U.S. Democracy, Carnegie Corporation Scholars Program, and Special Opportunities Fund. The last affords the Foundation an opportunity to make grants and appropriations outside its other defined program areas. Available as well are application guidelines and grant restrictions, a description of the Foundation's six special initiatives, full-text online versions of selected Carnegie publications, a listing of Foundation officers and trustees, links to other foundation and nonprofit resources on the Internet, and contact information.

Carnegie Endowment for International Peace (DC) (Operating foundation) (http://www.ceip.org)

The Carnegie Endowment for International Peace was established with a gift from Andrew Carnegie in 1910. It conducts programs of research, discussion, publication, and education in international affairs and U.S. foreign policy and publishes the quarterly magazine *Foreign Policy.* The Endowment and its associates seek "to invigorate and extend both expert and public discussion on a wide range of international issues," such as worldwide migration, nuclear non-proliferation, and regional conflicts. It also "engages in and encourages projects designed to foster innovative contributions in international affairs." The Carnegie Endowment also has a public policy research center in Moscow to promote collaboration among scholars and specialists in the United States, Russia, and other post-Soviet states. The Moscow Center holds seminars, workshops, and study groups and provides a forum for international figures to present their views to "informed Moscow audiences." The Endowment has Junior Fellows Program; Junior Fellows are research assistants to senior associates. Fellows are uniquely qualified graduating seniors and individuals who have graduated during the past academic year and are selected from a pool of nominees. The Web site offers information on this program as well as information about the various projects within the Global Policy and Russia/Eurasia programs and links to the Carnegie Moscow Center and its magazine, *Foreign Policy.* A media guide, library, downloadable publications and book summaries, and lists of associates and their biographies, junior fellows, and board of trustees are also available.

The Carnegie Foundation for the Advancement of Teaching (CA) (Operating foundation) (http://www.carnegiefoundation.org)

Andrew Carnegie founded The Carnegie Foundation for the Advancement of Teaching in 1905 "to do all things necessary to encourage, uphold and dignify the profession of teaching." Based in Menlo Park, California, the Foundation is a major national and international center for research and policy studies about teaching. The Foundation's work includes founding the Educational Testing Service and developing the Graduate Record Exam. It uses income from its endowment to support its research and publication activities and makes no grants. A small group of distinguished scholars generate, critique, and monitor advances in the theory and practice of education in the United States and worldwide. The Foundation's mission is to address "the hardest problems faced in teaching in public schools, colleges and universities: how to succeed in the classroom, how best to achieve lasting student learning and how to assess the impact of teaching on students." The site contains an annual report that further describes the work and programs of the Foundation, which include: Carnegie Academy for the Scholarship of Teaching and Learning, Preparation for the Professions Program, Higher Education and the Development of Moral and Civic Responsibility, and Cultures of Teaching and Learning in Higher Education. The site includes an online forum for conversations with teachers at all levels about problems they have solved; press releases and articles; resources page, with list of publications, surveys, information on various facilities at their Foundation, archives, and links; and contact information.

Carnegie Hero Fund Commission (PA) (Operating foundation) (http://www.carnegiehero.org/)

A coal mine explosion on January 25, 1904 near Harwick, Pennsylvania, and the death of the two men who died trying to rescue those inside the mine inspired industrialist and philanthropist Andrew Carnegie to establish the Carnegie Hero Fund Commission. Within three months after the explosion that claimed 181 lives, Carnegie set aside $5 million under the care of a commission to recognize "civilization's heroes" and to carry out his wish that "heroes and those dependent upon them should be freed from pecuniary cares resulting from their heroism." Ninety-five years later, their mission is still the same: "to recognize acts of civilian heroism throughout the United States and Canada" and "to provide financial assistance to the awardees and the dependents of those awardees who are killed or disabled by their heroic actions." The Pittsburgh, Pennsylvania–based foundation awards a bronze medal, a $3000 grant, and scholarship eligibility to all cases considered worthy. Visitors to the Web site can read about the history behind the Commission and about past awardees; find award guidelines, application instructions, and contact information; peruse a bibliography for additional information about the Commission; and find links related to Andrew Carnegie.

The Kristen Ann Carr Fund (NY) (http://www.sarcoma.com)

Originally founded as a division of the T.J. Martell Foundation for Cancer, Leukemia and AIDS Research, the Kristen Ann Carr Fund provides grants for cancer research and seeks to improve all aspects of cancer patients' lives with an emphasis on adolescents and young adults. The Kristen Ann Carr Fund honors the life of Kristen Ann Carr (1971–1993), "a remarkable young woman who sought life and love," who herself had sarcoma. The New York City-based Fund was established at her request and seeks to provide funding for research and treatment of sarcoma, provide funding for the education of young physicians, improve the quality of cancer patient life, and develop an adolescent care unit at Memorial Sloan-Kettering Cancer Center. Among the programs are the Sunshine Program, which attempts to grant the wishes of adolescent and young adult patients at Memorial Sloan–Kettering, with a particular emphasis on and interest in the music and entertainment industries, and the Post-Treatment Resource Program, a resource center which offers a wide variety of services assisting people in their adjustment to life as cancer survivors.

The Carthage Foundation (PA) (http://www.scaife.com)

Based in Pittsburgh, Pennsylvania, the Carthage Foundation is one of the Scaife Foundations and confines most of its grant awards to programs that will address public policy questions concerned with national and international issues. There are no geographical restrictions, but the Foundation does not make grants to individuals. Visitors to the site will find a downloadable annual report, which includes a grant list and financials; grant application instructions; links to other Scaife Foundations; and contact information.

Roy J. Carver Charitable Trust (IA) (http://www.carvertrust.org/)

The Roy J. Carver Charitable Trust was created in 1982 through the will of Roy J. Carver, an industrialist and philanthropist who died in 1981. Based in Muscatine, Iowa, "it is the largest private foundation in the state of Iowa," listing five funding areas: medical and scientific research, education, scholarship and awards, youth, and miscellaneous, which are grants that "for various reasons do no fall within the Trust's four primary program classifications" and "in many cases are grants awarded for projects within the Muscatine area that have received special consideration because of their location." The Trust has an annual grantmaking budget of over $11 million, and the majority of grants are awarded for initiatives in Iowa and a portion of western Illinois. Visitors to the site will find information about each of the five funding areas, grant lists, information about grant guidelines and application procedures, a downloadable application cover sheet, and contact information.

Mary Flagler Cary Charitable Trust (NY) (http://www.carytrust.org/)

The Mary Flagler Cary Charitable Trust is a New York City-based foundation that was created in 1968 by the will of its namesake, a great lover of music and the environment. The trustees work to continue supporting the interests of the founder, reevaluating what that means as times change. While much of the Trust's assets are committed to special commitments related to the institutes now housing the family art collection, there are three unrelated grant programs. The Music program "supports professional performance institutions that add to the vitality and diversity of New York City's musical life." There are also special, bi-annual funds that support the commission of new musical works and that support ensembles and nonprofit record companies to record living composers. The Urban Environment program "supports grassroots groups and helps develop local leadership to work on environmental problems within low-income neighborhoods in New York City. This program has also established funds at the Citizens Committee for New York City and the Trust for Public Land. The Conservation program primarily supports "collaborative efforts to protect natural resources, including barrier islands, estuaries and coastal wetlands at selected sites along the Atlantic coastline from Maryland to Florida." The Trust's Web site specifies the areas that the Trust funds and underlines that most awards go to local action groups or regional/national conservation groups that are active at these sites. Lists of trustees and staff, categorized lists of previous grantees, and basic financial information are provided online. The Trust requests that interested applicants submit letters of inquiry.

Annie E. Casey Foundation (MD) (http://www.aecf.org/)
Established in 1948 by Jim Casey, one of the founders of United Parcel Service, and his siblings, the Annie E. Casey Foundation is dedicated to fostering public policies, human-service reforms, and community supports that more effectively meet the needs of today's vulnerable children and families. Working with neighborhoods and state and local governments, the Foundation provides grants to public and nonprofit organizations to strengthen the support services, social networks, physical infrastructure, employment, self-determination, and economic vitality of distressed communities. Most grantees have been invited by the Foundation to participate in these projects. The Foundation does not make grants to individuals, nor does it support capital projects that are not an integral part of a Foundation-sponsored initiative. Visitors to the Foundation's Web site will find: KIDS COUNT, an interactive database with national and state-level indicators of children's well-being; publications, including on-line newsletters and the Casey magazine *AdvoCasey;* grant guidelines; and extensive information about its ongoing initiatives.

The Casey Family Program (WA) (Operating foundation) (http://www.casey.org)
Jim Casey, founder of United Parcel Service, created the Casey Family Program in 1966. His father died when he was a young boy, but the "guidance of a strong mother and support of his family kept him grounded." He sought ways to help those without the family life he felt was so important. The Casey Family Program was created to "provide planned, long-term out-of-home care to children and youth, with long-term family foster care as its core." Its mission: to equip "young people with the skills to form and sustain significant positive relationships, to effectively parent their own children, to participate responsibly in their communities, to sustain themselves economically, and to provide support to those children and youth who will follow them into the Program." The Program, "through national and local community partnerships, advocacy efforts, and by serving as a center for information and learning about children in need of permanent family connections aims to positively impact the lives of children," in addition to those the Program directly helps with foster care. Headquartered in Seattle, Washington, there are field offices in Arizona, California, Colorado, Hawaii, Idaho, Louisiana, Montana, North Dakota, Oklahoma, Oregon, South Dakota, Texas, Washington, and Wyoming. Visitors to the Web will find information on their programs, research services, annual reports, their strategic plan, locations, contact information, and links to sister organization and resources.

Harold K.L. Castle Foundation (HI) (http://www.castlefoundation.org/)
The Castle Foundation, Hawaii's largest private foundation, was founded in 1962 by Harold Castle, the owner of Kaneohe Ranch. A significant portion of Mr. Castle's real estate assets were bequeathed to the Foundation upon his death in 1967, and it is that asset base from which most of the Foundation's grants are made. Historically, the Foundation's

priorities have been private education, youth and family services, and health programs for windward Oahu. But the broad purpose of the Foundation allows it to respond to any current community concern. In the latest years, the Foundation made grants totaling $10 million annually in the areas of arts and culture, education, the environment, health, human services, science and technology, and youth services. The Foundation is also one of the few private funders that still awards large capital improvement grants. The Castle Foundation's Web site provides a brief history of the Foundation, an overview of its current priorities, proposal guidelines, a listing of recent grants, news briefs and related links, and contact information.

Samuel N. and Mary Castle Foundation (HI)
(http://fdncenter.org/grantmaker/castle/index.html)

For more than a century, the Samuel N. and Mary Castle Foundation and its precursor, the Samuel N. Castle Memorial Trust, have served the needs of the people of Hawaii. Over the years, the Foundation's grantmaking has focused primarily on the support of early education and child care, private education (elementary and high schools as well as colleges and universities), Protestant churches, and arts and cultural organizations with ties to the Castle family. In addition, through the Henry and Dorothy Castle Memorial Fund, the Foundation supports the health and human services sector, concentrating its funds on agencies directly providing services to young children and their families. Because Hawaii's population is concentrated on O'ahu, preference is given to organizations whose programs are O'ahu-based. The Foundation's folder on the Center's Web site provides a history of the Foundation and brief biographies of Samuel N. and Mary Castle, messages from the Foundation's president and executive director, a rundown of its grantmaking policies and application procedures, a list of grants awarded in previous years, and contact information.

The C.A.W. Foundation (CA) (http://www.pacificfoundationservices.com/caw/index.html)

The San Francisco-based C.A.W. Foundation was established in 1997 to support public charities in surrounding counties (including limited funding for San Luis Obispo, California, and Seattle, Washington). The Foundation's interests include children, youth, and adults in areas such as education, human services, health care, and homelessness. While primarily focusing on capital improvements and equipment acquisition, the Foundation will consider support for specific projects. The Foundation will not support annual appeals or endowments. At C.A.W.'s Web site, visitors will find specific application procedures, grant ranges, recent grants list, and contact information.

Century Foundation (NY) (Operating foundation) (http://www.tcf.org/)

The Century Foundation (formerly the Twentieth Century Fund) was founded in 1919 and endowed by Edward A. Filene to "undertake timely and critical analyses of major economic, political, and social institutions and issues." The Foundation is an operating rather than grantmaking foundation and does not award fellowships or scholarships, support dissertation research, or make grants to individuals or institutions. Similarly, it almost never supports large-scale data-gathering efforts or research designed primarily to develop theory or methodology. Currently, it welcomes proposals in four areas: improving living standards, restoring civil society and respect for government, reinvigorating the media, and identifying new foundations for American foreign policy. In addition to information on and excerpts from current and recently completed projects, visitors to the Foundation's Web site will find a mission statement and history of the Foundation, detailed program descriptions, proposal submission guidelines, the Foundation's recent annual report, press releases and a publications catalog, listings of the Foundation's board and staff, e-mail links to staff members, links to sites of interest, and contact information.

The Champlin Foundations (RI) (http://fdncenter.org/grantmaker/champlin/)

The aim of the Champlin Foundations is to "provide funds to tax-exempt organizations in Rhode Island who serve—or are able to serve—the broadest possible segment of the population." The Warwick, Rhode Island, foundation makes direct grants for capital needs such as the purchase of equipment, construction, and purchases of real property. They do not provide funds for facilities or equipment for agencies who engage in "program activities" such as counseling or day care. The Foundations do not rely solely on applications to allocate grants; they identify and make grants to many organizations that have not applied or may encourage those who have not to apply. Grantseekers can consult the Web site for guidelines and funding criteria, contact information, a list of members of the Distribution Committee, and a breakdown of recent grants.

The Chiang Ching-kuo Foundation for International Scholarly Exchange (VA) (Operating foundation) (http://www.cckf.org/)

The Chiang Ching-kuo Foundation for International Scholarly Exchange (the CCK Foundation) is headquartered in Taipei, Taiwan, ROC, with a regional office in McLean, Virginia. CCK Foundation was established in 1989 in memory of the late President of the Republic of China, Chiang Ching-kuo, who died in 1988. Its purpose is to promote the study of Chinese culture and society and to promote understanding between the Chinese and other people of the world, with the "ultimate goal of encouraging the integration of the best of Chinese culture with an emerging global culture." The scope of its programs includes Chinese cultural heritage, classical studies, the Republic of China, Taiwan area studies, and China-related comparative studies. Grants are made to institutions and individuals for institutional enhancement, research, conferences and seminars, subsidies for publication, and fellowships for graduate students and post-doctoral research. Visitors to the Web site will find details of each of its funding categories and programs, grant guidelines and deadlines, downloadable applications, contact information, a list of the board of directors and offices, and grant recipient lists.

Chiesman Foundation For Democracy, Inc. (SD) (http://www.chiesman.org)

Allene R. Chiesman founded the Chiesman Foundation for Democracy to promote and support the "greater awareness of the meaning of democracy and democratic ideals by its citizens." She was a philanthropist whose beliefs "were rooted in the fundamentals of hard work and giving back to society a fair share of what one gains through living in a democratic society." Based in Rapid City, South Dakota, the Chiesman Foundation supports institutes and programs that assist citizens to understand the meaning of American democracy; the importance of participatory citizenship; the principles of economic competitiveness and development and the role of government; scholars who research and publish results on sound government policy options that promote economic growth and productivity, participatory government, and U.S. constitutional law; and universities and colleges that establish centers for civic education and law-related education and establish forums for the education of students, faculty, and citizens. Visitors to the Web site will find more detailed information about its goals and purposes and its programs and endowments. Other points of interest are descriptions of its grant programs; application criteria and instructions; a biography of the founder; online viewing of its publication, *Chiesman Quarterly;* a listing of civic education resources; and contact information. In the future, its Web site will feature a Virtual Classroom, an online education center where meetings, conferences, and classses will take place.

The Christensen Fund (CA) (Operating foundation) (http://www.christensenfund.org)

Allen D. and Carmen M. Christensen formed the Christensen Fund in 1957 in Palo Alto, California. The Fund has become a sponsor and grantmaker in two main areas, each with its own particular focus: arts, by loaning the Fund's art collection to museums and educational institutions and supporting visual arts; natural sciences and education, by funding work in the natural sciences as well as supporting arts and science education at all levels. The Fund's Web site contains an overview of the Christensen Foundation's collection of fine art and artifacts, which are loaned out worldwide. Visitors will also find a form to request grant overviews, information on past grants and grant guidelines, links to other foundation and arts resources, and contact addresses.

The CINTAS Foundation (NY) (http://www.iie.org/fulbright/cintas)

The CINTAS Foundation, located in New York City, was established with funds from the estate of the late Oscar B. Cintas, a former Cuban ambassador to the United States and a prominent industrialist and patron of the arts. The CINTAS Foundation, Inc. awards fellowships annually to creative artists of Cuban lineage who currently reside outside of Cuba. Specifically, the fellowships are intended to acknowledge creative accomplishments and encourage the development of talented and creative artists in the fields of architecture, literature, music competition, the visual arts, and photography. The application form, recommendation form, and slide script form can all be downloaded from the Web site in PDF format. Deadlines and application guidelines are posted on the site as is contact information and a list of previous fellows.

Edna McConnell Clark Foundation (NY) (http://www.emcf.org/)

The Edna McConnell Clark Foundation seeks to improve conditions and opportunities for people who live in poor and disadvantaged communities. Through its grantmaking, the Foundation "assists nonprofit organizations and public agencies committed to advancing practices and policies that better the lives of children and families, [while supporting] initiatives that promise to help systems and institutions become more responsive to the needs of the people they serve." The current interests of the Foundation fall into four separate program areas, each with specific goals, strategies, and grantmaking priorities: the Program for Children, the Program for New York Neighborhoods, the Program for Student Achievement, and the Program for Tropical Disease Research. Applicants may want to read the Foundation's latest annual report to ensure that their projects fit within the above programs' very specific, site-based grantmaking strategies. Visitors to the Foundation's Web site will find detailed program descriptions, application guidelines, a recent grants list organized by program area, a report from the Foundation president, a list of Foundation-sponsored publications that can be obtained free of charge, board and staff listings, and contact information.

Robert Sterling Clark Foundation, Inc. (NY) (http://fdncenter.org/grantmaker/rsclark/index.html)

Incorporated in 1952, the Robert Sterling Clark Foundation has provided financial assistance to a wide variety of charitable organizations over the years. At present, it is concentrating its resources in the following fields: improving the performance of public institutions in New York City and State, strengthening the management of New York cultural institutions, and ensuring access to family planning practices. While most of its support will be allocated for these purposes, the Foundation has also begun to make funds available to protect artistic freedom and to educate the public about the importance of the arts in our society. Visitors to the Foundation's folder on the Center's Web site will find program guidelines, application procedures, and contact information.

The Clipper Ship Foundation (MA) (http://www.agmconnect.org/clipper1.html)

The Clipper Ship Foundation, based in Boston, Massachusetts, offers financial assistance to fulfill the goals and broaden the scope of human service organizations. Priority is given to organizations devoted to helping the homeless and ill-housed, the destitute, the handicapped, children, the elderly, or addressing the special needs of minority, low-income individuals and families. The foundation favors grants that will be matched or will stimulate giving by other donors and grants for the construction or renovation of physical facilities or other capital projects over operating grants. In general, grants are limited to human service organizations whose majority of individuals served reside in the Greater Boston area, but special consideration will be given to emergency disaster situations worldwide. Grants in support of the arts will be limited to those that expose children or disabled individuals to the arts without charge or at a significantly reduced cost. Visitors to the Web site will find more information about the Foundation, application information, and contact information for requesting grant guidelines and annual reports.

The Cloud Foundation (MA) (http://www.agmconnect.org/cloud.html)
The Boston-based, Cloud Foundation seeks to renew the confidence, ambition, and hope of youth at risk by supporting programs that provide immersion in a foreign culture and exposure to the arts in the rich mosaic of our city, country, and world. Major interests of the Foundation include exposing youth to cross-cultural experiences that can deepen self-awareness through an understanding of themselves in their world and offering youth the opportunity to fully participate in the arts: dance, drama, writing, music, and visual arts. The Foundation prefers to support projects that actively seek to involve under-served youth, combine artistic challenge with exposure to new cultures, deepen awareness of one's self through exposure to another culture, involve immersion in a foreign culture, foster confidence and trust in participants, encourage development of artistic skills for the purpose of self-expression, seek to build new leaders in both the proposing organization and participant group, and that local community groups initiate or support. The Cloud Foundation's Web site includes a list of previous years' grants, specific information on areas funded, application deadlines, application information, and contact information.

The Coleman Foundation, Inc. (IL) (http://www.colemanfoundation.org/)
The Chicago, Illinois-based Coleman Foundation was established in 1951 by Mr. and Mrs. J. D. Stetson Coleman, entrepreneurs with various holdings that included Fannie May Candies. Their desire was to "make the community aware of opportunities which could improve the quality of Life." The Coleman Foundation has four program areas: entrepreneurship awareness education; cancer research, care, and treatment in the Midwest; housing and education for the handicapped; and a wide range of other educational programs. The Coleman Foundation also considers "special needs associated with poverty and unemployment." Support is generally focused on organizations within the Midwest and particularly within the state of Illinois and the metropolitan Chicago area, although programs outside of this geographic area, but within the United States, are considered. Proposals are not solicited and grantseekers should first make contact through an inquiry letter. The Foundation's Web site contains information about its programs, grant eligibility, grant applications and procedures, grant lists, financial statements, and contact information.

The Colorado Trust (CO) (http://www.coloradotrust.org)
The mission of the Colorado Trust is to promote the health and well-being of the people of Colorado through the support of accessible and affordable health care programs and the strengthening of families. The Trust employs an initiative framework in which it identifies objectives, establishes workable approaches, and recruits interested organizations to implement programs. Visitors to the Trust's easy-to-navigate Web site will find descriptions of its initiatives in each of Colorado's counties as well as information about its approaches to grantmaking. Special features of the site include a funding opportunities mailing list and a program evaluation section titled Lessons Learned at the Colorado Trust.

Columbia Foundation (CA) (http://www.columbia.org)
Madeleine Haas and her brother, William, established the Columbia Foundation in 1940 "for the furtherance of the public welfare." This San Francisco-based foundation has had a long-standing interest in world peace, human rights, the environment, cross-cultural and international understanding, the quality of urban life, and the arts, though the board of directors set new priorities within these areas as conditions change. Currently, there are four program areas: arts and culture, whose goal is to enhance the quality of life through arts and cultural programs, with a geographic focus in the San Francisco Bay Area and London; human rights, whose goal is the protection of basic human rights for all, with a focus in the San Francisco Bay area and national programs; preservation of wildness ecosystems and biological diversity, whose goal is to protect and restore wild ecosystems, with a focus on northern California; and sustainable urban community development, with the goal of promoting the viability and quality of life over time without using up the natural processes and products on which life depends, with a geographic focus on the San Francisco Bay Area. The foundation also considers media projects. The Foundation's Web site provides grant and application guidelines, a summary of its screening process, information

about its funding and project priorities, a printable application cover sheet, grant lists, and contact information.

The Commonweal Foundation, Inc. (MD) (Operating foundation)
(http://www.commonweal-foundation.org)

The Commonweal Foundation supports education and programs in the Maryland and Washington, D.C., metropolitan area, with a focus on educational assistance for disadvantaged, at-risk youth. Current programs of the foundation are Pathways to Success Boarding School Scholarship Program, which awards scholarships to boarding schools; Afterschool and Summer Skills centers in low-income housing complexes; "I have a dream" class; and the small grants program. The Pathways to Success Boarding School Scholarship program has its own separate Web site describing the program and procedures for applying, but no other information about the other programs is provided on this Web site. However, contact information is provided for this Silver Spring, Maryland-based organization, complete with phone and fax numbers, street and e-mail addresses.

Commonwealth Fund (NY) (http://www.cmwf.org)

The Commonwealth Fund, a New York City-based organization, supports independent research on health and social issues and makes grants to improve health care practice and policy. The Fund is "dedicated to helping people become more informed about their health care, and improving care for vulnerable populations such as children, elderly people, low-income families, minority Americans, and the uninsured." The Commonwealth Fund awards grants in four major areas: international health care policy and practice, improving the quality of healthcare services, improving insurance coverage and access to care, and improving public spaces and services. Details about each funding area are available on the Fund's Web site. Prospective grantees should send a letter of inquiry via regular mail or e-mail. The Fund's Web site provides a detailed history of the organization, links to annual reports, and information about its staff and Board of Directors.

Community Technology Foundation of California (CA)
(http://www.partnership.pacbell.net/ctf.html)

Based in San Francisco, California, the Community Technology Foundation of California was established in 1998 to administer the $50 million Pacific Bell Community Technology Fund, a partnership between Pacific Bell and nine statewide community coalitions. The Fund was created to "ensure that all Californians have access to emerging technology." The grantmaking program supports programs that bring communications technologies to traditionally underserved populations. Targeted groups include low-income, inner-city, minority, disabled, limited-English speaking, and low-income senior communities. Funding may come in the form of matching or challenge grants or leveraged gifts. The Foundation's Web site offers grant applications and guidelines only when the applications are being accepted. The board of directors is listed, with biographies of each member, and contact information is given. The Web page is on a site with a number of other Pacific Bell partnerships.

Compton Foundation, Inc. (CA) (http://www.comptonfoundation.org)

Established as a trust in 1946, Menlo Park, California's Compton Foundation converted to a foundation in 1973. The organization's original mission was to "build the foundations for peace and to help prevent another world war" and has been expanded to include "support for welfare, social justice, and the arts in the communities where [Compton] family Board members live." These goals are achieved through a grant program that emphasizes peace and world order, population, and environment as its major categories and welcomes projects combining these issues. The program encourages prevention and research by preferring projects involving public education, education of policy makers and the media, advocacy and public activism, replicable demonstration projects, scholarly research, and fellowships to promising young scholars at selected institutions. The site expands on the Foundation's interests and involvement in each of the three major categories, offers a grant history, and gives application deadlines and guidelines including a proposal outline form that can be printed right from the screen. The site also includes staff and board lists and financial statements.

Connelly Foundation (PA) (http://www.connellyfdn.org)

Based in West Conshohocken, Pennsylvania, the Connelly Foundation develops programs with and directs its support to educational, human services, health, cultural, and civic organizations. Established in 1955 by Mr. and Mrs. John F. Connelly, who rose from the working class to prominent industrialists and philanthropists, its mission is to enhance the quality of life in the greater Philadelphia area. The foundation focuses its philanthropy on nonprofit organizations and institutions based in and serving the city of Philadelphia and the surrounding Delaware Valley region and prefers to support projects that receive funding from several sources. Of note is the founders' mandate, which specifies that a minimum sixty percent of funding be granted each year to organizations affiliated with the Roman Catholic Church or toward programs impacting its members. Visitors to the Web site will find application guidelines, grant summaries and breakdowns of grants by geographic concentration, short biographies of its founders, and contact information.

Conservation, Food & Health Foundation (MA)
(http://www.grantsmanagement.com/cfhguide.html)

The primary purpose of the Massachusetts-based Conservation, Food & Health Foundation is "to assist in the conservation of natural resources, the production and distribution of food, and the improvement and promotion of health in the developing world." The Foundation is especially interested in supporting projects that lead to the transfer of responsibility to the citizens of developing countries for managing and solving their own problems and in supporting self-help initiatives. Preference is given to organizations located in developing countries or to developed country organizations whose activities are of direct and immediate benefit to developing countries. The Foundation does not consider the states of the former Soviet Union or former eastern bloc countries as within its geographic focus, however. Visitors to the Foundation's Web site will find detailed application guidelines and eligibility requirements, a recent grants list, a form for submitting a concept paper to the Foundation (in advance of a final proposal), and contact information.

Cooper Foundation (NE) (http://www.cooperfoundation.org/)

The Nebraska-based Cooper Foundation restricts it support to organizations within its home state, primarily in Lincoln and Lancaster County. The Foundation's mission is to support innovative ideas that "promise substantial impact and encourage others to make similar or larger grants." To that end, it funds programs in education, human services, the arts, and the humanities. It does not fund individuals, endowments, private foundations, businesses, health or religious issues, travel, or organizations outside of Nebraska, and most of its grants are for program funding rather than general operating support. In addition, the Foundation accepts formal applications only from organizations that have already communicated with it and that have been asked to complete an application form. Visitors to the Foundation's Web site will find a brief history of the foundation, an equally brief description of program priorities, and contact information.

The Cooper Institute for Advanced Studies in Medicine and the Humanities (FL)
(Operating foundation) (http://www.cooperinstitute.org)

The Cooper Institute for Advanced Studies in Medicine and the Humanities, based in Naples, Florida, is a nonprofit educational foundation established in 1974 by Irving S. Cooper, who was an internationally renowned neurosurgeon, teacher, and author. The Institute is focused on the interests and well-being of health care consumers and is dedicated to bringing "clarity to the increasingly complex health care environment by organizing health care information in a manner that provides consumers with the tools to make informed decisions," thereby preparing and empowering patients for their "enhanced role as more active and assertive partners in the management of their health care." The Institute's view is that patient education will create choice and also encourage patient input in the debate over medical quality improvement. Visitors to the Web site will find information about the institute and its founder, links to databases of physician profiles, links to sites about health care policy, a survey, in-depth interviews with authorities in health care, and contact information.

The Aaron Copland Fund for Music, Inc. (NY) (http://www.amc.net/resources/grants)

The Aaron Copland Fund for Music, Inc. is one of the grant programs administered by The American Music Center (AMC), based in New York City. Aaron Copland was one of the founders of AMC in 1939, whose original mission was "foster and encourage the composition of contemporary (American) music and to promote its production, publication, distribution and performance in every way possible throughout the Western Hemisphere," and whose mission now is "building a national community for new American music." There are two programs under The Aaron Copland Fund for Music, the Performing Ensembles Program and the Recording Program. The objective of the Performing Ensembles Program is to support organizations whose performances encourage and improve public knowledge and appreciation of serious contemporary music, with grants ranging from $1,000 to $20,000. The objectives of the Recording Program are to document and provide wider exposure for the music of contemporary American composers, to develop audiences for contemporary American music through record distribution and other retail markets, and to support the release and dissemination of recordings for previously unreleased contemporary American music and the reissuance of recordings no longer available. Grants range from $2,000 to $20,000. Visitors to the Web site will find eligibility criteria, funding provisions, review procedures, application instructions, downloadable brochures and applications, and contact information for these two programs. Visitors will also find links to other grant programs administered by AMC and information about AMC.

Corman Foundation, Inc. (AL) (http://www.touch1.com)

The Corman Foundation of Atmore, Alabama, was created in 1989 by Jim and Jane Corman, the founders of the Touch 1 telecommunications company. The Foundation's goal is "to glorify God and make Christ known through effective stewardship of the resources entrusted to [the Foundation.]" The organization supports evangelical Christian groups with money, time, oversight, prayers, and encouragement. Grants are given to help efforts directly "aimed at securing the salvation of individuals, and providing for the discipleship and training of God's people for Christian witness." Groups that primarily address physical needs may apply if they have a strong secondary component that meets the description above. The site includes basic application guidelines and an outline of the application process. There is a list of helpful FAQs and a list of previous grant recipients.

S.H. Cowell Foundation (CA) (http://www.shcowell.org/)

The S.H. Cowell Foundation of San Francisco, California, was established in 1956. The organization "addresses the underlying causes of poverty and social problems, promotes neighborhood/civic participation and builds sustainable local resources in northern California." The grant program has four primary areas of interest: access to affordable housing, the abilities of families to care for and nurture their children, public school students' learning and parent involvement teacher support, and helping youth to make healthy and successful life choices. The Foundation also provides emergency funds and supports building efforts. Visitors to the site will find program guidelines and restrictions, a description of the application process, and lists of the staff and the board of directors.

Jessie B. Cox Charitable Trust (PA) (http://www.agmconnect.org/cox.html)

Jessie B. Cox, noted for her philanthropy, established the Jessie B. Cox Charitable Trust to continue that tradition following her death in 1982. The Boston, Massachusetts-based Trust funds projects in New England in the areas of health, education, environment, and philanthropy, with a particular interest in projects that will primarily benefit underserved populations and disadvantaged communities as well as projects that focus on prevention rather than remediation. It also has an interest in fostering collaboration among nonprofit organizations in New England and welcomes collaborative concept papers. Its goals are to improve the level of health; enhance educational opportunities and achievement, especially for underserved children and youth; protect and enhance the natural and urban environment and to conserve New England's natural resources; and to increase philanthropy in the area. Its Web site provides grant guideline policies and exclusions; application procedures; annual reports; grant lists; and contact information.

Crail-Johnson Foundation (CA) (http://www.crail-johnson.org/)

The Crail-Johnson Foundation of San Pedro, California, seeks to "promote the well being of children in need, through the effective application of human and financial resources." Priority is given to organizations and projects of benefit to residents of the greater Los Angeles area. In addition to awarding cash grants, the Foundation also provides technical assistance to select community-based projects benefiting children and families. No grants are made directly to individuals or for programs and projects benefiting religious purposes, university-level graduate and post-graduate education, research, cultural programs, sporting events, political causes, or programs attempting to influence legislation. Current areas of emphasis are health and human services, education programs, and neighborhood and community. Visitors to the CJF Web site can access the Foundation's annual report, which provides detailed grant application guidelines and limitations; a financial statement; information on selected grants; and a listing of officers and staff. The Web site also provides links to other grantmakers online, detailed descriptions of special Foundation projects, and contact information, including e-mail links to staff members.

Crotched Mountain Foundation (NH) (http://www.cmf.org/)

The Crotched Mountain Foundation is an umbrella organization comprised of the Crotched Mountain School and Rehabilitation Center and the Crotched Mountain Community Based Services, which extends throughout New Hampshire and into Maine and New York. Founded by businessman and philanthropist Harry Alan Gregg, the foundation traces its origins back to the New Hampshire Society for Crippled Children, established in 1936. Its mission is to "promote, encourage, and sponsor charitable health, rehabilitative, and educational services on behalf of children, adults, and elderly persons." The foundation "enables and empowers persons with physical, developmental, emotional or other health-related considerations to pursue their highest degree of physical, emotional, and social independence as may be individually possible." Based in Greenfield, New Hampshire, the Foundation's Web site contains its history, its programs for the disabled and elderly, a search engine for the Web site, links, and contact information.

Nathan Cummings Foundation, Inc. (NY) (http://www.ncf.org/)

Established by noted philanthropist and founder of the Sara Lee Corporation, Nathan Cummings, the Nathan Cummings Foundation is "rooted in the Jewish tradition and committed to democratic values, including fairness, diversity, and community. [The Foundation seeks] to build a society that values nature and protects ecological balance for future generations; promotes humane health care; and fosters arts to enrich communities." To that end, the Foundation focuses its grantmaking activities in five program areas: arts, environment, health, Jewish life, and "interprogram," which reinforces connections among the Foundation's core areas. Visitors to the Foundation's Web site will find detailed guidelines, grant lists for each program area, links to grantee Web sites, application procedures, staff and trustee listings, and various reports and publications, including the Foundation's most recent annual report.

Charles A. Dana Foundation, Inc. (NY) (http://www.dana.org/)

The Charles A. Dana Foundation is a private philanthropic foundation with principle interests in brain research and public education initiatives. The Foundation's Web site includes a statement of the Foundation's grantmaking policies and procedures; detailed application and program information, including recent major grants; information about the Charles A. Dana Awards, which honor innovators in neuroscience and education reform; the Dana Alliance for Brain initiatives, a nonprofit dedicated to educating the public about the benefits of brain research; a publications archive (including the Foundation's recent annual reports); Dana BrainWeb (annotated links to Web sites devoted to specific brain disorders, general health, and neuroscience); a listing of the Foundation's directors, officers, and staff; and press and contact information.

Lucy Daniels Foundation (PA) (http://www.ldf.org/)

Lucy Daniels is a writer and psychologist who says "Psychoanalysis saved my writing and my life." For this reason, Daniels established her Foundation in 1989; its goal is to support selected patients receiving psychoanalytic treatment. Daniels also heads the Lucy Daniels Center for Early Childhood, which applies psychoanalytic understanding to early childhood education. The Foundation provides psychoanalytic treatment, research, education, and outreach in conjunction with the Center. The Foundation is especially interested, however, in the treatment and research into the psychoanalysis of creative people; this project comprises the Foundation's central work. Although there is no specific information related to grants on the Foundation's Web site, there is an overview of the Foundation's programs and events as well as resource links and contact information.

The Davidson Foundation (NV) (http://www.davidsonfoundation.org/)

Located in Incline Village, Nevada, the Davidson Foundation was founded in 1997 by Bob and Jan Davidson and their children, Liz, Emilie, and John. Its mission is to "advance learning, enhance human potential and empower people to live lives of achievement and service," with a focus on supporting exceptionally gifted young people. To that end, one of their programs is the Davidson Young Scholars Pilot Program, whose mission is to "recognize, nurture and support the special needs of exceptionally gifted children." The program was launched in the spring of 1999 and provides a variety of resources, such as needs-assessment, personal planning, funding, mentoring, and fellowship to children between the ages of 4 and 12. The Foundation states that it is proactive in its grantmaking, and that the Foundation seeks out and investigates grantmaking opportunities with nonprofit organizations whose work supports their mission. It does not accept unsolicited grant proposals. Consult the Web site to learn more about the foundation, its focus on exceptionally gifted children, the Davidson Young Scholars Pilot Program, application procedures, information on exceptionally gifted children, annual report, grant list, and contact information.

Arthur Vining Davis Foundations (FL) (http://www.jvm.com/davis/)

The Arthur Davis Vining Foundations provide support nationally for five primary program areas: private higher education, secondary education, religion (graduate theological education), health care (caring attitudes), and public television. The Foundations do not make grants to individuals; institutions or programs outside the United States and its possessions; publicly governed colleges, universities, and other entities that are supported primarily by government funds (except in health care and secondary education programs); or projects incurring obligations extending over several years. Visitors to the Foundations' Web site will find descriptions of each program area, a recent grants list organized by program area, application procedures, a brief FAQ, and contact information.

Dr. G. Clifford & Florence B. Decker Foundation (NY)
(http://www.pronetisp.net/~deckerfn/index.html)

Dr. G. Clifford Decker established the Decker Foundation in 1979 with his wife, Florence, to assist charitable organizations servicing the residents of Broome County, New York. Located in Binghampton, New York, the Foundation focuses grantmaking on education, medical and medical research institutions, and cultural and human service organizations. Grants may be used for capital projects or new and innovative projects and programs. In general, it does not provide continuing or regular operating support, as its efforts are "directed toward helping organizations provide programs to earn income and thus become self-sufficient." Grant applications can be requested by phone, mail, or e-mail. "Interest in the Decker Foundation is welcome." Visitors to the Web site will find grant application guidelines, the Deckers' and Foundation's history, annual reports, a list of its board of directors, links to institutions that have received Decker Foundation grants, and contact information.

The Dekko Foundation, Inc. (IN) (http://www.dekkofoundation.org)

Chester E. Dekko created the Dekko Foundation in 1981 as a way to give back to the communities that had bred his success. He learned that education, hard work, and leadership could provide economic freedom for any individual that desired it; accordingly, the mission of his foundation is to "foster economic freedom through education." The Foundation's two broad program areas are education and community, with a geographic focus on communities in which Group Dekko International had plants or where Mr. Dekko had a presence prior to his death in 1992. Grant proposals are considered from counties in Indiana, Iowa and Alabama. Based in Kendallville, Indiana, its educational priorities are public and private schools and early childhood education; its community priorities are community foundations, libraries, museums, parks, festivals, summer camps, youth organizations, and organizations for the needy and disabled. In addition to these funding areas, Dekko Foundation also has four proactive programs in supporting education and community: Einstein Grants, for ideas that will stimulate excitement for education; Youth Initiative, to empower young people to serve their community and school through grantmaking; Early Education Programs, which develops partnerships with early childhood programs; and the Dekko Award for Teaching Excellence. Visitors to the Web site will find further information on the funding areas, proactive programs, geographic focus, grant guidelines and application instructions, the history of the foundation and its founder, and contact information.

The Barbara Delano Foundation, Inc. (CA) (http://www.bdfoundation.org)

The Barbara Delano Foundation (BDF) is a San Francisco-based foundation devoted to the protection of wildlife and its habitats and improving humankind's treatment of animals. The Foundation was established in 1985 by Barbara Delano Gauntlett, granddaughter of Dr. William E. Upjohn, founder of the Upjohn Company, as an expression of her life-long commitment to conservation and the survival of local people and communities. The Foundation currently considers applications for the support of the conservation and habitat protection of the following animals: large cats, great apes, rhinos, bears, elephants, marine mammals, sharks, and marine turtles. BDF also works for the humane treatment of domesticated animals. BDF seeks to assist grantees in obtaining further funding and with objective advice on campaigning and project management and offers to assist other foundations and private individuals in selecting international conservation programs to support. BDF offers monitoring and on-site visit reports to donors without administrative charge. The site contains proposal guidelines, grant recipient list and links to projects supported by the Foundation, and contact information.

Gladys Krieble Delmas Foundation (NY) (http://www.delmas.org/)

The Gladys Krieble Delmas Foundation promotes "the advancement and perpetuation of humanistic inquiry and artistic creativity by encouraging excellence in scholarship and in the performing arts, and by supporting research libraries and other institutions that preserve the resources which transmit this cultural heritage." The Foundation sponsors four distinct grantmaking programs: in the humanities, in the performing arts, for research libraries, and for Venetian research. Foundation trustees may also award discretionary grants outside of these specific programs. Visitors to the Foundation's Web site will find descriptions and recent grants lists for each program area, a list of grants for Independent Research in Venice and the Veneto, application procedures and eligibility requirements, and a listing of the Foundation's trustees, staff, and advisory board members.

The Rene & Veronica di Rosa Foundation (CA) (Operating foundation) (http://www.dirosapreserve.org)

The Rene & Veronica di Rosa Foundation operates the di Rosa Preserve, the vision of two devoted patrons of the arts, Rene and Veronica di Rosa. The Preserve is the public exhibition space for the di Rosa art collection, which consists of art produced in the greater San Francisco Bay Area during the latter part of the 20th Century. Visitors to the site can view a selection of images from over 1,600 works of art in the di Rosa Preserve online. The site also contains a short biography of the founders, contact information, and links related to art and the Napa, California, area where the Preserve is located.

William Orr Dingwall Foundation (CA) (http://www.wod.org/index.html)

Established in 1994 by Dr. William Orr Dingwall, the San Francisoco-based Dingwall Foundation has two primary goals: to provide financial assistance to persons of Korean ancestry to pursue undergraduate or graduate studies devoted to any subject offered by well-established universities throughout the world and to provide financial assistance to persons of any national origin to pursue graduate studies devoted to the neural bases of language. Every year the Foundation distributes one or more grants of up to $18,000 per year to students who meet its goals. The normal duration of the grant is three years but may be extended for up to one additional year. The Foundation's Web site provides a brief description of its one program and an electronic application form, in both English and Korean.

DJ & T Foundation (CA) (http://www.djtfoundation.org)

Television personality Bob Barker, of *Price is Right* fame, established the Beverly Hills, California-based DJ & T Foundation in 1995, which was named in memory of his wife, Dorothy Jo, and his mother, Matilda (Tilly) Valandra, who both loved all animals. Its goal is to help relieve animal overpopulation by funding low cost or free spay/neuter clinics all over the United States. The Foundation assists all qualified spay/neuter clinics, but it is most committed to making grants at the grassroots level to under-funded clinics that provide free or low cost spay/neuter services. Grants are only awarded to organizations operating a stationary and/or mobile clinic or who are in the process of creating one. Grant seekers can download an application or request one in writing after checking out grant guidelines and the FAQ sheet on their Web site.

Geraldine R. Dodge Foundation, Inc. (NJ) (http://www.grdodge.org/)

The Geraldine R. Dodge Foundation makes grants in five major areas: 1) elementary and secondary education; 2) arts, with a primary focus on New Jersey and on programs that seek to establish and improve education in the arts, foster conditions that promote public access to the arts, recognize the critical role of the individual artist, enable developing institutions to gain stability, and help major institutions realize long-term goals; 3) welfare of animals, especially projects with national implications that encourage a more humane ethic and lower the violence in the way we treat animals; 4) public issues, with a particular interest in New Jersey and the Northeast and focusing on ecosystems preservation, energy conservation, pollution prevention and reduction, education and communication efforts that lead to enlightened environmental policy, and projects that address population growth and family planning; and 5) local projects in Morris County, New Jersey. The Foundation's elegant Web site (frames-enabled browsers a must) provides concise program descriptions, application guidelines, a brief history of the Foundation, and contact information.

The Patrick and Catherine Weldon Donaghue Medical Research Foundation (CT) (http://www.donaghue.org)

The Patrick and Catherine Weldon Donaghue Medical Research Foundation, based in West Hartford, Connecticut, was created in the will of Ethel Frances Donaghue in memory of her parents. One of three trusts provided for in her will when she died in 1989 at the age of 93, the Medical Research Foundation was funded in May 1991 with over $50 million, the bulk of the proceeds of two generations' successful family endeavors in Hartford commerce and investment. One of Connecticut's first woman lawyers, she dedicated her substantial fortune to providing " financial assistance for research in the fields of cancer and heart disease and/or other medical research to promote medical knowledge which will be of practical benefit to the preservation, maintenance and improvement of human life." The Medical Research Foundation began in 1991 with three grant programs that focused on postdoctoral fellows and new investigators doing basic and pre-clinical research in cancer and heart disease and has since expanded to include research in community health, epidemiology and health services. The Foundation also "invites grant applications from investigators in mental health and neurodegenerative illnesses." There are currently three types of grant awards: Research in Clinical and Community Health Issues, Donaghue Investigator Program, and the Practical Benefits Initiatives. The Foundation focuses funding of research to health-related institutions and organizations located in Connecticut. Visitors to its Web site will find downloadable applications; information on its funding areas, grant award types, and grant guidelines and instructions; the founder's and the foundation's history; highlights of grantmaking and financial information; advisory board members; a downloadable newsletter, FAQs, and contact information.

William H. Donner Foundation, Inc. (NY) (http://www.donner.org/)

The William H. Donner Foundation, a small, family foundation based in New York City, was created in 1961 with the endowment originally established by Mr. Donner for the International Cancer Research Foundation, which he founded in 1932 to honor his son's memory after his death from cancer. In January 1999, the foundation adopted a policy that it would no longer accept unsolicited proposals; only applications invited by the Foundation are considered. In its grantmaking, the Foundation follows two philanthropic principals of its founder: "acceptance of clearly defined risks and the judicious use of incentive grants to advance thoughtful, creative projects." The Foundation's Web site contains a biography of its founder, a statement of its grantmaking policy, a listing of Foundation officers and staff, and contact information. A link to application forms is provided but requires a password for entry.

Dorot Foundation (RI) (http://www.dorot.org/)

Based in Providence, Rhode Island, the Dorot Foundation is a charitable family foundation with a strong tradition of commitment to Israel, the Jewish community in North America, and nurturing the relationship between them both. The Foundation sponsors the Dorot Fellowship in Israel, created to help build a knowledgeable and impassioned lay leadership for the Jewish community. Open to young Jewish persons in their 20s and 30s, it is a full-year fellowship made up of two major components: part-time Jewish studies and a part-time internship in the fellow's field of interest. Additionally, fellows must begin their year with the study of Hebrew at a summer Ulpan, share apartments with Israelis, and take part in Israeli life to the fullest extent possible. The Fellowship seeks to provide fellows with opportunities for development in the following areas: Hebrew competence, personal contact with Israelis and other future lay leaders, knowledge of Israeli society and institutions, Jewish studies, leadership skills, and understanding of issues vital to the Jewish community in Israel, North America, and throughout the world. Visitors to the site will find Fellowship information and application instructions, a downloadable application, and contact information for the Dorot Foundation, Ulpan, and other educational programs in Israel.

Do Right Foundation (CA) (http://www.doright.org/)

The broadly stated mission of the Do Right Foundation is to "address some of the current obstacles to a more joyful and rewarding society," and the Foundation's Web site is devoted to explaining this philosophy as it relates to the grantseeking process. The Foundation gives priority to grantseekers who focus on the application of new and improved management theories. Visitors to the site will find a biography of Dr. W. Edwards Deming, upon whose management concepts the Foundation's philosophies are based. Grants lists, a downloadable application, and contact information are also available. Prospects are encouraged to submit a pre-grant inquiry by e-mail before applying formally.

Gaylord and Dorothy Donnelley Foundation (IL) (http://www.gddf.org)

The Chicago, Illinois-based Gaylord and Dorothy Donnelley Foundation works to "fund efforts to promote healthy human communities and natural environments in the Chicago region and Lowcountry of South Carolina." The grant program awards funding to organizations working in the following categories: the environment and conservation, education, the arts and culture, and community welfare. While the Foundation prefers requests for specific projects, those for general operating support are accepted. The Foundation application can be downloaded in PDF format and includes guidelines and deadlines. The Foundation's Web site includes lists of board and staff members and lists of past grantees, grouped by the year that the grant was awarded. The Foundation is particularly interested in collaborative projects.

J.C. Downing Foundation (CA) (http://www.jcdowning.org/)

The San Diego-based J.C. Downing Foundation supports innovative efforts and original projects in five program areas: science and technology, sports and athletics, education and child development, wildlife research and preservation, and environmental research and economics. The Foundation awards grants to qualified nonprofit organizations with explicit, identifiable needs and does not place geographic or dollar restrictions on its grants (although the typical award falls between $5,000 and $50,000). The Foundation's Web site provides grantmaking guidelines and areas of exclusion, application procedures, a list of selected grants the Foundation has made since 1990, and a Resource section, which includes information about the grantseeeking process, a recommended reading list, and links to Web sites of interest.

Drachen Foundation (WA) (Operating foundation) (http://www.drachen.org/)

The Drachen Foundation is a nonprofit educational corporation founded in Seattle, Washington, in 1994 for the purpose of facilitating educational projects concerning historical, cultural, and artistic areas of kiting. Primary focus includes: artist-in residence programs, historical and cultural research, and educational publications. Projects are brought forth by the board of directors and advisory board for review, and awards are given based on the value and merit of the project. The Drachen Foundation does not solicit funding requests. Special attention is given to projects that demonstrate both the need that they propose to fill and their ability to fill it and that address one or more of the following criteria: support of educational workshops and lectures for the public through artist-in-residence programs and travel stipends; Support of research efforts in the area of cultural ties between kites and international histories; Support of educational exhibits with kites as the subject; Support of leading kite artisans through travel stipends, workshop/lecture opportunities, gallery exhibits, and traveling exhibitions; Preservation of artifacts unique to kiting history; Research and publication efforts with kites as the subject. All projects that the Foundation participates in must be educational in nature and benefit both the public at large and individuals already interested in kiting. The Foundation's well-designed Web site includes a brief history of kiting, board/staff listing, links to affiliates, and contact information.

Camille and Henry Dreyfus Foundation, Inc. (NY) (http://www.dreyfus.org/)

The principal aim of the Camille and Henry Dreyfus Foundation is to "advance the science of chemistry, chemical engineering and related sciences as a means of improving human relations and circumstances around the world." To that end, the Foundation makes grant awards to academic and other eligible institutions for the purposes of sponsoring qualified applicants in their education and research. The Foundation's Web site provides detailed descriptions of the Foundation's various programs, including eligibility requirements and application and nomination procedures and a listing of recent grantees. As an added convenience, requests for nomination forms can be submitted through the Foundation's Web site.

Joseph Drown Foundation (CA) (http://www.jdrown.org)

Joseph Warford Drown was involved with the hotel industry, notably as owner of Hotel Bel-Air in Los Angeles. He formed the Los Angeles, California-based Joseph Drown Foundation in 1953 to provide an organized means of charitable giving, both during his lifetime and after his death in 1982. The goal of his foundation is to assist individuals to becoming successful, self- sustaining, contributing citizens, and the foundation is interested in programs that break down barriers that prevent growth and learning. The Foundation has five main funding areas: education, community, health and social services, arts and humanities, medical and scientific research, and special projects, which are at the discretion of the board but still related to the mission of the foundation. Programs in the area of medical and scientific research are initiated by the Foundation; arts and humanities programs are a lesser priority and concentrate on outreach and education. Most of its grantmaking is limited to programs and organizations in California. Consult the Foundation's Web site for more information about each funding area, the grant application procedure, a list of sample grants, contact information, and related links.

The Peter F. Drucker Foundation for Nonprofit Management, Inc. (NY) (Operating foundation) (http://www.pfdf.org/)

Frances Hesselbein founded the Peter F. Drucker Foundation for Nonprofit Management in 1990, named for and inspired by the "acknowledged father of modern management." The mission of the New York City-based foundation is "to lead social sector organizations toward excellence in performance," through the presentation of conferences, the annual Peter F. Drucker Award for Nonprofit Innovation, the Frances Hesselbein Community Innovation Fellows Program, and the development of management resources, partnerships, and publications. The Foundation considers itself "a broker of intellectual capital, bringing together the finest leaders, consultants, authors and social philosophers in the world with the leaders of social sector voluntary organizations." The Peter F. Drucker Award for Nonprofit Innovation is given to a nonprofit organization in recognition of an innovative program and is accompanied by a $25,000 prize and a professionally-produced short video documentary of the winning project or program. The Frances Hesselbein Community Innovation Fellows Program recognizes the accomplishments and supports the professional development of social sector leaders who have a demonstrated record of leadership and entrepreneurial performance and who are engaged in projects or programs that demonstrate community innovation. Visitors to the Foundation's Web site will find guidelines and instructions for these two programs; downloadable applications, conference reports, quarterly newsletters and annual reports; schedules and printable registration forms to its events; an online feedback and information request form; descriptions of the Foundation's leadership publications, reader's guides, and links to order its publications; and contact information. The Foundation makes clear that it only provides programs and resources, does not make grants, and can not accept funding proposals.

The Dudley Foundation (WA) (http://www.dudleyfoundation.org)

Based in Bellingham, Washington, the primary goal of the Dudley Foundation is "to help alleviate unnecessary present and future suffering of all sentient beings by attempting to address its environmental and social roots." The Foundation's focus is on "over (human) population, intolerance, wanton consumption of resources (greed), and ecological destruction." The site contains application instructions and criteria, a printable cover page, a description of the evaluation procedure, a list of organizations funded, biographies of staff who evaluate proposals, and contact information.

Doris Duke Charitable Foundation (NY) (http://fdncenter.org/grantmaker/dorisduke/)

The New York-based Doris Duke Charitable Foundation was created in 1996, in accordance with the terms of the will of Doris Duke, to improve the quality of people's lives by preserving natural environments, seeking cures for diseases, and nurturing the arts. The Foundation currently pursues its mission through three grantmaking programs supporting performing artists in the creation and public performance of their work, the protection and restoration of the environment and promotion of the sustainable use of land and other natural resources, and medical research leading to the prevention and cure of heart disease, cancer, AIDS, and sickle cell anemia and other blood disorders. The Foundation's Web site—a folder on the Center's site—describes these programs in detail and provides guidelines to the grantmaking process. Visitors to the site will also find grants lists for the last three years, information about the Foundation's three non-grantmaking operating foundations, and a listing of trustees and staff.

The Duke Endowment (NC) (http://www.dukeendowment.org/)

The Duke Endowment, a charitable trust established in 1924 by North Carolina industrialist James Buchanan Duke, continues its founder's philanthropic legacy of giving to "educate students and teachers, to heal minds and bodies, to nurture children, and to strengthen the human spirit." As a trust, the Duke Endowment differs from a private foundation in that its principle donor named specific organizations or individuals eligible to receive funding. In the case of the Endowment, these are not-for-profit health care organizations in North and South Carolina; not-for-profit child care institutions in North and South Carolina; rural United Methodist churches and retired ministers in North Carolina; Duke, Furman, and

Johnson C. Smith universities, and Davidson College. Program areas are education, health care, childcare, and rural churches. The Endowment's Web site provides general program descriptions and application procedures, a grants list organized by area of interest, links to resources and grantee organizations, a searchable online catalog of library materials (the Endowment's library houses a Foundation Center Cooperating Collection), financial statements, a listing of Endowment trustees and staff, and contact information.

Jessie Ball duPont Fund (FL) (http://www.dupontfund.org/)

The Jessie Ball duPont Fund, a national foundation having a special, though not exclusive, interest in issues affecting the South, makes grants "to a defined universe of eligible institutions"—that is, any institution that received a contribution from Mrs. duPont between January 1, 1960 and December 31, 1964 (approximately 350 in total). Proof of eligibility is determined by the Fund from examination of Mrs. duPont's personal or tax records or by the applicant presenting written, verifiable evidence of having received a contribution during the eligibility period. The Fund's mission, "to address broad-based issues of communities and of the larger society that have regional, national, and international relevance," is achieved through programs in arts and culture, education, health, historic preservation, human services, and religion. Visitors to the Fund's Web site will find detailed program information and eligibility guidelines, a statement of the Fund's mission and core values, a biography of Mrs. DuPont, and contact information. The Fund also plans to post to its Web site excerpts from *Notes from the Field,* its publication devoted to philanthropic "best practices," in the following areas: access to health care, affordable housing for low-income families, inclusiveness in institutions of higher education, taking action and seeking justice, and creating healthy outcomes for children.

Durfee Foundation (CA) (http://www.durfee.org/)

Named in honor of the late Dorothy Durfee Avery who, with her husband, the late R. Stanton Avery, founded the Avery Dennison Corporation, a multinational manufacturing concern, the Durfee Foundation has awarded more than $13 million in grants since 1960 in the areas of arts and culture, education, history, and community development, primarily in Southern California. Programs currently supported by the Foundation include the American/Chinese Adventure Capital Program, the Durfee Community Fund, the Durfee Sabbatical Program, Student Challenge Awards, the Student Service and Philanthropy Project, and Durfee Artist and Music Fellowships. Although as a rule the Foundation does not review unsolicited proposals, one-page letters of introduction are welcome. Visitors to the Foundation's Web site will find program descriptions and criteria, project proposal guidelines, financial statements and a summary of grants from the Foundation's most recent annual report, a listing of the Foundation's trustees, and contact information.

The Dyson Foundation (NY) (http://www.dysonfoundation.org)

The New York-based, Dyson Foundation was established in 1957 supporting innovative programs and compelling causes. The Foundation focuses much of its grantmaking on child welfare; however, it also makes grants for specified areas in New York. The Dyson Initiative provides training services to pediatric professionals to help better serve their patients within the community. The Foundation also makes less specific grants to the Mid-Hudson Valley area, in the areas of social services, education, health, community development, and arts and cultural programs. The Foundation's Web site include recent grants, explicit application information, staff/board lists, financial data, and contact information.

The Eagle Sky Foundation, Inc. (CO) (Operating foundation)
(http://members.aol.com/_ht_a/eagleskyf/myhomepage/index.html)

The Eagle Sky Foundation (ESF) is a not-for-profit Foundation established "to create and build very high quality Christian Challenge Camp and Conference Centers in some of the most scenic areas of America, such as the Heart of the Rockies and the Ozarks." ESF is a non-denominational Christian foundation whose mission is to encourage Christians in their spiritual growth and development, which the Foundation believes is "more easily accomplished in certain environments, such as the Rocky Mountains and the Ozarks." Eagle Sky Christian Challenge Camp and Conference Center will be open to all Christians, Churches, and Denominations. The Eagle Sky of the Rockies' Ranch is located in the northern third of the Tennessee Park Valley in Lake County, Colorado.

echoing green foundation (NY) (http://echinggreen.org)

The New York City-based echoing green foundation was founded by venture capitalist Ed Cohen, who along with a group of investors created an organization that "applies venture capitalist principles to a social change sphere." echoing green, named after one of the poems of Eighteenth Century poet and artist William Blake, is a nonprofit foundation that offers full-time fellowships to emerging "social entrepreneurs" and applies a venture capital approach to philanthropy by providing seed money and technical support to individuals creating innovative public service organizations or projects with goals of positive social change. Investing in organizations and projects at an early stage where most funders are unwilling to do so, echoing green also provides them with support to help them grow beyond a start-up. The fellowship includes a two-year $60,000 stipend, health care benefits, online connectivity, access to echoing green's network of social entrepreneurs, training, and technical assistance. Proposed organizations and projects can be domestic or international and in all public service areas including, but not limited to, the environment, arts, education, youth service, civil and human rights, and community and economic development. Consult the echoing green Web site for information about the foundation and how to become a fellow, news and events related to the foundation, a resource center covering topics from organizational development to attracting resources to people development and for related links, a public forum for dialogue about fellows and projects, a database of profiles of fellows, and contact information.

Edah, Inc. (NY) (Operating foundation) (http://www.edah.org)

The mission of Edah, Inc. is to "give voice to the ideology and values of modern Orthodoxy and to educate and empower the community to address its concerns." The Edah, Inc. site is not yet live, but those interested can sign up to receive an e-mail when the site goes live. In addition, there is an advertisement for an upcoming conference titled "Modern Orthodoxy Begins in the Classroom." The program description and a registration form are available online.

The Educational Foundation for America (CT) (http://www.efaw.org/)

The Westport, Connecticut-based, Education Foundation for America was established in 1959 by Richard Prentice Ettinger and his wife, Elsie P. Ettinger. Mr. Ettinger was one of the founders of Prentice Hall Publishing. The Foundation is based on four principles that Mr. Ettinger felt were the most important to philanthropy: take risks; think globally, focus grants sharply; make grants short-term; and know how and where the money will be used. Areas of interest include, but are not limited to, the environment, energy, the crisis of human overpopulation and reproductive freedom, Native Americans, the arts, education, medicine, and social services. Visitors to the site will find some background information on the founders, letter of inquiry submission guidelines, deadlines, grant lists by area, board and staff listings, and contact information.

O.P. and W.E. Edwards Foundation, Inc. (NY) (http://fdncenter.org/grantmaker/edwards)

The O.P. and W.E. Edwards Foundation is located in the heart of New York City, Grants from the General Fund are made in two categories: annual support grants and trustee-directed grants to organizations serving children and their families who are severely disadvantaged economically. Grants from the W.E. Edwards Fund are distributed to organizations designated in the donor's will. The Arts and Astronomy Funds are donor-directed funds. The Foundation also makes investments in organizations committed to economic development, including community development banks and loans for low-income housing. The very simple Web site does offer an extensive list of previous grant recipients. The small, unstaffed Foundation does not accept unsolicited proposals.

EGBAR Foundation (CA) (http://www.egbar.org)

Located in Huntington Beach, California, the EGBAR Foundation was established in 1989 by Sunshine Makers, Inc., the manufacturers of Simple Green, an all-purpose cleaner. The Foundation's mission is to "assist individuals, as well as groups, in their efforts to improve the quality of our environment." More specific goals include educating children internationally on recycling and being environmentally conscious and addressing community clean-up needs. One primary way that the Foundation addresses these goals is through the EGBAR Environmental Curriculum. This collection of lessons and projects, many working in conjunction with newspapers, enhances science classes for fourth through ninth graders and is available online in PDF format. Participants in the curriculum are encouraged to take part in the annual EGBAR Clean-up Challenge and to submit essays to the EGBAR Environmental Essay Contest. The Foundation also distributes over 400,000 Family Environmental Surveys and then posts the results and analysis on the site. Visitors to the site can take the survey online. The extensive and attractive site includes related games and activities, an impressive set of links, and information on selected staff and board members.

El Pomar Foundation (CO) (http://www.elpomar.org/)

Founded in 1937 by copper mining magnate Spencer Penrose, El Pomar Foundation today has assets in excess of $475 million, making it one of the largest and oldest foundations in the Rocky Mountain West. The Foundation makes grants throughout the state of Colorado in the areas of human services, community development, the arts, health care, amateur athletics, and education. In addition to grant application guidelines and summary financial information for the latest year, visitors to the Foundation's Web site will find general information about the Foundation and its many operating programs: Fellowship in Community Service, a program designed to develop future leaders among recent college graduates; El Pomar Youth in Community Service (EPYCS); El Pomar Awards for Excellence, which reward outstanding nonprofit organizations in Colorado; the Foundation's Education Initiative; and El Pomar Center, which is dedicated to the recognition and promotion of excellence within the nonprofit community.

The Ellison Medical Foundation (MD) (http://www.ellison-med-fn.org/)

Headquartered in Bethesda, Maryland, the Ellison Medical Foundation funds basic biomedical research in multiple disciplines related to gerontology, the science of aging, through four programs. The New Scholars in Aging accepts applications by invitation only. The Senior Scholar Program, given to an established investigator, requires a letter of intent and cover page. There are listings of previous awardees of the Conferences and Workshops Program and the Infrastructure Award Program on the Foundation's Web site. Details of restrictions, deadlines and terms of funding through these four programs, as well as contact information and a general discussion of current research in gerontology are also available on the Foundation's Web site.

Energy Foundation (CA) (http://www.energyfoundation.org/)

Created in 1991 under the auspices of the MacArthur Foundation, The Pew Charitable Trusts, and the Rockefeller Foundation, the mission of the Energy Foundation is "to assist in the nation's transition to a sustainable energy future by promoting energy efficiency and renewable energy." Visitors to the Foundation's Web site will find program descriptions, application guidelines, lists of recent grant recipients, and downloadable application forms for each of the Foundation's seven program areas: utilities, buildings, transportation, renewable energy, integrated issues, U.S. Clean Energy Program, and The China Sustainable Energy Program. Also available online are essays devoted to the realities surrounding the Foundation's mission, a section for special Foundation reports, and a list of annotated links to energy-related Web sites.

Engineering Information Foundation (NY) (http://www.eifgrants.org)

The Engineering Information Foundation began its long philanthropical history as a public foundation indexing and abstracting engineering and technical literature in 1934. In 1994, EiF restructured itself as a private foundation dedicated solely to making grants to qualified not-for-profit organizations. Based in New York City, the Foundation's mission is to "[improve] worldwide engineering education and practice through information technology and the recruitment of women." To this end, the Foundation has three fields of interest: availability and use of information, women in engineering (projects directed by engineering educators), and developing countries. The EiF Web site outlines funding desires and limitations, as well as specific grant guidelines, criteria, terms and conditions. Recent grants are posted by year and program area. The Foundation's Web site also includes contact information as well as resources to facilitate communication among scholars with similar engineering interests.

Lois and Richard England Family Foundation, Inc. (DC)
(http://fdncenter.org/grantmaker/england/index.html)
Created in 1994, the Lois and Richard England Family Foundation is "committed to improving the lives of those in need in the Washington metropolitan area." Toward that end, the Foundation's grantmaking focuses on local human services, education, and arts and culture. The Foundation also supports programs to strengthen Jewish life and institutions locally, nationally, and in Israel. In addition to mission and goal statements, the Foundation's folder on the Center's Web site provides grant guidelines, an archive of grants lists, a listing of the Foundation's trustees, and contact information.

The Environmental Trust (CA) (http://www.tet.org)
Located in La Mesa, California, the Environmental Trust exists to "protect and preserve our natural resources for future generations . . . by acquiring land, establishing land banks and facilitating the monitoring and management of lands identified and set aside by individuals, agencies, and developers for protection." The Trust achieves its mission through varied means, from grants of money and land to facilitating the development of land bank systems and the management of property set aside as preserves or open space. Projects of interest focus on sensitive land planning concepts, the acquisition of natural lands and habitats for the enjoyment of Californians, and assisting every agency level in locating appropriate habitats for endangered species of plants and animals. The Web site includes information on presents and planned projects, a board lists, and means of contributing to the trust.

Esquel Group Foundation, Inc. (DC) (http://www.esquel.org)
Esquel Group Foundation, Inc. (EGF) is the United States-based member and coordinator for regional programs of the Grupo Esquel Network, a group of nonprofit, non-governmental organizations dedicated to promoting "alternative policies and programs which strengthen the role of civil society" and to promoting sustainable and equitable development in South America. The Washington, D.C.-based EGF provides a variety of services, including research; advocacy; technical cooperation and extensive advice regarding development in Latin America to non-governmental organizations, foundations, private corporations; and international development agencies working in Latin America and the Caribbean. EGF also works in collaboration with private sector entities to improve public policy for sustainable development with political, economic, social, and natural resource considerations in mind. EGF has five priority areas: legal framework for civil society; environment, especially in semi-arid and arid zones; rural development and agriculture; children and youth at risk; and "microenterprise development." Visitors to the EFG site will find reports on its work, list of publications and conferences participated in and organized by EGF, contact information for members of the EGF network, board and staff member profiles, a history of EGF, and information on its internship program.

The Fales Foundation Trust (WA) (http://fdncenter.org/grantmaker/fales/)
The Fales Foundation Trust was established in 1985 by Gilbert R. Fales, a long-time Seattle resident. The Foundation was established to provide financial support to social service agencies addressing issues of homelessness and hunger and to artistic and cultural organizations in the city of Seattle. The Foundation's funding is broken down between homeless and hungry and support for arts and culture. Visit the Foundation's folder on the Center's

Web site to find specific information on the Foundation's areas of interest, detailed Foundation policies, application procedures, and contact information.

Fassino Foundation (http://www.fassinofoundation.org/)

The Fassino Foundation supports community-based organizations in the Boston area by aiding homeless, abused, or disabled children and their families The Foundation also gives scholarships to specific area high schools. Visitors to the Fassino Foundation Web site will see grant guidelines and two applications: the application long form, for grants of $10,000–$50,000, and the application short form, for grants of $2,000 to $9,000; both are available as forms that can be e-mailed to the Foundation or printed from the Web site. Guidelines for attachments and contact information are also provided online.

Samuel S. Fels Fund (PA) (http://www.dvg.org/Fels/)

Samuel S. Fels was a Philadelphia philanthropist and civic leader who was president of Fels & Company, which manufactured Fels Naptha, a popular household soap. On December 17, 1935, the Samuel S. Fels Fund was incorporated to initiate and support projects of "a scientific, educational or charitable nature which tend to improve human daily life and to bring the average person greater health, happiness, and a fuller understanding of the meaning and purposes of life." Its mission is also to support projects "which prevent, lessen or resolve contemporary social problems." Based in Philadelphia, Pennsylvania, the foundation has four funding categories: arts and humanities, education, community programs, and health. Grants are restricted to organizations located in the city of Philadelphia or focused on local issues. An "ideal proposal to Fels is one that addresses positive social change." Grants range from $1,000 to $30,000, though larger grants are occasionally made in exceptional situations. Visitors to the Web site will find detailed grant application guidelines, a printable proposal cover sheet, recent grants list, list of trustees and staff, president's message, and contact information.

Hugh and Jane Ferguson Foundation (WA) (http://fdncenter.org/grantmaker/ferguson/)

The Hugh and Jane Ferguson Foundation, founded in 1987, is a family foundation that supports nonprofit organizations in the Pacific Northwest and Alaska. The Foundation is dedicated to the preservation and restoration of nature, including wildlife and their required habitats. It also supports the institutions that present nature and our rich cultural heritage to the public. Areas of interest to the Foundation include community-based projects working to restore habitat and wildlife by activating volunteers and local residents, collaborative and coalition projects involving a number of organizations working together to share strengths and maximize effectiveness, cultural and natural history institutions exploring the history and traditions of the greater Puget Sound area, and projects from Native American communities throughout the Northwest. Visit the Foundation's folder on the Center's Web site to view application guidelines, a listing of recent grantees, and contact information.

Fetzer Institute (MI) (Operating foundation) (http://www.fetzer.org/)

The Fetzer Institute of Kalamazoo, Michigan, was founded by John E. Fetzer, broadcasting pioneer, to support "research, education, and service programs exploring the integral relationships among body, mind, and spirit." The Institute usually does not accept unsolicited applications; instead, it works with other organizations, institutions, and individuals on various projects. A limited number of funding opportunities are available, however, in the Announcements section of the Institute's Web site. The Institute has a special interest in "how individuals and communities are influenced by the interactions among the physical, psychological, social, and spiritual dimensions of life, and how understandings in these areas can improve health, foster growth, and better the human condition." The Institute maintains funding programs in science, education for fellows and senior scholars, and emerging communities. Information on programs the Institute supports and works with, as well as scholarly public grants, are available online along with contact information.

FHL Foundation (NM) (http://www.fhlfoundation.com)

Located in Albuquerque, New Mexico, the FHL Foundation is a small, family foundation. The mission of this foundation is "providing collaborative support in the areas of discovery, education, and service, all with a focus on eliminating abusive systems which support abuse and oppression towards people and animals." The Foundation has specific guidelines and limitations for funding, which are described on its Web site. Grants are made in the general areas of education, discovery, and service, all relating to the subjects of abuse and oppression. There are three levels of grants—$1,000 and less, $1,000–$10,000, and $10,000–$25,000, and each level has different limitations, including geographic, although grants are limited in general to New Mexico and Colorado. The grant request process begins with the "first-step survey form," which is available online, as are the deadlines for grant requests and grant application guidelines.

Fields Pond Foundation, Inc. (MA) (http://www.fieldspond.org)

Created in 1993, the Fields Pond Foundation of Waltham, Massachusetts, works to "provide financial assistance to nature and land conservation organizations which are community-based and which serve to increase environmental awareness by involving local residents in conservation issues." Grants are made in four primary areas: trail making and other projects that give the public access to conservation lands, land acquisition for conservation, endowments to fund stewardship of conservation areas, and educational programs and publications. The Foundation does consider loan requests for the purpose of acquiring conservation lands and projects with a "demonstrated local impact in precollegiate education." The site offers full application guidelines and deadlines online and in PDF format. There are also lists of previous grants and links to related resources. The Foundation accepts the Common Proposal Format of the Associated Grantmakers of Massachusetts (AGM), for which there is a link on the Web site.

The Film Foundation, Inc. (NY) (http://www.cinema.ucla.edu/filmfoundation/)

Incorporated in New York City in 1990, the Film Foundation is headed by Martin Scorcese and nine other equally eminent directors. The group is "committed to fostering greater awareness of the urgent need to preserve motion picture history" and to "encouraging cooperative preservation projects between the archives and the industry and seeking to ensure that reliable preservation practices are in place for future productions." Funds are raised through national efforts and then distributed to the members' archives and affiliated organizations. The site offers a list of the board of directors, links to each member archive and affiliated organization, a list of films preserved or restored as a result of Foundation funds, and a list of the advisory council.

First Fruit Inc. (CA) (http://www.firstfruit.org)

First Fruit Inc., located in Newport Beach, California, "grants to Christian ministries in the developing world in the areas of leadership development, evangelism, and wholistic ministry." The organization does not fund individuals, nor does it consider sustained support. First Fruit's Web site provides Mandate and Trends That Guide Us sections, allowing visitors to examine the organization's guiding mission. No grant guidelines are available; instead, the organization requests that interested applicants send a two–page letter of inquiry. Information that should be included in the letter, as well as First Fruit's fax, e-mail, and mailing addresses, are provided online.

The Fitzpatrick Foundation (CA) (http://www.fitzpatrickfoundation.com/)

The Fitzpatrick Foundation of Burlingame, California, is primarily interested in supporting elementary and secondary school programs for students and educators, with a particular emphasis on programs serving economically disadvantaged youth in northern California. The Foundation supports a number of activities for students, including in-school and after-school programs that enhance academic achievement, arts education, athletics and recreation, technology skills, and leadership development. The Foundation concentrates its support on programs that support contemporary visual and performing arts, improve or save lives of domestic animals and endangered species, enhance family life and health, and foster advances in technology. The Foundation's Web site provides detailed information on the individual programs and contains grant guidelines and contact information.

Flinn Foundation (AZ) (http://www.flinn.org/)

The Phoenix-based Flinn Foundation primarily awards grants in the fields of health and health care but also sponsors a scholarship program for higher education and supports Arizona's arts organizations (by invitation only). The Foundation takes a proactive approach in its grantmaking; most grant recipients are chosen through Requests for Proposals or by invitation. The Foundation's activities are limited to the state of Arizona. In addition to brief biographies of Foundation founders Dr. Robert Flinn and his wife, Irene Pierce Flinn, visitors to the Foundation's Web site will find program descriptions, grant application procedures, a downloadable annual report, links to online resources, a publications order form, a listing of the Foundation's trustees and staff, and an online contact/grant proposal inquiry form.

The Ford Family Foundation (OR) (http://www.tfff.org/)

The Ford Family Foundation, of Eugene, Oregon, was created in 1956 to return good fortune to the community of southwest Oregon. The organization is committed to "helping individuals, through organized learning opportunities, to be contributing and successful citizens; and to supporting non-profit activities, agencies, and projects, with particular emphasis on midsize and small communities in the State of Oregon and Siskiyou County, California." Grants are made in four major categories: arts and culture, civic and community betterment, health and human services, and education. The Foundation prefers to support projects from well-established organizations that have already secured at least 50 percent of the necessary funding. Besides the grant program, the Foundation also awards scholarships. The Ford Scholars Program, the Ford Opportunity Scholarship Program for Single Parents, and the Scholarship Program for Sons and Daughters of Employees of Roseburg Forest Products Company each have their own guidelines and restrictions. Although the Foundation requires a pre-application letter for the grants program, the Web site does include application guidelines.

Ford Foundation (NY) (http://www.fordfound.org)

Founded in 1936 by Henry and Edsel Ford and operated as a local philanthropy in the state of Michigan until 1950, the Ford Foundation has since expanded to become a leading force in the world of national and international philanthropy. The Foundation's broadly stated goals are to "strengthen democratic values, reduce poverty and injustice, promote international cooperation, and advance human achievement." To realize its goals, the Foundation focuses its grantmaking in three program areas: asset building and community development; education, media, arts, and culture; and peace and social justice. The Foundation's comprehensive Web site provides visitors with grant guidelines, application procedures, a searchable grants database, worldwide contact and program information, and numerous publications to view online or order, including the Foundation's most recent annual report, its quarterly magazine, and an online form for ordering copies of print publications.

Edward E. Ford Foundation (DC) (http://www.eeford.org/)

Established by Edward E. Ford, an IBM director and independent businessman, in 1957, the Edward E. Ford Foundation is dedicated to encouraging and improving secondary education as provided by independent schools in the United States. To that end, the Foundation has awarded 1,648 grants totaling almost $52 million since its inception—the vast majority of them to National Association of Independent School (NAIS) member schools or NAIS member state and regional associations. The Foundation does not make grants to individuals. The initial step in the process of filing an application with the Foundation is to contact the Office of the Executive Director in Washington, D.C. for a preliminary telephone interview. The Foundation's Web site provides a brief history of the Foundation, proposal guidelines for schools and associations, a list of recent grants, a one-page financial statement, and contact information.

Thomas B. Fordham Foundation (DC) (http://www.edexcellence.net)

Thomas B. Fordham was a successful industrialist and prominent civic leader in Dayton, Ohio, who passed away in 1944. In 1953, his widow, Thelma Fordham Pruett, established the Thomas B. Fordham Foundation in his memory. During her lifetime, the Foundation aided diverse charitable organizations and educational institutions in the Dayton area, but upon her death in 1995, the trustees determined that reform of elementary/secondary school education would be their sole focus, as it was a long-time interest of Thelma Pruett. To that end, the Thomas B. Fordham Foundation supports research, publications, action projects of national significance in elementary/secondary education reform, and significant education reform projects in Dayton, Ohio, and vicinity. The Washington, D.C.-based foundation is proactive in approach, designing and conducting projects and seeking out partners to "further its mission of public awareness and education reform." It does not support unsolicited projects or consider unsolicited proposals. It is primarily interested in "projects leading to information that advances knowledge of effective education reform strategies consistent with the Foundation's principles." Visitors to the Web site will find further information on the Foundation's mode of operation, information on its national reform issues, links, viewable and downloadable publications and articles, ordering information, bibliographies of recommended books, and contact information.

Foundation for the Advancement of MesoAmerican Studies, Inc. (FL) (http://www.famsi.org)

Based in Crystal River, Florida, the Foundation for the Advancement of Mesoamerican Studies (FAMSI) was created in 1993 to foster increased understanding of ancient Mesoamerican cultures. The Foundation has three departments: Granting, Research, and Conference Facilities. The Granting Facility provides funds to support research projects that promise to make significant contributions to the understanding of ancient Mesoamerican cultures. The Foundation aims to assist and promote qualified scholars who might otherwise be unable to undertake or complete their programs of research and synthesis. Projects in the following disciplines are urged to apply: anthropology, archaeology, art history, epigraphy, ethnography, ethnohistory, linguistics, and related fields. Grant applications may be requested in writing or downloaded from the Web site, and visitors to the site will find grant reports, a summary of funding, and grant recipient lists. The Research Facility is composed of a Mesoamerican-oriented library, with access to the Kerr Photographic Archives, the Linda Schele Image Archives, and the John Montgomery Drawing Archive. The archives and a bibliography devoted to Mesoamerican studies can be accessed from the FAMSI Web site. The site also contains conference reports, links to Pre–Columbian sites, and contact information.

Foundation for Child Development (NY) (http://www.ffcd.org/)

The New York City-based Foundation for Child Development is dedicated to the principle that all families should have the social and material resources to raise their children to be healthy, educated, and productive members of their communities. The foundation makes grants nationally to nonprofit institutions for research, policy analysis, advocacy, leadership development, and a small number of program development projects. Three cross-cutting themes guide FCD's work: linking research on children and families for the formation of relevant programs and policies, identifying fresh approaches to crafting sound social strategies for children and families, and nurturing new generations of leaders in child development research and policy. The Foundation does not consider requests for scholarships or grants to individuals, capital campaigns, or the purchase, construction or renovation of buildings. The Foundation's Web site offers a brief history of the Foundation, its mission statement and application instructions, a searchable grants database, the FCD Working Paper Series in PDF format, listings of the Foundation's board and staff, and contact information.

Foundation for the Future (WA) (http://www.futurefoundation.org)

In 1996, Walter Kistler established Foundation for the Future, located in Bellevue, Washington. He is founder of Kistler Instruments Corporation, a world leader in the development of quartz sensors and is also the co-founder and Chairman Emeritus of Kistler Aerospace Corporation. The Foundation is focused on the long-term survivability of humanity and supports research and symposia whose purpose is to identify the most critical factors that may affect future human life on Earth. To that end, the Foundation has a research grant award program, the biannual Kistler Prize, and the Humanity 3000 symposium and seminars. The research grant award program provides financial support to scholars for research that is directly related to a better understanding of the factors affecting the quality of life for the long-term future of humanity. The Kistler Prize is awarded every other year to individuals and organizations for "outstanding achievement in identifying the genetic factors that may have a decisive impact on the survivability of a human population" and includes a $100,000 prize. The Foundation is also planning Humanity 3000, a major international symposium of "approximately 100 of the world's most prominent scholars" for discussion and debate of the factors affecting quality of human life in the future. Visit the Web site for more information about the Foundation's programs, application procedures, newsletter, links to other futurist organizations, and contact information. The site also has online submission of preliminary applications and an online feedback and information request form.

The Foundation for Hellenic Culture, Inc. (NY) (Operating foundation) (http://www.hri.org/FHC)

The New York City branch of the Foundation for Hellenic Culture was established in 1995; its headquarters, in Athens, Greece, was created in 1992. The organization's goal is to "promote and disseminate Greek culture and language outside of Greece." The Foundation sponsors art and visual art exhibitions, film screenings, concerts, lectures, theatrical productions, readings, and educational programs. The Web site includes a list of many of the sponsored activities in North America, the activities that are currently happening, and contact information for all of the Foundation branches. The FHC is an operating, not grantmaking, foundation.

Foundation for Microbiology (NY) (http://www.tiac.net/users/waksman/)

The purpose of the New York City-based Foundation for Microbiology is "to promote, encourage, and aid scientific research in microbiology; [and] to provide and assist in providing the funds and facilities by which scientific discoveries, inventions, and processes in microbiology may be developed." The Foundation does not offer conventional research, fellowship, or travel grants. Instead, its funds are used "for the support of lectureships, prizes, or courses related to the field of microbiology, as well as for unusual publications or other activities in this field poorly supported by the usual Government agencies." To qualify for support, any of these activities must be expected to address a national or an international audience. Innovative educational programs dealing with microbiological topics and making use of contemporary communication techniques are a special focus of interest, as are programs concerned with enhancing public awareness of science, including K–12 teaching programs that make use of microorganisms. Visitors to the Foundation's Web site will find financial information for fiscal year 1997, concise application guidelines and limitations, a list of grants and contributions made by the Foundation in 1997, and a directory of officers and trustees (complete with phone, fax, and e-mail info).

Foundation for Middle East Peace (DC) (http://www.fmep.org)

Located in Washington, D.C., the Foundation for Middle East Peace (FMEP) was created in 1979. The group is committed to "inform[ing] Americans on the Israeli-Palestinian conflict and assist[ing] in a peaceful solution that brings security for both peoples." The four main programs within the foundation are the Speakers Progam, the production of publications, media outreach, and grantmakers. The grantmaking program provides support for organizations and individuals working toward a solution of the Israeli-Palestinian conflict. The Web site serves as a resource for those interested in the issue. There are electronic versions of many publications, maps, charts, and a searchable database of statistics. The only mention of the grants program is in the About FMEP section.

Foundation for Seacoast Health (NH) (http://www.ffsh.org)
The Foundation for Seacoast Health, created in 1984, has become the largest private charitable foundation in New Hampshire. Its mission is to "support and promote health care in any one or more of the cities and towns in the New Hampshire/Maine Seacoast area and do any and all things in furtherance thereof, including providing goods, services and programs and fostering the provision of goods, services and programs and the study, promotion, demonstration and dissemination of ideas that promote public health and well-being." The Foundation accepts grants from both individuals and nonprofit organizations located in the Foundation's community. A Request for Proposal brochure explaining the grant application procedure can be obtained by calling, e-mailing, or writing the Foundation. The Foundation also has a scholarship program, which offers scholarships to assist qualified students who are residents of the Foundation's community and are pursuing a degree program in health-related fields of study at an accredited institution of higher learning. Scholarship applications can be requested from the Foundation. Deadlines for both grant and scholarship applications are posted on the Web site.

The Fourjay Foundation (PA) (http://www.fourjay.org)
The Fourjay Foundation, based in Willow Grove, Pennsylvania, supports organizations whose chief purpose is to improve health and/or promote education within Philadelphia, Montgomery, and Bucks Counties in southeastern Pennsylvania. The Foundation has a Cardiology Research Grant, which is open to cardiology fellows in training and faculty at the rank of associate and assistant professor level. Areas of focus include congenital heart disease in the adult, regression of arteriosclerosis, new technology applications in the diagnosis of heart disease, early detection and/or prevention of stroke, and new advances in the treatment of hypertension. Application procedures, grant recipient list, and printable application materials are available on the Foundation's Web site. The site also provides information on a Foundation initiative: the Healthlink Medical Center, which is an organization of volunteer physicians, dentists, nurses, dental hygienists, social service workers, and pharmacists who will provide free primary medical and dental care to individuals and families, employed, without health insurance, who live in Bucks and Montgomery Counties.

John Edward Fowler Memorial Foundation (DC) (http://fdncenter.org/grantmaker/fowler/)
The John Edward Fowler Memorial Foundation of Washington, D.C., was created in 1964 in memory of John Edward Fowler, a northern Virginia businessman. The Foundation is particularly interested in providing operating support in the areas of homelessness, hunger, at-risk children and youth, adult literacy, free medical care, seniors, and job training and placement. The Foundation prefers to support smaller, grassroots, neighborhood-based organizations. The Foundation prefers to focus its giving on organizations that serve disadvantaged people who live in the inner-city of Washington, D.C., and the close-in suburbs of Maryland and Virginia. Visitors to the Foundation's folder on the Center's Web site will find specific information on the Foundation's areas of interest, recent grants listings, recent financial statement, application procedures, printable application, and contact information.

Freedom Forum, Inc. (VA) (http://www.freedomforum.org)
Dedicated to "free press, free speech and free spirit for all people," the mission of the Freedom Forum is to help the public and the news media understand one another better. Primary areas of interest include First Amendment rights, journalism education, newsroom diversity, professional development of journalists, media studies and research, and international journalism programs. The Forum does not accept unsolicited grant applications and only makes limited grants in connection with its programs. Its Web site offers a range of information and features, including detailed descriptions of the Forum's programs and history; articles drawn from various Freedom Forum publications; links to the Gannett Center for Media Studies as well as dozens of related online resources; an online version of the Forum's 1997 annual report, with grant "highlights" organized by month; and a listing of the Foundation's trustees and officers.

Frey Foundation (MI) (http://www.freyfdn.org)

As heir to Union Bank and Trust and founder of Foremost Insurance Company, Edward Frey accumulated considerable wealth, which he and his wife, Francis, believed should be reinvested in the community. As a means to carry out their charitable interests, they established the Frey Foundation, based in Grand Rapids, Michigan. The Frey Foundation is "committed to working together to make a difference in the lives of individuals, families, organizations, and communities," and states that "as we strive to make a meaningful impact on the lives of people, we encourage creativity and excellence and expect accountability of ourselves and others." The Foundation has five funding categories: Enhancing the Lives of Children and Their Families, Protecting the Environment, Nurturing Community Arts, Encouraging Civic Progress, and Strengthening Philanthropy; and two special initiatives: Revitalizing Our Community and Supporting Our Children. Support is primarily given to the western side of Michigan's lower peninsula, with special emphasis on the greater Grand Rapids area and Charlevoix and Emmet Counties. Consult its Web site for more details about each funding category, grant application instructions, financial statements, available publications, contact information including an e-mail link, and links to other organizations in the community.

Friedman-Klarreich Family Foundation (OH) (http://members.aol.com/klarff/index.htm)

Established in 1992 by Susan Friedman Klarreich and her four daughters, Karin, Betsy, Kathie, and Beth, the Los Altos, California-based Friedman-Klarreich Family Foundation awards grants of up to $5,000 to innovative nonprofit organizations or properly qualified individuals dedicated to achieving educational and economic equality for girls and women and/or to enhancing the stability of families. The Foundation's simple Web site provides application guidelines and requirements, a listing of grants awarded to date, links to related sites of interest, and contact information.

The Frist Foundation (TN) (http://www.fristfoundation.org)

Formerly known as the HCA Foundation, the Nashville-based Frist Foundation was established in 1982 by Hospital Corporation of America. Following the merger of HCA with Columbia Healthcare Corporation in 1994, the Foundation became fully independent of the company and in 1997 changed its name to honor the philanthropic influence of its founding directors: Dr. Thomas F. Frist, Sr., gifted cardiologist, businessman, and philanthropist and Dr. Thomas F. Frist, Jr., who still serves as chairman. The Frist Foundation continues its mission to invest its resources in select not-for-profit organizations in metropolitan Nashville in order to strengthen their abilities to provide services. The Foundation's activities are mostly grantmaking, but it has also initiated special programs to enhance the community, some of which award grants. Grants are awarded to a variety of organizations in the fields of health, human services, civic affairs, education, and the arts and generally fall into three categories: sustaining (operating support), project and program, and capital. Consult the Foundation's Web site for more information on its special programs guidelines, funding guidelines, lists of directors and staff members, annual report, grant recipient lists, and contact information, including an e-mail link.

Lloyd A. Fry Foundation (IL) (http://www.fryfoundation.org/)

The mission of the Fry Foundation is to improve the quality of life for Chicago's disadvantaged residents by promoting solutions to problems associated with urban poverty. The Lloyd A. Fry Foundation was established in 1983 following the death of its founder and namesake, an entrepreneur in the roofing industry. Grants are made in the following fields: education, civic affairs and social service, arts and culture, and health. Grantseekers will find grant application guidelines, foundation history, board and staff listing, grants by area, latest copy of the Foundation's annual report, and contact information.

Helene Fuld Health Trust (NY) (http://www.fuld.org/welcome.htm)

Dr. Leonhard Felix Fuld and his sister, Florentine, created a foundation in honor of their mother in 1935, which was converted to the Helene Fuld Health Trust in 1965. This New York City-based Trust, dedicated to the support and promotion of the health, welfare, and education of student nurses, is the nation's largest private funder devoted exclusively to nursing students and nursing education. The Trust has three program areas: Curriculum and Faculty Development in Community-based Care, to prepare nursing students to work in a community or outpatient setting; Leadership Development, to develop the leadership ability of a new generation of nurses to provide inspiration and direction in the uncertain and "dramatically changing future" of the health care industry and of the "nursing profession in particular;" and Educational Mobility, to aid nursing students to earn higher degrees in nursing. Grants are not made to individuals but to nursing schools and educational programs or nonprofit organizations with programs that benefit nursing students and relate to nursing education. Visitors to the Web site can learn more about the Trust's program guidelines, application instructions, recent grants list, and contact information.

The Fuller Foundation (NH) (http://www.agmconnect.org/fuller1.html)

Alvan T. Fuller, state legislator, member of Congress, Lieutenant Governor, and two-term Governor of Massachusetts, founded the Fuller Foundation in 1936 so that his legacy of philanthropy would continue. This Rye Beach, New Hampshire-based Foundation's purpose is to support nonprofit agencies that improve the quality of life for people, animals, and the environment. It also funds the Fuller Foundation of New Hampshire, which supports horticulture and education programs for the public at Fuller Gardens, which is what remains of Fuller's summer estate. The Fuller Foundation seeks proposals in three focus areas of grantmaking: Youth at Risk; Wildlife, Endangered Species—Their Environment, and Animals Helping People; and the Arts. The geographic focus of its grantmaking is predominantly the Boston area and the immediate seacoast area of New Hampshire. New and "seed" organizations that do not have financial history will also be considered for support, as long as they have sound financial plans. Consult the Foundation's Web site for more details on focus areas, guidelines, application procedures, grant list, and contact information.

Fund for Astrophysical Research (NY) (http://fdncenter.org/grantmaker/fundastro/)

The New York-based Fund for Astrophysical Research makes small grants to support research in astronomy and astrophysics. Founded in 1936 by Charles G. Thompson and Alice Bemis Thompson, FAR has supported astronomical and astrophysical projects in the United States, Australia, and New Zealand through loans and gifts of funds and optical equipment. Grants are awarded for the acquisition of astronomical equipment, computer time, and computer hardware or software that will be used in research. The foundation's folder on the Center's Web site contains a brief history of the foundation, grant guidelines and recipients, a listing of officers and trustees, and a biography of Theodore Dunham, Jr., the founding scientific director of the foundation.

Fund for the City of New York (NY) (Operating foundation) (http://www.fcny.org/)

The Fund is an independent private operating foundation whose mandate is "to respond to the opportunities and problems of New York City; to improve the performance of the city's government and the quality of life of its citizens." The Fund's five primary grantmaking areas are children and youth, AIDS, community development and housing, the urban environment, and government and technology, but it also makes a limited number of grants that do not fall neatly into any of the above categories. Grants awarded are generally between $5,000 and $10,000, and the Fund provides both general and project support. It also operates the Cash Flow Loan Program, the Nonprofit Computer Exchange, and the Management Initiative, all of which address "the importance of this type of funding to maintain the management infrastructure needed to support an agency's programs." Visitors to the Fund's Web site will find detailed information on all of the Fund's programs and initiatives as well as contact information.

Fund for Nonviolence (CA) (http://fdncenter.org/grantmaker/fnv/)

The Santa Cruz-based Fund for Nonviolence was founded in 1997 to benefit "community based efforts whose aim is significant social change which moves humanity towards a more just and compassionate coexistence." In general, the Fund supports nonviolence in work for progressive social change, especially in the areas of women in poverty, children (with an emphasis on girls), and challenging state-sponsored violence (such as militarization and the death penalty). Funding priorities are for groups that focus on structural changes to root causes of injustice, reflect the spirit of nonviolence in their organizational structure and process, and demonstrate a vision grounded in reflective thought on actions taken. The Fund's folder on the Center's Web site provides the current topics of specific interest, which change periodically: guidelines for letters of inquiry, limitations to funding, a list of recent grants, and contact information.

The G & P Charitable Foundation (NY) (http://www.gpcharity.com)

The G & P Charitable Foundation, based in New York City, supports research that will lead to advances in the treatment of hematologic malignancies such as leukemia, lymphoma, and other such cancers. The following general approaches are funding priorities: Genetic Abnormalities, Signal Transduction Pathways, Cell Death Programs, Clinical Trial Research, Epidemiology and Prevention, Early Diagnosis, and Immune Prevention of Malignancy. The G & P Charitable Foundation seeks improvement of treatment through the development of novel therapeutic approaches that could replace or be used in conjunction with existing therapies, collaborative efforts between select leaders in different areas of biology and integrative medical research, to improve efficacy and reduce toxicity of cancer treatments, and to improve quality of life for patients. The Foundation was the vision of Gabrielle Rich Aouad, who died at the age of 27 from AML Leukemia. Her last wish was to create a foundation, named for herself and her husband, that would invest in research to find better treatment for leukemia and spare others from the suffering she endured. To that end, her husband, Philip Aouad, and her mother, Denise Rich, formed The G & P Charitable Foundation for Cancer Research. Consult the Web site for more information about each funding priority, goals, medical advances, and an online contact form.

The GAR Foundation (OH) (http://www.garfdn.org)

The GAR Foundation was established in 1967 to support organizations located in Summit County, Ohio. Organizations in adjoining counties (Cuyahoga, Medina, Portage, Stark and Wayne counties) are given secondary consideration. Interests of the Foundation include education, arts, social services, and other areas that are deemed supportive to the above communities. Visit the Foundation's Web site to find out how to apply for support. The site also contains guidelines for applying, a helpful FAQs section, information about special initiatives, and contact information.

Gates Family Foundation (CO) (http://www.gatesfamilyfdn.org)

In 1911, Charles C. Gates, Sr., educated as a mining engineer, bought the Colorado Tire and Leather Company for $3500 in response to a newspaper ad and founded the company known today as the Gates Corporation. By the time he transferred presidency to his son in 1961, the Gates Corporation had annual sales totaling $137 million. Charles C. Gates, Sr., along with members of the Gates family, established The Gates Foundation on November 6, 1946, whose name was later changed in December 1995 to the Gates Family Foundation. Its purpose is to "aid, assist, encourage, initiate, or carry on activities that will promote the health, well-being, security, and broad education of all people." Among their varied interests are the growth and development of independent schools and private colleges, historic preservation, the arts, urban and mountain parks and U.S. Forest Service trail systems, supporting organizations that promote free enterprise, and supporting programs that encourage individuals to improve and maintain their physical well-being. This Denver, Colorado, Foundation invests primarily in institutions, projects, and programs that will affect the people of Colorado, with special attention paid to the Denver metropolitan area. Consult the Web site for further details on the Foundation's major areas of funding interest, guidelines, application instructions, 1996 annual report with grant list, projects funded, resource links, and contact information.

Bill and Melinda Gates Foundation (WA) (http://www.gatesfoundation.org/)
The William H. Gates Foundation and the Gates Learning Foundation merged in August 1999 to become the Bill and Melinda Gates Foundation, which encompasses those two foundations and the Gates Center for Technology Access. The Gates Foundation ranks as one of the wealthiest private foundations in the world. Established by the Microsoft co-founder and CEO, the Seattle-based Foundation is led by Bill Gates's father, William Gates, Sr., and supports initiatives in education, technology and global health, and community giving in the Pacific Northwest. The Foundation requests that grantseekers submit letters of inquiry before submitting formal funding proposals. Visitors to the Foundation's Web site will find descriptions of the Foundation's various initiatives, grantmaking guidelines, press releases, a PDF version of the Foundation's most recent annual report, links to recent grantees, and contact information.

Carl Gellert and Celia Berta Gellert Foundation (CA) (http://home.earthlink.net/~cgcbg/)
Based in San Francisco, the Gellert Foundation promotes religious, charitable, scientific, literary, and educational activities in the nine counties of the greater San Francisco Bay Area (i.e., Alameda, Contra Costa, Marin, Napa, San Francisco, San Mateo, Santa Clara, Solano, and Sonoma Counties). Visitors to the Foundation's Web site will find a mission statement, application guidelines, a list of grants and contributions, and contact information.

General Service Foundation (CO) (http://www.generalservice.org/)
The General Service Foundation, founded in Illinois in 1946 by Clifton R. and Margaret Kulp Musser, is now based in Aspen, Colorado. The Foundation seeks to address the "world's basic long-term problems in four areas: international peace, reproductive health and rights, resources, and education" in new, innovative, or demonstrative projects. International peace programs address the need for peaceful, stable communities mainly in Mexico, Central America, and the Caribbean through education and policy analysis and formation. Comprehensive reproductive health care and education efforts comprise the reproductive health and rights area. Funds for resources are directed toward the preservation of aquatic and riparian ecosystems in the rivers and tributaries of the Western U.S. Educational projects are geared toward targeted communities, including Native American youth programs, and unsolicited proposals are not accepted. The Foundation's Web site provides complete grant guidelines and limitations, past grants in each area, application procedures, and contact information.

The George Foundation (TX) (http://www.thegeorgefoundation.org)
Based in Richmond, Texas, the George Foundation was established by Albert and Mamie George, who had a great love for Fort Bend County and its people. Before their death, they created the George Foundation as a "trust for religious, charitable, scientific, literary and/or educational purposes" to ensure that their wealth would continue to be administered to benefit the citizens of Fort Bend County and to preserve the heritage of the area. Current funding is directed towards providing programs in early childhood development and education to serve children and their families. The Foundation has student scholarships and student loans for Fort Bend County students attending Texas colleges and universities, which are administered by the individual educational institutions. The Foundation also has scholarships for high school students, which are administered by each Fort Bend school district. The Foundation does not provide financial support to students in elementary or secondary schools but does support special programs that are offered at Fort Bend elementary and secondary schools. The George Foundation set aside land for The George Ranch Historical Park, which includes the homes of the Georges. Authentic activities of a working Texas ranch are relived there, and the park serves as a center for community activities, a place for agricultural research, a site for cultural and charitable events, and a resource for research and education about the rich heritage of Fort Bend County. Visitors to the site will find grant application guidelines, contact information for the scholarship program, and grant lists.

The George Family Foundation (MN)
(http://www.users.uswest.net/~famphiladv/george.htm)
The Minneapolis-based George Family Foundation considers its mission "to foster human development—spiritual, intellectual, physical and psychological—and to enhance the work of people and organizations devoted to exemplary service in the community." Its funding interests lie in five main categories: integrated healing of mind, body, heart, and spirit; educational opportunities leading to personal growth, societal impact, and under-standing of the world and its diverse cultures; youth development of leadership and mentoring; overcoming barriers for women and people of color; and collaboration of peo-ple and organizations to address community needs. The Foundation's Web site includes application guidelines and limitations, a downloadable grant application cover page and past award recipient list (in Microsoft Word format), and contact information. Grant applications should be received by May 30th or October 30th for consideration.

The Gerber Foundation (MI) (http://www.gerberfoundation.org/)
The mission of the Gerber Foundation is to "enhance the quality of life of infants and young children in nutrition, care and development." The Foundation, located in Freemont, Michigan, was established in 1952 as the Gerber Baby Foods Fund by Dan Gerber and Gerber Products Company. Since 1994, the Gerber Foundation has been a separately endowed, private foundation. Although there are some grant programs that reflect the Foundation's ongoing commitment to the associates and communities of Gerber Products Company, the majority of the Foundation's grant dollars are distributed on a competitive basis to national programs within four areas of funding: education and training, science and research, infant and child, and special initiatives. Information on how to apply for a grant can be found on the Foundation's Web site. All applications must include an application form, which can be printed directly from the Web site. Annual reports, a listing of the board of trustees, and information about the Foundation's programs and research can all be found online.

Wallace Alexander Gerbode Foundation (CA)
(http://fdncenter.org/grantmaker/gerbode/index.html)
The Wallace Alexander Gerbode Foundation supports programs in the San Francisco Bay Area and Hawaii in the areas of arts and culture, environment, population, reproductive rights, citizen participation/building communities/inclusiveness, and strength of the philan-thropic process and the nonprofit sector. The Foundation generally does not support direct services, deficit budgets, general operating funds, building or equipment funds, general fundraising campaigns, religious purposes, private schools, publications, scholarships, or grants to individuals. In addition to general application and fiscal information, the Founda-tion's folder on the Center's Web site provides an archive of grants lists by program area and the most recent financial information.

J. Paul Getty Trust (CA) (Operating foundation) (http://www.getty.edu/grants/index.html)
The J. Paul Getty Trust, a private operating foundation dedicated to the visual arts and humanities, comprises a museum, four institutes, and a grant program. The purpose of the latter is to strengthen the fields in which the Trust is active by funding exceptional projects throughout the world that promote research in the history of art and related fields, advance-ment of the understanding of art, and conservation of cultural heritage. Grants may fund conceptual projects that take intellectual risks, or they may support more basic resources and activities. Funded projects include a wide variety of methodologies and subject matter, ranging through all historical periods and geographic regions. The Trust's Web site pro-vides a general overview of the Trust's grantmaking activities, extensive program informa-tion and guidelines, a list of grants recently awarded, and application and contact informa-tion. Applications for some Getty programs can be downloaded from the site.

Addison H. Gibson Foundation (PA) (http://www.gibson-fnd.org)
Addison H. Gibson was a pioneer in the oil and gas industry during the early twentieth cen-tury. Gibson specified in his will that the majority of his fortune be used to help improve

quality of life for needy western Pennsylvanians in higher education and medical care. The Pittsburgh-based Foundation has an education loan program and a medical trust, which provides medical treatment to needy, self-supporting patients who otherwise cannot afford the required medical aid. Visitors to the Web site will find further information on its programs, residency requirements, application information, a trustee and staff listing, and contact information.

The Harry Bramhall Gilbert Charitable Trust (VA)
(http://fdncenter.org/grantmaker/gilbert/)

The Harry Bramhall Gilbert Charitable Trust supports tax-exempt organizations that contribute to the health, education, and cultural life of the Tidewater, Virginia, region. The Trust currently and substantially funds nonprofits based in the cities of Norfolk, Chesapeake, and Virginia Beach, Virginia. Visitors to the Foundation's folder on the Center's Web site will find recent tax returns downloadable in PDF format, and contact information.

Price Gilbert, Jr. Charitable Fund (GA)
(http://www.wachovia.com/trust/pricegilbert_overview.asp)

The Price Gilbert, Jr. Charitable Fund of Atlanta was established under the will of Price Gilbert, Jr. in 1973. The purpose of the Fund is to support charitable and/or educational institutions focused on capital needs in the metropolitan Atlanta area. Visitors to the Fund's Web site will find information of the board, grant guidelines, a listing of recent grants, fiscal information, and contact information.

The Gill Foundation (CO) (http://www.gillfoundation.org)

Headquartered in Colorado Springs, Colorado, the Gill Foundation "serves as a catalyst and provides resources for communities in pursuit of justice and equality, while building awareness of the contributions gay men and lesbians make to American society." The Gill Foundation was established in 1994 by Tim Gill, one of two openly gay individuals on the 1997 Forbes 400 list and founder, Chairman, and Chief Technology Officer of Quark, Inc., a successful desktop publishing software company. It currently has three program areas: Gill Foundation Grantmaking, which funds organizations nationwide serving gay men, lesbians, bisexuals, transgendered individuals, and people living with HIV/AIDS; the Gay and Lesbian Fund for Colorado, which funds nonprofits in Colorado in the areas of social justice, children and youth, leadership development, arts and culture, public broadcasting, and excellence in communications; and the OutGiving Project, which aims to expand the base of support for gay, lesbian, bisexual, and transgender organizations by providing organizational development and fundraising training, and training for donors on how to give effectively, through both workshops and online resources. Visitors to the Web site will find more details about each program area, guidelines, application instructions, a sample of a successful grant proposal (downloadable and viewable), downloadable handouts from its OutGiving Project, online request forms (including one for borrowing publications from the foundation), links to other resources, and contact information.

Irving S. Gilmore Foundation (MI) (http://www.isgilmorefoundation.org/)

Irving Gilmore, a lifelong resident of Kalamazoo, Michigan, established the Irving S. Gilmore Foundation in 1972 as a way of giving back to the community he loved in perpetuity. The Foundation strives to sustain and, whenever possible, to improve the cultural, social, and economic life of greater Kalamazoo, with a focus (in order of importance) on the cultural and performing arts, human services, education and youth, community development, and health and well-being. The Foundation's trustees make all decisions concerning the funding of proposals and encourage grant applications from Kalamazoo area nonprofits whose work does, or will, benefit the community. The Foundation does not make grants to individuals. The Foundation's Web site provides a brief history of the Foundation and a description of its involvement in the community, grant application guidelines and procedures, and contact information.

Glaser Family Foundation (WA) (http://www.progressproject.org/foundation.html)
The Glaser Family Foundation was established by Rob Glaser, CEO and founder of RealNetworks, Inc. in Seattle, Washington. As part of the online Progress Project, a partnership of foundations with a common goal, the Glaser Family Foundation focuses on the areas of homelessness, animal rights, and socially-conscious media. The Foundation is "dedicated to stimulating and elevating public discourse on the broader concept of 'progress' in all its forms as we enter the next millennium." Through initiatives in education and communication, the Foundation promotes the understanding, advancement, mechanics and meaningful strategies of progress. A contact and e-mail address are provided on the Foundation's Web site.

Glazer Family Foundation (FL) (http://www.glazerfamilyfoundation.com/)
The Glazer Family Foundation, located in Tampa, Florida, is "dedicated to developing ways to assist charitable and educational causes—focusing primarily on youth—in the Greater Tampa Bay and Central Florida regions." The Foundation works with non-profit organizations to help identify and create programs that advocate positive social development in its community. It gives preference to programs focused on youth and families in the areas of general health, safety, education, and recreation. Deadlines for grant application are posted on the Web site. Applications can be requested by mail or downloaded in PDF format. The Web site also has information on programs the Glazer Family Foundation is involved is, as well as a photo gallery of events and details on the Board of Directors.

Glenn Foundation for Medical Research, Inc. (CA) (Operating foundation) (http://www.glenn.deco.net/)
The purpose of the Glenn Foundation is "to extend the healthful productive years of life through research on the mechanisms of biological aging." The Foundation neither solicits nor accepts charitable contributions, and it does not consider unsolicited grant applications or fellowship nominations. Its Web site, which was developed as a resource and point-of-access for scientists whose primary interest is the biology of aging, offers brief descriptions of the Foundation's programs, conferences, workshops, and numerous links to other organizations involved in aging research.

Goizueta Foundation (GA) (http://www.goizuetafoundation.org)
The Atlanta-based foundation was established in 1992 by Roberto C. Goizueta, Chairman of the Board of Directors and Chief Executive Officer of The Coca-Cola Company until his death in October 1997. The Foundation provides assistance to educational, cultural, religious, and charitable institutions. The primary focus of The Goizueta Foundation is to respond to the needs of families by assisting institutions that serve children, support families at risk, and create educational opportunities. Consideration may also be given to religious and cultural institutions that operate within the areas of education, community, and youth services. Preference is given to the southeastern states of Alabama, Florida, Georgia, North Carolina, South Carolina, and Tennessee. The Foundation's Web site contains grant proposal guidelines, links to other Foundation Resources, and contact information.

The Golden Rule Foundation, Inc. (TX) (http://www.goldrule.org)
The Golden Rule Foundation makes grants to arts, environment, and self-help social organizations. The Foundation does not fund unsolicited applications. Applicants may reapply after a three year period. The Foundation's Web site is in its formative stages.

Goldman Environmental Foundation (CA) (http://www.goldmanprize.org)
The Goldman Environmental Foundation, based in San Francisco, was founded by Richard N. Goldman, chairman of a major independent insurance brokerage firm, and Rhoda H. Goldman, who was a descendant of Levi Strauss. The Goldman Environmental Prize is a project of the Foundation, reflecting the Goldman family's longstanding commitment to both philanthropic endeavors and to environmental concerns. The Goldman Environmental Prize was established in 1990 to demonstrate the international nature of environmental problems, to draw public attention to global issues of critical importance, to reward

individuals for outstanding grassroots environmental initiatives and to inspire others to emulate the examples set by the Prize recipients. The Prize awards $125,000 annually to six environmental heroes from each of the inhabited continental regions. Nominated by a network of internationally known environmental organizations and a confidential panel of environmental experts, recipients are chosen for their sustained and important efforts to preserve the natural environment, including but not limited to protecting endangered ecosystems and species, combating destructive development projects, promoting sustainability, influencing environmental policies, and striving for environmental justice. There is no application for the Goldman Prize, and unsolicited nominations are not accepted. Visitors to the site will find recipient lists, a list of nominating organizations, press releases, and an online version of the Foundation's newsletters. The site can be viewed in six languages.

Richard & Rhoda Goldman Fund (CA) (http://www.goldmanfund.org/)

The Goldman Fund was established in 1951 by Richard and Rhoda Goldman to improve the quality of life in the San Francisco Bay Area, to protect the environment, and to promote a more just and sustainable world. The Fund is interested in supporting programs that will have a positive impact in an array of fields, including the environment, population, Jewish affairs, children and youth, the elderly, social and human services, health, education, and the arts. While the Fund is primarily interested in organizations and projects that have an impact on San Francisco and local Bay Area communities, it will consider inquiries from domestic organizations that provide support to Israel and national and international projects that address environmental and population issues. The Fund does not accept applications for research, grants or scholarships to individuals, conferences, documentary films, fundraisers, deficit budgets, or endowment campaigns; unsolicited proposals for support of arts organizations or institutions of primary, secondary, or higher education; or applications for the Goldman Environmental Prize. The Fund's Web site provides detailed application guidelines, limitation statements, recent grants lists organized by subject area, FAQs, summaries of recent Fund initiatives, a letter from Board Chair Richard Goldman, and a link to the Goldman Environmental PrizeWeb site.

Grable Foundation (PA) (http://www.grablefdn.org)

This Pittsburgh, Pennsylvania-based Foundation was founded in 1976 by Minnie K. Grable, widow of Errett M. Grable, the founder of Rubbermaid, Inc. The Grable Foundation's mission is "to help children and youth become independent, caring, contributing members of society by supporting programs critical to a child's successful development." The Foundation focuses its giving in four areas: education, families, community, and special areas. Education receives the majority of the Foundation's funding, in the areas of early childhood, school improvement and curriculum development, mentoring and out of school programs, arts in education, workforce training, and educational leadership and policy development. The Foundation's funding in special areas includes volunteerism, mental illness, and civic involvement. Visitors to the Foundation's Web site will find listings of the board and staff members, financial information, links, application guidelines, recent grants lists, and contact information. The Foundation also accepts the Common Grant Application for Grantmakers of Western Pennsylvania and includes a link to this form on its site.

Graham Foundation for the Advanced Studies in the Fine Arts (IL) (http://www.GrahamFoundation.org/)

The Graham Foundation was established by a bequest from Ernest R. Graham, a prominent Chicago architect who died in 1936. Since Graham died in the depths of the depression, the value of his estate was "severely depressed," and it took twenty years to rebuild his estate and implement his legacy. In 1956, the Graham Foundation for the Advanced Studies in the Fine Arts was established in Chicago, Illinois. The Foundation supports individuals and institutions undertaking work in architecture and with other arts and academic disciplines that are "immediately contributive to architecture." In the past, the Foundation has supported a variety of endeavors, including grants to sponsor fellowships, seminars, and symposia at universities, architectural publications, and grants for exhibitions. In addition to its general grantmaking program, there is also the Carter Manny Award to support doctoral candidates in their research for academic dissertations directly concerned with architecture. Points of interest on its Web site are grant descriptions and application instructions, lists of past supported projects and publications, annual report, list and biographies of trustees, list of and contact information for staff members, schedule of lectures and exhibitions, and a searchable database of past grantees.

William T. Grant Foundation (NY) (http://fdncenter.org/grantmaker/wtgrant/index.html)

The goal of the William T. Grant Foundation is to help create a society that values young people and enables them to reach their full potential. It pursues this goal primarily by investing in research in health; social and behavioral sciences, such as anthropology; economics; education; health services; political science; history; demography; sociology; in marketing and communications disciplines; and in those fields traditionally concerned with youth development and mental health, such as pediatrics, psychology, psychiatry, and social work. The Foundation supports three new programs of research: Youth Development, Systems Affecting Youth, and the Public's View of Youth. The Foundation is especially interested in interdisciplinary research, including policy analyses and strategic communications research. Additionally, the Foundation supports the development of promising junior (i.e., pre-tenure) scholars in tenure-track positions through its Faculty Scholars Program and youth-serving organizations in the New York City metropolitan area through its Youth Service Grants. The Foundation's folder on the Center's Web site offers general information about the Foundation and its programs; detailed application procedures; a downloadable cover sheet for letters of inquiry; officer, staff, and trustee listings; and online versions of the Foundation's past two annual reports.

The Grass Foundation (MA) (http://www.mbl.edu/grassfdn)

Based in Braintree, Massachusetts, the Grass Foundation supports independent research by young investigators in the field of neuroscience. The Grass Foundation was organized in 1955 by Albert and Ellen Grass, founders of Grass Instrument Co., and a group of eminent and dedicated medical and scientific researchers. The Foundation provides fellowships for scientists at the beginning of their careers, such as the Grass Fellowship in Neuroscience at the Marine Biological Laboratory and the Robert S. Morison Fellowship. The Foundation has supported additional programs including courses and lectureships and has made grants available to qualified institutions. The Grass Fellowship in Neuroscience at the Marine Biological Laboratory, Woods Hole, Massachusetts, supports research in the following areas: neurophysiology, membrane biophysics, integrative neurobiology and neuroethology, neuroanatomy, neuropharmacology, cellular and developmental neurobiology, cognitive neuroscience, and computational approaches to neural systems. Interested applicants can print applications and find a list of past recipients on the site. The Morison Fellowship provides support for an outstanding young clinician who wishes to invest one to two years in intensive, supervised research as preparation for a career as an academic clinician. Visitors to the site will find information on the Foundation's other activities and contact information.

William Casper Graustein Memorial Fund (CT) (http://www.wcgmf.org/)

The New Haven, Connecticut-based William Casper Graustein Memorial Fund was founded by Graustein's brother to continue the Harvard math professor's work in education reform. The Fund's current mission is to "work collaboratively to improve education for Connecticut's children by supporting school change, informing the public debate on educational issues, and strengthening the involvement of parents and the community in education." The three key funding areas are policy research and advocacy, community engagement and parental involvement, and educational change in schools. The last is administered by the Connecticut Center for School Change, and a link is provided to its own site, which provides application and grant specifics. Application instructions for the other two programs can be found at the Memorial Fund's site, along with grant lists, contact information, program reports, and electronic requests for free copies of assorted policy and research reports and their most recent biennial report.

Green Mountain Fund, Inc. (VT) (http://homepages.together.net/~gmfps/)
Located in Westford, Vermont, the Green Mountain Fund for Popular Struggle supports
organizations that actively organize for radical social change in Vermont and the Cham-
plain Valley watershed of New York. The Fund is "committed to revolutionary transformation toward a socialist-feminist society," a society that "requires the elimination of all
oppressions (such as oppressions by race, sex, class, sexual orientation, age, ability or species) and their basis in patriarchal, capitalist and imperialist structures." The Fund was set
up with a one-time donation of $500,000, and "recognizing that income-producing invest-
ments require the exploitation of labor, the fund has placed the money with nonprofit organizations in the form of no-interest loans." The loans are repaid on an annual basis over a
period of ten years, and these repayments provide funds to be granted to other groups.
Therefore, barring unsolicited donations, the Fund expects to dissolve by the year 2000. To
be eligible, organizations have to be eligible for tax-exempt status and no significant portion of their budget can come from government agencies, religious institutions or "establishment foundations" such as United Way and the Rockefeller Foundation. Consult the
Fund's Web site for a complete listing of the causes it supports, application guidelines and
instructions, application form and coversheet, contact information for each board member,
grant lists, and links to other resources.

Greenville Foundation (CA) (http://fdncenter.org/grantmaker/grnville/)
The Sonoma, California-based Greenville Foundation provides support for special projects
in the following areas: education, the environment, human and social issues, international,
and religion. The Foundation does not make grants for scholarships, individuals, venture
capital, capital improvements, endowments, general classroom-based environmental education programs, individual species preservation, health, food banks, or temporary shelter.
Because it is located in the West, "practicality dictates that proposals for domestic projects
be located west of the Rockies," although a limited number of grants may be made outside
the region. Grants for international programs are made only through United States-based or
affiliated nonprofit organizations and for projects as specifically defined by the Foundation's international and environment programs. The Foundation's folder on the Center's
Web site provides program descriptions, recent grants lists in each program area, application guidelines and procedures, a downloadable application cover sheet, a financial report
for the latest year, and contact information.

The Greenwall Foundation (NY) (http://www.greenwall.org/)
The Greenwall Foundation was established in 1949 by Frank and Anna Greenwall of New
York City in honor of their daughter and other family members. The Foundation mainly
supports work in medicine, education, arts, and humanities programs, while also providing
limited support for basic research in insulin dependent diabetes mellitus. These interests
break down into three specific program areas. The Interdisciplinary Program in Bioethics
funds micro and macro bioethics issues, especially pilot projects, and can include programs
that are sensitive or controversial in nature. The education program is geared toward the
professional development of New York City schoolteachers. The arts and humanities program provides funds for innovative and creative projects in visual, performing, and literary
arts to encourage the growth of New York City as a cultural center. The Foundation's Web
page includes application procedures and guidelines as well as a listing of past grants for
each of these programs. Applicants are encouraged to contact the Foundation well in
advance of the grant due date; contact information is provided online.

The Grotto Foundation, Inc. (MN) (http://www.grottofoundation.org/)
The Grotto Foundation, Inc. was established on December 31, 1964 by Louis Warren Hill,
Jr., eldest grandson of James J. Hill, the railway baron known as the "empire builder."
Believing that people were capable of improving their own lives in their own ways, the
foundation he created supports projects and programs that "empower people to chart their
own course." Located in St. Paul, Minnesota, the Foundation works with communities of
different ethnic groups and cultures who are "inspired by their sense of vision and possibility" and assists these communities as they move forward in the course they have

determined themselves. Its formal mission statement is "to benefit society by improving the education and the economic, physical, and social well-being of citizens, with a special focus on families and culturally diverse groups." It is further interested in "increasing public understanding of the American cultural heritage, the cultures of nations, and the individual's responsibility to fellow human beings." Visit the Web site for grant guidelines and instructions, a link to download the Minnesota Common Grant Application, biographies of the founder and founding director, recent grant list, financial information, list of board and staff members, contact information, and links to other resources. A printable version of their entire Web site is also available.

Harry Frank Guggenheim Foundation (NY) (http://www.hfg.org/)

The Harry Frank Guggenheim Foundation sponsors scholarly research on problems of violence, aggression, and dominance and encourages related research projects in neuroscience, genetics, animal behavior, the social sciences, history, criminology, and the humanities. The Foundation also awards research grants to established scholars and dissertation fellowships to graduate students. (Institutions, programs, and pure interventions are not supported.) Visitors to the Foundation's Web site will find a section on its research priorities, detailed application guidelines and procedures, a comprehensive listing of recent Foundation grants and fellowships, and an interactive form for requesting written application guidelines, and the Foundation's most recent annual report.

John Simon Guggenheim Memorial Foundation (NY) (http://www.gf.org/)

The John Simon Guggenheim Memorial Foundation awards fellowships for advanced professionals in all areas of the natural sciences, social sciences, humanities, and creative arts (except the performing arts). The Foundation selects its fellows on the basis of two separate competitions, one for the United States and Canada, the other for Latin America and the Caribbean. Only professional individuals are eligible for awards; the Foundation does not support students, organizations, or institutions. The Foundation's straightforward Web site provides general information about its programs, fellowship eligibility requirements, and application deadlines in English, Spanish, and Portuguese. Also available in English only is a listing of recent Guggenheim Fellows, a helpful FAQ, an interactive form for ordering application forms, a listing of Foundation officers and trustees, and contact information.

Josephine S. Gumbiner Foundation (CA) (http://www.gumbiner.com/jsgf/)

The Josephine S. Gumbiner Foundation was established in 1989 by Josephine Gumbiner, a noted philanthropist with an educational and professional background in social work. The Foundation strives to support nonprofit organizations that benefit women and children in the Long Beach area of southern California. Program areas that the Foundation considers for funding include day care, education, housing, recreation, the arts, and health care, with a special emphasis on intervention, prevention, and direct service. New and existing programs, general operating expenses, and technical assistance grants are most likely to be funded by the Foundation. Visitors to the Web site will find application guidelines, instructions, and an application that can be downloaded in Microsoft Word. The Foundation also provides a copy of its Form 990-PF that can be downloaded in PDF format, a review of the funding process, a list of past grantees, and an online e-mail response form.

George Gund Foundation (OH) (http://www.gundfdn.org/)

The George Gund Foundation was created in 1952 by Cleveland banker and businessman George Gund, who believed the private foundation structure provided the most positive, far-sighted vehicle for intelligent underwriting of creative solutions to social ills in a manner that would not be limited to his own lifetime. Today, the Foundation makes grants quarterly in the areas of education, economic development and community revitalization, human services, arts, environment, and civic affairs. The Foundation's Web site offers a biography of George Gund, program descriptions, grant application instructions and grant restrictions, contact information, and links to a handful of related Web sites.

Gunk Foundation (NY) (Operating foundation) (http://www.gunk.org/)

The Gunk Foundation is a charitable operating foundation established in 1994 "to provide a counterbalance to the recent, disturbing trends in funding for intellectual endeavors. . . ." It does this by supporting two types of projects—public arts projects, which are funded through the Foundation itself, and scholarly/artistic publications, which are funded through Critical Press, the Foundation's publishing arm. Grant amounts are small and usually fall in a range between $1,000 and $5,000. Visitors to "GunkWeb" will find grant application guidelines (for the Foundation), proposal guidelines (for Critical Press), and a grant archive. A component with links to public arts related resources is underconstruction.

Walter and Elise Haas Fund (CA) (http://www.haassr.org/)

The Walter and Elise Haas Fund was created in 1952. Walter Haas was president and later chairman of Levi Strauss and Co. The Haas's shared a commitment to the "basic values and pluralism of American culture, quality, ethical conduct, creative approaches to meeting human needs, leadership, public participation, and joining public good and individual initiative." The San Francisco-based foundation was created to provide support for the charitable causes consistent with these values and is interested in projects that demonstrate an ability to have wide impact and which demonstrate creative approaches toward meeting human needs. An overall goal is the development of leadership and professional competence in the fields of funding support, which are human services, arts, environment, professional ethics, education, Jewish life, citizenship and civic education, and the Creative Work Fund, which the Haas Fund along with three other funders support the collaboration between artists and nonprofit organizations to create new work. Each field of support has funding and geographic priorities, which are listed in the grant guidelines. Consult the Web site for grant guidelines; application instructions; grant request cover sheet; link to the Creative Work Fund, which has its own separate site and application instructions; grant list; President's Statement and Executive Director's Report; list of staff; and contact information.

Hagen Family Foundation (MI) (http://www.hagenfamilyfoundation.org)

The Hagen Family Foundation (THFF), located in Dearborn, Michigan, is a private family foundation established in 1999 for the purpose of operating and acting exclusively for charitable, religious, literary, or scientific purposes and/or to lessen the financial burdens of government by carrying out a grantmaking program in support of other tax-exempt organizations. THFF prefers to fund programs that seek start-up costs for creative new strategies, identify ongoing means for being self sustaining, promote prevention of social problems, demonstrate interagency cooperation, and empower targeted populations to meet their own needs more effectively. Interested parties should first send a letter of intent, which can be printed directly from the site. Should the letter of intent be favorably considered by the board of directors, organizations will be asked to generate a grant application; grant applications can be downloaded from the Web site in PDF format. Deadline information and a contact e-mail address can also be found on the site.

Halcyon Hill Foundation (NY) (http://www.hhf.org)

Halcyon Hill Foundation, located in Webster, New York, is a family foundation dedicated to the well-being of young children in Monroe County, New York, and in areas where the Foundation's directors live. Grants are made to programs and agencies that support and encourage education, health, justice, and the arts for preschool–age children. Grants to religious organizations are made only for nonsectarian programs, and no grants can be made to individuals. Visitors will find application procedures and a grant list.

Hall-Voyer Foundation (TX) (Operating foundation) (http://www2.1starnet.com/hallv)

The Hall-Voyer Foundation, originally established in 1940 as the David Graham Hall Trust and Foundation, bases its philanthropic activities in the community of Honey Grove, Texas. As an operating foundation, the organization does not make grants, instead financially supporting a number of institutions. The Foundation's projects of interest have changed over the years, but currently it is focused on the operation of the Bertha Voyer Memorial Library,

St. Mark's Episcopal Church, Hall-Voyer Exhibits Hall, and maintenance of the Bertha Voyer Park, all in Honey Grove, Texas. Additionally, the Foundation runs the 2020 Vision Program, which is funding the rehabilitation of the town to its original, historic state. The Foundation's Web site gives a lengthy history of the Foundation, its members, and past projects; its financial status; and contact address.

Luke B. Hancock Foundation (CA) (http://www.lukebhancock.org/)

Established in 1948 with a donation from pioneering oilman Luke B. Hancock, the Hancock Foundation received its principal assets from his estate in 1963 and later changed its name to the Luke B. Hancock Foundation in order to recognize its founder and first president. The Foundation funds community and economic development, youth and education, and special projects, and focuses its support on the Bay Area of northern California, in particular San Jose, and on grassroots neighborhood initiatives that benefit youth as well as the entire community. The Foundation's Web site provides application guidelines, its annual report, and a listing of the Foundation's board of directors.

Phil Hardin Foundation (MS) (http://www.philhardin.org/)

The Hardin Foundation was created in 1964 by Mississippi businessman Phil Hardin, who wanted to give something back to the people of the state. From the outset, the focus of the Foundation was on education. In 1997 it decided to further concentrate its efforts and resources on four goals: strengthening the capacity of communities in the state to nurture and educate young children, strengthening the capacity of higher education institutions to renew communities and their economies, strengthening the capacity of communities for locally initiated educational improvement and economic development, and strengthening policy and leadership at local and state levels. In addition to pursuing these goals, the Foundation also operates four programs: the Thomas R. Ward Fellows Program, which provides fellowships for experienced principals and those aspiring to principalship to attend the Harvard University School of Education's Principals' Center; the S.A. Rosenbaum Earthwatch Mississippi Teaching Fellows Program, which provides faculty of Mississippi schools (K–12) and community colleges the opportunity to participate in Earthwatch Expeditions to further their personal and professional development; the Mississippi Geography Education Fund, which is designed to improve the teaching of geography in Mississippi; and, with the John M. Olin Foundation, the George Washington Scholars Institute, which provides a one-week educational study program at Mount Vernon, in northern Virginia, for as many as 20 teachers from public and non-public schools. Visitors to the Hardin Foundation Web site will find detailed information about the Foundation's goals, programs, and strategies; application guidelines and a downloadable application form; a comprehensive set of links to related education resources; and contact information.

The Hartford Courant Foundation (CT) (http://www.hartfordcourantfoundation.org/)

The Hartford Courant Foundation of Connecticut "seeks to make a sustainable impact on the vitality of Connecticut's capital region by being a catalyst for hope, inspiration and creativity and by improving the lives of its people, especially its children." The Foundation makes grants primarily in support of education, the arts, community development, health, and social services, with an emphasis on programs benefiting children, youth, and families. Visitors to the Foundation's Web site will find information on the board and staff, grant guidelines, a listing of recent grants, information on the Foundation's grants program, a copy of the latest tax return downloadable in PDF format, and contact information.

John A. Hartford Foundation, Inc. (NY) (http://www.jhartfound.org/)

Established in 1929 by John A. and George L. Hartford, former chief executives of the Great Atlantic and Pacific Tea Company (A&P), the John A. Hartford Foundation is concerned with the improvement of healthcare in America. The Foundation focuses its grantmaking activities in the areas of aging and health and healthcare cost and quality and generally makes grants by invitation. Grantseekers are encouraged to familiarize themselves with the Foundation's program areas and guidelines—detailed information about which can be found at its Web site—before submitting a written letter of inquiry. The Web site also provides the Foundation's recent annual report, application information, a report from the chairman, Foundation trustees and staff, and contact information.

Charles Hayden Foundation (NY) (http://fdncenter.org/grantmaker/hayden/index.html)

The New York City-based Hayden Foundation seeks to promote the mental, moral, and physical development of school-aged youth in the New York and Boston metropolitan areas—the former defined as New York City and Nassau County, the southern portion of Westchester County, and, in New Jersey, all of Hudson and Essex Counties and the contiguous urban portions of Union, Passaic, and Bergen Counties; the latter as the City of Boston and adjacent municipalities located on the east side of an arc from Salem to Quincy that is roughly delineated by Route 128. Priority is given to institutions and programs serving youth most at risk of not reaching their full potential, especially youth in low-income communities, and that continuously provide opportunities and supports over many years. Visitors to the Foundation's folder on the Center's Web site will find a mission statement, recent grants lists, detailed application guidelines, and contact information.

John Randolph Haynes and Dora Haynes Foundation (CA) (http://www.haynesfoundation.org/)

Established in 1926, the Haynes Foundation supports study and research in political science, economics, public policy, history, social psychology, and sociology, favoring projects with specific application to California and, more particularly, the Los Angeles region. The Foundation also provides undergraduate scholarships, graduate fellowships, and faculty research fellowships in the social sciences to colleges and universities in the greater Los Angeles area. All support is made directly to institutions; no grants are awarded to individuals. A searchable bibliography of publications resulting from 70 years of Foundation support is available at the Foundation's Web site, along with detailed program information, recent grants, application guidelines, a listing of the Foundation's board of trustees and staff, and a history of the Foundation and the Haynes family.

Edward W. Hazen Foundation, Inc. (NY) (http://www.hazenfoundation.org)

The Edward W. Hazen Foundation of New York City was established in 1925 by Hazen, a state senator and retired publishing executive. The Foundation is committed to "assisting young people, particularly minorities and those disadvantaged by poverty, in achieving their full potential as individuals and as active participants in a democratic society." The grantmaking program focuses on public education and youth development. Within public education, grants are awarded to programs that deal with parent and community organizing, advocacy, and training and leadership building. The youth development program addresses youth organizing and leadership development, innovative programs at youth-service organizations, and school-based leadership development programs. Interested applicants first submit a letter of inquiry and then may receive the Foundation's application form in the mail. Application guidelines and lists of previous grantees can be viewed online or downloaded in PDF format from the Foundation's Web site. The site also includes trustee, board, and staff lists; links to related resources; and a helpful list of FAQs.

The Health Foundation of Greater Cincinnati (OH) (http://www.healthfoundation.org)

The Health Foundation of Greater Cincinnati is committed to "promoting the health of the people of Cincinnati and the surrounding counties in Ohio, Kentucky, and Indiana through investing in enduring projects that improve community health status, healthcare delivery, and access to healthcare for all." The grantmaking program is divided into five categories: primary care for the poor, children's health, substance abuse, severe mental illness, and other health related issues. Most funding in the first two categories goes toward strengthening primary care providers for the poor and school-based child health intervention. Eligible programs address issues including the improvement and stimulation of health care delivery, the coordination and creation of community health services, the education of healthcare providers, and the public's awareness of and access to community health services. Each of the five main categories has its own area of the elegant Web site with a program report and RFPs (Requests for Proposals) with deadlines for the area. Nonprofits within the twenty county service area interested in applying for a non-specified grant should call the Foundation with an initial inquiry before submitting a full proposal. Visitors to the Web site will find lists of each department staff and the board of trustees. There are also lists of recent grants, listed by the same categories as above, and a section with health statistics.

Healthcare Foundation of New Jersey (NJ) (http://www.hfnj.org/)

The Healthcare Foundation of New Jersey is firmly rooted in the strong tradition of delivering the highest standards of medical care, a tradition established by the Jewish community in Newark, New Jersey, and that began with the inauguration of the Newark Beth Israel Hospital in 1901. Formerly known as the NBI Healthcare Foundation, the private grantmaking foundation was founded in 1996 to alleviate the suffering of the most vulnerable members of the community. Its goal is to strengthen existing healthcare programs and provide seed money for innovative projects that address unmet healthcare needs. The foundation is interested in health-related proposals that address one of its four priority areas: vulnerable children and families of Newark, especially the South Ward; vulnerable members of the MetroWest Jewish community of northern New Jersey; medical education and humanism in medicine; and clinical research, especially at the Newark Beth Israel Medical Center. The foundation also has the Humanism in Medicine Award, which recognizes graduating medical students and faculty members who best exemplify humanism and compassion in medical care delivery, and the Humanistic Patient Care Awards, which recognizes healthcare workers at area hospitals and nursing homes for compassionate caregiving. Consult its Web site for grant guidelines, instructions, information on their programs, grant lists, financial information, and contact information.

Healthcare Foundation for Orange County (CA) (http://www.hfoc.org)

Based in Santa Ana, California, the Healthcare Foundation for Orange County was formed by the acquisition of United Western Medical Centers (UWMC), a not-for-profit hospital system, by OrNda Healthcare, a for-profit company. Funds in excess of UWMC's departments and other obligations were placed in the Foundation. The mission of The Healthcare Foundation for Orange County is to improve the health of the neediest and most underserved residents of Orange County, with particular emphasis on United Western Medical Center's historic service area of Central Orange County. One of its major initiatives is "Healthy Orange County," which is aimed toward programs that will improve maternal, child, and adolescent health through increased access to prevention and primary care services. Funding will emphasize expanding and developing services for low-income families in Santa Ana, Tustin, Orange, and Anaheim. Priority will be given to collaborative efforts that: empower parents with information, resources, and support to ensure the health of their children; bring culturally relevant services and information into all communities served; remove access barriers such as those due to transportation, language, cost, or location; stimulate innovative services and proven models for effectively addressing community health; establish priorities and identify delivery system gaps; and assess the changing health needs of pregnant women, children, and adolescents. Preference is given to programs that maximize existing resources and enable individuals and communities to take charge of their own health. The Web site provides grant application guidelines and a printable application cover page. Visitors will also find an online information request form, press releases, and a search function for the site.

William Randolph Hearst Foundations (NY) (http://hearstfdn.org)

The Hearst Foundation, Inc., was founded in 1945 by publisher and philanthropist William Randolph Hearst. In 1948, Hearst established the California Charities Foundation, the name of which was changed to the William Randolph Hearst Foundation after Mr. Hearst's death in 1951. The charitable goals of the two Foundations are essentially the same, reflecting the philanthropic interests of William Randolph Hearst: education, health, social service, and culture. The Foundations' proposal evaluation process is divided geographically: organizations east of the Mississippi River must apply to the Foundations' New York offices, while organizations west of the Mississippi are asked to apply through the Foundations' San Francisco offices. In addition to its grantmaking activities in the four program areas mentioned above, the Hearst Foundations make grants to students through the Hearst Journalism Awards Program and the United States Senate Youth Program. Visitors to the Foundations' Web site will find program guidelines, funding policies and limitations, a listing of recent grants, application procedures, and descriptions of both awards programs.

Heathcote Art Foundation, Inc. (CT) (http://www.artswire.org/ArtsWire/heathcote)

The Heathcote Art Foundation was established in New York in 1964 by Josephine Mercy Heathcote Haskell. It was originally an exhibiting foundation for Haskell's personal collection of eighteenth century English art and furnishings, but since its conversion to a grantmaking foundation in 1986, its purpose has been to support arts organizations that directly assist emerging artists of promise and that promote the creation of new and innovative work in all artistic disciplines. Located in Old Greenwich, Connecticut, the Foundation prefers to restrict its grantmaking to organizations in the New York City area with annual operating budgets no greater than $1 million, though exceptions are made at the discretion of the executive committee. Whenever possible, grants are passed through sponsoring organizations to benefit individual artists. Visitors to the Web site will find grant guidelines and instructions, a printable application form, some financial information, a grants list, and contact information.

The Heinz Endowments (PA) (http://www.heinz.org/)

The Pittsburgh-based Heinz Endowments, comprised of the Howard Heinz and the Vira I. Henz Endowements, support the efforts of nonprofit organizations active in the areas of arts and culture, education, children, youth and families, economic opportunity, and the environment, with an emphasis on programs either in southwestern Pennsylvania or of clear benefit to the region. A model of functional design, the Endowments' Web site offers a range of information, including broad and program-specific statements of philosophy; information about goals, grants, projects, and staff in each program area; application guidelines; FAQs; news; and brief biographies of Howard Heinz and Vira I. Heinz as well as various program officers and directors.

Clarence E. Heller Foundation (CA) (http://cehcf.org)

Founded by Clarence E. Heller in 1982 in San Francisco, the Clarence E. Heller Foundation's mission is "to protect and improve the quality of life through support of programs in the environment, human health, education and the arts." In the area of environment and health, the Foundation concentrates on programs that address the health risks of toxic substances and environmental hazards; the Management of Resources program focuses on the viability of communities and regions and sustainable agriculture; music programs promote symphonic and chamber music; education strives to give elementary and secondary students opportunities. Grants range from $5,000 to $600,000. The Foundation also funds select special projects. Visitors to the Web site will find past program highlights, past grants, application guidelines, and contact information for each grant.

The F.B. Heron Foundation (NY) (http://fdncenter.org/grantmaker/fbheron/)

The F.B. Heron Foundation was created in 1992 with the mission of helping people and communities to help themselves. The Foundation is interesting in "supporting organizations engaged in efforts to strengthen individuals, families, and communities as they face challenges and seize opportunities presented by contemporary society." The Foundation also makes program related investments (PRIs), mostly in respect to the social and economic impact on low-income families and communities. Visitors to the Foundation's folder on the Center's Web site will find detailed information on the Foundation's grant and PRI programs; application procedures; a copy of the latest annual report and Form 990-PF; a listing of the current directors, officers, and staff; and contact information.

Hershey Foundation (OH) (http://fdncenter.org/grantmaker/hershey/index.html)

Founded in 1986 by Jo Hershey Selden, the Hershey Foundation was established in honor of her late husband, Alvin A. Hershey. Located in Concord Township, Ohio, the Foundation is dedicated to providing "bridges of opportunity for the children of Northeast Ohio."

The Foundation aims to help schools, museums, cultural institutions, and other nonprofits develop and implement innovative programs that will improve quality of life, build self-esteem, enhance learning, increase exposure to other cultures and ideas, and encourage the development of independent thinking and problem-solving skills. Support is given to pilot projects that can be replicated in other settings, with priority given to alternative educational programs; arts, cultural, and science programs; and early childhood education programs. A particular funding focus is Montessori education and programs embodying the Montessori child-centered approach to learning. Grants are given for program development and special projects, equipment that brings new capabilities to an organization (but not computers), and capital campaigns and endowment of special projects. Visitors to the Web site will find grant guidelines and procedures, a grants list, financial information, and a history of the Hershey Foundation.

Fannie and John Hertz Foundation (CA) (http://www.hertzfoundation.org)
The Fannie and John Hertz Foundation was founded in 1957 by John Daniel Hertz, an Austrian emigrant who lived the American Dream. The Foundation, based in Livermore, California, is an expression of his gratitude for the country that afforded him so many opportunities. He sensed that the nation, "in order to survive, prosper, and lead, had to increase substantially the ranks of its most competent engineers and applied scientists" and felt that that Foundation could "perform a notable service to the nation by fostering the education and training of outstanding students in these areas." To that end, the Foundation provides fellowships for graduate work leading to a Ph.D. degree from three dozen universities in applications of the physical sciences: applied physics, chemistry, mathematics, modern biology, and all areas of engineering. Although a list of fields of study is provided on the Web site, it is up to the individual applicant to advocate his or her specific field of interest as an "applied physical science." Consult the Web site for information and application instructions for the Graduate Fellowship Program. Visitors to the Web site will also find a history of the foundation and a biography of John Hertz and his wife Fannie, a soon-to-be available FAQ page, links to other resources, and contact information. Applications may be submitted online and through traditional means.

William and Flora Hewlett Foundation (CA) (http://www.hewlett.org/)
The broadly stated mission of the Hewlett Foundation, established in 1966 by Palo Alto industrialist William R. Hewlett (of Hewlett-Packard fame), his late wife, Flora Lamson Hewlett, and their eldest son, Walter B. Hewlett, is "to promote the well-being of mankind by supporting selected activities of a charitable nature, as well as organizations or institutions engaged in such activities." The Foundation concentrates its resources on activities in the areas of education, performing arts, population, environment, conflict resolution, family and community development, and U.S.-Latin American relations, the latter an outgrowth of the Foundation's long-standing interest in U.S.-Mexico relations. The Foundation's Web site provides detailed program descriptions and application guidelines, a board and staff listing, a list of grants organized by program area, an online version of the Foundation's annual report, and contact information.

Allen Hilles Fund (PA) (http://www.dvg.org/Hilles)
The Allen Hilles Fund, located in Philadelphia, provides financial support in the areas of education, women's issues, economic development in disadvantaged communities, and activities of the Religious Society of Friends. The Fund was established by Edith Hilles Dewees in memory of her father, Thomas Allen Hilles, and began operation in 1983. Grants focus on the cities of Philadelphia and Chester, Pennsylvania, and Wilmington, Delaware. Visitors to the site will find a history of the founder, guidelines, a recent grants list, statistics, the Fund's tax return, a downloadable and printable application form, and contact information.

Conrad N. Hilton Foundation (CA & NV) (http://www.hiltonfoundation.org/)
The Conrad N. Hilton Foundation was founded in 1944 by hotel entrepreneur Conrad N. Hilton and is based in Los Angeles, California, and Reno, Nevada. The Foundation's

mission is to "alleviate the suffering of the world's most disadvantaged, with a special emphasis on children and support for the work of the Roman Catholic Sisters." This cause manifests itself through seven project areas: blindness, early childhood development, water, domestic violence, Catholic sisters, homeless mentally ill, and the College of Hotel and Restaurant Management. The Foundation also awards the Conrad N. Hilton Humanitarian Prize of $1 million to a nonprofit organization that has made an extraordinary contribution in alleviating human suffering. Additionally, the Foundation supports the Conrad N. Hilton Fund, a nonprofit organization that makes grants to specific organizations delineated in its charter, but it does not accept unsolicited proposals. The Foundation supplies further information on its finances, past Humanitarian Prize recipients and a description of the nomination process (with a nomination form that can be downloaded in Microsoft Word), news, conferences, a history of Mr. Hilton, and links to granting priority organizations.

Hoblitzelle Foundation (TX) (http://home.att.net/~hoblitzelle/)

The Hoblitzelle Foundation, based in Dallas, Texas, was founded by Karl Hoblitzelle in 1942. Karl Hoblitzelle had a successful entertainment business and investments in the oil, gas, real estate, and banking industries in Texas. The Foundation focuses its grantmaking on specific, non-recurring needs of the educational, social service, medical, cultural, and civic organizations in the state of Texas only, particularly within the Dallas Metroplex. Consult the Web site for application guidelines, links to additional information, a short biography of its founder, a listing of directors, a grant list, and contact information.

The Hoglund Foundation (TX) (http://www.hoglundfdtn.org)

Established in 1989, the Hoglund Foundation uses the "resources and abilities of the extended family of Forrest E. Hoglund and Sally R. Hoglund to generate and/or support activities that can make a positive difference in the lives of others." The primary focus of the Dallas-based foundation is to "promote interests and entities in education, health science and services, social services, and children's health and development." Priorities are organizations and programs that nurture, recognize, and reward individual initiative and responsibility; are innovative and promote creative solutions; have sound management and are efficient in the management of funds; and are collaborative in nature so that resources are shared and the impact of the grant is multiplied in the community. The Foundation's geographic focus is primarily Dallas and Houston, Texas, but grants are made outside of this area. Check the Web site for grant application guidelines, contact information, and links to other resources.

Horizon Foundation (MA) (http://www.horizonfoundation.org)

The Horizon Foundation is located in Ipswich, Massachusetts, and was founded in 1997. The Foundation supports "non-profit organizations that affect positive change among children, the adults who work with them, and the communities in which they live. Horizon supports projects and organizations that teach respect and care for the natural environment, encourage an appreciation and understanding of the significance of the arts and history, and promote leadership skills." The Foundation will only consider grant proposals from non-profit organizations that support projects in Cumberland, Franklin, Lincoln, and York Counties in Maine; Barnstable, Essex, and Middlesex Counties in Massachusetts; and Mercer County in New Jersey. The Foundation will consider proposals for youth-focused programs for children of elementary and secondary school age in the areas of the arts, the environment, history education, and leadership training. Information about restrictions, grant sizes, and types of funding is available on the Foundation's Web site as is a list of previous grants awarded. The Foundation does not accept unsolicited applications, but interested organizations may submit a letter of inquiry. Guidelines for the letter and the full proposal can be found on the site, along with deadline information.

Houston Endowment, Inc. (TX) (http://www.houstonendowment.org)

Founded in 1937 by Jesse H. Jones and Mary Gibbs Jones, and today the largest private philanthropic foundation in Texas, the Houston Endowment is dedicated to the support of charitable undertakings serving the people of the greater Houston area and the state of Texas and contributes to a broad spectrum of programs in education, health care, human services, cultural arts, and other areas. In addition to general information about the Foundation and its founders, visitors to the Web site will find descriptions of the Foundation's programs and grant eligibility criteria, application procedures, online versions of the Foundation's annual reports, recent grants lists, board and staff listings, and contact information.

Hunter's Hope Foundation, Inc. (NY) (http://www.huntershope.org/)

Created in 1997 by Former Buffalo Bills quarterback Jim Kelly and his wife after their son was diagnosed with Krabbes Disease, Hunter's Hope Foundation seeks to find a cure for all forms of Leukodystrophies. Krabbes, a specific form of Leukodystrophy, is caused by a genetic error that prevents proper nerve development in the brain, affecting breathing and body temperature—those things that are automatic body functions. Because these functions affect so many others, seizures occur, and digestion is inhibited. The body, without many of these basic functions, is subjected to a domino effect of other problems—poor muscle control being the one thing that inhibits these children most. The Foundation provides grants in three areas: Post-Doctoral Fellowships are provided for individuals who are within five years of receiving their degree in studying Krabbes or other Leukodystrophies; Pilot Studies support researchers testing new concepts and ideas to fight the disease; Major Research Grants are awarded to senior investigators who are studying either basic mechanisms or treatment approaches to Krabbes Disease. Visit the Foundation's Web site to learn more about Krabbes Disease and to obtain specific information on the Foundation's giving program and contact information.

Hut Foundation (CA) (http://www.hutfdn.org)

Based in San Francisco, the Hut Foundation was established in 1998 and funds projects in the areas of education, humanitarian issues, and the environment. The Foundation also seeks "to promote respect for others and to develop our commitment to family." Hut Foundation funds are used to target educational programs that serve both children and young adults and strengthen families. Within the area of education, the Hut Foundation's primary funding interests include children with autism and their families; animal assisted therapy for children and adults with disabilities; arts education with an emphasis on populations which are culturally, economically, or physically disadvantaged; and environmental education for children and young adults. Programs that encourage the development of self esteem and independence are preferred over direct service programs. Priority is also given to interactive, innovative programs that provide hands-on experience for those served. The Foundation has a special interest in supporting programs that not only serve those in need but also encourage those served to give back to the community at large. The Hut Foundation offers grants of $5,000–$10,000 to nonprofit organizations within the geographic areas where Foundation members live and work: the San Francisco Bay Area (counties of San Francisco, Alameda, Marin, and Sonoma), Maryland (counties of Montgomery and Prince Georges), The District of Columbia, and Virginia. The format for letters of inquiry may be printed from the site; letters of inquiry may also be submitted electronically. Visitors to the site will also find grant lists and contact information.

Hutton Foundation (CA) (http://www.huttonfoundation.org)

The Betty L. Hutton founded the Hutton Foundation in 1980. She was the widow of Harold C. Hutton, with whom she had built an international oil refining empire. The Foundation supports educational, health, and community organizations and acts as a catalyst to encourage development of new programs and services for future generations. Primary areas of focus include education; health and human services; child, youth, and family services; arts and culture; women's services; and civic and community development. Funding is primarily awarded to organizations in Orange, Riverside, and Santa Barbara Counties in California, with select international awards. In addition to donations and grants, the Foundation also offers Program Related Investments (PRI), which are loans to purchase buildings, make major tenant improvements on buildings owned by nonprofit organizations, and to refinance existing real estate or construction loans. The Foundation is headquartered in

Santa Barbara, California, with an additional office in Orange. Visit the Web site for grant application guidelines and instructions, further information about PRIs, information about the review and selection process, 1998 grants list, and contact information.

Hyde and Watson Foundation (NJ) (http://fdncenter.org/grantmaker/hydeandwatson/)

Formerly the Lillia Babbitt Hyde Foundation and the John Jay and Eliza Jane Watson Foundation, which were consolidated in January 1983, the Chatham Township, New Jersey-based Hyde and Watson Foundation supports capital projects such as purchase or relocation of facilities, building improvements, capital equipment, instructive materials development, and certain medical research areas. Broad fields include health, education, religion, social services, arts, and humanities. Currently grant support is focused primarily in the New York City metropolitan area and Essex, Union, and Morris Counties in New Jersey. The typical grant range is $5,000–$25,000. The foundation's folder on the Center's Web site provides a history of the foundation, grant guidelines, a grants list, financial statements, and information about the foundation's management.

The i2 Foundation (TX) (http://www.i2foundation.org)

The mission of the Texas-based i2 Foundation is to "promote advancements in education, technology, environmental practices, medicine, and economic opportunity through programs that improve the quality of life and create a healthier society." Created in 1997 by employees of i2 Technologies, the purpose of the Foundation is to give back to the community where the company operates. The Foundation supports projects and organizations all over the world. The Foundation also supports annual fundraising campaigns to benefit the organization, including the 5K Run/Walk for a Better World and i2 Cooks!, a cookbook that brings together recipes from i2er's from all over the world. "The major priorities of the Foundation include the development and education of children and youth, however also considers issues related to poverty, hunger, illiteracy, education, youth violence, violence against women, early child development, environmental preservation, scientific research, and improved healthcare." Visit the Foundation's Web site to find interesting information about the i2's mission, a FAQ page, grant application information, and contact information.

I Have a Dream Foundation (NY) (Operating foundation) (http://www.ihad.org)

The I Have a Dream Foundation (IHAD) was started by Eugene Lang, a New York businessman, who in 1981 made an extraordinary offer to a group of sixth graders at the East Harlem elementary school he had once attended. He promised partial college scholarships if they finished high school. Four years later, all the children were still in school, and widespread national attention and interest began to develop. In 1986, Eugene Lang organized the national I Have a Dream Foundation to help launch a new generation of IHAD projects across the country. Today, IHAD helps "children from low-income areas become productive citizens by providing a long-term program of mentoring, tutoring, and enrichment, with an assured opportunity for higher education." Its goal is to see that all the "Dreamers," as the children are called, graduate from high school "functionally literate and prepared either for fulfilling employment or further education." IHAD provides partial financial assistance for college, university, or accredited vocational school tuition. Local IHAD projects usually have 60 to 79 Dreamers who represent either an entire grade level from an elementary school or an entire age group from a public housing project, determined in consultation with local school officials, community-based organizations, and the national IHAD foundation. For this reason, students can not apply to be Dreamers. Visit the Web site for further information on the IHAD program. Visitors will find a history of the foundation, a FAQ sheet, locations and contact information for local IHAD projects, and information about how to get involved.

Institute of Current World Affairs, Inc. (NY) (Operating foundation) (http://www.icwa.org)

Established in 1925, the Institute of Current World Affairs of New York City is funded by its own Crane-Rogers Foundation and two other trusts. The organization's purpose is to "provide talented and promising individuals with an opportunity to develop a deep understanding of an issue, country or region outside the United States and to share that understanding with a wider public." The Institute offers two-year fellowships to people under 36 years of age for advanced study overseas. There are three different types of fellowships. The Target of Opportunity Fellowships are given in the fellow's field of choice or in one of the Fields of Interest selected by Institute members. The fields have included Korea, Japan, South America's southern cone, the seas, fresh water, and the status of women. The John Miller Musser Memorial Forest and Society Fellowships are awarded to people with graduate degrees in forestry-related fields to study the relationship between forest-resource problems and people. John O. Crane Memorial Fellowships are for the study of Eastern Europe and the Middle East. The straightforward Web site offers all that an applicant needs. There is a list of current Fields of Interest and information on fellowships available each year, sometimes including additional specialized programs. There are application instructions and deadlines and a list of past fellows. Visitors will also find trustee and staff lists and contact information. These are not scholarships but fellowships for those who have already received their degrees.

Institute of Mental Hygiene (LA) (http://www.imhno.org)

The Institute of Mental Hygiene (IMH) is located in New Orleans, Louisiana. The IMH is committed to "investing in children through its grantmaking programs, active involvement with grantees, and leadership in improving mental health programs and policies." Nonprofits in New Orleans are eligible to apply to three different grant programs. The Children's Mental Health Grants Program funds the testing of new ideas, works to ensure that effective programs are replicated, encourages projects addressing critical or emerging issues, and provides core support to reputable organizations. Programs involving very young children are especially encouraged to apply. The Early Childhood Mini-Grants Program supports organizations working with very young children and their families. Awards go toward seed money, leadership and training in the field, engaging parents as educators, and raising public awareness, among other issues. The Technical Assistance Grants Program makes grants to support management and capacity building in organizations. The IMH Web site includes more specific program descriptions and application deadlines. Grant guidelines and applications can be downloaded in PDF format. The site also includes contact information for select staff members and a list of previous grantees. IMH Evaluation Guidelines can also be viewed online.

Institute of Turkish Studies, Inc. (DC) (http://www.turkishstudies.org)

Created in 1982, the Institute of Turkish Studies is located at the Edmund A. Walsh School of Foreign Service at Georgetown University in Washington, D.C. The organization is "devoted solely to supporting and encouraging the development of Turkish Studies in American higher education through an annual grant program." The Institute supports the work of individuals and universities in the field of Turkish studies, the publication of books and journals that bring the field to the American population, and discussion of the history and current events of Turkey. The grant program offers scholarships and makes awards to institutes of higher learning. Individual awards include Travel-Research Grants in Turkey for post-doctoral scholars, Pre-Dissertation Graduate Fellowships, Dissertation Writing Grants, and Teaching Aid Grants for the development of resources. Institutions may receive library support, matching grants for conferences and lecture series, and matching seed money for new faculty positions. The Institute also funds a series of prizes distributed by the Turkish Studies Association. There is a page with specific application instructions, deadlines, and restrictions for each of the awards. The thorough site also includes a list of publications and information on public programs. Board members are listed in the Organization section, and there is information on contributing.

James Irvine Foundation (CA) (http://www.irvine.org/)

The San Francisco-based Irvine Foundation was established in 1937 as trustee of the charitable trust of James Irvine, a California agricultural pioneer, to promote the general welfare of the people of California. Today, it is dedicated "to enhancing the social, economic, and physical quality of life throughout California, and to enriching the State's intellectual and cultural environment." Within this broad mandate, the Foundation makes grants in seven program areas: the arts; children, youth, and families; civic culture; health; higher education; sustainable communities; and workforce development. The Foundation also makes room for special projects; in the recent past the Foundation has made a commitment to effective management and governance of nonprofits, initiatives to support community foundations, and enhanced the capacity of organized philanthropy. Visitors to the Foundation's Web site will find detailed program information, including priority goals and recent grants in each funding area; application guidelines; board and staff listings; numerous links to grantee organizations; an interesting feedback area; and contact information.

Irvine Health Foundation (CA) (http://www.ihf.org/)
Established in 1985, the Irvine Health Foundation provides support for prevention, service, research, and policy activities related to the health and wellness of the Orange County, California, community. The Foundation's Web site offers a mission statement, a listing of directors and staff, FAQs, press releases, grant highlights, a For Your Health feature, highlights from the IHF lecture series, grant application procedures with FAQs, and links to numerous related sites.

Irwin Foundation (MI) (http://comnet.org/irwin/)
The Irwin Foundation is located in Southfield, Michigan, and received its non-profit status in 1996. It provides funding for scholarships in veterinary education. Its mission is "the promotion of veterinary education, including the funding of student funding in schools, departments, or units accredited in veterinary medicine of veterinary technology, within a major university structure." The Foundation provides funding only to accredited schools within major universities. However, scholarship recipients are chosen by the universities themselves; the Irwin Foundation does not participate in, nor interfere with, the selection process. The Web site provides information about the future of the Foundation as well as links to information about the veterinary field.

Ittleson Foundation, Inc. (NY) (http://www.IttlesonFoundation.org)
Henry Ittleson, founder of CIT Financial Corporation, established the Ittleson Foundation in 1932. The New York City-based Foundation seeks to fund pilot projects, test and demonstration projects and applied research that would inform public policy, and "such projects [that] should have significance beyond the local area of implementation and [that] should result in an outcome of some consequence in the real world." Areas of particular interest are mental health, AIDS, and the environment. Although the Foundation funds broadly in each area, there are specific concerns of interest. In the area of mental health, the Foundation prefers projects that "cut across the entire field and those that address underserved populations." In the area of environment, it seeks to educate a new generation of environmentalists and has interests in urban environmental issues and efforts at resource protection. For AIDS, the Foundation focuses on prevention and mental health consequences of the disease. Visit the Web site for further information on each grantmaking area, application guidelines, viewable grant lists and summaries, a downloadable annual report, guidelines, and contact information.

Caroline Lawson Ivey Memorial Foundation, Inc. (AL) (http://www.mindspring.com/~climf/index.html)
Located in Auburn, Alabama, the Caroline Lawson Ivey Memorial Foundation was established in 1986 by Oliver Turner Ivey, a professor of history, to honor his wife. The organization works to "encourage, promote and sponsor the discipline of Social Studies at all grade levels, with special emphasis being placed on the preparation of persons who plan to enter the teaching profession." This is accomplished through the distribution of scholarships and grants and the sponsorship of workshops. Scholarships are offered to college juniors and seniors who are pursuing a career of teaching social studies in middle or secondary grades. Specific criteria are listed, and the application can either be printed from the screen or downloaded. Workshops teach the Cultural Approach teaching methods developed by the founder and are available to teachers in Alabama and west Georgia. Teachers attending the week-long summer workshops receive a stipend. The grants are also offered

to teachers in Alabama and west Georgia for curriculum planning and development, in-service training, the development of instructional materials for use in elementary and secondary schools, and other projects that focus on the Cultural Approach method of teaching. The site includes information on this methodology, biographical information on the founder and his wife, and a list of board members.

Janx Foundation (NJ) (http://fdncenter.org/grantmaker/janx/)

Based in Newark, New Jersey, the Janx Foundation funds programs that encourage the education of America's youth, especially in urban areas. It strives to provide "urban, underprivileged youth with positive opportunities to make evident to the world that they are productive, responsible members of society" in school, the workplace, and life in general. To this end, the Foundation prefers to fund nonprofits with youth development programs and gives preference to organizations in the greater New York and New Jersey metropolitan areas. The Foundation's folder on the Center's Web site provides an extensive explanation of its mission and goals. Grantseekers will also find letter of inquiry guidelines, grant submission guidelines, and contact information.

The Jaqua Foundation (NJ) (http://fdncenter.org/grantmaker/jaqua/)

The Jaqua Foundation of New Jersey is interested in collegiate education, welfare of animals, and performing arts. The Foundation does not makes grants to individuals. Visitors to the Foundation's folder on the Center's Web site will find a copy of the Foundation's latest Form 990-PF and contact information.

Martha Holden Jennings Foundation (OH) (http://www.mhjf.org)

The Martha Holden Jennings Foundation, founded in 1959, is dedicated to fostering "the development of young people to the maximum possible extent through improving the quality of education in secular elementary and secondary schools in Ohio." To that end, the Cleveland-based Foundation is eager to explore new frontiers in Ohio schools and to promote more effective teaching in those schools. The Foundation offers two specific grants programs, Grants-to-Administrators and Grants-to-Teachers, as well as an Open Grants program. Guidelines and limitations of these grants can be found on the Foundation's Web site. Visitors to the site will also find the Foundation's publication, *Pro Excellentia,* which can be downloaded in PDF format, and contact information.

Jerome Foundation (MN) (http://www.jeromefdn.org/)

The St. Paul-based Jerome Foundation promotes the careers and work of emerging artists in Minnesota and New York City through its support of programs in dance, literature, media arts, music, theater, performance art, visual arts, multidisciplinary work, and arts criticism. The Foundation places the emerging creative artist at the center of its grantmaking and gives funding priority to programs and projects that are artist driven. The Foundation's Web site provides program guidelines, application requirements and procedures, full descriptions of every grant awarded in recent years arranged alphabetically by program area or by date, answers to frequently asked questions, financial statements, contact information, and enough multimedia bits to keep you busy for hours.

Jewish Foundation for Education of Women (NY) (http://www.jfew.org/index.html)

The Jewish Foundation for Education of Women provides financial aid for higher education to women within a 50-mile radius of New York City. The Foundation is the successor to the historic Lower East Side Hebrew Technical School and provides two direct grant programs and numerous collaborative programs. Grants, usually in the amount of $5,000, can be renewed annually. Some larger grants, of $10–20,000, exist. The Foundation's direct grant programs are the Fellowship Program for Émgrés Training for Careers in Jewish Education and Scholarships for Émgrés in the Health Professions, both of which are for Émgrés from the former Soviet Union. Collaborative grants are through partnerships with various organizations in New York City. The JFEW Web site provides more information on these grants and partnerships as well as eligibility guidelines, a short application guide, a history of the Foundation, and contact information.

Jewish Healthcare Foundation (PA) (http://www.jhf.org)

The Jewish Healthcare Foundation (JHF) continues the tradition of its predecessor, Montefiore Hospital, a high-quality teaching hospital that pioneered advancements in medicine and public health and provided medical care in a kindly environment with an understanding of Jewish people and their needs. It was founded in 1908 by the Jewish community of southwestern Pennsylvania. In 1990, the board of trustees of Montefiore Hospital adopted a "plan of division" that separated the newly created Jewish Healthcare Foundation from the hospital. The mission of JHF is to "foster the provision of healthcare services, healthcare education, and when reasonable and appropriate, health care research, and it shall respond to the health-related needs of the elderly, underprivileged, indigent and underserved populations in Western Pennsylvania." The Pittsburgh, Pennsylvania-based JHF also supports and sometimes produces the research and publications necessary to inform others about new approaches to health problems. Grantmaking priorities are giving children the physical and mental health to succeed, preventing disease and disability, building healthy neighborhoods and communities, and improving public policies and systems of care. Visit the Web site for specific information on each grantmaking priority and for funding guidelines and application instructions. The Web site also features an online feedback form, site search function, a media contact center, a research report on foundations and philanthropy, an online publications order form, and contact information.

Johnson Foundation, Inc. (WI) (Operating foundation) (http://www.johnsonfdn.org/index.html)

The primary activity of the Wisconsin-based Johnson Foundation is planning and co- sponsoring conferences of public interest at Wingspread, its Frank Lloyd Wright-designed headquarters and conference center in Racine. The Foundation encourages conference proposals from nonprofit organizations in six areas of interest: supporting sustainable development; enhancing learning productivity at all educational levels; building civil and civic community; encouraging constructive adult engagement in the lives of children and youth; Keland Endowment conferences on the arts, the environment, and persons with disabilities; and southeastern Wisconsin. The Foundation does not award grants, fund programs, sponsor retreats or fundraisers, or rent its facilities. Visitors to the Foundation's elegant, earth-toned Web site will find a brief history of the Foundation and its mission; general descriptions of its program interests; a searchable Virtual Library with online versions of recent annual reports and conference proceedings, articles (in HTML and PDF formats) from back issues of the *Wingspread Journal,* and dozens of links organized by program interest; an Online Discussion area with both "open" and "closed" discussions; and detailed information about proposing a conference.

Helen K. and Arthur E. Johnson Foundation (CO) (http://www.johnsonfoundation.net)

The Denver, Colorado-based Helen K. and Arthur E. Johnson Foundation was established in 1948 in memory of Arther E. Johnson, Colorado oil entrepreneur, and his wife Helen, both noted philanthropists in the area. The Foundation strives to relieve suffering, provide basic human needs, promote self-sufficiency, and enrich the quality of life in local Colorado communities. Online, the Foundation's concise Web site provides application guidelines, contact information, and a brief history of the Johnson family.

Robert Wood Johnson Foundation (NJ) (http://www.rwjf.org/)

The mission of the Robert Wood Johnson Foundation is to improve the health and health care of all Americans. The Foundation's main funding goals are to ensure that all Americans have access to basic health care at reasonable cost, to improve the way services are organized and provided to people with chronic health conditions, and to reduce the harm caused by substance abuse–tobacco, alcohol, and illicit drugs. The Foundation's comprehensive Web site is a guide to its programs and activities and a substantial resource for the health care field. Visitors will find detailed program descriptions and application guidelines, grant outcomes and related publications, information about the Foundation's own programs and projects, a library of publications, current calls for proposals, and press releases and other media-related information. Visitors to the site will also find links to the Foundation's special resource sites: Last Acts (http://www.lastacts.org/), a call-to-action campaign designed to improve care at the end of life, and ChronicNet (http://www.chronicnet.org/), a resource for reporting on chronic health conditions and disabilities.

Walter S. Johnson Foundation (CA) (http://www.wsjf.org/)

The Walter S. Johnson Foundation supports programs in northern California and Washoe County, Nevada, that "help children and youth meet their full potential and rise to the challenges of our diverse and changing society." The Foundation's grants program is focused on three primary goals: ensuring the well-being of children and youth, strengthening public education, and assisting young people in the transition to adulthood. Within these broad goals, the majority of grants are likely to focus on positive youth development, the professional development of educators, or the transition from school to career. Grants are also made for families in crisis, integrated services, family support, and neighborhood development. The Foundation's straightforward Web site provides grantmaking guidelines and grants lists for each program area as well as application procedures and a listing of the Foundation's trustees and staff.

JoMiJo Foundation (CA) (http://www.jomijo.org/)

The JoMiJo Foundation's mission is to "aid disenfranchised persons or communities through targeted funding of grassroots projects that improve the quality of people's lives or preserve the earth's natural environment." To achieve this, the Foundation supports economically disenfranchised people and communities; provides aid in education and welfare of children, including those at risk; and supports social and economic justice for women and minorities. The Foundation currently supports organizations in the San Francisco Bay Area, Denver, and Chicago. Upon visiting the Foundation's Web site, visitors will find examples of projects that have earned program support, organizations and areas that are not supported, application information, an online letter of intent form, contact information, and links to a variety of local, regional, national, and Internet organizational resources.

Daisy Marquis Jones Foundation (NY) (http://www.dmjf.org)

The Daisy Marquis Jones Foundation, located in Rochester, New York, was established in 1968 by Daisy Marquis Jones and Leo Marquis Lyons as a way of giving back to the community. The foundation is "dedicated to improving the well-being of residents in Monroe and Yates Counties by funding programs that aid disadvantaged children and families." The Foundation grants time-limited support to nonprofit organizations with programs or projects that provide access to health care, attend to the needs of young children, or help families develop economic security. The Web site provides more detailed information about the types of programs the Foundation funds and gives a list of previous grants. To apply, you must first fill out an inquiry form, which can be completed directly on the Web site. Those who complete the form will receive a follow-up e-mail that details the next steps. The annual report and contact information can be found on the Foundation's Web site.

W. Alton Jones Foundation, Inc. (VA) (http://www.wajones.org/)

Established in 1944 by millionaire oilman "Pete" Jones, the W. Alton Jones Foundation "focuses on global environmental protection and the prevention of nuclear war [or disaster]." At present, the Foundation concentrates its efforts in two main areas: a Sustainable World Program, which "supports efforts that will ensure that human activities do not undermine the quality of life of future generations," and a Secure World Program, which "seeks to build a secure world, free from the nuclear threat." The Foundation's Web site combines a smartly efficient architecture with an array of features and content, including program descriptions; grants lists and links to grantee Web sites; a grants "almanac;" application procedures; a listing of trustees, officers, and staff; and extensive e-mail contact information.

Joukowsky Family Foundation (NY) (http://www.joukowsky.org/)

The Joukowsky Family Foundation of New York was established in 1981 with a primary purpose of supporting education. Other interests of the Foundation include cultural, social, archaeological, and historical activities. Visitors to the Foundation's Web site will find information on the board, grant guidelines, a listing of recent grants, information on the Foundation's scholarship program, a copy of the latest tax return downloadable in PDF format, and contact information.

The Joyce Foundation (IL) (http://www.joycefdn.org)

Beatrice Joyce Kean, whose family wealth came from the lumber industry, established the Joyce Foundation in 1948. The Foundation supports efforts to protect the natural environment of the Great Lakes, to reduce poverty and violence in the region, and to ensure that its people have access to good schools, decent jobs, and a diverse and thriving culture. It also support efforts to reform the system of financing election campaigns. Currently, the Foundation's program areas are education, employment, environment, gun violence prevention, money and politics, and culture. The Chicago-based foundation gives preference to organizations based in or who have a program in the Midwest, specifically the Great Lakes region: Illinois, Indiana, Iowa, Michigan, Minnesota, Ohio, and Wisconsin. A limited number of grants are made to organizations in Canada, and culture grants are restricted to the Chicago metropolitan area. Consult the Web site for further information on each program area and for grant application information and deadlines. The Web site also features downloadable application forms and guidelines; a downloadable newsletter and annual report; grants list; links to grantee organizations; a site search function; announcements and press releases; a listing of officers, directors, and staff; and contact information.

Henry J. Kaiser Family Foundation (CA) (http://www.kff.org)

The Kaiser Family Foundation is an independent philanthropy that seeks to be an independent, trusted, and credible source of information, analysis, and balanced discussion on the field of health, which the foundation recognizes as being otherwise dominated by large interests. The Foundation seeks to be this source of information to policymakers, the media, and the general public. The Foundation's work is focused on four main areas: health policy, reproductive health, HIV policy, and health and development in South Africa. Its Web site is primarily designed to be an information resource in its program areas; as such, it provides a wealth of health-related news, reports, and fact sheets. The Foundation makes few grants, but information about applying can be found in the About KFF section of the site.

Kansas Health Foundation (KS) (http://www.kansashealth.org/)

Established with the proceeds from the sale of the Wesley Medical Center in 1985, and with an endowment of more than $450 million, the Kansas Health Foundation makes grants to health organizations throughout the state aimed at improving the quality of health in Kansas. Although the majority of the Foundation's activity centers around Foundation-initiated partnerships and programs, it does provide funding each year through its Recognition Grant program "to support grass-roots organizations doing creative and innovative work to improve the health of Kansans." Recognition Grants fall into five primary categories: primary care education, rural health, health promotion and disease prevention, public health, and health policy and research. In addition to general information about the Foundation and its programs, visitors to the Foundation's Web site will find Recognition Grant program descriptions and funding guidelines.

Mitchell Kapor Foundation (CA) (http://www.mkf.org/)

The Mitchell Kapor Foundation, based in Bolinas, California, pursues its grantmaking with the mission of "improving human well-being and sustaining healthy ecosystems that support all life on earth." Established by Mitchell Kapor, the founder of the Lotus Development Corporation, the Foundation centers its funding interests in the areas of human health, the environment, and the impact of information technology on society. The Foundation's Web site provides detailed background descriptions of its two main grants: the

Environmental Health Program and the Program on the Impact of Information Technology. The latter does not accept outside funding requests; it is chosen on Foundation initiative. The former currently focuses on the issue of chemical contamination, and application instructions can be found through a link to the Jenifer Altman Foundation Web site. Contact information for the Kapor Foundation is provided.

The Karma Foundation (NJ) (http://www.karmafoundation.org/)
The New Jersey-based Karma Foundation was established in 1996 to provide grants to support organizations engaged in activities and programs in the areas of arts and culture, education and literacy, health and human services, and the development and enrichment of Jewish life. The Foundation's Web site provides grant guidelines, application procedures, restrictions, sample grants, and foundation trustees.

Ewing Marion Kauffman Foundation (MO) (http://www.emkf.org)
The Kansas City-based Kauffman Foundation is an operating and grantmaking foundation with a special interest in entrepreneurial leadership and youth development. In making grants, the Foundation aims to support "sustainable programs and projects that will lead to individual, organizational and community self-sufficiency." The Foundation accepts direct inquiries, not unsolicited proposals. Features of its Web site include program descriptions and application criteria, grant guidelines, contact information, and a brief biography of Ewing Kauffman.

The Kawabe Memorial Fund (WA) (http://fdncenter.org/grantmaker/kawabe/)
The Washington-based Kawabe Memorial Fund is a private foundation established under the will of Harry S. Kawabe. The purposes of the foundation are set forth in his will, which requires grants to be awarded in the areas of human services, religious institutions, and scholarships directed towards students graduating from Seward High School. Visit the Foundation's folder on the Center's Web site to find specific information on the Foundation's areas of interest, policies, geographical restrictions, application procedures, and contact information.

The Calvin K. Kazanjian Economics Foundation, Inc. (PA) (http://www.kazanjian.org)
Calvin K. Kazanjian established the Economics Foundation in his own name in 1947. A business owner for thirty years, he believed that social and political difficulties could be traced to economic illiteracy and that if people understood the basic facts of economics, "the world would be a better place in which to live." Therefore the mission of the foundation is "to help bring greater happiness and prosperity to all through better understanding of economics." Based in Dallas, Pennsylvania, the Foundation is interested in projects that present economics in an effective, thoughtful, and understandable way; encourage measurement of economic understanding more often, and/or more effectively; help otherwise disenfranchised youth and/or adults learn to participate in the economic system; and distribute high-quality economic education materials to regions of the world with emerging markets, though such projects represent a small portion of the annual grants budget. The Kazanjian Foundation is primarily interested in proposals that are national in scope and usually does not support regional or statewide programs. Visitors to the Web site will find application guidelines and procedures, information about the founder, links to other economic education resources, descriptions of some projects funded, and contact information.

The W.M. Keck Foundation (CA) (http://www.wmkeck.org/)
Established in 1954 by William Myron Keck, founder of the Superior Oil Company, the W.M. Keck Foundation focuses its grantmaking on the areas of medical research, science, and engineering. The Foundation also maintains a program for liberal arts colleges and the Southern California Grant Program, which provides support in the areas of civic and community services, health care and hospitals, precollegiate education, and the arts. According to the Foundation's guidelines, eligible institutions in the fields of science, engineering, medical research, and liberal arts are "accredited universities, colleges, medical schools, and major, independent medical research institutions." In the Southern California Grant

Program, "only organizations located in and serving the population of Southern California are eligible for consideration." Visitors to the Foundation's Web site will find general program descriptions, application criteria and guidelines, the Foundation's most recent annual report, grants lists organized by program area (no dollar amounts), a page devoted to the W.M. Keck Observatory on Hawaii's Mauna Kea volcano, and contact information.

W.K. Kellogg Foundation (MI) (http://www.wkkf.org/)

The mission of the W.K. Kellogg Foundation is to "help people help themselves through the practical application of knowledge and resources to improve their quality of life and that of future generations." The Foundation awards grants in three primary global regions: the United States; five southern Africa countries, including Botswana, Lesotho, South Africa, Swaziland, and Zimbabwe; and Latin America and the Caribbean. The U.S. program areas include; health, philanthropy and volunteerism, food systems and rural development, youth and education, and support for greater Battle Creek. In addition to thorough program descriptions, application guidelines, and the Foundation's latest annual report, the Foundation's sophisticated Web site offers a variety of useful features, including a state-of-the-art searchable grants database, an electronic version of the International Journal of the W.K. Kellogg Foundation, and individual listings of resources of interest in the Foundation's various program areas.

Henry P. Kendall Foundation (MA) (http://www.kendall.org/)

The Henry P. Kendall Foundation, based in Boston, Massachusetts, is dedicated to restoring and maintaining the ecological integrity of terrestrial, aquatic, and marine systems in the northeast and northwest regions of North America. The Foundation's current programs are focused on the "desire to integrate good science and local knowledge into environmental decision-making, to build capacity for sustained protection of natural resources, and to connect people and places by fostering stewardship of those resources." The Foundation's Web site includes application guidelines, recent annual reports (in PDF format), a publication listing, staff and trustee listings, and contact information.

Joseph P. Kennedy, Jr. Foundation (DC) (http://www.familyvillage.wisc.edu/jpkf/)

The Joseph P. Kennedy, Jr. Foundation has two major objectives: "to improve the way society deals with its citizens who have mental retardation, and to help identify and disseminate ways to prevent the causes of mental retardation." To that end, the Foundation provides seed funding that encourages new methods of service and supports and, through the use of its influence, promotes public awareness of the needs of persons with mental retardation and their families. The Foundation does not participate in capital costs or costs of equipment for projects or pay for ongoing support or operations of existing programs. Visitors to the Foundation's Web site will find information on the Foundation's various funding and award programs, detailed application guidelines, and an extensive listing of links to other online resources for mental retardation.

Kentucky Foundation for Women (KY) (http://www.kfw.org/)

The mission of the Kentucky Foundation for Women is "to change the lives of women by supporting feminist expression in the arts in Kentucky." The primary goal of the Foundation's grants program is to support the work of individual artists who live or work in Kentucky and "whose work embodies a feminist consciousness." Grants may also be awarded to organizations and for special collaborative projects that share the Foundation's goals. In addition to general Foundation information, application guidelines and procedures, and a list of recent grant recipients, visitors to the KFW Web site can learn about the Foundation's literary journal, *The American Voice,* and Hopscotch House, its rural retreat for women.

Charles F. Kettering Foundation (OH) (Operating foundation) (http://www.kettering.org/)

Established in 1927 by inventor Charles F. Kettering, the Kettering Foundation's objective is "to understand the way bodies politic . . . function or fail to function." The Foundation does not make grants; rather, it sponsors its own programs and participates in collaborative research efforts with other organizations to address the roles of politics and institutional structures as a dimension of everyday life. The results of the Foundation's research are published in study guides, community workbooks, and other exercises to help the public act responsibly and effectively on its problems. In addition to general information about the Foundation's activities and publications, a listing of Foundation trustees, and e-mail and contact information, visitors to the Foundation's Web site site can access a searchable database of more than 2,000 non-evaluative summaries of books and articles in the subject areas of governing, community, education, international, science, policy, and political philosophy.

Kettering Family Foundation (CO) (http://www.ketteringfamilyfoundation.org)

Located in Denver, Colorado, the Kettering Family Foundation was established in 1955 and currently is composed of 12 family members who elect 13 trustees annually. Priority is given to trustee-sponsored requests. Unsolicited proposals will be considered only after trustee-sponsored requests have been reviewed and funded. The Foundation considers unsolicited requests that fall under the following areas of interest: cultural/arts, education, environment, medical/health, and social/human services. Information about how to apply and where to send applications is available on the site. Deadlines, lists of previous grantees, and the Foundation's financial information are all available on the Web site.

The Sara H. and William R. Kimball Foundation (CA)
(http://www.pacificfoundationservices.com/kimball/index.html)

Founded in California in 1997, The Sara H. and William R. Kimball Foundation is committed to helping at-risk and disadvantaged individuals in the San Francisco Bay area to achieve the highest possible quality of life. Major program interests include education and the arts. Within the Education program, the Foundation focuses on higher education (undergraduate and graduate programs) specifically in areas of youth development, academic enrichment, tutorials, outdoor education, leadership development, vocational training and employment, learning disabilities, and sports/recreational activities for low-income youth. The arts program primarily focuses on youth groups. The Foundation also holds an interest in animal welfare and historic preservation, as well as capital support. Upon visiting the Foundation's Web site, visitors will find a most recent grants list, contact information, a board of directors list, and application procedures.

The Sidney Kimmel Foundation (PA) (http://www.kimmel.org/)

Located in Philadelphia, Pennsylvania, the Sidney Kimmel Foundation for Cancer Research is dedicated to "improving our basic understanding of cancer biology and to developing new methods for the prevention and treatment of cancer." The Foundation supports the research of those who concentrate on the following: basic cancer research, the rapid translation of basic science concepts into potential therapeutic applications, and/or clinical research with innovative treatment strategies. Grant recipients are chosen by a medical advisory board made up of distinguished cancer researchers. The Web site explains all of the grant guidelines and restrictions, as well as the rules and regulations. Each application must include a cover page, which can be printed from the site. Contact information, FAQs, and lists of previous grant recipients are all available on the site.

The Kimsey Foundation (DC) (http://www.kimseyfoundation.org)

Established in 1996 by James V. Kimsey, The Kimsey Foundation's mission is to level the playing field for economically disadvantaged Washington, D.C., youth. Subject areas of interest to the Foundation include education, computer technology, arts and culture, and domestic and international affairs. The Foundation primarily funds programs that benefit children in the Washington, D.C., area. The Foundation makes operating grants but prefers to fund established programs. Visit the Foundation's Web site to find areas not supported by the foundation and also to view grant application guidelines and contact information.

Charles and Lucille King Family Foundation, Inc. (NY) (http://www.kingfoundation.org)

The Charles and Lucille King Family Foundation, located in New York City and established in 1989, provides scholarships for undergraduate and graduate students in film and television production. Undergraduates must be entering their junior or senior year and demonstrate academic ability, financial need, and professional potential. Normally, outstanding undergraduate and graduate students at New York University, the University of California–Los Angeles and the University of Southern California, among other schools, receive funding of up to $2500 per year. The Foundation's Web site provides an FAQ, a list of past scholarship winners, and contact information. Applications are due annually on April 15th.

F.M. Kirby Foundation (NJ) (http://fdncenter.org/grantmaker/kirby)

The New Jersey-based Kirby Foundation believes that "private philanthropy, at its best, if provided compassionately and prudently, encourages self-reliance and diminishes government's role." The Foundation makes support mainly in the geographic areas of interest to the Kirby family members in the areas of education, health and medicine, the arts, and religious, welfare, and youth organizations. Visitors to the Foundation's folder on the Center's Web site will find more specific information on the Foundation's areas of interest, application procedures, specific restrictions, a listing of directors and officers, and contact information.

The Kirkwood Family Foundation (CA) (http://www.pacificfoundationservices.com/kirkwood/index.html)

Established in 1999, the San Francisco, California-based Kirkwood Family Foundation supports public charities serving children and families in the states of California, Oregon, and Washington. Qualified grantees are those organizations that "offer education or social services, and that promote resource conservation." The Foundation also plans to provide support for health care programs and civil projects. The Foundation's Web site outlines areas that will not be considered, a board of directors list, contact information, and application procedures.

The Klingenstein Third Generation Foundation (NY) (http://www.ktgf.org/)

Established in 1993 by the grandchildren of Joseph Klingenstein, one of the founding partners of Wertheim & Company (now Schroder & Company, Inc.), The Klingenstein Third Generation Foundation focuses their funding interests in the areas of childhood and adolescent depression and Attention Deficit/Hyperactive Disorder (ADHD). Their grants primarily fall under the categories of intervention and referral, prevention, public education/training, and infrastructure. The KTGF also awards a postgraduate research fellowship in clinical or basic research of depression. Letters of inquiry regarding grants may be sent via e-mail, though the KTGF does not accept unsolicited applications for the fellowship. Its thorough Web site includes application procedures, recent grants and published articles by grantees, its funding philosophy, contact information and links to mental health associations for grantseekers, and its mission and selection process for the fellowship.

John S. and James L. Knight Foundation (FL) (http://www.knightfdn.org/)

Established in 1950, the John S. and James L. Knight Foundation focuses its grantmaking activities on journalism, education, and arts and culture. The Foundation also supports organizations in 27 communities where the communications company founded by the Knight brothers publishes newspapers, and it "remains flexible enough to respond to unique challenges, ideas and projects that lie beyond its identified program areas, yet would fulfill the broad vision of its founders." Visitors to the site can access an array of information about the Foundation and its programs; application guidelines and restrictions, including a sample proposal and proposal cover sheet (in PDF format); Foundation news, including the most recent annual report; a listing of recent grants by program area; and an informative FAQ section.

Marion I. & Henry J. Knott Foundation (MD) (http://www.knottfoundation.org)

Marion and Henry Knott established the Knott Foundation in 1977 to nurture family unity in their Maryland Roman Catholic community. The Knott Foundation today provides funding in five areas: arts and humanities, Catholic activities, education (Catholic and nonsectarian private schools), health care, and social and human services. Grants are limited to organizations in Baltimore City and Allegany, Anne Arundel, Baltimore, Carroll, Frederick, Garrett, Harford, Howard and Washington Counties in Maryland. The Knott Foundation's Web site has a complete guide to its grant applications, including application guidelines, limitations, and an application form, available for downloading. The Foundation also provides a listing of previous grants and a balance sheet of the Foundation's assets.

Koinonia Foundation (MD) (http://www.koinoniafoundation.org/)

The Baltimore-based Koinonia Foundation supports projects that are consistent with its values of "a belief in oneness of life; a belief in the spiritual nature of the human individual, with respect for the integrity and wholeness of the person and the human race; a belief in the existence of a spiritual order designed and ordained by God, with a recognition of the wholeness and holiness of God's Creation." Its funding priorities are grassroots programs and actions that work for systemic change, empower small group action to influence large movements, and articulate a clearly defined goal or activity as part of a larger project or organizational effort. The site features detailed support guidelines, printable application forms, a listing of grant recipients, and contact information.

Kongsgaard-Goldman Foundation (WA) (http://www.kongsgaard-goldman.org)

The Kongsgaard-Goldman Foundation was formed in 1988 by Martha Kongsgaard and Peter Goldman. The Seattle-based private foundation supports a wide range of nonprofit organizations in the Pacific Northwest, specifically Washington, Oregon, Idaho, Alaska, Montana, and British Columbia, Canada. Primary funding areas are environmental conservation and restoration in the Pacific Northwest, civic development and civil rights in the Pacific Northwest, and artistic expression in the state of Washington. Another funding area, but of low priority, is Technical Assistance. Within these funding areas, the Foundation favors projects that reflect "a deep and broad level of citizen participation and leadership." Their priority is to help "fund the building of grassroots organizations with the power to change their communities and improve their lives." Visitors to the Web site will find further information on each funding area, downloadable guidelines, application instructions, grants lists with links or e-mail addresses of grantee organizations, links to related sites, and contact information.

Kopp Family Foundation (MN) (http://www.koppfamilyfdtn.org)

Lee and Barbara Kopp established the Kopp Family Foundation in 1986. The Edina, Minnesota Foundation, focused on youth, women, and the aging population, runs a grants management program and a scholarship program. Through its grants management program, it supports nonprofit organizations mainly within the Twin Cities, though it has donated to organizations throughout Greater Minnesota, in several other states, and internationally as well. The scholarship program provides funds directly to participating high schools for graduating seniors, enabling them to continue education at a post-secondary school of their choice. The other scholarship program is the Random Acts of Kindness (RAK) program, which provides funds to participating high schools for students who need help for unexpected emergencies. Visit the Web site for grant application instructions, scholarship program information, links to other foundation Web sites, and annual report and contact information. The site also features online reporting forms for schools that participate in the scholarship and Random Acts of Kindness programs.

Koret Foundation (CA) (http://www.koretfoundation.org/)

The Koret Foundation reflects the dreams and philosophies of its benefactors, Joseph and Stephanie Koret, Jewish immigrants from eastern Europe who "epitomized the American Dream." Founded in 1979, areas of funding interest include: San Francisco Bay Area

Jewish community projects (Jewish identity, linking Bay Area Jewry to Israel, enhancing Jewish communal organizations, Jewish education/Jewish studies, and émigré resettlement), San Francisco Bay Area community development and support (K–12 public education, cultural/community development, higher education, and public policy) and Israeli and international Jewish organizations (economic development/free market initiatives in Israel, higher education in Israel, and Jewish educational, cultural and communal activities in the former Soviet Union). Recipient organizations in the San Francisco Bay Area must serve the needs of one or more of the following Bay Area counties: San Francisco, Alameda, Contra Costa, Marin, San Mateo, or Santa Clara. In the area of Jewish funding, Koret will consider grant applications from throughout northern California and nationally on a selected basis. The San Francisco-based Foundation also has the Koret Jewish Book Awards in cooperation with the National Foundation for Jewish Culture, which serve to heighten the visibility of the best new Jewish books and authors. Visitors to the site will find downloadable guidelines and submission forms for the Jewish Book Awards, printable letter of inquiry coversheet, application instructions, financial information, selected grant lists, archive of news and press releases, and contact information.

Kresge Foundation (MI) (http://www.kresge.org)

Sebastian S. Kresge, founder of the S.S. Kresge Company that is now known as Kmart, established the Kresge Foundation in 1924. Its mission statement is simple: "to promote the well-being of mankind." The Kresge Foundation makes grants to build and renovate facilities, challenge private giving, and build institutional capacity among nonprofits, with goals of strengthening the capacity of charitable organizations to provide effective programs of quality. Located in Troy, Michigan, the Foundation has national geographic scope, occasionally international, and supports a range of organizations "reflecting almost the entire breadth of the nonprofit sector." Currently, there are five programs: Bricks and Mortar, which is a grant program to build facilities and challenge private giving and makes up about 80 percent of its grantmaking; Science Initiative, a challenge grant program to upgrade and endow scientific equipment; Detroit Initiative, grant program to support strategic investment in Detroit and southeastern Michigan; The Kresge Foundation Partnership to Raise Community Capital, a five-year grant program to develop permanent endowment assets for community foundations and nonprofit organizations; and The Kresge Foundation HBCU initiative, a five-year grant program that helps develop fundraising capacity at historically Black colleges and universities. Visit the Foundation's Web site for detailed information on each of its programs and application guidelines, latest annual report, FAQ page, history of the foundation, staff listing, and contact information.

Samuel H. Kress Foundation (NY) (http://www.shkf.org)

Samuel H. Kress, who made his fortune from S.H. Kress & Co. variety stores, established the Samuel H. Kress Foundation in 1929. With his fortune from his stores, Samuel Kress amassed a collection of over 3000 works of art, which he then donated to more than 90 institutions in 33 states. At the time of distribution, completed over three decades ago, the collection was valued at $100 million. Beyond its endowment of works of art, the Foundation has several Grant Programs for projects or programs focused on European art from antiquity through the early nineteenth century: the Resources of Scholarship, for development of essential resources for art historical research and the practice of art conservation; the Sharing of Expertise, projects in which art historians and conservators share their professional skills and experience; Art Conservation Research, scientific investigation of problems in art conservation; Conservation and Restoration Projects, which supports the care and conservation of works of art and the preservation of European monuments; and its Special Initiatives Program, which are projects that the Foundation takes an active role in developing and implementing. To advance the academic discipline of the history of art, the Foundation developed four Kress Fellowships: Conservation, Curatorial, Travel, and Two-Year Fellowships in the History of Art, which are for the completion of dissertation research. Further information and application information for its grant and fellowship programs is available on the Web site, along with further information on the Foundation and samples and locations of works from the Kress Collection.

Kronkosky Charitable Foundation (TX) (http://www.kronkosky.org)

The Kronkosky Charitable Foundation was established by a Trust Agreement in 1991 but did not receive its principle funding until 1997, some $295 million from the estate of Albert Kronkosky, Jr. The Kronkosky family was a significant shareholder in Merck stock and was involved in a number of successful local business ventures. Based in San Antonio, Texas, the Foundation's mission statement is "to produce profound good that is tangible and measurable in Bandera, Bexar, Comal, and Kendall counties in Texas by implementing the Kronkosky's charitable purposes." The focus of the Foundation is to "support programs, projects, and collaborative efforts that reach as many people as possible; involve the persons served in developing solutions; raise expectations; build self-esteem; develop personal and organizational capacity; encourage innovation; and make use of technology." Its funding areas are health and human services, including the elderly, youth, child abuse and neglect, and persons with disabilities; cultural activities; and other areas, such as wildlife preservation and animal issues. Consult the Web site for detailed information on each funding area, application information, a FAQ area, grants lists, tax information and annual reports, online feedback/contact form, and contact information.

Kulas Foundation (OH) (http://fdncenter.org/grantmaker/kulas/)

The Cleveland, Ohio-based Kulas Foundation was established in 1937. The Foundation supports various aspects of music, including musical education, institutions and performances, and other groups that have similar priorities to the founders. Besides supporting programs designated by the founders, the Foundation has a grantmaking program that distributes funds to Cleveland-area programs in four areas: arts and culture, education, social services, and community. The last three categories are still music-oriented, focusing on arts programs in schools, the musical needs of social service organizations, and music or arts components of community projects. The Foundation also supports research in music therapy. While applications must be requested from the Foundation, its folder on the Center's Web site does offer thorough program descriptions and application guidelines. The site also includes lists of trustees and officers, financial statements, and biographical information on the founders that provides important insight into the Foundation's grantmaking decisions.

Ronald and Mary Ann Lachman Foundation (IL) (http://www.lachman.org)

The Ronald and Mary Ann Lachman Foundation spawned from the Lachman Associates Foundation, founded in 1987, which was established with the proceeds of the sale of Lachman Associates, a Chicago consulting firm, to Eastman Kodak. The Foundation supports the causes of deaf education, especially literacy; technology for the deaf; technological development, especially for organizations which support technology education in computers or energy; and Jewish education. The Foundation seldom grants to unsolicited funding request, preferring to establish a long-term relationship with particular organizations. Currently funded donations and organizations are listed on the Foundation's Web site. A history of the Lachman family, grantmaking goals and interests, and an e-mail contact address are also available online.

LaFetra Private Operating Foundation (CA) (Operating foundation) (http://www.lafetra.org/)

The LaFetra Private Operating Foundation is located in Oakland, California, and supports an international fellowship program as well as an association of international volunteers. The Foundation's mission is to "[promote] international voluntary service that contributes to a greater sense of global responsibility." The LaFetra Fellows Program is comprised of a period of service in the San Francisco Bay Area followed by two to three months of volunteer work abroad. The program's overview, an online application, and past fellows and details of the program in years past are all accessible on the Foundation's Web site. The South-North Exchange Program is a grant for nonprofit organizations with international collaborations and alliances. The Foundation's Web site provides an online application cover sheet and guidelines. The Foundation posts numerous other resources for international volunteers—including conferences, links, and a professional association—on their Web site. Staff and contact information for the Foundation is also available.

Laird Norton Endowment Foundation (WA) (http://www.lairdnorton.org/)
The Laird Norton Endowment Foundation was initiated in 1940 by descendants of three men who formed the Laird Norton Company, a lumber business: William Harris Laird, Matthew George Norton, and James Laird Norton. Through the Foundation, the Laird Norton family seeks to honor and reflect a common heritage—the American forest and lumber industry—in programs of creative philanthropy. The mission of the Seattle-based Laird Norton Endowment Foundation is to fund distinctive programs in conservation and forestry education. The Foundation is currently concentrating its efforts on sustainable forestry: the practice of forestry that restores, enhances, and then sustains a full range of forest values, both ecological and economic. Visit the Web site for grant information, application materials and procedures, guidelines, grants lists, and contact information.

The Lalor Foundation (RI) (http://www.lalorfound.org)
The Lalor Foundation, based in Providence, Rhode Island, was established in 1935 from bequests from members for the Lalor Family. The goal of the Foundation is to give assistance and encouragement to capable investigators who have teaching and research careers in universities and colleges. The principal areas of support have been branches of life sciences "wherein applications of chemical and physical methods of research could be expected to give useful and fruitful results." Since 1960, however, the Foundation has concentrated its support on special aspects of reproductive physiology, which the Foundation considers of "pressing importance;" its Web site states that since resources must be conserved, "a finer understanding of all aspects of reproduction and the means to control population growth is an imperative." The program of research grants offered in 1999 were grants to institutions for "basic postdoctoral research in mammalian reproductive biology as related to the regulation of fertility." Visit its Web site for more information about the Foundation and its grant program, application instructions and printable application form, links to related sites, current grant awardees and their projects, and contact information.

Jacob and Valeria Langeloth Foundation (NY) (http://www.langeloth.org)
The Jacob and Valeria Langeloth Foundation has its roots in a bequest in 1914 from Jacob Langeloth, Chairman of the American Metal Co., Ltd. Langeloth left instructions for a convalescent home for professionals of modest means. Called Valeria Home in honor of his wife, it was open for six decades until it was closed and sold in 1977. Proceeds from the sale passed to the newly-named Jacob and Valeria Langeloth Foundation, which continues in the tradition of Langeloth's commitment to convalescence. The Foundation "supports programs designed to improve, speed, make more cost effective, and in other ways promote physical and emotional recovery from illness and accident." The New York City-based Foundation seeks proposals that include one or more of the following: innovative approaches or model programs that can be replicated; new community models that reach out to empower communities that may normally be beyond the reach of good medical care; interdisciplinary and interagency collaboration; programs that promote among patients greater knowledge of their illnesses, paths to recovery, and rights as consumers of medical care, as well as involving families in the convalescent process; applied research, which holds the promise of developing new knowledge and understanding about the field; and humanization of relations between medical professionals and those in their care. Consult its Web site for application procedures, sample budget template, history of the foundation and its founder, listing of staff, and contact information.

Lannan Foundation (NM) (http://www.lannan.org)
The Lannan Foundation, established in 1960, is headquartered in Santa Fe, New Mexico, and is dedicated to supporting contemporary artists and writers, as well as Native activists in rural indigenous communities. The Foundation has three program areas in which it gives awards and fellowships: contemporary visual artists; poets, fiction and nonfiction writers; and Native community activists. Funding for the last category must be for programs that are "consistent with traditional values in the areas of education, Native cultures, the revival and preservation of languages, legal rights and environmental protection." Descriptions of the specific funding available for each area (prizes, exhibitions, and grants), as well as

recipients of the awards, guidelines and procedures, are available on the Foundation's Web site. The Foundation also sponsors a large Prize for Cultural Freedom as well as a Residency Program, which gives artists, curators, writers, and Native community activists contemplative time to work. Applications and letters of inquiry are not accepted for these programs. The Foundation's Web site has very thorough details of all of its funding opportunities and links to other resources as well.

George A. and Dolly F. LaRue Trust (MO) (http://www.gkccf.org)

The George A. and Dolly F. LaRue Trust was established in 1971 after the death of its two founders. George A. LaRue was president of LaRue Printing Company, and he and his wife were active in charitable and civic programs in the Kansas City area. The Trust supports religious, charitable, scientific, and educational purposes and operates as an affiliated trust of the Greater Kansas City Community Foundation. The Trust can be contacted in care of the GKCCF or through the Community Foundation's Web site, and there is a brief introduction to the LaRue Trust in the online Annual Report, under Affiliated Trusts on the site.

Albert & Mary Lasker Foundation, Inc. (NY) (Operating foundation) (http://www.laskerfoundation.org/index.html)

The Albert & Mary Lasker foundation is known for its Albert Lasker awards. Philanthropists Albert and Mary Woodard Lasker first inaugurated these awards in 1946. The mission of the foundation is "to elevate and sustain medical research as a universal priority so that the foundation's goals—to eradicate life threatening disease and disabilities and improve health standards—are strongly supported by national and international policies and resources." An international jury of top medical researchers annually selects the Lasker Award recipients, who are scientists, physicians, and public servants who have made major advances in the understanding, diagnosis, treatment, prevention, and cure of human disease. Currently, three awards are presented each year: the Albert Lasker Basic Medical Research Award, Clinical Medical Research Award, and Award for Special Medical Research Achievement. In addition to its awards program, the Foundation also has a program of public education aimed at encouraging federal financial support for biomedical research. The primary beneficiary of the Foundation's support has been the National Institutes of Health. Visit the Lasker Foundation Web site for more information about its award programs, past recipients, a searchable library of materials related to the awards and its past recipients, and press releases.

The LEF Foundation (CA) (http://www.agmconnect.org/lef.html)

The LEF Foundation assists the "innovative efforts of individuals and organizations seeking to expand the boundaries of artistic expression and create new ideas and opportunities that affirm the constructive link between the arts and contemporary life." Funds are given for projects, programs, and services that encourage "a positive interchange between the arts and the natural urban environment" and may involve visual, media, performing, and literary art. Projects may also involve public and environmental art, architecture, and landscape architecture and be design and interdisciplinary collaborations. Within these areas, the Foundation also considers projects that address critical community needs. Located in Cambridge, Massachusetts, and St. Helena, California, the Foundation primarily sponsors projects in New England and northern California, although application may be open to relevant proposals outside of those areas. Consult the Web site for application instructions and guidelines and contact information.

Leeway Foundation (PA) (http://www.leeway.org/)

The Leeway Foundation was established in 1993 by artist Linda Lee Alter to promote the welfare of women and to benefit the arts. The Foundation's primary grantmaking program supports individual women artists in the Philadelphia area and encourages their increased recognition and representation in the community. The Foundation makes grants each year in a selected visual or literary discipline. Grants are awarded to artists who demonstrate exceptional creativity and vision in a body of work. In addition, two special grants recognizing artists at particular stages in their careers are available each year at the jurors'

discretion. The Bessie Berman Grant acknowledges the accomplishments of a woman artist fifty years or older. The Edna Andrade Emerging Artist Grant encourages a woman artist who exhibits great promise early in her artistic career. The Foundation's Web site
provides information about these programs as well as the Foundation's general program,
application instructions (including the dates and locations of Foundation-sponsored application workshops in the five-county Philadelphia metro region), the names of recent
grantees and examples of their work, listings of the Foundation's board and staff, and
contact information.

Levitt Foundation (NY) (http://fdncenter.org/grantmaker/levitt/)

The Levitt Foundation is an independent foundation incorporated in New York in 1949.
The Foundation is interested in the environment as it relates to children and youth living in
the five boroughs of New York City and on Long Island, New York. The Foundation supports programs that help young people understand the value of their environment and to
help young people build confidence and self-esteem and leadership skills. Visit the Foundation's folder on the Center's Web site to view information on the Foundation's interests, a
listing of recent grantees, and contact information.

Libra Foundation (ME) (http://www.librafoundation.org/)

Founded in Portland, Maine, in 1989, the Libra Foundation seeks to provide financial assistance and, in turn, provide hope and assurance to a broad spectrum of people in Maine. The
Foundation's lack of formal grant guidelines follows closely to its mission, that all areas
and people need support. Broad subject areas that have been supported in the past include
religion, health, education, human services, the arts, public/society benefit, and justice.
Libra accepts applications from all over the state of Maine and also supports all sectors of
Maine society. Information found on the Foundation's Web site includes a complete grant
history, list of trustees, specific grant exclusions, grant application procedures, and contact
information.

The Lifebridge Foundation, Inc. (NY) (http://www.lifebridge.org)

The Lifebridge Foundation's role is to bridge the "chasm between the spiritual and the
so-called mundane," and "facilitating the integration of an emerging holistic consciousness
into daily action." It believes that people all over the world, particularly in industrialized
Western societies, are searching for meaning and for "what is missing" in their lives.
Lifebridge Foundation believes that this missing part is the "ability to perceive our existence as part of the same life as the Earth and the Universe; as integral parts of an
ever-evolving co-creation." The Foundation, located in New York City, seeks to promote
the concept of "One Humanity and the Interconnectedness of all Life" and to foster a spirit
of "inclusiveness and global vision leading to transformative action." Grantees cover a
wide range of disciplines and social concerns and can be roughly divided into the following
fields: arts and culture, youth/education, environment, science, community service, world
goodwill, and "interdimensional." The Foundation generally pre-selects grantees but does
accept letters of introduction. Visit the Web site for grant guidelines, a list of grantees and
their e-mail and/or Web addresses, newsletter, links to related sites and projects, and contact information.

Agnes M. Lindsay Trust (NH) (http://www.cris.com/~amltrust/)

Located in Manchester, New Hampshire, The Agnes M. Lindsay Trust was founded when
Agnes M. Lindsay died in 1937 and left behind in her will the provisions for the establishment of a trust. The mission of the Trust is to provide grants in the areas of educating poor
and deserving students from rural communities and child welfare. Grants are restricted to
New Hampshire, Massachusetts, Maine, and Vermont. The Web site provides guidelines
and deadlines for grant applications as well as contact information.

Franklin Lindsay Student Aid Fund (TX) (http://www.franklinlindsay.org)

The Franklin Lindsay Student Aid Fund was provided for in the Will of Franklin Lindsay,
who died on May 3, 1954. He believed that "the greatest good that could be done for the

country and the world was to educate its people." Accordingly, he arranged for his $2 million estate to be held and managed in a Trust for loans to be provided for students to further their education. Located in Austin, Texas, the Fund makes loans to "worthy and deserving" students of either sex who wish to pursue an education at an institute of higher learning within the state of Texas. Loans are up to $3000 per academic year and are non-interest bearing for up to four months after the student's graduation, provided they maintain certain terms and conditions. Consult the Web site to learn more about the Fund's loan program, its terms and conditions and application procedures, and contact information. The site also features online forms to start the application process and for feedback about the site.

Albert A. List Foundation, Inc. (NY) (http://fdncenter.org/grantmaker/listfdn/index.html)

The New York City-based List Foundation achieves its mission of supporting and enhancing citizen participation within our pluralistic society through grantmaking in three major program areas: Democracy and Citizen Participation, Freedom of Expression, and New Problems/New Solutions. The Foundation currently funds organizations that foster citizen participation in the democratic process and that share its commitment to a society free of ageism, classism, homophobia, racism, religious prejudice, sexism, and discrimination against those who are physically or mentally challenged; community involvement; economic justice; involving youth in the process of social change; alliances that go beyond traditional, short-term coalition building around a specific action; progressive, proactive policies that speak to the needs of broad sectors of society; and solutions to ongoing and emerging problems that enable us to live more harmoniously with our natural environment and with each other. The Foundation's folder on the Center's Web site provides descriptions of its three main programs, eligibility requirements, application procedures, and contact information.

John M. Lloyd Foundation (CA) (http://www.johnmlloyd.org)

John M. Lloyd was committed to seeking the root cause of problems, not just treating their symptoms. His foundation, created at the time of his death from complications related to AIDS in 1991, strives to fund programs related to the prevention, care, and public awareness of AIDS. Based in Santa Monica, California, the Foundation supports three areas in the overall fight against HIV and AIDS: policy, education, and prevention; medical research; and healthcare and services. Previous grants in each category are listed on the Foundation's Web site, along with granting guidelines, an outline of the application process, and contact information.

The John Locke Foundation (NC) (Operating foundation) (http://www.johnlocke.org)

The John Locke Foundation is a non-partisan public policy institute that opened its doors in 1990. Based in Raleigh, North Carolina, the Foundation was named for the seventeenth century English philosopher whose writings on government and political freedom inspired the founding documents of this country and who played a major role in drawing up the Fundamental Constitution of Carolina in 1665. Locke was also a "great believer in the value of public debate and policy research." The name is fitting since the Foundation's purpose is to "conduct research, disseminate information, and advance public understanding of society based on the principles of individual liberty, the voluntary exchange of a free market economy, and limited government." The Foundation also seeks to "foster a climate of innovative thinking and debate on issues facing North Carolinians." It operates a number of programs and services to provide information and observations to legislators, policymakers, business executives, citizen activists, civic and community leaders, and the news media. Among its activities are producing newsletters, journals, and policy research reports; holding public policy events; making speeches; and responding to requests for information. Visit the Foundation's Web site to learn more about its services, the history of the Foundation and its namesake, and its goals and purposes and position on issues. The Foundation also has its publications online.

Carrie J. Loose Trust (MO) (http://www.gkccf.org)

The Carrie J. Loose Trust was established in 1931 by Harry Wilson Loose, the son of Carrie J. Loose and Joseph S. Loose, to further the Loose's philanthropic interests in the Kansas City community. The Trust operates as an affiliated trust of the Greater Kansas City Community Foundation and can be contacted in care of or through the Community Foundation's Web site. There is a very brief introduction to the Carrie J. Loose Trust in the online annual report, under Affiliated Trusts, on the GKCCF site.

Harry Wilson Loose Trust (MO) (http://www.gkccf.org)

Harry Wilson Loose created, from the estate of his father, Joseph S. Loose, a trust in honor of his mother (Carrie J. Loose) and in his name as well. The Harry Wilson Loose Trust was established in 1971 to serve the charitable needs of the Kansas City community. The Trust operates as an affiliated trust of the Greater Kansas City Community Foundation and can be contacted in care of or through the Community Foundation's Web site. There is a very brief introduction to the Harry Wilson Loose Trust in the online annual report, under Affiliated Trusts, on the GKCCF site.

Edward Lowe Foundation (MI) (Operating foundation) (http://www.lowe.org)

The focus of the Edward Lowe Foundation, a private operating foundation, is "on encouraging entrepreneurship throughout the United States." The Foundation does not make awards, grants, or loans to individual entrepreneurs or their businesses, nor does it consider unsolicited grant proposals or publish grant guidelines. In addition to its mission statement and a listing of officers and directors, the Foundation's Web site offers a history of its grants, detailed program information, and a number of electronic information services related to its mission.

George Lucas Educational Foundation (CA) (http://glef.org/)

The George Lucas Educational Foundation uses various media, including its Web site, to promote and share the latest strategies to change the K–12 educational system, especially those that integrate technology with teaching or learning. Those strategies are based on the filmmaker's belief that "education is the most important investment we can make to secure the future of our democracy." Visitors to the site can access *Edutopia,* the Foundation's newsletter and "Learn & Live," the Foundation's educational resource guide. Although the Foundation is a private operating entity and does not make grants, visitors are encouraged to contact the Foundation if they know of a program or resource that can advance the Foundation's mission.

Henry Luce Foundation, Inc. (NY) (http://www.hluce.org/)

Established in 1936 by the late Henry R. Luce, co-founder and editor-in-chief of Time Inc., the New York City-based Henry Luce Foundation today focuses its activities on the interdisciplinary exploration of higher education, increased understanding between Asia and the United States, the study of religion and theology, scholarship in American art, opportunities for women in science and engineering, and contributions to youth and public policy programs. Higher education has been a persistent theme for most of the Foundation's programs, with an emphasis on innovation and scholarship. The Foundation's elegant, bandwidth-friendly Web site provides detailed information about a range of programs, including the Luce Fund in American Art, the American Collections Enhancement Initiative, the Clare Booth Luce Program, the Henry R. Luce Professorships, the Luce Scholars Program, the United States-China Cooperative Research Program, and the Asia Project; general application guidelines, guidelines for specific programs, and grant restrictions; recent grants list organized by program area; a helpful FAQ; listings of the Foundation's board and staff; and contact information.

The Ludwick Family Foundation (CA) (http://www.ludwick.org/)

Founded in 1990, the Ludwick Family Foundation "seeks opportunities to encourage new and expanded projects and programs by providing grants to nonprofit organizations for new equipment, equipment replacement and modernization, improvements to facilities, and educational materials." The Foundation, which is located in Glendora, California, does not seek to provide continuing long-term support. Grants range from $5,000 to $50,000 and are limited to U.S. organizations or international organizations based in the United States. To apply for a grant, an organization must first provide a letter of inquiry and complete an information form, which is available online. Full proposals are only by invitation. Deadlines, contact information, and financial information are all available on the site.

Lumpkin Foundation (IL) (http://www.lumpkinfoundation.org)

The mission of the Illinois-based Lumpkin Foundation is "to provide leadership, individually and collectively, both locally and globally, to enrich [family members'] respective communities and in so doing preserve the tradition and goals of the [Lumpkin] family." The Foundation is dedicated to supporting education, preserving and protecting the environment, and fostering opportunities for leadership and gives special consideration to its heritage in east central Illinois. In addition to a mission statement and officer and committee listings, the Foundation's Web site provides grant application procedures and restrictions, a letter of conditions (for grant recipients), downloadable versions of its grant application cover sheet and post-evaluation grant report, and contact information.

Lyndhurst Foundation (TN) (http://www.lyndhurstfoundation.org)

The Chattanooga, Tennessee-based, Lyndhurst Foundation, was founded in 1938 by Thomas Cartter Lupton, a pioneer in the Coca-Cola bottling business. The foundation has gone through many transformations. Initially the Foundation focused on broad local and regional activities; however, upon the death of Mr. Lupton, the priorities then concentrated on giving to more specific areas including parks, inner-city neighborhoods, childhood development, education, and youth development. The Foundation's priorities inside Chattanooga include the development of Tennessee's state parks and natural environment, revitalization of inner-city neighborhoods, arts and culture, elementary and secondary public school education, housing, and urban issues. Outside of Chattanooga, the Foundation also holds an interest in preservation of the South Appalachian Mountains, supporting Tennessee charter schools, and other interests of the trustees. The Foundation's Web site includes a board/staff list, a three-year history of financial information, and contact information.

Lynn Charitable Foundation, Nancy L. (CA) (http://www.nllcf.org/)

The Nancy L. Lynn Charitable Foundation was established to assist organizations within southern California. The foundation focuses its funding on those organizations providing assistance in the following areas: cancer organizations providing direct services, child abuse organizations providing direct service and/or education; and organizations dedicated to helping those with HIV/AIDS. Specific grant guidelines and instructions are listed on the site. Applications can be downloaded in PDF format. There is a contact page that can be completed and sent from the site for those who wish to contact the Foundation staff. Additionally, the site has a list of previous grants awarded and a list of resources and links.

John D. and Catherine T. MacArthur Foundation (IL) (http://www.macfdn.org/)

The Chicago-based MacArthur Foundation recently revised most of its programs and guidelines and unveiled a redesigned Web site to help get the message out. With a broad goal of fostering lasting improvement in the human condition, the Foundation seeks the development of healthy individuals and effective communities, peace within and among nations, responsible choices about human reproduction, and a global ecosystem capable of supporting healthy human societies. The Foundation makes grants through two major integrated programs, Human and Community Development and Global Security and Sustainability, and two special programs. The former supports national research and policy work in Chicago and Palm Beach Counties, Florida, and direct local efforts. The program on Global Security and Sustainability focuses on arms reduction and security policy, ecosystems conservation, population, and on three cross-cutting themes: concepts of security and sustainability, new partnerships and institutions, and education about United States interests and responsibilities. The Foundation's two special programs are the General

Program, which undertakes special initiatives and supports projects that promote excellence and diversity in the media, and the MacArthur Fellows Program, which awards fellowships to exceptionally creative individuals, regardless of field of endeavor. Visitors to the Foundation's well-organized, bandwidth-friendly Web site will find a great deal of information, including brief biographies of John D. and Catherine T. MacArthur, detailed program descriptions and application guidelines, financial statements, links to philanthropy resources, contact information, and a variety of other materials.

The MacDonnell Foundation (CA)
(http://www.pacificfoundationservices.com/macdonnell/index.html)
The MacDonnell Foundation was founded in 1989 in San Francisco, California, to support disadvantaged youth and families in the areas surrounding San Francisco. The Foundation's primary interest centers on rewarding talent and achievement of low-income, disadvantaged youth in areas of education, recreation, and/or social activities. Interests of the Foundation include literacy and learning disabilities, as well as programs that enhance children's self-esteem and self-awareness. The Foundation will also support recreation and athletic programs, specifically for inner-city youth. Capital campaigns may also be considered by the Foundation on a limited basis. Upon visiting the Foundation's Web site, visitors will find a most recent grants list, contact information, a board of directors list, and application procedures.

The Maclellan Foundation, Inc. (TN) (http://www.maclellanfdn.org)
Dora Maclellan Brown, Robert J. Maclellan, and Robert L. Maclellan established the Maclellan Foundation, located in Chattanooga, Tennessee, in 1945. The original principle of the Foundation and its related trusts was in the form of Provident Life and Accident Insurance Company stock, a company founded by Thomas Maclellan, father of Robert J. Maclellan and Dora Maclellan Brown. The purpose of the Foundation is "to contribute to and otherwise serve strategic national and international organizations committed to furthering the Kingdom of Christ; to contribute to and otherwise serve select local organizations which foster the spiritual welfare of the community; and to serve by providing financial and leadership resources to extend the Kingdom of God in accordance with the Great Commission." The Foundation prefers to make project or seed grants, not operating grants. Visit the Web site for application instructions; information about their philosophy, policies, and guidelines; the grantmaking process, from board meetings to a site meeting checklist used by the Foundation; grantee responsibilities; and contact information. The site also features a letter from one of its founders on the ideals the Foundation was established upon, a grantmaking manual prepared by the Foundation, a public discussion forum and multimedia clips.

Josiah Macy, Jr., Foundation (NY) (http://www.josiahmacyfoundation.org/)
Established in 1930 by Kate Macy Ladd in memory of her father, the Josiah Macy, Jr., Foundation has been committed to "[improving] the education of health professionals in the interest of the health of the public, and to [enhancing] the representation of minorities in the health profession" since the 1960s. To this end, the Foundation funds numerous programs and research initiatives in the medical profession, as well as the yearly Macy Conference. Current and on-going programs are detailed on the Foundation's Web site, along with an e-mail contact address, grant guidelines, and recent publications and studies by the Foundation.

Maddie's Fund (CA) (http://www.maddies.org/)
Established in 1994 by David and Cheryl Duffield to honor the memory of their beloved miniature schnauzer, Maddie's Fund (formerly known as the Duffield Family Foundation) hopes "to revolutionize the status and well being of companion animals" by spending more than $200 million to help build, community by community, a "No-Kill Nation" in which "healthy, adoptable dogs and cats in animal shelters across the country are guaranteed loving homes." The Fund is particularly interested in supporting animal welfare organizations capable of building alliances and developing collaborative pet-related projects within their

communities. Successful projects will set forth comprehensive life-saving strategies that involve the participation of cooperating animal shelters, rescue groups, volunteer foster organizations, local animal control agencies, veterinarians, and others. In addition to a clear articulation of the Fund's philosophy and goals, the Maddie's Fund Web site provides detailed grant proposal guidelines and requirements, a hypothetical funding scenario, a downloadable application form in PDF format, a letter from the Fund's president, and contact information.

A.L. Mailman Family Foundation, Inc. (NY) (http://www.mailman.org)

Headquartered in White Plains, New York, the A.L. Mailman Family Foundation focuses its grantmaking activities on children and families, with a special emphasis on early childhood. The Foundation's current program is focused in the following areas: early care and education, family support, and moral education and social responsibility. Foundation grants generally are not awarded for ongoing direct services, general operating expenses, individuals, capital expenditures, endowment campaigns, or for local services or programs. Visitors to the Foundation's Web site will find general information and recent grant summary lists for each program area; grant application guidelines; a listing of directors, officers, and staff; and contact information.

Manitou Foundation, Inc. (CO) (http://www.manitou.org/mf_homepage.html)

The Manitou Foundation offers land grants in the Crestone/Baca area of Colorado to qualified U.S. nonprofit organizations in the following categories: religious organizations and spiritual projects, ecological and environmental sustainability projects, and related educational endeavors (youth and adult). The Foundation also administers a land preservation program and seeks to network with individuals and organizations locally, nationally, and internationally to facilitate its mission objectives. Visitors will find program guidelines and application procedures for the program, information on its Solitary Retreat Hermitage Building Project, and contact information with e-mail addresses.

John and Mary R. Markle Foundation (NY) (http://www.markle.org/)

The John and Mary R. Markle Foundation was established in 1927 "to promote the advancement and diffusion of knowledge and the general good of mankind." Today the Foundation focuses its activities on the ways that emerging communications media and information technology create unprecedented opportunity to improve people's lives. Most of the Foundation's current work is through the following programs: Public Engagement through Interactive Technologies, Policy for a Networked Society, Interactive Media for Children, and Information Technologies for Better Health. Visitors to the Foundation's Web site will find lots of information on its focus on communications and technology and current programs, grant guidelines, the history of the Foundation, board and staff listings, grants and investments since 1990, news, and contact information.

MARPAT Foundation (MD) (http://fdncenter.org/grantmaker/marpat/)

The Silver Spring, Maryland-based MARPAT Foundation provides support for organizations benefiting the greater Washington, D.C., metropolitan area. Projects related to education, healthcare, cultural affairs, and science constitute the Foundation's funding priority. The Foundation does not support endowment funds, individuals, medical research projects, or organizations based outside the United States. Visitors to the Foundation's folder on the Center's Web site will find an alphabetical listing of past grants, current grant guidelines and deadlines, a grant summary sheet that can be downloaded off the Web in HTML or PDF format, and contact information.

Carlos and Marguerite Mason Trust (GA)
(http://www.wachovia.com/trust/masontrust_overview.asp)

The Mason Trust was established in 1991 with the purpose to "improve the process of organ transplantation for Georgians through the making of grants to Georgia 501(c)(3) organizations associated with the transplantation process." The Foundation awards grants to qualified organizations and institutions. The Web site includes grant guidelines, grant application downloadable in PDF format, recent grants awarded, a listing of committee members, and contact information.

Charlotte Martin Foundation (WA) (http://www.charlottemartin.org/)

The Charlotte Martin Foundation, located in Seattle, Washington, is dedicated to enriching the lives of youth in the areas of athletics, culture, and education and also to preserving and protecting wildlife and habitat. The Foundation was established in 1987 and is committed to awarding grants, primarily in the Pacific Northwest Region, in two primary areas: youth (through athletics, culture, and education) and wildlife and habitat preservation. The Foundation's Web site provides detailed information about each program area. The site also explains how to apply for grants. The annual report, a list of previous grantees, and contact information can also be found on the site.

The Katharine Matthies Foundation (CT) (http://www.electronicvalley.org/matthies/)

Established in 1987 following the death of Katharine Matthies, the Foundation supports programs in education, social service, sports recreation, health care, culture, prevention of cruelty to children and animals, and other programs that benefit local residents and improve the quality of life in Seymour, Oxford, Beacon Falls, Ansonia and Derby, Connecticut. The Seymour, Connecticut-based Foundation is the legacy of Katharine Matthies, a lifelong Seymour resident whose family members were leading industrialists in Seymour. Visitors to the site will find application guidelines and submission requirements, a list of grants, a short biography of its founder, and contact information.

Edmund F. Maxwell Foundation (WA) (http://www.maxwell.org)

The Edmund F. Maxwell Foundation, located in Seattle, Washington, "believing in the importance of acknowledging the fine accomplishments of high-achieving young people," offers the Edmund F. Maxwell Foundation Scholarships to residents of western Washington who require financial assistance to attend independent colleges or universities. The Foundation's namesake, Edmund Maxwell, was the head of Blyth & Co., a premier investment firm in the region. Students who are residents of western Washington with combined S.A.T. scores of over 1200, a demonstrated financial need, and who meet other criteria are eligible for the scholarship, which is $3,500 for the 1999–2000 school year. Consult the Web site for a brief biography, application guidelines, printable forms, recipient list, and contact information. Forms are also available by mail.

The Faye McBeath Foundation (WI) (http://www.fayemcbeath.org)

The Faye McBeath Foundation of Wisconsin was established in 1964 to support the community in which Ms. Mcbeath was born and raised. Major areas of interest for the Foundation include children, the elderly, health care, health education, and civic/governmental affairs. Visitors to the Foundation's Web site will find detailed information on the program priorities, information on special programs, application information, a history of grantees, and contact information.

McCarthy Family Foundation (CA) (http://fdncenter.org/grantmaker/mccarthy/index.html)

The San Diego-based McCarthy Family Foundation makes grants in five primary program areas: secondary school science education; AIDS research, education, and support; assistance to homeless people; support for children and families in need; and environmental protection. The Foundation makes grants exclusively within California, with the typical grant award being between $3,500 and $40,000. The Foundation does not make grants for individuals, scholarship funds, sectarian religious activities, general fundraising drives, or programs supporting political candidates or to influence legislation. The Foundation's folder on the Center's Web site provides visitors with program guidelines, application instructions, and a recent grants list.

The Edna McConnell Clark Foundation (NY) (http://www.emcf.org/)

The Edna McConnell Clark Foundation seeks to improve conditions and opportunities for people who live in poor and disadvantaged communities. Through its grantmaking, the

Foundation "assists nonprofit organizations and public agencies committed to advancing practices and policies that better the lives of children and families, [while supporting] initiatives that promise to help systems and institutions become more responsive to the needs of the people they serve." The current interests of the Foundation fall into four separate program areas, each with specific goals, strategies, and grantmaking priorities: the Program for Children, the Program for New York Neighborhoods, the Program for Student Achievement, and the Program for Tropical Disease Research. Applicants may want to read the Foundation's latest annual report to ensure that their projects fit within the above programs' very specific, site-based grantmaking strategies. Visitors to the Foundation's Web site will find detailed program descriptions, application guidelines, a recent grants list organized by program area, a report from the Foundation president, a list of Foundation-sponsored publications that can be obtained free of charge, board and staff listings, and contact information.

Robert R. McCormick Tribune Foundation (IL) (http://www.rrmtf.org)

The Robert R. McCormick Tribune Foundation was established as a charitable trust in 1955 upon the death of Colonel Robert R. McCormick, longtime editor and publisher of the *Chicago Tribune,* and was restructured as a foundation in 1991, with an emphasis on four grantmaking areas: communities, journalism, education, and citizenship. Because each program has its own guidelines, geographic restrictions, and application procedures, grantseekers are encouraged to read carefully all information pertaining to their particular program of interest. In addition to the four program areas, the Foundation also provides annual support to Cantigny, the Colonel's former estate in Wheaton, Illinois, which is now operated as a park for the "education, instruction and welfare of the people of Illinois." The Foundation's Web site provides program descriptions, grant summaries, and grant guidelines where applicable.

McCune Charitable Foundation (NM) (http://www.nmmccune.org/)

Perrine D. McCune founded the McCune Charitable Foundation in Sante Fe, New Mexico, in 1989 to continue the philanthropic legacy that she and her husband, Marshall Lockhart McCune, had established during their lifetime. The couple was a significant part of the cultural and artistic life in the Sante Fe area and helped establish many organizations and institutions there. The mission of the Marshall L. and Perrine D. McCune Charitable Foundation is "to memorialize the donors through grants which enrich the cultural life, health, education, environment and spiritual life of the citizens of New Mexico." Funding is targeted for community-based, community-driven projects, with preference given to organizations that operate programs in Sante Fe or northern New Mexico. Visitors to the Web site will find grant application guidelines, staff listing, short descriptions of sample funded projects, and contact information.

James S. McDonnell Foundation (MO) (http://www.jsmf.org/)

The McDonnell Foundation was established in 1950 by aerospace pioneer James S. McDonnell, "to explore methods for developing a stable world order and lasting peace." Today the foundation awards $11 million in grants annually, primarily in the areas of biomedical and behavioral sciences and research and innovation in education. The three programs the Foundation currently supports are Bridging Brain, Mind, and Behavior; Studying Complex Systems; and Brain Cancer Research. The Foundation's Web site provides program information, application guidelines, a listing of grants and awards made by the Foundation, current Foundation financial reports, staff and board information, and contact information.

D.V. and Ida J. McEachern Charitable Trust (WA)
(http://fdncenter.org/grantmaker/mceachern/)

The D.V. and Ida J. McEachern Charitable Trust was established in 1969 to help give a better start in life to all children, both educationally and physically. The Foundation supports social service agencies that allow children and youth to attain their basic needs. Artistic and cultural programs are also of interest to the Foundation. Visitors to the Foundation's folder on the Center's Web site will find application guidelines, grant ranges, sample grants, restrictions, application deadlines, and contact information.

R.J. McElroy Trust (IA) (http://www.cedarnet.org/mcelroy)
R.J. McElroy was a pioneer Iowa broadcaster who founded the Black Hawk Broadcasting Company, put KWWL radio station, KWWL–TV, and several other radio and television stations on the air. When he died in 1965, a provision in his will provided for the establishment of a trust fund for the educational benefit of deserving young people. Located in Waterloo, Iowa, the R.J. McElroy Trust has since then funded a broad range of educational programs, such as scholarships, fellowships, internships, student loan funds, and other projects to benefit youth of all ages. Organizations located in the KWWL viewing area are preferred, and organizations located in Black Hawk County and the rural counties in that viewing area will receive higher priority. The Trust will also give higher priority to grants that fund program rather than capital projects. Consult the Web site for grant application guidelines, policies, and contact information, including an e-mail link.

William G. McGowan Charitable Fund (DC) (http://www.mcgowanfund.com)
The William G. McGowan Charitable Fund was established in 1992 in Washington, D.C., to further the vision of its founder, Bill McGowan. In 1968, McGowan organized the MCI Communications Corporation, effectively ending the telecommunications monopoly in the United States The Fund makes grants in the areas of health care and medical scientific research, the creation of educational opportunities, and the development of the gifts and talents of youth. Funding is limited to organizations in the following geographic areas: northeastern Pennsylvania; the Chicago area; western New York state; central and northern California; the Dallas/Houston/San Antonio region; Washington, D.C., and the Baltimore area; northern Virginia; and the Kansas City metropolitan area. Details on the grantmaking process, guidelines, and an application, which can be downloaded in Microsoft Word, Word Perfect and in plain text, are provided on the Fund's Web site. More information on the Fund and the vision and work of its founder is also available online.

McGregor Fund (MI) (http://www.mcgregorfund.org/)
Founded in 1925 by Michigan philanthropists Tracy and Katherine Whitney McGregor, the McGregor Fund was established to "relieve the misfortunes and promote the well being of mankind." The Fund presently awards grants in the areas of human services, education, health care, arts and culture, and public benefit. Only organizations located in the metropolitan Detroit area, or projects that significantly benefit that area, are eligible for support. The Fund does not award grants for individuals or student scholarships and generally does not support travel, conferences, seminars or workshops, film or video projects, or disease–specific organizations. Visitors to the Fund's Web site will find brief descriptions of each program area, application procedures and guidelines, grants list archive organized by program area, complete financial statements, a listing of Fund trustees and staff, and contact information.

The McInerney Family Foundation (NY) (http://www.McInerneyFoundation.org)
Established in 1997, the McInerney Family Foundation is committed to improving the lives of children living in underserved communities within the tri-state area. The Foundation believes "it is only through our children that the cycle of poverty can be broken. Communities that raise strong children thrive and prosper. Therefore, it is crucial to give young children a strong foundation." Visit the Foundation's Web site to view information on eligibility and application information. The site also contains contact information.

Robert E. and Evelyn McKee Foundation (TX) (http://www.mckeefoundation.org)
The Robert E. and Evelyn McKee Foundation was founded in 1952 in Texas. Robert E. McKee founded one of the nation's largest general contracting firms and, along with his wife Evelyn, was a noted local philanthropist. Their Foundation makes grants in the categories of civics, culture, and religion; education and scholarships; hospitals; medicine and medical research; welfare, rehabilitation, and mental health; the United Way; and youth

activities. Scholarships are made to select local high school and universities that distribute the funds to individual students. Grants are mainly limited to local nonprofit organizations or national organizations with local affiliates, and grants in the area of religion are directed toward local Episcopal churches. The Foundation's Web site provides a history of its founders, succinct grant guidelines, and contact information.

The McKnight Endowment Fund for Neuroscience (MN) (http://www.mcknight.org/neuroscience)

The McKnight Endowment Fund for Neuroscience is an independent organization established and funded by the McKnight Foundation in 1986 to oversee its neuroscience research awards program, which dates back to 1977, due to the success of the awards program and the recognition attained by the participants. The Fund has its own board of directors but is administered by the Foundation. This research program is a direct legacy of founder William L. McKnight, who was interested in the biology of the brain, particularly diseases affecting memory. The Endowment Fund has the following awards for research on memory: McKnight Scholar Awards, for scientists in the early stages of their research careers; McKnight Investigator Awards, for mid-career scientists exploring new ideas about the basic mechanisms of memory and disorders affecting memory; McKnight Technological Innovations in Neuroscience Awards, which provide seed funding for highly innovative projects to stimulate the development of novel approaches to exploring and understanding how the brain functions; and McKnight Senior Investigator Awards, of which 10 were given every three years from 1977 to 1999 to established neuroscientists and their associates. The board of directors makes funding decisions on the basis of recommendations by review committees. Visitors to the Web site will find downloadable application forms and guidelines, a list of awardees, announcements, a search engine for the site, and contact information.

The McKnight Foundation (MN) (http://www.mcknight.org)

The McKnight Foundation was established and endowed by William L. McKnight and Maude L. McKnight in 1953. William McKnight was one of the early leaders of 3M, as president and chief executive; however, the Foundation is independent of that corporation. The McKnight Foundation seeks to improve the quality of life for present and future generations; "supports efforts to improve outcomes for children, families, and communities; contributes to the arts; encourages preservation of the natural environment; and promotes scientific research in selected fields." The Foundation has the following funding areas: children, families, and communities; arts; environment; initiatives; international; and research and applied science. Located in Minneapolis, Minnesota, its primary geographic focus in its human services and arts grantmaking is the state of Minnesota. Consult the Web site for more information on grant and award programs for each funding area; downloadable guidelines (can also be ordered by phone); conditions and limitations; grants lists; financial information; online free publications request, including the annual report; and an online contact form.

Meadows Foundation, Inc. (TX) (http://www.mfi.org/)

The Meadows Foundation was established in 1948 by Algur H. and Virginia Meadows to benefit the people of Texas by "working toward the elimination of ignorance, hopelessness and suffering, protecting the environment, providing cultural enrichment, encouraging excellence and promoting understanding and cooperation among people." The Foundation provides grants in the areas of art and culture, civic and public affairs, education, health, and human services. In addition to examples of grants awarded in each area of giving, visitors to the Foundation's Web site can access grant guidelines (in Spanish and English); the Foundation's financial information; a listing of officers, directors; and staff; and links to local and national nonprofit organizations. The site also describes the Foundation's Wilson Historic District housing restoration project as well as its Awards for Charitable School project, which supports youth voluntarism.

Medina Foundation (WA) (http://www.medinafoundation.org/)

The Medina Foundation seeks to "aid in improving the human condition in the greater Puget Sound community by fostering positive change, growth and the improvement of people." The Foundation makes grants to qualified charitable organizations, particularly those offering direct service delivery. No grants are made to individuals. The Foundation supports four program areas: human services, education, persons with disabilities, and alcohol and drug abuse. The Foundation's Web site includes program and financial guidelines, funding parameters and geographical restrictions, application procedures, an overview of the Foundation's Management Excellence Awards Program, FAQs, and contact information.

Mega Foundation (CT) (http://www.megafoundation.org)

The Mega Foundation, located in Norwalk, Connecticut, works toward the development and community of severely gifted people and their ideas. "Severely gifted" is defined as someone with an IQ of 164 or above, and the Foundation posts some information about identifying these individuals. In order to keep severely gifted people from falling through the cracks of an educational system that may not nurture their "rage to learn," the Mega Foundation maintains a variety of programs and grants to encourage work by and about people who are severely gifted. The Foundation has three program areas: giftedness development, science, and visual, literary, and performing arts. Additionally, the Foundation runs Ultranet, a Web site creating community among the severely gifted, and a mentor program to encourage younger gifted individuals. The Foundation's Web site includes a form for more information and links to more resources.

Andrew W. Mellon Foundation (NY) (http://www.mellon.org)

Under its broad charter, the New York City-based Andrew W. Mellon Foundation currently makes grants on a selective basis in the following areas of interest: higher education, cultural affairs and the performing arts, population, conservation and the environment, and cost-effective uses of technology in teaching. Although the Foundation reviews proposals on a rolling basis throughout the year, "prospective applicants are encouraged to explore their ideas informally with Foundation staff (preferably in writing) before submitting formal proposals." The Foundation does not make grants to individuals or to primarily local organizations. In addition to a range of general information, visitors to the Foundation's no-frills Web site will find program descriptions, a list of Foundation trustees and staff, and online versions of two dozen Foundation reports from 1987 to present.

Richard King Mellon Foundation (PA) (http://fdncenter.org/grantmaker/rkmellon/)

Founded in 1947 by the financial giant, the Richard King Mellon Foundation is committed to improving the quality of life in Pittsburgh, Pennsylvania, and to national land and wildlife conservation. Grants have been given in the following program categories: civic affairs, conservation, cultural activities, medicine, education, and human services. The organization considers support for operations, capital projects, programs, and start-up and prefers not to be the only donor. Most funding is distributed in southwestern Pennsylvania, except for the sponsored national land conservation program. The site has grant application procedures and guidelines, including an application that can be printed in HTML (right from the screen). There is a grants list and lists of the staff and the board. The foundation also accepts the Grantmakers of Western Pennsylvania's Common Grant Application Form.

Merck Family Fund (MA) (http://www.merckff.org/)

Established in 1954, Merck Family Fund is a private family foundation with two goals: to restore and protect the natural environment and ensure a healthy planet for generations to come and to strengthen the social fabric and the physical landscape of the urban community. There are two areas of priority to help achieve a healthy planet: the protection of vital ecosystems in eastern United States and supporting the shift towards environmentally sustainable economic systems, incentives, and behaviors. The two areas of priority for strengthening the urban community are creating green and open space and supporting youth as agents of social change. The Milton, Massachusetts-based Fund limits grants to grassroots programs in New York City, Providence, Rhode Island, and Boston, Massachusetts. Visit the Web site for more information on its funding areas and priorities, grant application guidelines, financial information, grant lists with links to grantee organizations, related links, and contact information. The Fund urges grantseekers to use the common proposal format (for invited proposals only) and provides a link to a site where it can be downloaded.

The Merck Genome Research Institute (PA) (Operating foundation) (http://www.mgri.org)

The Merck Genome Research Institute, located in West Point, Pennsylvania, is dedicated to "[improving] techniques to the linkage of human genetic traits and [resolving] biological function of disease genes" and gives special interest to the "development of methods which tend to accelerate predictions of gene function independent of linkage." Associated with Merck & Co., the Institute provides funding for two types of grants: research proposals of one to two years' duration, with funding of $100,000 to $150,000; and pilot proposals for high risk projects of one year duration, with funding of up to $50,000. Grants are designed for M.D., Ph.D., or M.D./Ph.D. independent investigators, and the following specific research areas are of specific interest to the Institute: Merck Gene Index, Full Mammalian cDNA Cloning/Sequencing Technology, Bioinformatics, Disease Models, and Gene Expression/Function Assays. The Institute's Web page provides eligibility requirements, a description of the selection process, application guidelines, and terms of the grants. Contact information and more details about the Institute are also available at the site.

Joyce Mertz-Gilmore Foundation (NY) (http://www.jmgf.org/)

The Joyce Mertz-Gilmore Foundation makes grants to nonprofit organizations active in the areas of the environment, human rights, peace and security, and New York City civic and cultural life. The Foundation currently sponsors five grantmaking programs: environment/energy, human rights, peace and security, New York City human and built environment, and arts in New York City. The Foundation does not typically make grants for endowments or annual fund appeals; capital projects; political activities such as lobbying; conferences or workshops; sectarian religious concerns; individual scholarships, research, fellowships, loans, or travel; film or media projects; or publications. Visitors to the Foundation's Web site will find program guidelines and restrictions, a listing of selected grants by program area, recent financial statements, application instructions, and a listing of the Foundation' staff and board of directors.

Meru Foundation (MA) (http://www.meru.org) (Operating foundation)

The Meru Foundation is a private nonprofit research and educational corporation founded in 1983 to "study ancient alphabets and texts from a modern mathematical perspective, with emphasis on their self-organizing whole systems." Its work is based on 20 years of research by Stan Tenen into the origin and nature of the Hebrew alphabet and the mathematical structure underlying the sequence of letters of the Hebrew text of Genesis. Visit the Foundation's Web site for articles and papers describing Tenen's work.

Eugene and Agnes E. Meyer Foundation (DC) (http://www.meyerfdn.org/)

Founded in Washington, D.C. in 1944 by Eugene Meyer, owner and publisher of the *Washington Post*, The Eugene and Agnes E. Meyer Foundation invests in nonprofit entrepreneurs and community–based organizations that meet emerging social needs and strengthen the region's communities. The Meyer Foundation is interested in a variety of programs including arts and humanities, community service, education, health and mental health, law and justice, neighborhood development, and housing. The foundation also strongly supports the surrounding areas of Washington, D.C., metropolitan area, providing four types of support to local communities in the form of the Management Assistance Program, Cash Flow Loans, Technology Circuit Rider, and Sector Capacity-Building. The Foundation's Web site includes a well-built searchable database of grant recipients with extended profiles of each organization, a resourceful set of links and resources, staff/board listing, grant guidelines, grant applications, and contact information.

Meyer Memorial Trust (OR) (http://www.mmt.org/)

Founded by retail-store magnate Fred G. Meyer, the Portland-based Meyer Memorial Trust operates three grantmaking programs—General Purpose Grants, Small Grants, and Support for Teacher Initiatives—to benefit qualified tax-exempt applicants in Oregon and Clark County, Washington. The Trust does not provide grants, loans, or scholarships to individuals, nor does it provide assistance to for-profit businesses. Visitors to the Trust's Web site will find application guidelines, restrictions, and cover sheets (in PDF format) for each of its programs; grants lists by subject area for the latest years; a listing of trustees and staff; a brief biography of Trust founder Fred Meyer; and a short list of links to other online resources.

The Allen H. and Nydia Meyers Foundation (MI) (http://www.meyersfoundation.org/)

The Allen H. and Nydia Meyers Foundation, located in Adrian, Michigan, was founded in 1966 by the Meyerses to encourage, support, and stimulate scientific education, teaching, research, and related efforts such as engineering and aerospace study and design. The goal of the Foundation is to provide early financial support for young men and women interested in post–secondary education for aeronautics or scientific careers. Generally the Foundation grants awards to high school graduates residing in the Lenawee County, Michigan school district who have graduated from a Lenawee County, Michigan high school and who are planning college studies in the sciences and allied fields. The Foundation also makes grants to institutions of learning and research that are engaging in projects that will generally help fulfill the goals of the Foundation. Applications can be downloaded in PDF format. A detailed history of the Foundation is also posted on the Web site.

The Michelson Foundation (CA) (http://www.pacificfoundationservices.com/michelson/index.html)

Founded in California in 1991, The Michelson Foundation is committed to providing for disadvantaged individuals and families through education, human services, health care, and teen pregnancy prevention in San Mateo County. Other areas of interest include support for psychiatric disabilities and organizations that support the arts for youth. The Foundation will also consider requests involving capital improvements and equipment acquisitions. Upon visiting the Foundation's Web site, visitors will find the most recent grants, contact information, board of directors list, and application procedures.

Milbank Memorial Fund (NY) (http://www.milbank.org)

The Milbank Memorial Fund, based in New York City, supports nonpartisan analysis, study, research, and communication on significant issues in health policy and makes the results of its work available in meetings with decision-makers and in reports, books, and the *Milbank Quarterly,* a peer-reviewed journal of public health and healthcare policy. Access book titles, abstracts, and articles online on its Web site.

Milken Family Foundation (CA) (http://www.mff.org/)

Established in 1982 by Lowell and Michael Milken, the California-based Milken Family Foundation advances its mission of "helping people help themselves and those around them to lead productive and satisfying lives" by focusing its activities on education and medicine (specifically prostate cancer and epilepsy). The Foundation's Web site comes in Shockwave Flash and non-Shockwave versions. It has a number of interactive features and a good deal of information about the Foundation's areas of interest and programs. Among the latter are the American Epilepsy Society/Milken Family Foundation Epilepsy Research Award Grants and Fellowship Program, recognizing outstanding physicians and scientists working to improve the lives of people with epilepsy; Mike's Math Club, a mentoring program for fifth- and sixth-graders; and the Milken Family National Educator Awards, offering financial recognition to outstanding educators in schools affiliated with the Bureau of Jewish Education of Greater Los Angeles.

The Miller Foundation (MI) (http://www.willard.lib.mi.us/npa/miller)

The Miller Foundation was established in Battle Creek, Michigan, in 1963 by Robert Miller, newspaperman and noted philanthropist. The Foundation seeks to improve the Battle Creek community and serve as an example to other philanthropic groups. Through grants and partnerships with other organizations, the Foundation focuses on the areas of economic development, neighborhood improvement, improving educational outcomes for youth, and eliminating barriers to employment for all in Battle Creek, Michigan, and the surrounding area. The Foundation's Web site provides visitors with a short biography of founder Robert Miller, a list of past grantees, related links, and guidelines for the initial inquiry letter that should be sent to the Foundation by interested grantseekers. The Foundation strictly limits funding to the Battle Creek area; contact information is available online.

Minnesota Masonic Foundation, Inc. (MN) (http://www.mn-mason.org/found.html)

The Minnesota Masonic Foundation was created in 1970 to meet the needs of Minnesota Masonry. The St. Paul, Minnesota-based Foundation is focused on Minnesota's youth, matching local lodge scholarships up to a pre-set limit that varies from year to year. Local lodges administer their programs as they wish, and the Foundation augments the contributions to the education of young Minnesotans. Visitors to the site will find printable scholarship applications, links to contact information, and application instructions.

The Joan Mitchell Foundation (NY) (http://fdncenter.org/grantmaker/joanmitchellfdn/)

The mission of the New York-based Joan Mitchell Foundation seeks to demonstrate that painting and sculpture are significant cultural necessities. The Foundation provides grants, stipends, and scholarships for painters and sculptors. The Foundation also seeks out avenues to meet the needs of artists, such as colloquiums and workshops, classes, and other resource facilities. Each year the Foundation's giving program awards 20 grants to outstanding artists who are in need of financial aid. The Foundation also has established free art classes for artistically inclined young people in grades 7–12. Visit the Foundation's folder on the Center's Web site to learn more about the history of Joan Mitchell and the Foundation. Also at the site visitors will find further information about the scholarship programs, view recent grant recipient lists, and receive contact information.

L.R. Moffitt & L.Q. Moffitt Foundation (OH)
(http://community.ohio.com/realcities/moffittfdn)

The L.R. Moffitt & L.Q. Moffitt Foundation, based in Akron, Ohio, provides grants to institutions of learning, hospitals, religious organizations, and institutions of public charity. The Foundation does not have an application for grants; instead, a proposal is required and guidelines are provided on the Web site. Funding is considered twice yearly. An outline of general types of funding that the Foundation supports, a newsletter, a calendar of events, and contact information are available online.

The Monell Foundation, Ambrose (NY) (http://www.monellvetlesen.org/)

The Ambrose Monell Foundation's mission is: "Voluntarily aiding and contributing to religious, charitable, scientific, literary, and educational uses and purposes, in New York, elsewhere in the United States and throughout the world." Grants are made to qualified nonprofit organizations; no individual grants are given. Interested parties should submit a request for funding to the Foundation; guidelines and information about what should be included can be found on the Web site. The Foundation provides a copy of its Form 990–PF online, which can be downloaded in PDF format. Previous annual reports and lists of recent grants awarded are also available on the site.

The Burton D. Morgan Foundation (OH) (http://www.bdmorgan-fdn.com)

The mission of the Akron, Ohio-based Burton D. Morgan Foundation is to preserve and encourage "America's greatest asset, the free enterprise system." It was established in 1967 by Burton Morgan to support the private enterprise system. Other areas of interest include economics, education, and mental health. The Foundation prefers to make grants to organizations located in northeastern Ohio and does not make grants to social service organizations or programs. It is recommended that grantseekers contact the Foundation regarding any proposals before sending a formal grant request letter. Visitors to the site will find a brief history of the Foundation, grant application guidelines, and contact information.

Morino Foundation/Institute (VA) (http://www.morino.org)

Founded by business leader and "social entrepreneur" Mario Marino, the Morino Foundation/Institute is dedicated to "opening the doors of opportunity—economic, civic, health and education—and empowering people to improve their lives and communities in the communications age." Grants are normally made from the Morino Foundation, on behalf of the Institute, in support of initiatives or focus areas in which the Institute is actively engaged—youth advocacy and services, entrepreneurship, social networking, and community services. In all of its grantmaking activities, the Institute, which does not accept unsolicited proposals, emphasizes the emerging medium of electronic communications and how it can be applied to further positive social change and community improvement. The Institute's elegant Web site offers a good deal of interesting information about the Institute's core beliefs and funding philosophy, general program and grant information, links to a variety of Institute-sponsored projects and partners, and contact information.

The John Motley Morehead Foundation (NC) (http://www.moreheadfoundation.org)

Based in Chapel Hill, North Carolina, the John Motley Morehead Foundation sponsors the Morehead Award, a full four-year scholarship award to attend the University of North Carolina at Chapel Hill. It includes a stipend covering all educational and living expenses during the recipient's four years of undergraduate study as well as a summer enrichment program that gives the Morehead Scholars leadership training and hands-on experience during each of their four undergraduate summers. These undergraduate scholarship awards are designed to attract outstanding, well-rounded students to study at the University of North Carolina at Chapel Hill and are based solely on merit. Students must show the capacity to lead and motivate fellow students, scholastic ability and extracurricular achievement, moral force of character, and physical vigor as shown by participation in sports or in other ways. It is not possible to apply for the award; candidates are nominated by committees at their high schools. All high schools in North Carolina, seventy-three schools outside of North Carolina, thirty-one schools in Great Britain, and all high schools and cegeps in Canada are eligible to nominate students. A list of eligible schools are provided on the site. Visitors to the site will find eligibility criteria, a history of the award, and alumni directory and profiles, and contact information.

Charles Stewart Mott Foundation (MI) (http://www.mott.org/)

Established in 1926 by industrialist Charles Stewart Mott, the Flint, Michigan-based Mott Foundation makes grants in the United States and, on a limited geographic basis, internationally in four broad program areas: civil society; the environment; philanthropy in Flint, Michigan; and poverty. These programs, in turn, are divided into more specific areas: the civil society program focuses on the United States, South Africa, Central/Eastern Europe, Russia, and the newly created Republics; the environment program is devoted to reform of international lending and trade policies, prevention of toxic pollution, protection of the Great Lakes ecosystem, and special initiatives; the Flint program concentrates on institutional capacity building, arts and recreation, economic and community development, and education; and the poverty program focuses on building communities, strengthening families, improving education, economic opportunity, and cross-cutting initiatives. In addition to detailed application guidelines and a biography of Charles Stewart Mott, the Foundation's well-organized Web site offers a searchable grants database, dozens of links to grantee Web sites, a list of publications available through the Foundation, a copy of the latest annual report, and related stories in each broad program area.

MSMS Foundation (MI) (http://www.msms.org/msmsf/index.html)

The Michigan State Medical Society Foundation is sponsored by the Michigan State Medical Society. Its purpose is to "advance the field of health for the public good." Specifically, the Foundation works to support and/or initiate education, research programs, and projects in the field of health; encourage the advancement of healthy lifestyles and the prevention of disease; and develop and administer funds for the support of health education and research. The Foundation supports both research programs and demonstration programs with short-term or start-up costs. Contact information is provided for those interested in learning more about the grant program and deadlines. The Foundation accepts applications through the Council of Michigan Foundations Common Grant Application Form, which can be down-loaded in PDF format from the site. Instructions and information are included on the application. The Web site also provides information about the Foundation's board of directors, recent news about the Foundation, and a list of recent grant recipients.

M.J. Murdock Charitable Trust (WA) (http://www.murdock-trust.org/)

The Vancouver, Washington-headquartered M.J. Murdock Charitable Trust was estab-lished by the will of Melvin J. Murdock, co-founder of the Oregon electronic instruments company, Tektronix, Inc., in 1975. The Foundation focuses its grantmaking efforts in the five states of the Pacific Northwest: Alaska, Idaho, Montana, Oregon, and Washington, with emphasis on programs in education and scientific research, the arts, public affairs, health and medicine, human services, and people with disabilities. The Foundation makes grants in the four areas of education, scientific research, arts and culture, and health and human services. The Foundation's Web site provides ample instruction on the guidelines, limitations, and requirements for applications to these grants. There are five grant applica-tion forms that can be downloaded in PDF format: general, research, life sciences, Partners in Science Mentor, and Partners in Science High School Teacher Candidate Statement. Some of these programs are considered formal grants and are therefore by invitation-only. Each grant type is detailed online, along with a listing of recent grantees, a history of the Foundation, financial statements, and contact information.

John P. Murphy Foundation (OH) (http://fdncenter.org/grantmaker/jpmurphy/)

The John P. Murphy Foundation was established in 1960 in Cleveland, Ohio, by Murphy, a legal counsel whose mission for the Foundation was to provide funding for "charitable, educational, scientific, literary and religious purposes." The Foundation today continues to follow the pattern of giving established by Murphy when he was alive, supporting the areas of education, the arts and culture, social service, community, health, and religion. The Foundation's folder on the Center's Web site provides a short biography of John Murphy with more details on the spirit in which the Foundation makes grants. The site also includes grant application requirements and guidelines, a contact address, a list of board and officers of the Foundation, and financial statements.

Musicians Foundation, Inc. (NY) (http://www.musiciansfoundation.org)

The Musicians Foundation aims to foster the interests and advance the conditions and social welfare of professional musicians and their families in case of need. Based in New York City, the Foundation provides financial assistance to musicians who need help in meeting current living, medical, and allied expenses. Visitors will find a downloadable grant application in PDF format, links, and descriptions of related sites and contact information.

Musser Fund (MN) (http://www.musserfund.org)

The Laura Jane Musser Fund was established in 1989 in Minnesota. The Fund provides grants to qualifying organizations in areas where trustees live or have an interest and in rural areas including the Little Falls, Minnesota area where Laura Jane Musser made her lifelong home. The Fund makes grants in the domains of children and youth, music and fine art, intercultural harmony, rural life, and environment. The Fund places priority on organizations that are creative or innovative in approach, community based and/or commu-nity initiated, self-sustaining, offering replicable possibilities, and having smaller budgets. The Fund does not make grants toward general operating support. Visit the Foundation's Web site to find application guidelines and printable application.

The Mustard Seed Foundation (VA) (Operating foundation) (http://www.msfdn.org)

Dennis and Eileen Harvey Bakke established the Mustard Seed Foundation in 1983 as "an expression of their desire to advance the Kingdom of God through faithful stewardship." The Foundation provides grants to Christians who are engaged in or preparing for evangelism, stewardship, ministry, education, and relieving human suffering. Individuals and organizations receiving Mustard Seed grants must demonstrate personal faith in Christ and must desire "to serve and witness in His name." For the Foundation, "the gospel of Jesus Christ and the advance of His Kingdom are central to all that we are and all that we do." The Foundation places highest priority on funding projects that "seek to draw disciples to Jesus from every 'unreached' community, city, and culture and which attempt to redeem society's structures and institutions." The Foundation has the following funding categories: Acts of Mercy, Church Parenting, Empowerment, Unreached Peoples, and Christian Discipleship; and the following scholarships: Theological Scholarships, Bakke Scholars, and Harvey Fellows. Consult the Web site for more detailed information on each area of the Foundation's grant program and scholarship programs. The site features a downloadable application form and online contact forms. Visitors to the Web site will also find a description of its principles, its annual report, and financial information.

E. Nakamichi Foundation (CA) (http://www.enfoundation.com)

The E. Nakamichi Foundation was established in Los Angeles, California, in 1982 to "encourage the propagation and appreciation of baroque and other fine forms of classical music" that are generally not available on a commercial basis. The Foundation underwrites performances or broadcasts of performances on public television or radio. It does not make grants to individuals, nor does it make multi-year grants. Extensive information on the guidelines and limitations of funding are available at the Foundation's Web site. On the site, grantseekers may register their organization, then apply for a grant directly online; the Foundation allows applicants to check the status of their preliminary application online. Additionally, the Web site includes a list of previously funded organizations and institutions and contact information.

The National Academy of Education (NY) (Operating foundation) (http://www.nae.nyu.edu)

The National Academy of Education (NAE) was founded in 1965 to "promote scholarly inquiry and discussion concerning the ends and means of education, in all its forms, in the United States and abroad." The New York City-based Academy has sponsored a variety of commissions and study panels that have published proceedings and reports. In keeping with its mission, the Academy seeks to fund proposals that promise to make significant scholarly contributions to the field of education as well as to advance the careers of the recipients. NAE also administers a Postdoctoral Fellowship Program, funded by the Spencer Foundation, which is designed to insure the future of research in education by supporting young scholars working in critical areas of educational scholarship. Visitors to the site will find fellowship applications that can be downloaded in PDF format, grant application instructions and guidelines, and links to affiliated Web sites.

National Association of Chain Drug Stores Education Foundation, Inc. (VA) (http://www.nacds.org)

Based in Alexandria, Virginia, the chief purpose of National Association of Chain Drug Stores Education Foundation (NACDS) is to represent the views and policy positions of member chain drug companies. NACDS seeks to address pharmacy and health-related issues, promote the value and role of community retail pharmacy in the health care system, ensure that the community retail pharmacy perspective is communicated to and understood by legislators and policy-makers, provide appropriate forums for retailers to interact with their suppliers and business partners, create a favorable political and business climate in which NACDS member companies can carry out their business plans, and develop and promote policies and programs aimed at improving merchandise distribution and retail operations efficiency. NACDS provides members with a library, publications, meetings and conferences, and programs such as an interactive education for pharmacy technician training programs. Visitors to the site will find online membership applications.

National Video Resources, Inc. (NY) (Operating foundation) (http://www.nvr.org)

National Video Resources (NVR) was established in 1990 by the Rockefeller Foundation. Its goal is to "assist in increasing the public's awareness of and access to independently produced media & film and video as well as motion media delivered through the new digital technologies." NVR designs and implements projects that help enable individuals and organizations such as public libraries, colleges and universities, and other nonprofits to acquire and use independent film and video. NVR also commissions and publishes research on issues of concern to independent media makers, distributors, educators, activists, and individuals. Visitors to the site will find information on publications and projects. NVR manages the Film/Video/Multimedia Fellowships Program for the Rockefeller and MacArthur Foundations, which supports media artists from the United States (funded by Rockefeller) and Latin America (funded by Rockefeller and MacArthur). Fellowships are awarded through a nomination process; applications are not accepted. The NVR Web site features information on its programs and publications and an online publications order form.

Needmor Fund (CO) (http://fdncenter.org/grantmaker/needmor/index.html)

Established in Toledo, Ohio, in 1956, the Colorado-based Needmor Fund today works to change the social, economic, and political conditions that bar access to participation in a democratic society. The Fund is committed to the idea that "citizens should be free and equal to determine the actions of government and the terms of public policy" and thus assure their right to justice, political liberty, the basic necessities of life, an education that enables them to be contributing members of society, and the opportunity to secure productive work with just wages and benefits and decent working conditions. Visitors to the Fund's folder on the Center's Web site will find a statement of the Fund's mission and values, detailed application guidelines and restrictions, and a recent listing of grants.

The Nemours Foundation (FL) (http://www.nemours.org/no/)

The Nemours Foundation of Florida was created in 1936, following a bequest from Alfred I. DuPont. The Foundation's mission is to "execute prudently and effectively the Wills of Alfred I. duPont and [his brother-in-law] Edward Ball in perpetuity;" since 1940 this mission has manifested itself in the operation of health institutions. These institutions provide services for children in Delaware and Florida and the surrounding areas and for the elderly in Delaware. Foundation funding goes toward staff education and research. The organization also sponsors continuing medical education conferences throughout the country. The Foundation funds KidsHealth.org which is full of information on infections, behavior and emotions, food and fitness, and children's health. The site includes information on the history of the Foundation, each of the sponsored institutions, and the offered conferences.

New England Biolabs Foundation (MA) (http://www.nebf.org/)

Established in 1982, NEBF supports grassroots organizations working in the areas of the environment, social change, the arts, elementary education, and limited scientific research. Ordinarily, NEBF limits its domestic grantmaking to the greater Boston/North Shore area. But the Foundation does encourage proposals from or about developing countries with an emphasis on assisting community organizations in their endeavors. Due to its size, it restricts these activities to specific countries. Visitors to the NEBF site will find detailed application guidelines and reporting requirements, proposal tips from the Foundation's director, a list of awards made in 1996, and contact information. NEBF accepts the common grant application form sponsored by the National Network of Grantmakers.

New York Foundation (NY) (http://www.nyf.org)

One of the first foundations in the country, the New York City-based New York Foundation was established in 1909. The group's mission is to "support groups in New York City that are working on problems of urgent concern to residents of disadvantaged communities and neighborhoods [with a] particular interest in start-up grants to new, untested programs that have few other sources of support." The $20,000 to $50,000 grants are distributed four times a year. The types of programs that the Foundation likes to support include services and advocacy for various issues facing minority communities; education, hunger, and youth organizations; and coalitions of community groups. The Foundation holds regular meetings between its board and its grantees. The staff also supports the grantees through site visits and technical assistance. The site offers application guidelines; grant, staff, and board lists; and a news section. The Foundation accepts the New York-New Jersey Common Application Form.

New York Foundation for Architecture, Inc. (NY) (http://www.aiany.org)

The New York Foundation for Architecture is the sister organization of the New York Chapter of the American Institute of Architects. The two groups work together to provide scholarship and educational opportunities to students and the general public. The AIA New York Chapter offers two types of Grants: The Arnold W. Brunner Grant and the Stewardson Keefe LeBrun Travel Grant(s). Each year, the Chapter's Grant Selection Committee supervises the selection of scholarship recipients and distributes the awards. Information about these grants and how to apply is available on the Web site.

Newman's Own (CT) (http://www.newmansown.com/)

Established in 1982 in Westport, Connecticut, by actor Paul Newman, Newman's Own produces a wide variety of comestibles, donating 100 percent of the post-tax revenue to charity. From the sale of salad dressing, pasta sauce, salsa, and other food stuffs, Newman's Own funds grants and camps for children. The Hole in the Wall Gang Camp, for children with cancer and serious blood diseases, was founded by Newman with seed money from Newman's Own profits. Other camps that Newman supports are listed and linked to from the Newman's Own Web site. Grant guidelines and a grant application form, which can be downloaded in PDF format and should be attached to proposals, are available on the site. Visitors will be entertained by Newman's wacky sense of humor in the descriptions of the history of Newman's Own and its programs.

Samuel Roberts Noble Foundation (OK) (http://www.noble.org/)

Established in 1945 by oil industrialist Lloyd Noble in honor of his father, the Samuel Roberts Noble Foundation seeks "to assist humanity in reaching its maximum usefulness." To that end, the Ardmore, Oklahoma-based Foundation focuses on basic plant biology and agricultural research, consultation, and demonstration projects that enable farmers and ranchers to achieve their goals, enhancing plant productivity through fundamental research and applied biotechnology and assisting community, health, and educational organizations through grants and employee involvement. Among other offerings, the Foundation's Web site provides grant guidelines and procedures; an overview of activities in the Foundation's Plant Biology and Agricultural divisions; links to a variety of local, regional, and Internet resources; and contact information.

The Nokomis Foundation (MI) (http://www.nokomisfoundation.org/)

The Nokomis Foundation exists to "make a difference in the lives of women and girls by advocating for women-friendly policies, celebrating women's accomplishments, instilling economic self-sufficiency, and promoting healthy choices." The Foundation is located in Grand Rapids, Michigan, and primarily funds grants in the west Michigan area but will consider applications for programs with a state or national focus, provided they include a west Michigan component. The Foundation is particularly interested in pilot programs and gives priority to organizations that do not have access to traditional sources of funding. The Foundation funds programs that have similar focus to its mission, that show innovation and creativity, and that intend to foster collaboration among groups and accomplish long-term social change. To apply for a grant, an interested party should send a concise letter or e-mail describing the program; details are listed on the Web site. Lists of previous grants awarded are available on the site as is the most recent edition of the Foundation's newsletter.

Norcross Wildlife Foundation, Inc. (MA) (Operating foundation) (http://www.norcrossws.org/)

The Norcross Wildlife Foundation, Inc. was established in 1965 by Arthur D. Norcross, a native of Massachusetts and founder and manager of the Norcross Greeting Card Company. He established the Wales, Massachusetts-based Foundation to ensure the future well being of the Norcross Wildlife Sanctuary, which presently covers 4,000 acres but that had its beginnings with a 100-acre family woodlot-pasture Arthur Norcross inherited from his father in 1916. Around 1930, he began gathering nearby wooded acres, farmland, wetlands, and other parcels with the goal of establishing the Sanctuary. It was formally dedicated in 1939 as "a place where wildlife may be encouraged not just to survive but also to propagate and spread naturally, so that specific species, threatened with extinction, might again attain more normal distribution." In addition to maintaining the Sanctuary, the Foundation also has a grantmaking program. The Foundation prefers to place grants with organizations that ask for specific amounts, for example, to purchase and protect land, build nature centers and walkways, print and distribute educational materials—generally projects that have finite completion dates. Consult the Web site for grant request guidelines and contact information. Visitors to the Web site will also find a history of the Foundation and Sanctuary, descriptions of the programs and exhibits at the Sanctuary, schedules, and horticultural and animal facts.

Nord Family Foundation (OH) (http://www.nordff.org)

The Nord Family Foundation was originally the Nordson Foundation, a trust created in 1952 by Walter G. Nord, founder of the Nordson Corporation in Ohio. The Nordson Foundation was dissolved in 1988 and the Nord Family Foundation was created. In the tradition of its original founders Walter and Virginia Nord, the Foundation, located in Elyria, Ohio, seeks to build community by supporting projects that bring opportunity to the disadvantaged, strengthen family bonds, and improve quality of life. Grants are awarded in the fields of social service, health, education, the arts, and civic affairs. High priority is given to programs that address the needs of economically or socially disadvantaged families and projects that address the root causes of problems are of special interest. Most grants are made to organizations or for projects in Lorain County, Ohio, with a small number of grants to organizations in Cuyahoga County, Ohio; Denver, Colorado; Columbia, South Carolina; and to national organizations that address the Foundation's priorities. Consult the Web site for application instructions and contact information. The site is presently under construction, but the Foundation intends to post additional information in the future, such as copies of annual reports, press releases, and other public statements.

Norman Foundation (NY) (http://www.normanfdn.org/)

The New York-based Norman Foundation is committed to a strategy of seeking and supporting grassroots efforts that strengthen the ability of communities to determine their economic, environmental and civic well-being; promote community-based economic development efforts that are trying out new ownership structures and financing mechanisms; work to prevent the use of toxics and their disposal into the environment; build bridges across issues and constituencies and organize to counter the "radical right" in all its forms; promote civil rights by fighting discrimination and violence and working for ethnic, religious, and sexual equity and for reproductive freedom; challenge the power of money over our political process; and/or seek to improve governments' and businesses' accountability to the public and especially to those affected by their actions. The Foundation also seeks to address "the profound civic disengagement in society" and is particularly interested in strategies "on how to engage more Americans in their civic lives and how to increase their faith and involvement in community institutions." The Foundation's Web site provides a description of the application process; grant guidelines and restrictions; basic financial information; a list of the grants the Foundation recently awarded; listings of the Foundation's officers, directors, and staff; and contact information.

The Kenneth T. and Eileen L. Norris Foundation (CA) (http://www.norrisfoundation.org)
Kenneth T. and Eileen L. Norris owned Norris Stamping and Manufacturing Companies, later called Norris Industries. Kenneth Norris was a metallurgist who discovered a way to make steel casings for bullets, which led to a key role for the family business during World War II. The Norrises believed they had an obligation to give back to the community, so they established the Kenneth T. and Eileen L. Norris Foundation in 1963. The Foundation funds in the categories of medicine, education and science, youth, community, and cultural arts. Located in Long Beach, California, the Foundation funds organizations in he Los Angeles County area. Visitors to the Web site will find information about the founder, application guidelines, downloadable annual report, downloadable proposal information sheet, and contact information including e-mail links.

Northwest Area Foundation (MN) (http://www.nwaf.org/)
The Northwest Area Foundation was established in 1934 by Louis W. Hill, son of James J. Hill, the founder of the Great Northern Railroad, and renamed in 1975 to reflect its "commitment to the region that provided its original resources and its growth beyond the scope of the traditional family foundation." The Foundation's mission is to help communities most in need in an eight-state area—Minnesota, Iowa, North Dakota, South Dakota, Montana, Idaho, Washington, and Oregon—create positive futures economically, ecologically and socially. To implement that mission, the Foundation will help communities "work toward a balanced and sustainable system that will reduce poverty; stimulate economic growth; sustain the natural environment; and develop effective institutions, relationships, and individuals." In addition to contact information, a brief history of the Foundation, staff and trustee listings, and a copy of the most recent biannual report, the Foundation's Web site provides an overview of its new direction and the decision-making process that led to it.

Northwest Fund for the Environment (WA) (http://www.nwfund.org/)
The Northwest Fund for the Environment was established in 1971 with the initial purpose of functioning as a "pass-through" organization to allow small groups to receive tax deductible funding from grassroots supporters. When tax laws changed in the 1980s, the Foundation's purpose was to evaluate requests and make grants from an annual donation. In 1994, the Fund received a major bequest and became a private foundation with an endowment. The endowment is designated for "promoting change in the uses of natural resources which will increase their protection and preservation in the State of Washington," with special emphasis placed on "the protection of wild fish, native wildlife, natural forests, wetlands and shorelines, and the preservation of pure and free-flowing waters." Located in Seattle, Washington, the Fund supports actions to preserve threatened and endangered species and/or ecosystems, implement and enforce environmental laws and regulations, fund research directly relevant to Washington state on a limited basis, and strengthen the effectiveness of nonprofit environmental groups. Visit the Web site for grant guidelines, printable and downloadable application forms, selections from annual reports, a report of its grantmaking trends, and contact information.

Northwest Health Foundation (OR) (http://www.nwhf.org/)
The Northwest Health Foundation was founded in late 1997 from the proceeds of the sale of PACC Health Plans and PACC HMO. The Northwest Health Foundation exists to "advance, support, and promote the health of the people of Oregon and Southwest Washington." The Foundation supports innovative programs that address the following issues: health protection, quality of healthcare, access to healthcare, basic and applied biomedical, health, socio-behavioral research, education for health professionals and consumers, and mental health. In addition, the Foundation gives preference to projects that deal with children, rural communities, diverse communities, and specifically projects and programs that benefit Clackamas County. More details about the types of programs and projects funded are available on the Foundation's Web site as are lists of previous grants awarded. Those interested in applying should first send a letter of inquiry. Deadlines and information about

what should be included in the letter are listed on the site, and the application cover sheet can be downloaded in PDF format.

Jessie Smith Noyes Foundation, Inc. (NY) (http://www.noyes.org)

The Jessie Smith Noyes Foundation was established in 1947 by Charles F. Noyes as a memorial to his wife. Charles F. Noyes owned a real estate brokerage firm in New York City, and his most famous deal was the 1951 sale of the Empire State Building, "previously regarded as a white elephant," for the largest price at the time in real estate history. Located in New York City, the Foundation is committed to "protecting and restoring Earth's natural systems and promoting a sustainable society by strengthening individuals, institutions and communities pledged to pursuing those goals." Currently, the Foundation makes grants primarily in the areas of environment and reproductive rights, with the following program areas: toxics, sustainable agriculture, sustainable communities, reproductive rights, metro New York environment, and related interests, which are activities outside of the five areas but still further the Foundation's goals. Projects that receive preference are ones that address the connections between these concerns and their broader implications, have potential for widespread impact or applicability, and that address the connections between environmental issues and social justice issues. Visit the Web site for program and application guidelines, grants lists, annual reports, financial information, a staff listing, and contact information.

John M. Olin Foundation, Inc. (NY) (http://www.jmof.org/)

The John M. Olin Foundation was established in 1953 by the industrialist John Merrill Olin (1892–1982). Mr. Olin was committed to "the preservation of the principles of political and economic liberty as they have been expressed in American thought, institutions and practice." Accordingly, the purpose of the John M. Olin Foundation is to provide support for projects that "reflect or are intended to strengthen the economic, political and cultural institutions upon which the American heritage of constitutional government and private enterprise is based." Within this context, the Foundation has authorized grants in the areas of American institutions, law and the legal system, public policy research, and strategic and international studies. In each of these areas, it attempts to advance its objectives through support of research, institutional support, fellowships, professorships, lectures and lecture series, books, scholarly journals, journals of opinion, conferences and seminars, and, on occasion, television and radio programs. The Foundation's straightforward Web site provides general information about its programs, grantmaking policies, and application procedures; a schedule of the Foundation's recent grants; listings of the Foundation's trustees and staff; and contact information.

Onan Family Foundation (MN) (http://www.onanfamily.org/foundation.htm)

The Onan Family Foundation was founded by David Warren Onan, an entrepreneur in Minneapolis who wanted to give back to the community where his business thrived and where he lived. Located in Minneapolis, Minnesota, the Foundation has a strong interest in programs that focus on Minneapolis and St. Paul. Funding areas are education, social welfare, cultural and civic affairs, and religion. Consult the Web site for grant guidelines, a grants list, a staff listing, financial information, and contact information. Grant requests are to be made using the Minnesota Common Grant Application form, and a link is provided to the site where the form can be downloaded or printed.

The O'Neill Foundation, Inc., William J. and Dorothy K. (OH) (http://www.oneillfdn.org/)

The William J. and Dorothy K. O'Neill Foundation of Cleveland, Ohio was established in 1987. The Foundation strives to continue the family's philanthropy in a manner in which the founders would be proud. Gifts are made through three different channels. The first is through the focus program, Families. Through RFPs to institutions in cities where family members live, the Foundation is currently sponsoring "fathering" programs as part of its effort to find the root cause of the family unit's disintegration. The general grantmaking program supports groups that fall under the following areas of interest: family, health, education, employment, housing, poverty, children, and the elderly. Finally, there is a matching gifts program with organizations in which family members are active. The well-organized Web site includes application guidelines and deadlines, a grant lists, financial statements, and lists of trustees and officers.

Open Society Institute (NY) (http://www.soros.org)
The Open Society Institute "promotes the development and maintenance of open societies around the world by supporting an array of programs dealing with educational, social, and legal reform." There are Open Society Institutes in countries around the world that all share a similar mission: "to support the development of an open society." The Open Society in New York specifically works with the Open Society Institute in Budapest to assist the other organizations in the Soros Foundations network by providing programmatic, administrative, financial, and technical support. There are links to each Institute in every country on the site, along with contact information.

Ottinger Foundation (NY) (http://www.ottingerfoundation.org)
The Ottinger Foundation, located in New York City, supports "organizations that develop innovative public policy and new ways of grassroots organizing to build a movement for social change." The Foundation generally funds groups that promote grassroots citizen activism with national significance. Letters of inquiry are not accepted; the Foundation prefers proposals submitted to its mailing address. Grant guidelines and recent grantees are posted on the Foundation's Web site, along with contact information.

Pacific Northwest Foundation (OR) (http://www.pnf.org)
Established in 1988, the Pacific Northwest Foundation of Portland, Oregon, is a nonprofit venture capitalist. The organization's mission is to "respond quickly to unique nonprofit ventures, focusing particularly on their efforts to expand and become self-sustaining through broad support from within their respective communities." Recent multi-year grant recipients have included an organization that provides technical assistance and grants research information to those interested in nonprofit pursuits, a project alerting the public to latex sensitivities, and an environmental pollution project. The site includes a recent annual report and staff and board lists. The majority of the site is made up of features on informed individual giving and making the most of nonprofit boards, summaries of insurance and policy issues, and health reports based on two case studies on pollutants and allergies. The Foundation does not accept unsolicited applications.

Pacific Pioneer Fund (CA) (http://www.pacificpioneerfund.com)
The Pacific Pioneer Fund exists "to support emerging documentary filmmakers. The term 'emerging' is intended to denote a person committed to the craft of making documentaries, who has demonstrated that commitment by several years of practical film or video experience." Grants are limited to persons and organizations in California, Oregon, and Washington. Application forms may be printed out from the Web site and mailed to the address listed. Further details about restrictions and limitations are also available on this site.

David and Lucile Packard Foundation (CA) (http://www.packfound.org/)
The David and Lucile Packard Foundation was created in 1964 by David Packard (1912–1996), a co-founder (with his Stanford classmate William Hewlett) of the Hewlett-Packard Company, and his wife, Lucile Salter Packard (1914–1987). From its relatively modest beginnings–over the first dozen years of its existence the Foundation had only one employee and awarded just over $1 million in grants–the Packard Foundation has grown into one of the largest private grantmaking foundations in the country, with assets over $13 billion. The Foundation continues "to support nonprofit organizations with the hope that [it] can help people through the improvement of scientific knowledge, education, health, culture, employment opportunities, the environment, and quality of life." To that end, the Foundation makes grants nationally and internationally (with a special focus on the northern California counties of San Mateo, Santa Clara, Santa Cruz, and Monterey) in the following broad program areas: science; conservation; population; children, families, and communities; arts; organizational effectiveness; philanthropy; and Pueblo, Colorado

(David Packard's hometown). In addition to a history of the Foundation and a biography of David Packard, the Foundation's Web site provides detailed program descriptions and application guidelines, recent grants in a number of program areas, a listing of the Foundation's officers and trustees, Foundation contact names by program area, and the Foundation's annual report.

PADI Foundation (CA) (http://www.padi.com)
PADI's (Professional Association of Diving Instructors) headquarters are located in California, but there are PADI service offices around the world. PADI is the world's largest recreational diving membership organization, with a membership including diving businesses, resort facilities, academic institutions, instructor trainers, diving educators, divers, snorklers, and other watersports enthusiasts. PADI exists to "develop programs that encourage and fulfill the public interest in recreational scuba and snorkel diving worldwide." The PADI Foundation encourages and supports underwater science, environmental projects, and education. The Foundation funds projects that will enrich mankind's understanding of the aquatic environment and encourage sensitivity to and protection of the delicate ecological balance of underwater life. In addition, the Foundation funds projects to increase understanding of sport diving physics and physiology that will benefit the general diving public and add to the scientific understanding of man's relationship and ability to survive in the underwater environment. Instructions on how to apply for grants and whom to contact are available on this site, as is more information about other PADI programs, including its diving projects around the world.

Parker Foundation (VA) (http://www.parkerfoundation.org)
The mission of the Richmond, Virginia-based Parker Foundation "is to assist strategic international, national and local Christian organizations whose primary focus is advancing the Gospel of Jesus Christ." To this end, the Foundation has four general funding concerns: world evangelism, evangelical leadership development, Christian social relief, and public persuasion. The Foundation tends to support a few specific organizations already established as grant recipients, as well as some startup projects or organizations with special projects intended to increase their effectiveness. The Foundation's Web site includes grant guidelines and restrictions, links, a What's New page, contact information, and two documents that can be downloaded in Microsoft Word format: the Foundation's grant application and a self-evaluation form for grant requests.

Patrina Foundation (NY) (http://www.patrinafoundation.org/)
Established in 1990, the Patrina Foundation's mission is to expand women's educational opportunities and to create scholarship opportunities for women in the Northeast. The Foundation's interest focuses on research and in curriculum development. Recipients of the Foundation's giving are for the most part educational and cultural organizations, but the foundation also occasionally funds social service organizations that build on skills and leadership qualities. The Foundation does not make grants for general operating support, and it does not fund individuals. Visitors to the Foundation's limited Web site will find detailed applications procedures, guidelines, and contact information.

Alicia Patterson Foundation (DC) (Operating foundation)
(http://www.aliciapatterson.org)
The Alicia Patterson Foundation was established in 1965 in memory of Alicia Patterson, editor and publisher of *Newsday* for 23 years before her death in 1963. The Washington, D.C.-based Foundation has a fellowship program, in which one-year grants are awarded to working journalists to pursue independent projects of "significant interest." They spend that year traveling, researching, and writing articles based on their investigations for *The APF Reporter,* a quarterly magazine published by the Foundation. A stipend of $35,000 is provided for each fellow. The application form and instructions are available for downloading from the site, and past issues of *The APF Reporter* are available online. Visitors to the Web site will also find two biographies of Alicia Patterson, grant application instructions, a listings of past fellows, related links, and contact information.

Pegasus Foundation (MA) (http://www.pegasusfoundation.org/)

The Pegasus Foundation, established in 1997 for the purpose of "animal protection, environmental preservation and public education," mainly provides programs and funding in the West and Southwest (Montana and Arizona), Florida, and Cape Cod, Massachusetts. The Foundation partners with other not-for-profit environmental and animal protection groups to support various projects as well as to maintain three programs in wildlife protection, companion animal and equine rescue programs, and land conservation and preservation. No unsolicited proposals are accepted, as the Foundation works with projects where they have already established a personal connection. The Foundation's Web site provides a detailed description of each of its three projects, along with a listing of its partnership organizations and their Web sites, an annual report, and staff contact information.

William Penn Foundation (PA) (http://fdncenter.org/grantmaker/wmpenn/)

The William Penn Foundation, a private grantmaking organization created in 1945 by Otto Haas and his wife, Phoebe, strives to improve the quality of life in the greater Philadelphia area, particularly for its neediest residents. The Foundation makes grants ranging from a few thousand dollars to several million dollars in four main categories: children, youth and families; communities; arts and culture; and the natural environment. Within the first three categories, the Foundation's grantmaking is limited to the six-county Philadelphia area (Bucks, Chester, Delaware, Montgomery, and Philadelphia Counties in Pennsylvania and Camden County, especially the City of Camden, in New Jersey) unless initiated by the Foundation. Grants for school-based programs in Philadelphia are generally limited to the Martin Luther King, Jr. and West Philadelphia clusters. Grants in the natural environment category are awarded throughout a larger region extending from the Delaware Water Gap southeast along the northern border of Warren, Hunterdon, Mercer, and Ocean Counties in New Jersey to the Atlantic coast at Manasquan; south along the coast to the mouth of the Delaware Bay; west along the C & D Canal and the Susquehanna River to the Appalachian trail; and north along the trail to the Delaware Water Gap. See the Foundation's Web site for a map of areas considered for funding. The site also provides detailed program descriptions, application guidelines and restrictions, a searchable grants lists, statements of the Foundation's mission and grantmaking values, a history of the Foundation, board and staff listings, and contact information.

Pew Charitable Trusts (PA) (http://www.pewtrusts.com/)

The Philadelphia-based Pew Trusts are a group of seven individual charitable funds established by the children of Sun Oil Company founder Joseph N. Pew and his wife, Mary Anderson Pew. Each year, the Trusts make grants of about $230 million to between 300 and 500 nonprofit organizations in the areas of culture, education, the environment, health and human services, public policy, religion, and its Venture Fund. In addition to a strong national giving program, the Trusts maintain a particular commitment to their local community. The Trusts' well-organized Web site provides visitors with program guidelines and limitations, application procedures, searchable grants lists, grantee Web links, publications, news, and a staff list with phone numbers and e-mail addresses.

Gustavus and Louise Pfeiffer Research Foundation (NJ)
(http://fdncenter.org/grantmaker/pfeiffer/)

The Gustavus and Louise Pfeiffer Research Foundation, located in Denville, New Jersey, funds healthcare research. The Foundation's grant program supports "projects or programs carried out in the United States for advancement of medicine and pharmacy, including scientific research, post-graduate scholarship and fellowship assistance, and studies in nutrition, blindness, deafness and other physical disabilities." Funding for basic research is restricted to breast, ovarian, and prostate cancer. Projects involving animal experimentation are not funded. The Foundation publishes a biennial report that includes program descriptions and lists of grant recipients. Potential applicants can request a copy of the report. The Foundation's folder on the Center's Web site includes application guidelines and restrictions and instructions on submitting a letter of inquiry.

Ellis L. Phillips Foundation (MA) (http://www.agmconnect.org/epf.html)

The Ellis L. Phillips Foundation was established by its namesake, the president and founder of the Long Island Lighting Company, in New York in 1930. Now headquartered in Boston, the Foundation seeks to enhance the communities where the directors live and fields of particular interest to the Foundation. These include: informal and women's education, advanced training and institutional development in music and the visual arts, rural human services, rural historic preservation, and biodiversity conservation. Grants are usually made to organizations in New England. The Foundation includes guidelines for the grant application, evaluation criteria and process, and a list of past grant recipients on its Web site. Contact information is available online.

Louie M. and Betty M. Phillips Foundation (TN) (http://www.phillipsfoundation.org)

Located in Nashville, Tennessee, The Louie M. and Betty M. Phillips Foundation was established in 1978 after the death of Mrs. Phillips but was not fully funded until the death of Mr. Phillips in 1986. The Foundation "supports a variety of organizations in the fields of health, human services, civic affairs, education and the arts." Detailed information about the types of funding the Foundation will provide is available on the site. To apply for a grant, an organization should send a letter describing its program and the request; a description of what the application should include is available on the Web site. There is a form that can be completed online to request more information about the Foundation. In addition, the site includes details about previous grants awarded.

Pickett & Hatcher Educational Fund, Inc. (GA) (http://www.pickettandhatcher.org)

The Pickett & Hatcher Educational Fund was established in 1938 through the generosity of Claud A. Hatcher, president of the Nehi Corporation that later became the Royal Crown Cola Company. Located in Columbus, Georgia, the Fund is a private foundation that grants student loans to help students who otherwise might not be able to attend college. To be eligible, students should be United States citizens and legal residents of one of the following states: Alabama, Florida, Georgia, Kentucky, Mississippi, North Carolina, South Carolina, Tennessee, or Virginia. They should also have a minimum ACT of 20 or a combined SAT I of 950. Loans of up to $5,500 are made per academic year. Consult the Web site for complete eligibility requirements, loan limits, interest rates, renewal requirements, application instructions, and contact information. (Due to the success of this program, and the demand for student loans, applications for the 1999–2000 academic year are no longer available. The distribution of applications will resume January 3, 2000 for the 2000–2001 academic year.)

Pinkerton Foundation (NY) (http://fdncenter.org/grantmaker/pinkerton/)

The New York-based Pinkerton Foundation was established in 1966 with a mission of reducing the incidence of crime and to prevent juvenile delinquency. In order to work towards its mission, the Foundation makes grants to organizations that strengthen youth programs in poor communities. The Foundation seeks to support programs that develop individual competencies, instill values, and increase opportunities to participate in society. Visitor's to the Foundation's folder on the Center's Web site will find further information on the above program, a listing of recent grants, staff and board information, grant guidelines, and contact information.

The Piton Foundation (CO) (Operating foundation) (http://www.piton.org)

The mission of the Denver-based, Piton Foundation is to "help children and families in Denver move from poverty and dependence to self-reliance." The privately funded operating Foundation was established in 1976 and is principally funded by the Gary-Williams Energy Corporation. The Foundation provides support generally for public education, youth development, and neighborhood leadership. The Fund also maintains a scholarship program, the Charter Fund Scholarship, which supports Colorado students in their first year of undergraduate work. The Foundation also maintains a database on all 79 neighborhoods in Denver that includes maps and graphs on each neighborhood's population, housing, economic, and education characteristics. The database is available through the

Foundation's Web site, as well as many reports and articles from the Foundation down-loadable in PDF format.

Plan for Social Excellence, Inc. (NY) (Operating foundation) (http://www.pfse.org)

The Plan for Social Excellence, located in Mt. Kisco, New York, creates and supports inno-vative pilot projects in education in the United States that are fluid and responsive to the needs of individual schools and communities instead of programs that attempt to address needs through a system-wide process of reform. Supported projects take place at various levels, including early childhood education and higher education. The Plan pursues its goals through five major activities: grantmaking, "coinvestments" (collaboration and co-investment with other foundations and corporations in funding programs), technical assistance, scholarships, and dissemination. The Plan is primarily interested in funding replications of certain pilot programs but also considers grant requests for innovative projects that are designed for easy evaluation and can be replicated. Along with its grantmaking, technical assistance is provided to grantees and other educational organiza-tions and includes providing information and resources to support or enhance project goals. In addition, the Plan publishes and disseminates the results of many funded projects to organizations that may be candidates for replicating the project. The Plan also administers a last-dollar scholarship program for high school students who have participated in select Plan-supported projects. Consult the Web site for more complete information on its activi-ties and programs and for application information and instructions. A grant guideline request form is available online. Visitors to the site will also find downloadable quarterly newsletters, scholarship recipient lists, links to related resources, and contact information.

Carl and Eloise Pohlad Family Foundation (MN) (http://www.pohladfamilycharities.org)

Based in Minneapolis, Minnesota, the Carl and Eloise Pohlad Family Foundation is one-third of the Pohlad Family Charities. "The Foundation seeks to improve and enrich the lives of economically disadvantaged children, youth and families." Community Grants, Foundation Initiative Grants, and Family-Directed Grants are awarded each year to nonprofits in the state of Minnesota, with a focus on those serving the citizens of the Min-neapolis/St. Paul metropolitan area. Grants are made to human services, education, and enrichment programs for the economically disadvantaged. The Foundation does not fund research or demonstration projects or programs that will need ongoing support. Applica-tion guidelines and deadlines are available at the Foundation's Web site. Unsolicited appli-cations are not considered for Family-Directed Grants. The Foundation runs its own grantmaking initiatives or chooses a particular area of interest and posts RFPs (Requests for Proposals) for these projects online, such as a Summer Camp Scholarship Program. The site offers basic contact information and e-mail addresses for selected staff.

Polk Bros. Foundation (IL) (http://www.polkbrosfdn.org/)

Established from the Polk family's Chicago-based retail furniture and appliance stores, the Polk Brothers Foundation is helping to "strengthen the city's children and families [as well as] bolster social service, education, cultural and health care programs that provide direct service to low-income Chicagoans." The Foundation directs its funding toward specific areas within each of these four main categories: Social Service includes employment, fami-lies, and children and youth; Education funds programs in the classroom, beyond the class-room, and full service schools; Culture is directed toward school programming and neigh-borhood outreach; and Health funds facilities enhancement and mothers and newborns. All proposals should address the goal of increased access to services and the improvement of the quality of life for area residents. The Foundation has a large and small grants program, and applications are accepted year-round. Visitors to the Foundation's extensive Web site will find application guidelines, grant limitations, recent grantees, a pre-application form, an RFP, and the Foundation's financial report and contact information.

Pollock-Krasner Foundation, Inc. (NY) (http://www.pkf.org/)

Established by Lee Krasner, widow of the painter Jackson Pollock and a celebrated artist in her own right, the Pollock-Krasner Foundation's mission is "to aid, internationally, those individuals who have worked as professional artists over a significant period of time." Potential grant recipients must demonstrate a combination of recognizable artistic merit and financial need relating to either work, living, or medical expenses. The Foundation provides support exclusively to visual artists—painters, sculptors, and artists who work on paper, including printmakers—and will not accept applications from commercial artists, photographers, video artists, performance artists, filmmakers, crafts-makers, or any artist whose work primarily falls into one of these categories. Nor does the Foundation fund academic study or make grants to pay for past debts, legal fees, the purchase of real estate, relocation to another city, or the costs of installations, commissions, or projects ordered by others. The Foundation's Web site provides visitors with a brief history of the Foundation, application and selection procedures, a listing of officers and staff, and contact information.

Irwin Andrew Porter Foundation (MI) (http://www.iapfoundation.org/)
The Michigan-based, Irwin Andrew Porter (IAP) Foundation's mission is to "support projects and programs fostering connections to ourselves, our community, our environment, our world." IAP places primary importance in the areas of arts, education, environment, and social programs; however, it believes that the quality and innovativeness of the specific program is more important that broad topic areas. The Foundation does not provide funding for general operating funds, capital campaigns, fundraising events, political or religious causes, or to individuals. IAP gives preference to organizations within Minnesota, Wisconsin, Illinois, and Michigan. Visit IAP's limited Web site to find selected recent grants, more specific grant and geographic restrictions, grant application, a short list of important links, and contact information.

Pottruck-Scott Family Foundation (CA) (http://www.ps-ff.org/)
The Pottruck Scott Family Foundation (PSFF) was established in 1995 to "improve the lives of disadvantaged children and youth, and to support volunteer-driven organizations, with a primary focus in San Francisco." The Foundation funds organizations that support education, youth services, and civic/community initiatives. Visitors to the Foundation's Web site will find a listing of recent grants, a copy of the latest tax return downloadable in PDF format, a board and staff listing, and contact information.

Poudre Valley Hospital Foundation (CO) (http://www.pvhs.org)
The Poudre Valley Hospital Foundation's mission is to "philanthropically support and promote activities that best serve the health interests of the community." The Foundation receives, administers, and distributes funds for community health initiatives that target prevention, health promotion, wellness, disease management, educational, and charitable purposes. Visitors to the Foundation's Web site will find further information on the grantmaking program, a viewable copy of the Foundation's most recent tax return, staff listings, and contact information.

The Prospect Hill Foundation (NY) (http://fdncenter.org/grantmaker/prospecthill/)
The Prospect Hill Foundation was established in New York in 1960 by William S. Beinecke, former president and chairman of the Sperry and Hutchinson Company. In 1983, the Prospect Hill Foundation merged with the Frederick W. Beinecke Fund. The foundation has a broad range of philanthropic interests but recently has made grants to support organizations active in environmental conservation, nuclear weapons control, family planning in Latin America, and selected social service, arts, cultural, and educational institutions. The foundation's folder on the Center's Web site provides an introduction to the foundation, grants program description, grants list, and application guidelines.

Public Domain Foundation (VT) (http://www.pdfoundation.org)
The Public Domain Foundation (PDF) was founded in Vermont by folk artist Noel Paul Stookey of Peter, Paul, and Mary fame. In 1971, after having written the instant classic, "The Wedding Song," Stookey felt as if the inspiration came from some distant place. Because of this, Noel decided to donate all the royalties of this song to his new Foundation.

The Foundation's belief is that "into every songwriter's life comes a song, the source of which cannot be explained by personal experience." PDF encourages other folk singers who have had inspiration come from some unknown source to follow Stookey's lead. Visitors to the Foundation's site will find out how they can get involved and contact information.

Public Welfare Foundation, Inc. (DC) (http://www.publicwelfare.org/)

Established and incorporated in Texas in 1947 and reincorporated in Washington, D.C., in 1960, the Public Welfare Foundation is dedicated "to supporting organizations that provide services to disadvantaged populations and work for lasting improvements in the delivery of services that meet basic human needs." The Foundation's wide-ranging interests include community support (homelessness, low-income housing, low-income community and economic development, global security, countering hate-motivated activity and discrimination, immigration and refugees, international human rights, and technical assistance to grassroots community development efforts), criminal justice (community-based correctional options, institutional programming, legal representation of low-income persons, and violence prevention), the disadvantaged elderly (community-based long-term care), disadvantaged youth (early intervention; employment, training, and alternative education; teen parents and their children; violence prevention; and, youth empowerment and leadership development), the environment (global climate change, sustainable development, direct support, and technical assistance to grassroots organizations), health (health advocacy and reform, hunger and nutrition, mental health advocacy and services, occupational health and safety, and preventive and primary services), and population and reproductive health (AIDS prevention, education, and advocacy; international family planning; reproductive rights; reproductive health for teens; and emerging issues). A model of uncluttered, functional design, the Foundation's Web site provides a short history of the Foundation, FAQs, detailed program information, financial statements, application procedures, grants lists organized by specific funding area, contact information, and more.

The Puffin Foundation, Ltd. (NJ) (http://www.angelfire.com/nj/PuffinFoundation)

The Puffin Foundation was established in 1987, with the mission of "continuing the dialogue between art and the lives of ordinary people." The Foundation seeks to "open the doors of artistic expression to those who are often excluded because of their race, gender, or social philosophy" and to "ensure that the arts not merely survive, but flourish at all levels of our society." The Foundation provides seed grants to artists and arts organizations across the entire spectrum of visual and performing arts. It has established two exhibition, performance, and discussion spaces: the Puffin Room in SoHo, and the Puffin Cultural Forum in Teaneck, New Jersey, where the Foundation is located. It also has a publishing branch to produce books that "otherwise might not come to life." Consult the Web site for instructions on obtaining an application packet. Its site also contains a link to the site of the Puffin Cultural Forum, which provides a schedule of upcoming events.

Bernard and Audre Rapoport Foundation (TX) (http://www.rapoportfdn.org/)

The mission statement of the Bernard and Audre Rapoport Foundation is "meeting basic human needs while building individual and social resiliency." Located in Waco, Texas, the Foundation's current program priorities are education, in all its broad areas, but with a focus on early learning; cultural enrichment, especially programs that encourage the participation of children and the disadvantaged; healthcare, to improve the quality and delivery of services to all citizens, but especially women, children and the disadvantaged; community building, to improve quality of life and foster the growth and development of children; and building democratic opportunities and encouraging democratic citizenship, to make government more responsive and encourage citizens to take a more active interest and role in political life. Consult the Web site for grant application instructions, an update on the Foundation's activities, and contact information, including an e-mail link.

The Paul Rapoport Foundation (NY) (http://fdncenter.org/grantmaker/rapoport/)

The New York-based Paul Rapoport Foundation was established in 1987 in memorial to Paul Rapoport and his life. Paul was deeply committed to supporting the lesbian, gay, bisexual, and transgender (LGBT) communities, with a particular focus on efforts to eliminate homophobia and discrimination against gay men, lesbians, bisexuals, and transgendered persons. The Foundation supports projects in the greater New York City area concerned with areas of social services, healthcare and legal rights and issues for the LGBT communities. Visitors to the Foundation's folder on the Center's Web site will find more specific information on the Foundation's areas of interest, application guidelines, a grants list, a board listing, and contact information.

The Bill Raskob Foundation, Inc. (MD)
(http://www.dml.georgetown.edu/scholarship/raskob.html)

The Bill Raskob Foundation provides non-interest bearing loans to medical students. To apply for a loan, an applicant must be an American citizen, have completed their first year at an accredited medical school, and demonstrate financial need. There is a phone number for interested parties to call to receive an application and further information.

A.C. Ratshesky Foundation (MA) (http://www.agmconnect.org/ratshes1.html)

A.C. Ratshesky celebrated his 50th birthday in 1916 by establishing this charitable foundation in his own name. Currently, the Boston, Massachusetts-based Foundation has three program areas: human services, focusing on the well-being of children and families in inner-city neighborhoods; education/training/advocacy, including adult vocation, GED and literacy programs, school enrichment, parenting skills, reproductive freedom and reproductive health education, prevention of discrimination and racism, and community organizing and promotion of citizenship skills; and arts/culture, supporting school enrichment, performing arts, youth programs, and performance opportunities for young artists. Support is generally limited to Boston and adjacent communities and is focused on children, teens, immigrants, "linguistic minorities," the gifted and talented, and the Jewish community; support for programs that service disadvantaged Jewish populations or Jewish cultural institutions are of special interest, in accordance with the original declaration of trust. From time to time, the trustees may also give consideration to programs that fall outside of the usual geographic or program limitations. Visit the Web site for application procedures, a grants list, and contact information.

Michael Reese Health Trust (IL) (http://fdncenter.org/grantmaker/health/)

The Michael Reese Health Trust seeks to improve the health of people in Chicago's metropolitan communities through effective grantmaking in health care, health education, and health research. The Trust, which funds exclusively in metropolitan Chicago, with an emphasis on the city of Chicago, seeks to address the needs of the most vulnerable in society, particularly through programs that serve the medically indigent and underserved, immigrants, refugees, the elderly, mentally and physically disabled, children and youth. To emphasize the Trust's Jewish heritage, special consideration will be given to programs that serve those in the Jewish community who fall within these populations. The Trust does not fund programs operating outside of metropolitan Chicago, capital needs (such as buildings, vehicles, and equipment), endowment, fundraising events, debt reduction, individuals, or scholarships. The Trust's folder on the Center's Web site includes a mission statement, a recent grants list, program guidelines, application procedures, and contact information.

Paul E. & Klare N. Reinhold Foundation, Inc. (FL) (http://www.Reinhold.org)

Located in Orange Park, Florida, the Paul E. & Klare N. Reinhold Foundation was established in 1954. The organization's mission is to continue to support programs that are involved in the founders' areas of interests, including the church, youth, and healthcare. Awards are made to nonprofits in northeast Florida, with major emphasis in Clay and Duval Counties. The grants program makes gifts in six categories: healthcare, religion, children and youth services, music appreciation and education, art appreciation and education, and projects for public improvement and enjoyment. Applications are reviewed once a year by the board. Potential grantees will find short, basic application guidelines and can download an application cover letter in PDF format. The site, which is shared with Reinhold Corporation, also includes a list of most recent and all former grantees and basic contact information.

Research Corporation (AZ) (http://www.rescorp.org/)

Established in New York in 1912, making it one of the first private foundations in the United States, the Research Corporation is the only domestic foundation wholly devoted to the advancement of science and technology. Its unique philanthropic mission is to make inventions and patent rights "more available and effective in the useful arts and manufactures" and to devote any new resources therefrom "to provide means for the advancement and extension of technical and scientific investigation, research and experimentation" at scholarly institutions. The Foundation makes between 200 and 300 awards annually for original research in chemistry, physics, and astronomy at colleges and universities throughout the United States and Canada. Visitors to the Web site will find guidelines for seven Foundation-supported programs (Cottrell College Science Awards, Cottrell Scholars, Partners in Science, Research Opportunity Awards, Research Innovation Awards, Department Development Program, and General Foundation Awards), recent news releases, contact information, and the current issue of the *Research Corporation Bulletin* in PDF format.

Retirement Research Foundation (IL) (http://www.rrf.org)

The Chicago-based Retirement Research Foundation (RRF) is the nation's largest private foundation exclusively devoted to aging and retirement issues. Founded by the late John D. MacArthur, it makes approximately $9 million in grants each year to nonprofit and educational organizations to support programs, research, and public policy studies to improve the quality of life of older Americans. The Foundation operates a general grants program, two award programs (ENCORE and the Congregation Connection Program) open to Chicago-area nonprofits only, and the National Media Owl Awards, a national film and video competition. Visitors to RRF's Web site will find a variety of materials, including an overview of the Foundation and its funding interests, program descriptions, grants lists, program-related FAQs, a board/staff list, application information, and a number of press releases.

Reuter Foundation (OH) (http://www.reuterfdn.org)

Founded in 1988, the Cleveland, Ohio-based Reuter Foundation provides human services to the disadvantaged as well as to other organizations who share the same mission. The Foundation's primary charitable interest lies in "emergency assistance to individuals, services and rehabilitation for chemical dependencies, abused women, affordable daycare, low-cost housing, and innovative medical research." The Foundation maintains other funding interests as well, such as the First Credit Fund, which provides no-interest loans to individuals who do not qualify for bank loans, and the Women's Housing Corp. for women recently completing two-year chemical dependency programs. Guidelines for potential applicants, more specific details on grant awards, an annual report and contact information are available at the Foundation's Web site.

Kate B. Reynolds Charitable Trust (NC) (http://www.kbr.org)

Located in Winston-Salem, North Carolina, the Kate B. Reynolds Charitable Trust is named after the late Kate Gertrude Bitting Reynolds, wife of William Neal Reynolds, chairman of R.J. Reynolds Tobacco Company. She created the Trust in 1947 in her will, designating that one-fourth of the income from the Trust be used for the poor and needy in Winston-Salem and Forsyth County and that the remaining three-fourths be used for charity patients in North Carolina hospitals. These designations have become the Trust's two divisions: the Health Care Division and the Poor and Needy Division, which has an emphasis on those who need assistance with basic necessities. The Trust's grantmaking is limited to the state of North Carolina. Guidelines, applications, expenditure and program report forms (for grantees) are available for downloading, and there is an online contact form on the site. The Trust also has satellite offices in different areas of the state, to make themselves more accessible to those who can benefit most from their grantmaking and to help the Trust gather information on different areas of the state. Another component of its outreach effort is technical workshops, where organizations can learn about the Trust's objectives, the grant process, preparation of grant requests, and ask questions. Consult the Web site for information on the two divisions, the outreach programs, and special initiatives. Visitors will also find a grant lists, advisory board and staff listings, an FAQ sheet, press releases, and contact information.

Donald W. Reynolds Foundation (NV) (http://www.dwreynolds.org)

The Donald W. Reynolds Foundation was established in 1954 by Donald W. Reynolds, pioneer in the American communications industry and founder of Donrey Media Group. The Foundation's current programs, however, did not begin taking shape until 1993, when Mr. Reynolds died and left a generous bequest. The mission statement of the Las Vegas-based Foundation is to make grants in "Arkansas, Nevada, and Oklahoma to qualified charitable organizations which demonstrate a sustainable program, exhibit an entrepreneurial spirit, and assists those served to be healthy, self-sufficient and productive members of the community." The Foundation has five programs: capital grants, aging and quality of life initiative, clinical cardiovascular research, community services center program, and Donald W. Reynolds special initiatives. Some solicit applications and others are driven exclusively by trustee initiative. Guidelines for the capital grants and community services center programs are available. Consult the Web site for more information on its programs, for annual reports, a grant lists (including brief descriptions and contact information for grantee organizations), staff listings, and contact information, including e-mail links to staff members.

Z. Smith Reynolds Foundation (NC) (http://www.zsr.org/)

Created almost 60 years ago to serve the people of North Carolina, the Z. Smith Reynolds Foundation is the country's largest general purpose foundation with a mandate to make grants within a single state. The Foundation focuses its activities in the areas of pre-collegiate education, community economic development, environmental interests, minority issues, and women's issues but will consider proposals that fall outside these areas as long as they are consistent with the Foundation's mission. The Foundation's Web site provides general information about the Foundation, detailed grant application procedures, information on special publications and programs, a helpful FAQ section, a list of recent grants awarded, and links to grantee Web sites.

RGK Foundation (TX) (http://www.rgkfoundation.org)

Ronya and George Kozmetsky established the RGK Foundation in 1966 to support medical and educational research. Since then, the Austin, Texas-based Foundation has broadened its focus over the years and "community" is now the third component to its grantmaking. Grants in these three areas support research (the Foundation has sponsored studies in several areas of national and international concern, including health, corporate governance, energy, economic analysis, and technology transfer); conferences, which are designed to enhance information exchange as well as maintain an "interlinkage" among business, academia, community, and government; and programs that promote academic excellence in institutions of higher learning, raise literacy levels, attract minority and women students into the math, science, and technology fields, and promote the well being of children. There are no geographic limitations to its grantmaking. Visitors to the Web site will find application guidelines, a printable and downloadable application form, online contact form, grant lists, related links, a list of publications resulting from Foundation-sponsored research, financial data, staff listing, and contact information.

The Richards Foundation (GA) (http://www.rrichards.org/)

Located in Carrolton, Georgia, the Richards Foundation was established in 1990 by Roy Richards, Jr. to extend his Christian beliefs. The organization's mission is to "support programs which address the root causes rather than the symptoms of social needs." Areas of interest include art and culture; elementary, secondary, and higher education; human services for children and youth; medical and hospice care; and religion. The Foundation is looking for projects that will have a lasting effect on Carrolton and the surrounding areas and that will break the cycles that keep people deprived. Programs outside of Carrolton are considered if they fall strictly within the Foundation's goals. There is no application available online, but the Web site includes proposal guidelines and deadlines. Visitors will also find a list of past grant recipients and very basic Foundation financial data.

Smith Richardson Foundation, Inc. (CT) (http://www.srf.org)

H. Smith Richardson and his wife, Grace Jones Richardson, created the Smith Richardson Foundation in 1935. H. Smith Richardson helped build a "world-wide medicinal empire" with Vicks Family Remedies. Located in Westport, Connecticut, the Smith Richardson Foundation seeks to "help ensure the vitality of our social, economic, and governmental institutions" and "assist with the development of effective policies to compete internationally and advance US interests and values abroad." The Foundation has two grant programs: the International Security and Foreign Policy Program, which supports research and policy projects on issues central to the strategic interests of the United States, and the Domestic Public Policy Program, which supports research, writing, and analysis that informs the thinking of policy makers and the public on domestic issues. The Foundation also makes small grants to organizations in North Carolina and Connecticut that provide innovative services for children and families at risk, though the Foundation's governors customarily solicit these grants. Consult the Web site for information about the Foundation's grant programs, grant guidelines, proposal templates (for those who are invited to submit a proposal after an initial inquiry has been made), grant reporting requirements, an FAQ sheet, a staff listing, and contact information, including an e-mail link.

Sid W. Richardson Foundation (TX) (http://www.sidrichardson.org)

The Ft. Worth, Texas-based Sid W. Richardson Foundation was established in 1947 for the purpose of supporting organizations that serve the people of Texas. The Foundation provides grants primarily in the areas of education, health, human services, and the arts and humanities. Funding is limited to programs and projects within the state of Texas. Visit the Web site for grant guidelines, grants lists, a short biography of its founder, information on ordering annual reports and Foundation-sponsored reports, and contact information. Links are also provided to related resources, Sid W. Richardson's collection of western art, and to the Lee and Ramona Bass Foundation.

The Riordan Foundation (CA) (http://www.riordanfoundation.org)

Richard J. Riordan founded The Riordan Foundation in 1981 "to ensure that all children become successful readers and writers while they are still young." The Foundation also seeks to use its funds as a "catalyst to encourage a broad base of support for early childhood education." The Foundation charted Rx for Reading in 1989, a public foundation through which many donations are distributed, to enhance and support the goals of the Riordan Foundation. Through Rx for Reading, the Foundation makes challenge grants to schools that wish to participate in Writing to Read, Computers in the Classroom, and English Language Development grants. Outside donations are used to meet the terms of the challenge grants, and since the Foundation funds all administrative expenses, 100 percent of the contributions to Rx for Reading go directly toward funding projects. The Riordan Foundation also provides mini-grants, only available in Los Angeles County: Safe Place to Play, which are small grants to develop, improve, or enhance play areas; and Easy Access to Books for Recreational Reading, to develop or enhance classroom lending libraries. Visit the site for more information on the Foundation's grant programs, grant guidelines, FAQ sheet, and contact information. Schools interested in applying for grants administered through Rx for Reading can print application forms from the site or call to request applications.

Fannie E. Rippel Foundation (NJ) (http://fdncenter.org/grantmaker/rippel/index.html)

The Fannie E. Rippel Foundation's objectives are to support the relief and care of aged women, the erection and maintenance of hospitals, and the treatment of and/or research concerning heart disease and cancer. Although strict geographic limitations are not imposed, emphasis is given to institutions located in New Jersey and the greater New York metropolitan area, the general Northeast, and the middle Atlantic seaboard. The Foundation's folder on the Center's Web site serves as an online version of the Foundation's most recent annual report, which offers application guidelines, messages from the Foundation's president and chairman, recent grants listings, statements of financial position and activities, and a listing of its trustees and staff.

The Roberts Foundation (CA)
(http://www.pacificfoundationservices.com/roberts/index.html)
Established in 1985, the San Francisco-based Roberts Foundation encompasses distinct grant programs supporting northern California. The Roberts Foundation grant program supports children and youth services, education, higher education, and wildlife preservation and animal welfare. The Roberts Enterprise Development Fund (REDF) structures its grant program around the concept of "social purpose enterprise" that seeks to "raise the standards of excellence and integrity in the nonprofit and philanthropic community nationwide through the development and dissemination of innovative approaches to address critical social issues." While the Roberts Foundation grant program does accept proposals, the REDF does not. More information on these programs is provided at the Foundation's Web site. Also at the site, visitors will find the most recent grants, contact information, a board of directors list, and application procedures.

Robins Foundation (VA) (http://members.aol.com/robinsfdn)
The Richmond, Virginia-based Robins Foundation seeks to improve the lives and opportunities of Virginians through grants to nonprofit organizations. It is particularly interested in helping with emerging issues and underfunded areas where its grants can act as catalysts and also in helping established organizations sustain and build on past successes. Funds are given in the form of program support, capital expenditures, or endowment. Grantmaking is normally limited to the central Virginia area, but the Foundation may consider proposals from other areas of the commonwealth. Visit the site for viewable and downloadable guidelines, downloadable application materials, and contact information.

The David Robinson Foundation (TX)
(http://www.swbc-solutions.com/theadmiral/drf.htm)
The David Robinson Foundation is a Christian organization whose mission is to support programs that address the physical and spiritual needs of the family, in particular those programs that encourage educating children and developing positive values, especially strong faith lives. The San Antonio, Texas-based Foundation was established in 1992 by basketball player David Robinson and his wife Valerie to carry out their philanthropic interests. The private Foundation makes grants to charitable organizations and donations such as Spurs tickets, autographed basketballs, and other memorabilia for fundraisers. Special projects administered by the Foundation include Robinson's Neighborhood Students, a scholarship and mentoring program for local students; Feed My Sheep, a program for providing food to organizations that feed the hungry; and the Ruth Project, a program offering diapers and baby food to needy infants and toddlers through area agencies. In September 1997, the Robinsons announced a $5 million gift to establish The Carver Academy at San Antonio's Carver Center, a multicultural and multiethnic community center and arts presenter. Academy construction is underway as are specific plans for the school's curriculum and admission requirements.

Rockefeller Brothers Fund (NY) (http://www.rbf.org/index.html)
Since 1984, the main part of the Rockefeller Brother Fund's grantmaking program has been organized around ten programmatic areas: sustainable resource use, global security, nonprofit sector, education, health, arts and culture, New York City, South Africa, Pocantico programs, and the Ramon Magsaysay Award Foundation. The Fund's program interests are promoting and sustaining a vital nonprofit sector, both nationally and internationally; strengthening the numbers and quality of teachers in public education in the United States; and improving the quality an accessibility of basic education for children and adults in

South Africa. Visitors to the Fund's Web site will find program guidelines and comprehensive lists of recent grants, application procedures and grant restrictions, a list of Fund publications (available upon e-mailed request), a listing of trustees and officers, and links to the Fund's non-grantmaking programs and affiliations.

Rockefeller Foundation (NY) (http://www.rockfound.org/)

Endowed by John D. Rockefeller and chartered in 1913 for "the well-being of people throughout the world," the Rockefeller Foundation is one of America's oldest private foundations and one of the few with strong international interests. The Foundation focuses its activities on creativity and culture, food security, health equity, working communities, global inclusions, and a number of special programs all over the world. The balance of the Foundation's grant and fellowship programs support work in building democracy, international security, international philanthropy, and other special interests and initiatives. Visitors to the Foundation's comprehensive Web site will find information about the Foundation's programs, funding priorities, fellowships, recent grants, recent annual reports, a listing of the Foundation's trustees, and a letter from the Foundation's president.

Rockwell Fund (TX) (http://www.rockfund.org/)

The Houston, Texas-based, Rockwell Fund was established 1931 upon the death of James M. Rockwell, owner and manager of Rockwell Lumber Company. The Rockwell Fund is dedicated to the charitable purposes set forth by its founder and the Rockwell family. The Fund is most interested in education, although other areas such as the arts, health, civics, religion, and social services are also occasionally supported. The Fund awards most grants in Houston; however, giving is not completely limited to that singular area. The Fund makes grants in the form of scholarships (through schools, colleges and universities), general operating support, new buildings, building renovations, endowment, equipment, professorships, academic chairs, special projects, operation of existing programs, and seed money. Visit the Fund's Web site to find comparable financial information, most recent grant list, application guidelines, a printable application, and contact information.

Rosenberg Foundation (CA) (http://www.rosenbergfdn.org/)

The Rosenberg Foundation was established in 1935 by relatives and associates of Max L. Rosenberg, a San Francisco businessman and philanthropist. Since the 1940s, the Foundation has emphasized the health, education, and recreation of California's children and communities. Today, the Foundation accepts grant requests in three priority areas: the Changing Population of California, which includes activities that "promote the full social, economic, and cultural integration of immigrants and minorities into a pluralistic society;" Children and their Families in Poverty, which includes activities that "reduce dependency, promote self-help, create access to the economic mainstream, or address the causes of poverty among children and families;" and Child Support Reform, a multi-year initiative aimed at increasing "economic security for children, particularly children in low-income families, through the development of a public system that is effective in establishing paternity, fair in awarding support, efficient and effective in collecting and distributing payments, and build[s] toward a national program of child support assurance." Visitors to the Foundation's user-friendly Web site will find thorough program descriptions and recent grants lists by program area, application guidelines and procedures, current financial information, a brief history of the Foundation, and contact information.

Henry and Ruth Blaustein Rosenberg Foundation (MD)
(http://fdncenter.org/grantmaker/rosenberg)

The mission of the Henry and Ruth Blaustein Rosenberg Foundation is to "improve the human condition through promoting life-long educational opportunities, research advances and a spectrum of cultural programming." The Foundation focuses its grantmaking primarily in the Baltimore, Maryland area, providing support in three general program areas: education and adult self-sufficiency, arts and culture, and health and youth development. More details about grant guidelines and restrictions can be found online. Organizations interested in applying should submit a letter of intent or a short proposal. The site contains information about what details should be included and where the letter should be sent. The Web site additionally contains a list of previous grants awarded, including a description and dollar amount for each grant.

Sunny & Abe Rosenberg Foundation (NY) (http://www.rosenbergfoundation.org)

Founded in 1966 by Abraham Rosenberg, a successful New York City businessman, "to promote a wide variety of philanthropic interests both in New York and Israel," the Sunny & Abe Rosenberg Foundation mainly funds organizations in New York City but does consider worthwhile grant requests from other geographic areas. The Foundation concentrates its giving in six areas: health organizations include mental health programs, cancer research, programs for the young and elderly, and programs serving persons with physical or sensory impairments; education includes public education, libraries, and organizations that promote tolerance and combat discrimination; artistic and cultural programs include art museums, performing arts, and education in public schools; recreation includes city parks programs and youth camps; social services includes food distribution to the needy and elderly, AIDS prevention, family planning, youth employment services, and alcohol and drug rehabilitation programs; international includes schools, orphanages and libraries. The Foundation's concise Web site also provides some funding guidelines, contact information, and a limited number of links.

The Judith Rothschild Foundation (NY) (http://fdncenter.org/grantmaker/rothschild/)

Painter Judith Rothschild created a Foundation in her will "to stimulate interest in recently deceased American painters, sculptors and photographers whose work is of the highest quality but lacks wide recognition." The New York City-based Foundation makes grants to present, preserve, or interpret work of the highest aesthetic merit by lesser known American artists who have died after September 12, 1976, as stipulated in Rothschild's will. Rothschild's goal for the Foundation was "to increase the public understanding of such lesser known and insufficiently appreciated artists—affording their work the opportunity for public viewing, institutional acquisition, and critical reassessment." The Web site contains a description of the Foundation's mission, grant application instructions, a listing of grants, a short biography of Rothschild, and contact information.

The Shelley and Donald Rubin Foundation (NY) (http://www.sdrubin.org)

The New York City-based Shelley and Donald Rubin Foundation is dedicated to "encouraging and supporting policy analysis, advocacy, and research as well as educational and artistic activities that address issues around society's changing family structure and its cultural and ethnic diversity." The grant program's areas of interest include at-risk children, healthcare, AIDS and its effects, the environment, developing community identity, and preserving ancient Tibetan art. Interested organizations should contact the Foundation with a letter of inquiry in order to receive an application. Projects will be monitored by phone, correspondence, and site visits throughout the grant period. The site includes contact information, a list of grant recipients, and brief descriptions of many projects.

The Rudder Foundation, Inc. (KY) (http://www.rudderfn.org)

Located in Kentucky, the Rudder Foundation truly exists on the Web. The organization works to "steer development programs to move toward sustainable development" through a series of discussions and papers posted on the site. Still under construction, the site offers position papers on a series of topics including "NGO (Non-Governmental Organization) strengthening, sustainable community development, program evaluation, applications of digital video in community development, encouraging individual charity in action, and the role of library media centers in curriculum development." There will eventually be an annotated list of members and an Intranet available.

Rural Kentucky Medical Scholarship Fund (KY) (http://www.kyma.org/rural.stm)

Found on the Kentucky Medical Association Web site, the Rural Kentucky Medical Scholarship Fund has distributed millions of dollars to medical students since its establishment in 1946. The Fund works "to provide better distribution of physicians to rural areas of

Kentucky." This is done by awarding loans for a year of medical school for every year that the recipient practices in designated rural areas. Those who practice in rural areas receive very low interest rates, while those who practice in areas of critical need are forgiven their loans. Applicants can download the application in either Microsoft Word or rich text format, which can be read by most word processors. The site includes a table of the counties in Kentucky with designations of whether they qualify for this program.

Russell Family Foundation (WA) (http://www.russellfamilyfdn.org)

The Russell Family Foundation of Seattle, Washington, was established in 1994 by the founders of the Frank Russell Company, an investment management and advisory firm. The Foundation "exists to enhance family and improve community" in the Puget Sound region. While the grantmaking focus is on western Washington, the Foundation accepts proposals from nonprofits throughout the state that fall in its major funding categories: values-based education and a healthy, sustainable environment. Proposals are accepted from nonprofits outside of these categories that are located in Pierce County. The simple Web site includes application deadlines and instructions on the first step of the process: submitting a letter of inquiry.

Ida Alice Ryan Trust (GA) (http://www.wachovia.com/trust/idaryan_overview.asp)

The Ida A. Ryan Charitable Trust was established in Georgia after the death of Miss Ida Alice Ryan in 1953. The Trust supports charitable institutions in the vicinity of Atlanta, Georgia. The split-interest trust makes grants to metropolitan Atlanta nonprofits primarily for capital needs in the areas of health, human services, and community welfare. Special consideration is given to ministries of the Catholic Church. Visit the Trust's Web site to find grant guidelines, grant application downloadable in PDF format, recent grants awarded, and a listing of committee members.

Sachs Foundation (CO) (http://www.frii.com/~sachs)

The Sachs Foundation was established in Colorado Springs, Colorado, in 1931. The organization is committed to awarding scholarships to African-American graduating high school seniors who have lived in Colorado from at least five years. Applicants can not be currently attending college but may have graduated from high school within three years of applying. Applications are screened for both financial need and academic achievement, and the Foundation attempts to keep the ratio of men to women fairly even. The average scholarship is $4,000 a year and continues for the four years of college. The site includes an electronic application and a financial statements attachment, both of which must be printed and mailed to the Foundation for consideration.

Russell Sage Foundation (NY) (Operating foundation) (http://www.russellsage.org/)

The Russell Sage Foundation is dedicated "to strengthening the methods, data, and theoretical core of the social sciences as a means of improving social policies." It does this by conducting a visiting scholars program and by funding studies by scholars at other academic and research institutions. The Foundation currently is focusing on four areas: the future of work, immigration, literacy and disadvantaged children, and the psychology of cultural contact. Offerings at its Web site include program descriptions, grants lists, application guidelines, and information about projects of special interest to the Foundation. The site also offers a searchable listing of Foundation publications, that can be ordered online.

Sailors' Snug Harbor of Boston (MA) (http://www.agmconnect.org/ssh/sshhome.html)

The Sailors' Snug Harbor of Boston is a nonpofit organization that helps current and retired fishing families in Massachusetts achieve sustainable self-sufficiency during this period of transition in their industry. The organization was established in 1853 to provide homes to sailors who were "broken down by infirmities brought on by disease in foreign clinics, expenses, and hardships." In recent years, the organization has made grants to support the needs of low-income elderly sailors and their families. Since 1995, the trustees have focused funds specifically toward programs addressing the needs of Massachusetts fishing families, primarily in Gloucester, New Bedford, and Cape Cod. Visitors to the

Foundation's Web site will find a list of past grants, a list of trustees/staff, and contact information. Also available at the site is a grant proposal form downloadable in PDF format.

Salomon Family Foundation (NY) (http://fdncenter.org/grantmaker/salomon/)

The New York-based Salomon Family Foundation supports the treatment of child abuse, with special emphasis on sexual abuse and programs that provide the intensive and extensive treatment needed. The Foundation's folder on the Center's Web site states the Foundation's purpose and provides grant proposal guidelines and grant cycles.

The Fan Fox and Leslie R. Samuels Foundation, Inc. (NY) (http://www.samuels.org)

Although founded in Utah in 1959, The Fan Fox and Leslie R. Samuels Foundation is now located in New York City. The Foundation supports performing arts programs and organizations or projects working to improve the delivery of high quality healthcare throughout the metropolitan area. The healthcare program is focused on supporting elderly and chronically ill patients and making sure they receive the treatment to which they are entitled. Grants are made to support "demonstrations, evaluations, and other types of studies that directly impact the users of healthcare." The performing arts program supports the highest level companies and presenters, along with arts education programs in the public schools and support for those pursuing careers in the arts. Fields receiving support include dance, music, opera, and theater. Special project grants are made to support programs addressing important issues in the arts community. Application guidelines for each program are posted, and applicants must submit a letter of inquiry first. The site also includes lists of past grant recipients by category and a staff list.

The Sasakawa Peace Foundation (DC) (Operating foundation) (http://www.spf.org)

The Sasakawa Peace Foundation (SPF) was established in 1986 to promote international understanding, exchange, and cooperation. The Foundation, located in Tokyo, Japan, carries out a "diverse program of public-interest activities and initiatives steadfastly aimed at making tangible contributions to world harmony and peace." Its programs are both self-initiated and grant-funded and are classified under two major categories: Regular Projects, which address specific fields of international issues and concerns such as global policy issues and international networking concerns; and area-specific projects (Pacific island nations, China, central Europe, and Southeast Asia) conducted by special regional funds operating with SPF. Visitors to the Foundation's Web site will find program information, grant guidelines and application instructions, downloadable application cover sheet and organization information sheet, online feedback and information request forms, annual reports and financial information, newsletters, calendar of upcoming events, and contact information.

Sarah Scaife Foundation, Inc. (PA) (http://www.scaife.com)

Located in Pittsburgh, Pennsylvania, the Sarah Scaife Foundation is one of four Scaife Foundations. The Sarah Scaife Foundation's grant program is "primarily directed toward public policy programs that address major domestic and international issues." There are no geographical restrictions, but only nonprofit organizations are eligible for grants. To apply, organizations should initially send a letter with a brief description of the program and several supporting documents, which are described on the Web site. The site also has contact and mailing information as well as financial information about the Foundation, which can be downloaded in PDF format.

Scaife Family Foundation (PA) (http://www.scaife.com)

The Scaife Family Foundation is located in Pittsburgh, Pennsylvania, and is one of four Scaife Foundations. The Foundation awards grants to programs that "support and develop programs that promote the well-being of the family and traditional values." Applications for projects in southwestern Pennsylvania are given special priority. Initial inquiries to the Foundation should be in letter form, be signed by the organization's president or authorized representative, and have the approval of the board of directors. Specifics about the letter and necessary attachments are described on the Web site. Contact and financial information are also available on the site. Annual reports are downloadable in PDF Format.

Robert Schalkenbach Foundation (NY) (http://www.schalkenbach.org)

The Robert Schalkenbach Foundation of New York was created in 1925 to teach, expound, and propagate the ideas of Henry George as set forth in his book, *Progress and Poverty,* and other works. The Foundation and its supporters are convinced that the principles expounded by Henry George will, to the extent that they are enacted into law, give equal opportunity to all and lead to the betterment of society. These principles will free labor, exchange, and capital formation to create a world of greater abundance coupled with lesser demands on scarce natural resources, leading to the abolition of involuntary poverty. The Foundation makes grants to individuals and organizations that show an interest in progressing the public dialogue of Henry George's philosophy and ideas. Specific areas of interest are support for publications dealing with Henry George's ideas, support for individuals and organizations that educate the public in principles of economics and public finance related to Henry George's ideas, and for support of research towards a more just and productive society. Visitor's to the Foundation's site will find information on the grant program, a listing of Foundation directors and staff, and contact information.

The Karla Scherer Foundation (IL)
(http://www.comnet.org/local/orgs/kschererf/index.html)

Appalled by how badly she was treated during the proxy fight to sell her father's company in 1988, the result, she felt, of being a woman in a male-dominated business world, Karla Schere "resolved to do her utmost to enable more women to attain positions of power in business. With this resolve, and $4 million dollars from the sale of the company, the Karla Scherer Foundation was born." Located in Chicago, Illinois, The Karla Scherer Foundation awards scholarships to female students majoring in finance or economics with plans for a corporate business career. Applications must be requested in writing; the address and other necessary information are provided on the site. There are no geographic restrictions, and those awarded scholarships may apply for renewals.

The Scholarships Foundation (NY) (http://fdncenter.org/grantmaker/scholarships/)

The Scholarships Foundation, founded in 1921 by Maria Bowen Chapin, is based in New York and awards grants to undergraduate and graduate students enrolled in academic programs either full-time or part-time. Priority is given to students who do not fit into defined scholarship categories, and grants are based on merit and need. The foundation's folder on the Center's Web site states its mission and provides FAQs, including who should apply for a grant and how to do so.

Caroline & Sigmund Schott Foundation (MA) (http://www.schottfoundation.org/)

The mission of the Massachusetts-based Schott Foundation is to develop and strengthen the movement for equity in education and childcare. The Foundation believes that the maintenance of good health and good schools are the cornerstones of public responsibility. "A child's intellectual, emotional, social, and moral development is significantly shaped by the quality of their educational experiences." The Schott Foundation emphasizes three areas of education, including creating better public schools in underserved communities; making schools "gender healthy," by supporting professional development for teachers, counselors, and administrators to strengthen and expand the network of activists and advocates for gender equality; and to assure universal and accessible high quality early care and education. To meet the goals set by its mission, the Foundation's grant program assists in raising public awareness and increasing understanding of complex issues and strengthens grassroots advocacy networks. Specific areas of interest supported by the Foundation include leadership development programs, grassroots organizing, partnership with policy makers, media campaigns for public awareness, voter education, litigation, research, and coalition building. Visitors to the Foundation's Web site can view current organizations being supported within the three program areas, application information, staff information, and contact information.

The Eulalie Bloedel Schneider Foundation (WA)
(http://fdncenter.org/grantmaker/schneider/)

The Eulalie Bloedel Schneider Foundation of Seattle, Washington, is primarily interested in creative educational programs and community-based grassroots programs that contain in-depth experiential learning and skill training for family members of all ages. The Foundation also shows an interest in the environment, natural sciences, and artistic and cultural programs. Visit the Foundation's folder on the Center's Web site to view further information on the grants program, grant guidelines and restrictions, information on applying to the Foundation, and contact information.

The Arthur B. Schultz Foundation (NV) (http://www.absfoundation.org)

Located in Incline Village, Nevada, the Arthur B. Schultz Foundation supports "improved understanding between nations of previously differing political systems through trade in an interdependent global economy; education of a new generation of students within the framework of an interdependent global economy and environment; and organizations and initiatives promoting environmental protection and natural resource conservation." Grants support improved facilities and specific programs in "visionary educational institutions" and also support environmental conservation, with priority given to habitat protection. Visit the Web site for program areas, grant guidelines, grants lists, financial information, and contact information.

Charles and Lynn Schusterman Family Foundation (OK) (http://www.schusterman.org)

Located in Tulsa, Oklahoma, the Foundation was established by Lynn and Charles Schusterman in 1987 to support programs that enhance Jewish life in the United States, Israel, and the former Soviet Union. It also funds Oklahoma-based, non-sectarian charitable groups that focus on education, children, and community service. Visit the Web site for grant guidelines, online preliminary application form, news and media stories about the Foundation, contact information, and related links.

Schwab Family Foundation, Charles and Helen (CA) (http://www.schwabfamilyfdn.org/)

The San Mateo, California-based Schwab Family Foundation's original grant program began in 1993 with a trustee-directed scattered grant philosophy. In 1998, the Foundation redirected its energy and formed a specific grant program called Children, Youth and Family (CYF), following the mission that "every person has the potential to be productive and, within their individual capability, to contribute positively to their own well-being, to their family's well-being and the well-being of their community." Within this program the Foundation provides support in four basic areas: basic needs, behavioral health, youth development, and community economic development. Grant emphasis is placed on helping individuals and families achieve a sense of self-sufficiency. The Foundation's Web site describes the three types of grants made, provides specific application information, individual grant history, fiscal information, a staff/trustee list, and contact information.

Schwab Foundation for Learning (CA) (Operating foundation)
(http://www.schwablearning.org)

The Schwab Foundation for Learning is a nonprofit operating foundation founded by discount brokerage pioneer Charles R. Schwab and his wife, Helen O'Neill Schwab, in 1988. They established a resource center in San Mateo, California, that is dedicated to raising awareness and providing parents and teachers with information, resources, and support to improve the lives of children with learning differences. Questions about learning differences can be asked online for free, and more extensive help is offered if you become a member, which gives you access to personalized resources and addresses your specific concerns. The Web site also features a list of resources for parents and educators, online bulletin boards, an online feedback form, online membership sign-up, and contact information.

The Self Family Foundation (SC) (http://www.selffoundation.greenwood.net)

The Self Family Foundation has its roots in the Self Foundation, incorporated by James C. Self, founder of Greenwood mills, in 1942. Its goal then was primarily to build a hospital, which he referred to as a "debt of gratitude to the community that [had] been so good to [him]." Today, the Foundation's mission is "to encourage self-sufficiency in people and the communities in which they live." Its grantmaking program is concerned with enhancing life, encouraging self-sufficiency, and "providing cures rather than treatments," and has the following target areas: education, health care, and arts, culture, and history. The Foundation's primary geographic area of interest is Greenwood, South Carolina, where the Foundation is located, and the surrounding counties followed by the Upper Piedmont region. The Foundation will consider providing seed money for creative and innovative projects in other regions in South Carolina, if they have the potential to be replicated in or have a positive impact on the Greenwood area. Visit the Foundation's Web site for grant guideline and application procedures, grants lists, and contact information.

Sierra Health Foundation (CA) (http://www.sierrahealth.org)

The Sierra Health Foundation, headquartered in Sacramento, California, awards grants in support of health and health-related activities in a 26-county region of northern California. It was established in 1984 when Foundation Health Plan, now part of Health Net of California, converted from nonprofit to for-profit corporate status. The Sierra Health Foundation was created and endowed with the proceeds from the sale. The Foundation seeks to provide monetary support for local and regional health-related programs and services, influence public health policy and choices, and stimulate improvement in California's health care system. Currently, there are four grant programs: Health Grants, Community Partnerships for Healthy Children, the Conference Program, and brightSMILES, a special dental health grant for the Foundation's northern California region. Visit the Web site to view program information, grant guidelines, and recent awards; download applications; view and download publications; request information on line; and for contact information.

William E. Simon Foundation, Inc. (NJ) (http://www.wesimonfoundation.org)

The William E. Simon Foundation, Inc., located in Morristown, New Jersey, is named after its principal benefactor. It supports programs that strengthen the free enterprise system and "the moral and spiritual values on which it rests: individual freedom, initiative, thrift, self-discipline, and faith in God." The main charitable purpose of the Foundation is to assist those in need by providing the means through which they may help themselves; accordingly, the Foundation seeks to fund programs that promote independence and personal responsibility among those in need. Its funding areas include, but are not limited to, education, religion, youth welfare, athletics, social welfare, and special awards, which recognizes outstanding achievement and excellence in selected fields. Visit the Web site for information about funding areas and for contact information. Application procedures and instructions can be downloaded from the site.

Harry Singer Foundation (CA) (Operating foundation) (http://www.singerfoundation.org/)

The California-based Harry Singer Foundation focuses on promoting "responsibility and involv[ing] people more fully in public policy." As a private operating foundation, it supports and administers active programs but does not make grants. Current programs focus on government spending, personal responsibility, values, and emotional intelligence. The Foundation's Web site provides information about a range of Foundation programs, including current and past essay contests, a teacher's mentor program, a workbook series, and offers an electronic lending library. The site's archives have an interactive feature called "Match Maker," an electronic bulletin board designed to match worthy grantseekers with sponsors.

The Siragusa Foundation (IL) (http://www.siragusa.org/index.html)

The Siragusa Foundation was founded in 1950 by Ross D. Siragusa, a Chicago philanthropist whose charitable interests included child development, social services, education, health care, cultural endeavors, and the environment. The Siragusa Foundation follows the original interests of its founder in its funding today, basing most of its grantmaking in Chicago-area organizations. Currently, the Foundation is not accepting proposals; in general, the Foundation does not accept unsolicited proposals from outside the Chicago area. Visitors to the Foundation's Web site will find application guidelines; listings of past and recent grantees; the Foundation's annual report, which can be downloaded in PDF format; links to philanthropic resources; a history of the organization and its founder; and a general introduction to philanthropy. Contact information is provided for further details.

Skillman Foundation (MI) (http://www.skillman.org/)

Founded in December 1960 by Rose P. Skillman, widow of 3M vice president and director Robert H. Skillman, the Skillman Foundation seeks to improve the well-being of residents of southeastern Michigan and, in particular, the metropolitan Detroit area (Wayne, Oakland, and Macomb Counties). Developing children and youth to their maximum potential is the Foundation's primary goal, and to that end, it makes grants in the areas of child and family welfare, child and family health, education, juvenile justice, youth development, basic human needs, culture and the arts, and strengthening community and civic institutions. The Foundation's nicely laid out, no-frills Web site provides information about the Foundation's grantmaking policies and procedures, a list of grants organized by subject area, online versions of its most recent newsletter and reports and publications (under construction), an evaluation guide, a listing of the Foundation's trustees and staff, and contact information.

Alfred P. Sloan Foundation (NY) (http://www.sloan.org/)

Established in 1934 by longtime General Motors chairman and CEO Alfred P. Sloan, the New York City-based Sloan Foundation today concentrates its activities in four main areas: science and technology; standard of living, competitiveness, and economics; education and careers in science and technology; and selected national issues. Visitors to the Foundation's Web site will find detailed program descriptions, application procedures, a directory of Foundation officers and staff, and a brief biography of founder Alfred P. Sloan, Jr.

The Christopher D. Smithers Foundation (NY) (http://www.smithersfoundation.org)

R. Brinkley Smithers established the Christopher D. Smithers Foundation in 1953 in memory of his father, who was one of the founders of IBM and a major stockholder. A recovered alcoholic, R. Brinkley Smithers made alcoholism the focus of the Foundation's efforts. The Foundation, located in Mills Valley, New York, seeks to educate the public that alcoholism is a "respectable, treatable disease from which people can and do recover." It also encourages prevention programs and activities, with an emphasis on high-risk populations, and aims to reduce and eliminate the stigma associated with alcoholism. Visitors to the Web site will find a history of the Foundation and several biographies of its founder, related links, and contact information.

The William Snyder Foundation for Animals (MD) (http://www.wsfanimals.org)

The Web site currently contains no information on the Foundation or its grant making programs, as it was being updated. However, it does have the Foundation's address, phone and fax numbers, e-mail links to staff, and foundation and grant application information.

Sobrato Family Foundation (CA) (http://www.sobrato.com/foundation)

John A. Sobrato and his wife, Susan, established the Sobrato Family Foundation in 1996. The Sobratos are owners of the Sobrato Development Companies, which has led the real estate industry in innovation by developing and building facilities for more than 200 high-technology companies in Santa Clara Valley in California. The mission of the Cupertino, California-based Family Foundation is "to build a strong and healthy local community by creating opportunities that empower individuals to reach their full potential." Giving is focused on the following program areas: community and economic development, education, health and human services, and youth development. Grants are limited to three counties in northern California: Santa Clara and San Mateo and the cities of Newark and Fremont in Alameda County, since their goal is to meet the needs of the communities from which the Sobrato family business has benefited. Visit the Foundation's Web site for grant guidelines, grant program information, a grant lists with links to grantee organizations when available, a printable proposal abstract form, and contact information.

Society for Analytical Chemists of Pittsburgh (PA) (http://www.sacp.org/)

The Society for Analytical Chemists (SACP) of Pittsburgh, a nonprofit organization founded in 1943, is dedicated to "the advancement of analytical chemistry through science education." The SACP is a professional membership organization that provides educational opportunities for its members and the community. The SACP provides a number of educational and scholarship programs for college, high school, and elementary students. Brief descriptions are provided on the site. Those who are interested are encouraged to contact the SACP directly. The site also has information about membership, monthly meetings, and related links.

Sonoma Wings Foundation (CA) (http://www.sonomawings.org/)

Located in Sonoma County, California, the Sonoma Wings Foundation is dedicated to promoting accountability in the nonprofit sector. The foundation provides funds, expertise, and advice to organizations with proven results in promoting the fulfillment of individual potential. The Foundation supports nonprofit organizations that provide services or programs in literacy, technology, arts, and youth. The Web site provides more information about the Foundation's areas of focus and gives a contact phone number and e-mail address for those interested in learning more or applying for grants.

The Paul & Daisy Soros Fellowships for New Americans (NY) (Operating foundation) (http://www.pdsoros.org)

Operating out of New York City, the Paul & Daisy Soros Fellowships for New Americans was named after the founders who are "New Americans" themselves. The Fellowship was established "in recognition of the contributions New Americans have made to American life and in gratitude for the opportunities the United States has afforded the donors and their family." It provides opportunities to "continuing generations of able and accomplished New Americans to achieve leadership in their chosen fields and to partake of the American Dream." Annually, thirty fellowships consisting of grants for two years of graduate study in the United States are awarded to "New Americans" who have shown at least two of the following three attributes: potential in the fields for which they seek further education; a capacity for creativity, persistence, and work; and a commitment to the values of the U.S. Constitution and the Bill of Rights. A "New American" is an individual who is a resident alien or has been naturalized as a U.S. citizen or is the child of two parents who are both naturalized citizens. Visit the Web site for further program information and requirements, application instructions, printable application forms (application forms are also available by contacting them directly), profiles of past fellows, related links, and contact information, including e-mail links to staff members.

Soros Foundations Network (NY) (http://www.soros.org)

Supported by financier-turned-philanthropist George Soros, the Soros Foundations Network comprises 26 national foundations located in the countries of central and eastern Europe, the former Soviet Union, South Africa, and Haiti; and the Open Society Institute, which promotes connections and cooperation among the various Soros-sponsored foundations. The SFN's member organizations "help build the infrastructure and institutions necessary for open societies" by supporting programs for education, children and youth, media and communications, civil society, human rights and humanitarian aid, science and medicine, arts and culture, and economic restructuring. SFN's Web site, which serves as the information clearinghouse for the Network, offers a wide range of information, including general program categories and application guidelines, annotated bibliographies, newsletters, press releases, and contact info. Also of interest is the manner in which the SFN site integrates a Web interface with a central gopher database to allow for meaningful access by the broadest possible online constituency.

Spencer Foundation (IL) (http://www.spencer.org/)

Established by Lyle M. Spencer, founder of the educational publishing firm Science Research Associates Inc., the Spencer Foundation investigates "ways in which education, broadly conceived, can be improved around the world." To this end, the Foundation supports "high quality investigation of education through its research programs ... [and] strengthens and renews the educational research community through fellowship programs and related activities." Since 1968, the Foundation has made grants totaling approximately $180 million. Visitors to the Foundation's Web site will find descriptions, eligibility guidelines, and application instructions or contact information for each research grant program. The Foundation's latest annual report and a listing of its directors, advisors, and staff are also available.

The Stanley Foundation (IA) (Operating foundation) (http://www.stanleyfdn.org)

The Stanley Foundation is a non-partisan operating foundation based in Muscatine, Iowa. C. Maxwell and Elizabeth Stanley created the foundation in 1956 to pursue their long-time commitment to the effective management of global problems. The Foundation strives toward "provoking thought and encouraging dialogue on world affairs" and "striving for a secure peace with freedom and justice." It serves policy professionals through policy conferences, congressional staff programs, and conference reports; involved citizens through conferences, seminars, resource materials, and networking; and the wider public through "Common Ground," a weekly news radio program on world affairs, *World Press Review,* a monthly magazine, *The Courier,* a newsletter, and the foundation's Web site. Current topics are arms control and security, global economy and society, global education, human rights, regions and countries, United Nations, and U.S. foreign policy. Visitors to the Web site will find conference reports, radio transcripts and live broadcasts, online publications, publications ordering information, and an online contact form.

Starr Foundation (NY) (http://fdncenter.org/grantmaker/starr/)

Located in New York City, the Starr Foundation was created by insurance entrepreneur Cornelius Vander Starr in 1955. The Foundation focuses funding on education, while also generously supporting projects in medicine and healthcare, human needs, public policy, and culture. In addition to having endowed scholarships at over 80 colleges, universities, and secondary schools, the Foundation "funds organizations that provide need-based financial aid to students seeking to attend secondary and post-secondary schools" and occasionally supports foreign exchange programs. The Foundation does run scholarship programs specifically for children of American International Group employees; students who live in Brewster, New York; and students at specified high schools in downtown Manhattan. Funding in medicine and healthcare goes toward a variety of projects, including capital campaigns, research, and those providing care to underserved communities. Recipients of human needs awards range from literacy to housing to hunger programs. Outside of the tri-state area, most of this giving is done through community foundations. Public policy focuses on international relations and funds institutions all over the world. And culture grants have gone to large museums and to small, community-based groups but not to individual artists. There is no formal application and no deadlines, but the Foundation's folder on the Center's Web site lists proposal requirements and gives contact information.

Staunton Farm Foundation (PA) (http://www.stauntonfarm.org)

Located in Pittsburgh, Pennsylvania, the Staunton Farm Foundation was incorporated in 1937 as directed by the will of Mrs. Matilda S. McCready. She charged her executors to erect and maintain "a home for the treatment and care of persons suffering curable neurotic, mild mental and kindred ailments, wherein persons undergoing treatment may have the benefit of fresh air, sunshine and rural surroundings in ample grounds for work and recreation without being brought in contact with those suffering from incurable forms of the same trouble." In addition to the outpatient clinics that the Foundation has established, it awards grants in the field of mental health in southwestern Pennsylvania. The ten-county area is outlined on a map on the site. To apply for a grant, an initial letter of intent must be submitted. The Foundation accepts the Common Grant Application for Western

Pennsylvania, and provides a link to this application on its site. Application guidelines, recent grant recipients, and contact information are also available on the site.

Rudolph Steiner Foundation (CA) (http://www.rsfoundation.org)

Rudolf Steiner, the founder of Waldorf Education and a proponent of biodynamic farming, "worked for the basic human principles of freedom in cultural affairs, equality in political affairs, and interdependence in a sustainable economy." The Foundation that carries his name was formed in 1984 in San Francisco and upholds Steiner's vision as a progressive financial service organization supporting social and environmental change. Through gifts, grants, and loans, the Foundation supports education and the arts, science and caring for the earth, social responsibility and mutual support, medical and religious renewal, and associative economic relationships. The Foundation also runs advisory and educational services. Its Web site provides client profiles, a listing of specific funds, descriptions of projects funded, links to affiliated associations, and an e-mail contact form. The Foundation does not accept grant inquiries or proposals over e-mail, but a one-page grant request with a description of the program can be submitted through the address provided online.

Stern Family Fund (VA) (http://www.sternfund.org/)

The Arlington, Virginia-based Stern Family Fund "supports policy oriented government and corporate accountability projects. . . . [T]he Fund is committed to aiding citizens striving to guarantee the responsiveness of public and private institutions that wield substantial power over their lives." The Stern Fund seeks to achieve these goals through two distinct grant programs: the Public Interest Pioneer Program, which provides large seed grants ($50,000 to $100,000) to spark the creation of new organizations; and Strategic Support Grants, which are awarded to projects or organizations "at critical junctures in their development. . . ." With the exception of campaign finance reform proposals, the Fund generally limits its grants to organizations with annual operating budgets of less than $500,000. The Fund's Web site provides detailed program information, a list of grantees, application guidelines and procedures, FAQs on the Stern Grant Program, and a listing of the Fund's board members.

The Stuart Foundation (CA) (http://www.stuartfoundation.org)

The Stuart Foundation's "overarching purpose" is to help the children and youth of California and Washington become responsible citizens. Based in San Francisco, California, the Foundation's approach to this purpose is to help strengthen the public systems and community supports that contribute to children's development. There are three grant program areas: Strengthening the Public School System, Strengthening the Child Welfare System, and Strengthening Communities to Support Families. Visit the Web site for funding guidelines and program information, application guidelines and instructions, grant statistics and lists with short project descriptions and e-mail links to grantee organizations, lists of related links, an online feedback form, and contact information.

The Sudbury Foundation (MA) (http://www.agmconnect.org/sudbury1.html)

Longtime residents Herbert J. and Esther M. Atkinson established the Sudbury Foundation in 1952 to benefit the people of Sudbury, Massachusetts, and the organizations that serve them. The Atkinsons operated the Sudbury Laboratory, a successful business specializing in marine products and soil testing kits. Their Sudbury-based Foundation was one of the ways through which they shared their good fortune as the laboratory prospered. The Foundation operates two programs: the Atkinson Scholarship Program, which recognizes and assists local, college-bound students; and the Charitable Grants Program, which supports not-for-profit organizations whose work improves the quality of life for Sudbury residents and their neighbors in surrounding towns. Eligible students for the $5,000 per-year scholarship should have ties to Sudbury, have financial need, academic promise, and the desire and capacity to contribute to society. Preference in funding for the Charitable Grants Program is given to projects that foster individual and organizational self-sufficiency, help those in need, encourage volunteerism, and/or engender a spirit of pride and a greater sense of community. The Foundation also supports environmental programs of direct benefit to the

Sudbury area and also has a Regional Environmental Program, which supports organizations based in or active in the New England area that are working on issues of regional significance. Visitors to the Web site will find funding guidelines for the two main programs, grant lists with descriptions, application instructions, links to other sites of interest, and contact information.

Summerlee Foundation (TX) (http://www.summerlee.org/index.htm)

The Summerlee Foundation located in Houston, Texas, was established in 1988 to both support animal protection and preserve the history of Texas. The animal protection program emphasizes research and dissemination of information, including an emphasis on companion animals, cruelty investigations and rescue, feral cat issues, overpopulation, and reducing euthanasia. The Texas history program focuses on research. The Foundation also holds an interest in enhancing the programmatic needs of state agencies responsible for promotion, preservation, and interpretation of the history of Texas. Visit the Summerlee Foundation's Web site to view recent grant listings, grant guidelines, and contact information.

Surdna Foundation, Inc. (NY) (http://www.surdna.org/)

Established in 1917 by businessman John E. Andrus, the New York City-based Surdna Foundation concentrates its grantmaking activities in five programmatic areas: the environment, biological diversity and the human communities that depend on it, human systems, transportation and urban/suburban land use, and energy. The Foundation's Web site offers general information about the Foundation and its approach to grantmaking, as well as detailed program information, application guidelines, grant restrictions, a recent listing of grants, board and staff information, and contact information.

Swalm Foundation (TX) (http://www.swalm.org)

The Swalm Foundation, located in Houston, makes grants to human service organizations in Texas that serve the homeless, the educationally and economically disadvantaged, survivors of domestic violence, victims of child abuse and neglect, and the mentally or physically disabled. The Foundation is especially interested in assisting organizations in parts of Texas that have very limited resources, including small towns and rural areas. Guidelines and restrictions are explained on the Foundation's Web site. The application can be completed and sent online, although organizations will have to mail in attachments and additional forms.

John Templeton Foundation (PA) (http://www.templeton.org/)

The Templeton Foundation was established in 1987 by international investment manager John Templeton "to explore and encourage the relationship between science and religion." The Foundation's programs, which are primarily operating in nature, focus on five areas: spiritual information through science, spirituality and health, free enterprise, character development, and the John Templeton Prize for Progress in Religion. In addition to general program and contact information, the Foundation's Web site offers visitors a listing of the Foundation's officers and trustees, winners of the Templeton Prizes for Progress in Religion, information about other awards given by the Foundation, a list of recent grants, and a Request for Proposals for scientific studies in the area of forgiveness, with RFP application packets available for downloading in PDF format.

The Tiffany & Co. Foundation (NY) (http://www.tiffanyandcofoundation.org/)

The recently established Tiffany & Co. Foundation, based in New York City, supports the arts, including crafts education, arts education, preservation and conservation, decorative arts, performing arts, and visual arts, as well as environmental conservation. The Foundation's Web site lists grant proposal guidelines and limitations, the board of directors, and contact information.

Tinker Foundation, Inc. (NY) (http://fdncenter.org/grantmaker/tinker/index.html)

Created in 1956 by Dr. Edward Larocque Tinker, the Tinker Foundation has long focused its grantmaking activities on Latin America, Spain, and Portugal. More recently, it has included in its mandate the support of projects concerning Antarctica, "a region of significant interest on an international scale." Institutional Grants are awarded to organizations and institutions "that promote the interchange and exchange of information within the community of those concerned with the affairs of Spain, Portugal, Ibero-America and Antarctica." Within these parameters, the Foundation looks for innovative projects in the areas of environmental policy, governance, or economic policy that have a strong public policy component. The Foundation also awards Field Research Grants to recognized institutes of Ibero-American or Latin American Studies with graduate doctoral programs at accredited U.S. universities. The Foundation's folder on the Center's Web site offers descriptions of both programs; application instructions, reporting requirements, and a downloadable proposal cover sheet; a recent grants list for the Institutional Grants program; and a listing of Foundation officers and staff.

TKF Foundation (MD) (http://www.tkffdn.org)

Created in 1985 in Annapolis, Maryland, the TKF Foundation is committed to "creating urban greenspace, sponsoring public art, and championing urban agriculture with the goals of nurturing the human spirit and fostering a sense of community." Open to projects in the Annapolis and Baltimore, Maryland, and Washington, D.C., areas, the grants program has two major categories: Open Spaces/Sacred Places and Community Greening. The former funds projects such as community parks, healing gardens, recreation paths, and bay buffers that are available to a large segment of the population. The latter helps community-based initiatives with small-scale plantings and with funding for projects that include community-sustainable agriculture. The Foundation only funds new projects and considers constant evaluation a very important part of each project. Grantseekers are required to submit a letter of inquiry with a series of required attachments. If the group is advised to submit a proposal, the Foundation accepts the Association of Baltimore Area Grantmakers' common application. The Foundation's Web site includes application deadlines, previous grant recipients, and a monthly feature on a successful project.

The Randall L. Tobias Foundation, Inc. (IN) (http://www.rltfound.org)

The Randall L. Tobias Foundation, Inc. is a family foundation located in Indianapolis, Indiana. Established in 1994, the Foundation's primary emphasis is on providing support for its own initiatives, but grant proposals are "welcomed and encouraged." The Foundation is receptive to proposals in all areas, other than those that are excluded in its policy (consult the Web site for the list of exclusions). However, there are areas of funding priority: education, at all levels but with particular interest in K–12 education and education reform; culture and the arts, particularly enhancing its quality and availability in selected communities and developing the broadest possible interest in culture and the arts among individuals and groups of all ages; community development, to significantly advance the quality of life in selected communities; and innovation, to support and encourage new ideas and solutions to important issues of public interest in virtually any area of human endeavor. Consult the Foundation's Web site for funding guidelines, priorities, and contact information. The site features an online grant application and a printable brochure on the Foundation.

Tocker Foundation (TX) (http://www.tocker.org/)

The Tocker Founder was established in 1964 to implement the philanthropic interests of Phillip Tocker, a Texas businessman and attorney, and his wife, Olive. In 1992 the Foundation decided to focus its grantmaking on small rural libraries serving a population of 12,000 or less. The Foundation partners with community libraries to make their services more accessible to individuals who by reason of distance, residence, handicap, age, literacy level, or other disadvantage are unable to receive the benefits of public library services. In recent years the Foundation has made grants for outreach and "shut-in" programs, library automation, enhancement of services, adult reading classes, after school projects, bilingual material, and a variety of other projects initiated by community public libraries. Visitors to the Foundation's Web site will find a brief history of the Foundation, detailed grant proposal guidelines, a downloadable grant application form in PDF format, recent grants lists, a list of library automation projects in progress, and contact information.

The Trellis Fund (DC) (http://fdncenter.org/grantmaker/trellis/)

The Washington, D.C.-based Trellis Fund is "committed to making communities more responsive to and responsible for their residents and other constituents." The Foundation does not set specific funding focuses but is interested in supporting organizations that attempt to solve "complex problems." The Fund prefers to fund organizations within the District of Columbia, although it is interested in funding "extraordinary funding opportunities" outside the District. Trellis has a special interest in local arts institutions that sponsor artistic talent that alters, refines, critiques, or in any way extends thinking beyond the status quo. Therefore, a small portion of Trellis' annual budget will be made available to support the visual arts. Visitors to the Foundation's folder on the Center's Web site will find application guidelines, a staff listing, application procedures, deadlines, a copy of the Foundation's latest annual report, and contact information.

TriMix Foundation (RI) (http://www.trimixfoundation.org)

The TriMix Foundation of Warwick, Rhode Island, has created a simple Web site that is really a service to potential applicants. The Foundation "supports programs and initiatives designed to improve the lives of children and build cohesive neighborhoods and communities" all over the United States. The site offers clear descriptions of what programs fall in the four funding categories. In education, the Foundation supports projects concerning early childhood development, at-risk youth, scholarships, adult literacy programs, and other special initiatives. Health funding focuses on prebirth and childhood initiatives, supportive care and rehabilitation, and research on cancer, paralysis, blood diseases, and neuromuscular disease. Athletics includes sponsoring community teams and funding athletic complexes. Art funding supports programs for young artists and local art organizations. Qualifying applicants should submit a brief letter of inquiry. There is an electronic form on the site that can be used for this purpose.

The Trull Foundation (TX) (http://www.trullfoundation.org)

In 1967 the Trull Foundation was founded in Texas, continuing the legacy left by the B.W. Trull Foundation, which was originally founded in 1948 to support religious and educational purposes. The newly established Trull Foundation reprioritized and created a broader grant program supporting educational, religious, cultural, and social programs. The Foundation makes grants primarily in Texas. The Foundation's priorities center around health care, children and families, substance abuse, and agriculture and farming in Texas communities. The Foundation's Web site includes a board/staff listing, grant guidelines, a most current grants list, a printable proposal fact sheet, and contact information.

Tucson Osteopathic Medical Foundation (AZ) (Operating foundation) (http://www.tomf.org/about.html)

The Tucson Osteopathic Medical Foundation, based in Tucson, Arizona, is a "conversion" foundation that resulted from the sale of Tucson General Hospital to Summit Health, Ltd. Established in 1986, it is an operating foundation serving the seven counties of southern Arizona whose mission is to advance postgraduate osteopathic medical education, improve the public's understanding of osteopathic medicine, and "to elevate through education" the health and well-being of the community. It has two grant programs: the Founders Awards, which are loans to osteopathic medical students that become scholarships if the students graduate and practice in southern Arizona for a specific period of time, and Trustee Awards, which are grants to local charitable organizations that can achieve significant results with a small grant (it is unclear from the Web site whether grant proposals are accepted). Applicants to the Founders Award must be Arizona residents, and applicants from southern Arizona will be given special consideration. A printable application, criteria, and instructions for the Founders Award are available on the Foundation's Web site. Visitors to the site will also find information on its operating programs, information on osteopathic medicine, related links, a searchable directory of physicians, and a continuing education event calendar.

Turner Foundation, Inc. (GA) (http://www.turnerfoundation.org/)

The Turner Foundation supports activities directed toward preservation of the environment, conservation of natural resources, protection of wildlife, and sound population policies. The Foundation supports organizations that "provide education and activism on preservation activities and seek to instill in all citizens a sense of common responsibility for the fate of life on Earth." It does not customarily provide support for buildings, land acquisition, endowments, or startup funds. Nor does it normally fund films, books, magazines, or other specific media projects. The Foundation's Web site provides detailed program guidelines, lists of recent grants awarded in four main program areas (i.e., water/toxics, energy, forests/habitat, and population), application procedures and limitations, messages from Ted Turner and the Foundation's executive director, and an interactive form for feedback.

Turrell Fund (NJ) (http://fdncenter.org/grantmaker/turrell/index.html)

The main purpose of the New Jersey-based Turrell Fund is "to support social and educational activities that will contribute to the development of young people from families which could not afford these services without help." Programs that focus on children under the age of twelve are given highest priority; requests for capital support, while considered, are of secondary priority. The Fund supports programs in Vermont and in Essex, Hudson, Passaic, and Union Counties in New Jersey. Visitors to the Fund's folder on the Center's Web site will find a brief description of its program interests; application instructions; a listing of officers, trustees, and staff; FAQs; and a downloadable summary request form.

Isaac H. Tuttle Fund (NY) (http://www.tuttlefund.org)

Established in 1872, the New York-based Isaac H. Tuttle Fund's mission is to "provide temporal and spiritual welfare of aged persons." The organization supports both individuals and organizations that service the elderly population in the borough of Manhattan, with a goal of enabling these individuals to continue living in their own homes "so long as they are physically and mentally able to do so." Support is provided in two ways: through a stipendiary program that provides financial help to elderly persons whose financial stability had been eroded through illness, inflation, and other factors; and through the Foundation's grants to organizations program. Visit the Fund's Web site to find further details about its grantmaking initiatives, a brief history, a listing of recent grants, and contact information.

United States-Japan Foundation (NY) (http://www.us-jf.org/)

The principal mission of the United States-Japan Foundation, a private nonprofit grantmaking organization incorporated in 1980 in the State of New York, is "to promote greater mutual knowledge between the United States and Japan and to contribute to a strengthened understanding of important public policy issues of interest to both countries." The Foundation currently focuses its grantmaking in the areas of pre-college education and policy studies. It does not award grants as contributions to capital campaigns, endowment funds, deficit operations, for the construction or maintenance of buildings, or for the purchase of equipment. Visitors to the Foundation's Web site will find basic program descriptions, application procedures, a limitations statement, and contact information.

Until There's A Cure Foundation (CA) (http://www.utac.org/)

Until There's A Cure Foundation was established in 1993 by Dana Cappiello and Kathleen Scutchfield. When her best friend died of AIDS in 1992, Dana Cappiello began wearing a ring he left her shortly before he died, and the ring, "worn as a symbol of remembrance, and the devastation of his death, inspired the genesis" of the Foundation. The Foundation derives its funds from the sale of The Bracelet, a bracelet bearing the design of the AIDS ribbon. The Foundation has four priority areas: direct care services, prevention education, vaccine research development, and policy development. The Foundation also has a Partnership Program, in which qualified organizations receive 25 percent of total revenues they generate from sales of The Bracelet. Visitors to the Web site will find grant application instructions, grant lists, and contact information.

W.E. Upjohn Institute for Employment Research (MI) (Operating foundation) (http://www.upjohninst.org)

The W.E. Upjohn Institute for Employment Research has its roots in the W.E. Upjohn Unemployment Trustee Corporation, which maintained a cooperative farm for laid-off workers to maintain their income and their dignity. Dr. W.E. Upjohn, founder and head of the Upjohn Company, had conceived of the idea during the Depression in 1932, when he was concerned about the prospects of laying off his workers and the broader problem of the hardships of the unemployed. The farm program did not last long, but concern over unemployment remained a top priority. So in 1945 the trustees established the W.E. Upjohn Institute, located in Kalamazoo, Michigan, a research organization devoted to finding, evaluating, and promoting solutions to employment-related problems. The Foundation's grant program funds proposals to conduct policy-relevant research on employment issues. Although proposals on any policy-relevant labor market issue will be considered, the Foundation gives higher priority to proposals addressing employment relationships, low wages and public policy, and social insurance. Grants made under this program are expected to result in "research of a rigorous nature and a book published by the Institute that will be of interest to policy makers, practitioners, and academics." The Foundation also invites submissions for its Dissertation Award, an annual prize for the best Ph.D. dissertation on employment-related issues. Visit the Web site for grant and award program information, application instructions, a history of the foundation, information and publications on employment issues, and contact information.

Valley Foundation (CA) (http://www.valley.org/)

Formed in 1984 from the proceeds of the sale of the Community Hospital of Los Gatos, California, and Saratoga, Inc., the Valley Foundation provides funding for nonprofit organizations in Santa Clara County, with an emphasis in the medical field. Although the Foundation's primary interest is in medical services and health care for lower-income households, it also supports programs in the areas of youth, the arts, seniors, and general medical services. Visitors to the Foundation's Web site will find a listing of sample grants awarded in each of the program areas mentioned above, application procedures and limitations, a financial summary of the Foundation's activities, a listing of the Foundation's board, and an electronic application form.

van Ameringen Foundation (NY) (http://fdncenter.org/grantmaker/vanameringen/)

The van Ameringen Foundation is located in New York City and gives in the urban northeast of the United States. The organization "promotes mental health through preventive measures, treatment and rehabilitation and supports the field of psychiatry." Areas of interest are mental health, treatment, and mental health/crisis services. The very simple page has basic application instructions and deadlines. The Foundation does publish an annual report.

The Vetlesen Foundation, G. Unger (NY) (http://www.monellvetlesen.org/)

The G. Unger Vetlesen Foundation's mission is "Voluntarily aiding and contributing to religious, charitable, scientific, literary, and educational uses and purposes, in New York, elsewhere in the United States and throughout the world." The Foundation concentrates its grants in the fields of oceanographies, climate studies, and other earth sciences. Interested parties should submit a request for funding to the Foundation; guidelines and information about what should be included can be found on the Web site. The Foundation provides a copy of its Form 990–PF form online, which can be downloaded in PDF format. Previous annual reports and a listing of recent grants awarded are also available on the site.

Virginia Environmental Endowment (VA) (http://www.cvco.org/vee/)

Virginia Environmental Endowment aims to improve the quality of the environment by encouraging all sectors to work together to prevent pollution, conserve natural resources, and promote environmental literacy. It was created through a court order in 1977, when a portion of the fine that the Allied Chemical Corporation was ordered to pay for polluting the James River was used to create the Virginia Environmental Endowment. Grantmaking priorities encompass Sustainable Communities, Water Quality Protection and Management, and Environmental Education. Located in Richmond, Virginia, the Endowment currently limits awards for programs conducted in Virginia and in the Kanawha and Ohio River Valleys of Kentucky and West Virginia. Visit the Web site for grant application procedures, grant lists with links to grantee organizations, and links to other useful resources. The Virginia mini-grants program has downloadable application procedures.

Virginia Environmental Research Endowment (VA) (http://www.vee.org)

The Virginia Environmental Research Endowment was created in 1977 in Richmond, Virginia, stemming from the court order of fines imposed on the Allied Chemical Company for pollution infractions. The Endowment's mission is to "improve the quality of the environment by encouraging all sectors to work together to prevent pollution, conserve natural resources, and promote environmental literacy." Areas of interest for grants and mini-grants include sustainable communities, water quality protection and management, and environmental education. The Endowment limits its funding scope to Virginia and the Kanawha and Ohio River Valleys of Kentucky and West Virginia. Visitors to the Endowment's Web site will find program details, recent grants, links, a list of staff members, and contact information. Application guidelines for the grant and mini-grant program are different; both are provided online.

VNA Foundation (IL) (http://www.smallfoundations.org/webpage/vnahome.htm)

The Visiting Nurse Association of Chicago, an organization with a hundred-year history as an active health care service, is now a foundation dedicated to financing nonprofit organizations offering home and community-based health care to the underserved in Cook County, Illinois, and the surrounding area, with an emphasis on Chicago. Grants are given to groups working mainly in three areas: home health care services, prevention and health promotion, and early intervention. Priority is given to care services provided by nurses. The VNA Foundation's Web site provides a message from the executive director, grant guidelines, application procedures, a listing of past grants, a financial report, and contact information.

The Laura B. Vogler Foundation, Inc. (NY) (http://fdncenter.org/grantmaker/vogler/)

Established in 1959, the Laura B. Vogler Foundation awards one-time non-renewable grants for new programs in the areas of health, youth, child welfare, the disadvantaged, the elderly, and other related services. The Foundation favors specific programs or projects, rather than general operating support or capital programs. The Foundation does not make grants for conferences, seminars, or loans. The Foundation is a member of the New York Regional Association of Grantmakers and the Association of Small Foundations. Visitors to the Foundation's folder on the Center's Web site will find a brief description of its program interests, a listing of trustees, a sampling of recent grants, application instructions, and a copy of the New York Area Common Application Form.

The William J. Von Liebig Foundation, Inc. (FL) (Operating foundation) (http://www.vonliebigfoundation.com)

The William J. Von Liebig Foundation, based in Naples, Florida, "encourage[s] the movement of technical innovation and relevant clinical findings from the laboratory to the vascular surgical community." The Foundation awards a $10,000 prize to the resident or fellow with the best essay on a problem in general vascular surgery. $500 prizes are awarded to manuscripts with high ratings and $2,000 to the research mentors of award winners. The Foundation also presents research grants to universities and to noted presidents of vascular societies. The Foundation's Web site lists past residents and fellows award winners, general requirements for awards, links to vascular resources, and contact information to request application materials.

Waitt Family Foundation (SD) (http://www.waittfoundation.org/)
The Waitt Family Foundation was founded in 1993 by Ted and Joan Waitt; Ted Waitt is the founder of Gateway Computer Company. The Foundation is based in Sioux City, South Dakota, and the Waitts focus their funding on the surrounding Siouxland area, their home. The Foundation does fund some national programs, but the Foundation initiates its funding in the Siouxland area before branching out nationally. Funding areas include education, non-violence, child advocacy, and community enhancement. Through the Educational Fund Program, the Foundation grants scholarships, teacher-student recognition, and teaching training. PeaceWorks is a program to bring peace to the home, community, and world. The Foundation supports other programs and initiatives as well; there is a guide to grants and funding limitations, as well as an application request form, on the Foundation's Web site.

Wallace Global Fund (DC) (http://www.wgf.org)
The mission of the Washington, D.C.-based Wallace Global Fund is "to catalyze and leverage critically needed global progress towards an equitable and environmentally sustainable society." The Fund is guided by the vision of the late Henry A. Wallace, former Secretary of Agriculture and Vice-President under Franklin D. Roosevelt. It supports initiatives that advance globally sustainable development in some fundamental way. Grants have been made to a wide range of projects that address obstacles to a sustainable future, including but not limited to population growth, over-consumption, global climate change, imperfect economic policies and inadequate analytic tools, and deforestation. Visitors to the Web site will find program information, application procedures, grants lists with links to grantee organizations, financial information, staff and trustee listing, and contact information.

Wallace-Reader's Digest Funds (NY) (http://www.wallacefunds.org/)
Founded in 1987 as the Dewitt Wallace-Reader's Digest Fund and the Lila Wallace-Reader's Digest Fund, the Wallace-Reader's Digest Fund now operates under a common goal: "enriching community life through [the] support of education, arts and culture," while maintaining funding interests begun through the individual organizations. The Fund has pooled its resources to concentrate and continue its support of New York City programs in education, the arts, and communities. The Dewitt Wallace-Reader's Digest Fund focuses on education and career development of low-income youth, while the Lila Wallace Reader's Digest Fund focuses on making the arts part of our daily lives, promoting literacy programs for adults, and creating or improving urban parks. While continuing these programs, the new Wallace-Reader's Digest Fund will work to find more effective superintendents and principals to improve the quality of public schools, engage more people in the arts and cultural institutions, and promote informal learning for adults and children in low-income areas. The Fund's Web site contains past and present grant recipients, along with evaluations of these programs; annual reports and articles about the Fund's work, which can be downloaded in PDF format; links to related resources; and a form to contact the Fund.

Walton Family Foundation, Inc. (AR) (http://www.wffhome.com)
The Bentonville, Arkansas-based Walton Family Foundation was established by Sam M. (founder of Wal-Mart stores) and Helen R. Walton. The Foundation is principally involved in programs of its own initiative and does not accept unsolicited proposals, but from time to time grants are made to organizations whose work embodies one or more of the goals of the Foundation. Applicants are asked to send a brief letter of inquiry to the Foundation prior to submitting a complete application. The Foundation has a primary focus on education, specifically systemic reform, with special emphasis on primary and secondary education. The Foundation funds three scholarship programs, all for higher education (one for children of Wal-Mart Associates, one for high school seniors interested in pursuing a career in teaching, and one for low-income Central American students to study at three private Arkansas universities). Another Foundation program is the Charter School Grantmaking Program, whose purpose is to improve the quality of charter schools, strengthen the charter school movement, and bring the qualities of the charter concept to more public schools. Its

geographic focus is on Arkansas, where the founders lived. The Foundation also has a particular interest in the economic development and in the enhancement of educational opportunities for students and adults in the Mississippi River's delta region of Arkansas and Mississippi. Consult the Web site for program and scholarship information, funding guidelines, application procedures, links to programs they support and to other resources, and contact information.

The Andy Warhol Foundation for the Visual Arts (NY) (http://www.warholfoundation.org/)

The Andy Warhol Foundation for the Visual Arts was established in 1987 with the mission, in accordance with Warhol's will, of advancing the visual arts. The Foundation is committed to the idea that "arts are essential to an open, enlightened democracy" and seeks to foster innovative artistic expression and the creative process by encouraging and supporting cultural organizations that in turn, directly or indirectly, support artists and their work. Seeking to advance an "inclusive cultural dialogue," support is given for work of "a challenging and often experimental nature" and to organizations that support artists reflecting a diverse society. The Foundation also supports efforts to "strengthen" areas that directly affect the context in which artists work, such as freedom of artistic expression and equitable access to resources. Grants are made on a project basis to curatorial programs at museums, artists' organizations, and other cultural institutions to assist in innovative and scholarly presentations of contemporary visual arts. The creation of new work is also supported through "regranting" initiatives and artist-in-residence programs. The work of choreographers and performing artists occasionally receive funding when the visual arts are an inherent element. Consult the Web site of this New York City-based Foundation for grant guidelines, application information, and contact information. Visitors to the site will also find a brief biography of Andy Warhol; a calendar of funded projects; grant lists; a series of papers from its project on the arts, culture, and society (whose purpose is to ensure public debate about the global, economic, and societal forces affecting the arts); and a FAQ sheet.

Warren Memorial Foundation (ME) (Operating foundation) (http://www.javanet.com/~warren/board.html)

The Warren Memorial Foundation was established in 1929 with a bequest from Susan Warren, who was Samuel Warren's wife. Samuel Warren was the president of S.D. Warren Mill, and in 1879 he established a library in a small room over the company's main office for his employees. It was Susan Warren who carried on the library's work, a library that eventually became the Warren Memorial Library that is today housed in its own building. The Foundation is the sole funder of the Warren Memorial Library, which is free of charge for all residents and nonresidents of Westbrook, Maine, where the Foundation and library are located. The goal of the Warren Memorial Library is "to provide a collection of materials appropriate to meet the informational, educational, cultural and recreational needs of community residents." The Foundation is also a strong advocate of literacy and encourages reading as a family activity. The library has a program of services designed to encourage an interest in reading and learning in children and to facilitate the use of the library of senior citizens. Visitors to the Web site can read about the library's history, its programs and policies, and collections. Links to related sites and contact information are provided.

Washington Research Foundation (WA) (http://www.wrfseattle.org)

The Washington Research Foundation (WRF), based in Seattle, Washington, was established in 1981 to help Washington State research institutions capture value from their emerging technologies. WRF initially focused on patenting inventions and licensing them to companies. With its proceeds from licensing, WRF built a seed venture fund, managed by WRF Capital, which creates and invests in technology-based start-up companies that have strong ties to the University of Washington and other nonprofit research institutions in Washington State. It also established WRF Venture Center, which leases office space to technology-based start-ups and provides them with business support. The Foundation continues to pursue its licensing activities, and revenues generated from licensing and WRF Capital investments are used to make gifts to support scholarship and research at Washington State research institutions. Visit the Web site for information on the services offered by the Foundation, WRF Capital, WRF Venture Center, and for contact information. A list of the Foundation's past gifts is also on their site.

Washington Square Health Foundation Inc. (IL) (http://www.wshf.org)

The Washington Square Healthcare Foundation, Inc. grants funds in order to promote and maintain access to adequate healthcare for all people in the Chicago area. Located in Chicago, Illinois, the Foundation makes grants for medical and nursing education, medical research, and direct healthcare services. The Web site contains grantmaking policies and guidelines, annual reports, and grant listings. The site also provides online and downloadable grant applications and links to other Foundation resources.

The Thomas J. Watson Foundation (RI) (http://watsonfellowship.org/)

The Thomas J. Watson Foundation was founded in 1961 as a charitable trust by Mrs. Thomas J. Watson, Sr., in honor of her late husband. Based in Providence, Rhode Island, the Foundation initially used its resources in support of a variety of programs, but in 1968, in recognition of Mr. and Mrs. Watson's long-standing interest in education and world affairs, their children decided that the major activity of the Foundation would be to support a fellowship that would give college graduates of "unusual promise" the freedom to engage in a year of independent study and travel abroad after graduation. Administered in cooperation with fifty outstanding private colleges and universities throughout the United States, the Watson Fellowship provides a grant of $22,000 and an amount equal to twelve-months' payment of outstanding federally guaranteed student loans, "to ease the financial burden of Watson Fellows during their fellowship year and to provide encouragement for all students, regardless of student loan debt, to apply for Watson Fellowships." Individual colleges and universities participating in the Watson Fellowship Program establish their own procedures and deadlines for the application process. Visit the Web site for a list of links to participating colleges and universities and a list of recent fellows.

Weaver Foundation (NC) (http://www.weaverfoundation.com)

The Weaver Foundation was founded in 1967 by W. Herman Weaver and H. Michael Weaver with the intention of supporting activities and causes that benefit the greater Greensboro area. Since its establishment, the directors have been interested in supporting community improvement, environmental activities, educational development, helping the disadvantaged and advancing human and civil rights, racial tolerance, and diversity. Specifically, the Foundation's mission is to "help the Greater Greensboro community enhance and improve the quality of life and the economic environment for its citizens while developing a sense of philanthropy, civic education and commitment in current and future generations of the founders' families." The Weaver Foundation does not maintain a grant application cycle, nor does it accept unsolicited grant application. However, inquiries are welcome via phone, letter, and e-mail. All grants are limited to programs that are designed to help the greater Greensboro community. More details on the Foundation's grant program can be found online. Grant highlights, annual reports, IRS forms, and contact information can all be found on the Web site.

W.E.D. Educational Fund (VA) (http://members.aol.com/wedfund/index.html)

The William Ervant Docter Educational Fund (W.E.D.) was established in 1998 to help American citizens of Armenian ancestry to pursue studies and training in the United States or Canada. The Fund provides grants and/or loans of up to $5,000 to worthy students regardless of age, gender, or level of education or training. Visit the Fund's Web site to find information on eligibility, recent recipient listing, application information, and downloadable application in either Microsoft Word or PDF format. Contact information is also available.

Weeden Foundation (NY) (http://www.weedenfdn.org/)

From its inception in 1963, the New York City-based Weeden Foundation (formerly the Frank Weeden Foundation) embraced the protection of biodiversity as its main priority. More recently, the Foundation has sought "to equalize distribution of grants between conservation and population programs in order to more fully address the factors driving biological impoverishment." The Foundation's well-organized Web site offers visitors a mission statement, application guidelines, an index to and summary of its grant awards for the latest fiscal year, and contact information.

Kurt Weill Foundation for Music, Inc. (NY) (http://www.kwf.org)
The Kurt Weill Foundation for Music is chartered to preserve and perpetuate the legacies of composer Kurt Weill (1900–1950) and actress-singer Lotte Lenya (1898–1981). The Foundation awards grants to individuals and not-for-profit organizations "for projects related to Weill or Lenya" in the following categories: research and travel, publication assistance, dissertation fellowships, professional and regional performance and production, college and university performance and production, recording projects, and broadcasts. In addition to detailed guidelines, application information, and a listing of grants awarded by the Foundation from 1984–1997, visitors to the Web site can read about the Weill-Lenya Research Center, the Kurt Weill Edition (a collected critical edition of Weill's works), and the Kurt Weill Prize. Listings of Foundation staff and board members, information about copyright and licensing permissions, and contact information are also provided.

Weingart Foundation (CA) (http://www.weingartfnd.org)
The Weingart Foundation focuses its grantmaking efforts on programs serving children and youth in the southern California area, with secondary attention paid to institutions and agencies benefiting the southern California community in general. The Foundation's Web site serves as an online version of its current annual report and offers a biography of founder Ben Weingart, financial statements for both the current and past year, brief profiles of eight grantees, grant guidelines and application procedures, downloadable application forms, and descriptions of grants $25,000 or more paid in the following categories: crisis intervention, education, health and medicine, community youth programs, higher education, culture and the arts, and adult community services. Visitors to the site will also find a new bulletin board service for grantseekers.

The Robert A. Welch Foundation (TX) (http://www.welch1.org)
The Robert A. Welch Foundation was established in 1952 with the estate of Robert A. Welch, who made his fortune in oil and minerals. From his association with scientists, geologists, and petroleum engineers, Robert Welch determined over the course of his career and life that that the pursuit of chemistry and chemical research held "great potential for the vast good and would continue to have a valuable impact on business, industry, global leadership and the human condition." Accordingly, his Houston, Texas-based Foundation supports fundamental chemical research at educational institutions within the state of Texas. It has a research grant program, department grant program, and the Welch Award in Chemistry, which recognizes important chemical research contributions that have a significant, positive influence on mankind. Consult the Foundation's Web site for grant guidelines, application instructions, newsletter, and contact information.

Wellmark Foundation (IA)
(http://www.wellmark.com/community/wellmark_foundation/wellmark_foundation.htm)
The Wellmark Foundation, established in 1992 in Des Moines, Iowa, is a joint venture between the Wellmark Blue Cross/Blue Shields of Iowa and South Dakota, concentrating on health-related projects in those two states. The Foundation's mission is to "efficiently and effectively facilitate the continuous improvement of health status within Iowa and South Dakota communities," mainly by providing seed money to organizations that will establish or expand health care in local communities. Other specific areas of interest to the Foundation are quality care for chronic conditions, prevention of acute episodes of disease, cancer screenings, tobacco use, and immunizations. The Wellmark Foundation Web site includes an overview of the Foundation's activities, publications and conferences, and specific information for grantseekers: proposal review criteria, outline, and instructions; a list of past grantees; and contact information.

Wender-Weis Foundation for Children (CA) (http://www.wenderweis.org)

Based in Palo Alto, California, the Wender-Weis Foundation for Children was founded in 1994 by Amy Wender to provide charitable relief and assistance to at-risk, disadvantaged children throughout the San Francisco Bay Area. Visit the Web site for contact information.

Wenner-Gren Foundation for Anthropological Research, Inc. (NY) (Operating foundation) (http://www.wennergren.org)

The Wenner-Gren Foundation for Anthropological Research, Inc. was created and endowed in 1941 by Axel Leonard Wenner-Gren, and originally was known as The Viking Fund, Inc. Its mission is "to encourage significant and innovative research on the human species and to foster the development of an international community of anthropological scholars." The Foundation supports research in all branches of anthropology, including cultural/social anthropology, ethnology, biological/physical anthropology, archaeology, anthropological linguistics, and closely related disciplines concerned with human origins, development, and variation. It has five grantmaking program areas: Small Grants Program, for basic research in all branches of anthropology; Conference and International Symposium Program, which funds conferences; Developing Countries Training Fellowships, for scholars and advanced students from developing countries seeking additional training in anthropology to enhance their skills or to expand or develop their areas of expertise; Historical Archives Program, to encourage the preservation of unpublished records and other materials of value for research on the history of anthropology; and International Collaboration Research Grants, to assist anthropological research projects undertaken jointly by two (or more) investigators from different countries. The New York City-based Foundation also sponsors *Current Anthropology,* an international journal of general anthropology. Visit the Web site for further program information; application instructions; grant lists; contact information; listing of trustees, staff and advisory council; and list of related links.

Whitaker Foundation (VA) (http://www.whitaker.org/)

The Whitaker Foundation primarily supports research and education in biomedical engineering. Since its inception in 1975, the Foundation has awarded approximately hundreds of millions of dollars to colleges and universities for faculty research, graduate fellowships, and program development. In the field of biomedical engineering, the Foundation funds research grants, graduate fellowships, development awards, special opportunity awards, a teaching materials program, industrial internships, leadership awards, and conference awards. Visitors to the Foundation's Web site will find detailed program announcements and application guidelines with downloadable applications in PDF format; a copy of the most recent annual report, including lists of grantees; research grants program abstracts; and news from the Foundation. The site is searchable and provides links to BMEnet, the Biomedical Engineering Network, which is maintained at Purdue University under a grant from the Foundation.

The Ryan White Foundation (IN) (http://www.ryanwhite.org)

Ryan White was a hemophiliac who contracted HIV through blood-clotting products he received to treat his condition. He was ostracized by his community, but his fight against AIDS and against people's ignorance propelled him into the national spotlight before his death in 1990. In 1991, his mother, Jeanne White, and Phil Donahue founded the Ryan White Foundation to carry on his legacy. Located in Indianapolis, Indiana, the Ryan White Foundation was established to increase awareness of personal, family, and community issues related to HIV and AIDS. The Foundation seeks to increase understanding and acceptance of people with HIV/AIDS through education and to inform and educate target populations and community groups about HIV/AIDS. Its target populations include youth, parents, and schools. The Foundation's mini-grant program awards grants for nonprofit youth organizations across the country to develop HIV/AIDS awareness and education programs. Consult the Web site for grant information and printable application. Visitors to the Web site will also find Ryan White's story, facts on AIDS and HIV, educational materials, links and information on AIDS-related resources, and contact information.

Whitehall Foundation, Inc. (FL) (http://www.whitehall.org)
The Whitehall Foundation, located in Palm Beach, Florida, assists scholarly research in the life sciences. Currently, it is focused exclusively on assisting basic research (excluding clinical) in vertebrate and invertebrate neurobiology in the United States. Research should specifically concern neural mechanisms involved in sensory, motor, and other complex functions of the whole organism as these relate to behavior, and the overall goal should be to understand behavioral output or brain mechanisms of behavior. Funding is provided through the Research Grants and Grants-in-Aid Programs. Research grants are available to established scientists of all ages working at accredited institutions in the United States, range from $30,000 to $75,000 a year, and are provided for up to three years. Grants-in-Aid are designed for researchers at the assistant professor level who have difficulties in competing for research funds because they are not yet firmly established; Grants-in-Aid are also made to senior scientists. These grants are awarded for a one-year period and do not exceed $30,000. Applications will be judged on their scientific merit and innovative aspects. Consult the Web site for further program information, application procedures, grants lists, and contact information.

Helen Hay Whitney Foundation (NY) (http://www.hhwf.org/)
The Helen Hay Whitney Foundation was established and endowed by Mrs. Charles S. Payson, the former Joan Whitney, in 1943 and named in honor of her mother, Helen Hay Whitney. Originally established to stimulate and support research in the area of rheumatic fever and rheumatic heart disease, the Foundation later expanded its interests to include diseases of connective tissue and, ultimately, all basic biomedical sciences. The Helen Hay Whitney Foundation supports early postdoctoral research training in all basic biomedical sciences. To attain its ultimate goal of increasing the number of imaginative, well-trained and dedicated medical scientists, the Foundation makes grants of financial support of sufficient duration to help further the careers of young men and women engaged in biological or medical research. The Foundation's Web site includes a board list, biannual newsletter, a listing of fellowship recipients, eligibility information, and contact information.

Wilburforce Foundation (WA) (http://www.wilburforce.org/)
The Seattle-based Wilburforce Foundation awards grants in the areas of the environment and population stabilization to nonprofit organizations operating in the Pacific Northwest, Alaska, and the Canadian province of British Columbia. The Foundation's well-designed Web site offers detailed information on the types of grants and support awarded, grant proposal guidelines and application information, a list of the Foundation's 1997 grants, a map of the Foundation's funding regions and grants made in each geographic location, and a wide variety of useful links to organizations and online news articles about the planet.

Catherine Holmes Wilkins Foundation (WA) (http://fdncenter.org/grantmaker/wilkins/)
The Seattle, Washington-based Catherine Holmes Wilkins Foundation was created by the Will of Catherine Holmes Wilkins to provide charitable grants to qualified medical research and social service agencies in the Puget Sound region. Funding priorities of the Foundation include medical research and education, physically handicapped and mentally ill, and services for the needy. Visitors to the Foundation's folder on the Center's Web site will find specific information on the Foundation's areas of interest, Foundation policies, application procedures, and contact information.

Willary Foundation (PA) (http://www.willary.org)
The Willary Foundation, a small family foundation based in Scranton, Pennsylvania, makes grants for organizations and individuals in Lackawanna and Luzerne Counties. The Foundation seeks to foster both individuals and groups with unique, innovative, or unusual ideas and efforts and is disposed to leveraging the impact of its grants by encouraging efforts that could have a ripple effect in the community or by supporting projects in conjunction with other sources of funding. The Foundation is particularly interested in projects that support leadership and the development of leadership in business, the economy, education, human services, government, the arts, media, and research. In addition to

a mission statement, visitors to the Foundation's Web site will find a history of the Foundation's recent grantmaking activities and financial activity, the Foundation's online Form 990-PF, a discussion board, printable grant application and grant evaluation forms, a listing of the Foundation's board and staff, and contact information.

The Windham Foundation, Inc. (VT) (http://www.windham-foundation.org)

The Windham Foundation was established in 1963 by Dean Mathey, a prominent investment banker who had long family ties to Grafton, Vermont. The Grafton-based Foundation was established with "a three-fold purpose: to restore buildings and economic vitality in the village of Grafton; to provide financial support for education and private charities; and to develop projects that will benefit the general welfare of Vermont and Vermonters." Links are provided on the site to some of the Foundation's restoration projects. The Foundation awards scholarships to Windham County residents who are studying at the undergraduate level or who are high school graduates pursuing a certificate in a trade or technical setting. Application instructions and an electronic scholarship application are available on the Web site. The Foundation also maintains a grants program that supports elementary and secondary educational organizations in Vermont. Prospective applicants will find application instructions and a downloadable grant application cover sheet on the site. Visitors to the Web site will also find a history of the Foundation, its annual report, a search engine for the site, links to Foundation projects, and an online contact form.

The Wolf Aviation Fund, (PA) (http://www.wolf-aviation.org)

Located in Philadelphia, Pennsylvania, the Wolf Aviation Fund was created to help individuals work together to support general aviation. The Foundation's mission is to "promote and support the advancement of personal air transportation by seeking and funding the most promising individuals and worthy projects which advance the field of general aviation; by increasing the public's knowledge of aviation through publications, seminars, and other information media; by informing the aviation and scientific community of the existence and purpose of the Fund." The programs sponsored by the Fund include Developing Public Policy and Airports; Networking and Mutual Support; Development and Alternative Resources; Communications, Media, and Community Relations; General Aviation Technology, Safety, and Noise; Outreach: Improving Public Understanding and Perceptions; and Aviation and Space Education. The extensive text–filled Web site includes previous grants made, numerous related links, specific grant guidelines and procedures, staff/board members, and contact information.

The Wood Family Foundation (WA) (http://fdncenter.org/grantmaker/wood/)

The Wood Family Foundation of Seattle, Washington, was established in 1997 to enhance the lives of women and children. Specifically, the Foundation provides support for at-risk teens and young adults living in poverty, preventing domestic violence and sexual assault, improving lives of low-income women, and encouraging philanthropy among teens and young people. Visitors to the Foundation's folder on the Center's Web site will find application guidelines, a listing of officers, restrictions, application deadlines, and contact information.

Robert W. Woodruff Foundation, Inc. (GA) (http://www.woodruff.org/)

Known for the first fifty years of its existence as the Trebor Foundation, the Robert W. Woodruff Foundation was renamed in 1985 in honor of the man who, over six decades, guided the Coca-Cola Company from a regional soft-drink enterprise to a multinational conglomerate with one of the most recognizable trademarks in the world—and who, through the Foundation, gave generously to a wide range of charitable and cultural organizations in Atlanta, the state of Georgia, and nationwide. Today, the Atlanta-based Woodruff Foundation focuses its giving in the areas of elementary, secondary, and higher education; health care; human services, particularly for children and youth; economic development and civic affairs; art and cultural activities; and conservation of natural resources and environmental protection. It also has been seeking ways in which it can help achieve "systemic improvement in public education, health care access, and family, children, and youth services at the state and local levels." Most, but not all, of the Foundation's grantmaking is limited to tax-exempt organizations operating in Georgia, and organizations seeking support are encouraged to make an informal inquiry before submitting a proposal. Visitors to the Foundation's Web site will find general background information and a brief biography of Robert W. Woodruff, grant application guidelines, an analysis of the Foundation's recent grants, a copy of its latest Form 990-PF, and contact information.

Woods Charitable Fund, Inc. (NE) (http://www.4w.com/woods/index.html)
Based in Lincoln, Nebraska, the Woods Charitable Fund seeks to "strengthen the community by improving opportunities and life outcomes for all people in Lincoln. . . ." The Fund supports organizations that "are exploring creative alternatives and promoting more just, effective approaches to meet community needs." Within its limited geographic scope, the Fund's special funding interests are in the program areas of children, youth, and families; education; community development and housing; and arts and humanities. In addition to a history of the Fund and the affiliated Woods Fund of Chicago, the Fund's Web site provides general information on its funding interests and limitations, a summary of grants by areas of interest, and a listing of the Fund's board of directors.

David, Helen, and Marian Woodward Fund-Atlanta (GA) (http://www.wachovia.com/trust/woodward_overview.asp)
The David, Helen, and Marian Woodward Fund was established in 1974 in Atlanta to "benefit non-profit institutions, corporations, and associations which are located in Georgia or one of its neighboring states and which are organized and operated exclusively for religious, educational and charitable and scientific purposes and to governmental agencies to which contributions by individuals are made deductible from income by the Internal Revenue laws." The Web site includes grant guidelines, a grant application downloadable in PDF format, recent grants awarded, and a listing of committee members.

The Frank Lloyd Wright Foundation (AZ) (http://www.franklloydwright.org)
Frank Lloyd Wright, recognized as "one of the 20th Century's greatest architects," established this Foundation in 1940 to perpetuate the Taliesen Fellowship, a "self-sustaining community of apprentices and architects who would learn and practice the philosophy of organic architecture by sharing in architectural work, building construction and the related arts." Located in Scottsdale, Arizona, the Foundation is "committed to advancing the ideas and principles of organic architecture, organic education and conservation of the natural environment" and "seeks to preserve and enhance the lifetime contributions and ideas of Frank Lloyd Wright and make available to the public opportunities to study and experience organic architecture." The Foundation provides for the continued operation, maintenance and reservation of Taliesin (Spring Green, WI) and Taliesin West (Scottsdale, AZ), which were Wright residences during his life; architectural, educational, environmental and cultural centers; and sites of public outreach and apprenticeship programs. Taliesen and Taliesen West also serve as the campus of the Frank Lloyd Wright School of Architecture. Visit the Web site to learn more about the activities of the Wright Foundation, a biography of its founder's life and works, links to related sites, and contact information.

Xeric Foundation (MA) (http://www.xericfoundation.com)
Based in Northampton, Massachusetts, the Xeric Foundation was established by Peter A. Laird, co-creator of the Teenage Mutant Ninja Turtles and Planet Racers. The Foundation offers financial assistance to self-publishing comic book creators in the United States and Canada and to nonprofit organizations in western Massachusetts. The Xeric Foundation assists comic book creators with some of the costs of self-publishing their work, though "it is not the Foundation's intention to fully support an artist/writer through the entire process of self-publishing, but to encourage creators to experience the learning process involved in working towards such a goal." The Foundation provides funds to charitable and nonprofit organizations for unique projects or services and for leveraging other funds and does not assist with operating budgets or capital costs. Visitors to the site can find a grants list, application instructions and forms, and contact information.

Grantmaking Public Charities on the Web

AAA Foundation for Traffic Safety (DC) (http://www.aaafts.org)

Located in Washington, D.C., the AAA Foundation for Traffic Safety was founded in 1947 by the American Automobile Association. The group is committed "to [researching] why motor vehicle crashes happen and educate the public about how to avoid problems on the road." The Foundation site offers products, including videos and publications, addressing various areas of interest, research reports, and quizzes that test different relevant issues for drivers. The Foundation makes grants to support research and education. All projects must address traffic safety, including those focusing on problem behaviors, novice drivers, older drivers, and combating impaired driving. The Foundation suggests that interested grantseekers e-mail a one-page summary before preparing a full proposal. There are slightly different guidelines for solicited and unsolicited proposals, with all guidelines and deadlines available on the site. The Foundation's newsletter is available online, along with a staff list and individual contact information.

Abraham Fund (NY) (http://www.coexistence.org/)

The Abraham Fund promotes constructive coexistence between Jews and Arabs within Israeli society. Named for Abraham, the common ancestor of Jews and Arabs, the Fund was founded in 1989 as a funding source for programs—cultural, educational, health related, recreational, and vocational—aimed at developing coexistence opportunities. Visitors to the Fund's Web site will find a description of the Fund and its activities, a listing of coexistence projects (grants summary and list), newsletter excerpts, a message from the chairman, contact information for the Fund in the United States and Israel, links to related Web sites, and a quiz.

The Frederick B. Abramson Memorial Foundation (DC)
(http://www.abramsonfoundation.org)

Located in Washington, D.C., The Frederick B. Abramson Memorial Foundation was created in 1991 to honor the greatly-respected member of the local legal community. The purpose of the organization is to "honor and further Fred's mentoring roles to minorities and women; his belief in the importance of education; and his devotion to the cause of legal representation for disadvantaged individuals and the public interest." This is accomplished through the distribution of two scholarship funds. The Frederick B. Abramson Memorial Scholarships are awarded to District of Columbia public high school seniors to attend four-year institutions. Academic achievement, a commitment to progressive social change, and economic need are all considered in the award decision. The Frederick B. Abramson Public Service Award is a fellowship for graduating law students to help support a year's employment at a nonprofit or a public interest law firm. The Web site offers guidelines and deadlines for each and applications that can printed out straight from the screen. Visitors will also find a board list, lists of past recipients, and information on contributing and contributors.

Academy of American Poets (NY) (http://www.poets.org/)

The Academy of American Poets of New York City was founded in 1934 to "support American poets at all stages of their careers and to foster the appreciation of contemporary poetry." The Academy awards assorted prizes ranging from $1,000–$20,000 to poets in different career stages for various accomplishments. It also distributes university and college poetry prizes at over 160 schools. There is also the Atlas Fund, which supports the publication of poetry, and the American Poets Fund, which confidentially assists poets in event of an illness or other emergency. Applications are not accepted for the latter—selected Academy members can submit nominations. Each award has its own description and application guidelines, list of past recipients, and list of judges. Deadlines are posted in each of these sections.

ACMP Foundation (NY) (http://www.acmp.net)

The Amateur Chamber Music Players, Inc. created the ACMP Foundation of New York City in 1993. The Foundation funds the organization's goal of "fostering the playing and singing of chamber music by people of all ages and skill levels." Grants are given internationally in four program areas that reflect the goals of the organization: fellowships at existing adult chamber music workshops; weekend workshops for amateur players; community music schools, youth symphonies, and similar institutions; and special events. Current special projects include an effort to encourage touring professionals to hold workshops for adult amateurs and home coaching for amateur groups that are playing together regularly. The are lists of all the different boards and contact information in the About ACMP section of the site.

Adhesive & Sealant Council Education Foundation (MD) (http://www.ascouncil.org/educationfoundation/)

The Adhesive and Sealant Council Education Foundation was created in 1987 to support a partnership between the adhesive and sealant industries and the Virginia Tech Center for Adhesive and Sealant Science. The unique partnership creates a forum for "attracting and training bright potential new employees for the adhesive and sealant industry; ready access to an academic environment and state-of-the-art equipment dedicated to adhesive and sealant science; continuing education opportunities for future and current employees; the encouragement of research in adhesive and sealant science; and communication and exchange of ideas with academia." The Advancement Fund, an annual fundraising appeal, supports many elements of the program. This includes a scholarship program for summer, undergraduate, and graduate students. The Fund also supports conventions, educational programs, meetings, campus tours, and a summer employment program within the industry. The site includes a list of contributors, information on plans for the foundation, and a description of services to the industry.

Agape Foundation (CA) (http://www.agapefn.org)

The Agape Foundation, established by pacifists and anti-war activists in Palo Alto, California, in 1969, funds nonviolent, grassroots projects in the western United States. The Foundation strives to support "projects which challenge the root causes of war and bring fresh energy and new perspectives to the ongoing movement for peace and justice." Along with a loan program and select grants, the Foundation gives out a $500 maximum Emergency

Grant Fund, and the Emmy Lefson Memorial Fund for Peace, Social Justice, and Human Rights. The Agape Web site gives a brief history of the Foundation—including previous grantees—an annual report, funding priorities, details on the grant application process, and a short FAQ.

AHP Foundation (VA) (http://www.go-ahp.org/fdn.htm)

The AHP Foundation was established in 1974 as the charitable arm of the Association for Healthcare Philanthropy. The Foundation's main focuses are the study and dissemination of information regarding healthcare development, continuing education to healthcare resource development professionals, and grants to individuals and organizations. The Foundation also provides scholarships to members to attend the Association's annual conferences; scholarship applications can be downloaded online in PDF format. The Foundation's Web site also provides a number of publications on giving trends, information on the Pooled Income Fund for nonprofit healthcare organizations, and contact information.

Aid to Artisans, Inc. (CT) (http://www.aidtoartisans.org/)

Aid to Artisans, a nonprofit organization founded in 1976 to create economic opportunities for craftspeople around the world, offers design consultation, on-site workshops, business training, and links to markets where craft products are sold. It awards 30–40 grants, ranging from $500–$1,500, every year to emerging artisans and craft-based associations worldwide. Grant application information is located in the Description of Services directory. The ATA site also offers information about ATA's direct service programs, a bulletin board of events, a description of its work and projects, and listings of its officers, directors, and staff.

AIDS Foundation of Chicago (IL) (http://www.aidschicago.org)

The AIDS Foundation of Chicago was established in 1985, spurred by the local response to the AIDS epidemic by civic leaders and health professionals, and is now the largest private sector AIDS network in the Midwest. The Foundation works "to develop and support a comprehensive system of HIV prevention and care, bringing together public and private resources, advocating for sound and compassionate public policy, and coordinating the activities of AIDS service providers." The Foundation focuses on five main areas of funding interest: HIV service delivery systems, work with policy makers, technical support, AIDS service providers, and increasing private sector support. The Foundation's Web site contains a vast amount of information and links to resources on each of these topics and many others related to HIV/AIDS. In the Provider Services section of the site, the Foundation has made available a Request for Proposal for HIV-related programs and services; the application and guidelines can be downloaded in PDF format. Other publications and forms are also available, including the Emergency Client Assistance and Rent Subsidy Program forms. The Foundation's Web site is an excellent resource; contact and information on prevention, case management, and provider services, among other topics, is readily available.

Alabama Law Foundation, Inc. (AL) (http://www.alfinc.org/)

The Alabama Law Foundation was established in 1987 to be the recipient of funds generated by the Interest on Lawyers' Trust Accounts (IOLTA) program. The Foundation distributes IOLTA grants each March in support of legal aid to the poor, to help maintain public law libraries, and to provide law-related education to the public. It also administers the Cabaniss, Johnston Scholarship Fund and the Kids' Chance Scholarship Fund. The Foundation's Web site offers a brief description of its programs.

Alabama Humanities Foundation (AL) (http://www.ahf.net)

Based in Birmingham, Alabama, the Alabama Humanities Foundation was founded in 1975 as the state's affiliate of the National Endowment for the Humanities. The Foundation's mission is "to create and foster opportunities, through grants and AHF-conducted programs, for scholars and the public together to explore human values and meanings through the humanities." The Foundation sponsors a number of programs related to the humanities, including their grants for public humanities projects. Funding policies, grant categories, and application and budget instructions are provided on the Foundation's Web site, along with grant applications for large and small grants that can be downloaded in PDF format. The Web site also provides more information on other programs sponsored by the Foundation, upcoming events, and contact information.

Alabama Textile Education Foundation, Inc. (AL) (http://www.eng.auburn.edu/department/te/resources/scho.html)

The Alabama Textile Education Foundation is associated with Auburn University's Textile Engineering Department, whose mission is to perform research and prepare students for the textile industry. The Foundation, along with other textile companies and organizations, provides financial aid based on need to students in the field. Scholarship applications can be downloaded in Microsoft Word or PDF formats online. The Auburn University Textile Engineering home page also describes current careers, advancements, and available resources in the textile industry.

Alaska Humanities Forum (AK) (http://www.akhf.org/)

The Alaska Humanities Forum seeks to enrich the civic, intellectual, and cultural lives of Alaskans through the humanities. The AHF grant program funds a variety of innovative humanities-based projects, including publications, films, lectures, exhibits, conferences, scholarly research, and public discussions. The Forum's Web site provides information about AHF's activities, along with grant guidelines and application forms in PDF format, a listing of recent grant recipients, and a nice collection of links to related resources on the Web.

Albany-Schenectady League of Arts, Inc. (NY) (http://www.artsleague.org/)

Founded in 1946, the Albany-Schenectady League of Arts is the oldest continually operating regional arts council in the United States. It provides technical and administrative services to artists and arts organizations in the 11 counties of the Capital Region of New York State. Job listings, community calendars, and news from the art world can be found on the League's Web site. Grant opportunities are also posted on the site. Those interested in learning more about the grants are encouraged to call the League directly. Contact information is listed on the site.

Alliance for Quality Education (SC) (http://www.allianceforqualityed.org)

Established in 1985, the Alliance for Quality Education was created to improve the education in every public classroom in Greenville County, South Carolina. The grants program is made up of three components. The Mini-Grant Awards Program makes grants to districts, schools, and teachers to enhance student learning. Applications can be printed straight from the screen for all three, and the previous year's recipients are listed. The Professional Development Leadership Institute is a seminar run during the summer by the Alliance to create professional development plans for the improvement of student learning. School teams of five administrators and teachers can apply. Past attendees are listed, and the application is posted when ready each year. The Healthy Schools, Healthy Communities program makes school-wide grants to "improve the physical health of public school employees, and to increase the understanding among public school employees about the direct relationship between their health and their effectiveness in schools and the implications for students." The application and a list of past recipients are available online. The site also offers a list of staff and board members and links to related resources.

Alliance of Resident Theatres (NY) (http://www.offbroadwayonline.com/aboutartny.php3)

Founded in 1972, A.R.T./New York serves hundreds of not-for-profit theatres and related organizations. Its members serve millions of theatergoers annually, constitute the single largest source of new work entering the American repertory, and have produced 15 winners of the Pulitzer Prize for Drama. A.R.T. provides low-cost office space for theater organizations, management-related technical assistance grants to small and emerging theaters, capital financing, and more. Details about A.R.T.'s programs and funds are available on the site.

Those who wish to learn more or gain support from the organization are encouraged to call, write, or e-mail using the information provided on the Web site.

Allina Health System Foundation (MN) (http://www.allinahealthsystemfoundation.com/ahs/foundation.nsf)

The Minneapolis-based Allina Health System Foundation's mission is to "promote innovation that engages citizens and changes systems to improve the health of our communities." The Foundation maintains an extensive Web site that provides a wealth of information on a number of programs, including partnerships; violence prevention; community investment; Project Decide and Project Reach, with overviews of each project; current research; news; and reports. The Grant Inquiries section gives details on the Foundation's current funding interests as well as a contact address for potential applicants.

Alpha Omicron Pi Foundation (TN) (http://www.aoiifoundation.org/)

Based in Brentwood, Tennessee, the Alpha Omicron Pi Foundation was established in 1977 to support sisters in economic need. The organization's mission is to "fund programs, which promote the intellectual, ethical and leadership development of members of Alpha Omicron Pi Fraternity and, through its philanthropic efforts, benefit the larger society." The Foundation focuses on educational awards. The Diamond Jubilee Scholarships are given to sisters who need economic support and have achieved academically and in commitment to the community and the fraternity. The Ruby Fund supports sisters, usually alumni, in extreme financial need. Educational grants allow fraternity members and chapters to participate in educational, leadership, and programmatic training and events. Finally, Arthritis Grants are made to researchers in the arthritis field by the foundation. The site offers an opportunity to contribute online and includes lists of staff and board members.

Alpha One Foundation, Inc. (FL) (http://www.alphaone.org/main.htm)

The Alpha One Foundation is a not-for-profit Florida corporation founded in early 1995 by three individuals diagnosed with alpha1-antitrypsin deficiency (Alpha-1). The vision of the organization is to "advance the means to control and cure Alpha-1 and to improve the quality of life for those with the disorder." The Foundation is committed to close collaborations with medical experts, the National Institutes of Health, the Food and Drug Administration, and industry and other organizations to jointly resolve critical issues in the field of Alpha-1 research and treatment. A number of programs and activities support research in the field of Alpha-1. To learn more about the Foundation's research programs, visit its Web site. In addition to its research programs, the Foundation also gives out research grants in several different areas. Details about each program, along with listings of past grant recipients, can be found on the site.

Alzheimer's Association (IL) (http://www.alz.org/)

The Alzheimer's Association and its more than 200 local chapters across the United States work to eliminate Alzheimer's disease through the advancement of research, while enhancing care and support services for individuals and their families. The Research area of the Association's Web site outlines its Research and Conference Grants programs, lists past grant recipients by year and state, and provides contact information for interested grantseekers. The Association's grants activities are administered by the Ronald and Nancy Reagan Research Institute, which was established by the former president and his wife in 1995. The remainder of the Association's site is devoted to news, facts, and care and medical issues related to Alzheimer's disease.

American Academy of Family Physicians Foundation (KS) (http://www.aafp.org/aafpf/)

The American Academy of Family Physicians Foundation is located in Leawood, Kansas. As the philanthropic arm of the American Academy of Family Physicians, the group is committed to "enhancing the healthcare delivered to the American people by developing and providing philanthropic resources for the promotion and support of family practice." The Joint Grant Awards Program is run in conjunction with the parent organization and is the specialty's major grant program. Individual family physicians, family medicine organizations and residency programs, qualifying faculty, and healthcare institutions can apply for support for research projects on family medicine/practice. The site includes application guidelines and deadlines and an application that can be downloaded in PDF format. The Parke-Davis Teacher Development Awards are a cash award given to a recent graduate of an ACGME-approved family practice residency program who teaches or has plans to teach family medicine part-time. Those interested should contact the Foundation to receive an application packet. There is also a program that matches local grants to medical students to perform eight-week "externships" in family medicine. There is also the Resident Repayment Program (RPP), which assists selected residents by paying 75 percent of the interest that accrues on their medical school loans. The site offers a list of state chapters that have foundations, electronic versions of selected issues of *The Bulletin* (the Foundation newsletter), and contact information.

American Antiquarian Society (MA) (http://www.americanantiquarian.org)

Established in Worcester, Massachusetts, in 1812, the American Antiquarian Society is an independent research library. The Society is devoted to "documenting the life of America's people from the colonial era through the Civil War and Reconstruction, [using] collections that include books, pamphlets, newspapers, periodicals, broadsides, manuscripts, music, children's literature, graphic arts, genealogy and local histories." The group awards three different visiting fellowships. There are many different Visiting Academic Research Fellowships, varying from short-term to twelve months, with the shorter recommended for doctoral candidates and the longer for senior scholars or those in the middle of their careers. Brief descriptions of the different fellowships are listed, along with application deadlines and directions and lists of selected former recipients and their publications. The Mellon Post-Dissertation Fellowships are nine months long and intended to allow a scholar to pursue further research or prepare a dissertation for publication. Application deadlines are posted along with information on receiving an application packet. The Fellowships for Creative Artists and Writers are for historical research that will eventually be relayed to the American people through performance. There is a list of past recipients and information on applying. The site includes information on using the library and the programs and publications offered by the society. A link to the library's catalogs and collections is also included.

The American Architectural Foundation, Inc. (DC) (http://archfoundation.org/)

The American Architectural Foundation (AAF) is a public outreach and educational organization dedicated to helping people understand the importance of architecture in their lives. The AAF "envisions a society in which everyone uses the power of architecture to enrich their lives and transform their communities." In addition to its education efforts and programs, AAF gives scholarships and grants. Scholarships are given to students who are currently attending NAAB-accredited architecture programs in the United States and RAIC-accredited programs in Canada. Descriptions of each scholarship, along with nomination forms that can be downloaded in PDF format, are available on the site. The AAF Accent on Architecture Grant Program assists local architectural foundations, AIA components, and other local design and civic organizations in producing innovative public education programming. In addition to enhancing the visibility and public understanding of architecture, this program aims to strengthen long-term relationships between communities and local design groups. Deadlines, guidelines, and the application, which can be downloaded in PDF format) are all posted on the Web site.

American Association of Airport Executives Foundation (VA) (http://www.airportnet.org)

The Alexandria, Virginia-based American Association of Airport Executives was founded in 1928 to represent the interests of managers and directors of U.S. and International airports. The AAAE Web site covers the organization's mission, board and staff, membership information, and a brief history. There is no information about the Foundation on the AAAE Web site, although contact information is provided.

The American Association of Medical Assistants Endowment (IL)
(http://www.aama-ntl.org/)

The American Association of Medical Assistants promotes the professional identity of its members and members of the medical assistants profession through continuing education and credential programs. The AAMA Web site covers educational requirements for certifications in the field and the various programs and member organizations of the AAMA. There is no information on the Endowment online, but regional contact information and membership information is available.

American Association of Spinal Cord Nurses (NY) (http://www.aascin.org)

The Jackson Heights, New York-based American Association of Spinal Cord Nurses (AASCIN) is dedicated to promoting quality care for individuals with Spinal Cord Impairment (SCI). AASCIN advances nursing practice through education, research, advocacy, healthcare policy, and collaboration with consumers and healthcare delivery systems. Founded in 1983, AASCIN is "the only nursing organization devoted exclusively to promoting excellence in meeting the nursing care needs of individuals with SCI." The Association has an awards and research grants program. Its award program includes the Outstanding Contribution to SCI Nursing Award, given to an active member of AASCIN who has demonstrated outstanding contributions that impact nationally on this specialty practice; the Excellence in SCI Clinical Performance Award, which recognizes a nurse who is a role model in providing competent and compassionate nursing care to individuals with SCI; and the Distinguished Service Award, for those who show evidence of outstanding contribution to the AASCIN through one or more of the following: leadership skills, organizational abilities or public service, significant contribution to the growth and/or functioning of the AASCIN, and demonstrated dedication toward achieving excellence in the healthcare of individuals with SCI. In its research grants program, nurses are encouraged to conduct research related to SCI nursing practice and to evaluate the effectiveness of existing programs and delivery systems related to SCI. Research projects may be clinical, educational, or administrative. Priorities include, but are not limited to, community living, education, administration, health management, and innovative approaches to SCI nursing care. Interested applicants for awards or research grants programs can request application materials and guidelines through the Association's online form, as well as request publications. Visitors to the site will find legislative updates, position statements, information on upcoming conferences, information on membership, and contact information.

American Association of University Women (DC) (http://www.aauw.org/)

The American Association of University Women promotes education and equity for women and girls through a membership organization, the AAUW Educational Foundation, and the AAUW Legal Advocacy Fund. The Education Foundation funds research on girls and education, community action projects, and fellowships and grants for outstanding women around the globe. The Legal Fund provides funds and a support system for women seeking judicial redress for sex discrimination in higher education. AAUW's Web site clearly describes the organization's fellowships, grants, and awards and provides application instructions for each category. Visitors to the site will also find membership information, AAUW research, a detailed overview of public policy issues of concern to organization members, a call for papers, and contact information.

American Bar Foundation (IL) (http://www.abf-sociolegal.org/)

The Chicago-based American Bar Foundation supports basic empirical research into the theory and functioning of the law, legal institutions, and the legal profession. The Foundation sponsors in-residence fellowship programs for postdoctoral scholars, doctoral candidates, and minority undergraduate students. The Foundation's Web site outlines each of these programs in detail and provides a downloadable application form. The site also provides an overview of current areas of research, information for prospective donors, online versions of recent annual reports, and a directory of staff members with e-mail links.

American Cancer Society, Inc. (GA) (http://www.cancer.org/)

The American Cancer Society, the largest non-government funder of cancer research in the United States, has committed more than $2 billion to finding a cure for cancer since 1946. The ACS offers a variety of research grants, training grants for health professionals, fellowships, and a clinical research professorship. Detailed information on its programs, including application forms in multiple formats for downloading, is provided in the Research area of the ACS Web site. Visitors to the site will also find a listing (including e-mail addresses) of the extramural grants administrative staff, histories of funding by research area and by state, and a Cancer Resource Center, with information about different cancers and cancer treatments, statistics, alternative therapies, and a comprehensive set of links to related resources.

The American Berlin Opera Foundation, Inc. (NY) (http://www.operafoundation.org)

The New York City-based American Berlin Opera Foundation was created by opera enthusiasts in 1985. The organization was established to send promising Americans to study and perform opera in Berlin and to then pursue professional careers in Europe. The Curt Engelhorn Scholarship is awarded to an American between the ages of 18 and 20 who is beginning his or her professional career. The application can be downloaded in PDF format or requested through an electronic form. Finalists travel to New York City at their own expense to audition at the Metropolitan Opera. Applications are due at the beginning of February. The truly elegant Web site also includes information on the founders, the trustees, and the annual gala.

American College of Obstetricians and Gynecologists (DC) (http://www.acog.org/)

The American College of Obstetricians and Gynecologists (ACOG) is "the nation's leading group of professionals providing healthcare for women." It was founded in Chicago, Illinois, in 1951 and is now based in Washington, D.C. ACOG "serves as a strong advocate for quality healthcare for women; maintains the highest standards of clinical practice and continuing education of its members; promotes patient education and stimulating patient understanding of, and involvement in, medical care; and increases awareness among its members and the public of the changing issues facing women's healthcare." Visitors to the Web site will find membership information, a listing of ACOG events and seminars, and news releases.

American Council of Learned Societies (NY) (http://www.acls.org/jshome.htm)

The ACLS is a federation of 61 national scholarly organizations that seeks to "advance humanistic studies in all fields of learning in the humanities and the related social sciences and to maintain and strengthen relations among the national societies devoted to such studies." ACLS administers several grant and fellowship programs, which are explained in detail at its Web site. Visitors to the site can also request, through an electronic order form, a brochure on the current year's competitions and will find, in addition, information about ACLS affiliates and publications and a list of links to funding, research, and institutional resources.

American Council of the Blind (DC) (http://www.acb.org/index.html)

Founded in Washington, D.C., in 1961, the American Council of the Blind strives "to improve the well-being of all blind and visually impaired people." This mission is accomplished through a variety of programs and efforts in education, public awareness, rehabilitation, cooperation with lawmakers and institutions, and a general advocacy on behalf of the blind and visually impaired. Along with a number of other resources and services available through the ACB Web site, the Council offers scholarships to post-secondary students. Interested applicants should contact the Council directly.

American Diabetes Association (VA) (http://www.diabetes.org/research)

The Alexandria, Virginia-based American Diabetes Association was founded in 1940 as a nonprofit health organization providing diabetes research, information, and advocacy. The Association supports a large number of grants and awards for Diabetes investigations and innovative research strategies. The ADA Web site provides a wealth of Diabetes-related resources along with news on past grant recipients and deadlines for upcoming grants. Forms, applications and guidelines for funding can be downloaded in Microsoft Word 6.0 and rich text formats from the Web site. Contact information is provided for questions and more details.

American Digestive Health Foundation (MD) (http://www.gastro.org/adhf/)

The American Digestive Health Foundation was founded in 1994 to improve digestive health through financial support of scientific research, medical education, and consumer awareness. The Foundation funds many awards to individuals—all levels of students and established investigators—for research into gastroenterology and hepatology. The Foundation's Web site provides a searchable, online version of its current Research Awards Book, which includes application forms to print and mail, as well as information on industry scholar awards, awards for underrepresented minorities, award recipients, and the Foundation's research funding newsletter, *Research In Focus*. The Foundation's Web site also offers information on digestive health, news, and its annual report.

American Federation for Aging Research, Inc. (NY) (http://www.afar.org/)

Founded in 1981, the American Federation for Aging Research helps scientists launch and further their careers in aging research and geriatric medicine in order to promote healthier aging. To achieve its goal, AFAR administers eight grant programs a year: AFAR Research Grants; the AFAR/Pfizer Research Grants in Cardiovascular Disease and Aging Program, the Paul Beeson Physician Faculty Scholars in Aging Research Program, the Merck/AFAR Fellowships in Geriatric Clinical Pharmacology, the John A. Hartford Foundation/AFAR Medical Student Geriatric Scholars Program, the Glenn/AFAR Scholarships for Research in the Biology of Aging, the Merck/AFAR Research Scholarships for Medical and Pharmacy Students in Geriatric Pharmacology, and the John A. Hartford Foundation/AFAR Geriatrics Centers of Excellence Program. The site describes these programs in detail and provides an interactive form for requesting application forms. Visitors to the site will also find donor information, meetings and conference information, an electronic form for requesting publications, and a listing of AFAR's board members.

American Federation of Riders (OH) (http://www.afr1982.org/index.html)

The American Federation of Riders, founded in 1982 and based in Cincinnati, Ohio, is a federation of motorcyclists dedicated to helping needy, orphaned, handicapped, abused, and/or neglected children, which it does through support of individual children and organizations. AFR has provided trust funds for orphaned children, medical grants to families, Christmas gifts and meals, and recently started a scholarship fund for college-bound high school seniors. AFR's Web site describes its support in general terms, gives a history of the organization, and provides contact information.

American Floral Endowment (IL) (http://www.endowment.org/)

The American Floral Endowment funds research and educational development in floriculture and provides development funding for the advancement of the floral industry. The Endowment's research funding is focused on Thrips (TSWV/INSV control systems, post-harvest systems for fresh cut flowers, air/soil borne disease control systems for potted plants, and development of production protocols for Minor crops), potted plants, cut flowers, and bedding plants. The Foundation also offers scholarships and paid internships to horticulture students. Information about all funding programs, including some offered by related organizations, is provided at the Endowment's Web site, along with applications for downloading. The site also lists funded programs going back to 1991, the names of proposal reviewers, news, and donor information.

American Foundation (AZ) (http://www.americanfoundation.org)

The American Foundation of Phoenix, Arizona, was established in its present state in 1997. The organization's mission is to "energetically promote and help create vast amounts of new and more effective philanthropy." This is done in three ways: helping others to establish charitable trusts and foundations; helping these, and other, foundations become more successful and efficient; and building networks between the grantees, foundations, and donors. The Foundation does have a grantmaking program. Awards are given to assist charities in developing their governance and organizational structure, to improve equipment and facilities, and to improve human resources. Applicants fill out one application, which can be downloaded from the site in PDF format, for consideration by the Foundation and the American Family of Foundations, which is made up of the smaller grantmakers. Areas of interest include education, health, environment, religion, community development, and the arts and sciences. Grants are made throughout the United States and internationally. The site includes application restrictions and deadlines, a board of directors list, and information on selected staff. There is also a list of grant recipients, extensive information on establishing a private or corporate foundation, and a special area for advisors (attorneys, accountants, etc.) to nonprofits.

American Foundation for AIDS Research, Inc. (NY) (http://www.amfar.org/)

The American Foundation for AIDS Research works to prevent death and disease associated with HIV/AIDS and to foster sound AIDS-related public policies—a goal it seeks to achieve through support of scientific and social research, advocacy, and public information programs. Requests for proposals are posted at AmFAR's Web site, along with contact information for its grant programs. Visitors to the site will also find press releases, a publications catalog, information about upcoming events and conferences, and donor information.

American Health Assistance Foundation (MD) (http://www.ahaf.org)

For over 25 year, the American Health Assistance Foundation has been supporting important medical research. The organization's goals are "funding research on age-related and degenerative disease; educating the public about these diseases; and providing emergency financial assistance to Alzheimer's disease patients and their caregivers." The Foundation has five major programs. There are research programs for Alzheimer's disease, macular degeneration, glaucoma, heart disease, and stroke. These programs all fund research and work to disseminate the resulting information. There is also an Alzheimer Family Relief Program to "provide direct financial assistance and resources for the continued care and support of the Alzheimer's patients and their caregivers." These gifts can be as large as $500. The Web site includes a downloadable application for the Relief Program and applications for all of the research programs. Visitors need PDF Reader to download any of the publications. Those who are interested can also electronically request hard copies of the applications. There are also application guidelines for the research programs and a list of the review committee members for each one. The site features ample opportunities to donate money, a list of publications, and links to important organizations in each area of research.

American Heart Association (TX) (http://www.americanheart.org)

The American Heart Association provides education and information on heart disease and stroke and supports scientific research that will help fight these life-threatening medical conditions. The AHA offers numerous national and regional affiliate research programs. The Science and Professionals area of its Web site provides guidelines for all research programs and the application form for the national programs, which can be downloaded and/or submitted electronically. This large Web site provides a great deal of educational and scientific information on heart disease, links to AFA affiliates and other resources, online advocacy, and donor and volunteer information.

Americans Helping Americans, Inc. (IL) (http://www.helpingamericans.org/)

Located in Lorton, Virginia, Americans Helping Americans supports the needs of various communities in the United States, the Appalachian community in particular. Its mission is "to join communities, build and strengthen neighbor relations, and work side by side with residences to address local concerns, linking resources supportive of a healthy, safe and economically vibrant standard of living" through various charitable programs. Project areas include community housing, water, safe houses for victims of domestic abuse, disaster relief, and school supplies, among others. More details about the group's programs can be found online, along with contact information, current news and events, a kids' page, and letters from previous program recipients.

American Hotel Foundation (DC) (http://www.ei-ahma.org/ahf/ahf.htm)
The American Hotel Foundation serves the lodging industry by providing resources for projects that assure continued growth and opportunities for the industry. The Foundation awards scholarships to students pursuing an undergraduate degree in hospitality management and awards grants for research that will benefit the industry. The Foundation's scholarship programs are outlined at its Web site; however, scholarship recipients are selected by schools, not by the Foundation. The Foundation's research is described only briefly, but contact information is provided.

American Institute of Indian Studies (IL) (http://humanities.uchicago.edu/orgs/aiis)
Since 1961, the Chicago-based American Institute of Indian Studies has been instrumental in shaping American knowledge of India. This group is a "consortium of universities and colleges in the United States at which scholars actively engage in teaching and research about India." One primary function of the group is to supply fellowship support to scholars of all aspects of Indian culture, history, and contemporary life. Thirty-five scholars a year, ranging from graduate students to established scholars and specialists, are awarded these periods of study in India. The elite Advanced Language Programs Competition is based in India and the American Institute of Indian Studies. The Institute also offers research and training programs and a list of publications. The site includes a list of member organizations and a list of the trustees and committee heads. A variety of applications, forms, and checklists are available for download in PDF format.

American Jewish World Service, Inc. (NY) (http://www.ajws.org)
The American Jewish World Service was founded in 1985 "to help alleviate poverty, hunger and disease among the people of the world" regardless of religion or race. This mission is accomplished through programs that include technical support, humanitarian aid, emergency relief, and volunteer efforts in the areas of healthcare, education, economic development and agriculture reform. The AJWS Web site details its numerous programs worldwide, provides current news and relief efforts, and contact information.

American Kennel Club Canine Health Foundation, Inc. (OH) (http://www.akcchf.org/)
Located in Aurora, Ohio, the American Kennel Club Canine Health Foundation's mission is "to develop significant resources for basic and applied health programs with emphasis on canine genetics to improve the quality of life for dogs and their owners." The Foundation funds hundreds of grants for general research as well as investigation into molecular genetics and specific diseases that are listed by disease, breed, and university and are described online. Additionally, the Foundation provides current news, newsletters, upcoming events, links to more resources, and contact information on its Web site.

American Library Association (IL) (http://www.ala.org)
The Chicago-based American Library Association (ALA) "provides leadership for the development, promotion, and improvement of library and information services and the profession of librarianship in order to enhance learning and ensure access to information for all." The ALA has numerous areas of interest and activity, but its key action areas are diversity, reflected in its commitment to recruiting people of color and people with disabilities to the profession, and the promotion and development of library collections and services of all people; education and continuous learning; providing opportunities for the professional development and education of librarians, library staff, and trustees; equity of access, serving people of all ages, income levels, locations, or ethnicities; providing the full range of information resources needed to live, learn, govern, and work; intellectual freedom; defending the right of library users to read, seek information, and speak freely as guaranteed by the First Amendment; and 21st century literacy—assisting and promoting libraries

in helping children and adults develop the skills they need to seek and effectively utilize information resources in a global information society. Visit ALA's Web site for program descriptions, application criteria, instructions, and application forms for its numerous grant, scholarship, and award programs. Visitors to the site will also find an employment section with job listings, a listing of events and conferences, news and contact information.

American Medical Women's Association Foundation (VA) (http://www.amwa-doc.org/foundation2.html)

Founded in 1915, the American Medical Women's Association strives "to advance women in medicine and improve women's health." To accomplish the Association's charitable and education goals, the AMWA Foundation was established in 1990. The Foundation seeks to educate physicians, medical students, and the general public on the issues of women's health through a variety of programs and services, including scholarship funds, the Reproductive Health Initiative, and grants to affiliates of the Associations for projects associated with the Foundation's goals. The AWMA Foundation's Web site details specific funding and programs, provides links to the *Foundation Watch* newsletter, and includes e-mail addresses for more information.

American Meterological Society (DC) (http://www.ametsoc.org/ams)

Based in Boston, Massachusetts, the American Meteorological Society's Web site is a clearinghouse of information on the meteorological sciences. Information on upcoming conferences, current news and trends in meteorology, journals, and educational opportunities are available online. Under the Education Programs and Resources link, the Society details various links and information for programs and organizations that promote science literacy in the nation's schools. Much more information is available on the Society's Web site.

American Music Center, Inc. (NY) (http://www.amc.net/home.html)

Created in 1939 by a musical group headed by Aaron Copland, the American Music Center of New York City is still flourishing. The national service organization's historic mission is to "foster and encourage the composition of contemporary music and to promote its production, publication, distribution, and performance in every way possible through the Western Hemisphere," and its new, additional mission is to "build a national community for new American music." Grants are distributed for four distinct purposes. The Margaret Fairbank Jory Copying Assistance Program assists American composers with copying their compositions for premiere performances. The Live Music for Dance Program of the Mary Flagler Cary Charitable Trust is open to New York City dance companies for live music at their performances. The Aaron Copland Fund for Music Performing Ensembles Program supports the expansion of public appreciation of new American music. The Aaron Copland Fund for Music Recording Program helps document and spread the music of contemporary American composers. Each program has a very clear and extensive page of its own where applicants can download information and applications in PDF format. The attractive site also includes information on the Center's workshops, networking groups, publications, library, and many online communication opportunities. There are also staff and board lists and special features for members.

American Occupational Therapy Foundation (MD) (http://www.aotf.org)

The American Occupational Therapy Foundation (AOTF), based in Bethesda, Maryland, seeks to advance the practice of occupational therapy. AOTF "generates funds, manages assets, and marshals human resources to ensure that society and the nation's healthcare system recognize and value the benefits of occupational therapy." The goals of the AOTF are "to secure contributions and managed assets; to promote scientific inquiry; and to support excellence in education about occupation and occupational therapy." The AOTF offers scholarships to occupational therapy students studying at the associate degree, baccalaureate degree, post-baccalaureate certificate, professional master's degree, and post-professional master's degree levels. The AOTF also seeks to foster the development of researchers within the field of occupational therapy. The site provides a listing of scholarships and application instructions, a listing of additional sources of financial aid, information on its educational and research programs, and a listing of scholarship winners. The site also features a link to the Wilma L. West Library, a national clearinghouse of occupational therapy information for AOTA members and personnel. The contents, resources related to allied health, biomedical, and psychosocial literature as well occupational therapy, are indexed in an online database. Librarians can assist in performing literature searches, obtaining factual information for specific queries, providing guidance on additional sources of information, or sending photocopies of documents in compliance with copyright laws. The site also has a link to the Doctoral Network, which promotes excellence in occupational therapy. Visit their Web site for news, events, and contact information.

American Osteopathic Association (IL) (http://www.aoa-net.org)
The mission of the American Osteopathic Association (AOA) is "to advance the philosophy and practice of osteopathic medicine by promoting excellence in education, research, and the delivery of quality, cost-effective healthcare in a distinct, unified profession." The American Osteopathic Association Bureau of Research has funded research within the osteopathic profession for many years. The purpose of the research programs is "to investigate problems that will lead to a better understanding and a more effective application of the philosophy and concepts of osteopathic medicine, and to develop the research capacity of the osteopathic profession by supporting the training and research of career track investigators." AOA has various grant programs, research fellowships, and awards. Grant and fellowship applications can be downloaded from the site. Visitors to the site will find descriptions of its programs, information on internships and residency programs for students, links to external resources, the Bureau of Research annual report, press releases, publications, and contact information.

American Pharmaceutical Association Foundation (DC) (http://www.aphafoundation.org)
Based in Washington, D.C., the American Pharmaceutical Association Foundation was created in 1952 by the APhA. The group's mission is "to enhance the quality of consumer health outcomes that are affected by pharmacy, by positively affecting consumer health outcomes through research, public education, issue forums, and awards and recognition programs." The Pharmaceutical Care effort includes grants for research and the Advance Practice Institute, a weekend program teaching new techniques and perspectives. Application deadlines for both programs are available online, and interested parties can e-mail the Foundation to request an application. Participants in both of these programs must be members of the Practice-Based Research Network. The Foundation also includes a Quality Center that supports research and gives awards for various accomplishments. The Pinnacle Awards recognize contributions to healthcare quality improvement through the medication use process. The site includes a list of past recipients, information on the awards dinner, and instructions on contacting the Foundation in order to submit a nomination. The site also features research papers, descriptions of models developed from research projects, information on contributing, and a list of publications.

American Philosophical Society (PA) (http://www.amphilsoc.org)
Established in 1743 with the support of, among others, Benjamin Franklin, the American Philosophical Society is still located in Philadelphia, Pennsylvania. This scholarly organization "promotes useful knowledge in the sciences and humanities through excellence in scholarly research, professional meetings, publications, library resources, and community outreach." The Grants program supports research by residents of the United States, American citizens working for foreign institutions, and foreign nationals whose research can only take place in America. Awards include the general research program, the Clinical Investigator Fellowships for Patient-oriented Research, the Phillips Fund grants for Native American Research; the Sabbatical Fellowship for the Humanities and Social Sciences, the Slater Fellowship in the History of Twentieth-century Physical Sciences, and the Library Resident Research Fellowships. Interested parties should send a self-addressed envelope and the requested information to the given address in order to receive an application. Each

award has its own page that includes details on eligibility and requirements and offers a list of past recipients. The Society's site also includes announcements of upcoming meetings, a publications section, and information on the group's library.

American Physicians Fellowship for Medicine in Israel (MA) (http://www.apfmed.org/)

The American Physicians Fellowship for Medicine in Israel, established in 1950, is an organization of North American physicians and others dedicated to advancing the state of medical education, research, and care in Israel. The core of APF's funding is a fellowship program for Israeli physicians training in the United States and Canada—40 physicians currently receive APF fellowship support. In recent years, APF has expanded its support to include various awards and programs benefiting the medical community in Israel. Funding areas include research projects, a trauma program, training for Russian immigrant physicians and pathology technicians, the Solomon Hirsh Nurse Fund, programs focused on women's health, Jewish genetic diseases, and geriatric medicine. APF's Web site describes its programs and provides contacts for requesting more information. The site also provides information on recent APF fellows, news, donor and membership information, a discussion forum, and a listing of staff and board members.

American Psychiatric Association (DC) (http://www.psych.org)

The Washington, D.C.-based American Psychiatric Association was founded in 1844 and consists of a group of physicians who "specialize in the diagnosis and treatment of mental and emotional illnesses and substance use disorders." The Association's Web site consists mainly of current news and events for individuals in the field, including job postings, upcoming conferences, Current Action on the Hill, breaking news, links to books and journals, and a section for members of the Association. A feedback form is also available online.

American Psychological Foundation (DC) (http://www.apa.org/apf/)

Washington, D.C.'s American Psychological Foundation was created in 1953 to "to advance the science and practice of psychology for the understanding of behavior and the benefit of human welfare." The Foundation awards assorted scholarships to high school and graduate school students demonstrating achievement in areas of psychology. It also offers grants for research in specific areas and to reward outstanding research accomplishments. Finally, the Foundation distributes achievement awards for great contributions to both the field as a whole and in certain areas of interest. The APF also sponsors an annual lecture series. The site contains application instructions and restrictions for each of the scholarships and awards, a list of the board of trustees, and information on contributing to the Foundation.

American Society of Consultant Pharmacists Research & Education Foundation (VA) (http://www.ascpfoundation.org/)

The ASCP Research and Education Foundation of Alexandria, Virginia, was founded in 1982 by the American Society of Consultant Pharmacists to support educational programs and research. "The unique focus of the Foundation is the integration and application of knowledge regarding drug use in the elderly and long-term care facility residents and the practice of long-term care and consultant pharmacy to optimize healthcare outcomes." The Foundation funds research, traineeships, fellowships, clerkships, and conferences on different areas affecting pharmacology. The Foundation is made up of two institutes that each administer programs in their specific area of interest: the Niemerov Institute, which works on long-term care and consultant pharmacy practice, and the Geriatric Drug Therapy Research Institute, which supports the study of diseases that disable elderly people and the use of drugs to treat these conditions. Traineeships are competitive five-day programs in fields ranging from specific diseases (Alzheimer's, AIDS, etc.) to wound care. The site includes information on each traineeship, applications, and guidelines. The current guidelines are for 1999, and the deadlines have already passed. There is also information on electronic and print publications and a collection of press releases. The Facts section includes information on each of the awards and the basic application guidelines.

American Society of Health-System Pharmacists Research and Education Foundation (MD) (http://www.ashpfoundation.org)

The Bethesda, Maryland-based American Society of Health-System Pharmacists Research and Education Foundation was established in 1968 "to foster research and educational activities that enable health-system pharmacists to expand their capacity to help people make the best use of medicines." The ASHP places priority on projects that have a high impact on public health, and the Foundation funds various awards, grants, and traineeships. The ASHP Foundation Literature Awards Program has awards for researchers, pharmacy professionals, and students. The Foundation maintains a detailed list of current research grants and traineeships. Visitors to the ASHP Research and Education Foundation Web site will find guidelines, limitations, criteria, and funding aspects of its research grants program and traineeships, as well as past grants and current news and events from the Foundation.

American Society of Newspaper Editors Foundation (VA) (http://www.asne.org)

Based in Reston, Virginia, the American Society of Newspaper Editors is made up of directing editors of daily newspapers. The organization is "committed to fostering the public discourse essential to democracy; helping editors maintain the highest standards of quality, improving their craft and better serving their communities; and preserving and promoting core journalistic values, while embracing and exploring change." The associated Foundation, along with member contributions and a long-standing endowment, fund the group's writing awards, which are distributed by Florida's Poynter Institute. There are four $2,500 awards to recognized excellence in Non-Deadline Writing, Commentary/Column Writing, Editorial Writing, and Diversity. There are also two $10,000 awards given to an individual and a team being recognized for their Deadline Reporting. The site includes extensive information on ASNE, including a list of board members, copies of the board minutes, the bylaws of the groups, and archives of the annual convention. There is information on the annual convention, the group's newspaper, an events calendar, and links to related sites. There are background and position papers on ASNE's current special focus on diversity in the newsroom. There is an award application that can be printed from the screen and a list of past award recipients. The only direct mention of the Foundation is in the Foundation Board's minutes in the Kiosk section.

American Speech-Language-Hearing Association Foundation (MD) (http://www.ashfoundation.org)

The American Speech-Language-Hearing Association Foundation of Rockville, Maryland, was established in 1946 by Wendell Johnson. The organization's mission is to "advance knowledge about the causes and treatment of hearing, speech, and language problems." The three primary giving programs are Research Grants, Graduate Scholarships, and Clinical Recognition Awards. Research grants include $2,000–$5,000 awards for doctoral degree recipients researching speech communication and graduate and postgraduate students wanting to study audiology or early childhood language development. Graduate scholarships are offered for students demonstrating outstanding academic performance in the related fields—with specific grants for those with disabilities and for international/minority students. There is also a scholarship for minority students who are seniors in college who have been accepted in a graduate speech-language pathology or audiology program. Outstanding Lifetime Achievement, Outstanding Recent Achievement, and Outstanding Schools-Related Achievement Awards are given in the clinical recognition category. The site includes a contact address to order application materials as they become available. Visitors will also find a list of board members, opportunities to contribute, a list of current sponsors, and an events calendar.

American Symphony Orchestra League (NY) (http://www.symphony.org)

Established in 1942, and then chartered by Congress in 1962, the American Symphony Orchestra League is a member organization headquartered in New York City. The group is committed to "providing leadership and service to American orchestras while communicating to the public the value and importance of orchestras and the music they perform." The League organizes conferences, meetings, research and analysis, professional development, and career opportunities in and on topics appealing to its membership. In addition, the organization tracks and issues industry news, advocates for its constituent membership with the government, and offers orchestra products and services. The Orchestra Management Fellowship Program trains a limited number of highly qualified individuals to learn about being executive directors of orchestras. The applications can be filled in and then printed from the screen. The expansive site includes information on all of the above-mentioned membership benefits, a special section for kids, and links to other related sites created by the League.

Amit Women, Inc. (NY) (http://www.amitchildren.org)

Based in New York City, Amit Women was founded in 1925 to support Israel and the Jewish people. The organization's goals include "nurturing and educating Israel's children to become self-reliant and self-respecting; educating thousands of unprivileged youngsters throughout the length and breadth of Israel; instilling a love of Torah and Jewish tradition; providing children from dysfunctional homes with joy of real family life in family group homes; absorbing and training Ethiopian and Russian youngsters; and developing Israel's young scientific talent." The agency supports many schools and educational programs in Israel as a result of successful fundraising and organizing at chapters throughout the United States. The Web site offers addresses for the major branches and contact information for its headquarters. The Schools section lists and describes the schools being supported in Israel, grouping them by city. There are selected articles from the newsletter online, along with press releases and other news involving Amit.

Irene W. & Guy L. Anderson Children's Foundation (CA) (http://www.andersongrants.org)

The Anderson Children's Foundation was established in 1970 by Irene Anderson in memory of her late husband to serve the needs of the children of the Coachella Valley, near Palm Springs, California. The Foundation makes grants to a wide variety of nonprofit organizations serving children in the area, with maximum grants of $15,000. The Foundation's thorough Web site includes reports on recipients of past grants, grant-writing tips, current grants and application procedures, and contact information. Applications can be downloaded from the Foundation's Web site once an initial request is made.

ANGELCARE (CA) (http://www.angelcare.org)

Based in San Diego, California, ANGELCARE was incorporated in 1977 as Children's Aid International by a Vietnam War veteran who wanted to help the Vietnamese Boat People. The organization's goal is to "provide worldwide help to poor and needy children and families with food, clothing, medical care, medicines, parenting skills, schooling, and anti-drug programs through Child Sponsorship and emergency relief." One of the group's primary programs is its child sponsorship program. "Angels" donate $23 per month for the benefit of a particular child who receives food, education, health and dental assistance, and varied other support. A small percentage of each monthly donation goes toward administrative overhead and toward the family's medical care and community development projects. ANGELCARE has sponsorship programs in communities throughout the world, including Belarus (the victims of Chernobyl), Guatemala, and South Central Los Angeles, with benefits specifically catered to the needs of those people. The organization supports small, concentrated projects that might not be able to get funding otherwise. The Web site gives many opportunities for a visitor to donate a one-time gift or begin a sponsorship. There are also descriptions of the various projects, features on needy children, and information on volunteer opportunities. There is very basic financial information offered.

Ann Arbor Film Festival (MI) (http://aafilmfest.org)

The Ann Arbor Film Festival is a nonprofit arts organization that showcases 16mm independent and experimental films. Founded in 1963 by filmmaker/artist George Manupelli at the University of Michigan School of Art, it is the oldest festival of its kind in the United States. Now independent of the University and under the direction of Vicki Honeyman, the Ann Arbor Film Festival's mission is "to provide a worldwide public forum for 16mm film screenings, to encourage and showcase independent & experimental film artists, to promote film as art, and to offer educational outreach." The Ann Arbor Film Festival is open to films in all categories that demonstrate a high regard for film as an art form. Those interested in entering the festival must submit an application form and an entry fee along with their film. The entry form, which contains the Festival's mailing address, can be printed from the Web site. The site also contains contact information, deadlines and festival dates, and festival procedures.

Aplastic Anemia & MDS International Foundation (MD) (http://www.aamds.org/)

The Aplastic Anemia & MDS International Foundation works to find the causes of and cures for aplastic anemia, myelodysplastic syndromes, and other kinds of bone marrow failure. The Foundation funds scientific research into these conditions. A brief description of its Research Awards program is provided at AAFA's Web site with contact information for requesting an application packet. The site also offers a newsletter, donor information, and related Web links.

Appalachian Community Fund (TN) (http://www.korrnet.org/appafund/)

Created in 1986, the Appalachian Community Fund of Knoxville, Tennessee, supports organization in central Appalachia, eastern Kentucky, southwest Virginia, east Tennessee, and all of West Virginia. The fund is "a regionally based and controlled grant-making organization for work on economic, environmental, social and racial justice issues." Only programs that are directly tied to grassroots organizing for social change are eligible for funding. Grantees support diverse communities, including low and moderate income working class people, women, people of color, gay and lesbian persons, and people with disabilities." Areas of interest include workers' rights, race and affirmative action, gender and sexual preference issues; domestic violence, training indigenous leaders and young people as activists, environmental justice, and alternative arts and media. The site includes application guidelines, a list of grantees and features on other past grant recipients, information on contributing, and a staff list.

American Dietetic Association Foundation (IL) (http://www.adaf.org)

Established in 1966 to promote good nutrition, the American Dietetic Association Foundation focuses on public awareness, education, and research in the science of dietetics. The Foundation provides grants and scholarships to dietetics students and professionals in the United States and internationally. The Foundation focuses on a specific research interest yearly, outlined online. More details about scholarship and grant programs, current news and events at the Foundation, the *Insider's Report* publication, and contact information are also available at the Foundation's Web site.

Arizona Diamondbacks Charities, Inc. (AZ) (http://www.azdiamondbacks.com/community/index.shtml)

Arizona Diamondbacks Charities is a newly established nonprofit corporation that generates and distributes contributions to nonprofit organizations that provide services to promote positive growth and development for the residents of Arizona. The Diamondbacks is a baseball organization based in Maricopa County in Arizona. The charity directs its efforts to housing for the homeless and low-income residents, indigent healthcare, and children's programs of all types, including education. A 13-member board of team and county appointees is responsible for the approval of applications for financial assistance. Visit the Website for grant guidelines, an FAQ sheet, and a downloadable grant application.

Arizona Humanities Council (AZ) (http://www.azhumanities.org/)

The Arizona Humanities Council, founded in 1973 as the state affiliate of the National Endowment for the Humanities, directs and supports programs that promote understanding of human thoughts, actions, creations, and values. AHC provides support in four program areas: heritage, books and reading, community dialogue, and teacher education. In addition to its Competitive Grants Program, AHC award General Grants, Proposal Development Grants, Resource Center Grants, and Book Bucks. The programs are described at AHC's

Web site with contacts for requesting application instructions. AHC's site also features a list of Arizona humanities scholars, news, a calendar, resources, and donor information.

Arkansas Humanities Council (AR) (http://www.arkhums.org/)

The Arkansas Humanities Council, established in 1974 as the state affiliate of the National Endowment for the Humanities, promotes understanding, appreciation, and use of the humanities in Arkansas. To achieve its goal, the council awards grants to groups and organizations to plan, conduct, and evaluate projects in the humanities. Funding is provided for public programs, research, publications, media projects, and planning, as well as occasional matching grants. Thorough guidelines are provided at the Council's Web site; however, prospective applicants are encouraged to consult with council program staff before submitting grant applications. Visitors to the site will also find descriptions of materials held in the Council's Resource Center.

Art Omi International Art Center (NY) (http://www.artomi.org)

Located in Omi, New York, in the Hudson Valley, Art Omi is an "international arts center for visual artists, writers and musicians as well as the site for The Fields Sculpture Park, a year round public exhibition space for contemporary sculpture." The Center houses three residency programs: the Art Omi International Artists' Colony, the Ledig House International Writers' Colony, and the Music Omi International Residency, all of which are described in more detail on the Center's Web site. The Center also hosts public and educational programs throughout the year. Application guidelines, details on current residents and programs, and other fellowships and prizes associated with the Artists' and Writers' Colonies, along with contact addresses for completed applications, are provided online.

Arthritis Foundation, Inc. (GA) (http://www.arthritis.org/)

The Arthritis Foundation, which was organized in 1948 as the Arthritis and Rheumatism Foundation until its name was changed in 1964, generated initial research into arthritis and now supports research to help find causes, treatments, and ways to prevent and cure the condition. The grants, training awards, and career development awards provided by the Foundation are detailed at its Web site with an application form to download (in PDF format). The Research area of the Foundation's Web site also provides information on its peer review process, Study Section members (grant application reviewers), and the Lee C. Howley Sr. Prize for Research in Arthritis—awarded for excellence in research.

Arts and Cultural Council for Greater Rochester (NY) (http://www.artsrochester.org)

The Arts and Cultural Council for Greater Rochester was formed "to develop, promote and strengthen the cultural industry for the benefit of the people of the Rochester, (NY) region." There are three types of grants distributed. Community Arts Grants are given through two funds, one that supports groups and individuals in Monroe County who benefit the county, and the other that supports capacity-building projects for organizations with budgets less than $250,000. Guidelines and applications are available. Culture Builds Communities is a neighborhood art program in city neighborhoods. Special Opportunity Stipends (SOS) are given to individuals to "significantly benefit their work or career." Deadlines are listed, and a link is given to the New York Foundation for the Arts Web site, where the application can be downloaded. Each of the programs' pages lists the latest recipients. The site also offers information on the board, staff, membership, and current programs.

Arts and Education Council of Greater St. Louis (MO) (http://www.stlartsanded.org)

The Arts and Education Council of Greater St. Louis works to support and promote "song, dance, drama and creative energy in schools, on stages and in performances throughout the region." The very bare site does specify the development of an awareness campaign and reports on the initial findings of a focus group's thoughts on the arts in the area. There are also updates on past events, a list of member organizations, an events calendar, and a synopsis of the most recent annual report. There is contact information on the opening page for any visitors interested in more information.

Arts and Humanities Assembly of Boulder, Inc. (CO) (http://www.tesser.com/AHAB/)
The Arts and Humanities Assembly of Boulder, Colorado, is the only multi-disciplinary arts agency in the county. The group works to "provide leadership and resources for arts organizations, artists, educators and the Boulder County community." Grant support is distributed through four different programs. The AHAB Endowment Grant Program is the largest of these and is open to individuals and art organizations. The AHAB/Tesser Awards Program supports one to four artists or organizations presenting multi-disciplinary performances. The AHAB/Milash Award Program gives one annual grant to a visual artist working with paint or brushstroke. Finally, the AHAB/Addison Mini-Grant Program distributes about $9,000 between 30–40 people and groups. Applications for each program can be downloaded on the site in Microsoft Word format. Another major component of the Assembly is artist services. One-time technical assistance is given in the form of seminars. The agency serves as a sponsor for individuals who are not their own nonprofit organization and even makes e-mail and address lists available to artists needing to reach the community. The somewhat barren Web site has an extensive list of members (organizations and individuals) available in the Links section, including many e-mail links. There is a list of contributors and alerts for upcoming events.

Arts Council of Greater Kalamazoo (MI) (http://www.kazooart.org/)
The Arts Council of Greater Kalamazoo, founded in 1969, supports the arts in Kalamazoo County, Michigan. Funds are granted on the basis of high artistic quality and merit to artists and organizations in the region. The Council's Web site offers a list of grant programs and provides more detailed arts funding information in its *New You Can Use* newsletter—available in HTML or PDF formats. Visitors to the site will also find membership information, press releases, events, information on Council activities, an artists registry, and contact information.

Arts Council of Indianapolis, Inc. (IN) (http://www.indyarts.org)
The Arts Council of Indianapolis supports hundreds of arts organizations and artists. The group's mission is to "build the community through the arts by developing visibility, funding, audiences, information, and partnerships." The Council's grant program is made up of three different components: the Annual Grant Program for Organizations, the Mini-Grant Program, and the Creative Renewal Arts Fellowship Program for Professional Individual Artists & Arts Administrators. The first is the city's official means of supporting the arts and an application can be downloaded in Microsoft Word format from the Web site. The middle program is restricted to Marion County and the last is a unique program to support individual artists. The Web site offers information and tickets for art events throughout the city, details on workshops and seminars for organizations, and a relevant publications list.

The Arts Council of Northwest Florida, Inc. (FL) (http://www.artsnwfl.org/)
The Arts Council of Northwest Florida supports quality, diversity, and economic growth in the region's cultural community. The Council awards grants to organizations to improve, extend, preserve, create, and plan cultural programs. Grant guidelines, the application form, and a grants calendar are available for download from the Council's Web site in rich text and Microsoft Word formats. The site also provides information on the Council's activities and programs, links to northwest Florida cultural institutions, news articles, and donor information.

Arts Midwest (MN) (http://www.artsmidwest.org/)
Formed in 1985 through the merger of two organizations, the Affiliated State Arts Agencies of the Upper Midwest and the Great Lakes Arts Alliance, Arts Midwest provides funding, training, publications, information services, and conferences to arts and cultural organizations, artists, art administrators, and art enthusiasts in Illinois, Indiana, Iowa, Michigan, Minnesota, North Dakota, Ohio, South Dakota, and Wisconsin. Since its inception, the organization has distributed almost $8 million to artists and arts organizations through a variety of funding and training programs. At present, it manages four funding programs: the Performing Arts Touring Fund, Meet the Composer/Midwest, Jazz Satellite

Touring Fund, and the Jazz Master Awards. The latter serves individual artists in Arts Midwest's nine-state region. The other programs assist presenters in the region in bringing Midwestern artists as well as national artists to their communities. Visitors to the AM Web site will find a variety of program, application, conference, and publication information.

Arts United of Greater Fort Wayne, Inc. (IN) (http://www.artsunited.org)

The third-oldest united arts fund in the country, Arts United of Greater Fort Wayne (Indiana) was established in 1955. "The umbrella organization for the arts in northeast Indiana, [Arts United] raises funds and awareness of the area's many excellent cultural organizations." The organization raises money for a variety of funds through various annual appeals. Funding is given to member and affiliate organizations and is used towards the upkeep of Arts United's facilities. The site includes staff, board, and fundraising committee lists; a list of funded/affiliate organizations; and information on the assorted ways to contribute. There is also a page with links to related resources.

ArtServe Michigan (MI) (http://artservemichigan.org/)

The organization serves, supports, advocates for an enriched cultural environment, and promotes the arts as a valuable state and community resource. It assists and informs individuals and organizations in the state of Michigan through education, professional services, networking, support of artists and cultural organizations, volunteer assistance, and collaborations. Its Web site includes information on grants and awards for individual artists, a listing of the board of directors, news about arts advocacy, and more.

The ASCAP Foundation (NY) (http://www.ascapfoundation.org)

Located in New York City, the ASCAP Foundation is "dedicated to nurturing the music talent of tomorrow, reserving the legacy of the past and sustaining the creative incentive for today's musically gifted through a variety of educational, professional, and humanitarian programs and activities which serve the entire music community." The organization funds a series of scholarships for musically gifted students, ranging from high school seniors to graduate students. Each award has specific requirements, often for a specific high school and/or college, and is distributed by the school or conservatory. Therefore the Foundation does not accept applications for any of the scholarships. A series of awards are given by the Foundation to exemplary composers and songwriters. These awards range from a Lilith Fair award for female songwriters to a Richard Rodgers award for musical theater. Although about half of the awards only consider nominated entrants, many of the awards do have applications and deadlines (or links to those) available on the site. The Foundation sponsors workshops, development programs, and residencies in affiliation with institutions around the country. Various application directions and scholarship information is briefly mentioned in the descriptions. Finally, the Foundation organizes performances to entertain assorted elderly and sick audiences. There is a single page with a collection of the application instructions for each of the programs. A list of Foundation officers and board members is also offered.

Asia Foundation (CA) (http://www.asiafoundation.com/)

The Asia Foundation is a private, nonprofit, nongovernmental organization working to build leadership, improve policies, and strengthen institutions to foster greater openness and shared prosperity in the Asia-Pacific region. The Foundation currently has program priorities in four areas: State and Society, Opening Global Markets, International Initiatives, and Women in Politics. Visitors to the Foundation's Web site will find detailed information on the Foundation's programs in Bangladesh, Cambodia, China, Indonesia, Japan, Korea, Mongolia, Nepal, Pakistan, the Philippines, Sri Lanka, Taiwan, Thailand, and Vietnam as well as its U.S. administered programs, which are the Asian-American Exchange, Global Women in Politics, Books for Asia, Environmental Programs, and the Luce Program, which offers scholars work experience in Asia. The Web site provides contact information, including e-mail addresses, for representatives in each country and the United States; lists of trustees, officers, and senior staff in the United States; and Web resources in Asia.

The Asia Society (NY) (http://www.asiasociety.org/)
Founded in 1956 by John D. Rockefeller III, The Asia Society is headquartered in New York City. The nonpolitical educational institution was formed to "foster understanding between Asians and Americans" and has expanded to include programs affecting Asian American issues. The Society presents art exhibitions and performances, films, lectures, seminars and conferences, publications, and educational materials and programs that present different aspects of Asia to Americans. The very extensive Web site includes information on all the different current programs, forums for roundtable discussions, links to a huge number of sites concerning Asia, and information on contributing to the Society. The site also features speech transcripts, publications, and many other resources. The Asia Society is not a grantmaking organization.

Asian American Arts Alliance (NY) (http://www.aaartsalliance.org/)
The Asian American Arts Alliance, located in New York City, is committed to "increasing the support, recognition and appreciation of Asian American Arts." The Alliance sponsors some grant programs, such as the Asian American Arts Fund and the Chase SMARTS Regrant Program. Through its other programs and services—a resource directory and Asian American arts calendar—the Alliance strives to provide managerial and artist assistance, inform and educate the public, facilitate connections between artists and groups, and advocate for increased visibility and opportunities for Asian American artists and groups. More details on these programs, plus the arts calendar and resource directory for New York and New Jersey Asian arts organizations, and contact information for the Alliance are available on the Web site.

Asian and Pacific Islander Wellness Center (CA) (http://www.apiwellness.org)
The Asian and Pacific Islander Wellness Center in San Francisco, California, is committed to "educating, supporting, empowering and advocating for Asian and Pacific Islander (A&PI) communities—particularly A&PIs living with, or at-risk for HIV/AIDS." The group supplies many care services for HIV-positive Asian and Pacific Islanders, including treatment case management, peer advocacy, treatment advocacy, and counseling. The Center also sponsors support groups, prevention education, HIV testing, and many curricula from the research and technical assistance department on covering all the aforementioned services. The site includes information on all these services and opportunities to volunteer and contribute.

Asian Cultural Exchange (NY) (http://www.asianculturalcouncil.org)
Created as a grantmaking organization in 1963 by John D. Rockefeller III, the Asian Cultural Council is committed to "supporting cultural exchange in the visual and performing arts between the United States and the countries of Asia." With headquarters in New York City and regional offices in Tokyo, Hong Kong, and Taipei, the Asian Cultural Council's grants cover a large geographic area in Asia. The group provides grants, fellowships, service, and support to individuals working in traditional and contemporary arts. The ACC Web site contains specific information on fellowships and grants, information for new applicants, news on recent grantees and activities, and contact information.

Association of Trial Lawyers of America (DC) (http://www.atlanet.org/)
As the world's largest trial bar, the Association of Trial Lawyers of America (ATLA) "promotes justice and fairness for injured persons, safeguards victims' rights—particularly the right to trial by jury—and strengthens the civil justice system through education and disclosure of information critical to public health and safety." With more than 56,000 members worldwide, and a network of U.S. and Canadian affiliates involved in diverse areas of trial advocacy, ATLA provides lawyers with the information and professional assistance needed to serve clients successfully and protect the democratic values inherent in the civil justice system. Visit the site for information on ATLA's law student education programs, awards and scholarships, and ATLA events.

Astraea National Lesbian Action Foundation (NY) (http://www.astraea.org/)
The Astraea National Lesbian Action Foundation, established in 1977, provides financial support for organizations and projects that are lesbian-led or focused and work to promote the economic, political, educational, and cultural well-being of lesbians. Visitors to the site will find grant guidelines, membership and volunteer information, events, news, and contact information.

Atlas Economic Research Foundation (VA) (http://www.atlas-fdn.org/)
The Atlas Economic Research Foundation, incorporated in 1981, helps to create, develop, advise, and support independent public policy research institutes by providing "intellectual entrepreneurs" with advice, financial support, workshops, and access to a network of leaders who share a commitment to achieving a free society. The Foundation's Sir Antony Fisher International Memorial Awards for Public Policy Institutes recognizes institutes that combine the talents of the academic and the entrepreneur. Application information is provided at the Foundation's Web site, along with lists of previous winners going back to 1990. The site also provides best practices "Nuts & Bolts" for independent public policy institutes, a virtual phone book, and upcoming conference information.

Austin Film Society (TX) (http://www.austinfilm.org)
The Austin Film Society was incorporated in May 1986. The group's mission is to "make rarely-seen works of film accessible to the Austin community [and to] serve as a nucleus of support and information for regional media production." The Texas Filmmakers' Production Fund makes grants to emerging film and video artists throughout the state. The 32 grants in 1999 totaled $50,000. The society also has a fiscal sponsorship program, which can assist members in obtaining funding. The application for the next round of grants and application guidelines for the fiscal sponsorship program are posted on the Society's Web site. The group also sponsors exhibition programs and movie screenings. Visitors to the site will find a calendar of events, information on staff members, and an online edition of the group's newsletter, *Persistence of Vision*.

The Autism Foundation of New York (NY) (http://www.aaog.org/)
Based in Staten Island, the Autism Foundation of New York Advocacy and Outreach Group is comprised of family and friends of people afflicted with autism. The Foundation's goal is to "advocate for appropriate, scientifically proven treatments and educational methodologies to help these individuals achieve their fullest potential." To this end, the Foundation operates a number of events throughout the year and supports educational programs about autism. The Foundation's Web site lists upcoming events, regular recreation activities for autistic children, support groups for family and friends, links to resources on autism, and contact information.

Averitt Express Associates Charities (TN)
(http://www.averittexpress.com/AverittCares.htm)
Averitt Express, a delivery service located in Cookeville, Tennessee, supports local and national healthcare organizations and charities. The Averitt Cares area of the Web site provides details of recent contributions and a list of giving since 1987. Contact information is provided.

Bainbridge Foundation, Inc. (WA) (http://www.bainbridgefoundation.org/)
The Bainbridge Foundation supports community organizations on and near Bainbridge Island, Washington. The Foundation runs the "One Call for All" funding drive in order to support these agencies. The Foundation's Web site lists Island agencies and off-Island agencies that it funds and maintains an online feedback and pledge form for donors.

Bainbridge Island Arts & Humanities Council (WA) (http://www.artshum.org/)
The Bainbridge Island Arts and Humanities Council was established in 1986. The group's mission is to "provide access to the arts and humanities for every Island citizen, and to assist individuals and organizations delivering cultural services and programs" to the

Bainbridge Island, Washington, community. The elegant site includes a searchable database of cultural resources and artists in the area. There is also information on current exhibits and events, a calendar of cultural events in the community, a page of links to related sites, and a membership form. The site does not offer any information on applying for a grant.

Bainbridge-Ometepe Sister Islands Association (WA) (http://www.bosia.org)

Founded by Kim and Ela Esterberg in 1986, the Bainbridge-Ometepe Sister Islands Association forms a connection between Bainbridge Island, Washington, and the island community of Ometepe, Nicaragua. The Association's project to improve the quality of life in Ometepe, Nicaragua, includes the Sí a la Vida program and the sale of fair trade organic coffee from Ometepe. The Association publishes a quarterly newsletter; past and current issues of the newsletter and the Association's annual report can be downloaded in PDF format. More information on the history of the two sister cities, related links, and contact information can be found on the Association's Web site.

Banner Health Foundation of Arizona (AZ) (http://www.bannerhealthaz.com/Foundations/sf_main.html)

The Phoenix, Arizona-based Banner Health Foundation has been providing philanthropic support for Samaritan Medical Centers and acting as a steward for those funds for 25 years. The Foundation's mission is to improve the health and wellness of the community. The Foundation's Web site provides details for potential donors, a listing of special events, contact information, and details about the Banner Health Foundation's sister foundation, the Lutheran Foundation. The site is best viewed using the Internet Explorer browser.

Barberton Community Foundation (OH) (http://www.bcfcharity.org/)

The Barberton Community Foundation was created in September 1996 to improve the quality of life for the citizens of Barberton, Ohio. Grants are intended "for charitable endeavors, education, public health, public recreation and to lessen the burden of government." Grants are distributed quarterly, with a Small Grants Program administered every month. The Foundation awards scholarships to local students and has a business and home improvement loan program to invest in the community. It also sponsors assorted local philanthropic events. The site includes downloadable applications for grants, scholarship application guidelines, staff e-mail addresses, board of trustees meeting minutes, and information on donating to the Foundation. There are also links to other Barberton-related sites.

Barth Syndrome Foundation, Inc. (FL) (http://www.barthsyndrome.org/)

The Perry, Florida-based Barth Syndrome Foundation was established in 1997 by three families whose children have Barth Syndrome. The Foundation's goals include supporting boys afflicted with Barth Syndrome and their families, funding research, promoting awareness of the syndrome, and supporting other charitable causes with similar goals. The Foundation is also active in registering afflicted children and doctors with experience in treating Barth Syndrome in order to establish a database and promote understanding. The Foundation's Web site provides a wealth of information on the syndrome, its history and treatment, professional resources, links for families, and FAQs. Information on the Foundation's budget, goals, and programs can be downloaded in PDF format.

Bedford Community Health Foundation (VA) (http://www.bchf.org)

Organized in 1978, the Bedford Community Health Foundation serves the "health-related needs of the citizens of Bedford City and Bedford County, Virginia" through financial grants to nonprofit health service organizations serving the community. The Foundation provides general grants, grants from specific funds, and scholarship awards, all of which are described online. Additionally, the Foundation's Web site gives detailed instructions for potential applicants, a list of recent and past grants, and information for donors and volunteers. The Web site also provides a listing of health-related services in the Bedford community and contact information for the Foundation.

Belgian American Educational Foundation (CT) (http://www.baef.be/)

The Belgian American Educational Foundation began as part of the Commission for Relief in Belgium, created in 1914. Today, the Foundation is dedicated to "fostering the higher education of deserving Belgians and Americans" through its fellowships for Belgian citizens to study or perform investigations in the United States as well as for Americans to study in Belgium. The Foundation's Web site contains descriptions of the various fellowships, detailed instructions for applicants, and a preliminary online application. The Foundation also grants an Alumni Award for research in a variety of fields. A history of the Foundation and contact information are available online.

The Bernardine Franciscan Sisters Foundation (VA) (http://www.bfranfound.org/)

The Virginia-based Bernardine Franciscan Sisters Foundation, Inc. was established in 1996 to serve the counties of Newport News, Hampton, Poquoson, Gloucester and York. The Foundation "enables the Bernardine Sisters of the Third Order of St. Francis to continue and to increase its services to the poor." The Sisters mainly focus their giving in the area of healthcare, specifically care to the sick and injured, health promotion, general health in local communities, and resources for health restoration and disease prevention. The Foundation funds "organizations whose missions, philosophies and works are in keeping with the mission of the congregation." This mission is outlined on the Foundation's Web site, as are grantmaking policies and limitations, recent grants made, a list of the Foundation's directors and staff, and contact information for requesting a specific grant application and brochure.

Eric Berne Memorial Award of the International Transactional Analysis Association (CA) (http://www.ITAA-NET.org)

Eric Berne Memorial Award in Transactional Analysis is named after the founder of the psychological theory of transactional analysis. The award was established in 1971 and is to benefit "published original and significant contributions to transactional analysis in one of four award categories: theory; research; practice applications; and the comparison and/or integration of transactional analysis theory with other theories and approaches." Award nominees must have contributed their work on transactional analysis to a professional journal, book, or publication one year prior to their nomination and must be an ITAA member. The Award's Web site can be found under the Transactional Analysis link of the ITAA Web site, and includes a list of past award winners and their articles, contact information, and a history of Eric Berne and transactional analysis.

Betaseron Multiple Sclerosis Champions of Courage (DC) (http://www.championsofcourage.org/)

The Betaseron Multiple Sclerosis Champions of Courage Program intends to show that "quality healthcare, combined with a positive attitude and the support of others, can be empowering forces that enable people with MS to enhance their quality of life." The program funds a grant for up to $7,000 to recognize the achievements of people with Multiple Sclerosis and support their inspirational work in their communities. Grant applicants must be taking Betaseron®, participate in community service work, and outline how they would use the grant to demonstrate unique courage and inspire others with MS. The program provides a grant application for the Betaseron® Multiple Sclerosis Champions of Courage[SM] Program on its Web site in HTML or PDF format. FAQs about the Program, contact information, news, links, and past grant recipients and a description of their projects, are also online.

Bingham Program (ME) (http://www.megrants.org/BProgram.htm)

The Bingham Program was founded in 1932, in a partnership between philanthropist William Bingham II and a group of dedicated doctors, "to promote the advancement of medicine and healthcare in Maine." The Program grew from a strong need for rural doctors to be connected to the latest information and support services that are available in urban surroundings. The Bingham Program initiates funds and programs in three high priority areas: health profession development, community health programs, and public health policy development. Within these areas, the program also places special focus on underserved groups and the efficient delivery of appropriate and quality care to them. The Program does not make grants to capital campaigns, general overhead costs, or individuals. Visit the Program's Web page to view recent grants, grant guidelines, deadlines, proposal information, and contact information.

Mary Black Foundation, Inc. (SC) (http://www.maryblackfoundation.org)
Founded in 1985, the Mary Black Foundation serves Spartanburg County, South Carolina, with occasional support to upstate organizations that directly relate to the goals and mission in the county. The recently reconfigured Foundation has amended its charitable mission, "to promote and foster the uncompromising principles and virtues for which Black stood: honesty, industry, courage, and an unwillingness ever to acknowledge defeat," to primarily provide grants to health-related, nonprofit organizations in the community. The two major goals of the Foundation are to promote wellness and concentrate on preventive measures that address core challenges to the overall health of families and individuals. Unsolicited applications are accepted if they fall within these goals, but much grantmaking is done through Request For Proposals (RFPs) for long-term initiatives. The Foundation also distributes two annual leadership awards, which grant award money to the nominating organization. The site includes grant application guidelines, RFPs for two existing five-year health initiatives, information on the two awards, and a list of the trustees and staff.

Blue Cross Blue Shield of Michigan Foundation (MI) (http://www.bcbsm.com/foundation.shtml)
The BCBSM Foundation seeks to improve healthcare in Michigan by "enhancing the quality and appropriate use of healthcare; improving access to appropriate health services; and controlling healthcare costs." Its grant programs support research and community healthcare solutions, acknowledge excellence in research, and support medical education. The Foundation area of the BCBSM Web site provides clear and concise information on the Foundation's primary funding programs, including its Proposal Development Award, Matching Initiative Program, Physician- Investigator Research Award, Student Award Program, Request for Proposal Program, Excellence in Research Awards, and Investigator-Initiated Program. Applications for the above programs are available at the site in PDF format. The site also provides e-mail addresses of program administrators, a select list of links, and an online version of the Foundation's most recent annual report.

BoatU.S. Foundation for Boating Safety (VA) (http://www.boatus.com/foundation/)
In 1989, the BoatU.S. Foundation for Boating Safety began its Grassroots Grants Program, supporting community-based boating safety programs and services. The Foundation makes $5,000 grants to "local, volunteer organizations that use innovative approaches to educate boaters about safe boating practices." The Foundation's Web site hosts a wealth of resources for boaters and grantseekers, including news about boating safety, recent consumer reports relating to boating, a free service to locate local boating safety courses, a mailing list form to order grant applications, a lengthy history of past grant recipients, and limited contact information to request further details from the Foundation.

Boston Adult Literacy Fund (MA) (http://www.balf.net/home.htm)
The Boston Adult Literacy Fund was founded in 1988 to provide access to basic education for adults in the Boston metropolitan area and to raise awareness of the need for basic education and literacy. Grants are awarded to community-based literacy programs (ABE—Adult Basic Education, ESL—English as a Second Language, and high school credential programs, either GED or EDP). The Fund also awards scholarships to adults who have completed their basic education and wish to continue on to higher education or vocational training. In addition to descriptions of its programs, the BALF Web site provides a list of recent grant recipients, links to literacy-related Web sites, and contact information.

Boston Film and Video Foundation (MA) (http://www.bfvf.org)

The Boston Film and Video Foundation was established in 1976 to support local filmmakers. Today, the Foundation's mission is "to provide an organizational support system to artists for the understanding and the creation of new work, facilitate the discussion and critique of work and issues, and to pool human and equipment resources." To this end, the Foundation sponsors three programs: Massachusetts Media Fellowships, for exceptional work in independent film and video; BF-VF Fiscal Sponsorships, for film or video projects; and an Equipment Access Membership, for borrowing film and video equipment. The Foundation has application guidelines for each program posted on its Web site, as well as past recipients. There is an online application for the Equipment Access Membership and details of other programs and services, such as the Vision Award, that the BF-VF provides in the Boston filmmaking community.

Boston Foundation for Architecture (MA) (http://www.bfagrants.org/)

The Boston Foundation for Architecture was established in 1984 to support public education programs related to the field. It was created by the Boston Society of Architecture, a professional association that administers programs and provides resources to enhance the public and professional understanding of design and architecture. Through its grantmaking program, the Foundation encourages greater public awareness of the value of well-designed public places. Support is given to projects that further the understanding of design, such as educational programs about design, aimed especially at young people, that focus on the public realm; community forums or "charrettes" to discuss and debate public improvements to the communal environment; exhibitions of exceptional examples of public-facility design; recognition programs, awards programs, and other ways of enhancing the visibility of well-designed infrastructure and civic architecture; lecture series of topics relevant to the design of public buildings or spaces; ideas for competitions for future public buildings and improvements; and historic studies of public facilities that have been especially well designed. The Foundation seeks to "engender in current and future generations informed commitment to sensitive, well-designed, humanistic environments." Visit the Foundation's Web site to view grant guidelines and application, both of which are downloadable in PDF format.

Bread and Roses Community Fund (PA) (http://www.breadrosesfund.org)

The Bread and Roses Community Fund of Philadelphia, Pennsylvania, "is a unique partnership of donors and activists committed to building a permanent base for social change in the Delaware Valley." The fund gives out General Fund grants, Discretionary grants, and the Jonathan Lax scholarship. 1998 General Fund grants were given in the following categories to organizations that are working against a problem that affects many aspects of society: AIDS and health, arts and social change, community organizing, environment, human rights/civil liberties, international/peace, lesbian/gay rights, resources for organizing, women's rights, workers' rights, and youth empowerment. These grants are distributed once a year. Discretionary grants are distributed monthly for special projects, emergencies, technical assistance, and organizational development. The Jonathan Lax scholarship was created to "encourage gay men to obtain additional education, aspire to positions in which they contribute to society, be open about their sexual preference, and act as role models for other gay men with similar potential." Men who live in or attend school in the Delaware Valley are eligible for the $5,000 or $20,000 annual scholarships. The Web site includes applications in HTML format that can be printed straight from the site, application guidelines, a lists of staff members and grant recipients, and donor guidelines.

Brewster Education Foundation, Inc. (NY) (http://www.bef.org)

Based in Brewster, New York, the Brewster Education Foundation was established in 1984 to raise funds to foster, encourage, and promote pubic education programs for Brewster Central Schools. The concept for the Foundation was initiated by George Zupko, former Interim Principal and long-time Director of Student Services at Brewster High School. It was the first such foundation in New York to develop a public-private collaboration. The Foundation raises and disburses funds for projects beyond those supported by regular school sources and helps fill the gap that exists between the programs teachers would like to have and those available to them through district budgeting. The goal of the Foundation is to promote excellence in education by recognizing students for scholastic achievement, encouraging teachers to take innovative approaches to public education, and fostering community service. The Foundation also funds scholarships, financial aid counseling, a dinner recognizing academic achievement, a post-prom party, and workshops in poetry, writing, and training for peer helpers. Visit the site for contact information.

Broadcast Education Association (DC) (http://www.beaweb.org)

The Washington, D.C.-based Broadcast Education Association (BEA) was established in 1955 as the Association for Professional Broadcast Education and adopted its current name in 1973. BEA is an academic organization of approximately 1,500 faculty and professionals and approximately 250 university and college member institutions with a commitment to broadcast and electronic media education. Its purpose and slogan is "Educating tomorrow's electronic media professionals." BEA administers 15 scholarships annually to honor broadcasters and the broadcast industry. Unless otherwise specified, scholarships are awarded only to juniors, seniors, and graduate students at BEA member universities. Visitors to the Association's Web site will find scholarship application instructions, printable application materials, a scholarship recipient list, and links to additional scholarship sites. BEA also provides the new faculty research grant and travel grants, with printable application materials and instructions on its site. Visitors can also find information on joining BEA; publication subscription forms, printable and online; information on the Association's conventions; links to media sites; listings of industry and academic job openings; listings of individual, associate, and institutional members; a news archive; and contact information.

Broadway Cares/Equity Fights AIDS (NY) (http://www.bcefa.org/)

Founded in 1988, Broadway Cares/Equity Fights AIDS leverages the talents and resources of the American theater community to raise funds for AIDS-related causes in the United States. BC/EFA also awards grants, usually in January and September, for direct care and/or services to people with HIV/AIDS. Projects funded in the past have provided meals, shelter, transportation, emergency financial aid, emotional/practical support, and/or payment of non-reimbursable medical expenses. Information on BC/EFA's grants program can be requested by telephone or e-mail. In addition to information on its activities, the BC/EFA Web site provides a listing of its affiliates, links to Web resources, a password-protected electronic callboard, and an e-mail list for receiving information and updates.

Bronx Council on the Arts (NY) (http://www.bronxarts.org/)

The Bronx Council on the Arts serves the New York City borough of the Bronx by developing programs that provide for public participation in the arts, nurture arts organizations' development, publicize and promote the arts, and generate financial support and new initiatives. The Council offers several types of grants, all of which are described on the Council's Web site. The Community Arts Grants guidelines and application forms can be downloaded (in PDF format); however, grantseekers must contact the Council's Arts Services department for more information on the other programs. The site also outlines its arts activities and provides membership, funding, staff, and contact information.

The Brother's Brother Foundation (PA) (http://www.brothersbrother.com/)

Founded in 1958, The Brother's Brother Foundation (BBF) of Pittsburgh, Pennsylvania, donates needed resources to millions of people internationally—in over 100 countries on five continents. This disaster relief organization focuses its efforts on four programs: education, medical, humanitarian, and agriculture. The education program distributes donated books and supplies to support increased opportunity for advancement, with the largest program being Books Across Seas in the Philippines. The medical program ships contributions of products, functioning equipment, and funds in response to requests from all over the world. The agricultural program addresses the issue of hunger by sending vegetable seeds and food to needy individuals and families. All applicants must have offices overseas. The site includes an application form for grants, information and opportunities for organizations and individuals to donate money or in-kind goods, an archive of newsletters, and updates on the Foundation's response to many crises throughout the world. There is also a list of country recipients, a list of BBF accomplishments, and information on membership interaction.

Nicole Brown Charitable Foundation (CA) (http://www.nbcf.org/)

The Nicole Brown Charitable Foundation, formerly the Nicole Brown Simpson Foundation, of California helps to fund organizations that protect families from domestic violence and offer long-term solutions for those affected by it. The Foundation's Web site lists donor and volunteer information, news, Web resources, and a listing of shelters.

The Barbara Bush Foundation for Family Literacy (DC)
(http://www.barbarabushfoundation.com)

The Barbara Bush Foundation for Family Literacy has funded 204 family literacy programs in 42 states since it was launched by Barbara Bush in March 1989. The mission of the Foundation is "to establish literacy as a value in every family in America, by helping every family in the nation understand that the home is the child's first school, that the parent is the child's first teacher, and that reading is the child's first subject; and to break the intergenerational cycle of illiteracy, by supporting the development of family literacy programs where parents and children can learn and read together." A total of $500,000 is awarded each year, with no grant exceeding $50,000. The site contains a grants list, news releases, publications, descriptions of state literacy initiatives, and application information.

The Business and Professional Women's Foundation (DC)
(http://www.bpwusa.org/content/BPWFoundation/foundation_introtext.htm)

The Business and Professional Women's Foundation (BPW), established in 1956, promotes equity for working women through education, information, and research. Headquartered in Washington, D.C., the Foundation provides financial assistance to women seeking education to advance in their careers or reenter the workforce and also collects, conducts, and analyzes research on issues affecting women in the workplace. BPW also provides networking opportunities, resources, career positioning, educational programs, and visibility for its members nationwide. The site provides information on the following issues: sexual harassment, health and legal policy, domestic violence, affirmative action, and social security reform. Visitors to the site will find scholarship application instructions, a congressional vote database, chat room, search function for the site, a state and local affiliate search form, and contact information.

California Council for the Humanities (CA) (http://www.calhum.org/)

The California Council for the Humanities is a non-governmental affiliate of the National Endowment for the Humanities, which looks for ways to make the knowledge and insights of the humanities available to all Californians. The CCH Web site offers two options for joining in humanities discussions—a "Citizenship, Culture, and the Humanities" e-mail discussion list and a Web-based "Humanities Forum"—as well as a calendar-style listing of programs funded by grants from CCH.

California HealthCare Foundation (CA) (http://www.chcf.org/)

The California HealthCare Foundation was established in May 1996 as a result of the conversion of Blue Cross of California from a nonprofit health plan to WellPoint Health Networks, a for-profit corporation. The Foundation is one of two philanthropies created by the conversion—the other is the California Endowment—and is charged with responsibility for gradually divesting the Foundation of WellPoint stock and transferring 80 percent of the proceeds to the Endowment and for developing the Foundation's own independent grantmaking program with the remaining 20 percent of the funds. The Foundation's grantmaking is statewide and focuses initially on five program areas: managed care and special populations, California's uninsured, California health policy, consumer health information and education, and public health. CHCF's well-organized Web site provides general program information, grant guidelines and limitations, a list of recent grants, RFPs (in Microsoft Word and PDF format), an electronic form for ordering Foundation publications, a comprehensive set of links to health-related Web sites, a message from Foundation President Mark D. Smith, listings of the board and staff, and contact information.

Calvert Social Investment Foundation (MD) (http://www.calvertgroup.com/foundation)

The Calvert Social Investment Foundation's mission is to establish community investment as a new asset class in the financial services industry. The Bethesda, Maryland-based Foundation is a community investment facility offering options for individuals and institutions to invest in community lenders globally. By raising funds and making investments into community development finance institutions and other community development nonprofits, Calvert Foundation aims to "end poverty through investment." These investments serve as a bridge between disadvantaged communities and the financial markets, promoting economic justice and community development. Loans are made to community development loan funds, micro-enterprise and small business loan funds, affordable housing loan funds, community development banks and credit unions, nonprofit facilities funds, nonprofit enterprises, community development corporations, cooperatives, community development intermediaries, micro-finance institutions, and international financial intermediaries working in developing countries. The Foundation seeks to invest in community organizations that focus on low-income communities and individuals without access to traditional sources of capital; grow the local economy by expanding opportunity and promoting work-related activities, homeownership, or nontraditional business owners; support diverse communities in rural and urban settings, domestically and internationally; and demonstrate a consistent track record of repayment and the organizational management capacity to repay the investment. Requests for funding are considered throughout the year, and the Calvert Foundation Investment Committee makes investment decisions quarterly. The site contains application instructions and criteria. Visitors to the site will find annual reports, a resource center for community investing, and contact information.

Cancer Aid and Research Fund (AZ) (http://www.canceraidresearch.org/)

The Cancer Aid and Research Fund, based in Phoenix, Arizona, strives to give aid and support to victims of cancer and their families. The Fund has two main funding priorities: providing educational material about nutrition and alternative cancer treatments and providing medical equipment and supplies to clinics and hospitals that use alternative cancer treatments. The Fund also works to establish and maintain cancer support groups and to educate the public about preventative cancer measures. The Fund's Web page posts contact information and an online donation form.

Cancer Research Foundation of American (VA) (http://www.preventcancer.org/)

The Cancer Research Foundation of America, founded in 1985, supports education and research to help prevent cancer. Since its inception, the Foundation has funded more than 200 scientists at leading medical centers; It has also recognized scientific excellence, new and innovative projects, and young scientists interested in cancer prevention research. The Foundation's grant review process is approved by the National Institutes of Health. Grant and fellowship details, past recipients, and application forms can be printed or downloaded (in PDF format) from the Prevention Science and Research directory on the Foundation's Web site. The site also provides facts on preventing cancer, information on education programs, online versions of publications, and links to cancer resources on the Web.

Cancer Research Fund of the Damon Runyon-Walter Winchell Foundation (NY) (http://www.cancerresearchfund.org/)

The Cancer Research Fund was established in 1954 by radio personality Walter Winchell after his friend, journalist Damon Runyon, died from cancer. Winchell believed that "young scientists following their own best instincts would make the critical discoveries leading to the defeat of cancer." Following this belief, the Fund grants post-doctoral fellowships and scholar awards for biomedical scientists. The Fund's Web site provides detailed guidelines and application forms to view and print for both programs. The site also provides donor information and a Scientist Spotlight.

The Carter Center, Inc. (GA) (http://www.cartercenter.org/)

The Atlanta-based Carter Center, established by former President Jimmy Carter and his wife Rosalynn, is "guided by a fundamental commitment to human rights and the alleviation of human suffering; it seeks to prevent and resolve conflicts, enhance freedom and democracy, and improve health." The Center achieves these goals through numerous programs and initiatives, including Peace Initiatives, Health Initiatives and International Activities. Peace Initiatives address democracy, global development, Latin America and the Caribbean, conflict resolution, and human rights. Health Initiatives strive to fight disease and advance health. The Center's Web Site includes a list of countries and the issues the Carter Center has addressed there through its International Activities. The Center, in association with Emory University, also administers internship programs for students, and a Graduate Assistant Program, which supplies a $3,000 stipend for select interns. There are application procedures and more information on the internship program, including an FAQ, on the Center's Web site. The Center also solicits donors and runs events throughout the year. Extensive information is posted on the Center's Web site.

Cascadia Revolving Fund (WA) (http://www.cascadiafund.org)

Located in Seattle, Washington, Cascadia Revolving Fund is a community development loan fund that provides loans and technical support to small businesses that have been unable to access financing through traditional sources. The Fund lends to women, minority, and low-income entrepreneurs and to businesses that are located in distressed urban and rural communities that have a significant potential for job creation. It also loans to businesses that act to preserve or restore the environment. The Fund's goal is to help entrepreneurs start and grow successful businesses in an effort to bring much-needed jobs and economic prosperity to distressed communities throughout Washington and Oregon. In its 12-year history Cascadia has loaned nearly $10 million to more than 170 businesses, creating or preserving more than 700 jobs. Cascadia is funded by both donations and investments from the philanthropic community. Visitors to the Web site will find information on loan activity, successful borrowers, and descriptions of recent loans; loan application information and instructions; and contact information.

Catholic Campaign for Human Development (DC) (http://www.nccbuscc.org/cchd/index.htm)

Established in 1969 by the National Conference of Catholic Bishops, the Catholic Campaign for Human Development works to empower the poor and encourage their participation in the decisions and actions that affect their lives in order to move beyond poverty. It does this by supporting and funding community-controlled, self-help organizations, economic development projects, and transformative education. Guidelines for these projects are available on the CCHD Web site, as are a list of currently funded projects organized by state, local contact information (also by state), and a form for requesting more information.

Center for Ecoliteracy (CA) (http://www.ecoliteracy.org/)

The Center for Ecoliteracy is dedicated to fostering the experience and understanding of the natural world in the San Francisco Bay Area. The center was founded in 1995 to support a network of northern California organizations engaged in habitat restoration and agriculture-related programs. The grant program at the Center encourages school communities and educational organizations in the region to engage in the fostering and understanding of the natural world. The Center is a public foundation that sponsors donor-advised funds and shelters projects consistent with its mission. The Center also publishes resources that provide research and education about the mission and the state of today's environment. Upon visiting the Web site, you can view excerpts from many of these publications which are downloadable in PDF format. The Web site also provides a board list, grant application information, information on deadlines, previous grant recipients, and contact information.

The Center for Photography of Woodstock, Inc. (NY) (http://www.cpw.org)

The Center for Photography at Woodstock, Inc., was founded in 1977 and provides an artistic home for contemporary creative photographers. The Woodstock, New York-based Center sponsors programs in education, exhibition, publication, and fellowships. It also provides the following services: darkroom access, a library and archive, portfolio review, and computers. The site provides information on exhibitions and workshops, events, internships, links to other photo Web sites and resources, and contact information.

Center for the Study of the Presidency (DC) (http://www.thepresidency.org)

Situated in Washington, D.C., the Center for the Study of the Presidency was created in 1969, inspired by President Eisenhower's call for programs on the American presidency. As such, the Center is the foremost institution devoted to the study of the presidency and related governmental and political institutions. As a nonprofit, non-partisan institution, the Center provides educational resources on the presidency, some of which can be obtained on the Center's Web site, and ongoing events at the Center, the listings for which are also available online. The Center also grants a number of fellowships and travel grants, mainly for undergraduate students studying in related fields. The Center's Web site gives detailed descriptions of the fellowships and travel grants and contact information for potential applicants.

Central Minnesota Arts Board (MN) (http://www.cmab.org)

Based in St. Cloud, Minnesota, the Central Minnesota Arts Board (CMAB) was founded in 1977. The purpose of CMAB is to stimulate and encourage the creation, performance, and appreciation of the arts in the four-county area of central Minnesota: Benton, Sherburne, Stearns, and Wright Counties. CMAB funds local arts-producing and sponsoring organizations, educational institutions, or individuals and will also provide other assistance that will help further develop the arts in central Minnesota. Among its programs are project grants, which include furthering arts education and after-school and summer arts educational programming; the Technical Development and Education Fund, which provides training funds for nonprofit arts organizations staff to attend management workshops, seminars, or conferences; scholarships, designed to help graduating high school seniors further their education in music, dance, literature, the visual arts or performance art; individual artist awards; general operation support; an individual artist directory, which is an Internet listing of artists to increase awareness of artists in the area and to encourage schools, galleries, and performance and art centers to utilize their skills; and grant writing assistance. Visitors to the site will find an online quarterly newsletter, an online directory of artists, links to other arts–related sites, and contact information.

Chamber Music America (NY) (http://www.chamber-music.org)

Located in New York City, Chamber Music America is a national member organization that was created in 1978. The group's mission is "to make chamber music a vital part of American culture . . . [by] designing programs and services to help those who perform and present professional chamber music. . . [and by] the advancement of chamber music education." The CMA's six grant programs are only open to members of the organization. These programs are the Chamber Music Rural Residencies Program (looks for both communities and musicians), the Commissioning program, Consulting awards, the Ensemble Residency program, Opportunity awards, and the Presenter-Community Residency Program. Each program has its guidelines and applications available to be downloaded in Microsoft Word and PDF formats. There is a table with deadlines for each of the programs. The CMA also distributes awards recognizing excellence in teaching, service, and programming. Applications can be downloaded from the site. Visitors will also find information on membership, a calendar of events, a publication center, a membership directory available to members only, and lists of the board of directors and of the staff.

Changemakers Fund (CA) (http://www.changemakersfund.org)

Changemakers is a new national foundation that promotes community-based philanthropy through fundraising, grantmaking, donor education, and special programs. The Fund make grants to and collaborates with community-based public foundations, organizations that add diversity and strength to the philanthropic sector, and other organizations that help transform philanthropy, making it more responsive to grassroots groups working for social and economic justice, environmental sustainability, and equality for all. Community-based philanthropy breaks down the isolation of both funders and nonprofit groups by bringing donors, foundations, and grantees together to create a more conscious, compassionate, and strategic philanthropic sector. Changemakers funds are made available for strengthening organizations' existing infrastructures; organizations that meet the Fund's strategy "building, expanding, and transforming;" and for general support. Visitors to the Fund's Web site will find grant guidelines and specifications, a staff/board list, and contact information.

Harry Chapin Foundation (NY) (http://www.harrysfriends.com/hcf/)

The Harry Chapin Foundation, founded to "address the problems of the disadvantaged and promote educational programs that lead to a greater understanding of human suffering," provides funding for community education, arts in education, and agricultural and environmental programs. The Foundation favors programs in the New York region, although it will consider national programs. The Foundation's Web site provides funding guidelines and a contact for application requests, as well as a biography of Harry Chapin, memorabilia, and a listing of board members.

Chesapeake Bay Trust (MD) (http://www.chesapeakebaytrust.org)

The Chesapeake Bay Trust was created in 1985 by the Maryland General Assembly "to promote public awareness and participation in the restoration and protection of the Chesapeake Bay." The Trust funds groups and individuals who contribute to the restoration of the Chesapeake Bay and favors action-oriented activities. The Trust's priority areas are educational projects promoting behavior change toward the Bay and restoration projects that utilize volunteers. The Trust also sponsors the Ellen Fraites Wagner Award for an outstanding individual or organization that demonstrates the Trust's mission. Visitors to the Trust's Web site will find extensive grant guidelines, criteria and deadlines, a summary of operations, project suggestions for teachers and students, environmental and Chesapeake Bay-specific links, and contact information. The Trust's Web site also includes two printable grant application forms: one is a general form; the other is a special form for schools.

Chicago Foundation for Education (IL) (http://www.chgofdneduc.org)

Located in downtown Chicago, Illinois, the Chicago Foundation for Education was established in 1985. The organization is committed to "improving and enhancing the educational experiences provided to Chicago's public elementary school children by the educators who serve, guide, and teach them." One grant program, the Mentor and Adaptor Grants, give small grants to teachers who have developed a successful classroom project. That project is then described in a catalogue that all schools receive, and selected teachers are given small grants to enact the project. Applications are available at Chicago public schools, although they can be viewed online. The Small Grant program supports teachers with ideas for creative standards-based projects. Again, the applications can be viewed at the site. Lists of past recipients are available for both programs. Other efforts include the Takeoff Summer Technology Institutes in which teachers develop curricula that require students to seek out technology, Creative Classroom Workshops, and an effort to create a new Character Education Resource Book. The site offers visitors details on each project, a board list, and links to related resources. There is also a great section for volunteers, including an online survey.

Chicago White Sox Charities, Inc. (IL)
(http://www.chisox.com/community/sox_charities.cfm)

The Chicago White Sox Charities, established in 1990 by the professional baseball team, began primarily as a cancer research and treatment fund but grew into a charity to support youth education and athletic programs and senior citizen programs. Today, The Chicago White Sox Charities is committed to extending its circle of support to the less fortunate in its community and beyond, funding programs for "children, families and seniors in the greater Chicago metro area in the form of annual grants." Grants go towards programs and events that often involve the Chicago White Sox players in youth education, athletics, and at-risk programs. The Charities' Web site includes recent grantees, contact information, and details on some of the programs and events the organization hosts.

Child Abuse Prevention Foundation (CA) (http://www.capfsd.com/capf.htm)
The Child Abuse Prevention Foundation located in San Diego, California, was established in 1981 by a group of concerned citizens to help the area's abused children. The Foundation, working with community leaders and private citizens, has raised over $12 million to build a critically-needed emergency shelter for San Diego's children. The A.B. and Jessie Polinsky Children's Center has become a model for childrens' shelters nationwide. The Center attracts visitors from throughout the United States, Europe and the Middle East who are interested in building a similar facility for their dependent children. Visitors to the Foundation's Web site will find information on the board and staff, a printable information request form, and contact information.

Child Health Foundation (MD) (http://www.childhealthfoundation.org/)
The Child Health Foundation was established in 1985 to prevent and treat life-threatening communicable diseases in infants and children through support of clinical research, medical outreach, public education, and collaborative research partnerships. The Foundation's Web site provides excerpts from the CHF newsletter, an online version of the Foundation's most recent annual report, and general information about the Foundation's formal partnership agreements with a number of educational and medical organizations, including the University of Alabama, Hahnemann University (Philadelphia), City Hospital (Boston), Johns Hopkins Hospital and University (Baltimore), the University of Maryland (Baltimore), the Hospital Infantil Albert Sabin (Brazil), the International Centre for Health and Population Research (Bangladesh), the Instituto Investigacin Nutricinal (Peru), and the University of Virginia.

Children's Health Fund (NY) (http://www.childrenshealthfund.org)
The Children's Health Fund is committed to providing healthcare to the nation's most medically underserved children through the development and support of innovative primary care medical programs and the promotion of guaranteed access to appropriate healthcare for all children. Specifically, the fund works to ensure support of its flagship pediatric programs for homeless and underprivileged children in New York City, develop and support a national network of pediatric programs in some of the United States' poorest urban and rural communities, advocate for policies and programs to ensure access to medical homes for all children, and educate health professionals, policy makers, and the general public about the needs and barriers to healthcare experienced by disadvantaged children. The Foundation produces reports and sponsors public education and public service campaigns.

Children's Scholarship Fund (NY) (http://www.scholarshipfund.org)
The Children's Scholarship Fund seeks to expand educational opportunities for low-income families, by awarding up to 75 percent of a child's private or parochial school tuition. Founded by Ted Forstmann and John Walton in 1998, this national Fund intends to give disadvantaged families more options in their child's education. The Fund's Web site features a school search, which includes a database of 90 percent of American private schools, in Spanish and English. Application instructions and procedures, a contact form for more information, and a list of the members of the Fund's diverse National Board of Advisors, including members of Congress, CEOs, and education advocates from all walks of life, are available on the Fund's web site.

Chinook Fund (CO) (http://www.chinookfund.org/)

Created in 1988, the Chinook Fund of Denver, Colorado, supports cutting edge organizations throughout the state that "are working to address the root causes of social problems such as racism, sexism, homophobia, and discrimination against people with disabilities." Giving programs include standard and exceptional program grants, technical assistance grants, small emergency grants, special initiatives, and donor-advised grants. Funding is given to groups working for progressive social change, as opposed to those only performing direct service. The application, application guidelines, and newsletters are downloadable in PDF format. The site also includes comprehensive lists of grantee organizations (since 1995) and of board of director and committee members. There are also links to related resources on the Web, opportunities to donate to the fund, and information on the group's endowment. The fund does not make grants to organizations with annual budgets over $250,000.

Citizens Committee for New York City, Inc. (NY) (http://www.citizensnyc.org)

The Citizens Committee for New York City was established in 1975 by the late Senator Jacob Javits. The organization's goal is to "stimulate and support self-help and civic action that improves the quality of life in New York City and its neighborhoods." This is primarily achieved through work with over 12,000 associations representing over one million volunteers. The Committee distributes cash grants through three major directives: The Neighborhood Resources Department includes the self-explanatory Neighborhood Environmental Action Program; One City Awards to honor anti-poverty, anti-bias and HIV-AIDS related efforts; and the Building Blocks Awards for work in new organizing, communication, and model projects. The Neighborhood Anti-Crime Center includes the Reisenbach Neighborhood Awards for fighting drugs and crime in north Brooklyn and the CHASE Drug and Crime Prevention Awards that grant up to $1,000. The Youth Unlimited program includes the Mollie Parnis Dress Up Your School Awards for neighborhood beautification projects and Youth for Youth Incentive grants for youth-run groups addressing the city's problems. All of these grants are distributed once a year, except for the Building Blocks Awards, which are given every month. There is also the Strengthening Neighborhood Assets Program, a multi-year, ongoing award of technical and financial assistance. The site includes the Citizens Portal that offers links to a multitude of related organizations and information on fundraising campaigns.

Cleveland Education Fund (OH) (http://www.cleveland-ed-fund.org)

The Cleveland Education Fund began with funding from the Cleveland Foundation in 1984. "Through a wide range of innovative instructional initiatives, CEF furnishes teachers with current research and trends in their subject areas, encourages practices that have proven successful elsewhere, supports teachers who are themselves developing new instructional methods and makes monetary grants to innovative teachers and schools." Grants are given in two major categories. Leadership Grants are for teachers and collaborative teams to help implement instructional projects either in single classrooms or across grades, schools, or the city. Project Achieve Grants are "empowerment grants" for schools focusing on long-term capacity building. Interested parties are encouraged to write to the Fund for application guidelines and deadlines. The site does offer the list of recipients and the names of the selection committee members for the previous years' Leadership Grants. The focus of the Web site is the Fund's different projects. Many include supporting information and all demonstrate the goals of the fund. Visitors will also find lists of officers and funders and an events calendar.

Club Foundation (VA) (http://www.clubfoundation.org/)

The Club Foundation, a professional organization for the managers of private clubs, was established in 1988 to provide educational opportunities for future professionals of the club industry. Scholarships and grants are awarded to students enrolled in hospitality programs who are pursuing managerial careers in club management. The Foundation's straightforward Web site provides descriptions of its programs and contact information for requesting application forms.

Coalition for the Advancement of Jewish Education (NY) (http://www.caje.org)
The Coalition seeks to advance Jewish education by supporting Jewish teachers, encouraging young people to go into the field professionally, and running national conferences and local in-service programs. The Coalition's Web site provides information about its annual conference, a job bank, newsletters, membership, and advocacy. In addition, information and an application form (in Microsoft Word format) for the Spack Fellowship are available.

College Art Association (NY) (http://www.collegeart.org/)
The College Art Association, founded in 1911, promotes scholarship and teaching in the history and criticism of the visual arts and creativity and technical skill in the teaching and practices of art. CAA's Professional Development Fellowship Program helps artists to complete their M.F.A., Ph.D., or M.A. degree, to secure employment, and then subsidizes their first year's salary through matching grants to the institutions that hire them. CAA's Web site announces the current year's fellows in the News section and there provides information for requesting application forms. CAA's Web site also lists opportunities for artists' awards, calls for entries and manuscripts, grants and fellowships, internships, online opportunities, publications, and residencies—offered by various organizations. Publications, conference information, and job opportunities are also available online.

Colorado Endowment for the Humanities (CO) (http://www.ceh.org)
The Colorado Endowment for the Humanities, of Denver, was established in 1974. The group "sponsors and provides support for humanities programming throughout the state including local history exhibits, free public lectures, radio programs, and Chautauqua performances." The grants program is made up of three different components. The largest is the Program and Planning Grants, which are given to support lifelong learning in the humanities: literature, history, philosophy, ethics, languages, linguistics, jurisprudence, archaeology, comparative religion, and the history, theory, and criticism of the arts. Up to $1000 research grants are given on a matching basis. Packaged Program Grants facilitate events and programs including Chautauqua speakers and the Jefferson Hour Radio Program. Deadlines for each program are listed and application forms can be downloaded in Microsoft Word. The whole application process is outlined, with many steps electronically provided. Previous Program and Planning Grant recipients are listed. The Endowment also sponsors a Summer Teacher Institute and an annual publication prize. The Web site has an events calendar for projects around the state and features on assorted sponsored events.

Colorado Springs Osteopathic Foundation (CO) (http://www.csof.org)
The Colorado Springs Osteopathic Foundation and Family Medicine Center was founded in 1984. "The Foundation supports and promotes quality medicine, medical and public education, and a two year residency program in Family Practice." The Foundation offers a variety of programs to benefit the health of the medically indigent and low-income families of Colorado Springs. Projects include providing general health education, offering continuing medical education programs including an annual medical ethics conference, a speaker's bureau and physician referral service, and loans to Colorado resident osteopathic medical students. These are all in addition to the ambulatory clinic listed in the organization's name. The site includes information on all these services and programs, ways to make contributions, and new Web videos.

Columbus Medical Association Foundation (OH) (http://www.cmaf-ohio.org)
A health education foundation, the Columbus Medical Association Foundation was created by local physicians in 1958. The organization's mission is to "improve the health of the people of greater Columbus by focusing resources on health promotion, health education, and access to healthcare." The Foundation will accept proposals for projects whose proposed outcomes enable people to take actions and adopt behaviors, such as gathering and monitoring health–related statistics, that will give them better control over their own health and thus create a more health–conscious community. Basic application guidelines are outlined, but all interested groups should request the full application and guidelines. There is an electronic form to do so. This section includes information on selected previous grants.

The very extensive site also offers a step–by–step guide to submitting a proposal, a listing of the board of trustees, an electronic request for the annual report, information on specific initiatives, and a publications section.

Common Counsel Foundation (CA) (http://www.commoncounsel.org/)

The Common Counsel Foundation is an Oakland, California-based public charity that offers strategic philanthropic advisory services to a small group of family foundations and individual donors. Proposals are submitted to Common Counsel and are reviewed by staff members who keep in mind the member fund for which the proposal may be appropriate. Common Counsel also develops grantmaking programs that reflect the objectives of the member funds and individual donors. This group of family foundations and individual donors is committed to funding economic, environmental, and social justice initiatives seeking to "give voice" to the needs of low-income people, women, youth, people of color, and others working for justice, equity, and a healthy, sustainable environment. The member funds of Common Counsel have a special interest in organizations that are committed to the empowerment of their members through community organizing. Current member funds of the Foundation are the Abelard Foundation, the Acorn Foundation, and the Penney Family Fund. Common Counsel Foundation also administers the Grantee Exchange Fund and coordinates two retreat programs: one for writers and one for social-change community organizers and activists. The Web site contains information about the goals and funding areas of each of its member funds and retreat programs, contact information for developing your own grantmaking program, proposal guidelines, printable applications, grant lists, printable applications for the two retreat programs, and contact information.

Community Shares of Wisconsin, Inc. (WI) (http://communityshares.com)

Located in Madison, Wisconsin, Community Shares of Wisconsin works toward fundamental social change. The agency's mission is to "educate the community about, and encourage support of organizations working for social and economic justice." The Liesl Blockstein Community Grants are distributed to support organizations in south central Wisconsin. Projects should encourage cooperation between groups; work toward basic human rights for all; work toward the end of racial, sexual, and economic discrimination; and promote systemic change. Interested organizations can join the application mailing list by e-mail. The site includes staff biographies and contact information, board and committee lists, basic financial statements, and areas on ongoing projects. There is an electronic survey for visitor input and an organization events calendar.

Concern Foundation (CA)
(http://www.choicemall.com/cgi-bin/tame/concernfoundation/index.tam)

The Beverly Hills, California-based Concern (CONquer canCER Now) Foundation was created in 1968 by twenty-eight people whose lives had been effected by cancer. The group is "dedicated to funding promising cancer researchers in the fields of immunology, immunotherapy and other closely related areas of basic cancer research." The Foundation's grant program distributed awards of $100,000 over two years to investigators that are assistant professors or equivalent. The next application round will be in 2001 for consideration in 2002. Application guidelines from the last round can be viewed. The site also includes information on the 28 researchers currently being funded, information on becoming involved by volunteering or donating, and a list of the governing board members. The Cancer Immunology Research Foundation (CIRF) is a division of the Concern Foundation that raises money for the Medical Research Agencies of America. This money is distributed through the Concern Foundation's grant program.

Concerned Women for America (DC) (http://www.cwfa.org)

Located in Washington, D.C., Concerned Women of America was founded in 1979 in response to the vocal women of the National Organization of Women. Founder Betty LaHay's vision was to "restore the family to its traditional purpose and thereby allow each member of the family to realize their God-given potential and be more responsible citizens." The CWA awards two $1,000 scholarships annually to women attending a conservative, Christian college or university. Guidelines are listed in the About CWA area, along with an electronic application request. The organization offers extensive resources on topics that concern members, from education and religious freedom to United Nations and national sovereignty. Position papers and news on these topics are available in the online library. The group is also politically active, supporting and fighting national and state bills. The Legislative section of the site includes a chart of pending legislation in areas of interest and information on its status and where the group stands on it. LaHay has a daily radio show and visitors to the Web site can listen to broadcasts or read highlights.

Thomas L. Conlan Education Foundation (OH) (http://www.tlcfund.org/)

The Thomas L. Conlan Education Foundation, of Cincinnati, Ohio, was established by Thomas L. Conlan, Sr. who co-founded The Student Loan Funding Corporation with his oldest son, in 1981. Conlan established himself as a supporter of increased access to education, and his Foundation's mission is to "[further] universal access to educational opportunities." The Foundation maintains three program areas: college access for students underrepresented in education; outreach to increase the public's value of education; and school-to-career and early childhood development projects. Grant guidelines and highlights in these areas are provided online. The Foundation also sponsors the Financial Aid Enhancement Grant program, which provides funding to college and universities. In addition, the Foundation's operating programs provide college loans and run the Ohio College Access Network. An FAQ answers questions about the Foundation's programs, and contact information is available in the About the Grants section.

Connecticut Humanities Council (CT) (http://www.cthum.org)

A private foundation, the Connecticut Humanities Council was created in 1974 by the National Endowment for the Humanities. The organization's goal is to "to provide opportunities for all people in Connecticut to rediscover the joy of lifelong learning, to see themselves in the full context of their history and heritage, and to explore the infinite varieties of human thought and experience contained in our literature and expressed in our arts that give shape and direction to our lives." The Grant program distributes money through two programs: the Cultural Heritage Development Fund (CHDF) and the Connecticut Collaborations for Teaching the Arts and Humanities. The former is the larger and older program that funds projects that tell the story of the state's past, while the latter and newer program supports teaching arts and humanities in the public schools. Nonprofits throughout the state are eligible to apply for funding for public projects that deal with a humanities discipline (history, language, literature, linguistics, philosophy, etc.). The CHDF supports museums and cultural institutions with four types of grants: technical assistance, planning, implementation, and professional development. All applications and guidelines for both programs can be downloaded in Microsoft Word. There is also information on programs that the Council funds and runs including Time for Ideas in Libraries, a book discussion group program; the Connecticut Experience, a television program; and Connecticut Heritage, a publication series. Visitors to the site will find information on exhibits and events throughout the state, board and staff lists, and a list of recent grant recipients. There is also information on contributing and the Idea Depot section, which has extensive resources on the state.

The Conservation Alliance (WA) (http://www.outdoorlink.com/consall/)

The Conservation Alliance is a group of outdoor businesses that support grassroots citizen-action groups in protecting rivers, trails, and wild lands—natural areas where outdoor enthusiasts recreate. Grants are made to organizations for projects focused on direct action to protect and enhance natural resources for recreation—not education or scientific research projects. Guidelines and application instructions are provided at the Alliance's Web site, along with a history of grantmaking; however, grantseekers are asked to contact the Alliance before submitting a proposal. The Alliance site also provides success stories, news, and membership information.

Cooperative Development Foundation (DC)
(http://www.coopdevelopment.org/funds.html)

The Washington, D.C.-based Cooperative Development Fund maintains an unrestricted fund as well as a large number of specific funds that address needs such as rural development, welfare-to-work programs, and agricultural coops, among other areas. Funding categories include: consumer, general, housing leadership, rural, seniors and students. The Foundation provides a link to each of its specific funds with more details about the fund and descriptions of sample projects. A very general set of funding guidelines is included on the site, and the Foundation provides contact information for those interested in applying to a specific, named fund.

Cooperative Fund of New England, Inc. (CT) (http://www.cooperativefund.org)

The Cooperative Fund of New England is a community development loan fund whose mission is "to advance community based, cooperative and democratically owned or managed enterprises with preference to those that serve low income communities through: provision of prompt financial assistance at reasonable rates; provision of an investment opportunity that promotes socially conscious enterprise; and development of a regional reservoir of business skills with which to assist and advise these groups." Based in Hartford, Connecticut, the program loans are available only to organizations operated on a cooperative or nonprofit basis within the New England states of Massachusetts, Vermont, New Hampshire, Maine, Connecticut, and Rhode Island or within the adjacent parts of New York state. The site features a printable loan application.

Corporate Council for the Arts/ArtsFund (WA) (http://www.artsfund.org)

Located in Seattle, Washington, the Corporate Council for the Arts/ArtsFund have been supporting the city's nonprofit arts groups since 1969 and 1993 respectively. The former is funded by corporations, while the latter is a workplace giving program supported by individuals. The funds distribute annual sustaining grants and discretionary grants to groups in King and Pierce Counties. The areas throughout the Puget Sound receiving funding include the performing arts, the visual arts, and education. The site includes information on contributors, opportunities to contribute, the results of a study demonstrating the effectiveness of the funding, and lists of grant recipients. Lists of staff members and the board can be found under the Leaders heading.

Cottonwood Foundation (MN) (http://www.cottonwoodfdn.org)

The Cottonwood Foundation is "dedicated to promoting empowerment of people, protection of the environment, and respect for cultural diversity." The Foundation focuses its modest grantmaking activities on "committed, grass roots organizations that rely strongly on volunteer efforts and where foundation support will make a significant difference." The Foundation typically awards grants in the $500–$1,000 range to organizations in the United States and internationally that protect the environment, promote cultural diversity, empower people to meet their basic needs, and rely on volunteer efforts. In addition to general information about its activities, the Foundation's Web site provides grant guidelines, a downloadable grant application form, a list of recent grant recipients, and the Foundation's latest annual report.

Council of Independent Colleges (DC) (http://www.cic.edu/)

The Council of Independent Colleges, founded in 1956 and based in Washington, D.C., is an association of independent liberal arts colleges and universities that helps to enhance educational programs, improve administrative and financial performance, and increase institutional visibility. CIC offers funding and technical assistance programs, which are outlined in the Programs & Services area of its Web site. Additionally, CIC's Consortium for the Advancement of Private Higher Education (CAPHE) helps corporations and foundations stimulate meaningful reform by designing and administering directed grant competitions, offering technical assistance to funders, and disseminating ideas resulting from its programs. The Web site provides detailed information about CAPHE, membership and sponsor information, board and staff listings, and an online version of its most recent annual report (in PDF format).

The Covenant Foundation (NY) (http://www.covenantfn.org)

The Covenant Foundation was established in 1990 by the Crown Family Foundation and is located in New York City. The purpose of the Foundation is to build on existing strengths within the field of Jewish education in North America across all denominations and in all educational settings. The Foundation honors Jewish educators and supports creative approaches to programming in hopes of strengthening endeavors in education that perpetuate the identity and heritage of the Jewish people. The Foundation supports pre-collegiate, adult, and family education through awards, grants, and other activities. Information about grant programs and funding areas is available on the Web site. To apply for grants, organizations must first send a letter of inquiry. Details about what to include and whom to send the letter to are on the site. Additionally, the site contains information about the Foundation's award program, including how to apply and how to nominate individuals. Applications for the awards programs can be downloaded in PDF format. The site contains a list of the Foundation's board of directors as well as contact information.

Craft Emergency Relief Fund, Inc. (VT) (http://www.craftemergency.org)

Located in Montpelier, Vermont, the Craft Emergency Relief Fund was established in 1985. The group was created in order to "provide immediate support to professional craftspeople facing career threatening emergencies such as fire, theft, illness and natural disaster." Fund assistance is granted in the form of loans, booth fee waivers at craft shows, discounts from suppliers, and marketing and promotional assistance. Loan guidelines and application forms are available to be downloaded in PDF, Microsoft Word, and rich text formats. The site includes a list of the different funds and simple explanations of whom they support, from specific professions to specific ailments. Visitors will also find a list of the board of directors, press releases, information on selected staff, and an appeal for contributions. Loans range from $200–$2,000.

Jennifer Craig Memorial Fund for the Arts, Inc. (FL) (http://jcmfa.org/)

Established by a young musician's family and friends after her early death, the Jennifer Craig Memorial Fund for the Arts funds scholars and organizations in Florida. The fund is committed to spreading "Jenny's Song—a message of the joy that music [and the arts] can bring to its participants—that shall grow and involve as many young people as possible." A primary component of the giving program is an annual $10,000 scholarship for a southwest Florida high school senior who is going to attend the University of Central Florida to major in music. Other programs include loaning used instruments to students who can't afford them, small group lessons in oboe and bassoon at discounted rates, annual musical festivals, and a summer program for young, at-risk students. Assorted other grants are made to music-related organizations and projects. Interested visitors can contact the Fund by e-mail, fax, or phone.

CREATE Foundation (MS) (http://www.createfoundation.com)

Based in Tupelo, Mississippi, CREATE is an acronym for Christian Research, Education, Action, and Technical Enterprise and is a community foundation for northern Mississippi. CREATE awards grants to select organizations that target the community in the areas of community development, human development, and education. These areas are explained in detail on the CREATE Web site. Application instructions and guidelines, contact information, and details on CREATE's role as an endowment fund and its presence in northern Mississippi are available online.

Creative Capital (NY) (http://www.creative-capital.org/)

An outgrowth of the Andy Warhol Foundation, Creative Capital is oriented towards supporting individual artists in the visual, performing, and media arts. The organization provides audience development, marketing, and other forms of assistance tailored to individual projects in exchange for a share of the proceeds generated, which are then reinvested into the work of other artists. The organization's description, history, application and guidelines, and list of staff and advisors, and a selection of links to other arts resource organizations can all be found on its site. In addition, visitors may join a mailing list to receive updates.

Creative Time, Inc. (NY) (http://www.creativetime.org)

Based in New York City, Creative Time is an organization that supports the performing arts in public spaces in the five boroughs of New York City and nationwide. The Citywide Project Series provides funding for visual artists, architects, and performing artists in unexplored, underutilized, or abandoned public spaces in the five boroughs. Projects should challenge viewers and bridge cultures in its chosen public site. Extensive guidelines and requirements for these art projects are posted on the Web site along with previous projects. Although Creative Time's Web site does not provide a general overview of the organization, it does link to a number of projects and current events it sponsors. Opportunities for internships and to donate to Creative Time, an archive of past projects, and The Daily Dispatch with up-to-date news on the organization and the artists and projects it sponsors are all available online.

Crossroads Fund (IL) (http://www.crossroadsfund.org)

The Crossroads Fund is based in Chicago, Illinois. Its limited Web site details the backgrounds of its staff members and provides a list of previous grant recipients and the particulars of their programs. There is no contact information on the Web site.

Cruise Industry Charitable Foundation (DC) (http://www.iccl.org/foundation.htm)

The Cruise Industry Charitable Foundation (CICF) was established in 1998 by the International Council of Cruise Lines (ICCL), whose mission is to participate in the regulatory and policy development process of the cruise industry. The Washington, D.C.-based CICF works to improve the quality of life in the communities where the cruise industry has a presence by providing charitable grants to local programs. The Foundation supports programs designed to encourage job creation and training, improve access to community services, and provide youth and adult education, particularly for minority and disadvantaged students. The Foundation also focuses on programs designed to improve literacy, teach basic life skills, and provide mentoring services. Within these focus areas, the Foundation actively encourages and supports programs that meet the needs of "at risk populations within the following categories of individuals: the economically disadvantaged, the young, the elderly, people with disabilities, women, and minorities." Visit the Foundation's Web site for grant requirements and guidelines, links, press releases, and contact information.

Cystic Fibrosis Foundation (MD) (http://www.cff.org/)

Headquartered in Bethesda, Maryland, the Cystic Fibrosis Foundation was created in 1955 "to assure the development of the means to cure and control cystic fibrosis and to improve the quality of life for those with the disease." The group offers many research grants covering the many issues of cystic fibrosis. These include the new Therapeutics Development program that supports the development of drugs from the discovery through much of the evaluation phase. There are also training grants, which mostly support fellowships and post-doctoral funding. There are electronic applications available for most of the training grants and a link to the GEPPS system, where applicants can download research applications and find electronic cover sheets. The in-depth site offers visitors electronic publications, including the annual report; information on clinical trials; updates on relevant public policy and the Foundation's involvement in these efforts; and information on the cystic fibrosis pharmacy service. There are also facts on the disease and opportunities to contribute to the organization.

Dade Human Rights Foundation, Inc. (FL) (http://www.dhrf.com)

The Miami-based Dade Human Rights Foundation was established in 1994 to "advance education and public awareness with respect to GLBT [Gay, Lesbian, Bisexual, and Transgendered] issues and to support the local GLBT community." This is accomplished through twice-yearly community grants and the support of services dedicated to education, arts and culture, humanities, advocacy, and other community development projects. The Foundation's Web site includes grant guidelines, recent and previous grant recipients, a listing of related organizations, upcoming community events, and contact information.

Dance Films Association, Inc. (NY) (http://www.dancefilmsassn.org)

Dance Films Association (DFA) is a membership organization that acts as an information clearinghouse and meeting ground for the user, producer, and distributor of dance films and videos. Susan Braun founded the organization in 1956 after a futile search for films of her favorite dancer, Isadora Duncan. Ms. Braun devoted her life to finding, showcasing, preserving, and honoring dance films until her death in 1995. In addition to sponsoring publications, a film festival, and a touring program, the New York City-based Association serves as a "non-profit umbrella" for independent filmmakers seeking funding and supports documentaries. DFA has organized innumerable lectures, screenings, workshops, and panel discussions in institutions around the country and participated in competitions and festivals around the world. DFA accepts written proposals from dance filmmakers for post-production funding and will investigate discounts through post-production houses for members. Visit the Web site for a printable entry form for the Dance on Camera Festival and a printable membership form.

Deaconess Community Foundation (OH) (http://fdncenter.org/grantmaker/deaconess/)

Deaconess Community Foundation was created in 1997 following the sale of Deaconess Hospital of Cleveland in 1994 and two years of planning by Deaconess Health Systems. The Foundation provides resources that help organizations empower people in greater Cleveland, Ohio, to become self-sufficient and is guided by the spiritual traditions of the United Church of Christ. Grants are provided to nonprofit organizations for charitable, health, education, welfare, community, or social services. The Foundation's Web site gives the history of the foundation, grant guidelines and an application form, grants lists, and a listing of the board of trustees.

Deaconess Foundation (MO) (http://www.deaconess.org)

The Deaconess Foundation was established in 1972 as a supporting foundation for Deaconess Hospital. When the assets of Deaconess Incarnate Word Health System were sold in 1997, the proceeds were distributed to the Deaconess Foundation and Incarnate Word Health System; the Foundation no longer has any affiliation with the hospital. Based in St. Louis, Missouri, the Deaconess Foundation is a faith-based health foundation dedicated to the improved health of metropolitan St. Louis. The priority of the Foundation is to increase the well-being of vulnerable children in the core urban areas of the region. The Foundation defines the metropolitan St. Louis area as St. Louis City and St. Louis, Franklin, Jefferson and St. Charles Counties in Missouri and Madison, Monroe, and St. Clair Counties in Illinois. Visit the site for a description of the grant application process, grant listings, links to related sites, news releases, and contact information.

Deafness Research Foundation (NY) (http://www.drf.org)

The New York City-based Deafness Research Foundation (DRF) is a voluntary health organization committed to curing and preventing all forms of hearing loss and making lifelong hearing health a national priority. The Foundation's research grant program, the Otologic Research Grant Awards, aims to provide the "venture capital" for younger scientists for whom, in many cases, DRF is the only source of funds; support is also provided for established researchers. DRF recently launched the National Campaign for Hearing Health, a public outreach, professional education, and government relations initiative to ensure that all Americans, especially children, can benefit from these research breakthroughs and enjoy lifelong hearing. A principal goal of the campaign is to place into the national consciousness the idea and expectation that all hearing loss and tinnitus can be ended and that private funding for the research to achieve that end is an important national priority. The campaign's first focus is babies and children, promoting hearing tests and early intervention for all newborns; second, emphasizing the need to protect hearing by wearing ear protectors in noisy environments, practicing volume discipline, and advocating for toxic noise control policy; third, making all hearing devices available to all by pushing insurance companies to cover cochlear implants and other high-quality assistive hearing devices, especially for children; and fourth, expanding the field of otolaryngology and the supporting funding networks to greatly accelerate and increase research and encourage major scientific breakthroughs. Visitors to the site will find information on the awards program and the Foundation's initiatives, contact information, annual reports and the publications, related links, and information on hearing health.

Delaware Humanities Forum (DE) (http://www.dhf.org/)

The Delaware Humanities Forum, an adjunct of the Delaware Humanities Council, supports educational programs in the humanities through its own programs and sponsorship of a range of activities, including lectures, conferences, radio and television broadcasts, interpretive exhibits, and book and film discussions. Descriptions of the Forum's programs, which include a Speakers Bureau, a Visiting Scholars Program, an Annual Lecture, and Workplace Programs are available on the Forum's Web site, along with information about grant eligibility requirements and deadlines, frequently asked questions, and downloadable guidelines and application forms in PDF format. Visitors will also find a calendar of events, an interactive form for ordering Forum materials, and contact information.

Dental Fund (MI) (http://www.deltadentalmi.com/communityservice.htm)

Created in 1980, the Delta Dental Fund is the philanthropic arm of Delta Dental Plan of Michigan (DDPM). The Fund's mission is "to manifest the social responsibility of Delta Dental Plan of Michigan, its parent organization, and in doing so, make a positive impact on the quality of life in the community, placing a special emphasis on dental health." The Fund supports educational and research programs for the advancement of dental science, promotes the general oral health of the public through educational and service activities, encourages civic and cultural activities, and enhances the relationship between DDPM and its participating dentists. The Web site provides links to information about current programs that the Fund participates in. Contact information for the Delta Dental Plan is also available.

Denver Broncos Charities (CO) (http://www.denverbroncos.com/offthefield/index.php3)

Founded in 1994 by the Denver Broncos pro football team, the Denver Broncos Charities supports nonprofit organizations in Colorado. For every dollar the Denver Broncos Charity Fund spends, the Robert R. McCormick Tribune Foundation donates a matching dollar. The Fund supports programs in three areas: education, athletics, and life skills designed to impact disadvantaged and at-risk young people; programs devoted to physically and mentally challenged individuals; and programs for the hungry and homeless. On the Off-the-Field section of the Denver Broncos Web site, the Fund lists events that it has sponsored and its community partners. The Broncos Charities also sponsor a number of events, camps, and programs for the youth and families of Colorado, which are described in the Community Relations portion of the Web site. A four-year scholarship is also available to Colorado high school students who will be attending a Colorado college or university. An application in PDF format can be downloaded from the site.

Detroit Lions Charities (MI) (http://www.detroitlions.com/home.html)

Established by the NFL's Detroit Lions, the Detroit Lions Charities support education, civic affairs, and health and human services in the state of Michigan. Programs currently funded by the DLC include learning initiatives for youth, housing for less fortunate families, mentoring projects, domestic violence education, athletic programs for youth, substance abuse programs, and a visiting lecturer series at a creative studies center. Visitors to the Lions' Web site will find a description of the DLC and its activities, funding request deadlines, a press release on current grants and annual giving totals, and contact information.

Diana Princess of Wales Memorial Fund (DC) (http://www.usdianafund.org)

The mission of the Diana Princess of Wales Memorial Fund is "to help people in need and distress, especially those at the margins of society, in a manner that is consistent with the vision and lifework of Diana, Princess of Wales." The Fund was set up in response to thousands of letters and contributions from people around the world following the death of Diana, Princess of Wales in August 1997. The Fund seeks to continue Princess Diana's vision and life work by generating support for issues that have not yet received considerable funding or attention. The Fund provides financial assistance to U.S. nonprofit organizations doing local, national, or international work in the following general areas: support for disadvantaged individuals, families, and groups, including the homeless, the unemployed, the mentally ill, the physically disabled, the dying and bereaved, displaced people and refugees, and others who are under-served; support for people suffering from discrimination and prejudice, including women, children, and others who have been marginalized; support for land-mine victims and their families and other survivors of violence, including domestic violence; and support for health education and prevention, with a particular emphasis on AIDS. The Fund will seek to support organizations that have an innovative approach, that promote new and viable strategies or build upon existing positive models, and that have the potential to have long-term impact. Visitors to the site will find information on grants competitions, application information, downloadable application packets and forms, downloadable grant recipients list, contact information, and links to related sites.

Do Something, Inc. (NY) (http://www.dosomething.org/)

Founded in 1993, Do Something provides leadership training, guidance, and financial resources to young people committed to strengthening their communities. The organization annually honors 10 community leaders under the age of 30 with the "BRICK Award for Community Leadership." Do Something also awards grants of up to $500 to young people with an idea for a community project. Application forms for both programs can be printed from the Do Something Web site (the form for the latter program is also available on America Online by entering the keyword "Do Something"). In addition to information about the organization's activities, visitors to the colorful Do Something Web site can check out back issues of *Build,* the organization's online 'zine, and learn more about community networks, partnerships, and jobs.

The Dollywood Foundation (TN) (http://www.dollywood.com/Foundation.htm)

Founded in 1988 by Dolly Parton and the Dollywood Company, the Dollywood Foundation is in Pigeon Forge, Tennessee. "The Foundation develops and administers educational programs for the children of Dolly's native Sevier County, Tennessee, to inspire them to Dream More . . . Learn More . . . Do More . . . [and] Be More." The Foundation awards three scholarships each year at each of the three county high schools, one each in the areas of music, academics, and environment. The current main project is the Imagination Library, which distributes a sixty-volume collection of books to children in Servier County. They receive a book a month from birth until age three. The site includes a contact address and information on Dolly Parton's albums whose sales supply the Foundation funding.

Dranoff Foundation, Murray (FL) (http://www.dranoff2piano.org/)

Miami, Florida's Murray Dranoff Foundation was founded in 1987 by the late musician's wife. The Foundation is devoted to introducing, educating, and involving the largest possible audience in the renaissance and literature of four-hand chamber music for the piano. The Foundation hosts two annual two–piano competitions in Miami, one being a new competition for young players. The organization also sponsors an annual two–piano symposium, commissions new pieces to be played in competition finals, and sponsors a series of salon nights in preparation for the competition. The site includes deadlines and downloadable applications (in PDF format) for the competitions.

Drug Policy Foundation (DC) (http://www.dpf.org/)

The Drug Policy Foundation (DPF) of Washington, D.C., was founded in 1986 and represents over 24,000 supporters. DPF "is an independent, non-profit organization that develops and promotes innovative approaches to reduce the risk of drug use, the harms of drug abuse and the harms caused by the war on drugs." The Grant Program funds drug policy reform organizations in the United States and abroad. All proposals must be specifically for project, general, or technical support. Most funding goes toward project funding in one of three categories: model programs, advocacy efforts, or drug policy education. Grants rarely exceed $25,000 and address goals that span every aspect of drug policy. The Foundation's site has very detailed grant application instructions. Goals are succinctly listed, each type of support is clearly described, there is a highlighted grantee example, and a grantee list. Appendices supply guides for applications, planning, and writing a budget. The rest of the newly designed site offers press releases and papers describing the Foundation's stance and actions on current issues and descriptions of different bills going before legislators. The Annual Report and a list of board members are available.

The Dunn Foundation (RI) (http://www.dunnfoundation.org/)

The mission of The Dunn Foundation is to promote the quality of the visual environment as a guiding principle for the growth and development of America's communities through education and philanthropy. This mission is fulfilled through increasing public understanding of the contribution community appearance makes to our quality of life and by linking people to the tools they need to make positive aesthetic changes in their environment. Application guidelines, grants lists, grantmaking priorities, and information on the Foundation's "visual literacy" programs, Viewfinders and Suburban Streetscapes, are among the features offered on the Foundation's Web site.

Dystonia Medical Research Foundation (IL) (http://www.dystonia-foundation.org/)

The Dystonia Medical Research Foundation, based in Chicago, Illinois, supports research on dystonia, increases public awareness, and provides support to those affected by the disease. A brief description of the Foundation's research funding is provided at its Web site, along with information on its education and awareness activities, donor information, listings of its board of directors and scientific advisory board, and contact information. The Foundation also provides Spanish and French versions of its Web site.

The Education Enhancement Partnership (OH) (http://www.teep.org)

Created in 1989, The Education Enhancement Partnership is located in Canton, Ohio, and serves 95,000 students. The organization's mission is to "foster private sector efforts in education reform to improve learning for all children, from pre-school through twelfth grade, in Stark County, Ohio." The group supports schools that are committed to reform and are working in conjunction with their administration and community. TEEP works toward reforms including those that hold all students to high standards and judge effectiveness by the quality of students' work and educators' practice. Projects include: Science Education Enhancing the Development of Skills (SEEDS), a $3 million elementary school program; a summer arts institute for teacher development; a small grants program to increase family involvement; SAMM (Science and Math in Motion) Project, which brings high–tech science equipment and training into the classroom; and a series of programs bringing computer technology into the schools. The Web site includes staff and board lists and a page of very helpful, related links. The Partnership serves as the reviewing agency for the Partners in Education on grant requests dealing with education reform.

Education Foundation National Restaurant Association (IL) (http://www.edfound.org)

The National Restaurant Association Educational Foundation is a not-for-profit organization "dedicated to providing educational and training solutions that serve the needs of the entire restaurant and hospitality industry (national and international): corporations, associations, schools, independent operators and trainers." Established in 1987 through a merger between the National Restaurant Association's educational department and the National Institute for the Foodservice Industry (NIFI), the Foundation is the primary resource for industry career development at all levels. The Foundation gives scholarships to senior high school students, undergraduate students, and educators who are committed to furthering their education and enhancing their careers in the restaurant and foodservice industry. To receive an application, interested parties can either e-mail or call the Foundation or complete an online application using the link provided on the Web site. In addition to giving scholarships, the Foundation also conducts research, sets industry training standards, and organizes and conducts training seminars. More information about the Foundation's work is available on the site.

The Electrical Contracting Foundation, Inc. (MD) (http://www.ecfound.org)

Located in Bethesda, Maryland, the Electrical Contracting Foundation (ELECTRI21) has been supporting the goals of the National Electrical Contractors Association (NECA) since it was established in 1988. The organization's mission is to "strengthen the fabric of the electrical industry through the development of information which will positively affect the future of the electrical industry and its service to the public." Research grants are made to accomplish this mission. Projects of particular interest involve career awareness, productivity enhancement, organizational development, and technology transfer. The group posts Requests for Proposals on its site that include deadlines, guidelines, and specific project interests. There is also an electronic form for visitors to submit research topics for the next year. The site includes information on becoming a member of the Foundation, descriptions of ongoing research, and finished research reports. There is a also a news section, a calendar of events, and an online version of the annual report.

Emergency Nursing Foundation (IL) (http://www.ena.org/foundation/)

The Emergency Nursing Foundation was founded by the Emergency Nursing Association in 1991 and is based in Des Plains, Illinois. The Foundation's mission is to "enhance emergency health services available to the public through education and research," in order to benefit emergency nurses, emergency patients, and the public. The Foundation favors grants that promote emergency nursing, enhance professional development, educate healthcare professionals and the public on subjects relating to emergency care, and provide research grants and scholarships. Scholarships are available for undergraduates and graduates; the Foundation provides an application form that can be downloaded in PDF format from its Web site. Grants are made for special projects/program development and research; the Foundation's Web site includes guidelines and applications for each grant in PDF and Microsoft Word formats that can be downloaded and in an online form that can be printed. The Web site also includes news, a contribution form, an FAQ, and contact information.

Enterprise Foundation (MD) (http://www.enterprisefoundation.org/)

Launched by visionary developer Jim Rouse and his wife Patty in 1982, the Enterprise Foundation focuses its activities on providing "all low-income people in the United States . . . the opportunity for fit and affordable housing . . ." The Foundation's Web site offers extensive information about the plethora of loans, investments, training programs, and technical assistance supported by the foundation and its subsidiaries. Visitors to the site can also access information on the Foundation's annual Network Conference; read various Foundation publications, news releases, and newsletters; and search the Best Practices Database, which shares experiences, strategies, and techniques for assisting low-income people.

The Entertainment Industry Foundation (CA) (http://eifoundation.org)

Formed in 1942 by Samuel Goldwyn as the Motion Pictures Charity Committee, the Entertainment Industry Foundation of Los Angeles, California, is still thriving. The Foundation works "to coordinate the philanthropy of the entertainment industry to achieve maximum social impact in the community." Funding is given to organizations in the greater Los Angeles area. The Education and Prevention Program includes funds for creative and performing arts, environment, literacy and education, family care and welfare, substance abuse prevention, and youth welfare. The Health and Human Services Program fund includes children's health and care, medical research and healthcare, HIV/AIDS, hunger/homelessness, and seniors issues. Grant guidelines are extensive and explicit, and interested parties must call the Foundation to have a grant application sent. In the Beneficiaries section there is a list of organizations supported by each fund. There are also opportunities to contribute to the Foundation, a list of corporate sponsors, and special events that it sponsors. The Foundation was formerly known as Permanent Charities.

Entomological Foundation (MD) (http://www.entsoc.org/foundation/)

The Entomological Foundation of Lanham, Maryland, was created in 1991 as the resource development arm of the Entomological Society of America. This scientific, educational group is "dedicated to the acquisition and dissemination of scientific knowledge within the field of entomology." The Foundation awards fellowships to researchers, college scholarships for students around the world to study entomology, and sponsors hands-on activities through the United States and Canada through the traveling Insect Expo. The assorted fellowships, awards, and scholarships each have their own descriptions and qualifications. They range from travel stipends to research grants in biodiversity inventory, integrated pest management, and the identification and biology of new insects. Each description includes application guidelines and deadlines and information on the sponsors of the grant. The site includes a board list, donor lists, and information on donor-advised funds.

Entrepreneurs' Foundation (CA) (http://www.the-ef.org/)

The Entrepreneurs' Foundation was created in 1998 to encourage entrepreneurs in the Silicon Valley/Bay Area to reinvest in their communities. The Foundation works with young companies to help them develop and facilitate a three-year community involvement plan. In return, each company gives equity stock to the Foundation, which invests the capital gains from the appreciated stock in nonprofit leaders who engage in "venture philanthropy" practices—the application of venture capital strategies to philanthropic giving. The Foundation collaborates with existing funders to provide capital for expanding education and youth development programs. The EF Web site provides a helpful FAQ on the Foundation's brand of philanthropy, information about sponsors and participants, links to related "venture philanthropy" resources, and contact information.

Environmental Research and Education Foundation (DC) (http://www.erefdn.org)

The Environmental Research and Education Foundation of Washington, D.C., was established in 1992. The group's goal is to "develop environmental solutions for the future through research and education." Grants are focused in four areas of interest: new technological safety measures for the waste service industry, public education on the industry, discoveries and research that advance the industry, and scholarship programs for doctoral candidates in environmental science. Applications can be requested by mail or downloaded in PDF format. The site also includes the annual report, which provides a board list, and a list of recent grant recipients.

Equipment Leasing and Finance Foundation (VA) (http://www.leasefoundation.org/index.htm)

The Equipment Leasing and Finance Foundation was established in Arlington, Virginia, in 1989 as a means to "promote the growth and effectiveness of equipment leasing and finance" through the development and enhanced recognition of the lease financing industry. The Foundation makes grants to organizations and programs whose proposed grant subject has a practical application to professionals in the leasing and finance business. Internships in the industry are also available; more information is provided on the Foundation's Web site. Grant guidelines, publications and industry resources (some specifically for members of the Equipment Leasing Association), and contact information are also provided online.

Equity Foundation, Inc. (OR) (http://equityfoundation.org/)

Based in Portland, Oregon, the Equity Foundation works to promote the welfare of the gay, lesbian, bisexual, and transgendered communities and of the people of Oregon in general by providing support to nonprofit organizations throughout the state. The Foundation provides funding through its annual granting cycle and community outreach grants as well as through the administration of individual donor-advised funds and scholarship programs. Key issues for the Foundation include improving acceptance, understanding, and cooperation among people and eradicating homophobia and other forms of discrimination; providing support for youth and family programs that strengthen GLBT families; health and social services; and support for arts and cultural organizations whose programs are in alignment with the Foundation's mission and that enrich the entire community. The Foundation's Web site provides a thorough description of its grantmaking activities, a list of recent grants, information for donors, FAQs, brief biographies of the Foundation's board and staff, and contact information.

Boomer Esiason Foundation (NY) (http://www.esiason.org)

Based in New York City, the Boomer Esiason Foundation was founded by the football great in 1993 after his son was born with cystic fibrosis. The organization is committed to "heightening awareness of cystic fibrosis and to providing a better quality of life for those affected by cystic fibrosis." The Foundation supports research, makes sure that doctors have access to the most innovative treatments, educates the public on the disease, helps patients combat the disease, and supports students' and hospital staff's effort to create a tradition of quality healthcare. The Web site includes updates on related legislative issues, news on medical research, and a basic definition of the disease. Visitors will also find board and staff lists and links to both fundraising and cystic fibrosis resources. There is a calendar of events, primarily fundraisers, and also a list of corporate partners. Information for students interested in interning for the Foundation is also included.

Eurasia Foundation (DC) (http://www.eurasia.org/)

The Washington, D.C.-based Eurasia Foundation is a privately managed grantmaking organization dedicated to funding programs that build democratic and free market institutions in the newly independent states of the former Soviet Union: Armenia, Azerbaijan, Belarus, Georgia, Kazakstan, Kyrgyzstan, Moldova, Russia, Tajikistan, Turkmenistan, Ukraine, and Uzbekistan. The Foundation concentrates its support in eight priority areas: business development, business education and management training, economics education and research, public administration and local government reform, NGO development, rule of law, media, and electronic communications. Visitors to the Foundation's Web site will find program descriptions and application guidelines; a searchable database of grants; a directory of Foundation offices, staff, and board members; links to Web sites of interest; job opportunities; news; and contact information.

Lettie Pate Evans Foundation, Inc. (GA) (http://www.lpevans.org)

Lettie Pate Evans was the wife of Joseph Whitehead, one of the original bottlers of Coca-Cola. She became one of the first American women to serve as a director of a major American corporation when she was appointed to the Board of Directors of the Coca-Cola Company in 1934, a post she held for 20 years. In 1945, Lettie Pate Evans created a foundation in her own name, for the "promotion of charity," with a grant program reflecting a strong emphasis in private secondary and higher education, arts and culture, and museums and historic preservation. Grants awarded by this Atlanta, Georgia-based foundation are generally limited to institutions in Georgia and, from time to time, institutions in Virginia favored by Lettie Pate Evans during her lifetime. Preference has traditionally been given to one-time capital projects. Grant proposals submitted to the Foundation may also be considered by one or more of the four other foundations sharing staff and offices with the Lettie Pate Evans Foundation; therefore, it is unnecessary to communicate separately with more than one of these foundations when seeking information or grant support. Points of interest on the Web site include grant application guidelines; analysis of 1998 grants; financial information; a list of officers and trustees; contact information, including an e-mail link; a link to other foundations; and a short biography of the founder.

Experimental Television Center, Ltd. (NY) (http://www.experimentaltvcenter.org)
Founded in 1971, the Experimental Television Center's mission is "to support the creation of new work using electronic media technologies," through programs, grants, and services that encourage education, research, and preservation. The Center offers a residency program as well as four types of grants to artists: Electronic and Film Arts Grants, Finishing Funds, Presentation Funds, and the Media Arts Technical Assistance Fund. The Residency program and each grant type is explained in greater detail on the Center's Web site, along with grant guidelines for potential applicants. Applications for the four grants can be downloaded in PDF format. A history of the Center, introduction to its facilities, and a contact e-mail address are also available online.

Family Office Exchange Foundation (IL) (http://www.foxfoundation.org)
Based in Oak Park, Illinois, the Family Office Exchange Foundation (known as the FOX Foundation) is committed to lifelong family learning and a family-centered curriculum based on human, intellectual, financial, and social capital. These areas of interest are explained in more detail on the Foundation's Web site, along with an outline of the Foundation's curriculum, with course descriptions and syllabi for each course. There is contact information on the site for further details about the FOX Foundation and current class schedules.

Farm Foundation (IL) (http://www.farmfoundation.org)
Created in 1933, the Farm Foundation of Oak Brook, Illinois, is an operating foundation. The organization's mission is "to improve the economic and social well-being of U.S. agriculture and rural people by helping private and public sector decision makers identify and understand forces that will shape the future." The Foundation provides proactive leadership in projects that it supports, which frequently focus on educational outreach or forums for the population that the Foundation serves. The very diverse projects fall in the following categories: globalization, environmental and natural resource issues, new technologies, the role of agricultural institutions, consumer issues, and rural community viability communications and leadership. Projects range from conferences and seminars to research projects and policy surveys. The Foundation does award Extension Fellowships to state and federal cooperative extension employees pursuing additional training. Applications can be requested from the Foundation and are due annually at the beginning of March. The site offers the results of many research projects, an extensive area of public policy education, lists of the board and staff members, and online versions of Foundation publications, including the annual report in PDF format.

Fidelity Investments Charitable Gift Fund (MA) (http://www.charitable-gift.org/)
The Fidelity Investments Charitable Gift Fund is a new way for individuals to make tax-exempt donations to their favorite nonprofit organization. There are two programs: a donor-advised fund and a Pooled Income Fund. Grants are made to organizations that investors select. There is no application process, as participants are encouraged to research areas of interest to find a grantee. The company's annual report is available.

Film Arts Foundation (CA) (http://www.filmarts.org)
The Film Arts Foundation (FAF) was founded in San Francisco, California, in 1976 and has served the Bay Area community ever since. The organization is committed to supporting the development of independent films with equipment and education, screening independent films, and supporting the community that creates these films. Since 1984, FAF has distributed grants through the Film Arts Foundation Grants Program. The Fund for Independent Cinema gives cash grants to Bay Area residents to "encourage new and diverse works by film and video artists who have little likelihood of being supported through traditional funding sources." The Cash Awards Program makes grants of $4,000 for personal works in film or video that can be produced for the grant amount and makes grants of $8,000 to artists who need just this amount to distribute their film. The Blazing Paradigm Completion Grants gives one filmmaker the use of an Apple Final Cut Pro. The Robin Eickman Feature Film Award, materials and services valued at $48,000, is given to

one feature–length narrative film budgeted under $200,000. Finally, STAND (Support, Training, and Access for New Directors) awards are given to directors from under-represented communities. Applications and application guidelines are available in PDF format, along with lists of previous years' recipients. The site includes information of screenings, the annual film festival, and an extensive list of seminars.

Fine Arts Work Center in Provincetown, Inc. (MA) (http://www.fawc.org)
The Fine Arts Work Center in Provincetown was established in Massachusetts in 1968 by a group of artists who wanted to support talented artists at the beginning of their careers. This greatly esteemed organization is "devoted to encouraging and supporting young artists and is built on the belief that freedom and community are the best means and natural conditions for artistic growth." The Center's predominant program is the seven-month Winter Fellow-ship, which brings ten writers and ten visual artists to Provincetown for a residency in a his-torically supportive community. The site offers application guidelines and deadlines and a printable online application. There is an impressive list of past recipients and awards. The Center also sponsors ten weeks of Summer Programs each year, with week-long and week-end courses taught by former fellows and committee members. Assorted other program include long-term and short-term intensive residencies for former fellows and a program for older (over 50) writers, speakers, and exhibitions. The site includes an events calendar, staff and board lists, and organization updates.

First Nations Development Institute (VA) (http://www.firstnations.org/)
The First Nations Development Institute was formed in 1980 to help Native American tribes build sound, sustainable reservation communities by linking grassroots projects with national programs. Through its Eagle Staff Fund: A Collaborative For Native American Development, the Institute offers grants in support of "holistic" economic development projects that consider communities' economic, environmental, spiritual, cultural, political, social, and health needs. In addition, the Institute's Oweesta Program provides technical assistance to communities in creating and controlling capital assets for financing reserva-tion and community development. Detailed information on these programs, a list of related links, and contact information are available at the First Nations Web site.

FishAmerica Foundation (VA)
(http://www.asafishing.org/programs/conservation/fishamerica/)
The philanthropic arm of the American Sportfishing Association, the FishAmerica Foun-dation was established in the mid-1970s in Alexandria, Virginia. The goal of the organiza-tion is to "help industry and citizens put something back into the fishery resources that make their businesses profitable and their spare time so enjoyable." The Foundation offers grants to encourage volunteer activity and to support the programmatic efforts of grassroots organizations in all fifty states and Canada. Areas that the Foundation supports include: habitat improvement, streambank stabilization, reef projects, silt removal, fish passages, litter cleanups and prevention, and hands-on education. Visitors to the Web site can print out an application or a membership form and watch a video. Application must be accompa-nied by a letter of support from the appropriate state resource agency.

Alisa Flatow Memorial Scholarship Fund (NJ) (http://www.alisafund.org/)
The Alisa Flatow Memorial Scholarship Fund of Whippany, New Jersey, was created to "encourage others to follow in Alisa's footsteps by studying Judaism at schools in the State of Israel." Scholarships are granted for post-high school study combining secular and Jew-ish study at institutions in Israel—recipients are allowed to simultaneously earn credits for a university. Applicants can apply online or request a print copy of the application. The site also contains a list of present and past scholarship recipients. The scholarship is adminis-tered through the Jewish Community Foundation of MetroWest.

A.J. Fletcher Foundation (NC) (http://www.ajf.org/)
Originally formed to provide operating support for A.J. Fletcher's Grass Roots Opera, which later evolved into the National Opera Company, the A.J. Fletcher Foundation today

supports a broad range of "nonprofit organizations in their endeavors to enrich the people of North Carolina." The Foundation makes grants in five areas: Arts and Humanities, Organizational and Administrative Development, Education, Programs Benefiting Children and Youth, and Community Initiatives and Human Services. The Foundation's Web site provides a description of the foundation, a biography of A.J. Fletcher, grants lists by giving area, grant guidelines, and a downloadable application form. Visitors to the site can also read about the National Opera Company and another major beneficiary, the Fletcher School of Performing Arts.

Florida Humanities Council (FL) (http://www.flahum.org/)
Since its founding in 1971, the Florida Humanities Council has awarded more than eight million dollars to community and educational organizations in support of public programs centered in the following disciplines: philosophy, ethics, comparative religions, history, art criticism/art history, jurisprudence, literature, languages, linguistics, archaeology, cultural anthropology, and folklore/folklife. FHC's grantmaking is divided into three main categories: Major Grants (all requests for more than $2,000, with an upper limit of $25,000 per grant), Mini Grants (grants up to $2,000), and Scholar/Humanist Fellowships (grants to individual scholars or humanists for research on humanities topics or themes announced by FHC). In addition to detailed program information and information about FHC activities and membership, visitors to the FHC Web site will find downloadable application and independent evaluator forms, a calendar of FHC-sponsored and -funded events, and links to dozens of state humanities councils and humanities resources on the Web.

The For All Kids Foundation, Inc. (NJ) (http://www.forallkids.org)
The For All Kids Foundation of Allendale, New Jersey, was established in 1997 by talk show host, Rosie O'Donnell. Its mission is to "help support the intellectual, social and cultural development of disadvantaged children throughout the United States." The Foundation focuses on supporting at-risk children through childcare, healthcare, and education programs in underserved communities. A key interest is in organizations that provide direct childcare services. The site includes application guidelines, a list of grant recipients, and a link to the online auction site that raises money for the Foundation.

Foundation For Cancer Survival (CT) (http://www.foundationforcancersurvival.com)
The Foundation for Cancer Survival was established in April 2000 to honor the life and experiences of Lisa Liscomb, who was diagnosed with a malignant brain tumor at the age of 24. Through Lisa's journey, the founders of the Foundation saw that "proper information and funding can lead to cancer survival." The Foundation, based in Tolland, Connecticut, is currently in its formative stages, actively seeking donations and links to cancer resources for its Web site. A contact address is provided for further information.

Foundation for Chiropractic Education & Research, Inc. (IA) (http://www.fcer.org)
The Foundation for Chiropractic Education and Research was established in 1944 and now has offices in Des Moines, Iowa (administrative); Brookline, Massachusetts (research); and Bremerton, Washington (editorial). The group is committed to "promoting the public's health by encouraging and supporting research and education relative to the field of chiropractic care, and serving the needs of practicing chiropractors worldwide." Research grants are made in a number of major categories including: the effectiveness of chiropractic care in the management of conditions beyond low-back pain; the identification of new groups of patients; basic and educational research; verification of instruments, design, and data processing techniques; and economic and practice patterns of chiropractic care. Application guidelines and restrictions are given in "The Development and Funding [Care and Feeding] of a Research Proposal: A Review of the Process of Grant Applications to FCER." Applications can be requested from the Foundation, and lists of previous grantees are offered. The site also includes lists of staff and board members and a Products area where publications are offered.

Foundation for National Progress (CA) (http://www.motherjones.com)

Located in San Francisco, the Foundation for National Progress was established in 1975 "to educate and empower people through media to work toward progressive change." Along with a training program for interns in investigative journalism and the Mother Jones International Fund for Documentary Photography, the Foundation has been publishing the magazine *Mother Jones* since 1976. The acclaimed publication focuses on issues of social justice, the environment, politics, and popular culture. Along with its bimonthly print edition, the Foundation publishes a Web-based version of *Mother Jones* free of charge. The site includes Web-exclusive articles, discussion groups, and breaking news. Applicants interested in the Photography Fund can find more details and previous grant recipients in the site's FAQ section, while contact information for the Foundation for National Progress can be found in the About Us section of the site.

Foundation for Physical Therapy (VA) (http://www.apta.org/Foundation)

The Foundation for Physical Therapy, located in Alexandria, Virginia, was established in 1979 as a national, independent, nonprofit corporation to support the physical therapy profession's research needs in three areas: scientific research, clinical research, and health services research. Its mission is to "advance the physical therapy profession through support for doctoral education and sponsorship of clinically relevant research." Specifically, the Foundation aims to assist clinicians, researchers, and academicians in their doctoral programs; expand funding for emerging researchers; support clinically relevant research; and strengthen the Foundation's capacity to promote the profession's research agenda. For research funding assistance, interested parties are encouraged to contact the Foundation to learn more about application procedures and deadlines. Contact information, a listing of staff members and the board of directors, and information on the most recent grant and scholarship awardees can all be found on the Web site.

Foundation for Saline Area Schools (MI) (http://server.saline.lib.mi.us/fsas/)

The Foundation for Saline Area Schools was established in 1987 to "generate, for distribution, financial and other resources to the schools for enrichment programs and other projects aimed at enhancing the quality of education and educational opportunities." Its purpose is to fund innovative educational programs, activities, and events that supplement basic school programs not provided by existing school budgets. Specifically, the Foundation promotes student learning opportunities, encourages excellence and growth of all staff, and facilitates community/school partnerships. It receives and reviews grant proposals from Saline Area Schools. The Web site provides e-mail and regular mail addresses for those interested in receiving an application or learning more. It also provides the list of Board members and advisors, along with lists of previous grants awarded.

The Foundation for Technology Education, Inc. (VA) (http://www.iteawww.org/I1.html)

Based in Reston, Virginia, the Foundation for Technology Education was created in 1986 by the International Technology Education Association (ITEA). The organization's straightforward mission is to "support the advancement of technology education through teacher scholarships and grants." The Foundation distributes two grants: the Hearlihy/FTE Grant is given to a K–12 teacher who has integrated quality technology education into the curriculum and the Howard and Virtue Gerrish/FTE Technology Education Graduate Fellowship for Leadership Development goes to a member of the ITEA for professional development. The Foundation also offers three scholarships. The Litherland/FTE Scholarship is given to an undergraduate student majoring in technology education teacher preparation, the Maley/FTE Technology Teacher Scholarship supports a successful teacher who is attending graduate school, and the Undergraduate Scholarship is given to an exemplary student. All of these scholarships are only open to members of the ITEA. All five of these programs have application deadlines and guidelines listed. The Foundation's Web site also features pages on other scholarships and a series of awards given by the ITEA.

Frameline, Inc. (CA) (http://www.frameline.org/fund_home.html)

Frameline is dedicated to the exhibition, distribution, promotion, and funding of lesbian and gay film and video and presents the annual San Francisco International Lesbian & Gay Film Festival. Frameline's grant program is called the Completion Fund, which helps artists to complete their film and video projects. Fund guidelines are provided at Frameline's Web site. Visitors to the site will also find information about the festival, Frameline Distribution, membership, events, and resources.

FRAXA Research Foundation (MA) (http://www.fraxa.org)

The FRAXA Research Foundation supports in-depth research leading to the treatment or a cure for Fragile X Syndrome, a genetic cause of mental retardation. The Foundation funds grants and fellowships that research timely and practical treatment of Fragile X, especially "preclinical studies of potential pharmaceutical and genetic treatments and studies aimed at understanding the function of the FMR1 gene." The FRAXA Web site provides an informative Q & A on Fragile X, as well as information on joining FRAXA, publications, events, and links to other resources. Grants and fellowships made by the Foundation are for up to $35,000 per year of postdoctoral study. Past fellows and grantees, with abstracts of their work, are listed on the site. Grant guidelines, including the application process and obligations of fellows, are also provided online.

Milton & Rose D. Friedman Foundation (IN) (http://www.friedmanfoundation.org/)

The Milton & Rose D. Friedman Foundation, established in September 1996 by two economists concerned about the quality of public schools, works to restructure the education system to encourage competition in the market for educational services and give parents more choices about the schools their children attend. The Foundation promotes the use of "educational vouchers"—providing to parents who wish to send their children to private schools "a sum equal to the estimated cost of educating a child in a government school, provided that at least this sum was spent on education in an approved school." The Foundation funds research into the judicial and legislative decisions on school choice and the social and economic impact of voucher programs. The Foundation's Web site offers opinions and answers to questions on this issue and provides donor information, related Web sites, and an e-mail contact.

Frontier Village Foundation (CO) (http://rmmc.org/mcmc/FVF/FVF.main.htm)

The Frontier Village Foundation is based in Palmer Lake, Colorado, and focuses its giving in the Rocky Mountain region. The Foundation is associated with the Mountain Community Mennonite Church and mainly grants one-time startup funding for programs that follow the Foundation's mission: "to fund community service programs of a preventive nature which reflects our collective understanding of Jesus Christ's teaching to reach out to those in need among us." The FVF Web site includes grant guidelines, past grant recipients, the Foundation's guiding philosophy, and a link to the Foundation's parent church, where more contact information is available.

The Fund for American Studies (DC) (http://www.TFAS.org)

The Fund for American Studies, located in Washington, D.C., is dedicated to "preparing young people for honorable leadership by educating them in the theory, practice, and benefits of a free society." This is done by sponsoring summer institutes that take place all over the world for college students on economic concepts, political systems, and moral philosophy. The topics of the six rigorous courses are political and economic systems/studies, business and government affairs, political journalism, and philanthropy and voluntary service. The competitive, international programs each have their own page with details on that specific institute that may include a downloadable application, an application status check, and testaments from former participants. The site also includes the most recent Fund newsletter (available in PDF or plain text formats), a list of the board, a list of corporate sponsors, organization news, and a link to an alumni Web site.

Fund for an Open Society (PA) (http://www.libertynet.org/~open)
The Fund for an Open Society is a Philadelphia-based national nonprofit mortgage fund and a Pennsylvania mortgage broker, providing financially advantageous loans to qualified borrowers purchasing owner-occupied housing where it will help sustain or promote racially integrated neighborhoods. Civil rights legend James Farmer and pro-integrative housing developer Morris Milgram organized OPEN in 1975 to promote racial integration in housing. Loans are made to people of color and whites buying where their races are underrepresented. Visit the site for loan guidelines and requirements, newsletters, articles, and brochures, related resources, and contact information. A mortgage loan prequalification form can be printed from the site or submitted online.

Fund for Santa Barbara (CA) (http://www.fundforsantabarbara.org/)
Created in 1980, the Fund for Santa Barbara supports progressive social change. The organization is "dedicated to finding solutions to current and emerging social problems and issues that challenge our society as a whole." The Fund encourages groups in South Santa Barbara County that focus on one of its areas of interest to apply for cash grants and/or technical support. Areas of interest include: discrimination based on race, sex, age, religion, economic status, etc.; the rights of workers; self-determination in low-income communities; the environment; and operating in a democratic manner. Grants are made for up to $4,000. The site includes application guidelines, limitations, and deadlines; online applications; information on contributing; a grant history; a newsletter; and contact information.

Fund for Southern Communities (GA) (http://www.fex.org/south/south.html)
The Fund for Southern Communities, of Decatur, Georgia, was created in 1981. The founders' goals were to "build safe, equitable communities that are free of oppression and that embrace and celebrate all people," and these goals are being met today through grants to groups in Georgia, North Carolina, and South Carolina. The grant program supports organizations including those that work against discrimination, support the rights of workers, promote self-determination in low-income communities, and protect the environment. The site includes extensive funding guidelines and application deadlines, grant lists, and information on donor involvement.

The Fund for Wild Nature (OR) (http://www.fundwildnature.org/)
The Fund for Wild Nature, of Portland, Oregon, believes in the importance of healthy ecosystems. The organization's mission is "to fund grassroots projects that protect biodiversity, which would not otherwise be funded through mainstream sources." The Fund is looking for projects that address issues not being given enough national attention, involve an alliance of related groups within the field, and may lead to long-term systemic change. General areas supported by the group include wilderness defense, teaching the ethics of biocentrism, human population growth and commodity consumption reduction efforts, cultural arts that encourage action, and indigenous peoples' activism. The Web site includes application guidelines and restrictions, grant lists, and selected portions of the most recent annual report.

Funding Exchange (NY) (http://www.fex.org)
Funding Exchange is a network of 15 community foundations throughout the United States, with a national office in New York City. These foundations support community-based efforts addressing a wide range of social problems, with emphasis on grass-roots organizing. According to the organization's Web site, "Groups that are denied support from traditional funding sources because they are too small, too new, too outspoken or too controversial are welcome applicants." The group seeks to fund projects that work for a more equitable distribution of power and wealth in society; organize in communities and workplaces around basic economic and social issues; work for a society without discrimination on the basis of race, gender, sexual orientation, or age; operate in a democratic manner and involve the constituencies they serve; and have relatively little access to traditional sources of funds. Visitors to the site will find links to its member organizations, grant lists, and contact information.

Gamma Mu Foundation (FL) (http://www.GMFOUND.org)

Established in 1989 by the Gamma Mu Fraternity, the Foundation supports the unmet needs of the gay community on a nationwide and continuing basis, providing graduate–level scholarships to college and university students whose degree programs have a positive influence on gay acceptance in the community at large, and providing financial assistance for the needs of individuals suffering from HIV/AIDS in rural America. The site contains a grant listing, application instructions, and an e-mail link.

Gay and Lesbian Medical Association (CA) (http://www.glma.org/)

The Gay and Lesbian Medical Association, of San Francisco, California, was formed in 1981 to "promote quality healthcare for LGBT and HIV-positive people; to foster a professional climate in which our diverse members can achieve their full potential; and to support members challenged by discrimination on the basis of sexual orientation." Grant programs include the Lesbian Health Fund, which supports research and advocacy in creating better healthcare for lesbians and their families; the Medical Expertise Retention Plan, which addresses the issue of HIV-positive healthcare workers; and scholarships for medical students to attend the annual symposium. There are application guidelines and a downloadable cover sheet for the Lesbian Health Fund and a downloadable application form for the medical scholarships. The site also includes information on membership, publications, conferences, and a list of the board of directors.

General Health System Foundation (LA) (http://www.generalhealth.org/)

Based in Baton Rouge, Louisiana, the General Health System Foundation is committed to improving that community's access to healthcare services. GHS provides opportunities for education and assistance, as well as support for affiliates of the General Health System, a network of healthcare providers. The Foundation is described briefly on a page of the GHS Web site.

Georgia Humanities Council (GA) (http://www.georgiahumanities.org/)

The Georgia Humanities Council, the state affiliate of the National Endowment for the Humanities, was founded in 1970 to support and conduct local and statewide educational programs in the humanities. In addition to descriptions of and guidelines for its four grant programs—Special Program Grants, Community Program Grants, Conference Program Grants, and Teacher Enrichment Grants—the site also provides information about a range of humanities resources (Web sites, book discussion groups, video resources, etc.) and contact information.

The German Marshall Fund of the United States (DC) (http://www.gmfus.org)

The German Marshall Fund of the United States was created in 1972 by the German people to memorialize post-WWII aid from the Marshall Plan. Headquartered in Washington, D.C., in the United States and in Berlin in Germany, the Fund's goal "is to promote cooperation and networking between the United States, Western Europe and the newly democratic countries of Central and Eastern Europe in the areas of political, economic, and environmental reforms." The Fund's main areas of funding interest are economics, environment, immigration and integration, and policy and opinion leaders. Funding is made through grants and fellowship programs, both of which are detailed extensively on the Fund's Web site and are designed to involve people and efforts on both sides of the Atlantic. Fellowships include the Research Support Program, Marshall Memorial Fellowship, Community Foundation Fellowship, Resident Fellows Program and the Journalism Program. The Fund's grantmaking "promotes the study of international and domestic policies, supports comparative research and debate on key issues, and assists policy and opinion leaders' understanding of these issues." Past grant and fellowship recipients, guidelines and limitations to funding, transatlantic resource links, the annual report (downloadable in PDF format), and board and staff information are all available on the Fund's Web site.

Gifts In Kind International (VA) (http://www.GiftsInKind.org/)

Gifts In Kind helps businesses to effectively and efficiently donate their products to charities. Its donation programs include Clothe & Comfort, Healthy from the Start, Housing the Homeless, Youth Programs, Emergency Relief, Office Smart, Recycle Technology, and the Retail Donation Partner Program. Gifts In Kind's Web site asks those seeking product donations to locate a Coordinating Agency Partner (CAP) in their geographic region; the site provides a listing by state. For those unable to locate a CAP, an online application form can be filled out and submitted electronically. The site also provides donor and partnership information as well as new products, programs, and reports.

Elizabeth Glaser Pediatric AIDS Foundation (CA) (http://www.pedaids.org/)

The Elizabeth Glaser Pediatric AIDS Foundation is dedicated to identifying, funding, and conducting basic pediatric HIV/AIDS research, with the goal of reducing HIV transmission from mother to newborn, prolonging and improving the lives of children living with HIV, and eradicating HIV from infected children. The Foundation conducts its own targeted research and awards several grants for individual research, including the Elizabeth Glaser Scientist Awards, Basic Research Grants, Scholar Awards, Short-Term Scientific Awards, and Student Intern Awards, all of which are briefly outlined at the Foundation's Web site. Visitors to the site will also find a brief history of the Foundation, facts about pediatric AIDS, listings of the Foundation's staff and various boards, Foundation-related news, and information for donors.

The Glaucoma Foundation (NY) (http://www.glaucoma-foundation.org/)

Established in 1984 by Dr. Robert Ritch, the Glaucoma Foundation is dedicated to glaucoma research and public education worldwide. The New York City-based Foundation's mission is "to create a world without blindness." The Foundation funds research specifically in the areas of optic nerve rescue and restoration and the molecular genetics of glaucoma, striving to enhance understanding of how to prevent and treat glaucoma. The Foundation also has many other outreach and educational programs designed to raise awareness about prevention of the disease and assist those who have been diagnosed with glaucoma. Research grant applications can be printed from the site. Visitors to the site can read and obtain free copies of literature for doctor's offices through online request forms; read online versions of the Foundation newsletter, *Eye to Eye,* which contains stories about individual case histories, recent research developments, grant announcements, answers to medical questions from readers, announcements of upcoming Glaucoma Foundation events, and advice on planned giving; and find further information on glaucoma. The site also contains a calendar of events, press releases, and information on signing up for an e-mail support/discussion list for youths with glaucoma.

Glaucoma Research Foundation (CA) (http://www.glaucoma.org/)

The Glaucoma Research Foundation funds research to find a cure for glaucoma. Funding goes to research in the United States and in other countries, particularly collaborative projects across disciplines. Current research explores such subjects as genetic links to glaucoma, optic nerve analysis, new medications, and laser treatments. The Research area of the Foundation's Web site provides the grants policy, grantees list, program details, and information about its fellowship program. Visitors to the Web site will also find information on the disease, donor information, an interactive forum, a link to online donation opportunities, and contact information.

Global Fund for Women (CA) (http://www.globalfundforwomen.org)

The mission of the Global Fund for Women is to listen to the concerns of women's groups globally, provide women's groups with financial and other resources, increase support for women's efforts globally, develop and strengthen links among women's groups worldwide, and heighten awareness of the needs and strengths of women. It strives to do this through its support of issues as diverse as literacy, domestic violence, economic autonomy, and the international trafficking of women. It does not fund in the United States, however, nor does it fund individuals. As a non-endowed foundation, it relies on the annual support of individuals, foundations, corporations, and other nongovernmental and multilateral organizations. The Fund's Web site provides program descriptions, a FAQ section, grant application guidelines and criteria, a listing of the Fund's board of directors and advisory council, detailed accounts of many of its recent activities, dozens of links to nonprofit resources and sites concerned with women's issues, and an electronic donation pledge form.

Global Greengrants Fund (CO) (http://www.greengrants.org/)

The Boulder, Colorado-based Global Greengrants Fund is an international environmental grantmaking fund of The Tides Foundation, a public foundation in San Francisco. The Fund was established in 1993 to enable private foundations and individual donors to collaborate in support for the grassroots environmental movement in developing countries. The Fund supports a wide range of community-based initiatives that protect the environment in the most underserved and threatened regions on Earth. Grants are made to pre-selected organizations recommended by regional advisory committees comprised of local environmental leaders who can make the most effective use of the limited resources available in their particular region. The Advisory Board is comprised of leaders from five of the world's foremost global networks of grassroots environmental organizations: Earth Island Institute, Friends of the Earth, International Rivers Network, Pesticide Action Network, and Rainforest Action Network. The Web site contains a grants list based on region, background information on members of the advisory board with links to their organizations, international organizations' donor links, contact information, and the option to have any page on the site translated into French, German, Italian, Spanish, or Portuguese.

The Arnold P. Gold Foundation (NJ) (http://www.humanism-in-medicine.org/)

Drs. Arnold and Sandra Gold, to "foster humanism in medicine" and emphasize the tradition of compassion in the doctor-patient relationship, established the Arnold P. Gold Foundation in Englewood, New Jersey, in 1988. The founders are colleagues at the Columbia University College of Physicians and Surgeons, where Dr. Arnold P. Gold is Professor of Clinical Neurology and Professor of Clinical Pediatrics. The Foundation raises funds that have resulted in significant advances in the development, implementation, evaluation, and replication of innovative medical educational programs and projects that are influencing the way physicians are trained. There are medical student, resident, educator, and research programs through which the Gold Foundation supports annual commencement awards, provides assistant and associate professorships, sponsors student-initiated programs, and conducts research of medical students' attitudes toward humanism. Grant applications will be considered from medical schools and organizations and will not be accepted from individuals. Visit the Foundation's Web site for information about its programs, grant application procedure, printable grant request form, past award recipients, public forum and bulletin board, and contact information.

Golden Apple Foundation (IL) (http://www.goldenapple.org/)

Chicago, Illinois's Golden Apple Foundation was created in 1985 to recognize excellence in teaching. The goal is to "publicly honor excellent (Pre K–12) teachers and provide them the means to have an impact on their profession." The Foundation recognizes ten outstanding teachers a year, who then become fellows that participate in programs that the Foundation runs. These include a program to prepare young people to teach in schools with high need, the only teacher-taught alternative teacher certification program, and science workshops for Chicago area students. Nominating forms and/or guidelines are available online for both teacher and student recognition programs. The site also supplies a calendar of upcoming events, press releases, and lists of past and current honorees.

Good Samaritan Foundation, Inc. (KY) (http://www.gsfky.org/)

Started in 1888, the Good Samaritan Foundation of Lexington, Kentucky, has been committed to "initiating, participating in, and supporting activities which focus on improving the health status of Kentuckians." Programs supported by the Foundation include countywide surveys and localized and statewide needs assessment programs, rural and urban healthcare programs, nursing scholarships and internships, and various clinics. The

Foundation funds school health education programs and the Good Samaritan Foundation, Inc. Nursing Center at the University of Kentucky College of Nursing. It has also endowed chairs at the University of Kentucky. The site includes grant guidelines, an electronic form to request a grant application, a list of the officers and trustees, and information about Foundation publications.

Greater Seattle Business Association Scholarship Fund (WA) (http://www.the-GSBA.org)

Based in Seattle, the Greater Seattle Business Association (GSBA), "sometimes called the 'Gay and Lesbian Chamber of Commerce,' includes over 800 members who join together to promote and support the lesbian and gay business and professional community." It is an association that includes business owners, professionals, working people, and retirees who have joined together for the purpose of networking and members come from all sexual orientations, races, political affiliations, and professions. Its primary goals are to strengthen and expand business and career opportunities for members and to aid in creating a strong advocate for the Gay/Lesbian community. The GSBA Scholarship Fund targets undergraduate residents of Washington who demonstrate need and potential leadership for the lesbian, gay, bisexual, and transgender community. Scholarships are available for college, creative or vocational training, or other post-secondary education and are open to residents of Washington, Oregon, Idaho, Montana, and Alaska. Visitors to the site will find information on the Association's other activities and also will be able to access a business and community resource directory.

Great Lakes Fishery Trust (MI) (http://www.glft.org/)

The Great Lakes Fishery Trust was created in 1996 as a part of a court settlement for fish losses at the Ludington Pumped Storage Project hydroelectric facility jointly owned by Consumers Power Company (now Consumers Energy) and the Detroit Edison Company. Its mission is to "provide funding to enhance, protect, and rehabilitate Great Lakes fishery resources." The Great Lakes Fishery Trust provides funding to nonprofit organizations, educational institutions, and government agencies for projects related to Great Lakes fisheries to provide mitigation for fish losses. Its funding categories include education, research on Great Lakes Fisheries and population rehabilitation, fishing access, fisheries habitat protection and restoration, special projects, and the Muskegon River Initiative. The Web site provides detailed information about each funding category, along with deadlines and applications, which can be downloaded in PDF format. The site also provides lists of previous grants awarded, information about trustees and the advisory team, and recent press releases. Annual reports can be downloaded in PDF format.

Great Lakes Protection Fund (IL) (http://www.glpf.org/)

Great Lakes Protection Fund was established by the Council of Great Lakes Governors and the Center for the Great Lakes in 1989 as a "permanent environmental endowment that supports collaborative actions to improve the health of the Great Lakes ecosystem." Headquartered in Chicago, the Fund maintains state programs in Michigan, New York, Pennsylvania, Wisconsin, Ohio, and Minnesota. Through preproposals and supplemental requests for preproposals, which address issues of the applicants' choosing and topics of special interest, respectively, the Fund finances projects that lead to tangible improvements in the health of the Great Lakes ecosystem, promote the interdependence of healthy ecological and economic systems, and are innovative, creative, and venturesome. The Fund is able to provide financial support for nonprofit organizations (including environmental organizations, trade associations, and universities), for-profit businesses, government agencies, and individuals. Visitors to the Fund's Web site will find project guidelines and funding principles; numerous past annual reports that can be downloaded in PDF format; an extensive archive of past grants, with the details of the project and contact information for each; and links to other resources and contact information for the Chicago-based organization and the state programs.

The Greater Houston Women's Foundation (TX) (http://www.ghwf.org/)

The Greater Houston Women's Foundation located in Bellaire, Texas, wants to help women achieve economic self-sufficiency. To do its part, the Foundation acts a catalyst to increase awareness of the needs of women and girls in the community, fosters prevention and early intervention in problems affecting women and girls, and emphasizes support for and enrichment of programs for women and girls. The goals of the Foundation are to help women become economically self-sufficient, to encourage prevention and early intervention of problems affecting women and girls, to support programs that help to develop and improve life skills, to actively involve women in philanthropic decision-making, and to educate women about charitable giving. Grants have been given for programs on literacy, job readiness and training, parenting skills, and health education including violence prevention, among others. The Foundation also conducts research and provides education, in the hope of providing additional resources that explain issues "affecting the well-being of women and girls." The Foundation's Web site provides a list of previous grants, explanation of the Foundation's research and educational programs, and contact information.

Greensboro Justice Fund, Inc. (MA) (http://www.gjf.org)

Based in Haydenville, Massachusetts, the Greensboro Justice Fund is dedicated to the service of those fighting for human dignity against bigotry in the South today. The GJF was originally founded as a civil rights and legal organization in response to the murders of five labor and anti-racist organizers at an anti-Klan demonstration in Greensboro, North Carolina, on November 3, 1979. It won a major civil rights law suit against the City of Greensboro, Greensboro Police Department, and Ku Klux Klan. Widows and victims of the November 3rd massacre donated the proceeds of the civil rights suit to the Greensboro Justice Fund to support others working for social justice. The Fund supports grassroots organizations and activists in the South that work for economic justice, workers' rights, political empowerment, an end to racism, homophobic discrimination and violence, religious intolerance, police brutality, right wing attacks, and environmental injustice. The GJF particularly supports groups that seek to address root causes of economic and social injustice and that develop links between issues and across diverse communities. Projects must be located in Virginia, North Carolina, South Carolina, Georgia, Florida, Alabama, Mississippi, Kentucky, Tennessee, Louisiana, or Arkansas. Visitors to the site will find downloadable grant applications, related links, an online newsletter, and contact information.

Group Health/Kaiser Permanente Community Foundation (WA)
(http://www.ghc.org/web/about_gh/comm_involvement/index.jhtml)

The Group Health/Kaiser Permanente Community Foundation was founded in 1984 to support health research, clinical innovations, health promotion/education programs, and community-based public health projects that focus on healthcare for homeless families, infant mortality, immunizations, and the prevention of violence. The Foundation's Group Health Web site provides examples of research grants, information on its endowment, and a listing of its board members.

Hawai'i Committee for the Humanities (HI) (http://www.planet-hawaii.com/hch/)

The Hawai'i Committee for the Humanities was founded in 1972 to promote and support public awareness in Hawaii of the humanities (defined on the HCH's Web site as studies examining philosophy, ethics, comparative religion, history, archaeology and anthropology, literature, languages, and art history). HCH offers grants primarily to nonprofit organizations that operate humanities programs, although a limited number of smaller grants are temporarily available for research by individuals and preservation and publications projects by nonprofits. The Web site provides detailed information about its grant programs and downloadable applications and instructions in PDF format. The site also lists humanities resources and links to those with Web sites, information on Hawai'i History Day and other programs, and contact information.

Hawaii Tropical Botanical Garden (HI) (http://www.htbg.com)

The Hawaii Tropical Botanical Garden (HTBG), of Papaikou, Hawaii, first opened to the public in 1985. The goal of the HTBG is to "serve as a nature preserve and sanctuary. The Garden is dedicated to the collection and display of the world's tropical plants, and to the education of both children and adults about the plight of the world's rainforests." The operating foundation that supports the institute was founded by Dan and Pauline Lutkenhouse to continue the vision they have worked toward for years; the Lutkenhouses even donated the land that makes up the preserve to the organization. The Web site offers a virtual tour of the garden, a history of the HTBG and Onomea Bay, and a market area where visitors can order flowers from the gift shop.

Haymarket People's Fund (MA) (http://www.haymarket.org/)

The Haymarket People's Fund of Boston, Massachusetts is committed to "putting money behind groups of local people who believe change is possible . . . Who work for innovative solutions that go to the root of social problems." The Fund's mission is to support meaningful jobs at a living wage, childcare, healthcare, the clean-up of toxic dumps and more. The Web site provides more information for donors and grantees.

Headwaters Fund (MN) (http://www.fex.org/headwater/headwate.html)

Founded on the belief that the capacity for fundamental social change lies in the hands of ordinary people, the Headwaters Fund provides financial and organizational resources to grassroots organizations in the Minneapolis/St. Paul metropolitan area. The Fund tends to support smaller organizations (i.e., with budgets under $200,000) whose programs address the root causes of social, political, environmental, and economic injustice, and its grantmaking decisions are made by community activists, including people of color, women, poor and working class individuals, gays and lesbians, and people with disabilities. Visitors to the Fund's Web site will find grant guidelines, information about donor opportunities, and contact information.

Health Foundation of South Florida (FL) (http://www.hfsf.org/)

The Health Foundation of South Florida was created in 1993 to improve the community's health. Its mission is to "fund a range of community endeavors that have the greatest impact on the wellness of South Floridians . . . [by] selecting initiatives that promote improved health and healthcare delivery for the medically underserved." Initiatives that the Foundation is currently funding involve the homeless, school-based healthcare, nursing scholarships, medical research and health education, teenage pregnancy prevention, violence prevention, and women's health screening. It is now looking to fund early childhood development programs. The site offers a list of grant recipients, application guidelines and information for requesting an application, updates on special event fundraisers, and the Foundation's newsletter.

Health Trust of Santa Clara Valley (CA) (http://www.healthtrust.org/)

The Health Trust of Santa Clara Valley was formed in 1996 with proceeds from the sale of the Good Samaritan Health System. The Health Trust makes grants to nonprofit organizations that provide direct preventive health and wellness services and operates community health programs that fill gaps in current health prevention services. General support (i.e., "Good Samaritan") grants are limited to ten percent of the funds distributed by the Trust; the other 90 percent of its giving is initiated through an RFP process and invited proposals. Good Samaritan grants support community-based health, prevention, and wellness projects, particularly for medically indigent children; the elderly; and vulnerable adults. The Health Trust Web site outlines the organization's various activities and grant programs (including those involving restricted funds) and also provides donor and volunteer information, a listing of board and staff members, and contact information.

HealthONE Alliance (CO) (http://www.health1.org/)

Located in Denver, the HealthONE Alliance is dedicated "to excellence in healthcare by supporting medical education, research and philanthropy and by representing the community as an equal partner in Denver's largest healthcare delivery system." The Alliance carries out this mission through programs such as Adult Day Care, the Mother's Milk Bank and the Lactation Program, as well as education and research support. With an overall focus on healthcare education, the Alliance funds community groups and activities committed to this need. The HealthONE Alliance Web site provides descriptions of current programs and priorities, an online form to request grant guidelines, and more information about the organization's philanthropic endeavors.

Jimi Hendrix Family Foundation (WA) (http://www.jimihendrix.org)

The Jimi Hendrix Family Foundation funds charitable, religious, and educational organizations with programs concentrating on education, inner city assistance, international humanitarian aid, and Christian outreach. The Foundation's Web site includes contact information and details about its annual Electric Guitar Competition, its mission, and its board of advisors.

Hispanic Federation of New York City (NY) (http://www.hispanicfederation.org)

The Hispanic Federation of New York City, a membership organization of health and human services agencies, serves Latinos in the tri-state area of New York, New Jersey, and Connecticut. The Federation's mission is "to build and strengthen community-based organizations which provide Latinos with a host of services, including immigration services, healthcare, economic development, job training, AIDS prevention, youth services, leadership development, and housing." The Federation maintains three areas of support: fund development and grantmaking, advocacy, and technical assistance for non-profits through the Hispanic Enterprises Launching Programs (HELP). The Hispanic Federation's Web site offers extensive resources for nonprofits and individuals alike. The Big Board contains over a hundred recommended links relating to Latinos and beneficial services. The Federation also provides a local arts calendar, links to member organizations, for-sale publications, and contact information.

Hispanic Scholarship Fund, Inc. (CA) (http://www.hsf.net/)

The Hispanic Scholarship Fund, Inc. of San Francisco, California, was established in 1975. The organization's goal is to "recognize and reward outstanding Hispanic students in higher education throughout the United States and Puerto Rico." Scholarships are given in three major categories to American citizens and permanent residents of Hispanic background. The College Retention/General Program is for students at four-year colleges who are full-time and have already earned at least 15 credits. These scholarships can be for specific areas of study, etc., depending on the donor. The High School Program supports graduating seniors who have been accepted at a college for the fall. The Community College Transfer Program is for community college attendees or graduates who have the potential to succeed at a four-year college. There is also an additional Professional program, which awards to pre-professional majors in selected areas. Applications are available online for the General Program, while application guidelines, deadlines, and a phone number and e-mail address for applications are available for the other programs. The site also includes information on general college aid, a list of other organizations offering scholarships to Latino students, a list of internship programs that seek Latinos, and a list of the board of directors and staff of the fund. There is also information on CyberCampus, which has resources for Latino students looking for a college, donating to the fund.

Hogg Foundation for Mental Health (TX) (http://hogg1.lac.utexas.edu/Default.html)

Since 1940, the mission of the Hogg Foundation has been "to develop and conduct a broad mental health program of great benefit to the people of Texas" through education and grants supporting mental health service projects and research efforts. The Foundation gives priority to projects in the areas of children and their families, youth development, and minority mental health; it does not make grants for projects located outside the state of Texas. Offerings at the Foundation's Web site include a short history of the Hogg family, grant restrictions and application guidelines for its mental health service and research programs, grants listings, a publications list, a staff listing with e-mail addresses, and information about its Regional Foundation Library, a longtime member of the Foundation Center's Cooperating Collections network.

Holy Land Foundation for Relief and Development (TX) (http://www.hlf.org/index.shtml)

Formed in 1989 in Richardson, Texas, the Holy Land Foundation for Relief and Development "is dedicated to finding practical solutions for human suffering through humanitarian programs in the area of emergency relief, healthcare, social welfare, education and community development." The Foundation supports social programs, orphan sponsorship programs, health services, educational services, and emergency relief and community development programs in the United States and throughout the Middle East. The Web site is dominated by opportunities to contribute and to become sponsors of different programs. Visitors can also find details on each program area, a newsletter, and chat rooms.

Hospice Foundation of America (FL) (http://www.hospicefoundation.org/)

The mission of the Hospice Foundation of America is to "provide leadership in the development and application of hospice and its philosophy of care for terminally ill people, with the goal of enhancing the American healthcare system and the role of hospice within it." The Foundation designs and implements programs that assist hospices and the terminally ill and makes grants that are supportive of hospice concepts. Grants are not normally awarded for endowments, debt reduction, religious efforts, or to individuals. Priority is given to those communities from which the Foundation collects donations. However, the Foundation has temporarily suspended grantmaking. The Web site serves as an online resource for hospice care, providing excerpts from the Foundation's own publications in addition to numerous links to online hospice resources. The online version of the Foundation's 1996 annual report provides descriptions of grant programs, grant guidelines, a listing of 1996 grants, Foundation history, board and staff lists, and contact information. Visitors to the site will also find information on an array of Foundation projects as well as interactive order and donation forms.

Hospice Foundation for the Central Coast (CA) (http://www.hffcc.org)

The Monterey, California-based Hospice Foundation for the Central Coast "helps hospice care providers close the gap between decreasing healthcare reimbursement from insurance payers, such as Medicare, and the cost to provide this specialized, highly personal form of care." The Foundation raises and disperses funds to support hospice care in Monterey and San Benito Counties. These funds go toward hospice organizations that enhance the quality of life or allow death with dignity for individuals with life-threatening illnesses and to family support services. The Foundation holds a number of special events and community education programs throughout the year. Visitors to the Hospice Foundation Web site will find guidelines, priorities, limitations and deadlines for grants, information on current grant recipients, a form to request publications from the Foundation, and contact addresses.

The Whitney Houston Foundation for Children (NJ) (http://www.whfoundation.com/)

The Whitney Houston Foundation for Children is dedicated to promoting a positive self-image in children and youth by providing opportunities for them to learn and express themselves in safe, supportive environments. The Foundation's Web site includes grant guidelines, application instructions, and donor information.

Houston Regional HIV AIDS Resource Group, Inc. (TX) (http://hivresourcegroup.org)

The Houston Regional HIV AIDS Resource Group was created in 1993 and is the largest community based HIV/AIDS agency in Texas. The organization's mission is to "maximize all possible medical, psychosocial and educational resources to help persons affected by or at risk of HIV/AIDS in the ten county area surrounding Houston, Texas." The Resource Group provides services and information to the community through a number of programs. One primary way to do this is to offer contact information for the many surrounding groups. The Web site includes pages with links and/or phone numbers for general HIV services, specific services for women and families, and programs for adolescents. The Houston Multiple Diagnosis Initiative (MDI), integrates "housing services, drug/alcohol treatment, and treatment for mental illness into the HIV continuum of care for homeless persons living in Harris County." The Web site offers information on eligibility, service providers, and funders for this program. Elsewhere on the site is an electronic form that providers can fill out to become part of the group's database. The site also includes information on rural services and a forum for case managers to submit unique experiences. Another electronic form is offered for clients to comment on the services offered.

Hudson River Foundation (NY) (http://www.hudsonriver.org)

The Hudson River Foundation of New York City was established in 1981 "under the terms of an agreement among environmental groups, government regulatory agencies and utility companies seeking the constructive resolution of a long series of legal controversies concerning the environmental impacts of power plants on the Hudson River." The organization supports scientific and public policy research, education, and public access projects involving the Hudson River, with a focus on making scientific research integral in any decisions made about the River. The organization's grantmaking program is made up of three funds: the Hudson River Fund, supporting "scientific, ecological, and related public policy research on issues and matters of concern to the Hudson Rivers, its tributaries and its drainage basin, with emphasis given, but not limited to . . . the factors related to the abundance and structure of fish populations" and the river's ecosystem, with geographic focus on estuarine portion; The Hudson River Improvement Fund, which funds projects that enhance public use and enjoyment of the River with areas of interest including the improvement of facilities that allow public access, educational facilities, and habitat repair, restoration, and creation; and the New York City Environmental Fund, supporting the more general area of the city and Westchester County's public resources. Funded projects have included those in the following categories: increasing access to natural areas and promoting their appropriate use, educating people about the value of natural resources and environmental protection, and/or addressing and responding to the environmental effects of ConEd's operations. The site offers an extensive application packet for the Hudson River Fund. This can be downloaded in PDF format, with certain pages available in Microsoft Excel. This packet includes a list of the board and select staff members. It includes specific deadlines, guidelines, and restrictions and the specific RFPs (Requests for Proposals) for each year. The other two funds each have their own page with basic application guidelines and restrictions.

Howard Hughes Medical Institute (MD) (http://www.hhmi.org/)

In addition to supporting more than 60 medical research laboratories worldwide, the Howard Hughes Medical Institute, the nation's largest philanthropy, awards both institutional and individual grants to strengthen education in medicine, biology, and the related sciences. HHMI's grants program also supports the research of biomedical scientists outside the United States. Although portions of this large site are under construction, visitors will find detailed program descriptions; application guidelines and requirements; a short history of the organization; press releases and the HHMI Bulletin; online versions of 1994, 1995, and 1996 annual reports; a map of HHMI locations; and an interactive form that allows for direct communication with HHMI staff.

The Humana Foundation, Inc. (KY) (http://www.humanafoundation.org/)

Based in Louisville, Kentucky, the Humana Foundation is the philanthropic arm of Humana, Inc., one of the nation's largest managed healthcare companies. Established in 1981, the Humana Foundation supports charitable organizations and institutions that promote education, health and human services, community development, and the arts in communities where Humana has a business presence. In 1991 the Foundation started its scholarship program, designed to recognize and honor academic excellence and to assist Humana families in meeting the cost of sending children to colleges of their choice. A scholarship application can be downloaded from the site, and grant applications can be downloaded and printed. Visit the site for application guidelines and instructions, aid recipient list, a breakdown of fund distribution by area, descriptions of projects, and contact information.

Humanities Council of Washington, D.C. (DC) (http://www.humanities-wdc.org)

The Humanities Council of Washington, D.C., is the District's affiliate of the National Endowment for the Humanities. The Council annually supports 60–70 humanities programs in the nation's capitol through its grants program. The Council's Web site provides grant information and deadlines, contact information, a calendar of events, information about its activities, newsletter subscription information, and donor information.

Humanities Iowa (IA) (http://www.uiowa.edu/~humiowa/)

Humanities Iowa, based in Iowa City, was founded in 1971 to enhance the civic life, culture and identity of Iowans. Humanities Iowa supports "history, literature, philosophy, law, and other humanities fields, [and] it fosters life-long learning, critical thinking, and community connections." Along with sponsored readings, discussions, and speakers, Humanities Iowa has four types of grants: mini, regular, and major, all of which share the same downloadable application and instruction form, and media grants, which has a separate downloadable instruction and application form. Humanities Iowa provides one-to-one matching funds for these grants. Visitors to the Web site will find extensive application FAQs with eligibility, criteria, requirements, and deadlines; a calendar of events; and other humanities resources and publications.

Huntington's Disease Society of America, Inc. (NY) (http://www.hdsa.org)

Huntington's Disease Society of America, Inc. is a national health agency located in New York City. The organization's mission is to "promote and support research to find a cure for HD, help those affected by the disease and their families, and educate the public and healthcare professionals about HD." The Society offers fellowships and grants in two main areas: laboratory research and clinical and epidemiological research testing. Research Grants are given to innovative projects with the expectation that they will attract other funders. Research Fellowships are for postdoctoral investigators in the early part of their career. And the Research Initiative Grants are given to projects—with relatively little preliminary data—for an immediate boost. Extensive guidelines are available online along with the three applications, which can each be printed straight from the screen or downloaded in Microsoft Word. The expansive site includes information on current and past research reports, educative information about HD, a calendar of events, and information on local chapters. There are opportunities to contribute and to order products. There is a board of trustees list and lists of national staff.

Idaho Humanities Council (ID) (http://www2.state.id.us/ihc/)

The Idaho Humanities Council partners with civic groups, citizens, and educators to expand public humanities programs in the state. It accomplishes this mission by supporting educational programs for the general public as well as various target audiences. Although the Council's Web site offers comprehensive information on its grants programs, applicants are "strongly advised to seek more detailed information through staff consultation before completing and submitting grant proposals," and an e-mail contact is provided for this purpose. The Council's Web site also provides news, information on programs for teachers, humanities resources and links of interest, and contact and donor information.

Illinois Humanities Council, Inc. (IL) (http://www.prairie.org)

The Illinois Humanities Council, located in Chicago, was established by the National Endowment for the Arts in 1974. The Council is "dedicated to fostering a culture in which the humanities are a vital part of the lives of individuals and communities . . . [and] promoting greater understanding of, appreciation for, and involvement in the humanities by the citizens of Illinois, regardless of their economic resources, cultural background or geographic location." The Grants Program awards Mini (up to $2,000) and Major (up to $10,000) Grants to Illinois nonprofit organizations and institutions. To be eligible, a project must be rooted in at least one humanitarian discipline, involve a humanities scholar, be for the public, include an evaluation plan, and the sponsoring group must cover at least half of the total budget. Categories that past recipients have explored include African American heritage, arts in context, ethnicity, Illinois heritage, living history, Native American culture, rural life, storytelling, and understanding music and theater. Applications can be downloaded in PDF format, and there is page with a breakdown of the distribution of past grants. Organizations developing media projects, Web sites, local and community or oral histories, exhibits, or repeat funding should contact the office to discuss applying. The very extensive Web site, entitled "Prairie," also includes information on ongoing projects such as the Speakers Bureau, summer seminars for teachers, and Choices for the 21st Century, a library discussion group program. Visitors will also find lists of the board of directors and the staff, an events calendar, maps, links, and information on exhibits and programs throughout the state.

Illinois State Historical Society (IL) (http://www.prairienet.org/ishs)
Created in 1899 to support libraries, writing, and research on Illinois, the Illinois State Historical Society is based in Springfield, Illinois. The organization's mission is to "foster in citizens a deeper understanding of and appreciation for all Illinois history through programs and publications" and coordinate and support programs that further this goal. The Centennial Awards Programs recognizes and honors businesses that have been open for a hundred years. There is an electronic application that follows the description. The Society also offers a series of educational awards. The Verna Ross Orndorff Scholarship is given to a high school senior who has written an exemplary article on Abraham Lincoln or the Civil War. There are four other awards given to exceptional high school history students and one to an elementary teacher who is doing a particularly good job in teaching about the state's past. The group also distributes the King V. Hostick Award to a graduate student in history or library sciences who is studying a topic related to Illinois. The Web site offers an events calendar, lists of books and other related publications, lists of directors and staff, and information on becoming a member.

Immune Deficiency Foundation (MD) (http://www.primaryimmune.org/)
The Towson, Maryland-based Immune Deficiency Foundation was founded in 1980 with the mission: "to improve the diagnosis and treatment of patients with primary immunodeficiency diseases through research and education." The Foundation funds two grants: The Fellowship of the Immune Deficiency Foundation, a one-year $25,000 stipend for MD or Ph.D. fellows researching in clinical and laboratory aspects of the Primary Immune Deficiency Diseases and/or related areas, and the Novartis Scholarship Program to help fund post-secondary education of a student with Primary Immune Deficiencies. There is contact information on the Foundation's Web site for more information about these grants. The Foundation is also a clearinghouse for information and services to families, patients, and researchers of Immune Deficiency Diseases. Services such as consultations, advocacy groups, discussion groups, and expert advice all appear on the Foundation's extensive Web site.

Independent Accountants International Educational Foundation (FL) (http://www.iai.org/education/)
The Independent Accountants International Educational Foundation administers the Robert Kaufman Memorial Scholarship Fund to assist young people pursuing education in the field of accountancy. The scholarship program is described on the Foundation's page of the Independent Accountants International Web site; the page also provides links to the scholarship application form and a list of last year's award winners.

Independent Television Service (CA) (http://www.ITVS.org)
The San Francisco-based Independent Television Service (ITVS) was created by Congress to be an independent provider of public television programs. ITVS' mission is to "create and promote independent media that will expand civic participation by bringing new voices and expressiveness into the public discourse," especially by addressing the needs of under-served minority and youth audiences. ITVS funds, distributes, and promotes new programs that show diversity and a range of subjects, viewpoints, and forms. They fund various new programs yearly, and an application and guidelines—downloadable in PDF format—for these grants can be obtained on the ITVS Web site. The LINCS (Local

Independents Collaborating with Stations) Fund provides an incentive or matching funds for partnerships between public television stations and independent producers. Along with other grant opportunities, ITVS provides a production manual, links to other resources, and descriptions of recently produced ITVS programs on its Web site.

Indiana Humanities Council (IN) (http://www.ihc4u.org/)
The Indiana Humanities Council supports the humanities in Indiana in cooperation with educational, cultural, and community organizations. IHC grant programs include International Awareness Grants, Humanities Initiative Grants, Indiana Heritage Research Grants, and Historic Preservation Education Grants. IHC's Web site offers brief descriptions of its programs, listings of recent grant recipients, and e- mail contacts for requesting more information. The IHC site also provides information on the organization's activities, articles about the humanities, and a listing of humanities resources—exhibits, books, films, speakers, performances, and curricula—available to Indiana residents.

Initiative Foundation (MN) (http://www.ifound.org)
Based in Little Falls, Minnesota, the Initiative Foundation was established in 1986 by the Knight Foundation to improve the quality of life for residents, families, and communities in central Minnesota through integrated community planning, promoting leadership training, and addressing barriers to economic development. The Foundation is "Central Minnesota's nonprofit resource for grants, business investments, community planning and donor services." The Foundation acts as a "gap" lender, providing business loans, loan guarantees, and seed investments, with the goal of creating and retaining quality jobs with liveable wages and benefits essential to improving and maintaining a high quality of life in central Minnesota. Among the Foundation's programs is the Healthy Communities Partnership, which provides training, grant support, and technical assistance to help communities meet their challenges and plan for their futures, and the Healthy Lakes Program, where up to eight lake associations in Crow Wing County will be selected to receive training and grants of up to $2,400 to create and begin implementation of Lake Management Plans. The Foundation has a service area of Cass, Chisago, Crow Wing, Isanti, Kanabec, Mille Lacs, Morrison, Pine, Sherburne, Stearns, Todd, Wadena, and Wright Counties, which include 160 communities. Visitors to the site will find FAQ sheets, links, and downloadable grant applications for each of their programs. The site also provides an online contact form as well as traditional contact information.

Initiative Fund of Southeastern and South Central Minnesota (MN) (http://www.semif.org/)
The Initiative Fund is a regional economic and community development fund serving 20 counties in southeastern and south central Minnesota. The Fund awards program grants up to $30,000 twice a year and mini-grants up to $2,000 on a monthly basis. The Fund also runs a loan program to help finance new business start-ups and to expand existing businesses. The Fund's Web site provides grant and loan guidelines and staff e-mail contacts for requesting more information. The site also provides online versions of publications, links to special projects, and resources.

Institute of International Education, Inc. (NY) (http://www.iie.org/)
Created in 1919, the renowned Institute of International Education (IIE) is headquartered in New York City, but it has offices all over the country and internationally. The organization's purpose is "strengthening international understanding and cooperation by enabling men and women of talent and enterprise to study, conduct research, and receive practical training outside their own countries." Created in 1946, the Fulbright Program is principally administered by the U.S. Department of State. Grants are made to Americans and residents of other participating countries for university teaching, advanced research, graduate study, and teaching in elementary and secondary schools. There are post-baccalaureate, post-doctoral, and mid-career fellowships. Each category has an area for U.S. and non-U.S. citizens, with extensive descriptions of the program, application guidelines and deadlines, and information of competitiveness. Applications can be received from U.S. institutions or

applied for from the IIE. The Institute also administers over 250 programs internationally, many with the Department of State. The site offers a list of these programs and online aspects of many of them. The Services area of the site includes a list of publications, information on membership, and statistical and policy research. The About IIE section offers a list of the board of trustees and annual reports, available in PDF format either in their entirety or by section. The Web site, IIE Online, is growing rapidly and offers information on countless programs and initiatives.

The International Association of Culinary Professionals Foundation (KY) (http://www.iacp.com)

The International Association of Culinary Professionals Foundation was established in 1984 in Louisville, Kentucky, as the philanthropic partner of the IACP. The IACP Foundation provides "funds for educational, and charitable work related to the culinary profession" in five program areas: research, scholarships, library resources, world-hunger alleviation, and children's educational workshops. Scholarships are the main interest of the IACP; the Foundation funds partial tuition costs and provides limited application instructions on its Web site. The Foundation also maintains a number of special funds, listed on the site. Contact information is posted for more information about all of the IACP funding opportunities.

International Center for Research on Women (DC) (http://www.icrw.org/)

The International Center for Research on Women, founded in 1976, focuses its funding and activities on women's productive and reproductive roles, family status, leadership in society, and management of environmental resources in developing countries. Funds are primarily available through the Promoting Women in Development (PROWID) Program and the ICRW's Fellows Program, which gives development researchers and practitioners from developing countries the opportunity to spend time in Washington, D.C., to conduct independent research, meet policymakers, and refine their skills in data analysis, computer applications, and program development. The ICRW's Web site provides fellowship details and an application form to submit electronically. Contacts are provided for those interested in the PROWID Program. The ICRW site also provides news, information on its activities, publications, and listings of board, staff, and partners.

International Youth Federation (MD) (http://www.iyfnet.org/)

The International Youth Foundation promotes the positive development of children and youth, ages 5–20, around the world by supporting programs that focus on such areas as vocational training, health education, recreation, cultural tolerance, environmental awareness, and the development of leadership, conflict resolution, and decision-making skills. The Foundation's Web site provides recent grants lists, a listing of international partners, IYF programs, an e-mail contact, and detailed information about its work.

The Izumi Foundation (MA) (http://www.izumi.org/)

Based in Boston, Massachusetts, the Izumi Foundation was created in hopes of alleviating human suffering through improving and extending healthcare to all living creatures. The Foundation follows the goals of Shinnyo-En USA, a Buddhist order that is based on the last teachings of Gautama Buddha. The Foundation's goals are "to address the root causes of human suffering, to increase compassion and caring among all human beings, and to promote a society that respects all living things." Support is given to projects that address the underlying causes of disease and persistent healthcare problems, use innovative and creative solutions to promote sustainable outcomes, recognize the inter-relationship between disease and poverty, develop/strengthen leadership in healthcare, and promote collaboration and partnership between healthcare providers. The Web site includes information on application procedures and contact information.

The Henry M. Jackson Foundation (WA) (http://www.hmjackson.org/)

Seattle, Washington's Henry M. Jackson Foundation was created in honor of the late senator in 1983. The Foundation's mission is to address issues that were important to the senator, including "promoting dialogue between the academic and policy worlds, between the public and private sectors, and between citizens and their government." The Foundation makes grants in four program areas. Most funding in the Education and Advanced Research in International Affairs goes to the Henry M. Jackson School of International Studies at the University of Washington and the National Bureau of Asian Research, with any other grants going to organizations in the former Soviet Union, the Pacific Rim countries, and the Middle East. Environment and Natural Resources Management covers "national land use planning and metropolitan growth management programs and the development of sound public policy in this field." The Public Service category includes programs that encourage college and post-college-aged youth to pursue careers in civil service. Finally, Human Rights funding is primarily awarded to Russia to help ease the transition from communism, with a small amount of support going to American organizations that are active in Russia. The site includes grant guidelines and deadlines and grant lists by category. There is an area of the site in Russian.

Jefferson Foundation (CO) (http://www.jeffersonfoundation.org)

The Jefferson Foundation is based in Lakewood, Colorado, and is a public education foundation serving Jefferson County. The Foundation provides various grants within the Jefferson school district: Venture grants for teachers, to provide new ideas and creative programming, and general grants to students. The Foundation also provides various programs and funding under its Columbine Funds, for the students and educators at Columbine High School. The Foundation's Web site includes a listing of past grants and an online application for current grants.

Jewish Communal Fund (NY) (http://www.JewishCommunalFund.org)

The Jewish Communal Fund serves a broad spectrum of philanthropic objectives, including the fields of health, education, welfare, science, and cultural and religious affairs. The Fund also supports sectarian and nonsectarian institutions that serve the community of greater New York City, and the nation. Upon visiting the Fund's Web site, you will find downloadable files in PDF format and contact information.

Jewish Community Federation of Cleveland (OH) (http://www.jewishcleveland.org/)

The Jewish Community Federation of Cleveland raises money and distributes it to member organizations in order to meet the various needs of the local Jewish community. "Primary Federation functions include community planning and research, community relations, leadership development, philanthropic planning and endowment programs." The Federation's Endowment Fund supports emergency needs and community projects. The largest grantee of the Federation is United Jewish Communities, which works in partnership with The Jewish Agency for Israel and The American Jewish Joint Distribution Committee. In the latest year, the organization supported 16 local community service groups and more than 20 national and international groups. The Web site is directed at potential donors and people looking to learn about the Jewish community in Cleveland. There are e-mail addresses for each of the committees that make up the Federation, including the Community Relations Committee and the Endowment Fund Committee. There is also a guide to Jewish Cleveland, a page of links to Jewish resources, and pages for many of the specific departments within the Federation. The site also contains an HTML version of the latest Annual Report.

Jewish Community Foundation of MetroWest (NJ) (http://www.ujfmetrowest.org)

Located in Whippany, New Jersey, the Jewish Community Foundation of MetroWest was established in 1993. The organization's mission is to "enhance the life of the MetroWest community and to create a Jewish future rooted in religious heritage and nourished by dreams." Over half of the awarded funds are donated annually to the United Jewish Appeal of MetroWest, but the remaining grants go to Jewish and non-Jewish charities. Grants support research, special projects and new programs, assist the United Jewish Federation of MetroWest beneficiaries and other local Jewish institutions, and awards made in support of nonsectarian causes where appropriate. The Foundation is made up of over 400 funds, some restricted and others designated for specific program or fields of interest. The site includes information on key staff members and information on creating a fund or endowment.

Jewish Family and Children's Services of San Francisco, the Peninsula, Marin, and Sonoma Counties (CA) (http://www.jfcs.org)

Jewish Family and Children's Services was founded in 1850 to serve the west Bay Area of California. Located in San Francisco, the JFCS provides "professional and volunteer services for the purposes of developing, restoring and maintaining the competency of families and individuals of all ages." The JFCS runs literally hundreds of services for adults and families, children and youth, people with special needs, new Americans, and older adults. These programs and services are staffed by JFCS volunteers and are delineated on the organization's Web site. The JFCS maintains a set of core values to which it adheres its varied support systems: maintaining, developing, strengthening, and restoring the competency of families and individuals; reaching out to children, the aged, the alienated, and the dependent; assisting in the resettlement and acculturation of refugees and immigrants; and promoting Jewish continuity within the context of historic Jewish values. The organization's Web site includes a number of resource guides with area services, an FAQ, a feedback form, and a featured service organization.

Jewish Federation of Metropolitan Detroit (MI) (http://www.jfmd.org)

The Jewish Federation of Metropolitan Detroit plays the leadership role in identifying needs within the Jewish community and in mobilizing human and financial resources, engaging in communal planning and allocation and advocating to meet those needs. It is committed to ensuring the continuity of the Jewish people in Detroit, Israel, and around the world. The Federation works with numerous agencies to accomplish its mission and provides services for many people in the Detroit Jewish community, including the elderly and youth. Monies raised by the Federation through its annual campaign are distributed to many Detroit agencies and several national organizations. The Federation does not accept grant proposals. Each year the Federation goes through a local Campaign allocation process involving committees of community volunteers as well as Federation professional staff. These committees balance available resources against community priorities. The Federation also has a number of programs and divisions that focus on different efforts; the Web site describes each in detail. Contact information, descriptions of missions and trips, and a community calendar can also be found on the site.

Jewish Foundation of Greater Los Angeles (CA) (http://www.jewishfoundationla.org)

The Jewish Foundation of Greater Los Angeles is a clearinghouse for Jewish philanthropists in southern California, directing funds toward a variety of nonprofit organizations and services in Los Angeles, the community at large, and Israel. Through Legacy Grants, the Foundation supports the areas of social service and health agencies, art and cultural institutions, educational institutions, and synagogues, among others. Comprehensive Development Grants and Partnership Grants pair the Foundation with other organizations or family foundations mainly focused on Jewish identity and affiliation for youth. Family resources, information for donors, program and grant details, news and publications, and a FAQs page are available at the Foundation's Web site. The site provides extensive descriptions of specific grants, along with funding guidelines, previous recipients, and application procedures.

Jewish Fund for Justice (NY) (http://www.jfjustice.org)

Founded in 1984, the Jewish Fund for Justice of New York City works with community-based organizations across the country to address poverty and its causes. The organization's mission is to "act on the historic commitment of the Jewish people to tzedakah (righteous giving) and tikkun olam (repair of the world) . . . [by] combating poverty in the U.S., and the injustices underlying it." This is done by making grants to grassroots organizations, sponsoring awareness programs directed at Jewish Americans, and encouraging direct Jewish involvement. The grants program focuses on the following fields of interest:

economic justice, building community, investing in youth, and assisting new Americans, women in poverty, and Jewish social justice groups. Applicants' projects must directly involve and benefit low-income people and should be community-based. While the site offers application guidelines and deadlines, potential grantees must speak to a Fund staff member before submitting proposals. There are additional guidelines and restrictions for the Synagogue Challenge and Jewish Social Justice Projects. The site includes staff and board lists and a set of curriculum to teach related lessons during many Jewish holidays.

Elton John AIDS Foundation (CA) (http://www.ejaf.org/)

The London and Los Angeles-based Elton John AIDS Foundation was founded in 1992 by entertainer Elton John to fund programs that "provide services to people living with HIV/AIDS and educational programs targeted at AIDS prevention, and/or elimination of prejudice and discrimination against HIV affected individuals." Services supported by the Foundation include food banks and meal programs, legal aid, hospice and housing, counseling and support groups, education outreach programs, at-home care, and pediatric treatment centers. The Foundation's Web site provides a description of its programs, contact information for those seeking grants, and areas for purchasing merchandise or otherwise contributing to the Foundation.

Magic Johnson Foundation (CA) (http://www.magicjohnson.org/)

Originally established to raise funds for HIV/AIDS educational and prevention programs, the Magic Johnson Foundation now awards grants to community-based organizations involved with educational, health, and social programs for inner-city youth. The Foundation recently launched a National Breast Cancer Awareness Initiative that targets African-American Women, and it also operates a number of programs to support youth. These include the Youth Entrepreneurial Project, the Education Program, and the Fashion and Merchandising Scholarship Program. Grant guidelines and scholarship information are provided in the About area of the Foundation's Web site, and online application and request-for-information forms are promised in the near future. The site also provides HIV/AIDS and general health information, a calendar of upcoming events, and donor and contact information.

Kansas Humanities Council (KS) (http://www.cc.ukans.edu/kansas/khc/mainpage.html)

The Kansas Humanities Council of Topeka, Kansas, was created to "promote understanding of the history, traditions, and ideas that shape our lives and the communities in which we live." The Council has two main grant programs. The Humanities Program supports programs that make the humanities accessible to all Kansans, whether through live or filmed presentations, exhibits, or Web sites. The Heritage Programs offer grants to community groups that preserve Kansas' history, including through oral history projects. The Web site is extensive and offers many instructions and support for potential grantees. Each of the grant programs has project categories and examples, application guidelines and deadlines, and advice on contacting Council staff in regard to each project. The site also includes A Calendar of Events in Kansas section and features on many sponsored programs taking place across the state. There is a list of the board of trustees and Council staff and information on making a gift to the Council.

Kelly For Kids Foundation (NY) (http://www.jimkelly.com/kelly_for_kids.htm)

Jim Kelly of the Buffalo Bills founded the Kelly For Kids Organization (KFK) in 1987. KFK is a not-for-profit organization committed to providing funding and support to those organizations that operate for the benefit of specially challenged youth. Visit the Web site for information.

John F. Kennedy Center for the Performing Arts (DC) (http://www.kennedy-center.org)

The Kennedy Center for the Performing Arts, located in Washington, D.C., serves as one of the nation's premier arts facilities. The Center "strives to commission, produce, and present performances reflecting the highest standards of excellence and diversity indicative of the world in which we live, and to make those performances accessible to the broadest possible audience through arts education." Known for its command performances, education and arts outreach programs are a high priority for the Kennedy Center, a leader in national performing arts education policy and programs. The Center runs professional development programs for teachers, administrators, arts supervisors, and schools; provides paid internships for college students; supplies teaching resources, such as the Alliance for Arts Education Network and ArtsEdge on a national level; teaches courses and classes, some through distance learning; and supports school and community initiatives in the metropolitan D.C. area. Additionally, the Kennedy Center awards a number of prizes to artists annually, as well as awarding grants through the Kennedy Center Fund for New American Plays. The Kennedy Center Web site hosts a wealth of information on all of the Center's programs and performances, application guidelines for the New American Plays award, information on internships and educational opportunities, and events calendars.

John F. Kennedy Library Foundation (MA) (http://www.cs.umb.edu/jfklibrary/index.htm)
Boston's John F. Kennedy Library Foundation was founded in 1984 and retains the same mission as the Library itself: "To capture, preserve and exhibit for scholars and visitors of future generations the history and essence of President Kennedy's life and career, and to encourage understanding, respect for and participation in public service." The Foundation's Profile in Courage Award, inspired by the Pulitzer Prize-winning book of the same name by John F. Kennedy, awards $25,000 to a current or former elected official who demonstrates the kind of political courage outlined in the book. The Profile in Courage Essay, open to high school students, covers the same theme. Additionally, the Foundation funds research grants to defray costs incurred while researching in the library and an archival internship in the library. Information and an online application for these grants can be found on the Foundation's Web site. The Foundation sponsors other community outreach activities and posts its newsletter online with further details of activities and awards.

Kentucky Humanities Council (KY) (http://www.uky.edu/~vgsmit00/khc/khc.htm)
The Kentucky Humanities Council, an independent, nonprofit affiliate of the National Endowment for the Humanities, provides grants and services to nonprofit organizations seeking to foster greater understanding of the humanities. The sort of programs traditionally funded by the Council include, but are not limited to, conferences, lectures, radio and video productions, exhibits, teacher training and development of curricular materials, interpretive programs for festivals, book discussions, and planning for future projects. Visitors to the Council's Web site will find grant guidelines as well as information about its speakers bureau, living history performances, book discussion programs, a listing of board and staff members, and contact information.

Susan G. Komen Breast Cancer Foundation (TX) (http://www.komen.org/)
Founded in 1982 and best known as the sponsor of the 5K Race for the Cure runs to raise funds for national and local breast cancer initiatives, the Susan G. Komen Breast Cancer Foundation is the largest private funder of research dedicated solely to breast cancer in the United States. The Foundation's National Grant Program awards grants and fellowships in basic and clinical research as well as grants for breast cancer education, treatment, and screening projects for the medically underserved. Descriptions of the Foundation's programs and downloadable application forms are available on the Web site, as is a list of Komen affiliates who award grants locally. Visitors to the site will also find information about Race for the Cure; an online version of the Foundation's annual report; and a link to breastcancerinfo.com, which provides general health and breast cancer news and information; an online forum; and a calendar of events.

Kosciuszko Foundation, Inc. (NY) (http://www.kosciuszkofoundation.org/)
Headquartered in New York City, the national Kosciuszko Foundation, Inc. was founded in 1925. The goal of the organization is to "promote educational and cultural exchanges between the United States and Poland and to increase American understanding of Polish culture and history." The Foundation offers graduate school scholarships to Americans of Polish descent and Americans whose studies primarily relate to Polish subjects. The

Foundation also administers these scholarships for other Polish groups. The group awards scholarships for American undergraduate and graduate students to spend a year abroad in Cracow and another for American graduate students or faculty to study and/or research in Poland. There are a series of grants and scholarships available to Polish citizens to study in the United States. There is also a voice competition, a piano competition, and the Metchie J.E. Budka Award to recognize scholarly works on subjects of interest to the Foundation. The site includes deadline information, application guidelines, and application forms for the many scholarships and awards. There is also information on current events, cultural events, and summer programs in Poland.

Landscape Architecture Foundation (DC) (http://www.asla.org/nonmembers/laf_section.cfm)

The Landscape Architecture Foundation, located in Washington, D.C., is the philanthropic arm of the American Society of Landscape Architects, whose mission is to "lead, to educate and to participate in the careful stewardship, wise planning and artful design of our cultural and natural environments." The Foundation offers a variety of fellowships and scholarships to undergraduate and graduate students in the landscape architecture field. Deadlines and details about how to apply are posted on the Foundation's Web site. The Web site also has information about the Foundation's officers, its recruitment Web site aimed at bringing in new people to the landscape architecture field, and other initiatives. The most recent Foundation report can also be read on the site.

Leadership for Learning Foundation (a.k.a. American Association of School Administrators) (VA) (http://www.aasa.org/)

The Leadership for Learning Foundation, part of the American Association of School Administrators, an international professional organization for educational leaders, focuses on preparing schools and school systems for the 21st century, on connecting schools and communities, and on enhancing the quality and effectiveness of school leaders. AASA offers numerous awards and scholarships, which are listed and described in various degrees of detail in the Awards and Scholarships area of ASAA's Web site. The organization also operates three programs (Healthy School Environments, School Health, and Options for Pre-Teens) and provides general descriptions of and contact information for each program on its site.

Legal Foundation of Washington (WA) (http://www.legalfoundation.org)

The Legal Foundation of Washington, established in Washington State in 1984, seeks to fund legal and educational programs for low-income persons. The Washington Supreme Court mandated the creation of the Foundation to administer the Interest on Lawyer's Trust Accounts (IOLTA) and provide "free access to justice in civil cases for the poorest and most vulnerable families throughout Washington State." The Foundation also supports community and education programs for lawyers, social service providers and the public toward greater knowledge about and defense of civil legal assistance for the poor. The Foundation's Web site provides a list of staff, financial information, a history of grants, information on IOLTA, events, information on internships at the Foundation, community links, and contact information.

Leukemia Research Foundation (IL) (http://www.leukemia-research.org)

Located in Sonoma County, California, the Sonoma Wings Foundation is dedicated to promoting accountability in the nonprofit sector. The foundation provides both funds and expertise and advice to organizations with proven results in promoting the fulfillment of individual potential. The Foundation supports nonprofit organizations that provide services or programs in literacy, technology, arts, and youth. The Web site provides more information about the Foundation's areas of focus and gives a contact phone number and e-mail address for those interested in learning more or in applying for grants.

The Leukemia & Lymphoma Society (NY) (www.leukemia-lymphoma.org)

In addition to sponsoring a broad range of public conferences about leukemia treatment and research, the Leukemia Society of America supports worldwide research efforts—both in the lab and clinical applications—toward controlling and finding a cure for leukemia, lymphoma, and myeloma. Grant information, guidelines, and application forms are downloadable in Microsoft Word and PDF formats and are available in the Research area of the Society's Web site.

The Liberace Foundation (NV) (http://www.liberace.org/foundation.html)

Located in Las Vegas, Nevada, the Liberace Foundation for the Performing and Creative Arts was founded by the pianist and showman in 1976. The Foundation is made up of a Scholarship and a Community Arts Fund. The Scholarship Fund funnels support through accredited colleges, universities, and conservatories to talented students in disciplines including music, theater, dance, and the visual arts. The institution selects a junior, senior, or graduate school student for the award. The Community Arts Fund supports students attending accredited institutions that offer non-degree training in the performance and creative arts by making grants for scholarships to the institutions. Guidelines are identical to those of the Scholarship Fund. Although there are expansion plans, this program currently only funds programs in Las Vegas. The site includes funding guidelines for each award and a history of the Foundation. The Foundation Grants Coordinator's contact information can be found in the Contact Us area.

Liberty Hill Foundation (CA) (http://www.libertyhill.org/)

Created in 1976, the Liberty Hill Foundation of Santa Monica, California, "promotes progressive social change by funding grassroots community organizations in Los Angeles that empower the disenfranchised and challenge the institutions and attitudes which create economic, social and racial inequalities." The Seed Fund is to help new organizations or programs become community advocates and leaders. The Fund for a New Los Angeles supports established groups working for racial equality, economic justice, and community development that are ready to take the next step in expansion. The Environmental Justice Fund supports grassroots organizations that are working in low-income areas or communities of color to decrease exposure to toxic substances. The Social Entrepreneurial Fund offers grants, technical assistance, and volunteer support to nonprofit organizations with viable business plans that lead to social benefits. The Lesbian and Gay Community Fund supports existing and new programs and services for the gay community. The Special Opportunities Fund offers funding to a variety of groups that need immediate financial help. Each fund's application guidelines can be downloaded in PDF format. The site also offers an electronic version of the annual report, an events calendar, and information on contributing, including, and establishing a donor-advised fund.

Library of Michigan Foundation (MI)
(http://www.libofmich.lib.mi.us/foundation/foundation.html)

The Library of Michigan Foundation "supports major projects of the Library of Michigan, promotes library resources and services for all of the citizens of Michigan, and accepts private gifts to finance projects for local libraries throughout Michigan." The Foundation runs several programs, including Read Indeed!, which works to fund adult literacy efforts, and the Michigan Rare Book Room Project. Details about the Read Indeed! Grant Program and how to apply are available on the site, as is a list of previous awardees. The Foundation also works to conserve and preserve rare books and Michigan's printed heritage, enhance library services for the blind and physically handicapped, and support the Abram's Genealogy Collection and its use. Information about Foundation publications and staff and contact information can also be found on the Web site.

Libri Foundation (OR) (http://www.teleport.com/~librifdn/index.html)

The Libri Foundation of Eugene, Oregon, was established in 1989. The Foundation is dedicated to "helping rural libraries acquire quality children's books they could not otherwise afford to buy." Through the Books for Children program, selected libraries raise and contribute between $50 and $350, which is then matched 2:1 by the Foundation. Librarians can then choose new hardback books from the extensive list that will most benefit the children of their community. Interested libraries can e-mail the foundation for an application. Most selected libraries serve a population under 5,000, but those serving communities of up to 10,000 are considered. There is a specific Mississippi Delta Books for Children program. This two-year program support libraries in Arkansas, Louisiana, and Mississippi. There is a Web page for this project that lists the eligible counties. The site also includes a list of grant recipients, information on featured books from the Foundation's list, and suggestions for library fundraisers. Visitors will also find a list of the four-member board of directors.

LIFEbeat, Inc. (NY) (http://www.lifebeat.org)
Record executive Daniel Glass and late music industry manager/promoter Bob Caviano founded LIFEbeat in 1992. Located in New York City, the Foundation is an AIDS resource and awareness organization dedicated to mobilizing the talent of the music industry in order to provide grants to community-based service organizations, establish innovative ways to disseminate information on HIV/AIDS and AIDS-related services, and empower members of the music industry living with HIV/AIDS by offering access to information, services, and financial assistance. There is contact information provided for those who are interested in learning more about the organization and its grants.

Charles A. and Anne Morrow Lindbergh Foundation (MN) (http://www.lindberghfoundation.org)
The Lindbergh Foundation awards grants to individuals whose "initiative and work in a wide spectrum of disciplines furthers the Lindberghs' vision of a balance between the advance of technology and the preservation of the natural/human environment." The Foundation pursues its mission through three major programs: the presentation of Lindbergh Grants of up to $10,580 (a symbolic amount representing the cost of the Spirit of St. Louis), presentation of the Lindbergh Award to an individual for his or her lifelong contributions to the Lindberghs' shared vision, and the sponsoring of educational programs and publications which advance the Lindberghs' vision. In addition to a brief history of the Foundation, contact information, and application guidelines, the Foundation's Web site offers visitors a grant application to view, print, or download in Microsoft Word format; a list of Lindbergh Grants awarded in recent years; an online version of the Foundation's most recent annual report; a listing of the Foundation's officers, board, and staff; and links to other sites.

LMC Community Foundation (CO) (http://www.lmccf.org/)
Formerly the Lutheran Medical Center Foundation, the LMC Community Foundation of Wheat Ridge, Colorado, was created in 1975 to "help people and communities help themselves achieve better health in all dimensions." The Connecting Neighbors program distributes grants up to $3,000 to support activities working for the health and well-being of their communities. There is an electronic application available. Annual Healthy Community Awards are given out to recognize community groups that have stood out in promoting health in children twelve and under, in providing service for the health of seniors, and for promoting intergenerational "connectedness," as well as businesses that have contributed to the health of the community. The 1999 award recipients are now posted. The site provides a list of the board of directors, features on grant recipients, options of organizations donors can support, and opportunities to donate. There is also an area to register for Foundation listservs and information on volunteering.

Local Initiatives Support Corporation (NY) (http://www.liscnet.org)
Begun by a grant from the Ford Foundation and six Fortune 500 companies in 1979, the Local Initiatives Support Corporation is committed to revitalizing neighborhoods through community services and affordable housing. LISC channels "grants, investments, and technical support to community development corporations (CDCs) rebuilding neighborhoods and rural areas throughout the country." The reinvigoration of the south Bronx community

in New York is one of LISC's first projects, showcased as a model of LISC's work. LISC incorporates various program initiatives in the 41 cities and communities it serves, including Public Housing Initiatives, Rural LISC, the Community Investment Collaborative for Kids, the Retail Initiative, and the Community Building Initiative, all detailed on the LISC Web site. The site also includes more information about LISC's funding sources and projects, as well as a form to request more information on grants and programs.

The Loft, Inc. (MN) (http://www.loft.org/)

The Loft was formed in Minneapolis, Minnesota, in 1974 by a group of writers who gathered together to give each other feedback, guidance, and support. The Loft is now one of the nation's largest, most comprehensive literary centers. The mission of the Loft is "to foster a writing community, the artistic development of individual writers, and an audience for literature." The Loft offers a variety of contests, grants, and fellowships, all of which are described on its site along with the guidelines for applications. Submissions will be accepted for Loft competition and grant programs only during the annual submission periods specified in the program guidelines. Grants and fellowships are given to writers, poets, and organizations and individuals that promote literature. In addition to information about grants and contests, the Web site provides comprehensive information about the organization's history and mission, staff contact information, and a calendar of Loft events.

Terri Lynne Lokoff Child Care Foundation (PA) (http://www.childcarefoundation.org)

Located in King of Prussia, Pennsylvania, the Terri Lynne Lokoff Child Care Foundation was founded in 1986 by the parents of the Foundation's namesake, who died in a tragic car accident. In honor of Terri Lynne Lokoff's life as a childcare teacher, the Foundation's mission is to "improve the quality of child care for all children; support and elevate the status of child care teachers and providers; raise awareness of the need for affordable, quality child care; and partner with business and government in making child care a priority." Programs supported by the Foundation have included Federation Day Care Services; Montgomery County Early Learning Center; Best Friends, a division of United Cerebral Palsy; and Children's Village. It is looking to start supporting programs outside of the Philadelphia area. The Foundation is also committed to helping parents find quality day care, and much of the Web site is dedicated to this effort. Visitors will find a page of questions to ask child care providers and what to look for in a program. The site also includes features on Foundation events and information on contributing or becoming a member. The site does include basic contact information.

Los Angeles Women's Foundation (CA) (http://www.lawomen.org)

The Los Angeles Women's Foundation is a community-based foundation with a 15-year history of promoting women's philanthropy and granting funds to community–based organizations to support services to women and girls in the greater Los Angeles area. The Foundation's initiatives have been created to help increase access and use of existing health services, to improve the quality of health services, and to bring visibility to the issue of healthcare for women and girls. Grants are made for programs that support economic literacy and justice, prevention of violence, self-determination, and technical assistance. Visit the Foundation's Web site to find further details on areas supported, a history of the Foundation, and contact information.

Louisiana Endowment for the Humanities (LA) (http://www.leh.org/)

The Louisiana Endowment for the Humanities was founded in 1971 to foster a deeper understanding and appreciation of the humanities throughout Louisiana and to broaden Louisianans' access to history, literature, philosophy, language, and culture. To that end, LEH develops its own projects and makes grants to nonprofit organizations for public projects such as documentary films, museum exhibits, radio programs, conferences, lecture series, library reading programs, books, and interpretive folklife festivals. The LEH Web site provides brief descriptions of its programs and provides an interactive form for requesting more detailed information, including grant guidelines.

The Lutheran Church-Missouri Synod Foundation (MO) (http://www.lfnd.org/)

The LCMS Foundation of St. Louis, Missouri, was created in 1958 and is the fundraising arm of The Lutheran Church-Missouri Synod. The organization allows donors, organizations, or individuals to set up funds to provide assistance to the ministries that the LCMS also supports. The site includes services and advice for donors and potential donors, a newsletter that can be downloaded in PDF format, and a feature on a monthly success story. There is information for Lutheran organizations that are interested in fundraising assistance and gift management investment advice. This is not a "granting" foundation.

Lutheran World Relief (MD) (http://www.lwr.org)

Located in Baltimore, Maryland, the Lutheran World Relief "extends the hand of Christian love to people overcoming poverty and injustice in 50 countries." While the Web site provides financial and contact information, a history of the organization, and stories about the work the organization does around the world, it does not mention grantmaking.

Lymphoma Research Foundation of America, Inc. (CA) (http://www.lymphoma.org/)

Founded by non-Hodgkins lymphoma survivor Ellen Glesby Cohen in 1991, the Lymphoma Research Foundation of America funds lymphoma research and educational information for lymphoma patients. Research grants are awarded annually to third-year researchers, and applications can be requested via e-mail through the Foundation's Web site, where the LRFA grants program is described and past recipients are listed. The site also provides information on the Foundation's activities; information about clinical trials; an online version of *Lymphoma Update,* the organization's newsletters and links to various lymphoma-related resources on the Internet.

James Madison Memorial Fellowship Foundation (DC) (http://jamesmadison.com/)

Established by Congress in 1986, The James Madison Memorial Fellowship Foundation seeks to "strengthen secondary school teaching of the principles, framing, and development of the U.S. Constitution" and works to foster the spirit of civic participation in teachers and students. The Foundation annually awards fellowships for graduate study of the principles, framing, and history of the U.S. Constitution to teachers of American history, American government, and social studies in grades 7–12, as well as to college seniors and college graduates who plan to become secondary school teachers of these subjects. At least one junior or senior fellow is selected from each state every year. The Foundation's Web site provides a thorough description of the application process and allows visitors to sign up to be notified electronically when new applications are posted to the site for downloading. The site also offers a password protected Fellows Only area; news announcements; a listing of staff, trustees, academic advisors, and faculty representatives by state; and contact information.

Maine Humanities Council (ME) (http://www.mainehumanities.org)

The Portland-based Maine Humanities Council was founded in 1975 to promote "community programs in cultural heritage, contemporary issues, reading and literacy, as well as enrichment programs for teachers." Some of the programs the Council sponsors are outlined on its Web site: Reading & Discussion/Family Literacy: The Maine Center for the Book; Teacher Enrichment Programs: The Maine Collaborative; Heritage Programs, to study the history and heritage of Maine's towns; and the current contemporary issue, Literature and Medicine, which allows healthcare providers to reflect on their professional work and how it relates to their patients. The Council provides more information on the Literature and Medicine program on its web site, as well as helpful links and contact information to learn more about their other grant programs.

Maine Women's Fund (ME) (http://www.mainewomensfund.org/)

The Maine Women's Fund, founded in 1988, "envisions a world where women and girls have achieved political, economic and social equality." To help achieve this goal, the Fund supports policy, programs, and practices that help empower girls and women of Maine. The Fund supports start-up expenses, projects, programs, and general operating support of organizations that promote the empowerment, advancement, and full participation of women and girls in society. The priorities of the Fund include economic justice, health, prevention of violence, and self-determination. The Fund's Web site includes recent grants, descriptions of program areas, a board list, and contact information.

Manhattan Neighborhood Network (NY) (http://www.mnn.org)
The Manhattan Neighborhood Network administers public access television in New York City's borough of Manhattan. The Network looks for programming that supports First Amendment rights and promotes the social, political, ethnic, and artistic diversity apparent in Manhattan. The MNN Web site provides programming schedules as well as information on taking advantages of MNN's television production resources. MNN's grants "assist Manhattan non-profit organizations and individuals to provide training and support for community video productions." Grants are mainly for producers; grant guidelines and cover sheets can be downloaded in PDF format from the site. Past grant recipients and the details and images from their projects are also provided on the site.

MAP International (GA) (http://www.map.org/)
MAP International is a Christian relief and development organization whose mission is to promote the total health of people living in the world's poorest communities. Founded over 45 years ago as an arm of the Christian Medical Society, MAP (Medical Assistance Programs) moved to its permanent location in Brunswick, Georgia, in 1985. MAP's three-fold mission is to provide essential medicines, prevent and eradicate disease, and promote community health development. MAP is currently focusing three primary program activities: Provision of Essential Medicines, Promotion of Comprehensive Community Health, and Prevention of HIV/AIDS. It also has a fellowship program, the MAP International/Reader's Digest International Fellowship program (MAP- RDIF), which "encourages lifelong involvement in global health issues by providing selected medical students firsthand exposure in a Christian context to the health, social and cultural characteristics of a developing world community." The fellowship provides 75 percent of the fellow's round–trip airfare to the destination. Students pay room and board as well as the remaining 25 percent of travel costs. Visit the site to obtain further information on programs in Africa and Latin America, to obtain application instructions for the fellowship program, and for press releases, newsletters, and contact information.

March of Dimes Birth Defect Foundation (NY) (http://www.modimes.org/)
President Franklin D. Roosevelt created the March of Dimes in 1938 at the height of the polio epidemic. With the advent of the polio vaccine in the late 1950s, the focus of the organization shifted to the reduction of birth defects and infant mortality rates through advocacy, education, support of community programs, and research in genetics and neurobiology. The Foundation's Web site provides detailed information about its grants, scholarships, and application guidelines. Unique and useful features of the site include an interactive form for contacting a local chapter of the March of Dimes and free access to MedLine, a medical information database. The site also offers a great deal of information (some of it in Spanish) about the Foundation's advocacy and education efforts (including Walk America) and about various health issues affecting infants.

Mariners Care (WA) (http://www.mariners.org/community/default.html)
Mariners Care is a nonprofit foundation of the Baseball Club of Seattle. It is dedicated to serving the community, especially young people. Its mission is to support youth-oriented community service programs and other worthy projects in the Pacific Northwest. Visitors to the site will find descriptions of the numerous programs the Foundation is involved in, a monthly newsletter, and contact information.

Mary's Pence (NJ) (http://www.igc.apc.org/maryspence/)
Mary's Pence is dedicated to furthering the self-empowerment of all women and, through women's growth, the self-improvement of all humanity. In support of these goals, it provides seed money for creative programs designed to bring about systemic change in church

and society, especially programs that are likely to help dismantle oppressive structures and to have liberating and long lasting results. Support is reserved for ministries in the Americas that have been created and are managed by women, that are not sponsored by parishes or dioceses, and that do not receive significant funding from other sources. In addition to a detailed description of the organization's funding philosophy, the Mary's Pence Web site provides grant guidelines, a list of past recipients, information on how to get involved, and e-mail contact information.

Maryland 4-H Foundation, Inc. (MD) (http://www.agnr.umd.edu/CES/4H/)

The Maryland 4-H Foundation is part of the programs and services offered by the Maryland 4-H organization. 4-H programs provide education and enrichment for children of diverse regions of the United States Programs in workforce skills, citizenship, public speaking and other activities are offered for children, with a focus on the needs of youth of rural America. The Foundation supports 4-H members through scholarships, which are "made available through an endowment established by the 4-H families and friends of those for whom the scholarships are named." The Maryland 4-H Web site includes information on the varied activities of the group. Information on the Foundation itself is scarce, and can best be found by searching the site.

Maryland Humanities Council, Inc. (MD) (http://www.mdhc.org)

Based in Baltimore, the Maryland Humanities Council supports programs and individuals working in the humanities: history, philosophy, languages, literature, ethics, linguistics, archaeology, comparative religion, and jurisprudence; the history, theory, and criticism of the arts and architecture; and those aspects of the social sciences employing historical or philosophical approaches. The Council strives to promote these areas of the humanities in Maryland through public programs, including lectures and courses, grants, and awards. Two types of grants are available through the Council: minigrants, for up to $1,200, and regular grants, for up to $10,000. The Council's Web site provides extensive information on grant deadlines, limitations, regulations, guidelines, application outlines, and benefits. The Eisenberg Prize for Excellence in the Humanities rewards an individual who has contributed to the public understanding and appreciation of the humanities in Maryland. More information on upcoming events and the Council's programs, plus contact information, are available online.

Massachusetts Environmental Trust (MA) (http://www.agmconnect.org/maenvtr1.html)

The Massachusetts Environmental Trust was established in 1988 through the settlement of a federal lawsuit over the pollution of Boston Harbor. The Trust funds grassroots environmental programs that will restore, protect, and improve the quality of Massachusetts waterways. The Trust recommends that grantseekers apply for funds within one of its eight defined grant programs but will accept unsolicited proposals that do not fit within those parameters. Guidelines are provided at the Trust's Web site with links to the Massachusetts Common Proposal Format, which is required for at least two of the programs. Recent grant awards and contact information are also provided at the Trust's site.

Massachusetts Foundation for the Humanities, Inc. (MA) (http://www.mfh.org)

Founded in 1974 as the Massachusetts arm of the National Endowment for the Humanities, the Massachusetts Foundation for the Humanities strives to bring the humanities out of the classroom and into the community. Its mission is to "foster critical inquiry; promote understanding of our diverse cultural heritages; and provide forums for the citizens of [Massachusetts] to engage actively in thoughtful public discourse about matters of individual choice and collective responsibility." The Foundation has numerous programs: mini grants, up to $2,500; major grants, which include media grants; planning; grants for humanities resource centers; reading and discussion funding; research inventory grants; special places grants; and scholar in residence funding, for the study of history in Massachusetts historical organizations, museums, and libraries. The Foundation's current special considerations are on Massachusetts women and the millennium. Its Web site includes an extensive download library, with all types of applications and guidelines available to download in

Microsoft Word. The Foundation's Web center additionally provides resources, links, contact information, and definitions of the humanities.

Mathcounts Foundation (VA) (http://www.mathcounts.org/About/about.html)

The Mathcounts Foundation, based in Virginia, is a national organization that has promoted math excellence among middle school students since 1984. The Foundation's mission is to "increase interest and involvement in mathematics among all intermediate school students in order to assist in developing a technically literate population essential to U.S. global competitiveness and the quality of life." Visit the Foundation's Web site to view a copy of the Foundation's annual report, downloadable in PDF format, a listing of board and staff, information on how the program is funded, and contact information.

The Joseph Matteucci Foundation (CA) (http://www.jmf4peace.org)

The Castro Valley, California-based Joseph Matteucci Foundation is dedicated to youth nonviolence. Its mission is to "[support] young people who teach, live and stand for peace." Joseph Matteucci was the victim of a senseless act of violence when another youth mistakenly hit him with a baseball bat after a Little League game dispute. The Foundation that bears his name strives to sponsor programs that promote nonviolence, especially in sports. Through meditation programs in schools; the Sports Emblem Program, which raises awareness of nonviolence; the Stand for Peace workshop; and a speaking program, the Foundation's staff and supporters seek to use Joseph's story for positive change. The Foundation's Web site provides more information on these programs, events, links to further resources for youth nonviolence, and contact information.

McClennan Scholarship Fund, W.H. (Howie) (DC) (http://www.covenantfn.org)

The McClennan Scholarship Fund is one of the many charities of the International Association of Fire Fighters. Named after IAFF President Emeritus Howie McClennan, the scholarship exists to help the sons and daughters of fire fighters who have been killed in the line of duty. The annual award can be used by the recipient toward the expenses of any university, accredited college, or school of higher learning in the United States or Canada. Scholarships are awarded each year and can be renewed up to four years, providing that the winners maintain satisfactory academic standards. Guidelines and details on how to apply for the scholarship are posted on the Web site. The application and scholarship rules can be downloaded from the site in PDF format.

Ronald McDonald House Charities (IL) (http://www.rmhc.org)

The Ronald McDonald House Charities, based in Illinios, is committed to "lifting children to a better tomorrow." The charity provides comfort and care to children and their families by supporting Ronald McDonald Houses in communities around the world and by making grants to other not-for-profit organizations whose programs help children in need. Ronald McDonald House Charities has a network of over 174 local charities serving in 32 countries. McDonald's Corporation is committed to giving something back to the community by supporting RMHC initiatives. The Charity's Web site offers information for families who need a place to stay, volunteer opportunities, a history of Ronald McDonald Houses, information on grantmaking programs, and contact information.

McKenzie River Gathering Foundation (OR) (http://www.mrgf.org/)

The McKenzie River Gathering Foundation was established in 1976 to provide funding in Oregon to grassroots groups challenging social, economic, and political inequities. The Foundation's grantmaking focuses on human and civil rights, racial justice, economic justice, environmental protection, peace, and international solidarity, with grant amounts in the $3,000–$5,000 range. The Foundation's Web site describes its mission and provides grant guidelines and contact information for administrators of its programs, donor information, and a link to the Funding Exchange Network, of which it is a member.

McStain Enterprises, Inc. (CO) (http://www.mcstain.com/ecology/grants.htm)

As a Colorado land developer and homebuilder, McStain Enterprises maintains a community involvement program that seeks to find long-term solutions and establish educational programs dealing with land-use and environmental issues. To this end, McStain grants to "land-use related programs which support preservation and/or improvements to open space, innovative solutions to transportation or recycling issues or provide education connected to land-use topics" in the communities where McStain builds homes. The McStain Web site details these goals and provides criteria for eligibility, a funding timeline and final proposal guidelines, and a contact e-mail address for further information.

Media Alliance, Inc. (NY) (http://www.Mediaalliance.org)

Based in New York City, Media Alliance is a resource for media amateurs and professionals; its mission is to "[advance] independent media—video, film, audio, radio, and computers—in New York State by expanding resources, support, and audiences for the media arts." Media Alliance has an extensive listing of resources, including New York State arts organizations, video preservation services, equipment and facilities, publications, funding, and residency programs on its Web site. Media Action grants—cash awards for the organization of conferences, workshops, and events—are given by the Alliance "to promote media arts networking at the statewide level by enabling organizations and individuals to initiate activities that directly serve upstate communities." Recent grant recipients are posted online, as are grant guidelines and requirements prior to the next grant cycle. Contact information and a wealth of links to further arts resources are all available online.

Meet the Composer (NY) (http://www.meetthecomposer.org/)

Meet The Composer was founded in 1974 as a project of the New York State Council on the Arts to increase artistic and financial opportunities for American composers, which it does by providing composer fees to nonprofit organizations that perform, present, or commission original works. Meet the Composer has several funding programs, which are detailed on its Web site with downloadable application forms and guidelines (in PDF format). Visitors to the site will also find news, free publications to order, links to related Web sites, and donor and contact information.

Michigan AIDS Fund (MI) (http://www.michaidsfund.org/)

The Michigan AIDS Fund, of Grand Rapids, Michigan, was established in 1990 to address the AIDS epidemic in the state. The organization aims to pool resources "to support efforts to stop the spread of HIV/AIDS and to alleviate the suffering of those infected and affected by the AIDS epidemic." The fund gives money to groups that provide AIDS/HIV prevention and services. The grants include cash as well as other support from the fund. There are annual conferences for grantees, and recipients get technical support and peer reviews. The site includes an address to contact with funding requests. There is also information on the history of the AIDS epidemic in Michigan and on making donations to the fund.

Michigan Humanities Council (MI) (http://mihumanities.h-net.msu.edu/)

The Michigan Humanities Council, the state's affiliate of the National Endowment for the Humanities, encourages and supports activities that bring humanities scholars and the public together to promote understanding and appreciation of the humanities. The Council's grants program funds collaborative projects that use the disciplines of the humanities to explore community issues, particularly in communities with limited humanities programming and resources. Grant guidelines and application forms, are provided at the Council's Web site, along with grant announcements, a note from the director, Council newsletters, resources and events, and grants lists.

Michigan Women's Foundation (MI) (http://comnet.org/mwf)

Founded on the anniversary of the ratification of the 19th Constitutional Amendment, which gave women the right to vote, in 1986, the Grand Rapids-based Michigan Women's Foundation is committed to the interests of women and girls in Michigan. The Foundation's goal is to "expand economic options for low-income women, to promote financial education for women, to sponsor leadership programs for women and girls, to help non-profit organizations serving women and girls become more effective and efficient and to increase women's participation in the philanthropic process." This goal manifests itself in projects dedicated to employment and economic development, management of nonprofits serving Michigan women and girls, leadership development, and personal well-being of Michigan women and girls. The Foundation's Women's Health Funding Initiative includes grants for collaborative partnerships, access, and change. The Young Women for Change program allows a diverse group of Michigan girls to assess the needs of local girls and grant approximately $20,000 in funds. Visitor's to the Foundation's Web site will find a number of resources: funding criteria, a project budget worksheet, a listing of past recipients, the archives of the Foundation's two newsletters—*Road Map* and *Trillium*, donor information, current events sponsored by the Foundation, links to further resources, and a listing of the board and staff members with contact information.

Mid Atlantic Arts Foundation (MD) (http://www.midatlanticarts.org)

One of six regional arts organizations in the continental United States, the Mid Atlantic Arts Foundation addresses the support of the arts in a multi-state region comprised of Delaware, the District of Columbia, Maryland, New Jersey, New York, Pennsylvania, the U.S. Virgin Islands, Virginia, and West Virginia. The Foundation, which is primarily concerned with providing increased access to quality arts programs, provides financial support, technical assistance, and information to artists and arts organizations through a variety of programs and services. Visitors to the Foundation's Web site will find general program descriptions for the visual arts, performing arts, jazz, and traditional and folk arts; some recent grant awards and descriptions; listings of the Foundation's board and staff; links to the nine Mid-Atlantic state arts agencies' Web sites; and an online version of *ARTSINK,* the Foundation's newsletter.

Million Dollar Round Table Foundation (IL) (http://www.mdrtfoundation.org/)

The Million Dollar Round Table is an association of sales professionals in life insurance-based financial services. The MDRT Foundation was established by this organization in 1959 to "improve the quality of life." The Foundation promotes volunteerism among its members, charitable giving to organizations throughout the world, and funds a number of grants. Grants fall into three categories: Quality of Life, National/International, and Local/Regional. An alphabetical listing of past National/International and Local/Regional grants appears on the Foundation's Web site. Also included is current news and Foundation events and contact information. Future additions to the site will include grant applications, fundraising programs, and resources.

John Milton Society for the Blind (NY) (http://www.jmsblind.org)

The John Milton Society (JMS) was created in 1928 to provide nonsectarian religious material for the blind, in response to a demand for a wider selection of brailed religious literature than was available. Based in New York City, JMS was named for the English Christian poet who lost his sight soon after he turned forty and who was blind when he wrote the epic poem "Paradise Lost." JMS seeks to fulfill the vision of founding member Helen Keller by providing "Christian nurture to persons worldwide who cannot see to read regular print, and to those who serve them, through free religious literature and educational scholarships, regardless of denominational affiliation." JMS currently has two scholarship programs that aim to both educate and expand services. One program provides an annual scholarship to a blind student in the New York area. The society's second program, administered through two U.S. schools for the blind (Perkins School in Watertown, Massachusetts, and Overbrook School in Philadelphia, Pennsylvania), provides international scholarships to individuals to study in the United States so that they can return home to teach and promote resources for blind persons there. The site contains descriptions of its scholarship programs, a printable publications order form, a list of scholarship resources for the blind and visually impaired, links to related resources, and a downloadable reference handbook of religious materials in Microsoft Word, Word Perfect, and rich text formats.

Minnesota Humanities Commission (MN) (http://www.thinkmhc.org/grants.htm)

The Minnesota Humanities Commission (MHC) is dedicated solely to promoting excellent humanities education throughout Minnesota. The MHC Grant program provides funding for Minnesota groups and organizations conducting public projects in the humanities. MHC grants are intended to foster connections among humanities scholars, cultural organizations, and community groups. Through its grants program, MHC promotes an appreciation of learning, thoughtfulness, dialogue, and tolerance. Priority is given to senior citizen organizations, minority organizations, multi-site projects serving hard-to-reach audiences, and greater Minnesota organizations. Visitor's to MHC's site will find specific information on the MHC's program, application guidelines, recent grants, and contact information.

Minnesota Twins Community Fund (http://www.pohladfamilycharities.org/mtcf.html)

Founded in 1991, the Minnesota Twins Community Fund supports Minnesota nonprofits through direct funding and the volunteer efforts of Minnesota Twins baseball players and their families. Financial support is mainly directed toward youth recreation and education programs, particularly area baseball and softball leagues. The Fund also makes in-kind donations of tickets and memorabilia to aid area nonprofit organizations. Further details and funding guidelines for the Fund's programs are available online, along with general information for nonprofits, news releases, printer-friendly versions of documents, and contacts. Application materials can be downloaded in PDF format from the site.

Mississippi Humanities Council (MS) (http://www.ihl.state.ms.us/mhc/index.html)

The Mississippi Humanities Council encourages and supports activities that make the humanities accessible to the people of Mississippi, primarily by awarding grants to nonprofits that plan and sponsor humanities activities. The Council's Web site provides grant program descriptions, guidelines, and contact information, as well as information about the Council, a calendar of events, and links to humanities resources and funding sources on the Web.

Missouri Humanities Council (MO) (http://www.umsl.edu/community/mohuman/)

The Missouri Humanities Council promotes community, citizenship, and learning through humanities programs. The Council makes grants primarily for family reading programs, cultural heritage development, Chautauqua programs (a form of history theater), and local initiatives. Guidelines and an application to print and mail are provided at the Council's Web site. The site also provides information on the humanities and the Council's activities, links to Missouri Web sites, a listing of board members, and contact information.

The Mockingbird Foundation (NY) (http://www.phish.net/mockingbird/)

The Mockingbird Foundation, located in Saratoga Springs, New York, was founded in 1997 by fans of the band Phish. It was originally founded to produce the most factually accurate and literary book on Phish's music. While the book is the main focus of the Foundation, it now seeks to produce a wider range of resources for fans, including a Phish tribute album. Additionally, the Foundation uses the proceeds from its books and albums to offer competitive grants to schools and nonprofit organizations with in the United States that effect improvements in areas of importance to the Phish fan community. These areas include music, education, and children. Grant guidelines, details about how to apply, and deadlines are all available on the Mockingbird Foundation Web site.

Montana Committee for the Humanities (MT) (http://www.umt.edu/lastbest/)

The Montana Committee for the Humanities, the state's affiliate of the National Endowment for the Humanities founded in 1972, offers grants for public programs in history, literature, philosophy, and other disciplines of the humanities and awards fellowships for humanities research relating to Montana. MCH provides guidelines for these programs and for its "Packaged Programs," a speakers bureau and media collection, in the Grant Info area of its Web site, along with contacts for requesting additional information. The site also provides news, MCH committee information, and a listing of humanities resources.

Mr. Holland's Opus Foundation, Inc. (CA) (http://www.mhopus.org)

The Sherman Oaks, California-based Mr. Holland's Opus Foundation was inspired by the movie of the same name and was founded by the movie's creative team: composer Michael Kamen, actor Richard Dreyfuss, and director Stephen Herek. The Foundation is committed to "promoting instrumental music nationwide by partnering with businesses, schools, and communities to provide new and refurbished musical instruments to qualified schools and individual students." Three grants programs help attain this mission: the Melody Program, which supports school music programs threatened by budget cuts; the Solo Program, which grants instruments to financially limited student musicians; and the Special Project Program, providing funding for community schools of the arts, hospitals, nursing homes, music therapy programs, and school districts. The Foundation's Web site includes grant information, criteria and requirements, past grant and instrument recipients, and contact information for grant applications.

Ms. Foundation for Women (NY) (http://www.ms.foundation.org/)

The Ms. Foundation for Women, founded in 1972, supports the efforts of women and girls to govern their own lives and influence the world around them by funding women's self-help organizing efforts and supporting changes in public consciousness, law, philanthropy, and social policy. The Foundation awards grants through special RFP initiatives in three issue areas—Women's Economic Security, Women's Health and Safety, and Girls, Young Women, and Leadership—and offers Movement Building Grants in two grant cycles. Grant guidelines, RFPs, and the application form for Movement Building Grants are provided in the Women & Philanthropy area of the Foundation's Web site. The site provides information on the Foundation's activities, "Take Our Daughters to Work Day," and collaborative funding information.

The Mt. Sinai healthcare Foundation (OH) (http://www.mtsinaifoundation.org)

The mission of the Cleveland, Ohio-based Mt. Sinai healthcare Foundation is to "assist greater Cleveland's organizations and leaders to improve the health and well-being of the Jewish and general communities now and for generations to come." The Foundation's grantmaking program specifies four areas relating to its work within the health field. Areas of interest include child development, the elderly, organizations, and the community. The foundation also considers proposals not covered within its specific areas to deserving applicants. Visit the Foundation's Web site to find more details regarding the specific program areas. The site also provides details on submitting proposals, restrictions, news on the Foundation, and contact information.

Multiple Sclerosis Foundation, Inc. (FL) (http://www.msfacts.org/)

Based in Ft. Lauderdale, the Multiple Sclerosis Foundation (MSF) was founded in 1986 to provide both "complementary and conventional healthcare options to address the varied symptoms associated with MS." Among the services provided by the Foundation are toll-free phone support, home care assisted program (which provides temporary non-medical home care to people with MS who financially qualify for the relief), newsletters, MS updates, an in-house library, networking and referral services, and donated medical equipment program. The MSF provides gifts for research into the cause, treatment, prevention, and eventual cure of MS. The Foundation also provides scholarships for student studies and special projects in the areas of quality of life and healthcare issues related to MS. Visitors to the site will find related links, a directory of products and services provided by people with MS, and contact information.

Muscular Dystrophy Association (AZ) (http://www.mdausa.org/)

The Muscular Dystrophy Association seeks to find the causes of and cures for 40 neuromuscular diseases through sponsorship of 400 research projects worldwide. MDA provides research grants to professionals or faculty members who are qualified to conduct and supervise a program of original research at appropriate educational, medical, or research institutions. Grant guidelines are provided at the MDA Web site along with an application form. The site also lists current research grantees and projects, research developments, clinical trials, and scientific meetings, symposia, and workshops.

A.J. Muste Memorial Institute (NY) (http://www.nonviolence.org/ajmuste/)

The A.J. Muste Memorial Institute explores the link between nonviolence and social change by applying its resources to the nonviolent struggle for social justice and a peaceful future. The Institute awards grants for projects promoting its mission through peace and disarmament, social and economic justice, racial and sexual equality, and the labor movement. It also provides funding through its International Nonviolence Training Fund. Grant guidelines are available at the Institute's Web site along with contact information for interested grantseekers, a list of grantees since 1994, and details of its fiscal sponsorship program. The site also describes the "Peace Pentagon"—low-cost office space in New York City for activists—and provides information on publications, contributions to the Institute, and a biography of A.J. Muste.

NAACP Legal Defense and Educational Fund, Inc. (NY) (http://www.ldfla.org)

The NAACP Legal Defense and Educational Fund was established in 1940 under the leadership of Thurgood Marshall, who became the first African-American Supreme Court Justice. The Fund is now based in New York City, with its Western Regional Office located in Los Angeles. The Fund "fights for equality and empowerment for African Americans and other disenfranchised groups in the areas of education, employment, criminal justice, voting rights, housing, healthcare, and environmental justice" through litigation and educational programs. The work of the Western Regional Office is publicized through the Fund's Web site, where information on current cases and issues of interest to the Fund are described. Case-related documents can be downloaded in Word Perfect format from the site. Petitions for potential cases for the Fund can be sent in writing to the contact address provided online, where a feedback form is also available.

National Alliance for Autism Research (NJ) (http://www.naar.org)

Created by parents in 1994, the National Alliance for Autism Research (NAAR) is based in Princeton, New Jersey. NAAR is "dedicated to finding the causes, prevention, effective treatment and, ultimately, cure of the autism spectrum disorders." To this end, NAAR funds, promotes, and supports biomedical research into autism. Under the Research Funding heading of its Web site, NAAR details current and past research projects it has funded. Current Requests for Proposals, applications, and grant guidelines are also available for downloading in PDF format, along with a bibliography of NAAR-funded research. A wealth of autism-related information is available on the NAAR Web site, including current news on research, upcoming events and meetings, and related links.

National Alopecia Areata Foundation (CA) (http://www.naaf.org)

Based in San Rafael, California, the National Alopecia Areata Foundation's (NAAF) mission is "to support research to find a cure or acceptable treatment for alopecia areata, to support those with the disease, and to educate the public about alopecia areata," a skin disease of the autoimmune system that results in the loss of scalp and body hair. This mission is accomplished through public education, research funding, and advocating for those afflicted with the disease. The Foundation's Web site offers announcements on current research, recent grant recipients, and grants instructions and application forms that can be downloaded in PDF format. The Web site also provides a form for further information on alopecia areata, news and events, and upcoming conference information.

National Association for the Exchange of Industrial Resources, Inc. (IL) (http://www.naeir.org)

NAEIR was founded in January, 1977 by Norbert C. Smith, a former aircraft parts manufacturing executive. While working as a charitable gifts consultant to major corporations, he discovered that many companies have millions of dollars worth of new, excess inventory in their warehouses. He founded the National Association for the Exchange of Industrial Resources (NAEIR), based in Galesburg, Illinois, a nonprofit organization that collects and processes donations of new, top quality merchandise from American corporations, then redistributes those goods to qualified schools and nonprofits across the United States. Schools and nonprofit organizations pay a membership fee to participate in NAEIR. The merchandise must be used for the care of the ill, the needy, or minors and cannot be bartered, traded, or sold. The merchandise can be given directly to the qualifying individuals an organization serves or used in the administration of the organization. The materials are offered to NAEIR members through a variety of programs, such as the catalog program. NAEIR publishes five catalogs per year, filled with such items as office supplies, arts and crafts items, maintenance and janitorial supplies, clothing, and health and beauty items. Visitors to the site will find an online membership application and details on how the program works.

National Association of Child Advocates (DC) (http://www.childadvocacy.org)
The National Association of Child Advocates was created in 1984 in Washington, D.C., as a national network of child advocacy organizations. NACA operates under the principles that the United States has the resources to "lift all children out of poverty; end childhood hunger and homelessness; and ensure quality healthcare, early childhood and school programs for every child." Ongoing initiatives include child welfare, early care and education, and health and income supports. The group's Web site provides a primer on child advocacy, information on membership and benefits to related nonprofit organizations, a listing of current NACA members, and links and publications, including *Child Advocates Making a Difference* which can be downloaded online in PDF format.

NAFSA: Association of International Educators (DC) (http://www.nafsa.org)
NAFSA, a membership organization created in 1948, promotes the international exchange of students and scholars through training workshops and in-service training grants, grants for professionals to travel to NAFSA conferences, and a variety of overseas opportunities. The Education and Training area of the NAFSA Web site provides information on these programs. Visitors to the site can also find information on or about financial aid and re-entry job searching, funding programs for study abroad, and upcoming conferences and publications by NAFSA members.

National 4-H Council (MD) (http://www.fourhcouncil.edu)
Headquartered in Chevy Chase, Maryland, the National 4-H Council is an organization that promotes the 4-H "youth development movement to build a world in which youth and adults learn, grow, and work together as catalysts for positive change." The National 4-H Council maintains programs, grants, curriculums and publications, initiatives, and projects in a variety of areas, including workforce preparation; the environment; health, wellness, and safety; community development; and the Youth Changing Their Community program. Current youth grants are detailed on the site, along with instructions and applications that can be downloaded in PDF format. The Council's Web site provides extensive information about National 4-H programs, current events, a discussion board, membership opportunities, and the Council's annual report, which is also downloadable online.

National AIDS Fund (DC) (http://www.aidsfund.org)
The Washington, D.C.-based National AIDS Fund pools its efforts with local community partners to lead community-based prevention, care, and support programs for people with HIV/AIDS. It seeks to "[provide] financial support, technical assistance, and compassionate guidance to communities seeking to build programs and services that meet the needs of local people hardest hit by the epidemic." The Fund maintains various programs under six broad areas: community, workplace, nutrition, youth initiatives, women's initiatives, and prevention. Through these specific programs, which are detailed on the Fund's Web site, the National AIDS Fund strives to fill unmet needs, assist marginalized populations, and contribute to the national fight against HIV/AIDS. The Fund's Web site also contains workplace resources and newsletter archives that can be downloaded in PDF format.

The National Alliance for Research on Schizophrenia and Depression (NY) (http://www.mhsource.com/narsad/)

The National Alliance for Research on Schizophrenia and Depression (NARSAD), located in Great Neck, New York, was incorporated in 1986 through the combined efforts of several mental health organizations. Today NARSAD is the largest non-government, donor-supported organization that distributes funds for brain disorder research. Specifically, NARSAD's purpose is to raise and distribute funds for scientific research into the causes, cures, preventions, and treatments of severe mental illnesses, primarily schizophrenia and depression. NARSAD has three award programs: Young Investigator Award, Independent Investigator Award, and Distinguished Investigator Award. Descriptions, deadlines, and guidelines for each are available online. Face sheets, which must be included with each application, can be downloaded from the site in rich text format. The Foundation's Web site provides a great deal of information about the organization and its mission, including press releases, details about symposia and other events, and a detailed description of NARSAD's role. A list of staff contacts with e-mail addresses can also be found on the site.

National Ataxia Foundation, Inc. (MN) (http://www.ataxia.org/)

The Minneapolis, Minnesota-based National Ataxia Foundation (NAF) was established in 1957 by John W. Schut, a physician who dedicated his life to research into the cause and cure of the hereditary ataxias. NAF's mission is to support research into the causes and mechanisms of hereditary ataxia, improving diagnosis, and developing treatment models. There are more than 45 affiliated chapters and support groups throughout the United States and Canada. NAF also works to locate families affected by ataxia or at risk for ataxia in order to offer information and education, identify needs and services for purposes of referral, create and disseminate educational programs, and increase public awareness. Visitors to the site will find a listing of NAF chapters and support groups, a chatroom, an online information request form, related links, and a sampling of the Foundation's publication, *Generations.*

National Blood Foundation of the American Association of Blood Banks (MD) (http://www.aabb.org/About_the_AABB/Nbf/nbf2.htm)

The National Blood Foundation was established in 1983 as a program of the American Association of Blood Banks to fund "basic and applied scientific research, administrative/research projects, professional education, technical training, and public education in all aspects of blood banking, transfusion medicine, and tissue transplantation." NBF's 1999 Scientific Research Grant Program provides $30,000 grants for projects dealing with scientific, administrative, or educational aspects of blood banking and transfusion medicine. Application forms (in PDF format) can be downloaded from the NBF Web site or requested via phone or e-mail. In addition to information on the Research Grant program, visitors to the site will find a list of grant recipients, donor information, and board and staff listings.

The National Catholic Community Foundation (MD) (http://www.nccfcommunity.org/)

Created in May 1997, The National Catholic Community Foundation, based in Maryland, is a group of donor advised funds. The organization was established to "address the needs of persons and organizations who wish to engage in philanthropic activities which support the ministries of the Catholic Church, but do not have the ability to organize a traditional private foundation." Donations can be made specifically to Catholic organizations or to groups that support the Gospel in a larger way. The site includes a list of the individual funds, a list of grant recipients, a catalog of possible recipients for donors, and testimonials from donors and grant recipients. Visitors will also find a list of the board of trustees, information on how to establish a fund, and advice on all areas of giving. There is also a news and events section and a helpful set of FAQs.

National Center of Small Communities (DC) (http://www.natat.org/ncsc/Default.htm)

The National Center of Small Communities was formed in 1976 to serve the leaders of America's smaller communities. The NCSC's programs and services strive to support smaller communities by reorienting and expanding their economies and employment opportunities, developing skilled elected leadership, finding additional funding, complying with federal regulations, protecting rural and small-town character, and soliciting and receiving government and private grants. The Center also administers an American Hometown Leadership Award and works with the Environmental Protection Agency to protect small town water sources. The NCSC Web site includes links to its member town Web sites, updates on its National Conference, publications, and contact information.

National Children's Cancer Society (MO) (http://www.children-cancer.com)
The St. Louis-based National Children's Cancer Society was created in 1987 to help children suffering from cancer and their families with emotional and financial support. The Society's Web site offers information geared toward adults, as well as a special section for kids with cancer. Questions about financial support are addressed in the FAQ section of the Web site, and information for patient and family services, donations, volunteerism, special events, links, and contact information are also available online.

National Community Pharmacists Association (VA) (http://www.ncpanet.org)
Established in 1898 as the National Association of Retail Druggists, NCPA is located in Alexandria, Virginia. Elements of the membership organization's mission include "representing the professional and proprietary interests of independent retail pharmacists and vigorously promoting and defending those interests; restoring, maintaining, and promoting the health and well-being of the public we serve; and ensuring the ability of independent retail pharmacists to compete in a free and fair marketplace." The association offers a series of scholarships to its student members. The NCPA Foundation Presidential Scholarship applicants must be full-time pharmacology students with excellent academic and leadership qualities. The J.C. and Rheba Cobb Memorial Scholarship, which is awarded along with a trip to the annual awards dinner, is given to a student with community and government affairs experience and leadership and academic excellence. There is also an internship program offered. Information on all of these can be found in the Student Affairs section, along with the scholarship application, which can be downloaded in PDF format. The NCPA Foundation funds research grants for pharmacology school faculty each year. RFPs are distributed each year to all schools and colleges of pharmacology, but a list of past recipients can be found online. The extensive site includes information on the annual conference, association publications, current public policy issues, and upcoming meetings.

National Council of La Raza (DC) (http://www.nclr.org/)
Established in 1968 in Washington, D.C., the National Council of La Raza is committed to reducing poverty and discrimination and improving life opportunities for all Hispanic national groups in all regions of the United States. NCLR's mission is twofold: to provide assistance to support and strengthen Hispanic community-based organizations and to provide applied research, policy analysis, and advocacy with a Hispanic perspective. Additionally, the NCLR maintains public information sources, media activities, and special national and international projects. It also runs the NCLR Policy Analysis Center, considered the premiere Hispanic "think tank." Much of this information is available on the extensive NCLR Web site, a resource providing a listing of current Council-sponsored events, the Council's publications, news, recent studies, and an FAQ.

National Council for the Social Studies (DC) (http://www.ncss.org/awards/)
Founded in 1921, the National Council for the Social Studies supports social studies education—geography, economics, political science, sociology, psychology, anthropology, and law-related education—at all levels. NCSS awards excellence in teaching, curricula, research, writing, and service. Grantmaking programs include the Grant for the Enhancement of Geographic Literacy, the Fund for Advancement of Social Studies Grant, and the Christa McAuliffe Reach for the Stars Award. Application information is provided at NCSS's Web site for these programs and for the Council's service and writing awards. This site is also a social studies resource offering information on NCSS's activities, professional

development, publications, a discussion board, membership information and a Members Only area, curriculum standards, state and local councils, and teaching resources.

National Endowment for Democracy (DC) (http://www.ned.org)

Founded in 1983, the National Endowment for Democracy (NED) is a grantmaking organization created to strengthen democratic institutions around the world. Funded by an annual congressional appropriation, the Endowment's grants program assists organizations abroad working for democratic goals. The Endowment's programs encourage democratic political development primarily in three major functional areas: pluralism, democratic governance, and education, culture, and communications. The Endowment created the International Forum for Democratic Studies in 1994 to respond to the need for sustained and serious study of democracy's problems and prospects throughout the world. The International Forum consists of the Democracy Resource Center, whose mission is to collect, organize, and disseminate information and analysis produced by and about the organizations working to strengthen democracy around the world, a Research and Conferences Program, a small Visiting Fellows Program, and the Journal of Democracy. Visitors to the site will find application instructions, information on its various programs, a searchable databases of grants made by NED, an online publications catalog on democracy, a democracy experts database, news, an archive of electronic mailing lists, and contact information.

National Environmental Education and Training Foundation (DC) (http://www.neetf.org/)

Launched in Washington, D.C., the National Environmental Education and Training Center is committed to "helping America meet critical national challenges through environmental learning." In 1999 the Center awarded Challenge Grants in three areas: health and the environment, safe water, and environmental education excellence. These grants must be matched 2:1 by a third party within a year. Other areas of interest to the organization include: business and the environment and National Public Land Day. The Center has ongoing projects in all of these areas and sponsors conferences and training sessions with assorted partners to further address them. The Center also distributes the National Environmental Education Achievement Awards to organizations that "enhance environmental knowledge for day-to-day local and national decision-making." Visitors to the site will find downloadable (in PDF and Microsoft Word formats) application guidelines for the Challenge Grants, grant lists, lists of award recipients, and links to related resources.

National Film Preservation Foundation (CA) (http://www.filmpreservation.org)

The National Film Preservation Foundation was created by the Congressional National Film Preservation Act of 1996 to save America's film heritage. Based in San Francisco, the NFPF supports "preservation activities nationwide that ensure the physical survival of film and improve access to film for study, education and exhibition." The Foundation funds three types of grants for organizations or individuals involved in the process of restoring and disseminating early American film work: Access grants, for the purpose of sharing preserved films with the public; Laboratory grants, funding "in-kind" laboratory preservation work; and Partnership grants, for distributing preservation services. The NFPF also sponsors various yearly projects, including the Treasures of American Film Archives and Saving the Silents. This appealing Web site presents background material on the necessity and process of preserving films, as well as examples of projects the Foundation has funded in the past, such as the preservation of Groucho Marx's home movies. There are grant eligibility and application guidelines, a preservation assessment checklist, and more information on the board and film archive members across the United States.

National Fish and Wildlife Foundation (DC) (http://www.nfwf.org/)

The National Fish and Wildlife Foundation was established by an act of Congress in 1984 to help conserve and sustain natural resources in the United States, which it accomplishes through conservation education, natural resource management, habitat protection, ecosystem restoration, and public policy development. The Foundation makes "Challenge Grants" with federal funds matched by private dollars through five initiatives—Conservation Education, Fisheries Conservation and Management, Neotropical Migratory Bird

Conservation, Wetlands and Private Lands, and Wildlife and Habitat—and through special programs funded by corporate partners. The Foundation's Web site provides grant guidelines for its challenge grants; the Unified Request for Proposals describes its special programs and provides an application form in various word-processing formats. The site also provides news and donor information.

National Foundation for Advancement in the Arts (FL) (http://www.nfaa.org/)

The Miami-based National Foundation for Advancement in the Arts was founded in 1981 to identify emerging artists and assist them at critical junctures in their educational and professional development and to raise appreciation for and support of the arts in American society. The NFAA operates five programs in support of individual artists: the Arts Recognition and Talent Search, Presidential Scholars in the Arts, the Scholarship List Service, Career Development for NFAA Artists, and Career Advancement of Visual Artists. The NFAA Web site provides e-mail contacts for all five programs and online registration for two, news items of interest, and employment opportunities.

National Foundation for the Improvement of Education (DC) (http://www.nfie.org/)

The National Foundation for the Improvement of Education, created in 1969 by the National Education Association, provides grants and technical assistance to improve student learning in public schools. The NFIE's Leadership Grants underwrite professional development opportunities for teachers, education support personnel, and higher education faculty and staff to prepare them for collegial leadership. The Foundation's Web site provides guidelines for this grant program and an application form to print out and mail. Visitors to the site will also find detailed information on other NFIE initiatives, recent Leadership grantees, and a newsletter on a Microsoft partnership program called Road Ahead.

National Foundation for Infectious Diseases (MD) (http://www.nfid.org/)

The National Foundation for Infection Diseases supports research toward understanding the causes of infectious diseases, preventing and curing them, and supporting educational programs. In addition to its own research and education activities, the Foundation awards grants and fellowships for research and specialization in infectious diseases and the microbiological/immunological/epidemiological sciences. Detailed information about the Foundation's fellowship and grant programs can be found in the Fellowships area of its Web site. Visitors to the Web site will find various sources of information on infectious diseases (some areas are for members only), as well as publications, conferences and press conferences, and contact information.

National Foundation for Jewish Culture (NY) (http://www.Jewishculture.org)

Based in New York City, the National Foundation for Jewish Culture (NFJC) was founded in 1960 by the Council of Jewish Federations. The NFJC works with artists, scholars, cultural institutions, and community agencies to enrich local Jewish life, enhance educational opportunities, and foster a dynamic Jewish identity in a multicultural society. The NFJC also sponsors the annual Jewish Cultural Achievement Awards in Scholarship and publishes articles on trends in Jewish studies. Other grant programs are the Fund for Jewish Documentary Filmmaking, New Play Commissions in Jewish Theater, and Doctoral Dissertation Fellowships in Jewish Studies. Visitors to the site will find information on its various programs and contact information. Application forms are available to be printed online.

National Gallery of Art (DC) (http://www.nga.gov/resources/casva.htm)

The Center for Advanced Study in the Visual Arts is a research institute founded in 1979 as part of the National Gallery of Art. The Center fosters study of the production, use, and cultural meaning of art, artifacts, and architecture from prehistoric times to the present. The Center encourages study of the visual arts from a variety of approaches by historians, critics, and theorists of art as well as by scholars in related disciplines of the humanities and social sciences. The Center has several fellowship programs: Predoctoral Fellowship Program for Summer Travel Abroad for Historians of American Art, Paired Fellowship

Program in Conservation and Art History/Archaeology, Predoctoral Fellowship Program, Senior Fellowship Program, Frese Senior Fellowship Program, and the Starr Foundation Visiting Senior Research Fellowship Program for Scholars from East and South Asia. Interested applicants can obtain application instructions, information for the fellowship programs, and contact information on the site. Fellows have access to resources such as the collections of the National Gallery, its library and photographic archives, as well as the Library of Congress and other specialized research libraries and collections in Washington. Lectures, colloquia, and informal discussions complement the fellowship program. Other features of the site are online museum tours, information on current exhibits, programs, and events at the National Gallery of Art, and links to research resources.

National Gardening Association (VT) (http://www.garden.org)
The official Web site of the National Gardening Association, an organization established in 1972 in Burlington, Vermont, is home to a wealth of gardening advice for people of all ages. The Association's goals today focus "on children and the ways that gardening enhances education and helps build environmentally responsible adults." This is accomplished through a number of Web sites and media products geared toward children, such as Kidsgardening. The Association's Web site provides free services for gardeners, including regional garden reports, how-to instructions, online courses and discussion boards, among other community and gardening resources.

National Geographic Society Education Foundation (DC)
(http://www.nationalgeographic.com/foundation/)
The National Geographic Society Education Foundation currently awards more than three million dollars in grants annually to programs nationwide in support of its mission "to revitalize the teaching and learning of geography in the nation's K–12 classrooms." Ninety percent of the Foundation's grants budget is "earmarked for a state-based network of geographic alliances, grassroots organizations of classroom teachers and university geographers dedicated to improving geography education." In addition to funding the alliances, the Foundation awards grants to individual teachers who work with the alliances to implement innovative educational strategies relating to geography. The Foundation also funds an urban initiative program, which awards grants to address the special needs of urban schools, and offers discretionary grant endowments for geography education in Colorado, Mississippi, and Oklahoma. Visitors to the Foundation's Web site will find detailed descriptions of the Foundation's programs, application guidelines, a list of sample teacher grants, a downloadable teacher grant application form, and a contact list for each state alliance.

National Hemophilia Foundation (NY) (http://www.hemophilia.org/)
The National Hemophilia Foundation is dedicated to preventing, treating, and finding the cures of inherited bleeding disorders through education, advocacy, and research. The Foundation's Web site provides information on its Nursing Excellence and Judith Graham Pool Research fellowships in the Resources directory under Programs & Services. Contact information and a downloadable application form for the research fellowship are provided. The Foundation's Web site also provides information on bleeding disorders, events, publications, an online version of its annual report, a listing of board members, and related Web sites.

National Heritage Foundation (VA) (http://www.nhf.org/)
The Heritage Foundation of Falls Church, Virginia, helps people to establish their own foundations. Its "purpose is to undertake projects whose aim is to restore, maintain and extend our heritage of 'people making peoples' lives more meaningful.'" Donor/Applicants are provided with administrative, tax filing, and fundraising support. For established organizations seeking funding there is a list of foundation links and one of foundation profiles. The site does not include information on applying to member organizations for grants. The very extensive site includes applications for support from NHF, information on how the

fund can assist different types of organizations, information on legal issues, and opportunities for members to make requests for their foundation's giving.

National Hispanic Scholarship Fund, Inc (CA) (http://www.hsf.net/)

Established in 1975, the National Hispanic Scholarship Fund, located in California, helps pave the way for young Latinos to gain access to higher education. Since its inception it has "awarded more than 36,000 scholarships totaling nearly $38 million." The Web site covers all aspects of searching for scholarships and includes financial aid advice. Applicants can apply online for awards. In addition to the Scholarship portal, there is a portal for Cyber Campus. This site provides a complete career counseling section in both English and Spanish. A list of the board of directors and links to other resources for scholarships can be accessed.

National Italian American Foundation, Inc. (DC) (http://www.niaf.org/)

The goal of the National Italian American Foundation, established in 1975, is to serve as an advocate for the 15 million Italian Americans in the United States. Through scholarships and grants, the Foundation hopes to "preserve and protect Italian American heritage and culture." The Foundation maintains a long list of scholarships for high school seniors through graduate students, available on the Scholarships and Grants section of its Web site. Grants are available in five areas: research, literary, film, programs, and conferences and lecture series. In each area, the Foundation has specific program objectives, all of which somehow promote, help, or discuss Italian Americans. The Foundation's Web site lists these specific objectives along with past grant winners. The Foundation's site also provides instructions, online applications, and a keyword search for both scholarships and grants.

The National Latina/o Lesbian Gay Bisexual & Transgender Organization, Inc. (DC) (http://www.llego.org/)

The National Latina/o Lesbian Gay Bisexual & Transgender Organization, or LLEGÓ, was established in 1987 after the National March in Washington for Gay and Lesbian Rights. LLEGÓ seeks to "build and strengthen the national network of Latina/o Lesbian, Gay, Bisexual and Transgender (LGBT) community-based organizations and to build their capacity to serve their local constituency." The Organization and its Web site is a clearinghouse for information and services for Latino/a men and women, with listings of publications, conferences, and organizations geared toward specific population groups, such as Latino men, young Latinos, and Latinos living with HIV/AIDS. The site is in English and Spanish and contains numerous resources for varied population groups within the gay, bisexual, and transgender Latino community.

National Medical Fellowships, Inc. (NY) (http://www.nmf-online.org)

Established in 1946, National Medical Fellowships is committed to "improving the health of underserved communities by increasing the representation of minority physicians, educators, researchers, and policymakers in the United States" through the special training of minority medical students and education on the health needs of underserved populations. NMF is based in New York City, with regional offices in San Francisco and Washington, D.C., and offers need-based scholarships, fellowships, grants, and prizes to students. The NMF Web site provides a fact sheet on the program's funding opportunities, as well as instructions and applications for need-based scholarships, all of which can be downloaded in PDF format.

National Music Foundation, Inc. (MA) (http://www.nmc.org/)

The National Music Foundation is dedicated to American music and the people who bring it to us. Its mission is to educate the public about American music in order to preserve our nation's musical heritage and to provide for the retirement of professionals from the fields of music and recording, with provision made for those who cannot afford to retire on their own. Its mission will be fulfilled through building the National Music Center. The Center occupies a sixty-three acre campus in Lenox, Massachusetts, and will have educational facilities that will include an interactive museum, performance centers, a library and archive, a radio broadcast facility, and a recording studio. The Center will include a residence where professionals from music, radio, and recording can retire among their peers and provide a core faculty for the Center's educational and mentor programs. Workshops and classes in all forms, styles, and genres of American music will be presented. Through scholarships, grants, and mentor programs the Center will encourage students to pursue studies of American music at all educational levels. In addition to the Center, the Foundation also maintains the American Music Education Initiative, which is a program designed to identify, recognize, and support the creative educational endeavors of teachers who are using American Music with their students. Awards are made to teachers to be used for teaching resources and materials. The site contains award guidelines and printable application forms. Visitors to the site will also find a newsletter, links to sites featuring American music genres and music resources, a schedule of concerts and festivals, and contact information.

National Park Foundation (DC) (http://www.nationalparks.org/)
The National Park Foundation was established in 1967 to help conserve, preserve, and enhance U.S. National Parks and to support education and outreach programs. The Foundation's Competitive Grants program funds conservation, preservation, and education efforts; funds are distributed to parks as seed money or challenge grants. Grant guidelines are provided in the NPF Programs directory of the Foundation's Web site, along with sample grants and a contact for requesting more information. This area of the site also details the Foundation's research, education, and other special initiatives.

National Press Foundation, Inc. (DC) (http://www.natpress.org/)
The National Press Foundation of Washington, D.C., was established by journalists and communicators in 1975. The purpose of the organization is to "offer issue-oriented professional development programs and awards for journalists" without prejudice or bias. In order to encourage excellence, the Foundation annually distributes a set of very prestigious awards for American journalism. Traditional awards, which are presented at an annual fundraising dinner, include the Sol Taishoff Award for Excellence in Broadcasting, the Distinguished Contributions to Journalism Award, the George Beveridge Editor of the Year Award, the Kifford K. and James T. Berryman Cartoonist of the Year Award, and the Everett McKinley Dirksen Awards for Congressional Reporting. The Foundation is now accepting submissions for the Thomas L. Stokes Award for writing on energy. The Foundation also offers competitive fellowships for working journalists to attend seminars run by both the Foundation and by other groups. The site includes application guidelines for the scholarships and instructions for submitting entries for any open awards. There is a list of the board and one of the NPF staff. There is also information on the current and past award recipients and an archive of winning political cartoons.

National Repertory Theatre Foundation (CA) (http://www.nrtf.org)
The National Repertory Theatre Foundation (NRTF) was founded by Michael Dewell and Frances Ann Dougherty in 1961. NRTF is a theatre development agency based in Los Angeles that encourages new talent, creates new programs, and sponsors new organizations vital to the growth of American theatre. NRTF sponsors the Classical Theatre Lab, an innovative group of 70 professional actors dedicated to the exploration, preservation, and celebration of the classics. The Foundation also sponsors the Educational Community Outreach Theatre (ECOT), which brings youth to the theatre through their study of source material in schools, and the National Play Award (NPA), which grants a $5,000 cash prize for an unproduced, unpublished full–length play. Consult the Web site to learn more about the NRTF, for NPA guidelines, and contact information.

National Restaurant Association Educational Foundation (IL) (http://www.edfound.org)
The National Restaurant Association Educational Foundation was formed in 1987 through a merger between the National Restaurant Association's educational department and the National Institute for the Foodservice Industry (NIFI). The NRA Education Foundation works to provide training and enrichment for individuals in the restaurant and hospitality

industries. The Foundation runs various programs, seminars, and research projects, which are detailed on its Web site. Additionally, the Foundation provides four types of scholarships for students of the restaurant and hospitality profession: Undergraduate Merit for high school seniors, Undergraduate Merit for college students, Graduate Degree Scholar, and Teacher Work/Study grants. There are instructions and contact information for applying to each of these scholarships on the Web site, along with resources on careers and training in the field.

National Society of Accountants Scholarship Foundation (VA) (http://www.nsacct.org/)
The NSA Scholarship Foundation, created in 1969 to ensure the future of the accounting profession, awards annual scholarships to second-, third-, and fourth-year college accounting students. The scholarship program is outlined at NSA's Web site, along with application instructions.

National Society of Professional Engineers (VA) (http://www.nspe.org)
Founded in 1934, the National Society of Professional Engineers "promotes the ethical and competent practice of engineering, advocates licensure, and enhances the image and well-being of its members." This mission is accomplished through a variety of programs, conferences, awards, and educational services. In 1960, the Society established the NSPE Education Foundation, which currently grants scholarships to high school, college, and graduate student engineers. The Society's Web site includes online applications for these scholarships. Additionally, the site provides a listing of firms, news and information related to engineering, links, and membership information.

National Tourism Foundation (KY) (http://www.ntfonline.org)
The Lexington, Kentucky-based National Tourism Foundation's mission is "to benefit society through the support of education and research contributing to the values of travel and tourism, including personal enrichment, community development, heritage and natural preservation, and cultural understanding." To this end, the Foundation maintains services in the areas of education and research, including scholarships, internships, conferences, and development programs. The Foundation funds a wide variety of scholarship programs, including general and state-specific educational funding. Application requirements and guidelines for each scholarship are provided online, as is information on visiting scholars, internships, research opportunities, and upcoming conferences, among other tourism-related resources.

National Trust for Historic Preservation (DC) (http://www.nthp.org/)
The National Trust for Historic Preservation, founded in 1949, provides leadership, education, and advocacy to save diverse historic places and revitalize communities. The Trust gives several awards recognizing excellence in preservation and restoration. The Awards page of the Trust's Web site provides a brief description and contact telephone number for each award. Visitors to the site will find a wealth of information on historic preservation, news, membership and donor information, and online publications.

National Urban League, Inc. (NY) (http://www.nul.org)
The National Urban League was founded in New York City in 1910; its mission is "to enable African Americans to secure economic self-reliance, parity, power and civil rights." These goals are obtained through a variety of programs, such as Bridge the Digital Divide and the Black Executive Exchange Program; services; community mobilization; advocacy; and research. The National Urban League's Web site features employment resources, current publications and speeches, a listing of Urban League Affiliates, more details on the League's programs and special events, and an Audio/Visual archive.

National Wildlife Federation (VA) (http://www.nwf.org)
Headquartered in Reston, Virginia, the National Wildlife Federation's mission is "to educate, inspire and assist individuals and organizations of diverse cultures to conserve wildlife and other natural resources and to protect the Earth's environment in order to achieve a

peaceful, equitable and sustainable future." The Federation was founded in 1936 as a network of grassroots environmental organizations and today combines action and education to further its mission. NWF operates a number of regional offices, carries environmental concerns to governmental institutions, and creates science-based educational materials for a greater appreciation of nature. The Federation's Web site provides nomination packets for the National Conservation Achievement Award and lists previous winners of the award. The site also features job opportunities, information on conferences, the NWF's annual report, and a page where visitors can take action on specific environmental issues, among other resources.

The NATSO Foundation (VA) (http://www.natsofoundation.org)

The NATSO Foundation was established in 1990 in Alexandria, Virginia, as "the research, education and public outreach affiliate of America's travel plaza and truckstop industry." The Foundation provides services and support in three areas: research, to benefit the travel plaza and truckstop industry and secure its future; education, to provide opportunities to industry employees; and public outreach, through programs that benefit the general public and enhance the industry. Research programs include the University Research Grant, for up to $10,000; the NATSO Foundation Library; and the Call for Papers to be submitted to the Journal of Transportation Research. Education encompasses the Bill Moon Scholarship Program and the Distance Learning program. The Foundation sponsors such public outreach projects as the Drive to Save Lives and the NATSO Foundation Disaster Relief Program. The NATSO Foundation Web site lists research grant areas of interest, guidelines, and an application that can be downloaded. Also included on the site are lists of current funders, information on NATSO leadership, news and publications, links, and contact information.

Nebraska Humanities Council (NE) (http://lincolnne.com/nonprofit/nhc)

Founded in 1972, the Nebraska Humanities Council "works with numerous groups throughout the state to create high-quality programs that add to the understanding and appreciation of Nebraska and the world, and that foster a better understanding of the humanities." The Council gives out a variety of different types of grants, all of which are described on the site. Grant applications may be downloaded in PDF format directly from the site.

Nellie Mae Foundation (MA) (http://www.nelliemae.com/nmf/)

The Nellie Mae Foundation of Braintree, Massachusetts, was launched in 1998 to "promote accessibility, quality and effectiveness of education from preschool through postsecondary levels, for all ages, especially for underserved populations." The Foundation will support educational institutions, foundations, government programs, and other community organizations as long as their programs or services promote education. Higher education for disadvantaged populations continues to be a priority. Technical assistance is an important part of the Foundation's giving program. Funding is limited to New England states. The site offers funding guidelines, which can be downloaded in PDF format, and links to press releases concerning major grants. The Foundation also funds and conducts major policy analyses and research on educational delivery and access. This aspect of the Foundation is not limited to New England.

Nevada Humanities Committee (NV) (http://www.unr.edu/nhc/index.html)

The Nevada Humanities Committee was established in 1971. Based in Reno, Nevada, the Committee exists to "enrich the lives of all Nevadans through the humanities. The humanities brings people together so that they may learn from each other, and explore and celebrate the cultures of our state and our world." The grants program is designed to provide financial support to organizations for exemplary public humanities programs. The Web site provides information about the scope of projects the Committee funds; the grant proposal guidelines, downloadable in PDF format; deadlines; and staff contact information. The site also contains a grant application cover sheet that can be printed online, to be completed and submitted with all grant applications.

New England Forestry Foundation (MA) (http://www.neforestry.org/)

Created in 1944, the New England Forestry Foundation is located in Groton, Massachu-setts. The organization "encourages and demonstrates responsible management of working forests for the benefit of land owners and the public." The Foundation works to conserve New England's privately owned forests through permanent protection through ownership, educating people about forest stewardship and land planning, managing Foundation land as models, supporting regional policy that encourages private ownership, and conserving a working landscape to best benefit New England. The Current Projects section lists and describes a number of existing programs. The site also includes a clothing and publications marketplace and a membership/donations section, which has an electronic application form.

New England Foundation for the Arts (MA) (http://www.nefa.org/)

One of six regional arts organizations in the continental United States, the New England Foundation for the Arts links the public and private sectors in a regional partnership to sup-port the arts in Connecticut, Maine, Massachusetts, New Hampshire, Rhode Island, and Vermont. Organized on a "community foundation" model, the Foundation has three pro-gram areas: the Culture in Community Fund, to strengthen the role the arts play in commu-nity development; the Connections Fund, to expand knowledge concerning the roles, prac-tices, and social impact of the arts; and the Creation and Presentation Fund, to enable the development and presentation of high–quality, artistic work. Most grants are made through the Creation and Presentation Fund's New England Arts Access programs, which provide support to artists for art-making and to arts organizations for presenting activities in the New England area. NEFA's Web site provides descriptions of the Foundations programs; grant program descriptions, guidelines, and deadlines; a calendar of events; newsletter; links to other Web sites related to the arts; and a staff list with e-mail addresses.

The New Israel Fund (DC) (http://www.nif.org/)

The New Israel Fund was founded in 1979 to strengthen Israeli democracy and promote social justice. This is achieved through grants and technical assistance to Israeli public interest groups and public education programs in North America, Israel, and Great Britian about the challenges of democracy in the Israeli state. Through its offices worldwide, the NIF focuses its efforts on a "network of non-government organizations in Israel that safe-guard civil and human rights, promote Jewish-Arab equality and coexistence, advance the status of women, foster tolerance and pluralism, bridge social and economic gaps, pursue environmental justice, and encourage government accountability." The Fund's Web site includes information on the programs and services it supports, including study tours, events, and SHATIL—technical assistance to social change organizations in Isreal—among others. Criteria for new grants and a list of grantees can be found in the More About NIF section.

New Jersey Council for the Humanities (NJ) (http://www.njch.org/)

The New Jersey Council for the Humanities of Trenton, New Jersey, was created in 1973 as a state council of the National Endowment for the Humanities. The organization "supports the public's use of the humanities to enrich personal and community life in New Jersey" by "developing, supporting, and promoting projects that explore and interpret the human experience, foster cross-cultural understanding and engage people in dialogue about mat-ters of individual choice and public responsibility." The Council's grant program supports humanities programs involving interpretive and critical thinking, collaboration between organizers or scholars and audiences, and/or the public distribution of materials that serve an adult or intergenerational audience primarily in New Jersey. The Council distributes awards for excellence to teachers, schools, companies, authors, and individuals. It also runs the New Jersey Teacher Institute Seminars for the development of K–12 teachers each sum-mer. Available on the site are downloadable copies of the grants program application and budget form and extensive support for the applicant. There are also nomination/application instructions for the annual awards and a number to call to receive an application for the summer seminars. The site also includes a newsletter, features on current programs, information on volunteering, and links to related sites.

New Jersey Historic Trust (NJ) (http://www.njht.org/)

Founded in 1967 in Trenton, the New Jersey Historic Trust was created by state law "to advance the preservation of the state's historic properties through financial, educational, and stewardship programs." The Trust supports numerous programs and initiatives; its main grantmaking programs are The Garden State Historic Preservation Trust Fund, the Historic Preservation Bond Program, the Emergency Grant and Load Fund, the Revolving Loan Fund, the Preservation Easement Program, and New Jersey Legacies. The Trust's expansive Web site provides detailed descriptions of each program, with links to other resources and related topics. Applications can be downloaded in PDF format. Guidelines, a listing of funded projects, and a featured project are also provided. Additionally, the Trust's Web site features news, links to other history-focused sites, and online publications in PDF format. Contact information is presented on the home page.

New Mexico Endowment for the Humanities (NM) (http://www.nmeh.org)

The New Mexico Endowment for the Humanities was established in 1972 in partnership with the National Endowment for the Humanities. The organization "encourages and supports the humanities in New Mexico [by] seeking out and funding quality humanities programs for presentation to public audiences throughout the state." The Endowment achieves its goal through the distribution of grants and through its Humanities Resource Center and Speakers Bureau. There is an online application for groups desiring a visit from one of the humanities experts to speak or perform as a historical person. There are grant guidelines and deadlines in the funding section and a list of currently funded programs in the project area. The site includes a list of the board of directors, information on available materials and resources, and opportunities to donate to the endowment.

New Orleans Jazz & Heritage Foundation, Inc. (LA) (http://www.nojhf.org)

The New Orleans Jazz & Heritage Foundation, Inc. is a Louisiana nonprofit corporation organized "to promote, preserve, perpetuate and encourage the music, arts, culture, and heritage indigenous to the New Orleans area." To accomplish its goals, the New Orleans Jazz & Heritage Foundation presents the New Orleans Jazz & Heritage Festival. All profits go to support the Foundations' programs, including grantmaking. The Web site gives a list of previous grants awarded and information and archives of music and cultural resources in the New Orleans area. The Foundation also runs music classes and clinics and provides seed money to economically disadvantaged Louisiana businesses. To find out about how to apply for grants, the site provides contact information.

New Schools Venture Fund (CA) (http://www.newschools.org)

Based in Redwood City, California, the New Schools Venture Fund pools the resources of New Economy pioneers to improve "public K–12 education by supporting a growing community of education entrepreneurs." The New Schools network of supporters includes education entrepreneurs and organizations in which the fund has invested. The Fund's Web site includes requirements for educational entrepreneurial teams in which the Fund will invest, links to recommended reading and related educational resources, news and events (including New Schools conferences), and contact information.

New Visions for Public Schools (NY) (http://www.newvisions.org/)

New Visions for Public Schools works with the New York City school system, the private sector, and the New York community to improve the educational achievements of children. New Visions' programs include creating new schools, renovating school libraries, bringing technology to classrooms, and training teachers in innovative instruction. Visitors to the New Visions Web site will find descriptions of the organization's programs, some of which award grants; an online version of its most recent annual report; a public bulletin board; a statistical snapshot of the New York City school system; and an excellent set of links to education-related (local and national) resources.

New World Foundation (NY) (http://www.newwf.org)

The New World Foundation has been supporting "organizations working to strengthen and expand civil rights and the active participation of citizens in American democracy" since 1954. Based in New York City, the Foundation maintains four main areas of grantmaking: Political Participation (including the California Initiative and Southern Organizing programs), Environmental Justice, Economic Justice (comprised of the Phoenix Fund), and Media and Democracy. The Foundation's Web site includes more detailed descriptions of its programs, as well as information for donors and potential grantees, financial information about the Foundation, and an e-mail contact address. The New World Foundation does not accept unsolicited proposals.

New York Foundation for the Arts (NY) (http://www.nyfa.org)

The New York Foundation for the Arts serves individual artists, promotes their freedom to develop and create, and provides the broader public with opportunities to experience and understand their work. NYFA accomplishes this by offering financial and informational assistance to artists and arts organizations, by supporting arts programming in the schools and local communities, and by building collaborative relationships with others who advocate for the arts in New York State and throughout the country. NYFA's programs include Artists' Fellowships in 16 disciplines: fiscal sponsorship of artists' projects and emerging organizations; grant initiatives that support career advancement, organizational development, technology planning, and arts-in-education projects; informational services including the Visual Artists Information Hotline and *FYI*, a quarterly news journal; and technical assistance workshops. NYFA's Web site offers detailed program information, contact information, downloadable application forms, and a number of links to other grantmakers in the arts.

The New York Women's Foundation (NY) (http://www.nywf.org)

The New York Women's Foundation is located in New York City. It is a "cross-cultural alliance of women helping low-income girls and women in our city to achieve sustained economic self-sufficiency and self-reliance." The Foundation funds programs within the five boroughs of New York City in five areas: sustainable economic self-sufficiency and self-reliance for low-income women, community organizing and advocacy, multi-year capacity building, collaborative activity, and positive development programming for girls. The Foundation has an annual grantmaking cycle; deadlines and other dates are posted on the site and the application can be downloaded in Microsoft Word format.

Newspaper Association of America Foundation (VA) (http://www.naa.org/foundation/index.html)

Located in Vienna, Virginia, the Newspaper Association of America Foundation helps to "develop tomorrow's readers by encouraging students to acquire and value information from newspapers and new media." The NAA Foundation accomplishes these goals through three main programs—Newspaper in Education, youth content, and student newspapers. The Foundation also sponsors a number of conferences and publications, many of which are available at its Web site, and administers the McCormick Fellowship Program to "provide the media with a diverse braintrust of executives to lead the way in a changing future." For more information about specific grants and how to apply, contact information is provided on the Web site.

1939 Club (http://www.1939club.com)

Taking its name from the year in which Hitler invaded Poland, the Los Angeles-based 1939 Club is an organization of Holocaust survivors promoting Holocaust education, documentation, and justice. The Club maintains strong ties to UCLA, where it sponsors lecture series through the Holocaust Studies Program, and to Chapman University in Orange County, California. The Club's Web site lists previously honored survivors, along with a wealth of resources on Holocaust survivors and related materials, including links to articles, recommended reading, other Holocaust-related nonprofit organizations and activities, and membership and contact information.

Nonprofit Facilities Fund (NY) (http://www.nffusa.org)
Established in 1980 to help New York City nonprofits with energy conservation, the Nonprofit Facilities Fund is now a nationwide community development financial institution. The Fund provides financial and advisory services to nonprofits across the country. The Fund's Web site lists organizations the Fund supports, as well as partners in funding. There is contact information for the Fund's national offices in New York and regional offices in Chicago, Boston, Philadelphia, and San Francisco.

The Nonprofit Sector Research Fund of the Aspen Institute (DC)
(http://www.nonprofitresearch.org/)
Established by the internationally respected Aspen Institute in 1991, the Nonprofit Sector Research Fund is based in Washington, D.C. The Fund's purpose is to "enhance both the quantity and quality of nonprofit research by increasing the legitimacy and visibility of nonprofit scholarship; encouraging new investments in sector research; supporting the exploration of tough, neglected questions and enlarging the number of creative scholars and practitioners interested in pursuing nonprofit studies." General topics of interest to the Fund include cross-sector comparisons, market-oriented activity of nonprofits, the impact of welfare reform changes, nonprofit advocacy and civic participation, and the performance and accountability. The various grant programs, which include a national program, programs in California and Michigan, and a scholarship for minority students, all have specific interests within those general topics. The site offers proposal guidelines and applications that can be printed for all active programs. The site also includes reports on funded research studies, a publication list, contact information, and lists of the staff and the board.

North Capitol Neighborhood Development, Inc. (DC) (http://www.ncnd.org)
Since 1984, North Capitol Neighborhood Development (NCND), a nonprofit community development corporation, has been developing affordable housing, promoting small business, and empowering the community to improve neighborhoods in Washington, D.C. NCND takes a comprehensive approach to neighborhood revitalization by forecasting, planning, influencing, and executing programs that stimulate housing and economic development in our service areas. Visit the NCND's Web site to find out more about its residential, community, and business development programs and to find contact information.

North Star Fund (NY) (http://www.northstarfund.org/)
The North Star Fund works for progressive social change in New York City. Goals that fall within their mission include "an equitable distribution of wealth and resources; the realization of democratic process through the exercise of political power by historically disempowered peoples and communities; the well-being of people and the environment above profit; peaceful and just settlements of conflict; and freedom from institutional, cultural, and economic discrimination based on class, race." Grants are given to New York City organizations that organize low-income or working people to make a lasting change, are structured democratically and held accountable by their communities, and correct different forms of oppression. Regular, interim, and emergency grants are distributed, in addition to a $5,000 revolving loan. The site includes grant guidelines, a list of staff, and information on contributing to the fund.

Northern California Community Loan Fund (CA) (http://www.ncclf.org)
The Northern California Community Loan Fund, which was established in 1987 and is located in San Francisco, is a nonprofit lender "dedicated to strengthening the economic base of low income and minority communities." The Fund lends to nonprofit organizations that serve communities with limited access to financing from traditional lenders. The Fund supports projects throughout northern California and gives out two types of loans: term and bridge financing for project development and lines of credit for operating cash flow needs. In order to begin the application process, an organization must call or e-mail the Fund. All of the contact information is available on this site, along with information about the types of programs and organizations to which the Fund has previously made loans.

Northland Foundation (MN) (http://www.northlandfdn.org/)

The Northland Foundation, located in Duluth, Minnesota, seeks to address economic, social, and human needs in a rural seven-county area of northeastern Minnesota to accomplish greater self-sufficiency for communities, organizations, families, and individuals. The Foundation achieves these goals through grants and business loan programs. Grants are awarded in four areas: Connecting Kids and Community, Aging With Independence, Economic Diversification, and Opportunities for Self-Reliance. The Foundation's Web site provides this information and e-mail contacts for interested grantseekers, information on its other activities, and a staff listing with e-mail links.

Northwest AIDS Foundation (WA) (http://www.nwaids.org/)

The Northwest AIDS Foundation, founded in 1983 and located in Seattle, Washington, provides case management, housing assistance, emergency grants to people with AIDS, wellness information, prevention education, public policy advocacy, and grants to associate agencies and to other AIDS service organizations throughout Washington State. The Foundation's Web site provides information on financial advocacy and assistance for people with AIDS. Also at the site: AIDS legislation and education, volunteer and donor information, links to related Web sites, and contact information.

Northwest Danish Foundation (WA) (http://www.nwdf.org)

The Northwest Danish Foundation has two branches: one in Portland, Oregon, and one in Seattle, Washington. The Foundation is a human service organization "whose goal is to promote and preserve Danish heritage and social interaction in the Danish communities of Oregon and Washington through a variety of intergenerational cultural, educational, social and support programs." The Foundation awards scholarships each year to persons of Danish descent who participate in the Danish community or demonstrate interest in preserving the Danish heritage. Applications may be downloaded in Microsoft Word format or requested by e-mail, phone, or mail. All contact information is available on the Web site.

Northwest Osteopathic Medical Foundation (OR) (http://www.nwosteo.org/)

The Northwest Osteopathic Medical Foundation serves people of the northwest United States (Alaska, Idaho, Montana, Oregon, and Washington) by providing resources for osteopathic education. Currently, the Portland, Oregon-based Foundation has four grant programs: professional grants, funding osteopathic professional enhancement; community IMPACT grants, supporting the health and safety of families; osteopathic education, a student scholarship program; and the rural rotation program, which makes $500 grants to assist osteopathic medical students who seek an experience in rural medicine in the Pacific Northwest in elective rotations. Osteopathic medical students from all states are eligible to apply. The site contains descriptions of each of its programs and includes online applications, guidelines, and information request forms for its rural rotation and osteopathic education programs. Visitors to the site will also find osteopathic links, an events page, and an online contact form.

The NRA Foundation, Inc. (VA) (http://www.nrafoundation.org/)

Since 1990, the NRA Foundation, Inc. of Fairfax, Virginia, has "supported a wide range of firearm-related public interest activities of the National Rifle Association of America and other organizations that defend and foster the Second Amendment rights of all law-abiding Americans." Funding goes toward promoting firearm and hunting safety, supporting marksmanship for shooting sport participants, and educating the public on firearms. Grants are distributed in the following categories: Youth Programs, Range Improvement and Development, Public Safety, Education and Training, Wildlife and Natural Resource Conservation, and Constitutional Research and Education. The grants are given on the recommendation of the 49 State Fund Committees. Potential applicants can contact their local committee through the national Web site. The site also includes a list of the board of trustees, descriptions of selected programs in each grant area, and opportunities to make donations.

Oklahoma State Medical Association-Education and Research Foundation (OK) (http://www.osmaonline.org/)

Created in 1906, the Oklahoma State Medical Association is committed to the advancement of "science and the art of medicine for the betterment of Oklahoma physicians and the public they serve." The Association's Web site provides current health news, access to the *OSMA Journal* and other publications, and information for patients and potential members. Contact information is available online.

100 Black Men of Greater Charlotte, Inc. (NC) (http://www.100blackmenofcharlotte.org)

The idea of 100 Black Men was born in New York City in 1963, when a body of successful men from the fields of business, industry, public affairs, government, and the professions decided to pool their skills, experiences, and resources to improve the quality of life for Blacks and other minorities. In the 1970's, individual chapters in cities were established. The primary focus of the 100 Black Men of Greater Charlotte, Inc., based in Charlotte, North Carolina, is "The Movement of Youth," a structured one-on-one and group mentoring program for at-risk middle school students. The organization seeks to assist African American male students in developing high self-esteem and an appreciation for the value of a good education by providing citizenship, leadership development, motivational workshops, cultural enrichment, and community activities. In addition, the organization also has a job shadowing program, a scholarship program, and a service-learning program.

Optical Society of America (DC) (http://www.osa.org)

The Washington, D.C.-based Optical Society of American serves as a resource for an association of optical scientists, engineers, and technicians worldwide. The Society's Web site hosts a wealth of resources for those in the field, including optics in the news, an industry calendar and the *Optics & Photonics News* publication. Additionally, the Society offers a wide variety of funding for students, researchers, and technicians in the optical sciences. Funding takes the form of specifically named awards, grants, fellowships, and scholarships and travel grants for students, all of which are explained in greater detail online. Nomination forms for awards and fellowships, grant applications, and contact e-mail addresses for more information, are all available online.

Order of the Alhambra Charity Fund, Inc. (MD) (http://www.OrderAlhambra.org)

The Order of the Alhambra Charity Fund "provides assistance, education and residences for persons developmentally disabled by mental retardation; identifies, marks, preserves, and commemorates Catholic historical places, events and persons of international or regional importance; and promotes fraternalism and sociability among its members and their families." While the Charity Fund is located in Baltimore, Maryland, William Harper Bennett founded the original Order of the Alhambra in Brooklyn, New York, in 1904 as a fraternal and social organization. The Fund awards scholarships to undergraduate students who apply and are approved by a scholarship committee. In addition, the Fund has a project entitled the Alhambra House Project and finances a medical research program dedicated to finding the causes of mental retardation. To find out more about the organization and its programs, contact information is available on the Web site.

Oregon Law Foundation (DC) (http://www.osbar.org/Governance/OregonLawFoundation/OLF.html)

The Oregon Law Foundation is the charitable arm of the Oregon State Bar. The Foundation makes grants to provide legal aid to low income Oregonians, to law school scholarships, and other law–related charitable programs. Visit the Foundation's site for further information.

Oregon Lions Sight and Hearing Foundation, Inc.(OR) (http://www.orlions.org)

The Oregon Lions Sight and Hearing Foundation was founded by the Lion Clubs of Oregon in 1959 with the mission "to improve the quality of life in the areas of sight, hearing, diabetes and positive youth development." The Foundation is based in Portland, Oregon, and supports research to find the causes and cures of blindness and deafness. The

Foundation runs various programs, including the Lions Eye Bank and The Vision Research Laboratory, in addition to making grants for sight, hearing, and diabetes research and related projects. The Foundation's Web site provides details of projects and events, some information on past grant recipients, and contact information for more details about funding.

Orthopaedic Research and Education Foundation (IL) (http://www.oref.org/)

The Orthopaedic Research and Education Foundation of Rosemont, Illinois, was established in 1955 to build a base of research and clinical practices for the orthopaedic community. The mission of the organization is to advance "knowledge concerning the prevention and treatment of conditions affecting the musculoskeletal and related systems and the maintenance of the general physical well being of the individual." Individuals at American institutions are eligible for grants and awards for research, career development (for those who have finished orthopaedic residencies), clinical and resident research, and a fellowship in health services research. There are also awards recognizing individuals who have conducted "outstanding clinical research related to musculoskeletal disease or injury" and for excellence in bone allograft research. Institutional grants include research in orthopaedic treatment, educational awards, and lectureships and honorariums for speeches. The site includes deadlines and downloadable applications for all of the above and lists of past winners. There are also lists of the boards and the staff, information on member organizations, and opportunities to donate to the foundation.

Osteogenesis Imperfecta Foundation, Inc. (MD) (http://www.oif.org)

The Osteogenesis Imperfecta Foundation, located in Gaithersburg, Maryland, began in 1970 when a small group of parents from around the nation met in Chicago to discuss OI (osteogenesis imperfecta) and its problems. The Foundation's mission is to "improve the quality of life for individuals affected by OI through research to find a cure, education, awareness, and mutual support." The Foundation provides funding for postdoctoral fellowships to encourage new investigators to begin a career in OI research and for seed grants for preliminary research. The Foundation also puts on a biennial conference, provides information and research to the public, and hosts support groups. For information on funding, a contact address is available on the Web site.

Overture to the Cultural Season (LA) (http://www.overtureneworleans.org)

Formed in 1968, Overture to the Cultural Season is a nonprofit organization dedicated to supporting "the vitality of the arts in the New Orleans area by generating public awareness and involvement in the activities and performances of cultural organizations." Overture is a volunteer organization that maintains community programs, special events, and scholarship and award opportunities to primary, secondary, and college students in the arts. Overture's Web site provides descriptions of the organization's arts programs and events, along with information on membership, member activities, and an e-mail address for further details.

Oxfam America (MA) (http://www.oxfamamerica.org)

Initiated in 1970 in Boston, Oxfam America is dedicated to social and economic justice in communities worldwide. The organization's mission is to create "lasting solutions to hunger, poverty, and social injustice through long-term partnerships with poor communities around the world." To this end, Oxfam America operates emergency relief programs and humanitarian aid projects and advocates for policy change. Specific programs include the Fast for a World Harvest and Fair Trade Coffee campaigns. The Oxfam America Web site provides descriptions of particular programs and campaigns, current news and humanitarian emergencies, a youth action page, details on global programs, opportunities for individuals to get involved, and contact information.

Packaging Machinery Manufacturers Institute Education and Training Foundation (VA) (http://www.packexpo.com/AboutPMMI/about_pmmi.cfm)

Located in Arlington, Virginia, the Packaging Machinery Manufacturers Institute Education and Training Foundation is the philanthropic arm of the PMMI. The Foundation strives to "provide support for technical and educational programs and advances in packaging machinery through grants and scholarships," as well as increase student awareness of opportunities in the packaging machinery profession, conduct relevant research, and enhance the knowledge and capabilities of the industry. The Foundation funds four programs: Scholarships/Grants through the Claude S. Breeden Fund, PMMI Member Employee Scholarships, Industry Workforce and Training Research, and Partners in Education Program. Contact information for the PMMI Education and Training Foundation can be found on the About Us section of the PMMI Web site.

Pact, Inc. (DC) (http://www.pactworld.org)

Pact began in 1971 as a membership organization for private and voluntary organizations and nongovernmental organizations. In 1992 Pact revised its bylaws, dissolved its membership, and established itself as an independent international nonprofit corporation. While its headquarters are located in Washington, D.C., Pact runs development programs and has field offices in countries around the world. Pact's mission is to "contribute to the growth of civil societies—where citizens acting together can express their interests, exchange information, strive for mutual goals and influence government." Pact offers NGOs and nonprofits a number of services, including low employee insurance rates, subgrants management, strategic communications, and publication production and distribution. The Web site contains detailed descriptions of such services and information about Pact projects throughout the world.

Page Education Foundation (MN) (http://www.page-ed.org)

In 1988, Alan Page, NFL Hall of Fame pro football player, established the Page Education Foundation to encourage Minnesota youth of color to continue their education beyond high school. The Foundation grants scholarships to high school students of color who might otherwise not continue their schooling. These students in turn serve as mentors and role models to Minnesota youth in service-to-children projects. Scholarships are given for post-secondary institutions in Minnesota and are linked with mentoring and service projects. Scholarships may be renewed annually. Adult volunteers serve as mentors to the scholarship recipients, and there is a form on the Foundation's Web site to apply to be a Senior Mentor. The site also includes scholarship guidelines, which can be found in the Mechanics section; an FAQ; a history of the Foundation and its scholarship recipients; and a response/contact form for more information.

Pan-Icarian Foundation (PA) (http://www.pan-icarian.com/pan_icarian_foundation.htm)

The Pan-Icarian Foundation was established in 1961 as the charitable giving arm for the Philadelphia-based Pan-Icarian Brotherhood, the oldest Hellenic organization in the Western Hemisphere. The Foundation makes charitable donations in the form of "medical aid, scholarships, disaster relief, and other charitable causes in North America and Greece." A list of current officers of the Foundation, contact information, and more details about the Pan-Icarian Brotherhood can be found online.

Paralysis Project of America (CA) (http://www.paralysisproject.org)

The Paralysis Project of America was formed in 1987 in Los Angeles, California, "to accelerate progress toward finding a cure for paralysis caused by spinal cord injury (SCI)." The Project works toward its mission by funding select scientific and clinical studies researching spinal cord injuries and regeneration. The Project's Web site is sponsored by the Entertainment Industry Foundation and is geared toward spinal cord injury researchers and clinicians. To this end, the Foundation's site maintains a Call for Applications section, with information on specific grants and funding, as well as past and current grant recipients with the scientific abstracts from their projects, links to other SCI resources, and information on other funding sources.

The Park Nicollet Foundation (MN)
(http://www.parknicolletfoundation.org/Grants/grants.html)

The Park Nicollet Foundation is committed to improving the health of children and adults in the communities of Minneapolis and its suburbs. To this end, the Foundation provides community grants to organizations that address local health needs and "programs for families or children (newborn to young adult) that improve health, partner with schools and build developmental assets." The Foundation's Web site provides extensive application guidelines and procedures, funding eligibility, a list of developmental assets, descriptions of previous grantees, and a community grant application that can be downloaded in PDF format.

Pasteur Foundation (NY) (http://www.pasteur.fr)

The Pasteur Foundation was originally known as the Rapkine Fund, which for over thirty years generously supported French science. In 1985, the name of the fund was changed to the Pasteur Foundation to underscore its most enduring affiliation—to the Institut Pasteur. The Pasteur Foundation exists to raise money for scientific research conducted at the Institut Pasteur, as well as to "introduce the Institute's rich history and current research developments to the American public." The Pasteur Foundation has a special fund to award grants to finance the work of young American and British scientists at the Institut Pasteur. In addition, the Foundation has distributed scholastic materials about the work of Louis Pasteur that have reached thousands of American high school French and science students. Interested educators and scientists should contact the Pasteur Foundation for more information about its materials and grants. Contact information is available on the Web site.

The Gary Payton Foundation (WA) (http://www.gpfoundation.org/)

Established in 1996 by Gary Payton, an All-Star NBA point guard and Olympic Gold Medalist, the Foundation's mission is to benefit underprivileged youth. Funding is currently within the greater Seattle area. The Foundation supports opportunities in the areas of education, recreation, and overall wellness to at-risk youth who are deprived of basic options in life. Grant recipients, grant guidelines, a list of the board of directors, and a section on Foundation events can be found on the Web site.

Peace Development Fund (MA) (http://www.peacefund.org/)

Started in 1981, the Peace Development Fund of Amherst, Massachusetts, partners with organizations sharing a common vision. That vision is to "strengthen a broad-based social justice movement that embodies, embraces, and honors many cultures to create the new systems and institutions essential to building a peaceful, just, and equitable world." Grants address three major issues: the relationship between the United States and other countries and people, relationships between people and groups within the United States, and the relationships between institutions, those who run them, and those that they serve. Funding is given to "organizations and projects working to achieve peaceful, just and interdependent relationships among people and nations" by working against an injustice or inequality in their community. The site includes instructions on letters of intent, lists of grantees, a list of the activist board and the staff, and donation opportunities. The Fund does not accept uninvited proposals.

Pediatric Brain Tumor Foundation of the United States, Inc. (NC) (http://www.pbtfus.org)

The Pediatric Brian Tumor Foundation of the United States seeks to find the cause of and a cure for childhood brain tumors, aid in the early detection and treatment of such tumors, and provide hope to the families of children afflicted with brain tumors. The Foundation also supports the development of a national database on all primary brain tumors and provides funding for research on new therapies designed to extend the lives of stricken children. Although the Foundation's Web site is geared toward attracting new donors and participants in Ride 4 Kids, a motorcycle fundraising event started in 1984 in Atlanta, Georgia, it does provide a list of recent grant recipients and contact information.

PEN American Center, Inc. (NY) (http://www.pen.org)

The New York-based PEN American Center, Inc. is a membership association of literary writers and editors who seek "to defend the freedom of expression wherever it may be threatened, and to promote and encourage the recognition and reading of contemporary literature." To this end, the PEN American Center funds literary prizes in the areas of literary translation, creative nonfiction, poetry, drama, children's literature, and editing and publishing. The Prison Writing Program awards prizes to prisoners for works of poetry, fiction, drama, and nonfiction. The Center also sponsors programs such as the Readers and Writers Program, which sends writers and their books to low-income populations with little access to literary culture, and Open Book, a program to promote racial and ethnic diversity within the literary and publishing community. The Center also grants two emergency funds: the PEN Writers Fund and the PEN Fund for Writers and Editors with HIV/AIDS, both of which grant up to $1,000 to combat serious financial difficulties. The PEN American Center Web site provides detailed information on all of these grants and programs, as well as information on membership and contacting the Center. From the site, interested visitors can also order the Center's *Guide to Grants and Awards Available to American Writers.*

Pen & Brush, Inc. (NY) (http://www.penandbrush.org)

Pen & Brush, Inc. is the oldest organization of women in the arts in the United States. Located in New York, it was founded in 1892 when Janet and Mary Lewis invited a group of eight writers and three artists to their studio. Today, the activities of this club are numerous and varied. Schedules and upcoming events are posted on the home page of the site. Activities include concerts, play readings, and exhibitions. All events are open to the public and are free of charge. You can also view works of art by club members on the site.

PEN/Faulkner (DC) (http://www.penfaulkner.org)

The PEN/Faulkner Award was established in Washington, D.C., in 1980 by writers to honor their peers. It is the largest juried fiction award in the United States, awarding prizes to five authors of exceptional published works of fiction each year. The winner of the PEN/Faulkner Award receives $15,000, and the four other outstanding authors receive $5,000. PEN/Faulkner also sponsors the Writers in Schools Project, which brings authors into an area high school to give a reading and teach for a day. The PEN/Faulkner Web site includes a calendar of readings, the current and past winners of the award, submission guidelines, and contact information.

Pennsylvania Humanities Council (PA) (http://www.pahumanities.org)

The Pennsylvania Humanities Council, the state affiliate of the National Endowment for the Humanities, conducts and supports "public humanities programs for adults who seek lifelong learning in history, philosophy, literature, and related subjects." The Council provides qualified nonprofit organizations with resources for developing humanities programs, including speakers, grants, and access to local scholars. The PCH Web site offers a brief description of its grant program and interactive forms for requesting more information or grants counseling.

Perfect Storm Foundation (MA) (http://www.perfectstorm.org/)

The Perfect Storm Foundation, located in Gloucester, Massachusetts, was founded by author Sebastian Junger. He was inspired by the fisherman of Gloucester while writing his international best seller, *The Perfect Storm.* Junger wanted to give their children the kinds of opportunities he experienced growing up that made it possible for him to write *The Perfect Storm.* The mission of The Perfect Storm Foundation is to "provide educational and cultural opportunities to young people whose parents make their living in the commercial fishing industry and in working maritime communities." Complete information about grant applications and the applications themselves are available on the site in PDF format. The Web site also provides a list of scholarships available and contact information.

The Pet Care Trust (WA) (http://petsforum.com/petcaretrust/)

The Pet Care Trust seeks to enhance public and professional understanding of companion animals and their value. The Trust awards grants to direct service programs to improve the health and welfare of pets; to research programs exploring various aspects of the health, care, and possession of companion animals; and to education programs that enhance the public's knowledge and professionalism among pet care professionals. The Trust's Web site lists grant recipients and provides contact information for further grant information. The site also provides a listing of the board of trustees and selected program video clips.

Petroleum Research Fund (DC) (http://www.acs.org/prf/)

Established in 1944 by seven major oil companies, the Fund exists to further "advanced scientific education and fundamental research in the 'petroleum field,' which may include any field of pure science which . . . may afford a basis for subsequent research directly connected with the petroleum field." Grants are made to nonprofits in the United States and other countries. To apply, interested parties must either request information from the Petroleum Research Fund or submit a request form via e-mail; contact information is listed on the site. In addition to information about its funding program, the Petroleum Research Fund site offers research assistance, databases, and links to other educational resources.

Pharmaceutical Research and Manufacturers of America Foundation (DC) (http://www.phrmafoundation.org/)

The PhRMA Foundation promotes public health through support of scientific and medical research into improved medicines. The Foundation's funding helps to develop the careers of young scientists and researchers; establish an infrastructure of expertise in biomedical technology, scientific research, and outcomes measurement; and build alliances between industry and academic scientists. Foundation grants, fellowships, and faculty awards are available in the areas of clinical pharmacology, basic pharmacology, bioinformatics, pharmacology-morphology, pharmaceutics, and pharmacoeconomics. Guidelines and application forms can be downloaded (in various formats) from the Foundation's Web site, which also provides listings of the Foundation's board, advisory committees, and benefactors.

Philanthrofund Foundation (MN) (http://www.scc.net/~philanth/)

The Philanthrofund Foundation provides financial and fundraising support to organizations that serve the needs and enhance the quality of life of the gay, lesbian, bisexual, transgender, and allied communities of the northern Midwest—primarily in the state of Minnesota. Typical grants range from $1,000–$2,000, and the Foundation keeps its definition of who is eligible for funding intentionally broad. The Foundation's Web site provides grant guidelines and application instructions, along with a listing of board members and last year's grant recipients.

Philanthropic Ventures Foundation (CA) (http://www.venturesfoundation.org/)

Established in 1991, the Philanthropic Ventures Foundation (PVF) is located in San Francisco, California. PVF is a public charity that "works with individuals, families, businesses, and foundations to create innovative giving programs to match the specific interests of donors." PVF works with donors to maximize their philanthropic potential. However, organizations cannot apply to PVF for grants because the Foundation initiates the projects it is involved in to customize giving to donors. However, contact information is available for those interested in learning more about PVF or discussing their goals and giving interests.

Phoenix Suns Charities, Inc. (AZ) (http://www1.nba.com/suns/community/)

The Phoenix Suns Charities, Inc. "takes great pride in making contributions to help improve the quality of life in Arizona." The organization offers various resources to nonprofits to help them fulfill their missions, such as item donations, celebrity appearances, and financial donations. To qualify for a Suns Charity grant, an organization must be a nonprofit and the program must be youth or family related. A phone number is available for those interested in receiving a grant application. In addition, there is staff contact information for all of the other programs the Suns Charities is involved in. The Web site also includes articles and information about previous and current philanthropic and community events that the Suns Charities has initiated or in which it has participated.

Phoenixville Community Health Foundation (PA)
(http://www.dvg.org/Phoenixville/index.html)
The Phoenixville Community Health Foundation was established in 1987 through a merger of the Phoenixville Hospital with the University of Pennsylvania Health System. By providing services to the townships of Chester County, the Foundation seeks to improve the health and quality of life of the community. Grants are focused on the areas of community and personal health, as well as the overall civic, social, and economic health of the community. The Foundation's Web site provides a grantmaking overview, grant guidelines, request for contribution forms, previously awarded grants and the Foundation's annual report. All necessary forms, the annual report, and *The Keystone Kommunicator* publication can be downloaded in PDF format.

Pioneering Partners Foundation, Inc. (IN) (http://www.pioneeringpartners.org/)
The Pioneering Partners Foundation is "dedicated to identifying and supporting the best classroom practices where technology is used to prepare children to be productive in both citizenship and in the workforce." Created in 1992 in cooperation with the Council of Great Lakes Governors, the program was transitioned to a nonprofit foundation in 1995 and receives lead support from Ameritech and additional support through GTE and IBM. The Foundation helps teams of educators, community officials, and government leaders to improve learning, strengthen schools, and benefit students. These teams are given grant funding, specialized training, and ongoing support to disseminate their technology-based innovations to ever-wider audiences of students, teachers, parents, and community leaders. Grantseekers will find grant information, guidelines, information on its projects, and an online contact form.

The Ploughshares Fund (CA) (http://www.ploughshares.org/)
Founded at a time when global nuclear conflict seemed a real and immediate possibility, the Ploughshares Fund was designed to provide financial support to people and organizations working to eliminate the threat of nuclear war. Ploughshares now focuses its support on combatting the burgeoning trade in conventional weapons, the explosion of regional conflict in the aftermath of the Cold War, and the growing danger of nuclear weapons proliferation following the breakup of the Soviet Union. Ploughshares has made over 1,000 grants totaling more than $15 million. Visitors to the Foundation's Web site will find detailed information on its main areas of interest: banning land mines, preventing armed conflict, restraining the weapons trade, cutting Pentagon waste, cleaning up our radioactive environment, and fighting nuclear terrorism and proliferation. A grants list—with links to grantee Web sites—is available, along with grant application guidelines, an interactive subscription form for the Foundation's free newsletter, board and staff lists, and contact information.

PKR Foundation (MO) (http://www.pkdcure.org/index.html)
Founded in Kansas City, Missouri, in 1982, the PKR Foundation is "devoted to determining the cause, improving clinical treatment and discovering a cure for polycystic kidney disease (PKD)." The Foundation supports funds for PKD research, peer-approved biomedical research projects, and National Institute of Health magnet centers of research. The Foundation also disseminates a wealth of information on the disease, much of which is accessible via their Web site. There are complete listings of the staff and board of the Foundation, as well as the Scientific and Friends Advisory Committees. The site includes a financial report, membership and donor information, and news items on PKD research. In its effort to provide patient education about the disease, the Foundation lists numerous and wide-ranging links to other resources on the site.

Points of Light Foundation (DC) (http://www.pointsoflight.org/)

Created in 1990, the Points of Light Foundation is located in Washington, D.C. Supported by a network of over 500 Volunteer Centers, the organization is a "nonpartisan nonprofit organization devoted to promoting volunteerism." The Foundation distributes a series of recognition awards, including the Awards for Excellence in Corporate Community Service, the President's Service Award, the President's Student Service Award, the Romney Volunteer Center Excellence Award, and the Family Matters Award. The Foundation partners with corporations and private foundations to run national programs encouraging volunteerism. Two featured programs are Family Matters, which encourages and links families to volunteer opportunities and acknowledges outstanding efforts, and Connect America, which works to "build national public awareness about the power of connections through advertising, the media, and recognition efforts while demonstrating the outcomes of connections in addressing local social problems." The organization offers training, products, and consultations in engaging volunteers in community service efforts to organizations and volunteers, including an annual conference. The site includes links to local Volunteer Centers, a volunteer marketplace, information on training and products, and a small feature on the Daily Points of Light Award recipient. The annual report is online, in addition to a board list and staff directory. There are nomination forms for the different awards and lists of past recipients. There is also information on contributing and on many opportunities to volunteer. There are presently applications for the National Community Service Conference and an online National Volunteer Week Kit.

Police Foundation (DC) (http://www.policefoundation.org)

The Washington, D.C., based Police Foundation was established in 1970 by Ford Foundation President McGeorge Bundy. The organization's mission is "to help the police be more effective in doing their job, whether it be deterring robberies, intervening in potentially injurious family disputes, or working to improve relationships between the police and the communities they serve." The Foundation offers research, publications, and training in the most up-to-date and relevant areas of interest to the field. This includes crime management, risk analysis management, and technical assistant and technology. The Foundation runs the Police Fellowship Program, which brings people with expertise in different areas in to the Foundation's office to work for a specific amount of time with the leaders in the field. Applications and details on this program can be found online. The site also includes lists of the staff and board members, opportunities to order publications, information on the Foundation's Center for Police and Civil Disorder, and an update on research projects.

The Roscoe Pound Foundation (DC) (http://www.atla.org/rpf.ht)

The Roscoe Pound Foundation was established in 1956 by trial lawyers to honor and build upon the work of Roscoe Pound, Dean of the Harvard Law School from 1916–1936. Based in Washington, D.C., the Foundation strengthens the practice of trial law through its programs, publications, and research grants, which help judges, academics, and others understand a balanced view of the U.S. civil justice system. Among its programs are the Elaine Osborne Jacobson Scholarship for Women Working in healthcare Law, given each year to a female law student who is committed to a career in healthcare law; the Pound Award for Excellence in Teaching Trial Advocacy as an Adjunct, awarded annually to an individual who balances a trial practice and teaching trial advocacy as an adjunct professor of law; Pound Foundation Grants to Legal Scholars, which are grants for research on a variety of topics of concern to the trial bar awarded by a jury of academics, jurists, and lawyers; the Roscoe Hogan Environmental Law Essay Contest, which annually honors a law student's writing ability in the area of environmental law; the Richard S. Jacobson Award for Excellence in Teaching Trial Advocacy, awarded annually to an outstanding law professor; and Trial Advocacy Training for Law Students, a program that provides free advocacy training. Visit the site for further descriptions of the programs, contact information, and links to other resources.

The Pride Foundation (WA) (http://www.pridefoundation.org/)

The Pride Foundation of Seattle, Washington, is devoted to "strengthen [the] lesbian, gay, transgender, and bisexual community today, and building an endowment fund for tomorrow." Grants are primarily given in Washington, but programs in Oregon, Montana, Idaho, and Alaska are also funded. The Pride Foundation and the Greater Seattle Business Association (GSBA) Scholarship Programs give grants of up to $3,500 to individuals attending any sort of post-secondary school. Scholarships include those for gay, lesbian, bisexual, and transgender youth and adults; children raised in gay or lesbian families; and leaders and activists in promoting the rights of sexual minorities. Past grant recipients have fallen in two categories: programmatic support for education and advocacy, AIDS education and support, arts and recreation, youth and family services, lesbian health, and other health and community service and general operating support focused on small, grassroots organizations. Grant applications are not currently online but will be posted soon. There is an address to contact for scholarship applications. The site includes links to related sites and funding opportunities, information on contributing and volunteering, a calendar of events, and a grants list from 1991 to the present.

Princess Grace Foundation-USA (NY) (http://www.pgfusa.com/)

Established in 1982 in memory of Princess Grace of Monaco, the Princess Grace Foundation-USA supports emerging young artists nationwide in the the fields of theater, dance, and film. Students in their last year of schooling or training are eligible for tuition assistance through scholarships, while young artists working in the areas of theater and dance qualify for apprenticeships and fellowships. The Foundation, which has awarded over $1.6 million in grants since 1984, also recognizes exceptional and continuing professional achievement through the awarding of Princess Grace Statuettes, its highest honor, to two or three recipients annually. The Foundation's Web site provides a fact sheet and background information about the Foundation, application guidelines, a list of recent grantees, and contact information.

Pro-Choice Resources (MN) (http://www.sff.net/people/RobinR/pcr.htm)

Located in Minneapolis, Minnesota, Pro-Choice Resources was founded in 1967 to provide information and referral services for women facing an unwanted pregnancy. Its mission today is to "provide financial and educational resources to ensure access and expand reproductive options for all women including the right to choose and obtain a legal abortion." As educating the public is one of Pro-Choice Resources' primary goals, the organization provides numerous materials and resources to interested parties, including a speaker's bureau. The Hersey Abortion Assistance Fund provides grants or loans to women seeking abortions who cannot afford them, do not have insurance, or are faced with other difficult situations. The HLHV Medical Scholarship Fund provides tuition assistance for first through fourth year medical students who will provide abortions as part of their practice. The application form for this scholarship can be printed out from the Web site and completed. Contact information is provided on the site.

Professional Tennis Registry Foundation (SC) (http://www.usptr.org/foundation.htm)

Based in Hilton Head Island, South Carolina, the Professional Tennis Registry Foundation was established in 1981 as the charitable arm of the United States Professional Tennis Registry (USPTR). The Foundation raises, administers, and distributes funds for charitable activities. USPTR members donate to the Foundation along with their membership renewals. These funds are pooled and used for various charitable and research activities. The Foundation's primary focus is to bring tennis instruction and tennis equipment to children in inner cities and rural areas where the opportunity may not otherwise be available to them. Through the Foundation, tennis programs (in low-income housing projects), after school latch-key programs, at-risk youth programs, and wheelchair tennis rehabilitation programs have been developed. More information on programs and grant qualification requirements can be obtained by writing to the Foundation. Visit the Web site for contact information.

Prosthetics for Diabetics Foundation (GA) (http://www.expage.com/page/pfdfoundation)

The Prosthetics for Diabetics Foundation was created in May 1999 in Monroe, Georgia, by a man whose nephew had lost a leg to diabetes. The organization works "to realize the needs of amputees and their families by providing them with not only prosthetics, but also rehabilitation and long term care as well." The Foundation is currently focused on three areas. The first is helping those who can't cover the 20 percent of the cost of prosthetic limbs that Medicaid/Medicare doesn't cover. The Foundation will also help the family to raise any other money that they need for the related medical expenses. The second is educating school children on diabetes and teaching them to understand and help those who suffer from diabetes and other diseases. The third effort is to work with similar organization to increase awareness of diabetes throughout the country. The site offers links to related organizations and basic contact information.

Public Entity Risk Institute (VA) (http://www.riskinstitute.org/)

The Public Entity Risk Institute of Fairfax, Virginia, began working in 1997 "to serve public, private, and nonprofit organizations as a dynamic, forward thinking resource for the practical enhancement of risk management." All grants must fall within one of the three major goals. These goals are facilitating the delivery and development of training on risk management, serving as a clearinghouse and resource center for risk management information, and stimulating innovative programming in its areas of interest. There is a focus on smaller, nonprofit organizations. The grant program looks at five elements: the furthering of PERI's goals, meeting an unmet need, providing leveraged and long-term benefit for small groups, transferring or replicating to benefit others, and otherwise not having the resources to occur. The site includes directions on submitting a letter of inquiry and a description of the entire application process. There is a list of current grantees and a section with features on many of them. There is also a news center and an area reporting on a recent symposium.

Pulmonary Fibrosis Foundation (CO) (http://www.pulmonaryfibrosis.org)

The Pulmonary Fibrosis Foundation, located in Denver, Colorado, originated as a result of the dedication and generosity of Albert Rose, a prominent Denver, Colorado, businessman who was informed that he was afflicted with Pulmonary Fibrosis. The Foundation's primary purpose is to provide funding for research and treatment of Pulmonary Fibrosis. The Foundation aims to "empower scientists and physicians to sufficiently increase biomedical knowledge to the point where having Pulmonary Fibrosis no longer implies a death sentence." The Foundation is also an educational resource, providing access to the most recent studies on the disease. The Foundation's Web site does not provide information about applying for grants, but it does have contact information for those interested in learning more. Additionally, the site has more information on Pulmonary Fibrosis, resource links, and a listing of the Foundation's board members.

PVA Spinal Cord Research Foundation (DC) (http://www.pva.org/scrf/)

Paralyzed Veterans of America was established after World War II to help those who had incurred a spinal cord injury during the war reenter mainstream society. Since then, its membership and resources have grown, as has the scope of its work. Its mission is to "support research to alleviate, and ultimately end, the medical and functional consequences of paralysis." In 1975, PVA added the Spinal Cord Research Foundation to carry out the responsibility of supporting research. In addition to supporting work that aims to find a cure to spinal cord dysfunction, the Foundation also "supports grants designed to improve the current treatment and care for acute and chronic spinal cord dysfunction, develop innovative rehabilitative therapies and assistive devices for paralyzed individuals, and train talented researchers to focus on the problem of spinal cord dysfunction." Institutions interested in applying for a grant must be located in the United States or Canada, but investigators and fellows are not limited geographically. All applicants must have a professional degree and must apply for the fellowship within four years of obtaining this degree. An e-mail address is provided for those interested in receiving information about guidelines and applications. The Web site also contains financial information, conference information, and lists of past awardees.

Queens Council on the Arts (NY) (http://www.queenscouncilarts.org)

The Queens Council on the Arts was founded in 1966 to promote, support, and develop the arts in Queens County, New York. Specifically, its mission is to "provide services to cultural organizations and individual artists and to promote our many diverse cultural activities on a county wide level to the two million residents of our borough, as well as to visitors and tourists to our New York City region." The Council invites Queens artists and arts organizations to apply for funding to help them pursue their artistic dreams. Applications and guidelines can be obtained from the Council office (contact information listed on the site) or downloaded in PDF format. New applicants are required to attend an application seminar. Dates and locations are posted on the Web site. The site also has a list of special events, publications and videos, and a comprehensive calendar of performances and exhibitions throughout Queens.

Radio and Television News Directors Foundation (DC) (http://www.rtndf.org)

The mission of the Radio and Television News Directors Foundation (RTNDF) is to "promote excellence in electronic journalism through research, education and professional training in four principal program areas: journalistic ethics and practices; the impact of technological change on electronic journalism; the role of electronic news in politics and public policy; and cultural diversity in the electronic journalism profession." RTNDF offers a variety of internships, scholarships, and fellowships. All of these programs are described on the site, and applications for each program may be downloaded in PDF format. To apply for a scholarship, applicants must be at least of sophomore standing. Contact information and a list of FAQs are available. The Web site also has a great deal of information about the Radio and Television News Directors Association, its programs, awards, and upcoming convention.

Rainforest Alliance, Inc. (NY) (http://www.rainforest-alliance.org)

The Rainforest Alliance is an international nonprofit organization dedicated to the conservation of tropical forests. It was founded by Daniel Katz, a 24 year old China specialist for a Wall Street law firm. He attended a small rainforest workshop in New York City and came up with the idea for the Rainforest Alliance. The mission of this New York City-based organization is to develop and promote economically viable and socially desirable alternatives to the destruction of this endangered resource. The Alliance pursues this mission through education, research in the social and natural sciences, and the establishment of cooperative partnerships with businesses, governments, and local peoples. Its grant programs seek to increase the effectiveness of community-based conservation initiatives around the world. Among its conservation programs is the Catalyst Grants program, which assists promising community-based forest conservation initiatives in tropical countries. Catalyst Grants provide grants of under $3,000, with priority given to groups that are out of the "funding loop" of international or local sources due to size or geographic location. In recognition of the pivotal role women have as conservationists and maintainers of the environment, the program places special emphasis on women's issues. To date, Catalyst Grants have supported over 70 projects in 16 countries. Another of its programs is the Kleinhans Fellowship, which aims to promote research into the practical means of managing and using tropical forest resources without destroying the integrity of the forest ecosystem. The research will synthesize elements of conservation and business and must lead to the development of a product or marketing technique that can provide income for community-based groups living in or near tropical forest areas. The Kleinhans Fellowship research area is restricted to Latin America, though projects that can eventually be replicated in other parts of the world are encouraged. Visit the Alliance's Web site for information on grant programs, annual reports, rainforest resources and facts, news, links to other resources, and contact information.

Rainforest Cafe Friends of the Future Foundation (MN)
(http://www.rainforestcafe.com/RFC/lFriends.asp)
The Rainforest Cafe Friends of the Future Foundation, located in Hopkins, Minnesota, is dedicated to supporting environmental causes and causes that enrich the lives of children, the families, and the communities in which the Rainforest Cafe operates. To apply for a grant, organizations must complete and mail in a grant application. Instructions on how to complete a grant application and what information to include can be found on the Web site. The mailing address for the Foundation is also available online.

Ayn Rand Institute/The Center for the Advancement of Objectivism (CA)
(http://www.aynrand.org/)
The Ayn Rand Institute was founded in 1985 by philosopher Leonard Peikoff to advance Objectivism, Ayn Rand's philosophy of reason, egoism, individualism, and laissez-faire capitalism. The Institute influences the public through opinion pieces and its own media projects; runs the Campaign Against Servitude, which opposes volunteerism; sponsors essay contests; supports college and university campus clubs; and produces materials and training on Objectivism. The Institute's Web site provides a fair amount of information on Objectivism and Ayn Rand and describes the activities of the Institute.

Rapides Foundation (LA) (http://www.rapidesfoundation.org/)
The Rapides Foundation is centered in an 11-parish service area in central Louisiana. Founded in 1994, the Foundation funds "opportunities that strengthen health and well-being, education, and the arts and humanities" in the form of three types of grants. Initiative grants address community health, arts, education, and development. Responsive grants fund innovative and effective approaches not covered in the Initiative grants. Mini-grants provide funding of less than $10,000 for short-term projects. The Foundation's Web site provides current newsletters and an application coversheet, both downloadable in PDF format; grant guidelines and limitations; contact information; and news on current Foundation events in Louisiana.

Ravens Foundation for Families, Inc. (MD) (http://www.baltimoreravens.com/community)
The Baltimore-based Ravens Foundation for Families "seeks to help change fundamental ills with which Baltimore and area families must deal with in the pursuit of healthy and productive lives for themselves and their community." Established by the Baltimore Ravens, of the NFL, the Foundation's funding priority is the physical and mental health of youth and the creation of environments for their positive social development. The Foundation's objective is to attack core problems that, when ignored or untreated, could foster other social ills. Foundation resources will be applied to programs creating motivational and educational opportunities for youth. Visit the Web site for contact information, a partial list of grant recipients, and information on other charitable foundations established by Baltimore Ravens football players.

Reaching Heights (OH) (http://www.chuh.net/reachingheights)
Founded in 1989 by the community and school district, Reaching Heights is a "citizen organization that supports the public schools serving Cleveland Heights and University Heights, Ohio." The organization's goal is to enhance local public education to meet the challenges of the 21st Century. Reaching Heights provides three types of grants to students and educators: School Team grants, for up to $1500 for innovative school initiatives; Community Connection, for up to $250 to educate and involve the public in the school system; and the Podis-Weiskopf Music Fund, for up to $400 for music education projects. Community involvement projects are detailed on the organization's Web site, along with grant guidelines, past grant recipients, links, and contact information.

Reading Musical Foundation (PA) (http://www.readingmusicalfoundation.org/)
The Reading Musical Foundation, located in Reading, Pennsylvania, works to support local music enrichment and education. The Foundation supports numerous music groups—both professional and amateur—in the Reading area. Additionally, the

Foundation's main manner of philanthropic funding is through five named music scholarships. While the majority of these scholarships are for Berks County high school students preparing to pursue music through higher education, some scholarships are intended for younger music students, including those of elementary and middle school age. Details of each scholarship, plus application guidelines and a printable application form, can be found online. The Foundation also sponsors two music education programs: Music-in-the-Schools and Blues-in-the-Schools. The Web site provides information on these programs, a schedule of concerts, listings of musical ensembles in the area, and contact information.

Red Ribbon Charitable Foundation, Inc. (FL) (http://www.red-ribbon.org/)
Red Ribbon Charitable Foundation, Inc. was endowed in 1995 by Dr. Garry P. Bergeron to support healthy and responsible living through community initiatives for persons living with HIV and AIDS. Based in Pensacola, Florida, the Foundation raises and provides funds for activities that reduce the impact of HIV and AIDS on the community. The site contains a grant recipient list and contact information.

Donna Reed Foundation for the Performing Arts (IA) (http://www.donnareed.org/)
The Donna Reed Foundation for the Performing Arts was formed in 1987 in Denison, Iowa, to memorialize Ms. Reed's achievements and to perpetuate the actress's belief in the importance of education and the pursuit of one's dreams. The Foundation supports talented youth through national, state, and local scholarships; conducts workshops by industry professionals; and promotes stage plays, concerts, and other cultural activities. The Foundation's Web site provides information about the Donna Reed Scholarships for students of the performing arts, including a downloadable application form. The site also provides details and registration information for workshops, membership information, and press releases about the Foundation and its activities.

Christopher Reeve Paralysis Foundation (NJ) (http://paralysis.apacure.org/)
The American Paralysis Association (APA) and the Christopher Reeve Foundation (CRF) merged in April 1999 to form the Christopher Reeve Paralysis Foundation. Founded in 1982, APA had established an international leadership role in funding spinal cord research. CRF, founded in 1996, directed 75 percent of its funding to APA's research programs and 25 percent to quality of life awards for disability organizations. The Christopher Reeve Paralysis Foundation (CRPF) encourages and supports research to develop effective treatments and a cure for paralysis caused by spinal cord injury and other central nervous system disorders. The Springfield, New Jersey-based Foundation also allocates a portion of its resources to grants that improve the quality of life for people with disabilities, with primary consideration given to programs that deal with spinal cord injury and other afflictions of the central nervous system. The quality of life program has the following fields of interest: children, arts, sports/recreation, education, advocacy, accessibility and practical service/needs. Its two types of funding are Quality of Life awards of $25,000 for programs that are wide in scope and Direct Effect Awards of $5000, for smaller, community-based nonprofits that will have an immediate and positive impact on their ability to deliver services to their communities. Its two research programs are the CRPF Consortium on Spinal Cord injury, which focuses the expertise and scientific tools of a group of international neuroscientists on developing therapies for recovery from chronic spinal cord injury, and individual awards, which are two-year research grants of up to $50,000 a year. Visit the site for downloadable applications, application guidelines and instructions, and publications, including annual reports and *Progress in Research,* a report on scientific breakthroughs, researcher profiles, and abstracts of CRPF-funded grants. Visitors can also find facts on spinal cord injuries, press releases, and contact information.

The Reinvestment Fund (PA) (http://www.trfund.com)
Based in Philadelphia and founded in 1985, the Reinvestment Fund is a community development financial institution that uses investments from individuals and institutions to make loans and equity investments in the areas of affordable housing, community facilities, small

businesses, workforce development programs, and sustainable energy. The Fund also offers consulting and technical assistance in real estate development services and neighborhood planning. The mission of the Fund is to alleviate poverty and create economic opportunity in a 21-county, three-state region centered in Philadelphia. Visit the site for contact information on each of the Fund's lending areas, detailed information on each program area, and application instructions.

Resist, Inc. (MA) (http://www.resistinc.org)

Dating back to Vietnam War resistance in 1967, Resist, Inc. of Somerville, Massachusetts, works for social change and against injustice. This group is "a different kind of funding organization seeking out groups that withstand reactionary government policies, corporate arrogance, and right-wing fanaticism through organizing, education and action." There are three different types of grants. The general grant program includes programs that organize people to take action, build human or physical capacity to take action, encourage collaboration between groups, and promote organizational longevity. Areas of interest include "community organizing and anti-racism projects; economic justice; environmental protection; the struggle for gay, lesbian, bisexual and transgendered rights; health, AIDS and disability issues; labor; progressive media and culture resources; Native Americans/native peoples; peace/anti-militarism; prisoners; women; and youth." The site includes application guidelines and restrictions and a downloadable application, which can be accessed after filling out a questionnaire. There are also lists of past grantees, the board, and the staff. Visitors are offered information on contributing and volunteering and a publication for grantseekers.

Rex Foundation (CA) (http://www.rexfoundation.org/index.html)

The Rex Foundation, a charitable foundation established by members and friends of the Grateful Dead, "aims to help secure a healthy environment, promote individuality in the arts, provide support to critical and necessary social services, assist others less fortunate than ourselves, protect the rights of indigenous people and ensure their cultural survival, build a stronger community, and to educate children and adults everywhere." Virtually all the Foundation's grant recipients are preselected; therefore, unsolicited requests are not considered. Visitors to the Foundation's Web site will find the the most recent annual report, a listing of grant recipients, profiles of selected Foundation beneficiaries, a listing of board bembers, and information about the most current Rex Awards: the Jerry Garcia Award, which honors and supports those working to encourage creativity in young people; the Bill Graham Award, which is designated for those working to assist children who are victims of political oppression and human rights violations; and the Ralph. J. Gleason Award, which recognizes individuals making outstanding contributions to culture.

Riverside Community Health Foundation (CA) (http://www.rchf.org)

The Riverside Community Health Foundation, in partnership with the Community Health Corporation, "provides and facilitates programs and services to improve the health" of Riverside, California, community residents. The Foundation participates in a wide range of funding to nonprofit organizations that share a similar mission of health improvement in the community. Past grants are listed on the Foundation's Web site. The Foundation runs a number of programs, services, and events, all of which are posted on the site. Visitors interested in applying for grants may download an application, which includes grant evaluation criteria, in PDF format. Contact information and links to related resources are also available online.

Jackie Robinson Foundation (NY) (http://www.jackierobinson.org/)

The Jackie Robinson Foundation, founded in 1973 by Rachel Robinson, helps young people in financial need reach their potential through education. The Foundation awards four scholarships annually to minority students enrolled in higher education studies and offers personal and career counseling and assistance obtaining employment. The Foundation's Web site provides scholarship guidelines and alumni and donor information.

Rockefeller Family Fund, Inc. (NY) (http://www.rffund.org/)

The New York City-based Rockefeller Family Fund makes grants in five major program areas: citizen education and participation, economic justice for women, the environment, institutional responsiveness, and self-sufficiency. The Fund supports tax-exempt organizations engaged in educational and charitable activities of national significance. It does not usually fund projects pertaining only to a single community. In addition to general program descriptions, visitors to the Fund's Web site will find a list (by program and alphabetically) of recent grantees and links to those with Web sites, application procedures, a letter from the Fund's president, a listing of the Fund's trustees and staff, and information about the Rockefeller Technology Project, which helps grantees to learn about and effectively use new communication technology.

Rocky Mountain Elk Foundation, Inc. (MT) (http://www.rmef.org)

The Rocky Mountain Elk Foundation (RMEF) of Missoula, Montana, was created by four hunters in 1984. The apolitical organization's mission is to "ensure the future of elk, other wildlife and their habitat." This is accomplished through a number of educational outreach and conservation programs. The site is full of information that is targeted to different audiences: the general public, teachers, and hunters. RMEF distributes the Wallace Fennell Pate Wildlife Conservation Award annually to a person who personifies the goals of the organization. In addition, the group awards ten Wildlife Leadership awards to undergraduate wildlife students. Each of these comes with a $2,000 scholarship. Scholarship applications can be printed from the site or filed electronically at Free Scholarship Search (http://www.fastweb.com). The extensive site includes membership information, related contests, links, news, and board and staff lists.

Rose Community Foundation (CO) (http://www.rcfdenver.org/)

The Rose Community Foundation of Denver, Colorado was created in 1995 from the sale of Rose Medical Center. The organization "dedicates its resources towards enhancing the health and well being of the Greater Denver community." The Foundation funds programs in five basic categories and has specific areas of interest within each. The Aging program is interested in public awareness and education, support for caregivers, and coordination of independent living services. Early childhood development and family self-sufficiency are the focuses within the Child and Family Development category. The Education program addresses quality teaching and systemic change in individual schools and in public education. Health includes primary prevention, access to care for those who can't afford it, and leadership capacity on health issues. Finally, Jewish Life includes outreach to unconnected Jews, organizational and leadership development, and experiences that promote Jewish growth. The site includes very explicit application guidelines, a letter of invitation to potential applicants, information on contributing, a set of FAQs, and information on Rose Biomedical, an organization existing within the Foundation.

The R.O.S.E. Fund (MA) (http://www.rosefund.org)

The ROSE (Regaining One's Self Esteem) Fund is located in Boston, Massachusetts. The organization is devoted to "ending violence against women and assisting women survivors of violence to regain their self-esteem and rebuild their lives ... by helping women to achieve a positive sense of self-esteem." Programs include public education, work with individual women, awards, and scholarships. The Heinz Family Foundation ROSE Achievement Award is given annually to a "woman survivor of violence for her work and achievements in the area of ending violence against women" and includes a cash gift to the nonprofit of the recipients choice. The New England Patriots ROSE Award goes to the victim of a violent crime who is working to overcome the situation and includes a cash gift to help her move on. The nomination packet can be downloaded in Microsoft Word and includes guidelines and deadlines. The Fund does not accept self-nominations. The Fund also offers four scholarships for survivors of abuse. Some scholarships are for particular schools, including Northeastern University, University of Massachusetts, and Pine Manor, and each have their own restrictions. Applications and guidelines can be downloaded in Microsoft Word. The site includes information for women that have been abused, educational information on rape and domestic abuse, a list of items being auctioned at the next fundraiser, lists and biographies of past award recipients, and a staff list.

The Rosenberg Fund for Children (MA) (http://www.rfc.org/)

In 1953 Ethel and Julius Rosenberg were controversially accused and executed for allegedly giving top-secret data on nuclear weapons to the U.S.S.R. The Rosenberg Fund for Children was founded by their son, Robert Meeropol, in Springfield, Massachusetts, "to provide for the educational and emotional needs of children in this country whose parents have been targeted in the course of their progressive activities," and have been imprisoned, physically or emotionally disabled, unemployed, or have died. The Fund supports activists' children in the following areas: school tuition, camp tuition, counseling, cultural lessons, outdoor programs, after-school programs, and the Carry it Forward program, which supports young adults in paying for college or a similar program. The Fund's Web site provides a listing of recent and on-going grants, grant guidelines, limitations, a printable grant application in both Spanish and English, and contact information.

Rotary District 6360 Foundation (MI) (http://www.district6360.com/foundation.htm)

The Rotary District 6360 Foundation, located in Delton, Michigan, was founded at the 1992 Rotary District conference and is governed by a board of thirteen trustees who are members of Rotary clubs located in the District. It was created to assist the Rotary District 6360 Club with service projects involving education, vocation, community, and international objectives. The Foundation assists the District Club by providing encouragement and funding. Applications for grants must be made to the Foundation board in writing. A formal application outlining needed information can be requested from Foundation trustees or the district governors; this information is available on the site. Applications must indicate the needs and goals of the proposed service project as well as the plan for meeting those objectives. This Foundation only gives grants to Rotary Clubs.

Rotary Foundation of Rotary International (IL) (http://www.rotary.org/foundation/)

As the philanthropic arm of Rotary International, the Rotary Foundation supports efforts to "achieve world understanding and peace through international humanitarian, educational, and cultural exchange programs." The Foundation sponsors activities in two main areas: the Humanitarian Programs, which fund projects designed to improve quality of life, primarily in the developing world, and the Educational Programs, through which the Foundation provides funding for students to study abroad each year, for university professors to teach in developing countries, and for exchanges of business and professional people. In addition to general program descriptions, visitors to the Foundation area of Rotary International's Web site will find information on the Foundation's history, support, governance, and a list of trustees.

Albert B. Sabin Vaccine Institute, Inc. (DC) (http://www.sabin.org)

The Albert B. Sabin Vaccine Institute was established to promote "rapid scientific advances in vaccine development, delivery and distribution worldwide." (Albert B. Sabin developed the original polio vaccine.) In the field of vaccine development, the Institute supports the academic development of scientists and physicians; provides grants for research, development, and testing; advocates for the integration of scientific advances and public policy; and promotes public awareness of vaccine research and the development of educational materials. The Institute's Web site offers brief descriptions of its programs and activities and provides contact information.

St. Louis Rams Foundation (MO)
(http://go.stlouisrams.com/Community/RamsFoundation/)

The St. Louis Rams Foundation, which was established in 1997, is just one arm of the St. Louis Rams football team's outreach program. The Foundation "supports efforts and organizations that inspire positive change in the greater St. Louis area with an emphasis on youth." Primary areas of interest include education/literacy, recreation, health, and human services. The Foundation is looking to establish partnerships. The ideal application will request involvement and support beyond just a cash grant. Application guidelines and deadlines are available online. In addition, applications and guidelines can be downloaded in PDF format. There is a list of Foundation "partners," or past support recipients, and press releases on events and recent projects.

St. Luke's Charitable Health Trust (AZ) (http://www.sltrust.com/)

The St. Luke's Charitable Health Trust, located in Phoenix, Arizona, invests in the development and support of activities, programs, and organizations that improve the health of people in the Phoenix metropolitan area. In its grantmaking, the Trust places emphasis on prevention programs for children, youth, and families; delivery of health services to the underserved; and building the capacity of communities to help themselves. The Trust awards community grants, "Bridge" grants for emerging programs, individual medical financial assistance, and issues RFPs for special initiatives. Application information for grants is provided at the Trust's Web site, along with a listing of recently awarded grants, proposal tips, and evaluation criteria.

Saint Lukes Foundation of Cleveland Ohio (OH) (http://stlukesfoundcleveland.org/index.html)

The Saint Lukes Foundation of Cleveland, Ohio, was created from the sale of Saint Lukes Medical Center in 1997. The organization's mission is to "foster and improve the health status and well-being of the people of Northeast Ohio, with special emphasis on those living in the areas traditionally served by Saint Luke's Medical Center . . . [by] providing funding support for initiatives focused on general health and wellness, health and medical education, medical research, and healthcare delivery." The grantmaking program focuses giving on neighborhoods suffering from poverty, joblessness, and a lack of quality medical care. Areas of interest include community involvement and ownership, healthy behaviors and lifestyles, increased and improved healthcare, educating healthcare professionals, and public education. The Foundation accepts letters of inquiry from qualified organizations throughout the year. A letter must be approved before an application is submitted. Application guidelines and deadlines can be found on the site. Visitors will also find contact information and lists of past grant recipients.

San Angelo Health Foundation (TX) (http://www.sahfoundation.org)

Established in 1995, the San Angelo Health Foundation focuses its support and funding on "community health in its broadest form" in San Angelo and the Concho Valley area of Texas. To this end, all community services are eligible for funding, but the trustees of the Foundation make health-related services a priority. The Foundation's Web site provides detailed guidelines for potential grant applicants, recent grants, significant achievements, Foundation publications that can be requested via e-mail, and contact information.

San Diego Foundation for Change (CA) (http://www.foundation4change.org/)

Created in 1994, the San Diego Foundation for Change began as a group of volunteers working under the auspices of Los Angeles' Liberty Hill Foundation. The organization's mission is to "promote positive, permanent change to end discrimination, lack of opportunity, poverty and environmental degradation in the San Diego/Tijuana border region by empowering small, community-based organizations with funding and technical assistance." One unique aspect of the foundation is that grant awards are decided by a community grantmaking committee that is made up of community leaders, activists, and donors. Grant applications are distributed and awards are announced annually. This socially progressive groups' areas of interest include ending discrimination, halting pollution, immigrant rights, racial equality, women's rights, youth projects, and domestic and community violence. Applicants must have a significant community organizing component. There are also two special awards given: the San Diego Lesbian, Gay, Bisexual and Transgender Pride Awards and the James Mitsuo Cua Award for Lesbian, Gay, Bisexual and Transgender San Diegans. The application guidelines can be downloaded in PDF format, and applications can be requested by e-mail, phone, or fax. The site includes a board list, a list of recipient organizations, information on contributing, and links to related resources.

Save-the-Redwoods League (CA) (http://www.savetheredwoods.org)

Created in 1918, the Save-the-Redwoods League of San Francisco, California is committed to conserving the ancient forests of its state. The group's mission is "to rescue from destruction representative areas of primeval redwood forests, and to cooperate with state and national park services in establishing redwood parks." This is accomplished through four program areas. The Redwood Land Purchase supports buying and protecting redwood forests. Memorial and Honor Groves allow donors to create a living memorial by dedicating a grove. The organization plants new redwoods through the Tree Planting Program. The Granting Program supports research on redwoods and projects that inform people about the cause. Areas of interest include trail maintenance, interpretation, research, exhibits, and books on redwood and sequoia trees and ecosystems. The site includes information on each program, including application guidelines for the grants. Visitors will also find resources on redwoods and their environment, a description of the Master Plan for redwoods that the League is developing, online copies of the semi-annual newsletter, and all press releases.

Stanley J. Sarnoff Endowment for Cardiovascular Science, Inc. (VA) (http://www.SarnoffEndowment.org/)

The mission of the Stanley J. Sarnoff Endowment is to interest medical school students in careers in cardiovascular research. The Endowment administers a Fellowship Program, which is open to students currently attending medical school, and a Scholars Program, which is open to former Sarnoff Fellows. Details of both programs are outlined on the Endowment's Web site, along with information about current and past Sarnoff Fellows and Scholars. The Fellowship application along with sample essays from previous applicants, can be downloaded in PDF format. The site also provides a brief biography of Dr. Sarnoff, information about the Endowment's scientific board and board of directors, and contact information.

Detlef Schrempf Foundation (WA) (http://www.detlef.com)

Formed at the beginning of 1996, the Detlef Schrempf Foundation of Seattle, Washington was created to involve the basketball player and his wife further in their community. The goal of the organization is "to strengthen the lives of children and families in the northwest by raising funds for various children's charities and youth organizations." Organizations that educate and support children in the Pacific Northwest are potential grantees. The site includes a list of grantees and links to those on the Web. There is an electronic response page where visitors can contact the Foundation, although applying for grants is not one of the listed options. There is also an events calendar with features on upcoming and past fundraisers.

Schumpert Medical Center Foundation (LA) (http://www.schumpertfoundation.org/)

The Schumpert Medical Center Foundation of Shreveport, LA was established in 1992 to join in the humanitarian efforts of the Sisters of Charity of the Incarnate Word. The group's mission is to "to further the Sisters' mission, and to support new and innovative healthcare programs for the benefit of our community, without regard for an individual's ability to pay." Projects supported by the Foundation include the Schumpert Cancer Treatment Center, Health System Hospice Care, Physical Medicine and Rehabilitation Programs, and women and children's health and radiology centers. There are also specific funds to support asthma/allergy education research and colon and rectal disease research and treatment. There are detailed descriptions of each project available online, along with information on current fundraisers, ways to contribute, and a list of the board of directors.

Schwab Fund for Charitable Giving (CA) (http://www.schwabcharitable.org/)

The San Francisco-based Schwab Fund for Charitable Giving strives "to increase charitable giving in the United States by providing useful information, unbiased guidance, and advantageous ways to give." The Fund supports philanthropists' search for the most appropriate charitable giving plan, through a variety of programs and services. The Fund's Web site details seven principles of charitable giving and administers a Charitable Gift Fund and a Philanthropy Fund. A grant nomination form can be downloaded in PDF format from the site, in conjunction with a contribution to the Charitable Gift Fund. Funds given to the Philanthropy Fund are used for grants at the discretion of the Schwab Fund. Also available from the Fund's Web site is a charity search, provided by Guidestar; links to further resources on charitable giving; online account services; and contact information.

Securities Industry Foundation for Economic Education (NY) (http://www.sia.com/about_sia/html/sifee.html)

Located in New York City's Wall Street district, the Securities Foundation for Economic Education has existed for over two decades and was established by the Securities Industry Association to fulfill its mandate to foster economic education. Its mission is "to promote economic education and financial literacy among children and adults." The Foundation's largest program is the Stock Market Game, a stock market simulation program designed for students of all ages. The Stock Market Game program has become the major teaching resource for economic education and investment principles for 25,000 teachers in every state and in 15 countries worldwide. On the site, annual reports are available in PDF format, and there are links to latest issues of newsletters and upcoming events.

Seedco and Non-Profit Assistance Corporation (NY) (http://www.seedco.org)

Established in 1986 with a grant from the Ford Foundation, the New York City–Seedco and Non-Profit Assistance Corporation is a community development intermediary. The organization works to "provide technical and financial assistance to community-based organizations and local anchor institutions that are working in partnership to revitalize low-asset communities." Seedco, which affiliated with the Non-Profit Assistance Corporation in 1998, is now collaborating with universities, hospitals, community health centers, community foundations, youth-serving agencies, workforce development organizations, and government entities to catalyze partnerships in disadvantaged neighborhoods. The site includes a brief description of the organization, contact information, an electronic form to join an e-mail list of organization updates, news updates, and a link to the Seedco newsletter, *Fieldnotes.*

Selena Foundation (TX) (http://www.q-productions.com/selenaf.htm)

The Selena Foundation was established in 1995 with the funds donated to Selena's family following the death of the Tejano singer and songwriter. Based in Corpus Christi, Texas, the Selena Foundation operates under the mission to "offer the motivation that every child needs to complete their education, to live moral lives, to love their families, to respect human life and to sing whatever song they were born to sing." The Foundation's Web site provides information mainly for donors and lists a number of corporations that have provided funding. Contact information is available on the site.

Sertoma Foundation (MO) (http://www.sertoma.org)

Sertoma International is a volunteer civic service organization with about 27,000 members who belong to clubs in the United States, Canada, and Mexico. Based in Kansas City, Missouri, Sertoma stands for Service To Mankind. The Foundation's primary service project is helping the more than 42 million people with speech and hearing disorders. The Sertoma Foundation was established in 1960 to "raise, invest and distribute funds to support the approved charitable programs of Sertoma and LaSertoma International." The Foundation depends upon annual membership gifts from individuals and clubs and earnings from endowment gifts to support its charitable works. The Web site provides information on the latest club news, upcoming events and service projects, information on how to join or make a gift, and contact information.

Seva Foundation (CA) (http://www.seva.org/)

The Seva Foundation, located in Berkeley, California, was founded in 1978 by a group of people who had powerful experiences in the work that led to the eradication of small pox. The Foundation "is dedicated to finding skillful means to relieve suffering." While the Foundation is not guided by any specific ideology or religious affiliation, it does have some principles that it follows, such as affirming the rational and the intuitive in its work and respecting the spiritual and cultural roots of the individuals and communities it seeks to help. The Foundation began as an organization working on international health problems; now, the Foundation's programs address the needlessly blind in India and Nepal; indigenous culture, sustainable agriculture and micro enterprise in Guatemala and Chiapas; and the epidemic of diabetes on Native American reservations. More information on the Foundation's vision and the specific programs in each international area is available on the site.

Share Our Strength (DC) (http://www.strength.org/)

Share Our Strength was started in the basement of a row house on Capitol Hill in 1984 by a group of people who organized chefs to volunteer to cook for fundraisers. Today, it is one of the nation's largest anti-hunger, anti-poverty organizations. The organization "mobilizes individuals and industries to use their talents to raise funds and awareness for the fight against hunger and poverty." The organization has a broad range of programs and events, all of which are described in detail on the organization's Web site. One of the most recent undertakings of Share Our Strength is Community Wealth Ventures, which began in 1997 and provides strategic counsel to corporations, foundations, and nonprofit organizations interested in creating community wealth (resources generated through profitable enterprise to promote social change). The focus of Share Our Strength is on both short–and long–term solutions to the hunger and poverty issues. The site includes more information about its programs and partnerships.

Shinnyo-En Foundation (CA) (http://www.sef.org/)

Also known as Buddhists for World Harmony, the Shinnyo-En Foundation is based in San Francisco, California, and was founded in 1994 as the grantmaking arm of the Shinnyo-En U.S.A. Order. The Foundation's mission is to "bring forth deeper compassion among humankind, to promote greater harmony, and to nurture future generations toward building a more ethical society." The Foundation's Web site includes an overview of its funding process: the Foundation does not accept unsolicited proposals but welcomes letters of inquiry from potential applicants. Additionally, the Web site lists recent and active grants, as well as recent small contributions that detail specific areas of interest for the Foundation. More information about Shinnyo-En, contact information, and a map of the Foundation's location are available online.

The Sierra Club Foundation (CA) (http://www.sierraclub.org/foundation/)

The Sierra Club Foundation funds charitable, scientific, artistic, and educational endeavors of the Sierra Club and other environmental organizations. The page of the Sierra Club's Web site devoted to the Foundation offers a description of the organization and examples of funding projects.

Silicon Valley Realtors Charitable Foundation (CA) (http://www.siliconvalley-realtors.org)

The Silicon Valley Realtors Charitable Foundation is located in Los Altos, California. It is a trust that makes grants available from donations made by members and friends. The Foundation is committed to "the welfare and prosperity of the communities where we live and work" and aims to "help create more productive and enriched communities." The Foundation considers applications from all nonprofit organizations operating within the jurisdictional boundaries of the Silicon Valley Association of Realtors. Special consideration is given to those organizations involved in housing or education issues. The Foundation's Web site can be reached through a link on the Silicon Valley Association of Realtors homepage. Guidelines and deadlines are available online, along with information about the application, which can be downloaded from the Web site in PDF format.

The Sisters of Charity Foundation of South Carolina (SC) (http://www.sistersofcharitysc.com)

The Sisters of Charity Foundation is a faith-based organization, deeply rooted in the principles of the Gospel and the Catholic Church. It is a ministry of the Sisters of Charity of St. Augustine. The Foundation is committed to "efforts which help build a sustainable, healthy economy; promote educational success; support stronger families; and contribute to long-term community development." The Foundation uses its own resources, including making grants to eligible organizations. It also mobilizes the resources of others, especially through partnerships, to confront the fundamental causes of poverty and reduce its impact in South Carolina. Nonprofit organizations located in South Carolina whose programs and projects coincide with the mission of the Foundation are encouraged to apply for grants. A list of the types of grants the Foundation awards, along with contact information for those interested in learning more about or applying for grants, is available on the site. The Foundation's Web site also provides links to other organizations, related publications, and a calendar of events.

Social Science Research Council (NY) (http://www.ssrc.org/)

The Social Science Research Council of New York City was founded in 1923. The international association is devoted to "the advancement of interdisciplinary research in the social sciences . . . through a wide variety of interdisciplinary workshops and conferences, fellowships and grants, summer training institutes, scholarly exchanges, and publications." Fellowships and grants are given out on the pre-dissertation, dissertation, and post-doctoral levels and short-term programs are sponsored for younger students. The subject areas vary from European to Middle Eastern countries and from sexuality and migration to economics. Each of the fellowships and grants works with a committee or program of the Council's. There are descriptions, guidelines, and application deadlines for each of the scholarships. There are also descriptions of each of the programs throughout the world. The site includes a staff list with phone numbers and e-mail addresses, and a publications list.

Society of Manufacturing Engineers Education Foundation (MI) (http://www.sme.org/cgi-bin/smeefhtml.pl?/foundation/homepg.htm&SME&)

The Society of Manufacturing Engineers is a professional membership organization for career development. SME's Education Foundation makes grants of $50,000–$500,000 that target "competency gaps" in manufacturing identified by SME's Manufacturing Education Plan. Programs should involve local industry and encompass interdisciplinary university education. The Education Foundation area of SME's Web site provides an outline of its grant program, including guidelines; an application form; recent funding results; a list of board members; donor information; related links; and contact information.

Sons of Italy Foundation (DC) (http://www.osia.org/public/foundation.htm)

The Sons of Italy Foundation, established in 1959, supports programs to preserve Italian-American culture, encourage educational excellence, and support transatlantic initiatives for diplomatic, economic, and educational exchanges. The Foundation's Web site provides information on its National Leadership Grant Competition—comprising several scholarship programs—along with application forms to download and profiles of last year's scholarship winners. The Foundation's other philanthropic activities, described briefly on the site, include medical research for genetic diseases, provision of homes for orphans, aid to victims of natural disasters, forums on international issues, strengthening of communities through law enforcement projects, and sponsorship of special programs of national and international significance.

South Dakota Humanities Council (SD) (http://web.sdstate.edu/humanities/)

The South Dakota Humanities Council of Brookings, South Dakota, was created by the National Endowment for the Humanities in 1972. The Council's goal is to "explore and promote state, and national programs focusing on ideas, history, and culture." The main areas of grant activity are the Humanities Discussion Group, in which the out-of-school public and scholars in the humanities take part in a participatory learning experience about issues of interest to the general citizenry, and the Humanities Institutes for Schoolteachers, which bring together humanities scholars and elementary school teachers to deepen the teachers' humanities teaching experience. The Media Program funds all phases in the development of a product that will encourage public outreach in the humanities. The Research Program for Humanities Scholars encourages scholarly research on topics relating to the history and culture of South Dakota. The Council Initiatives include literacy, support for the state's American Indians, and programs for older state citizens. Special "Council Conducted Programs" include the Speakers Bureau, which funds visits from leading state authorities to groups throughout the state to speak about the humanities, and the Significant Literature Reading Series, which takes place in libraries throughout the state. Visitors to the Web site will find application deadlines and guidelines, an electronic application form, and a budget form. Grant program information can be found under the Publications headline in the Program Guidelines section. There is a separate application for the Speakers Bureau. The extensive site also includes a list of publications, a directory of scholars, links to the NEH and other state councils, and a list of the board members. There are grant lists as well as opportunities to make donations.

Southern Arts Federation (GA) (http://www.southarts.org)

The Atlanta-based Southern Arts Federation is itself supported by the National Endowment for the Arts and holds as its mission to "[enhance] the professional skills of southern arts organizations and artists, and [broaden] the appreciation and support of the arts in the South among policy makers and audiences." The Federation's commitment is to arts education, multiculturalism, and indigenous southern arts and underserved communities through its efforts in five areas: arts partnerships, professional development, southern arts and culture, arts education, and art advocacy. The Federation has two main funding categories focused on advocacy, information and communication, and training: the NEA/SAF Regional Touring Program and Meet the Composer/South. Extensive program guidelines and grant applications for these programs can be downloaded in PDF format from the Federation's Web site. Links, further funding information, and contact information are also available online.

Southern Education Foundation (GA) (http://www.sefatl.org/)

The Southern Education Foundation was formed in 1937—through the merger of four funds committed to developing educational opportunities for minorities and disadvantaged citizens following the Civil War—to help achieve equal educational opportunities for minority students. The Foundation operates programs with funding partners that focus on teacher preparation, student opportunity and performance, educational equity and opportunity, socioeconomic factors affecting equity, and community enrichment. The Foundation supports programs in collaboration with funding partners, which are listed at its Web site (with links to those with Web sites). Grant lists are provided for each program, along with information on the Foundation's activities, history, and contact information.

Southwest Minnesota Foundation (http://www.swmnfoundation.org/)

The Southwest Minnesota Foundation (SWMF) was created in the early 1980s through an idea of the McKnight Foundation after a realization that communities in greater Minnesota were in need of support due to declining farming and mining economies. The mission of SWMF is to be a catalyst, facilitating opportunities for economic, social, and cultural growth by promoting philanthropy, leadership, innovation, and collaboration for the 18 counties of southwest Minnesota. Program interests include people of color, youth initiatives, aging, family support, and business development. SWMF also has a number of loan programs aimed at start–up or expanding businesses that will create employment by generating new wealth and diversifying the economy of southwest Minnesota. Visit the Foundation's elegant Web site to view specific program information, grant guidelines, restricted grant areas, specific areas of support, board/staff listings, and contact information.

Special Libraries Association (DC) (http://www.sla.org/)

The Special Libraries Association seeks to be "a catalyst in the development of the information economy, and a strategic partner in the emerging information society." To that end, SLA has set research goals related to the topics of futures, current/user issues, measures of productivity and value, client/user satisfaction measures, and staffing. SLA awards grants through the Steven I. Goldspiel Memorial Research Fund to support research on and advancement of library sciences. SLA's Web site provides guidelines, an application form to print out, and information on recent recipients and their projects, publications, and links to other funding sources. Contact information for Research as well as the SLA Scholarship, can be found in the Association Information: SLA Unit Leadership: SLA Committees section.

Spirits of the Land Foundation (OK) (http://greatspirit.earth.com/)

The Spirits of the Land Foundation supports education and activities benefiting state and federally recognized Indian tribes, bands, and nations and supports scientific research to benefit humanity and Earth. The Foundation's Web site provides news, Indian resources and business opportunities, Indian attractions in Oklahoma, and mailing addresses of tribes and leaders. Although the site doesn't provide much detail on the research it supports, contact information is provided.

Sponsors of Musical Enrichment, Inc. (CA) (http://www.someinc.com)

Sponsors of Musical Enrichment, Inc. was founded in California in 1978. It exists for the purpose of "supporting local youth organizations and the performing arts on a continuing basis." The Sponsors of Musical Enrichment also provide deserving students of the musical and performing arts with programs like the Drum Corps International, national scholarships, and competitions. There is a list of the types of scholarships given, as well as a mailing and e-mail address for those interested in learning more. In addition, the site has a calendar of events with upcoming concerts and information on how to obtain tickets.

State Medical Society Foundation, Inc. (WI)
(http://www.wismed.com/foundation/found.htm)

The State Medical Society Foundation was charted by the Wisconsin State Medical Society in 1955 as a nonprofit corporation to enable physicians and other friends of the profession to support projects vitally affecting scientific medicine and public health. Since then, its financial resources and scope have grown immensely. Today, its mission is to "direct its leadership toward assisting deserving medical students though the student loan program and scholarships, to fostering the knowledge and development of worthy educational, charitable, research and scientific projects which lead to improved public health and medical care." The Foundation's Web site lists all of the loans and scholarships that students are eligible to apply for, along with information about applications and deadlines. Note that some awards are limited to those attending school in Wisconsin. The Foundation also awards grants for public healthcare initiatives; descriptions and guidelines are listed on the site.

Rudolf Steiner Foundation (CA) (http://www.rsfoundation.org/)

Established in 1984, the Rudolf Steiner Foundation is a progressive financial service organization that supports social and environmental change, particularly the kinds of change inspired by Rudolf Steiner, best known as the founder of Waldorf Education and biodynamic farming. The Foundation's basic work is to connect philanthropists and investors with worthy projects in need of grants or loans. The areas in which the Foundation supports research and activities include education and the arts, science and caring for the earth, social responsibility and mutual support, medical and religious renewal, and associative economic relationships. The Foundation, located in San Francisco, California, carries out its charitable activity on a worldwide basis through its gift, grant, and loan fund programs. The Web site provides contact information for those interested in learning more about the Foundation's programs and services.

Sundance Institute (UT) (http://www.sundance.org)

Established in 1981 at the behest of Robert Redford, the Sundance Institute has administrative and programmatic offices in Salt Lake City, Utah, and Los Angeles, California, while most events take place in Park City, Utah. The organization is "dedicated to the support and development of emerging screenwriters and directors of vision, and to the national and international exhibition of new, independent dramatic and documentary films." Although many associate the name Sundance only with the annual independent film festival that it sponsors, the Institute also sponsors competitive laboratories, fellowships, and screenings and lectures. The major program areas that these components fall under are feature film, international, theater, Native American, composing, and writing. Each of these topics includes a variety of elements. Each category has its own page with descriptions of each program, applications that can be printed from the screen, application guidelines and deadlines, and lists of past recipients/participants. The site also includes information on the Sundance archives at UCLA, volunteering at events (with applications online), and a calendar of events. There is also a special area on Sundance Kids, a youth initiative that includes internships and teacher training.

Suntory Water Group, Inc (GA)
(http://www.suntorywatergroup.com/about_us/cor1515_inthecom.asp)

The Atlanta, Georgia-based Suntory Water Group maintains ties with the community by sponsoring a number of healthy living events nationwide. These events include programs for Drink to Your Good Health Month, inaugurated in 1999, regarding drinking the proper amount of water each day; the Good Health Advisory Board, providing experts for health and medical advice; and a bottle recycling program. More information about these community contributions are available on the Suntory Water Group's Web site, which is best viewed using the Netscape browser.

Surfrider Foundation (CA) (http://www.surfrider.org/)

The Surfrider Foundation is a non-profit environmental organization "dedicated to the protection and enjoyment of the world's oceans, waves and beaches for all people, through conservation, activism, research and education." Surfrider, founded in 1984 and based in San Clemente, California, now has well over 40 chapters located along the East, West, Gulf, Puerto Rican, and Hawaiian coasts and over 25,000 members in the United States; in addition, International Surfrider chapters and affiliates have been established in 4 foreign countries: Japan, Brazil, France, and Australia. Surfrider has several programs, among which is the Thomas Pratte Memorial Scholarship fund, named after the Foundation's co-founder and established to promote academic research of the coastal environment. The Foundation also has a national bimonthly publication, *MAKING WAVES,* which can be found online and is an additional public outreach and educational outreach tool the Foundation uses. Articles published in *MAKING WAVES* cover subjects such as current coastal issues, Surfrider Chapter news, and coastal scientific reports. Descriptions of all of its programs, contact information, a feedback page, links to chapters, publications, and the Foundation's strategic plan, can be found on its Web site. Among other items in this packed site is an Education section, which helps visitors perform research and find information.

TAPPI Foundation, Inc. (GA)
(http://www.tappi.org/public/foundation/foundation_main.asp)

Created in 1990 by the Technical Association of the Pulp and Paper Industry to support research and education, the TAPPI Foundation awards research grants to scientists and engineers for projects that will assist in securing the future of the paper and pulp industries. Research needs of the industry are available for download in PDF format on the Foundation's Web site. The Foundation encourages proposal submissions from newcomers to the industry. The site also provides guidelines, the application in PDF format, 1997 award recipients, grant executive summaries, and a funding evaluation form.

R.J. Taylor, Jr. Foundation (GA) (http://www.taylorfoundation.org/)

The R.J. Taylor, Jr. Foundation, based in Atlanta, was founded in 1971 to "promote genealogical research and study in Georgia in conjunction with the Georgia Genealogical Society and the Georgia Department of Archives and History." The Foundation is dedicated to the promotion of genealogical research and study in Georgia by the use of public and private records and the methods of indexing, abstracting, and historical research. The Foundation's goal is to preserve and publish these genealogical works. Visitors to the Foundation's Web site will find grant requirements, guidelines for producing publications, an application that can be filled out online and printed, a publication search guide, and links and library resources for more information.

A Territory Resource Foundation (WA) (http://www.atrfoundation.org/)

Based in Seattle, Washington, A Territory Resource Foundation strives to "create a more equitable, just, and environmentally sound society for all" by providing limited financial support to activist, community-based organizations in the states of Idaho, Montana, Oregon, Washington, and Wyoming. In addition to grant guidelines and a list of recent grantees, visitors to the ATR Web site will find a brief history of the Foundation, a copy of the director's report, a short essay on socially responsible investing, and donor information.

Texas Bar Foundation (TX) (http://www.txbf.org)

The Texas Bar Foundation, located in Austin, is dedicated to "promoting the ends of justice through education and charitable activities which improve the administration of our legal system . . . which advance public education and understanding of our judicial system . . . and which are sensitive to the needs of the public as well as the legal profession." The Foundation funds four program areas: legal assistance to the poor and disadvantaged, legal and public education on the court system and legal process, legal aid facilities, and experimental projects in an area that needs seed money. The Foundation's Web site includes application guidelines, deadlines and restrictions, and the application itself, which can be printed from the screen. Visitors will also find a list of various board and committee members, lists of previous grantees, and a thorough page of related links. For an interesting view into the Foundation's mission, the Texas Lawyer's Creed is also posted.

Texas Council for the Humanities (TX) (http://www.public-humanities.org/)

The Texas Council for the Humanities, established in 1972, works with the National Endowment for the Humanities to encourage the people of Texas to engage in "critical reflection on their individual and collective lives by providing opportunities for lifelong learning in the humanities." TCH's grant program provides financial support to nonprofit organizations and institutions for public educational humanities programs through Packaged Programs and Speakers Grants, Community Projects Grants, General Grants, and Media Grants. TCH's Web site provides guidelines and a printable form for ordering application forms by mail or fax. The site also provides information about its activities, publications, and donors, as well as listings of board and staff members and related links.

Theatre Communications Group (NY) (http://www.tcg.org/)

Theatre Communications Group was founded in 1961 to provide artistic, administrative, and information services to theaters and independent theater artists. TCG collaborates with the National Endowment for the Arts to offer a residency program for playwrights and career development programs for directors and designers. Guidelines for these programs are provided at TCG's Web site. TCG also offers extended collaboration grants to fund research and developmental time for playwrights and collaborating artists, as well as National Theatre Artist Residency grants. Although information at the site on these programs and about the Foundation in general is limited, contact information, including e-mail, is provided.

Third Wave, Inc. (NY) (http://www.thirdwavefoundation.org)

Third Wave is a New York City-based association of activist young women and me connecting young women to "the resources necessary to counter attacks on their personal freedoms," striving to combat inequalities and to become a nationwide foundation supporting young women's activism. Third Wave funds scholarships and organizing and advocacy grants with the general interests of reproductive rights, economic education and microenterprise, philanthropic education, and leadership training. Scholarships are intended for college students or future college students, age 30 or younger, who are activists, artists, or cultural workers active on issues of inequality. There is an online general information form to apply for scholarships. Grants are intended for nonprofit organizations headed by women 15–30 years old, with an emphasis on low-income women, differently-abled women, women of color, and lesbian and bisexual women. An application is available on Third Wave's Web site for grants consideration, as is contact information for further inquiries.

The TIA Foundation (DC) (http://www.tia.org/whatsTIA/found.stm)

The TIA Foundation was founded in 1990 to benefit the U.S. travel industry by supporting education and research vital to the concerns of the industry. The Foundation awards yearly graduate and undergraduate scholarships. Although the Foundation's Web site does not provide application information, it does list its board members and contact information.

The Tides Foundation (CA) (http://www.tides.org/)

The Tides Foundation of San Francisco, California, was established in 1976 and is part of the Tides family of organizations. The group "partners with donors to increase and organize resources for social change. We facilitate effective grantmaking programs, create opportunities for learning, and build community among donors and grantees." Grants are made from Donor Advised Funds that the Foundation manages. Each fund supports organizations in its donor's area of interest, from civic participation, economic development, environment, and HIV/AIDS to Native American communities, women's issues/reproductive health, and youth programs. Less than five percent of unsolicited proposals are funded. The site includes a list of the board of directors, a list of key staff, information on donations, and basic application guidelines, including a letter of inquiry cover sheet. There is also currently an RFP for and information about the Community Clinics Initiative, which works to "to strengthen community clinics' information systems throughout California." Visitors can also find Foundation newsletters and a calendar of events.

The Touch 'em All Foundation (CO) (http://www.touchemall.com)

Based in Denver, Colorado, the Touch 'em All Foundation was co-founded by country music performer Garth Brooks in 1999. Teaming with over a hundred major league baseball players, the Foundation makes grants and donations based on game performance (for instance, specific dollar amounts are donated for home runs, strikeouts, etc.). The Foundation's emphasis is on children's charities, mainly in health; education; and inner city needs. The Web site provides an overview of the Foundation's operations, with listings of the major league baseball players and celebrities involved; grant guidelines; limitations; and a listing of board and staff members. Donations to the Foundation can be made online or through the purchase of a special credit card or phone card. There is currently no contact information provided on the site.

Trust Fund for Children with Special healthcare Needs (MI)
(http://www.mdch.state.mi.us/msa/cshcs/)

The Trust Fund for Children with Special healthcare Needs began in 1944 with a generous bequest of Dow Chemical Company stock by Dr. and Mrs. James T. Pardee; Dr. Pardee was the founder of Dow Chemical Company. The Trust Fund "helps pay for services and projects for children with special healthcare needs not provided by other healthcare funds." The fund supports unique services and programs for special needs children and their families and caregivers that promote optimal health and development. Specifically, the Fund has three areas of giving: services for children, assistance to groups, and improving service systems. Details about each giving area are available on the site. Only Michigan residents can apply for funding. Families with a child enrolled in or eligible to enroll in the Children Special healthcare Services Program can apply. Organizations or groups serving children with special healthcare needs may also apply for grants. To apply, you must contact the Fund; phone numbers are listed on the Web site. The site also gives details on the Fund's history, as well of a listing of the Fund's Committee members.

Turner Amyotrophic Lateral Sclerosis Foundation, Les (IL) (http://www.lesturnerals.org/)

The Les Turner Amyotrophic Lateral Sclerosis Foundation of Skokie, Illinois, was created in 1977 by a patient and his family. The organization is "devoted to the treatment and elimination of amyotrophic lateral sclerosis (ALS), better known as Lou Gehrig's disease . . . and supports the ALS community in Chicago and its suburbs." Among other grantees, the Foundation funds research, the Lois Insolia ALS Center (a clinic affiliated with Northwestern University Medical School), a tissue bank, support groups, and many educational programs. The Web site includes information and links to more resources on ALS, information on the low-cost services the Foundation offers, and updates on different research projects. There are also features on relevant legislation and alerts for special events. There are descriptions of different programs funded by the Foundation and ample opportunities to contribute.

Uncommon Legacy Foundation, Inc. (NY) (http://www.uncommonlegacy.org/)
Uncommon Legacy Foundation was founded in 1990 to enhance the visibility, strength, and vitality of the lesbian community. The Foundation awards scholarships to openly lesbian students with leadership potential and funds projects and organizations that contribute to the health, education, and culture of the lesbian community. The Foundation's Web site provides grant guidelines and a downloadable application form in PDF format, scholarship guidelines and a list of most recent scholarship recipients, an online version of the Foundation's newsletter, and information for prospective donors.

Union League Civic & Arts Foundation (IL) (http://www.ulcc.org/)
The Union League Civic & Arts Foundation, one of three philanthropic efforts of the Union League Club of Chicago, was established in 1949 to contribute to the cultural and civic well being of the Chicago metropolitan area. The Foundation awards grants to community organizations and scholarships to young people enrolled in visual arts and music programs; in recent years its grantmaking activities have totaled roughly $140,000 annually. The Foundation's single page on the Union League Club Web site gives a brief description of its activities and a telephone number to call for more information.

United Board for Christian Higher Education in Asia (NY) (http://www.unitedboard.org)
The United Board for Christian Higher Education in Asia was chartered by the Regents of the University of the State of New York to assist with higher education in Asian countries. From its origins in 1922, the board's mission has always been "the support of higher education in Asia from the perspective of the Christian faith." The Board works with selected schools in Asia to support, among many programs, scholarly exchanges within Asia and between Asia and the West; academic training for faculty; strengthening libraries, curricula, and research; and professional development for administrators. The very informative site includes lists of supported schools, the board and staff, selected programs, and information on a major alumni program. There is information on contributing and contact information, including directions. The board does not accept unsolicited proposals.

United Hospital Fund (NY) (http://www.uhfnyc.org/)
Created in 1879, the United Hospital Fund of New York City is the oldest federated charity in the country. The group is a "health services research and philanthropic organization that addresses critical issues affecting hospitals and healthcare in New York City." There are a variety of grant programs for hospitals, nursing homes, and healthcare, academic, and public interest organizations. The Palliative Care Initiative is in its second year in five major hospitals. The Families and healthcare Project distributes funds to support the development of innovative programs and resources for assisting family caregivers. Gifts from the Special Project Fund are "intended to increase access to and use of appropriate, high quality, and efficient healthcare services, especially for low-income and other vulnerable persons." The Hospital Auxiliary and Volunteer Program encourages projects that involve adults and youth in volunteer activities that promote better health. General Support funding is divided between not-for-profit hospitals, depending on their ambulatory and inpatient statistics. The Nursing Home Grant Program is an initiative to support quality-of-life improvements. The Fund also supports research and policy initiative. The Special Projects Fund is currently open for applications. Guidelines and deadlines are available online and an application can be downloaded in PDF format. There are grant lists for each program, the annual report, and staff and board lists. The site offers a publications list and information on contributing.

United Nations Foundation (DC) (http://www.unfoundation.org)
The United Nations Foundation, located in Washington, D.C., was founded by Ted Turner "to support the goals and objectives of the United Nations and its Charter, in order to promote a more peaceful, prosperous and just world—with special emphasis on the UN's work on behalf of economic, social, environmental and humanitarian causes." The Foundation has four areas of particular interest: women and population, children's health, the environment, and humanitarian causes. The Foundation engages in four primary activities in pursuit of its mission: providing additional funding for programs and people served by UN agencies, strengthening UN institutions and encouraging support for the UN and UN causes, sponsoring or conducting outreach efforts aimed at educating the public about the UN, and raising new funds to support UN programs and purposes. The Foundation works collaboratively with the UN in program development and does not accept unsolicited proposals. Visitors to the Web site will find information about the United Nations Foundation's priority issues, projects, grant lists, on line news briefings about the UN, links to the UN and its agencies, and an online contact form.

United States Institute of Peace (DC) (http://www.usip.org/)
The Washington, D.C.-based United States Institute of Peace was established in 1984. The organization's mission is "to strengthen the nation's capabilities to promote the peaceful resolution of international conflicts." Grants support research, education, pilot projects and training, and the dissemination of information on international peace and conflict resolution. The group's two major grant programs are solicited and unsolicited grants. The four topics being funded through the solicited program in 2000 are "Great Power Relations: The United States, China, and Russia;" Intervention and Humanitarian Assistance; Africa; and Training. The unsolicited grants cover varied areas of interest, including international conflict and its resolution, issues of nonviolence, and human rights. The Institute also sponsors the Jennings Randolph Program for International Peace, which offers Senior Fellowships and Peace Scholar Dissertation Fellowships to people conducting research on important issues concerning international conflict and peace. The site includes grant guidelines and deadlines and downloadable applications for all three of the aforementioned programs. There is a database of past grants and a description of the review process. There are lists of former fellows, their products, and information on being a research assistant. The site also offers a list of publications, descriptions of the education and training programs, and links to related resources.

US Soccer Foundation (DC) (http://www.ussoccerfoundation.org/)
Based in Washington, D.C., the US Soccer Foundation was created in 1993 and began distributing funds in 1995. The organization's mission is to "enhance, assist and grow the sport of soccer." Grants are focused in three major areas: urban programming, field development, and player development. Within these categories, the Foundation looks for programs that will work to establish a high level of soccer for the long-term; develop the sport where it didn't have a strong presence; encourage gender equity and participation by the economically disadvantaged, physically challenged, and mentally disadvantaged; and teach health and physical education through soccer. Organizations that fall within these goals will find the application online, along with guidelines and helpful FAQs. There are lists of the staff, board of directors, and recent grantees available. The site also features a Resource Center that includes support for developing a soccer project.

Utah Humanities Council (UT) (http://www.utahhumanities.org)
The Utah Humanities Council, the state affiliate of the National Endowment for the Humanities, promotes learning through the humanities. UHC provides grants and technical assistance to nonprofit organizations and a limited number of individual grants to teachers and scholars. Grant programs include competitive grants to nonprofits up to $5,000, "quick grants" for smaller projects, Teacher Incentive Program grants of $500, and an annual $3,000 research fellowship. Guidelines and application forms (in PDF, Word Perfect, and Microsoft Word formats) can be viewed and downloaded at UHC's Web site. Visitors to the

site will also find online versions of the most recent annual report (in PDF format) and newsletter, details of UHC's activities, and contact and donor information.

V Foundation (NC) (http://www.jimmyv.org/)
Founded by the late Jim Valvano and ESPN, the cable sports network, the V Foundation seeks to raise awareness of and support for cancer research. Although grant information on the Foundation's Web site is limited to a list of recent grant recipients, visitors to the site can read about the life and times of Jimmy "V," learn more about events staged in support of the Foundation, and sign up for e-mail updates about the Foundation and its activities.

Vanguard Public Foundation (CA) (http://www.vanguardsf.org)
Created in 1972, the Vanguard Public Foundation is located in San Francisco, California. This "partnership of community activists and donors has distributed [funds] to organizations and projects that work to achieve a more equitable distribution of power and resources in our society." Grantees are located in northern California, in counties north of Monterey. The Foundation is interested in programs that try to change the underlying causes of injustice and poverty, involve the self-determination of low-income and working class people, work toward a prejudice-free society, and incorporate affirmative action practices. Areas of interest include issues of civil rights, economic justice, workers' rights, women's rights, education, disability, health, housing, environment, cultural activism, indigenous peoples' rights, and international solidarity. The site includes application guidelines and instructions, information on donating to the Foundation, and a staff list.

Virginia Foundation for the Humanities (VA) (http://www.virginia.edu/vfh)
Established in 1974, the Virginia Foundation for the Humanities is based at the University of Virginia in Charlottesville. The organization is "dedicated to developing and supporting research, education, and public programs in the humanities . . . [and how this] contributes to the interpretation and understanding of cultural traditions, and to the understanding of current policy debates." The VFH Grant Program supports organizations in Virginia, or those that will have an impact on a large population of Virginians, that are involved in areas of humanities, including the study of history, literature, ethics, philosophy, culture, religion, and folk traditions. The Foundation is looking for projects that increase humanities-based public programs that respond to a demonstrated need in the community. The Grant Program has special categories for film and video, teacher institutes, digital media, and discretionary grants. The site includes application guidelines, deadlines, and application forms and coversheets that can be downloaded in PDF format. There is also the African-American Heritage Trails Program, which includes a grant program specifically for projects related to African-American history in the state. Another division of the Foundation, the Virginia Center for the Humanities, includes a scholar-in-residence program. These fellowships support scholars who conduct their own research while also contributing to the Foundation's work. The fellowship application and a schedule of public presentations by fellows can be downloaded in PDF format. The Web site is attractive and full of information on programs, grant opportunities, and ongoing research projects. There is a list of featured grant recipients and links to the regional councils and bureaus throughout the state.

Virginia healthcare Foundation (VA) (http://www.vhcf.org/)
The Virginia healthcare Foundation (VHCF) funds local public-private partnerships that increase access to primary healthcare services for uninsured and medically underserved residents of the commonwealth. The VHCF promotes and funds local public-private partnerships that increase access to primary healthcare services for medically underserved and uninsured Virginian's. VHCF supports projects that offer innovative primary care service delivery, increase primary care providers in target areas, incorporate telemedicine initiatives, and/or replicate VHCF's "Models That Made It"—programs that have proven to be cost effective and capable of sustaining themselves. The VHCF Web site offers descriptions of the Foundation's funding categories, FAQs, grant guidelines, a listing of board and staff members, and information for donors.

Visual Aid Artists for AIDS Relief (CA) (http://www.visualaid.org)
An arts nonprofit, Visual Aid of San Francisco is committed to "encouraging visual artists with life-threatening illness to continue their creative work by providing a variety of direct services." These services include a Voucher Program, which distributes certificates that can be redeemed at participating art and photo supply stores; the ArtBank, which distributes donated art supplies; the Studio Assistant Program, which connects volunteer helpers with artists; and the Arts Services Program, which organizes relevant workshops. The organization's Web site includes lists of contributors, an events schedule, and information on volunteering.

Wampum (WA) (http://www.wampum.org/)
Wampum of Spokane, Washington, is a nonprofit public charity interested in making the arts a part of everyday life to the people of Spokane. Annually around 20 Spokane area arts and culture organizations receive grants from the charity. Wampum is also dedicated to providing opportunities for children in the community to participate in and realize the value of the arts. All grants made by Wampum are unrestricted and can be utilized for any purpose that supports the mission of grantee's organization. For many arts and cultural organizations, this type of support is often critical to their continuing survival. Wampum's Web site includes a listing of officers and trustees, a historical look at past presidents, a listing of past grant recipients, and contact information.

Washington AIDS Partnership (DC) (http://www.wrag.org/rfp.html)
Founded in 1989, the AIDS Partnership in now housed and administered by the Washington, D.C., Regional Association of Grantmakers (WRAG). The group is a "collaboration of grantmaking organizations whose goals are to mobilize and sustain private funding to address the AIDS epidemic in the Washington metropolitan area, to improve coordination and communication between key players in the fight against HIV/AIDS, and to provide support and technical assistance to community-based organizations working in HIV/AIDS prevention and care." Priority is given to organizations that effectively educate targeted, culturally-appropriate populations on HIV prevention. Underfunded service groups and groups needing technical assistance are also considered. The site includes a list of funding partners and past application guidelines and deadlines.

Washington Commission for the Humanities (WA) (http://www.humanities.org/)
The Washington Commission for the Humanities supports humanities projects—which it defines as "the stories, ideas and writings that help us make sense of our lives and enhance our ability to think creatively and critically about our world"—in Washington State. Grants are awarded for a range of programs and activities, including exhibits, public forums, school programs, reading and discussion series, and cultural events. The WCH Web site provides grant guidelines—applicants are encouraged to contact WCH before applying—along with information about past recipients. WCH also gives two annual awards: the Washington Humanities Award and the Governor's Writers Award. Eligibility requirements are provided on the site.

Washington Health Foundation (WA) (http://www.whf.org)
Based in Olympia, Washington, "the Washington Health Foundation exists to improve health and access to quality healthcare for the people of Washington through leadership in education, research and services." This mission is achieved through affiliations with the Washington State Hospital Association, Washington Hospital Services, the Association of Washington Public Hospital Districts, and the Health Information Program. The Foundation administers healthcare access programs throughout the state to help people get the care that they need and the resources to pay for it. The Foundation offers details and application information on state-sponsored and privately run programs, including the AIDS/HIV Care Access Project, the Basic Health Plan, Community Access programs, and a kids health initiative. The Foundation also supports the state's rural hospitals and has created a resource center of relevant information and links. The WHF publishes a bi-monthly newsletter, much of which is available online; county health statistics; and other newsletters and

brochures on project subjects. The Web site includes a survey for visitors to track their health, selected information from annual reports, and a list of staff members, including their e-mail addresses.

Washington Software Foundation (WA) (http://www.wsf-wa.org/)
The Washington Software Foundation is committed to closing the technology gap in Washington State at-risk schools and communities. Programs seek to introduce technology in the lives of students, parents, and teachers who may not have access in their daily lives. The Foundation supports a New Technology Partnership grant and an Innovation in Teaching Award and Fellowship. Both of these programs are detailed on the Foundation's Web site, along with funding guidelines, sample projects, an application that can be downloaded in PDF format for the grant, and guidelines and an application in rich text format for the award and fellowship. Examples of other projects undertaken by the Foundation and contact information are also available online. Visitors should be aware that funding is limited to Washington State.

Water Environment Research Foundation (VA) (http://www.werf.org)
Based in Alexandria, Virginia, the Water Environment Research Foundation (WERF) was created in the late 1980s with a loan from the Water Environment Federation. The organization works to help improve the quality of water by supporting research and educating the public. The Foundation accomplishes this by funding research and publishing the findings and by sponsoring workshops, newsletters, reports, papers, computer programs, and video presentations to disseminate the results. Research is performed by individual organizations or teams of researchers from utilities, universities, industrial and commercial firms, and the government. There are six research categories listed in the requests for proposals: unsolicited research, solicited research, emerging technologies, targeted collaborative research, peer review, and cooperative research. Requests for proposals for all of these categories are regularly posted on the Web site. Visitors to the site can also find in-depth information on submitting a proposal, along with the necessary forms, all of which can be viewed online or downloaded in PDF format. The Web site also has a section on the Foundation's publications and a great Visitor's Gallery, which includes contact information, board and staff lists, and information on volunteering. There is a special Clean Water Central area for WERF subscribers, which includes special data and research results online.

Wender-Weis Foundation for Children (http://www.wenderweis.org/)
Based in Palo Alto, California, the Wender-Weis Foundation for Children was founded in 1994 by Amy Wender to provide charitable relief and assistance to at-risk, disadvantaged children throughout the San Francisco Bay Area. Visit the site for contact information.

West Central Minnesota Initiative (MN) (http://www.wcif.org/)
The West Central Initiative was created to enhance the viablity of the west central Minnesota region through six funding initiatives: quality employment, workforce, housing, community, family, and economic development. The WCI Web site thoroughly details these initiatives and also provides more than a dozen downloadable application forms in PDF format. Where applications are not available, e-mail links are provided for requesting the forms via regular mail. In addition to its funding programs, the WCI site provides a variety of regional information, including links to community home pages.

Western States Arts Federation (CO) (http://www.westaf.org/)
The Western States Arts Federation, also known as WESTAF, supports state arts agencies, arts organizations, and artists in the western United States to promote creative advancement and preservation of the arts. Its current work centers on arts policy research, information systems development, and the convening of arts experts and leaders. Most program information is available in the News section of WESTAF's Web site. WESTAF also publishes *ArtJob,* a bi-monthly publication of national and international listings of arts employment and related opportunities in the Arts, which is available by subscription online or by regular mail.

The WHA Foundation, Inc. (WI) (http://www.wha.org/www/foundation/index.htm)
The WHA Foundation, based in Madison, Wisconsin, was established in 1968 to support health education activities. Foundation programs include scholarships for Native American students at the University of Wisconsin-Madison; a conference on bioethics and production of a videotape designed to improve physician/patient communication; the WHA Foundation's annual Global Vision Community Outreach Award, which recognize Wisconsin healthcare organizations for innovative approaches in addressing demonstrated community needs; and activities designed to encourage healthcare leadership opportunities for minorities. Visit the site for a complete overview of the Foundation's programs. Visitors to the site will find a grants list, downloadable and viewable Foundation reports, related links, and contact information.

WHAS Crusade for Children, Inc. (KY) (http://www.whas-crusade.org)
Based in Louisville, Kentucky, the WHAS Crusade for Children was first created in 1954. It is the "most successful single station telethon in the United States," raising money to aid in the care and treatment of handicapped children in Kentucky and southern Indiana. The Crusade is centered on a 30–plus hour broadcast on WHAS11 the first weekend in June, though donations are accepted year-round and are presented on "Crusade Weekend." Nonprofit agencies help special children apply for funds once a year from the Crusade. Each application is considered by a group of seven ministers, and a meeting is arranged with a representative of the agency. The ministers alone make the decision on how to fund each agency. Visitors to the site will find donation and contact information; a "report to the people," detailing which organizations received assistance; downloadable audio and video clips form past crusades; and a list of upcoming events.

Wheat Ridge Ministries (IL) (http://www.wheatridge.org/)
Wheat Ridge is an independent Lutheran charitable organization that provides seed money grants for new church-related "health and hope" ministries that address health-related issues through Christian service or prevent conditions that keep people from living full lives. Wheat Ridge awards Major Grants, Special Short-Term Grants, and Congregation Health and Hope Grants. The Ministries' Web site provides proposal guidelines; grantwriting resources; a list of grant recipients; news; Web, video, and fax resources; a listing of Wheat Ridge awards winners; and a listing of board and staff members.

Joseph B. Whitehead Foundation (GA) (http://www.jbwhitehead.org)
Joseph B. Whitehead, Jr. established the Joseph B. Whitehead Foundation in 1937 as a memorial to his father, one of the original bottlers of Coca-Cola. The Foundation was established to support charitable activities in Atlanta, Georgia, where the Foundation is located. The Foundation's grant program has a particular interest in basic human services, especially organizations and programs that benefit children and youth in metropolitan Atlanta; a recent focus is improving public education and family, children, and youth services. Preference is given to one-time capital projects. The Foundation shares offices and administrative staff with four other foundations (Robert W. Woodruff Foundation, Inc., Lettie Pate Whitehead Foundation, Inc., Lettie Pate Evans Foundation, Inc., and Ichauway, Inc.), so grant inquiries and proposals may be considered by one or more of the other foundations in this arrangement; it is also unnecessary to communicate separately with these foundations. Visitors to the Web site will find grant guidelines and application procedures, grants lists, links to other foundation resources, a brief biography of Joseph B. Whitehead, and contact information.

Lettie Pate Whitehead Foundation, Inc. (GA) (http://www.lpwhitehead.org)
Conkey Pate Whitehead, influenced by the generous example of his parents, provided in his will for the creation of the Lettie Pate Whitehead Foundation as a memorial to its namesake, his mother. The Foundation was chartered in 1946 to aid "poor and needy Christian girls and women" in nine states: Georgia, North Carolina, South Carolina, Virginia, Louisiana, Mississippi, Alabama, Tennessee, and Florida. Support is given in the form of grants to educational institutions in the nine states to fund scholarships for the education of

women. While most of the grants are used for undergraduate higher education, a significant number of grants are used to support education in the medical, nursing, and allied healthcare fields. In addition, operating grants are provided to a few select institutions serving the needs of elderly women in Georgia, Virginia, and North Carolina. Applications for individual scholarship aid should be made directly to the institutions. All inquiries from institutions eligible for Foundation support should be made to the president of the Foundation. Visit the Web site for more information about the Foundation's grant programs, a list of participating institutions, a biography of the founder and of its namesake, links to other foundations with which the Lettie Pate Whitehead Foundation shares a common administrative arrangement, links to other resources, and contact information.

The Elie Wiesel Foundation for Humanity (NY) (http://www.eliewieselfoundation.org)

The Elie Wiesel Foundation for Humanity was established by Elie Wiesel and his wife, Marion, after he was awarded the 1986 Nobel Prize for Peace. Based in New York City, the Foundation's mission, rooted in the memory of the Holocaust, is "to advance the cause of human rights by creating forums for the discussion and resolution of urgent ethical issues." In addition to international conferences and seminars that bring together leading scholars, artists, scientists, politicians, humanists, and young people from all over the world, the Foundation also sponsors an annual undergraduate essay contest. In Israel, the Foundation continues to expand its after-school centers, which are helping Ethiopian-Israeli children and adults achieve the educational standards needed to build successful lives. Through all its activities, the Foundation seeks to combat indifference, intolerance, and injustice. Guidelines and forms for the essay contest, both viewable and downloadable, are available on the site.

Woodrow Wilson National Fellowship Foundation (NJ) (http://www.woodrow.org/)

The Woodrow Wilson National Fellowship Foundation encourages excellence in education by developing and funding programs that target the needs of new teachers and scholars, that encourage cooperation between academia and other sectors of society, that improve the status and representation of minority groups and women, and that maintain the vitality of teachers. The Foundation offers numerous fellowships, grants, and scholarships in the humanities, public policy and international affairs, women's studies, children and women's health, and teacher development, all of which are described in detail at its Web site. Visitors to the site will also find an online version of the Foundation's most recent annual report, information about upcoming Foundation-sponsored conferences, press releases, listings of board and staff, and contact information.

The Wilson Research Foundation (MS) (http://www.mmrcrehab.org)

The Wilson Research Foundation is the research arm of the Jackson-based Mississippi Methodist Hospital & Rehabilitation Center. Established in 1988, the Foundation's mission is "to enhance the quality of life for the catastrophically disabled through medical, clinical and educational research." This is done through strategic grants to fund major scientific studies. More information can be obtained by contacting the Foundation from the address and e-mail provided on the Research portion of the Mississippi Methodist Rehabilitation Center site or by registering with MMRC.

The Windstar Foundation (CO) (http://www.wstar.org/)

Created in 1976 by singer/songwriter John Denver and Aikido master Tom Crum, the Windstar Foundation of Snowmass, Colorado, is an environmental education organization. The group works toward spreading "a holistic approach to addressing environmental concerns." Foundation funding goes toward the Windstar Connections Program, which supports regional, grassroots outreach programs that allow interested people to meet, network, and work together on projects addressing environmental awareness and leadership potential in citizens. It also supports an annual Educators Week conference for teachers to learn from environmental specialists. Information and registration for the 2000 conference is now online. The Foundation also produces educational materials that can be ordered through the site. Visitors will find information on the group's philosophy, founders, and the

Windstar Land Conservancy. There are opportunities to contribute and information on a nonviolence award received in 1999.

Wireless Foundation (DC) (http://www.wirelessfoundation.org/)

The Wireless Foundation of Washington, D.C., helps communities use wireless phones to enhance safety. The organization's goal is to "initiate and oversee strategic corporate philanthropic programs utilizing wireless communications to make communities safer, families more secure and teachers more effective." The group has three ongoing projects. A Call to Protect distributes wireless phones to victims of domestic violence and the professionals who support them. The victim's preprogrammed phones call for help at the push of one button. The site includes information on how to apply for a phone, how to donate a phone, and resources on domestic violence. Through ClassLink, wireless phones and airtime are donated to classrooms without access to telephones in order to advance the in-class learning. The site offers examples of how the phones are used in the classroom, results from successful projects, and contact information to request an application. Communities on Phone Patrol (COPP) donates wireless phones and airtime to volunteer neighborhood watch groups to increase the effectiveness of their efforts. Interested neighborhood watch groups can download an application in PDF format from the Web site. The Foundation is also currently sponsoring Wireless HELP for Disaster Relief, which sends a transportable, self-contained wireless network to locations suffering from disasters. The site also includes board and staff lists, a list of contributors, and a password–protected area for members.

Wisconsin Community Fund (WI) (http://www.wisconsincommunityfund.org/)

The Madison and Milwaukee-based Wisconsin Community Fund was founded in 1982 with the mission to "raise and disburse money to progressive groups working for democracy, justice, and social & economic equality." The Fund donates to a wide variety of social, political, and environmental programs throughout Wisconsin and operates with four grant types: project grants, general operating expense grants, special opportunity grants, and donor advised grants. For further details on organizations the Fund has supported in the past, grant guidelines and limitations, links to progressive organizations and grantmaking resources, and contact information, the Fund's Web site is an excellent resource.

Wisconsin Health & Hospital Association Foundation (WI) (http://www.wha.org/www/foundation/index.htm)

The Wisconsin Health & Hospital Association Foundation was founded in 1968 in Madison and is now known as the WHA Foundation. The Foundation "supports healthcare education efforts by providing grants to Wisconsin-based healthcare organizations." Along with an annual Global Vision Community Outreach Award, the Foundation provides grants in the form of seed money, usually $2,000 or less, to startup organizations. There is no specific application for these grants, though the Foundation's Web site includes application guidelines that can be found on the pull-down menu on the WHA Foundation Grants page. The Foundation's site also includes past grant and award recipients, donor information, contact information, and recent Foundation reports, which are available for downloading in PDF format.

Wisconsin Humanities Council (WI) (http://www.danenet.wicip.org/whc/)

Created in 1972 by the National Endowment for the Humanities, the Wisconsin Humanities Council is located in Madison. The organization supports "projects that deepen public knowledge of and appreciation for the humanities, encourage dialogue between humanities scholars and members of the general public, and build bridges between diverse groups of Wisconsin citizens." The Council gives out three types of grants to Wisconsin nonprofits: $500 proposal development grants, mini-grants of up to $2,000, and major grants. Project topics include history, philosophy, language, literature, cultural anthropology, jurisprudence, and religious studies. Most funded projects do include at least one humanities scholar with a graduate degree in an appropriate discipline, although this can be waived when there is a qualified specialist involved. Application guidelines and deadlines are available on the site, along with downloadable applications in PDF format. There is information on the Resource Center, which provides pre-packaged humanities programs at a low cost, and the Speakers Bureau, which organizes expert speaker presentations throughout the state. There are links to resources for educators, an electronic copy of the Council's newsletter, and a calendar of activities. The Council cannot fund more than one-half of a program's budget.

Women's Community Foundation (OH) (http://www.wcfcleveland.org/)
Based in Cleveland, Ohio, the Women's Community Foundation (WCF) was established in 1981 with $30,000 in proceeds from the Cleveland exhibit of the artist Judy Chicago's *The Dinner Party*. The WCF raises money and makes grants to groups serving women and girls in Cuyahoga County, Ohio. Its stated mission is "To invest in the dreams of girls and the power of women through philanthropy, grantmaking, and education." WCF grantmaking is based on the principle that women should have the freedom to make choices in all aspects of their lives: employment, religion, health, sexual orientation, family life, reproduction, education, and residence. The intention is to fund and assist women organizing on their own behalf. Any project seeking support from the WCF must protect and expand the choices women and girls make in their lives. Emphasis is placed on programs that work toward eliminating gender discrimination faced by women and girls, especially projects that serve those most affected by economic, social, and physical oppression: women of color, lesbians, low-income women, older women, girls and teenagers, and women with disabilities. WCF also administers the Creative Philanthropy Award, greater Cleveland's annual tribute to a woman who has demonstrated outstanding leadership in supporting programs that serve women and girls. Visitors to the site will find award and grant recipient lists and contact information.

The Women's Foundation (CA) (http://www.twfusa.org)
Based in San Francisco, The Women's Foundation (TWF) "is the oldest and largest philanthropic fund for women in the western United States." Created in 1979 in response to the inequity of funding directed towards women and girls throughout the United States, TWF supports organizations that serve low-income women and girls throughout 50 counties in northern and central California and, more recently, the Mexico side of the U.S./Mexico border. TWF funds programs for the prevention of violence against women and girls, girls' leadership, health, and economic justice and targets programs that promote and protect the human rights of women and girls in the civil, political, economic, and social arenas. In addition to grantmaking, TWF develops collaborations between individuals, organizations, and institutions who can combine their efforts towards creating the changes necessary to achieving gender equality and social justice. Visit the Foundation's Web site to read about programs and partnerships and its various grantmaking funds. The site features a downloadable grant application, site map, related links, and contact information.

The Women's Foundation of Colorado (CO) (http://www.wfco.org)
The Women's Foundation of Colorado, established in 1987, "works to create communities in which women's talents and abilities are valued as important assets in building a vital and strong society." The Foundation serves the areas of Denver, Colorado Springs, Boulder, Fort Collins, and the intermountain region in Colorado. Its grantmaking focuses on removing barriers for girls and women in three areas: girls' futures; education, employment, and training; and technology. Grants are made yearly, and the Foundation provides grant guidelines and an application in PDF format that can be downloaded from the Foundation's Web site. The Foundation also provides current reports and research, previous grants, and news and events online.

Women's Funding Alliance (WA) (http://www.wfalliance.org/)
The Women's Funding Alliance of Seattle, Washington, was created in 1983. The organization's mission is to "promote justice, health and opportunities by investing in the future of women and girls." The Alliance distributes financial support to its eleven member groups that address topics including poverty, domestic violence, and welfare rights. Grants are also distributed through the Community Fund to Washington State nonprofits with women in

leadership positions and/or that prioritize diversity in projects and agencies. A scholarship program was enacted for the first time in 1999. The BrenMar Scholarship "supports women and girls in any activity that helps them dream, speaks to their soul, and otherwise enriches them personally or professionally." The scholarship is open to women who are active in one of the Alliance's member organizations. The site includes an address for scholarship applications, an e-mail address to contact in order to receive requests for proposals, information on current scholarship recipients, and information on member organizations and past and present grant recipients. Visitors will also find information on making donations or volunteering and features on special events. There are lists of the board of directors and the staff. Organizations receiving Community Fund grants cannot have annual budgets exceeding $300,000.

Women's Sports Foundation (NY) (http://www.womenssportsfoundation.org/)
The Women's Sports Foundation, founded in 1974 by Billie Jean King and other female athletes, is dedicated to increasing opportunities for girls and women in sports and fitness through education, advocacy, recognition, and grants. Visitors should follow the Funding link on the Web site's athletic shoe navigation tool to find detailed information on numerous grant and scholarship programs, some of which provide downloadable application forms.

Women's Studio Workshop, Inc. (NY) (http://www.wsworkshop.org/)
The Women's Studio Workshop, located in Rosendale, New York, was begun in 1974 by four women artists committed to developing an alternative space for female artists to create new work and share skills. The Workshop now supports a number of grants, fellowships, and special initiatives, most of which take place at the Studio in Rosendale, with facilities for printmaking, papermaking, book arts, and clay and photographic media. Grants include the Artists Book Residency and the Artists Book Production Grant, for which there is an application in PDF format that can be downloaded from the WSW Web site. Fellowships are generally for a reduction in cost of studio time at the WSW and are either for general purposes or clay. Special Initiatives include Residency for New Jersey Artists, Visiting Artist Project, Art- in-Education, and Emerging Artist Project. The Workshop also sponsors six internships throughout the year. The WSW Web site includes details on the resources available to artists at the studio, a literary journal, more information on programs and grants, current news and events at the Workshop, and a contact form.

Women's Way (PA) (http://www.womensway.org)
Formed in 1977 by a conglomerate of local women's agencies, Women's Way serves the greater Philadelphia area, including Delaware Valley and southern New Jersey. Through its discretionary funds, Women's Way supports programs that are run by and serve women and that agree with the Women's Way mission: to "advocate freedom from violence, guarantee equal opportunity, challenge discrimination in all forms, foster economic self-determination, and affirm reproductive freedom." The Women's Way Web site includes numerous listings of events and news, links to resources for women, and examples of some of the recent programs and services the organization has funded.

The Woods Foundation, Inc., Tiger (OH)
(http://ww1.sportsline.com/u/fans/celebrity/tiger/course/foundation.html)
Golfer Tiger Woods created the Reynoldsburg, Ohio, Tiger Woods Foundation in December 1996. The Foundation "actively encourages and promotes parental responsibility and involvement in the lives of children and celebrates the spirit of inclusion in all aspects of human existence." The Foundation runs youth golf clinics in urban settings and distributes grants associated with children, family health and welfare, education, parenting, and youth development in urban communities. There are four specific grantmaking areas. Child and Family Health and Welfare includes infant and maternal health support, prevention of substance abuse, family violence and neglect, and giving families access to life's necessities. Education objectives involve school readiness through programs for parents, projects helping youths move from school to work, and school organization and management programs.

Parenting objectives include strengthening the role of parents in their children's lives, the importance of parents accepting full parental responsibilities, and improving communication between parents and children. Finally, the youth development category supports programs that "build self-esteem, life skills, positive values and expand life option opportunities." There are also two college scholarships given by the Foundation: one for graduates of Minerva High School and one for an Atlanta metropolitan area high school senior recognizing moral character, leadership, and academic potential. The site offers extensive grant application procedures and guidelines, a phone number to call for information on the scholarships, and a page that will soon have information on the clinics taking place in 2000. There is a list of grant recipients in the Year in Review section and information on the staff and the board of directors.

World Studio Foundation, Inc. (http://www.worldstudio.org)
World Studio Foundation provides scholarships to minority and economically disadvantaged students who are studying the design/arts disciplines in American colleges and universities. One of the Foundation's primary aims is to increase diversity in the creative professions and to foster social responsibility in the artists and designers of tomorrow. Scholarship recipients are selected for their ability, need, and demonstrated commitment to giving back to the larger community. Visit the site for downloadable applications and information about the Foundation's mentoring program. Its publication is also available online.

World Wildlife Fund (DC) (http://www.worldwildlife.org/)
The World Wildlife Fund, the largest privately supported international conservation organization in the world, directs its conservation efforts toward two global goals: protecting and saving endangered species (e.g., elephants, pandas, rhinos, tigers, whales) and addressing global threats to wildlife (e.g., global warming, worldwide deforestation, overfishing). The Fund's beautiful Web site provides a great deal of information on its activities around the world as well as on issues related to conservation. While grant information does not fall into a particular area of the site, recent grants lists can be found by entering the word "grant" into the site's search engine.

Wyoming Council for the Humanities (WY) (http://www.uwyo.edu/special/wch/)
The Wyoming Council for the Humanities fosters interaction between the public and humanities scholars on questions related to the "significant dimensions of our existence—personal, social, cultural, and political—from local, national, and international perspectives." The Council awards grants to Wyoming nonprofits to support public presentations that examine the humanities. Programs supported by WCH generally comprise lectures, panel discussions, conferences, seminars, exhibits, historical dramatizations, and/or community forums. Visitors to the WCH Web site will find information on the Council's activities, grant guidelines and downloadable application forms, a database of humanities scholars, an online newsletter, and information for prospective donors.

The Kristi Yamaguchi Always Dream Foundation (CA) (http://kristi.yahoo.com/)
The Oakland, California-based Kristi Yamaguchi Always Dream Foundation was founded by the former Olympic—now professional—figure skater, Kristi Yamaguchi. The Foundation "[supports] organizations that have a positive influence on children and youth living in economically and socially disadvantaged environments" through a number of events, programs, and the Fulfilling Dreams grant. This grant supports children's organizations by either donating a "dream list" of much-needed items for the children they serve or by sponsoring special outings or trips that provide an educational and life-enriching experience. Funds must go to an organization located in California, Nevada, or Hawaii. The Foundation posts grant guidelines, details of past programs and events, and contact information on its Web site.

APPENDIX D

Community Foundations on the Web

ALABAMA

Calhoun County Community Foundation (http://www.cccfoundation.org)

Located in Anniston, Alabama, the Calhoun County Community Foundation (CCCF) is a family of funds that serve as a permanent endowment for the long-term benefit of Calhoun County in northeast Alabama. The CCCF exists to "support nonprofit organizations targeting the most discernible needs and most promising opportunities within Calhoun County, Alabama." The CCCF has three funds: Stringfellow Health, Preventative Healthcare, and the E.D. King Family Fund. Each has its own guidelines and application, all of which can be found on the Foundation's Web site. Applications can be downloaded in PDF format. The site also has information about investments, planned giving opportunities, and Foundation news.

The Community Foundation of Greater Birmingham
(http://www.foundationbirmingham.org)

Established in 1959, The Community Foundation of Greater Birmingham is made up of more than 180 grantmaking funds established by individuals, families, nonprofit agencies, private foundations, and businesses. Its mission is to connect caring people and key resources with communities in need, today and tomorrow. The Women's Fund of Greater Birmingham, a component fund of The Community Foundation of Greater Birmingham, is dedicated to improving the status and quality of life for women and girls in the Greater Birmingham area through purposeful philanthropy and the establishment of a permanent endowment. Visitors to the Foundation's Web site will find a brief history of the Foundation, application guidelines and procedures, information on becoming a donor, a listing of the Foundation's board of directors and staff, FAQs, and contact information.

ALASKA

Alaska Conservation Foundation (http://www.akcf.org)

Established in 1980, the Alaska Conservation Foundation receives funds and makes grants to protect the integrity of Alaska's ecosystems and to promote sustainable livelihoods among its communities and peoples. Areas of interest for ACF include advocacy, community development, public communications, public policy, and rural affairs. The Foundation's guidelines favor approaches that convene diverse constituencies, promote citizen participation in public process, provide forums for increasing environmental awareness, and build capacity to implement sustainable futures. The Foundation's Web site offers a mission statement, a brief history of the Foundation, facts about the state of Alaska, a board and staff listing, program descriptions, grant guidelines and application procedures, a section on ways to give to ACF, and contact information.

ARIZONA

Arizona Community Foundation (http://www.azfoundation.com)

The Phoenix-based Arizona Community Foundation was established in 1978 by a trio of local businessmen and has since become one of the fastest-growing public charities in the nation. Through its grantmaking activities, the Foundation aims to improve the lives of children and families and strengthen neighborhoods and communities across the Grand Canyon State. Of special interest to the Foundation are programs that respond to the needs of low income and vulnerable older persons; disadvantaged and underserved children and youth, with an emphasis on "the early childhood years and/or prevention and early intervention strategies that reduce the likelihood or mitigate the severity of negative outcomes for 'at risk' groups;" education; neighborhood- and community-based economic and social development; social justice, with a focus on ways to mediate community conflict and promote appreciation and understanding of cultural diversity in Arizona; and the environment, in particular projects "that preserve and protect habitat for humans, animals, and plant life." In addition to general information about the Foundation's programs, visitors to the ACF Web site will find a listing of its board of directors; information for potential donors, including FAQs and a section called Estate Planning News; and contact information for its affiliates in Flagstaff, the Green Valley Area, and Page, Scottsdale, Sedona, Tempe, and Cochise, Graham, and Yavapai Counties.

ARKANSAS

Arkansas Community Foundation, Inc. (http://www.arcf.org)

The Arkansas Community Foundation, located in Little Rock, was started in 1976 with an $8,000 contribution and now has over $21 million worth of assets. The group's mission is to "provide and promote leadership as the premier builder of philanthropic funds to meet Arkansas's diverse grantmaking needs and challenges." The Foundation's giving program has three major components. The largest is the basic grant program, which makes modest, one-time grants to nonprofits throughout the state. Emphasis is placed on projects that benefit rural and urban communities, those that promote philanthropy throughout the state, and projects that partner nonprofits together. The Foundation is particularly looking for projects that will have a long-term effect and can be replicated. There is a list of scholarships for students in post-secondary schools online, including the very specific qualifications for each. Each has a contact listed, mostly at the state universities or local high schools. Other programs include the ACF Board Partner Fund, which is a discretionary fund for board members, and the Women's Foundation of Arkansas, an alliance of women working to support issues of importance to them as a group and to foster philanthropy and leadership in women. The Foundation prefers a letter of inquiry as an initial approach. The site offers visitors lists of the Foundation staff and board and information on contributing or starting a fund. There is also an electronic form to request Foundation publications.

Foundation for the Mid South (http://www.fndmidsouth.org/)

The Foundation for the Mid South makes grants "to build the capacity of communities, organizations, and individuals" throughout the states of Arkansas, Louisiana, and Mississippi. Grants are made within the three primary program areas of economic development, education, and families and children. In addition to general information about the Foundation, visitors to the Web site will find detailed program descriptions, including types of funding provided within each program area; downloadable application forms in PDF format; and an interactive bulletin board through which regional grantseekers and grantmakers can communicate. Selections from the Foundation's annual report, including listings of grants by program area, are also available.

CALIFORNIA

Berkeley Community Fund (http://www.netwiz.net/~bcf/)

The Berkeley Community Fund was established in 1992 to address local social problems. It seeks to narrow the inequities within the community, create hope and opportunity for disadvantaged youth, enhance cultural and intellectual diversity while building consensus to address common problems, and stimulate public and private investments to raise the quality of community life. The Berkeley, California-based Fund connects people and organizations to enhance planning and resource sharing, provides technical assistance, makes cash grants to community groups, gives college scholarships to deserving Berkeley High School seniors, and brings "public and private resources to bear on efforts that support the mission of the fund and the needs of the community." Visitors to the Web site will find grantmaking criteria, a grantmaking FAQ sheet, descriptions of some of the Fund's current projects, contact information, a listing of the board of directors and staff, and contact information.

California Community Foundation (http://www.calfund.org/)

Established in 1915, the California Community Foundation was Los Angeles's first grantmaking institution and is the country's second-oldest community foundation. The Foundation makes grants to organizations serving the greater Los Angeles region in the following areas: human services, community development, civic affairs, community health, early education, and arts and culture. Visitors to the Foundation's Web site will find a range of general information as well as grant guidelines and a downloadable version of the Foundation's grant application form, a list of recent grants, brief biographies of selected donors, a list of Foundation-sponsored publications, and a calendar of upcoming Foundation-related events and special initiatives.

Claremont Community Foundation (http://www.claremontfoundation.org/)

The Claremont Community Foundation was established in 1989 to serve the community of Claremont, California, a town within the larger Los Angeles metropolitan area. The Foundation supports projects oriented at preserving the local cultural heritage and has awarded grants to programs and special projects for the arts, health, welfare, education, and history. The Foundation can be contacted with inquires about application guidelines from its Web site.

Community Foundation for Monterey County (http://www.commfdnmc.org)

The Community Foundation for Monterey County seeks to be the leader in increasing charitable giving to improve the quality of life for all residents of Monterey County and to strengthen the institutions that help build healthy communities. Based in Monterey, California, the Foundation encourages applications that provide significant benefits to the community in the areas of arts and culture, social and community services, health, education, and the environment. Visitors to the site will find application materials that can be downloaded in Microsoft Word format, downloadable program guidelines, and other funding sources. The Foundation also has a Management Assistance Program designed to improve and expand access to management assistance services and resources for not-for-profit

organizations in Monterey and San Benito Counties. Workshops, management, and technical assistance grants are available to nonprofits.

Community Foundation of Santa Cruz County (http://www.cfscc.org)
The Community Foundation of Santa Cruz County was established in 1982 with the purpose of making "greater Santa Cruz County a better place to live, now, and in the future."
To accomplish its mission, the Foundation builds permanent endowed funds contributed by
individuals and institutions. The Foundation's grants are made to organizations that hold an
interest in health, human services, education, arts and humanities, historic preservation,
community development, or the environment. The Foundation also maintains a scholarship
fund. Visitors to the Foundation's Web site will find more information on the grants program, board and staff listings, financial data, and contact information.

Community Foundation Silicon Valley (http://www.siliconvalleygives.org/)
The Community Foundation Silicon Valley (formerly the Community Foundation of Santa
Clara County) changed its name in November 1997 to better reflect the entrepreneurial
spirit, creativity, and diversity of the community it serves. The Foundation supports programs that benefit the residents of Santa Clara County and southern San Mateo County in
the following areas: arts and humanities, community and social services, education, the
environment, and health. In addition, the Foundation's Neighborhood Grants Program promotes "the development of healthy and self-reliant neighborhoods by supporting residents
to unify for action, actualize their collective power, and create community-based solutions
to physical, social, and economic challenges." Low-to-middle-income neighborhoods in
Santa Clara County receive priority. The Foundation's Web site provides general program
information, application guidelines, a Foundation calendar, a list of recent grants, an electronic form for ordering copies of the Foundation's print publications, related links, and
e-mail contact information. Visitors can also access results of the latest Corporate Community Involvement Study as well as an introduction to the Foundation's Mayfair Neighborhood Improvement Initiative.

East Bay Community Foundation (http://www.eastbaycf.org/)
Founded in 1928, the Oakland-based East Bay Community Foundation (EBCF) is a permanent endowment of charitable funds dedicated to improving the human condition and
enhancing the quality of life of the residents and communities of Alameda and Contra
Costa Counties in California. Grantmaking is focused on collaborative approaches to
issues such as violence prevention, school reform, homelessness, youth development, community arts, and neighborhood empowerment. EBCF has the following grant programs:
community building, a competitive grants program; education mini-grants, which are $500
maximum grants for education enrichment activities in schools, nonprofits, and public
agencies serving preschool through eighth grades; the APEX program, for arts education
projects; and healthy communities, for community building activities such as neighborhood cleanups and arts and cultural activities. Application guidelines and procedures can
be downloaded from the Foundation's Web site. The Foundation also sponsors such projects as Art Education Initiative, promoting arts education for local school children and
bringing together artists, teachers, parents, schools, community groups, and businesses to
create sustainable arts education programs; East Bay Land Recycling Initiative, a joint project of the California Center for Land Recycling and the Foundation to help redirect growth
from greenfields on the urban fringe of Alameda and Contra Costa to the core of the East
Bay metropolitan region; East Bay Public Safety Corridor Partnership, seeking solutions to
the problems of local public safety; Management Assistance Partnership Project, designed
to enhance technical assistance and training for local nonprofit organizations; and Oakland
Child Health and Safety Initiative, a collaboration focusing on the health and safety of
Oakland's youth. Visit the site for a listing and links to affiliate funds, contact information,
and links to a gift planning guide site.

Glendale Community Foundation (http://www.cwire.com/GCF/)

Founded in 1956 as part of Glendale's 50th anniversary celebration, the Glendale Community Foundation exists to improve the quality of life for the people of the greater Glendale community—Glendale, La Crescenta, La Caada, Flintridge, Montrose, and Verdugo City—by leveraging community assets. The Foundation administers gifts and grants according to donors' wishes and uses the income from unrestricted gifts to fund hard asset acquisitions (i.e., capital equipment and improvements) and programming for local charities to make them more efficient and effective. Visitors to the Foundation's Web site will find general information on community foundations, a brief history of the Foundation itself, grant application guidelines and procedures, recent issues of the Foundation's quarterly newsletter, and information on ways to give and the benefits of giving to donors.

Great Valley Center, Inc. (http://www.greatvalley.org)

Based in Modesto, California, the Great Valley Center is a non-partisan organization committed to activities and organizations that support the economic, social, and environmental well-being of California's Great Central Valley. The Great Valley Center was established to foster collaboration, seek solutions, and be a voice for California's Great Central Valley. The Center awards monetary grants to nonprofit groups, community organizations, and local governments that are working to improve the well–being of the Great Central Valley through initiatives in the areas of land use, the environment, growth, agriculture, conservation, and investment. The Center also has a fellowship, the Institute or the Development of Emerging Area Leaders (IDEAL) Fellowship Program, whose goal is to provide access and information to emerging area leaders on issues relating to Central Valley land use, economics, agriculture, and conservation. The program is targeted to reach underrepresented groups, minorities, and local leaders from small rural communities. The site features downloadable applications, information on the counties in the Greater Valley Area, related links, and contact information.

Humboldt Area Foundation (http://www.northcoast.com/~hafound/welcome.html)

The Humboldt Area Foundation was established in 1972 as a vehicle of and for the citizens of the north coast of California—that is, Humboldt, Del Norte, and parts of Trinity and Siskiyou Counties. In addition to general information about the Foundation itself, its Web site provides detailed grant application guidelines and an overview of the resources available to nonprofit organizations at the Foundation-operated William T. Rooney Resource Center.

Los Altos Community Foundation (http://www.losaltoscf.org/)

The Los Altos Community Foundation serves Los Altos, Los Altos Hills, and the surrounding area "by promoting community building—those activities and facilities that give the community its favorable character, making it a desirable place to live and work." Community building includes projects that strengthen values, preserve the community's physical heritage, and enhance community based philanthropic activities. The Foundation makes grants to local programs, builds an endowment, and manages philanthropic activities for other organizations and individuals. The Web site provides a description of the Foundation's programs, information about the criteria for grantmaking, and the Foundation's financial statement. While grant proposal guidelines and dates are not provided, there is contact information available on the site.

Marin Community Foundation (http://www.marincf.org/)

The Marin Community Foundation strives to encourage and apply philanthropic contributions to help improve the human condition, embrace diversity, promote a humane and democratic society, and enhance the community's quality of life. The Foundation focuses its grantmaking activities in the following areas: the arts, with an emphasis on arts in the community and arts education; community development; education and training, with an emphasis on drop-out prevention, improving literacy and basic skills, school restructure and redesign, and lifelong learning; the environment; human services; and religion. The MCF Web site provides detailed program descriptions and application guidelines for the above; additional information about the Foundation's various community programs, donor-advised funds, and loan program; FAQs about MCF's funding reference library; and a handful of links to related sites.

Orange County Community Foundation (http://www.oc-communityfoundation.org/)
In addition to approximately $2 million in donor-advised funds, the Irvine-based Orange County Community Foundation (OCCF) makes discretionary grants in the following areas: children and youth, with a focus on ensuring the safety of young people in their homes and neighborhoods, child and foster care, early childhood development, school preparedness, arts and classical music education, and building self-esteem; family relationships, with a focus on improving family impact on children and youth, parenting, family economic self-sufficiency, and family violence; and diverse communities, with a focus on the promotion of mutual respect and understanding among diverse groups in Orange County. The Foundation also awards a limited number of scholarships to high school juniors and seniors who are continuing their education in an accredited institution, are graduating from an Orange County high school, and are residents of Orange County. OCCF also administers a program called the XOXO Fund, which was created by an anonymous donor to provide food, health, and social services to those most in need. The OCCF Web site provides information on all its grantmaking activities, application guidelines and recent grants, separate FAQs for grantseekers and potential donors, a summary of Foundation publications, and contact information.

Pasadena Foundation (http://www.pasadenafoundation.org/)
Founded in 1953, the Pasadena Foundation serves as a leader, catalyst, and resource for philanthropy in the community it serves. The Foundation seeks to improve the lives of children, the disabled, and seniors in the Pasadena, Altadena and Sierra Madre areas of California. Regular grants of up to $8,000 and major grants of up to $50,000 are available; grant guidelines and a complete listing of past grants are available on the Foundation's Web site. The Foundation also sponsors various initiatives, including a Christmas present program for underprivileged children called Yes, Virginia. Donor services, including the Fellows Program, as well as a message from the chairman and contact information are all available online.

Peninsula Community Foundation (http://www.pcf.org/)
Created by residents of the San Francisco peninsula in 1964, the Peninsula Community Foundation today provides funding for nonprofit groups in San Mateo and Santa Clara Counties that address the needs of children, youth, and families or that work in the areas of education, health and human services, housing and homelessness, the arts, or civic and public benefit. Through its Center for Venture Philanthropy, the Foundation is also forging partnerships of donor/investors "to make long-term, focused investments in complex programs . . . [such as] as school reform and welfare reform." In addition to information for potential donors, visitors to the PCF Web site will find general program information, current grantmaking guidelines, a list of recent grants, board and staff listings (including e-mail links), a calendar of deadlines and events, a section devoted to the Foundation's Strategic Philanthropy Initiatives (i.e., the Center for Venture Philanthropy, the Peninsula Partnership for Children, Youth and Families, the Prenatal to Three Initiative, and the Neighborhood Grants program), and contact information.

Sacramento Regional Foundation (http://www.sacregfoundation.org)
The Sacramento Regional Foundation is the community foundation for Sacramento, El Dorado, Placer, and Yolo Counties. It is committed to implementing donors' charitable wishes according to their directives and creating an everlasting gift that will benefit the Sacramento area for generations. Among its grant programs and scholarships is Operation Graduation, a five-year initiative to "increase the number of Sacramento-area students who graduate from high school prepared to pursue happy, successful lives." Visitors to the site will find examples of their grantmaking and contact information.

San Diego Community Foundation (http://www.sdcf.org/)

The mission of the San Diego Community Foundation (SDCF) is "to assist donors to build and preserve enduring assets for charitable purposes in the San Diego Region; to monitor and assess changing needs and to meet those needs through financial awards and organizational support." Incorporated in 1975, the SDCF has assets of more than $138 million in some 300 separate funds. Approximately nine percent of the Foundation's endowments generate discretionary income, which is distributed through a community grants program. The Foundation also operates the Funding Information Center, a Foundation Center Cooperating Collection, which provides free access and technical assistance to anyone seeking nonprofit or educational funding. In addition to general information, visitors to the Foundation's Web site will find descriptive lists of its 1996 spring grant awards, excerpts from recent Foundation newsletters, staff and board listings, and contact information.

The San Diego Foundation (http://www.sdfoundation.org)

The San Diego Foundation, of San Diego, California, is a community foundation that was established in 1975. The organization's mission is to "improve the quality of life within all of our communities by promoting and increasing responsible and effective philanthropy." The expansive grantmaking program supports projects that encompass arts and culture, economic development, education, the environment, healthcare and human services, and religious endeavors. Interested organizations must submit a letter of intent and any requested additional information. While some funding is unrestricted, there are funds established to support specific areas, including the Civil Society Initiative, the Teachers Fund, and Community Endowment Grants. Applications and guidelines are posted as grants become available. The Foundation also administers a large number of scholarships. These are listed in two categories: those that accept a common application and those with their own application. The latter include contact information to receive an application. The common application and a list of necessary supporting documents are listed online. Board and staff lists and financial information can be found in the About SDF section. Much of the site is dedicated to encouraging donations and educating visitors on donation options.

The San Francisco Foundation (http://www.sff.org/)

With more than $680 million in assets and annual giving in excess of $50 million, the San Francisco Foundation is one of the largest community foundations in the country. As the community foundation serving Alameda, Contra Costa, Marin, San Francisco, and San Mateo Counties, it partners with diverse donors and organizations to mobilize resources in the promotion of vibrant, sustainable communities throughout the Bay Area. The Foundation, which marks its fiftieth anniversary this year, awards grants to nonprofit organizations in the fields of arts and humanities, community health, education, the environment, neighborhood and community development, social services, and philanthropy. The Foundation's easy-to-navigate Web site provides a good deal of information about Foundation activities, past and present; its grantmaking, including program priorities, selected grants in each program area, and grantee profiles; information about the Koshland Civic Unity Awards, the Foundation's Special Awards Program, and the Foundation's Community Initiative Funds; information for prospective donors; FAQs; a short list of Foundation publications available upon reuquest; and contact information.

Santa Barbara Foundation (http://www.sbfoundation.org)

The Santa Barbara Foundation was established in 1928 by Major Max Fleischmann, who gathered a group of local citizens to create a permanent endowment to support free band concerts for the community. The Santa Barbara-based Foundation supported band concerts for several years, but its mission was soon broadened to include projects that would "benefit the public good." The Foundation funds the fields of the arts, education, recreation, the environment, community enhancement, health, human services, and youth. It also works to promote partnerships to address important community issues and leverage resources to meet community needs. In addition to grantmaking, the Foundation also has several student aid programs in the form of loans and scholarships. Visit the Web site for grant application guidelines and contact information, with e-mail links to Foundation staff.

Shasta Regional Community Foundation (http://www.shastarcf.org/)

Located in Redding, California, the Shasta Regional Community Foundation works to "enhance the quality of life of Shasta and Siskiyou Communities through facilitating the everlasting gift intentions of donors." The grant program is defined by the ongoing needs of the community and the challenges the community is facing. Nonprofits serving the residents of either or both of the counties are eligible to apply for funding. The Foundation's Web site offers application guidelines and suggests that interested programs e-mail the Foundation in order to receive the application and coversheet by mail. Deadlines and restrictions are listed as is a description of the required application. The site also includes a staff list. The Foundation houses the Grant and Resource Center of Northern California, a funding research library. Information on the Center's hours and resources is available online.

The Sonoma County Community Foundation http://www.sonomacf.org/

The Sonoma County Community Foundation (SCCF) administers and awards grants from a permanent endowment to eligible nonprofit organizations based and operating in Sonoma County, California, in the areas of health, social well-being, economy, environment and culture. The Foundation manages and distributes monies from several individual funds established to support the specific philanthropic interests of their donors. Also, the SCCF scholarship program offers financial assistance to Sonoma County residents pursuing higher education through over 15 separate scholarship funds. In addition to substantial information about the Foundation, the Foundation's Web site provides visitors with a listing and brief description of all individual funds, listings of the board of trustees and major donors, a helpful FAQ section, and contact information.

Sonora Area Foundation (http://www.sonora-area.org/)

Established in 1989, the Sonora Area Foundation strives "to enhance the community and the quality of life of its residents through facilitating the philanthropic intentions of donors, and the needs of the surrounding communities." The Foundation awards approximately a few dozen grants annually to nonprofit and public agencies throughout the Tuolumne County, California, area. Grants have been made in the past in the areas of recreational services, education, social service programs, and education. The Foundation does not make grants to individuals. The Foundation's Web site offers a short history of the Foundation, brief descriptions of the programs it funds and the individual donor funds administered by the Foundation, a grants listing, grant application policies and instructions, a listing of Foundation board members, and contact information.

Truckee Tahoe Community Foundation (http://ttcf.net/)

The Truckee Tahoe Community Foundation, located in Truckee, California, is committed to "matching philanthropic interests with charitable needs to enhance the quality of life in the Truckee-Tahoe community." The Web page offers basic contact information.

Ventura County Community Foundation (http://www.vccf.org)

Headquartered in Camarillo, California, the Ventura County Community Foundation (VCCF) "provides grantmaking opportunities for programs meeting the needs of children, youth and families or programs focusing on education, health and human services, housing and homelessness, the arts and civic and public benefit." The VCCF funds nonprofit organizations serving Ventura County as well as individuals through its scholarship program. Though the VCCF maintains a variety of funds, its grants focus on five main programs: The Women's Legacy Fund, The Community Needs Response Fund, Destino 2000, Swift Memorial Healthcare Foundation, and the Martin V. and Martin K. Smith Foundation. The VCCF Web site provides a list of the specific cities the Foundation serves, a guide for grantseekers with limitations and deadlines, the Foundation's Resource Center for Nonprofit Management, information regarding the annual report, nonprofit links, and contact information.

COLORADO

Aspen County Community Foundation (http://www.avcfoundation.org.)
Incorporated in Colorado in 1986, the Aspen County Community Foundation was established by the Aspen Skiing Company in 1980. Formerly known as the Aspen Foundation, the organization's goal is to "provide services and support to valleywide residents and to expand its base of community participation." The grant program funds nonprofits in the areas of health and human services, education, and community that support families and strengthen the community. Emphasis is placed on programs that eliminate risks to children and families and that create a permanent change in the way people live. Programs in Pitkin, Garfield, and west Eagle Counties are eligible to apply. Application guidelines, deadlines, and specific descriptions of each funding category, along with lists of previous grantees, are located in the Program area of the site. Visitors will also find board and staff lists, the latter with e-mail addresses, and articles from the Foundation newsletter. There is also a section devoted to the Executive Service Corps, a program that links retired professionals who volunteer their time as consultants with nonprofit programs.

Community Foundation Serving Boulder County
(http://bcn.boulder.co.us/community/found/)
Established in 1991, the Community Foundation Serving Boulder County generally supports the community of Boulder County, Colorado, however, "several donors have interests elsewhere which they fund through The Community Foundation." The Foundation's areas of interest include arts, environment, education, health, and human services. The Foundation's Web site is aimed primarily at donors, but basic contact information is included.

Community Foundation Serving Northern Colorado (http://www.fortnet.org/CF/)
Established in 1975, the Community Foundation Serving Northern Colorado is located in Fort Collins, Colorado. The group's mission is to "build an endowment to meet the diverse needs of [the] community by attracting, managing, and distributing funds entrusted by donors." The Foundation supports diverse projects throughout the region through its endowment and donor-directed funds. The very simple Web page includes contact information and a general description of the Foundation's contribution to different populations (donors, community, and nonprofits).

The Denver Foundation (http://www.denverfoundation.org/)
With an endowment of nearly $185 million, the 75-year-old Denver Foundation supports a range of community-based programs that make the metropolitan Denver area a better place to live. In the recent year, the Foundation awarded more than $11 million in grants in the areas of arts and culture, community development, education, and health and human services to more than 600 nonprofit organizations in Adams, Arapahoe, Boulder, Denver, Douglas, and Jefferson Counties. In addition, some donor funds help nonprofit organizations throughout Colorado and beyond. The Foundation's Web site provides a mission statement, general program information, grant guidelines and application procedures, an FAQ section for grantees, information for potential donors, an electronic order form for Foundation publications, and extensive contact information.

The Summit Foundation (http://www.summitfoundation.org)
Established in 1984 as the Breckenridge Development Foundation by the Breckenridge Ski Area, the Summit Foundation added support from Copper Mountain, Keystone, and Arapahoe Basin ski resorts and assumed its current name in 1991. Based in Breckenridge, Colorado, the Summit Foundation is dedicated to improving the quality of life for residents and guests of Summit County. The Foundation funds other Summit County nonprofit agencies providing programs and services in arts and culture, health and human services, education, the environment, and sports. The site contains an online contact form and contact information.

Yampa Valley Community Foundation (http://www.yvcf.org/)
The Yampa Valley Community Foundation serves the residents of Routt County, Colorado. It was originally established in 1979 under the name of Yampa Valley Foundation to save Alpine College, Colorado. The new name, with the word "community" in it, was adopted in 1994 to reflect a reorganization and broadening of focus. The Foundation's present areas of interest include arts and culture, education, health and human services, recreation, and the environment. Detailed application guidelines, FAQs, and a form for requesting more information can be found at the Foundation's Web site.

CONNECTICUT

Community Foundation for Greater New Haven (http://www.cfgnh.org/)
Founded in 1928, the Community Foundation for Greater New Haven manages charitable funds in its 20-town region of Connecticut. The mission is to "to strengthen and protect the community's varied assets; to increase respect, understanding and collaboration among its diverse stakeholders; and to enhance the quality of life for all." The Foundation supports a wide range of interests through many distinct endowments funds including the areas of education, health, youth development, community development, regionalism, and capacity building. The Foundation's latest annual report, current newsletter, and grant guidelines can be obtained by visiting the Foundation's Web site.

The Community Foundation of Southeastern Connecticut (http://www.cfsect.org/)
The Community Foundation of Southeastern Connecticut, located in New London, Connecticut, focuses its giving in the areas of arts, education, environment, health, and social services. High priority goes to those programs that: "strengthen families; improve access to area resources, especially for underserved populations; encourage residents to participate in the cultural life of the community; and add to the general well being of the community." The Foundation's special initiatives include technical assistance grants, a family grant program, after-school programs, and a women and girls fund. Additionally, the Foundation provides numerous scholarships for college-bound students: a complete list of scholarships and applications, both in PDF format, can be downloaded from the Foundation's Web site. Grant guidelines and limitations, a grant application in PDF format, a listing of the southern Connecticut towns served by the Foundation, donor information, and contact information to request publications are all available online.

Fairfield County Foundation (http://www.fcfoundation.org/)
Located in Wilton, Connecticut, the Fairfield County Foundation "promote[s] the growth of philanthropy to fulfill donor interests and strengthen the communities of Fairfield County." The Foundation identifies and responds to the needs of the community through specific initiatives, partnerships with funders, and strategic grantmaking. The Foundation's expanding Web site provides phone and e-mail contact information for further details.

The Greater Bridgeport Area Foundation, Inc. (http://www.gbafoundation.org)
Based in Bridgeport, Connecticut, the mission of the Greater Bridgeport Area Foundation is "to participate actively in shaping the well-being of the region by: raising resources entrusted to the Foundation; distributing income effectively to arts and entertainment, education, health and human services, and other charitable organizations serving the community; and identifying the pressing needs of the community and responding with appropriate initiatives and financial support." The Foundation primarily serves the communities of Bridgeport, Easton, Fairfield, Milford, Monroe, Shelton, Stratford, Trumbull, and Westport. The site contains grant guidelines, instructions, and application materials; scholarship listings, instructions, and application materials; a listing of scholarship recipients; and contact information.

Hartford Foundation for Public Giving (http://www.hfpg.org)
Established in 1925 to serve the changing needs of the residents of Connecticut's Capitol Region, the Hartford Foundation ranks among the largest of the country's community foundations. The Foundation provides grants and other support to a broad range of nonprofits, helps donors make effective charitable giving decision, and brings people together to discuss important community issues. The Foundation's Web site provides general information about the Foundation and its programs, information for nonprofits including the Foundation's grantmaking policies and a consultant database, information for donors about charitable giving, and a college scholarship directory and application form for students. Organizations interested in applying for a grant are encouraged to visit the Foundation's Web site or call the Foundation for a copy of its Grantee Guidelines and to discuss their interests with a member of the Foundation's program staff.

The Waterbury Foundation (http://www.waterburyfoundation.org/)
The Waterbury Foundation, headquartered in Waterbury, Connecticut, "makes grants to support programs that improve the quality of life for residents of the Central Naugatuck Valley and Litchfield Hills." The Foundation funds grants, a nonprofit management assistance initiative, and scholarships. Grants dealing with arts and humanities and youth growth and development are given priority. The Foundation's Nonprofit Assistance Initiative provides consulting or funding to help strengthen nonprofits in northwestern Connecticut. Scholarships are intended for residents of the 21-town service area of the Foundation, listed on the Web site. The Foundation also provides scholarship application guidelines and forms, which can be downloaded in PDF format, on the site. Grant guidelines and limitations, as well as information on donor services and a reply form to request more information from the Foundation can be found on the Web site as well.

DELAWARE

(http://www.delcf.org/)
Established in 1986, the Delaware Community Foundation (DCF) today has over $130 million in charitable assets and distributes close to $2 million annually from more than 345 restricted and unrestricted funds. The Foundation focuses its unrestricted grantmaking resources on building a stronger community, in large part by supporting disadvantaged populations. Program grants have been awarded to address some of Delaware's most pressing challenges, including affordable housing, homelessness, healthcare, arts stabilization, adolescent needs, and violence prevention. Unrestricted fund grants are distributed to qualified nonprofit organizations twice annually: in the winter for program support and in the summer for capital needs. The easy-to-navigate DCF Web site provides application guidelines and deadlines for grantseekers; information for potential donors, friends, and supporters; general information on starting an endowment; selections from recent DCF newsletters and an HTML version of the Foundation's most recent annual report; a listing of the Foundation's board and staff; and contact information.

DISTRICT OF COLUMBIA

The Community Foundation for the National Capital Region (http://www.cfncr.org)
The Community Foundation for the National Capital Region was founded in 1973. Its mission is to build philanthropic capital and improve the quality of life in the metropolitan Washington, D.C., area. It works to strengthen the region's nonprofit organizations and fund projects that offer new solutions to community needs. The Foundation assists individuals with philanthropy by helping them to invest time, money, and commitment in building a stronger, better region. The Foundation and its regional affiliates house hundreds of different funds, and each has its own set of guidelines for grantmaking. The Web site provides specific details about each fund's deadlines and application processes. The Foundation also provides services to nonprofit organizations, including planned giving tools. The Web site

also gives information about the Foundation's staff, history, and prior grantmaking and provides contact information. The annual report can also be found on the site.

FLORIDA

Community Foundation of Broward (http://www.cfbroward.org)

Based in Ft. Lauderdale, Florida, the Community Foundation of Broward (CFB) was incorporated in December 1984 and exists to enhance the quality of life for all residents of Broward County. The Foundation's focus areas are "Building our community through strengthening families," which means supporting programs that assist individuals, children and families in need through strengthening the effectiveness of community organizations and systems by developing healthy physical, cultural and social environments; animal welfare; arthritis research and cancer research/patient care; and adult literacy. The site also has a link to the Foundation's Nonprofit Resource Center, whose mission is "to provide varied resources for more efficient and effective nonprofit management, now and in years to come." Visitors to the site will find a nonprofit job bank, an online discussion forum for topics related to nonprofit organizations, a resource library, and nonprofit links. Visitors will also find a printable application form and contact information.

The Community Foundation for Palm Beach and Martin Counties
(http://www.cfpbmc.org/)

Founded in 1972 by Michael and Winsome McIntosh, "a community-conscious couple from New York," the Community Foundation for Palm Beach and Martin Counties (CFPBMC) today is a thriving enterprise with a $50 million endowment representing the gifts and commitments of many people. The Foundation applies the income from its assets to a wide range of community needs, including human and race relations, arts and culture, education, community development, health, human services, the environment, and the conservation and preservation of historical and cultural resources. In addition to a mission statement, a brief history of the Foundation, and listings of the Foundation's board, officers, and staff, the CFPBMC Web site provides program descriptions and information about the Foundation's Dwight Allison Fellows Program, grant guidelines and eligibility requirements, a selection of recent grants, a section on ways to give to the Foundation, and information about its Funding Resource Center.

The Community Foundation of Sarasota County (http://www.sarasota-foundation.org)

The Community Foundation of Sarasota County supports a variety of worthy causes throughout the west coast of Florida, including the arts and culture (increasing audiences for local artistic pursuits), community development (encouraging access to and use of community-based development methods), education (early childhood development, primary education through completion of high school and preparation for employment), the environment (promoting ways to conserve resources, encourage responsible animal welfare, and protect wildlife), health (basic medical, dental, and mental health needs), and human services (families, youth, seniors, the disabled, and the disadvantaged). The Foundation also administers 14 scholarship funds designated for students in Charlotte, Manatee, and Sarasota Counties, Florida. Scholarship recipients are selected on an objective, competitive basis that takes into account academic and non-academic factors plus demonstrated financial need. Visitors to the Foundation's Web site will find application guidelines, a current grants list, scholarship information, and information for donors.

Community Foundation of Tampa Bay (http://www.cftampabay.org)

The Community Foundation of Tampa Bay awards creative grants with the goal of fostering positive changes in the lives of area citizens. Program interests of the Foundation include arts and culture, community enablement, education, environment and animals, health and human services, history, neighborhoods, senior citizens, and youth and families. The primary area to be served by the Foundation is Hillsborough and Pinellas Counties, Florida. Visit the Foundation's Web site to see specific programs and areas not considered for funding, grant guidelines, grant application downloadable in PDF format, and contact information.

Jacksonville Community Foundation (http://www.jaxcf.org)

Jacksonville Community Foundation (JCF) is a grantmaking foundation that receives gifts or bequests from individuals, families, or organizations interested in providing, through the Foundation, financial support for charitable and public causes or institutions. Its goals are to strengthen families with children, improve services to infants and young children, strengthen neighborhoods, encourage conversation on community values, and foster vitality in the arts. JCF serves residents of the First Coast Region of northeast Florida, a five-county area including Baker, Clay, Duval, Nassau, and St. Johns Counties. Visit the Web site for application instructions, a description of the review process, contact information, and an FAQ page.

Mount Dora Community Trust (http://www.fnbmd.com/_docs/com_trust.htm)

The Mount Dora Community Trust of Mt. Dora, Florida, is committed to supporting "community activities and charitable organizations providing services to our community." Two major grant categories are schools and the public. The schools category includes grants for scholarships, classroom equipment, computers, and sports teams. The public category encompasses libraries, parks, the arts, and public festivals. The site includes a list of the members of the distribution committee, a list of past grants given, and an electronic request form for more information.

Pinellas County Community Foundation
(http://fdncenter.org/grantmaker/pinellas/index.html)

The purpose of the Pinellas County Community Foundation is to distribute the investment income from donated funds (or principal when directed by a donor) to recognized charitable organizations located in Pinellas County, Florida. If designated by a donor, charities located outside of the county can be beneficiaries of donated funds or income earned on those funds. The Foundation carefully screens charities in the county that request funding through discretionary grants and favors those that assist persons with handicaps, low or moderate incomes, or those who are trying to become self-sufficient. Also favored are nonprofit organizations that assist persons who have been abused or neglected or have special needs. The Foundation does not make grants to cultural groups, schools, or colleges; to organizations that are largely taxpayer or government funded; or to organizations that have large endowments or have significant fundraising staffs or abilities. The Foundation's folder on the Center's site provides information about the Foundation's structure, guidelines, donor funds, and financials; recent grants lists; reports from the Foundation's chairman and executive director; and contact information.

The Southwest Florida Community Foundation, Inc. (http://www.floridacommunity.com)

Located in Fort Meyers, Florida, the Southwest Florida Community Foundation was established in 1976 and is now composed of over 100 funds. The organization was created to "serve the charitable needs of Charlotte, Lee, Glades, Hendry, and Collier Counties, Florida." Areas of interest to the Foundation include arts and culture, education, environment, health and human services, community development, and historical and cultural resources. Of particular interest to the Foundation are projects that demonstrate an innovative approach to a community problem that has measurable outcomes. Besides its major grant program, the Foundation also distributes the Good Samaritan Fund, which addresses one-time emergencies that are not covered by any other funding. The extensive Web site includes a partial electronic application, the rest of which can be printed from the screen. There are detailed guidelines and deadlines and a list of past grantees. There is a board list and descriptions of the different types of funds that make up the Foundation. In addition, there is information on contributing to and joining the Foundation.

GEORGIA

The Community Foundation for Greater Atlanta, Inc. (http://www.atlcf.org/)

The Community Foundation for Greater Atlanta (CFGA) was established in 1951 for the purpose of improving the quality of life in the metropolitan Atlanta area. Today the Foundation manages 500 individual funds and more than $400 million in assets for the benefit of residents in a 22-county region (i.e, Barrow, Bartow, Butts, Carroll, Cherokee, Clayton, Cobb, Coweta, DeKalb, Douglas, Fayette, Forsyth, Fulton, Gwinnett, Hall, Henry, Newton, Paulding, Pickens, Rockdale, Spalding, and Walton Counties). The Foundation's Unrestricted Grants Program considers and funds proposals in seven major program areas: arts and culture, civic affairs, education, health, religion, social services, and community development. The Foundation emphasizes two of these areas each year (children, youth and families, and community capacity building in 2001). In addition to its application guidelines, the CFGA Web site provides information about the Foundation's community scholarships, information for donors and professional advisors (including a planned giving design center), press releases, and contact information.

Community Foundation of Central Georgia (http://www.cfcgonline.org)

The Community Foundation of Central Georgia is located in Macon, Georgia. It helps individuals, families, businesses, and nonprofit organizations meet their charitable goals by providing technical expertise and charitable giving services and by connecting donors with the projects and organizations that serve their interests. The Community Foundation grants benefit the entire central Georgia community. Currently, grant applications and guidelines can only be obtained by calling the number available on the site, although they will eventually be available directly on the Web site. The site also has a list of all the Foundation's funds, board members, and staff.

The Gwinnett Foundation (http://www.gwinnettfoundation.org)

Established in 1985, the Gwinnett Foundation strives to better the quality of life for the people of Gwinnett County, Georgia, by serving as a "catalyst for constructive programs and initiatives." The Foundation focuses on the areas of education, health and human services, community service, and the arts. Visitors to the Foundation's Web site will find a complete listing of specific funds available, some of which are linked to longer descriptions about the funds. Additionally, the Foundation provides financial information; information for donors; grant policies, restrictions, and deadlines; and information on the Foundation's philanthropic advising programs. All inquiries should be directed to the contact address and e-mail provided on the site.

North Georgia Community Foundation (http://www.ngcf.org/)

Established as the Gainesville Community Foundation in 1985, the North Georgia Community Foundation (NGCF) today provides grants and serves donors in an eight-county area (Hall, Banks, Dawson, Forsyth, Habersham, Jackson, Lumpkin, and White Counties). The Foundation is interested in organizations that can demonstrate that they have planned their projects in light of overall community need and that the projects can be replicated by other nonprofit organizations in other areas. The Foundation generally does not provide funding for annual fund campaigns, lobbying activities, ongoing operating support, or to individuals. Visitors to the NGCF Web site will find very general information about the Foundation and its activities, grant application guidelines, and a few words for potential donors.

HAWAII

Hawai'i Community Foundation (http://www.hcf-hawaii.org)

The Hawai'i Community Foundation was established in 1916, making it one of the oldest community foundations in the United States. The Foundation supports nonprofit organizations in the following areas: culture and art, natural resources conservation, education, health and medical research, human services, disability, mentoring and media, and neighbor island assistance. The Foundation also supports Hawaiian individuals through various scholarships. The Foundation's Web site lists a phone number and e-mail address to contact regarding each area of funding interest. Also available on the Web site are grant guidelines, a list of past grantees, a calendar with applicable deadlines, and resources the Foundation offers for Hawaiian nonprofits.

ILLINOIS

The Aurora Foundation (http://fdncenter.org/grantmaker/aurora/)
Established in 1948, the Aurora Foundation provides scholarships to students and grants to nonprofit organizations in the greater Aurora, Illinois, area, including the Tri-Cities and Kendall County. The Foundation's folder on the Center's Web site includes a mission statement and a "letter to the community;" information on ways to give and benefits to donors; a statement of principal transactions for the fiscal year ended September 30, 1996; a summary of grants awarded in 1996; and a listing of directors, officers, and staff.

The Chicago Community Trust and Affiliates (http://www.cct.org)
The Chicago Community Trust was established in 1915 to benefit the greater Chicago area. The Trust focuses on five main areas: arts and humanities, civic affairs, education, health, and social services. All funding is restricted to organizations that serve Cook County, Illinois, and its residents. Additionally, the Trust maintains two programs—the Human Resource Grant Program and the Management/Organizational Development (MOD) Grant Program—as well as a number of awards for community service and service to developmentally disabled individuals. The Trust's easy-to-use and thorough Web site includes details of each award and program, recent grants and news, an overview of the Trust organization, an FAQ, application procedures, and contact information.

DuPage Community Foundation (http://www.dupagecommfdn.org)
The DuPage Community Foundation of Wheaton, Illinois, was created in 1986 by longtime DuPage residents. The organization's goal is "to develop and channel philanthropy to meet the emerging, changing and ongoing needs of the people of DuPage County." Foundation funds include those supporting the arts, basic human needs, children and youth, the environment, health, and an operating fund to support the Foundation. There are also a variety of donor-advised funds, scholarship programs, and an agency endowment fund for a local children's chorus. The Foundation's Web site includes ample information on the history of community foundations and opportunities to create or contribute to a fund. The site also offers lists of the board of trustees and of all existing funds, including the founding donors for each one. There is basic contact information and an electronic form to submit inquiries.

Oak Park-River Forest Community Foundation (http://www.oprfcommfd.org)
The Oak Park-River Forest Community Foundation was established in 1958 "to provide a tangible, permanent contribution" to the residents of Oak Park and River Forest, Illinois. The Foundation focuses on supporting educational, cultural, and charitable organizations. The Foundation also provides scholarships and awards. Grant guidelines, FAQs, and contact information can be found at the Foundation's Web site.

INDIANA

Brown County Community Foundation (http://www.brownco.org/bccf.htm)
The Brown County Community Foundation, headquartered in Nashville, Indiana, is committed to improving the quality of life for its residents. The Foundation was established in 1993 with the help of a $500,000 Eli Lilly G.I.F.T. (Giving Indiana Funds for Tomorrow) Initiative grant. The Foundation supports such community programs as the Brown Literacy Fund, the Humane Society Fund, and scholarships to local students. The Web page outlines

the Foundation's mission, focusing mainly on details for donors, and includes contact information for perspective grantseekers.

Central Indiana Community Foundation (http://www.cicf.org/)
The Central Indiana Community Foundation (CICF) is the product of a collaborative effort between community foundations serving Marion and Hamilton Counties. The founding partners of CICF—the Hamilton County Legacy Fund and the Indianapolis Foundation—are "committed to a structure that sustains local engagement, leadership and capacity while supporting an expanded level of philanthropic service and growth for the region." In addition to assisting the community in "convening, consensus building and problem solving," the Foundation supports and coordinates a variety of special projects, including the Neighborhood Preservation Initiative, the Youth, Sport and Fitness Network, the Library Fund, Project Hi-Net, the Marion County Education Foundation Network, and the Partnership for National Service. Visitors to CICF's well-organized Web site will find a wealth of information about the Foundation's mission, donor services, programs, and initiatives, as well as links to resources of interest.

Community Foundation of Boone County (http://www.bccn.boone.in.us/cf/index.html)
The Community Foundation of Boone County was established in 1992 to serve residents of Boone County, Indiana. With a mission of providing a central philanthropic vehicle for donors of various interests and purposes, building and managing community capital, and serving a broad base of human service organizations, the Foundation was established to make a difference in the life of Boone County residents. The Foundation's main areas of interest are education, youth, culture, health and human services, civic affairs, environment, and recreation. The Foundation gives both to individuals and to nonprofits. Detailed application guidelines and deadlines are included at the Foundation's Web site, as well as contact information.

Community Foundation of Grant County (http://www.nxco.net/community)
The Community Foundation of Grant County, located in Marion, Indiana, was established in 1984 to serve as a vehicle through which "those of us who have lived our lives and earned our livelihoods in Grant County could pool our resources for the benefit of our own community." The Foundation offers financial support for several fields of interest, such as such as community development, community services, education, health, and human services. Grant and scholarship applications can be downloaded from the site, and visitors can read the Community Foundation report online.

The Community Foundation of Howard County, Inc. (http://www.carlnet.org/foundation)
The Community Foundation of Howard County was incorporated in 1991 in Kokomo, Indiana. The organization's mission is to "serve the interest of donors of enduring charitable gifts" and serve as a "catalyst for stimulating and funding initiatives that improve the quality of life for citizens of Howard, Carroll and Clinton Counties, Indiana." The grants program concentrates giving in the following areas: health and medicine, social services, education, cultural affairs, and civic affairs. The Foundation prefers to make gifts with an emphasis on seed money and considers making grants of technical or staff assistance. Potential grantees should send a letter of inquiry to the Foundation. All applicants must be pre-qualified to submit an application. This includes attending a community grants meeting and filing specific organizational information. Once a project has been approved to apply, there is an application packet that can be printed from the site. The Foundation also manages scholarship funds: award amounts and restrictions vary by fund, but each is simply described online. Interested students can print the application form online for many of these or can find contact information on applying for the rest. Basic grant application guidelines and restrictions are offered on the site, along with lists of past grantees and scholarship recipients. Visitors will also find board and staff lists, lists of funders, and information on creating a fund.

Community Foundation of St. Joseph County (http://www.cfsjc.org/)
The Community Foundation of St. Joseph County was established in South Bend, Indiana, in 1992 with the support of the Eli Lilly Endowment G.I.F.T. (Giving Indiana Funds for Tomorrow) Initiative. The Foundation is a "charitable endowment to improve the quality of life for the citizens of St. Joseph County and their succeeding generations." The Foundation maintains a number of grant programs and initiatives, including the Leighton Award for Nonprofit Excellence, African American Community Fund, Northern Indiana Partnership for Arts, and Special Project Challenge Grant. The Foundation provides application information on its Web site that can be downloaded in PDF format on the Partnership for Arts and Challenge Grant. Additionally, scholarships for high school seniors bound for Indiana colleges include: Lilly Endowment, Indiana University South Bend, Purdue University, Field of Interest, and Corporate Scholarships. A guide and application are provided for downloading in PDF format off the Web site. Visitor's to the site will also find the Foundation's Form 990-PF and attachments in PDF format, a financial statement, a list of recent grants, sites for professional advising and charitable donor information, a calendar of events, and a form to request more information.

Community Foundation of Wabash County (http://www.cfwabash.org)
The Community Foundation of Wabash County serves the residents of Wabash County, Indiana. The Foundation areas of interest include social services, education, civic affairs, cultural affairs, health and medical, recreation, and environment. The Foundation can be contacted directly from its Web site, where one can also find information on becoming a donor, application guidelines, board and staff lists, and contact information.

Dearborn County Community Foundation (http://www.dearborncounty.org/dccf)
The Dearborn County Community Foundation, based in Lawrenceburg, Indiana, makes grants in the fields of community service, social service, education, health, environment, and the arts. The Foundation's Web site contains descriptions of various grant and scholarship programs, downloadable grant applications, and contact information.

Elkhart County Community Foundation, Inc. (IN) (http://www.elkcocommfdn.org)
The Elkhart County Community Foundation (ECCF), located in Elkhart, Indiana, exists to create permanent endowment funds, make grants in the community, address the charitable needs of the community, and serve as a leader in meeting those needs. Specifically, the Foundation provides funding in the following areas: arts and culture, community development, education and health and human services. The Foundation accepts applications from organizations located in Elkhart County. ECCF funds innovative programs or projects that address problems to be solved or opportunities to be seized in Elkhart. The Foundation gives priority to programs that involve community collaboration where organizations work together towards a shared goal with shared responsibility and accountability. Grant application deadlines and guidelines are available on the Foundation's Web site. The site also lists the necessary materials to apply for a grant and has information for donors about different funds, planned giving, and current events.

Hancock County Community Foundation, Inc. (http://www.hccf.cc/)
The Hancock County Community Foundation, established in Greenfield, Indiana, in 1992, seeks "to build and improve the quality of life within the community through culture, education, physical and mental healthfulness, art, social services, social awareness and economic vitality." These goals are met through scholarships for post-secondary education, through specific Hancock County high schools, and grants. Grants fall into the following categories: health and human services, education, arts and culture, civic affairs, and youth. The Foundation's Web site offers grant guidelines, an online printable application form, and an outline of the grant review process. The site also includes a complete listing of scholarships, sorted by high school where they are available; information for donors; and a contact address.

Henry County Community Foundation, Inc.
(http://www.newcastlein.com/hccf/default.asp)

The mission of the Henry County Community Foundation, which is located in New Castle, Indiana, is to "help where the needs are the greatest and the benefits to the community and its citizens are most substantial, and to provide public-spirited donors a vehicle for using their gifts in the best possible way now and in the future as conditions inevitably change, and to provide excellent stewardship of those gifts which it receives." The Foundation awards grants in the areas of health and medicine, social services, education, cultural affairs, and civic affairs. Those interested in applying for a grant should first submit a letter of inquiry; details are available on the Foundation's Web site.

Indianapolis Foundation (http://www.cicf.org/About/fsetif.htm)

The Indianapolis Foundation was created in 1916—as one of the first such trusts in the United States—to serve the residents in and around Indianapolis, Indiana. The Mission of The Indianapolis Foundation is "to help where the needs are greatest and the benefits to our community and its citizens are most substantial; and to provide public spirited donors a vehicle for using their gifts in the best possible way now and in the future as conditions inevitably change." The Foundation funds programs in Marion County, and grants from its unrestricted Community Endowment Fund are made in the areas of arts, culture and humanities, civic and community development, education and libraries, health and human services, and information and technology. Grant guidelines, a list of the board of trustees, and the Foundation's financial statement are provided at its Web site. The Foundation partners with the Hamilton County Legacy Fund in the Central Indiana Community Foundation.

Kosciusko County Foundation (http://www.kcfoundation.org)

The Kosciusko County Foundation was first organized in Warsaw, Indiana, in 1968, as the Greater Warsaw Community Foundation under the sponsorship of the Warsaw Chamber of Commerce. In 1973 the Foundation was renamed for the county in which it is located. With help from the Indiana-based Lilly Endowment in 1990, the Foundation's assets grew significantly. Grants are given in civic services, education, health, culture, environment, and social services. Grant guidelines, financial information, and contact information can be found at the Foundation's Web site.

Lawrence County Community Foundation (http://www.kiva.net/~lccf/)

The mission of the Lawrence County Community Foundation is to "enhance the quality of life for the citizens of Lawrence County, Indiana, in the areas of education, health and human services, civic and historical affairs, the arts and culture, and recreational activities." The Foundation achieves its goals by attracting charitable donations from the community, managing those funds, and helping donors turn their philanthropic desires into reality. The Foundation works closely with other community organizations to meet the needs of the community, generally funding projects in the areas of arts and cultural activities, civic and historical affairs, education, recreation, and health and human services. A more detailed description of the types of projects the Foundation typically funds is available on the Foundation's Web site, as is information about how to apply and contact information. The actual application can be printed from the site. The site also provides financial information about the Foundation and lists of past grants awarded.

Legacy Fund of Hamilton County (http://www.cicf.org)

The Legacy Fund was founded in 1991 as a community foundation for the Hamilton County area. The Legacy Fund's mission is to "strengthen the Hamilton County community by attracting charitable endowments, maximizing benefits to donors, making effective grants, and providing leadership to address community needs." The Legacy Fund awards grants in the areas of arts and culture, health and human services, education, and civic affairs. The Fund's Web site provides financial statements and a list of the board of directors and staff for the Fund. The site also provides information about grant restrictions and limitations, as well as more in-depth descriptions of the types of programs the Fund supports and deadline information. The application may be downloaded in Microsoft Word format directly from the site.

Madison County Community Foundation (http://members.aol.com/mccf32in)

The Anderson, Indiana-based Madison County Community Foundation supports the arts and culture, education, health, human services, economic development, and civic affairs locally in order to enhance the quality of life of Madison County residents. The Foundation provides funding in the support of various named grants and scholarships. Information on grants, including grant procedure; an online grant cover sheet; application questions; and an evaluation form are available on the Foundation's Web site. These can be printed directly from the screen or submitted electronically. Scholarship application forms are available for downloading in either Miccrosoft Word or PDF formats from the site. The latest annual report includes listings of past grantees and scholarship recipients, financial information, recent events, and programs at the Foundation. The Web site also contains a newsletter and a contact e-mail address.

Montgomery County Community Foundation (http://www.mc-cf.org/)

The Crawfordsville, Indiana-based Montgomery County Community Foundation (MCCF), established in 1991, splits its funding between grants and scholarships in the local community. The Foundation's grants interests fall in five categories: health and medical; social services; education; arts, local history, and historical preservation; and civic affairs. The MCCF Web site includes a grants policy, with limitations and a schedule of funding, as well as details of recent grants. The Foundation also provides an MCCF Scholarship Central page with information on scholarships to students attending colleges in Indiana, a list of applicable institutions, and an application form that can be downloaded in PDF format. The Foundation's site also provides information for potential donors, a listing of the board and staff members, and contact information.

Noble County Community Foundation (http://www.kpcpages.com/?nccf)

The Noble County Community Foundation's primary mission is to improve the quality of life for the people of Noble County, Indiana. The Foundation holds interests in children and youth development, jail intervention programs, and operating funds for organizations within Noble County. The Foundation's limited Web site includes contact information and a listing of publications available through the Noble County Community Foundation.

The Portland Foundation (http://www.portlandfoundation.org)

Created in 1951, the Portland Foundation is the second oldest community foundation in Indiana. The organization works to "promote and assist donors in realizing their philanthropic intentions through the establishment of permanently endowed funds designed to address the ever-changing needs of the community." The Foundation's grant program funds nonprofits that serve the citizens of Jay County in areas including community improvement, arts and culture, health and human services, youth, economic development, and education. Funding usually is awarded to provide start-up funds for new programs, to address one-time needs or projects, or for capital needs. Proposal guidelines and applications can be printed straight from the Web page or downloaded in Microsoft Word format. The Foundation also awards scholarships to area students attending post-secondary schools. Applicants are judged by "academic accomplishment, financial need and resources available to the student, and activity and involvement in school, work and the community." Applications can be printed from the screen or downloaded in Microsoft Word format. The site offers excerpts from the most current Foundation newsletter, selections of the annual report, information on creating a fund, and an electronic message form for visitors to contact the Foundation staff.

Steuben County Community Foundation (http://www.steubenfoundation.org/)

The Steuben County Community Foundation serves the residents of Steuben County, Indiana. "The Foundation makes grants to support programs and projects in arts and culture, community development, education, health and human services and other charitable purposes. It also helps community groups develop and manage resources in the areas of special collaborative projects." Grant guidelines and contact information can be obtained at the Foundation's Web site.

Unity Foundation of LaPorte County (http://www.alco.org/orgs/unity/index.html)
The Unity Foundation of LaPorte County is based in Michigan City, Indiana. The Foundation supports the areas of the arts, education, health and human services, the environment, and the community in general for the benefit of the citizens of LaPorte County, Indiana. With various types of funds, including donor advised funds and endowments, the Foundation is able to support a wide range of programs and services. Grant guidelines and a contact address are provided for potential applicants on the Foundation's Web site. The site also includes a number of links and explanatory resources about community foundations in general.

Wabash Valley Community Foundation, Inc. (http://www.wvcf.com)
Established in 1991, the Wabash Valley Community Foundation is a public charity whose mission is "to improve the quality of life in the Wabash Valley." The Foundation receives gifts and administers an endowment comprised of numerous funds, large and small, from which it makes grants for community betterment. Grant and scholarship applications can be downloaded from the site in PDF format. The site also has deadline information, the opportunity to provide feedback or contact the staff, and information about upcoming community events.

Washington County Community Foundation (http://www.blueriver.net/~wcegp/foundation/wccf4.html)
Located in Salem, Indiana, the Washington County Community Foundation was created "to encourage philanthropy and the fostering of responsibility for the public good." The Foundation seeks and accepts donations from public and private sources and manages these funds for the purpose of distributing the earned assets, which are used to provide grants to community enhancing projects. The Washington Community Foundation is a collection of separate, charitable funds, each created by varied donors to fulfill a different purpose. To apply for a grant, interested organizations should submit a letter of inquiry. If the Foundation is interested, it will mail a grant application to be completed by the applicant. The Web site provides a list of grants approved in previous years as well as information about the types of funds that donors can create or contribute to.

IOWA

Greater Cedar Rapids Community Foundation (http://www.gcrcf.org)
The Greater Cedar Rapids Foundation, based in Cedar Rapids, Iowa, is a collection of more than 100 permanent and pass-through funds whose assets provide support to hundreds of nonprofit organizations and programs annually throughout Linn County. The mission of the Greater Cedar Rapids Foundation is "to assist in identifying unfulfilled needs of the community and to be a catalyst for solutions that have long-lasting impact." The Foundation considers requests for funding in seven broad areas: arts and culture, health, community affairs and development, historic preservation, education, human services, and the environment. The site contains a funds chart with specific information on priorities, areas of interest, and application deadlines for each fund. The site also provides information on the Iowa Community AIDS Partnership, a collaboration with the National AIDS Fund, which focuses on HIV/AIDS education, prevention, and direct services in Iowa communities. One–year grants are made to organizations headquartered in or serving Johnson, Linn, or Black Hawk Counties. Visit the site for printable application materials, grant lists, and contact information.

KANSAS

Greater Kansas City Community Foundation (http://www.gkccf.org/)

Established in 1978 and today comprised of more than 1,200 charitable funds, the Greater Kansas City Community Foundation strives "to make a positive difference in the lives and future of the people in Greater Kansas City"—Jackson, Clay, and Platte Counties in Missouri and Johnson and Wyandotte Counties in Kansas— "through grant making, advocacy, support of the not-for-profit sector and promotion of philanthropy for the benefit of the community." In addition to a listing of the Foundation's board and officers, contact information, and links to other sites of interest, visitors to the site will find general descriptions of the Foundation's programs, a listing of scholarships available through the Foundation, information about important Foundation initiatives in the areas of early childhood education and homelessness, application guidelines, a list of publications, an online copy of the annual report, upcoming events, and a section devoted to the services the Foundation provides to donors. The Foundation also maintains a searchable scholarship database that allows the individual grantseeker to locate participating funds that support or are devoted to specific educational scholarships.

KENTUCKY

Blue Grass Community Foundation (http://www.bgcf.org/)

The Blue Grass Community Foundation is a permanent community endowment built with gifts from individuals, families, foundations, businesses, and organizations committed to meeting the changing needs of the many communities surrounding central and eastern Kentucky. The Foundation holds several types of funds that provide grants for the community annually, makes scholarships, and provides funds to schools and universities. Funds can be set up in the form of discretionary funds, field of interest funds, scholarship funds, donor advised funds, designated funds, agency endowment funds, and affiliate funds. Upon entering the Foundation's Web site, visitors will find a copy of the latest tax return, a board listing, specific information about the available funds, application requirements, and contact information.

The Community Foundation of Louisville, Inc. (http://www.cflouisville.org/)

With nearly $180 million in assets, established in 1984, the Community Foundation of Louisville (CFL) promotes philanthropy in the Louisville area by enriching the quality of life of individuals and serving as a catalyst within the local community. The Foundation supports the programs of more than 1,000 charitable organizations with grants totaling over $30 million dollars annually. In addition to its unrestricted grantmaking, the Foundation awards community grants in support of programs designed to break the cycle of poverty in the Louisville neighborhoods of Algonquin, California, Chickasaw, Limerick, Old Louisville, Park DuValle, Park Hill, Parkland, Portland, Shawnee, and south Louisville; field of interest grants in the areas of the visual arts, crafts, theater, and historic preservation; donor endowment grants; nonprofit organization endowment grants; and scholarships. The CFL Web site provides a brief overview of the Foundation's activities, general program and application information, a list of recent community grants, an electronic order form for requesting print materials and application forms, a list of the Foundation's board and officers, and contact information.

LOUISIANA

Baton Rouge Area Foundation (http://www.braf.org)

The Baton Rouge Area Foundation, established in 1964, "seeks to enhance the quality of life for all citizens now and for generations to come." The Foundation makes grants in eight categories of interest, all of which are detailed on the Foundation's Web site: arts and humanities, community development, education, environment, human services, medical health, religion, and scholarships. Visitors to the site will find most information available as

PDF documents to be downloaded, including guidelines for specific named grants; the annual report; *Currents,* the Foundation's quarterly newsletter; and financial reports. Additionally, the Foundation provides donor and membership information, a list of recent grants, and contact addresses online.

Community Foundation of Shreveport-Bossier (http://www.comfoundsb.org/)

The Community Foundation of Shreveport-Bossier, established in 1961 in Shreveport, Louisiana, supports nonprofit organizations that serve the people of the Caddo and Bossier Parishes. Areas of funding include education, the environment, arts, youth services, programs for the elderly, and other social and cultural areas as determined by donors to the Foundation. Grants are made from a pool of funds: unrestricted, field of interest, designated, donor advised, and scholarships. The Foundation's Web site gives more specific information on these funds, including a list of past grants; guidelines, limitations, instructions, and the procedure for the application; and the structure of the eventual proposal. Foundation events, a guide for donors, the annual report, and contact information are also provided online.

Foundation for the Mid South (http://www.fndmidsouth.org/)

The Foundation for the Mid South makes grants "to build the capacity of communities, organizations, and individuals" throughout the states of Arkansas, Louisiana, and Mississippi. Grants are made within the three primary program areas of economic development, education, and families and children. In addition to general information about the Foundation, visitors to the Web site will find detailed program descriptions, including types of funding provided within each program area; downloadable application forms in PDF format; and an interactive bulletin board through which regional grantseekers and grantmakers can communicate. Selections from the Foundation's annual report, including listings of grants by program area, are also available.

The Greater New Orleans Foundation (http://www.gnof.org)

Founded in 1983 as successor to the Community Chest, the Greater New Orleans Foundation "improves the quality of life for all citizens of our area, now and for future generations." It serves as a catalyst and resource for philanthropy by awarding grants that invest in leaders and systemic change, building permanent endowments for the community, and serving as a vehicle for philanthropists to invest in the community. The Foundation makes grants primarily to nonprofit organizations in the broad program categories of arts and culture, education, health, human services, and public/society benefit. The Web site provides information about grant application guidelines and deadlines, as well as staff contact information.

MAINE

Maine Community Foundation (http://www.mainecf.org/)

The Maine Community Foundation (MCF) administers a variety of individual funds established to support a wide range of organizations and programs within the state of Maine. Funds may be restricted by their donors to support specific programmatic or geographic interests, while others are unrestricted and distributed at the Foundation's discretion. Discretionary grants are not awarded for lobbying or religious activities and are not generally awarded for endowment purposes, equipment, annual campaigns, regular operations, or capital campaigns. The Foundation also manages scholarship funds, provides technical assistance to guide grantseekers through the fundraising process, and is involved with a number of initiatives that provide major support to address specific issues within Maine. Visitors to the MCF Web site will find general information about the Foundation, application procedures, a staff listing, donor information, a community leadership section, scholarship information, a news and events section, and contact information for other Maine-based philanthropic organizations.

MARYLAND

The Baltimore Community Foundation (http://www.bcf.org/)

The Baltimore Community Foundation is a permanent collection of more than 270 different charitable funds supported by the general public and serving the greater Baltimore region. Each fund was established with a unique mission and purpose, which the Community Foundation is pledged to carry out in perpetuity. The Foundation is committed to helping donors plan and carry out their charitable giving, making grants that respond to community needs, and building a permanent source of charitable funds for the Baltimore region. The site gives further detail about the Foundation's mission, its donors, and board of directors.

The Columbia Foundation (http://www.columbiafoundation.org/)

The Columbia Foundation, the community foundation of Howard County, Maryland, was founded in 1969 by James W. Rouse. "The [organization's] purpose is to enhance the quality of life in Howard County by helping to meet diverse needs and building a more caring, creative and effective community." Grants are made in four major categories: human service, culture, education, and community affairs. Gifts are made in three different categories. A project grant supports the development of innovative, new programs. Operation grants go to groups that have existed for at least three years and during that time received and successfully used a grant from the Foundation. Finally, contingency grants are given to assist with unanticipated situations and crises. The site includes application guidelines and deadlines and an application and checklist for project grants that can be printed online. There are lists of past grantees and the board of directors, information on making contributions, and updates on news and events at the Foundation.

Community Foundation of Frederick County (http://www.cffredco.org)

Founded in 1986 in Frederick, Maryland, the Community Foundation of Frederick County "strive[s] to build a lasting legacy of financial support for human services, civic causes, scholarships, healthcare, the arts, education and historic preservation." The Foundation focuses its giving on scholarships, given to full-time students who are residents of Frederick County, and a variety of grants, which are distributed in the fall of the year. The Foundation posts extensive descriptions of its specific grant and scholarship funds, as well as contact information, on its Web site. The site also provides scholarship applicants with guidelines and deadlines and a printable application form. Grant application deadlines and guidelines, a detailed FAQ page with donor information, and other items of interest are available on the Foundation's site.

Community Foundation of the Eastern Shore (http://www.intercom.net/npo/commfnd/)

The Community Foundation of the Eastern Shore is dedicated to improving the quality of life in Worcester, Wicomico, and Somerset Counties, Maryland. The Foundation manages and distributes monies from individual funds in the areas of education, health and human services, arts and culture, community development and conservation, and historic preservation. Grants are awarded to nonprofit organizations located within or serving the three counties for three general purposes: "as seed funding for special projects that meet priority needs; as expansion funding to enable successful programs to serve broader constituencies; and to strengthen small and moderate sized nonprofit agencies that are providing exemplary services within [Foundation] areas of interest." Grants are usually not made for long-term operating support, building and endowment projects, budget deficits, sectarian programs, or direct assistance to individuals, other than through scholarship funds. Visitors to the Foundation's Web page will find general information about the Foundation, application guidelines and instructions, and contact information.

Prince George's Community Foundation, Inc. (http://www.pgcf.org/)

Incorporated in 1981 as the Prince George's County Parks and Recreation Foundation, in 1994 it became the Prince George's Community Foundation. It serves the residents of Prince George County, Maryland. The Foundation awards grants and services to community-based nonprofit groups, schools, and social services organizations that offer programs in the areas of human services, education, and children and youth. Contact information as well as application guidelines and a community resource directory can be found at the Foundation's Web site.

MASSACHUSETTS

The Boston Foundation (http://www.tbf.org/)
Founded in 1915, the Boston Foundation is one of the oldest and, with an endowment of more than $700 million, one of the largest community foundations in the country. The Foundation comprises more than 600 separate funds that have been established by hundreds of donors either for the general benefit of the community or for special purposes, such as giving that is targeted to a special need or the yearly support of specific nonprofit organizations. The current focus of the Foundation's discretionary grantmaking is the Building Family and Community Initiative, which gives priority to community-building strategies that help children and their families overcome poverty. Special funding initiatives include the Boston Foundation Arts Fund, the Vision Fund, the Fund for Preservation of Wildlife and Natural Areas, the Boston Schoolyard Initiative, and the Bruce J. Anderson Foundation. In addition to information about these initiatives and the Foundation's discretionary grantmaking, the Foundation's Web site provides application procedures and guidelines (in English and Spanish), a selection of recent grants, excerpts from past issues of the Foundation's quarterly newsletter, and information for donors.

Community Foundation of Cape Cod (http://www.capecodfoundation.com/)
Established in 1989, the Community Foundation of Cape Cod serves the community of Cape Cod, Massachusetts. The mission of the Foundation is to improve the quality of life for the people of Cape Cod through the support of educational and charitable programs. Areas in which grants are made include the arts, education, health and human services, conservation, the environment, and community development. The Foundation also provides scholarships for local students through a number of scholarship funds. The Foundation's Web site provides news, grant guidelines, a list of scholarship funds, grants lists, staff and board information, and a form through which to request additional information.

Community Foundation of Southeastern Massachusetts
(http://www.agmconnect.org/cfsem1.html)
The Community Foundation of Southeastern Massachusetts was established in the early 1990s. The Foundation "is not dedicated to one specific cause, it can aid local charities and nonprofit organizations in a variety of areas—from the arts to education, from the environment to helping the needy." Contact information can be found at the Foundation's Web site.

Greater Lowell Community Foundation (http://www.agmconnect.org/glcf.html)
The Greater Lowell Community Foundation seeks to improve the quality of life in the greater Lowell, Massachusetts, community. The Foundation is a "resource which attracts funds, distributes grants, makes loans, and serves as a catalyst and leader among funders, agencies and individuals to address identified and emerging community needs." It seeks to strengthen the administrative and program management capacity of nonprofits so they can more effectively address their mission, in a wide variety of fields, including health and social service, arts and culture, education, community development, recreation, and the environment. Available on its Web site are grant guidelines, a printable proposal summary form, and contact information.

Greater Worcester Community Foundation (http://www.greaterworcester.org)
The Greater Worcester Community Foundation is a permanent charitable resource to build healthy and vibrant communities in central Massachusetts. The Foundation achieves its mission by working with donors on tailored giving programs, by distributing grants to projects conducted by local nonprofit organizations, by convening people with shared goals to

solve problems, and by safeguarding the assets in its trust. Grants are made to a broad range of organizations including those involved in arts and culture, the environment, health and human services, youth, and community development. The Foundation also administers a scholarship program. For individuals, businesses, and private foundations the Greater Worcester Community Foundation offers low-cost stewardship of gifts, professional grants management, and the most generous tax benefits provided by law. The web site includes information for donors, grant guidelines and applications, lists of scholarships, and recent grants. Direct e-mail to staff is also available.

MICHIGAN

Albion Community Foundation (http://www.albionfoundation.org/)

The Albion Community Foundation has been serving the philanthropic needs of the Albion area since 1969. Its mission is to promote philanthropy, build a permanent community endowment, address community needs through grantmaking, and provide leadership on key community issues. The Foundation's Web site includes a grant application and cover sheet in PDF format, deadlines, recent grants, and contact information.

Alger Regional Community Foundation
(http://www.algercounty.com/communityfoundation/)

The Alger Regional Community Foundation was established in 1992. Located in Munising, Michigan, the Community Foundation provides financial support through grants to qualified tax-exempt organizations for projects aimed at solving community problems or enhancing life in Alger County. Grants are made in the field of cultural arts, community service, education, the environment and conservation, health and human services, youth, and scholarships. Grant requests must have direct relevance to the residents of Alger County. The Foundation makes no grants to individuals; in general, requests for sectarian religious purposes, budget deficits, routine operating expenses of existing organizations, and endowments are not funded. Visit the Web site for grant guidelines, instructions, and contact information. The site features a printable grant application.

Ann Arbor Area Community Foundation (http://www.aaacf.org/)

Since 1963, the Ann Arbor Area Community Foundation has been an agent for positive change in the Ann Arbor community. Specifically, its mission is to "enrich the quality of life in the greater Ann Arbor area." The Foundation achieves this goal by building a permanent endowment for the community, providing a flexible vehicle for donors with varied philanthropic interests, and acting as a leader of the local philanthropic community. The Ann Arbor Area Community Foundation administers over 100 funds and is most interested in funding projects that focus on education, social service, environmental awareness, culture, community development, or health and wellness; details about the Foundation's funding focus as well as information about special programs the Foundation is involved in can all be found online. The Foundation welcomes grant applications from organizations in Ann Arbor and the surrounding area. Prospective grant applicants are encouraged to contact the Foundation to discuss their proposal and obtain more information about the grantmaking process. Applications can be downloaded directly from the Web site in PDF format.

Baraga County Community Foundation (http://www.cmif.org/baraga.htm)

Baraga County Community Foundation was established in 1995 to serve the needs of Baraga County. The Foundation focuses its funding in the areas of cultural arts, community service, education, the environment and conservation, health and human services, and youth and scholarships. Visitors to the Foundation's Web site will find a newsletter and a listing of past grantees in Microsoft Word format, grant guidelines, and an online grant application form.

Barry Community Foundation (http://www.barrycf.org)
Established in July of 1995, the Hastings, Michigan-based Barry Community Foundation "bridges community needs with donor interests, granting dollars to programs, projects and organizations that fit our vision, to be a trusted resource for positive change." The Barry Community Foundation awards grants throughout Barry County for a wide variety of programs and projects that positively impact the lives of its residents. Visit the Web site for a grants list, printable application materials and instructions, a listing of funds, links to related sites, and contact information.

Battle Creek Community Foundation
(http://www.willard.lib.mi.us/npa/bccf/bccfindx.html)
The Battle Creek Community Foundation supports organizations in the Battle Creek area through four grant categories: unrestricted, the BCCF Health Fund, special funds, and scholarships. The Foundation funds programs and services in areas such as education, health, human services, arts, public affairs, and community development with grants of $250–$10,000. A Youth Alliance Committee, comprised of local high school students, reviews youth grant requests. The Foundation's Web site contains a page with instructions on accessing an online database of scholarships. The Web site also provides funding guidelines and limitations. Visitors should contact the appropriate Foundation department for an application packet.

Bay Area Community Foundation (http://www.bayfoundation.org/)
The Bay Area Community Foundation was created in 1982 by an endowment from the Kantzler Foundation. The Foundation serves to improve the quality of life in the Bay Area community. Visit the Foundation's Web site for more information.

Berrien Community Foundation (http://www.qtm.net/~bcf)
The Berrien Community Foundation is a public charity established in 1952 to improve the quality of life for the people of Berrien County, Michigan. It is a permanent, growing endowment built by gifts both large and small from individuals, families, organizations, and businesses. The Community Foundation promotes, builds, and maintains a permanent collection of endowment funds used to shape effective responses to community issues and opportunities. The Foundation manages and awards grants from more than 65 individual endowments ranging from field-of-interest funds to donor advised funds. Grants are awarded in the general areas of the arts and culture, community development, education and scholarships, health and human services, restoration and preservation of historical resources, sustainable development, youth leadership and development, and strengthening the family—with an emphasis on the needs of young children and women. Visitors to the Foundation's Web site will find information about grants, guidelines, and a wide range of donor services.

Cadillac Area Community Foundation (http://www.netonecom.net/~cavb/CACF.htm)
The Cadillac Area Community Foundation, established in 1988, supports the areas of arts and culture, education, healthcare, environment, human service, economic development, and youth and recreation in the Cadillac community. The Foundation's Web site gives some information on past grantees and contains contact information for further details.

Capital Region Community Foundation (http://www.crcfoundation.org/)
The Michigan-based Capital Region Community Foundation's mission is to serve the charitable needs and enhance the quality of life in Ingham, Eaton, and Clinton Counties. The fields of interest to the Foundation include the following areas: humanities, education, environment, healthcare, human services, and public benefit. Visit the Foundation's site to find out a history of the Foundation, how to become a donor, grant guidelines, and contact information.

Community Foundation for Muskegon County (http://www.cffmc.org/)

The Community Foundation for Muskegon County was established in 1961 to serve Muskegon County, Michigan, residents. The Foundation supports projects in the areas of arts, education, community development, health, human services, and youth issues, and operates its own performing arts center. The Foundation's Web site includes contact information, a detailed description of the different types of support it provides, and a brief description of application guidelines. Potential applicants are encouraged to contact the Foundation.

Community Foundation for Southeastern Michigan
(http://comnet.org/comfound/index.html)

The Community Foundation for Southeastern Michigan serves the residents of seven counties in southeastern Michigan. Its main areas of interest are education, arts and culture, health, human services, community development, and civic affairs. The Foundation has an informative Web site, that includes very specific application guidelines and a list of the types of support the Foundation does not provide. The Foundation has major interest in improving the already existing cultural and economic infrastructure of its geographic area. Contact information, including a telephone number, is included at the Web site.

Community Foundation of Greater Flint (http://www.flint.lib.mi.us/cfflint/)

Through its support of "projects aimed at solving community problems or enhancing life in the county," the Community Foundation of Greater Flint is committed to improving the quality of life in Genesee County, Michigan. The Foundation makes grants through more than 100 funds in the fields of arts and humanities, advancing philanthropy, community services, education, conservation and the environment, and health, human, and social services. The Foundation also makes limited grants from discretionary funds, with special priority given to programs addressing issues of persistent and pervasive poverty and children under the age of ten. The Foundation does not make grants to individuals, for sectarian religious purposes, budget deficits, routine operating expenses of existing organizations, or endowments. Visitors to the Foundation's simple, straightforward Web site will find general information about the Foundation and its funding priorities, application guidelines, and information for potential donors.

Community Foundation of Greater Rochester (http://www.cfound.org/)

The Community Foundation of Greater Rochester was established in 1983 by Richard Huizenga, a local educator and leader. The Foundation is "dedicated to enhancing the quality of life for the citizens of the Greater Rochester Area in the following ways: asset development; . . . providing a perpetual source of income to help meet the charitable needs of our community; . . . and managing funds and awards." The organization distributes grants from restricted fund to designated groups and makes awards to applicants through unrestricted funds. Grants are given to innovative projects that support art, culture, youth, and other philanthropic activities. Interested nonprofits in the area can send a letter of intent to the Foundation at any time. A staff member will then notify the group of the next step. The Foundation also awards a series of scholarships to local high school seniors. Interested students can download scholarship descriptions, applications, and the required appraisal form in PDF format. The site also includes extensive information on contributing to or starting a fund, a list of existing funds, and a list of the board and staff.

The Community Foundation of the Holland/Zeeland Area
(http://www.macatawa.org/~cfothza)

Formerly the Holland Community Foundation, the mission of the Community Foundation of the Holland/Zeeland Area is to make the greater Holland-Zeeland area a better place to live and work by enhancing the quality of life for all its citizens. The Holland, Michigan-based Foundation is a community foundation that manages endowments, using the income to "meet the needs and enhance the quality of life in ways that are compatible with the wishes of the donor and the goals of the community" through a wide variety of funds and scholarships. Areas of interest to the Foundation are arts and culture, education, health, recreation, youth, elderly, affordable housing, social needs, environment, and natural resources. Grants are focused on capital projects and "new, creative endeavors." Visitors to the Web site will find grant guidelines, application instructions, an online application (and one that can be downloaded in Microsoft Word format), a detailed listing of managed funds, past grants, and contact information.

Dickinson County Community Foundation (http://biz-comm.com/dcacf)

The Dickinson County Area Community Foundation is an independent, nonprofit organization located in Iron Mountain, Michigan. Established in 1995 for the area of Dickinson County and surrounding Wisconsin communities, the Foundation encourages philanthropic investment in the Dickinson County area by building and managing permanent endowments and utilizing the income to enhance the community's quality of life. The Foundation states that it "is not designed to compete with, nor duplicate, the efforts of other agencies which provide ongoing support for charitable organizations and services;" rather, it provides "one-time-only and start-up funding, support for innovative projects when there is an identified need that cannot be met by other means, and programs that enhance the quality of life in [the] community." While the Foundation supports a broad range of activities, its current grantmaking focus is on youth. Visit the Web site for a printable grant application. The Foundation's site also provides contact information and press releases.

Forest Park Community Fund (http://www.cmif.org/forest.htm)

The Forest Park Community Fund serves the philanthropic needs of the Crystal Falls, Amasa, and Alpha areas in the cultural arts, community service, education, the environment and conservation, health and human services, and youth and scholarships. The Fund strives to solve community problems and enhance community life. Visitors to the Fund's Web site will find a detailed list of current funds, local links of interest, application guidelines, and an online grant application form.

Four County Community Foundation (http://www.4ccf.org/)

The Four County Community Foundation serves the northeast corner of Oakland County, the southeast corner of Lapeer County, the southwest corner of St. Clair County, and the northwest corner of Macomb County, Michigan. The Foundation is dedicated to bringing together human and financial resources to support progressive ideas in education, health, community, youth, and adult programs. Visit the Foundation's Web site to find a brief history, a staff listing, specific information on the grant program, and contact information.

Fremont Area Foundation (http://www.tfaf.org/)

The Fremont Area Foundation serves the community interests of Newaygo County, Michigan, through a variety of grants, scholarships, and initiatives. Areas of interest for funding include health, education, social welfare, civic responsibilities, arts and culture, character building, and rehabilitation—all for the benefit of Newaygo residents and services. The Foundation's Web site includes guidelines, instructions for grant applications, and an online cover sheet, to be used for all funds. Other programs that the Foundation supports include a Summer Youth Initiative, to organizations providing summer youth programs; scholarships, with detailed descriptions of each and an online application form; and other initiatives (detailed on the Web site), such as Leadership in Newaygo County (LiNC), Newaygo County Youth Initiative (with a grant application), and Salute to Educators (with a nomination form). The Foundation's Web site also includes links and contact information.

The Grand Rapids Foundation (http://www.grfoundation.org/)

Established in 1922, the Grand Rapids Foundation serves Grand Rapids, Michigan, and its surrounding communities. With a mission to build and manage the community's permanent endowment and lead the community to strengthen the lives of its people, the Foundation's fields of interest include education, arts and culture, health, environment, and human services. The foundation offers grants and scholarships and provides detailed information about both at its Web site. Applications can be downloaded and contact information is provided.

Grand Traverse Regional Community Foundation (http://www.gtrcf.org/)

The Grand Traverse Regional Community Foundation is committed to enhancing the quality of life in it regions. Specifically, the Foundation serves Antrie, Benzie, Grand Traverse, Kalkaska, and Leelan Counties, all located in Michigan. It facilitates philanthropy by providing leadership that coordinates the use of resources for community improvement. The Foundation establishes and develops permanent endowment funds; involves regional volunteers in developing, managing, and distributing income; develops an understanding of the role of philanthropy in helping the community; and empowers individuals to make a difference through grantmaking and leadership. The site has a FundFinder that allows users to learn about the types of funds the Foundation houses and also has a search feature that allows users to locate funds either by county or keyword. The site provides information about the Foundation's staff and financials. The annual report, Foundation calendar, and recent press releases can also be found on the site.

The Jackson County Community Foundation (http://www.jacksoncf.org/)

The Jackson County Community Foundation was founded in 1948 for the purpose of assisting the residents of Jackson, Michigan. The Foundation provides support to the programs and services of nonprofits in areas such as the arts, community development, education, health, and human services. It "serves as a convener of individuals and organizations for the purpose of identifying community-wide challenges and opportunities as well as the resources to address both."Application guidelines and contact information are available at the Foundation's Web site.

Keweenaw Community Foundation (http://www.cmif.org/keweenaw.htm)

Established in 1994, the Keweenaw Community Foundation supports the counties and communities of Houghton and Keweenaw. The Foundation's funding interests address the areas of arts and culture, community and economic development, education, environment, and historic preservation. Current funds include the Portage Lake Endowment, the Portage Health Endowment, and the Youth Endowment, which is one of the Foundation's main focuses. The Foundation's Web site includes a list of current funds, information for donors and applicants, and contact information.

Les Cheneaux Community Fund (http://www.cmif.org/lescheneaux.htm)

The mission of the Les Cheneaux Community Fund, established in 1997, is "to provide opportunities for [the] community to invest in its future." The Foundation concentrates its giving in the areas of education and cultural enrichment, environment, scholarships, youth, and for the development of a library and cultural resource center for the Les Cheneaux area. The Foundation's Web site lists current endowment funds, information for donors and applicants, and contact information for more details.

Mackinac Island Community Foundation (http://www.micf.org)

Established in 1994, the Mackinac Island Community Foundation serves the general well-being of Island residents and visitors. The Foundation, through a number of specific funds, supports the arts, health, social sciences, humanities, education, youth, senior citizens, beautification, the environment, and the conservation and preservation of historical and cultural resources. The Foundation's Web site details current funds, provides donor and grant applicant information, and posts contact information for further resources.

M & M Area Community Foundation (http://www.cmif.org/mm.htm)

M & M Area Community Foundation strives to promote the spirit of philanthropy and meet the needs of the people of Menominee County, Michigan, and Marinette County, Wisconsin. A variety of funds provide support in the areas of education, the environment, and cultural, recreational, and charitable purposes. The Foundation's Web site provides a list of current funds, donor and applicant information, and contact information for more details.

Marquette Community Foundation (http://www.cmif.org/marquette.htm)

The Marquette Community Foundation, founded in 1988, follows its mission: "to enhance the charitable, educational, cultural, recreational, environmental, and social welfare needs of the Greater Marquette Area." The Foundation's Web site lists its current funds and affiliate funds. Also available online is information for grant applicants and donors, and contact information for further details.

Michigan Gateway Community Foundation (http://www.mgcf.org)

The Michigan Gateway Community Foundation was established to strengthen south Berrien and Cass Counties. The Foundation supports organizations that strengthen families and youth by providing prevention-oriented social action programs; that assist families and youth to find quality of life in the arts, beautification, recreation and other diverse family programs; and that help solve community problems. Visit the Foundation's Web site to view detailed information on the programs the Foundation supports, deadlines, recent grants recipients, financial information, and contact information.

The Midland Foundation (http://www.midlandfoundation.com)

The 25-year-old Midland Foundation promotes and enables community-wide philanthropic giving to enrich and improve the lives of residents throughout the greater Midland County area. Now the eighth-largest of the community foundations in Michigan, the Foundation restricts its discretionary grantmaking to 501(c)(3) nonprofit, educational nonprofit, or governmental nonprofit organizations and to projects that have a direct relevance to the people of Midland County and the surrounding area. While the Foundation does not make grants directly to individuals, it does administers two student loan funds and a general scholarship program for Midland County high school seniors or college students, as well as for adults who are resuming undergraduate work or who are retraining to enter the job market. All grant requests must be submitted on the Foundation's grant application form, and applicants are encouraged to discuss their proposal with the Foundation's executive director prior to completing the application form. Visitors to the Foundation's Web site will find general information about the Foundation and its activities; general grant, student loan, and scholarship application forms in three formats (Microsoft Word, WordPerfect, and PDF); relevant application deadlines and a deadline calendar; information for donors; and contact information.

Norway Area Community Fund (http://www.cmif.org/norway.htm)

The Norway Area Community Fund is committed to meeting "the social, recreational, educational, historical and cultural needs of the Norway Area, now and in the future." The Fund serves the City of Norway and surrounding townships. The Foundation's Web site provides information for donors and potential applicants, a list of current funds, and contact information for more details.

Paradise Area Community Foundation (http://www.cmif.org/paradise.htm)

The Paradise Area Community Foundation was established in 1983 and became an affiliate of Upper Peninsula Regional Community Foundation, allowing it to share in the UPRCF's substantial resources. The Paradise Area Community Foundation's mission is "to support community programs and services and to enhance the historic, cultural and sociological assets for the Paradise area and nearby communities not served by other community foundations in Chippewa and Luce Counties." The Foundation supports the areas of cultural arts, community service, education, the environment and conservation, health and human services, and youth and scholarships. Endowment Funds include community service, education, community development, library support, and emergency services. The Foundation's Web site lists information for donors and potential applicants, current funds, and contact information for more details.

**Petoskey-Harbor Springs Area Community Foundation
(http://www.petoskey-harborspringsfoundation.org)**

The Petoskey-Harbor Springs Area Community Foundation, founded in 1991 in Petoskey, Michigan, is a "permanent pool of flexible resources [addressing] new and ongoing needs in our area to build a stronger community." The Foundation supports programs in areas such as human services, health, the environment, economic development, the arts, and education. The Foundation's Web site provides information for donors and contact information for those interested in more details.

Saginaw Community Foundation (http://www.SaginawFoundation.org/)

The Saginaw Community Foundation (SCF) is dedicated to improving the quality of life in Saginaw County, Michigan. Its donors are individuals, families, corporations, and organizations who establish permanent charitable funds within the Foundation. From arts and education to human services and the environment, SCF supports all types of community projects. Guided by the wishes of its donors, SCF makes grants and awards scholarships to a wide variety of nonprofit organizations and individuals throughout Saginaw County. Visitors to the SCF Web site can find detailed information about its grants, downloadable grant applications, board and staff listings, and information on the Foundation's scholarship program. In addition, there is a special section for professional advisors.

Sault Area Community Foundation (http://www.cmif.org/sault.htm)

The Sault Area Community Foundation was founded in 1994 "to benefit the Eastern Upper Peninsula for charitable, educational, cultural, recreational, environmental, and social welfare purposes in a manner which promotes the spirit of philanthropy and utilizes the talents and abilities of its youth." Visitors to the Foundation's Web site will find information for donors and potential applicants, a list of current funds, and contact information—with current Foundation officers—for more details.

Southfield Community Foundation (http://www.scfmi.org)

The Southfield Community Foundation was established by philanthropically active business, civic, and community leaders in 1989 to enhance the lives of those who work and live in Southfield and Lathrup Village. To accomplish this mission, the Foundation focuses on four areas: Service to Donors, Grants to the Community, Community Building Activities, and The Promotion of Philanthropy. Through the development of permanent funds made by donations from individuals, corporations, and foundations, the Foundation creates a flexible base of financial, informational, and human resources that can be used to effectively address the community's changing needs. Visit the Foundation's Web site to find a brief history, FAQs, specific information on the grant program, and contact information.

St. Ignace Area Community Fund (http://www.cmif.org/stignace.htm)

The St. Ignace Area Community Fund is dedicated to improving the quality of life in the St. Ignace area through the support of nonprofit programs and services. The Fund considers grants in the general categories of cultural arts, community service, education, the environment and conservation, health and human services, and youth and scholarships. Visitors to the Fund's Web site will find an annotated list of current funds, information for donors and potential applicants, and contact information for more details.

Upper Peninsula Community Foundation (http://www.cmif.org/upcfa.htm)

The Upper Peninsula Community Foundation, based in Galdstone, Michigan, provides financial support through grants to qualified tax-exempt organizations for projects aimed at solving community problems or enhancing life in the community. The Foundation serves as a catalyst for change, an innovator to solve problems, a partner with other community organizations, and as a resource for solutions to emerging community needs. Grants are made in the fields of cultural arts, community service, education, the environment and conservation, health and human services, and youth and scholarships. Visit the site for contact information.

MINNESOTA

Duluth-Superior Area Community Foundation
(http://www.dsacommunityfoundation.com)

Incorporated in 1982, the Duluth-Superior Area Community Foundation strives to improve the quality of life for the residents of Duluth, Minnesota; Superior, Wisconsin; and the surrounding areas. The Foundation supports local projects and organizations in the arts, civic projects, education, environment, and human services. Information on specific named grants and general grants, as well as previous grantees in each area of interest, is available on the Foundation's Web site. Scholarships are also granted, and more information can be obtained by contacting the Foundation. The Foundation's site provides recent annual reports online, donor information, a contact form, a short history of the Foundation, and a list of its staff and board.

The Minneapolis Foundation (http://www.mplsfoundation.org/)

Created more than 80 years ago to encourage and facilitate philanthropy in the Minneapolis-St. Paul area, the Minneapolis Foundation today seeks to improve the quality of life in the Twin Cities by making program or project-specific support grants, operating support grants, and capital support grants in the following areas: children, youth, and families in poverty; public policy research; neighborhood capacity building; economic development and employment; low-income senior citizens; people with disabilities; healthcare for low-income citizens; and medical research and services for children's chronic diseases. Program details are fully explained in the Foundation's grant guidelines, which can be ordered from the Publications area of the Foundation's Web site. The site also offers brief descriptions of a dozen of the Foundation's programs and projects; press releases and a regional events calendar; information for prospective donors; financial statements and a copy of the Foundation's Form 990–PF for the latest year; listings of the Foundation's staff, board, and trustees; and contact information.

The Minnesota Foundation (http://www.mnfoundation.org/)

The primary mission of the Minnesota Foundation is to assist individuals, organizations, and communities statewide in developing local charitable trusts. The Foundation is affiliated with the Saint Paul Foundation, which, generally speaking, serves the east metropolitan area of the Twin Cities. The Foundation does not make grants on a general unrestricted basis and, therefore, does not publish grant guidelines or application forms. Professional financial advisors will appreciate the link to the Planned Giving Design Center, which was created by the two organizations to provide financial advisors with resources they can use to advise their clients in matters of charitable gift and estate planning. The site also has a section for potential donors and provides contact information for those who'd like to learn more about the Foundation and its programs.

Northwest Minnesota Foundation (http://www.nwmf.org)

Established in 1986, the Northwest Minnesota Foundation's mission is "to improve the quality of life for the residents in the twelve counties of northwest Minnesota." The Foundation, which is located in Bemidji, Minnesota, provides grants to nonprofits, governmental units, and public institutions. Grants are awarded in the areas of technical assistance, youth entrepreneurship, and general grants. Grants are awarded only to organizations that work within the twelve county area described on the Web site. To be considered for a grant, an organization must first submit a pre-proposal, which can be printed online.

The Saint Paul Foundation (http://www.tspf.org/)

The Saint Paul Foundation was established in 1940 with a $5,000 bequest from a Lithuanian immigrant named Annie Paper. Today, it's the largest community foundation in the state of Minnesota and a major philanthropic force in the city of Saint Paul. The Foundation exists to help create a healthy and vital community in which all people have the opportunity to enhance the quality of their lives and the lives of others. To achieve its mission, the Foundation makes grants in eight fields of interest: arts and humanities, civic affairs, education, environment and nature, health, human services, religion, and scholarships. Visitors to the Foundation's Web site will find grant and application guidelines for grantseekers, grant listings, information on starting a fund, information for scholarship seekers and prospective donors, a separate section on the Foundation's Diversity Endowment Funds initiative, and contact information.

St. Croix Valley Community Foundation (http://www.pressenter.com/~scvcf/)
Founded in 1995, the St. Croix Valley Community Foundation serves the communities of St. Croix Valley in Wisconsin and Minnesota. Its fields of interest include education, arts, environment, civic affairs, and emergency human needs. The Foundation's Web site includes its annual report, board and staff lists, and a form to request more information.

MISSISSIPPI

Foundation for the Mid South (http://www.fndmidsouth.org/)
The Foundation for the Mid South makes grants "to build the capacity of communities, organizations, and individuals" throughout the states of Arkansas, Louisiana, and Mississippi. Grants are made within the three primary program areas of economic development, education, and families and children. In addition to general information about the Foundation, visitors to the Web site will find detailed program descriptions, including types of funding provided within each program area; downloadable application forms in PDF format; and an interactive bulletin board through which regional grantseekers and grantmakers can communicate. Selections from the Foundation's annual report, including listings of grants by program area, are also available.

MISSOURI

Greater Kansas City Community Foundation (http://www.gkccf.org/)
Established in 1978 and today comprised of more than 1,200 charitable funds, the Greater Kansas City Community Foundation strives "to make a positive difference in the lives and future of the people in Greater Kansas City"—Jackson, Clay, and Platte Counties in Missouri and Johnson and Wyandotte Counties in Kansas— "through grant making, advocacy, support of the not-for-profit sector and promotion of philanthropy for the benefit of the community." In addition to a listing of the Foundation's board and officers, contact information, and links to other sites of interest, visitors to the site will find general descriptions of the Foundation's programs, a listing of scholarships available through the Foundation, information about important Foundation initiatives in the areas of early childhood education and homelessness, application guidelines, a list of publications, an online copy of the annual report, an upcoming events list, and a section devoted to the services the Foundation provides to donors. The Foundation also maintains a searchable scholarship database that allows the individual grantseeker to locate participating funds for that support are devoted to specific educational scholarships.

MONTANA

The Lower Flathead Valley Community Foundation (http://www.lfvcf.org/)
The Lower Flathead Valley Community Foundation serves the community of Flathead Valley, Montana. The Foundation's purpose "is to bring tribal and non-tribal members together to work on projects preserving and conserving the cultural, natural and human resources of the region, with special emphasis on meeting the needs of children." The Foundation's fields of interest include education, preservation and conservation, culture, arts, health, human services, and civic improvement. Contact information can be found at the Foundation's Web site.

Montana Community Foundation (http://www.mtcf.org/)
Established in 1988, the Montana Community Foundation is a statewide charitable organization that administers more than 420 private and public funds encompassing the whole spectrum of philanthropy. The Foundation makes grants totaling more than $200,000 annually in five focus areas—arts and culture, basic human needs, economic development, education, and natural resources and conservation—and two additional categories: leadership development and tolerance. The MCF Web site provides a good overview of the Foundation and its activities; descriptions of its General Grants, Leadership Development, and Fund for Tolerance programs; grant application procedures and a grant application cover sheet; information for potential donors; a list of board members and staff; links to sites of interest; and contact information.

NEBRASKA

Grand Island Community Foundation (http://www.gicf.org/)
The Grand Island Community Foundation (GICF) was established in 1960 to make a lasting difference in the quality of life for greater Hall County area citizens. The Foundation does not operate charitable programs itself, but, through partnering and coordination, it assists in orchestrating charitable activities within the greater Hall County community. The principle vehicle for its activities in this area is the GICF "wish list," which leverages the GICF Web site and other emerging communications technologies to bring potential donors together with worthwhile charitable causes and organizations. In addition to the still-developing "wish list" and general background information, the GICF Web site provides information about a number of endowed scholarship funds established by people and organizations wanting to assist Grand Island and Hall County area students in continuing their education beyond high school.

Lincoln Community Foundation (http://www.lcf.org/)
Established in 1955, The Lincoln Community Foundation makes grants to enrich the quality of life in Lincoln and Lancaster Counties, Nebraska. The Foundation administers and disperses monies from a permanent unrestricted endowment, responding to emerging and changing community needs and sustaining existing organizations through grants for education, arts and culture, health, social services, economic development, and civic affairs. The Foundation also manages a number of individual funds established by donors with specific philanthropic interests. Visitors to the Foundation's Web site will find general discretionary funding guidelines and restrictions, application instructions (including the common application form accepted by a number of area grantmakers), information for donors interested in establishing funds, and a staff listing. Visitors will also find a listing of recent grants, excerpts from the latest annual report, and a full description of its grantmaking focus and programs.

Nebraska Community Foundation (http://www.nebcommfound.org/)
The Nebraska Community Foundation was established in 1993 to provide financial management, strategic development, and education/training services to communities, organizations, and donors throughout Nebraska. The Foundation provides affiliated fund status (allowing communities or organizations to achieve nonprofit charitable status without forming their own nonprofit corporation) and strategic development assistance in nearly 180 communities throughout Nebraska. The Foundation also maintains a special initiative called the Rural Entrepreneurship Initiative that attempts to build stronger rural development strategies employing entrepreneurial opportunities. Visitors to the Foundation's Web site will find information on how to start or support a current fund, a recent annual report, a listing of recent grant recipients, and contact information.

Omaha Community Foundation (http://www.omahacf.org/)
The Omaha Community Foundation (OCF) was created to enhance the quality of life for the citizens of the greater Omaha community by identifying and addressing current and

anticipated community needs, as well as raising, managing, and distributing funds for charitable purposes in the areas of education, health, and civic, cultural, and social services. The Foundation's three primary grantmaking programs are the Fund for Omaha, Neighborhood Grants, and the Women's Fund Community Initiated Grants. Each program has a different process and timetable, though all limit their grants to organizations, not individuals, serving the greater Omaha area. In addition to general information about the Foundation's grantmaking, visitors to the OCF Web site will find a Planned Giving Design Center with resources that can be used in matters of charitable gift and estate planning, an electronic publications request form, and staff contact information.

NEW HAMPSHIRE

New Hampshire Charitable Foundation (http://www.nhcf.org)
The New Hampshire Charitable Foundation, headquartered in Concord, was founded in 1962, making it the first community foundation in northern New England. The Foundation incorporates five regional chapters: Greater Piscataqua, Lakes Region, Monadnock, northern New Hampshire, and Upper Valley Community Foundations. The New Hampshire Charitable Foundation's Web site includes links to the sites of each of these regional foundations, with particular information on their specific grants and programs. For general grant information, visitors must contact the Foundation by phone or e-mail. Contact information is included on the Web site. The Foundation has an extensive scholarship program for New Hampshire graduate, adult, undergraduate, and graduating high school students. The Web site includes a scholarship application guide, a listing of specific scholarships, and some program application forms that can be downloaded in PDF format. Further information for donors, through the Foundation's Planned Giving Design Center, can also be accessed through the site.

NEW JERSEY

Princeton Area Community Foundation (http://www.princetonol.com/groups/pacf/)
The Princeton Area Community Foundation (PACF) was established in 1991 to bring the services of a community foundation to the greater Mercer County area. Today, the Foundation seeks "to enter into partnerships with nonprofit organizations that are actively involved in developing their community," while supporting "groups working to coordinate resources and strengthen relationships between residents, businesses and institutions in a neighborhood." In addition to a brief history of the Foundation and information about the New Jersey AIDS Partnership, the PACF Web site provides application guidelines; a listing of the Foundation's various unrestricted, donor-advised, memorial, and scholarship funds; recent grants lists; brief trustee and associate profiles; and information for prospective donors.

Westfield Foundation (http://www.westfieldnj.com/wf/index.htm)
The Westfield Foundation, established by local citizens and H. Emerson Thomas, former Mayor of Westfield, New Jersey, in 1975, strives to improve the quality of life for the residents of its community. Grants are made in the areas of education; the arts and other cultural activities; civic, health, and human services; community development; and the conservation and preservation of historic resources. The Foundation's Web site provides financial statements, grant guidelines and limitations, information for donors, an extensive list of the named funds available, a printable application form, and contact information.

NEW MEXICO

Albuquerque Community Foundation (http://www.albuquerquefoundation.org/)
The Albuquerque Community Foundation (ACF) manages a pool of charitable funds whose income is used to benefit the greater Albuquerque, New Mexico, community through grants to nonprofit organizations, educational programs, and scholarships. The

general policy of the Foundation is to allocate funds to nonprofits (including educational institutions) whose purpose and continuing work is in the areas of arts and culture, education, health and human services, and environmental and historic preservation. ACF's well-organized Web site provides information about its grant policies and restrictions, detailed proposal guidelines, a section for prospective donors, board and staff listings, useful links to regional and national nonprofit resources, and contact information.

New Mexico Community Foundation (http://www.nmcf.org/)

Established in 1983, the New Mexico Community Foundation supports residents of the state of New Mexico, primarily in rural areas. The Foundation's focus is on "entrepreneurial enterprises which address environmental, water-related, youth service or other community resource use issues," as well as technical assistance in the forms of organization and business development, marketing design, and financial management. The Foundation's very informative Web site contains detailed application guidelines and contact information.

Santa Fe Community Foundation (http://www.santafecf.org/)

Founded in 1981, the Santa Fe Community Foundation serves the general area of Santa Fe, New Mexico. Although priority is placed on projects and programs in the Santa Fe area, proposals from Rio Arriba, Los Alamos, Taos, San Miguel, and Mora Counties are also eligible. The Foundation's fields of interest include arts, civic affairs, education, environment, and health and human services; it also offers technical assistance grants and lesbian and gay initiative grants. The Foundation's Web site provides detailed grant guidelines, a calendar with proposal deadlines, and contact information.

NEW YORK

Chautauqua Region Community Foundation (http://www.crcfonline.org)

Established in 1978, the Chautauqua Foundation seeks to enrich the quality of life in the Chautauqua region. With more than 300 separate funds, the Foundation provides grants for a wide variety of arts, education, social service, and other noble purposes. Scholarship funds are available for students, primarily from the Chautauqua region, attending secondary, post-secondary, and graduate education programs. Awards may be for individuals pursuing a variety of educational pursuits, those demonstrating scholastic achievement, those demonstrating financial need, or any combination thereof. Instructions for applying are available on the site, as is a PDF version of the application. The Foundation also gives out several different types of grants. Descriptions of each, along with deadlines and applications (available in PDF format) can be found on the site. Additionally, the Foundation gives out annual awards; details and applications can be found on the Web site. The site also provides information about the board and staff and links to previous newsletters and annual reports.

Community Foundation for the Capital Region (http://www.cfcr.org/)

The Community Foundation for the Capital Region was established in 1968 to serve residents of in the area of Albany, New York. The Foundation gives grants to nonprofits and scholarships to individuals. The Foundation is primarily interested in funding for health services, technology, and AIDS, but other areas are not excluded. The Foundation also makes donor-advised funds. The Foundation's Web site includes detailed descriptions of its grantmaking activities, as well as thorough contact information and application guidelines.

Community Foundation of Greater Buffalo (http://www.cfgb.org)

Established in 1919, The Community Foundation of Greater Buffalo serves the area of western New York. The Foundation's mission is "to strengthen and improve the quality of life in the Greater Buffalo area by supporting and enhancing philanthropy and charitable activities." The Foundation's areas of interest include education, humanities, civic needs, community development, health, environment, science, and social needs. The Foundation also has created a special initiative called the 21st Century Fund. The Foundation's Web site contains grant guidelines and deadlines, information on scholarships, contact information, and a staff listing.

Long Island Community Foundation (http://www.licf.org/)
Founded in 1978, the New York-based Long Island Community Foundation serves as the Long Island arm of The New York Community Trust for the citizens of Nassau and Suffolk Counties. The Foundation "prefers supporting efforts that: start, change, or accomplish something specific and concrete; solve problems rather than alleviate their symptoms; address the needs of people who are disadvantaged, economically or otherwise; address problems that have significance for large numbers of people; are undertaken by smaller organizations with limited access to other resources; use the resources of the community to accomplish self-sustaining change." In addition, the Foundation believes "that strong arts organizations form an integral part of healthy communities." Answers to FAQs, detailed application guidelines, and contact information can be found at the Foundation's Web site.

New York Community Trust (http://www.nycommunitytrust.org)
The New York Community Trust, established in 1924, "help[s] New Yorkers fulfill their charitable goals and make[s] grants that respond to the needs of our city." The Trust is comprised of over 1,300 charitable funds established by an individual, family, or business and administers assets of more than $1.7 billion. The Trust's Web site contains introductory information and resources for donors, including a guide to giving; a handbook for donor advisors; financial statements; and a listing of the Trust's board. Grantseekers are encouraged to contact the Trust for more information, using the contact information provided online.

Northern Chautauqua Community Foundation
(http://fdncenter.org/grantmaker/nccf/index.html)
The mission of the Northern Chautauqua Community Foundation is to enrich the area it serves. To that end, the Foundation, which was established in 1986, has five primary goals: to be a catalyst for the establishment of endowments to benefit the community both now and in the future, to provide a vehicle for donors' varied interests, to promote local philanthropy, to serve as a steward of funds, and to provide leadership and resources in addressing local challenges and opportunities. The Foundation's folder on the Center's Web site provides lists of recent grants and scholarships awarded by the Foundation, brief descriptions of the many funds it administers, financial statements, a short section on "How to Become a Community Philanthropist," and a roster of the Foundation's board, staff, and members.

Rochester Area Community Foundation (http://www.racf.org/)
Established in 1972, the Rochester Area Community Foundation manages more than 750 funds that provide grants for a wide variety of arts, education, social service, and other civic purposes in the Genesee Valley region of upstate New York (including Orleans, Genesee, Monroe, Wayne, Livingston, and Ontario Counties). The Foundation also administers over 75 scholarships mostly to students originating in the same geographic areas. Visitors to the Foundation's Web site will find the most current annual report, grant guidelines, downloadable application and request forms, staff and board listings, and contact information.

NORTH CAROLINA

Community Foundation of Greater Greensboro (http://www.cfgg.org/)
The Community Foundation of Greater Greensboro (CFGG) "promotes philanthropy, builds and maintains a permanent collection of endowment funds, and serves as a trustworthy partner and leader in shaping effective responses" to issues and opportunities in the greater Greensboro, North Carolina, community. Geared more to potential donors than grantseekers, the Foundation's attractive Web site provides general information about the various funds and endowments managed by CFGG, grants information organized by

category (grants from unrestricted endowment funds, grants from special interest endowment funds, and permanent revolving loan funds), FAQs, general financial information, profiles of recent donors and grant recipients, listings of the Foundation's board and staff, and current and previous issues of *Horizon*, the Foundation's seasonal newsletter.

The Community Foundation of Western North Carolina (http://www.cfwnc.org/)

Established in 1978 to benefit 18 mountain counties, the Community Foundation of Western North Carolina comprises more than 550 charitable funds with combined assets of over $87 million. The Foundation currently makes grants to support activities benefiting the arts, education, the environment, human services, and civic improvements. Typically, grants are made for one-year projects or programs and fall into two categories: seed grants that help an organization provide a new level of service to the community and "signature" grants that show potential for producing significant long-term benefits for western North Carolina. In addition to a good deal of information about the Foundation's programs and affiliates, including the Cashiers Community Fund, the Fund for Haywood County, the Highlands Community Foundation, the McDowell Foundation, the Rutherford County Foundation, the Transylvania County Endowment, and the Yancey Foundation, the Foundation's Web site provides detailed application guidelines and procedures, recent grants lists by category, information for donors, an online version of the Foundation's quarterly newsletter, a calendar of upcoming events, staff and board listings, and contact information.

Foundation for the Carolinas (http://www.fftc.org/)

With assets in excess of $200 million and annual giving of $30 million, established in 1958 the Foundation for the Carolinas (FFTC) is the one of the largest community foundations in the South. Building A Better Future, the Foundation's major grantmaking program, awards grants only to organizations located in or serving the greater Charlotte area. Other grant opportunities are available through affiliated community foundations serving the Lexington area; Blowing Rock, Cabarrus, Cleveland, Iredell, and Union Counties in North Carolina; and Cherokee, Lancaster, and York Counties in South Carolina. Specialized grants programs operated by FFTC include the Salisbury Community Foundation (Salibury and Rowan counties), the African American Community Endowment Fund (Charlotte-Mecklenburg and surrounding communities), the Cole Foundation Endowment (Richmond County area), HIV/AIDS Consortium Grants (13 Charlotte area counties), and the Medical Research Grants program (North and South Carolina). In addition to a good deal of information aimed at potential donors, the Foundation's well-organized Web site provides general program information, guidelines, and deadlines; listings of senior management and board members; an electronic form for requesting copies of the Foundation's publications; and contact information.

North Carolina Community Foundation (http://www.nccommf.org/)

The North Carolina Community Foundation, established in 1988, is a statewide foundation seeking gifts from individuals, corporations, and other foundations to build endowments and ensure financial security for nonprofit organizations and institutions throughout the state. Based in Raleigh, North Carolina, the Foundation also manages 48 community affiliates throughout North Carolina that make grants in their communities in the areas of human services, education, health, arts, religion, civic affairs, and the conservation and preservation of historical, cultural, and environmental resources. The Foundation also manages over 50 scholarship programs statewide. Check the site for contact information.

Outer Banks Community Foundation (http://www.obcf.org)

The Outer Banks Community Foundation was organized in 1982 as a public charity to help meet local needs in Dare County and all of the Outer Banks communities from Corolla to Ocracoke Island in North Carolina. The Foundation manages charitable funds for individuals and agencies and targets grants toward the community's most pressing needs and promising opportunities. Located in Kill Devil Hills, North Carolina, the Outer Banks Community Foundation was organized to provide assistance to the Outer Banks areas of Dare

County, Currituck County, and Ocracoke Island (Hyde County). The Foundation makes grants to qualifying nonprofit organizations, churches and government agencies, and to individuals for designated purposes through named funds established by donors. Grants are awarded in one of four categories: Mini-Grants, ranging from $500–$2,000; Vision Grants, ranging from $2,000–$8,000; the Major Initiative Grant (only one annually), ranging from $10,000–$15,000; and Contingency Grants, which are mostly for emergency purposes. Each scholarship fund has its own criteria for selection, such as academic ability, career choice, financial need, athletic interests, or geographic location. Visit the Web site for more information on the Foundation's grant and scholarship funds, grantmaking policy, grant recipient list, and contact information. The site features printable grant application forms and printable scholarship application forms.

Triangle Community Foundation (http://www.trianglecf.org/)
The mission of the Triangle Community Foundation is to expand private philanthropy in the communities of the greater Triangle area, including Wake, Durham, and Orange Counties, North Carolina. The Foundation is comprised of more than 230 individual philanthropic funds with combined total assets currently exceeding $34 million. The Foundation also distributes discretionary monies for new initiatives or one-time special projects in cultural affairs and the arts, community development, education, environmental issues, health, social services, and other areas that benefit residents of the region. Visitors to the Foundation's Web site will find eligibility guidelines, application procedures, a recent grants list, and featured articles from its current newsletter. Visitors can also download an application form in Microsoft Word format.

The Winston-Salem Foundation (http://www.wsfoundation.org)
The Winston-Salem Foundation is a community foundation dedicated to building a permanent pool of philanthropic funds to benefit the community. Based in Winston-Salem, North Carolina, the Foundation provides resources and leadership to improve life for all people in the greater Forsyth County area. Visitors to this brief site will find contact information.

NORTH DAKOTA

Fargo-Moorhead Area Foundation (http://www.areafoundation.org/)
The Fargo-Moorhead Area Foundation, established in Fargo, North Dakota in 1960, supports nonprofit organizations that serve the local community in the fields of the arts, civic affairs, education, health, and human services. Grants are made from a pool of funds, including unrestricted, field of interest, advised, designated, and organizational. Interested grantseekers should write or call the Foundation for a grant application and guidelines. Visitors to the Web site will find charts detailing the Foundation's finances, a newsletter, and contact information.

OHIO

Akron Community Foundation (http://www.ohio.com/nonprofit/acf/)
The Akron Community Foundation (ACF) was established in 1955 to serve the communities of Summit County, Ohio, through grantmaking in civic affairs, culture and the humanities, education, and health and human services. Today it comprises more than 150 charitable funds holding a combined $73 million in assets. A number of those funds, such as the Women's Endowment Fund and the Medina County Fund (MCF), have been created to address the needs of distinct populations or a specific region. The former, ACF's first affiliated fund, focuses on creating opportunities to support the educational, physical, emotional, social, artistic, and personal growth of women and girls. The MCF, another affiliate fund, is laying the groundwork for the establishment of a Medina County community foundation in the future. In addition to an overview of the Foundation's activities, the ACF Web site provides application guidelines, FAQs, information about its donor services, press

releases and a calendar of Foundation-sponsored events, links to sites of interest, and contact information.

Bowling Green Community Foundation (http://www.wcnet.org/~bgcf/)

The Bowling Green Community Foundation was created in 1994 to provide a perpetual endowment to support worthwhile projects benefiting the community and its citizens. The Foundation has a diversified grant program supporting a variety of organizations within the Bowling Green area. The Foundation also maintains a scholarship fund for students within the county. The Foundation's Web site features grant guidelines, a board of trustees list, a list of the Foundation's current funds, information about upcoming events, and contact information.

The Cleveland Foundation (http://www.clevelandfoundation.org/)

Founded in 1914, The Cleveland Foundation is the nation's oldest community foundation. The Foundation gives grants in support of projects in greater Cleveland or that benefit greater Clevelanders directly in the following categories: arts and culture, education, education development, health, neighborhoods and housing, and social services. It does not give grants to individuals, nor does it give support for membership drives, most fundraising projects, travel, police and fire protection, government staff positions, publications or audiovisual programs (unless they're part of a larger project), most requests for buildings, land or equipment, or religious organizations for religious purposes. (It does support religious organizations' non-religious programs, such as hunger centers or job training or childcare.) In addition to detailed program guidelines and application procedures, the Foundation's Web site provides information for donors and a planned giving design center, an electronic publications order form, information about the Anisfield-Wolf Book Awards (which recognize books that address issues of racism or expand our appreciation for human diversity), a listing of the Foundation's board and executive staff, and contact information.

The Columbus Foundation (http://www.columbusfoundation.com)

A partnership of donors, nonprofit organizations, and the community, the Columbus Foundation was established in 1943. The group's extensive mission is in part "to serve as a leader, catalyst, and center for education on philanthropy; to broaden the base of philanthropic giving in central Ohio; to preserve and grow an endowment to address changing community needs in partnership with all stakeholders; and to strive for measurable community improvement through strategic grantmaking in the arts, community development, education, health, social services, and other community needs." Key grant categories include arts and humanities, conservation, education, health, social services, urban affairs, and advancing philanthropy. Programs should reach a diverse population, have an innovative take on their field, receive other funding from the public or the government, encourage the beneficiaries to help themselves, and strengthen the applicant organization. All potential applicants are instructed to request the *Information for Grant Applicants* brochure and encouraged to sign up for a grant application workshop (this can be done online). The site has a number of featured grant recipients, grant coversheets that can be downloaded in Microsft Word or PDF formats, a staff directory, and lists of committee members. There is a publication section with the Foundation's newsletter online, information, and opportunities to donate.

Community Foundation of Greater Lorain County (http://www.cfglc.org/)

The Community Foundation of Greater Lorain County was established in 1980 to serve the residents of Lorain County, Ohio. Every year the Foundation gives numerous contributions to the community through many funds. The Foundation's areas of interest include arts and culture, civic affairs, education, health, and social services. Diversity grants are awarded through its African American Community Fund and Hispanic Fund. The Foundation also awards scholarships and tries to address "gaps in services" through funds for program development, capacity building, preventive endeavors, and "projects that enhance greater self-sufficiency" for individuals and organizations. Application forms can be downloaded from its Web site.

Community Foundation of Sidney and Shelby County (http://www.commfoun.com/)

The Community Foundation of Sidney and Shelby County was established in 1952 to improve the quality of life in the Sidney-Shelby County, Ohio area. The Foundation supports education, arts, healthcare, and youth projects. A general fund was also established early in the Foundation's history for the promotion of education and advancement of learning, for the improvement of the health and physical well-being, for the enrichment of the moral and spiritual life, and for the betterment of community relationships. The Foundation also makes scholarships to individuals. Visitors to the Foundation's Web site will find further information on its giving program, a brief history, a listing of trustees, and contact information.

Coshocton Foundation (http://www.coshoctonfoundation.org/)

The Ohio-based Coshocton Foundation was created in 1967 to "lend a helping hand" to the community of Coshocton County. The Foundation makes grants to organizations that support areas of community improvement, literacy and education, encouragement of the arts, health and welfare, and parks and recreation. Visitors to the Foundation's Web site will find a listing of officers and trustees, summary of recent grants, information on how to apply, a printable application, and contact information.

Dayton Foundation (http://www.daytonfoundation.org/)

Established in 1921, the Ohio-based Dayton Foundation is "a community foundation designed for permanence and for the benefit of the Dayton/Miami Valley region." The Foundation supports a wide range of interests. Its goal is to support projects "not addressed by existing organizations or to support special efforts of already-established nonprofit organizations in the Miami Valley." Grantseekers are encouraged to call for application guidelines; the telephone number is given at the Foundation's Web site.

Foundation for Appalachian Ohio (http://www.appalachianohio.org/)

Established in 1998, the Foundation for Appalachian Ohio serves the residents of 29 Appalachian counties in Ohio. The Foundation addresses a wide range of local needs, among which are employment opportunities (job creation, retention, and training), overcoming effects of poverty, education and training, human services, healthcare and prevention services, affordable-accessible housing, physical infrastructure (roads, bridges, power, communications, water, and sewer), preserving and improving the natural environment, enhancing arts and cultural opportunities, increasing philanthropic/charitable capital and leadership, and reducing out migration of human, capital, and natural resources. FAQs, contact information, and Ohio Appalachian resources and links can be found at the Fund's Web site.

The Greater Cincinnati Foundation (http://www.greatercincinnatifdn.org/)

The Greater Cincinnati Foundation (GCF) is a charitable organization that builds and preserves endowment funds, identifies opportunities to enhance the quality of community life, and responds with grants addressing six key areas: arts and culture, community progress, education, the environment, health, and human services. Formed in 1963, GCF provides philanthropic leadership to eight counties in the Ohio-Kentucky-Indiana region. The site contains contact information for GCF representatives, each of whom can provide information on applying for grants and on grant opportunities.

Greater Wayne County Foundation, Inc. (http://gwcf.net/)

Based in Wooster, Ohio, the Greater Wayne County Foundation was established in 1978 to accept contributions, create and administer funds, and make grants for the benefit of the people of the greater Wayne County area. Grants are paid to a wide variety of organizations in the areas of arts, culture, and humanities; capital campaigns; civic and community; conservation and environment; education; health and wellness; human services; religion; and scholarships. Grant guidelines and applications can be downloaded from the Foundation's Web site or requested by e-mail. The site also has a descriptive listing of scholarships and contact information for each scholarship fund.

Middletown Community Foundation (http://www.mcfoundation.org/)

Founded in 1976, the Middletown Community Foundation funds scholarships and grants in the Middletown, Monroe, Trenton, Franklin, Madison and Lemon Townships, Ohio. Scholarships are available for area high school and adult students, some through particular high schools; applications are available through these local institutions. Foundation grants focus on the arts, education, health, social services, recreation, and community development, among other needs. Brief grant guidelines are provided online. Additionally, the Foundation gives the Crystal Apple Teacher Recognition Award, a prize for which area educators can be nominated using a form available from the Foundation. The Summertime for Kids Award, a mini-grant program, funds nonprofit organizations that have activities catering to youth during the summer. The Foundation's Web site provides charts on the organization's growth, membership and donor information, links to other resources, and contact information.

Muskingum County Community Foundation (http://www.mccf.org/)

The mission of the Muskingum County Community Foundation, established in 1985 in Zanesville, Ohio, is to "improve the quality of life and to serve the charitable needs of the community by attracting and administering Charitable Funds." The Foundation's Web site lists numerous available scholarships, with past recipients and contact information specific for each one; grants, with a list of past grantees; and named funds. A list of restricted funds also details recent donors. Additionally, the Foundation provides a listing of staff and officers, a report on its financial position, a strategic plan and donor guide, an online version of its newsletter, a nomination form for the Thomas Community Service Award, and contact information.

Parkersburg Area Community Foundation (http://home.wirefire.com/pacf/)

The Parkersburg Area Community Foundation (PACF) is committed to serving the people of the Mid-Ohio Valley—Wood, Pleasants, Tyler, Ritchie, Doddridge, Gilmer, Wirt, Calhoun, Roane, Jackson, and Mason Counties in West Virginia and Washington County in Ohio—by linking community resources with community needs. PACF focuses its grantmaking in the following areas: arts and culture, education, health and human services, recreation, and youth and family services. To be eligible for a grant from the Foundation, an applicant must be a private, nonprofit, tax-exempt organization under section 501(c)(3) of the Internal Revenue Code, or the applicant must be a public institution. The Foundation also administers more than 40 different scholarship funds, the majority of which are designated for students in Wood County, West Virginia. The Foundation's Web site provides general information about the Foundation, detailed application guidelines and scholarship information, and general information about becoming a donor to the Foundation.

Sandusky/Erie County Community Foundation (http://www.sanduskyfoundation.org/)

The Sandusky/Erie Community Foundation was created in 1996 to enable people and organizations to make a positive impact on the Erie County community. The Foundation is particularly interested in providing seed money for new programs that work to meet emerging needs of the community or to expand successful programs. Program areas of interest to the Foundation include arts and culture, community development, education, environmental services, parks and recreation, safety, social services, and youth services. Visitors to the Foundation's Web site will find information on the grant programs, news from the Foundation, a listing of recent grants by subject area, FAQs, and contact information.

OKLAHOMA

Oklahoma City Community Foundation, Inc. (http://www.occf.org)

Established in 1969 the Oklahoma City Community Foundation serves the area of Oklahoma City, Oklahoma. The Foundation's areas of interest include arts, culture, education, rural development, and others. The Foundation's Web site provides FAQs, board of trustees listing, contact information, and community program descriptions with a telephone number for requesting guidelines.

OREGON

The Oregon Community Foundation (http://www.oregoncommunityfound.org)

The Oregon Community Foundation, established in 1973, funds a variety of grants, scholarships, and a special initiative program. The Foundation's funding objectives for grants fall into four areas, all geared toward Oregonians: nurturing children, strengthening families, and fostering self-sufficiency; enhancing educational experience; increasing cultural opportunities; and preserving and improving Oregon's livability through citizen involvement. OREGON! Ready to Learn is the Foundation's five-year initiative program to raise the literacy level, language development, and educational experience of young children. The Foundation also funds a scholarship program for college-bound graduates of Oregon high schools or returning adults. The Foundation's Web site provides extensive information on all of these funding opportunities, including grant and scholarship guidelines, limitations and deadlines, recent grants and scholarships, FAQs, and forms and instructions that can be downloaded in PDF format. The site also provides a list of the Foundation board and staff, related links, information for potential donors, and contact information.

PENNSYLVANIA

Berks County Community Foundation (http://www.bccf.org)

Established in 1994, the Reading, Pennsylvania-based Berks County Community Foundation seeks "to improve the quality of life of the residents of the county by providing funds to meet existing and emerging needs." The Foundation disperses funds to social, educational, environmental, and cultural programs in Berks County. Visit the Foundation's Web site for an overview of its grant activities, descriptions of its special programs and initiatives, a grants list, a list of established funds, news and press releases, links to related resources, downloadable financial information, and contact information.

Big Ben Foundation (http://www.lehigh.edu/~inifc/bbf/bbf.html)

Founded at Lehigh University in February 1995, the Big Ben Foundation is a cooperative between members of the Allentown, Bethlehem, and Easton, Pennsylvania, communities and the students of Lehigh University. The purpose of the Foundation is "to raise and distribute funds to other nonprofit community-based organizations or individuals with specific economic hardships." The Foundation provides nonprofits with supplemental funding, "so they in turn can maintain existing programs and provide new and better services for their local communities." The Foundation does not accept applications. It operates its own programs and raises funds from the general public and local businesses.

Chester County Community Foundation (http://www.chescocf.org/)

The Chester County Community Foundation's (CCCF) mission is to maintain and enhance the quality of life in Chester County, Pennsylvania. CCCF is made up of more than 110 separate funds whose combined assets total $10 million (80 percent of which is endowed). The vast majority of grants that the Foundation makes are donor advised were they believe grants should be made from the restricted fund that they have established. There are four grant making funds for the Foundation: the Fund for Chester County; Scholarships; Individual or Family Donor Advised Funds; and the Chester County Fund for Women and Girls. Visit the Foundation's Web site to learn more about the foundation's grantmaking programs, a list of available funds, areas CCCF does not support, a board/staff list, and contact information.

Greater Harrisburg Foundation (http://www.tghf.org)

Established in 1920 by Donald McCormick, the Greater Harrisburg Foundation serves the five-county area of Cumberland, Dauphin, Lebanon, Perry, and Franklin in south central

Pennsylvania. Field of interest funds held by the Foundation include funds that specify the arts, services for children, education, homelessness and hunger, health, the environment, dental care for the disadvantaged, head and spinal injury prevention, services to girls, mental health, mental retardation, and services for the needy, among others. The Foundation's Web site provides FAQs, information on regional foundations, grant guidelines, and contact information.

The Luzerne Foundation (http://www2.epix.net/~luzerne/)

The Luzerne Foundation, located in Wilkes-Barre, Pennsylvania, works to enhance and improve the Luzerne County community through permanent endowment funds. Areas of funding interest to the Foundation include human services, health, education, arts and culture, and the beautification and enhancement of the environment. Funds are distributed through various donor-advised grants, scholarships, and general grants. The Foundation provides information and benefits for donors and contact information for interested grantseekers.

The Philadelphia Foundation (http://www.philafound.org/)

Established in 1918, The Philadelphia Foundation serves as a vehicle and resource for philanthropy in Bucks, Chester, Delaware, Montgomery, and Philadelphia Counties. It does this by developing, managing, and allocating community resources in partnership with donors and grantees; by building on community assets; and by promoting empowerment, leadership, and civic participation among underserved groups. The Foundation makes grants from over 350 individually named charitable trust funds, with assets totaling $220 million. Grant distributions are made according to the charitable interests and specifications of the individual fund donors, but the Foundation also identifies emerging needs in the community and sets policies and priorities for distributing unrestricted dollars in the areas of children and families, community organizing and advocacy, culture, education, health, housing and economic development, and social services. To be eligible for any funding through the Foundation, organizations must have 501(c)(3) tax exempt status and based in one of the five counties of southeastern Pennsylvania. The Foundation's Web site offers application guidelines, detailed information about the various individual funds under the Foundation's auspices, the Foundation's financial management policies, and listings of recipient organizations, its board of managers, and staff. The Foundation's Web site also includes a What's New? section, which contains recent press releases and a donor information section.

The Pittsburgh Foundation (http://www.pittsburghfoundation.org)

The Pittsburgh Foundation was established in Pennsylvania in 1945 "to provide individuals, families, organizations, and corporations with an avenue for their charitable giving and to benefit the world around them—especially the people in the communities where they live." The Foundation promotes the betterment of the greater Pittsburgh community and the quality of life for all its citizens. At its Web site, visitors will find general information about the Foundation, guidelines and applications, donor information and how to establish a fund, supporting organizations, and a link to the Planned Giving Design Center created to provide professional advisors with resources to advise clients in matters of charitable gift and estate planning.

Scranton Area Foundation (http://www.scrantonareafoundation.org)

The Scranton Area Foundation was founded in 1954 as a private foundation, becoming a community foundation in 1988, to serve Scranton and Lackawanna Counties, Pennsylvania. The Foundation's mission is to "enhance the quality of life for all people in Lackawanna County through the development of organized philanthropy." Areas of funding interest include education, human service, environment, and civic, arts, and cultural organizations. The Foundation has a variety of grants and provides information for prospective donors and grantees on its Web site. Also available online is an FAQ about the Foundation, links, and contact information to request a grant application.

Three Rivers Community Fund (http://trfn.clpgh.org/trcf/)

Established in 1989 by five donors, The Three Rivers Community Fund (TCRF) is based in Pittsburgh, Pennsylvania, and helps the communities of Southwestern Pennsylvania. The Foundation "identifies and funds alternative methods of dealing with barriers in society that hinder education, employment opportunities and community development." The Foundation generally supports smaller groups not supported by the government or other foundations. Its funding interests include children, youth, and families; global neighbors; progressive organizing; public accountability; racial divisions and racial pride; health concerns; and gay and lesbian issues. A newsletter, calendar of events, information about the TRCF proposal writing workshop, grant guidelines, past grant recipients, application information, and contact information can be found at the Foundation's Web site.

PUERTO RICO

Puerto Rico Community Foundation (http://www.fcpr.org)

Through its support of self-directed development of Puerto Rican community groups, the Puerto Rico Community Foundation "seeks to contribute to the growth of a healthier community, [acting] as a catalytic agent in fostering new and innovative solutions to the Island's problems." Although the Foundation concentrates its efforts on the needs of Puerto Ricans on the island, it collaborates with Puerto Rican communities in the United States as well. Visitors to the Foundation's Web site will find descriptions of its various programs, including the General Fund, the Permanent Fund for the Arts, the Community Housing Development Organizations Program, the Middle School Renewal Initiative, and the Institute for the Development of Philanthropy; a listing of the Foundation's board of directors and staff; and links to other philanthropic resources and organizations of interest on the web.

RHODE ISLAND

The Rhode Island Foundation (http://www.rifoundation.org/)

Established in 1916 with a gift of $10,000, the Providence-based Rhode Island Foundation has grown to become one of the largest community foundations in the United States, with an endowment of more than $400 million. The Foundation focuses its discretionary grantmaking in the areas of children and families, economic/community development, and education, although it views those designations more as starting points than as hard and fast categories with fixed parameters. Visitors to the Foundation's Web site will find a history of the Foundation, detailed program descriptions, recent grants in each program area, application guidelines and eligibility requirements, information for donors, a financial overview of the Foundation, listings of the board and staff, and contact information.

SOUTH CAROLINA

Community Foundation of Greater Greenville (http://www.greenvillefoundation.org)

Located in Greenville, South Carolina, the Community Foundation of Greater Greenville "exists to enhance the quality of life of the citizens of Greater Greenville by linking philanthropic leadership, charitable resources and civic influence with needs and opportunities in the community." The Foundation makes grants to tax-exempt organizations to enhance community life through the support of a broad range of services: health, education, religion, arts and humanities, and the environment. Some grants follow an open application process under published guidelines. Other noncompetitive grants reflect the charitable priorities of individual donors. While the site does not provide an application or specific grant guidelines, there is a contact page that can be completed and sent online. The site also contains the latest news about the Foundation and a list of previous grantees.

The Community Foundation Serving Coastal South Carolina (http://www.communityfoundationsc.org)

The Community Foundation Serving Coastal South Carolina was founded in Charleston in 1974 to serve the eight coastal counties of South Carolina. The Foundation provides funding in various programs areas, including arts, education, basic human needs, neighborhood and community development, health, conservation, historical preservation, and animal welfare. Grants are available in a wide array of categories, including Open Grants, Teacher Mini-Grants, Rural Development Initiative, Expansion Arts, and various scholarships. Grant descriptions, guidelines, and applications for each type of grant can be downloaded in PDF format from the Foundation's Web site. A complete listing of scholarships and applications in PDF format are also available online. The Foundation additionally provides a detailed list of past grants, news and events, a donor guide, a publication order form, and a regional map covering funding possibilities in surrounding areas on its Web site.

Foundation for the Carolinas (http://www.fftc.org/)

With assets in excess of $200 million and annual giving of $30 million, established in 1958, the Foundation for the Carolinas (FFTC) is the one of the largest community foundations in the South. Building A Better Future, the Foundation's major grantmaking program, awards grants only to organizations located in or serving the greater Charlotte area. Other grant opportunities are available through affiliated community foundations serving the Lexington area and Blowing Rock, Cabarrus, Cleveland, Iredell, and Union Counties in North Carolina, and Cherokee, Lancaster, and York Counties in South Carolina. Specialized grants programs operated by FFTC include the Salisbury Community Foundation (Salibury and Rowan Counties), the African American Community Endowment Fund (Charlotte-Mecklenburg and surrounding communities), the Cole Foundation Endowment (Richmond County area), HIV/AIDS Consortium Grants (13 Charlotte area counties), and the Medical Research Grants program (North and South Carolina). In addition to a good deal of information aimed at potential donors, the Foundation's well-organized Web site provides general program information, guidelines, and deadlines; listings of senior management and board members; an electronic form for requesting copies of the Foundation's publications; and contact information.

Hilton Head Island Foundation, Inc. (http://www.hhif.org)

South Carolina's Hilton Head Island Foundation, established in 1994, is "dedicated to the principles of fairness and caring stewardship so that [it] may provide opportunities of enduring value for the Hilton Head Island community area." The Foundation supports a wide variety of grants as well as two specific programs: the Endowment Challenge 2000, a three-year matching funds program for local nonprofit organizations, and the Scholarship Coalition, making awards to area high school students. The Foundation's extensive Web site incorporates a donor guide, a legal and financial advisors guide, news and events, a list of recent grants, related links, contact information for the Foundation's staff and board, grant guidelines and deadlines, and a reply form to request more information.

SOUTH DAKOTA

Sioux Falls Area Community Foundation (http://www.sfacf.org)

The Sioux Falls Area Community Foundation is located in Sioux Falls, South Dakota, and works to support the needs of the surrounding region. The Foundation is committed to "serving as a resource and catalyst for charitable purposes; building an endowment fund for the future; serving donors with many different interests; and assessing and responding to community needs." The simple Web page includes basic contact information, e-mail addresses for key staff, and encouragement to use them.

TENNESSEE

Community Foundation of Greater Chattanooga (http://www.cfgc.org)

Established in 1962, The Community Foundation of Greater Chattanooga "encourages and invests in creative and long-term solutions to improve the community and the lives of its citizens." The Foundation now holds over 160 funds making grants in many forms, including community funds, scholarship funds, project funds, agency funds, field of interest funds, designated funds, and donor advised fund. Visit the Foundation's Web site to view an archive of grant history, grant guidelines and procedures, a board listing, information on scholarships, a link library of interesting resources, and contact information.

Community Foundation of Greater Memphis (http://www.cfgm.org/)

The Community Foundation of Greater Memphis was established in 1969 to serve communities in eastern Arkansas, northern Mississippi, and western Tennessee. The mission of the Foundation is to strengthen the community through philanthropy. The Foundation supports a wide variety if causes through several funds. Among those listed are serving children with disabilities and visually impaired individuals, organizing children's summer camps, and providing humane contraception for animals. This list is not exhaustive. Contact information, application guidelines, and staff and board listings can be found at its Web site.

The Community Foundation of Middle Tennessee (http://www.cfmt.org/)

The Community Foundation of Middle Tennessee was created to enhance the quality of life in the 39 counties of middle Tennessee. In order to serve this community, the Foundation has identified several broad categories in which needs exist and in which grant requests are encouraged. These categories include arts and humanities, civic affairs and community planning, conservation and environment, education, employment and training, health, historic preservation, housing and community development, and human services for citizens of all ages. The Foundation is particularly interested in ideas that shed new light on the needs and aspirations of middle Tennesseans, with emphasis on providing long-term solutions. The Foundation does not award grants for fundraising events, annual campaigns, capital campaigns (unless there is compelling evidence that such support is vital to the success of a program), general operating funds (unless similar evidence is presented), individuals, private schools, religious/sectarian causes, private foundations, debt retirement or restructuring, fundraising feasibility studies, biomedical or clinical studies, lobbying or political activities, advertising, trips and/or conference attendance, or to organizations or for purposes outside its service area. The Foundation's Web site provides a considerable amount of information about the Foundation's various funds (e.g., discretionary, donor-advised, scholarship, etc.), grant application guidelines, financial policies, listings of its staff and board of directors, and contact information.

TEXAS

Amarillo Area Foundation (http://www.aaf-hf.org/)

The Amarillo Area Foundation of Texas was established in 1957 to meet the needs of underserved communities in the northernmost 26 counties of the Texas Panhandle. As a community foundation, the Amarillo Area Foundation does not limit its discretionary grantmaking to a particular area of interest. Rather, it seeks to support the entire range of human needs in the Panhandle. The Community Foundation manages over 200 fund in the form of donor advised funds, scholarships, unrestricted funds, and project funds. In General, the Foundation does not fund religious or political causes; private of parochial schools; national, state, or local fundraising activities; or general operating support for United Way agencies. At the Foundation's Web site, you will find a detailed history of the Foundation by decade, a board/staff list, explicit grant application criteria, application guidelines, a printable application form, deadlines, and a helpful list of FAQ's.

Communities Foundation of Texas, Inc. (http://www.cftexas.org/)

Based in Dallas, the Communities Foundation of Texas was formed in 1981 from the Dallas Community Chest Trust Fund, which was established in the 1950's. The Foundation carries out the objectives of its donors through 650 funds as well as various external charitable projects and branch offices throughout Texas. The Foundation's major areas of distribution include education, religion, cultural and historical, social services, youth, and inner city/community. The Foundation gives locally in Texas and across the United States. Its Web site caters mainly to donors but includes a year in review; listings of the board, advisory council, and staff members; profiles of grant recipients; a financial report; application guidelines; and a newsletter, all of which are helpful for grantseekers as well.

Community Foundation of Abilene (http://www.abilene.com/communityfoundation)

The Community Foundation of Abiline was created in 1985. The group's mission is multi-part: "to establish permanent charitable endowments; to provide a vehicle for donors' varied interests; to promote local philanthropy; and to provide leadership and resources in addressing local challenges and opportunities." The Foundation's giving program also has many components, including a grants program, scholarships, and a community leadership program. Grants, generally $1,000–$5,000, are distributed to nonprofits in Abiline twice a year. The Foundation is looking for projects that benefit the community, with particular interest in those that promote volunteerism and community involvement, address emerging needs, include cooperation between nonprofits, and address prevention in addition to assistance. The site offers basic guidelines, restrictions, and deadlines. The scholarship program makes awards to area students at a variety of colleges. The Foundations administers 31 scholarships, and local colleges award the rest. The site includes a list of many of these scholarships with brief descriptions and qualifications. Interested students should speak with their high school counselor. In the Community Leadership area, the Foundation offers a resource center and planning support. The site also offers staff and board lists, a grants history, and the current newsletter.

The Community Foundation of North Texas (http://www.cfntx.org/)

Established in 1981 as a branch of the United Way, the Community Foundation of North Texas, located in Ft. Worth, Texas, was known as the Community Foundation of Metropolitan Tarrant County until 1999. The Foundation provides "efficient charitable fund administration" for many individual donors in the area. The Foundation's Web site includes an area for one specific fund, the Community Investment Fund. This Fund supports projects in the following categories: the aged, the arts, the environment, children/youth services, and social services. The page includes information on the fund's donors, application guidelines and deadlines, and other helpful facts. The Foundation's site also includes board and staff lists and ample information on the funds: how to establish one and descriptions of the different types.

The Dallas Foundation (http://www.dallasfoundation.org)

The Dallas Foundation was established in 1929 to support the charitable causes of the city and the county of Dallas. Based in Dallas, the Foundation awards grants for a broad array of charitable purposes that improve the moral or social well-being of the residents of the city and county of Dallas in the areas of the arts, education, health, social services and general community. The site contains grant guidelines, grant lists, financials, an FAQ sheet, links, news and press releases, and contact information. Certain publications can be downloaded from the site, and information is provided on ordering others, such as an annual report.

El Paso Community Foundation (http://www.epcf.org/)

The El Paso Community Foundation (EPCF) was established in 1977 to address community challenges in the southwest Texas border region. Today, it awards funds twice a year (in May and November) to grant applicants from area nonprofit organizations or from community activist groups in the following areas of interest: arts and humanities, civic affairs/public benefit, environment/animal welfare, education, health and disabilities, and human services. Priority is given to 1) more effective ways of doing things and ideas that require risk-taking, 2) projects where a moderate amount of grant money can have an impact, and 3) projects that show collaboration with other organizations. Generally speaking, the Foundation does not fund capital campaigns, fund raising events, projects of a religious nature, medical or academic research, annual appeals, membership contributions, organizations that are political or partisan in purpose, travel for individuals or groups, ongoing requests for general operating support, or requests from organizations outside the El Paso geographic area. Visitors to the EPCF Web site will find a rundown of the various funds under its management, detailed grant guidelines, a listing of the volunteers who serve as the Foundation's board of directors, and contact information.

Lubbock Area Foundation, Inc. (http://www.lubbockareafoundation.org)

The Lubbock Area Foundation (LAF) was created in 1981 to help Texas South Plains residents realize their long-term philanthropic goals. The Foundation manages a pool of charitable funds, the income from which is used to benefit the South Plains community through grants to 501(c)(3) nonprofit organizations, educational programs, and scholarships. Grants, which typically range from $500–$2,500, are made for start-up funding, general operating support, program support, and/or demonstration programs. The Foundation does not make grants to individuals, for political purposes, to retire indebtedness, or for payment of interest or taxes. The LAF Web site offers information for grantseekers, including funding priorities and application procedures, as well as prospective donors; a list of endowed scholarship funds within LAF; general information about the Foundation's Mini-Grants for Teachers Program and its Funding Information Library (a Foundation Center Cooperating Collection); and contact information.

San Antonio Area Foundation (http://www.saafdn.org/)

The San Antonio Area Foundation (SAAF) was established in 1964 as a memorial to local community leader, visionary, and philanthropist Nat Goldsmith. Today it manages more than $100 million in assets distributed among 288 component funds and one support foundation. The Foundation does not state its areas of interest on its Web site. It only reviews proposals from applicants whose Letters of Intent—submission of which is the first step in the Foundation's grant application process—have been approved. In addition to a brief history of and general information about the Foundation, visitors to the SAAF Web site will find scholarship and grant application instructions, information for donors, and a listing of the Foundation's board of directors.

The Waco Foundation (http://www.wacofdn.org/)

Established in 1958, the Foundation serves the residents of Waco and McLennan Counties in Texas. Its fields of interest include childcare, medical facilities, education, art, and culture. Through its Mac Grant Scholarship Fund, the Foundation helps local high school graduates attend a community college. Grant application forms and guidelines can be downloaded from the Foundation's Web site, which also provides contact information.

VERMONT

Vermont Community Foundation (http://www.vermontcf.org/)

The Vermont Community Foundation (VCF) was established in 1986 to address the needs of Vermont now and in the future by building charitable capital and by providing services, resources, leadership, and encouragement to donors and to the nonprofit sector. In its role as a grantmaker, the Foundation will consider any project that meets a clearly defined community need in Vermont. Categories of support include, but are not limited to, the arts and humanities, education, the environment, historic resources, health, public affairs and community development, and social services. The Foundation emphasizes small (typically under $10,000), one-time grants rather than continuing support. It does not make grants for endowments, annual operating or capital campaigns, religious purposes, individuals, or equipment (unless it is an integral part of an otherwise eligible project). In addition to detailed grant guidelines, lists of recent grants, information for potential donors, and a list of links to related resources, the VCF site provides general information about the Vermont Women's Fund and various TAP-VT technical assistance programs.

VIRGIN ISLANDS

Community Foundation of the Virgin Islands (http://fdncenter.org/grantmaker/cfvi/)

The Community Foundation of the Virgin Islands (CFVI), based on the island of St. Thomas, was established in 1990 to "enhance the educational, physical, social, cultural and environmental well-being of the islands' people." The Foundation works to improve the quality of life for people in the Virgin Islands through programs and initiatives, as well as funds and scholarships. The CFVI's folder on the Center's Web site lists its numerous programs and specific funds, including the Technical Assistance Program; mini-grants which benefit children and families; and scholarship and scholar awards. The Foundation's Web site also provides donor information, CFVI news, a directory of Virgin Islands community services organizations, listings of recently funded programs and scholarships, and contact information to apply for funding.

VIRGINIA

The Community Foundation Serving Richmond and Central Virginia (http://www.tcfrichmond.org/)

The Community Foundation Serving Richmond and Central Virginia was established in 1968 to enhance the lives of the citizens of central Virginia. Located in Richmond, the Foundation "provides effective stewardship of philanthropic assets entrusted to its care by donors who wish to enhance the quality of community life." Grantseekers will find grant application guidelines for its competitive grantmaking programs: Strengthening Families—Strengthening Communities; the programs of the Jenkins Foundation, an organization whose mission is to support effective healthcare programs and improved healthcare in the greater Richmond area; the R.E.B. Awards for Teaching Excellence, sponsored by the R.E.B. Foundation, which serve to identify, recognize, and promote excellence in classroom teaching in area public schools; and the Youth Philanthropy Project, which encourages student volunteerism and philanthropy by engaging young people in decision making about the distribution of grant dollars. The Foundation also has several student scholarship funds and provides information on each individual fund as well as application instructions. The site also provides highlights; grant list; listing of community foundations in Virginia by area, with contact information for each; press releases; and contact information.

Greater Lynchburg Community Trust (http://www.lynchburgtrust.org)

The Greater Lynchburg Community Trust was founded in 1972 by the Fidelity American Bank. It is located in Lynchburg, Virginia, and serves the cities of Lynchburg and Bedford and the counties of Amherst, Bedford, and Campbell. The trust exists "to promote local philanthropy and to simplify the process of giving." It provides for the administration and the investment of gifts and bequests. Needs served are broad in scope, including human services to children, youth, the needy, and the elderly; education; health; the arts; and the humanities. Grant application deadlines and information are provided on the Web site, as well as contact information. The Trust will consider applications from nonprofit organizations that work to help the communities the Trust serves.

The Norfolk Foundation (http://www.norfolkfoundation.org)

The Norfolk Foundation is a "permanent endowment created by the community for the community." Established in 1950, the Foundation is dedicated to improving the quality of life in Norfolk and surrounding cities. As the oldest community foundation in Virginia, the Foundation includes over 100 separate funds. Grants are made to students for financial aid and to nonprofit organizations in qualified communities within Virginia. Two important initiatives of the Foundation are the Business Consortium for Arts Support, providing operating support to dozens of arts organizations in the community, and the Planning Council's Homeless Prevention Program. The Web site outlines extensive qualifications for those areas considered and those that are not. The site also includes detailed application information, recent grants, and contact information. Finally, the site also has a section for potential donors and provides contact information for those who would like to learn more about the Foundation and its programs.

Staunton Augusta Waynesboro Community Foundation (http://personal.cfw.com/~sawfdtn/)

The mission of the Staunton Augusta Waynesboro Community Foundation (SAW Foundation) is to "provide for the enrichment of the quality of life in the community by developing a permanent endowment in order to assess and respond to changing community needs today and in the future, and serving as a mechanism for donors at all levels of charitable giving." Local industrialist H.D. Dawbarn founded the SAW Foundation in 1992. Its area of service extends to the city of Staunton, county of Augusta, city of Waynesboro, and surrounding communities; the Foundation itself is located in Waynesboro, Virginia. In addition to building endowments for the community, the SAW Foundation does award grants. Its areas of funding interest are education, health and human services, civic and community initiatives, arts and culture, and the environment. All grant guidelines and deadlines are explained on the site. Those interested in receiving a grant are encouraged to first contact the Foundation for direct assistance.

The Virginia Beach Foundation (http://fdncenter.org/grantmaker/vbf/index.html)

The Virginia Beach Foundation is a community foundation serving the people of Virginia Beach and their neighbors. Founded in 1987, The Virginia Beach Foundation's mission is to stimulate the establishment of endowments to serve the people of Virginia Beach now and in the future; respond to changing, emerging community needs; assist donors in achieving their charitable giving objectives; and serve as a resource, broker, catalyst and leader in the community. At the site you will find a history the foundation, FAQs, words from foundation supporters and grantees, and donor information.

WASHINGTON

Community Foundation for Southwest Washington (http://www.cfsww.com/index.html)

The Community Foundation for Southwest Washington, located in Vancouver, has been assisting the surrounding community since 1984. The group's mission is to "shape the future of Southwest Washington through philanthropy . . . [by] supporting worthy projects in the areas of social and human services, arts and culture, education, and quality of life." Nonprofits serving the communities of Cowlitz, Clark, Skamania, and West Klickitat Counties are eligible to receive funding. Areas of funding interest include social services, civic affairs, health, education, children's issues, and arts and cultural affairs. The site offers an application that can be printed right from the screen, along with application guidelines and deadlines. The public charity also hosts a series of special initiatives. These include a program to address recent reductions in welfare reform laws, assistance with electric bills during the winter, a sculpture garden, and a fund to support innovative ideas in the classroom. The straightforward site includes an extensive list of board members and a calendar of events. There is also a section devoted to soliciting donations.

The Seattle Foundation (http://www.seattlefoundation.org/)

Established in 1946, the Seattle Foundation today works to improve the quality of life for people in the Puget Sound region by nurturing a greater sense of community in the region and serving as a catalyst for dialogue within the area's nonprofit community. The Foundation manages an endowment of more than $235 million and in the most recent year made grant distributions totaling almost $19 million. Grants are awarded quarterly to organizations in the areas of arts, culture, and the humanities; health; human services; the environment; and public/society benefit. All applicant organizations must qualify as tax-exempt under section 501(c)(3) of the IRS Code and be located primarily in King County. Visitors to the Seattle Foundation's Web site will find general information about the Foundation and its activities, PDF versions of the Foundation's discretionary grant guidelines and latest annual report, an electronic form for requesting other Foundation publications, information for potential donors, and contact information.

WEST VIRGINIA

Parkersburg Area Community Foundation (http://home.wirefire.com/pacf/)

The Parkersburg Area Community Foundation (PACF) is committed to serving the people of the Mid-Ohio Valley—Wood, Calhoun, Doddridge, Gilmer, Jackson, Pleasants, Ritchie, and Roane Counties in West Virginia and Washington County in Ohio—by linking community resources with community needs. PACF focuses its grantmaking in the following areas: arts and culture, education, health and human services, recreation, and youth and family services. To be eligible for a grant from the Foundation, an applicant must be a private, nonprofit, tax-exempt organization under section 501(c)(3) of the Internal Revenue Code, or they must be a public institution. The Foundation also administers more than 65 different scholarship funds, the majority of which are designated for students in Wood County, West Virginia. The Foundation's Web site provides general information about the Foundation, detailed application guidelines and scholarship information, and general information about becoming a donor to the Foundation.

WISCONSIN

Community Foundation for the Fox Valley Region (http://www.cffoxvalley.org)

Incorporated in 1986, The Community Foundation for the Fox Valley Region "exists to enhance the quality of life for all citizens" in the region of Wisconsin from Neenah to Appleton to Kaukauna and into surrounding areas. The Foundation's grants support five program areas: human services, arts and culture, healthcare, education, and community development. The Foundation maintains information on the programs they have supported in the past on their Web site, along with current grant guidelines and limitations and a printable common grant application. Visitors to the Foundation's site can also find a list of the staff and board members, financial information, news releases, donor information, and related links.

Dickinson County Community Foundation (http://biz-comm.com/dcacf)

The Dickinson County Community Foundation was established in 1995 to address the community needs, using local resources, of Dickinson County, Michigan, and the surrounding Wisconsin communities. The Foundation focuses on youth programs and services, among other areas. For more details, the Foundation lists contact information, and information for donors, on its Web site.

Duluth-Superior Area Community Foundation (MN/WI)
(http://www.dsacommunityfoundation.com)

Incorporated in 1982, the Duluth-Superior Area Community Foundation strives to improve the quality of life for the residents of Duluth, Minnesota; Superior, Wisconsin; and the surrounding areas. The Foundation supports local projects and organizations in the arts, civic projects, education, environment, and human services. Information on specific named grants and general grants, as well as previous grantees in each area of interest, is available on the Foundation's Web site. Scholarships are also granted, and more information can be obtained by contacting the Foundation. The Foundation's site provides recent annual reports online, donor information, a contact form, a short history of the Foundation, and a list of its staff and board.

The Eau Claire Area Foundation (http://www.ecareafoundation.org)

The Eau Claire Area Foundation, in Wisconsin, is committed to enriching area life by strengthening the community, encouraging volunteer participation and collaboration, and helping people help themselves. The Foundation considers funding in the following five areas: education, culture, the environment, recreation, and social concerns. This concise Web site includes a grant application form (with application guidelines), the annual report, and the Foundation's Form 990–PF, all of which can be downloaded in Microsoft Word or PDF formats. Phone and fax contact numbers are included.

Fond du Lac Area Foundation (http://www.fdlareafoundation.com)

Established in 1976, the Fond du Lac Area Foundation funds community endeavors in education, health and human services, youth services, arts and culture, and the environment. A number of named scholarships are available for area students and are listed on the Foundation's Web site. Grants are made to provide practical solutions to community problems, promote cooperation and volunteerism, stimulate stability and effectiveness, and encourage prevention as well as remediation. The Foundation lists current financial information, grant guidelines and limitations, an FAQ, recent Foundation news, and links to additional resources online. There is ample donor information, including a contributions form in PDF format, and a contact form to request an application for further information.

La Crosse Community Foundation (http://www.laxcommfoundation.com)

The La Crosse Community Foundation seeks to enrich the quality of life in the greater La Crosse, Wisconsin area. The Foundation supports "programs and activities of economic, educational, social and cultural nonprofit organizations" through grants and scholarships. During the quarterly Foundation meetings, an issue of primary concern is decided upon, and grants strive to address this focus. Grantseekers should use the Foundation's online contact form to receive news of the current issue. The Foundation's Web site includes a complete list of specific scholarships for individuals, as well as donor and financial information.

M & M Area Community Foundation (MI/WI) (http://www.cmif.org/mm.htm)

M & M Area Community Foundation strives to promote the spirit of philanthropy and meet the needs of the people of Menominee County, Michigan, and Marinette County, Wisconsin. A variety of funds provide support in the areas of education, the environment, and cultural, recreational, and charitable purposes. The Foundation's Web site provides a list of current funds, donor and applicant information, and contact information for more details.

Milwaukee Foundation (http://www.milwaukeefoundation.org)

Established in 1915, making it one of the first community foundations in the United States, the Milwaukee Foundation today comprises nearly 600 individual funds with a combined $275 million in assets. The Foundation makes grants in six areas: arts and culture, education, employment and training, health and human services, community economic development, and conservation and historic preservation; and limits its grantmaking "to projects that offer a significant improvement" to the lives of the people living in Milwaukee, Waukesha, Ozaukee, and Washington Counties. Grants made outside this area are based upon donor recommendations. Detailed criteria in each of these funding areas is available from the Foundation upon request. In addition to general information and a history of the Foundation, visitors to the Web site will find application procedures, examples of recent grants, a variety of information for prospective donors, an electronic form for requesting guidelines and the Foundation's annual report, and contact information.

St. Croix Valley Community Foundation (http://www.pressenter.com/~scvcf/)

Founded in 1995, the St. Croix Valley Community Foundation serves the communities of St. Croix Valley in Wisconsin and Minnesota. Its fields of interest include education, arts, environment, civic affairs, and emergency human needs. The Foundation's Web site includes its annual report, board and staff lists, and a form to request more information.

Wausau Area Community Foundation (http://wacf.org/)

Wisconsin's Wausau Area Community Foundation was created in 1987 "to serve Wausau and the surrounding areas by creating an endowment dedicated to enriching the quality of life for present and future generations." The Foundation focuses on five program areas—education, the arts, health, social services, and conservation and preservation of resources (including historical and cultural resources)—and supports programs that uphold its mission. Grant guidelines and limitations are available at the Foundation's Web site, as is donor information. Beyond Pencils/Crayons is a Foundation-supported program that strives to enhance and reward innovative teaching, learning, and special motivational activities through grants of up to $2,000. Past grant recipients and programs are listed on the Web site. For more information, including financial reports and grant applications, the Foundation provides a reply form on its site.

WYOMING

Community Foundation of Jackson Hole (http://www.cfjacksonhole.org/)

The Community Foundation of Jackson Hole is committed to "enhance[ing] philanthropy and strengthen[ing] the sense of community in the Jackson Hole [Wyoming] area [by providing] a permanent source of funding and other support for nonprofit organizations and scholarship recipients." The Foundation assists donors in maximizing the impact of their charitable giving, manages permanent endowments in response to donors' wishes, provides and monitors competitive grants, and holds workshops for local nonprofit organizations. The Foundation's Web site provides general fiscal information, comprehensive listings (alphabetically and by subject category) of Jackson Hole-area charitable organizations, and contact information for grantmaking guidelines and application forms.

Wyoming Community Foundation (http://www.wycf.org)

The Wyoming Community Foundation, established in 1989, strives "to ensure and enhance the quality of life for present and future generations of Wyoming people." The Foundation focuses its grants in the general areas of arts and culture, civic projects, education, conservation and natural resources, and health and human services. Awards range from $500–$5000, and the Foundation favors giving in two areas: prevention and early intervention for high-risk children and families and community based organizations that address physical, social, and economic issues at the grassroots level. Visitors to the Foundation's Web site will find application guidelines, information for donors, a list of the Foundation's board and staff, related links, and contact information to request additional resources directly from the Foundation.

APPENDIX E

Corporate Grantmakers on the Web

Abbott Laboratories Fund (IL)
(http://www.abbott.com/community/community_relations.html)
The Abbott Laboratories Fund makes grants to nonprofit organizations operating in "Abbott Communities" in the areas of human health and welfare; elementary, secondary, and higher education; and culture, the arts, and civic activities. Priority is given to institutions that provide education or service to present or potential Abbott employees and to organizations with activities directed toward support of professions that provide healthcare or other services in the fields related to Abbott's primary areas of operation. The Fund generally favors requests for one-time contributions and for programmatic and operating purposes; its guidelines preclude it from making grants for individuals, purely social organizations, political parties or candidates, religious organizations, advertising, symposia and conferences, ticket purchases, memberships, or business-related purposes. In addition to general facts about the Fund's giving, the site contains general program guidelines, application instructions, and contact information. Visitors to the site will also find information about Abbott Laboratories and its products.

The Ackerley Group, Inc. (WA)
(http://www.ackerley.com/ackerley_corporate/cgbody.html)
The Ackerley Group of Seattle, Washington, has a Corporate Giving Program that supports nonprofit organizations in communities where its properties conduct business. The company supports strong community partnerships through financial and in-kind support in four areas: youth, the arts, family services, and civic and community affairs. The succinct page includes application guidelines and restrictions, and an e-mail and street address to contact with questions. The program does not accept unsolicited applications.

ADC Telecommunications (MN)
(http://www.adc.com/main_template/1,1034,25,00.html?contcat=0)
Based in Minneapolis, Minnesota, ADC is a leading global supplier of voice, video, and data systems and solutions for television, cable television, Internet, broadcast, wireless, and private communications networks. ADC "works in partnership with others in service to

the community, responding and listening to them, and acting and following the values of the ADC Way—service, high performance, continuous improvement, integrity, respect and spirit." The Foundation seeks to improve the future of society by supporting excellent science and technology education, expanding telecommunications access for the disadvantaged, and improving the quality of life in core cities and municipalities where ADC's people live and work. ADC matches gifts by its employees or supports organizations its employees give time to through the ADC Foundation Dollars for Doers Program. Those interested in applying for a grant can find a link to the Minnesota Common Grant Application Form on the Foundation's site, as well as grant recipient lists, the annual report, and contact information.

Adobe Systems, Inc. (CA) (http://www.adobe.com/aboutadobe/philanthropy/main.html)
Adobe's corporate giving is centered around its Philanthropy Council, a representative group of Adobe employees committed to supporting programs that improve the quality of life for everyone. The San Jose, California, company specifically supports nonprofit organizations that service "disadvantaged youth, the homeless, people with disabilities, minorities, the elderly, and victims of abuse; provide disaster relief, medical and hospice care, and meal services; provide education and literacy programs; support human rights; support the arts; protect the environment; and support animal rights." Cash grants, equipment donations, and volunteer support for activities such as walkathons and service projects are available. Adobe also has a Teach the Teacher program where free training is provided to educators on Adobe products. The page devoted to the company's philanthropic activities provides visitors with a brief description of its individual programs and application guidelines, downloadable application forms and annual report, and contact information. The site also has a test to determine if an organization is eligible for a cash grant or volunteer support.

Aetna Foundation (CT) (http://www.aetna.com/foundation/)
As the Hartford-based insurance giant's primary philanthropic vehicle, the Aetna Foundation focuses its activities in the areas of children's health, where it looks for initiatives that "focus on cardiac disease prevention and detection initiatives; and education, where it favors college preparation, school-to-career initiatives, and entrepreneurial education . . . for middle school students whose parents actively participate in the programs." The grant awards made by the Foundation reflect a geographic emphasis on organizations and initiatives in selected communities of strategic importance to Aetna Inc. and are limited to proposals submitted by invitation. Grant proposals are accepted year-round and must be submitted in writing. In addition to detailed application guidelines, visitors to the Foundation section of the company's Web site will find general program information, profiles of successful Foundation-sponsored initiatives, and a section devoted to the company's Voice of Conscience Award, created as a tribute to the late Arthur Ashe. Additionally, the Foundation makes grants to participants in its Academic Medicine and Managed Care Forum for research that will directly improve practices impacting the quality of care and health outcomes for patients.

Agilent Technologies, Inc. (CA) (http://www.agilent.com/philanthropy/)
Palo Alto, California-based Agilent Technologies' corporate giving programs are focused on healthcare and pre-university education. Its healthcare initiatives provide critical resources to partners who make the dream of healthcare self-sufficiency a reality. Its pre-university education programs are designed to improve student achievement in science and math education and encourage technical fields of study for women and minorities. Descriptions of specific initiatives and programs, such as the Individual Self-Sufficiency Program, are available on the Agilent Web site. Agilent Technologies does not accept unsolicited applications, but contact information is provided for those who wish to provide an idea to be considered in the future. The Web site also contains information about the University Grants Programs and Employee Funds Matching Programs.

Agrilink Foods/Pro-Fac Foundation (NY) (http://www.agrilinkfoods.com/corp/about/community)

Agrilink Foods, Inc. is a food processing and marketing cooperative headquartered in Rochester, New York. The Agrilink Foods/Pro-Fac Foundation provides grants to nonprofit organizations operating in communities where Agrilink has facilities or where Pro-Fac members are located. Primary giving areas are health, community services, education, youth, agricultural research, and cultural programs. Grant guidelines, restrictions, and contact information for various divisions and locations are included in the Philanthropy and Community Service section of the Web site.

Alcoa Foundation (PA) (http://www.alcoa.com/community/community_foundation.asp)

The Alcoa Foundation is the philanthropic arm of Pittsburgh, Pennsylvania-based Alcoa, the world's leading producer of primary aluminum, fabricated aluminum, and alumina. The Foundation's goals include "enhancing the quality of life and optimizing human potential in those communities around the globe that Alcoa calls home." Primary areas of giving are education, health and human services, the environment and ecology, civic and community improvements, and cultural endeavors, with over 60 percent of funding going to programs falling in the first two categories. While interested national and international organizations should contact the Foundation in Pittsburgh, local nonprofits should contact their local Alcoa facility in order to be recommended for a grant. The site includes a page with features on selected grant projects throughout the world.

The Aleut Foundation (AK) (http://www.aleutcorp.com/found.html/)

The Aleut Foundation is the scholarship program of The Aleut Corporation (TAC), which was established in 1972 under the terms of the Alaska Native Claims Settlement Act. Formed in February of 1988, the primary goal and objective of the Anchorage, Alaska-based Foundation is to serve the economic and social needs of the shareholders of TAC, their descendants, spouses, and ex-spouses with minor children. Visitors to the site will find detailed eligibility criteria, application instructions, and information on The Aleut Corporation and Aleut culture.

Alliant Energy (WI) (http://www.alliantenergy.com/community/charity.htm)

Alliant Energy's Corporate Foundation is committed to "contributions that benefit the citizens of the communities served by Alliant Energy." The Foundation partners with communities in which it has an interest to improve the quality of life for its members. While Alliant's corporate headquarters and Wisconsin charitable operations are located in Madison, Wisconsin, the Alliant Foundation also maintains a Cedar Rapids, Iowa, office for charitable work in Illinois, Iowa, and Minnesota. The Foundation focuses on the following areas: human needs, education, culture and the arts, civic service, and nature. Specific descriptions of the types of projects the Foundation will fund are available on its Web site. To apply for a grant, visitors must complete an application for funding, which is available on the site and downloadable in PDF format. In addition, financial statements, contact information, and information about the Foundation's geographic boundaries are available online.

The Allstate Foundation (IL) (http://www.allstate.com/foundation/)

Founded in 1952, The Allstate Foundation is an independent corporation funded by contributions from Allstate Insurance Company. Based in Northbrook, Illinois, the Foundation has field offices in numerous states. The Foundation works in concert with Allstate by aligning with the company's major focus areas: automobile and highway safety, which advocates seat belt usage and infant and child car seat awareness; anti-drinking and driving; educational awareness for new drivers; car theft prevention and traffic court monitoring; personal safety and security, which works to make the community a safer place to live by raising awareness of poverty, child abuse, drugs, and violence prevention; and homes and neighborhoods, which emphasizes urban neighborhood revitalization, home fire prevention, security information against burglary, accident prevention, and small business safety awareness. The Allstate Foundation prefers to support specific programs within the focus areas, rather than making general operating grants. The site contains grant application instructions and guidelines, a grant recipient list, and contact information for all of the Foundation's field offices.

Ameren Corporation (MO) (http://www.ameren.com/community/community.asp)

Ameren, an energy provider based in St. Louis, Missouri, supports community groups and organizations through the Ameren Corporation Charitable Trust and a direct corporate giving program. Contributions focus on education; services for youth, the elderly, and the environment; and scholarships offered at Missouri and Illinois colleges and universities to eligible customers in Ameren service territories. Ameren also supports organizations with grantss where their employees volunteer. The Community Services area of Ameren's Web site describes the Trust's giving policy and provides grant application information, information on scholarship eligibility, and has an online information request form. The site also provides information on non-grantmaking charitable activities and environmental programs.

American Express Foundation (NY)
(http://home3.americanexpress.com/corp/philanthropy/)

The New York City-based philanthropic program of the American Express Company includes the activities of the American Express Foundation and a direct corporate giving program and encompasses both U.S. nonprofits as well as organizations outside the United States that can document nonprofit status. The company makes grants in three program areas: community service, with funding primarily supporting the volunteer efforts of employees and advisors in their local communities; cultural heritage, with the twin themes of protecting "the built and natural environment" and supporting "art and culture unique to countries and regions;" and economic independence, with an emphasis on supporting initiatives that "encourage, support or develop economic self-reliance." In addition to general program information and application guidelines, visitors to the company's Web site will find a list of grant recipients and descriptions of major programs to which the company has recently made grants.

American Express Minnesota Philanthropic Program (MN)
(http://home3.americanexpress.com/advisors/about/giving/)

Based in Minneapolis, Minnesota, the American Express Minnesota Philanthropic Program works to support the communities in which employees live and work. The three-part program is made up of community support, philanthropic giving, and a volunteer program. Community support includes donations to the United Way and supporting the community-oriented nonprofit efforts of financial advisors across the country. The grant program awards gifts in three areas of interest to nonprofits in the Twin Cities and throughout greater Minnesota: economic independence, particularly programs serving youth, building awareness of career and job options, and educating people on the basics of business and economics; art/cultural heritage, focusing on arts and major cultural institutions and projects; community service grants support employee volunteer efforts and selected service groups. The volunteer program supports employee volunteer efforts and organizes their participation. The site includes very clear application guidelines, restrictions, and deadlines.

American Power Conversion Corporation (RI)
(http://www.apcc.com/corporate/contributions.cfm)

Based in West Kingston, Rhode Island, the American Power Conversion Corporation's Contributions Program supports organizations and services in its community. The Program's main funding interest is technological education for primary, secondary, and university students, supported through financial aid to area school districts, equipment donation, and specific educational program support. The Corporation's Web site provides funding criteria, limitations, and an online funding request form.

American Savings Bank Foundation (CT) (http://www.americansavingsbank.com/)

The American Savings Bank Foundation was born through actor Paul Newman's 1999 recruitment of *Fortune* 500 CEOs to form a new organization dedicated to the encouragement of corporate philanthropy. The Foundation's program priorities consist of education, human services, and arts and culture. Additionally, the Foundation awards scholarships to college students who are residents of one of the 47 Connecticut towns served by the American Savings Bank. Scholarship applications can be downloaded in PDF format. Grant guidelines, recent scholarship and grant recipients, and contact information are also provided on the Foundation's Web site.

AMP Foundation (PA) (http://www.amp.com/about/foundation/)

Supported and run by the world's leading supplier of electrical and electronic connectors and interconnection systems, the AMP Foundation supports programs nationally, in communities where the company has employees. It "is dedicated to fostering a society which enhances the quality of life and in which all people can participate." This is accomplished through four programs: matching employee grants to schools and supporting programs that encourage pre-college math and science education, community service agencies that promote personal growth, career opportunities and economic self sufficiency, and community-wide arts organizations that solicit and allocate funds for a number of arts groups and institutions. The grant application can be downloaded in Microsoft Word format, and there is an additional set of questions for anyone requesting more than $2,500. Also available are addresses for inquiries, financial statements, and extensive information on matching programs for employees. The Foundation accepts applications through the year and makes decisions on a quarterly basis.

AMR/American Airlines Foundation (TX) (http://www.amrcorp.com/corp_fdn.htm)

The AMR/American Airlines Foundation supports nonprofit organizations in the communities that AMR Corporation serves, particularly its hub cities of Dallas/Fort Worth, Texas; Chicago, Illinois; Miami, Florida; and San Juan, Puerto Rico. The Texas-based Foundation provides organizations with air transportation and monetary support, which is focused on four areas: community development, arts and culture, education, and health and welfare. The company's Web site provides grant guidelines, instructions for proposal submission, and contact information.

AOL Time Warner Foundation (NY) (http://www.aoltwfoundation.org/)

The AOL Time Warner Foundation, based in New York City and Dulles, Virginia, "seeks to use the power of media, communications and information technology to serve the public interest and strengthen society." The Foundation engages AOL Time Warner's unique resources to build innovative and sustainable programs in four priority areas: Equipping Children for a Better Future, Extending Internet Benefits to All, Engaging Communities in the Arts, and Empowering Citizens and Civic Participation. Details about each program, including descriptions of specific initiatives, can be found on the Web site. Solicitations for funds must be made in writing or by e-mail. Guidelines and deadlines are posted on the site, as is contact information.

Apple Computer (CA)
(http://www.apple.com/education/k12/leadership/funding/index.html)

The primary philanthropic activity of Apple Computer is the donation of new computer equipment to K–12 schools. In the area of higher education, Apple helps institutions to use technology more effectively "to deliver learning experiences that are rich in communication, collaboration and construction of knowledge." The Cupertino, California-based company does not fund religious groups, political groups, or individuals and does not make donations in support of raffles, fundraising events, auctions, or door prizes. The Education section of the Apple Web site offers general information about Apple's support of K–12 and higher education; information about the Apple Education Grants program, the Apple Distinguished Schools initiative, the Apple Classroom of Tomorrow (ACOT) project, and other education-oriented intiatives; and a helpful FAQ section with, among other things, specific guidelines for contacting the company about its philanthropic programs.

Applied Materials, Inc. (CA) (http://www.appliedmaterials.com/about/community.html)
Applied Materials, Inc. of Santa Clara, California, created a corporate philanthropy program to benefit its community. The goal of the program is to make a positive social contribution in areas where the company has major operations. Grants are focused in three giving areas: education, civics, and arts and culture. Besides the grant program, there is a University Partnership Program and an in-kind Office and Computer Donations component, which primarily gives to K–12 public schools. The site includes grant guidelines and a partial list of grantees under the Grants link. There is an address to send inquiries to, including a second address solely for applicants in Austin, Texas.

Aramco Services Company (TX)
(http://www.aramcoservices.com/inside/public/communitycont.html)
Aramco Services Company's assistance program focuses on contributing to local charities and nonprofit organizations in educational, cultural, environmental, and community efforts that enhance the city of Houston, where Aramco Services Company is located. Aramco Services is involved in several ongoing projects, including the support of an adult learning center for the Houston READ Commission, the involvement in the local Private Sector Initiative, and the support for a local inter–city Headstart Program

Ashland Inc. (KY) (http://www.ashland.com/community)
Ashland is a diversified company headquartered in Covington, Kentucky, with operations in specialty chemical production and distribution, motor oil and car care products, and highway construction. The In Our Communities area of Ashland's Web site outlines its charitable efforts, which are focused on education, arts and culture, the environment, and health and human services in cities where the company operates. The online Community Relations Annual Report provides detailed information on Ashland's giving in each area. The site also contains application instructions, a downloadable application form, and contact information.

Aspect Telecommunications Corporation (CA)
(http://www.aspect.com/newsinfo/community/community_comm.htm)
Aspect Telecommunications, a supplier of call center products headquartered in San Jose, California, created the Aspect Community Commitment Fund, a direct corporate giving program, to support local nonprofits and schools (public and private) to help better educate children and youth. The primary focus is on programs and projects that build capabilities in science, math, or technology. The Fund awards grants of $1,000–$10,000 for projects that encourage "positive and healthy" learning by children at the K–9 level and primarily targets minorities, low- or no-income populations, and the physically or mentally challenged. The Community Commitment area of the company's Web site details the company's corporate giving program, explains grant eligibility, and provides application instructions.

AT&T Foundation (NY) (http://www.att.com/foundation/)
As the principal philanthropic arm of AT&T Corp., the AT&T Foundation makes grants in the program areas of education, arts and culture, and civic and community service. While the scope of the Foundation's activities is global, the majority of its funds support U.S.-based institutions. The Foundation also maintains a local program to focus support on cities and regions with large concentrations of AT&T employees and business operations. The company's Web site includes a separate area for Foundation information where visitors will find detailed program descriptions, application guidelines and procedures, complete grants listings for each program area, and an interactive form for requesting additional information.

Attachmate Corporation (WA) (http://cooljobs.attachmate.com/community.asp)

The Attachmate Corporation was founded in 1982 as a supplier of enterprise information and to create management software and services to major corporations and government agencies worldwide. The Corporation's mission in the community is to provide qualifying organizations that are worthy, relevant, and have a tangible impact on the community with the support they need to continue their good work. Attachmate Corporation has a history of giving back to the community through programs such as its Corporate Matching Fund Program, the EXTRA! Reward Program, and its Corporate Contributions Program. Attachmate supports many different nonprofit organizations, mostly concerned with health, social services, education, the environment, the arts, and others. Visit Attachmate's Web site to find a listing of some of the recent organizations supported and contact information.

Autodesk, Inc. (CA) (http://www3.autodesk.com/adsk/index/0,,304882-123112,00.html)

The design resource service Autodesk, located in San Rafael, California, established its Community Relations program in 1989. Autodesk provides grants, product donations, and encourages employee volunteerism to area nonprofit organizations focused on art and culture, civic and community issues, education, the environment, and health and human services. The Autodesk Web site gives guidelines for financial and product grants, along with contact information. Potential applicants may also download a Product Grant application in PDF format from the site.

AutoZone, Inc. (TN)
(http://www.autozone.com/aboutUs/CommunityAction/body_communityaction.html)

Memphis-based AutoZone focuses its philanthropic efforts on various community organizations and programs based in the areas where the company's branches are located. These contributions vary in scope, from funds toward the National Civil Rights Museum, to sponsorship of the AutoZone Invitational Golf Tournament. AutoZone's participation in a number of these programs and events is detailed on the company's Web site. Charitable giving guidelines, funding limitations, and contact information are provided online as well.

Aventis Pharmaceuticals Inc. (PA)
(http://www.aventispharma-us.com/community_involvement.htm)

Aventis Pharmaceuticals is actively committed to the improvement of public health. The company supports activities in the communities in which it operates and its employees live. Aventis Pharmaceuticals believes that philanthropy works best through active support of projects that encourage self-sufficiency to build a stronger community. Specifically, Aventis participates in activities that encourage leadership in existing agencies or programs and projects that forge community coalitions or establish business and nonprofit partnerships. The company also provides direct financial support for programs and donates its associates' time, skills, and talents through volunteerism. The site does not provide specific details about the company's philanthropic activities, but the site does provide the ability to contact the company online.

Avon Products Foundation, Inc. (NY)
(http://www.avon.com/about/women/foundation/foundation.html)

The Avon Products Foundation, located in New York City, supports organizations addressing the needs of women worldwide. Funding is provided for women's programs that focus on health, education, community and social services, and arts and culture. Although the Foundation accepts unsolicited proposals, funds are more commonly awarded to pre-selected organizations. Guidelines are provided in the Foundation section of Avon Products, Inc.'s Web site, along with a sampling of grant recipients.

The AXA Foundation (NY) (http://www.axa-financial.com/aboutus/foundation.html)

The AXA Foundation is the philanthropic arm of AXA Financial. Its mission is to direct "charitable and volunteer activities on behalf of the many communities in which [it does] business." The AXA Foundation manages three programs that comprise its broad-based response to meeting community needs. These programs are direct grants, the employee Matching Gifts Plan, and an annual United Way campaign. In terms of grantmaking, the Foundation is committed to playing a leadership role in maintaining and improving the quality of life in its headquarter city, New York. Grantmaking in this area focuses on youth service organizations and the principal arts institutions. The Foundation is also committed to supporting the communities in which it does business by funding programs that focus on the pressing issues that face such communities. In addition, the Foundation supports interests in eldercare and programs that assess the needs of family caregivers and that disseminate eldercare information and resources. To apply for a grant, interested parties should submit an introductory letter; details are listed on the Foundation's Web site. Information about the Matching Gift program and the United Way campaign are also available online.

Baltimore Gas and Electric Company (MD) (http://www.bge.com/community/)
Based in Baltimore, Maryland, the Baltimore Gas and Electric Company (BGE) seeks to enhance the quality of life in the communities in which it operates. Major giving areas in its contributions program are early childhood development, education, health and welfare, hospitals, culture, civics, and the environment. BGE also seeks to provide support for organizations that have designated management and employee involvement. Visit BGE's Web site for application guidelines, giving history, and contact information. More information on BGE's grantmaking can be requested through e-mail.

Bally Total Fitness Holding Corporation (IL) (http://www.ballyfitness.com/company/comm/comm_main.asp)
The Bally Total Fitness Holding Corporation began its Stronger Communities initiative in 1997. The initiative involves donating reconditioned fitness equipment, fitness apparel, and memberships to Bally Total Fitness in communities adjacent to the Corporation's Fitness Clubs. The Corporation also provides training services to the organizations to which it donates equipment. Recent recipients of the Stronger Communities initiative are detailed in the Communities portion of the Bally Total Fitness Web site.

Bank of America Foundation (NC) (http://www.bankofamerica.com/foundation/)
The Bank of America Foundation directs charitable giving on behalf of the Bank of America corporation. The Bank of America Foundation contributes financial assistance to non-profit institutions and organizations that "enhance the quality of life and promote public interest in the areas where the company conducts business." The Foundation gives grants in the following areas of interest: education, community development, health and human services, and arts and culture. To apply for a grant, interested organizations should send a letter to the local Bank of America office in the city where the organization is based. Information about what to include in the letter is available on the Foundation's Web site. The site also contains contact information for contribution managers in each state where Bank of America is located. The Foundation has several other programs in addition to general grantmaking: volunteer grants, educational partnerships, matching grants, and scholarships. Further details are listed online.

C.R. Bard Foundation (NJ) (http://www.crbard.com/about/foundation.html)
The C.R. Bard Foundation, established in Murray Hill, New Jersey, in 1987, supports charitable organizations that benefit the community where Bard is located, as well as Bard's employees, their families, and organizations in which they are active. The Foundation's funding priorities lie in three categories: healthcare and social welfare, education and arts, and cultural and community life. healthcare focuses are in vascular, urology, and oncology. Bard also sponsors a corporate donations program and matching gifts. Some of the Bard employee-led projects are described on the Foundation's Web site. Contact information is available in the Contact & Support section of the site.

Eddie Bauer, Inc. (WA) (http://eddiebauer.com/about/eb_philanthropy.asp)
Based in Redmond, Washington, Eddie Bauer, Inc. has created a strong community relations/corporate giving program. Grants and in-kind donations are made to organizations

fitting into one of three categories. Education programs include the newly created Eddie Bauer Scholars program with scholarships to institutions including Howard University-School of Business, University of Washington-School of Business, The College Fund-UNCF, and the Hispanic College Fund. The environment category concentrates on the universal benefit of trees. The last area deals with programs that empower unemployed or underemployed women. There is also a "community volunteering" element of the program that encourages employees to volunteer in their communities. The site includes very brief application instructions.

Baxter International Inc. (IL) (http://www.baxter.com/investors/citizenship/index.html)

Baxter International, located in Deerfield, Illinois, develops therapies and technologies for treating life-threatening conditions of the blood and circulatory system. Its principal philanthropic vehicle, the Baxter Allegiance Foundation, supports healthcare and social service systems and providers internationally and is committed to environmental awareness. The Foundation's grantmaking program awards funds to improve healthcare in the United States, Europe, Latin America, and Mexico, with plans to expand its geographic reach to Japan and Asia. The company's Web site describes the Foundation, offers examples of grantmaking, and provides contact information.

Bayer Foundation (PA) (http://www.bayerus.com/about/community/com_foundation.html)

Bayer Corporation, headquartered in Pittsburgh, Pennsylvania, develops healthcare products, chemicals, and imaging technologies. The Bayer Foundation supports the communities where the company is located and awards grants in three areas: civic and community programs, science education and workforce development, and the arts, arts education, and culture. The company's Web site provides detailed grant guidelines, application instructions, and deadlines.

Bechtel Foundation (CA) (http://www.bechtel.com/bechfoun.html)

Bechtel Group, Inc., located in San Francisco, California, develops and manages capital projects and facilities worldwide. The Bechtel Foundation supports communities where the company has offices or major projects. Grants are typically directed to youth and educational programs—particularly math and science education—and engineering and business programs at selected colleges and universities. Although most grant recipients are pre-selected by Bechtel's office and project managers, the Foundation section of the company's Web site provides proposal guidelines for grantseekers whose projects fall into the Foundation's funding areas. Visitors to the site will also find highlights of the Foundation's recent giving.

BellSouth Foundation (GA) (http://www.bellsouthfoundation.org/)

The BellSouth Foundation seeks to improve outcomes and stimulate active learning for students in elementary and secondary education in nine southern states - Alabama, Florida, Georgia, Kentucky, Louisiana, Mississippi, North Carolina, South Carolina, and Tennessee. In its current grantmaking cycle (i.e., 2001–2005), the Foundation focuses its efforts in three areas: reforming high schools, supporting college students' persistence and success, and closing the gap for communities that are caught in the digital divide. BellSouth's Web site offers visitors a broad range of information about the activities of its Foundation, including online versions of two reports on the Foundation's grantmaking initiatives; detailed program descriptions; application guidelines, deadlines, and restrictions; recent grants, and an interactive application form.

The Ben & Jerry's Foundation (VT) (http://www.benjerry.com/foundation/index.html)

The Ben & Jerry's Foundation works "to make the world a better place by empowering Ben & Jerry's employees to use available resources to support and encourage organizations that are working towards eliminating the underlying causes of environmental and social problems." The Foundation offers competitive grants to nonprofit, grassroots organizations throughout the United States that facilitate progressive social change by addressing the underlying conditions of societal and environmental problems. Projects supported by the

Foundation must "help ameliorate an unjust or destructive situation by empowering constituents; facilitate leadership development and strengthen the self-empowerment efforts of
those who have traditionally been disenfranchised in our society; and support movement
building and collective action." The Foundation's parent company, Vermont-based Ben &
Jerry's Homemade, Inc., makes quarterly donations at the discretion of its board of approximately 7.5 percent of its pre-tax profits. A portion of those funds goes to the Foundation,
while the rest is earmarked for employee-led community action teams (CATs), which distribute small grants to community groups in Vermont. Visitors to the Foundation area of
the Ben & Jerry's site will find detailed information about the Foundation's funding guidelines, interests, and restrictions; application instructions; a downloadable letter of interest
cover page; recent grants lists; and online versions of the Foundation's five most recent
annual reports.

Berlex Foundation, Inc. (NJ) (http://www.berlex-foundation.org/)

The Hackensack, New Jersey-based Berlex Foundation was established in 1986 as a nonprofit organization dedicated to fostering education and encouraging innovative research in
the field of reproductive medicine. The Foundation's programs are funded by an endowment from Berlex Laboratories, Inc., a firm with a well-founded record of commitment to
reproductive research. The Foundation supports a wide spectrum of awards and educational programs, including the Berlex Scholar Award in Basic Science Research, an annual
fellowship dedicated to encouraging and enabling clinician-investigators to continue to
work on meritorious research projects in the area of reproductive medicine; the Berlex
Scholar Award in Clinical Research, which supports clinical research by young investigators in the areas of diagnosis, treatment, and prognosis in obstetrics and gynecology; the
Berlex Faculty Development Award, which provides individuals with the opportunity to
participate in a week-long intensive workshop concentrating on epidemiology, clinical trial
design, and statistical analysis; and the Reproductive Scientist Development Program
(RSDP), a national postdoctoral career development program designed for young obstetri-
cian-gynecologists who are committed to careers in academic medicine. In addition, each
year the Berlex Foundation sponsors the C.D. Christian Lectureship at the annual meeting
of the Society for Gynecologic Investigation, which has made it possible for internationally
distinguished scientists to share their insights and experiences with colleagues in the area
of reproductive medicine. Visit the site for related links and contact information.

Best Buy (MN)
(http://www.bestbuy.com/About/CommunityRelations/index.asp?m=435&cat=439)

Minneapolis-based Best Buy supports organizations in the communities where Best Buy
stores are located. The company's two main grant programs are the Community Service
Grants Program, which asks children ages 8–14 to suggest grant ideas that will benefit their
community, and the Best Buy Children's Foundation, which seeks to improve the quality of
life for school-aged children in the communities where Best Buy is located. Additionally,
Best Buy has numerous alliances through its corporate giving programs, promoting youth
education and enrichment and social service organizations. The Community Relations portion of the Best Buy Web site includes online applications, criteria and restrictions for the
two grant programs, and news of Best Buy's recent corporate giving.

Best Western International, Inc. (AZ) (http://www.bestwestern.com/about/donation.html)

Best Western International does not have a charitable foundation but does consider requests
for cash sponsorships and room nights. Requests are carefully considered and evaluated
based on the organizational benefits realized, the proposed financial commitment, the thoroughness of the proposal, and the amount of exposure the company receives from the sponsorship. Details about how to apply and where to send the proposals can be found on the
site.

BI-LO Inc. (SC) (http://www.bi-lo.com/web4/community)

The BI-LO chain of grocery stores centers its charitable giving in four southern states:
South Carolina, North Carolina, Georgia, and Tennessee. BI-LO focuses on supporting

food banks and pantries through the BI-LO Bags Hunger Campaign, especially during the summer months, when more food is needed for children who are out of school. The BI-LO Boosters are customers who partner with the grocery store to donate funds to three of their favorite schools, churches, or community organizations. BI-LO Charities, Inc. is the organization that manages BI-LO's corporate giving and also runs an annual golf tournament, benefiting children's charities; programs that feed the hungry or disabled; and programs that provide educational opportunities. Contact information for BI-LO in South Carolina and more details of BI-LO's charitable campaigns are provided on the company's Web site.

Blimpie International, Inc. (NY) (http://www.blimpie.com/content/more/community.php)
The Blimpie sandwich franchise makes local community contributions in the form of charitable events, trust funds, and other community involvement. Since 1992, Blimpie has supported the Boys and Girls Club of America through its Doing Well by Doing Good program. Blimpie has established strong ties to the Boys and Girls Club of America by organizing fund-raising events, donating food, coordinating volunteer time, and donating a percentage of its beverage sales to the Club. These efforts are described on the Blimpie Web site in greater detail, along with a spotlight on other community projects and events.

Blockbuster Inc. (TX) (http://www.blockbuster.com/co/community.jhtml)
Blockbuster, nationally based in Dallas, Texas, is committed to philanthropic giving that is in some way related to film or video and to programs that demonstrate clearly defined and evaluated goals. Locally and nationally, Blockbuster supports programs in the classroom, with projects that combine film and video with an educational motive; in the community, in minority communities, and in the film industry, through local film festivals. Blockbuster's Web site gives examples of specific funding in each interest area, in addition to guidelines and limitations for funding. Requests for funding should be directed depending on regional or national relevance to one of the various regional contact addresses provided on the site.

Blue Cross and Blue Shield of Minnesota Foundation, Inc. (MI) (http://www.bluecrossmn.com/community/index.shtml)
Blue Cross and Blue Shield of Minnesota began operations in 1933 and is Minnesota's oldest health plan and the nation's second oldest Blue plan. The St. Paul, Minnesota-based Foundation focuses its community resources on activities that help prevent and reduce health risks. The Foundation's priorities are to reduce tobacco use by helping communities take action to prevent youth tobacco use; help people with chronic illnesses or unique cultural needs navigate the healthcare system; promote individual physical activity, nutrition, and safety; and increase early childhood immunization rates through targeted community initiatives and the development of regional immunization registries. Visit the Foundation's Web site for descriptions of its programs. The site contains a self-assessment questionnaire to determine eligibility, instructions for letters of inquiry, and guidelines for full grant proposals, if the applicant is invited to submit one. The site also contains a grants list, a link to download the Minnesota Common Grant Application, instructions on how to obtain a community involvement report, and contact information.

The Boeing Company (WA) (http://www.boeing.com/companyoffices/aboutus/community/)
The Seattle-based Boeing Company is the world's largest manufacturer of commercial jetliners and military aircraft and is the nation's largest NASA contractor. Boeing aims to strengthen the communities where its employees live and work with four main areas of support: education, health and human services, arts and cultural organizations, and civic and environmental organizations. Education receives the largest portion of company contributions. In K–12 education funding, Boeing works in partnership with public school districts located near major Boeing facilities to identify and meet local needs. Cash grants are given to colleges and universities for numerous purposes, including scholarships, curriculum development, fellowships and endowed chairs, capital construction, and various in-kind support. In addition to company contributions, Boeing also has the Employees

Community Fund, "the world's largest employee-owned and -managed charitable fund," which mainly supports health and human services organizations. Employees at each Boeing site determine how their contributions are used. Visitors to the Web site will find information on Boeing's giving activities, grant guidelines, a breakdown of contributions by area of support and by region, links to supported organizations, downloadable citizenship and environmental reports, and contact information for the nearest community relations office. The site also contains information about another of its programs, Boeing International Relief Delivery Flights, which in concert with airlines and relief organizations uses empty space on new airplanes to carry food, medical supplies, clothing, books, and bandages to hurt, hungry, and homeless people all over the world.

Boston Globe Foundation, Inc. (MA)
(http://www.boston.com/extranet/foundation/home.stm)

The Boston Globe Foundation, one of the principal charitable arms of the Boston- based Globe Newspaper Company, focuses its grantmaking on children and youth who live primarily in low-income neighborhoods in the Massachusetts cities of Boston, Cambridge, Somerville, and Chelsea. It considers requests in arts and humanities, education, urban environment, healthcare, and community service. The Foundation seeks to decrease racism and bias and promote inclusion and cross-cultural understanding. The Foundation's Reactive Grantmaking program accepts grant proposals for program and operating support, particularly for programs targeted towards youth at a societal disadvantage due to race, class, ethnicity, disability, gender, or sexual orientation. Visitors will find application instructions, financial audit information (in PDF format), FAQs, a description of Foundation initiatives, and links to related Web sites.

The Bristol-Myers Squibb Foundation, Inc. (NY)
(http://www.bms.com/aboutbms/content/data/ourple.html)

The Bristol-Myers Squibb Foundation provides financial support in keeping with Bristol-Myers Squibb Company's commitment to extending and enhancing human life. The New York City-based Foundation supports the following program areas: biomedical research, women's health education, math and science education, AIDS/HIV research and outreach, donations of pharmaceutical products to developing countries and victims of natural disasters and civil unrest, and international local/community support where the pharmaceutical company has a presence. The Foundation area of the company's Web site contains the Foundation's most recent charitable giving report in PDF format, which includes grant lists, information about the Foundation's programs, and grant and application guidelines.

The Brooklyn Union Gas Company (NY) (http://www.bug.com/commune/bunewy.htm)

Brooklyn Union's corporate giving program supports education and community service programs in the New York metropolitan area. The Educational Services Grants Program funds nonprofit, community-based organizations for programs "in line with the company's corporate education agenda." Other educational programs include the Ambassadors for Education program, the Brooklyn Union Engineering Explorer Program, and the Science In Industry Summer Academy. The company's community service support includes toy donations, employee volunteerism, and support of more than 1,800 local organizations involved in the arts and culture, health, education, and community development. Businesses interested in expanding in or moving to Brooklyn Union's service area may find the company's economic development programs a good resource. Brooklyn Union's Web site details its various programs and provides contact information.

Brookshire Grocery Co. (TX) (http://www.brookshires.com/company/community/)

The national Brookshire Grocery Company, based in Tyler, Texas, has a page on its Web site that outlines its philanthropic activities. The company sponsors assorted community service projects. The list of supported programs includes Adopt-a-School programs, which include employee/volunteers, food pantries, anti-drug programs for students, various youth programs, arts and museums, volunteer fire departments, law enforcement agencies, homeless shelters, and programs for abuse victims. There is a phone number given for anyone interested in receiving more information. Support is given in areas where Brookshire stores operate.

Burger King Corporation Contributions Program (FL)
(http://www.burgerking.com/community.htm)

The Burger King Corporation Contributions Program (BKCCP) sponsors the Burger King Academies, a national network of 24 academies designed for students who have already dropped out of school, who are functioning below their potential in a traditional school setting, or who have encountered problems with the juvenile justice system. Burger King also participates in Second Harvest by donating food products and paper goods and cups. BKCCP also seeks to impact welfare reform and is interested in promoting diversity by working with minority, civil rights, education, business, and trade organizations that advocate for and assist minorities in realizing the American Dream. Burger King also has a College Football Scholarship Program, "the single largest corporate commitment of its kind in the sport of college football." In addition to information on its various programs, the Web site also provides a link to The Burger King/McLamore Youth Opportunities Foundation, whose mission is to provide educational opportunities to deserving youth in the spirit of Burger King co-founder, the late James McLamore. The Foundation has a scholarship program in partnership with the National Association of Secondary School Principals, which provides scholarships to hard-working high school seniors throughout the United States, Puerto Rico, and Canada.

Cablevision Systems Corporation (NY) (http://www.powertolearn.com/scholarship)

The Cablevision Systems Corporation, located in the Bronx, New York, distributes the Power to Learn Scholarship to qualified high school seniors going on to an accredited two- or four-year institution of higher learning. Applicants must live in a community serviced by Cablevision and show scholastic achievement, extracurricular activities, community involvement, teacher and guidance counselor recommendations, and financial need; all criteria are weighted equally. Applications for the scholarship, which is awarded in May, are available on the Power to Learn Web site.

Cadence Design Systems (CA)
(http://www.cadence.com/company/com_svc_I2_index.html)

Cadence Design Systems of San Jose, California, funds a number of projects through its community affairs program, the majority of which are based in the Santa Clara Valley area. General information on grant guidelines, applications, and the review process are available on the company's Web site. Additionally, Cadence Design sponsors a Matching Gift program for organizations located where employees live and work that focuses on the areas of K–12 education, higher education, arts and culture, health and human services, the environment, and animal rights and welfare. Stars and Strikes funds local programs through an annual bowling tournament. University donations and scholarships benefit institutions or departments that are engineering–, math–, or science–based and that improve access to education for traditionally underrepresented students. More details on each portion of the community affairs program, plus contact information, is available online.

California Pizza Kitchen, Inc. (CA) (http://www.cpk.com/cpk.cfm?page=about)

As part of its community relations program, California Pizza Kitchen (CPK) offers school programs, from restaurant tours to incentive awards for outstanding accomplishments. CPK provides schools with Student of the Month certificates and Pizza Passes, which can be used to award exceptional students throughout the year. Additionally, California Pizza Kitchen helps schools raise money through CPkids Fundraising events. Interested parties should contact the manager at the nearest location; a list of locations can be found on the Web site.

The Candle Foundation (CA)
(http://www.candle.com/about_candle/candle_foundation/index.html)

Candle Corporation is in the business of helping companies achieve "eBusiness at the speed of light." The corporation makes contributions to the community through two organizations: The Candle Foundation and PC Works. Based in El Segundo, California, the Foundation awards grants for community investment, education and information dissemination, hunger and homelessness, preventive healthcare and medical research. Through the PC Works program, Candle contributes computer equipment to help educate the Los Angeles community's youth. The program also provides training in IT skills to high school students. Both organizations donate computer equipment in Los Angeles and in other North American communities where Candle remote offices are located. Visit the Candle Web site for an online application.

Canon U.S.A. Inc. (NY) (http://www.usa.canon.com/cleanearth/index.html)

Since 1990, Canon U.S.A. Inc. has been supporting environmental efforts through its Clean Earth Campaign, based in Lake Success, New York. The program supports programs in four areas. Recycling is primarily addressed through the Canon Cartridge Recycling Program, which keeps empty ink cartridges from being placed in landfills or similar facilities. Exhibition into the Parks teaches conservation to old and young through research methods using donated Canon products—cameras, camcorders, binoculars, etc. The Science category is for science-based conservation programs. Finally, the Outdoor Appreciation heading encompasses three educational awards: the Canon National Parks Science Scholars is a three-year scholarship for doctoral students doing environmental research on national park ecosystems, the Envirothon is a year-long environmental curriculum culminating in a competition for high school students, and the program sponsors the PBS Nature series. The site includes a section of Good News press releases detailing the company's giving.

Capital City Bank Group Foundation (FL) (http://www.ccbg.com/)

The Capital City Bank Group of Tallahassee, Florida, created its foundation in 1983 to support organizations in the Big Bend area. Funding goes toward "special projects and community needs." Visitors to the Foundation's Web site should select the Community Investment tab. The site includes application guidelines and an application form, which can either be e-mailed or mailed to the foundation.

The Cargill Foundation (MN) (http://www.cargill.com/commun/found.htm)

Cargill Corporation's business includes providing a range of high quality, competitively priced products and services to help farmers increase their productivity and profitability, supplying basic ingredients used in food production, and operating a network of mini-mills. Cargill has a tradition of supporting charitable organizations that improve the lives of people living in the communities where it conducts business. Since 1953, the Cargill Foundation has focused its resources in the Twin Cities area, home to Cargill's world headquarters. The Minneapolis, Minnesota-based Foundation targets youth in the Minneapolis area and funds organizations and programs that focus on educational success and the development of necessary life skills that "enable socio-economically disadvantaged young people to work and thrive in a rapidly changing world." The Foundation's priorities are to prepare children for school, improve academic achievement, build character and positive identity, teach life skills, and create healthy, supportive family systems. Cargill also has a Higher Education Initiative, whose purpose is to build mutually beneficial relationships with key schools. Selected projects are supported with significant strategic grants. As part of its overall commitment to education, Cargill also supports three distinct scholarship programs: supporting students from farm families, students living in or around communities where Cargill has a presence, and sons and daughters of Cargill employees. Cargill also has a corporate volunteer policy to allow employees reasonable time off from work to participate in company-sponsored projects and also has many partnerships with regional and national nonprofits. Visitors to the site will find application instructions for the Foundation's various programs, a printable application sheet for its grantmaking program, and contact information.

Carolina Power & Light Co. (NC) (http://www.cplc.com/community/)

The Carolina Power & Light Co. (CP&L), located in North Carolina, has both a corporate giving program and the CP&L Foundation. By choosing Grant Programs from the left column of the page, visitors can read that the Foundation focuses giving in three areas: education, economic development, and the environment. The Foundation gives in the company's area of service and there is a phone number for interested applicants. The corporate giving program gives to organizations in those same categories and geographic area—the same phone number is listed for funding information. The site also features pages on each area of giving that highlight the different groups and programs that the Foundation and company support, often including the size of the grant.

Central Illinois Light Company (IL) (http://www.cilco.com/OurCommunity/1Our_Community/Corporate_Contributions.asp)

The Central Illinois Light Company's Corporate Contributions Program is committed to "efforts that enhance communities' economic vitality, improve the quality of life for residents, strengthen educational opportunities and attract businesses and residents to our service territory." The program focuses on two main funding areas: educational programs for individual self-sufficiency and health and human services. Interested applicants should call the Company directly. The phone number is provided online.

Ceridian Corporation (MN) (http://www.ceridian.com/who_schools.asp)

The primary emphasis of Ceridian's corporate giving program is on innovative policy initiatives and programs that help people balance the growing demands of work and home life. The Minneapolis-based information services and defense electronics company also emphasizes giving in the areas of health, education, and the arts. The In the Community section of the company's Web site provides general program information as well as application guidelines and an interactive application form. Visitors to the site can also access an online version of the company's annual report.

Chevron Corporation (CA) (http://www.chevron.com/community/index.html)

Chevron, the San Francisco-based petroleum and chemicals concern, has a long history of supporting communities where it does business and where its employees live and work. Those communities are scattered around the globe—from the Americas (Bolivia, Canada, Mexico, and the United States), to Europe and Africa (Angola, Scotland, Wales, and Zaire), to Asia and the Pacific (Australia, China, Indonesia, Kazakhstan, Papua New Guinea). Currently, the company focuses its giving in the areas of math and science education, with an emphasis on K–12; environmental conservation, with an emphasis on habitat preservation, wildlife protection, and environmental education programs; crime; and substance abuse. The Community section of the Chevron Web site offers a good deal of general program information, grant guidelines, a recent grants list organized by program area, FAQs, and a simple interactive application form.

CIGNA Corporation (PA) (http://www.cigna.com/general/about/community/index.html)

A national company based in Philadelphia, Pennsylvania, and Hartford, Connecticut, CIGNA Corporation's CIGNA Contributions Program has the mission to "strengthen CIGNA by supporting organizations and activities that improve the overall climate for business. More specifically, the Program focuses its attention on activities of direct concern to CIGNA and the healthcare, insurance and financial services industry." The program considers applicants in four categories: health and human services, education, community and civic affairs, and culture and the arts. Health issues get primary consideration and funding goes to communities where Cigna employees live. There is a page on each of these categories that explains the philosophy behind the giving, and each page gives examples of programs that are supported. Visitors to this site can find a grant list, full application directions, and the corporate annual report in the About Us section.

Cinergy Foundation, Inc. (OH)
(http://www.cinergy.com/about_cinergy_corp/community_involvement/
cinergy_foundation/default.asp)
Cinergy Foundation is the philanthropic organization of Cinergy Corp. The Foundation seeks to improve the quality of life in Indiana, southwestern Ohio, and northern Kentucky communities by supporting arts and culture, community development, education, and health and social services. The company's Web site provides thorough program descriptions and grant guidelines, application forms to download (in Microsoft Word and PDF formats), geographic considerations, examples of exemplary projects, a listing of Foundation officers, and contact information.

Cisco Systems Foundation (CA) (http://www.cisco.com/warp/public/750/fdn_home.html)
Created in 1997 with a gift from California's Cisco Systems, Inc., the Cisco Foundation's mission is to fund "organizations in the community that provide education, generate and sustain community service, or meet basic human needs." The Foundation gives primarily to education, including K–12 programs; career training for disadvantaged adults; and arts in education. The Foundation also gives a smaller percentage of its grants to community service, shelter, food, and health organizations. Recipients must be within 50 miles of San Jose, California; Research Triangle Park, North Carolina; Chelmsford, Massachusetts; or New York City. The site includes grant guidelines, a downloadable checklist that must be submitted with proposals, grant lists, and information on the education initiative, for which grants are made by invitation.

Citigroup Foundation (NY)
(http://www.citigroup.com/citigroup/homepage/fndtion/index.htm)
The Citigroup Foundation, created by a merger of the Traveler's Foundation and the former Citicorp Foundation, helps to build communities in their wide array of international markets. The Foundation supports community development corporations and financial institutions that revitalize low-income neighborhoods, microlenders that provide access to credit, and programs that assist in starting or expanding businesses. Support is also provided for educational resources to encourage financial literacy and the digitization of archives such as the Library of Congress, the American Museum of Natural History, and the New York Public Library. The Foundation's page on the corporate site gives a brief overview of its priorities and a summary of gifts and grants.

Citizens Banking Corporation Contributions Program (MI)
(http://www.cbclientsfirst.com/community/)
The Citizens Banking Corporation's purpose is to provide superior service to its clients and to contribute to the well being of the community it serves (Michigan and Illinois) through active participation in civic and charitable organizations and through charitable giving. The Bank's Web site provides detailed descriptions of previous community activities as well as information about previous Corporate Citizenship Award winners. This program recognizes one outstanding volunteer from Citizens Bank's markets in Michigan and Illinois and makes a donation to the winner's charity of choice.

Clorox Company Foundation (CA) (http://www.clorox.com/company/foundation/)
The Clorox Company Foundation is dedicated to improving the quality of life in communities where employees of the Clorox Company live and work—primarily in 23 "Clorox Cities" in the United States, Canada, and Puerto Rico. The Foundation focuses its grants on programs that serve youth, core cultural and civic organizations, plant programs, and organizations in which Clorox employees are involved. Grants typically support innovative programs in their developmental stages. The company's Web site offers a brief description of the Foundation's philanthropic interests and activities, contact information, and links to the Web sites of organizations receiving support from the Foundation.

CNET, Inc. Community Involvement Program (CA)
(http://www.cnet.com/aboutcnet/0-13620.html)

Located in San Francisco, California, the CNET Community Involvement Program is the philanthropic effort of CNET, Inc., a leading source of information and services relating to computers and technology. The program is committed to "assisting nonprofit organizations that are striving to improve the education and computer skills (in communities where our employees live and work)." Funding is concentrated on education, health and human services, arts and culture, and civic affairs and community service. Most contributions are made to San Francisco area organizations, while some support goes to national groups. CNET does not provide large financial donations because there is not an existing corporate contributions program. The site offers basic application guidelines. The board of directors list and financial information can be found in the Investor Relations section. Key executives are listed in the Company profile area.

The Coca-Cola Foundation, Inc. (GA)
(http://www2.coca-cola.com/business/community/foundation.html)

The philanthropic arm of the Coca-Cola Company, the Coca-Cola Foundation, is located in Atlanta, Georgia. The Foundation's goal is to "provide youth with the educational opportunities and support systems they need to become knowledgeable about the world in which they live and better able to give back to their communities." Since 1989, funding has been focused on education, particularly in these three categories: higher education, classroom teaching and learning, and global education. Programs include scholarship programs, teacher development, international exchange programs, and minority advancement. Visitors will find an outline of the desired program description and an application that can be printed right from the screen. There are lists of previous grant recipients organized by year and a list of the board. The Web site also offers a series of reports covering the three main funding topics.

Colonial Pipeline Company (GA) (http://www.colpipe.com/ab_com.asp)

The Colonial Pipeline Company believes in reinvesting in the communities it serves. Colonial Pipeline focuses its giving efforts on the environment, giving grants to environmental organizations in its communities and through support of its Earth Year Fund. Decisions about grants to local organizations and activities are made by Colonial employees. While the site does not give details about grant applications, contact information is listed.

Columbia Gas of Pennsylvania and Maryland (PA)
(http://www.columbiagaspamd.com/community_outreach/community_outreach.htm)

Columbia Gas of Pennsylvania and Maryland features its Corporate Contributions Program in the Community Service section of its Web site. The company considers its gifts to be investments in the communities that it serves. The goal of the program is to "provide cash contributions and volunteerism to deliver hope to deserving individuals and organizations." Giving is focused in three key areas. Community development and safety includes safe and healthy communities, tourism, historic preservation and beautification, and main street revitalization. Health and human services encompasses United Way annual campaigns, United Way resource allocation/review, Days of Caring, and fuel funds assistance. Finally, Humanities in Education covers English, history, and the arts. Available on the site are application guidelines, which encourage use of common grant applications from regional grantmaker associations; a description of the company's in-kind Wish List program; and helpful FAQs. The only way to reach any of these features is to click the blue words in the text.

Columbia Gas of Virginia, Inc. (VA) (http://www.cgva.com/commit/commit.htm)

Columbia Gas of Virginia's Community Support program focuses on three main areas of interest: energy, education, and environment. Columbia Gas of Virginia supports charitable organizations through donations, employee volunteerism, and community service. The company's Web site lists some of the organizations that it funds, including those that assist economic, environmental, cultural, social health, and educational programs for the benefit of the community. More information for potential beneficiaries is available by calling the phone number provided online.

Comcast Corp. (PA)
(http://www.comcast.com/defaultframe.asp?section=in_the_community)

Telecommunications giant Comcast Corp. runs a substantial corporate giving program out of its headquarters in Philadelphia, Pennsylvania. The program was created to "support initiatives both on a corporate level and regionally that allow communities [where their customers live and work] to thrive." Financial support and in-kind gifts are categorized in five areas. In the Education area, Comcast is interested in innovative uses of cable technology and services in schools. Civic and Community Issues addresses quality-of-life issues. Culture and Arts supports the performing arts and a limited number of museums. Health and Human Services funds are primarily given to the United Way. Finally, there is special consideration given to employee requests for organizations they are active in. The site includes application guidelines and restrictions, features on programs funded in each category, and a list of programs funded in the Philadelphia area.

Compaq Computer Corporation (TX) (http://www.compaq.com/corporate/community/)

Compaq is a personal computer manufacturer headquartered in Houston, Texas, where it currently focuses its grantmaking in the areas of education, health, social services, and the arts. Its current grantmaking strategy is described in the Community Relations area of the company's Web site along with success stories for each giving category and guidelines.

Computer Associates International, Inc. (CA) (http://www.cai.com/charity/)

Computer Associates International, Inc., headquartered in Islandia, New York, has an active giving program. Individual employees, through a corporate giving program and a Matching Charitable Gifts program, distribute support. Grants include worldwide emergency relief, support to create affordable housing, and efforts on behalf of missing and exploited children. The Community Relations section of the company's site is made up of a collection of press releases on philanthropic gifts. The annual report may be downloaded in PDF format on the company's home page.

ConAgra, Inc. (NE) (http://www.conagra.com/conagra_foundation.jsp)

Through its company-sponsored foundation, ConAgra, a diversified international food company based in Omaha, Nebraska, seeks to improve the quality of life in communities where the company's employees work and live. To that end, the ConAgra Foundation focuses its resources in the areas of education, health and human services, arts and culture, sustainable development, and civic and community betterment. The ConAgra Web site provides very general information about the Foundation's guidelines, restrictions, and deadlines, as well as contact information for written requests only.

The Connecticut Light and Power Company (CT)
(http://www.cl-p.com/community/partners/indexpartners.asp)

The Hartford-based Connecticut Light and Power Company maintains a corporate giving arm to support the communities that the Company serves. Areas of focus include education; energy conservation, safety, and environmental stewardship; programs for special-needs customers; employee volunteerism; and charitable contributions. These charitable aims are accomplished through a number of programs, including educational grants; corporate grants in the areas of education, civic service and community, human services, the environment, and culture and the arts; and participation in the Northeast Utilities Foundation for grants over $5,000. Information about these specific programs as well as grant applications in PDF format are available on the Company's Web site. The site also details the other charitable efforts of the Company and provides contact information.

The Consumers Energy Foundation (MI)
(http://www.consumersenergy.com/community/foundation/index.html)
The Consumers Energy Foundation, based in Jackson, Michigan, is the philanthropic arm of Consumers Energy. The Foundation supports nonprofit organizations in six main categories: education, the environment, Michigan growth and enhancement, culture and the arts, social services, and emerging issues. The Volunteer Investment Program and Matching Gifts Program also allow company employees and retirees to contribute to the Foundation's funding. Visitors to the Foundation's Web site will find grant eligibility and limitations, application guidelines, and an address where written funding requests can be sent. The Foundation also publishes the *Community Forum* newsletter, available on the site.

Cooper Industries (TX) (http://www.cooperindustries.com/about/index.htm)
Houston-based Cooper Industries, a diversified manufacturing company with 40,000-plus employees in 24 countries, makes contributions through the Cooper Industries Foundation and a direct corporate giving program in the areas of community development, the environment, education, health and human services, arts and culture, and workplace safety in communities where it has a strong presence. The company's Web site provides a good deal of information about charitable activities, including guidelines and application procedures, grants of $1,000 or more arranged by program area, a listing of the communities in which Cooper Industries has operations, and an online version of the company's annual report.

Corning Foundation (NY) (http://www.corning.com/inside_corning/foundation.asp)
The Corning Foundation was founded in 1952 in Corning, New York, and works to "develop and administer projects in support of educational, cultural, community and selected national organizations." Within education, the foundation funds all kinds of schools, from elementary to higher learning, with support for student community service organizations, curriculum enrichment, scholarships, facilities, and instructional technology projects. The cultural groups are just as varied, including arts organizations, libraries, museums, and public broadcasting stations. The community service category covers hospitals, hospices, community foundations, youth and women's centers, and local chapters of some prominent national groups. There is a special Corning Foundation Higher Education Program that specifically supports women and ethnically under-represented engineering students, pre-doctoral science fellowships in some specific areas of study, and selected special projects. Visitors can find application directions, lists of restrictions, and a description of the Matching Gifts Program. To find this information choose Search at the bottom of the page and enter "foundation."

Credit Suisse First Boston Foundation Trust (NY)
(http://www.csfb.com/company_info/html/company_foundation_trust.shtml)
The Credit Suisse First Boston Foundation Trust of New York City supports educational initiatives and programs for inner-city youth. This very sparse page presents basic application directions and states that proposals are considered on a quarterly basis. The annual review can also be accessed electronically.

Curriculum Associates, Inc. Excellence in Teaching Cabinet Grant Program (MA)
(http://www.curriculumassociates.com/cabinet)
Curriculum Associates, Inc. of North Billerica, Massachusetts, sponsors the Excellence in Teaching Cabinet Grant Program, which acknowledges outstanding K–8 teachers. The Teachers Who Publish award provides three cash and materials grants each year to teachers who then serve in the company's Cabinet of Resource Educators. Teachers submit proposals for innovative projects that are judged for their "creativity, educational goals and objectives, ability to incorporate technology and print materials, and ease of implementation." The site includes Official Rules, a list of past award recipients, information, and updates on Curriculum Associate's projects. Application guidelines and deadlines are included.

DaimlerChrysler Corporation Fund (MI) (http://www.fund.daimlerchrysler.com)

The DaimlerChrysler Corporation Fund is headquartered in Auburn Hills, Michigan, and strives to improve the communities and businesses where DaimlerChrysler is located. The Fund centers its giving in southeastern Michigan as well as parts of Alabama, Arizona, Delaware, Illinois, Indiana, Missouri, Ohio, and Wisconsin. The Fund supports four main areas: future workforce, community vitality, employee and Chrysler involvement, and marketplace and public policy leadership. There are more detailed descriptions of recent grants and grantmaking philosophies on the Fund's Web site. Visitors to the site can find grant guidelines, limitations, and contact information. They can also apply for a DaimlerChrysler grant online with a form on the Web site, request publications with the comment form, and download the Corporation's annual report in PDF format.

Dakota Telecommunications Group, Inc. (SD)
(http://www.dtg.com/corpinfo/communitydev)

Dakota Telecommunications Group, Inc. (DTG) is committed to helping with economic development and community service projects in the communities it serves. DTG sponsors youth activities and civic organizations and events. DTG also assists communities in using the McLeodUSA Distance Learning Network for community development and adult education. Details about the distance learning program and McLeodUSA contact information can be found on the DTG Web site.

Datatel Scholars Foundation (VA) (http://www.datatel.com/scholars.htm)

The Datatel Scholars Foundation is the philanthropic organization of Datatel, Inc., a provider of information service solutions to higher education. The Foundation awards scholarships to students planning to attend higher learning institutions that are Datatel client sites. The Foundation area of the company's Web site describes the Datatel and Angelfire scholarships and provides application instructions and contact information.

John Deere & Company (IL)
(http://www.deere.com/deerecom/_Company+Info/Contributions/default.htm)

Through the John Deere Foundation and a direct corporate giving program, Deere, also known as John Deere, awards grants and gives support to a variety of nonprofit organizations nationwide, with an emphasis on human services, community development, educational issues, and cultural opportunities. The Corporate Contributions Program page of John Deere's Web site provides general information about the company's contributions program, Foundation policies and procedures, and contact information. A link to the JD Journal provides a somewhat more detailed look at the scope and impact of various Foundation-sponsored initiatives. HTML and/or PDF versions of John Deere's annual report are also available at the site.

Deloitte and Touche Foundation (CT) (http://www.dttus.com/us/believe/dtfounda.htm)

Funded by the accounting, tax, and consulting firm, the Deloitte and Touche Foundation "supports teaching and research in accounting, business, and related fields." Within these areas, the Foundation funds projects that encourage excellence in teaching and pedagogy, cooperation among experts in the field, and research and that involve research and teaching. Funding recipients include the fellowship program and many conferences and consortiums. The Foundation's Web site includes news releases on many Foundation projects and gifts and contact information for interested visitors. There is also an archive of case studies that have been featured through the years at the Foundation-funded Trueblood Seminars for Professors.

Dell Foundation (TX) (http://www.dell.com/us/en/gen/corporate/vision_foundation.htm)

Founded in 1995, the Dell Foundation funds organizations in Central Texas that involve "collaborative and innovative solutions to community and children's issues." Funds are focused on children's programs in many categories, including art, collaboration, education, health and human services, and innovation. Each of these areas has its own page with examples of supported programs and links to the sites of funded organizations. Follow the link to the list of recent grant recipients to find a press release that contains the most recent round of grantees and information on receiving an application and application deadlines. Grants are made quarterly.

Delta Air Lines Foundation (GA) (http://www.delta-air.com/inside/community/index.jsp)

The Delta Air Lines Foundation, based in Atlanta, was established in 1968 as Delta's company-managed giving system to contribute to the well-being of the communities Delta Air Lines serves. The Foundation's focus is on organizations that support families with young children, foster cultural understanding (primarily in the visual and performing arts), and build strong communities (alleviating social ills like unemployment and poverty). The Delta Foundation also manages an employee matching gift fund that matches employee contributions to educational institutions. Visitors to the site will find grant application instructions, links to some of the organizations supported by the Foundation, and information on Delta's other giving programs: the Employee Giving Program, Corporate Contributions, and Delta Community Partners.

Deluxe Corporation Foundation (MN) (http://www.dlx.com/foundation.cfm)

The Deluxe Corporation Foundation was founded in 1954 and gives grants to qualified organizations located near Deluxe Corporation facilities. The Foundation's funding programs are focused on education, human services, culture, and its employee-matching program. Grants are normally designated for operating or program support, equipment, and capital needs. To apply for grants, organizations should first send a letter of inquiry to the address posted on the site. A name and phone number is provided for those who have questions about the application process. Details about the Employee Matching Gift Program are also available on the Web site.

Dermody Properties Foundation (NV)
(http://www.dermody.com/1-800-775-SITE/Dermody/Foundation.cfm)

Dermody Properties specializes in industrial real estate. Based in Reno, Nevada, the employee-directed Foundation seeks to give back to the communities in which it does business through volunteer support and financial donations to nonprofit causes. The Foundation's primary focus areas are family and children, education, services for seniors, and the arts. The site contains contact information and a listing of some organizations that have received Foundation support.

Detroit Edison Foundation (MI)
(http://www.detroitedison.com/discover/community/foundation.html)

Detroit Edison Foundation, the principal philanthropic vehicle of the primary energy supplier of southeastern Michigan, supports civic and community organizations, cultural activities, education programs, and health and human service agencies. The Foundation area of the Detroit Edison Company's Web site offers a brief description of the Foundation and an online version of its annual report, available in PDF format.

Detroit Tigers, Inc. (MI)
(http://tigers.mlb.com/NASApp/mlb/det/community/det_community_programs.jsp)

Through the Tigers Care organization, the Detroit Tigers baseball team operates a number of charitable operations, including donations of tickets and memorabilia, the Ambassadors for Education program, and the support of hundreds of charitable organizations in the Detroit metropolitan area. Every player and coach of the Detroit Tigers is involved in a local nonprofit organization. The Community Outreach section of the Tigers Web site includes a complete listing of charitable groups affiliated with the team as well as information for fans about upcoming events and contact information for potential recipients.

Disney Learning Partnership (CA) (http://disney.go.com/disneylearning/)

The Disney Learning Partnership grew from the Disney American Teacher Awards, begun in 1989, to recognize "creative, innovative teaching strategies." The Partnership focuses on three program areas: teacher recognition and professional development, collaborative school-wide learning initiatives, and strengthened parent-teacher connections. The Disney American Teacher Awards are given annually to creative teachers across the United States. Disney's interactive Web site contains a nomination form for the award, past honorees, and profiles of former winners and schools. The Partnership also funds the Creative Learning Communities (CLC) grant for public elementary schools that are exploring creative teaching strategies and improving student performance. The site contains an FAQ on the CLC grants, and the Teacher Center, a Web site with resources for creative teaching.

Dollar Thrifty Automotive Group, Inc. (OK) (http://www.dtag.com/indexcommunity.html)

Dollar Thrifty Automotive Group (DTG), located in Tulsa, Oklahoma, supports its employees' desire to enrich the lives of others. DTG employees are immersed in community activities—from coaching little league teams to working with the elderly. Additionally, each year DTG provides financial gifts to deserving nonprofit organizations. These contributions typically provide quality of life enhancements or help improve the economic well–being of the neighborhoods where DTG's employees and customers live. The site does not give specific information about these gifts or how to apply for financial assistance from DTG. However, there is a contact page on the site that allows interested parties to request information from DTG. Annual reports and company information can also be found on the site.

R.R. Donnelley & Sons Company (IL) (http://www.rrdonnelley.com/public/community)

R.R. Donnelley & Sons, an international printing and information management company headquartered in Chicago, Illinois, supports activities that promote the written word, serve children and youth at risk, and enhance the quality of life in communities served by the company. The company's Web site provides descriptions of its funding areas, grant guidelines, application instructions, a listing of R.R. Donnelley & Sons geographic locations, an online version of the community relations annual report (in PDF format), and contact information.

The Dow Chemical Company Foundation (MI) (http://www.dow.com/about/corp/corp.htm)

The Dow Chemical Company is a worldwide provider of chemicals, plastics, energy, agricultural products, consumer goods, and environmental services. The Dow Chemical Company Foundation focuses its funding on community needs in locations where Dow Chemical has a presence; pre-college science education; university-level science, engineering, or business programs; and improving the environment. Preferential treatment is given to charitable contributions requested by Dow Chemical employees, but the Foundation does accept unsolicited proposals. The company's Web site describes the Foundation and provides instructions for submitting a proposal.

The Dow Jones Newspaper Fund, Inc. (NJ) (http://www.dj.com/newsfund/)

The Dow Jones Newspaper Fund was founded in 1958 by editors of *The Wall Street Journal* to improve the quality of journalism education and the pool of applicants for jobs in the newspaper business. Based in Princeton, New Jersey, the Fund is a nonprofit foundation supported by the Dow Jones Foundation, Dow Jones & Company, Inc., and other newspaper companies. The Foundation provides internships and scholarships to college students, career literature, fellowships for high school journalism teachers and publications' advisers, and training for college journalism instructors. The Fund also accepts grant applications for programs that further its mission. Visitors will find program descriptions and guidelines, grant application guidelines, and contact information.

Duke Energy Corporation (NC)
(http://www.duke-energy.com/internet/stewardship/stewardship.asp)

Charlotte, North Carolina-based Duke Energy Corporation has a commitment to stewardship focused on volunteerism, the environment, community issues, and philanthropic giving. Through its interest in community issues, the Corporation centers on citizenship, partnership, and service through a variety of programs. The Duke Energy Foundation operates as a nonprofit organization making charitable contributions to communities. Additionally,

Duke Energy runs a matching gifts program, scholars program for undergraduate study, an annual grant, a community volunteers grant, global service events, and the Share the Warmth program, helping low-income customers with heating bill assistance. The Corporation's Web site outlines the application procedure for the annual grant: areas of interest for grantmaking are education, community development, and volunteerism. The site gives more detailed information on all of Duke Energy's programs, some examples of past initiatives, and information on the Corporation's involvement with environmental issues. A contact address is provided for the Foundation.

E.I. du Pont de Nemours and Company (DE) (http://www.dupont.com/corp/social/index.html)

This international company with operations throughout the United States is "committed to improving the quality of life and enhancing the vitality of the communities in which we operate throughout the world by supporting community sustainability efforts." The giving program concentrates on three areas. Community social progress and economic success refer to giving people access to opportunity, including helping children, youth and families revitalize neighborhoods, and help people develop self-sufficiency. Support is given to environmental programs that can show significant and proven results, with special consideration going to those that involve non-cash leverage and collaborative work between government and the private sectors. Finally, educational aid is given to colleges and universities worldwide and programs that improve education for K–12, especially for learning readiness, science and math, workforce readiness, and teacher preparation. Visitors will find a page that outlines the application process and deadlines, as well as a page of restrictions. Financial information can be found in the For Investors section.

Eastman Kodak Company (NY) (http://www.kodak.com/US/en/corp/community.shtml)

Eastman Kodak, an imaging company headquartered in Rochester, New York, designs its philanthropic programs and initiatives to instill employee pride, build public trust, foster education, respond to community needs, and enhance the company image. The company's primary funding areas include community revitalization, education, and health and human services. The Community Relations and Contributions area of Eastman Kodak's Web site thoroughly describes its corporate giving program and provides grant guidelines, highlights of giving in Rochester, recent quarterly recipient lists, special projects and awards, scholarship information, and information on the company's support for diversity and volunteerism.

Eaton Corporation (OH) (http://www.eaton.com/about/report.html)

Eaton, headquartered in Cleveland, Ohio, is a manufacturer of products for industrial, vehicle, construction, commercial, and semiconductor markets. Eaton's corporate giving program comprises cash grants, a matching gifts program, and support of the United Way. Grants are focused on education and community improvement. Organizations considered for funding include educational, health, human service, civic, arts, and cultural organizations and accredited colleges and universities. The company's Report of Contributions, available in PDF format, details its giving activities and funding areas and provides guidelines, a listing of company communities, staff and corporate contributions committee lists, a letter from the chairman, and information on volunteerism.

eBay Foundation (CA) (http://pages.ebay.com/aboutebay98/foundation/)

Created in June 1998, the eBay Foundation supports "organizations that provide tools, hope, and direction to those who seek new skills" and "organizations that implement programs that have long-term implications and maximize the ability to do good in the world." The foundation gives grants each quarter in different categories. These categories are kids, adults, community, and global impact. The areas include everything from education and job retraining to economic revitalization and the environment. The Web site guides you through a narrative that outlines the foundations' mission, the application deadlines, and restrictions and gives instructions on letters to request an application. There is also a list of grants for the past two years and information on online charity auctions and the Giving Board, where needs are posted and met.

Educational Communications Scholarship Foundation (IL) (http://www.eci-whoswho.com/highschool/scholar/)

The Educational Communications Scholarship Foundation was created in 1968 to offer financial support to those students being recognized in *Who's Who Among American High School Seniors.* The foundation is primarily funded by the book's publishing company. There are 250 scholarships of $1,000, each offered annually. Application is restricted to those students appearing in the book. They receive applications automatically. The site includes a list of the decision-making committee and a searchable database of past award recipients.

Electronic Data Systems Corporation (TX) (http://www.eds.com/foundation/index.shtml)

Electronic Data Systems, an information technology provider headquartered in Plano, Texas, primarily supports education efforts in communities where the company has a presence and makes cash, volunteer, and technology contributions. In addition to awarding grants to organizations in local communities, grants are provided through the Technology Grants program, which provides $1,500 to teachers wishing to purchase information technology products, training, or services. The company's Web site describes these programs and provides application instructions for each, as well as a recipient list for Technology Grants. Visitors will also find information on volunteer activities and technology contributions.

Eli Lilly and Company (IN) (http://www.lilly.com/about/community/foundation/index.html)

The Indianapolis, Indiana, Eli Lilly and Company Foundation was created in 1968 and now "the direction of the foundation's charitable efforts is evolving in concert with the company's increasing global commitment and transformed business strategy." The Foundation has a number of different funding programs. Through the product donation program, pharmaceuticals are distributed all over the world, largely through the Lilly Cares Patient Assistance Program and the Disaster Assistance and International Relief program. Fifty percent of cash distributions are employee-matching gifts. The rest of the cash is distributed through a discretionary fund that is given through two programs. The Company-Aligned giving goes to public policy research, health and human services aligned with major therapeutic interests, and academic relations. The Community-Aligned giving, which is distributed to groups in Indianapolis and other cities where the company has a strong representation, gives to community development, local healthcare organizations, fencerow neighborhood groups, and programs dealing with diversity. The site includes application procedures and descriptions of what organizations should apply. There is a separate index for product donation.

Ernst & Young Foundation (NY) (http://www.ey.com/global/gcr.nsf/US/Foundation_-_About_E&Y_-_Ernst_&_Young_LLP)

The Ernst and Young Foundation of New York City was founded in 1937 by the accounting, tax, and consulting firm. The Foundation is currently focusing on "supporting institutions of higher education primarily in accounting, information systems, tax, and other business areas." Most funding to higher education is distributed through the Matching Gifts program. Direct grants are given to schools with a few alumni within the company that attract outstanding minority talent to relevant fields and to outstanding tax research programs. The Foundation distributes the Ray M. Sommerfield Outstanding Tax Educator Award and sponsors short conferences on tax issues and annual symposiums on management information systems and the future of business education and professional services. There is also an in-kind services program that partners employees with reorganizing schools as well as multitudes of professorships sponsored by the Foundation. Visitors to the site will find a partial grants list and an address to contact for more information.

ExxonMobil Corporation (TX) (http://www.exxonmobil.com/community)

ExxonMobil supports charitable organizations in the United States through a direct corporate giving program and the ExxonMobil Education Foundation. Direct contributions concentrate on the following program areas: the environment; public policy and public research; health; united appeals and civic and community-service organizations; minority and women-oriented service organizations; arts, museums, and historical associations; and education. The ExxonMobil Education Foundation provides funds to launch new activities or to expand existing programs in mathematics education, elementary and secondary education, and undergraduate science, technology, engineering, and mathematics. ExxonMobil's Web site offers a list of corporate sponsorships as well as major ExxonMobil communities, funding guidelines and limitations, and contact information for both the direct corporate giving program and the ExxonMobil Education Foundation.

Fannie Mae Foundation (DC) (http://www.fanniemaefoundation.org/)

The mission of the Fannie Mae Foundation is "to expand decent and affordable housing opportunities and improve the quality of life in communities throughout the United States." The Foundation supports national and local nonprofit organizations dedicated to helping more families afford homes, provides prospective buyers and immigrants with information on the home-buying process, conducts local home-buying fairs as well as research on a broad range of housing and urban issues, and supports organizations addressing housing and community development issues across the country. In addition to detailed information on the Foundation's initiatives, the Web site provides complete grant program guidelines, current RFPs, and information about the Maxwell Awards for Excellence. Grant applications can be downloaded in PDF format or requested through an interactive form. An online version of the Foundation's annual report provides lists of program-related investments; national and local grants; Washington, D.C., grants; and officers and board members.

Farmers Insurance Group (CA)
(http://www.farmers.com/FarmComm/content/CC010153.jsp)

Farmers Insurance Group of Los Angeles, California, has a corporate giving program devoted to "keep[ing] its promise to restore our customers' lives to order when the unexpected occurs" and to contributing to the communities where its people live and work. The company does not list specific interests, but in 1998 it distributed $4.3 million dollars with 24 percent going to education, 37 percent to safety, 10 percent to health and human services, 25 percent to civic, and 4 percent to arts and culture causes. The site includes features on some of the organizations sponsored by the company, a grants list, application guidelines and information, and a list of the company's activity and educational giving by state. Its annual report can also be found under the All About Farmers section. The Aid to Education Program gives annual gifts to colleges and universities attended by employees who have been with Farmers for at least four years. Farmers also has an Agents' Community Sponsorship Fund that funds organizations nominated by the company's agents and district managers. All applications must be accompanied by a budget, annual report, or financial statement.

Federated Department Store Foundation (OH)
(http://www.federated-fds.com/community/)

The mission of the Federated Department Store Foundation is based on the belief that "stronger, healthy, and more vibrant communities provide better environments for our stores to do business and for our employees and customers to live and work." The program funds charitable organizations, civic programs, community projects, and educational institutions in hundreds of communities across the country. Women's issues and HIV/AIDS are two areas of special focus for the Federated Department Stores. The Foundation has a matching gift program and places a strong emphasis on volunteerism. More information, including contact addresses, is available by reading *Responsibility in Action: A Report to the Community,* which is available in its entirety online.

Fieldstone Foundation (CA) (http://www.fieldstone-homes.com/foundation/)
As the philanthropic vehicle of the Fieldstone Group, a home builder based in southern California, the Fieldstone Foundation is primarily interested in programs serving children and families. The Foundation funds capacity building of nonprofits through leadership programs, school retention programs, the prevention of drug and alcohol abuse, child abuse, and community violence. It also supports organizations that provide child care services, emergency assistance for youth and families, positive alternatives for youth, and positive responses to diversity. Contributions are made primarily within southern California, and to national organizations that earmark Foundation funds for use in these communities. Visitors to the Foundation's Web site will find a listing of the Foundation's recent grants; grant guidelines and criteria; information on the Fieldstone Leadership Network, which provides technical and management training to nonprofits in Fieldstone communities; a listing of the Foundation's staff and board members; and contact information.

First Union Regional Foundation (PA) (http://www.firstunion.com/involve/contributions/)
First Union Regional Foundation was founded in 1998 by First Union Corporation, the nation's sixth largest banking company based on assets as of September 1999. The Pennsylvania-based Foundation is targeted specifically to the tri-state region of New Jersey, Delaware, and eastern Pennsylvania. It funds grants that "enable individuals to overcome barriers to self-sufficiency and to revitalize the communities in which they live." Emphasis is given to projects that lead to long-term sustainable change and help rebuild communities. Visitors to the Web site will find information on the Foundation's total contributions and community involvement; information on the First Union Foundation, another grantmaking body of First Union; and a downloadable community report.

FirstEnergy Companies (OH) (http://www.firstenergycorp.com/communitysupport)
Based in Akron, Ohio, FirstEnergy Companies outlines its Giving Window program on the Community Support section of its Web site. Through its philanthropic contributions it strives to ensure the safety and health of the community, promote economic development, advance professional development, and support employee involvement and investment. FirstEnergy achieves these goals through its Matching Gifts Program, which matches employee contributions, and its FirstEnergy Foundation grants. The Foundation considers and supports nonprofit, tax-exempt health and human services agencies; educational organizations; cultural and arts programs and institutions; and civic groups in the areas of Ohio and Pennsylvania served by FirstEnergy's electric companies. Visitors to the site will find details of the Matching Gifts Program, instructions on how to apply for Foundation grants, limitations, and contact information.

Fleet Bank (MA) (http://www.fleet.com/about_inthecommunity_overview.asp)
Fleet Bank offers a full line of banking products and services, including consumer and commercial banking, mortgages, consumer lending, asset-based lending, and investment management. The goal of its charitable giving program is to help build and sustain strong, successful communities that serve Fleet's members well. Fleet funds community-based agencies and other nonprofit organizations to support programs and create opportunities in low-to-moderate income areas, especially for children, families, and individuals. It also provides resources to support community and economic development, education, healthcare, human services, and the arts and humanities. Its charitable contributions program supports a variety of nonprofit organizations, from small grass-roots groups to large institutions. Fleet Bank makes both charitable donations and sponsorships. Grant applications can be downloaded from the site. While Fleet is based in Boston, Massachusetts, completed proposals should be sent to the community relations/contributions contact in the applicant's region. Contact information is provided on the site.

FMC Foundation (IL)
(http://www.fmc.com/en_US/Contents/About_FMC/index.cfm?scrn=fmc_foundation)
Chicago-based FMC is one of the world's leading producers of chemicals and machinery for industry, government, and agriculture. The company's charitable-giving arm, the FMC

Foundation, contributes more than $1.5 million annually in five major areas—health and human services, education, community improvement, urban affairs, and public issues—to nonprofit organizations in FMC communities, as well as to national organizations working on issues relevant to FMC's businesses. Visitors to the parent company's Web site will find brief descriptions of the Foundation's philosophy and purpose, program descriptions and guidelines, detailed submission requirements, and basic contact information.

Ford Motor Company Fund (MI) (http://www2.ford.com/default.asp?pageid=238)

The Ford Motor Company Fund of Detroit, Michigan, was established in 1949 with the goal to "support initiatives and institutions that enhance and/or improve opportunities for those who live in communities where Ford Motor Company operates." Funding is given to organizations that directly impact communities where Ford operates and can be used as models for other communities. Grants are given in seven major areas. Forty percent of funding in 1998 went toward education. The fund supports various programs from colleges and universities, with continued support for historically black programs, to special schools and programs for students in Detroit, among others. Environmental efforts work to "promote environmental responsibility and help maintain the Earth's rich biodiversity," including a strategic alliance with Conservation International. Arts and humanities funding goes toward "projects that have a community interest, offer educational opportunities, are accessible to a wide audience and are not restricted to any person based on culture or physical limitations." Many civics grants go through local community relations committees to organizations that work for youth, safety, and minority opportunities. Funding in health and welfare goes toward extensive research and development in healthcare. Public policy includes programs about labor, schools, and new market areas. The United States/International Relations category encompasses groups in the United States that conduct research on or solicit funds for relief in other countries. The site includes strict application guidelines for the Fund, the corporate giving program, and the corporate sponsorship program. There is also an electronic version of the annual report, a list of distributions for the last few years, and detailed descriptions on funding in five of the categories.

Freddie Mac Foundation (VA) (http://www.freddiemacfoundation.org)

The Freddie Mac Foundation, the principal charitable arm of Federal Home Loan Mortgage Corporation, is dedicated to helping children, youth, and families at risk. The Foundation provides funds to nonprofit organizations in the Washington, D.C., area and in cities where regional offices are located and supports programs with a national scope. Giving areas include building strong families, developing the early child, foster care and adoption, building constituencies for children, assisting teen parents, and expanding childcare. The Foundation's Web site provides grant guidelines, geographic locations of the company, information on special leadership initiatives and volunteerism, news, the Foundation's annual report (in PDF format), and a message from the chairman.

Frito-Lay, Inc. (TX) (http:www.frito-lay.com/company/responsibilities)

The Frito-Lay corporation focuses its charitable giving on communities located near its headquarters in Dallas, Texas. Its corporate contributions target programs and organizations with results-oriented approaches and direct community benefits. The company is particularly interested in worthwhile causes that further the education of youth, the economic development of communities, and improved interracial relations. Its community service includes direct program funding as well as active involvement by employees and expert counsel provided by executives serving on community boards in volunteer roles. The Web site does not provide information about how to apply for funding or whom to contact for questions.

Gannett Foundation, Inc. (VA) (http://www.gannettfoundation.org)

The Gannett Foundation, the philanthropic organization of Gannett Co., Inc., a news and information concern headquartered in Alexandria, Virginia, funds programs to improve the education, health, and quality of life of people living in company communities. The Foundation seeks to fund programs that provide creative solutions to the issues of education and neighborhood improvement, economic development, youth development, community problem solving, assistance to disadvantaged people, environmental conservation, and cultural enrichment. The Foundation page of Gannett's Web site provides grant guidelines, an application form, a list of company locations, recent grantees, and contact information.

Gap, Inc. (CA) (http://www.gapinc.com/community/community.htm)

Based in San Francisco, California, the philanthropic efforts of Gap, Inc. feature the Gap Foundation. The Foundation is dedicated to supporting youth and AIDS prevention programs. The former effort is accomplished by "supporting youth learning programs that help kids develop self-esteem, stay in school, become inspired by dynamic teachers and visionary leaders, and succeed academically so they can grow up to lead rewarding and fulfilling lives." The latter effort focuses on AIDS-prevention programs that address underserved youth. Besides making monetary grants, the Gap, Inc. also donates T-shirts and gift certificates to selected groups working toward the described goals. In addition to the Foundation, the Gap's community relations program includes the company's efforts to be environmentally correct, through a Code of Conduct for manufacturers throughout the world, and against sweatshops. These projects are described on the Web site, where visitors can also find the company's annual reports in PDF format.

GATX Corporation (IL) (http://www.gatx.com/affairs.html)

Chicago-based GATX's Community Partnership Program seeks to "proactively select and support significant issues relevant to the economic viability of our local communities nationwide." The Program's major initiatives include Success through Education, which provides educational support for economically disadvantaged children; Caring for our Environment, which provides support for environmental causes, including pollution control and conservation efforts; and Strengthening Families, which supports programs that strengthen the family. These initiatives are described in greater detail on the program's Web site. Also included on the site are specific geographic limitations, grantmaking criteria, application procedures, contact information, and application form downloadable in PDF format.

GE Fund (CT) (http://www.gefund.org)

The GE Fund places education at the crux of its international grantmaking efforts, with support to programs in the areas of science and engineering, pre-college education, public policy, international programs, management, and arts and culture. An online version of the Fund's annual report, featured within General Electric Company's well-organized Web site, includes a letter from the Fund's president, profiles of the Fund's major initiatives, program descriptions, grants lists, and application guidelines.

Genentech, Inc. (CA) (http://www.gene.com/gene/about_genetech/responsibility)

Genentech is a biotechnology company headquartered in San Francisco, California, that uses human genetic information to develop, manufacture, and market pharmaceutical products. The company makes charitable contributions through the Genentech Foundation for Biomedical Sciences, the Genentech Foundation for Growth & Development for research and science education, and through a direct corporate giving program supporting Genentech communities. The Corporate Responsibility area of the company's Web site provides a brief description of its programs and contact information for each. Additionally, a Material Request Form can be filled out and submitted online by researchers wishing to receive proteins and antibodies free of charge through the Research Contracts and Reagents Program.

General Communications, Inc. (AK) (http://www.gci.com/about/corpgive.htm)

General Communications, Inc. (GCI), an Alaska-based communications company, "supports worthwhile charities and organizations which contribute to the quality of life for all Alaskans." GCI's Corporate Giving program is especially interested in organizations in which its employees are involved, as well as Alaska's youth and programs benefiting the deaf, hard-of-hearing, and speech-impaired communities. A listing of current and past funding beneficiaries, grant application guidelines, and contact information are provided on GCI's Web site.

General Mills, Inc. (MN) (http://www.generalmills.com/explore/community/)

Through the General Mills Foundation and a direct corporate giving program, General Mills focuses its funding on four areas: arts and culture, education, family life, and health and nutrition. The Community Involvement area of the company's Web site provides a description of the Foundation's objectives, a report on corporate citizenship, an overview of grant allocations, a directory of staff and General Mills locations, and a downloadable application form (in PDF format).

General Motors Corporate Giving Program (MI)
(http://www.gm.com/company/beliefs_policies/philanthropy/home.html)

Founded in 1976, the GM Foundation of Detroit, Michigan, aims to "ensure that we maintain our leadership position as a valued, responsible corporate citizen by enhancing the quality of life in the communities where we do business, consistent with our corporate goals and objectives." The Foundation focuses its giving in six areas: education, health, community relations, public policy, arts and culture, and environment and energy, with a strong commitment to diversity in all areas. Education receives the most funding; higher education and K–12 programs both receive support. Health and human services is the other primary category (together they receive well over 50 percent of cash contributions)—cancer research is a major concern. Additionally, the Foundation is concerned with motor vehicle safety. The site includes application guidelines under the Addendum heading, the philanthropic annual report, a list of distribution history, and descriptions of programs funded in each major category. Special initiatives which are also covered include the GM Cancer Research Foundation (GMCRF), Academic Research Partnerships, and marketing sponsorships.

Giant Food Inc. (DC) (http://www.giantfood.com/community.htm)

Giant Food, located in Washington, D.C., supports and heads community service efforts in the communities where Giant is located. Through charitable contributions, major partnerships, and donated food for events, among other areas, Giant tackles homelessness and providing food for people in need, contributions to locally based neighborhood activities, and support for young people. Potential applicants are provided with basic application guidelines and limitations, and a contact address for proposals (which are not accepted by fax or email) on the Giant Web site.

Giant Food Stores, Inc. (PA)
(http://www.giantpa.com/afunplacetoshop/communityevents.html)

The Pennsylvania-based Giant Food Stores focuses its charitable giving and fund raising campaigns on feeding the hungry, helping sick children, and supporting community groups. Through in-store donations and funding drives, Giant Food Stores raises money for numerous children's hospital charities in and around Pennsylvania. Additionally, the stores support anti-hunger campaigns and distribute benches made out of recycled store bags to local schools during Earth Week. This Web site mainly outlines Giant Food Stores' giving campaigns; there is no information for grantseekers on the site.

The Goodyear Tire & Rubber Company Giving Program (OH)
(http://www.goodyear.com/us/community/index.html)

Based in Akron, Ohio, the Goodyear Tire & Rubber Company "seeks to be a socially aware and responsive global citizen, wherever it operates or does business." Goodyear participates in organizations that seek to elevate the aspirations of and provide opportunities for the young and disadvantaged through summer work-study programs, scholarships, recreational offerings, and employment opportunities. Visitors to the site can read about some of the programs.

Green Bay Packers Foundation (WI)
(http://www.packers.com/community/foundation.html)

The Green Bay Packers Foundation, located in Green Bay, Wisconsin, was established December 30, 1986. The Foundation was created to assist charitable and worthwhile causes throughout the state of Wisconsin. It assists in a wide variety of activities and programs that benefit education, civic affairs, health services, human services, and youth-related programs. The Web site provides information about the types of grants the Foundation makes and the deadlines for applications. It also provides contact information to request an application. Details about past grants awarded are also available on the Foundation's Web site.

GROWMARK, Inc. (IL) (http://www.growmark.com/gmk/youth/ycap/ycap_start1.htm)

GROWMARK, located in Bloomington, Illinois, sponsors the Young Cooperator Award Program, geared toward youth and young farmers (35 or under) in Illinois, Iowa, Wisconsin, and Ontario, Canada. Goals of the program include identifying future cooperative leaders, increasing cooperative awareness, recognizing cooperative supporters, and increasing young producer involvement. The GROWMARK Web site provides a list of contest incentives, eligibility requirements, and details on recent winners of the Young Cooperator Award. A contact phone number and email address are available online.

GTE Corporation/Foundation (TX) (http://www.gte.com/AboutGTE/Community/index.html)

The GTE Foundation, one of the country's 20 largest corporate philanthropies, gives nearly $25 million annually to educational, scientific, and charitable organizations on behalf of GTE and its business units. As a corporation, the telecommunications giant is concerned about America's ability to produce a well-educated, highly productive workforce and has committed significant resources to improving education, with special emphasis on mathematics and science. The GTE Web site offers information about GTE's philanthropic efforts in education, health and human services, the arts, and community involvement. A brief description of the Foundation itself, including contact information, is also available.

The H&R Block Foundation (MO) (http://www.hrblock.com/about/community/index.html)

The H&R Block Foundation focuses giving in the Kansas City, Missouri area, where the tax firm is headquartered. "The goal of the Foundation is to build stronger communities by focusing funding on the arts, education, health and human service and volunteerism." Support generally falls in the following categories: artistic and cultural endeavors, education as a lifelong activity, healthcare services, opportunities for youth other than negative situations, community initiatives involving collaboration between diverse groups, and volunteerism. Visitors to the Web site can find a telephone number for the Foundation and a link to the company's cancer foundation in the FAQs section (quick access is through the site search).

Hach Company (CO) (http://www.hach.com/corporate/acommrel.htm)

Hach Company's community relations and contributions programs provide equipment or dollars to qualified and approved grant requesters. The community relations program is focused to instill employee pride, respond to local community needs, provide educational experiences, and enhance the company's image around the world. Grant guidelines for both the equipment and contributions programs can be found on the Hach Company Donations Request Form, which can be downloaded in PDF format. Those interested in applying for a donation must complete the form and send it to the Community Relations and Contributions department. Contact information is available on the Web site.

John Hancock Mutual Life Insurance Company, (MA)
(http://www.johnhancock.com/company/community/index.html)

John Hancock, headquartered in Boston, Massachusetts, focuses its funding on Boston's public schools and inner-city and minority youth. Its funding priorities are affordable housing, education, emergency shelters, employment and job training, intercultural/interracial relations, performing arts, social services, transitional and permanent housing, violence prevention, and youth development. The Community Relations area of John Hancock's Web site describes its funding activities in some detail and provides application instructions and brief descriptions of its special initiatives.

Hannaford Bros. Company (ME) (http://www.hannaford.com/community/index.htm)

The Hannaford Bros. Company, a chain of grocery stores based in Portland, Maine, provides charitable contributions in a number of areas. The Company sponsors nonprofit youth athletic leagues, school events, and environmental and health organizations in the communities where Hannaford does business. Stores in Maine, New Hampshire, Vermont, Massachusetts, New York, North Carolina, South Carolina, and Virginia donate funds and sponsor events through community giving kiosks, located in stores, and bottle and can donations. Grantseekers interested in funding for local community charitable causes should speak to a store manager. Hannaford also provides numerous annual college scholarships to employees and children of employees. More information on the Company's programs and regional contact phone numbers is available at its Web site, through the Community Service Information link under FAQs.

Hasbro Foundation (NY) (http://www.hasbro.org)

The Hasbro Foundation, the Foundation of the Hasbro Corporation, is located in New York City. The mission of the Hasbro Children's Foundation is to "improve the quality of life for disadvantaged children, birth through age 12, through the support of innovative, model direct service programs in the areas of health, education and social services." The Foundation also funds universally accessible play spaces. Specifically, The Hasbro Children's Foundation supports the development and/or expansion of programs located in the United States and that provide direct service to children. Requests for funding must include a cover sheet and a brief proposal. Instructions on how to apply are available on the Web site. A list of FAQs, a year–end report, and contact information can all be found on the site.

Hawaiian Electric Industries Charitable Foundation (HI) (http://www.hei.com/heicf/heicf.html)

The philanthropic arm of Hawaiian Electric Industries, the HEI Charitable Foundation was created in Honolulu in 1984. The organization's mission is "to assume leadership in making our community a better place in which to live for all of Hawaii's people." The grants program distributes gifts in four primary areas: community development, education, environment, and family services. The Foundation prefers to give awards to projects that exist in communities where HEI has—or plans to have—a significant presence, that will provide recognition and goodwill for the company, and that are actively supported by volunteers from within the company. The board of directors meets twice a year to discuss grants over $10,000, while requests for less than that amount are presented monthly. The company also encourages employees to volunteer with associated programs. The Web site is based around the *HEI Charitable Foundation Report on Corporate Citizenship*. Included in this are a message from the company president, a list of featured grant recipients in each of the major categories, and basic application guidelines and deadlines.

Hewlett-Packard Company (CA) (http://webcenter.hp.com/grants/)

Hewlett-Packard's Web site offers application guidelines and selection criteria for the primary components of its corporate giving program: the University Grants Program, which emphasizes the donation of equipment over cash; the National Grants Program, primarily supporting K–12 education; U.S. Education Matching, which provides cash matching to universities and equipment matching to educational institutions of all levels; U.S. Local Grants, which support local organizations and K–12 education; and the European Grants Programs, designed to help fulfill Hewlett-Packard's European citizenship objective. Visitors to the site will also find a corporate philanthropy overview and annual report, program and application guidelines, grant and product request forms to download as PDF or text files, and philanthropy contacts at Hewlett-Packard.

Hilton Hotels Corporation (CA) (http://www.hilton.com/corporate/charitable/index.html)
Located in Beverly Hills, California, the corporate philanthropy program of Hilton Hotels Corporation gives funds to national organizations and programs in communities where company employees live and work. Giving is focused in four areas: education, health, youth programs, and civic affairs and public policy. In-kind contributions of hotel room nights or the like are considered by general managers of local hotels. Visitors to the site will find an application form that can be printed out and application guidelines and restrictions. Annual reports may be downloaded in PDF format from the Company Information section of the site.

Hitachi Data Systems Corporation (CA) (http://www.hds.com/community)
The Santa Clara, California-based Hitachi Data System's Corporation maintains a corporate giving arm "to promote corporate citizenship in the communities in which Hitachi Data Systems operates." This mission is accomplished with volunteerism, funding, and in-kind donations through two programs: the Community Action committees, for volunteer services and grants up to $5000, and Corporate Donations, for larger grants. Corporate Donations focus on the areas of science and technology education, civic and community development, health and human services, and arts and culture. The Community Action Committees center on community-based charitable events. The Hitachi Web site provides information for potential applicants, a listing of community events, and a contact email address for further information.

The Hitachi Foundation (DC) (http://www.hitachi.org/)
The Hitachi Foundation, established in 1985 by Hitachi, Ltd. of Tokyo, Japan, centers its U.S. operations in Washington, D.C. The Foundation's mission is to "[promote] social responsibility through effective participation in global society." This is achieved through the Foundation's three programs. Grants and Program Related Investments support non-profit organizations in the United States in the areas of community development, education, and corporate citizenship. This program does not accept unsolicited proposals. The Foundation's corporate Community Action Committees/Matching Funds strive to improve the community through financial, volunteer, and in-kind contributions. The Yoshiyama Award for Exemplary Community Service provides a scholarship on the basis of exemplary service and community involvement. Applicants must be nominated. The Foundation's Web site provides guidelines for the Yoshiyama Award as well as a nomination form that can be downloaded in either Microsoft Word or PDF formats. Visitors to the site can also find guidelines for grantseekers, further information on the Foundation's three programs, and contact information for the board and staff of the Foundation.

The Hoechst Foundation (NJ) (http://www.hoechst-foundation.org)
The Hoechst Foundation was established in 1996 by the Danish Hoechst AG company. The organization has two goals: "to provide a forum to think about general questions relating to responsibility and communication and to develop sustainable answers; [and] to be an example of crossing boundaries and a model for encounters." The foundation's grant program supports mostly large, international, multi-year projects in the humanities, science, politics, or any other area that falls within the mission. Multidisciplinary projects are preferred. There are three additional funds administered by the Foundation. The Study Support Foundation supports gifted, underprivileged young people for professional and cultural gain and also loans money to students. The Karl Winnacker Foundation supports scientific projects and advanced scientific education. The Rolf Sammet Foundation sponsors guest lecturers and professors of natural sciences at Goethe University in Frankfort. Visitors to the site will find featured grantees under the Promoted Projects heading, annual reports, a list of the board of trustees, and an option to download the site's text in PDF format. The site has complete versions in English and in Dutch.

Hoffmann-La Roche Inc. Corporate Giving Program (NJ)
(http://www.rocheusa.com/about/responsibility.html)
The Hoffmann-La Roche Inc. Corporate Giving Program, based in Nutley, New Jersey, seeks to "enhance the quality of life for [its] employees and residents of the communities where Roche has a significant presence or interest." Funding is considered for domestic, charitable institutions whose initiatives closely align with the business initiatives of Hoffman-La Roche. The areas of primary interest in the giving program are health promotion and health education with an emphasis on Cardiology, Dermatology, Infectious diseases, Metabolic diseases, Neurology, Oncology, Transplantation, and Virology/HIV; and education, especially K–12 science and mathematics focusing on teacher enrichment. Funding exclusions and application guidelines are detailed online. Hoffmann-La Roche accepts only written requests for applications (not emailed or faxed); a contact address is provided on the Web site.

The Home Depot, Inc. (NC) (http://www.homedepot.com)
The Home Depot, a chain of home improvement stores headquartered in Charlotte, North Carolina, focuses its charitable giving on affordable housing, at-risk youth, and the environment. The Community Involvement area of the company's Web site provides a social responsibility report that outlines the corporate giving program and provides application instructions, a list of charitable activities by program area, and a description of the company's environmental program.

Honeywell Foundation (MN) (http://www.honeywell.com/merger/page_3_2.html)
Honeywell founded the Foundation in 1957 to support the communities in which it operates. Support is given through corporate contributions and partnerships. Honeywell has an interest in supporting housing issues based on the philosophy that home ownership leads to a stronger sense of community, resulting in economic security for the people within the neighborhood. The Foundation has an international partnership with Habitat for Humanity to support the construction of nonprofit homes for low-income families, through employee volunteers, energy-saving home thermostats, and annual donations for construction material. The community program is determined by employees as well, who can apply for community grants.

The Humana Foundation, Inc. (KY) (http://www.humanafoundation.org/)
Based in Louisville, Kentucky, the Humana Foundation is the philanthropic arm of Humana, Inc., one of the nation's largest managed healthcare companies. Established in 1981, the Humana Foundation supports charitable organizations and institutions that promote education, health and human services, community development, and the arts in communities where Humana has a business presence. In 1991 the Foundation started its scholarship program, designed to recognize and honor academic excellence and to assist Humana families in meeting the cost of sending children to colleges of their choice. A scholarship application can be downloaded from the site, and grant applications can be downloaded and printed. Visit the site for application guidelines and instructions, aid recipient list, a breakdown of fund distribution by area, descriptions of projects, and contact information.

IBM Corporation (NY) (http://www.ibm.com/IBM/IBMGives/index.html)
International Business Machines, also known as IBM, is guided by a new corporate strategy that aims to combine the company's "technology and people in effective partnerships to bring solutions to the systemic problems that impact society, business, and our quality of life." The four key elements in all new contributions are IBM technology and service, IBM expertise, IBM partnerships, and rigorous measurement. The Philanthropy section of Big Blue's Web site offers a listing of recent events (i.e., press release-style narratives about the company's recent charitable endeavors); a statement of the company's new corporate giving strategy and a summary of its current philanthropic initiatives, including K–12 education, reinventing education, workforce development, adult education and job training, and

the environment; and examples of funding to IBM communities worldwide. An online version of the company's annual report is also available.

ICG Communications, Inc. (CO) (http://www.icgcomm.com/profile/community.asp)

ICG Communications, based in Englewood, Colorado, "encourages community support and the spirit of volunteerism to enrich the lives of children, bringing together technology and education through cooperation, communication and collaboration." ICG's programs are centered in the communities where it does business. Additionally, ICG sponsors a number of charitable community events, which are detailed online. Potential grantees should send proposals in writing to the contact address provided on ICG's Web site.

IKOS Community Involvement Program (CA) (http://www.ikos.com/company/community/)

IKOS Systems, an electronics company in Cupertino, California, has a Community Involvement Program involving employee volunteers and a grants program. "As a technology leader in high performance design verification solutions, [IKOS] values the importance of investing in community solutions that accelerate positive change." Primary areas of interest are education, human/social services, health/healthcare, and the environment. Awards are made to nonprofits and schools in areas where IKOS employees work and live. Grants are usually under $1,000 and never over $5,000. The site includes application guidelines and deadlines. There is an electronic application form that the potential grantee fills out, attaches the necessary documents, and then submits online. If the applicant cannot attach the necessary papers, the files may be e-mailed separately or sent via the mail. Financial statements and board lists can be found in the Investor Relations area.

Illinois Power Company (IL) (http://www.illinoispower.com/ip.nsf/web/OurCommunity)

The Illinois Power Company is one of Illinois' primary sources for energy, providing service for many of the larger counties throughout the state. While being one of the larger service providers companies in the state, Illinois Power has been providing philanthropic services to the community for over 75 years. The company's community relations program supports qualified organizations based in Illinois with the potential to revitalize their communities. Illinois Power's Bright Ideas campaign focuses on pre-collegiate education, minority issues, economic development, and the environment. Grants are made only to those communities in areas of company operations. The company's Web site includes grant guidelines (including explicit exclusions and inclusions for those funded), a printable grant application, and contact information.

Ingram Book Company (TN)
(http://www.ingrambook.com/Company_Info/HR0523/html/philantropy.asp)

The Ingram Book Company encourages community interaction. Both the organization as a whole and Ingram associates as individuals participate in all levels of local and national community action programs. The company provides volunteers, time, supplies, funds, and creativity to various charities with a focus on helping people. Ingram also conducts a yearly United Way campaign and provides nine monthly Days of Caring. Participants in Days of Caring receive eight hours paid release time to spend the day performing corporate community service at a local nonprofit organization. The Ingram Community Access Network (ICAN) consists of independent teams of Ingram associates at each Ingram distribution center location as well as at Ingram Book Group headquarters in LaVergne, Tennessee. The team members encourage local community involvement for Ingram associates by sponsoring the Ingram Community Leadership Award. This award is given on a quarterly basis to an Ingram associate for extraordinary community volunteerism. The team also supervises the Ingram Book Group's Day of Caring program and allocates the corporate contribution budget.

Inland Paperboard and Packaging, Inc. (IL) (http://www.iccnet.com/com/com.html)

Indianapolis-based Inland Paperboard and Packaging, a wholly-owned subsidiary of Temple-Inland, Inc., places a substantial emphasis on action-oriented social responsibility. The company embraces the values of its founder, entrepreneur and philanthropist Herman

Krannert, and his wife, Ellnora, who were committed to improving educational and cultural opportunities for all people. The Inland Foundation, established in 1951, makes grants in the areas of health and welfare, education, art and culture, and civic issues. Inland's Web site provides visitors with a strong sense of the company's mission, its activities vis-à-vis its stewardship of the environment, and initiatives that comprise its Partners in Education program.

Independence Community Foundation (NY) (http://www.icfny.org)

The Independence Community Bank of Brooklyn, New York, founded the Independence Community Foundation in 1998 to "build strong partnerships with communities and support local efforts to improve neighborhoods through geographically targeted grant making and investments." The Foundation funds three major categories: neighborhood renewal; education, culture and the arts; and community quality of life initiatives. Neighborhood renewal and revitalization is the primary goal and receives half of the available funding. Programs addressing issues like "economic development, job readiness, housing, open space, community facilities, and health and human services" are supported. Almost 40 percent of funding goes towards education, arts, and culture, with a focus on projects that will help people and organizations establish financial independence. Small, local community service organizations receive the remaining ten percent of the funds. The site includes application guidelines, a downloadable common application, and a list of officers and trustees.

Inspiration Software (OR) (http://www.inspiration.com/scholarship.html)

Located in Portland, Oregon, Inspiration Software develops and supports visual learning and thinking tools. To this end, the company funds yearly Inspired Teacher Scholarships for Visual Learning to encourage teachers' professional development in visual learning and education technology. The Inspiration Software Web site provides a more detailed explanation of the company's visual learning philosophy, a listing of teachers recently awarded the scholarship, and an e-mail address for more information.

Intel Corporation (CA) (http://www.intel.com/intel/community/)

The focus of Intel's giving and outreach programs is on bettering education, supporting Intel communities, improving life with technology, and protecting the environment. The Intel Foundation funds programs that "advance math, science and engineering education, promote women and under-represented minorities entering science and engineering careers, and increase public understanding of technology and its impact on contemporary life." All information on the company's philanthropic activities is provided at its Web site under the heading Intel's Community Involvement. The Grant Information section in this area offers grant guidelines, downloadable application materials (in Microsoft Word format), additional information on local community grant programs, and links to information on research grants, scholarships, and fellowship programs. An online version of Intel's annual report is also available.

International Paper Company (NY)
(http://www.internationalpaper.com/our_world/outreach_frame.html)

The New York-based, International Paper Company is the world's largest paper and forest product company, producing printing paper, packaging, building materials, and chemical products. The Foundation concentrates the bulk of its grantmaking priorities on youth programs, education, and environmental awareness. The company's Web site includes a brief section on its Foundation. Here you will find a short description of funding priorities including a few recent grants. No other information on the Foundation is provided.

Intimate Brands, Inc. (OH) (http://www.intimatebrands.com/who/philanthrp.asp)

Intimate Brands, Inc.'s corporate contributions program, located in Columbus, Ohio, gives grants to "nonprofit organizations placing emphasis on projects and organizations relating to women, children, education and the community." The company's Web site provides brief grant requirements, a mailing address for those interested in applying for a grant, an alphabetical list of all the organizations Intimate Brand contributes to, and contact information for further inquiries.

IPALCO Enterprises, Inc. (IN)
(http://www.ipalco.com/ABOUTIPALCO/Community/Community.html)

IPALCO, a multi-state energy company headquartered in Indianapolis, Indiana, supports programs that focus on education, the environment, health and welfare, and the arts. IPALCO administers the Golden Apple Award, which recognizes outstanding teachers who integrate math, science, and technology into classroom subjects. The company's Golden Eagle Grants program funds projects aimed at resource conservation and environmental awareness. IPALCO's charitable efforts are briefly described at its Web site.

ITT Industries, Inc. Corporate Giving Program (NY)
(http://www.ittind.com/new/NEW-COMM.HTM)

Headquartered in White Plains, New York, ITT Industries sponsors an international Corporate Giving Program. The company's "firm commitment to good corporate citizenship" includes sponsoring important global environmental activities, as well as local activities where employees live and work. The company was part of the effort to found the Engineering Alliance, working to "improve public awareness, understanding, and recognition of the engineering profession and to addressing the crisis with respect to the number of U.S. students pursuing engineering degrees." It also sponsors international awards recognizing issues related to the world's use of water and community policing. The company's annual report and a list of the board of directors can be found in the Overview section.

Jacksonville Jaguars Foundation, Inc. (FL) (http://www.jaguarsnfl.com/)

The Jacksonville Jaguars Foundation, based in Jacksonville, Florida, is committed to serving the greater Jacksonville area through strategic financial, networking, and volunteer support benefiting economically and socially disadvantaged youth and families. Created by the National Football League team, the Foundation's primary objective is to "help meet the needs of disadvantaged youth, striving to address the causes of those needs wherever possible, and therefore prevent problems before they begin." The Foundation also seeks to support efforts to build understanding among different groups and promote cooperation. The Foundation's Web site contains grant lists and downloadable guidelines and application forms for its grantmaking program. The Foundation also has several programs, including Honor Rows, which rewards youths with game seats for academic achievement, behavioral improvement, and providing public service (the site contains downloadable guidelines, applications, and an honor list for this program), and the NIKE/Jaguars Foundation Community Scholars program, a scholarship program with full tuition and mentor support at the University of North Florida for select inner-city high school students who have participated in the Honor Rows or Let Us Play Camp program and have demonstrated a commitment to public service. Potential applicants can call the number provided on the site for information.

J.P. Morgan & Co., Inc. (NY)
(http://www.jpmorgan.com/Home/AbtMorgan/Community_f.html)

J.P. Morgan & Co., the global financial services firm established more than 150 years ago, makes charitable contributions to a wide range of organizations involved in the arts, education, the environment, health and human services, international affairs, and urban affairs through both the J.P. Morgan Charitable Trust and the firm's offices and subsidiaries around the world. Morgan's Community Relations and Public Affairs Department, which is responsible for the firm's relationships with nonprofit organizations, supports "recognized and competent groups" with financial grants, donations of equipment, volunteer services, technical advice, and other services. The department also supports Morgan's efforts to comply with the Community Reinvestment Act. The J.P. Morgan Web site offers general information about the firm's charitable activities; back issues of *Capital Ideas,* a biennial newsletter; and contact information.

Johnson & Johnson Corporate Giving Program (NJ)
(http://www.johnsonandjohnson.com/who_is_jnj/sr_index.html)

The Johnson & Johnson Corporate Giving Program in New Brunswick, New Jersey, works to "improve the health and welfare of children around the world." Significant worldwide funding goes towards programs assisting mothers and children, with support also going to programs in "the fields of health, family, education, employment, the environment, culture and the arts." The site offers the last three contributions annual reports. The program does not accept or respond to unsolicited proposals.

S.C. Johnson Wax Fund (WI) (http://www.scjohnsonwax.com/community/)

S.C. Johnson, headquartered in Racine, Wisconsin, is a manufacturer of home cleaning, storage, personal care, and insect control products and a supplier of products and services for commercial, industrial, and institutional facilities. Through the S.C. Johnson Wax Fund, Inc., and a direct corporate giving program, the company supports programs focused on education; medical, health, and environmental protection; and social, cultural, and community concerns. Scholarships and fellowships are also provided. The Building Better Communities area of the company's Web site briefly describes its giving initiatives.

KeySpan Foundation (NY) (http://www.keyspanenergy.com/foundation/index.cfm)

The KeySpan Foundation, located in Hicksville, New York, was established in 1998 by endowment to serve as a compliment to KeySpan Energy's Corporate Giving Program. The Foundation's funding focuses lie in the areas of health and human services, education, environment, community development, and arts and culture. The Foundation centers its grantmaking in KeySpan Energy's service territories, making occasional international grants, or grants in communities where KeySpan conducts business. The Foundation's Web site contains grant guidelines and limitations, details on the granting process, and complete application instructions. The Foundation will accept the New York/New Jersey Common Application form. Contact information is also available online.

King Pharmaceuticals, Inc. (TN)
(http://www.kingpharm.com/primary/public_rel_prim.htm)

King Pharmaceuticals focuses its philanthropic efforts in the areas of health, education, arts and culture, community improvement, youth development, and ministerial programs. Through monetary grants and employee community service projects, the company seeks to "improve the life, health, and welfare of the community." General information about King Pharmaceuticals' charitable programs and contact information is available online.

Kmart Corporation (MI) (http://www.kmartcorp.com/corp/community)

Located in Troy, Michigan, Kmart Corporation has four grantmaking arms: the Kmart Fund for Kids, which contributes to nonprofit organizations that help children live happier, healthier lives; the Kmart Fund for Communities, which supports nonprofit organizations in Kmart store communities nationwide with preference given to organizations that involve Kmart associate volunteer activities; the Kmart Fund for Metropolitan Detroit, which provides support to nonprofit organizations that directly benefit children and families in Macomb, Oakland, and Wayne Counties; and the Kmart Family Foundation, whose purpose is to educate, prevent, and fight against drug abuse by youth nationwide. The site provides application procedures, printable application forms, and contact information. The site also contains information on its partnership and scholarship program with the March of Dimes.

Knoll Pharmaceutical Company (NJ)
(http://www.basf.com/knoll/community/community.htm)

Mount Olive, New Jersey's Knoll Pharmaceutical Company focuses its philanthropic endeavors on "establishing and building healthy relationships with the communities in which its employees live and work." The Company maintains charitable programs in the areas of healthcare, health education, higher education, women's health, and elder services. "Making a Difference Days" pairs employees with community volunteer projects, the

Indigent Patient Program provides select pharmaceutical products to the financially disadvantaged, and Knoll also donates its products worldwide to communities struck by disaster or economic hardships. More information on these programs and the Company in general, along with e-mail addresses for more detail, is available on the Knoll's Web site.

Koch Industries, Inc. (KS) (http://www.kochind.com/community.asp)

Koch Industries, Inc., based in Wichita, Kansas, "supports a wide variety of nonprofit organizations that share [their] values and market-based philosophy." Koch funds organizations in communities where it has employees and facilities that fall into three categories. The company prioritizes education programs that apply scientific and economic principles to problem solving. The company supports environmental stewardship—programs that use innovative techniques to address environmental issues in their community—human services "projects that promote self-sufficiency, individual responsibility, tolerance, and respect for others." The site includes application guidelines, a list of communities that the company serves, and a partial grant list.

Kohl's Corporation (WI)
(http://www.kohls.com/kohls_in_the_community/kohls_in_the_community_intro.htm)

The Menomonee Falls, Wisconsin-based Kohl's Corporation, with Kohl's Department Stores located across the state, supports a number of community-based philanthropic activities. The Kohl's Kids Who Care Scholarship Program funds young people who volunteer in their communities; the Fundraising Gift Card provides profits from electronic gift cards to nonprofit community organizations; and the Children's Hospital Program donates proceeds from select merchandise sold during holiday seasons to benefit area children's hospitals. The Kohl's Web site provides more information on these programs, online forms to apply for the Gift Card Program, and contact information for further details.

Komag, Inc. (CA) (http://www.komag.com)

Located in San Jose, California, Komag runs a number of charitable giving programs under the heading of Corporate Citizenship on its Web site. These include Corporate Giving Community, Matching Gifts Program, and Komag Kids Scholarships, all of which are centered in the communities where Komag employees live and work. Komag also funds the United Way, environmental initiatives, and programs between factories and schools in support of education. More details about funding are available online, and contact information can be found on the Info section of the site.

The KPMG Foundation (NJ) (http://www.kpmgfoundation.com/)

The KPMG Foundation, established in 1968, is committed to enhancing business education for four groups of people: primary and secondary students, undergraduates, graduates, and faculty. For primary and secondary students, the Foundation funds SIFE (Students in Free Enterprise) and LEAD (Leadership Education and Development), mainly for minority high school students interested in a Summer Business Institute program. The Foundation funds scholarships, internships, and Ph.D. programs for minority undergraduate and graduate students in business. Faculty teaching, research, and development gains support through sponsored professorships, conferences, and associations. On the KPMG Foundation's Web site, specific programs are described in detail and linked to individual Web sites. The Foundation also promotes corporate volunteerism and community service and provides some contact information regarding these programs.

Lanoga Corporation (WA) (http://www.lanoga.com/community.htm)

Lanoga is a privately held company with a long and proud history in the building materials business. Lanoga Corporation and its regional subsidiaries and divisions believe in being involved in, and contributing to, the "communities where we operate. We think this is best accomplished at the local level where the needs are best known. Contributions by our subsidiaries and divisions most often are in the form of in-kind contributions and employee involvement." The Corporation focuses on Habitat for Humanity, food banks, medical needs, educational opportunities, endowments for the arts, and children and community services. Visit the Corporation's site to find information on the company, information on Lanoga's involvement in the community, and contact information.

Levi Strauss & Co. (CA) (http://www.levistrauss.com/index_community.html)

The Levi Strauss Foundation was created in 1952 and, along with a corporate giving program, is part of Levi Strauss and Company's commitment to its communities. Giving is focused in four areas: AIDS prevention and care; economic empowerment for disadvantaged and minority, especially female, populations; youth empowerment through advocating positive change among peers and communities; and those in social justice working to "break down barriers that prevent disenfranchised people from realizing their basic human rights." There are extensive grant guidelines and deadlines. In 1999 the Foundation did not accept unsolicited proposals from many countries, including the United States. A list of countries from which unsolicited proposals are welcome can be found on the site. There are grants lists divided by geographic area and information on employee volunteer and matching gifts programs.

The Limited, Inc. (OH) (http://www.limited.com/philanthropy/)

The Limited supports organizations that respond to the needs of women, children, education, and communities where the company is located. The Philanthropy section of the company's Web site provides descriptions of grant categories, grant guidelines, contact information for making inquiries, and listings of grant recipients.

Lincoln Benefit Life Company (NE) (http://www.lbl.com/info/community.asp)

Lincoln, Nebraska's Lincoln Benefit Life Company is involved in supporting the communities in which it is based. Along with encouraging employees to contribute time and resources to community organizations, the Company strives to provide "direct services or deliver effective solutions to improve the quality of life." Organizations that Lincoln Benefit Life supports are listed on the Company's Web site; contact information for further detail is available elsewhere on the site.

Lincoln Financial Group (IN) (http://www.lfg.com/f_main.htm?/who/communit.htm)

Lincoln Financial Group of Ft. Wayne, Indiana, gives money through corporate giving programs and through the Lincoln National Foundation in order to "assist philanthropic programs which enhance the quality of life in communities where Lincoln Financial Group employees live and work." Funds are distributed in three areas: arts and culture, education, and human services. Employee Gift Committees exist at company affiliates to best support local organizations. All of this information can be found under the Community Involvement link. Visitors will find applications guidelines and descriptions of some past and ongoing grants.

The Lincoln National Foundation, Inc. (IN) (http://www.lfg.com/f_main.htm?/who/grant.htm)

The Lincoln National Foundation "assists philanthropic programs which enhance the quality of life in communities where Lincoln Financial Group employees live and work." The Foundation has established three priority areas for funding: arts and culture, education and human services. Only 501(c)(3) organizations that have programs in areas where the Lincoln Financial Group has a presence are encouraged to apply. The Web site does not have grant guidelines or applications. Interested parties are told to contact a member of Corporate Public Involvement for application materials and current deadlines.

Lubrizol Foundation (OH) (http://www.lubrizol.com/Foundation/default.htm)

The Lubrizol Corporation of Wickliffe, Ohio, created the Lubrizol Foundation to "complement and support the interests and values of The Lubrizol Corporation by awarding financial support to educational institutions and charitable organizations in communities primarily within the United States where Lubrizol operates major facilities." Funding is distributed in the greater Houston, Texas, and Cleveland, Ohio, areas. The site includes application guidelines and an e-mail address to which inquiries can be sent. The latest annual report can be downloaded in PDF format.

Lucent Technologies Foundation (NJ)
(http://www.lucent.com/news/about/community/foundation.html)
Lucent Technologies, Inc., a communications technology company headquartered in Murray Hill, New Jersey, supports education and community needs through the Lucent Technologies Foundation. The company's Web site briefly describes the Foundation's giving objectives and provides a collection of articles and press releases about the support it offers.

Lyondell Chemical Company (TX) (http://www.lyondell.com/html/FR_community.html)
The community services portion of the Lyondell Chemical Company, headquartered in Houston, Texas, seeks to "[protect] the health and safety of [its] employees and neighbors and the environment." The Company sponsors numerous community events, initiatives, programs, and services, each of which detailed on the Community Highlights portion of the Web site. Funding priorities are pre-college education, environmental quality, and community sustainability. These areas are combined in the Explore Science program for local students, in which company employees conduct classroom experiments in an effort to make science, chemistry in particular, more exciting. Lyondell describes its contributions policy and funding limitations online and provides several contact addresses for more information.

Maritz Inc. (MO) (http://www.maritz.com/maritz/about/asp/community.asp)
Maritz and its employees dedicate time, talent, and financial support to civic and charitable projects in communities around the world. Examples of Maritz community involvement are listed on the Web site. Annual reports, worldwide location information, and corporate headquarter details can all also be found online.

Marsh Supermarkets, Inc. (IN) (http://www.marsh.net/ce_index.html)
Marsh Supermarkets contributes to the communities in which it operates. Specifically, Marsh supports food banks with both financial contributions and in-kind donations. Additionally, Marsh participates in nutrition programs that provide free hot meals for underprivileged children. Operating grants or project support are given to human service agencies that provide services to people in need in its communities. Marsh also supports organizations that provide direct service to a large number of individuals in the community, provide services to families, and meet multiple needs of its clients. Priority is given to projects that directly benefit children, promote the education of children, or encourage the positive development of children. Marsh Supermarkets also supports cultural and arts organizations along with local, grassroots organizations that focus on improving the community. Those interested can request donations via mail. Details and contact information are available on the Web site.

Master Brewers Association of the Americas Scholarship Foundation, Inc. (WI)
(http://www.mbaa.com/scholarship.html)
In 1887, the Master Brewers Association of the Americas (MBAA) was formed for the purpose of promoting, advancing, improving, and protecting the professional interest of brew and malt house production and technical personnel. Located in Wauwatosa, Wisconsin, MBAA disseminates technical and practical information, promotes training, encourages cooperation and interaction, and furthers knowledge through the exchange of ideas. The Association provides scholarships for members in a scientific course of study directly related to the technical areas of malting and brewing, including production, research, quality assurance, engineering, and beer packaging. Visitors to the site will find an online application, scholarship provisions, and contact information.

Materials for the Future Foundation (CA) (http://www.materials4future.org/)

The Materials for the Future Foundation was founded in San Francisco in 1992 by a group of Bay Area funders and recycling advocates. The Foundation's mission is to "support community-based initiatives that integrate the environmental goals of resource conservation through waste prevention, reuse, and recycling with the economic development goals of job creation/retention, enterprise development, and local empowerment." The Foundation focuses on low-income communities, communities of color, and communities with high numbers of unemployed persons, especially in the San Francisco Bay Area. The Foundation accomplishes its goals through grantmaking, loans, providing business and technical assistance, referral services, and community education. Three types of grants are awarded: Reclaim Grants, Enterprise Grants, and Deconstruction Grants. There are descriptions and guidelines for each grant on the Web site. For those grants that require an application, a phone number and email address is provided. The Web site also has information about the Foundation's other projects, as well as past and current programs and grant recipients.

MathSoft, Inc. (MA) (http://www.mathsoft.com/education/grant.htm)

Cambridge, Massachusetts-based MathSoft Inc. develops, markets, and supports technical calculation and data analysis software productivity tools for professionals, students, and educators. The MathSoft's StudyWorks Innovative Teaching Grant Program awards productive and innovative teachers with the use of Mathsoft products to better serve their classes. Within this program those teachers who find creative uses for the company's software are rewarded with complete student sets of these skill-building products. MathSoft Conference Presenter Grants provides stipends for educators chosen to present at local or national conferences in the areas of math, science, and/or technology with the use of MathSoft products. The company's Web site describes specific grant qualifications for both grant programs. At the site, visitors will also find an e-mail application, contact information, and complete product information.

Mattel Children's Foundation (CA)
(http://www.mattel.com/corporate/company/mattel_foundation/)

Based in El Segundo, California, the Mattel Children's Foundation—the philanthropic arm of Mattel, Inc.—promotes the spirit of philanthropy and community involvement among its employees and makes charitable investments aimed at furthering Mattel's goal to better the lives of children in need. The board of directors made a decision in the early 1990s to direct the majority of its philanthropic resources toward national Foundation-sponsored initiatives that creatively address relevant children's issues. Funding priorities include the construction of the Mattel Children's Hospital at UCLA and sustaining the Mattel Family Learning Program, which establishes computer learning labs worldwide. Due to funding limitations, applications for new Mattel Family Learning Program sites or site upgrades are not currently being accepted. The Foundation also has volunteer grants, matching gifts, scholarships for the children of Mattel Employees, and toy donations.

Mazda Foundation (DC) (http://www.mazdafoundation.org)

The Mazda Foundation in Washington, D.C., was established in 1990 to uphold the company's social responsibility. A major thrust of the Foundation is to support youth. The Foundation also strongly supports environmental conservation, cross-cultural understanding, and social well-being. The Mazda Foundation encourages innovative programs to meet these needs, forming partnerships with existing programs that promote academic excellence, civic responsibility, community service, leadership training, and literacy. The Foundation supports nonprofits that are national in scope and interested in promoting education and literacy, environmental conservation, building cross-cultural understanding and social welfare, and upholding scientific research. One of Mazda's programs is Reading is Fundamental, which provides children with free books and motivational activities to inspire them to read more. Visit the Foundation's Web site to view specific application procedures, grant restrictions, deadlines, and contact information.

McGraw-Hill Companies (NY) (http://www.mcgraw-hill.com/community/community.html)
The McGraw-Hill Companies, based in New York City, switched its philanthropic entity in 1998 from a foundation to a Corporate Contributions and Community Relations Program. The Program's mission is to "support innovative programs that increase the abilities of people around the world to learn, to grow intellectually, to master new skills, and to maximize their individual talents for school, work and community." Priority consideration is given to educational programs; initiatives to advance knowledge, home and work skills, and technology; and organizations trying to expand globally or set up models for others. The Program does not make grants to individual schools. The site includes application guidelines and restrictions; a section on the Virtual Volunteer program, which allows professionals to be economic experts for classes, and descriptions of community activities. There is also a section with information on strategic partners who work with the Program on funding and running select projects.

McKesson HBOC (CA)
(http://www.mckesson.com/webpage_templates/brochure_frame.php3)
McKesson HBOC, headquartered in San Francisco, California, is a provider of healthcare products and services to retail pharmacies, hospitals, and healthcare networks. The company's principal charitable arm, the McKesson Foundation, Inc., supports health-related, social, educational, civic, and cultural projects, located in the San Francisco Bay Area, primarily focused on youth. The company's Web site describes the Foundation's funding philosophy, provides grant guidelines and sample grants, and offers information on educational matching gifts, scholarships, special youth initiatives, and volunteering.

Medtronic Foundation (MN) (http://www.medtronic.com/foundation/index.html)
The Medtronic Foundation is the principal worldwide philanthropy and community affairs vehicle of Minneapolis-based Medtronic, Inc., a manufacturer of medical equipment and devices. Most of the Foundation's grant dollars are spent in three areas: education, with an emphasis on K–12 science education through its STAR (Science and Technology Are Rewarding) program; health; and community affairs, which includes human services, civic, and arts grants. In all three areas, priority is given "to programs that benefit people of color and those who are socioeconomically disadvantaged." The company's Web site offers program descriptions, grant guidelines and application procedures, an application form to print out, a list of Foundation grants, a listing of Medtronic communities, a selection of press releases, and an interactive correspondence page. Visitors can also browse an online version of Medtronic's annual report.

Meijer, Inc. (MI) (http://www.meijer.com/pr)
From the beginning, Meijer Superstores has been concerned with the needs of the communities it serves. This sense of community responsibility has led Meijer to spend millions of dollars each year helping others. The company donates money to dozens of organizations annually that serve areas of company operation. Meijer also holds a strong commitment to education and to the youth of its communities. The company actively seeks opportunities to support learning programs in local schools. Some of the programs include honor roll rewards, a teacher of the month program, athlete/scholar of the month, and an alcohol awareness program that rewards students with financial incentives for abstaining from alcohol during homecomings and proms. Visit the company's Web site to find specific information regarding its programs, an interesting history, and comments from community members who have benefited from the charity of Meijer.

Merck & Co., Inc. (NJ) (http://www.merck.com/philanthropy)
Merck & Co. maintains a variety of philanthropic programs through which the company supports education and healthcare and select social service, art and cultural, civic, and environmental programs. Merck's charitable giving was established in 1957, mainly to "support biomedical science training and education and to improve healthcare worldwide." Specific programs provide funding in math and science education in elementary and secondary schools; the advancement of science education at the undergraduate, graduate, and

postdoctoral levels; training and research in health policy; and the development of functional genomics research technologies and resources. Merck's philanthropic arms include Corporate Contributions, Merck Co. Foundation, Merck Institute for Science Education, Merck Medical Outreach Program, the Merck Genome Research Program, and matching gift/employee giving programs. Grants guidelines are available upon request, using the contact information provided on the Merck Web site; more details about Merck's various programs and funding strategies are available through its *Corporate Philanthropy Report.*

Merrill Lynch & Co., Inc. (NY) (http://www.ml.com/woml/phil_prog/index.htm)

Merrill Lynch, a global financial management and advisory company headquartered in New York City, promotes education by supporting scholastic programs and academic institutions and supports cultural arts, environmental, human service, health, and civic organizations. Grants are awarded to regional programs in New York State and to national organizations. The Corporate Responsibility area of the company's Web site provides an overview of Merrill Lynch's charitable activities, a global record of giving, grant guidelines, information about scholarships and employee programs, success stories, and news.

Mervyn's California (CA) (http://mervyns.com/giving/)

Mervyn's California stores have a corporate philosophy to "build a better world community by community through financial support, volunteer activities, and involvement in local nonprofit initiatives." Current grantees and partners include the California Missions Garden Restoration Project, to restore and preserve California's landmarks and history; Pet Partners, a Delta Society program that takes animals to visit nursing homes, hospitals, etc.; and Kristi Yamaguchi's Always Dream Foundation. The Web site does not provide any information on the application procedure.

Metropolitan Life Foundation (NY)
(http://www.metlife.com/Companyinfo/Community/Found/index.html)

MetLife's Web site provides visitors with detailed program guidelines and limitations, application procedures, and contact information for the insurance giant's three distinct giving programs: the Metropolitan Life Foundation, which awards grants in the areas of health, education, culture, civic affairs, and anti-violence; MetLife's Social Investment Program, which provides aid primarily in the form of loans to help "local and national groups build stronger communities across the country;" and the Targeted Suppliers Program, which is "designed to increase MetLife's purchasing of goods and services from minority and women-owned firms."

Fred Meyer Stores, Inc. (OR) (http://www.fredmeyerstores.com/contributn001.shtml)

Fred Meyer Stores, located in the western United States and based in Portland, Oregon, maintains two charitable programs: the Fred Meyer Corporate Contributions program, and the Fred Meyer Foundation. The Corporate Contributions program focuses on four areas of interest in communities where Fred Meyer Stores are located: youth development, community development, environmental programs, and cultural programs. The program provides for community services and participates in local and regional activities. The Foundation's goal is to improve the quality of life in the areas surrounding Fred Meyer Stores, in the general categories of family, children, and communities. A list of recent grants and a sketch of the grant process through the Foundation is provided in the Contributions section of the company's Web site, along with further details about the Corporate Contributions program and contact information.

MicrobiaLogic LLC (AZ) (http://www.microbialogic.com/donation.html)

Based in Phoenix, Arizona, MicrobiaLogic initiated a product donation program in 1999 to donate the company's outdoor toilet products to nonprofit organizations in need that "maintain high standards of environmental stewardship." The recipients of these products include research facilities, schools, and conferences and are detailed on the MibrobiaLogic Web site. Also available on the site is an online questionnaire form for potential applicants to the product donation program. Contact and company information is available elsewhere on the site.

Micron Technology, Inc. (ID)
(http://www.micron.com/content.jsp?path=/About%20Micron/Foundation)

Established in 1999, the Micron Foundation is committed to the "advancement of education, with emphasis on science and technology, and to the support of civic and charitable institutions" in the communities of Idaho, Utah, California, Minnesota and Texas where Micron offices are based. The Foundation operates a number of grants, including Education Grants for Higher Education, community grants, and the Science and Technology Scholars Program. Grants are made three times a year, and the Foundation's Web site includes specific information about each program, as well as press releases, community grant instructions and applications (available for downloading in PDF format), and the Foundation's downloadable Form 990–PF.

Microsoft Corporation (WA) (http://www.microsoft.com/giving/)

The Microsoft Corporation supports organizations in its communities of operation, primarily the Puget Sound region of Washington State, where its headquarters are located and where most of its employees reside. Community grants are made in the areas of human services, education, arts and culture, the environment, access to technology, and civic activities. The world's largest software manufacturer also makes cash and in-kind contributions nationally to K–12 and higher education institutions. The Community Affairs section of Microsoft's Web site offers brief program descriptions, application guidelines, giving highlights, and information on its employee giving and Libraries Online! programs.

Millipore Foundation (MA) (http://www.millipore.com/corporate/mf.nsf/docs/42YSSX)

The Millipore Foundation's objectives are to foster advances in science and technology related to Millipore Corporation business objectives, which include developing purification products for the microelectronic, biopharmaceutical, and analytical laboratory markets; to improve the quality of life in those communities in which Millipore employees live and work, particularly in its headquarters city of Bedford, Massachusetts; and to stimulate volunteerism and active community involvement by Millipore employees. Through its Grants Program, the Foundation supports projects in the areas of education and research, social services, healthcare, and the arts. Visitors to the company's Web site will find a brief overview of the Foundation, program guidelines, application instructions, and contact information. There is an online version of the company's annual report, and the Foundation's annual report is available for downloading in PDF format.

Minnesota Mining & Manufacturing company (3M) (MN)
(http://www.mmm.com/profile/community/)

The 3M Company of St. Paul, Minnesota, works to "affect people's lives in meaningful ways to build on successes in our communities everywhere." Funding is primarily given in four areas. Education grants mainly go toward science, technology, and business higher education. Health and human services funding supports agencies or programs dealing with service delivery systems, especially for youth, parenting, and strengthening families. Arts funding is given to major arts organizations that help people learn about the world around them. Community funding is generally operating and program grants for organizations in 3M communities. The site has a page on each category with a featured grantee and searchable archives of past features. There is an e-mail address listed for inquiries.

Mitsubishi Electric America Foundation (MEA) (DC) (http://www.meaf.org/)

The MEA Foundation is dedicated to the "improvement of quality of life and the empowerment of disabled youth." Its Web site details the Foundation's history and mission and includes extensive program descriptions, application guidelines, and recipient information on grants awarded by the Foundation. Visitors to the site will also find a list of Foundation staff and officers and Foundation contact information.

Montana Power Company (MT)
(http://www.mtpower.com/community/cm_foundation.htm)

The Montana Power Foundation of Butte, Montana, is funded by the Montana Power Company to "provide a method for the Company to be a welcomed neighbor and active participant in the communities [it] serves." The foundation has five major areas of giving. The primary focus is on education, with grants mostly going to scholarship and university programs, employee matching gifts, and some funding to local colleges, primary, and secondary schools. Health and human services covers organization like the United Way, youth homes, and programs for community health and safety. Civic and community grants encompass improvement projects, special events, and youth and senior organizations. Culture and the arts grants go to local institutions. Finally, resource conservation funding supports habitat preservation and fish and wildlife protection. Visitors will find downloadable copies of the foundation application (in Microsoft Word format) and the Community Relations Report (in PDF format). There are also application guidelines and examples of programs that the corporate giving program funds.

MONY Foundation (NY) (http://www.mony.com/AboutMONY/InsideMONY/Foundation/)

The MONY Foundation of New York is funded by The MONY Group in order to support "innovative, strategically effective, community-based programs." Foundation funding goes to communities where MONY employees live, work, and do business. Major contributors to the AIDS cause and great supporters of education, the Foundation also focuses on fostering the active involvement of company employees. The site offers very general and basic information. Financial statements can be found for the company elsewhere on the site.

Morton International, Inc. (IL) (http://www.mortonsalt.com/como/prflcomo.htm)

Morton contributes to the community through financial and educational support as well as the energy and talents of its employee volunteers. Examples of some of the programs Morton is involved with are listed on the company's Web site, including the Morton Arboretum, an employee matching gifts program, work on combating iodine deficiency disorders, and United Way partnerships. The Morton site does not include specific information on grants.

The Motley Fool, Inc. (VA) (http://www.fool.com/foolanthropy/foolanthropy.htm)

The Motley Fool is an internet portal dedicated to educating, enriching, and amusing its visitors on the topics of personal finance and investing. Foolanthropy, the Motley Fool's charitable drive, seeks charitable organizations that also educate, enrich, and amuse. Through Foolanthropy, the Motley Fool provides funds and seeks cash or stock donations (which can be made online) from its patrons during an annual funding drive. Readers nominate charities that are then featured on the site during the drive, and the Motley Fool provides discussion boards for visitors to discuss the charities. Charitable organizations should hold long-term expectations, provide complete details of finances, look for sustainable solutions, and involve the public in charitable programs. The Foolanthropy drives usually take place toward the end of the year, and The Motley Fool provides complete information on how and why to contribute online.

Motorola, Inc. (AZ) (http://www.motorola.com/GSS/SSTG/MOTinAZ/giving.html)

Motorola, Inc. incorporates the Motorola Foundation and local United Way partnerships in its corporate giving program. Additionally, the Scottsdale, Arizona-based Motorola Community Relations Council provides funding and sponsorships, equipment donations, radio loans, and requests for volunteer support to Arizona-based nonprofit organizations. A proposal checklist is included on the Motorola Web page for the Arizona program. The Motorola Foundation was founded in 1953, primarily to support universities in the United States. Today, the Foundation provides funds for higher education, primary and secondary education, and assistance to health and human services delivery systems, primarily through support of local United Way organizations. The Foundation focuses its grantmaking in communities where Motorola has a major manufacturing presence or an education program with a national scope. At the Motorola Web site visitors will find funding priorities and limitations, application instructions, a proposal checklist, and regional contact addresses where all application materials should be sent.

The Nalco Foundation (IL)
(http://www.nalco.com/About_Nalco/AN-Foundation/an-foundation.html)
Nalco Chemical Company, based in Naperville, Illinois, produces specialty chemicals and services for water and industrial process treatment. The Nalco Foundation makes grants to nonprofit organizations in the areas of education, community and civic affairs, health, and culture and arts. Geographic regions eligible for grants include Illinois, mainly the metropolitan Chicago area and DuPage County; Carson, California; Freeport and Sugar Land, Texas; Garyville, Louisiana; Jonesboro, Georgia; and Paulsboro, New Jersey. The Foundation area of the company's Web site offers a brief description and contact information for requesting grant guidelines.

National Semiconductor Corporation (CA) (http://www.national.com/community)
The National Semiconductor Corporation (NSC), based in Santa Clara, California, supports a number of corporate philanthropy programs and initiatives, with the common goals of improving education and addressing critical community needs in the communities nationwide where National Semiconductor is located. NSC's commitment to education focuses on grades K–12, in the areas of school volunteers, and technical assistance and equipment. Two initiatives the Corporation undertakes are the Internet Training Initiative and the Thin Client@School Initiative, both of which work to improving technical education and facilities in schools. Employee volunteers, matching gifts, and community grants are all integral parts of the NSC giving program. More details are available on these programs and initiatives on the NSC Web site, along with grant criteria and limitations for the community grants. A contact e-mail address is provided for more information.

Nationwide Foundation (OH) (http://www.nationwide.com/about_us/involve/fndatn.htm)
Nationwide is one of the largest diversified financial and insurance services providers in the United States. Based in Columbus, Ohio, the primary goal of the Foundation since 1959 has been to provide financial support for organizations whose programs address basic human needs within the following categories: health and welfare, education, culture and arts, civic and community services, and religious organizations. The Foundation's Web site provides links to other supported organizations and contact information.

NEC Foundation of America (NY) (http://www.necus.com/company/foundation)
The NEC Foundation was established in 1991 by NEC and its U.S. subsidiaries to promote NEC's corporate philosophy: the integration of computers and communications to help societies worldwide move toward deepened mutual understanding and fulfillment of human potential. The particular focus of the Foundation is on organizations and programs with national reach and impact in one or both of the following areas: science and technology education, principally at the secondary level, and/or the application of technology to assist people with disabilities. Visitors to the parent company's Web site will find extensive information about the Foundation's activities, including funding guidelines, application procedures, deadlines, and restrictions; a list of recent grant recipients indexed by organization type, geographic location, and grant purpose; and a financial statement.

New Century Energies Foundation (CO)
(http://www.ncenergies.com/CommunityProjects/Community.Asp)
Located in Denver, Colorado, New Century Energies created its Foundation to demonstrate its commitment to charitable giving. The Foundation focuses "on creating communities that are well-educated, affordable, economically sound, and that reflect the involvement of NCE employees." The New Century Energies Foundation provides grants in the areas of affordable living, workforce readiness, and classroom connection. To be considered for a grant, a nonprofit organization must complete the Request for Proposal (RFP) process. The Web site provides contact information for those who are interested in learning more about the process.

New England Financial (MA) (http://www.nefn.com/Content/AboutUs/comminv.cfm)

New England Financial, an insurance and investment company headquartered in Boston, Massachusetts, supports public education and makes grants to nonprofit organizations in the areas of education, healthcare, social service, housing, and culture. The Community Involvement area of the company's Web site provides a brief description of its funding strategy, examples of organizations awarded grants, and contact information.

New York Life Foundation (NY) (http://www.newyorklife.com/foundation/)

New York Life Insurance Company created the New York Life Foundation in 1979. The organization is intended to support groups in many categories, including health and human services, education, civic and community affairs, and arts and culture. The Foundation is currently focusing on programs that support children in specific areas: mentoring; creating safe places for kids, specifically afterschool and latchkey programs; and family oriented programs including educational enhancement, tutoring, and remedial education. The Foundation also has an educational matching gift program for employees, a local area volunteer program, and a special $5,000 grant given annually to 20 programs submitted by employees. The organization prefers national programs that allow it to work in local communities where employees live and considers programs in New York City, where it is based. Application guidelines and an electronic version of the annual report can be found on the site.

Newport News Shipbuilding (VA) (http://www.nns.com/about/aboutnns.htm)

Newport News Shipbuilding, based in Newport News, Virginia, supports educational and cultural arts programs, as well as civic, health, and human services organizations. Grants are generally made in the geographic locations of company plants, primarily in the state of Virginia. The Community Affairs area of the company's Web site describes its giving strategy, provides a breakdown of charitable giving, and lists grant recipients in various categories.

Nike, Inc. (OR) (http://www.nikebiz.com/social/index.shtml)

The mission of the philanthropic effort of the Portland, Oregon-based Nike, Inc. is "to lead in corporate citizenship through proactive programs that reflect caring for the world family of Nike, our teammates, our consumers, and those who provide services to Nike." The community responsibility program is divided into three areas: labor, global community, and environment. Labor efforts include disclosing the location of every factory manufacturing products for specific colleges, an extensive non-discrimination policy on gender, and other special initiatives and standards. The global community area includes the Nike Foundation, which is dedicated to "investing globally in youth action [by] giving them tools, resources, and opportunities." This is a new mission and direction for the Foundation, and new application guidelines will be posted after the transition. The current site does include a list of selected recipients of past grants and examples of groups that have received in-kind donations of excess inventory, sample products, and used office equipment. The mission of the environmental program is to "secure intergenerational quality of life, restoring the environment, and increasing value for our customers, shareholders, and business partners." The company accomplishes this through extensive internal efforts and many public programs, including Reuse-a-Shoe, which allows people to recycle used shoes to benefit underprivileged children. A special site specifically on the environmental program details each effort and offers a fact sheet on each project. Visitors to the site should place the cursor over the green Responsibility box on the top of the page to see the pull-down menu that will offer all these resources.

Nissan Motor Corporation (CA) (http://www.nissan-na.com/1.0/1-1-4.html)

The Nissan Motor Corporation supports a variety of community service endeavors, including community action, corporate contributions, employee matching gifts, and volunteerism. The Nissan Foundation is a five-year $5 million grant program established after the civil unrest in the South Central neighborhood of Los Angeles in 1992. The Foundation's goal is to "improve the social and economic quality of life in South Central Los Angeles by building partnerships with service groups and organizations already working in the area to promote economic development, job creation and community-building activities." The Nissan Motor Corporation's Web page, through the Community Service link, provide information about these programs and contact information.

Nordson Corporation Foundation (OH) (http://www.nordson.com/corporate/grants.html)

The Nordson Corporation Foundation was founded in 1988 when the Nordson Foundation was reorganized to create the Nord Family Foundation and The Nordson Corporation Foundation. The Nordson Corporation Foundation consolidates philanthropic resources dedicated by Nordson Corporation to address community needs. Like its predecessor, The Nordson Corporation Foundation "operates on the belief that business, as a corporate citizen, has a social responsibility to share its success with the communities where it operates and draws employees." The Foundation's four areas of interest are education, civic, human welfare, and arts and culture. The Web site gives more information about each specific area of interest. The Foundation makes grants to organizations based in geographic areas where Nordson facilities and employees are located— Cuyahoga and Lorain Counties in Ohio; the Greater Atlanta, Georgia area; and Monterey and San Diego Counties in California. Applications for grants can be obtained by contacting a Foundation staff member or by completing the form available on the Web site in PDF format.

North Carolina Electric Membership Corporation Bright Ideas Grant Program (NC) (http://www.ncemc.com/bright_ideas)

Sponsored by the North Carolina electric cooperatives, the Bright Ideas Grant Program "supports innovative projects to improve classroom instruction across the state." The Program began in 1994 and is open to all North Carolina school educators serving grades K–12 and supports programs in all disciplines. The grants underwrite innovative instructional projects the schools could not otherwise afford. Applications are available on- line and may be either printed out or submitted directly on the Web site. Staff contact information is also available on this site.

Northeast Utilities System Corporate Giving Program (CT) (http://www.nu.com/partners/commun.htm)

Located in Hartford, Connecticut, the Northeast Utilities System Corporate Giving Program works in partnership with community groups and public officials to build healthier communities and address vital community problems. Its goal is "enhancing the very quality of life in the homes and communities of the customers we serve and the quality of our environment." There is an environmental community grant program; downloadable applications in PDF format and guidelines are available on the Web site. In addition, the Program supports community programs such as soup kitchens, shelters and food banks, housing for low-income families, and civic and cultural activities. Educational speakers and programs, environmental tours, and support for recreational areas are also projects the Program supports. To find out more about funding and grant programs, contact information is available on the site.

Northrop Grumman Corporation (CA) (http://www.northgrum.com/who_we_are/who_community.html)

The Northrop Grumman Corporation, located in Los Angeles, California, looks to support programs that improve education, human services and culture, and address diversity. More specifically, the Corporation's Corporate Giving program supports such areas as pre-college education, domestic violence and child abuse, dropout prevention, childcare, housing and the homeless, youth and family counseling, health services, the arts, job training and employment, and welfare–to–work. The Northrop Grumman Web site provides grant guidelines and contact information through which to submit proposals. The Corporation also encourages community activities and volunteerism, giving select employee volunteers and their organizations awards for service. The site includes recent award recipients and more detailed information on the programs the Corporation supports.

Northwestern Steel and Wire Company (IL)
(http://www.nwsw.com/northwestern_and_community.htm)

The Northwestern Steel and Wire Company (NSW) makes donations to a variety of causes, both monetary and through employee involvement. Included are donations to help educate young people and to support programs sponsored by the local police and fire departments. Northwestern employees also show compassion toward the needy children of the Sterling/Rock Falls area and surrounding communities through their generosity at Christmas. Descriptions of how NSW helps local schools and other needy causes can be found on the Web site.

Novell, Inc. (UT) (http://www.novell.com/careers/college/cr)

The Novell, Inc. Corporate Giving Program is the philanthropic arm of Novell, Inc. The Corporate Giving Program is located in Utah, and its mission "is to enable nonprofit organizations to develop and realize their visions through the power of technology." Nonprofit organizations whose missions focus on education, homeless and hungry, and/or arts and culture are encouraged to apply. The Program makes grants in areas where its employees live and work and has three main programs: CYBERgrant, Software Donation, and Cash Grant. Application criteria and guidelines are listed for each program, as are lists of previous awards and contact information.

Oracle Corp. (CA) (http://www.oracle.com/corporate/giving/)

Based in Redwood Shores, California, the Oracle Corporation's corporate philanthropy is made up of three components. The Oracle Volunteers program supports employee volunteer efforts and is open to requests for volunteer support. The corporate giving program funds four major areas: medical research in the areas of cancer, AIDS, and neuroscience; endangered animal protection; environmental protection, specifically for education and the preservation of important open space; and K–12 education, specifically for math, science, and technology programs. Oracle's Promise is a $100 million initiative created in 1997 that is committed to students having Internet access. It grants network computers and teacher materials, development, and support to underfunded K–12 public schools. The site includes application guidelines for all three programs. There is an application that can be printed right from the page for the corporate giving program and an application that can be downloaded in PDF format for the Promise. There are lists of giving program grant recipients and sponsors and a page of statistics on Promise participants. The annual reports can be found in the About Us section under Corporate Relations.

The Orchard Foundation (MA/ME) (http://www.orchardfoundation.org)

Created in 1990, the Orchard Foundation of South Portland, Maine, supports New York and New England groups that work with the environment, children, youth, and families. The Foundation also invites state and local campaign finance reform groups to apply for a smaller grant program. Unsolicited proposals are considered in the board grants category. Applying organizations must fall into one of the two program areas. Environmental organizations, particularly those involved in advocacy, are encouraged to apply. The children, youth, and families category includes child and family advocacy, enrichment, parenting skills and support, and pregnancy prevention. The site includes application guidelines and grant lists for each category.

Osram Sylvania Inc. (MA) (http://www.sylvania.com/aboutus/corpgiving/)

Headquartered in Danvers, Massachusetts, Osram Sylvania is a manufacturer of lighting products whose philanthropic mission is to give back to the communities in which the company is based. Osram Sylvania's main philanthropic focus is math and science education for vocational and community colleges and K–12 students. Additionally, the company is interested in supporting health and human services, youth and safety-centered civic organizations, arts and culture, and the environment. The company's Web site provides information on grant guidelines and restrictions, as well as online initial applications for funding in each region where Osram Sylvania facilities are located.

Pacific Gas & Electric (CA)
(http://www.pge.com/007_our_comm/007b_giving_to_comm.shtml)
Through its corporate contributions program, Pacific Gas & Electric (PG&E) makes grants exclusively to nonprofit organizations in northern and central California, primarily in two areas: 1) job training and economic development and 2) education. It also makes a limited number of grants for emergency preparedness and response, environmental stewardship, and civic and cultural activities. Although the company prefers to fund special projects and new or existing programs, it does makes grants for general operating support and, on a limited basis, for capital campaigns. In addition to a general description of PG&E's philanthropic programs, visitors to the company's Web site will find a rundown of its grant application procedures and contact information.

The PacifiCorp Foundation (OR) (http://www.pacificorp.com/paccomp/commsvc/)
The Portland, Oregon-based PacifiCorp Foundation, created in 1988 as the philanthropic arm of PacifiCorp, states that its objective "is to link company and community goals to determine—and then fulfill—our responsibility to improve the quality of life in areas we serve." These areas include the communities served by Pacific Power and Utah Power in Idaho, Utah, California, Oregon, Washington, and Wyoming. The Foundation funds in the broad areas of civic and community organizations, culture and arts, health and human services, education and research, and other areas including the environment and safety. Visitors to the Web site will find a list of all the communities served by the Foundation, as well as funding guidelines and limitations, details of the application process and deadlines, and contact information.

Pacific Life Foundation (CA) (http://www.pacificlife.com/About/commun/Community.htm)
Pacific Life, founded in 1868, provides life and health insurance products, individual annuities and group employee benefits, and offers a variety of investment products and services to individuals, businesses, and pension plans. Through its Newport Beach, California-based foundation, grants are made to organizations that address a broad spectrum of social problems: health and human services, education, arts and culture, and civic and community services. A considerable portion of its budget is directed to five to seven pre-determined issues, identified by the Foundation's board of directors in December of each year and researched and funded throughout the following year, that receive special attention and larger grants. These focus programs are highlighted in the *Pacific Life/Pacific Life Foundation Report on Community Involvement,* which can be obtained by writing the Foundation. Focus programs highlighted in the report this year are children and television, ethnic tension reduction, marine mammals, family stability, innovation in education, and youth and family fitness. Contributions are made primarily in areas with large concentrations of Pacific Life employees, and some California and national organizations also receive support. Visitors to the Web site will find funding guidelines, a downloadable grant application, and contact information.

Padilla Speer Beardsley Inc. Corporate Giving Program (MN)
(http://www.psbpr.com/whoWeAre/whoe_comm.html)
Padilla Speer Beardsley (PSB) is a top, independently–owned public relations firm with offices in Minneapolis and St. Paul, Minnesota, and New York City. Each year, its corporate giving program selects two organizations to receive special assistance in public relations programming. In addition, PSB responds to emerging community needs by contributing public relations expertise and financial support to many organizations that strive to improve the quality of life for all people. PSB primarily supports programs and organizations that encourage the development of health and social services, youth development, education, and the arts. The firm encourages employees to invest time by providing public relations support at no charge. The Web site contains contact information and detailed descriptions of previous programs PSB has funded.

Palm, Inc. (CA) (http://www.palm.com/about/corporate/donations.html)

Palm, Inc. established its Palm Products Donation Program in 1998 to support nonprofit organizations that serve community needs through donated Palm products. The Palm, Inc. Web site lists organizations that have benefited from the program, and allows potential applicants to fill out an online application with step-by-step instructions.

The Panasonic Foundation (NJ)
(http://www.panasonic.com/MECA/foundation/foundation.html)

Headquartered in Secaucus, New Jersey, the Panasonic Foundation was established in 1984 because "human beings are our most precious natural resource, [and] the Foundation is dedicated to the development of that resource through the enhancement and improvement of public education in the United States." The Foundation's flagship program is the Panasonic Partnership Program, which involves helping public school districts restructure their education systems. The site includes a list of the systems currently taking part in the program, descriptions of the two Foundation newsletters, and a form to request either of the newsletters.

Patagonia, Inc. (CA) (http://www.patagonia.com/enviro/)

Patagonia, Inc. of Ventura, California, established the Environmental Grants Program in 1985. The goal of the program is to protect undomesticated lands and waters. 1999 Grants recipients fell in one of the following categories: biodiversity, forests, media/publications, resource extraction/alternative energy, social activism/environmental education, sustainable agriculture, and water/marine. The site includes a list of these 1999 recipients, with a description of each grant and contact information. There is also an R & D section that presents the results of different environmental research and development projects. The Take Action section includes a Tool Box for Activists for potential grassroots organizers and a page of links to all grant recipients for the last two years. There is an address to contact for application guidelines.

J.C. Penney Company (TX) (http://www.jcpenney.net/company/commrel/index.htm)

J.C. Penney makes grants to national organizations in the areas of health and welfare, education, civic betterment, and arts and culture. Special attention is given to the support and promotion of voluntarism and the improvement of pre-college education, with a focus on the areas of K–12 reform, restructuring, and dropout prevention. Funding emphasis is given to projects that serve a broad sector of a particular community, national projects that benefit local organizations across the country, organizations that provide direct services, and organizations with a proven record of success. Grants for projects with a local scope, hospitals, museums, and individual colleges and universities are made by local units of the company. Visitors to the Community Involvement area of the parent company's Web site will find general funding guidelines, application procedures and limitations, detailed information on support for education, Golden Rule and National Volunteer Awards, and the company's *Community Partners Annual Report.*

Pennzoil-Quaker State Company (TX)
(http://www.pennzoil-quakerstate.com/about/I3_corp_contributions_fs.htm)

Based in Houston, Texas, the Pennzoil-Quaker State Company supports communities where its employees live and work through charitable contributions in the areas of education, health, culture, civic services, and other charitable organizations whose programs promote well-being and vitality. The Company also provides matching gift donations with employees, shareholders, and company directors to accredited colleges and universities. An e-mail contact address for community relations can be found in the General section of the Contact Us portion of the Web site.

Pfizer, Inc. (NY) (http://www.pfizer.com/pfizerinc/philanthropy/)

Through its Venture Philanthropy program, pharmaceutical giant Pfizer Inc. makes grants to nonprofit organizations within the broad categories of health, education, and community and cultural affairs. Through both product donations and cash grants, Pfizer's health program seeks to "expand access to compassionate, high-quality healthcare, especially for those most at risk of poor health outcomes." The goal of its education programs is to "excite students, primarily K–12, about science and to increase their understanding of scientific principles and the importance of scientific progress." And the company's community and cultural affairs program "is committed to strengthening and enhancing the quality of life in communities" where Pfizer operates, particularly New York City. Visitors to the philanthropy section of the Pfizer Web site will find extensive descriptions of the company's philanthropic philosophy, general program descriptions, listings of selected grant recipients in each program area, and application instructions.

PGE-Enron Foundation (OR) (http://www.pge-enronfoundation.org/)
Formed in 1997, the Portland-based PGE-Enron Foundation is a corporate foundation permanently endowed by Portland General Electric and Enron Corp. The Foundation is committed to improving the quality of life for Oregonians. The Foundation's giving program centers on education, healthy families, arts and culture, and the environment. Recently, PGE-Enron also created a special initiative called, Community 101, which "helps high school youth experience the value of community service learning and philanthropy." Visitors to the Foundation's Web site will find detailed information on the Community 101 program and other grant initiatives, application information, a copy of the latest annual report downloadable in PDF format, an archive of recent press releases and news on the Foundation, board and staff listing, and contact information.

Philadelphia Newspapers, Inc. (PA) (http://home.phillynews.com/pni/giving)
The corporate giving program of Philadelphia Newspapers centers on the areas of human services, arts and culture, and particularly education. The company makes charitable contributions through scholarships, grants to nonprofit organizations and larger annual donations to the United Way. Grants are limited to organizations, in specific counties in Pennsylvania and New Jersey, enumerated on the Philadelphia Newspapers Web site. Also available online are previous grant recipients, funding guidelines and limitations, application procedures and deadlines, and contact information.

Philip Morris Companies Inc. (NY) (http://www.philipmorris.com/pmcares/)
Philip Morris has been helping to support local, national, and international communities since 1956 with its corporate contributions program. Headquartered in New York City, Philip Morris strives to help people in need through "a tradition of giving back to the communities where [they] do business, and a demonstrated commitment to excellence, innovation and diversity." Philip Morris' main funding concerns are hunger relief, assistance to victims of domestic violence, and culture. In addition, they have significant programs in the areas of the environment, AIDS education, and humanitarian assistance. Details of each funding area, as well as organizations Philip Morris has funded and in-depth articles on each program, can be found on the Philip Morris Web site. For grantseekers, the Web site provides an address to write in order to request a brochure on a specific program or on applying for a grant from Philip Morris.

The Pillsbury Company Foundation (MN)
(http://www.pillsbury.com/about/foundation.asp)
The Pillsbury Company Foundation, the grantmaking organization of food supplier Pillsbury, awards grants to programs that help prepare and empower economically disadvantaged young people in company communities. Grants support direct service programs that fall into two categories: Caring Adults and Kids and Skills for Self-Sufficiency. The Foundation area of Pillsbury's Web site describes these funding initiatives and provides a phone number for more information.

Pizza Hut, Inc. (KS) (http://www.pizzahut.com/news/community/)
Pizza Hut Corporate Giving is centered around the BOOK IT! program, which encourages children in K–6 to read. Since 1984, Pizza Hut has sponsored the BOOK IT! program, rewarding students for reading books on a monthly reading list with free pizza and

recognition for their achievements. The Pizza Hut Corporate Web site contains a link to the BOOK IT! site where parents and teachers will find background information on the program, reading lists, sample verification forms that can be downloaded in PDF format, and links to other organizations that encourage reading. Contact information for the Wichita, Kansas-based program is available on the site.

Playboy Foundation (IL) (http://www.playboy.com/corporate/foundation/index.html)

Through the Playboy Foundation, a direct corporate giving program despite its name, Playboy aims "to pursue, perpetuate and protect the principles of freedom and democracy" and "seeks to foster social change by confining its grants and other support to projects of national impact and scope involved in fostering open communication about, and research into, human sexuality, reproductive health and rights; protecting and fostering civil rights and civil liberties in the United States for all people, including women, people affected and impacted by HIV/AIDS, gays and lesbians, racial minorities, the poor and the disadvantaged; and eliminating censorship and protecting freedom of expression." The company also awards grants for post-production and distribution of documentary films and videos that address issues of social change. It has established the Freedom of Expression Award given at the Sundance Film Festival each year to honor the documentary film that best educates the public on an issue of social concern. Playboy's Web site provides visitors with general program guidelines, grant application and award nomination guidelines and limitations, a selected grants list, and contact information.

Polaroid Foundation, Inc. (MA) (http://www.polaroid.com/polinfo/foundation/index.html)

Polaroid Foundation is the philanthropic organization of Polaroid Corporation, a manufacturer of instant imaging products headquartered in Cambridge, Massachusetts. The Foundation supports programs in the Massachusetts communities of greater Boston and greater New Bedford that help disadvantaged children and adults develop measurable skills. The Foundation area of the company's Web site provides guidelines and an application form for grant proposals. Visitors will also find information on the Foundation's Volunteer Action Fund, college scholarships for children of employees, product donations, and matching gifts.

Polo Ralph Lauren Corporation (NY) (http://www.polo.com/about/philanthropy.asp)

The Polo Ralph Lauren Corporation maintains a charitable giving arm to support the communities where the Corporation and its employees live, work, and do business. Polo's specific programs support a variety of causes and organizations (from breast cancer research to the National Trust for Historic Preservation and educational support on parenting to the disadvantaged). These programs are discussed in more detail on the Corporation's Web site. Proceeds from the sale of Philanthropy Items, including clothing and other merchandise, support the Corporation's charities. These items can be purchased online.

PowerQuest Corporation (UT) (http://www.powerquest.com/givingpolicy)

Located in Orem, Utah, the PowerQuest Corporation's charitable giving arm focuses on software donations and contributions to organizations that have an on-going relationship with the Corporation. These organizations should serve the ill, needy, or youth. PowerQuest gives priority to charities focusing on education, health, and human services that are located along Utah's Wasatch Front and in Austin, Texas. Within the Giving Policy section of the PowerQuest Web site, the Corporation includes contact information for its programs and guidelines for organizations interested in applying for software donations or cash contributions.

PricewaterhouseCoopers (NY) (http://www.endowment.pwcglobal.com)

PricewaterhouseCoopers provides a full range of business advisory services, including audit, tax, and legal advice; management, information technology, and human resource consulting; financial advisory services, including corporate finance and litigation support; and business process outsourcing services to leading global, national, and local companies and public institutions. The company's corporate giving program supports higher education in the field of accountancy. The company makes grants to four-year and post-graduate degree-granting colleges and universities for aid to teachers, scholarships, fellowships, and student loans.

Principal Financial Group (IA) (http://www.principal.com/about/giving)

The Principal Financial Group Foundation Inc. was created in 1987 by the Principal Financial Group of Des Moines, Iowa. The charitable grants program focuses on four giving areas: health and human services; education; arts and culture; and environment, recreation, and tourism. Grants in each category are distributed once per year. The company also has a matching gifts program for employees and runs a volunteer network. The site includes application guidelines and deadlines and an application form that can be downloaded in PDF format. There is also a report to the community that can be downloaded in PDF format. All grants will be given in communities where Principal Financial Group has a strong employee presence.

Procter & Gamble Fund (OH)
(http://www.pg.com/about_pg/corporate/community/community_submain.jhtml)

Procter & Gamble (P&G) makes charitable contributions worldwide in excess of $50 million annually. Roughly 60 percent of the company's annual contributions support education, through grants to colleges and universities; public policy research programs; economic education organizations; and P&G's scholarship program for employee children. P&G also makes grants to health, social service, civic, cultural, and environmental organizations. Visitors to the Community Activity section of the P&G Web site will find a brief description of the company's philanthropic interests and a brief accounting of its contributions by interest area.

Prudential Insurance Co. (NJ) (http://www.prudential.com/community)

Founded in 1875, New Jersey-based Prudential today relies on three vehicles to further its philanthropic goals: the Prudential Foundation, which awards grants in support of early childhood education, professional development for teachers, school leadership development, school-based health and human services, arts education and conflict resolution, youth development, and the teaching of job entry skills; a Social Investments Program, which initiates and manages neighborhood revitalization and minority entrepreneurship projects; and a Local Initiatives program, which coordinates efforts by Prudential employees to address needs in specific communities. Information about the company's philanthropic activities is gathered in the Community Center section of the Prudential Web site, which also offers areas devoted to the company's Spirit of Community Initiative, the goal of which is to encourage young people to become involved in making their communities better places to live; and the Helping Heart Program, which helps voluntary emergency medical service squads purchase semi-automatic cardiac defibrillators.

Public Service Electric and Gas Company (NJ)
(http://www.pseg.com/community/index.html)

The Public Service Electric and Gas Company's (PSE&G) community giving programs seek to "improve people's lives and the economic vitality of New Jersey." Through resources for schools, employee contributions, community initiatives, and corporate contributions, PSE&G supports children's issues, economic development, and the environment in the areas of New Jersey that the company serves. Education grants for teachers help incorporate environmental education into the classroom. There is also a traveling education program. Employees of PSE&G donate time as volunteers, as well as through monetary gifts. PSE&G has a number of grants for these volunteers and their recipient organizations. Additionally, corporate contributions are made in a variety of areas, including pre-collegiate education, environmental education, job readiness, and urban revitalization. Recent grant recipients and programs through each of the four methods of charitable giving are detailed on the Company's Web site. Learning resources in The Electric Universe, grant guidelines and limitations, and an application in Microsoft Word format for the corporate contributions program are also online.

QUALCOMM Incorporated (CA) (http://www.qualcomm.com/cda/about/community)
Based in San Diego, California, QUALCOMM creates digital wireless communications products and services. Through QUALCOMM's Corporate Giving Program, the company provides cash donations, company products, used computers and electronic equipment, Internet and network wiring, and volunteers to a variety of qualifying nonprofit organizations. Program support is limited to areas of company location with strong interests in math and science education, arts and culture, and health and human services. Visitors to QUALCOMM's Web site will find grant guidelines, contact information, and more detailed information about its specific programs.

Quantum Corporation (CA)
(http://www.quantum.com/quantum/corporate/community/community.htm)
The Quantum Corporation, located in Santa Clara Valley, California, created its Community Relations Program in an effort to "to leverage resources by joining with others to address critical issues and support broadly backed solutions." The Foundation supports organizations in communities where the company has facilities and employees, including the greater Santa Clara Valley in California; Shrewsbury, Massachusetts, and nearby communities; Colorado Springs and Boulder, Colorado; and areas of Europe and Asia. Giving is funneled through two programs. Capacity for the Extraordinary grants go to a broad range of programs that are devoted to K–12 teacher/professional development. The Capacity for Caring program is administered by local Employee Advisory Committees and gives money to local organizations working on issues including the arts, health and human services, and the environment. The site includes grant guidelines and a proposal summary sheet.

QuikTrip Corporation (OK) (http://www.quiktrip.com/community/contributions.html)
Quiktrip is a chain of convenience stores and gas stations that contributes five percent of its profits each year to community organizations. Contributions are intended to "help bring about change to curb the increasing problem of individuals in our society who depend on the support of others." The contributions are intended to encourage others to build a better community. Visit the Web site to learn more about Quiktrip Corporation and its contributions Program.

Raytheon Company (MA) (http://www.raytheon.com/community)
The Corporate Giving Program of Raytheon, a national technology company, "is committed to improving math and science education, increasing access and opportunity for minorities, women, the physically disabled and economically disadvantaged, and improving the environment on an ecosystem basis." The Raytheon grant programs serve communities with Raytheon facilities; there is a map of these facilities on the Web site. Raytheon focuses on grants in math and science education, access and opportunity, and environmental stewardship and runs various initiatives in these areas. Raytheon's Web site, under the Community Connections link, provides an informative funding FAQ and resources links for more information. There is also an application—in PDF format—on the site.

RealNetworks (WA) (http://www.realnetworks.com/company/giving/)
RealNetworks, Inc., located in Seattle, Washington, is strongly committed to charitable responsibility. Since 1995, it has been donating software to charitable organizations. Additionally, in 1998, it created RealImpact, a RealNetworks division that provides online technical services at cost to progressive organizations. RealNetworks is now committed to donating approximately five percent of its annual net income to charitable organizations. RealNetworks focuses its giving on programs that enable alternative voices to foster the right of free speech throughout the world, broaden access to technology in underserved communities throughout the world, and enhance the quality of life in areas where RealNetworks employees live and work. RealNetworks contributes to charitable endeavors through several programs, including the RealNetworks Foundation, its corporate giving program, software and product donations, the employee gift matching program, and its employee volunteer program. Details about each, including how to apply, are available on

the Web site. Contact information for those who have questions or wish to learn more is also listed on the site. The RealNetworks Foundation Grant Guidelines, which include deadlines and funding parameters, can be viewed in PDF format.

Regence BlueShield (WA) (http://www.wa.regence.com/ioc/ioc_index.html)

Based in Tacoma, Washington, Regence BlueShield's corporate giving program focuses on the areas of health and human services and community-based programs, with preference given to organizations in which employees of the company are involved. The Regence BlueShield Web site describes the criteria and guidelines for potential applicants, and funding limitations. Additionally, the site provides a listing of recently supported Washington nonprofit organizations and contact information for further details.

Reynolds Metals Company Foundation (VA)
(http://www.rmc.com/gen/about/foundation.html)

The Reynolds Metals Company Foundation of Richmond, Virginia, supports a variety of organizations in communities where Reynolds Metals Company has a presence, with a focus on education. The Foundation is primarily interested in "education as it relates to preparing students for the business world. The Foundation places special emphasis on the support of business and engineering course curriculums in order to attract more of the best students and to train them for the workplace." Additionally, the Foundation funds organizations for health and human services, arts and culture, and civics. The site includes applications guidelines, a list of the board of trustees, and an e-mail address ordering printed Foundation guidelines.

Reynolds and Reynolds Company Foundation (OH)
(http://www.reyrey.com/about/commun.html)

The Reynolds and Reynolds Company Foundation currently confines its grantmaking to Dayton and Celina, Ohio, to "areas which promote a healthy environment and ensure the quality of life for the people in local communities." The Foundation focuses on four areas of funding interest: arts and culture, K–12 education, community benefit, and health and human services. The Reynolds and Reynolds Association Foundation concentrates on charitable health and human service organizations by organizing employee volunteers and making grants to select groups and programs. Recent grant recipients for both divisions of the Foundation are listed online. For grantseekers, there is contact information and an e-mail address to request applications and more information.

Rite Aid Corporation (PA)
(http://www.riteaid.com/company_info/citizen_ra/citizen_frameset.html)

Rite Aid, a chain of pharmacies headquartered in Harrisburg, Pennsylvania, supports programs and projects in communities served by the company. Funding is focused on health and medical programs, social services, education, the arts, and civic services. The In the Community area of the company's Web site provides funding criteria and request procedures.

Rohm and Haas Company (PA) (http://www.rohmhaas.com/company/CSI/index.html)

A leader in chemical technology, Rohm and Haas Company of Philadelphia, Pennsylvania, is committed to being "a valued corporate citizen and good neighbor." To follow through on this, the company supports its employees' volunteer efforts and has a corporate giving program. Grants are primarily given in the areas of health, human service, and education, but additional funds are distributed in civic and community improvement and culture and arts. Investments are made in communities where employees live and the company does business. The site includes application guidelines. The annual report is available in the Investors area of the site.

Romic Environmental Technologies Corporation Charitable Contributions Program (CA) (http://www.romic.com/romcomty.html)

Romic Environmental Technologies Corporation is located in East Palo Alto, California. Its corporate giving program is designed to support effective local programs that enable the local community to develop its own long-term solutions for meeting residents' needs. It is "an investment in the community's most important resources—its people and its environment." Romic focuses on funding programs that aim to keep children in school and build self-esteem, introduce youth to computers, provide after-school tutoring, match mentors with at- risk youth, and keep teenage mothers in school. It also funds programs that develop marketable job skills or job opportunities and abate drug abuse and crime. The Web site gives further detail about the types of programs and organizations that Romic makes contributions to and gives contact information for those interested in receiving more information and/or an application.

SAFECO Corporation (WA) (http://www.safeco.com/safeco/about/giving/giving.asp)

The Seattle, Washington, insurance company, SAFECO Corporation, is committed to "supporting business goals, enhancing SAFECO's reputation as an active community partner, contributing to healthy economic development, and demonstrating [their] commitment to social responsibility by placing resources back into [their] communities." The company has four main funding areas. Efforts to "create safe and vigorous neighborhoods" include educating residents about community safety and safe transportation and supporting neighborhoods suffering from natural disasters. "Maintaining engaged and proud neighborhoods" includes celebrating diversity through cultural events, youth-driven community projects, and building "human capital" through organizational development and leadership training. "Supporting economically secure and prosperous neighborhoods" encompasses increasing affordable housing and encouraging at-risk students to stay in school. Finally, "promoting stable and friendly neighborhoods" includes individual and family support for crucial transitions and increasing literacy. The Strengthening America's Neighborhoods page has application restrictions and instructions on receiving application guidelines for groups in Seattle as well as instructions on contacting local Community Relations representatives for those outside of Seattle.

The St. Paul Companies, Inc. Corporate Giving Program (MN) (http://www.stpaul.com/wwwcorporate/html/communities.html)

The St. Paul Companies, Inc, a property-liability insurance company located in St. Paul, Minnesota, has a multi-program corporate giving program. The entire program's mission is to "support people and institutions to reach their full potential, thereby creating strong, healthy, vital communities." All support is focused in four areas: education, community development, arts and culture, and advancement of the nonprofit, voluntary sector. Means used to extend this support include a foundation, an employee charitable-fund drive, employee and retiree volunteer programs, a grassroots program that encourages local leaders to develop yearlong projects that involve them in the Twin Cities, in-kind contributions, and social purpose investments. Created in 1999, the St. Paul Companies, Inc. Foundation shares the mission and focus areas of the larger program. Grants are given to nonprofits in the Twin City and Baltimore areas, specific regions in the United Kingdom, and select other communities where the Company has a significant business presence. The Web site offers specific descriptions of giving in each category and lists deadlines and extensive restrictions. First-time applicants are advised to submit a letter of inquiry. Previous grant recipients can directly request application materials from Foundation staff. The site includes a list of selected grantees, a list of principles that the Foundation works to follow, a list of the company's specific areas of employee involvement, and LIN, the Leadership Initiatives in Communities Program. The latter includes application deadlines and guidelines.

Salt River Project Agricultural Improvement and Power District (AZ) (http://www.srpnet.com/community/involvement.asp)

Salt River Project (SRP) Agricultural Improvement and Power District Points of Light Foundation and Volunteer Center National Network supports groups committed to working for a positive future for Arizona. Grantees include schools, human services groups, the arts, and environmental organizations, among others. The Community Giving section of SRP's Web site details the organizations and events that the Foundation will fund. Contact information is available elsewhere on the site.

Samsung Semiconductor, Inc. (TX) (http://www.sas.samsung.com/com_rel.html)

The Austin, Texas-based Samsung Semiconductor corporation supports community organizations in the areas of education, health and human services, arts and culture, and the environment through its corporate giving program. The company's Web site provides descriptions of each of these funding areas, along with information on the company's volunteer services. Instructions, guidelines, deadlines, and limitations for grants are detailed on the site, and interested organizations can download a grant application in PDF format.

San Diego Gas & Electric (CA) (http://www.sdge.com/community/)

The San Diego Gas & Electric Company Community Center is the philanthropic arm of this Southern California energy company. The Center's goal is to "provide funds for programs that allow us the opportunity to build partnerships with organizations, businesses and community leaders to meet community needs." Grants are made in five main categories: education, the environment, business and community development, health and human services, and civic and community affairs. Application guidelines are available and an electronic submission form is being developed. Visitors will find lists of grant recipients in each category. The site includes a list of cities and counties that the companies serves and supports. The program also includes a Speakers Bureau, a Tree Smart program, and a Virtual Powerplant to teach visitors about the company. Because the company is a subsidiary, its financial information is available on the Web site of its corporate owner.

The San Jose Sharks (CA) (http://www.sj-sharks.com)

The Sharks Foundation is "dedicated to meeting the educational, social and cultural needs of our community." The San Jose Sharks and the Sharks Foundation support a broad range of community programs but are especially focused on the community's youth. To apply for a grant, an organization must be located in Santa Clara County and must support local youth. The grant application may be printed from the Web site and mailed to the address listed on the site. The Web site also provides descriptions of the community programs that the Sharks are involved in and contact information for those requesting merchandise donations. In addition, the site has descriptions of all the Sharks Foundation community-based programs, which include golf tournaments, street hockey programs, and food, toy, and book drives.

Sara Lee Corporation (IL) (http://www.saraleefoundation.org/)

The Sara Lee Foundation of Chicago, Illinois, was founded in 1981 to, along with the company's corporate giving program, support groups that best serve the needs of communities where Sara Lee Corporation facilities and employees are located. The Foundation focuses its giving in four areas. The first is programs that personally and professionally benefit women. The Foundation runs the Frontrunner Awards to honor four women each year, while the Corporation supports local organizations. Forty-four percent of cash grants in 1999 went toward organizations that make art meaningful and available to a lot of people. The last two areas are hunger and people in need, which includes job placement and drug prevention programs. In addition to the Frontrunner Awards, the Foundation also awards the Chicago Spirit Award "to recognize and support nonprofit organizations that demonstrate innovative leadership in improving life for disadvantaged people in Chicago" and the Leadership Award for innovative organizations serving people in need. The site includes application guidelines, a list of current sponsorships, lists of past winners, and specific applications for each of the awards.

SAP America, Inc. (PA) (http://www.sap.com/usa/aboutsap/corpgive.asp)

The SAP America Corporate Giving program seeks to help worthwhile causes that enhance the quality of life for everyone. It focuses on "generosity, making life a little better by contributing to selected charities and organizations within human services and the arts and sciences in ways that can enrich our communities." Examples of SAP Corporate Giving can be found on the Web site. Interested parties can also complete an information request form online.

SAS Institute, Inc. (NC) (http://www.sas.com/corporate/philanthropy/)

Cary, North Carolina-based SAS Institutes Inc. has a Corporate Philanthropy program that supports "the spirit of SAS Institute as a supportive, caring environment in the community." Giving is focused in two areas: organizations working with children and families in crisis and the education of children and adults. SAS also has extensive projects that involve employees in volunteerism in the community. Information can be found by selecting the Corporate Culture heading. The company's annual report is available online.

SBC Foundation (TX)
(http://www.sbc.com/Community/SBC_Foundation/0,2951,7,00.html)

The SBC Foundation, the philanthropic unit of SBC Communications, Inc., seeks to help "communities search for lasting solutions to critical and complex problems." To that end, the Foundation focuses on education, community economic development, health and human services, and arts and culture. Most grants are directed toward regions served by SBC companies (Arkansas, California, Connecticut, Nevada, Missouri, Oklahoma, and Texas), but the Foundation does support a number of relevant initiatives that are national in scope. The SBC Web site provides visitors with a thorough, user-friendly overview of the grantseeking process, including grantmaking guidelines, a grant application form, and contact information.

Scripps Howard Foundation (OH) (http://www.scripps.com/foundation)

Established in 1963, the Scripps Howard Foundation is the corporate foundation of the E.W. Scripps Company. Its mission is to "advance the cause of a free press through support of excellence in journalism, quality journalism education and professional development." The Foundation's programs and projects include National Journalism Awards, a National Roundtable, scholarships and internships for journalism students, fellowships for practicing journalists, and a collegiate reporting competition. The Foundation also has an employee program, which includes matching gifts and scholarship awards. There are links for each program, which provide details, articles, and lists of past awards. Contact information for those interested in program/grant guidelines, annual reports, and more materials on the Foundation is available on the Web site.

Seagate (CA) (http://www.seagate.com)

Seagate Technology is "committed to being a good corporate citizen in the communities in which its employees live and work." The company demonstrates its support through donations of funds, furniture, computer and office equipment, and by encouraging employee volunteerism. Seagate focuses its giving on science and technology initiatives that enhance creativity and diversity in grades K–12. Seagate also gives special consideration to programs that offer employee-volunteering opportunities and funds programs that affect communities in which Seagate operates or its employees live. Grant requests must be submitted in letter format, following the guidelines listed on the site. The Web site also has a list of contacts in different parts of the country and the world for those who need more information. There is also a scrapbook on the site, which contains photos from different projects and programs that Seagate has been involved with around the globe.

Sears, Roebuck and Co. (IL) (http://www.sears.com)

In the Community segment of the For the Public section of the About Sears area of Sears, Roebuck and Company's Web site is information on the Chicago, Illinois-based merchandise giant's corporate philanthropy efforts. As part of the national America's Promise campaign, the company is encouraging and enabling employees to volunteer with local nonprofits. In 1999, Sears partnered with the Backstreet Boys and Youth Service America to award the Larger Than Life Award to young people aged 9–20 "who demonstrate a commitment to community service and dedication to volunteer spirit." The company also supports Gilda's Club, a center where people living with cancer, their families, and their friends can go for free social and emotional support.

Sega Foundation (CA) (http://sega.com/foundation/)

The Sega Youth Education & Health Foundation, also known as the Sega Foundation, is committed to improving the lives of young people and has a particular interest in children's education and health. The Foundation area of Sega of America, Inc.'s Web site offers a good deal of information about Foundation-funded projects and initiatives past, present, and future. The Foundation initiates most of its funding discussions with nonprofit organizations, but it accepts unsolicited proposals for small grants, typically ranging from $500–$2,500. Visitors will find thorough funding information, a grant application, eligibility guidelines, and lists of grants.

Sempra Energy (CA) (http://www.sempra.com/community)

Located in San Diego, California, the Sempra Energy Corporate Giving Program is "dedicated to taking a leadership role in promoting health, furthering education and environmental protection, and stimulating economic vitality, while enhancing the quality of life in communities where we do business." To receive the most recent grantmaking guidelines, click on the link provided and complete a form over the Internet. The Sempra Energy Corporate Giving Program also includes an employee matching program and a volunteer incentive program for employees. The site includes an email and mailing address for those interested in more information.

Seneca Foods Corporation (NY) (http://www.senecafoods.com/corp_affairs.htm)

Seneca Foods Corporation of Pittsford, New York, owns such major food labels as Libby's, Aunt Nellie's, and Blue Boy. The only mention of the Seneca Foundation is in the list of addresses to contact with questions in the Mail section.

Service Corporation International (TX)
(http://www.sci-corp.com/html/sci_community.html)

The philanthropic arm of the Houston, Texas-based Service Corporation International (SCI), a company of funeral homes and cemeteries, seeks to "protect families from the senseless tragedies that sometimes lead them" to use the Corporation's services. SCI supports four community service programs: Escape School, teaching children how to avoid abduction; Smart & Safe Seniors, providing seniors with information on a variety of criminal activities of which they are targets; support for a traveling Vietnam War Memorial; and free funeral services for police officers and fire fighters. SCI's Web site provides contact information and more details on these programs.

Shadowline Inc. (NC) (http://www.shadowline-lingerie.com/donate.asp)

Shadowline, as a maker of women's intimate apparel, focuses its charitable contributions program on organizations that deal with women's issues. The Morganton, North Carolina-based company has established its Because We Care donation program in order to assist a large number of nonprofit organizations and charities centered on women. Through its Because We Care program, Shadowline donates gift certificates for women's merchandise to nonprofit fundraisers. An application for organizations interested in these donations can be downloaded in PDF format from the Shadowline Web site.

Shaw's Supermarkets (MA)
(http://www.shaws.com/about_us/community_commitment.html)

Shaw's Supermarket Community Commitment program supports the quality of life in the six New England states of company operation. Although Shaw's Supermarkets primarily makes donations to specified organizations on an annual basis, the company does make other grants. Shaw's supports numerous organizations in the company's market area by participating in charitable grants, community relations activities, sponsorships and public relations activities. There are set priorities, funding sources, guidelines, and goals for each of these specific programs. The company's Web site is limited and does not give any specific information on the company's formal grantmaking program.

Shell Oil Company (TX)
(http://www.countonshell.com/community/involvement/shell_foundation.html)
Founded in 1953, the Shell Oil Company Foundation of Houston, Texas, "focuses on making a difference in the communities where Shell people work and live." Broad-based support is given to organizations falling in several areas. There is a health and human services category, with a focus on the United Way and hospitals that service large numbers of Shell employees. Much educational support goes to university departmental programs, matching grants, and secondary education. Money for culture and the arts is distributed to various established symphony, opera, and theater groups; museums; libraries; and zoos. Civic contributions go to local and national organizations involved in community improvement, justice and law, and research and conservation. The Foundation also supports groups working for equal opportunity. The Shell Web site is available in Shockwave, Flash, and HTML. Once visitors arrive at the home page, they should select Community and Environment to find information on community relations. The page on the Foundation includes an address to contact for more information or to submit applications. There is also information on employee volunteer programs, a list of selected grants under Constituent Relations, and information on the Shell Youth Training Academy, which provides Los Angeles high school students with post-secondary career opportunities and training.

Siemens Foundation (NY) (http://www.siemens-foundation.org)
The Siemens Foundation of New York City "embodies the Siemens commitment to education and research and builds on the Company's history of encouraging and supporting young talent throughout the United States." These goals are accomplished by awarding scholarships for higher education to gifted science, math, and technology students in the United States. Foundation programs include an Advanced Placement Award, which gives scholarships to students scoring highest on the Advanced Placement tests for math and science courses and to schools that have greatly improved their scores. It also runs the Siemens Westinghouse Science and Technology Competition, which gives hundreds of thousands of dollars in scholarships to the winners of this research-based competition. There are extensive descriptions of each program, announcements and profiles of past winners, and lists of what each award entitles.

Silicon Graphics, Inc. (CA) (http://www.sgi.com/company_info/community/)
A leader in high performance computing technology, SGI of Mountain View, California, is dedicated to "being an active partner in the continuous improvement of our community . . . [through] strategic investments in health and human services, education, the arts, and the environment." The Employee Matching Gift program matches employees' contributions to education organizations up to $2,500 a year, 100 percent of gifts to health and human services, and 50 percent of gifts to the arts and the environment. The company also has a program to support volunteerism in its employees and internal environmental and diversity efforts. SGI and the Tech Museum of Innovation distribute the B.R.I.T.E. (Breakthrough Results Integrating Technology and Education) award annually to recognize a teacher and a school district that have developed a technology program with positive, replicable results in topics such as increasing student attendance, retention, and academic achievement. There is a downloadable PDF file with the award application. The giving program does not consider unsolicited proposals.

Skadden Fellowship Foundation (NY) (http://216.44.201.143/skadweb/siteindex.htm)
Created in New York City in 1988, the Skadden Fellowship Foundation was formed to "affirm the firm's commitment to public interest law." The program awards 25 fellowships a year to graduating law students and outgoing judicial clerks. The fellows find a sponsoring public interest organization that they will spend two years working for. These organizations serve clients including the poor, elderly, homeless, disabled, and those deprived of their human or civil rights. The fellowships are awarded in December and begin the

following fall. The site includes a description of the application process, a number to call for more information, a list of the trustees, a demographic breakdown by law school and by sponsoring organization, and a list of fellows.

SLM Holding Corporation (VA) (http://www.salliemae.com/community/index.html)

SLM Holding Corporations, better known as Sallie Mae, owns and manages loans for college students. Sallie Mae's philanthropic mission continues to be that of "making college accessible because it strengthens relationships within our communities and touches society as a whole." Based in Reston, Virginia, the company has loan servicing centers in Killeen, Texas; Panama City, Florida; Lawrence, Kansas; and Wilkes-Barre, Pennsylvania. These are the communities where Sallie Mae tends to center its community giving. The Sallie Mae Trust for Education focuses on education about financing higher education, promoting volunteerism, and encouraging community service. Grant guidelines for the Trust are provided on the Sallie Mae Web site. The Corporation's community support takes the form of school mentoring, United Way campaigns, and fund raising sporting events. The Sallie Mae Cup rewards athletic and academic achievement in the form of block scholarship funds to area high schools in Washington, D.C.; Philadelphia; Pennsylvania; and Kansas City, Missouri. More information about specific programs and contact information is available online.

Solectron (CA) (http://www.solectron.com)

Solectron, a worldwide provider of electronics manufacturing services, has locations around the world, but its corporate headquarters are in Milpitas, California. Solectron's commitment extends "beyond customers, into its communities, demonstrating the company's belief in social responsibility [and] striving to be an asset to its communities." The company's Web site has a list of organizations and programs Solectron works with and supports in the areas of education, human services, the environment, and the arts. The site provides contact information for the corporate offices but does not have any information about applying for grants or receiving more information.

SOM Foundation (IL) (http://www.som.com/html/som_foundation.html)

The SOM Foundation of Chicago, Illinois, is the philanthropic arm of Skidmore, Owings & Merrill LLP. The Foundation's mission is "to help young architects and engineers broaden their professional education, instill in them a heightened sense of their responsibility to improve the quality of the built and natural environments, and encourage them to appreciate the influences that place-making, culture, and technology have on the design of buildings and their settings." This end is met by awarding traveling scholarships to undergraduate and graduate students of accredited architecture schools. The Architecture Traveling Fellowship, the Interior Architecture Traveling Fellowship Program, the Urban Design Traveling Fellowship, and United Kingdom Award grant different size awards to students of these disciplines. The Foundation also awards the Chicago Institute for Architecture and Urbanism Award, which "encourage(s) writing and research on the question of how architecture, urban design, and physical planning can contribute to improving the quality of life of the American city." Applicants must be nominated by their accredited school. There is a phone number for inquiries about program specifics.

Sonoco Products Company (SC) (http://www.sonoco.com/sonoco_foundation.htm)

The Sonoco Foundation, the philanthropic conduit for South Carolina-based Sonoco Products Company, focuses its giving on education, health and welfare, arts and culture, and the environment in locations where the company has operations. The majority of its grants are awarded to U.S. institutions with a local, rather than a national, perspective. Visitors to the company's Web site will find general policy, program, and application guidelines, the grant application format, program and support limitations, and contact information.

Southwire Company (GA) (http://www.southwire.com/community)

Southwire, a wire and cable manufacturer, supports education and environmental programs in several counties in Georgia, Illinois, Mississippi, Alabama, and Kentucky. The company's Web site describes its education grant and environmental award programs and provides online application forms.

Sovereign Bank Foundation (PA)
(http://www.sovereignbank.com/welcome/community/apply4grant.html)
In 1988, the Sovereign Bank Foundation was incorporated in Reading, Pennsylvania, to "Improve the quality of life in communities served by Sovereign Bank, Improve community services available to customers, employees, shareholders and vendors, and strive to be known as a vital, ethical corporate Foundation with a positive vision for the future of our communities." The primary interest of the Foundation is housing for at-risk children and families in the Foundation's areas of operation. However, the Foundation also supports health/hunger relief, social services, community culture, development of minority populations, and micro-business lending in urban environments. The Foundation places a higher priority on special programs that are not a part of the ongoing maintenance or operation of the organization. Also, the Foundation is interested in granting seed money for pilot programs with potential to be self-sufficient programs, capital projects that stimulate or provide leverage for additional funding, and capital and equipment needs. The Foundation's Web site lists detailed sections on application procedures, granting policies, obligations of grant recipients, deadlines, and contact information.

Sprint Corporation (KS) (http://www3.sprint.com/sprint/overview/commun.html)
Commitment to community, with an emphasis on "support of local and regional organizations in which the corporation has a major presence," is the basis for Sprint's corporate philanthropy. Through the Sprint Foundation and its direct corporate giving program, Sprint supports education, arts and culture, community improvement, and youth development. The Community Service area of the company's Web site includes information on Sprint's employee giving programs, a brief overview of the Sprint Foundation's activities, application guidelines, and contact information. An online version of the company's annual report is also available and can be downloaded as a PDF file.

Stage Stores, Inc. (TX) (http://www.stagestoresinc.com/companyinfo/community.htm)
Stage Stores, Inc supports the communities in which it operates and its employees live. Stage co-sponsors a variety of local events, sports teams, state fairs, and rodeos. The company also makes donations to children's organizations, schools, hospitals, and medical research programs. Stage Stores occasionally creates fashion-related events to help raise money for charitable causes. Stage Stores, Inc. also supports United Way and helps in disaster relief efforts in its communities. Those interested in seeking support from the company can either contact a local store manager or e-mail or call one of the contacts listed on the Web site.

Stahl Construction Company (MN)
(http://www.stahlconstruction.com/pages/community_connection1.htm)
The charitable giving arm of the Stahl Construction Company was formed in 1998 in Minnetonka, Minnesota. The Stahl Giving Program's goals are to "impact the image of the company in the community, enhance employee relations, keep our community vital, and achieve results within the organizations that receive our contributions." As a member of the Minnesota Keystone Program, Stahl donates a percentage of its profits to charitable, educational, and cultural organizations, and plans and performs a yearly special service project. Organizations impacted by the Stahl Giving Program are listed on the company's Web site along with a contact email address for more information about the Program.

The Starbucks Foundation (WA) (http://www.starbucks.com/aboutus/csr.asp)
The Starbucks Foundation, based in Seattle, Washington, was launched in 1997 with an initial contribution of $500,000 from Starbucks chairman and CEO Howard Schultz. It is supported in part by donations from Starbucks Coffee Company, donations from the general public, and Schultz's earnings from his book. "Mindful of the historical connections between drinking coffee and enjoying a good read," and understanding the essential role

reading skills play in our daily lives, the Foundation's first area of service is literacy. In addition to monetary support of literacy initiatives, the Foundation has also built its giving program around the participation of Starbucks partners by asking them to apply for grants on behalf of local community literacy organizations. The Foundation is also involved in the Doonesbury program to create products that will benefit local literacy programs across America, where all net proceeds are donated to local literacy programs through the combined efforts of The Starbucks Foundation, the Trudeau-Pauley Foundation, and the Andrews McMeel Universal Foundation. The Foundation also supports Starbucks' efforts to provide assistance to coffee growing countries of the world.

State Farm Companies Foundation (IL)
(http://www.statefarm.com/foundati/foundati.htm)
The State Farm Companies Foundation of Bloomington, Illinois, was created in 1963 to address the many requests from nonprofits for financial support that State Farm was receiving. Now the Foundation focuses its giving on scholarships and grants to colleges and universities, although it does award limited support to other organizations in locations with large employee populations. Scholarship programs include those for doctoral students writing dissertations on insurance and/or risk management, high potential business-related college students, and high school seniors demonstrating excellence whose parents work for State Farm. Other scholarships are fully administered by other national organizations, including the Hispanic, Native American, and National Merit related scholarships. Non-educational grants are given to community, human service, and health agencies that benefit large populations of State Farm employees. Application guidelines for grant consideration are listed. Scholarship eligibility is described and applications are online for those awards administered by the Foundation. Contact information is provided for outside organizations that administer Foundation scholarships.

State Street Foundation (MA)
(http://www.statestreet.com/stst/statestreet.nsf/Framesets/CommunityAffairs)
The State Street Foundation is the nonprofit corporate giving program of State Street that has been providing grants to qualifying charities in the Boston area since 1977. State Street was founded in 1792 and provides information services, custody, securities lending, investment management, performance and analytic measurement, cash management, and recordkeeping. The Foundation manages the allocation and distribution of most of the company's corporate contributions. Its primary mission is to help the urban poor build a better future. In an effort to globalize its corporate philanthropy, the Foundation has a Global Philanthropy Program, which addresses the local needs of the communities at State Street's worldwide locations. The Global Philanthropy program provides grants primarily for education and job skills training, affordable housing development and neighborhood revitalization, youth programs, and to address other community needs that its local sites deem appropriate. The Foundation's Web site contains a summary of community support.

Sun Microsystems (CA) (http://www.sun.com/corporateoverview/corpaffairs/giving.html)
Through its Community Development Grants Program, the Sun Microsystems Foundation, Inc. "invests in communities that are often characterized by low income, high unemployment, and disturbing school drop-out rates." Grants are awarded in the areas of education (grades 7–12 in the United States and secondary schools S1-S6 in Scotland) and employment and job development in the southern San Francisco Bay Area, California, the Merrimack Valley of Massachusetts, and the West Lothian District of Scotland. Visitors to the company's Web site will find information on the Program's funding criteria (including limitations), application guidelines, and an online version of the company's annual report.

Symantec Corporation (OR) (http://www.symantec.com/corporate/community.html)
Headquartered in Eugene, Oregon, the Symantec Corporation sponsors four areas of charitable giving: corporate grants, software donations, matching employee gifts, and used equipment donations. Begun in 1995, these programs are designed to provide aid locally in communities where Symantec is located, in the areas of education, community, social and

human services, the arts and humanities, and the environment. Symantec provides complete grant and donation guidelines, instructions and limitations for each type of support, and a contact address for proposals on its Web site.

Target Foundation (MN) (http://www.targetcorp.com/community/targetfoundation.asp)

The Minneapolis, Minnesota-based Target Foundation is the philanthropic arm of the Target Corporation, formerly known as the Dayton Hudson Corporation. The Target family of stores—including Mervyn's, Dayton's, Marshall Field's, and Hudson—has been supporting community programs through corporate contributions since 1962. The Target Corporation's contribution program divides its grantmaking between national and local programs and by areas of interest within those programs. Nationally, the Foundation supports assorted institutions, from the Washington Monument Restoration to St. Jude's Children's Research Hospital. Locally, giving is centered in three areas: making the arts more accessible; providing education initiatives to help students, teachers, and schools; and supporting agencies that strengthen family life. Additionally, the Target Foundation funds arts and social action programs in local Target communities, with a special emphasis on the Minnesota and the Twin Cities area. Applications for grants are filed with and distributed by individual stores and are due between February 1st and November 1st. Currently the company is focusing local giving on family-oriented arts experiences and programs that prevent family/domestic violence. Select Target Stores under the Community Involvement menu to access corporate giving information, application guidelines for local giving, and descriptions of selected national grants.

Tesoro Petroleum (TX) (http://www.tesoropetroleum.com/community.html)

The Tesoro Corporate Contribution Committee is the charitable giving arm of Tesoro Petroleum Corporation and its subsidiaries, including Tesoro Hawaii, Tesoro Northwest, and Tesoro Alaska. Based in San Antonio, Texas, the Tesoro Corporate Contribution Committee brings attention to the needs of the communities it serves and the programs it supports by focusing the available resources. The Tesoro Corporate Contribution Committee is made up of a cross-section of employees with subsidiary committees for local decisions. Tesoro supports programs that focus on the environment and education and are located in the communities in which the company has business interests. The Committee awards grants for both program and capital improvement projects. Deadlines and application procedures are available on the Tesoro Web site, as is a contact information list. The site also provides information about Tesoro community partnerships and employee volunteer programs.

Texaco Inc. (NY) (http://www.texaco.com/support/index.html)

Texaco, a provider of energy and energy products worldwide, supports programs that prepare children for the study of math and science. The Texaco Foundation makes grants through two specific programs: Education and Music and Science Discovery. A third, broad program provides funding for arts and culture, primary healthcare for children, the environment, and economic education in countries where Texaco operates. The company's Web site describes the Foundation's giving philosophy, provides guidelines and application instructions, and includes press releases of recent donations and scholarships.

Texas Instruments Foundation (TX)
(http://www.ti.com/corp/docs/company/citizen/foundation/index.shtml)

The Texas Instruments Foundation is the principal charitable vehicle of Texas Instruments Incorporated, a digital signal processing solutions company based in Dallas, Texas. The Foundation supports educational and research institutions, as well as organizations and projects in communities where the company has major facilities. In addition to education and research, funding is available for health, welfare, civic, and cultural projects committed to systemic change. The Foundation area of the company's Web site describes the Foundation's giving strategy, provides grant guidelines, and offers examples of funded programs.

Textron Inc. (RI) (http://www.textron.com/profile/community.html)

The Providence, Rhode Island-based Textron Corporate Giving Program works to "help make [its] community a better place for employees to live and work." Through programs and services that serve the educational needs of women and minorities, strengthen communities, improve race relations, and fund educational facilities, for example, Textron strives to give back to its communities. The Community Service portion of the Textron Web page presents a select number of examples of projects and funding the corporation supports; contact information is available in the Fast Facts area of the site.

Thomson Financial Services (MA) (http://www.tfn.com/community/index.html)

Founded in November of 1980, the Boston-based Thomson Financial Services is a leading provider of quality financial information, research, analysis, and software products to the worldwide investment and corporate communities. Its work in the community focuses primarily on child and youth development, learning, and leadership development. Education initiatives include forming partnerships with primary and secondary schools, and internships and after-school jobs at the secondary school and higher education levels in the communities where Thomson does business. Thomson also donates used computers and other office equipment to local public schools, builds technology infrastructures that make local public schools Internet-ready, and creates volunteer programs and opportunities that facilitate employee community involvement, such as a matching gifts program and a paid day of leave for volunteerism. Visit Thomson's site for more information on its programs, contact information, and an online feedback form.

3Com Corporation (CA) (http://www.3com.com/inside/comm_affairs)

3Com is a leader in computer networking that connects people and organizations around the world. As a logical extension of its business mission, 3Com seeks to reinforce connections where communications and community intersect. 3Com manages this by donating networking equipment, sharing the company's expertise, and encouraging community investment where 3Com employees live and work. 3Com also maintains an active employee-matching program called Share Our Success, where U.S. employees have the opportunity to have any annual gift up to $1,000 matched by the company. Finally, the company makes many donations of company product to qualifying organizations. Visit the company's Web site to view selected past grants, grant specifications, application procedures, and contact information.

Tom's of Maine, Inc. (ME) (http://www.tomsofmaine.com/mission/grants.htm)

The family-owned company, Tom's of Maine, produces natural toothpaste and other health and beauty products. The Kennebunk, Maine-based company's mission is to "address community concerns in Maine and around the globe, by devoting a portion of our time, talents, and resources to the environment, human needs, the arts, and education." The community giving program focuses on the environment, human need, arts, and education. Grants usually range from $500–$5,000, however larger grants are sometimes awarded. The company also encourages its employees to use up to five percent of their paid workweek volunteering in a nonprofit setting. The Foundation's Web site will allow you to view previous grants lists, detailed grant guidelines, interesting information about the company and its products, and contact information.

Tops Markets, Inc. (NY) (http://www1.topsmarkets.com/About_Tops/communit/communit.htm)

Tops Markets, in Williamsville, New York, centers its philanthropic giving in the communities in New York, Philadelphia, and Ohio where it does business. Much of Tops Markets' charitable donations are to food banks and pantries; a form on its Web site can be printed out to request or make donations. Additionally, Tops Markets runs a number of community initiatives, such as the Good Neighbor Award, limited to the Niagara County community in New York state; donations for collected register receipts; and a program providing schools with funds in exchange for recycled plastic grocery bags. The Tops Markets Web site provides visitors with descriptions of each of these programs, links to community resources, and contact information for further details.

Toshiba America Foundation (NY) (http://www.toshiba.com/about/taf.html)

As the principal charitable arm of Toshiba America, Inc., a leading consumer electronics company, the Toshiba America Foundation focuses on the improvement of classroom teaching in grades 7–12, especially in the areas of science, mathematics, and technology. Although the Foundation welcomes proposals from communities across the United States, it "feels a special responsibility toward those communities where the Toshiba America group companies have a corporate presence." In addition to information about the Foundation's current program interests, the company's attractive, well-organized Web site provides a summary of projects funded by the Foundation during the last 12 months, detailed instructions on preparing a grant application, a proposal format outline and sample proposal cover page, and contact information.

Toyota USA Foundation (CA) (http://www.toyota.com/html/about/community_care/)

With a primary emphasis on improving the teaching and learning of mathematics and science, the Toyota USA Foundation is committed to improving the quality of K–12 education in the United States. Grants are made to accredited colleges, universities, community colleges, vocational or trade schools, and to nonprofit organizations engaged in pre-collegiate math and/or science education; K–12 public and private schools may not apply directly to the Foundation, though they may be the recipient of an independent nonprofit agency's funding request. In addition to contact information and a general overview of its activities, visitors to the Foundation's Web site will find detailed application guidelines and restrictions, highlights of recent grants and a list of past Foundation grantees, and a grant application form.

Trimble Navigation (CA) (http://www.trimble.com)

Trimble is committed to "supporting the community. Trimble responds to societal needs, challenges, and opportunities by providing assistance to responsible nonprofit organizations of many kinds." Trimble contributes funds to local organizations that work in Silicon Valley communities. Trimble also supports global environmental, educational, and social programs through product donations. The site provides a contact address for those interested in learning more about the program. There are also several articles on the site about Trimble projects and interests.

TRW Foundation, Inc. (OH)
(http://www.trw.com/about/main/1,1015,1_1152_1182^3^1182^1182,00.html)

The TRW Foundation, located in Cleveland, Ohio, is the primary philanthropic arm of TRW, Inc. It supports organizations of interest to its operations, customers, and employees by serving the needs of the public in its communities. TRW contributions are primarily aimed to advance the well-being and the quality of life of employees and neighbors in TRW communities, stimulate economic and social progress, foster new knowledge through research, help to increase the quality and availability of education, and promote public understanding of the economic system and the role of private enterprise in that system. The three major elements of the Foundation's giving program are support of education with a particular emphasis on early childhood education, support of United Way, and support of community-based organizations. Grant guidelines and deadlines are detailed on the site. To apply, organizations must send a brief letter of proposal. Information on what to include can be found on the Web site. Additionally the site contains a list of communities that define the geographic scope of TRW and contact information for the Foundation staff.

Tupperware U.S., Inc. (FL)
(http://www.tupperware.com/company/headlines/giveachild.asp)

Tupperware established its charitable giving arm, Give a Child a Chance, in 1995. The mission of the organization is "to provide children, especially those from disadvantaged situations, with resources to combat the negative affects of poverty, neglect and abuse."

Tupperware's objective is to establish long-term alliances with children's groups in a number of countries: in the United States, it supports the Boys & Girls Clubs of America. The Tupperware Give a Child a Chance Web site is best viewed with the Netscape browser.

Union Pacific Foundation (NE) (http://www.up.com/found/)

Union Pacific Foundation is the philanthropic arm of Union Pacific Corporation and its subsidiaries, Union Pacific Railroad and Union Pacific Technologies. Originally created as the Union Pacific Railroad Foundation, the Foundation has distributed funds since 1959 to organizations for the improvement of quality of life in communities served by Union Pacific. To this end, the Omaha, Nebraska-based Foundation focuses activity in geographic areas where there is a significant Union Pacific presence. Areas of interest include education, health and human services, community and civic, and fine arts. Since organizations must be located in communities served by Union Pacific to be considered for funding, the site contains a downloadable map of operations. Visitors to the site can also request grant application forms via e-mail and find press releases and contact information.

United Airlines Foundation (IL) (http://www.ual.com/site/primary/0,10017,1367,00.html)

The United Airlines Foundation of Chicago, Illinois, was formed in 1952 to "support charitable organizations, as well as programs and activities that improve the communities where [their] customers and employees live and work." Giving is focused in five areas: education, health, arts and culture, volunteerism, and diversity. The foundation suggests that interested organizations become familiar with the succinct descriptions and partial grants lists that are included for each of these categories in order to discover whether the goals are truly compatible. Giving is concentrated in the airlines' six U.S. hubs: Chicago, Illinois; Denver, Colorado; Los Angeles, California; New York City; San Francisco, California; and Washington, D.C. The site includes application guidelines and restrictions, mail and e-mail addresses to send applications to, and descriptions of the philanthropic areas of interest.

United Parcel Service of America, Inc. (GA) (http://www.community.ups.com)

The United Parcel Service (UPS) is committed to making a difference in communities throughout the country. The company has a number of different programs to address this goal. The UPS Foundation, located in Atlanta, Georgia, was founded in 1951 and funds "programs that support family and workplace literacy, food distribution and increased nationwide volunteerism." The Region/District Grant Program is one in which UPS employees nominate local organizations, some of which eventually receive grants between $10,000 and $100,000. The Neighbor to Neighbor volunteer program has created volunteer banks at every UPS branch across the country. The company is a major supporter of literacy programs and has contributed greatly to a national network dedicated to distributing food to the needy. The UPS Community Service Scholarship Program grants $5,000 scholarships to needy students who, in return, perform 150 hours of community service. Many internal programs include the Community Internship Program, an intense four-week community service training for managers, and a large Welfare to Work program. The site includes a list of organizations that the company has partnered with, a Speakers Bureau collection of executive speeches, features on many internal award winners and programs, and an online application to volunteer for one of the funded groups.

United Technologies (CT) (http://www.utc.com/commun/index.htm)

United Technologies (UTC), a diversified $23 billion Fortune 500 conglomerate, makes grants to tax-exempt 501(c)(3) organizations in the areas of education, human services, cultural arts, and civic involvement. UTC focuses its grantmaking in communities where it has a substantial corporate presence. The application form available on the Web site must be filled out and submitted by June of the current year for projects to be considered for the next year's budget. The Community Involvement area of the United Technologies Web site provides visitors with general descriptions of each area of support, guidelines and limitations for grant and matching gift programs, summaries of funded projects in UTC's program areas, and appropriate contact information.

Unocal Corporation (CA) (http://www.unocal.com/responsibility)

The Unocal Corporation, based in El Segundo, California, includes its Unocal Foundation Programs on the Community Support and Humanitarian Assistance page of its Web site. Unocal sponsors various programs: Sons & Daughters Scholarship Program, Education Matching Program, and other national and international education initiatives, including fellowships and 4-H after school programs. In the United States, these programs mainly benefit the children of Unocal national employees. The Corporation's Web site does not include specific grant information for grantseekers, though there is a Corporate Responsibility Report with further details on Unocal's corporate giving.

U.S. Bancorp Piper Jaffray Companies Inc. (MN) (http://www.piperjaffray.com/pj/pj_ci.asp)

U.S. Bancorp Piper Jaffray, an investment firm based in Minneapolis, Minnesota, contributes to civic and charitable causes through the U.S. Bancorp Piper Jaffray Companies Foundation and a direct corporate giving program. The Foundation awards general operating and capital grants for programs that support families working toward self-sufficiency and the development and education of children. The Community Involvement area of the company's Web site describes its philanthropic activities and provides Foundation grant guidelines, an application form (in PDF format) to download, and contact information.

USX Foundation, Inc. (PA) (http://www.usx.com/corp/usxfoundation/usxfound.htm)

USX Corporation, headquartered in Pittsburgh, Pennsylvania, is a producer of oil, natural gas, and steel products. The USX Foundation was founded in Delaware in 1953 as the United States Steel Foundation to support educational, scientific, charitable, civic, cultural, and health needs. The Foundation awards grants to organizations for education, health and human services, and public, cultural, and scientific affairs. The Foundation area of USX's Web site provides a summary of giving, including financial statements; describes grant programs and lists recipients by giving category; includes grant application guidelines; and lists trustees, officers, and staff.

Verizon Foundation (NY) (http://foundation.verizon.com/)

Verizon Communications was founded in New York through a conglomeration of Bell Atlantic and GTE in hopes of creating a new standard in communications. Shortly after, The Verizon Foundation was formed with a mission of "transforming the way the private, public, and non profit sectors work together in building collaborative partnerships." The Foundation's grantmaking program is divided into four areas. E-Solutions is a program that focuses on training, education, and understanding of new and innovative communication software. The Good Citizen's program encourages past and present employees to put their natural skills to use in the community and lend a hand to issues facing today's nonprofit. The in-kind gift program provides donated computer and other office equipment to qualifying organizations. Finally, the Grant program makes monetary grants to innovative and original organizations or programs that hold a strong interest in literacy, mathematics and science. Visitors to the Verizon Foundation's bilingual (English and Spanish) Web site will find information on e-training and e-partners, a series of best-in-class technology success stories, and a comprehensive technology resource guide with links to more than 350 online resources supporting technology applications. The Verizon Foundation Web site also includes grant guidelines, an online grant eligibility quiz, and a technology needs assessment section to help nonprofits in applying for grants online, which is the only way applications may be submitted.

Vulcan Scholarships, Inc. (AL) (http://www.vulcaninc.com/plt0p04.htm)

Vulcan Scholarships, Inc. was created in 1984 by Vulcan Inc. of Foley, Alabama, to "influence qualified Foley and Robertsdale High School students' career paths by providing financial assistance in the pursuit of study in a qualified engineering curriculum." Official applications are available to graduating seniors at the two specific high schools in mid-February of each year. There are three scholarships awarded each year, and they are determined by academic achievement, leadership, extracurricular activities, demonstrated commitment to engineering, and demonstrated financial need. The site includes past and current recipients, applications guidelines, and details on each scholarship.

Walgreen Co. (IL) (http://www.walgreens.com/about/community/)

The corporate headquarters of pharmacy chain Walgreen Co. is in Deerfield, Illinois. The company is "committed to improving our customers' lives across America." Major grants have been made to health-related national organizations, such as the American Heart Association, the American Cancer Society, the Juvenile Diabetes Foundation, and the United Way. The company makes donations to support education, helps communities after disasters, and sponsors a tutoring program called Walgreen's One-On-One in five cities across the country. This mentoring and educational assistance program benefits both from financial support and from large numbers of employee volunteers. The Web site includes a selected grants list, information on contacting the One-On-One program near you, and a general address for all corporate inquiries.

Wal-Mart Foundation (AR) (http://www.walmartfoundation.org/)

The Wal-Mart Foundation of Arkansas "serves Wal-Mart Stores, Inc. with stewardship, compassion and integrity: by developing and implementing programs that support children and families through education, health, and economic development in our local communities." Ninety-seven percent of funding is distributed locally through Wal-Mart stores and SAMs Clubs. Currently, that funding is being focused in four areas: education, health and human services, economic involvement, and environment. Education includes assorted scholarships, mostly given out by each store, for area students; Wal-Mart employees; and exceptional technology and manufacturing students. There are also Teacher of the Year awards and a Vocational and Career Training program. Economic development includes business and leadership awards, support for women and minority-owned businesses, and programs to attract new industry to communities. Environmental efforts include two grants available from stores; one for clean air and water and the other for schools. Visitors to the site will find application guidelines for specific scholarships and programs and descriptions of many current projects. It is made clear that a majority of grants are given by local stores, and potential applicants should contact their stores to see if they are participating.

Wells Fargo & Company (CA) (http://www.wellsfargo.com/cra/craltr1.jhtml)

Wells Fargo, the San Francisco-based banking and financial services concern, directs the bulk of its corporate giving to three areas: community development, especially programs that provide affordable housing, provide job training, revitalize or stabilize low– and moderate– income communities, or promote economic development; pre–K–12 education, with a focus on math, literacy, and the history of the American West; and human services, especially organizations whose work in child care, health services and education, and basic needs assistance benefits low– and moderate– income individuals. Geographically, the company's grantmaking is concentrated west of the Mississippi in the states of Arizona, California, Colorado, Idaho, Nevada, New Mexico, Oregon, Texas, Utah, and Washington. Visitors to the Community Reinvestment section of the Wells Fargo Web site will find general program information, application guidelines and procedures, and contact information. The site also offers information about the company's $45 billion/10-year Community Reinvestment Lending and Investment Leadership Pledge.

Wendy's International, Inc. (OH)
(http://www.wendys.com/community/community_frame.html)

Wendy's In Touch with the Community program holds a number of varied programs to support communities nationally. Established in 1992, the Dave Thomas Foundation for Adoption works to raise awareness for the more than 100,000 children waiting for adoption and to educate prospective parents about the adoption process. Dave Thomas was adopted at birth and has become a national advocate for the cause. Wendy's High School Heisman program seeks to recognize America's most outstanding and well-rounded high school seniors in America. The company's Web site lists past recipients of the Heisman reward and information on how to get involved.

West Group Community Partnership Program (MN)
(http://www.westgroup.com/newsinfo/community/Welcome.html)
West Group is "the foremost provider of information to the U.S. legal market" and is head-quartered in Eagan, Minnesota. The company makes charitable contributions and encourages community involvement of employees in communities where West Group has major facilities and a substantial employee presence. West Group awards contributions to non-profit organizations; builds community partnerships; makes in-kind contributions of products, property, and services; has a matching gifts program; sponsors charitable fund drives; and encourages volunteerism among employees. Special emphasis is given to the Twin Cites of Minneapolis and St. Paul and surrounding communities, and priority consideration is given to nonprofits involving West Group employee volunteers. Visitors to the site will find application instructions for cash grants and contact information.

Westinghouse Foundation (PA) (http://www.westinghouse.com)
Located in Pittsburgh, Pennsylvania, the Westinghouse Charitable Giving Program "serves as the principal funding entity for the company's social investments. The Program makes charitable contributions to nonprofit organizations in Southwestern Pennsylvania and other communities throughout the United States where Westinghouse has a presence." Its areas of focus are health and welfare, education, and civic and social services. Within these areas, Westinghouse encourages programs that meet the needs of special populations, such as the disadvantaged, the young, and the elderly. The site explains the specifics in the areas West-inghouse funds and the restrictions of the grants. There is a list of information to be included by those applying for a grant, as well as an address to mail the completed materials to.

Weyerhaeuser Company Foundation (WA) (http://www.weyerhaeuser.com/community)
Weyerhaeuser Company, a supplier of forest products based in Washington State, established the Weyerhaeuser Company Foundation in 1948 to improve the quality of life in company communities and to increase understanding of forests and the products they provide. The Foundation supports education and programs that promote responsible natural resource management and dedicates 30 percent of its giving to industry-related projects. The Foundation area of the company's Web site describes these giving activities and provides guidelines, a list of eligible locations, and an electronic application form.

Whirlpool Foundation (MI)
(http://www.whirlpoolcorp.com/whr/foundation/foundation.html)
Through the Whirlpool Foundation, Whirlpool Corporation, the appliance manufacturer, seeks to "improve the quality of family life primarily in [Whirlpool] communities, world-wide." The Foundation particularly likes to partner with "organizations that target women and family life issues." Visitors to the company's Web site will find general descriptions of the Foundation's areas of interest, information on the Foundation's women's studies research, a sampling of recent grants, and contact information.

WHO Foundation (TX) (http://whofoundation.org)
The WHO Foundation of Dallas, Texas, was created in 1993 by the chairman of BeautiControl, Inc. The mission of the Foundation is to: "encourage women everywhere to help others through local community service; support organizations dedicated to women and children; and educate individuals about health and education issues." The Foundation publishes two booklets on health and beauty issues for cancer patients that are donated to cancer patients and cancer related organizations and distributed to others for a suggested donation. The Foundation also awards grants to specific projects and programs dealing with educational and health issues of women and children. The site offers application guidelines, a downloadable application in PDF format, and information on Foundation publications. The Foundation does not accept electronic applications and will next be accepting applications for the 2001 grant period.

Whole Foods Market, Inc. (TX)
(http://www.wholefoodsmarket.com/company/99contributions.html)

Located in Austin, Texas, Whole Foods contributes to nonprofit and educational organizations and compensates team members for time spent in community service. Past donations have been to organization such as public radio stations, museums, river and creek cleanups, hospices, literary councils, schools, recycling organizations, soup kitchens, playground rebuilding projects, and organizations promoting organic agriculture. The company's Web site also has descriptions of some of the programs Whole Foods has been involved with in the past. In the Community & Contributions section of its Web site, Whole Foods details a number of representative projects and causes it has funded and presents a brief financial table. Contact information is posted under the Store Locations link.

Wild Oats Markets, Inc. (CO) (http://www.wildoats.com/take_action/wild_giving.html)

The Wild Oats Markets Giving Program, located in Boulder, Colorado, is "dedicated to helping nonprofit, grassroots organizations who have small budgets & big hearts." The Program focuses on motivated innovative groups who strive to make the world a better place, which is defined as a place where the environment is preserved and replenished, the community is strong, health is a priority, organic farming is cherished, and where all living beings are respected. Wild Oats is particularly interested in supporting organizations within its communities whose philosophies are similar to those of Wild Oats. The Giving Program prioritizes environmental, educational, agricultural, animal rights, health, humanitarian, and international organizations. The Web site explains a variety of store-level and national programs that the Program offers, but no contact or application information is provided.

The Windermere Foundation (WA)
(http://home.windermere.com/about/foundation/foundationhome.htm)

The Windermere Foundation was created by Windermere Real Estate for the purpose of raising and providing funds to support homeless assistance programs throughout the Northwest. Since 1989, more than $3 million has been raised to provide shelter, clothing, food, and other services to homeless families. Every time a Windermere Real Estate associate sells a home, a portion of the commission is donated directly to the Foundation. Additional contributions are generated through donations from Windermere agents, employees, owners and managers, as well as from the public. Social services agencies that help homeless families can apply for funds by contacting their neighborhood Windermere office for information. Visit the Web site for a grant recipient list and contact information.

Working Assets Corporate Giving Program (CA) (http://www.workingassets.com)

Working Assets Funding Service, based in San Francisco, is a long distance, credit card, Internet services and broadcasting company "that was created to build a world that is more just, humane and environmentally sustainable." Created in 1985, Working Assets Funding Service donates a portion of its revenue to nonprofit groups working for peace, human rights, equality, education, and the environment. The company also serves as a strong political force, dedicated to giving its customers the opportunity to speak out on critical public issues. A percentage of Working Assets' revenue is placed in a donations pool for annual distribution. Donations come from sales, not profits; therefore, donations are made whether or not Working Assets makes a profit. Customers can nominate nonprofit groups to receive funding each year. After an independent foundation evaluates the effectiveness of the hundreds of nominees, Working Assets Funding Service employees and board of directors select 60 groups for the annual donations ballot. At the end of the year, customers vote on how to distribute the donations among the 60 groups. The site contains information about groups' programs and services. Visitors can also access WorkingForChange, an information portal where people can access news, shopping (five percent of the purchase price is donated to nonprofits when a product is purchased from one of the online merchants), donation, activism, volunteer, and broadcasting services through a central online hub. Visitors to the site will find a list of donation recipients and contact information.

WSFS Financial Corporation (DE) (http://www.wsfsbank.com/communityservice.asp)

The Wilmington Savings Fund Society focuses its charitable contributions and volunteer programs in the Wilmington and Delaware Valley areas of Delaware. The Corporation is mainly interested in supporting education, health, adult and child services, and the arts. General descriptions and details on some of the specific programs that the Society funds, as well as contact information, are available at the WSFS Web site.

xyz.net (AK) (http://www.xyz.net/corpgiving.shtml)

Xyz.net, located in Anchorage, Alaska, is an Internet service provider. Xyz's corporate giving program helps nonprofit organizations through small cash donations and gifts of products and services for the betterment of the Alaskan community. Xyz focuses its giving on youth and youth sports, technical and medical research, women's issues, education, arts and culture, and volunteerism relating to any of the aforementioned giving areas. Eligibility criteria and funding policies are explained on the Web site. Instructions on how to apply and contact information are also available on the site. Additionally, a Corporate Giving Application, which must accompany any application, can be completed on the site and submitted electronically.

Nonprofit Organizations on the Web

Categories Used in the Center's Links to Nonprofit Resources

The following is a presentation of the organization currently used in the Center's Links to Nonprofit Resources, but we reserve the right to change this structure as new sites are established and new Internet trends take hold.

Philanthropy Resources
General
Regional Associations of
    Grantmakers (RAGs)

Fundraising Resources
General
Charity Monitoring Organizations
Education
Online Giving
Professional Associations

Nonprofit Sector Information and News
General
Nonprofit Membership Organizations
Online Publications and Newsgroups

Nonprofit Resources, by Program Area
Aging
Arts
Children, Youth and Families
Community Development
Crime Prevention
Disabilities
Disaster Relief
Education, General
Education, Elementary and
    Secondary
Education, Higher
Environment
Gay/Lesbian
Health

HIV/AIDS
Hunger
Military/Veterans
Multicultural/Minorities
Science
Social Change
Substance Abuse
Women and Girls

**Nonprofit Management and
Staffing Resources**
General
Boards
Job Opportunities
Program Evaluation
Voluntarism

Nonprofit Technology Resources

International Resources
General
Africa
Asia
Canada

Europe/Eurasia
Germany
India
Ireland
Israel
Italy
Japan
Latin America
Russia
United Kingdom

**General Resources (Nonprofit,
Private, and Public Sector)**
Business and Industry
The Internet
Library Links
Public Interest and Policy
Reference

Government Resources
General
Federal Agencies
State Agencies

Philanthropy Resources

GENERAL

American Association of Fund-Raising Counsel (http://www.aafrc.org/)
The American Association of Fund-Raising Counsel (AAFRC) is a membership organization composed of consulting firms that advise nonprofits on fundraising matters. The Web
site leads visitors to useful data regarding trends in philanthropy, detailing giving information by source, recipient, and location. A particularly helpful feature on the site is its "8
Steps to Choosing Fundraising Counsel" area, which elucidates various factors to consider
in selecting the right firm.

**Association for Research on Nonprofit Organizations and Voluntary Action
(http://www.arnova.org/)**
The Association for Research on Nonprofit Organizations and Voluntary Action
(ARNOVA) describes itself as "an international, interdisciplinary network of scholars and
nonprofit leaders fostering the creation, application, and dissemination of research on voluntary action, nonprofit organizations, philanthropy, and civil society." Its main forms of
outreach are an annual conference, a variety of publications, and electronic discussions and
seminars. ARNOVA's Web site includes information about these various activities, as well
as a signup option for an e-mail-based discussion group.

Association of Small Foundations (http://www.smallfoundations.org)
The goal of the Association of Small Foundations (ASF) is to help foundations with few or
no staff. The ASF Web site offers links to members' sites, a listing of members by state, and
an online version of the ASF newsletter. The ASF has nearly 2,500 member foundations
and provides them with a password-protected area of the site.

Charities Today (http://www.charitiestoday.com/)

Serving as a guide to individual charity organizations and the field of philanthropy as a whole, the Charities Today site includes its Encyclopedia of Charities, which profiles individual charity organizations (organized by category), and its World of Philanthropy, which contains news and information of general interest to the public and charitable sectors.

Charity Channel (http://charitychannel.com)

Charity Channel is a rich Web site featuring reviews written by a volunteer community of nonprofit-sector professionals from the fundraising field of nonprofit periodicals, books, and software; free discussion forums with more than 45,000 participants; and an online career search feature.

The Chronicle of Philanthropy (http://philanthropy.com/)

Like its biweekly print analog, *The Chronicle of Philanthropy*'s Web site is full of useful information for fundraisers, grantmakers, nonprofit managers, and others. The site is organized into broad topic areas—Gifts and Grants, Fund Raising, Managing nonprofit Groups, and Technology—and includes a summary of the contents of the *Chronicle*'s current issue, with an archive of articles from the past two years, a listing of award and RFP deadlines, job opportunities in the nonprofit sector, a listing of upcoming conferences and workshops, and annotated links to other nonprofit resources on the Internet. Visitors also can sign up for free e-mail updates about changes at the site as well as breaking news stories. Some of the material is available only to *Chronicle* subscribers.

Council on Foundations (http://www.cof.org/)

The Council on Foundations (COF) is a membership organization for grantmakers, providing assistance to foundation staff, trustees, and board members through one-to-one technical assistance, research, publications, conferences and workshops, legal services, and a wide array of other services. The COF Web site offers a wealth of information for and about foundations. These include: Legal and Government Affairs with excerpts from select publications and special articles on legal issues of concern to foundations; Resources for Foundations, including career and professional development, publications, and a set of useful links for grantmakers; examples of successful grantmaking; resources to aid in starting a foundation or corporate giving program; *Foundation News & Commentary,* the Council's flagship magazine; a Professional Advisors Network section; and a set of links to a wide range of grantmaking resources, with a listing of more than 30 affinity groups of grantmakers.

Council on Foundations—Affinity Groups Listing
(http://www.cof.org/links/affinityindex.htm)

Affinity groups are coalitions of nonprofits focused on a specific area of interest and tend to be oriented towards grantmakers who want to fund efforts in those particular areas. Some groups primarily engage in networking and information exchange among members, while others emphasize advocacy efforts centered around an issue or cause within philanthropy and beyond. The Council on Foundations site includes a list of affinity groups in a variety of fields, along with a summary of their work, key staff member contact information, and links to their individual Web sites.

Council on Foundations—Community Foundation Locator
(http://www.cof.org/community)

This extremely useful tool from the Council on Foundations provides links to foundations that provide aid to specific communities in all 50 states and Australia, Bermuda, Canada, Costa Rica, The Dominican Republic, England, Germany, Jamaica, Japan, Kazakstan, Mexico, The Philippines, Poland, Portugal, Taiwan, and Turkey.

Gift Planning Resources Center (http://www.cam.org/~gprc/)

The Gift Planning Resources Center Web site provides an alphabetical listing of links (in English, with some information provided in French) to organizations in the United States and Canada that deal directly with planned giving or to sites that offer planned giving information. A short description of the linked resource is provided.

GuideStar (http://www.guidestar.org)

Produced by Philanthropic Research, Inc., GuideStar offers a searchable database of more than 700,000 U.S. nonprofit organizations; nonprofit sector news; an online marketplace to find requests for donations, in-kind gifts, or volunteers; job postings; a conference calendar; and a resource exchange. Nonprofits that register with GuideStar are automatically included in the charity searches at several other philanthropic-related Web sites.

Helping.org (http://www.helping.org)

Helping.org is an AOL Time Warner Foundation-sponsored Web site, designed as a one-stop online resource to help people find volunteer and giving opportunities. Visitors to the Web site can locate and donate to a charity, using the GuideStar database of over 700,000 nonprofit organizations; find a volunteer opportunity by searching Helping.org's volunteer database; or find nonprofit tools and resources to assist in utilizing the Internet in their strategic planning, recruiting, and fundraising.

Independent Sector (http://www.independentsector.org/)

Independent Sector (IS) is committed to promoting philanthropy, volunteering, and citizen action and brings together nonprofit organizations, foundations, and corporate giving programs. The Web site gives an overview of IS programs and includes a section on the basics of lobbying by charitable organizations, facts and figures on the size and scope of the nonprofit sector, and a statistical overview of the IS 1999 survey on giving and volunteering. The NonProfit Pathfinder, designed for scholars, researchers, practitioners, funders, and the media, is an information resource for civil society organizations. The Giving Voice to Your Heart Initiative includes five tools kits—Messages and the Media, Volunteering, Trust, Giving, and The Nonprofit Mosaic—to aid in promoting communication.

International Meeting of Associations Serving Grantmakers (http://www.imag.org/)

Sponsored by the Council on Foundations, the International Meeting of Associations Serving Grantmakers seeks to bring together grantmakers from around the world to increase communication with each other, pool resources, and raise awareness of global issues. The site includes a discussion forum, associations list, announcements of upcoming activities, pertinent articles, contact information for coordinating committees, and useful links.

Internet Prospector (http://www.internet-prospector.org/)

Internet Prospector is a nonprofit service produced by volunteers nationwide who search the Web for prospect research information for nonprofit fundraisers and the prospect research community, but anyone seeking tools for accessing corporate, foundation, biographical, international, and online news sources will find this Web site useful. You'll find an online newsletter and archives of past issues, search engine prospecting and test results, tips for foundation searches, international audio and video Web content, and Using Zip Code Demographics For Prospecting, a specialized Internet research tool.

National Center for Charitable Statistics—Resources on Nonprofits and Philanthropy (http://nccs.urban.org/resource.htm)

The National Center for Charitable Statistics serves as the national repository of statistical information from the Internal Revenue Service (IRS) and other sources on the nonprofit sector. Visitors to this Web site can download data on nonprofit organizations, view or download database documentation and classification schemes, and download blank IRS forms from which most of the data is collected.

National Center for Family Philanthropy (http://www.ncfp.org)

Established in 1997 by a group of family foundations, the goal of the National Center for Family Philanthropy (NCFP) is to serve as a resource for family philanthropists by publishing books, conducting research, and offering educational seminars on family foundations.

The Web site includes useful FAQs about family foundations and a set of links to family foundations' Web sites. It also includes links to resources on foundations and nonprofit organizations. The NCFP's publications can be ordered online.

National Committee for Responsive Philanthropy (http://www.ncrp.org/)

The National Committee for Responsive Philanthropy (NCRP) promotes philanthropy that addresses the unmet needs of disadvantaged populations through action research, providing technical assistance to nonprofits, and engaging in policy advocacy. NCRP's reform activism targets foundations, corporations, individual donors, and workplace fundraising. In addition to information about the Committee's projects and publications, the NCRP Web site has the current issue of the committee's newsletter, *Responsive Philanthropy;* selection of articles from past issues; and information about its advocacy programs.

Philanthropy News Network Online (http://www.pj.org/)

Philanthropy News Network (PNN), the online version of the *Philanthropy Journal of North Carolina,* is a comprehensive source of nonprofit news, information, and resources for all segments of the nonprofit world. Features on the Web site include a set of links to Private, Corporate, and Community foundations, and a Meta-Index of Nonprofit Organizations. *PNN Alert,* a twice weekly newsletter, has philanthropy news, updates, conference information on nonprofits, technology and fundraising, and national nonprofit job listings.

Philanthropy Roundtable (http://www.philanthropyroundtable.org/)

The Philanthropy Roundtable is an association of grantmakers founded on the principle that "voluntary private action offers the best means of addressing many of society's needs, and that a vibrant private sector is critical to creating the wealth that makes philanthropy possible." The Web site features synopses of articles from current and past issues of *Philanthropy,* a journal that covers relevant topics in the philanthropy field, and provides information about the Roundtable's publications and its conferences and events.

Quality 990 (http://www.qual990.org/)

Quality 990 is dedicated to improving the quality of IRS Forms 990 filed by nonprofit organizations. With new regulations and wider, simpler access to a nonprofit's tax form, this site offers many resources to assist the community involved in filing this form. There is information on forming or joining a Nonprofit Accountability Collaborative (990 NAC) for accountants, nonprofit managers, and regulators. Comprehensive guides to the form are available, along with links to other sites that help in understanding the form itself, and the rules to its disclosure.

Women's Philanthropy Institute (http://www.women-philanthropy.org)

The Women's Philanthropy Institute is a nonprofit educational institute that brings together philanthropists, volunteers, and professional funders to educate and empower women as philanthropists, donors, and volunteers. The Web site has a Resources & Articles section; a Bureau of Speakers and Trainers, which includes philanthropists, financial advisors, educators, fund raisers, and foundation trustees; and a schedule of upcoming presentations.

REGIONAL ASSOCIATIONS OF GRANTMAKERS (RAGS)

Associated Grantmakers of Massachusetts (http://www.agmconnect.org/)

The Associated Grantmakers of Massachusetts, Inc. (AGM) is a regional association of corporate and foundation grantmakers, whose mission is to support the practice and the expansion of effective philanthropic giving. The Association's Janet C. Taylor Library, a Foundation Center Cooperating Collection, maintains an extensive collection of publications that focus on local and national grantmaking, fundraising, and nonprofit management. AGM's Web site offers detailed descriptions of the services it provides to grantmakers and nonprofit organizations, an events calendar, the AGM annual report, a catalogue of AGM books and videos for sale, and extensive links to nonprofit and philanthropy resources.

Association of Baltimore Area Grantmakers (http://www.abagmd.org/)

The Association of Baltimore Area Grantmakers (ABAG) members include representatives of a majority of those private foundations and corporations in the Baltimore area with strategic, ongoing philanthropic programs. The ABAG Web site has links to the Web sites of its 90 members, member services, current projects, ABAG Affinity Group information, ABAG publications, a calendar of events, a listing of job openings in grantmaking organizations, and links to other job postings.

Conference of Southwest Foundations (http://www.c-s-f.org/)

The Dallas-based Conference of Southwest Foundations (CSF) holds two major meetings yearly and presents several educational programs throughout the year, at different locations in the region, for its 230 member foundations from Texas, Oklahoma, Colorado, Arizona, New Mexico, Nevada, and Arkansas. The one-page CSF Web site offers a short history of the Conference, an overview of its services to grantmakers, and a calendar of upcoming Conference-sponsored events.

Connecticut Council for Philanthropy (http://www.ctphilanthropy.org/)

The Connecticut Council for Philanthropy (CCP) includes more than 90 members from family, independent and community foundations, corporate foundations and giving programs, and federated funds, with a mission to support and promote effective philanthropy. CCP's Web site provides information about its services; news from and about its members; conference and meeting information; Connecticut Giving Project information, which includes advisor resources links; a short list of publications the Conference makes available to the public; a set of links to other philanthropic organizations on the Internet; and a listing of open positions at member organizations.

Council of Michigan Foundations (http://www.cmif.org/)

The Council of Michigan Foundations (CMF) is comprised of more than 490 foundation and corporation members. CMF's mission to enhance, improve, and increase philanthropy in Michigan is accomplished through the Council's primary focus of assisting Michigan grantmakers in their work. The Web site provides links to its members' Web sites and special materials developed by and for community foundations, including a list of certified Michigan community foundations and their affiliates; a searchable youth grantmakers database; and resources for entrepreneurs. The online bookstore has more than 60 CMF manuscripts, newsletters, booklets, videos, and audio tapes on Michigan's philanthropic issues and events.

Council of New Jersey Grantmakers (http://www.cnjg.org/)

The Council of New Jersey Grantmakers (CNJG) is comprised of independent foundations, community foundations, corporate foundations, corporate giving programs, and federated funds, whose mission is to strengthen effective grantmaking by increasing the impact of organized philanthropy in New Jersey and to act as a "synergist among and between New Jersey's public and private sectors to promote effective philanthropy." The Web site provides a list of some programs that are available to members, CNJG's newsletter, a philanthropy-related links page, a job bank, and a bulletin board that includes information regarding scheduled programs. Common Application and Report Forms for the New York/New Jersey Area are also available.

Delaware Valley Grantmakers (http://www.libertynet.org/%7Edvg/)

Delaware Valley Grantmakers (DVG) is a membership organization comprised of private, corporate, and community foundations; charitable trusts; corporate giving programs; and grantmaking public charities promoting philanthropy in the Delaware Valley area. It serves to educate grantmakers and the general public about the role of private philanthropy in improving the quality of life for all persons. In addition to basic information about DVG, the Web site provides a list of members, with links to their Web sites; resources for advisors; and descriptions of "great grants" that have made a real difference in people's lives and that are replicable by other nonprofits or grantmakers.

Donors Forum of Chicago (http://www.donorsforum.org/)

The Donors Forum of Chicago, with more than 160 grantmaking Members and 900 nonprofit Forum Partners, promotes effective philanthropy through its educational, collaborative, and networking efforts. The main offering at the Forum's Web site is a database of more than 40,000 grants awarded from 1994 through 1997, which is searchable by foundation name, recipient, beneficiary type, support type, neighborhood, and grant purpose.

Donors Forum of Wisconsin (http://www.dfwonline.org/)

The Donors Forum of Wisconsin is a membership association of independent and family foundations, community foundations, corporate foundations, and corporate giving programs, whose mission is to improve the quality, expand the scope, and enhance the understanding of philanthropy by providing continuing education and professional support to its members and by facilitating information exchange between grantmakers and the larger nonprofit community. The Web site has a calendar of events; a searchable directory of contact information for organizations; a section for grantseekers that includes training information and statistics on individual, foundation, and corporate giving; a Common Grant Application form; and a listing of contact information on community foundations in Wisconsin.

Forum of Regional Associations of Grantmakers (http://www.rag.org/)

The Forum of Regional Associations of Grantmakers is a membership association of 28 RAGS across the country that help more than 3,400 local grantmakers practice more effective philanthropy in their communities. The Forum assists RAGs in providing local leadership to grantmakers on the issues of public policy, promoting the growth of new philanthropy, technology, and measuring effectiveness and impact. The Forum of RAGs site includes a section that lists contact information for each individual RAG in the United States; a section on New Ventures in Philanthropy, a multi-year project that aims to create new foundations and corporate giving programs implemented and managed by the Forum of Regional Associations of Grantmakers; and a section on building communications and technology capacity.

Grantmakers of Western Pennsylvania (http://www.gwpa.org)

The Grantmakers of Western Pennsylvania (GWP) is an association of grantmaking foundations, corporations, and charitable trusts whose mission is to improve the effectiveness of its members to meet the needs of the people, organizations, and communities of 26 counties in western Pennsylvania. The GWP Web site offers an overview of the organization's services to grantmakers, basic funding resource information, a downloadable version of GWP's common grant application form, a calendar of upcoming GWP-sponsored events, and contact information.

Indiana Grantmakers Alliance (http://www.indonors.com/)

The Indiana Grantmakers Alliance is a membership association that serves Indiana's grantmaking community by facilitating communication and collaboration and by encouraging new opportunities for giving and volunteering. Offerings at its Web site include a mission statement; a calendar of Alliance workshops for grantmakers and grantseekers; information about its directories of Indiana and Kentucky foundations; a newsletter, annual report, and other publications; and links to more than 90 Indiana community foundations and affiliated funds, with information on how to support them.

Metropolitan Association for Philanthropy (http://www.mapstl.org/)

The Metropolitan Association for Philanthropy (MAP) is a regional association of 61 foundations, corporations, and trusts with more than 200 nonprofit organizations participating as Library Partners. The Association's Web site offers information about MAP programs for grantmakers and grantseekers, the MAP library (a Foundation Center Cooperating Collection), listings of MAP members and publications available from the Association, and an interactive Nonprofit Profile Form.

Minnesota Council on Foundations (http://www.mcf.org/)

Founded in 1969, the Minnesota Council on Foundations (MCF) is a regional membership association of public, private, and corporate foundations dedicated to strengthening and increasing participation in organized philanthropy throughout Minnesota and neighboring states. The MCF Web site is a good starting point for the latest news and information on grantmaking organizations, people, and trends in Minnesota; general grantseeking resources; listings of nonprofit events and grantmaker job opportunities in the region; and links to other online resources. The site also offers a downloadable version of the Minnesota Common Grant Application Form.

National Network of Grantmakers (http://www.nng.org/)

The National Network of Grantmakers (NNG) is an organization of 400 members (individual donors, foundation staff, board, and grantmaking committee members) involved in funding social and economic justice by supporting organizations working for economic and social change. The Web site provides program information, including NNG's research study on diversity in philanthropy and its 1% More for Democracy campaign; a section with information on events, meetings, and networking activities organized around specific themes or topics; and a section with nonprofit links, job lists, publications available to purchase, and a Common Grant Application Form. The current issue of the quarterly newsletter also is available and is free to members and nonmembers.

New York Regional Association of Grantmakers (http://www.nyrag.org/)

The New York Regional Association of Grantmakers (NYRAG) is a membership organization of grantmaking foundations and corporations in the New York metropolitan area. NYRAG's goals include improving the practice of philanthropy, increasing and diversifying philanthropy, and providing and encouraging leadership for collaborative action. NYRAG's Web site includes information on membership, peer networks and standing committees, its 2000 annual report and 2000 audited financial statements, its 2001–2005 strategic plan, information about programs it co-sponsor for nonprofits, legislative outreach and monitoring, and City Connect, NYRAG's initiative to foster information-sharing and coalition-building among city government, private funders, and the nonprofit community. The site also includes highlights of recent activities, announcements of job openings at member organizations, and resources for nonprofits.

Northern California Grantmakers (http://www.ncg.org/)

Northern California Grantmakers (NCG) provides its members with a forum for collaborative action, a resource for grantmaker effectiveness, a source for information, and a voice for philanthropy. Special events include educational programs, briefings, seminars, and workshops. NCG also administers a collaborative funding program, through which interested grantmakers pool resources to tackle important community needs.

Ohio Grantmakers Forum (http://www.ohiograntmakers.org/)

The Ohio Grantmakers Forum (OGF) is a membership association of private and family foundations, community foundations, corporate foundations, corporate giving programs, health-focused philanthropies, and other grantmaking public charities whose mission is to make philanthropy in Ohio more effective through more efficient communication, enhancing grantmakers knowledge and skills, encouraging the growth of philanthropic entities, and advocating for philanthropy. The Web site provides a list of OGF services, including a calendar of events with detailed information regarding workshops, seminars, and conferences; a news and publications section; a legislative update page that provides a summary of bills of interest to the philanthropic sector; and a nice list of links to philanthropy-related Web sites.

Philanthropy Northwest (http://www.pngf.org/)

Philanthropy Northwest (formerly the Pacific Northwest Grantmakers Forum) is a professional association of organizations and individuals funding in the Northwest states of Alaska, Idaho, Montana, Oregon, Washington, or British Columbia, Canada. Its Web site has a current list of members with links to their Web sites, information on the types of funding Philanthropy Northwest members provide, a summary of giving by Philanthropy Northwest members, conference and training information, a section for grantseekers with tips on grantwriting and a form that can be used as a boilerplate for proposals, and information on finding resources and technical assistance.

Rochester Grantmakers Forum (http://www.grantmakers.org/)

The Rochester Grantmakers Forum (RGF) is a professional association of foundations, corporations, government representatives, philanthropic organizations, and individuals currently serving grantmakers in Monroe, Orleans, Livingston, Wayne, Ontario, and Genesee Counties in New York. RGF's primary purpose is to provide networking opportunities, educational programs, publications, information/referral services, and consultations for grantmakers. The Web site provides an outline of programs, a calendar of member events, information regarding special projects, and links to philanthropy-related Web sites. Publications available on the site include Common Application and Report Forms; a Logic Model Packet for use in program planning, development of proposals, reporting, and evaluation; and a directory of area evaluators.

Southeastern Council of Foundations (http://www.secf.org/)

The Atlanta-based Southeastern Council of Foundations (SECF) is a membership association of grantmaking foundations and programs that seeks to advance the expansion and effective stewardship of the Southeast's philanthropic resources. The SECF Web site provides an overview of the Council's services to grantmakers; a description of member benefits, including *Interchange,* the Council's monthly newsletter; SECF programs and special projects, including a program archive; a calendar/announcements section; and links to member Web sites and other sites of interest.

Southern California Association for Philanthropy (http://www.scap.org/)

The Southern California Association for Philanthropy (SCAP) is a membership of over 145 organizations, which include corporations, family foundations, private foundations, community foundations, and independent foundations. SCAP members reflect the broad diversity of the southern California grantmaking community. SCAP's Web site offers general organizational information; a listing of its member organizations, member guidelines, and services; and a directory of local resources for grantseekers.

Washington Grantmakers (http://www.wrag.org)

Washington Grantmakers (WRAG) is a network of funders, partnering with nonprofits and governments, that is committed to improving the area in and around the District of Columbia by touching lives and changing communities. The WRAG web site provides grantmaker resources; grantseeker resources, which includes the Common Grant Application Form, and a list of grantmakers that accept the Form; and announcements of current job openings at its member organizations, with a special section on jobs in the nonprofit sector and links to other job listings. In addition, the site also has a listing of programs and trainings, including workshops and initiatives to help funders develop informed and strategic grantmaking programs.

Fundraising Resources

GENERAL

ChangingOurWorld (http://www.changingourworld.com)

ChangingOurWorld is a for–profit company that provides fundraising, philanthropic, and Internet services to nonprofit and corporate clients. Services include Web hosting, capital campaigns, major gift efforts, planned giving, and fundraising counseling. Donations can be made to selected organizations through iCampaigns. The company's biweekly newsletter is free of charge.

The Chronicle of Philanthropy (http://philanthropy.com/)

Like its biweekly print analog, *The Chronicle of Philanthropy*'s Web site is full of useful information for fundraisers, grantmakers, nonprofit managers, and others. The site is organized into broad topic areas—Gifts and Grants, Fund Raising, Managing nonprofit Groups, and Technology—and includes a summary of the contents of the *Chronicle*'s current issue, with an archive of articles from the past two years, a listing of award and RFP deadlines, job opportunities in the nonprofit sector, a listing of upcoming conferences and workshops, and annotated links to other nonprofit resources on the Internet. Visitors can also sign up for free e-mail updates about changes at the site as well as breaking news stories. Some of the material is available only to *Chronicle* subscribers.

Columbus Foundation Donor Connection
(http://www.columbusfoundation.com/donor_connection_pub_dec/index.html)

The Columbus Foundation Donor Connection is an online publication from the Columbus Foundation of Ohio, designed to link donors to selected programs of nonprofits in central Ohio. The Foundation accepts funding suggestions from donors via e-mail.

Community Foundation Silicon Valley Giving Center
(http://www.allcharities.com/npo/Login.jsp)

The Community Foundation Silicon Valley Giving Center lets potential donors search more than 5,500 Silicon Valley nonprofit organizations by name and location. Information on nonprofits includes clients, budgets, staff, needs, success stories, and more.

CyberGrants (http://www.cybergrants.com)

CyberGrants is a for-profit company that works to bring nonprofits and grantmaking organizations together via the Internet. The site offers nonprofits the opportunity to research grant guidelines and create online proposals that are submitted directly to member grantmakers. Participating private foundations and corporate giving programs, which pay a fee, are provided with access to a grantmaking and reporting system that facilitates online proposal review.

David Lamb's Prospect Research Page (http://www.lambresearch.com)

Lamb, a former development officer at the University of Washington, has attempted to "separate the wheat from the chaff" in describing truly useful Internet sites for researching corporations, foundations, and individual donors. The site includes links to directories of doctors, dentists, lawyers, and airplane owners, as well as to online news sources and public records databases. What's nice about the Prospect Research Page is that Lamb has distilled the overwhelming number of potential sources of information on the Internet into a relatively small selection of sites, which he has thoughtfully annotated. The casual visitor can tell that he or she is in capable hands.

donordigital.com (http://www.donordigital.com/site/HomePage)

donordigital.com (formerly Fundraising Online) is a for-profit group offering an "online strategy" for improving online fundraising, advocacy, and marketing. The Web site includes links to online fundraising resources, general nonprofit information, information on developing and managing a Web site, and case studies of organizations successfully raising funds online.

enews.com's Not-for-Profit Newsstand (http://www.enews.com/nonprofit/)

The Not-for-Profit Newsstand, a free affiliate program targeted to nonprofits and school groups, enables fundraisers to choose magazines that directly relate to their organization's mission and sell them at a discount, earning 21 percent of the revenue for all subscriptions placed through their organization's Web site.

Foundations On-Line (http://www.foundations.org/index.html)

Foundations On-line contains a directory of links to various foundations and grantmakers, fundraising software vendors and consultants, not-for-profit attorneys, and related sites.

Free Management Library (http://www.mapnp.org/library/)

The Free Management Library is a complete library of resources for nonprofit and for-profit organizations. The library is designed to be as user–friendly as possible, with a focus on providing free, online management resources to organizations. Visitors to this well-organized Web site can conduct a category search of free, self-directed management courses in topics such as board roles and responsibilities, communications skills, finance and taxes, program development, program evaluation, and consultants.

Fund-Raising and Foundation Research (http://www.usc.edu/dept/source/found.htm)

The Fund-Raising and Foundation Research Web site is sponsored by the University of Southern California's Development Research Department as part of its selected sites for prospect research on the Web. The site features a list of links to Web sites that pertain to fundraising, foundation research, and philanthropy news.

Fund-Raising.com (http://www.fund-raising.com)

A service of NicheNET, Fund-Raising.com provides nonprofits with information about creative ways to generate contributions. Resources include fundraising-oriented products, a Web-based fundraising competition, related links, and an Idea Bank that features suggestions from site visitors.

Fund-Raising Forum (http://www.raise-funds.com/forum.html)

The Fund-Raising Forum contains information related to annual campaign fundraising and nonprofit organizations. The Web site features the Fund-raising Forum Library, where fundraising information can be found under several categories: planning for fundraising, funding sources and prospects, organizing a campaign, managing a campaign, post-campaign activity, and developing the development team.

Fundsnet Services Online (http://www.fundsnetservices.com/)

Fundsnet Services Online is a comprehensive and searchable directory of funders, funding resources, and scholarship opportunities on the World Wide Web. Most links are annotated, and the Web site also includes a section organized by subject area.

GB3 Group Nonprofit Marketing (http://www.nonprofitmarketing.org)

GB3 Group, a member of the Association of Fundraising Professionals, is a marketing, communications, publicity and public relations, and fundraising consulting and training firm that services clients across the United States. The company provides training, consulting, coaching, and resources in marketing, communications, and fundraising to nonprofit and education managers, staff, and volunteers. The GB3 Group Web site offers a variety of topical reference material and information about workshops, books, and related job openings in the field.

Giving USA (http://www.aafrc.org)

Giving USA is the Web site of the American Association of Fundraising Counsel Trust for Philanthropy (AAFRC). AAFRC was founded in 1935 "to advance professional and ethical standards in philanthropic fundraising consulting and to promote philanthropy in general." The member firms of the AAFRC provide fundraising direction and counsel to nonprofit organizations throughout North America. The Web site has AAFRC's "eight step" plan to follow in selecting fundraising counsel and its statement of standards of membership and professional conduct.

GrantsDirect.com (http://www.grantsdirect.com/)

GrantsDirect.com was designed to help fundraisers research Washington, D.C., and Maryland grantmakers and their grant lists. For an annual subscription fee, grantseekers can access a searchable database of more than 1,375 Maryland and D.C. Grantmakers that have given away billions to nonprofit organizations and a companion guide to the funders titled *The Maryland/DC Foundation Directory Online.* The database is easily searchable by subject, name, or specific text. Visitors to the site can "test drive" a reduced database to get a sense of the services.

The Grantsmanship Center (http://www.tgci.com/)

The Grantsmanship Center (TGCI) is a clearinghouse of fundraising information and training in grantsmanship and proposal writing for nonprofit organizations and government agencies. In addition to a training program and schedule information, TGCIs Web site offers grant source information on community foundations and federal, state, and international funding; current Federal Register grant funding information, including a daily summary; TGCI's online magazine; and a listing of publications for fundraisers, including the Grantsmanship Center's proposal writing guide. The Web site also has a new resource, Winning Grant Proposals Online, with examples of effective proposal writing models for designing programs, consisting entirely of recently funded, top-ranked grant proposals in a wide variety of subject areas.

Grantmatch (http://www.grantmatch.com/)

Grantmatch is a for-profit company that allows charities and nonprofit organizations to inform potential donors about their work and match donations to specific projects. Grantseekers can post grant proposals or donation requests by category and make updates or deletions online.

GrantScape

(http://nonprofituniverse.com/gscape/lpext.dll/?f=templates&fn=main-h.htm&2.0)

Part of the Web site of Aspen Publishers, Inc., GrantScape is a guide to grantseeking, taking the grantseeker through the grantseeking process step-by-step, from initial research to accepting the grant or dealing with rejection. The site includes a brief how-to section on proposal fundraising. Also at this site is an annotated links page to other online fundraising instructional resources and Aspen's own catalog of fundraising titles.

GrantsWeb (http://www.srainternational.org/cws/sra/resource.htm)

Aimed at the academic/scientific research community, the GrantsWeb section of The Society of Research Administrators' Web site contains a comprehensive links resource for locating government research grant opportunities and information related to private funding. The links are categorized by general resources, U.S. federal agencies, Canadian resources, and by international resources, which include Australia, Europe, Great Britain, and Israel.

Guide to Proposal Writing and Planning (http://www.oryxpress.com/miner.htm)

Oryx Press is a privately held publishing company with headquarters in Phoenix, Arizona. *The Guide to Proposal Planning and Writing* is a condensed version of its publication *Proposal Writing and Planning.* The guide covers the grants marketplace, motivations of grantmakers, steps to follow in successful grantseeking, and information on finding out about public and private grants.

Internet Nonprofit Center's "How Can We Use the Internet for Fundraising?" (http://www.nonprofits.org/misc/981027em.html)

This is a comprehensive 1998 report by Eric Mercer designed to provide "an introduction and a classification scheme to help readers learn to effectively evaluate alternative methods of online fundraising."

Internet Prospector (http://www.internet-prospector.org/)

Internet Prospector is a service provided by volunteers nationwide who research the Web for corporate, foundation, and biographical information in order to find leads on prospects for nonprofit fundraisers. This service is invaluable for the prospect research community, but anyone seeking international or online news sources will find this Web site useful. You'll find an online newsletter and an archive of past issues, a guide to search engine prospecting with sample search results, tips for foundation searches, international audio and video Web content, and "Using Zip Code Demographics for Prospecting," a specialized Internet research tool.

Michigan State University Grants and Related Resources (http://www.lib.msu.edu/harris23/grants/grants.htm)

The amount of information available on these pages is nearly overwhelming, but Jon Harrison of the University of Michigan Libraries has created a site that is well organized and cleanly designed. You won't get lost. Most valuable here are the annotated lists of resources (print, electronic, and online) for grant information in particular subject areas, from Arts and Cultural Activities to Religion and Social Change. For each subject area, Harrison gives abstracts of useful print resources, descriptions of databases, and links to online information. There is a substantial section of information on grants to individuals, including financial aid. Harrison also has assembled an impressive bibliography, with links, on grantsmanship techniques, including lots of information on fundraising research and proposal writing.

Nonprofit Charitable Orgs "Online Donation Sites" (http://nonprofit.about.com/business/nonprofit/msubdonl.htm)

Stan Hutton, the About.com guide for Nonprofit Charitable Organizations, provides a list of Web sites accepting online donations and a list of online shopping malls.

The Nonprofit Coordinating Committee of New York (http://www.npccny.org/)

The Nonprofit Coordinating Committee (NPCC) of New York is a membership corporation of social service, educational, arts, religious, advocacy, health services, and community development groups, as well as foundations and individuals. The Web site includes information on advocacy, lobbying, government/tax issues, financial matters, fundraising, governance and organizational issues, health, disability insurance, workers' compensation, organizational insurance, personnel management, postal issues, and NPCC events, projects and editorials. Members can also sign up to receive automated targeted notices on funding availability and to access selected articles from NPCC's bimonthly newsletter.

Online Fundraising Mailing List (http://www.gilbert.org/fundraising/)

Online Fundraising Mailing List, the Gilbert Center's mailing list for online fundraising, provides a learning environment for fundraisers at all levels of experience. Visitors to the Web site can also subscribe to receive the weekly e-mail mirror of the Gilbert Center online news Web site.

Online Fundraising Resources Center (http://www.fund-online.com/)

The Online Fundraising Resources Center is a collection of online fundraising resources from the book *Fundraising and Friend-Raising on the Web*. The Web site includes excerpts from the book, with updates, and a good set of successful Web site examples. The site also has a list of links that include some general nonprofit, fundraising, and charity review sites; essays and published articles related to "cyber fundraising;" and teaching materials from Internet fundraising classes.

Peninsula Community Foundation's Philanthropy Center
(http://www.philanthropycenter.org/)

The Center for Venture Philanthropy, a program of the Peninsula Community Foundation, created this site to serve as a gateway for local community investors who want to educate themselves about the charitable sector in San Mateo and Santa Clara Counties, California. Private nonprofit organizations are represented in listings that include budget and funding information, number of staff or volunteers, a statement on immediate needs, scope and purpose of the agencies' services, and a vignette about the clients served.

Quality 990 (http://www.qual990.org/)

Quality 990 is dedicated to improving the quality of IRS Forms 990 filed by nonprofit organizations. With new regulations and wider, simpler access to a nonprofit's tax form, this site offers many resources to assist the community involved in filing this form. There is information on forming or joining a Nonprofit Accountability Collaborative (990 NAC) for accountants, nonprofit managers, and regulators. Comprehensive guides to the form are available, along with links to other sites that help in understanding the form itself and the rules to its disclosure.

Resources for Fundraising Online
(http://www.nonprofits.org/npofaq/misc/990804olfr.html)

Resources for Fundraising Online is compiled by Putnam Barber, of the Internet Nonprofit Center, and is a comprehensive list containing annotated links to a wide range of online fundraising sites, with an Edit Log at the end of the document to make it easier for repeat visitors to track changes.

Seliger & Associates—Free Grant Information (http://www.seliger.com/freeservices.cfm)

Seliger & Associates, a grantwriting consulting firm, provides access to two types of free grant availability information: the online Seliger Funding Report, which lists available federal, state, local, foundation, and corporate giving grant opportunities, and e-mail Grant Alerts. Registration is required.

UK Fundraising (http://www.fundraising.co.uk/software.html)

Howard Lake's highly regarded UK Fundraising site has a section on fundraising software that lists nearly 100 software services and products. A brief description of the product, links to developers' Web sites, and links to sites with additional information on software for nonprofits are also included. The Web site also has a listing of grant-seeking services for fundraisers, located in the United Kingdom and North America.

University of Virginia-Prospect Research
(http://www.people.virginia.edu/~dev-pros/webresources.html)

Assembled by the prospect researchers at the University of Virginia, this site includes sections on biographical information, corporate information, asset location and evaluation, nationwide listings of property assessors, public records and more.

Virtual Foundation (http://www.virtualfoundation.org/)

Virtual Foundation is an online program, founded in 1996 by ECOLOGIA, that supports grassroots initiatives around the world. The foundation screens and posts on its Web site, where they can be read by potential donors, small-scale proposals initiated by non-governmental organizations in the fields of environment, sustainable development, and health.

VirtualGiving.com (http://www.VirtualGiving.com)

VirtualGiving.com specializes in the development of planned giving Web sites that are tailored to the needs of the nonprofits they serve, integrating each organization's "look and feel" with enhanced marketing/promotional and information dissemination capabilities online.

CHARITY-MONITORING ORGANIZATIONS

Evangelical Council for Financial Accountability (http://www.ecfa.org)

Comprised of charitable, religious, missionary, social, and educational organizations, the Evangelical Council for Financial Accountability (ECFA) serves as a "Christian Better Business Bureau" by making appropriate public disclosure of its more than 900 members' financial practices and accomplishments and by developing and maintaining standards of accountability. The Web site has a directory of ECFA members, which can be searched by name, state, or ministry type. The site also has statement of responsible stewardship for charities to follow, and a "bill of rights" for donors.

Minnesota Charities Review Council (http://www.crcmn.org)

The Minnesota Charities Review Council is an independent, nonprofit organization that develops accountability standards for charities that solicit funds in Minnesota and conducts reviews based on those standards. The review information is provided to the potential donors and to the charitable organization without charge. The Web site includes the Council's accountability standards, organized by public disclosure, governance, financial activity, and fundraising, and a "giving guide" that contains the list of charities that have been reviewed, with information on ordering a full report. The site also has information for donors, resources for nonprofits, and a good set of links to charity-monitoring related Web sites.

Operation Missed Giving (http://www.ftc.gov/bcp/conline/edcams/giving/index.html)

The Federal Trade Commission's (FTC) Operation Missed Giving Web site provides information to help donors "give wisely." Included on the site are a list of cases filed by the FTC, a set of links to other charity-monitoring organizations, and FTC's brochure, *Charitable Donation$ Give or Take,* which provides a "charity checklist" to follow in order to avoid making contributions to fraudulent charities.

Philanthropic Advisory Service (http://www.bbb.org/about/pas.asp)

The Philanthropic Advisory Service (PAS), a program of the Council of Better Business Bureaus' Foundation, maintains files on hundreds of national and international soliciting organizations. The Web site provides donor education information that includes reports, articles, and publications that provide "tips" to the potential donor. The Better Business Bureau Wise Giving Guide is a new publication that combines the latest charity evaluation information completed by both the National Charities Information Bureau and PAS.

EDUCATION

The Council for Advancement and Support of Education (http://www.case.org)

The Council for Advancement and Support of Education (CASE) is an international association of education advancement officers, including alumni, administrators, fundraisers, public relations managers, publications editors, and government relations officers at more than 3,000 colleges, universities, and independent elementary and secondary schools. The CASE Web site contains job postings, discussion groups, information about CASE's awards and fellowships, training courses, member services, related merchandise, the online magazine *CURRENTS,* and news about issues related to institutional advancement at colleges, universities and independent schools around the world.

The Chronicle of Higher Education (http://chronicle.com/)

Published weekly, *The Chronicle of Higher Education* has news and information for college and university faculty and administrators. Subscribers who register can receive access to the entire Web site and to regular e-mail news updates. The Web site includes a daily briefing on developments in higher education; reports on developments in information technology, including links to Internet resources for higher education; daily updates on grant opportunities; and the full text of the current issue of *The Chronicle,* with a fully searchable archive going back more than ten years. Much of the Web site is available only to subscribers, but some parts of the site are free, including an open forum and online discussion on issues in higher education, a section with advice on careers; job announcements, and some articles, especially those about information technology and distance education.

GrantsNet (http://www.grantsnet.org)

GrantsNet is an online, searchable database of funding opportunities, sponsored by the American Association for the Advancement of Science, specifically geared towards scientists-in-training. The Web site also provides tips from grant reviewers, profiles of successful grantseekers, and monthly news highlighting brand new awards.

ONLINE GIVING

4Charity.com (http://www.4charity.com/)

This is a direct-donation site where users are guaranteed that 100 percent of their donations go to the nonprofit of their choice. The site earns revenue by offering advanced Internet tools and services to nonprofits and corporations.

AllCharities.com (http://www.allcharities.com/)

AllCharities.com is a searchable database of charities and nonprofits that channels 100 percent of online donations to recipient organizations. The Web site also sells Web-based services to nonprofits and provides a mechanism for organizations to securely receive donations.

California Community Foundation's Online Giving Center
(http://www.calfund.org/html/online_giving_center.html)

The California Community Foundation's Online Giving Center Web site allows donors to make online contributions to nonprofit organizations and endowment funds committed to improving conditions in communities across Los Angeles County. The Online Giving Center accepts credit card donations of as little as $25.

CharityWave (http://www.charitywave.com)

CharityWave.com provides an online donation service for selected charities. The selection process includes nonprofit status, a Web site that lists the organization's program and budget, a readily available Form 990, and recommendation by CharityWave's board of advisors. Organizations are listed alphabetically and by category. Profiles of the organizations are also available to help the donor make informed decisions. An annual audit is conducted to ensure that 100 percent of every donation goes to the charity for which it was intended.

CharityWeb.com (http://www.charityweb.com/)

CharityWeb is an online marketplace that offers nonprofit clients options for online purchasing and online donations, made directly to their different departments or programs, in real-time.

eGrants.org (http://www.egrants.org/)

Created in 1999 by the Tides Foundation, eGrants is a forward-looking organization that works to help other progressive nonprofits increase their financial support by fundraising online. eGrants provides online donation catalogs of social change nonprofits and allows individuals, organizations, and businesses to donate money through online transactions. The Web site encourages interested organizations to contact eGrants to either establish an online presence or add their tool to an existing site.

FundraisingAuctions.com (http://www.fundraisingauctions.com)

FundraisingAuctions.com, the nonprofit sector's answer to eBay, capitalizes on the popularity of online auctions to help nonprofit organizations raise money. Sellers donate the proceeds of their items to a nonprofit of their choice; additionally, nonprofits who wish to convert in-kind gifts received to cash can use FundraisingAuctions.com to do so. Product listing is free, and for a limited time, auction closing fees will be waived.

iGive.com (http://www.igive.com/)
iGive.com is an online shopping mall that donates up to 15 percent of an item's price to charity.

Independent Charities of America (http://www.independentcharities.org/)
Independent Charities of America is a nonprofit organization that prescreens and certifies the charities it presents to potential donors via Web-based giving, workplace giving programs, and other low-cost fundraising methods. Charities are reviewed and certified annually.

Independent Givers of America (http://www.givedirect.org)
The Independent Givers of America is a "nonprofit tax-exempt charitable organization whose mission is to bring together generous people and deserving causes, principally but not exclusively by developing workplace-based and Internet-based systems that reduce the cost and increase the productivity of charitable solicitation." This site gives philanthropists the opportunity to set up a personal, private, online foundation and make contributions to it at any time. This site also facilitates contributions to any IRS-recognized charity, church, or school.

Local Independent Charities of America (http://www.lic.org)
Local Independent Charities of America is a federation of more than 500 local nonprofit organizations in 19 states. The Web site provides an online giving service. Potential donors can conduct a keyword search to access information on member charitable organizations. Information provided includes the mission statements, programs offered, and links to the Web sites of various nonprofit charitable organizations.

ShopForChange.com (http://www.shopforchange.com)
An online initiative of Working Assets Long Distance, ShopForChange.com donates five percent of the revenue from its products to "progressive causes." Past recipient organizations include Human Rights Watch, Friends of the Earth, Stand for Children, RainForest Action Network, and Doctors Without Borders.

WebCharity.com (http://www.webcharity.com)
WebCharity.com is a Web site where nonprofit organizations can transform in-kind gift donations to cash. Individuals or companies can "pledge" new or used items, which will then be sold via an auction or retail sale format, to one of the several hundred WebCharity members, with 100 percent of the donation going to the nonprofit organization. The list of member organizations is organized by category, with a description of each charity, including contact information.

PROFESSIONAL ASSOCIATIONS

American Association of Fund-Raising Counsel (http://www.aafrc.org/)
The Web site of the American Association of Fund-Raising Counsel, whose membership is composed of consulting firms that advise nonprofits on fundraising matters, leads visitors to useful data regarding trends in philanthropy and the distribution of the types of sources and recipients of giving. A particularly helpful feature on the site is its "8 Steps to Choosing Fundraising Counsel" area, which elucidates various factors to consider in selecting the right firm.

American Association of Grant Professionals (http://www.grantprofessionals.org/)
The American Association of Grant Professionals serves grant developers who work for public or private organizations. According to its mission statement, the association "offers

professional certifications, maintains a code of ethics, promotes the public image of professional grant developers, enhances grant developers' relationships with funders and employers, and advances educational opportunities."

AssociationCentral.com (http://www.associationcentral.com/)

Serving as a portal site for professional associations, nonprofit networks, and special interest organizations, AssociationCentral.com is structured in a similar fashion to many popular search engines, breaking down its listings according to industry categories and providing advanced search capabilities. Additionally, visitors have the opportunity to find out about upcoming industry-specific events and current news.

Association of Fundraising Professionals (http://www.afpnet.org)

The Association of Fundraising Professionals (AFP) is comprised of 25,000 individual members who work to advance philanthropy through education, training, mentoring, research, credentialing, and advocacy in 159 chapters throughout the United States, Canada, and Mexico. Visitors to this Web site will find extensive information on nonprofit philanthropy and AFP's activities and publications, including its professional advancement programs and course information, the full text of its Code of Ethical Principles and Standards of Professional Practice, and the principles of an E-Donor Bill of Rights, created to address concerns and challenges arising from e-philanthropy. In addition, job opportunity and member services modules are made available to AFP members.

Association of Professional Researchers for Advancement (http://www.APRAhome.org/)

The Association of Professional Researchers for Advancement (APRA) Web site has information about APRA's mission, membership, and events; "Web Resources for Advancement Research" links; and APRA publications and conference information.

National Committee on Planned Giving (http://www.ncpg.org)

The National Committee on Planned Giving is the association for planned giving professionals. The Web site includes the Leave A Legacy program, which was created by the Central Ohio Planned Giving Council to be distributed nationally to encourage estate gifts to local charities. The site also includes information regarding education and training programs, planned giving conferences, and subscription information for ordering *The Journal of Gift Planning.*

Nonprofit Sector Information & News

GENERAL

About.com Guide to Nonprofit Charitable Organizations (http://nonprofit.about.com/index.htm)

This is a mini-Web site within the comprehensive About.com site (formerly the Mining Company) that serves as a useful guide to resources and information about nonprofit organizations, foundations, jobs, educational opportunities, and the latest developments in the field. Visitors to the Web site can search feature archives as well as the entire About.com site, participate in chats, and receive newsletters via e-mail.

AScribe (http://www.ascribe.org/)

AScribe is a low-cost national public interest newswire that includes more than 200 members—universities, foundations, nonprofit organizations, and other institutions in the independent sector—in 30 states that are sending news and information to the news media, Web sites, portals, and online services. News releases can be organized around specific topics or from particular institutions and can be customized for geographical regions or demographic groups. AScribe's Web site has an example of its Live Newswire, with news releases that have been issued by members during the past seven days.

Association for Research on Nonprofit Organizations and Voluntary Action (http://www.arnova.org/)

The Association for Research on Nonprofit Organizations and Voluntary Action (ARNOVA) describes itself as "an international, interdisciplinary network of scholars and nonprofit leaders fostering the creation, application, and dissemination of research on voluntary action, nonprofit organizations, philanthropy, and civil society." Its main forms of outreach are an annual conference, a variety of publications, and electronic discussions and seminars. ARNOVA's Web site includes information about these various activities, as well as a signup option for an e-mail-based discussion group.

Contributions Magazine (http://www.contributionsmagazine.com)

Contributions Magazine offers current and archived feature articles of this bimonthly print publication on the Web site and an index of the current issue's other articles available by subscription. The site also contains a list of articles pertaining to nonprofit issues, book reviews of its own current fundraising publications, and a "descriptive forum" of links to sites that offer services or products related to the nonprofit sector.

The Chronicle of Philanthropy (http://philanthropy.com/)

Like its biweekly print analog, *The Chronicle of Philanthropy*'s Web site is full of useful information for fundraisers, grantmakers, nonprofit managers, and others. The site is organized into broad topic areas—Gifts and Grants, Fund Raising, Managing nonprofit Groups, and Technology—and includes a summary of the contents of the *Chronicle*'s current issue, with an archive of articles from the past two years, a listing of award and RFP deadlines, job opportunities in the nonprofit sector, a listing of upcoming conferences and workshops, and annotated links to other nonprofit resources on the Internet. Visitors can also sign up for free e-mail updates about changes at the site as well as breaking news stories. Some of the material is available only to *Chronicle* subscribers.

Fundsnet Services Online (http://www.fundsnetservices.com/)

Fundsnet Services Online is a comprehensive and searchable directory of funders, funding resources, and scholarship opportunities on the World Wide Web. Most links are annotated, and the Web site also includes a section organized by subject area.

GuideStar (http://www.guidestar.org/index.html)

Produced by Philanthropic Research, Inc., GuideStar offers a searchable database of more than 700,000 U.S. nonprofit organizations, nonprofit sector news, an online marketplace to find requests for donations, in-kind gifts, volunteers, job postings, a conference calendar, and a resource exchange. Nonprofits that register with Guide Star are automatically included in the charity searches at several other philanthropic-related Web sites.

HandsNet (http://www.handsnet.org/)

HandsNet is a membership organization of more than 5,000 public interest and human services organizations. Web site features include articles and action alerts, providing daily news updates on human services issues and legislation; the Webclipper news and delivery service, with human services headlines from hundreds of Web sites; and information on training programs, including a mobile technology classroom, management seminars, and strategic planning workshops for nonprofit professionals.

Idealist (http://www.idealist.org)

Idealist, in English and Spanish, has a searchable network of 20,000 nonprofit and community organizations in 150 countries, which can be searched or browsed by name, location, or mission; a searchable list of volunteer opportunities; and hundreds of job and internship listings, events, and publications.

ImpactOnline (http://www.impactonline.org)

With Volunteer Match, ImpactOnline helps individuals nationwide find on-site volunteer opportunities posted by local nonprofit and public sector organizations. Volunteers can search the online database of thousands of one-time and ongoing opportunities, including walk-a-thons, beach day cleanups, tutoring, home building, and meal deliveries by zip code, category, and date, then sign up automatically by e-mail for those that fit their interest and schedule. The Web site also has an online newsletter, and a listing of "virtual volunteering" opportunities for individuals, including those with disabilities, who wish to contribute time via e-mail.

Interactive Knowledge for Nonprofits Worldwide (http://www.iknow.org/)
Developed and maintained by Raffa & Associates, P.C., Interactive Knowledge for Nonprofits Worldwide (IKNOW) is a collection of online resource links to information regarding business services, education, fringe benefits, fundraising, governance, human resources, an Internet resource directory for nonprofit organizations, legal issues, legislation, strategic planning, and volunteerism.

Internet Nonprofit Center (http://www.nonprofits.org/)
A project of the Evergreen State Society in Seattle, Washington, the Internet Nonprofit Center is oriented toward providing information to and about nonprofit organizations. The Web site has an extensive Nonprofit FAQ, with information on a wide range of topics of interest to leaders and managers of nonprofit organizations; a Library that offers longer essays and analysis of the nonprofit sector; a Unified Registration Statement which streamlines the process for nonprofits needing to register in multiple states in order to solicit contributions; and current nonprofit news.

Internet Resources for Nonprofits (http://www.ucp-utica.org/uwlinks/directory.html)
Amassed by the United Cerebral Palsy Association of the greater Utica, New York, area, this sizable collection of annotated links to resources all across the United States is divided into more than 20 subcategories. In addition, there is a Featured Web Sites section and a News and Views section, which features topical articles selected by the site editors.

IUPUI University Special Collections (http://www-lib.iupui.edu/special/)
The Special Collections department at the University Library of Indiana University-Purdue University Indianapolis (IUPUI) encompasses the manuscript collections, university archives, rare books, and the Joseph and Matthew Payton Philanthropic Studies Library. The Web site has The Philanthropy Collections, which includes the historical records of organizations and individuals that have worked as advocates for the nonprofit sector, fund raising firms that help nonprofit organizations raise money, foundations and individual philanthropists, and nonprofit organizations that provide social services, particularly in central Indiana.

National Center for Charitable Statistics (http://nccs.urban.org)
Visitors to this site can download data on nonprofit organizations, view or download database documentation and classification schemes, and download blank IRS forms from which most of the data is collected.

Nonprofit Prophets
(http://www.kn.pacbell.com/wired/prophets/prophets.res.topics.html)
The Nonprofit Prophets Web site features a comprehensive index of annotated links to resources for investigating problems, organized by topic. Categories include the environment/ecology; trees and animals; global conflict/politics; family issues; homelessness, hunger, and poverty; disasters; and major online news sources.

Nonprofit Times (http://www.nptimes.com)
The *NonProfit Times* is a biweekly print publication covering nonprofit management issues. Selected articles and features are available online at the Web site from current and archived past issues of the publication. Also included are a classified employment advertisement section and a resource directory that lists names and addresses of service-related organizations.

The Nonprofit Zone (http://www.nonprofitzone.com)
Staffed by volunteers, the Nonprofit Zone provides "free tools and resources to help nonprofits work better, smarter and faster." The Answers Database feature of the Web site contains a library of "interactive" answers and links to articles related to issues typically encountered by nonprofits, including topics added by participants. Some of the free services provided to nonprofit organizations include fundraising, volunteer classifieds, media, career, lobbying, public relations, marketing, management and technology, and a donations database for donating materials to organizations.

Planned Giving Today (http://www.pgtoday.com)
Planned Giving Today offers resources, including excerpts from its monthly print newsletter and a list of planned giving resources, for gift-planning professionals. Visitors can also subscribe online to the 12-page print version. The Web site also includes the current month's table of contents of the Canadian edition of the newsletter *Gift Planning in Canada,* and instructions on ordering the publication.

NPO MEMBERSHIP ORGANIZATIONS

AssociationCentral.com (http://www.associationcentral.com/)
Serving as a portal site for professional associations, nonprofit networks, and special interest organizations, AssociationCentral.com is structured in a similar fashion to many popular search engines, breaking down its listings according to industry categories and providing advanced search capabilities. Additionally, visitors have the opportunity to find out about upcoming industry-specific events and current news.

Colorado Association of Nonprofit Organizations (http://www.canpo.org/)
The Colorado Association of Nonprofit Organizations (CANPO) provides leadership and services to strengthen nonprofits' ability to build and sustain healthy communities in Colorado. The CANPO Web site contains a directory of its members and links to their sites, an online version of its newsletter, information about current legislation, links to helpful resources online, and a calendar of local events and forums.

Independent Sector (http://www.independentsector.org/)
Independent Sector (IS) is committed to promoting philanthropy, volunteering, and citizen action and brings together nonprofit organizations, foundations, and corporate giving programs. The IS Web site gives an overview of its programs and includes a section on the basics of lobbying by charitable organizations, facts and figures on the size and scope of the nonprofit sector, and a statistical overview of the IS 1999 survey on giving and volunteering. The NonProfit Pathfinder, designed for scholars, researchers, practitioners, funders, and the media, is an information resource for civil society organizations. The Giving Voice to Your Heart Initiative includes five toolkits—Messages and the Media, Volunteering, Trust, Giving, and the Nonprofit Mosaic—to aid in promoting communication.

Michigan Comnet (http://comnet.org/index.html)
Michigan Comnet, a community of individuals and organizations concerned with increasing communication and information sharing within the state's nonprofit public service sector, offers free Web hosting to nonprofit organizations. The Web site has a searchable directory of key individuals and nonprofit organizations in the state, a list of nonprofit directories, and a news and announcements forum.

Minnesota Council of Nonprofits (http://www.mncn.org/)
The Minnesota Council of Nonprofits, a statewide organization of more than 1,100 nonprofit and associate members, works to provide information and services to Minnesota's nonprofits by sharing information, services, and research in order to educate its members and the community. The Council's Web site is chock-full of useful links and resources,

including a weekly Minnesota legislative update, a nonprofit job board, and links to a number of searchable databases.

National Council of Nonprofit Organizations (http://www.ncna.org)

The National Council of Nonprofit Organizations is a network of 41 state and regional associations ranging from large to small, well established and starting up, and in all areas, including social service, education, health and cultural activities. Their Web site contains information on the various state associations, their conferences and meetings, as well as projects with which they are currently involved.

National Voluntary Organizations Active in Disaster (http://www.nvoad.org/)

National Voluntary Organizations Active in Disaster coordinates the planning efforts of many state and national voluntary organizations and assists these organizations in their efforts to work with government agencies in responding to disaster. The Web site has a list of links to member organizations, its annual report, and a "natural disasters topic" of the day news story.

Tech Soup (http://www.techsoup.org/)

Tech Soup is a Web-based resource center that offers technology assistance and solutions for small to mid-size nonprofit organizations. The site offers information on where to find donated or discounted software and equipment, computer training, advice on technology funding, technology planning, and listings of available volunteers and consultants. The Web site also has a free, monthly publication, *By the Cup,* with features articles related to nonprofit technology.

ONLINE PUBLICATIONS & NEWSGROUPS

Board Cafè (http://www.boardcafe.org)

Board Cafè, published by CompassPoint Nonprofit Services, is a monthly electronic newsletter for members of nonprofit boards. Each issue includes a menu of information, opinion, news, and resources, with numerous "little ideas" and one "big idea" that can be applied to board work. The Web site also has a summary of past issues.

Charity Channel (http://charitychannel.com)

Charity Channel is a rich Web site featuring reviews written by a volunteer community of nonprofit-sector professionals from the fundraising field of nonprofit periodicals, books, and software; free discussion forums with more than 45,000 participants; and an online career search feature.

The Chronicle of Philanthropy (http://philanthropy.com/)

Like its biweekly print analog, *The Chronicle of Philanthropy*'s Web site is full of useful information for fundraisers, grantmakers, nonprofit managers, and others. The site is organized into broad topic areas—Gifts and Grants, Fund Raising, Managing nonprofit Groups, and Technology—and includes a summary of the contents of the *Chronicle*'s current issue, with an archive of articles from the past two years, a listing of award and RFP deadlines, job opportunities in the nonprofit sector, a listing of upcoming conferences and workshops, and annotated links to other nonprofit resources on the Internet. Visitors can also sign up for free e-mail updates about changes at the site as well as breaking news stories. Some of the material is available only to *Chronicle* subscribers.

Internet Prospector (http://www.internet-prospector.org/)

Internet Prospector is a nonprofit service produced by volunteers nationwide who search the Web for prospect research information for nonprofit fundraisers and the prospect research community, but anyone seeking tools for accessing corporate, foundation, biographical, international, and online news sources will find this Web site useful. You'll find an online newsletter and archives of past issues, search engine prospecting and test results, tips for foundation searches, international audio and video Web content, and Using Zip Code Demographics For Prospecting, a specialized Internet research tools.

Kern, DeWenter, Viere, Ltd.'s Nonprofit Updates (http://www.kdv.com/agendas.html)

While Kern, DeWenter, Viere, Ltd. gears its accounting, tax, and management consulting services to clients located primarily within Minnesota, they also provide two free newsletters: *KDV Nonprofit Update,* a monthly e-zine featuring nonprofit reports, guest articles, news briefs, announcements, and links of interest to the nonprofit community, and *Nonprofit Agendas,* a bimonthly publication with articles covering new regulations, tax legislation, finance, and governmental issues. Topics include management, fundraising, technology, and employee compensation issues for nonprofit organizations.

Nonprofit FAQ (http://www.nonprofit-info.org/npofaq/)

Nonprofit FAQ is an online resource of information and advice about nonprofits taken from discussions on e-mail lists, in UseNet, and other sources. This frequently asked questions file has five main categories: organization, management, regulation, resources, and development, as well as several sections with a more specific focus.

Nonprofit Issues (http://www.nonprofitissues.com/)

Don Kramer's *Nonprofit Issues* is a newsletter that addresses legal developments and events that affect nonprofit organizations and employees. Visitors to the Web site can read selected highlights from past issues and access Ready Reference Pages, which summarize the rules and regulations governing various aspects of nonprofit organization. Trial and regular subscription orders can be placed online.

Online Fundraising Mailing List (http://www.gilbert.org/fundraising/)

Online Fundraising Mailing List, the Gilbert Center's mailing list for online fundraising, provides a learning environment for fundraisers at all levels of experience. Visitors to the Web site can also subscribe to receive the weekly e-mail mirror of the Gilbert Center online news Web site.

Philanthropy News Digest (http://www.fdncenter.org/pnd/)

The *Philanthropy News Digest* (*PND*) contains abstracts of news, surveys and reports, and other items related to the world of philanthropy. *PND* is published to the Web every Tuesday evening, with daily updates, and includes the RFP Bulletin, which provides a brief overview of current funding opportunities; Connections, a weekly guide to Web sites containing cutting-edge issues related to philanthropy; the NPO Spotlight, highlighting the activities of a different nonprofit organization or NGO each week; Newsmaker interviews; book and Web site reviews; a Conference Calendar; the Job Corner; and the searchable *PND* archive. *PND,* the RFP Bulletin, and the Job Corner Alert are all available as free weekly listservs.

Philanthropy News Network Online (http://www.pj.org/)

Philanthropy News Network (PNN), the online version of the *Philanthropy Journal of North Carolina,* is a comprehensive source of nonprofit news, information, and resources for all segments of the nonprofit world. Features on the Web site include a set of links to private, corporate, and community foundations, and a meta-index of nonprofit organizations. *PNN Alert,* a twice weekly newsletter, has philanthropy news, updates, conference information on nonprofits, technology and fundraising, and national nonprofit job listings.

Nonprofit Resources, by Program Area

AGING

Administration on Aging (http://www.aoa.dhhs.gov/)

The Administration on Aging is an exhaustive online resource, which provides a resource directory, statistics on aging, an Eldercare Locator, and links to related sites for senior citizens.

American Association of Retired Persons (http://www.aarp.org/)

Helping older Americans achieve lives of independence, dignity, and purpose, the American Association of Retired Persons (AARP) advances the interests of its members through advocacy efforts on issues related to Medicare, health insurance, housing, consumer rights, social security, tax reform, and transportation. AARP has added an entire section devoted to Computers & Technology to its Web site.

The National Council on the Aging (http://www.ncoa.org/)

The National Council on the Aging (NOCA) is an association of organizations and professionals—including senior centers, area agencies on aging, adult day services, faith congregations, senior housing, health centers, employment services, and consumer organizations—that help community organizations enhance the lives of older adults. The Web site has NOCA's latest annual report, news, detailed conference information, and links to other Web sites containing information about elderly Americans, including some reports issued by the U.S. government. The site's advocacy section includes current legislative alerts and general information about the legislative process and related issues.

Project on Death in America (http://www.soros.org/death/)

Dedicated to transforming the culture of dying in the United States, The Project on Death in America (PDIA) focuses on several major initiatives, while maintaining a commitment to education and training for healthcare professionals. The PDIA Web site provides information about project initiatives, press releases and research, amicus curiae briefs, and an excellent annotated list of links to other sites.

SeniorNet (http://www.seniornet.org/)

Provides training for and access to computer technology for older adults (age 50 plus). The site offers online courses on a variety of technology-related topics, virtual round-table discussion groups, discounts on computer hardware/software, a Showcase where members can describe various computer- and online-supported projects and display original digital works of art, and links to sites of interest.

SPRY Foundation (http://www.spry.org/)

The SPRY Foundation's information-rich site helps older adults plan for a healthy and financially secure future by conducting research and developing education programs.

ARTS

Alliance of Artists' Communities (http://www.artistcommunities.org/)

The Alliance of Artists' Communities is "a national service organization that supports the field of artists' communities and residency programs . . . by encouraging collaboration among members of the field, providing leadership on field issues, setting professional standards, raising the visibility of artists communities, and promoting philanthropy in the field." Site resources include background information about the Alliance and artists' communities, contact information for member programs, a multiple-categorized list of links to individual communities, information about the organization's directory, job opportunities, and other related links.

Americans for the Arts (http://www.artsusa.org/)

A creation of the American Council for the Arts, Americans for the Arts supports the arts and culture nationwide through resource, leadership, public policy development, information services, and education.

Art Deadlines List (http://www.xensei.com/adl/)

Art Deadlines List is a monthly e-mail newsletter listing art contests and competitions, art scholarships and grants, juried exhibitions, art jobs and internships, calls for entries/proposals/papers, writing and photo contests, residencies, design and architecture competitions, auditions, casting calls, fellowships, festivals, funding, and other opportunities (including some that take place on the Web) for artists, art educators, and art students of all ages. Two versions are available: free and paid subscription.

ArtQuarry (http://www.artswire.org/artquarry/)

ArtQuarry is a database of arts-related Web sites in a wide range of fields. Searchable by category, keyword, etc. Arts Webmasters can submit information on new or renovated sites using automatic registry forms.

Arts & Culture Indicators in Community Building Project
(http://www.urbaninstitute.org/nnip/acip.html)

Arts & Culture Indicators in Community Building Project is an experimental effort to develop arts and culture neighborhood indicators for use in local planning, policymaking, and community building. The Web site includes descriptions of the concepts, research framework, and current activities of the project.

ArtsEdNet (http://www.artsednet.getty.edu)

ArtsEdNet, the J. Paul Getty Trust's arts education Web site, offers an extensive array of resources, including lesson plans, image galleries, and information on professional development programs for teachers.

Arts International (http://www.artsinternational.org/)

Arts International supports and promotes global connections and exchanges between the international performing and visual arts communities. The Web site's "knowledge base" offers helpful tools and resources for artists seeking to expand into the international arena. Visitors can obtain embassy and visa information as well as reports and links to organizations all over the world.

Artsnet (http://www.artsnet.org/)

Artsnet is part of the Center for Arts Management & Technology, a research service and training center at Carnegie Mellon University devoted to the use of computer and information technology in the arts management process. The Artsnet Web site offers information on and links to development resources, career services, discussion forums, arts management resources, and art sites on the Internet.

ArtsWire (http://www.artswire.org/)

ArtsWire, funded and operated by the New York Foundation for the Arts, is a comprehensive "self-service" database of cultural resources on the Web. Offerings for artists and arts organizations include workshops, programs, telecommunications, and a forum for online art. Membership privileges include Web space and an e-mail account.

Association for Independent Video and Filmmakers
(http://www.aivf.org/index_enhanced.html)

The Association for Independent Video and Filmmakers (AIVF) is a national service organization for independent media, with nearly 5,000 members, serving as a clearinghouse for information on all aspects of filmmaking. The organization sponsors events nationwide, publishes several books and a monthly trade magazine called *The Independent,* and engages in advocacy efforts. The AIVF Web site has online discussion areas, information on AIVF Regional Salons (member-organized, member-run get-togethers that provide the opportunity to network, exhibit, and advocate for independent media in local communities) based in cities across the country, and links to useful film-related Web sites.

California Lawyers for the Arts (http://www.calawyersforthearts.org/)
California Lawyers for the Arts provides lawyer referrals, dispute resolution services, educational programs, publications, and a resource library to the state's artists and arts organizations.

Community Arts Network (http://www.communityarts.net/canabout.html)
The Community Arts Network promotes information exchange, research, and dialogue within the field of community-based arts. The Web site includes a monthly newsletter, a directory of trainers and training services in community-based artmaking, and an extensive list of links to related sites.

Connecticut Commission on the Arts (http://www.cslnet.ctstateu.edu/cca/vla.htm)
Connecticut Commission on the Arts offers matching grant programs, professional development programs, and a number of services to Connecticut artists, cultural, and other nonprofit organizations. The Web site offers opportunities for artists, resources for schools, and programs for organizations. The site also features a directory of more than 180 Connecticut-based performing artists and ensembles to provide employment opportunities for artists who specialize in public performances, classroom residencies, and curriculum development.

Eloquent Evidence: Arts at the Core of Learning
(http://www.nasaa-arts.org/new/nasaa/nasaanews/ee.pdf)
Eloquent Evidence: Arts at the Core of Learning is a downloadable brochure providing an overview of the issues involved in integrating the arts into a K–12 curriculum. Designed for, and to be used by, parents, teachers, administrators, school board members, and other stakeholders interested in promoting the case for arts education in the schools.

The Estate Project for Artists With AIDS (http://www.artistswithaids.org/)
The Estate Project is part of the Alliance for the Arts, a nonprofit arts service organization dedicated to policy research, information services, and advocacy for the arts in New York State. The Project's Web site offers information on arts news, artists' resources, specific strategies for arts preservation, lists of grants that have been awarded in the arts, and information and/or links to relevant arts organizations, many of which are national in scope. The site is geared toward the special needs of artists with AIDS but provides information useful to others involved with the arts communities and information on how to donate to the project.

Fundsnet Services List of Arts & Culture Funders
(http://www.fundsnetservices.com/arts01.htm)
Fundsnet Services List of Arts & Culture Funders is an online listing of grantmakers and funding opportunities, providing a solid and useful alphabetized compilation of arts and culture funders including corporations and private foundations.

Intermedia Arts (http://www.intermediaarts.org/index.html)
The mission of Minneapolis-based Intermedia Arts, a nonprofit multi-disciplinary art center, is to help "build understanding among people through art" by providing artist support, programs, and community education in the upper Midwest region. Among other features, visitors to the Web site will find an artist opportunities page that offers guidelines for fiscal sponsorship and a list of funding opportunities nationwide.

International Society for the Performing Arts (http://www.ispa.org/)
The International Society for the Performing Arts (founded 1949) is an organization of executives and directors of concert and performance halls, festivals, performing

companies, and artist competitions; government cultural officials; artists' managers; and others with a professional involvement in the performing arts from more than 50 countries in every region of the world and in every arts discipline. The Web site has a searchable membership directory.

National Alliance for Media Arts and Culture (http://www.namac.org/)

Founded in 1980, National Alliance for Media Arts and Culture (NAMAC) is a nonprofit association of organizations whose purpose is to further the media arts in all its forms—film, video, audio, and online/multimedia arts—and to promote the cultural contributions of individual media artists. The Web site has profiles of the nation's major media arts groups, current news and useful resources, job and event listings, advocacy information of relevance to the field, and an archive of NAMAC's quarterly newsletter.

National Arts Stabilization (http://www.artstabilization.org/)

National Arts Stabilization (NAS) is a nonprofit organization dedicated to helping strengthen arts organizations through the development of managerial and financial skills. This new Web site offers NAS journal resources and other information about the organization's programs and consulting services.

National Assembly of State Arts Agencies (http://www.nasaa-arts.org)

The National Assembly of State Arts Agencies (NASAA) is the membership organization of America's state and jurisdictional arts agencies. The Web site's Arts Over America section provides a directory of links to state arts agencies and regional arts organizations, an annotated list of arts-related Web sites, and links to major funders in the arts. The Artworks section has information on trends, issues, and activities influencing decision makers in the arts and government. The Web site also has publications, including a strategic planning toolkit, as well as NASAA news and legislative updates.

National Endowment for the Arts (http://arts.endow.gov/)

The National Endowment for the Arts (NEA) Web site serves as a comprehensive resource for the arts community and its supporters. This elegant Web site includes a "gateway" for nonprofits in search of information about grants, government services, regulations, and taxes and also posts announcements of grants, competitions, awards, arts-related news and interviews, and legislative updates. NEA publications—many of which are free—can be ordered through the site.

National Endowment for the Humanities (http://www.neh.fed.us/)

The National Endowment for the Humanities (NEH) supports learning in history, literature, philosophy, and other areas of the humanities through its support of research, education, documentaries, museum exhibits, and preservation. The information-packed NEH Web site is a good place to find out about funding opportunities, cultural events, and publications and exhibits of interest nationwide.

National Gallery of Art (http://www.nga.gov/home.htm)

Created in 1937 for the people of the United States, the National Gallery of Art (NGA) began with the private art collection of financier and art collector Andrew Mellon and today houses a growing number of world-class art collections. The NGA's elegant Web site is an outstanding example of the marriage of good design with compelling information. Art scholars can visit the Academic Programs section, which includes the Center for Advanced Study in the Visual Arts, to explore available fellowships. A variety of volunteer and internship opportunities are also available.

Nebraska Arts Council (http://www.nebraskaartscouncil.org/)

The Nebraska Arts Council (NAC) promotes the arts, cultivates resources, and supports excellence in artistic endeavors for all Nebraskans. The NAC Web site provides general information about its grant programs and application requirements; an artists directory;

links to other art councils (community and state), state organizations, and art museums on the Web; and contact information.

North Carolina Arts Council (http://www.ncarts.org/)

The mission of the North Carolina Arts Council is to enrich North Carolina's cultural life by supporting the arts. The Council is a catalyst for the development of arts organizations and awards grants and offers technical guidance statewide. The Council's colorful Web site provides, among other items, program and grant information and links to various arts organizations, government agencies, and regional and national arts partners.

North Dakota Council on the Arts (http://www.state.nd.us/arts/)

Established in 1967 by the state legislature, the North Dakota Council on the Arts (NDCA) is responsible for the support and development of the arts and artists in North Dakota. In addition to making grants based on recommendations from artists and arts administrators, the Council administers the Cultural Endowment Fund, through which it secures private and public funds to enhance existing programs. The Council's Web site provides program information, application instructions, grant-writing tips, related arts resource links, and contact information.

Ohio Arts Council (http://www.oac.state.oh.us/home.html)

Established in 1965 to "foster and encourage the development of the arts and assist the preservation of Ohio's cultural heritage," the Ohio Arts Council (OAC) funds programs to make arts activities available to the public and also supports Ohio artists through 25 different grant programs. The Council's Web site provides information about all OAC programs, complete grant guidelines, an impressive search engine, links to both state and national arts resources, and e-mail links to staff members.

Open Studio: The Arts Online (http://www.openstudio.org/)

Open Studio: The Arts Online is a national collaborative project of the Benton Foundation and the National Endowment for the Arts. Open Studio is focused on building community through public service media by providing access to the arts via the Internet, helping local arts groups and artists to become information providers online, and by providing Internet access and training to artists and nonprofit arts organizations around the country.

Philadelphia Volunteer Lawyers for the Arts (http://www.libertynet.org/pvla/)

Philadelphia Volunteer Lawyers for the Arts provides pro-bono legal assistance and basic business counseling to area artists and cultural organizations. The Web site offers a set of online informational pamphlets on legal issues and a partial listing of the many publications the group offers for sale.

Sources for Information on the Arts and Civic Engagement (http://www.ksg.harvard.edu/saguaro/sources7.html)

The Sources for Information on the Arts and Civic Engagement is a bibliography of publications and Web links on the arts and civic engagement from the Saguaro Seminar: Civic Engagement in America at the John F. Kennedy School of Government at Harvard University.

South Dakota Arts Council (http://www.state.sd.us/state/executive/deca/sdarts/)

The South Dakota Arts Council (SDAC) encourages and supports artists, strengthens arts organizations and arts education programs, and increases South Dakotans awareness of the arts. As a state agency of the Department of Education & Cultural Affairs, the Council makes grants to schools, individuals, and arts organizations. Grantseekers will especially appreciate the Council's online program guide, which includes detailed grant application guidelines and a handy glossary of terms.

Volunteer Lawyers for the Arts (http://www.vlany.org/)
Established in 1969, the New York City-based Volunteer Lawyers for the Arts works to help the arts community understand and deal with its legal problems. The Web site provides information on the group's educational and advocacy work, a schedule of upcoming seminars, a publications listing, news and events updates, and contact info for a legal advice hotline.

VSA Arts (http://www.vsarts.org/resources/webresources/index.html)
VSA Arts creates learning opportunities through the arts for people with disabilities. The organization operates arts-based programs in creative writing, dance, drama, music, and the visual arts, and its Web site offers an extensive database of Web resources for artists with disabilities.

Warshawski Fundraising Bibliography (http://www.warshawski.com/bibliography.html)
Morrie Warshawski's Fundraising Bibliography provides information related to fundraising in the arts. His bibliography is organized by books on fundraising, books on independent film/video, booklets and guides, magazines and newsletters, miscellaneous publications, information services, software, fundraising web sites, and mailing lists.

World Wide Arts Resources (http://wwar.com/artslocator/)
World Wide Arts Resources is a gateway site providing access to artists, museums, galleries, art history, arts education, performing arts, classified ads, resume postings, arts forums, news, and more. The Web site's Artslocator provides information on organizations and agencies in cities around the world.

CHILDREN, YOUTH, & FAMILIES

Administration for Children and Families (http://www.acf.dhhs.gov/)
The Administration for Children and Families Web site has information on the vast array of programs and services offered by this division of the Department of Health and Human Services, dedicated to promoting the economic and social well-being of families, children, individuals and communities.

Catholic Charities USA (http://www.catholiccharitiesusa.org)
The mission of Catholic Charities USA is to reduce poverty, help families become self-sufficient, build communities, and to advocate for justice in social structures. Some of the services Catholic Charities provides include after-school programs, youth centers, parenting classes, job training, and technical assistance. The Web site has programs and advocacy information, news releases, conference information, a media page, and a disaster response section. Its monthly newsletter is available to members. The site also has a section about Catholic Charities programs featured on PBS' Visionaries Documentary Program.

Child Welfare League of America (http://www.cwla.org)
The Child Welfare League of America (CWLA) is devoted to the well-being of America's children and their families. In addition to an advocacy section, statistics, and information about work the organization is doing, the CWLA Web site offers links, organized by region, to more than 1,100 member agencies.

Children Now (http://www.childrennow.org/)
Children Now is a colorful, well-organized Web site devoted to the nurturing, safety, and rights of children offers news, job listings, volunteer opportunities, and a wealth of related links, many of which lead to funding opportunities in children's issues.

Children, Youth and Family Consortium (http://www.cyfc.umn.edu)
The Children, Youth, and Family Consortium's Electronic Clearinghouse at the University of Minnesota is an electronic bridge to information and resources on children, youth, and

families. Among other things, visitors to the Web site will find a listing of events and activities, an experts' file, a list of Consortium publications, discussion groups, and links to related resources.

Children's Charities of America (http://www.childrenscharities.org)

Children's Charities of America (CCA) is a coalition of national nonprofit organizations dedicated to meeting the needs of children through heightened public awareness of children's issues and the solutions to their problems and by helping raise funds mainly through participation in workplace campaigns. CCA pre-screens and certifies national charities working to protect and assist children in the United States and internationally and then presents this information to potential donors. The Web site provides contact information, mission statements, e-mail and Web site links for each member organization, and the option of making an online donation.

Children's Defense Fund (http://www.childrensdefense.org/)

A leader in child advocacy, Children's Defense Fund provides a wealth of information and news about children's issues at its Web site. The Web site also offers state-by-state statistics and the Parents Resource Network, a collection of links to Web sites that offer parents information on caring for their own children and on getting involved in group efforts to help children in their communities or states.

Connect for Kids (http://www.connectforkids.org/)

Connect for Kids (CFK), a project of the Benton Foundation, was developed for parents, educators, and policy-makers. The site also provides solutions-oriented coverage of critical issues for children and families in more than 30 topics, including arts and youth development, out-of-school time, foster care, welfare reform, and oral health. The Web site has a free weekly e-mail newsletter, a news archive, and a features section that contains highlights of CFK programs. The Reference Room has information and resources related to children that can be searched by scope of work and includes reports, public opinion data, and book reviews.

HandsNet (http://www.handsnet.org/)

HandsNet is a membership organization of more than 5,000 public interest and human services organizations. Web site features include articles and action alerts, providing daily news updates on human services issues and legislation; the Webclipper news and delivery service, with human services headlines from hundreds of Web sites; and information on training programs, including a mobile technology classroom, management seminars, and strategic planning workshops for nonprofit professionals.

KidsHealth (http://kidshealth.org/)

Created by the medical experts at the Nemours Foundation, the KidsHealth Web site offers numerous interactive educational features and up-to-date health and medical information for the parents of children and teens.

Mediascope (http://www.mediascope.org)

The aim of Mediascope is to sensitize researchers, the government sector, and the producers and consumers of film, television, the Internet, video games, and music to social and health issues, particularly as they relate to children and adolescents, and to promote the production of constructive and responsible work without compromising creative freedom. The organization's Web site features sections for parents and educators, journalists, entertainment industry professionals, and public policymakers, researchers, and activists. The Media Research Library has more than 6,000 titles on a diverse range of media-related topics and is a good resource for researchers, screenwriters, journalists, teachers, legislators, and public policy analysts.

National Center for Youth Law (http://www.youthlaw.org/)

The National Center for Youth Law (NCYL) is a California-based private, nonprofit law office serving the legal needs of children and their families. The organization focuses particularly on children living in poverty and advocates for their protection from abuse; access to housing, healthcare, and public benefits; and improved methods of collecting child support. NCYL works towards these goals by publishing articles, manuals, books, and its bimonthly journal, *Youth Law News;* providing technical assistance and training; assisting legal advocates who represent poor children; and conducting administrative and legislative advocacy. Its Web site includes pertinent news, an overview of the organization, online articles, analyses, and publications, and links to related resources.

National Parent Information Network (http://npin.org/)

National Parent Information Network (NPIN) (a project of the ERIC system) provides access to research-based information for parents and those who work with parents, with a focus on family involvement in education. The "virtual library" includes a search engine to full-text resources, book summaries, descriptions of newsletters and magazines, and a collection of full-text resources for urban/minority families. NPIN features AskERIC, a question and answering service for educators, librarians, and parents. In addition, the site has an Internet discussion group and publishes a bimonthly magazine.

Quest International (http://www.quest.edu/)

The focus of Quest International is on programs serving young people ages five through 19 in school-based and community settings, providing adults with effective tools for helping youth develop positive personal and social skills and character traits. The organization's founder, Rick Little, was honored by the Council of Foundations with the 1997 Robert W. Scrivner for creativity and risk-taking in grantmaking. The Quest Web site offers extensive information about the organization itself, including partners and supporting organizations, a collection of articles on and about community-based service-learning, a bulletin board for threaded discussions, and links to relevant Web sites.

Save the Children (http://www.savethechildren.org/)

Save the Children works in 19 states across the United States and in more than 45 developing countries around the world to provide education and aid to communities in need. Areas of focus include health and nutrition, education, economic opportunity, and emergencies.

Starting Points (http://www.carnegie.org/starting_points/index.html)

Starting Points: Meeting the Needs of Our Youngest Children is an abridged version of the 150-page full report of the Carnegie Task Force on Meeting the Needs of Young children. The Web site includes a table of contents and information about how to order the full text version of the report.

UNICEF (http://www.unicef.org/)

The United Nations Children's Fund (UNICEF) advocates and works for the protection of children's rights by collaborating with other United Nations bodies, governments, and non-governmental organizations (NGOs) to offer community-based services in primary healthcare, basic education, and sanitation in developing countries. In addition to organizational information, UNICEF's excellent Web site provides program highlights, statistics, and job postings, among many other features.

COMMUNITY DEVELOPMENT

Catholic Charities USA (http://www.catholiccharitiesusa.org)

The mission of Catholic Charities USA is to reduce poverty, help families become self-sufficient, build communities, and to advocate for justice in social structures. Some of the services Catholic Charities provides include after-school programs, youth centers, parenting classes, job training, and technical assistance. The Web site has programs and advocacy information, news releases, conference information, a media page, and a disaster response section. Its monthly newsletter is available to members. The site also has a section about Catholic Charities programs featured on PBS' Visionaries Documentary Program.

Closing the Digital Divide (http://www.digitaldivide.gov/)

Maintained by the Commerce Department's National Telecommunications and Information Administration (NTIA), this site is a central clearinghouse of data about the digital divide. The Web site offers useful, detailed government reports on the subject and the *Digital Divide* newsletter.

Coalition for Healthier Cities and Communities (http://www.healthycommunities.org/)

The Coalition for Healthier Cities and Communities (CHCC)is a network of hundreds of community partnerships working to improve the health and quality of life of the country's communities. Through its Web site, CHCC is compiling a database of people, organizations, and initiatives dedicated to the sustenance of healthy communities around the nation. The Web site also offers a library of materials, tools, resources, press releases, and a calendar.

Communities by Choice (http://www.CommunitiesbyChoice.org)

Communities by Choice is a national network of individuals and communities committed to learning and practicing sustainable development. The Web site has a resources section that is organized by community, household, business, and public policy and can be searched by topic or keyword. The site's Community Center includes a calendar where members can add conferences, workshops or other events that are open to the public and that deal with sustainable development, a section for working groups to conduct online planning and discussions around sustainable development issues, and a resources exchange list of community group related tools and processes.

Community Technology Centers' Network (http://www.ctcnet.org)

The Community Technology Centers' Network (CTCNet) is a national membership organization that promotes nonprofit and community-based efforts to provide equal access to technology skills and usage to the general public and to disadvantaged populations. The Web site has address and contact information for the more than 400 community technology centers in the United States, Ireland, Scotland, Spain, and the United Kingdom, where access to computers and computer-related technology is available. The site also has relevant news and conference and resources sharing information.

Department of Housing and Urban Development (HUD) (http://www.hud.gov)

Department of Housing and Urban Development (HUD) has information about various types of grants, including community development, affordable housing, and research.

The Digital Divide Network (http://www.digitaldividenetwork.org/)

The Digital Divide Network (DDN) is from the Benton Foundation, in association with the National Urban League. Visitors to the Web site can search for all content stored within the DDN Web site, including news about efforts going on across the country and research organizations and corporations involved in those efforts to bridge the gap.

Digital Partners (http://www.digitaldivide.org/)

Digital Partners is a research institute based principally in Seattle, Washington, with chapters in New York City; Dehli, India; and Vancouver, British Columbia. Digital Partners fosters a global leadership movement in which IT entrepreneurs are linked with the poverty-alleviation activities of social entrepreneurs, foundations, and development institutions. The Web site has an overview of current projects and initiatives.

Habitat for Humanity International (http://www.habitat.org/)

Habitat for Humanity International aims to eliminate homelessness and poor housing conditions around the world by building and rehabilitating simple, decent houses with the help of volunteer labor and tax-deductible donations of money and materials. Habitat houses are sold to homeowner families at no profit and financed with affordable, no-interest loans. The Web site features basic information about the organization in 11 languages, a list of local affiliates, testimonials from Habitat volunteers and homeowners, news, and events.

National Center on Poverty Law (http://www.povertylaw.org/)

The National Center on Poverty Law (NCPL) develops its advocacy agenda in accordance with the needs of the low-income communities that it serves. Through policy, advocacy, and legal resources, the organization "identifies, develops, and supports creative and collaborative approaches to help achieve social and economic justice." The major clearinghouse on poverty law, the NCPL offers visitors to the Web site access to an enormous collection of publications and case studies. Over 500,000 documents from over 50,000 case studies are searchable by substantive area. A subscription to the site ($25 monthly or $200 annually) is required for access to the many databases.

National Congress for Community Economic Development (http://www.ncced.org)

The National Congress for Community Economic Development is a membership organization of more than 3,600 community development corporations (CDCs), which support their communities' economic development through grants, loans, donations, and income-generating projects. The Breaking News section lists funding opportunities and awards programs, and the State Associations section gives contact information for state-based coalitions of CDCs across the nation.

National Low-Income Housing Coalition (http://www.nlihc.org)

The National Low-Income Housing Coalition (NLIHC) seeks to address America's affordable housing crisis through education, organization, and advocacy. The Web site contains citizen action alerts, news, publications, recommended reading, events, legislative committees and reports, a state coalition directory, FAQs, and related links.

NeighborWorks Network (http://www.nw.org/)

The NeighborWorks Network site "promotes the creation of healthy communities through affordable housing, home ownership and investments in neighborhood revitalization through local partnerships of residents, nonprofits, lenders, business community and local government." Comprehensive and well-organized, the site includes extensive information about a range of programs, coalitions, and organizations, including the Neighborhood Reinvestment Corp., the Neighborhood Housing Services of America, and the NeighborWorks Network. A handy table of contents, site-wide search engine, conference calendar, and a library of links organized alphabetically and/or by category round out the features at this very useful site.

CRIME PREVENTION

Join Together Online (http://www.jointogether.org/)

Join Together, a project of the Boston University School of Public Health, is a national resource for communities working to reduce substance abuse and gun violence nationwide through the dissemination of public policy and community action information. The Web site offers news releases, grant announcements, and JTO Direct E-mail, with up to date news, funding information, resources, facts, and Web links for both substance abuse and gun violence subscribers.

Minnesota Center Against Violence and Abuse (http://www.mincava.umn.edu/)

The Minnesota Center Against Violence and Abuse (MINCAVA) is an electronic clearinghouse for violence-related resources available online. Links to information are organized by category, including child abuse, elder abuse, hate crimes, multimedia resources, speakers and trainers, and violence prevention. Additional resources are available in the areas of education, healthcare, criminal justice, and social service. The Web site provides a variety of searching mechanism for locating clearinghouse material. The site also has an events calendar; a news group, discussion lists, and electronic newsletters section; and a What's New section that features some of the "best new material and sites."

Partnerships Against Violence Network (http://www.pavnet.org/)

Partnerships Against Violence Network (PAVNET) is a coalition of federal agencies, including the U.S. Departments of Agriculture, Education, Health and Human Services, Housing and Urban Development, Justice, and Labor that provides an online library of information about anti-violence programs. The Web site also has a calendar of events that lists conferences, workshops, seminars, and other information related to juvenile and criminal justice, crime victimization, and drug control policy; a page of links to other anti-violence resources on the web; and a video library.

The Wilder Foundation's Violence Prevention Publications (http://www.wilder.org/pubs/index.html#Violence)

Although the Amherst H. Wilder Foundation publishes materials on widely ranging topics, its offerings in the area of violence prevention and domestic abuse are especially substantial. Along with its titles that can be purchased online, the foundation gives visitors the opportunity to download its Little Book of Peace for free, over 200,000 copies of which are in use in schools, homes, churches, businesses, and prisons to increase awareness and open discussion of violence and abuse issues.

DISABILITIES

AbilityNet (http://www.abilitynet.co.uk)

This Microsoft-sponsored UK-based site provides an abundance of information regarding various forms of adaptive technology for people with a wide range of disabilities.

National Cristina Foundation (http://www.cristina.org/)

The National Cristina Foundation provides computer technology and solutions to give people with disabilities, students at risk, and economically disadvantaged persons the opportunity, through training, to lead more independent and productive lives.

Office of Disability Employment Policy (http://www.dol.gov/dol/odep/)

The Office of Disability Employment Policy is a new office of The Department of Labor. Programs and staff of the former programs of the President's Committee on Employment of People with Disabilities have been integrated in this new office. The Web site provides programs and services information, technical assistance materials, publications, and an extensive list of for-profit companies interested in employing people with disabilities.

W3C Web Accessibility Initiative (http://www.w3.org/WAI/)

The World Wide Web Consortium's (W3C) Web Accessibility Initiative (WAI) promotes a high degree of usability for people with disabilities and, in coordination with organizations around the world, pursues accessibility of the Web through five primary areas of work: technology, guidelines, tools, education and outreach, and research and development. The site provides resources to aid in making a Web site accessible, including Web site evaluation, curriculum for Web content accessibility guidelines, and training and technical references. The Web site also has information on the Protocols and Formats Working Group, which reviews all W3C technologies for accessibility; the working groups that produce guidelines for Web sites, Web authoring tools, and browsers; a list of contacts, including information on how to reach WAI staff; a list of events; and a participation page that explains how to participate in WAI interest groups and working groups.

WebABLE! (http://www.webable.com/)

WebABLE! provides disability-related Internet resources and services that make it easier for people with disabilities to access the Web. The Web site lists workshops and conferences, links to white papers, articles, plans, standards, reference guidelines, journals that focus on accessibility and adaptive technology for people with disabilities, and a discussion board. WebABLE's extensive database of resources can be searched by topic, organization type, and geography.

DISASTER RELIEF

The American Red Cross (http://www.redcross.org)
The American Red Cross serves to aid disaster victims in the United States and abroad. Its Web site contains information on the services offered, current and archived news of worldwide disasters, a calendar of events, and links to local chapters.

DUO (Do Unto Others) (http://www.duo.org)
Do Unto Others works to ease the suffering of people who have suffered war, natural disaster, famine, or epidemic by screening and certifying charities with similar goals and helping donors to find charities whose work they wish to support. This site provides links to those charities' Web sites and/or e-mail.

EDUCATION—GENERAL

Council for Advancement and Support of Education (http://www.case.org)
The Council for Advancement and Support of Education (CASE) is an international association of education advancement officers, including alumni, administrators, fundraisers, public relations managers, publications editors, and government relations officers at more than 3,000 colleges, universities, and independent elementary and secondary schools. The CASE Web site contains job postings, discussion groups, information about CASE's awards and fellowships, training courses, member services, and related merchandise, the online magazine *CURRENTS,* and news about issues facing institutional advancement at colleges, universities and independent schools around the world.

International Reading Association (http://www.reading.org)
The International Reading Association, a professional membership organization with members and affiliates in 99 countries, is dedicated to promoting high levels of literacy for all by improving the quality of reading instruction, disseminating research and information about reading, and encouraging the lifetime reading habit. The organization's Web site includes a nice listing of grant opportunities.

EDUCATION—ELEMENTARY & SECONDARY

Children's Educational Opportunity (CEO) AMERICA (http://www.ceoamerica.org)
Children's Educational Opportunity AMERICA is the national clearinghouse of information on privately funded voucher programs—providing support services ranging from administrative training to programmatic consulting, to technical support, including resourcing existing programs and new programs with videotapes, how-to manuals, software, brochures, and other material.

Computers 4 Kids (http://www.c4k.org/)
Computers 4 Kids accepts donated computers, refurbishes them, and donates them to schools and organizations in need. The Web site has a list of needed equipment, grant information, downloadable application forms, and news of upcoming events.

Education Week (http://www.edweek.org/)
Education Week is a clearinghouse of information about education reform, schools, and the policies that guide them, brought to you by Editorial Projects in Education Inc., the publishers of *Education Week* and the monthly *Teacher Magazine.* The site offers online

versions of both publications, a Daily News section (access to the best articles written about education in newspapers around the country), a series of special reports, and a great links section of the major organizations involved in education.

Education Zone (http://szone.berlinwall.org/educational.html)

Education Zone has resources, scholarships, grants, education news, and free home pages for teachers and educators.

ERIC: Clearinghouse on Elementary and Early Childhood Education (http://ericeece.org/)

This site out of the University of Illinois at Urbana-Champaign provides access to the Educational Resources Information Center (ERIC), a comprehensive national database of education-related literature administered by the National Library of Education.

LETSNet (http://commtechlab.msu.edu/sites/letsnet)

LETSNet (Learning Exchange for Teachers and Students Through the Internet), a product of the Michigan State University College of Education, helps teachers to effectively harness the World Wide Web's instructive potential in the K–12 classroom. Resources include lesson plans, curriculum standards and guides, pointers to e-mail discussion lists, and many other online materials from teachers who have successfully utilized the Internet as a way to fulfill their teaching objectives.

National Education Association (http://www.nea.org/)

The National Education Association is America's oldest and largest organization committed to advancing the cause of public education. The site offers links to local and state affiliates and new school-based Web sites, information on school funding and grants for study abroad, pilot programs, TV specials, and education in cyberspace.

Teaching and Learning (http://www.techlearning.com/)

Teaching and Learning is an interactive publishing forum for the K–12 community where participants can read, write, and talk about educational technology.

EDUCATION—HIGHER

American Council on Education (http://www.ACENET.edu/)

The American Council on Education offers news about training, fellows programs, international initiatives, women and minorities in education, upcoming events, and products and services.

American Association of Community Colleges (http://www.aacc.nche.edu/)

The American Association of Community Colleges (AACC) works with other higher education associations, the federal government, and other national associations that represent the public and private sectors to promote the goals of community colleges and higher education. The Web site includes the 2000 AACC Online Membership Directory, searchable by state.

Beyond Bio 101: The Transformation of Undergraduate Biology Education (http://www.hhmi.org/BeyondBio101/)

This site features a colorful, well-designed report from the Howard Hughes Medical Institute based on the experiences of many of the 220 colleges and universities that, since 1988, have been awarded grants by the Institute's Undergraduate Biological Science Education Program.

The Chronicle of Higher Education (http://chronicle.com/)

Published weekly, *The Chronicle of Higher Education* has news and information for college and university faculty and administrators. Subscribers who register can receive access to the entire Web site and to regular e-mail news updates. The Web site includes a daily briefing on developments in higher education; reports on developments in information technology, including links to Internet resources for higher education; daily updates on grant opportunities; and the full text of the current issue of *The Chronicle,* with a fully searchable archive going back more than ten years. Much of the Web site is available only to subscribers, but some parts of the site are free, including an open forum and online discussion on issues in higher education; a section with advice on careers; job announcements; and some articles, especially those about information technology and distance education.

The College Board (http://www.collegeboard.com)
The College Board is an association of schools, colleges, universities, and other educational organizations dedicated to putting college within the reach of all students. The Web site includes College Search, with information on about 3,500 schools, online applications, and much more information designed to aid in planning and paying for college.

College Is Possible (http://www.CollegeIsPossible.org)
College Is Possible offers guidance about preparing for, choosing, and paying for college. This site serves parents, students, and education professionals on behalf of the Coalition of America's Colleges and Universities.

EDUCAUSE (http://www.educause.edu/)
EDUCAUSE is an international membership association whose mission is to help shape and enable transformational change in higher education through the introduction, use, and management of information resources and technologies in teaching, learning, scholarship, research, and institutional management. Visitors to the Web site can learn about award and fellowship opportunities, upcoming conferences, and current policy initiatives; post appropriate job openings; download extended excerpts from relevant print publications; and join any of 30 or so online discussion lists.

Federal Information Exchange, Inc. (http://content.sciencewise.com/fedix/index.htm?)
Federal Information Exchange, Inc. (FEDIX) is an online information retrieval service of federal opportunities for the education and research communities. The Web site also offers FEDIX Opportunity Alert, a free e-mail service that automatically delivers research and education funding opportunities in specific areas of interest.

FinAid: The Financial Aid Information Page (http://www.finaid.org/)
FinAid is a comprehensive collection of links to information about student financial aid on the Web. The site includes name and subject indexes as well as links to mailing lists and newsgroups, financial aid calculators, and FastWEB, a free scholarship search service.

International Research & Exchanges Board (http://www.irex.org)
The International Research & Exchanges Board (IREX) is an international nonprofit organization that administers programs between the United States and the countries of Eastern Europe, the New Independent States, Asia, and the Near East. With its traditional base in the university research community, and in collaboration with partners from the policy, corporate, media, and private foundation sectors, IREX sponsors and supports programs of advanced field research, professional training, international conferences, seminars, and comparative analysis.

National Science Foundation (http://www.nsf.gov/)
The National Science Foundation Web site is comprehensive and well-organized, with program and grants information in biology, education, engineering, the geosciences, math and the physical sciences, polar research, and the social and behavioral sciences.

PEP Directory of Computer Recycling Programs
(http://www.microweb.com/pepsite/Recycle/recycle_index.html)
Sponsored by Children's Software Revue and Custom Computers for Kids, the PEP (Parents, Educators, and Publishers) directory on the Web is a comprehensive guide to organizations that supply low-cost or donated computer equipment to nonprofits and schools. The annotated index is arranged by state and also includes national and international listings.

Science's Next Wave (http://nextwave.sciencemag.org/ca/)
Billed as "an electronic network for the next generation of scientists," the Next Wave site features profiles of and practical career advice for young scientists, as well as links to numerous scientific organizations and funding sources. The site features lots of material written by and of interest to Canadian scientists.

ENVIRONMENT

Amazing Environmental Organization WebDirectory (http://www.webdirectory.com)
The name says it all. The Amazing Environmental Organization WebDirectory is an enormous searchable directory of environmental organizations on the Web. It includes thousands of links to sites from 100 countries, organized into topics folders. The Web site also has a bulletin board and a list of other places to search for environment-related information.

Conservation Action Network (http://takeaction.worldwildlife.org/)
Conservation Action Network is an electronic advocacy network created by the World Wildlife Fund. The network disseminates concise information on issues such as endangered species, global warming, forest protection, and fisheries conservation and uses emerging communications technologies to facilitate communication between concerned individuals and members of Congress, state legislators, newspaper editors, corporations, foreign government leaders, and international agencies.

Earth Pledge Foundation (EPF) (http://www.earthpledge.org)
The Earth Pledge Foundation creates media projects and organizes special events to promote sustainable architecture and sustainable cuisine. Offerings include eco-friendly print design, new media, events, educational seminars and workshops, community affairs, and public relations.

Earth Share of Washington (http://www.esw.org/)
Earth Share of Washington is a federation of more than 80 environmental organizations working to conserve and protect the environment internationally, nationally, and locally in Washington State. The user-friendly Earth Share Web site provides eco tips, information on workplace giving and volunteer opportunities, and links to member organizations.

EcoNet (http://www.igc.org/igc/gateway/enindex.html)
Econet provides news on environmental issues and timely Action Alerts on opportunities for public involvement.

EELink (http://www.eelink.net)
EELink, whose focus is "Environmental Education on the Internet," presents on its site a vast array of useful resources for the classroom, for students and professionals, jobseekers and grantseekers, organizations in the field, and for those in search of relevant news and data. EELink also offers Web site design, development, and hosting services and Internet, intranet, and extranet consulting, targeted specifically to the needs of environmental education organizations and projects.

EnviroLink (http://www.envirolink.org/)
The EnviroLink Network is an environmental information clearinghouse that unites hundreds of organizations around the world. The EnviroWeb program offers Web site and

domain name hosting, automated mailing lists, interactive bulletin boards, and e-mail accounts free of charge to nonprofit organizations within the environmental and animal rights communities.

Environmental Defense (http://www.edf.org/)

Founded in 1967, Environmental Defense represents more than 300,000 members interested in a broad range of regional, national, and international environmental issues. The Environmental Defense Web site has information about its extensive programs, reports, brochures, fact sheets, and newsletter. Also included are practical suggestions for taking "action" to make a difference in solving environmental problems, and a special section for children called "Earth2Kids."

Environmental Grantmaker Association (http://www.ega.org)

Environmental Grantmakers Association (EGA), an affinity group of the Council on Foundations, is a voluntary association of foundations and giving programs concerned with the protection of the natural environment. The Web site provides brief information on membership, EGA working groups, and member-initiated projects.

Environmental "NewsLink" (http://www.caprep.com/index.htm)

Environmental "NewsLink" has a comprehensive list of links to government agencies and is an excellent place to track environmental legislation.

Environmental News Network (http://www.enn.com/)

Environmental News Network has daily news updates on all aspects of environmental activity on the Web.

Environmental Protection Agency (http://www.epa.gov)

The Environmental Protection Agency Web site includes material on virtually every aspect of U.S. environmental policy and protection.

Goldman Environmental Prize (http://www.goldmanprize.org/)

This is a small but elegant site devoted to the world's largest prize program honoring grassroots environmentalists. Founded in 1990 by philanthropists Richard and Rhonda Goldman, the Goldman Environmental Prize and $100,000 is awarded annually to an activist from each of the planet's six inhabited continental regions.

National Audubon Society (http://www.audubon.org/)

The Audubon Society is dedicated to conserving and restoring natural ecosystems for the benefit of humanity and the earth's biological diversity.

The Nature Conservancy (http://www.tnc.org/)

The Nature Conservancy operates the largest private system of nature sanctuaries in the world and preserves threatened species by buying and putting into trust the habitats they need to survive. This is a great "green" site.

One/Northwest (http://www.onenw.org/)

ONE/Northwest (Online Networking for the Environment) describes itself as "a nonprofit organization helping the conservation community in the Pacific Northwest (Alaska, British Columbia, Idaho, Montana, Oregon, and Washington) protect the environment through the effective use of electronic networking technologies." Useful resources on the site include the organization's background information, an activist toolkit, technical assessment forms, support for setting up e-mail discussion lists, a searchable directory of over 1200 Northwest conservation groups, job and volunteer opportunities, updates and bulletins, and e-mail based training workshops.

TreeLink (http://treelink.org)
Created to provide information, research, and networking for people working in urban and community forestry, TreeLink serves the field online through its various educational materials, a research database, discussion forums, a quarterly Webzine, a comprehensive link list of national and local resources, current news, and interactive tools for tree identification and selection.

The Wilderness Society (http://www.wilderness.org/)
The Washington, D.C.-based Wilderness Society is dedicated to fostering an American land ethic and to preserving wildlife and natural ecosystems in the United States, including prime forests, parks, rivers, deserts, and shorelands. The organization's Web site includes hot topics and news, multiple levels of links to original educational content, coast to coast conservation information, an annual report, job openings, and links to related sites.

GAY/LESBIAN

Human Rights Campaign (http://www.hrcusa.org)
Human Rights Campaign promotes lesbian and gay rights. The Web site offers tools for political activism as well as a section devoted to coming-out resources.

PrideNet (http://www.pridenet.com)
PrideNet is a clearinghouse of resources around the world for lesbian, gay, bisexual, and transgendered individuals.

HEALTH

Agency for healthcare Research and Quality (http://www.ahcpr.gov/)
The Agency for Healthcare Research and Quality (AHRQ) research provides evidence-based information on healthcare outcomes, quality, cost, use, and access (formerly Agency for healthcare Policy and Research). The Web site contains information on consumer health, research findings, data and surveys, and quality assessments. The Funding Opportunities section of the Web site includes an overview of AHRQ's research agenda, grant announcements, policy notices, grant award resources, contract solicitations, and research training information.

Centers for Disease Control and Prevention (http://www.cdc.gov/)
The Centers for Disease Control and Prevention (CDC) serves as the national focus for developing and applying disease prevention and control, environmental health, and health promotion and education activities designed to improve the health of the people of the United States. The Web site includes comprehensive program and application information for the CDC's many health-related funding opportunities.

Dana Alliance—BrainWeb (http://www.dana.org/brainweb)
The Brain Web has a vast collection of links to sites recommended by professionals containing information on various brain diseases and disorders.

Department of Health and Human Services (http://www.os.dhhs.gov/)
The Department of Health and Human Services Web site provides consumer and policy information, searchable databases, employment opportunities, and links to related government agencies.

Families USA (http://www.familiesusa.org/)
Families USA is a national nonprofit dedicated to the achievement of high-quality, affordable healthcare for all Americans. Families USA works to provide the consumer perspective in national and state debates on healthcare policy. The Web site provides several

resources including state-by-state information, the media center, and the legislative action center.

Healthfinder (http://www.healthfinder.gov/)
Healthfinder is a free Web portal to reliable consumer health and human services information developed by the U.S. Department of Health and Human Services. Healthfinder can lead you to selected online publications, clearinghouses, databases, Web sites, and support and self-help groups, as well as the government agencies and nonprofit organizations that produce reliable information for the public.

Health Resources and Services Administration (http://www.hrsa.dhhs.gov/)
The Health Resources and Services Administration provides an overview of programs, services, and grant opportunities from the Department of Health and Human Services agency.

Indian Health Service (http://www.ihs.gov/)
Indian Health Service, an agency within the Department of Health and Human Services, is responsible for providing federal health services to American Indians and Alaska Natives. The Web site provides information on the agency's activities and serves as an online resource for Native American communities.

Kaisernetwork.org (http://www.kaisernetwork.org/)
Kaisernetwork.org, a project of the Henry J. Kaiser Family Foundation, is a free webcasting and news summary service intended to keep users informed about critical health policy issues. Web site features include daily reports from major newspapers, Healthcast (live and archived webcasts of major health policy events and speeches), and the searchable AdWatch and Health Poll Search features.

KidsHealth (http://kidshealth.org/)
Created by the medical experts at the Nemours Foundation, the KidsHealth Web site offers up-to-date health and medical information for the parents of children and teens as well as numerous interactive educational features.

Medicare.gov (http://www.medicare.gov/default.asp?ScreenReaderOn=False)
Medicare.gov is the official U.S. Government Web site for Medicare information, including coverage, joining, the Medicare card, and address changes. The Web site also has information on choosing a nursing home, publications that can be downloaded, fraud and abuse information, a Health Information section, and search tools for locating health plans, nursing homes, dialysis facilities, Medigap policies, contacts, Medicare events, participating physicians, and prescription assistance programs.

MedWeb (http://WWW.MedWeb.Emory.Edu/MedWeb/)
Created and maintained by the staff of the Robert W. Woodruff Health Sciences Center Library of Emory University, MedWeb is billed as a biomedical Internet resource. Its vast database has the ability to custom-generate keyword search results within the parameters of a primary and secondary subject area, such as Grants and Funding—Cardiology.

National Coalition on healthcare (http://www.nchc.org/)
The National Coalition on healthcare, founded in 1990, is comprised of almost 96 groups, employing or representing approximately 100 million Americans working to improve America's healthcare. The Coalition members include large and small businesses, labor unions, consumer groups, religious groups, and primary care providers.

National Health Information Center (http://www.health.gov/nhic/)
Established in 1979 by the U.S. Department of Health and Human Services' Office of Disease Prevention and Health Promotion, the National Health Information Center (NHIC) is a health information referral service that puts health professionals and consumers who have health questions in touch with those organizations that are best able to provide answers.

NHIC's Health Information Resource Database includes 1,100 organizations and government offices that provide health information upon request. Entries include contact information, short abstracts, and information about publications and services the organizations provide.

National Institutes of Health (http://www.nih.gov/grants/)

The National Institutes of Health (NIH) is the federal government's principle biomedical research agency and a terrific online resource for NIH grant and fellowship programs information, policy changes, and access to the CRISP database. CRISP (Computer Retrieval of Information on Scientific Projects) is a searchable database of federally funded biomedical research projects conducted at universities, hospitals, and other research institutions. Links are also provided to a contracts/RFP page, the *NIH Guide for Grants and Contracts,* and the home pages of NIH Institutes, Centers, and Divisions.

New York State Conference of Local Mental Hygiene Directors (http://www.clmhd.org/)

The New York State Conference of Local Mental Hygiene Directors is a statewide membership organization composed of local mental hygiene directors and commissioners throughout all 57 New York state counties and New York City. Its Web site provides a listing of members and their counties, a page of useful related links, and a "members only" section.

Office of Minority Health Resource Center (http://www.omhrc.gov/omhrc/index.htm)

The Office of Minority Health (OMH) Resource Center offers a large amount of easily navigable material, including news releases, online publications, OMH funding announcements, a searchable funding database, requests for proposals, requests for applications, internships awards program announcements, additional funding resources, and OMH's newsletter, *Closing the Gap.*

University of Maryland's Center for School Mental Health Assistance (http://csmha.umaryland.edu/)

The Center for School Mental Health Assistance (CSMHA) provides technical assistance and leadership to facilitate learning and promote positive mental health in children, adolescents, mothers, caregivers, and families. It works toward the development of programs that are accessible, family-centered, culturally sensitive, and responsive to local needs. The web site features a bulletin board announcing news and upcoming Center events, online access to some of its materials, an examination of critical issues, electronic editions of its newsletter, and a list of related links.

World Health News (http://www.worldhealthnews.harvard.edu/)

World Health News is an online news digest from the Center for Health Communication at the Harvard School of Public Health. The Web site covers critical public health issues from around the world and is designed to be a resource for an international audience of policy makers and journalists as well as public health researchers, practitioners, and advocates.

HIV/AIDS

Bailey House (http://www.baileyhouse.org/)

Bailey House, the second-oldest AIDS organization in New York City, provides safe, comfortable, and permanent housing through its two nationally recognized housing programs, Bailey-Holt House and the Supportive Housing Apartment Program, and offers vocational education, job training, and placements. In addition to information about its programs and services, the Web site has links to sites with information about HIV and AIDS.

The Body (http://www.thebody.com)

The Body is a comprehensive HIV/AIDS information site offering information on giving and getting help, as well as treatment information from experts, policy updates, and bulletin board communities.

CDC HIV/AIDS Resources (http://www.cdcnpin.org/hiv/start.htm)

CDC HIV/AIDS Resources provides searchable access to all current and past year volumes of the *CDC Morbidity and Mortality Weekly Report* for articles on HIV/AIDS, sexually transmitted diseases, or tuberculosis; additional information; and resources. There are FAQ's, free online publication orders, links to a national hotline, and the latest information on clinical trials and treatment programs.

The Estate Project for Artists With AIDS (http://www.artistswithaids.org/)

The Estate Project (EP) is part of the Alliance for Arts, a nonprofit arts service organization dedicated to policy research, information services, and advocacy for the arts in New York State. EP's Web site offers information on arts news, artists' resources, specific strategies for arts preservation, lists of grants that have been awarded in the arts, and information and/or links to relevant arts organizations, many of which are national in scope. The site is geared toward the special needs of artists with AIDS but provides information useful to others involved with the arts communities and information on how to donate to the project.

Gay Men's Health Crisis (http://www.gmhc.org)

Founded by volunteers in 1981, Gay Men's Health Crisis (GMHC) offers AIDS education and political advocacy nationwide and direct services to men, women, and children with AIDS, as well as their families, in New York City. GMHC's Web site is divided into three areas: Drugs, Sex, and HIV; Living with HIV; and Take Action. Each area summarizes the issues specific to it and directs visitors to practical information.

God's Love We Deliver (http://www.godslovewedeliver.org/)

A New York City-based organization, God's Love We Deliver is a corps of volunteers and staff that cook and deliver meals to AIDS patients throughout the metropolitan area. Meals are delivered free of charge, regardless of financial situation, within 24 hours of the necessary registration call. The site supplies this phone number and information on volunteering in many areas of the organization. There are also nutritional and counseling guides and tips and information on contributing to the group.

The Oasis Foundation (http://mysiteinc.com/fightaids/)

Baltimore, Maryland's Oasis Foundation supplies temporary and long-term housing and services for people living with HIV/AIDS or other developmentally limiting conditions, senior citizens, and others needing a continuum of care. The group buys, renovates, and rehabilitates downtown buildings in order to rent them, at affordable prices, to the specified groups. The site offers links to other AIDS, AIDS housing, and advocacy sites; features on successful projects; an events calendar; and information on contributions.

HUNGER

America's Second Harvest (http://www.secondharvest.org/)

As the nation's largest domestic hunger relief organization, America's Second Harvest offers an extensive array of resources related to hunger issues via its newly redesigned Web site. Features include hunger statistics and profiles of hungry Americans, public policy updates and research studies, contact information for its 189 food banks arranged by state, guidelines for making financial contributions and donating food, current news, and announcements of volunteer and lobbying opportunities. Visitors can also sign up to receive updates on hunger-related issues.

Hunger Site (http://www.thehungersite.com)
The Hunger Site allows donors to benefit the world's hungry while shopping online. For every dollar spent at one of the more than 80 online retailers, one cup of food is donated to the United Nations World Food Program at no extra cost.

MILITARY/VETERANS

Military, Veterans, & Patriotic Service Organizations of America (http://www.mvpsoa.org)
The Military, Veterans, & Patriotic Service Organizations of America is a nonprofit organization that prescreens and certifies national charities working to assist military personnel, veterans, and their families. The Web site provides links to the sites of other nonprofit organizations as well as postal addresses and telephone and fax numbers. Potential donors can perform a "charity search" using this site.

MULTICULTURAL/MINORITIES

Coalition for Asian-American Children and Families (http://www.cacf.org)
Established to challenge myths, break barriers, and advocate for change, the Coalition for Asian-American Children and Families Web site contains a valuable directory of resources for members of the Asian-American community.

Council of Latino Agencies/Consejo de Agencias Latinas (http://www.consejo.org)
Composed of approximately 37 member organizations in the nation's capital, the Council of Latino Agencies promotes awareness of available services geared towards bettering the quality of life in the Latino community.

Foundation Funding Sources for Tribal Libraries (http://www.u.arizona.edu/~ecubbins/founfund.html)
This site provides links to funding sources for North American Indian tribal libraries.

Indian Health Service (http://www.ihs.gov/)
Dedicated to raising the health status of American Indians and Alaska Natives, the Indian Health Service Web site provides information on the agency's activities and serves as an online resource for Native American communities.

Internet Resources for Urban/Minority Families (http://eric-web.tc.columbia.edu/families/other.html)
Internet Resources for Urban/Minority Families provides links to several different resources that are of interest to urban and minority families. Links include facts for families, families and work institute, and the Administration for Children and Families.

Medlineplus Health Information (http://www.nlm.nih.gov/medlineplus/)
The Medlineplus Health Information Web site provides specific health information for African American, Asian American Pacific Islander, American Indian, and Hispanic populations.

National Association for the Advancement of Colored People (http://www.naacp.org)
National Association for the Advancement of Colored People is the largest civil rights organization in the United States serving to ensure the political, educational, social, and economic equality of minority group citizens. The Web site includes a description of programs, news releases, and links to relevant Web sites.

NativeWeb Resource Center (http://www.nativeweb.org/resources)
NativeWeb Resource Center is a comprehensive collection of Web links oriented towards the Native American community and those who want to learn about Native culture.

Office of Minority Health (http://www.omhrc.gov)
The Office of Minority Health (OMH) Web site offers a large amount of easily navigable material, including news releases, online publications, grants announcements, a funding resource guide, news of upcoming events and conferences, links to OMH databases for funding opportunities, and organizations and programs.

SCIENCE

American Association for the Advancement of Science (http://www.aaas.org)
The American Association for the Advancement of Science provides up-to-date information on scientific research and education and links to science funding organizations in the United States and around the world.

Beyond Bio 101: The Transformation of Undergraduate Biology Education (http://www.hhmi.org/BeyondBio101/)
Bio 101: The Transformation of Undergraduate Biology Education is a colorful, well-designed report from the Howard Hughes Medical Institute based on the experiences of many of the 220 colleges and universities that, since 1988, have been awarded grants by the Institute's Undergraduate Biological Science Education Program. The 88-page report can be read online, or it can be downloaded to your hard drive and read offline.

National Science Foundation (http://www.nsf.gov/)
The National Science Foundation Web site is comprehensive and well-organized, with program and grants information in biology, education, engineering, the geosciences, math and the physical sciences, polar research, and the social and behavioral sciences.

Science's Next Wave (http://nextwave.sciencemag.org/ca/)
Billed as "an electronic network for the next generation of scientists," the Next Wave site features profiles of and practical career advice for young scientists, as well as links to numerous scientific organizations and funding sources. The site also features lots of material written by and of interest to Canadian scientists.

SOCIAL CHANGE

Changemakers (http://www.changemakers.net)
Changemakers is an initiative of Ashoka Innovators for the Public, a global nonprofit organization. It focuses on the world of social entrepreneurship. Its mission is "to provide inspiration, resources, and opportunities for those interested in social change throughout the world." The Changemakers Web site is composed of sections including the *Changemakers Journal,* library, and creative resourcing.

National Network of Grantmakers (http://www.nng.org/)
The National Network of Grantmakers (NNG) is an organization of 400 members (individual donors, foundation staff, board, and grantmaking committee members) involved in funding social and economic justice by supporting organizations working for economic and social change. The Web site provides program information, including NNG's research study on diversity in philanthropy and its "1% More for Democracy" campaign; a section with information on events, meetings, and networking activities organized around specific themes or topics; and a section with nonprofit links, job lists, publications available to purchase, and a Common Grant Application Form. The current issue of the quarterly newsletter is also available and is free to members and nonmembers.

SUBSTANCE ABUSE

The Alcoholic Beverage Medical Research Foundation (http://www.abmrf.org)

The Alcoholic Beverage Medical Research Foundation supports research on the effects of alcohol on health, behavior, and prevention of alcohol-related problems. The site provides grant guidelines, a journal on the issue, and links to related organizations and to sites with various information concerning alcohol research.

Join Together Online (http://www.jointogether.org/)

Join Together, a project of the Boston University School of Public Health, is a national resource for communities working to reduce substance abuse and gun violence nationwide through the dissemination of public policy and community action information. The Web site offers news releases, grant announcements, and JTO Direct E-mail, with up to date news, funding information, resources, facts, and Web links for both substance abuse and gun violence subscribers.

National Institute on Alcohol Abuse and Alcoholism (http://www.niaaa.nih.gov/)

The National Institute on Alcohol Abuse and Alcoholism Web site provides grants information, news notes and upcoming events, and links to related publications and databases.

Phoenix House (http://www.phoenixhouse.org/)

Phoenix House, the nation's leading nonprofit drug abuse service organization, has developed this comprehensive Web site loaded with news and links to related resources.

Substance Abuse and Mental Health Services Administration (http://www.samhsa.gov/)

Substance Abuse and Mental Health Services Administration (SAMHSA) awards grants in the areas of substance abuse treatment and prevention, collects and analyzes relevant statistics and data, and makes public and private policy recommendations to finance substance-abuse related services. The Web site has information about SAMHSA's programs, funding, statistics and data, public information, and grant, contract, and job opportunities.

WOMEN & GIRLS

Feminist Internet Gateway (http://www.feminist.org/gateway/master2.html)

The Feminist Internet Gateway is a comprehensive list of women's Web sites, maintained by The Feminist Majority, and arranged by subject: general women's issues, global feminism, violence against women, women and work, affirmative action, women and girls in sports, women in politics, women's health, abortion rights, and women's studies and centers.

Grants for Women/"The Grant Lady (http://www.grantlady.com)"

Shakurra Amatulla, the self-named "Grant Lady," publishes the *For Us Women* newsletter monthly. An annual subscription, available for $25, gets you a copy of this collection of grants being offered to women. Each issue allows subscribers to search in 17 subject areas for new listings. There are also articles to guide a grantseeker through the process and through news on the funding world.

Institute for Women's Policy Research (http://www.iwpr.org/)

The Institute for Women's Policy Research is a public policy research organization working with policymakers, scholars, and public interest groups to design, execute, and disseminate research that illuminates economics and social policy issues affecting women and famillies. The Web site is an excellent resource on issues of poverty and welfare, employment and earnings, work and family issues, the economic and social aspects of healthcare and domestic violence, and women's civic and political participation.

National Women's Health Information Center (http://www.4woman.gov/)
Sponsored by the Office on Women's Health of the U.S. Department of Health and Human Services, the National Women's Health Information Center provides access to information on all areas of women's health. The information on the Web site is obtained from a variety of federal and private sector resources and can be searched by health topic or by keyword. The site includes press releases, a news archive, a good set of links to online medical dictionaries and journals, and a Hot Topics in Congress section that has women's health-related legislation in the U.S. Congress.

Women's Funding Network (http://www.wfnet.org/)
Describing itself as an "international association of public and private women's foundations, federations, funds in community foundations, individual donors, and supporting institutions," the Women's Funding Network was established to support women and girls by encouraging collaboration among women, donors, communities, and institutions. The site provides visitors with an introduction, news, activities and programs, member links, and investment opportunities.

WomensNet (http://www.igc.org/igc/gateway/wnindex.html)
WomensNet supports women's organizations worldwide by providing and adapting tele-communications technology to enhance their work. The Web site includes news updates and action alerts.

Women's Philanthropy Institute (http://www.women-philanthropy.org)
Women's Philanthropy Institute is a nonprofit educational institute that brings together philanthropists, volunteers, and professional funders to educate and empower women as philanthropists, donors, and volunteers.

Nonprofit Management & Staffing Resources

GENERAL

Alliance for Nonprofit Management (http://www.allianceonline.org)
The Alliance for Nonprofit Management members include management support organizations, individual professionals, and a range of national, regional, umbrella, research and academic, publishing, and philanthropic organizations that provide training and consulting to nonprofits. The Alliance Web site contains a new Alliance Resource Center, which features Web sites, books, videos and other valuable resources relating to nonprofit management and governance; the Alliance online newsletter; a job bank; and a database of Alliance member providers, searchable by geographic area, name, state, types of assistance offered and by types of services offered.

Aspen Institute (http://www.aspeninstitute.org)
The Aspen Institute is a global forum for leaders from various disciplines to address critical issues that affect societies, organizations, and individuals. The Aspen Institute Web site provides information on the seminars and policy programs that the institute offers, application guidelines, special initiatives, publication content and summaries, research abstracts, a list of grant recipients, and links to nonprofit resources.

Association of Fundraising Professionals (http://www.afpnet.org)
The Association of Fundraising Professionals (AFP) consists of 25,000 individual members in 159 chapters throughout the United States, Canada, and Mexico working to advance philanthropy through education, training, mentoring, research, credentialing, and advocacy. Visitors to AFP's Web site will find extensive information on nonprofit philanthropy and the Association's activities and publications, AFP's professional advancement programs and course information, the full text of its Code of Ethical Principles and Standards

of Professional Practice, and the principles of an E-Donor Bill of Rights, created to address concerns and challenges arising from Internet charitable giving. In addition, job opportunity and member services modules are made available to Association members.

The Chronicle of Philanthropy (http://philanthropy.com/)

Like its biweekly print analog, *The Chronicle of Philanthropy*'s Web site is full of useful information for fundraisers, grantmakers, nonprofit managers, and others. The site is organized into broad topic areas—Gifts and Grants, Fund Raising, Managing nonprofit Groups, and Technology—and includes a summary of the contents of the *Chronicle*'s current issue, with an archive of articles from the past two years, a listing of award and RFP deadlines, job opportunities in the nonprofit sector, a listing of upcoming conferences and workshops, and annotated links to other nonprofit resources on the Internet. Visitors can also sign up for free e-mail updates about changes at the site as well as breaking news stories. Some of the material is available only to *Chronicle* subscribers.

CompassPoint Nonprofit Services (http://www.supportcenter.org/sf/)

Funded by foundations, corporations, and individuals, CompassPoint provides affordable management consulting, training, and information to the San Francisco Bay Area nonprofit sector. Web site visitors can access its Nonprofit GENIE (Global Electronic Nonprofit Information Express), a list of FAQs developed by the staff. Categories include strategic planning, financial management, and board development. A free biweekly newsletter is also available.

Coro (http://www.coro.org)

Coro is a nonprofit leadership training organization that offers related workshops, internships, fellowships, and youth programs to the nonprofit community. With centers in seven different U.S. cities, the Sacramento, California-based company's reach extends across the nation. Its alumni include professionals in a variety of sectors, such as government, business, media, and nonprofit.

Peter F. Drucker Foundation for Nonprofit Management (http://www.pfdf.org)

The Peter F. Drucker Foundation supports leadership in the nonprofit sector by awarding honors of distinction and supplying intellectual resources to promising nonprofit leaders.

Executive Service Corps of Southern California (http://www.escsc.org)

The Executive Service Corps of Southern California is an innovative organization that links retired executives and professionals with nonprofit organizations to serve as management consultants and board members on a volunteer basis. These services bring experience and knowledge to help the groups receiving them function more effectively. The site includes information on volunteering, highlights current projects, and offers links to other sites relating to the nonprofit world in California.

Free Management Library (http://www.mapnp.org/library/)

The Free Management Library is a complete library of resources for nonprofit and for-profit organizations. The library is designed to be as user-friendly as possible, with a focus on providing free, online management resources to organizations. Visitors to this well-organized Web site can conduct a category search of free, self-directed management courses in topics such as board roles and responsibilities, communications skills, finance and taxes, program development, program evaluation, and consultants.

The Grantsmanship Center (http://www.tgci.com/)

The Grantsmanship Center (TGCI) is a clearinghouse of fundraising information and training in grantsmanship and proposal writing for nonprofit organizations and government agencies. In addition to training program and schedule information, TGCI's Web site offers grant source information on community foundations and federal, state, and international funding; current Federal Register grant funding information, including a daily summary; TGCI's online magazine; and a listing of publications for fundraisers, including The TGCI proposal writing guide. The Web site also has a new resource, Winning Grant Proposals Online, which includes examples of effective proposal writing models, consisting entirely of recently funded, top-ranked grant proposals in a wide variety of subject areas.

Hauser Center for Nonprofit Organizations (http://www.ksghauser.harvard.edu)

The Hauser Center for Nonprofit Organizations is a Harvard University research center focusing on nonprofit policy and leadership.

The Institute for Not-for-Profit Management
(http://www.gsb.columbia.edu/execed/INM/index.html)

The Institute for Not-for-Profit Management (INM) at Columbia Business School provides graduate-level management training to executives of not-for-profit organizations through a variety of programs: the Executive Level Program, Middle Management Programs, and Leadership Development Program. Each of these takes the form of an intensive, several-day course rather than lasting a full semester. Customized programs for individual organizations are available, as are scholarships for eligible applicants whose agencies are unable to sponsor them fully.

Interactive Knowledge for Nonprofits Worldwide (http://www.iknow.org/)

Developed and maintained by Raffa & Associates, P.C., Interactive Knowledge for Nonprofits Worldwide (Iknow) is a collection of online resource links to information regarding business services, education, fringe benefits, fundraising, governance, human resources, an internet resource directory for nonprofit organizations, legal issues, legislation, strategic planning, and volunteerism.

The Learning Institute for Nonprofit Organizations (http://www.uwex.edu/li)

Sponsored in part by the W.K. Kellogg Foundation and the United Way, the Learning Institute assists nonprofit organizations by offering educational programs and materials concerning nonprofit administration. The site includes a section of links to topical online articles and to related sites.

The Management Center (http://www.tmcenter.org)

The Management Center is a resource for nonprofit management support in northern California. The mission of the Management Center is to help nonprofit organizations achieve their full potential through effective consulting, training, and information resources, with a membership option that includes discounts on Management Center services. The Web site has a program catalog, an events calendar, executive search services, and consulting services.

Mandel Center for Nonprofit Organizations (http://www.cwru.edu/mandelcenter/)

The Mandel Center for Nonprofit Organizations, affiliated with Case Western Reserve University, has been the standard-setter in graduate education for leaders of nonprofit organizations in the United States. The Center's site contains information about its academic programs, conferences and lectures, career and alumni services, publications (including abstracts), faculty, and links to related sites.

National Teacher Recruitment Clearinghouse (http://www.recruitingteachers.org/)

The National Teacher Recruitment Clearinghouse is a "one-stop shop" for information and resources about teacher recruitment and retention. Developed through a planning grant from the U.S. Department of Education, and hosted by Recruiting New Teachers, the Web site offers practical resources for recruiters, teachers seeking jobs, prospective teachers, and others looking for information about how to become a teacher and how to improve teacher recruitment and retention efforts. The Clearinghouse has links to and profiles of hundreds of job banks, in addition to other resources, with new job banks and postings being added on a daily basis.

The Nonprofit Coordinating Committee of New York (http://www.npccny.org/)

The Nonprofit Coordinating Committee (NPCC) of New York is a membership corporation of social service, educational, arts, religious, advocacy, health services, and community development groups, as well as foundations and individuals. The Web site includes information on advocacy, lobbying, government/tax issues, financial matters, fundraising, governance and organizational issues, health, disability insurance, workers' compensation, organizational insurance, personnel management, postal issues, and NPCC events, projects and editorials. Members can also sign up to receive automated, targeted notices on funding availability and access to selected articles from NPCC's monthly newsletter.

Non-Profit Nuts & Bolts (http://www.nutsbolts.com)

Non-Profit Nuts & Bolts provides nonprofit professionals with management tips that will help build better organizations. The Web site includes articles, reports, and resources that pertain to nonprofit management.

Nonprofit Resource Center (http://www.not-for-profit.org)

The Nonprofit Resource Center is designed for managers, board members, and volunteers of nonprofit or tax-exempt organizations. The Web site contains links to resources for nonprofits, listed by category. Categories include legal links, fundraising, and books for nonprofits.

The Online Nonprofit Information Center
(http://www.socialworker.com/nonprofit/nphome.htm)

The Online Nonprofit Information Center provides tools to help nonprofit organizations. The Web site provides purchasing information for five different nonprofit handbooks, along with content summaries of each handbook. The site also features an annotated nonprofit links page.

Texas Nonprofit Management Assistance Network (http://www.texasnetwork.org)

The Texas Nonprofit Management Assistance Network, established in 1999, develops and connects centers and organizations that provide information, libraries, workshops, consulting services, and publications to the nonprofit sector. The Web site has membership criteria and benefits information; a list of current members, with links to their Web sites; news and events; and links to Web sites of Texas educational institutions that have programs that include the study of nonprofits or volunteerism.

BOARDS

Board Café (http://www.boardcafe.org)

Board Café, published by CompassPoint Nonprofit Services, is a monthly electronic newsletter for members of nonprofit boards. Each issue includes a menu of information, opinion, news, and resources, with numerous "Little Ideas", and one "Big Idea" that can be applied to board work. The Web site also offers a summary of past issues.

Board Match Plus (http://www.boardmatchplus.org)

Board Match Plus is a program designed to introduce qualified candidates to nonprofit boards of directors. Visitors to the site can join a nonprofit board or get advice on board service. The site also contains a "board classifieds" section, which allows visitors to browse board openings and submit experience information to boards with openings.

Free Management Library (http://www.mapnp.org/library/)

The Free Management Library is a complete library of resources for nonprofit and for-profit organizations. The library is designed to be as user-friendly as possible, with a focus on providing free, online management resources to organizations. Visitors to this well-organized Web site can conduct a category search of free, self-directed management courses in topics such as board roles and responsibilities, communications skills, finance and taxes, program development, program evaluation, and consultants.

National Center for Nonprofit Boards (http://www.ncnb.org)

Established in 1988 by the Association of Governing Boards of Universities and Colleges and Independent Sector, the National Center for Nonprofit Boards (NCNB) provides resources, programs, and services to the nonprofit community and publishes material on nonprofit governance, including more than 100 booklets, books, videos, and audiotapes. Visitors to the NCNB Web site will find membership, training, education, and consulting services; NCNB's Board Information Center, a free information clearinghouse on board-related topics; and *Board Member Online,* an abridged version of *Board Member,* the members-only periodical of the NCNB.

JOB OPPORTUNITIES

ACCESS (http://www.accessjobs.org)

Established just as public use of the Internet was beginning to explode, ACCESS continues to serve as a clearinghouse for employment, internships, volunteering, and career development in the nonprofit sector.

Action Without Borders—Nonprofit Internships (http://www.idealist.org/ip/internshipSearch?MODULE=INTERNSHIP)

Action Without Borders is a one-stop shopping source for internship opportunities around the United States and around the world. Visitors can conduct a keyword search of the database and subscribe to an internship mailing list for daily updates on new postings.

Charity Channel (http://charitychannel.com)

At Charity Channel's Job search feature, you can search for positions by title, location, organization, or classification. Updated daily.

CareerBuilder.com (http://www.careerbuilder.com/)

Combining the classified sections of several leading newspapers across the United States with Web postings from individual employers, this site is one of the hottest destinations for jobseekers with Internet access.

CharityCareers.com (http://www.charitycareers.com)

Serving nonprofit professionals across Canada, CharityCareers.com features current positions, a client list, a bookstore, online newsletters and reports, charity news, and career tips.

CharityJobs (http://www.charityjobs.co.uk/)

CharityJobs matches employers with jobseekers in the United Kingdom's nonprofit sector free of charge, offering advertising space, a weekly e-mail digest of charity vacancies, career advice for beginners, and links to other related helpful sites.

The Chronicle of Higher Education Career Network (http://chronicle.com/jobs/)

A valuable resource for professionals seeking employment in the field of higher education, this site contains job announcements that are updated weekly and offers career-related advice.

The Chronicle of Philanthropy—Job Openings (http://www.philanthropy.com/jobs/)

Like its biweekly print analog, *The Chronicle of Philanthropy*'s Web site is full of useful information for fundraisers, grantmakers, nonprofit managers, and others. Job-hunters can also benefit from searchable online position listings at a variety of nonprofit organizations in each issue.

Community Career Center (http://www.nonprofitjobs.org)

The Career Center provides a place for employers and prospective employees in the non-profit sector to find each other. Employers can post jobs, and candidates can submit their credentials. The site also provides information on other services available for nonprofit managers.

Idealist—Nonprofit Jobs (http://www.idealist.org/ip/jobSearch?MODULE=JOB)

This is a searchable database of nonprofit jobs around the world. Visitors can search the database and subscribe to a free e-mail job list, and nonprofits can register and post job openings at no charge.

Monster.com (http://monster.com/)

One of the first and biggest online job boards, Monster.com allows jobseekers to search nationwide listings by geographic location, field of interest, company, or keyword and even contains international listings. In addition, users can receive custom job-tracking and can store their resumes and cover letters online.

Nonprofit Career Network (http://www.nonprofitcareer.com)

Created to fill the needs of the nonprofit sector, the Nonprofit Career Network is a "one-stop resource center" for job seekers looking for employment within a nonprofit organization and for nonprofits seeking qualified candidates. Visitors can post jobs or resumes, search national job listings, consult a nonprofit organization directory and corporate profiles, and find out about job fairs, conferences, and workshops going on around the country. Internships and volunteer information for a handful of nonprofit organizations is also available.

Opportunity NOCs (http://www.opportunitynocs.org)

Job seekers can conduct free searches through a large database of available nonprofit jobs online, and nonprofit organizations can post help wanted classified ads. *Opportunity NOCs* also features a nonprofit library and career resource center. This is a resource for those seeking careers in the arts, health, social services, education, and other public sector or social enterprise jobs. *Opportunity NOCs* has been published by the Management Center of San Francisco since 1986.

SERVEnet (http://www.servenet.org/)

SERVEnet, a program of Youth Service America, was designed to encourage community involvement through volunteering by providing volunteer-based nonprofit organizations with the best resources available to them in a quick and easy manner and to match the skills, experience, and enthusiasm of dedicated volunteers with nonprofit organizations who need their participation. Visitors to the Web site can post and find volunteer and career opportunities, service news, events, and other resources. Volunteer opportunities are listed by location and can be searched by entering a zip code.

PROGRAM EVALUATION

American Evaluation Association (http://www.eval.org/)

The American Evaluation Association (AEA) is an international professional association of evaluators who assess the effectiveness of programs, policies, personnel, products, and organizations. The AEA Web site offers a variety of evaluation-related resources, including information about the AEA's annual conference and other related events; special interest groups; published books and journals; the full-text of key documents for evaluators; a list of job postings and training institutions in the field; links to other sites of interest; and the EVALTALK Listserv, an open discussion list devoted to issues in the field of evaluation. The AEA member newsletter, first published in the winter of 2001, is also accessible from the Web site.

InnoNet (http://www.inetwork.org/)

Innovation Network, Inc. (InnoNet) is dedicated to building evaluation skills, knowledge, and processes within public and nonprofit organizations through the use of participatory evaluation. The InnoNet Web site provides a free, innovative "Workstation" tool to guide nonprofits and public agencies through a planning and evaluation process, resulting in a blueprint for designing, evaluating, and implementing a successful program and corresponding work plan.

United Way Outcome Measurement Resource Network
(http://www.unitedway.org/outcomes/)

This branch of the United Way of America provides an online resource library, which contains excerpts from its manual, *Measuring Program Outcomes: A Practical Approach,* the full text of selected papers and newsletter articles, and links to other resources on the Web, subdivided by category.

VOLUNTARISM

Association for Research on Nonprofit Organizations and Voluntary Action
(http://www.arnova.org/)

The Association for Research on Nonprofit Organizations and Voluntary Action (ARNOVA) describes itself as "an international, interdisciplinary network of scholars and nonprofit leaders fostering the creation, application, and dissemination of research on voluntary action, nonprofit organizations, philanthropy, and civil society." Its main forms of outreach are an annual conference, a variety of publications, and electronic discussions and seminars. ARNOVA's Web site includes information about these various activities, as well as a signup option for an e-mail-based discussion group.

Cybervpm.com (http://www.cybervpm.com)

Cybervpm.com is an Internet resource for volunteer programs. The Web site offers a newsletter on volunteer management, advice for volunteers, and links to other resources for volunteer programs. The Web site also includes an online discussion group for volunteer program managers, as well as an online library that is categorized by the types of resources available.

Energize (http://www.energizeinc.com/)

Energize, Inc. is an international training, consulting, and publishing firm that specializes in all types of organizations with their volunteer efforts. The Web site has a free Job/Internship Bank, which includes members, interns, and community service participants; a volunteer management library of articles and books; and volunteerism information sources and links, with listings of conferences, classes, resource centers and Web sites, magazines, and products and services.

Federal Department of Housing and Urban Development Volunteer Center
(http://www.hud.gov/volunter.html)

The Federal Department of Housing and Urban Development Volunteer Center provides a listing of volunteer opportunities, including federal, national, and local volunteer programs. The Web site also includes links to volunteer publications.

Points of Light Foundation (http://www.pointsoflight.org)

Dedicated to encouraging community service, the Points of Light Foundation provides assistance to businesses that institute employee volunteer programs, youth organizations that promote involvement in the welfare of their community, and nonprofit groups that recruit and coordinate volunteer efforts.

SERVEnet (http://www.servenet.org/)

SERVEnet, a program of Youth Service America, was designed to encourage community involvement through volunteering by providing volunteer-based nonprofit organizations with the best resources available to them in a quick and easy manner and to match the skills, experience, and enthusiasm of dedicated volunteers with nonprofit organizations who need their participation. Visitors to the Web site can post and find volunteer and career opportunities, service news, events, and other resources. Volunteer opportunities are listed by location and can be searched by entering a zip code.

Service Leader's Virtual Volunteering Project (http://www.serviceleader.org/vv/)

Launched in 1996, the Virtual Volunteering Project (VVP) works to encourage and assist in the development of volunteer activities that can be completed off-site via the Internet. VVP publishes *VIRTUAL VERVE,* an electronic newsletter on virtual volunteering.

Volunteer For Our Children (http://www.child.net/volunteer.htm)

Volunteer For Our Children was created as part of Youth and Children Net. Volunteer For Children provides ideas on what can be done and where time can be contributed to help children. Additional volunteer opportunities are added to the site on the first of every month.

Volunteer Match (http://www.impactonline.org)

A service of ImpactOnline, Volunteer Match helps individuals nationwide find on-site volunteer opportunities posted by local nonprofit and public sector organizations. Volunteers can search the online database of thousands of one-time and ongoing opportunities—including walk-a-thons, beach day cleanups, tutoring, home building, and meal deliveries—by zip code, category, and date, then sign up automatically by e-mail for those that fit their interest and schedule. The Web site also has a listing of "virtual volunteering" opportunities for individuals, including those with disabilities who wish to contribute time via e-mail.

VoxCap Network (http://www.voxcap.com/)

VoxCap.com is an interactive community devoted to online activism. From education to the environment to international relations, this site offers up-to-date information on issues that involve people and politics. There are many opportunities for a visitor to express an opinion or just learn more about a huge array of subjects. There are also chances to take action online, from e-mailing a politician to writing a letter to an editor of a paper.

Washington State University's Volunteer Management Certificate Program (http://vmcp.wsu.edu/)

The Volunteer Management Certificate Program is a Web-based learning opportunity encompassing the training, recruiting, management, and recognition of volunteers. Prospective students visiting the site will find program and enrollment information, a description of program instructors, and a skills assessment self-test. Registered students have their own point of entry into the site, and have easy access to online help and support as needed.

Nonprofit Technology Resources

Benton Foundation's Nonprofits & Communities (http://www.benton.org/Nonprofits)

Benton Foundation's Nonprofits & Communities provides information to nonprofits and charities about useful technology updates and programs. The Web site offers a nonprofit toolkit and useful links to related services, articles, and other organizations.

CharityFocus (http://www.charityfocus.org/)

CharityFocus is a California nonprofit that organizes over 850 volunteers to create and market Web sites for nonprofit organizations, free of charge. The Web site also has a list of organizations and resources for nonprofits, as well as a list of resources for volunteers designing Web pages

Charity Village (http://www.charityvillage.com/)

The Canadian-based Charity Village Web site has news, jobs, information, and resources for nonprofit managers, staffers and fundraisers, donors, and volunteers. Visitors to the Web site can access a searchable directory of annotated links to Canadian charities and nonprofit organizations, more than 10,000 positions in Canadian nonprofit organizations, an online directory of products and services especially for nonprofit executives, and a listing of educational programs and professional development opportunities, including Charity Village's own workshops and online tutorials, and links to dozens of courses available across the country.

Closing the Digital Divide (http://www.digitaldivide.gov/)

Maintained by the National Telecommunications Information Administration, this Web site is a central clearinghouse of data about the digital divide. The Web site offers useful audio/video excerpts from the December 1999 Digital Divide Summit and detailed government reports on the subject.

Community Connector (http://databases.si.umich.edu/cfdocs/community/index.cfm)

This is a Web site for community-service organizations, funders, academics, and students who are using technology to improve their local communities. Offerings include news updates, research reports, articles, handbooks, an original journal, a directory of community networks, and links to relevant resources.

Community Technology Centers' Network (http://www.ctcnet.org)

The Community Technology Centers' Network (CTCNet) is a national membership organization that promotes nonprofit and community-based efforts to provide equal access to technology skills and usage to the general public and to disadvantaged populations. The Web site has address and contact information for the more than 400 community technology centers in the United States, Ireland, Scotland, Spain, and the United Kingdom, where access to computers and computer-related technology is available. The site also has relevant news, conference and resources sharing information.

CompuMentor (http://www.compumentor.org)

CompuMentor works to provide technology resources—person-to-person services, low-cost software, and online resources—to nonprofits and schools serving low-income communities. The Web site has software packages that can be ordered online for a fraction of the retail cost to organizations that qualify, a mentor matching program that matches skilled technical volunteers with community organizations and schools, a consulting program that includes technology planning for small and mid-size nonprofits, and information for nonprofits interested in developing a community technology center to provide access and training to low-income or disadvantaged communities.

Computer Recycling Resource List
(http://www.pnnonline.org/technology/computerrecycle1.cfm)

The Computer Recycling Resource List is a comprehensive list of organizations located in the United States that recycle and/or donate computers. The list is compiled by Lauren Matthews for Philanthropy News Network.

The Digital Divide Network (http://www.digitaldividenetwork.org/)

The Digital Divide Network is a product of the Benton Foundation, in association with the National Urban League. Visitors to the Web site can search for news about efforts going on across the country and research organizations and corporations involved in those efforts to bridge the gap.

Download.com (http://www.download.com)

Hosted by CNET, the Download.com Web site serves as a virtual warehouse of software and shareware of all kinds. Application types include business, education, games, home and personal, internet, multimedia and design development tools, utilities, drivers, PC, Mac, PalmPilot, Windows CE, and Linux.

ebase (http://www.ebase.org)

ebase is an integrated database template based on File Maker Pro that helps nonprofits effectively manage interactive communications with their members, donors, citizen activists, and volunteers. The database is available for downloading free of charge from the Web site.

The Electronic Development and Environment Information System (ELDIS) (http://nt1.ids.ac.uk/eldis/eldis.htm)

The Electronic Development and Environment Information System (ELDIS) offers the latest information on development and environmental issues. ELDIS provides descriptions and links to various sources of information including Web sites, databases, library catalogues, bibliographies, map and newspaper collections, and research project information. ELDIS also offers a database hosting service.

Flatiron WebWorks (http://www.flatiron.org/)

Located in New York City, Flatirons WebWorks is an organization dedicated to creating and promoting affordable Internet presence and customized Web pages for nonprofit organizations and small businesses. It was conceived by a team of professionals who see the Internet as an innovative and exciting means for nonprofits and small enterprises to get their messages out to a global audience. Web site offerings include a mission statement, client list, and detailed price sheet.

Gifts in Kind International (http://www.giftsinkind.org/)

Gifts In Kind International links corporations and their product donations and services, including software and computer training, with a network of more than 50,000 nonprofit organizations. Gifts In Kind, a free global online system, matches company volunteers with nonprofits needing assistance such as community rebuilding, mentoring, coaching, technology planning, and other critically needed support.

iComm (http://www.icomm.ca)

iComm is a nonprofit Internet service provider that donates its services to other nonprofits, community organizations, and charities all over the world.

Knowledge in Technology (http://www.nyfa.org/kit/index.html)

Knowledge in Technology is a pilot program of the New York Foundation for the Arts' (NYFA) online communication service Arts Wire. This project provides small to mid-sized nonprofit arts organizations with workshops, technical assistance, and an online magazine aimed to help these groups communicate and prosper in the face of new technologies.

Making the Net Work (http://www.makingthenetwork.org/)

Making The Net Work, a British-American initiative led by David Wilcox, Drew Mackie, and Terry Grunwald, aims to help those planning to get their organization or neighbourhood online or create local technology centers. The Web site offers a toolbox that provides information for communities and organizations seeking an online presence.

Morino Institute (http://www.morino.org/)

The Morino Institute is a nonprofit organization that explores the opportunities and risks of the Internet and the New Economy to advance social change by stimulating entrepreneurship, advancing a more effective philanthropy, closing social divides, and understanding the relationship and impact of the Internet on our society. The Web site has speeches and publications, information on the Institute's programs and venture philanthropy partners, and additional resources.

National Cristina Foundation (http://www.cristina.org/)

The National Cristina Foundation provides computer technology and solutions to give people with disabilities, students at risk, and economically disadvantaged persons the opportunity, through training, to lead more independent and productive lives.

The Nonprofit Software Index (http://www.npinfotech.org/tnopsi/index.htm)

Hosted by Seton Hall University's Center for Nonprofit Service, this low-graphics, frames-based site lists software packages in a variety of categories, including fundraising, financial, grants management, matching gifts, personnel, planned giving, and volunteer management. Each entry includes a detailed description of the software, system requirements, and company contact information.

Pew Internet & American Life (http://www.pewinternet.org/)

A project of the Pew Research Center for People and the Press, the Tides Center and the Pew Charitable Trusts, the Pew Internet & American Life Project explores the growth of the Internet and its societal effects on families, communities, and work environments. The Web site provides research reports, a useful listing of links, and a two-week archive of relevant news stories about society and the Internet.

Philanthropy News Network/Nonprofits & Technology
(http://www.pnnonline.org/technology/)

This free online journal offers new articles daily and includes a technology section detailing updates on technology in the nonprofit sector.

Seeking Solutions to the Digital Divide (http://www.digitaldivide.org/)

The Seeking Solutions to the Digital Divide Web site is designed to create solutions for bridging the digital divide and features links to various discussion forums, corporations, nonprofit organizations, and Web sites.

SeniorNet (http://www.seniornet.org/)

SeniorNet is a national nonprofit organization dedicated to building a community of computer-using seniors who use their new skills for their own benefit and to benefit society. The site provides a listing of SeniorNet Learning Centers by state, roundtable discussions and e-mail pen pals, information on computer discounts, and information on SeniorNet's educational programs.

TechRocks (http://www.techrocks.org/)

TechRocks (formerly the Technology Project), encourages and enables foundations, advocacy groups, and leading activists to use technology to achieve their goals. Visitors to the TechRocks Web site will find a free downloadable software program (ebase) that enables nonprofit organizations to manage their relationships with their members, donors, activists, and volunteers; an online organization program; and additional information on cutting edge products or services to nonprofit organizations.

Tech Soup (http://www.techsoup.org/)

Tech Soup is a Web-based resource center that offers technology assistance and solutions for small to midsize nonprofit organizations. The site offers information on where to find donated or discounted software and equipment; computer training; advice on technology funding; technology planning; and listings of available volunteers and consultants. The Web site also has a free, monthly publication, *By the Cup,* with features articles related to nonprofit technology.

Technology Grant News (http://www.technologygrantnews.com)
Technology Grant News, published four times a year, covers upcoming grant announce-ments by government, technology funders, trade associations, and private foundations. Among the technology funding opportunities covered are creating an Internet presence for educational purposes, electronic publishing, and global nonprofits and emerging technol-ogy outreach. The Web site has a sample issue with links to featured grant sites and a Grants Index sampling. A discounted subscription is offered to nonprofits.

Technology Resource Consortium (http://www.igc.org/trc/)
The Technology Resource Consortium is an association of nonprofit technology assistance organizations that provide education about and access to information technology to private and public nonprofit organizations.

Technology Tip Sheets for Nonprofits (http://www.coyotecom.com/tips.html)
Technology Tip Sheets for Nonprofits was created by Jayne Cravens, of Coyote Communi-cations, to help nonprofit and public sector organizations reap money-saving, pro-gram-enhancing benefits from technology. Most of the material is geared to commu-nity-based organizations, but some materials are for a broader audience. The Web site includes a What's New section.

The Web Developer's Toolkit (http://www.fund-online.com/alabook/links/resource.htm)
The Web Developer's Toolkit has authoring, design, graphics, and other resources for developing a Web site, from *Fundraising and Friend-Raising on the Web: A Handbook for Libraries and Other Nonprofit Organizations.*

Web Page Design for Designers (http://www.wpdfd.com/wpdres.htm)
The Web Page Design for Designers Web site serves as a portal to a vast array of free Web design-related resources on the Internet. The information on the Web site is searchable, and the links are broken down by subject area. Each link is annotated with a brief description.

World Wide Web Consortium (http://www.w3.org/)
Under the direction of Tim Berners-Lee, the World Wide Web Consortium (WC3) has played a leading role since 1994 in developing and articulating the specifications and pro-tocols at the heart of the Web. The W3C develops interoperable technologies (specifica-tions, guidelines, software, and tools) to lead the Web to its full potential as a forum for information, commerce, communication, and collective understanding. The Web site has W3C news as well as links to information about W3C technologies and getting involved in W3C.

International Resources

GENERAL

American Councils for International Education (http://www.actr.org)
American Councils for International Education is a nonprofit organization that specializes in education, training, and consulting, with a focus on the countries of Eastern Europe, Russia, and Eurasia. The organization's programs include academic exchange, professional training, institution building, research, materials development, and technical assistance. The Web site includes information about grant and fellowship opportunities for both U.S. and New Independent States (NIS) citizens.

Ashoka (http://www.ashoka.org)
Arlington, Virginia-based Ashoka searches the world for the best new ideas championed by the most capable, innovative social entrepreneurs and invests in them financially and pro-fessionally by selecting them to be Ashoka Fellows. The organization currently has fellows

in Africa, Asia, Central Europe, Latin America, the United States, and Canada working in a range of fields, including learning/education, environment, health, human rights, economic development, and civic participation. The Ashoka site offers information on selection procedures, a link to Chankemakers.net (one of its initiatives), job and volunteer opportunities, and an online donation form.

Charities Aid Foundation (http://www.charitynet.org/index.html)
Charities Aid Foundation, a British nonprofit whose aim is to encourage charitable giving in the United Kingdom as well as internationally, sponsors the CharityNet Web site, "a resource centre for the nonprofit sector and its contributors." The site includes contact information for thousands of charities and serves as a technical assistance provider to both funders and nonprofits. Of special interest is the site's Corporate Community Involvement Network, an alphabetical list of links to more than 250 corporate (U.S.-based and multinational) Web sites with charitable giving information.

Cross-Cultural Solutions (http://www.crossculturalsolutions.org/)
Cross-cultural Solutions is a nonprofit organization that utilizes humanitarian volunteer action in the interest of empowering local communities, fostering cultural sensitivity and understanding, and furthering social progress in China, Cuba, India, Ghana, Peru, and Russia. Information on the Web site includes an introduction to the organization, its operating philosophy, program descriptions, FAQs, comments from the press, the organization's newsletter, and a list of related links.

Disaster Relief.Org (http://www.disasterrelief.org/)
Disaster Relief.Org is an easy-to-navigate clearinghouse for worldwide disaster aid and information.

Grantmakers Without Borders (http://www.internationaldonors.org/)
Grantmakers Without Borders is a collaborative project of the International Donors' Dialogue and the International Working Group of the National Network of Grantmakers, working to expand and enrich progressive international philanthropy and to support international projects by providing free advice, alternative sources of information, and increased opportunities for communication among donors. The Web site has an annotated set of links to resources for international philanthropy, organized by category: donor organizations, organized philanthropy, international news, economics and finance, statistics, and think tanks.

Idealist (http://www.idealist.org)
Idealist, in English and Spanish, offers a searchable network of 20,000 nonprofit and community organizations in 150 countries, which can be searched or browsed by name, location, or mission. There is also a searchable list of volunteer opportunities and hundreds of job and internship listings, events, and publications.

International Foundation for Election Systems (IFES) (http://www.ifes.org/)
IFES promotes democracy worldwide and serves as a clearinghouse for information about democratic development and elections by conducting research and providing nonpartisan technical assistance in more than 100 countries. The organization's Web site features a calendar of elections around the world, information about its library holdings and current projects, links to related organizations, past issues of its newsletter, contact information for its various field offices, and job opportunities.

International Law Institute (http://www.ili.org)
The International Law Institute works toward finding practical solutions to the legal, economic, and financial problems of the international community. Its mission is carried out through scholarly research, publishing, and practical legal training and technical assistance regarding various components of international law, economic policy, and practice. The

organization's site features news, descriptions of its courses and publications, and includes a long list of related links, broken down by subject area.

International Meeting of Associations Serving Grantmakers (http://www.imag.org/)

Sponsored by the Council on Foundations, this initiative seeks to bring together grant-makers from around the world to increase communication with each other, pool resources, and raise awareness of global issues. The site includes a discussion forum, associations list, announcements of upcoming activities, pertinent articles, contact information for coordi-nating committees, and useful links.

International Reading Association (http://www.reading.org)

The International Reading Association, a professional membership organization with members and affiliates in 99 countries, is dedicated to promoting high levels of literacy for all by improving the quality of reading instruction, disseminating research and information about reading, and encouraging the lifetime reading habit. The organization's Web site includes a nice listing of grant opportunities.

International Research & Exchanges Board (http://www.irex.org)

The International Research & Exchanges (IREX) Board is an international nonprofit orga-nization that administers programs between the United States and the countries of Eastern Europe, the New Independent States, Asia, and the Near East. With its traditional base in the university research community and in collaboration with partners from the policy, cor-porate, media, and private foundation sectors, IREX sponsors and supports programs of advanced field research, professional training, international conferences, seminars, and comparative analysis.

Internet Law & Policy Forum (http://www.ilpf.org/)

The Internet Law & Policy Forum (ILPF) is dedicated to promoting global growth of e-commerce by contributing to a better understanding of the particular legal issues that arise from the cross border nature of the electronic medium. ILPF offers a spectrum of resources to lawyers and legal policy experts and provides a neutral forum for discussion of legal and policy issues that will effect the growth of global electronic commerce.

Internet Prospector (http://www.internet-prospector.org/)

Internet Prospector is a nonprofit service produced by volunteers nationwide who search the Web for prospect research information for nonprofit fundraisers and the prospect research community, but anyone seeking tools for accessing corporate, foundation, bio-graphical, international, and online news sources will find this Web site useful. You'll find an online newsletter and archives of past issues, search engine prospecting and test results, tips for foundation searches, international audio and video Web content, and Using Zip Code Demographics For Prospecting, a specialized Internet research tools.

NGO Global Network (http://www.ngo.org)

The NGO Global Network is a Web site for non-governmental organizations associated with the United Nations. The Web site has information about weekly briefings, UN confer-ences and observances and other activities at the UN and throughout the NGO community, and a nice set of links to Web sites of NGOs associated with the UN.

Novartis Foundation for Sustainable Development (http://www.foundation.novartis.com)

Established in December 1996, and formerly known as the Ciba-Geigy Foundation for Cooperation with Developing Countries, the Novartis Foundation supports a variety of pro-jects in developing countries in the areas of agriculture, healthcare, and social development.

Organization for Economic Cooperation and Development (http://www.oecd.org/)

The Organization for Economic Cooperation and Development, an international think tank whose headquarters are located in Paris, France, incorporates 30 member countries within an organization that provides governments a setting in which to discuss, develop, and perfect economic and social policy. Its Web site includes statistics, news and events, publication information, an online bookstore, and a site-wide search engine.

The Peace Corps (http://www.peacecorps.gov/home.html)
The Peace Corps, a volunteer aid organization, currently serves 78 countries and includes programs in education, the environment, health, business, agriculture, and other fields.

ReliefWeb (http://www.reliefweb.int)
ReliefWeb is a project of the United Nations Office for the Coordination of Humanitarian Affairs. It strives to improve humanitarian relief efforts through the timely dissemination of reliable information on prevention, preparedness, and disaster response. In addition to current news regarding international emergencies, the Web site provides financial figures on humanitarian assistance over the last five years, a list of recent natural disasters worldwide, job openings, and a directory of humanitarian organizations.

Soros Foundations Network (http://www.soros.org)
The Soros Foundations Network is a clearinghouse of information about and gateway to the dozens of Soros programs and organizations that support the development and maintenance of "open societies" in countries around the world.

Trickle Up Program (http://www.trickleup.org/)
Based in New York City, the Trickle Up Program encourages poor people (with special outreach to women, youth, and other disadvantaged groups) in Africa, Asia, and the Americas to start their own businesses by providing seed capital and teaching them basic business skills. The Trickle Up Web site includes success stories from the field, copies of its recent annual reports and financial statements, back issues of its online newsletter, and an online donation area.

The United Nations (http://www.un.org/)
The United Nations, an umbrella organization of international agencies, committees, and task forces, conducts worldwide efforts encompassing peace and security, economic and social development, international law, human rights, and humanitarian aid. Its vast, multilingual Web site provides detailed information about various facets of the organization and its work, a list of conferences and events, access to several of its online databases and documents, news, and a publications index.

United States Agency for International Development (http://www.info.usaid.gov)
The United States Agency for International Development (USAID) is an independent government agency that provides economic development and humanitarian assistance to advance U.S. economic and political interests overseas. The USAID Web site offers numerous links to governmental and non-governmental organizations concerned with international development.

Village Banking (http://www.villagebanking.org)
Village Banking is a program of the Foundation for International Community Assistance (FINCA), which supports the economic and human development of families trapped in severe poverty by creating "village banks" peer groups of 30 to 50 members, predominantly women, based on microcredit. The site offers a detailed explanation of how the program works, program locations and statistics, news, and job opportunities and internships.

The World Bank (http://www.worldbank.org)
The sometimes-controversial World Bank strives to reduce poverty and improve living standards by promoting sustainable growth and investment in developing countries. The World Bank Group includes the International Bank for Reconstruction and Development, the International Development Association, the International Finance Corporation, the Multilateral Investment Guarantee Agency, and the International Centre for the Settlement

of Investment Disputes. The Bank's Web site offers an imposing smorgasbord of economic facts and general information about the dozens of countries in which the Bank and its sister institutions do business.

AFRICA

ACCORD (African Centre for the Constructive Resolution of Disputes) (http://www.accord.org.za/)

ACCORD was founded with the goal of ending the political and social turmoil ravaging South African countries in the wake of apartheid. By making efforts to popularize and institutionalize the process of peaceful negotiation and by creating partnerships between members of society, government, and the business sector, the organization strives to facilitate the progression towards a stable democracy.

AllAfrica Global Media (http://allafrica.com/)

AllAfrica Global Media posts more than 500 new stories daily from over 80 African media organizations and from its own reporters. The Web site is a one-stop source for up-to-date information on all of Africa, with reports from Africa's leading newspapers, magazines, and news agencies. This site is an invaluable resource.

Novartis Foundation for Sustainable Development (http://www.foundation.novartis.com)

Established in December 1996, and formerly known as the Ciba-Geigy Foundation for Cooperation with Developing Countries, the Novartis Foundation supports a variety of projects in developing countries in the areas of agriculture, healthcare, and social development.

ASIA

Asia Pacific Center for Justice & Peace (http://www.apcjp.org/)

The Asia Pacific Center for Justice & Peace works to promote the realization of the full range of rights—including economic justice, political freedom, and genuine security—for the peoples of Asia and the Pacific. The Web site has information about the Center's programs, action alerts, events, and publications.

Asia Society (http://www.asiasociety.org/)

Founded in 1956 by John D. Rockefeller III, the Asia Society builds awareness of the more than 30 countries broadly defined as the Asia Pacific region through a range of programs, including major art exhibitions, performances, international corporate conferences, and policy programs.

Bridge to Asia Foundation (http://www.bridge.org/)

Bridge to Asia, a San Francisco-based nonprofit, supports education and research in developing countries in Asia through the donation of books and journals to universities, research services, and the development of in-country libraries and computer networks.

National Bureau of Asian Research (http://www.nbr.org/)

Founded in 1989 with a major grant from the Henry M. Jackson Foundation, the Seattle-based National Bureau of Asian Research conducts advanced research on policy-relevant issues affecting Asia.

CANADA

Canadian Centre for Philanthropy (http://www.ccp.ca/)

The Canadian Centre for Philanthropy is "dedicated to advancing the role and interests of the charitable sector for the benefit of Canadian communities." Web site resources include a foundation and grants directory of over 1,600 foundations that are actively granting in Canada; information about the Centre's publications; membership information, including the Centre's annual symposium; results of various research studies, including volunteering statistics, trends, and comparative studies; and an overview of the Centre's "Imagine" initiative, which promotes public and corporate giving, volunteering, and community support on a national level.

CharityCareers.com (http://www.charitycareers.com)

Serving nonprofit professionals across Canada, CharityCareers.com features current positions, a client list, a bookstore, online newsletters and reports, charity news, and career tips.

Charity Village (http://www.charityvillage.com/)

The Canadian-based Charity Village Web site offers news, jobs, information and resources for nonprofit managers, staffers and fundraisers, donors, and volunteers. Visitors to the Web site can access a searchable directory of annotated links to Canadian charities and nonprofit organizations; more than 10,000 positions in Canadian nonprofit organizations; an online directory of products and services especially for nonprofit executives; and a listing of educational programs and professional development opportunities, including Charity Village's own workshops and online tutorials, as well as links to dozens of courses available across the country.

In Kind Canada (http://www.inkindcanada.ca)

In Kind Canada, in English and French, functions as an intermediary between registered charities, Canadian corporations, charitable foundations, and other interested parties by facilitating the process by which the granting of goods and services in support of philanthropic initiatives at the local, regional, or national level can take place in an efficient and cost effective manner.

London Community Foundation (http://www.lcf.on.ca)

The London Community Foundation is a registered charity dedicated to enhancing the quality of life in the Ontario communities of London, Middlesex, Oxford, and Elgin. The Foundation solicits and accepts charitable gifts from individuals, corporations, and private foundations to establish permanent endowment funds. The interest earned from the prudent investment of this capital is disbursed throughout these communities in support of arts and culture, education, the environment, health and physical activities, and various social services.

Ontario Arts Council (http://www.arts.on.ca/)

The Ontario Arts Council (OAC) supports artists and arts organizations throughout the province of Ontario and awards grants based upon a unique peer assessment process that "gives artists and arts organizations a voice in how funds are distributed." Visitors to the OAC Web site will find a thorough description of its grant programs, application procedures, eligibility requirements, and deadlines.

Science's Next Wave (http://nextwave.sciencemag.org/ca/)

Billed as "an electronic network for the next generation of scientists," the Next Wave site features profiles of and practical career advice for young scientists, as well as links to numerous scientific organizations and funding sources. The site features lots of material written by and of interest to Canadian scientists.

The Trillium Foundation (http://www.trilliumfoundation.org/)
The Trillium Foundation was established in 1982 "to ensure that a portion of the proceeds of the Ontario Lottery Corporation is directed toward social issues" in Ontario. The focus of the foundation is on "the development of a new social vision which provides opportunity, and promotes both individual and collective responsibility." Through its grants program, the foundation encourages innovation and experimentation, cross-sectoral collaboration, citizen participation, and systemic change." The site is available in English- and French-language versions.

EUROPE/EURASIA

European Foundation Centre (http://www.efc.be/)
The European Foundation Centre (EFC) promotes and underpins the work of foundations and corporate funders active in and with Europe. Established in 1989 by seven of Europe's leading foundations, the EFC today has a membership of more than 160 independent funders and serves a further 7,000 organizations linked through networking centers in 35 countries across Europe. The Web site has a listing of member events; information on EFC's projects, activities, and publications; and the EFC newsletter, *Bookshelf.*

Funders Online (http://www.fundersonline.org)
An initiative of the European Foundation Centre, Funders Online seeks to promote and strengthen philanthropy in Europe by facilitating access to online independent funding and information resources. The site's fully searchable Funders Online Directory contains approximately 150 profiles of funder Web sites and interests.

International Research & Exchanges Board (http://www.irex.org)
The International Research & Exchanges (IREX) Board is an international nonprofit organization that administers programs between the United States and the countries of Eastern Europe, the New Independent States, Asia, and the Near East. With its traditional base in the university research community, and in collaboration with partners from the policy, corporate, media, and private foundation sectors, IREX sponsors and supports programs of advanced field research, professional training, international conferences, seminars, and comparative analysis.

NGONet (http://www.ngonet.org)
NGONet provides information to, for, and about non-governmental organizations (NGOs) active in Central and Eastern Europe. Visitors to the NGONet site will find resources for funders, grantseekers, organizations looking for project partners, and job seekers.

Regional Environmental Center for Central and Eastern Europe (http://www.rec.hu/)
The Regional Environmental Center (REC) for Central and Eastern Europe is a comprehensive Web site offering information on REC's programs and grantmaking activities, as well as several searchable databases.

GERMANY

German Charities Institute (http://www.dsk.de)
This site features more than 31,000 pages on German charity, philanthropy, and volunteering, including extensive listings of German and international nonprofit resources. It is available in German and English versions.

German Foundation Index (http://www.stiftungsindex.de/)
A joint project of the Federal Foundation Association of Germany, the University of Goettingen, and the Koerber-Foundation, the IDS (*Index Deutscher Stiftungen*) serves as a one-stop source of information about German foundations, with more than 650 links to German foundation Web sites, recommendations for students applying for grants,

addresses of foundation researchers, and links to a variety of international resources, including the Council on Foundations and the Foundation Center.

INDIA

Foundation of Occupational Development (http://www.xlweb.com/food)
Selected as a finalist for the Ericsson Internet Community Award, the Foundation of Occupational Development (FOOD) strives to foster sustainable development among the poor through projects encompassing sustainable agriculture, health, education, social development, employment, and empowerment. The organization also contributes to the field of development policy through community participation and dissemination of analyses relating to sustainable development. FOOD includes a women's network whose goal is to curtail the discrimination and abuse faced by women in India.

JAPAN

Japan Center for International Exchange (JCIE) (http://www.jcie.or.jp/)
This is an independent nonprofit organization dedicated to strengthening Japan's role in international networks of policy dialogue and cooperation. Major components of the Center's Web site include Global ThinkNet, a cluster of Japan Center for International Exchange-sponsored activities designed to broaden policy research and dialogue on issues pertaining to Japan's relationships with other countries, and CivilNet, which is designed to advance the cause of the nonprofit sector in the Asia Pacific region, with a special emphasis on the development of civil society in Japan. The CivilNet portion of the site is the gateway to information about the Asia Community Trust (ACT), a Japan-based charitable trust committed to financially supporting the grassroots efforts of NGOs involved in sustainable social and economic development across Asia.

LATIN AMERICA

ACCION International (http://www.partners.net/)
Tucson-based ACCION International is dedicated to fighting poverty and bringing financial services to poor but enterprising businessmen and women—street vendors, seamstresses, sandal makers—through the practice of microlending. In addition to its programs in a number of U.S. states, the organization operates a Latin American network of 18 microlending institutions that serves 450,000 clients in Argentina, Bolivia, Brazil, Columbia, Ecuador, Guatemala, Honduras, Mexico, Nicaragua, Panama, Paraguay, Peru, and Venezuela.

Organization of American States (http://www.oas.org/)
The Organization of American States (OAS), composed of 35 member countries from North, Central, and South America, seeks to strengthen and maintain peace and security in the Americas by making efforts to "promote and consolidate representative democracy, with due respect for the principle of nonintervention; to prevent possible causes of difficulties and to ensure the pacific settlement of disputes that may arise among the Member States; to provide for common action on the part of those States in the event of aggression; to seek the solution of political, juridical and economic problems that may arise among them; to promote, by cooperative action, their economic, social and cultural development; and to achieve an effective limitation of conventional weapons [so that it is] possible to devote the largest amount of resources to the economic and social development of the Member States."

MIDDLE EAST

Abraham Fund (http://www.coexistence.org/)

Headquartered in New York City and Jerusalem, the Abraham Fund works to foster increased dialogue, tolerance, and understanding between the Jewish and Arab citizens of Israel through advocacy and awareness campaigns and by sponsoring coexistence projects.

American Near East Refugee Aid (http://www.anera.org/)

Washington, D.C.-based American Near East Refugee Aid's mission is to reduce poverty and relieve suffering in the West Bank, Gaza Strip, and Lebanon, thereby improving the lives of all people in the Middle East. The organization coordinates health, education, and economic development projects in cooperation with local institutions and also provides humanitarian aid and relief to Palestinian refugees in Lebanon.

Economic Research Forum for the Arab Countries, Iran and Turkey (http://www.erf.org.eg/)

This independent regional network of economists, policy makers, and businesspeople initiates, funds, and facilitates policy-relevant economic research on the Arab Region, Turkey and Iran.

Foundation for Middle East Peace (http://www.fmep.org/)

Established in 1979, the Washington, D.C.-based Foundation for Middle East Peace (FMEP) works to promote a just solution to the Israeli-Palestinian conflict that brings peace and security to both peoples. In addition to its role as an information clearinghouse, FMEP awards grants to organizations and projects that contribute significantly to a solution to the Israeli-Palestinian conflict.

Giving Wisely: The Internet Directory of Israeli Nonprofit and Philanthropic Organizations (http://www.givingwisely.org.il)

This site is the companion to the print directory, *Giving Wisely.* The site has browsable listings of Israeli foundations and nonprofit organizations. In addition to browsing, you can use the searchable database to view foundation or nonprofit profiles in full or partial format. The search features work in both Hebrew and English.

Middle East Media and Research Institute (http://www.memri.org/)

The Middle East Media and Research Institute is an independent, U.S.-based nonprofit that provides translations of stories in the Arab media as well as original analysis and research on developments in the Middle East.

Middle East Policy Council (http://www.mepc.org/)

The Middle East Policy Council was founded in 1981 to expand public discussion and understanding of issues affecting U.S. policy in the Middle East.

Middle East Research and Information Project (http://www.merip.org/)

The Washington, D.C.-based Middle East Research and Information Project provides news and perspectives about the Middle East not available from mainstream media outlets.

RUSSIA

EcoLine—Russia (http://www.ecoline.ru/)

EcoLine is a program of the Socio-Ecological Union that provides resources on the environment and Third Sector development in Russia. In order to view the site, you will need to download Pan-European Text Display Support, which will take anywhere from two to twelve minutes. The site includes Internet and print resources, advice on funding sources, and news in related fields. Much of the site is in Russian, but there are English options for some of the sections.

The Non-Governmental Organization Development Center of Russia (http://www.spb.ru/ptchela/ndc.html)
Formerly known as the Russian-German Exchange (Russky-Nemetsky Obmen), the Non-Governmental Organization Development Center of Russia (NDC) is a Russian nonprofit that is committed to forwarding the formation and development of the Third Sector, specifically in the northwest region, of Russia. The country is experiencing a steady growth in the number of NGOs but needs knowledge and financial support in order to see the organizations function. The NDC is interested in partnering with international groups for purposes including expanding the expertise available to Russian groups and publicizing international events throughout Russia. The site is a simple page with e-mail and other contact information.

UNITED KINGDOM

Charities Aid Foundation (http://www.charitynet.org/index.html)
Charities Aid Foundation, a British nonprofit whose aim is to encourage charitable giving in the United Kingdom as well as internationally, sponsors the CharityNet Web site, "a resource centre for the nonprofit sector and its contributors." The site includes contact information for thousands of charities and serves as a technical assistance provider to both funders and nonprofits. Of special interest is the site's Corporate Community Involvement Network, an alphabetical list of links to more than 250 corporate (U.S.-based and multinational) Web sites with charitable giving information.

Oxfordshire Community Foundation (http://www.oxfordshire.org/)
The Oxfordshire Community Foundation was established in 1995 to raise funds locally to support the work of local voluntary groups and support programs in education, disability, poverty, and health within Oxfordshire County.

UK Fundraising (http://www.fundraising.co.uk)
UK Fundraising is a comprehensive resource for charities and nonprofit fundraisers in the United Kingdom and Ireland, Europe, North America, and the Pacific.

The Wellcome Trust (http://www.wellcome.ac.uk/)
The Trust spends £600 million annually on research in biomedical science and the history of medicine, making it the largest non-governmental source of funds for biomedical research in Europe. Grants are made to researchers in the United Kingdom for a variety of purposes, including programmatic, training, travel abroad, and equipment.

General Resources
(Nonprofit, Private, & Public Sectors)

BUSINESS & INDUSTRY

AssociationCentral.com (http://www.associationcentral.com/)
Serving as a portal site for professional associations, nonprofit networks, and special interest organizations, AssociationCentral.com is structured in a similar fashion to many popular search engines, breaking down its listings according to industry categories and providing advanced search capabilities. Additionally, visitors have the opportunity to find out about upcoming industry-specific events and current news.

Better Business Bureaus (http://www.bbb.org/)
Besides serving as a gateway to more than 150 local Better Business Bureaus throughout the United States and Canada, the BBB Web site provides instant access to business and consumer alerts, charity reports and standards (through its Philanthropic Advisory

Service), and other helpful resources. It also has begun to accept consumer complaints, which it forwards to the appropriate local BBB. This is an important service, and a nice site.

BizMove.com (http://www.bizmove.com)

BizMove.com is a vital online resource for entrepreneur. This small business information clearinghouse includes extensive content areas dealing with virtually every aspect of successfully starting and managing a small business. Site visitors may also subscribe to a free online newsletter containing relevant tips and tricks.

Business for Social Responsibility (http://www.bsr.org/)

Business for Social Responsibility (BSR) serves companies around the world that work towards promoting ethical values, people, communities, and the environment while sustaining commercial success. BSR helps its members create value for investors, customers, employees, local communities, and other stakeholders by providing professional assistance with socially responsible business policies and practices. One of the BSR Web site's outstanding features is its Global Business Responsibility Resource Center, a free service to site visitors that contains basic information regarding a wide range of corporate responsibility topics, along with company examples and links to other helpful sites.

EDGAR Database of Corporate Information (http://www.sec.gov/edgarhp.htm)

The Securities and Exchange Commission's EDGAR (Electronic Data Gathering, Analysis, and Retrieval) system is a goldmine of basic, but often hard-to-find, corporate information (e.g., fiscal data, officers, subsidiaries, recent M&A activity, et cetera). EDGAR on the Web allows visitors to retrieve publicly available filings submitted to the SEC from January 1994 to the present.

Hoover's Online (http://www.hoovers.com/)

Hoover's Online, the Austin, Texas-based publisher of corporate information, may not be the "Ultimate Source for Company Information," as it bills itself, but it sure is a good one. The site's offerings come in two flavors, free and fee-based. The former center around Hoover's Company Capsules, which provide news and information—company profile, key personnel, full stock quote, selected press coverage—on thousands of public and private enterprises. Subscribers (two options: personal or multi-user) get the same—in much greater depth and detail.

Inc.com (http://www.inc.com/)

Brought to you by the folks at *Inc.* magazine, the award-winning *Inc. Online* is a great resource for entrepreneurs and small business owners who are serious about growing their businesses. In addition to the most recent edition of *Inc.* and an archive of more than 5,000 articles on a wide variety of topics, the site offers interactive worksheets, case studies, online tutorials, a searchable database of America's 500 fastest-growing companies, and great links to other small business-related resources on the Net.

US Small Business Administration (http://www.sbaonline.sba.gov/)

As an independent agency of the U.S. government, the US Small Business Administration assists small businesses in order to encourage free enterprise and improve the nation's overall economy. Visitors to the site can retrieve exhaustive information about what the agency offers, including a variety of financial assistance programs. Concise descriptions explain the variety of routes available to financing a small business.

THE INTERNET

Download.com (http://www.download.com)
Hosted by CNET, the Download.com Web site serves as a virtual warehouse of software and shareware of all kinds. Application types include business, education, games, home, internet, multimedia and design development tools, utilities, and drivers.

Electronic Frontier Foundation (http://www.eff.org/)
The not-for-profit Electronic Frontier Foundation is a high-profile clearinghouse for news and information about Internet-related issues such as free speech, encryption, privacy, and intellectual property rights.

Internet Economy Indicators' Internet Organizations List (http://www.internetindicators.com/organizations.html)
The Internet Economy Indicators' Internet Organizations List contains links to major organizations that have arisen out of a need within the field of Internet-related technology for standardization, collaboration, and a relationship with government.

Internet Law & Policy Forum (http://www.ilpf.org/)
The Internet Law & Policy Forum was conceived as "a neutral venue in which to develop solutions to the challenging legal and policy questions of the Internet." Issues currently being addressed by the Forum include online certification of commercial transactions, digital signatures, and content blocking and regulation.

The Open Source Initiative (http://www.opensource.org/index.html)
The Open Source Initiative (OSI) is dedicated to the proposition that computer source code developed in an open, non-proprietary environment is chiefly responsible for the global popularity of the Internet. OSI maintains a list of open source licenses that conform to the Open Source Definition, have been through public scrutiny, and have been approved by OSI. The Web site lists successful software products that have these properties, as well as copies of approved open source licenses. The Open Source page explains the roots of the movement and where it's headed.

World Wide Web Consortium (http://www.w3.org/)
Under the direction of Tim Berners-Lee, the World Wide Web Consortium (WC3) has played a leading role since 1994 in developing and articulating the specifications and protocols at the heart of the Web. The W3C develops interoperable technologies (specifications, guidelines, software, and tools) to lead the Web to its full potential as a forum for information, commerce, communication, and collective understanding. The Web site has W3C news as well as links to information about W3C technologies and getting involved in W3C.

LIBRARY LINKS

American Library Association (http://www.ala.org/)
The 61,000-member American Library Association promotes intellectual freedom and quality library and information services in areas ranging from copyright to professional development. The site includes news; events; online summits; career leads; listings of awards, grants, and scholarships; FAQs, and an online bookstore and magazine stand.

Association of Research Libraries (http://www.arl.org)
The programs and services of the Association of Research Libraries promote access to and use of recorded knowledge in support of teaching, research, scholarship, and community service. The site includes a list of member libraries, partnerships, archives, career resources, training, and links to related publications.

EDUCAUSE (http://www.educause.edu/)
EDUCAUSE is a membership organization dedicated to managing and using information resources in higher education.

Foundation Center Historical Foundation Collection—IUPUI Special Collections (http://www.ulib.iupui.edu/special/mss005.html)
The Historical Foundation Collection, covering materials for the period 1896–1996, collected by the Foundation Center, was established as a manuscript collection of The Ruth Lilly Special Collections and Archives at the Indiana University-Purdue University Indianapolis (IUPUI) in 1997. The site generally describes the four components of the collection: IRS tax documents, historical information files, annual reports, and sets of Foundation Center directories, and it provides a detailed list of the available annual reports.

Institute of Museum and Library Services (http://www.imls.gov/)
An independent federal agency created in 1996, the Institute of Museum and Library Services (IMLS) supports libraries and museums through a national grantmaking program. The goals of the organization include encouraging community-wide access to resources and innovation in lifetime learning. IMLS also serves as a clearinghouse on information about library and museum events and advances research in the field. The site provides links to member organizations and to Web sites and online projects the Institute has funded. Visitors can also access IMLS publications in PDF format and find lists of grants available in each state.

IUPUI Special Collections—Philanthropy Studies (http://www-lib.iupui.edu/special/ppsl.html)
The Ruth Lilly Special Collections and Archives houses the Joseph and Matthew Payton Philanthropic Studies Library among its Manuscript Collections. Reference queries can be made by telephone, e-mail, or from the Web site. It also compiles and maintains the Philanthropic Studies Index, an online, searchable bibliography to literature, primarily periodicals and research reports, on voluntarism, nonprofit organizations, fund raising, and charitable giving.

Library of Congress (http://lcweb.loc.gov/)
The entire Library of Congress catalogue is searchable online, as well as information on the library's programs and services.

Libri Foundation (http://www.teleport.com/~librifdn/index.html)
The Libri Foundation is a national nonprofit organization that donates new hardcover children's books to small, rural public libraries in the United States through its Books for Children program.

PUBLIC INTEREST & POLICY

The Brookings Institution (http://www.brook.edu/)
The Brookings Institution holds conferences and conducts and publishes independent research, analysis, and criticism related to public policy, bringing new knowledge to the attention of decisionmakers and enhancing scholarly insight into public policy issues. Its economic studies, foreign policy studies, and governmental studies departments form the core of its program. The Brookings site includes a list of current scholars, publications, policy briefs, a calendar of events, and a search feature.

The Carter Center (http://www.cartercenter.org/)
The Carter Center's goal is to help alleviate the suffering that results from war, disease, famine, and poverty by advancing peace and health in neighborhoods and nations worldwide. Towards this end, the Center brings warring parties to the negotiating table, monitors elections, safeguards human rights, fights disease, increases crop production, promotes

preventive healthcare, and builds strong democracies through economic development in the United States and abroad. The Center is affiliated with Emory University.

Center for Responsive Politics (http://www.opensecrets.org/home/index.asp)

The Center for Responsive Politics is a Washington, D.C.-based research group that tracks money in politics, and its effect on elections and public policy. The Center's site offers a searchable database of political donors and "soft money" donations; the site can also be searched by state and politician.

HandsNet (http://www.handsnet.org/)

HandsNet is a membership organization of more than 5,000 public interest and human services organizations. Web site features include articles and Action Alerts, providing daily news updates on human services issues and legislation; the WebClipper news and delivery service, with human services headlines from hundreds of Web sites; and information on training programs, including a Mobile Technology Classroom, management seminars, and strategic planning workshops for nonprofit professionals.

Hoover Institution on War, Revolution and Peace (http://www-hoover.stanford.edu)

Before he became 31st president of the United States, Herbert Hoover founded the Hoover Institution, a public policy research center at Stanford University devoted to the advanced study of domestic and international affairs. Recognized as one of the first "think tanks" in the United States, the Institution boasts one of the world's most complete libraries on political, economic, and social change in the 20th century. The Hoover Institution Web site offers information on the organization's research program, publications, and library collections, as well as subscription information for its electronic mailing lists.

National Association for Public Interest Law (http://www.napil.org)

The National Association for Public Interest Law provides an extensive listing of links to online public interest law resources.

National Center for Youth Law (http://www.youthlaw.org/)

The National Center for Youth Law (NCYL) is a California-based private, nonprofit law office serving the legal needs of children and their families. The organization focuses particularly on children living in poverty, advocating for their protection from abuse; access to housing, healthcare, and public benefits; and improved methods of collecting child support. NCYL works towards these goals by publishing articles, manuals, books, and its bimonthly journal, *Youth Law News,* providing technical assistance and training, assisting legal advocates who represent poor children; and conducting administrative and legislative advocacy. Its Web site includes pertinent news, an overview of the organization, online articles, analyses, publications, and links to related resources.

National Center on Poverty Law (http://www.povertylaw.org/)

The National Center on Poverty Law (NCPL) develops its advocacy agenda in accordance with the needs of the low-income communities that it serves. Through policy, advocacy, and legal resources, the organization "identifies, develops, and supports creative and collaborative approaches to help achieve social and economic justice." The major clearinghouse on Poverty Law, the NCPL offers visitors to the Web site access to an enormous collection of publications and case studies. Over 500,000 documents from over 50,000 case studies are searchable by substantive area. A subscription to the site ($25 monthly or $200 annually) is required for access to the many databases.

National Institute for Research Advancement World Directory of Think Tanks (http://www.nira.go.jp/ice/tt-info/nwdtt99/)

The Japan-based National Institute for Research Advancement provides a no-frills site with basic information on more than 250 policy organizations in 65 countries. Information available for each organization can include executive personnel, organizational history, areas of research, geographic focus, availability of research findings, and funding sources.

Contact information is also available, as are individual Web site links (when available). Although the site lacks a master index, this is an excellent place to start for those interested in policy institutes and their work.

National Issues Forum (http://www.nifi.org/)

The National Issues Forum (NIF), a voluntary, nonpartisan, nationwide network of forums and study circles, is rooted in the notion that citizens need to come together to deliberate about common problems in order to act on them. The NIF Web site offers free access to NIF reports; discussion guides on such topics as physician-assisted suicide, drug use and policy, and the American family; a forum materials list; and a Talk Back area.

NetAction (http://www.netaction.org/)

Dedicated to promoting the use of the Internet for effective grassroots citizen action campaigns and to educating the public, policymakers, and the media about technology policy issues, the NetAction site provides the Virtual Activist, an online training program; NetAction's Online Buyer's Guide; and additional reports focusing on cyber action issues.

Nonprofit Sector Research Fund (http://www.nonprofitresearch.org/)

A program of the Aspen Institute in Washington, D.C., the Nonprofit Sector Research Fund makes grants for researching and disseminating information about nonprofit activities, impacts, and values, and promotes the use of that information to enhance nonprofit practices and inform public policy. The Fund also seeks to bolster nonprofit research by increasing the legitimacy and visibility of nonprofit scholarship, thereby attracting more investors and researchers to the field. The organization's site includes application guidelines, special initiatives, publication content and summaries, research abstracts, a list of grant recipients, and links to nonprofit resources.

Policy.com (http://www.policy.com)

Policy.com is a comprehensive non-partisan resource covering research, opinions, and events shaping public policy. The Web site provides links to hundreds of think tanks, advocacy groups, and other policy-orientated organizations and also features daily updates and briefings.

ProgressivePubs.com (http://www.progressivepubs.com/)

ProgressivePubs.com was created in 1997 to supply activists, policymakers, and other interested parties with print and electronic resources that can assist in enacting progressive change. Publications of collections of this information are on sale with all proceeds being reinvested in social change. The Web site offers access, after free registration, to a database of hundreds of foundations that support progressive efforts. There is also an online bookstore that sells hard-to-find works of progressive thinkers and organizations.

Project Vote Smart (http://www.vote-smart.org/)

Project Vote Smart researches, tracks, and provides independent factual information on over 13,000 candidates and elected officials. The site offers a searchable database of voting records, campaign issue positions, performance evaluations by special interests, campaign contributions, previous experience, and contact information.

Public Agenda Online (http://www.publicagenda.org)

Public Agenda Online is a nonpartisan resource for journalists and researchers interested in public opinion and public policy. The Web site features a collection of public opinion data on important issues facing the country, including crime, the economy, the environment, gambling, healthcare, illegal drugs, the right to die, abortion, education, the family, the federal deficit, immigration, medicare, race, social security, welfare, and America's role in the world. The Web site also offers guidance on using survey research and links to particularly interesting facts and findings.

RAND (http://www.rand.org)

RAND (an acronym for Research and Development) researchers assist public policymakers at all levels, private sector leaders in many industries, and the public at large in efforts to strengthen the nation's economy, maintain its security, and improve its quality of life. RAND's Web site offers information about the organization's research activities, technical capabilities, publications, educational opportunities, and board of trustees, along with a Hot Topics in RAND Research area.

The State Public Interest Research Groups (http://www.pirg.org)

Composed of state-based, member-supported public interest "watchdog" groups, the non-partisan State Public Interest Research Groups (PIRG) aim to protect consumers, preserve the environment, and encourage citizen participation in the democratic process. The site's most valuable offerings include complete voting records for the delegates of each state and a listing of other Internet resources pertaining to State PIRG issues.

WebActive (http://www.webactive.com)

WebActive is a weekly publication designed to offer progressive activists an up-to-date resource for locating organizations and individuals with similar values and interests. The Web site features: *RadioNation,* the weekly broadcast edition of *The Nation* magazine; *Pacifica Network News,* available every day; *Democracy NOW!,* available every weekday; and *Hightower Radio,* with Jim Hightower's daily two-minute commentaries on politics and progressive issues. The Web site also has an annotated, searchable directory of 1,250 progressive organizations.

REFERENCE

Ask.com (http://www.ask.com)

This unique site combs the Web for answers to specific questions posed by the user. In addition to its own indexed links, it also retrieves results from four major search engines.

InfoPlease.com (http://www.infoplease.com)

A colossal online reference center, InfoPlease.com empowers users to conduct keyword searches that retrieve facts from its almanacs, encyclopedia, and dictionary. Topics include current events, "today in history," science and technology, people, the United States and world, business and economy, lifestyles and interests, entertainment and sports, and society and culture.

National Center for Charitable Statistics—Resources on Nonprofits and Philanthropy (http://nccs.urban.org/resource.htm)

Visitors to the National Center for Charitable Statistics—Resources on Nonprofits and Philanthropy Web site can download data on nonprofit organizations, view or download database documentation and classification schemes, and download blank IRS forms from which most of the data is collected.

The Ultimates (http://www.theultimates.com)

The be-all-end-all of contact information directories, The Ultimates Web site offers visitors the chance to simultaneously search multiple Internet-based White Pages, Yellow Pages, and e-mail directory databases. It also includes access to several online mapping services for travel route planning.

U.S. Census Bureau (http://www.census.gov/)

The U.S. Census Bureau's sprawling Web site is *the* source of social, demographic, and economic information about the United States on the Web. Offerings include Census Bureau publications, listed by subject; statistical profiles for states, congressional districts, and counties; current economic indicators; state and county maps created on the fly; and much more.

Government Resources

GENERAL

Catalog of Federal Domestic Assistance (http://www.cfda.gov/)

The *Catalog of Federal Domestic Assistance* has information on a wide variety of financial and non-financial assistance programs, projects, services, and activities. The Web site provides access to a searchable database of all federal programs available to state and local governments (including the District of Columbia); federally-recognized Indian tribal governments; Territories (and possessions) of the United States; domestic public, quasi-public, and private profit and nonprofit organizations and institutions; specialized groups; and individuals.

Federal Information Exchange, Inc. (http://content.sciencewise.com/fedix/index.htm?)

Federal Information Exchange, Inc. (FEDIX) is an online information retrieval service of federal opportunities for the education and research communities. The Web site also offers FEDIX Opportunity Alert, a free e-mail service that automatically delivers research and education funding opportunities in specific areas of interest.

Federal Register (http://www.access.gpo.gov/su_docs/aces/aces140.html)

The no-frills Federal Register Web site provides access to presidential documents, executive orders, rules, and proposed rules from federal agencies and organizations. Visitors to the Web site can search the database in a variety of ways, including using the "browse feature." Detailed instructions and sample searches are provided to facilitate the process. The exhaustive information on governmentally funded projects and funding availability is especially helpful.

Grants Information Service (http://infoserv.rttonet.psu.edu/gis/)

Grants Information Service is a collection of links to (mostly) government sources of funding for research, instruction, and continuing education projects from Penn State's Office of Sponsored Programs.

Notices of Funding Availability (Empowerment Zone/Enterprise Communities Community Toolbox) (http://ocd.usda.gov/nofa.htm)

Notices of Funding Availability (NOFAs) are announcements that appear in the Federal Register which is printed each business day by the U.S. government. The Web site allows users to generate customized listings.

OMB Watch's Nonprofits' Policy and Technology Project (http://www.ombwatch.org/npt)

The goal of the Nonprofits' Policy and Technology Project is to improve communications linkages within the nonprofit sector to strengthen public policy participation. OMB Watch's Nonprofits' Policy and Technology Project provides information resources on nonprofit use of technology for public policy.

THOMAS: Legislative Information on the Internet (http://thomas.loc.gov/)

THOMAS: Legislative Information on the Internet is a service of the Library of Congress, offering up-to-date information on the legislative activities of both Houses and searchable databases of current and historical legislative documents of the U.S. Congress.

United States Government and Grant Resources (http://pegasus.uthct.edu/OtherUsefulSites/Govt.html)

United States Government and Grant Resources is a thorough meta-index of links to politicians and government agencies and departments.

United States House of Representatives (http://www.house.gov/)
United States House of Representatives is the official U.S. House Web site, providing House schedules, a directory of members, links to individual House offices' Web sites, a searchable database of U.S. code, and the House Internet Law Library.

United States Senate (http://www.senate.gov/)
United States Senate is the official U.S. Senate site, providing information on Senate activities and Committees, a complete directory of members, and a searchable calendar of business.

U.S. Small Business Administration (http://www.sbaonline.sba.gov/)
As an independent agency of the U.S. government, the U.S. Small Business Administration assists small businesses in order to encourage free enterprise and improve the nation's overall economy. Visitors to the site can retrieve exhaustive information about what the agency offers, including a variety of financial assistance programs. Easy to navigate, concise descriptions explain the variety of routes available to financing a small business.

WWW Virtual Library: U.S. Federal Government Agencies
(http://www.lib.lsu.edu/gov/fedgov.html)
WWW Virtual Library: U.S. Federal Government Agencies is a meta-index of federal agencies on the Internet.

WWW Virtual Library: U.S. Government Resources (http://iridium.nttc.edu/gov_res.html)
WWW Virtual Library: U.S. Government Resources is a searchable meta-index of federal agencies on the Internet.

FEDERAL AGENCIES

Administration on Aging (http://www.aoa.dhhs.gov/)
Administration on Aging is an exhaustive online resource for senior citizens, providing a resource directory, statistics on aging, an Eldercare Locator, and links to related sites.

Administration for Children and Families (http://www.acf.dhhs.gov/)
Administration for Children and Families has information on the vast array of programs and services offered by this division of the Department of Health and Human Services, dedicated to promoting the economic and social well-being of families, children, individuals and communities.

Agency for healthcare Policy and Research (http://www.ahcpr.gov/)
Agency for healthcare Policy and Research is a grantmaking DHHS agency, dedicated to generating and disseminating information that improves the healthcare system.

Centers for Disease Control and Prevention (http://www.cdc.gov/)
The Centers for Disease Control and Prevention Web site includes comprehensive program and application information for the CDC's many health-related funding opportunities.

Department of Health and Human Services (http://www.os.dhhs.gov/)
The Department of Health and Human Services Web site provides consumer and policy information, searchable databases, employment opportunities, and links to related government agencies.

Department of Housing and Urban Development (http://www.hud.gov)
The Department of Housing and Urban Development (HUD) has information about various types of grants, including community development, affordable housing, and research.

Environmental Protection Agency (http://www.epa.gov)
The Environmental Protection Agency Web site includes material on virtually every aspect of U.S. environmental policy and protection.

Health Resources and Services Administration (http://www.hrsa.dhhs.gov/)
The Health Resources and Services Administration Web site has an overview of programs, services, and grant opportunities.

Indian Health Service (http://www.ihs.gov/)
Dedicated to raising the health status of American Indians and Alaska Natives, the Indian Health Service Web site provides information on the agency's activities and serves as an online resource for Native American communities.

Internal Revenue Service (http://www.irs.ustreas.gov/prod/)
The highly regarded Internal Revenue Service Web site provides comprehensive tax information and has a site-wide search engine.

National Endowment for the Arts (http://arts.endow.gov/)
The National Endowment for the Arts (NEA) Web site serves as a comprehensive resource for the arts community and its supporters. This elegant Web site includes a "gateway" for nonprofits in search of information about grants, government services, regulations, and taxes, and also posts announcements of grants, competitions, awards, arts-related news and interviews, and legislative updates. NEA publications—many of which are free—can be ordered through the site.

National Endowment for the Humanities (http://www.neh.fed.us/)
The National Endowment for the Humanities (NEH) supports learning in history, literature, philosophy, and other areas of the humanities through its support of research, education, documentaries, museum exhibits, and preservation. The information-packed NEH Web site is a good place to find out about funding opportunities, cultural events, and publications and exhibits of interest nationwide.

National Institute on Alcohol Abuse and Alcoholism (http://www.niaaa.nih.gov/)
The National Institute on Alcohol Abuse and Alcoholism Web site provides grants information, news notes and upcoming events, and links to related publications and databases.

National Institutes of Health (http://www.nih.gov/)
The National Institutes of Health (NIH) is the federal government's principle biomedical research agency and a terrific online resource for NIH grant and fellowship information, policy changes, and access to the CRISP database. CRISP (Computer Retrieval of Information on Scientific Projects) is a searchable database of federally funded biomedical research projects conducted at universities, hospitals, and other research institutions. The Web site has links to a contracts/RFP page, the "NIH Guide for Grants and Contracts," and the home pages of NIH Institutes, Centers, and Divisions.

National Science Foundation (http://www.nsf.gov/)
The National Science Foundation Web site is comprehensive and well-organized, with program and grants information in biology, education, engineering, the geosciences, math and the physical sciences, polar research, and the social and behavioral sciences.

National Telecommunications & Information Administration (http://www.ntia.doc.gov/)
The National Telecommunications & Information Administration Web site includes application guidelines and a listing of recent grants awarded through its Telecommunications and Information Infrastructure Assistance Program.

Oak Ridge Institute for Science and Education (http://www.orau.gov/orise.htm)
The Oak Ridge Institute for Science and Education supports national and international pro-grams in education, training, health, and the environment.

Office of Disability Employment Policy (http://www.dol.gov/dol/odep/)
The Office of Disability Employment Policy is a new office of The Department of Labor. Programs and staff of the former programs of the President's Committee on Employment of People with Disabilities have been integrated in this new office. The Web site provides programs and services information, technical assistance materials, publications, and an extensive list of for-profit companies interested in employing people with disabilities.

Office of Minority Health (http://www.omhrc.gov)
The Office of Minority Health (OMH) Web site offers a large amount of easily navigable material, including news releases, online publications, grants announcements, a funding resource guide, news of upcoming events and conferences, links to OMH databases for funding opportunities, and organizations and programs.

Office of Telecommunications and Information Application
(http://www.ntia.doc.gov/otiahome/otiahome.html)
Office of Telecommunications and Information Application (OTIA), a part of the National Telecommunications and Informative Administration, was created to help all kinds of orga-nizations best use telecommunications and information technology to provide public ser-vices. There are descriptions of, and links to, the Technology Opportunities Program (For-merly, Telecommunications and Information Infrastructure Assistance Program) and the Public Telecommunications Facilities Program (PTFP). These programs provide matching grants for dissemination equipment and demonstration information infrastructures throughout the country. The linked sites have applications, lists of past recipients, and more specific requirements and descriptions.

Substance Abuse and Mental Health Services Administration (http://www.samhsa.gov/)
Substance Abuse and Mental Health Services Administration (SAMHSA) awards grants in the areas of substance abuse treatment and prevention, collects and analyzes relevant statis-tics and data, and makes public and private policy recommendations to finance sub-stance-abuse related services. The Web site has information about SAMHSA's programs, funding, statistics and data, public information, and grant, contract, and job opportunities.

U.S. Census Bureau (http://www.census.gov/)
The U.S. Census Bureau's sprawling Web site is *the* source of social, demographic, and economic information about the United States on the Web. Offerings include Census Bureau publications, listed by subject; statistical profiles for states, congressional districts, and counties; current economic indicators; state and county maps created on the fly; and much more.

STATE AGENCIES

Nebraska Arts Council (http://www.nebraskaartscouncil.org/)
The Nebraska Arts Council (NAC) promotes the arts, cultivates resources, and supports excellence in artistic endeavors for all Nebraskans. The NAC Web site provides general information about its grant programs and application requirements; an artists directory; links to other art councils (community and state), state organizations, and art museums on the Web; and contact information.

North Carolina Arts Council (http://www.ncarts.org/)
The mission of the North Carolina Arts Council is to enrich North Carolina's cultural life by supporting the arts. The Council is a catalyst for the development of arts organizations and awards grants and offers technical guidance statewide. The Council's colorful Web site

provides, among other items, program and grant information and links to various arts organizations, government agencies, and regional and national arts partners.

North Dakota Council on the Arts (http://www.state.nd.us/arts/)

Established in 1967 by the state legislature, the North Dakota Council on the Arts (NDCA) is responsible for the support and development of the arts and artists in North Dakota. In addition to making grants based on recommendations from artists and arts administrators, the Council administers the Cultural Endowment Fund, through which it secures private and public funds to enhance existing programs. The Council's Web site provides program information, application instructions, grant-writing tips, related arts resource links, and contact information.

Ohio Arts Council (http://www.oac.state.oh.us/home.html)

Established in 1965 to "foster and encourage the development of the arts and assist the preservation of Ohio's cultural heritage," the Ohio Arts Council (OAC) funds programs to make arts activities available to the public and also supports Ohio artists through 25 different grant programs. The Council's Web site provides information about all OAC programs (complete grant guidelines), an impressive search engine, links to both state and national arts resources, and e-mail links to staff members.

South Dakota Arts Council (http://www.state.sd.us/state/executive/deca/sdarts/)

The South Dakota Arts Council (SDAC) encourages and supports artists, strengthens arts organizations and arts education programs, and increases South Dakotans awareness of the arts. As a state agency of the Department of Education & Cultural Affairs, the Council makes grants to schools, individuals, and arts organizations. Grantseekers will especially appreciate the Council's online program guide, which includes detailed grant application guidelines and a handy glossary of terms.

Bibliography: Suggestions for Further Reading

Compiled by Sarah Collins

The following is a reading list of books and periodical articles that supplements the information in *Grantseeking on the Web*. Citations have been selected from the Foundation Center's bibliographic database, available on our Web site as *Literature of the Nonprofit Sector Online*. Be sure to check *LNPS Online* (http://lnps.fdncenter.org) regularly to keep abreast of new publications. Simply input the terms "Internet" or "Fundraising—computer aided" from the subject index.

Books

Bergan, Helen. *Where the Information Is: A Guide to Electronic Research for Nonprofit Organizations.* Alexandria, VA: BioGuide Press, 1996.

> Bergan explains in nontechnical language how electronic resources can help nonprofit organizations identify and cultivate potential donors, find grant funding, and manage daily operations. Chapters cover CD-ROMs, DIALOG, CompuServe, America Online, e-mail, using the Internet, and Internet resources of interest to nonprofits. Provides sections that list the names and addresses of vendors and groups that are involved in making electronic technology available for use by nonprofit organizations.

Corson-Finnerty, Adam, and Laura Blanchard. *Fundraising and Friend-Raising on the Web.* Chicago, IL: American Library Association, 1998.

> Intended for library administrators, but with approaches that will succeed for any nonprofit, the book offers advice on such topics as developing and measuring the impact of a Web site; creating donor recognition in cyberspace; delivering your site directly to potential donors on disk or CD-ROM; and fundraising with digital cash. Throughout, examples currently on the Web are provided. A CD-ROM disk is included.

E-Philanthropy v2.001: From Entrepreneurial Adventure to an Online Community. Battle Creek, MI: W. K. Kellogg Foundation, 2001.

> This Web-based publication updates the foundation's first report "e-Philanthropy, Volunteerism, and Social Changemaking" and expands the number of Web sites included in a searchable database. The report interprets the changes that have occurred in e-philanthropy, suggests a structural guide for the various types of Web sites, offers insights into the future, and provides a listing of additional resources. Available as PDF file at http://www.actknowledgeworks.net/ephil/red_cover.

Grobman, Gary M. and Gary B. Grant. *The Non-Profit Internet Handbook.* Harrisburg, PA: White Hat Communications, 1998.

> Comprehensive information about the uses of the Internet for nonprofits, devoting one chapter to fundraising. Includes case studies, issues to consider, and citations and reviews of numerous Web sites.

Grobman, Gary M. *The Nonprofit Organization's Guide to E-Commerce.* Harrisburg, PA: White Hat Communications, 2001.

> The book discusses how nonprofits can capitalize on the Internet for marketing, fundraising, maintaining contact with members and donors, and publicity. Appendices include a glossary, information about copyright, and a sample code of ethics.

Grobman, Gary M. and Gary B. Grant. *The Wilder Nonprofit Guide to Getting Started on the Internet: How to Use the Internet's Best Features to Uncover Valuable Information and Help Your Nonprofit Be More Profitable.* St. Paul, MN: Amherst H. Wilder Foundation, 1999.

> Basic handbook with information about the Internet, how to connect, use e-mail, join mailing lists, newsgroups, and other online tools. Includes glossary.

Grobman, Gary M., Gary B. Grant, and Steve Stoller. *The Wilder Nonprofit Guide to Fundraising on the Internet: How to Use the Internet to Raise Funds and Sharpen Your Fundraising Skills.* St. Paul, MN: Amherst H. Wilder Foundation, 1999.

> Handbook lists Web sites and Internet tools that assist in fundraising efforts. Instructions on how to join listservs, access journals, conduct prospect research, use e-mail to solicit support, and create a Web site are included. Subsequent chapters list and review useful foundation and charity sites.

Gross, Marilyn L. *300 Top Web Sites for Fundraisers.* Suffern, NY: Educational Funding Strategies, 1999.

> Organized into broad categories, such as capital campaigns, prospect research, and international grantseeking, each entry provides a synopsis of the content of the Web site and its URL. Introduction by the author provides guidance about the Internet as a research tool.

Gstalder, Steven, ed. *Government Information on the Internet*, 4th ed. Lanham, MD: Bernan Press, 2001.
> Covers nearly 3,000 U.S. government Internet resources. Organized by eighteen subject categories, and indexed by primary and alternative access URLs, Superintendent of Documents number, publication title, agency, and subject.

Johnston, Michael. *The Nonprofit Guide to the Internet: How to Survive and Thrive*, 2nd ed. New York, NY: John Wiley & Sons, 1999.
> Surveys the hardware and software needed to get online and discusses reasons for nonprofits to utilize the Internet. Explores and gives examples of fundraising, and fundraising research online. Explains how to use a Web site for marketing and public relations purposes. Includes a resource list, glossary, and index.

Lane, Carole A. *Naked in Cyberspace: How to Find Personal Information Online.* Edited by Helen Burwell and Owen B. Davies. Somerville, MA: Pemberton Press Books, 1997.
> Includes chapter on prospect research that indicates how to use public records, telephone directory databases, motor vehicle records, news and biographical databases to search for wealthy prospects.

Moran, Amanda M., ed. *CyberHound's Guide to Associations and Nonprofit Organizations on the Internet.* Detroit, MI: Gale Research, 1997.
> Provides entries for 2,500 Web sites of associations and other nonprofit organizations. Entries contain the URL; site description; updating frequency; site establishment date; geographic area and time span covered; language; target audience; contact information; and ratings of site content, design, and technical merit. Includes bibliography, glossary of Internet terms, and indexes of organization name, contact person, and subject.

Mudd, Mollie, ed. *The Grantseeker's Handbook of Essential Internet Sites*, 4th ed. Gaithersburg, MD: Aspen Publishers, 2000.
> Contains descriptions of more than 750 Internet sites of interest to grantseekers. Each description includes the resource's address and login or subscription instructions where applicable. Sites are arranged in the following categories: corporations, foundations and associations, government, research, and resources.

Articles

ONLINE FUNDRAISING

Barth, Steve. "Pulling Gifts into Your Web." *Currents*, vol. 24, September 1998, p. 32–7.
> Analyzes the practice of fundraising via the Internet on college campuses. Also includes some tips on successful Internet fundraising.

Blum, Debra E. "Charities Fail to Tap Internet's Potential to Spur Action and Giving, Study Finds." *Chronicle of Philanthropy,* vol. 11, September 23, 1999, p. 32.
> Discusses the findings of a new survey of "socially engaged Internet users" and "online activists," which indicates that charities are not utilizing the full potential of the Internet to stimulate giving and activism.

Demko, Paul, and Jennifer Moore. "Charities Put the Web to Work." *Chronicle of Philanthropy*, vol. 10, October 8, 1998, p. 1, 41–4.
>   Nonprofit organizations are increasing their use of the Internet to tell their stories, and also in their day-to-day operations.

Dickey, Marilyn. "E-mailing for Dollars." *Chronicle of Philanthropy*, vol. 10, September 10, 1998, p. 23–4.
>   Recounts successful fundraising efforts accomplished through various uses of e-mail.

Dickey, Marilyn. "Sold, to the Man at the Mouse." *Chronicle of Philanthropy*, vol. 11, October 22, 1998, p. 23–5.
>   Nonprofit organizations are beginning to use Internet auctions as a way to raise money and to reach people globally who have never supported their organization. Experts also offer advice on ways to avoid problems.

Frenza, JP and Leslie Hoffman. "Fundraising on the Internet: Three Easy Strategies for Nonprofits." *Nonprofit World*, vol. 17, July–August 1999, p. 10–3.
>   The suggested strategies are to become a nonprofit beneficiary of one of the "shop for a cause" Web sites; to establish a simple but secure Web page with a one-page form for collecting donations; and to create an online catalog to sell products.

Fuisz, Joseph. "Internet Causes Dramatic Changes in Fund Raising World." *Fund Raising Management,* vol. 30, October 1999, p. 22–4.
>   Discusses the impact of the Internet on fundraising, and explores the possibility of partnerships between nonprofits and online commercial enterprises.

Greer, Gayle. "Online Fundraising: The Time Is Now." *Fund Raising Management,* vol. 30, August 1999, p. 26–9.
>   Encourages nonprofit organizations to utilize the Internet as a fundraising tool and a means of building relationships with donors.

Hair, Dr. Jay D. "Fund Raising on the Internet: Instant Access to a New World of Donors." *Fund Raising Management,* vol. 30, October 1999, p. 16–8.
>   Discusses the advantages of having an online shopping village attached to a nonprofit organization's Web site.

Lewis, Nicole. "You've Got a Charity Solicitation." *Chronicle of Philanthropy*, vol. 13, November 30, 2000, p. 25–8.
>   E-mail can be an effective and cost-efficient way to maintain contact with donors, potential donors, alumni, and other interested parties. Techniques for online solicitation via e-mail, however, differ from those for traditional methods for direct mail, and suggestions are given here.

Lyttle, Jeni. "New Dimensions for Fundraising." *Nonprofits & Technology,* vol. 2, October 1999, p. 1, 3.
>   Some fundraisers are creating virtual tours of their planned facilities in order to raise capital funds.

Moore, Jennifer. "A Web of Confusion." *Chronicle of Philanthropy,* vol. 11, October 21, 1999, p. 37, 39.
>   Discusses the annual meeting of the National Association of State Charity Officials, at which nonprofit representatives urged charity regulators to clarify federal and state requirements regarding fundraising on the Internet.

Moore, Jennifer. "Internet Appeals and the Law: State Charity Regulators Issue Guidelines on When Charities That Solicit Online Must Register Locally." *Chronicle of Philanthropy*, vol. 12, September 7, 2000, p. 21–3.
> Article describes proposed guidelines by the National Association of State Charity Officials on the monitoring of online fundraising appeals.

"Old-Line Charities Succeed with New Approaches to Attracting Donors." *Chronicle of Philanthropy,* vol. 12, November 4, 1999, p. 49.
> Some of the charities in the 1999 Philanthropy 400 are using newer techniques for fundraising, including the Internet, payroll deduction plans, and inventive means of solicitation.

Roufa, Mike. "Can Nonprofits Really Raise Money on the Internet?" *Nonprofit World,* vol. 17, May–June 1999, p. 10–2.
> Explains what e-commerce is and how nonprofit organizations are using the Internet to raise funds.

Schwinn, Elizabeth. "Click and Easy." *Chronicle of Philanthropy*, vol. 13, December 14, 2000, p. 27–9.
> The pros and cons of online marketing and fundraising arrangements are revealed. Nonprofits are recognizing the appeal of their credibility to corporations, but may be naive in forging deals and handling the complicated ancillary issues of online promotional campaigns with for-profits.

Vimuktanon, Atisaya. "Non-Profits and the Internet." *Fund Raising Management,* vol. 28, October 1997, p. 25–8.
> Explores the use of the Internet to increase visibility and enhance fundraising for nonprofit organizations.

Williams, Grant. "Guidelines Show Charities How to Work with Internet Companies on Fund Raising." *Chronicle of Philanthropy*, vol. 13, November 2, 2000, p. 67.
> Discusses a report published by the Association of Fundraising Professionals entitled "Internet Transaction Guidelines." This report outlines a set of 22 guidelines that nonprofits can follow when working with Internet companies to raise money through Web-based resources. The guidelines can be located at http://www.afpnet.org/tier3_cd.cfm?folder_id=868&content_item_id=1260.

PHILANTHROPY PORTALS

Berger, Jeff, et al. "Nonprofit Sector Not Immune from 'Dot-Bombs'." *NonProfit Times*, vol. 15, March 2001, p. 27–30.
> Some of the dot.coms serving the nonprofit world have folded, including OnGiving, KickStart.com, Zoom2Net.com, ACUSA.com, IReachOut.com, and some others are struggling or changing their focus. Meanwhile ePhilanthropyFoundation.org has issued a code of ethics, reprinted here.

Demko, Paul. "On-Line Solicitors: Tangled Web." *Chronicle of Philanthropy*, vol. 10, January 29, 1998, p. 23–4.
> Discusses the Web sites that are raising money for charities through the Internet, and the subsequent questions about whether they should be regulated.

"The Dot-Com Shakeout: Where Does It Leave E-Philanthropy?" *Advancing Philanthropy,* vol. 8, May–June 2001, p. 14–5, 17-8, 41–3

> The demise of Charitableway and other dot-coms reinforces the fact that nonprofit alliances with philanthropy portals can be risky. Details about the dissolution are given by observers and Charitableway CEO Pete Mountanos. Offers suggestions for maintaining an Internet presence through application service providers (ASPs), and recommends several companies. Also provides guidelines for selecting a technology partner and adds several real-world examples.

Ford, Eugene. "Virtual Philanthropy Gets Needed Funds to Remote Countries." *Nonprofits & Technology,* vol. 2, September 1999, p. 6.

> Profiles the Virtual Foundation, an online philanthropy program that supports international grassroots initiatives. The Virtual Foundation posts project proposals on its Web site, where they can be read and funded by online donors. It was founded in 1996 by ECOLOGIA, an international nonprofit that focuses on environmental issues.

Hall, Holly. "A Brave New World of Giving." *Chronicle of Philanthropy,* vol. 12, June 15, 2000, p.1, 33–7.

> The rise of Internet donation portals, or "philanthropy portals" includes both nonprofits and businesses that seek to connect donors with charities. America Online Foundation, which established Helping.org, is one of the most active sites, but there are numerous competitors vying to register the big-name nonprofits. A comprehensive list describes the major giving portals.

Martin, Nita L. "You've Got Donations." *Corporate Philanthropy Report,* vol. 15, January 2000, p. 1–3, 5.

> Examines online cause related marketing, and the relationship between e-philanthropy companies and nonprofit organizations. Profiles the e-philanthropy Web sites Shop2Give, IGive.com, GreaterGood.com, and Helping.org. Sidebar provides tips to nonprofits that seek to do fundraising on the Internet or to partner with e-philanthropy companies.

PROSPECT RESEARCH

Allen, Nick. "Fundraising on the Internet: Using E-mail and the Web to Acquire and Cultivate Donors." *Grassroots Fundraising Journal,* vol. 19, June 2000, p. 3–5.

> Discusses seven ways to raise money on the Internet—and which are working best.

Barber, Putnam. "Looking for New Supporters? Look Again—Try Forging New Connections with the Friends You Already Have." *Advancing Philanthropy,* vol. 8, September–October 2000, p. 34–6, 38.

> Article describes ways that nonprofits can improve their online communications to current supporters via the Internet.

Dickey, Marilyn (comp.) "Internet Sites that Click for Charity Researchers Seeking Donors." *Chronicle of Philanthropy,* vol. 11, September 23, 1999, p. 30–1.

> Listing of Web sites useful to fundraisers.

Dickey, Marilyn and Holly Hall. "The Pitfalls of Mining the Internet." *Chronicle of Philanthropy,* vol. 11, September 23, 1999, p. 29, 32.

> Discusses current issues surrounding prospect research on the Internet. Experts remark that although the Internet is making it easier and less expensive to obtain information on potential donors, many charities are not utilizing it as effectively as they could. The increasing involvement of professional researchers in fundraising efforts and the issue of donor privacy are also discussed.

Robinson, Andy. "Direct Mail Alternatives: Finding New Donors in Manageable Numbers." *NonProfit Times*, vol. 13, April 1999, p. 45–6.

> Discusses techniques for small community organizations for recruiting new contributions.

TECHNOLOGY

"2001 Non-Profit Software Guide." *Fund Raising Management,* vol. 30, October 2000, p. 25–37.

> Annual guide to fundraising software for nonprofits.

Billitteri, Thomas J. "Technology and Accountability Will Shape the Future of Philanthropy." *Chronicle of Philanthropy*, vol. 12, January 13, 2000, p. 10, 16, 20.

> Various observers predict how new technology, including the Internet, will change the daily work of nonprofits and foundations, and their relationships with each other.

Feller, Gordon. "Latest High-Tech Trends: One Giant Leap for Nonprofits." *Nonprofit World*, vol. 19, January–February, 2001, p. 25–9.

> Recommends that nonprofits partner with application service providers (ASPs) as a way of keeping their Web sites current without the expense of hiring their own technical staff. Explains further benefits of such an arrangement and how to locate more information.

VOLUNTEERING

Ellis, Susan J. "Virtual Volunteering." *501(c)(3) Monthly Letter,* vol. 19, September 1999, p. 3, 5.

> Discusses virtual volunteering, through which individuals can contribute their time and expertise to nonprofit organizations via the Internet. Gives detailed examples of the types of technical assistance and direct client services that can be provided by virtual volunteers.

APPENDIX H

Glossary of Web-Related Terms

Adobe Acrobat*   A program that lets you capture a document and then view it in its original format and appearance. To view an Acrobat document, which is called a Portable Document Format (PDF) file, you need Acrobat Reader. The Reader is free and can be downloaded from Adobe (http://www.adobe.com/products/acrobat/readstep.html).

Architecture   The structuring paradigms, style and patterns that describe or make up either software systems or Internet/intranet systems. In particular, architectures can be overall structures for systems.

Bookmark   A bookmark is considered by some to be the best thing about surfing the Web. By bookmarking a Web site while you visit it, you can easily return to it at a later time with a simple mouse selection rather than remembering or typing in the URL.

Browser   Short for Web browser, it's the tool (program) that allows you to surf the Web. The most popular Web browsers are Netscape Navigator and Internet Explorer.

Bulletin Board System (BBS)   An electronic service that can be accessed via the Internet. BBS typically includes collections of files, notes from other computer users, and many other services.

Button   A graphic that a user can click to do something, such as download a program, submit information, or go to another Web page.

Adapted from the High Density.com online glossary (except as otherwise designated) at http://www.high-density.com/glossary.html. Used by permission of High Density Computing.
*Adapted from whatis.com's online encyclopedia at http://whatis.techtarget.com/whome/0,,sid9,00.html. Copyrighted by and used by permission of whatis.com and TechTarget, Inc.

Cache A file on your computer where the system stores a copy of things asked for recently. Then, if you ask for the same thing again, instead of issuing another Internet request, your computer can simply use the copy from the cache. This has to do with trying to speed things up, since every request you send over the Internet for a picture or text takes time.

Command A way of telling an application or Windows to perform a major chore, such as running an application or utility program. Usually an option from an application's menus. Also refers to commands typed in from a command-prompt session or from the Run dialog box from the Start Menu in Windows.

Cookie The most common meaning of "cookie" on the Internet refers to a piece of information sent by a Web server to a Web browser that the browser software is expected to save and to send back to the server whenever the browser makes additional requests from the server. Cookies might contain information such as login or registration information, online "shopping cart" information, user preferences, etc.

Cursor The representation of the mouse on the screen. It may take many different shapes.

Database A file or group of related files that are designed to hold recurring data types as if the files were lists.

Desktop The screen area on which the windows are displayed.

Dial-up connection The most popular form of Internet connection for the home user, this is a connection from your computer to a host computer over standard telephone lines.

Dialog box An on-screen message box that conveys or requests information from the user.

Digital divide* Describes the fact that the world can be divided into those who do and do not have access to, and the capability to use, modern information technology.

Discussion group A group of people who exchange messages about particular topics. Often associated with newsgroups, discussion groups can also take the form of interactive message boards, thread message forums, and e-mailing lists.

Domain name The unique name that identifies an Internet site. Domain names always have two or more parts, separated by dots. The part on the left is the most specific, and the part on the right is the most general. (See also Suffix.)

Download The transfer of information from the Internet to your computer. Every time you instruct your computer system to retrieve your e-mail, you are downloading your e-mail to your computer.

Drop list or drop-down menu	A list of options that drops down when you click on a down arrow button.
E-commerce*	The buying and selling of goods and services on the Internet, especially the World Wide Web.
E-mail (electronic mail)	Messages, usually text, sent from one person to another via computer. E-mail can also be sent automatically to a large number of addresses. (See Mailing list.)
Encryption	A way of making data unreadable to everyone except the receiver. An increasingly common way of sending credit card numbers over the Internet when conducting commercial transactions.
Extranet	The connecting of two or more intranets. If you think of an intranet as a company's internal Web site which allows users inside the company to communicate and exchange information, imagine connecting that virtual space with another company's intranet, thus allowing these two (or more) companies to share resources and communicate over the Internet in their own virtual space. This technology greatly enhances business to business communications.
FAQ (Frequently Asked Questions)	FAQs are documents that list and answer the most common questions on a particular subject.
Forms	An HTML page that passes variables back to the server. These pages are used to gather information from users.
Forum	See Discussion group.
Frames	A term used to describe a viewing and layout style of a World Wide Web site, it refers to the simultaneous loading of two or more Web pages at the same time within the same screen.
Gateway	See Portal.
Hit	A search result.
Home page	This has several meanings; originally, the Web page that your browser is set to use when it starts up. The more common meaning refers to the main Web page for a business, organization, person, or simply the main page out of a collection of Web pages.
HTML (hypertext markup language)	The coding language used to create hypertext documents for use on the World Wide Web.
Hyperlink	A link in a document that, when activated (often by clicking it), links or jumps to another document or graphic. (See also Link.)

Icon   A small graphic symbol used to represent a folder, program, shortcut, resource, or document.

Internet connection   The way one gains access to the Internet. For the average person a simple phone line is used. This is also known as a dial-up connection.

ISP (Internet service provider)   An organization that provides access to the Internet in some form, usually for a fee.

Javascript   A scripting language for Web pages. Scripts written with Javascript can be embedded into HTML documents. With Javascript you have many possibilities for enhancing your Web page with interesting elements.

Keyword   A word you might use to search for, or on, a Web site.

LAN (local area network)   A computer network limited to the immediate area, usually the same building or floor of a building.

Link   A link will transport you from one Internet site to another with a click of your mouse. Links can be text or graphic. Text links usually will be underlined and often a different color than the rest of the text on the screen. A graphic link usually has a frame around it. (See also Hyperlink.)

Listserv   The most common kind of electronic mailing list.

Logon   The process of connecting to a network or remote system.

Mailing list   A discussion forum where participants subscribe to a list and receive messages by e-mail.

Menu   A list of available command options.

Menu bar   Located under the title bar on a Web site's home page, the menu bar displays the names of all available menu lists.

Moderated mailing list   A mailing list where messages are first sent to the list owner for review before they are distributed to all subscribers.

Navigate   To move around on the World Wide Web by following hypertext paths from document to document.

Navigation bar   See Menu bar.

Newsgroup   The name for discussion groups on Usenet.

Password   A code used to gain access to a locked system.

PDF format   See Adobe Acrobat.

Personalization*   The process of tailoring Web pages to individual users' characteristics or preferences.

Portal*   A term, generally synonymous with gateway, for a World Wide Web site that is or proposes to be a major starting site for users.

Post   Means the same as "to put up." It can refer to subscribers to newsgroups or mailing lists sending or posting their articles or comments online. It is also used to indicate content added to or "put up" on a Web site.

Posting   A single message entered into a network communications system, such as to a newsgroup or a message board.

Search engine   A databased Web site containing information that can be used to find other sites of interest.

Server   A computer, or a software package, that provides a specific kind of service to client software running on other computers. The term can refer to a particular piece of software, such as a WWW server, or to the machine on which the software is running.

Site (Web)   A location on the Internet containing HTML documents that visitors can view using a browser.

Site map*   A visual model of a Web site's content that allows users to navigate through the site to find the information they are looking for.

Suffix (domain name)   The three-digit suffix of a domain can be used to identify the type of organization. Suffixes include, but are not limited to:
.com = commercial
.edu = educational
.int = international
.gov = government
.mil = military
.net = network
.org = organization

Surf   To browse or "look at" information on the World Wide Web by pointing and clicking and navigating in a nonlinear way.

Text file   A file containing only ASCII text characters. ASCII text is a basic form of electronic communication.

Thread   A group of related messages on an electronic bulletin board system or Web discussion group.

Thumbnail   Describes the size of an image you frequently find on Web pages. Usually a photo or picture archive will present a thumbnail version of its contents (which makes the page load quicker), and when a user clicks on the small image, a larger version will appear.

URL (uniform resource locator)   The standard way to give the address of any resource on the World Wide Web. URLs typically begin with http:// or www.

Usenet	Often referred to as simply "newsgroups," Usenet is a distributed bulletin board system supported mainly by UNIX machines.
User ID (user name)	This is the unique identifier (like your logon name) that you use to identify yourself on a computer.
Virtual	Simulation of the real thing. This term appears before various computer terms to indicate simulation technology that enables you to cross boundaries and experience something without needing its physical presence.
Web board	A discussion group or forum which is accessed via the World Wide Web.
Web host	The computer or hard drives where Web sites are hosted and accessible through the World Wide Web.
Web page	A document on the World Wide Web. Each Web page has its own unique URL. Every time you are on the World Wide Web, you are looking at a Web page.
Web site	A home page or group of pages either owned by an individual or a company and placed on the Web.
World Wide Web (WWW or the Web or W3)	A global (worldwide) hypertext system that uses the Internet as its transport mechanism. In a hypertext system, you navigate by clicking hyperlinks, which display other documents, which also contain hyperlinks. The Web relies upon the hypertext transport protocol (http), an Internet standard that specifies how an application can locate and acquire resources stored on another computer on the Internet. Most Web documents are created using hypertext markup language (html).

Index